Date **E**

COMPARATIVE ECONOMIC SYSTEMS
Organizational and Managerial Perspectives

Kanji Haitani

State University of New York
College at Fredonia

Prentice-Hall, Englewood Cliffs, New Jersey 07632

Library of Congress Cataloguing-in-Publication Data

HAITANI, KANJI.
  Comparative economic systems.

  Includes bibliographies and index.
    1. Comparative economics.   2. United States—
Economic policy.   3. Soviet Union—Economic policy.
4. Japan—Economic policy.   I. Title.
HB90.H35   1986   330.12   85-19409
ISBN   0-13-154063-7

Editorial/production supervision: Kim Gueterman
Cover design: Wanda Lubelska Design
Manufacturing buyer: Ed O'Dougherty

Printed in the United States of America

10 9 8 7 6 5 4 3 2 1

ISBN   0-13-154063-7   01

PRENTICE-HALL INTERNATIONAL (UK) LIMITED, *London*
PRENTICE-HALL OF AUSTRALIA PTY. LIMITED, *Sydney*
PRENTICE-HALL CANADA INC., *Toronto*
PRENTICE-HALL HISPANOAMERICANA, S.A., *Mexico*
PRENTICE-HALL OF INDIA PRIVATE LIMITED, *New Delhi*
PRENTICE-HALL OF JAPAN, INC., *Tokyo*
PRENTICE-HALL OF SOUTHEAST ASIA PTE. LTD., *Singapore*
EDITORA PRENTICE-HALL DO BRASIL, LTDA., *Rio de Janeiro*
WHITEHALL BOOKS LIMITED, *Wellington, New Zealand*

To the Memory of R.A.L.

Contents

v

2

Value Orientations and Ideologies   27

3

Social Relations and Social Stratification   51

4

The Political System   79

PART 2   THE THREE MAJOR ECONOMIC SYSTEMS

5

The Soviet Economy: Organization and Management   115

6

The Soviet Economy: Problems of Imbalance and Inefficiency   149

7

The American Economy: Macroeconomic Organization and Public Policy 182

8

The American Economy: Corporate Organization and Management   225

9

The Japanese Economy: Industrial Organization and Economic Policy   258

10

The Japanese Economy: Corporate Organization and Management   289

PART 3   SELECTED TOPICS AND CONCLUSIONS

11

The Chinese Economy   320

12

Market and Planning   341

13

Managers and Workers 369

14

Concluding Assessments 397

Index 404

Preface

This book is about comparing economic systems in today's industrialized world. Its focus is on the sociocultural and political dimensions of the ways different societies organize and manage their economic activities. I have tried to avoid the two major pitfalls of the conventional approaches to comparative studies of economic systems, namely, engaging in pedantic discourses on the grand "isms," and parading in front of the reader superficial descriptions of more than a dozen different national economies. Instead, I have chosen to analyze in some depth the economic systems of the world's three foremost industrial powers— the United States, the Soviet Union, and Japan. These systems have been chosen not only because of their relative importance in the global economy but also their remarkable differences from each other. I have provided thorough discussions of the social, cultural, ideological, and political dimensions of these three societies. I have then related these dimensions to the organization and management of the economic systems, not only at the macroeconomic level but also at the industrial and enterprise levels. Beyond the intensive examination of these three economic systems, I have also included discussions on some aspects of the following economies in order to illustrate the diversity of economic systems: Great Britain, France, West Germany, China, Hungary, and Yugoslavia.

The purpose of this book is threefold. First, it demonstrates that different economic systems function in markedly different sociocultural and political environments, each with its own internal logic, and that relative strengths and weaknesses of each system arise from those differences in environment and logic. Second, this book is designed to provide the reader with a world view and a cross-cultural perspective that are difficult to acquire unless he or she lives abroad. As it examines the sociocultural, political, and economic institutions of other societies, this book will provide the reader with a good substitute for overseas travel. Such an experience has a practical benefit. In an emerging world of increasing internationalization of business, it is becoming increasingly likely that most of us will at some time be dealing with someone from another economic environment, or even be living and working in an environment totally different from our own. In the second half of the 1980s and into the 1990s, an international perspective will no doubt be as important to the successful decision maker as communications skills and computer literacy. The third purpose of the book is to deepen the reader's understanding of the system in which he or she lives and works. A comparative economic study is a broadening experience not only because we learn more about others but, perhaps more importantly, because we begin to understand ourselves better.

Part 1 of the book examines some of the more important environmental factors of an economic system, namely, values and ideologies, social relations, social stratification, the educational system, the legal system, and the political system. Part 2 analyzes in some detail the organization and management of the national economy, industry, and productive enterprise of the three major economic systems. Part 3 discusses some selected issues of macroeconomic and enterprise management. At the end of each chapter I have provided a set of questions which I hope will not only encourage review of the chapter's material but also provoke new ideas and thoughts.

I have not followed the conventional practice of presenting little or no information on the American system; such a practice appears to be based on the mistaken notion that American readers know their system well. The truth is that most of the American readers have not examined their own system *in comparison to other systems.* I have described the American system with the eye of an outsider, on the premise that a degree of detachment is a prerequisite to genuine understanding. My hope is that this approach will enable the readers to gain a deeper understanding not only of their own system but of others as well.

I am grateful to Professors Thomas Bonsor, Jan Prybyla, and John Stevens for their incisive critiques of the manuscript of this book. Several significant changes have been made in response to their very helpful comments. I wish to thank my son Robert for providing research assistance on some chapters. I would also like to thank my wife, Masako, for her moral support. In a sense, the work on this book was as much hers as mine.

CHAPTER 1

Introduction to Economic Systems

The subject matter of this book is a comparative study of national *economic systems*, or different national forms of economic *organization* and *management*. Our interest lies in comparing the ways in which peoples of diverse sociocultural and political backgrounds organize and manage their economic affairs at both national and productive-enterprise levels.

WHY COMPARE ECONOMIC SYSTEMS?

What do we hope to gain from a comparative study of economic systems? Our endeavor in uncovering similarities and differences that exist among various national economic systems may bring several benefits.

First, a comparative study of a variety of economic systems is one of the best antidotes for nationalistic chauvinism. Most peoples in the world believe that their own culture is superior to others, and they use it as a basis for judging other societies. Sociologists refer to this belief in the inherent superiority of one's own culture and society as *ethnocentrism*. We become relatively free from the grip of economic ethnocentrism when we discover that there are many different ways of managing economic affairs and that our own practices are not necessarily the best in the world. Exposure to different economic philosophies, institutions, and practices tends to free us from our preconceived notions about other peoples.

The second benefit is more practical than the first. We live in a world in which nation states are in constant competition with each other economically, politically, and even militarily. In dealing effectively with other nations, it is important that we fully understand their behavior and motives. In the coming decades of increasing internationalization of business, it is likely that most of us will at some time be dealing with, or even living and working in, another economic environment. Comparative economic studies will help us equip ourselves with a much needed world view and intercultural perspective.

There is yet another reason why we should study economic systems. Comparing economic systems will give us ideas about possible ways of improving the performance of our own system. If our own ways of doing certain things have not worked well, perhaps we should try some other ways found successful elsewhere. For this purpose, we need to identify what has worked under what conditions and in what type of environment. Such knowledge is of great practical value in our efforts to identify and select alternative courses of action toward the betterment of our own system.

Lastly, and perhaps most importantly, comparative studies of economic systems will help us better understand the organization and practices of our own economic system that we otherwise tend to take for granted. Our familiarity with our own system and our uncritical acceptance of it tend to breed ignorance as to which aspects of this system are unique or specific to it and which aspects are common or universal to all systems. The ability to distinguish the specific from the universal, however, is vitally important if we are to fully understand our own system *and ourselves*. It is precisely because the French manage their economic affairs differently from the British that the French and British systems differ. What defines the French economic system uniquely as such are the specifically French ways of doing things. And the important point is that the French will never find out what aspects of their institutions, policies, and so on are uniquely French and what aspects are common to all nations unless they *compare* their system objectively and critically with other systems. It is a fundamental fact of life that we can truly know ourselves only by studying others.

Common to all these benefits of comparative studies is the fact that *we gain a relative orientation by comparison*. Vaclav Holesovsky stated this fact most lucidly when he wrote

Comparison is a source of insight and understanding. It kills static certitudes of isolation; it breeds abilities of relative orientation. Relativism leads to rationality. Wasn't travel always considered broadening? Comparative studies are a substitute for travel. They make it harder both for uncritical self-congratulations and for naïve admiration of the unknown and the exotic to hold sway. They make us skeptical. They also make us sensitive to the possibilities of new options.[1]

THE NATURE OF AN ECONOMIC SYSTEM

So that we know exactly what we are studying, let us first agree on some key definitions and relationships. Specifically, we shall define the term *economic system*, and explain the relationships between an economic system and its environment, and among the goals, behavior, and performance of an economic system.

The Definition of an Economic System

First, let us consider the word *economic*. Most simply put, the term refers to the material well-being of people. Since resources are limited and human needs and wants are unlimited, we must make wise choices in using resources by carefully weighing the costs and benefits involved in the choices. Thus, an idea, activity, behavior, or organization is *economic* if it involves considerations of costs and benefits of using scarce resources in our efforts to maximize our material well-being. (By contrast, the term *political* refers to *power* relationships among people.)

Second, consider the word *system*. A system is simply any set of interrelated parts. The parts may be objects, ideas, activities, or human beings. When these parts or elements are combined, arranged, or united in such a manner that there exists some form of regular or recurrent relationships, there is a system. Thus, a human body, an automobile, this book, the Interstate Highway System, the National Football League, the Medicare program, and Economics 101 are all systems.

Systems exist in hierarchies. The larger systems to which a given system belongs constitute its *environment*. The smaller systems contained within its boundary are its components, constituent parts, or subsystems. The relationships between a system's environment and its components, and the relationships among the components, uniquely determine the nature and character of the system.

---

[1]Vaclav Holesovsky, *Economic Systems: Analysis and Comparison* (New York: McGraw-Hill Book Company, 1977), p. 11.

In analyzing a social system, it is important to identify the ways in which the constituent parts are interrelated. We often speak of the "structure" or "organization" of a system. Every system has structure, but a system does not necessarily have organization. *Structure* is simply a relatively fixed or regular relationship among parts. Thus, we may speak of the structure of a house, a human body, or an economics course. *Organization,* by contrast, is a regular and recurrent relationship among component parts *requiring coordinated action toward a common purpose.* Thus, a few scrap pieces of wood put together by a child with nails has structure, but there is no organization among the wood pieces and nails. But a boat has organization since its parts are put together for the purpose of carrying objects over water, and its parts are related to each other in a coordinated manner. Similarly, there is an informal social structure among the employees who happen to find each other at a coffee break every morning in front of a coffee-vending machine, but there is no social organization among them. If, however, these people decide to buy their own coffee-making machine and take turns making coffee for the group, there emerges social organization among them.

Note that the term *organization* can be used in either abstract or concrete sense. In an abstract sense, a business firm *has organization;* that is, its component parts are related to each other in a coordinated and purposive manner. The concrete object being thus organized is often referred to as *an organization.* For example, General Motors and the National Hockey League are concrete social organizations, and each of them has its own unique organization.

A nation's economic system consists of the patterns of interaction among the people (participants of the system) and their various groupings (i.e., social organizations such as business firms, households, schools, trade unions, and government agencies). We may now formally define the term *economic system* as follows: *An economic system is a complex of organizational patterns among individuals and groups engaged in activities of fulfilling human material needs.*

Note that an economic system is not synonymous with an *economy,* although the two terms are often used interchangeably. The concept of economic system does not entail tangible objects such as land, mineral deposits, or buildings. Rather, it refers to the ways people "do their economic things." For example, crude oil deposits are part of the Saudi Arabian *economy* but they are not included in the Saudi Arabian *economic system,* or the ways in which the Saudi Arabian economy is organized and managed. In this book, comparison is made between economic systems of different nations, not between *concrete national economies.* The latter belongs to the field of economic *area study.*

The Environment of an Economic System

An economic system is a subsystem within a larger framework of a social system. The other subsystems—for example, the political, educational, and legal systems—comprise the *environment* of the economic system. It is important that we understand well the nature of the relationships among these subsystems. Their interrelationships are like those among the electrical system, the fuel system, and the engine of an automobile; or among the muscular, nervous, and circulatory systems in a human body. Each of the social subsystems represents some aspect of the social system; they are coextensive with the latter. They are so intertwined with each other that they cannot function individually. For example, the human circulatory system cannot function without the muscular and nervous systems, and an automobile engine cannot work without the electrical and fuel systems. Similarly, we can analyze an economic system apart from other social subsystems only as a mental exercise; to be realistic, we must always keep in mind the close working relationships among the economic, political, educational, and other social subsystems.

The environment of an economic system shapes its character and affects its behavior and performance. It is important to remember that no economic system functions in a vacuum, and that the behavior and performance of a given economic system are really those of the total social system as they manifest themselves primarily in the economic sphere. The descriptions and discussions of the economic system's environment contained in the next three chapters, therefore, are not merely preliminary matters that need be disposed of before we get to the main part of this book; on the contrary, they are very much an integral part of our study of economic systems.

The Goals, Behavior, and Performance of an Economic System

Implicit in our definition of an economic system as a social organization is a realization that the actions of its participants (individuals and groups) are coordinated with purpose. The purpose of organized activity is to achieve certain goals or objectives of the organization. An organization's behavior, which is coordinated toward its goals with different degrees of efficiency, produces outcomes that can be evaluated to measure the performance of the system. The relationships among the various aspects of organizational behavior of an economic system are depicted in Figure 1–1.

The choice of *goals* for an economic system—what goals are included and how they are rank-ordered—depends on the values and ideologies of the participants of that system and the nature of the information they have concerning the system's environment. Given those goals, the system *behaves;* that is, it acts, chooses, and decides. Behavioral decisions may be strategic, tactical, or routine in nature, and range in type from a single act to policies, programs, and plans.

The system's decision-making behavior produces *outcomes*. The outcomes of a national economic system may be the level of output, the rate of price or output stability, the rate of employment of resources, the degree of national prestige and power, and so on. The outcomes of the organizational behavior of a business firm may include the rate of profits, the job security of its employees, the rate of increase in its sales volume, the price of its shares on the stock market, and so forth.

A system's *performance* can be determined by evaluating its outcomes by reference to the *performance criteria*, which are derived from the goals of the system. For example, if rapid industrialization is the

FIGURE 1–1   The goals, behavior, and performance of an economic system

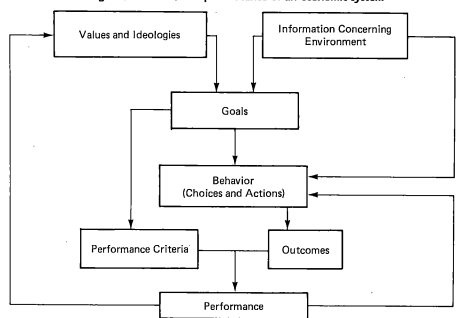

goal of a national economic system, an annual rate of increase of 10 percent in industrial production may be accepted by the participants in the system as a standard of excellence. If the actual outcome of the system's behavior is anything less than this norm, then the system's performance can be said to be poor or substandard. The participants must take necessary measures—that is, change their behavior—to produce a better outcome. In other words, performance affects behavior through a feedback loop. Feedback from performance also affects values and ideologies, leading to revisions in goals.

Evaluation of the performance of a national economic system *as a whole* is beset with many practical, theoretical, and philosophical problems. In the first place, the economic system is not the only factor affecting the overall performance of a nation's economy. The level of the country's economic development, the quantity and quality of economic resources in the country, and the various social environment of the economic system—legal, ideological, political, cultural, and so on— all influence the total performance of the economy. Since all these factors are closely intertwined with the economic system and with each other in their operation, it is next to impossible to isolate the contribution of the economic system to the total performance of the economy. Second, we must recognize that a given economic system must pursue multiple goals simultaneously. Multiplicity of goals lead to multiplicity of performance criteria. For example, performance criteria that are considered important in most national economic systems include, among others, efficiency in resource allocation, rate of growth of output, degree of consumer satisfaction, economic freedom, pattern of income distribution, national security, and stability of output and prices. Evaluation of the total performance of a system is possible only if the relative importance of these criteria can be unequivocally established; that is to say, if all the criteria are unequivocally weighted and rank-ordered. Without such a ranking, it is impossible to determine whether or not a system that excels in criterion A but does poorly in criterion B is doing better or worse than another system that does well in criterion B but fails in criterion A. The ranking of various criteria, however, depends on the value preferences of the evaluator, and, as such, cannot be unequivocally established by reference to rational calculus.

In this book we do not pursue the question of *total* performance of an economic (or social) system for the reasons discussed above. Instead, we shall use the term *performance* to mean the *specific* performance of a system, that is, evaluation of outcome by reference to a single performance criterion. For example, we may state that the Soviet economic system is performing poorly with respect to the criterion of allocative efficiency, or that the U.S. economic system has difficulties in maintaining a high level of employment. Such an evaluation is relatively free of the complexities discussed above since it only requires a societal agreement on the method of measuring an outcome by reference to a commonly accepted criterion.

The fact that a *comprehensive* evaluation of the performance of an economic system is virtually impossible does not mean, however, that comparing the performance of economic systems is a fruitless exercise. The performance of different systems can be meaningfully compared by reference to specific performance criteria. The difficulty associated with diverse preference standards can be minimized by approaching evaluation from the point of view of the cultural values of the evaluator. To illustrate, let us assume, for the sake of argument, that the United States economic system is experiencing a low rate of productivity gain (say, 1 percent per year), whereas in Japan the comparable rate is much higher (say, 4 percent per year). An American evaluator, following his or her own value preferences, *may* conclude that the Japanese system is performing better than the American system as far as this specific performance criterion is concerned. This does not necessarily mean that a Japanese evaluator views Japan's productivity performance superior or regards the rate of productivity gain as an important criterion in gauging the performance of an economic system. Certainly neither the Americans nor the Japanese can conclude that the Japanese system performs better, overall, than the American system; this is because of the problems of weights and rank-orders of multiple performance criteria and of the noneconomic factors affecting the performance, as discussed earlier.

Single-criterion comparison of different economic systems is useful if the evaluator interprets the result carefully by making judicious allowances for the noneconomic factors influencing the performance. For example, in our present illustration involving the difference in productivity gain between the United States and Japan, the American evaluator can ask what factors, in each country, are responsible for the respective outcomes, and which of these factors are specific to the economic and the noneconomic aspects of the two social systems. If, after due allowances are made for all the noneconomic factors, there still exists a residual difference in performance that can only be explained by differences in the economic systems, the evaluator can then ask why such a difference exists. Although comparisons based on specific performance criteria cannot resolve the question of superiority of one economic system to another, they nonetheless are quite helpful, if done judiciously, in suggesting ways of improving one system by borrowing some features from other systems.

ORGANIZATIONAL STRUCTURE

Most social structures are organizational in character. For example, the structure of a business firm involving the relationships between superior and subordinate and between divisions and departments is purposeful and coordinated. Hence the firm is said to be *organized*, and the structure of this organization is referred to as *organizational structure*.

The Three Dimensions
of Organizational Structure

Neuberger and Duffy, in what they call a decision-making approach to comparative economic studies, propose the use of a three-dimensional conceptual framework of organizational structure based on (1) the decision-making structure, (2) the motivation structure, and (3) the information structure.[2]

The *decision-making structure* of organization refers to the ways an organization's decision-making authority is allocated to its various participants (individuals and suborganizations). Who has authority over what types of decisions, who issues orders and who obeys them, and what the sources of decision-making authority are—these are the aspects of the decision-making structure. The authority relations between participating units give rise to a *hierarchy*, which is defined as individuals or organizations arranged in successive orders, with dependency or superior-subordinate relations between the orders. We find a hierarchy of constituent parts in a business corporation, ranging from the chief executive officer at the top down to the first-line operatives and clerical employees at the bottom. In the Soviet Union, the whole society is hierarchically structured, with the Politburo of the Communist party at the top and ordinary workers and peasants at the bottom.

The decision-making structure allocates decision-making authority to various participants within an organization. Each of the decision-making units makes decisions by exercising its authority, but also tries to influence other units' decisions to suit its own objectives. The acts of influencing others' decisions to suit one's own wishes by such means as coercion, moral suasion, and monetary rewards constitute the *motivation structure* of an organization.

The decision-making agents within an organization, having authority to make certain decisions as well as means to secure compliance

---

[2]Egon Neuberger and William J. Duffy, *Comparative Economic Systems: A Decision-Making Approach* (Boston: Allyn and Bacon, Inc., 1976), pp. 23–29.

of other agents with the decisions, need to have information concerning the system's environment and the actions of other decision-making agents in the system. The mechanism and channels for transmitting information among and within the participating units is called the *information structure*. It is the overall communications network within the organization.

In order for all the decision-making units within a social organization to make *rational* decisions—which are defined as decisions whose consequences best serve the overall interests of the organization—the decisions made by each unit must be *coordinated*. Coordination of decision making is necessary because the decisions of an organization's constituent parts are likely to be interrelated; that is, each part affects the choices of and consequences for all other parts. For example, if the Soviet steel mills do not produce enough steel to satisfy the combined needs for steel of the other industries, some steel users' choices will be adversely affected. Or, in a manufacturing firm, if one salesperson succeeds in getting a very large order, the consequences of the sales efforts of all other salespersons are likely to be poor. The information structure of the organization provides a mechanism for coordination of decisions.

The three aspects of organizational structure—decision making, motivation, and information—are closely intertwined. For example, if middle-level managers of a corporation are given authority to make substantive decisions on sales activities, but are not provided with sufficient information to make intelligent decisions and are not appropriately rewarded for making the right decisions for the company, they cannot be expected to make decisions that are in the best interest of the organization. In other words, there must exist a high degree of congruence among the three dimensions of organizational structure.

Vertical and Horizontal Organizational Structures

The relationship between the parts and the whole of a social organization is either vertical or horizontal in orientation.

A *vertical organizational structure* involves decision-making, motivation, and information structures aligned in a hierarchy, with high-echelon agents having authority to limit the decision-making authority of lower-echelon agents. This authority is naturally accompanied by the higher levels' authority to influence the motivation of the lower levels, as well as by vertical flows—up and down—of information. As noted earlier, the Soviet society is vertically organized. Vertical organization is also found in almost all productive enterprises in both capitalist and socialist countries.

In a vertically structured social organization, there often is found stratification of constituent parts. For example, we find the decision-making units in a large corporation hierarchically structured in three or four recognizable layers—for example, the top management, the middle management, the supervisory personnel, and the blue- and white-collar workers at the operating level. A national economic system, too, is stratified. At the top level of the hierarchy are the social organizations known as *ruling organizations.* These organizations issue rules that constrain the decisions of other participants in the system. The units and agencies of the government are ruling organizations in most countries. In the Soviet Union, the Communist party is an integral part of the country's ruling organizations. Moving down the hierarchy of a national economic system we find *middle-layer organizations* like enterprise groupings, producers' associations, professional associations, national trade unions, and other special interest groups. At the lowest level there are *basic organizations,* which include households, business firms, farms, hospitals, schools, agricultural cooperatives, and trade union locals.

A *horizontal organizational structure* exists when decision-making authority is not hierarchically arranged. For example, the three branches of the United States government—the executive, the legislative, and the judiciary—are related to each other in a circular and horizontal manner. Each has authority to constrain the others' decision-making authority, but this authority does not run in a one-way, downward direction. Another example of a horizontal organizational structure is found in the theoretical model of perfect competition in a market system. There, a large number of independent and autonomous decision makers constrain and motivate each other horizontally through relationships of voluntary exchange. Information also flows horizontally between the system's participants. When the market becomes imperfect, for example in a monopolistic or oligopolistic situation, vertical relationships develop between economic units of greater and lesser economic power.

Centralization, Decentralization, and Concentration

Centralization of decision making means that all the decisions in the system are made by a constituent part called the center. All the other participants, down the hierarchy, merely carry out, passively and mechanically, the orders emanating from the center. In a truly centralized form of authority structure, there is no room for decision making, even in the most trivial matters, at the lower levels.

The extreme opposite of perfect centralization is perfect *decentralization* where decisions are made autonomously by each and every constituent part of the organization. In making decisions, the participating units take into account only their own objectives, as well as the state of their environment. No directive is received from above. There is no vertical flow of information. There is no hierarchy in the structure of either decision-making authority or motivational control. The decision-making units, however, may exchange information and influence each other's motivation horizontally.

In real-life social organizations, particularly in very large social organizations like national economic systems, neither perfect centralization nor perfect decentralization is likely to be found. An actual economic organization is likely to have a mixed authority structure in that it exhibits a blend of centralization and decentralization in authority relations. Two types of the mixture may be identified.

In the first case, we start with a structure of complete centralization. Since it is technically not feasible for the center to make *all* decisions, it *delegates* decision-making authority to lower echelons of the hierarchy. In doing so, the center normally retains the relatively more important types of decisions. Broader, more general, and strategic decisions are retained by the center, and more specific, technical, and routine decisions are delegated downward. Often the decisions retained at the top (center) are the types that constrain or frame the decisions to be made by the lower units.

Downward delegation of decision-making authority is often a matter of dire technical necessity. Since a great deal of information is needed to execute directives from above, and since the center cannot have and provide all the required information in sufficient detail, considerations of efficiency dictate that lower-level units be given as much decision-making authority as possible without jeopardizing the center's control over the organization. This type of centralized structure may be called *centralization with downward delegation.*

In the second case, perfect decentralization is the starting point. The complexity of modern industrial organizations and economic systems make it next to impossible for the constituent parts to make all decisions autonomously. The need to delegate decision-making authority *upward* arises because many problems can be solved only through collective action.[3] For a variety of problems, collective and joint action by participating units is more economical than each unit trying to solve its own problems independently. For example, a group of farmers may form an agricultural cooperative that markets their products and purchases fertilizers and other inputs for all the members. Or individual manufacturers in a community who find it difficult to solve the problem of environmental pollution by themselves may form a suprafirm organ

---

[3]Holesovsky, *Economic Systems*, p. 22.

to which they delegate, upward, authority to compel individual producers to reduce the quantity of pollutants and to police violations of the antipollution rules. The economic systems of the Western, capitalist societies are largely based on this type of *decentralization with upward delegation of decision-making authority*.

A variant of the decentralization model—or perhaps it should be called a hybrid centralization decentralization model—is the *concentration* model. In industrial organization theory, we identify three basic types of market structure: monopoly, perfect competition, and oligopoly. Perfect centralization in organizational structure corresponds to perfect monopoly in industrial organization; perfect decentralization corresponds to perfect competition; and concentration corresponds to oligopoly. In the concentration model of organizational structure, we start with decentralization but recognize that for some economic reasons—for example, economies of scale—some economic decision-making units acquire concentrated economic (and perhaps political) power by growing larger or by merging or colluding with other units. Here and there, among a large number of decentralized economic decision makers, we find concentration of decision-making authority. If these large and powerful economic units merge into a single unit, then the economic system becomes centralized. If the centripetal move is blocked, say by an effective antitrust policy, the economic system is one with a concentrated but decentralized organizational structure. Most of the industrialized capitalist societies of the West today have this form of organization.

Sources of Decision-Making Authority

Why would some individuals and groups have authority to make decisions and enforce them over their subordinates? *Authority* is defined as *legitimate power* (see Chapter 4). What are the possible bases for such power? Neuberger and Duffy distinguish four *primary* sources of authority—tradition, coercion, ownership, and information—from *derived* sources based on delegation.[4]

Tradition and custom give some decision-making agents authority over others. For example, in a biological family, parents traditionally have authority to discipline their children. In a large Japanese corporation, much (but not all) of the authority of seniors over subordinates is based on the traditional respect for age and seniority.

Coercion—or constraint by threat or use of force—is another important source of authority. The monopoly of political power in the

---

[4]Neuberger and Duffy, *Comparative Economic Systems*, pp. 34–36.

Soviet Union by the Communist party is maintained by the coercive force of the police and the troops.

Property ownership is the major source of authority in the private sector of capitalist countries. Ownership gives owners the right to make decisions concerning the use and disposition of the property, as well as the right to enjoy the income from the property. The decision-making authority that the employer (or superiors in an enterprise) exercises over the employees (or subordinates) is based on the right of property ownership.

Another important source of authority is monopolization of specialized *information*. The decision-making authority of the group of specialists in professions—the group that John Kenneth Galbraith referred to as the *technostructure* (see Chapter 8)—is becoming increasingly more important with the advance of modern, complex technology of production and administration. In a large, technologically complex social organization like a large productive enterprise, the substantive decision-making authority based on tradition, coercion, and property becomes markedly weakened relative to the authority of the technostructure. For example, in the Soviet Union, the authority of party leadership is becoming increasingly eroded by the authority of the technostructure in the party administrative apparatus, the economic bureaucracy, and the military. In a large capitalist corporation, top management often yields in its decision making to the professional judgment of specialists in production, engineering, finance, and law. It is important to note, however, that the decision-making authority of those who have monopoly of information does not normally replace the authority of those who have power to make strategic decisions based on other sources. It is the *influence* of the technostructure over the substantive decision makers that is becoming increasingly great.

Some decision-making agents have authority that is not based directly on the four primary sources listed above, but is *delegated* to them by those who have primary authority. For example, hired professional managers of a large corporation who occupy the top management positions have authority over their subordinates not because of property ownership but because of the authority delegated downward to them by the shareholders. The authority that the middle managers exercise over their subordinates, in turn, is delegated to them by top management. In democratic societies, elected public officials exercise authority that is delegated upward to them by the electorate.

Motivation and Incentive Structures

We noted earlier that the structure of decision-making authority must be congruent with the structure of motivational control. What is the exact nature of the motivation structure in an organization? How can a decision-making agent manipulate the motivation of other agents so that they can be made to comply with the decisions made? In order to be able to answer these questions, it is necessary for us first to learn some basics of human motivation. As we shall discuss further in Chapter 3, human beings have both primary or biological needs (food, shelter, and so on) and secondary or social needs (security, social recognition, and so forth). In modern industrial societies where human biological needs are at least minimally satisfied, various forms of secondary or social needs become relatively more important as sources of human motivation. In concrete terms, the factors that motivate individual decision makers in modern industrial societies are likely to be some combinations of the following seven motives.

1. Coercion, or fear of being deprived of personal freedom
2. Social obligation, or fear of being rejected or ostracized by the group
3. Money and material privileges
4. Social recognition, or respect and approbation of peers
5. Power, or ability to influence others' choice and action
6. Self-achievement, or desire to actualize one's potential to the fullest extent
7. Group solidarity, or desire to contribute to the welfare of the group

Note that in the first six of these seven factors, the motivating force is egocentric or based on the self-interest of the decision-making agent.

Given these motivations of individual decision makers, how can another decision maker (the controlling agent) manipulate them in order to exercise control over them (the target agents)? Two means are available. First, the controlling agent can offer either positive or negative *incentives* to the target agents in order to influence their choice and/or behavior. For example, the top management may offer a bonus (a positive material reward) to middle managers in order to induce them to perform better. Or top management may threaten them with the possibility of a demotion or dismissal (a combination of negative incentives—coercion, loss of material privileges, loss of power, loss of face). Second, the controlling agent may try to change the motivations of the target agents from one of the egocentric motives (items 1 through 6 on the above list) to group solidarity (item 7). For example, Soviet leaders may appeal to nationalism and "socialist morality" of Soviet workers, or Japanese managers may stress the importance of group harmony (*wa*) among the employees, in order to enhance their productivity. To the extent that such attempts are successful, the controlling agents need no longer be concerned with the workers' motivations since they would spontaneously make decisions that would serve the best interest of the collective.

The foregoing discussion brings us to the most important issue in the comparative study of economic systems, namely, that of *harmony of interests*. Casual empiricism suggests that individual decision makers tend to follow courses of action that serve their self-interests rather than the interests of other persons or groups. Under what circumstances, and for what reasons, would they be willing to sacrifice their own personal objectives for the larger objectives of their group or society? The reader will find that this question is the recurrent theme of the remainder of this book.

MANAGEMENT

In any social organization—be it a productive enterprise or a national economic system—the activities of the participants must be organized, planned, coordinated, and controlled by a ruling organization toward the achievement of common goals. This vital function of a social organization is called *management*. For a national economic system, the management function is called *government*, and the ruling organization is called *the government*. In a productive enterprise, the comparable terms are *management* and *the management*.

In studying national economic systems and their subsystems, it is useful to distinguish between three types or levels of management: enterprise management, industrial management, and macroeconomic (or macro-) management.

Enterprise management refers to the management of human activities in a productive enterprise. For the enterprise to succeed in achieving its goals, it is necessary that its goals be defined; that tasks be assigned; that authority and responsibility relations be clearly defined; that plans be formulated; that day-to-day activities be coordinated, controlled, and monitored; and that personnel be recruited, trained, motivated, evaluated, and rewarded. These functions of management are found in every production organization—large or small, capitalist or socialist.

Industrial management is defined as the management of the productive activities of a specific industry (e.g., steel industry, automobile industry, textile industry, and so on). The roles of senior industrial managers may be played by trade association officials, senior executives of leading corporations in the industry, or government officials.

Macroeconomic management refers to the management of economic activities of an entire national economy. The output of an economy (goods and services produced for consumption and investment) is a consequence of human efforts applied to the society's material and financial resources. For the system to succeed in achieving its goals, human activities throughout the economy must be organized, planned, coordinated, controlled, motivated, and rewarded. Government performs these functions by such means as laws, regulations, policies, plans, administrative guidances, taxes, subsidies, and so on. In capitalist societies, the degree of participation by representatives of private industries is, as a rule, considerable, but varies from country to country. In the Soviet-type socialist countries, enterprise and industrial managers are likely to be lower-level government officials. As such, their participation in the top-level management decision making is limited.

The pattern of interlocking of these three levels of economic management varies from country to country. For example, in the Soviet Union, the three levels of management form a continuum; both enterprise management and industrial management are submerged in macromanagement. For that reason, it makes little sense to try to differentiate between the three levels of management when we study the Soviet economic system. (Often the term *industrial management* is used to refer to the entire management system of the Soviet-type economic system.) In the United States, by contrast, industrial management is characteristically feeble, and macromanagement provides a constraining environment for enterprise management, which is responsible for the great bulk of economic decision making that takes place within the system. In Japan, the two lower levels of management are much more autonomous than their counterparts in the Soviet Union, but the three levels are rather smoothly integrated.

We stated earlier that every hierarchically structured organization is headed by a central, rule-making group called the ruling organization. The top management and/or the board of directors is the ruling organization of a large capitalist corporation, and the central government is the ruling organization of a nation-state. The ruling organization is the highest-level decision-making organization in the system, and, in that capacity, defines objectives and sets goals for the system. A question arises as to the underlying motives of the ruling group in setting goals for the organization as a whole. Are the members of the ruling organization motivated by their own individual or group self-interest, or are they sincerely trying to promote the overall interest of the social organization they head? In setting national objectives for the Soviet Union, are Soviet leaders genuinely concerned about the best interest of the Soviet people? Are the top managers of a U.S. corporation more interested in the welfare of the employees, consumers, and local residents than in their own bonuses and stock options when they make the company's investment and production decisions? These questions, of course, must be answered on a case-by-case basis. The point being made here, however, is merely that the goals that are set and the decisions that are made by the ruling group of a social organization may or may not be consistent with the general interest of the organization. Here, again, we encounter the issue of the possible conflict between individual self-interests and the general interest of the collective.

APPROACHES TO COMPARING
ECONOMIC SYSTEMS

There are many alternative approaches to the method of classifying and comparing national economic systems. Traditional methods of classifying national systems include capitalism-socialism and market-command dichotomies. The *market-oriented* economic systems are those in which horizontal economic relationships of voluntary exchange and individualized choice predominate. Very crudely put, *capitalism* is a market-oriented economic system in which productive properties are predominantly privatized and individualized. The *command-oriented* economic systems are those in which economic activities are organized predominantly along vertical lines of authority relationships between superiors and subordinates. Command-oriented economic systems combined with social ownership and control of productive assets are commonly referred to as *socialism.*

Setting aside the question of classificatory schemes for a moment, let us ponder the question of which, and how many, national economic systems can be compared most profitably in a comparative study such as this. Obviously, the greater the number of systems we compare, the greater the system-to-system variation, and therefore the more interesting the comparison will be. The larger the number, however, the more superficially each system must be treated. A shallow treatment of a large number of systems is not likely to produce a good understanding of the essential differences and similarities that exist among economic systems. Also, we must realize that there is a law of diminishing returns of a sort working in our endeavor. Beyond a certain point, each additional economic system introduced would give us progressively less additional insight.

For heuristic purposes, it is necessary to select a few important economic systems that are truly different from each other in terms of their key characteristics. Comparisons among those systems are more meaningful, the greater the range of variation they exhibit not only in economic traits but also in sociocultural, ideological, and political dimensions. These considerations have led to the selection of the United States, the Soviet Union, and Japan for comprehensive examination in this book. Besides being the three largest national economic units in the industrialized world today in terms of total national output, these three economies happen to differ from each other in most fundamental ways.

According to the generally accepted scheme of classifying economic systems, we may label both the American and the Japanese systems as market-oriented, capitalist economies, and the Soviet system as command-oriented socialism. Applying a common label of "market-oriented, capitalist economies" to the economic systems of both the United States and Japan, however, involves a very serious oversimplification of the important differences between the two systems. On the level of *political economy*, the two systems appear very much alike. On the *sociocultural* level, however, the two are poles apart. Whereas American capitalism is rooted in individualism, the Japanese variety of capitalism exhibits strong characteristics of groupism. It is the central theme of this book that this individualism-groupism dichotomy observed within the capitalist world is just as important and crucial to our understanding of economic systems as the capitalism-socialism or market-command dichotomy.

In the following three chapters, we shall examine some of the more important environmental factors of the economic systems of the United States, the Soviet Union, and Japan (hereafter referred to simply as "the three economic systems"). These environmental factors include values and ideologies, social relations, social stratification, the educational system, and the political system. In the six chapters of Part 2 we shall describe and analyze, on a country-by-country basis, the organization and management of the three economic systems on both the national and enterprise levels. Part 3 will have a freer form, presenting some selected topics and concluding remarks.

BRIEF HISTORIES OF SOVIET RUSSIA AND JAPAN

An awareness of what has taken place in the past is indispensable for a good understanding of what is happening now. For this reason, it is advisable that the readers be familiar with at least the main currents of the histories of Soviet Russia and Japan (and, of course, the United States) over the last century or so. Unfortunately, to provide an adequate account of the histories of these countries would require too much of the book's limited space. Those readers who are unfamiliar with the recent histories of the Soviet Union and Japan are urged to look up some introductory materials in a library. Encyclopedias often provide brief but quite adequate accounts of a nation's history. Introductory books on Soviet and Japanese societies and economies usually have a good summary of the country's history.

In what follows we present very brief historical surveys of Russia and Japan over the last few centuries. Only the topics that have a bearing on what appears in this book are discussed. Non-American readers who have little or no knowledge of the history of the United States are similarly urged to familiarize themselves with a rudimentary knowledge of American history.

A Brief History of Soviet Russia

Russia before the Revolutions of 1917 was basically a feudal state with a large peasant population and a small minority of landed nobility. Agriculture was primitive and its productivity was low, and even among the peasants there was a wide variation in living standards. Although serfdom was officially abolished in 1861, many peasants in the early 1900s lived a wretched life not much better than that of a serf. The seeds of Russian industrialization had been planted by Peter the Great (1689–1725) in the early eighteenth century. Prompted by a desire to modernize Russia and build up its military strength, Peter undertook an ambitious industrialization program utilizing imported technologies and technicians. This tradition lasted until the end of the tsarist period, with the Russian industry being developed primarily in heavy industries, serving military needs, under a predominance of foreign investments and technologies. There was, however, little development of small and middle-scale light industries serving domestic needs of finished manufactured goods. Nor was there an accompanying development of a prosperous middle class. The living conditions of urban Russian workers were very low by the Western standards of the time. In the 1890s, Russia's economy grew spectacularly, spurred by railway construction and development in related industries of coal, iron, oil, and steel. Thus, in spite of the unbalanced industrial growth and the dire poverty of the large agrarian and urban masses, the Russian economy on the eve of the 1917 revolutions was one that had already completed its economic "takeoff."

The political instability rooted in antitsarist sentiment came to the surface with the humiliation of the Russian defeat in the Russo-Japanese War of 1905, and contributed to the worsening of conditions in Russia. The tsarist regime was overthrown in the March (1917) Revolution staged largely by moderate revolutionaries. The aspirations of peasants and urban workers coupled with deteriorating economic conditions resulted in conditions of chaos and disorder during the year. In November 1917, the Bolsheviks, led by Lenin, staged a successful coup d'état and seized power.

The Civil War that erupted after the Bolshevik takeover and the military intervention by the capitalist powers compelled the new Bolshevik government to adopt a series of extreme economic measures known as War Communism. All factories and trading were nationalized, and all market transactions based on money were replaced by direct decrees by the government. The economy nearly broke down, generating serious inflationary pressures. Food supplies were requisitioned by force from peasants so that soldiers and industrial workers could be fed. By the end of the Civil War in 1921, conditions had deteriorated so much that strikes and uprisings were increasingly common.

In 1921, Lenin made a complete turnaround and reinstated the market mechanism in a program known as the New Economic Policy (NEP). The free markets were restored in all aspects of the Soviet economic life. Small business firms were denationalized, and the remaining nationalized firms were made free to follow market signals. The NEP was highly successful in restoring order to the Soviet economy and preparing it for further development. Naturally the basically "capitalist" nature of the NEP was not received well by many of the ideological purists among the Communists, and a Great Industrialization Debate raged among the top leaders of the party during most of the 1920s. The leftists (the superindustrializers) argued that an all-out effort to industrialize the country was the only sensible strategy for the country, which was being plagued by the continued threat of foreign intervention and the peasants' refusal to provide enough food to the new regime. The rightists (the moderates) argued that the NEP should be continued indefinitely, and that the country should be developed under a program of mixed public and private initiatives. They advocated motivating peasants and workers with material incentives. In the midst of the debate, Lenin died in 1924.

The question of the post-NEP developmental strategy was decided by Joseph Stalin who ruled the country as dictator from 1928 until his death in 1953. Stalin adopted the superindustrialization route, and ordered collectivization of peasants in 1929 while launching the First Five-Year Plan. Peasants fought back the collectivization drive bitterly, and millions of them were shot or exiled to Siberia. Stalin also eliminated a large number of his political enemies. The bloody and costly methods used by Stalin, however, accomplished one thing: they completely eliminated political opposition to his total control over the Soviet society and economy. Using this power of control, Stalin succeeded in turning the Soviet economy into the world's second largest industrial power by the eve of World War II.

Nikita Khrushchev who led the Soviet oligarchy during the period between 1955 and 1964 denounced Stalinist excesses and introduced some half-hearted and confusing reform measures. His overambitious promises and disorganized reorganizations of the economic system became the main causes of his downfall in 1964. Leonid Brezhnev, who succeeded Khrushchev and stayed in power until his death in 1982, was able to remain in power for so long largely by not rocking the boat. Brezhnev "bought" the support of the party functionaries, government bureaucrats, and military leaders by giving them a great deal of power and privilege. Yuri Andropov and Konstantin Chernenko who succeeded

Brezhnev did not live long enough to leave their imprints on the power structure of the Soviet system. The new leader, Mikhail Gorbachev, appears to be consolidating power smoothly, but he seems to face heavy odds in trying to bring about fundamental reforms in the Soviet economic system.

A Brief History of Japan

Japan in the 1500s was a centralized feudal state, with the emperor residing in the ancient capital city of Kyoto without exercising real power of control over the nation. The country was divided into a number of military camps controlled by warring lords and fighting chronic civil wars among themselves. In 1600, one of the warring lords, Ieyasu Tokugawa, won a decisive battle and unified the country. Three years later, Ieyasu was granted the title of *shogun* (hereditary military governor) by the emperor, thereby launching 250 years of peace, law, and order in Japan under the Tokugawa Shogunate.

With its capital in Edo (now Tokyo), the Tokugawa Shogunate maintained a tight control over all aspects of the country's social life through a rigid system of centralized feudalism. The country was divided into about 270 provinces, each of which was ruled by a feudal lord who pledged allegiance to the shogun. Each of the provinces was in turn ruled by the lord and his clan with their own systems of centralized administration. The shogunate government's primary objective was to perpetuate the Tokugawa family's control over the country by preserving the status quo of the social order. It imposed a rigid classification of the population into four hereditary social classes: the warrior-bureaucrat (samurai), the peasant, the artisan, and the merchant. Particularly, the distinction between the samurai class and the three commoner classes was enforced strictly by government decrees prescribing permissible manners, articles of clothing, and foods that could be consumed for members of each social class. The samurai, who, with their families, comprised about 6 percent of the population of the country, constituted the elite class of the Tokugawa Japan. The tradition of centralized decision making by the state over the nation's economic activities was firmly established during the 250 years of the Tokugawa rule.

Although stability in social order was maintained during the Tokugawa period by the government's rigid socioeconomic policies, the era was by no means without significant social changes. Particularly noteworthy was growth and maturity in the fields of education, commerce, and arts and crafts.

The *terakoya*, or "temple school for children," was widespread throughout the country toward the end of the Tokugawa period. In these schools children of commoners, between the ages of 7 and 10, received rudimentary training in reading, writing, and arithmetic. Three quarters of the schools had enrollments of fewer than 50 children. People from a variety of walks of life served as teachers of the terakoya. As a result of terakoya education, about a quarter of children in Japan at the end of the Tokugawa period had elementary reading, writing, and arithmetic skills.[5]

The *hanko*, or "provincial school for samurai youths," was a school established in a feudal province by the clan administration for the purpose of educating the clan's youths in Chinese classics, particularly in the classics of Confucianism. By the end of the Tokugawa era, over 200 of the feudal provinces had a hanko in their castle towns. These schools were modeled after the shogunate's own school of Confucian studies, the Confucian Academy. The curriculum in the hanko also included studies in Japanese classics and medicine.

At the beginning of the Tokugawa era, the great majority of samurai were illiterate. By 1850, however, as a result of hanko education, virtually every member of this class was not only literate but was also familiar with the rudiments of Chinese and Japanese classics.

As each of the feudal clans was required by the shogunate to maintain its formal residence in Edo, there developed a huge consumption culture in that city. About one-half of the population of Edo, which approached 1 million at the end of the Tokugawa period, making it the largest city in the world, was samurai and their families. To support its official residence in Edo, each feudal clan sold rice in the national rice market located in the seaport city of Osaka. A nationwide system of commodity and money exchanges developed with centers in Edo and Osaka. To support the nearly half a million nonproductive samurai population in Edo, there developed a culture of conspicuous consumption requiring the services of a large number of artisans and craftsmen. Many large merchant houses emerged in Edo, Osaka, and other large cities, and by the end of the Tokugawa period much of the economic power of the samurai class had shifted to the emerging merchant class.

In spite of the increasing commercialization of the national economy, the conservative shogun government tried to maintain the status quo by policies of continuing static feudal controls. The dynamic pressures of economic change had become so strong by the middle of the nineteenth century that the Tokugawa government began to lose effective control over the country. Finally, in 1867, a coalition of several progressive clans openly challenged the hegemony of the Tokugawa family by advocating the restoration of the imperial rule. After a brief

[5]Susumu Ono, "The Japanese Language and Modernization in Japan," *Look Japan*, May 10, 1979, p. 14.

civil war, the Tokugawa Shogunate fell. The imperial rule was restored, and the nation under the young emperor Meiji launched on a massive industrialization program under the slogan of "rich country, strong military." To catch up with the West in science, technology, and industrial production became a national obsession.

Upon defeat in the Pacific War in 1945, Japan was occupied by the Allied Forces headed by General Douglas MacArthur. The Allied Occupation, which lasted nearly seven years, brought to the country many sweeping reforms that would have been impossible if the nation had been left to its own devices. The country was "democratized" both politically and economically. A new constitution, drafted by the Americans and adopted by the Japanese parliament, declared the equality of men and women and renounced "war as a sovereign right of the nation and the threat or use of force as a means of settling international disputes" (Article 9).

During the 20-year period between the end of the Allied Occupation in 1952 and the early 1970s, Japan's economy, blessed with a stable political environment under the conservative government and the free-trade environment abroad, achieved a spectacular growth that came to be known as "the Japanese miracle." Sometime toward the end of the 1960s, Japan became the world's third largest economic unit, surpassed only by the United States and the Soviet Union. In terms of total output per capita, Japan now far exceeds the Soviet Union. Japan's industrial success, however, began to generate frictions with its trading partners starting in the 1960s, and the situation appears to be getting worse in the 1980s.

The series of "oil shocks" of the 1970s jolted the complacency of the Japanese who realized the fragility of their mammoth economic machine built on the foundation of scarcity of natural resources and a heavy reliance on overseas markets. Under the pressures of high costs of energy and environmental protection, the growth rate of the economy has slowed down noticeably in the late 1970s and into the 1980s.

QUESTIONS

1. What does a *system* consist of? What is the relationship between a system and its environment? How do the relationships *among* the constituent parts of a system differ from those *between* the constituent parts *and* the elements outside the system?

2. Consider the circulatory system of a human body. What is its environment? What does the environment consist of? What are the constituent parts of the circulatory system? Is it possible to study the circulatory system without understanding how the collateral systems in the environment work? Does a change in the muscular system affect the functioning of the circulatory system?

3. Answer Question 2 by replacing the following words: *circulatory* by *economic, human body* by *society,* and *muscular* by *political.*

4. For each of the following social organizations, lettered (a) through (f), give examples of (i) *values or ideologies,* (ii) a *goal* chosen under the given values or ideologies, (iii) a *behavior* toward the chosen goal, and (iv) an *outcome* of the behavior: (a) the American political system, (b) the Ford Motor Company, (c) a mom and pop grocery store, (d) a college economics course, (e) a local television station, (f) a student body government.

5. In a social organization is it possible for information to flow horizontally toward or away from the center? Is it possible for decision-making authority to be structured horizontally?

6. Do you visualize the American business community as forming a pyramidlike hierarchy with small firms at the bottom and smoothly integrated upward toward the center (top) where the ruling business organization speaks with one voice with the center of public power? What difficulties do you have with this description?

7. Describe the three dimensions of organizational structure (decision making, motivation, and information) for each of the following social organizations: (a) a college economics course; (b) a family consisting of the parents and two teenagers, organized to execute household chores; and (c) the U.S. Federal Reserve System, organized to execute monetary policy.

8. Describe the sources of each of the following types of authority: (a) college professors over their students, (b) parents over their children, (c) prison guards over prisoners, (d) plant manager over blue-collar workers, and (e) farmer over hired hands.

9. What is the difference between a *motive* and an *incentive?*

10. In what sense is the word *management* used in this book? If the American economic system were perfectly competitive with a large number of small buyers and sellers competing with one another, would it be possible for us to use the expression "the management of the U.S. economic system"? (Make your own assumption about the role of government in this competitive economy.) How about the expression "the organization of the U.S. economic system"?

11. What do you think are the advantages and disadvantages of organizing a study of comparative economic systems using the following conceptual frameworks: (a) capitalism versus socialism, (b) market versus planning, (c) centralized versus decentralized decision-making systems?

12. What do you think Holesovsky means by his sentence, "Relativity leads to rationality"?

SELECTED READING

ECKSTEIN, ALEXANDER, Ed. *Comparison of Economic Systems: Theoretical and Methodological Approaches.* Berkeley, Calif.: University of California Press, 1971.

GROSSMAN, GREGORY. *Economic Systems* (2nd ed.). Englewood Cliffs, N.J.: Prentice-Hall, Inc., 1974.

HOLESOVSKY, VACLAV. *Economic Systems: Analysis and Comparison.* New York: McGraw-Hill Book Company, 1977.
NEUBERGER, EGON, and WILLIAM J. DUFFY. *Comparative Economic Systems: A Decision-Making Approach.* Boston: Allyn and Bacon, Inc., 1976.

CHAPTER 2

Value Orientations
and
Ideologies

The organization, behavior, and performance of an economic system are decisively affected by the culture of the society in which it exists. *Culture* is defined as the sum total of learned behavior that is inherited by communicative interaction and shared by the members of a society. Specifically, culture includes values, norms, beliefs, attitudes, knowledge, arts, myths, customs, rituals, and technologies of a given society. Broadly defined, it is the socially inherited way of life of a people.

Of all the elements of culture, of particular interest to us are value orientations and a special type of value orientation known as ideology. Value and ideological orientations of a given society are perhaps the most important determinants of the nature of the relationships between the individual and society, and therefore of the ways in which that society's economic systems—both macro and micro—are organized and managed.

VALUES, BELIEFS, ATTITUDES,
AND IDEOLOGIES

A value *orientation*, a value *system*, and a value *complex* are all used to mean the same thing—a complex of values with associated beliefs and attitudes. A special type of value orientation is called *ideology*. Each of these concepts will be briefly explained below.

Values

A *value* is any end or means that is regarded as desirable. It is a general and abstract principle—or standard of desirability—that guides human choice and action. Efficiency, stability, wealth, beauty, power, freedom, equality, justice, honesty, courage, human life, and achievement are examples of values that are regarded highly in many societies.

Some values represent goals and purposes of individuals and societies, while others are related to the means by which the ends are pursued. Freedom, justice, and peace are examples of goal or end values; whereas cooperation, due process, and organizational growth are examples of values that are related to means. These two types of values— goal values and instrumental values—are often difficult to distinguish from each other since some means are pursued as worthy goals while some goals are pursued as the means to yet other, more important goals. For example, rapid industrialization—which is essentially a means by which achievement of some goal values may be facilitated—is often pursued as a goal in its own right. On the other hand, such values as power, wealth, and autonomy may be pursued in order to facilitate the realization of yet other goals.

Personal values, when shared by a number of individuals, become group (or community or social) values. Social values exist in a hierarchy, with values rank-ordered along a continuum from the most important (dominant) to the least important (subordinate) values. Dominant values are those that are shared by the majority of people with a high degree of intensity over a considerable length of time. To identify the dominant values of a nation is to describe its national character. For example, competition and personal achievement are dominant American values, whereas cooperation and group harmony are subordinate values. In Japan, by contrast, cooperation and harmony are dominant values.

Beliefs

A *belief* is what people accept as true or real about the world around them; it is their *perception* of how the world actually is. A belief may be an uncritical conviction; that is, it may not pass the test of a critical examination. That God exists is a belief; that God does not exist also is a belief. To say that one cannot tell whether God exists or not is a belief, too. Some may believe that the earth is flat, while others may be convinced that free trade benefits the national economy.

Values and beliefs interact with each other. A value may distort the perception (belief) of those who embrace the value. For example, domestic producers who value the welfare of their industry more highly than that of consumers in general may believe that imports hurt the national economy. The converse may also be true; a belief—critical or uncritical—may lead to a value. Those who believe in life after death may value salvation of the soul. (If there were no life after death, there would be no soul to save.) Values and beliefs are thus closely intertwined in a given value-belief complex; it is often impossible to determine the cause-and-effect direction between the two.

Attitudes

An *attitude* is a predisposition of mind to respond, favorably or unfavorably, to a specific object or situation. Examples of attitudes include ethnocentrism, skepticism, extremism, sexism, racism, idealism, as well as predispositions toward such controversial issues as private property, capital punishment, abortion, divorce, religion, and deficit spending.

An attitude is broader in concept than an opinion, which is a concrete expression on a specific issue or question. An attitude, on the other hand, is narrower than a value; whereas a value is a general principle whose application transcends specific objects or situations, an attitude concerns a specific object or situation. The nature of predisposition is determined by the values and beliefs that are embodied in a given attitude. If my *attitude* toward cats is so hostile as to cause me always to act meanly toward them, that may be because I *value* loyalty highly and I *believe* cats are not loyal to their human masters.

Ideologies

The term *ideology* has been used in a bewildering variety of ways by different writers. The narrowest of the definitions sees an ideology as a concrete program or plan for political action. The broadest equates ideology with value orientation. The meaning of the word used in this book falls somewhere between these polar definitions.

We define an ideology as *a value orientation that advocates or legitimizes a relationship of political power and/or economic interests between social groups.* Here, a *social group* may consist of but one individual, or may be as large as the entire humanity. Proponents of liberalism as an ideology, for example, advocate that society should not interfere with the free choice and action of individuals. "The American way" as an ideology is a complex of many ideologies and value orientations, notable among which are individualism, pluralism, democracy, and free enterprise. Running through these values and ideologies is a common theme concerning the place of the individual in society. Marxism as an ideology originally advocated that the propertyless majority should strive to gain control over the capitalist minority because the economic interests of the two classes were deemed fundamentally at odds with each other. Marxism in the Soviet Union today is used by the Soviet power elite to legitimize its exercise of total power over the rest of the population. When we speak of the management ideology of Ford Motor Company, we refer to the quality of authority relationships between the management and its various constituencies as legitimized by the management.

In all the examples of ideology given above, we find that political and/or economic relationships between social groups are promoted, justified, rationalized, or legitimized. The persuasive or promotional effect of an ideology is aimed not only at the members of a group whose interests are being served, but also at individuals in other groups. In the case of Marxism in the Soviet Union today, an ideology is advanced by one group (the power elite) to be believed by individuals in other groups (the populace), who thereby unintentionally serve the interests of the elite.

An ideology is a rather loosely organized, open-ended complex of values, beliefs, and attitudes. It is basically a value system, except that it has a unique effect of guiding and inspiring individuals and groups in their collective choice and action. A value system that is merely held or shared by people becomes an ideology when it is endowed with an advocative quality. For example, racism may be a simple value orientation, but it becomes racist *ideology* when racist values, beliefs, and attitudes are appealed to with the intent of advocating a certain action either for or against a specific racial group, or of legitimizing certain power relationships between racial groups.

An ideology does not always have a logically consistent and self-contained structure. Its components may be only moderately coherent. The beliefs and attitudes embodied in a given ideology may be less than totally rational. Its cognitive content—that is, the knowledge it contains about reality—may be nothing but what its adherents perceive, or want others to perceive, to be the reality. Often it is the emotive content of the ideology that works as a glue to hold together its illogical, irrational, and deceptive elements.

Ideologies vary greatly in size and complexity. Some ideologies—for example, Marxism, democracy, and capitalism—are large and well-articulated systems of values that transcend single societies. At the other end of the scale are the narrowly circumscribed "miniideologies" of specific social groups or organizations, such as the ideology of faculty-student relationships in a high school or the management ideology of a corporation.

In the remainder of this chapter, the major value and ideological orientations of the United States, Japan, and the Soviet Union will be examined. We shall find that, among these three societies, not only does the nature of values and ideologies differ greatly from society to society, but the relationships between each society's major values and ideologies also vary markedly.

THE VALUES AND IDEOLOGIES
OF THE UNITED STATES

The dominant values of U.S. society are individualism, equality, competition, and personal achievement. These value orientations have produced uniquely American ideologies of pluralistic democracy, liberal capitalism, and a brand of nationalism called "the American way of life." (In this book when we use the words *America* and *American* we are referring to the United States and its people, customs, and economy-related factors.)

Individualism

At the heart of American value and ideology systems is the supreme virtue of individualism. *Individual* freedom, responsibility, achievement, competition, equality, and creativity—these are fundamental values that guide choices and actions of Americans in their social, economic, and political relations. Conversely, Americans tend to reject collectivism of all sorts; unitary government, centralized public power, and concentrated business power are anathemas to the American vision.

Individuals are the basic units of society, which is nothing but an aggregation of individuals. Society is viewed merely as a means by which individuals realize their objectives. All individuals are considered intrinsically of supreme worth, and therefore as morally equal. The notion of equality of individuals may also be traced to America's Puritan background: if all individuals are equal before God, then they must be equal to each other. Each individual must earn salvation of his or her soul through hard work and self-realization.

Success in the American context means the success of an individual, not of a group. Both successes and failures are ultimately attributed to individuals; they, and not any groups, are ultimately responsible for their actions.

Since individuals know their conditions, capabilities, and preferences better than anyone else, their interests are best served if they are left free to pursue their own objectives. Any control exercised over them by society diminishes the welfare of society. Free competition among self-reliant individuals results in their personal fulfillment and maximum social well-being. These views were given moral assurance by Adam Smith's theories. In *The Wealth of Nations*, published in 1776,

Smith convincingly demonstrated that the sum total of all individuals pursuing their own self-interests results in the greatest collective good. The belief in the efficacy and moral superiority of free exchange has produced a strong bias for the free-enterprise system with a minimum of government intervention.

The belief in the moral equivalence of all individuals leads to the ideology of political democracy, which accords to each individual an equal right to participate in the decisions of government. The stress on individuals' freedom of choice and action leads to the ideology of political liberty with emphases on limited government and the due process of law. The principle of inviolability of the individual accords to individuals certain basic rights, including the right to life, property, dignity, and privacy. The belief in the supremacy of individualized choice and action leads to a strong commitment to the ideology of political and economic pluralism that rejects centralized and concentrated power, both public and private.

These are the basic elements of the individualistic value orientation of the American people. Although it is true that not all Americans embrace all of these tenets with equal intensity, it is also true that the overwhelming majority of Americans are strongly affected—consciously or otherwise—by the individualistic way of thinking in their personal and social behavior.

Individualism as a social and political philosophy first emerged in seventeenth-century England in the writings of Thomas Hobbes and John Locke. In the eighteenth century, this philosophy found its fullest expression in Adam Smith's doctrine of the "invisible hand." The term *individualism*, however, did not appear in use until the middle of the nineteenth century. Most writers credit a work by the French historian–political scientist Alexis de Tocqueville, *Democracy in America*, published in 1880, as its birthplace, although other writers in France and Germany had used the term earlier.[1] It is worth noting that the term individualism became part of the vocabulary of the English language as a result of its use by Tocqueville in describing what he considered to be the central element of America's national character. Whereas individualism was observed in some aspects of social and personal behavior in Europe, nowhere else but in America was it a dominant national value orientation. The individualism Tocqueville found in America was a totally new type of individualism—an indigenous American variety; it was not the European variety transplanted in the New World.

One possible reason for the uniqueness of American individualism was suggested by historian Frederick Jackson Turner. According to Turner,

---

[1] Yehoshua Arieli, *Individualism and Nationalism in American Ideology* (Cambridge, Mass.: Harvard University Press, 1964), p. 194.

what gave American individualism its ruggedness was the frontier experience of the American people. Turner vividly described American individualism as follows:

> That coarseness and strength combined with acuteness and inquisitiveness; that practical, inventive turn of mind, quick to find expedients; that masterful grasp of material things, lacking in the artistic but powerful to effect great ends; that restless, nervous energy; that dominant individualism, working for good and for evil, and withal that buoyancy and exuberance which comes with freedom—these are traits of the frontier, or traits called out elsewhere because of the existence of the frontier.[2]

Conflicts between Individualism and Collectivism

The balance between the natural rights of the individual and the political authority of the collective—or the balance between private initiative and public power—is a central problem of political philosophy. The ideology that is diametrically opposed to individualism is *collectivism*, which sees the individual as being subordinate to a social collectivity such as a corporation or the nation-state. By value and ideological orientation, Americans are born individualists; collectivism is fundamentally alien to their way of thinking.

In a modern, complex society, however, it is not possible to remain ideological purists. Human activities seldom take place in isolation; many of the activities take place in a community of one type or another ranging from a family to a nation. And many of the problems that arise in the process are shared, community-wide problems. For their solution, individual actions working through the market are often inadequate or sometimes even harmful to the collective interest; community-wide problems require community-wide (i.e., collective) solutions. To act collectively, however, individuals must surrender a certain amount of decision-making power to the collective. Herein lies the fundamental dilemma of American social organization. The real issue is not that Americans must choose between pure individualism and total collectivism but, rather, the character, extent, and means of individual participation in collective problem solving.

What the United States needs is to find an *optimum mix* of individualism and collectivism. There are two alternative paths leading from atomistic to collective social organization. One is the vertical path. Society can be organized in a pyramidlike hierarchy with a ruling group

---

[2]Frederick Jackson Turner, *Frontier and Section* (Englewood Cliffs, N.J.: Prentice-Hall, Inc., 1961), p. 61.

on the top and the masses at the bottom, and the dictates of those in positions of authority can flow downward from the top through the hierarchical channel of command. This is basically how large American corporations are organized. The complexity of modern industrial society requires that the national economy, too, be organized in this vertical manner for at least some of its functions. The underlying ideological bias toward individualism dictates that in the United States the use of hierarchical organization and upward delegation of decision-making authority be kept to an absolute minimum.

The second path from the individual to the collective is more congruous with the basic ideological orientation of American society. This is the horizontal path. Individuals can strengthen their ties with their communities and the nation by forming horizontal networks of communication, cooperation, and exchange. The complexity of modern technologies may require that the decentralized networks of horizontal decision making develop subcenters of concentrated economic power here and there, but the individualistic bias again dictates that the relationships among these subcenters of power be horizontal and decentralized. As we shall see in a later chapter, the organizational structure of the American politico-economic system is a mixture of vertical pyramiding and horizontal networking, with the latter predominating and making a minimum concession to the former.

American Ideology
and Nationalism

Foreigners who observed the American republic in its early years, including Alexis de Tocqueville, asked how it was possible for the fiercely individualistic Americans with diverse cultural backgrounds to forge a new nation of a high degree of unity and solidarity. Tocqueville's answer was that it was democracy that gave cohesion and unity to the nation.[3] Yehoshua Arieli, in his 1964 book, took Tocqueville's idea a step further and argued that American ideals of individualism, democracy, and free enterprise are, at the same time, the very essence of American *nationalism*. Nationalistic fervor in all other lands draws its strength from parochial, ethnic, and geographic values and beliefs. Nationalism in America, by contrast, is a set of *universal principles*. Such ideological systems as socialism, communism, and Marxism are also sets of universal principles, but they are not limited by national boundaries or interests. Only in the United States do ideology and nationalism coincide. "*This coincidence . . . ,*" concludes Arieli, "*is the fundamental datum of American nationality and of the structure of its consciousness.*"[4] Ac-

---

[3]Arieli, *Individualism and Nationalism*, p. 20.
[4]Ibid., p. 25. Arieli's italics.

cording to Arieli's thesis, then, individualistic Americans are willing to uphold a collective—the American nation-state—for the very reason that that collective has been created for the purpose of protecting the individual.

This coincidence of ideology and nationalism in the United States is one of the most significant facts of our time. For the first time in the history of human society, there has emerged a nation-state that is a "personification" of a set of universal principles. To be a good American is to believe in these principles—the American way. By contrast, to be a good Soviet citizen is to be loyal to the party, and to be a good Japanese is to observe the rules of social behavior. In this sense, then, we can say that the United States in its makeup is more ideological than the Soviet Union or Japan.

THE VALUES AND IDEOLOGIES OF JAPAN

The fundamental difference between the American and Japanese world outlook centers on two interrelated dichotomies in social philosophy—individualism versus collectivism and universalism versus particularism. As we observed in the preceding section, individualism is the basic tenet of American ideology. *Universalism* is a corollary of individualism. As we shall see in Chapter 3, universalism in social relations means that individuals are, and should be, related to each other on the basis of a set of universal principles such as promises, contracts, or business dealings, and not by particularistic considerations as loyalty, love, or blood relations.

The individualistic and universalistic world outlook is alien to the group-oriented Japanese. In Japan, a person's self-image is defined by his or her identification with a group. Groups, too, are identified by their affiliation with larger groups. All the individuals and groups, if they are Japanese, are ultimately identified with the largest group—the nation-state of Japan. For the members of a group, the group's goals take precedence over their private goals. A group's values are the highest values for its members, and devotion and loyalty to one's group is the highest value in Japanese society. Since a group's values are the highest values, and since the nation is the largest group, there is no room for any alien values to take precedence over the indigenous values of the Japanese nation. The Japanese national consciousness is impervious to any universal principles that transcend the highest national values.

The origins of the group orientation of the Japanese people can be traced back to the economic hardships their ancestors suffered in trying to eke out a meager output from the limited natural resources. In peasant farming in rural villages where starvation was a constant threat, cooperation and mutual aid was often the only way of escaping mass starvation. There was little room for individualism to thrive under these circumstances. Aversion to conflicts within a group, hostility to outsiders, and fierce rivalry with other groups are collateral consequences of the paucity of natural resources. This explanation of Japan's groupism, it may be noted, is the direct opposite of Turner's frontier thesis accounting for American individualism.

Familism

If the national character of Americans is defined essentially by individualism, the Japanese character is best described by *familism*, a uniquely Japanese variety of particularistic collectivism. In this social philosophy, the relationships between individuals and social groups, between social groups, and between groups and the nation, are viewed as having traits similar to those found among members of a biological family. When applied to the Japanese nation as one big family, these traits include a pyramid-shaped hierarchy, time continuity, age/seniority progression, vertical orientation, mutuality of social obligations, and diffuse and particularistic relationships. (Some of these traits will be explained in the next chapter in the discussion of social relations in Japan. In this chapter, our interest is limited to the overall organization of society.)

Japan is an island nation located in the North Pacific Ocean off the east coast of the Asian Continent. Because of its isolated location, surrounded by water, the Japanese have had little contact with the rest of the world for most of its 2,000 years of recorded history. This historical fact has produced a people with an unusually high degree of homogeneity in racial stock, culture, language, and customs. The Japanese have strong affinity toward their fellow Japanese, and share among themselves a strong sense of uniqueness and separateness from the rest of the human community. This sense of uniqueness and isolation is accompanied by a high degree of ethnocentrism, a belief that foreigners, being non-Japanese, simply cannot understand the soul of Japan.

Most Japanese have an image of their nation as one big family, organized in a pyramidlike hierarchy with the emperor—the father figure—at the top. The imaginary family tree is pyramid-shaped not only at a given moment in time, but tracing back past generations into history. Every Japanese has a vague awareness that, if one could trace the primogenitary line far back into history, say for 2,000 years, one might reach the ancestors of the present imperial house, or come close to them. The Japanese national family is thus viewed not only as a hierarchy of families but also as an *ethnohistorical continuum*. The sense of moving up toward the top and the center of the hierarchy is inescapable, whether one moves up toward the present emperor or back in history toward the mythical promogeniture of the nation-family. This *temporal* aspect of the Japanese-style hierarchy is worth noting. In a typical Japanese social organization, those at the top are likely to be older and more senior than those at the bottom. As a rule, new members are "born into" (that is, recruited into) the organizational family at the lowest level, usually fresh from schools or universities, and rise in rank and authority within the organization as they grow in age and seniority. We might note that this is the natural pattern observed in a biological family.

Japanese society is best described as an ethnohistorical hierarchy. Against this overwhelming sense of ethnic collectivity and time continuity, the image of self as a sovereign being pales. Philosophically, the individual in the strict Western sense does not exist. Individual members of a family, a corporation, and other social groups are mere nexuses of mutual obligations within the organic community. Solidarity of the community is expressed through selfless loyalty and devotion of the members to the common purpose. Harmony within the group is a cardinal virtue. Vigorous competition within the group is allowed, but the nature of competition is limited to the kind that helps achieve the group goal.

In Japan's familistic groupism, authority relationships are understood to be largely a function of age and seniority. In a large, complex organization such as a corporation or government agency, some persons out of necessity must assume positions of authority and exercise power, just as parents must exercise control over children in a family. Power is not absolute; it is merely entrusted to the most senior (among the most capable) members of the group. As younger and junior members grow in age and seniority, they, too, will assume greater authority and power. Japan's familistic collectivism, thus, is much more organic in character than the absolute collectivism of the Soviet Union.

Japanese Ideology and Nationalism

Earlier we observed that the dominant ideologies of the United States are rooted in universal principles, which define America as a nation. Thus, in America, ideologies shape the character of nationalism. The relationship is reversed in Japan; there, nationalism shapes the character of the dominant ideology.

As we noted earlier, the highest value in Japan is that of the group. No value or principle can transcend that of the group. There can be no ideologies based on universal principles, since these principles are not bound by the values and interests of particular groups. Such ideologies as Confucianism, democracy, and free enterprise lose their universality when they are adopted by the Japanese; they become particularistic ideologies that apply only to Japan—that is, they are embraced by the Japanese only to the extent that they help Japan achieve its goals.

For example, *democracy* in Japan means that those who hold minority views are given every opportunity to voice their views, and that efforts are made to incorporate their positions in the consensus that arises out of group discussions. For another example, *free enterprise* means joint business-government initiatives, a degree of cooperation among sellers, and the right of the government to assume a tutelary role in the nation's economic development process. Other words that signify universal principles outside of Japan—for example, *equality, freedom, competition, achievement, law, justice,* and *God*—all mean something uniquely Japanese within Japan, and their meaning changes as the needs and circumstances of Japanese society change.

Those ideals that serve as dominant goal ideologies in the United States—for example, liberalism, democracy, and free enterprise—can serve only as instrumental and subordinate ideologies in Japan because they cannot transcend the particular interests of the Japanese nation. What, then, is the dominant ideology in Japan, if any? Such an ideology must be one that (1) transcends every other value and goal, and (2) serves the interests of the Japanese nation. The only ideology that satisfies both of these requirements is Japan's familistic nationalism, namely, the value orientation that advocates that individuals work toward achievement of the goals of their groups, and in the largest societal context, individuals and groups make their best efforts to achieve the goal of the nation, which is its survival and maximum well-being. This dominant ideology is a nationalistic or *ethnospecific* ideology inasmuch as it applies only to the Japanese and their relationships to their nation. We may call this Japan-specific ideology *Japanism.* Its elements are the Japanese people's national-familistic values, beliefs, and attitudes, which are rooted in their shared history and culture, as well as their shared sense of being unique and isolated in the community of nations.

THE VALUES AND IDEOLOGIES OF THE SOVIET UNION

The dominant ideologies of the present-day Soviet Union are authoritarian centralism, Marxism-Leninism, and patriotism. The first is the effective ruling ideology; the last two legitimize and reinforce the first. The dominant value orientation underlying these ideologies is authoritarian collectivism of the Russian people. (In this book we use the word *Russian* to refer to all the nationalities in the Soviet Union.)

The term *dominant ideology* means different things in different political systems. In a democratic society, it means an ideology that is shared by the great majority of people with high intensity. In an autocratic society like the Soviet Union, however, a dominant ideology can exist without a mass support; it may be an ideology of a minority power group imposed upon the majority by means of propaganda or intimidation.

Three types of dominant ideology may be identified within the Soviet context. First, the ideology of authoritarian centralism is promulgated by the elite power group, imposed on the majority, and maintained by political repression. Second, the ideology of Marxism-Leninism serves as a façade ideology. It is no longer a truly active ideology of the ruling power group, but is propounded under the pretext that it serves the interests of the people. When believed by the people, such an ideology provides a cover—or façade—of respectability and legitimacy to the Soviet regime. Third, Russian patriotism is an ideology that is genuinely held by both the ruling minority and the ruled majority. Such an ideology not only explains at least some aspects of the behavior of the political leadership, but also helps enhance its legitimacy.

Authoritarian Collectivism

The Russians have traditionally been authoritarian and collectivist in their social value orientation. They have lived for centuries under one form of autocratic rule or another. Unlike many peoples in Western (and some Eastern) Europe, Russians have never developed the notion of the individual as a sovereign being. (In this respect, Russians and Japanese are alike.) The collectivist orientation of Russians is often attributed to the thought patterns of the Mongols who ruled Russia for over two centuries (1237–1452).

The Mongol Empire was basically a tribal empire, built upon the principle of absolute subordination of the individual to the interests of the state. This political philosophy of the Mongols, according to some scholars, left a deep imprint on the Russian national psyche. Historian George Vernadsky described the Mongol impact on Russia as follows:

> What was of considerable importance was that the people were trained by the Mongols to take orders, to pay taxes, and to supply soldiers without delay. They continued to perform the same duties for their own grand duke, who became their leader in the national struggle against the Mongols. This change in attitude gradually resulted in a new concept of state and society. The old free political institutions were replaced by the authority of the grand duke. The free society was gradually transformed into a network of social classes bound to state service. The new order took definite shape in the post-Mongol period but its beginnings are to be found in the changes introduced into Russia by the Mongols or as a result of their rule.[5]

[5]George Vernadsky, *A History of Russia*, 4th ed. (New Haven, Conn.: Yale University Press, 1954), p. 80.

Following the Mongol tradition, each of the Russian tsars before the Bolshevik Revolution ruled Russia as an absolute ruler with the right of unlimited authority derived from God. The landed aristocracy in Russia never acquired an independent source of wealth that would have given it a power base for forming an effective opposition to the monarch. Tsarist Russia was ruled under the principle of universal obligatory services of all social classes to the needs of the state.

The Russian tradition of obedience to authority is alive and well in the present-day Soviet society. The average Soviet citizens are characterized by their unquestioning obedience to authority, their rank consciousness, and their authoritarian collectivist mentality. What is stressed is not the rights of individuals vis-à-vis the state, but rather their duties in the service to the state. They readily accept the authority of the collective, or the *kollektiv*—whether it is a factory, farm, or school—and find security in staying in their proper places and maintaining a low profile.

The Soviet government makes every effort to instill the proper spirit of collectivism in the minds of people. Individualism is officially denounced as being equal to egotism, bourgeois mentality, and self-aggrandizement. Children are taught in school to develop a collective zeal and suppress individuality. Note, however, that the Soviet government's indoctrination efforts have not *created* the collectivist orientation of the Russian people; rather, they have merely preserved, nurtured, and expanded the traditional collectivism that has been developed by centuries of living under autocratic rules.

The Ideology of Centralized Control

The effective ruling ideology of the Soviet Union—that is, the value orientation that guides choice and action of the Soviet rulers—is the *authoritarian centralism* of the Soviet ruling elite. This ideology is never explicitly articulated. Its true nature, therefore, can only be deduced from the behavior of the Soviet government and the Communist party.

The ideology of authoritarian centralism advocates that all major decisions in the Soviet Union must be made at the center—that is, by the Communist party leadership—and must be faithfully carried out by the state administrative apparatus under specific instructions from above. This political philosophy is justified on grounds that only the party—the "vanguard of the proletariat"—has the requisite wisdom and foresight to guide the development of society in proper directions.

The authoritarian centralist ideology, however, also serves a deeper interest of the ruling group. Self-perpetuation of this group, which has never been popularly elected, requires that the party and the state maintain a tight control and constant vigilance over the social and economic life of the people. Since social and economic instability can threaten the party's grip over the people and its monopoly of political power, the control over the thought, behavior, and lifestyle of the people must receive the highest priority in the domestic policy of the government.

Patriotism as an Ideology

In the Soviet Union, patriotic nationalism is a pervasive and powerful force binding all Soviet citizens of diverse ethnic and social backgrounds. Unlike Japanese nationalism, however, Soviet nationalism is not primarily ethnic in origin. The ethnic and linguistic diversity of the complex empire prevents ethnic affinity from becoming a powerful unionwide ideology. Rather, Soviet nationalism is an uncritical and unbridled patriotism, a passion for *rodina,* the motherland. The love for Mother Russia has been reinforced by the memories of World War II— the Great Patriotic War—in which millions of Soviet citizens perished. Foreign observers often report, with a sense of wonderment, the overwhelming emotive impact of the word *rodina* on the Soviet people. Even those Russians who are generally critical of the system seem unable to escape the spell cast by rodina.[6]

Soviet patriotism has the effect of cementing together all the segments of Soviet society and commanding their devotion and loyalty to the country. This is a powerful ideology in and of itself. More importantly, however, the ideology serves the interests of the Soviet ruling elite by legitimizing its monopoly of power. The Soviet rulers take a calculated advantage of the Soviet citizens' patriotic fervor by equating loyalty to the motherland with loyalty to the system.

MARXISM-LENINISM

In the popular mind, Marxism-Leninism is *the* ideology of the Soviet Union. This may have been true in the early years of the Soviet regime, for a few years after the Bolshevik Revolution. Over the last decade or two, however, Marxism-Leninism has lost much of its relevance and vigor. Today, it no longer shapes the direction of socioeconomic change in the Soviet Union. But the ideology is not completely dead. For the following reasons, it must still be considered a major ideological system at work in the Soviet Union today. First, the country's economic system still has many features that were originally developed within the Marx-

[6]David K. Shipler, *Russia: Broken Idols, Solemn Dreams* (New York: Times Books, 1983), p. 287.

ist-Leninist framework. In order for us to understand how the system works, what steps should be taken to reform parts of the system that are not working well, and why the reforms are difficult to carry out, we must first understand the nature of the ideology that gave rise to the features in question. Second, although the ideology no longer shapes the direction of change in the Soviet economic system, it nevertheless molds the perception of the Soviets in interpreting the events around the world. Third, Marxism-Leninism serves as a façade ideology providing legitimacy to the monopoly of power and social purpose by the Communist party.

Marx's Theory of History and Society

Marx rejected idealism—the outlook that holds that the principal driving force of historical process is ideas—and held instead that reality exists essentially as a material world following its own law that operates outside and independently of the human mind. Marx applied materialistic views to the analysis of historical development of societies, and produced a novel hypothesis that has come to be known as *historical materialism.*

Marx argued that the fundamental substance of life is labor. Labor, in combination with the means of production, generates the *mode of production* that forms the material base of human society. The material base of society consists of two components: the *forces of production* (technology and productive assets) and the *relations of production* (organization of production, including the patterns of ownership of the productive property). This material or economic base of society *determines* the superstructure of society—that is, its laws, political institutions, and ideologies. In this view, the economic subsystem shapes the nature and character of all other subsystems of society. For this reason, Marxist historical materialism is often referred to as *economic determinism.*

To Marx, all value—that is, economic value—is derived from labor. Only labor creates value. The capitalist, however, is driven by inexorable economic laws to pay the lowest wages possible and thereby make maximum profits. The excess of the fruit of labor over the wages workers receive—the *surplus value*—accrue to the capitalist. The capitalist expropriates part of the product of labor by merely being the owner of the productive assets, which—according to the labor theory of value—are nonproductive. Thus, in a capitalist society, the relations of production (i.e., the ownership of the productive property) gives rise to social classes—the capitalists (the ruling class) who exploit the surplus value of workers, and the workers (the exploited class) who create value but are prevented from receiving the full reward for their labor. Thus, according to Marx, the relationship between the social classes is one of irreconcilable antagonism: what is a gain for the one class is necessarily a loss for the other.

Marx predicted that the antagonistic conflict between the social classes will be resolved as revolutionary change is brought about by political action of the proletariat. Capitalist institutions—the private ownership of the means of production, production for private profit, and employment of wage labor—which have contributed immensely to the development and maturity of the capitalist economic system, will also become the causes of its own demise. Capitalist productive forces will outgrow the system's capacity to absorb its ever-growing output. While goods are overproduced, effective demand is kept low because wages are kept low; and an increasingly larger share of national income accrues to the wealthy capitalists whose capacity to consume goods is limited. Increasing inequality in the distribution of income and wealth, increasing impoverishment of industrial workers, and worsening economic conditions and social unrest—all these will provide conditions for revolution, a violent overthrow, by industrial workers, of the capitalist social order.

In the postrevolution era, the means of production will be socially owned, and the workers themselves will control their uses and share their output. Social classes will cease to exist since there no longer will be a group of people (i.e., capitalists) who have monopoly of the ownership and control of productive assets. With the change in the economic base of society, the character of the superstructure will be radically altered, allowing citizens to fully realize their creative potentials and to work in harmonious cooperation for the good of all.

At the heart of Marxist thought is the idea of *equality;* society without economic and political equality cannot be a just society. The sine qua non of equal society is the abolition of private property, for it is private property that allows a group of human beings to exploit others and create antagonistic social classes. Consequently, the *collective ownership of the means of production* is the first prerequisite of socialism. An important corollary of social ownership of productive resources is the *absence of hired labor.* Since workers themselves collectively own the means of production, they no longer have to sell their labor for wages. Instead, they work for themselves, just as capitalist entrepreneur-owners of business firms work for themselves. Under socialism, goods are provided "from each according to his abilities, to each according to his work."

Marx's ultimate aim was the creation of full communism, the highest form of socialism in which the "new man" lives and works in harmony with one another in a totally "classless" environment. In such society, wealth will be created and distributed "from each according to his abilities, to each according to his needs." Politically, communism means a new era of "stateless" society. To Marx the state apparatus was nothing more than an executive committee for the ruling class, or a protector of the property and interests of capitalists. In a classless society, therefore, there will be no need for a state; the state as a coercive institution will cease to exist.

Soviet Modifications of Marxism

Marxism, a nineteenth-century social and political theory, was embraced by Communists in different parts of the world in this century. The basic Marxist doctrine has gone through considerable transformation as it has been interpreted and modified by Marxist practitioners in light of conditions existing in their respective time and place. The most far-reaching modifications have been made in the Soviet Union, principally by V. I. Lenin, the leading architect and theoretician of the Bolshevik Revolution. The modifications of Marxism by Lenin and his successors fall largely into three categories: the theory of revolution, the theory of imperialism, and the theory of the organization of the state and the party. Only the last theory is directly relevant to our analysis of the Soviet economic system. The theory of government in Marxism-Leninism will be briefly discussed below. We shall find that Marx's theory of social and economic development was turned into a political theory of power and control by the Soviet ideologues.

Marx believed that government under socialism would be in the form of a "dictatorship of the proletariat." The task of destroying the last remnants of capitalism and of building a classless society had to be carried out by the proletarian majority exercising its dictatorship over the rest of society. Marx expected this form of government to be a temporary one, and assumed that there would be democratic participation within the proletarian majority.

Lenin made significant additions to Marx's theory of society in transition between capitalism and communism. Lenin did not believe that Russian industrial workers would spontaneously develop a class consciousness that represented their own true interests. Left to their own devices, Lenin said, many workers would only develop a "trade union consciousness" of seeking short-term gains and marginal improvements. The important task of articulating a revolutionary class consciousness and leading the fight to build full communism, Lenin argued, could be accomplished only by a highly organized political party led by dedicated revolutionaries including members of the intelligentsia with proletarian consciousness. Only the party—the vanguard of the proletariat—will articulate and protect the true interests of the working class.

An important question had to be answered by Lenin regarding the political power structure within the Communist party. On the one hand, there was a need to maintain firm leadership and strict membership discipline. The prospect of continued struggles with the enemies of the proletarian class necessitated a monolithic control of the party membership. On the other hand, Marxist ideals required a measure of political democracy within the party. Lenin's solution was to reconcile these conflicting needs in the doctrine of *democratic centralism.* Under this principle of party organization, a measure of limited democracy was allowed. Leaders were chosen by indirect election, and party policy decisions were made by open debate among the party members. However, no criticism of the leaders or debate on policies was allowed between elections and after policy decisions were made.

With Lenin's democratic centralism, the dictatorship of the proletariat came to mean the dictatorship of the Communist party over the working class. The effective power became even more centralized with the advent of the Stalinist era. The party itself was now controlled by a dictator. With Khrushchev's repudiation of the Stalinist excesses in the late 1950s, the dictatorship by one man (the cult of personality) was formally rejected, but the dictatorship over the state and the population by the party was not changed. The one-party dictatorship is now justified on the logically shaky ground that there is no need for opposing political parties now that conflicting class interests have been eradicated from Soviet society.

The Soviet Constitution of 1936 made only a brief reference to the Communist party of the Soviet Union (CPSU). It stated, in Article 126, that the party was "the vanguard of the working people" and "the leading core of all organizations of the working people." The new 1977 Constitution is more explicit. Its Article 6 states, in part: "The Communist Party of the Soviet Union is the leading and guiding force of Soviet society, and the nucleus of its political system and of state and public organizations." The fact that the Constitution mentions no other political parties implies that it is the only legal political party in the country. Furthermore, the CPSU is the de facto source of law (and the Constitution) in the Soviet Union, making ineffectual the other provision of the 1977 Constitution that states, in Article 108: "The Supreme Soviet of the USSR is the highest organ of state power in the USSR."

A careful examination of the rules of the Communist party reveals that there is very little "democracy" as understood in the West. Election of party leaders is indirect, lower-level members electing higher-level members in a pyramidal system. Decisions of higher bodies take precedence over those of lower bodies, and even the results of elections can be overruled by higher-level leaders. In other words, democratic centralism is more centralist than democratic; it is essentially authoritarian centralism. There exists merely an appearance of democratic participation; in reality, the leaders "have felt it necessary to devise a subtle system of counterweights to prevent an overturn of their leadership and an adoption of policies contrary to their desires."[7]

The Legitimizing Effect
of Marxism-Leninism

Earlier in this chapter we referred to the concept of façade ideology—an ideology that is used to provide a façade of legitimacy. The Marxist-Leninist ideology in the Soviet Union today is such an ideology. Two areas of glaring discrepancy between the ideological claims and the reality are noted: (1) the discrepancies between the ideological (and constitutional) claims of political democracy and the repressive realities of the police state, and (2) the inordinate amount of power and privileges enjoyed by the ruling elite in contrast to the drab life of the ordinary citizen.

According to the Soviet Constitution, the citizens are guaranteed all the political and civil rights enjoyed by citizens in democratic societies. As we noted earlier, the Soviet Constitution declares that the Supreme Soviet is the highest organ of state power in the USSR. In reality, however, the "highest organ of state power" is the Communist party's Politburo. The Supreme Soviet meets infrequently, and merely rubber-stamps the decisions already made by the party leaders.

The Soviet Constitution guarantees direct, equal, and universal elections of Soviet deputies by secret ballot. It is a well-known fact, however, that elections in the Soviet Union do not abide by these guarantees; citizens can cast yes or no votes only for candidates who are nominated by party organizations. Furthermore, as we shall see in Chapters 3 and 4, the party has the right to appoint all the key public and semipublic posts in the country through the system of *nomenklatura*.

The Constitution of 1977 also guarantees various basic freedoms of the citizen: freedom of speech, freedom of the press, freedom of assembly, freedom of mass demonstration, right to unite in mass organizations, inviolability of the person and freedom from unwarranted arrests, and inviolability of the homes of citizens and privacy of correspondence. These freedoms, however, are to be exercised "in conformity with the interests of working people and the socialist system."

Here again, it is well known that these civil rights are almost routinely violated by the agents of the Soviet state. The state exercises absolute power, being intolerant of plurality of political ideas. Dis-

---

[7]John N. Hazard, *The Soviet System of Government*, 5th ed. (Chicago: University of Chicago Press, 1980), p. 16.

senting views and criticisms of the leaders are efficiently and mercilessly repressed. Dissidents of all kinds are herded into camps and asylums along with common criminals.

To add insult to injury, the Soviet leaders who will not allow basic political and human rights to their citizens also constitute, among themselves, an elitist group that enjoys an inordinate amount of material privileges that are beyond the wildest dreams of the ordinary citizen (see Chapter 3).

One would be tempted to ask why these glaring discrepancies between the ideological claims and the realities continue to exist. Why do the Soviet leaders continue to claim that they conform to the ideals of equality and democracy in the face of such an overwhelming chasm between what things are and what things are supposed to be? In other words, why cling to the façade ideology? The answer, simply, is that they must; they need it as a means to provide the much needed *legitimacy* for the regime's existence and practices.

In 1917, by a brilliantly executed coup d'état, the Bolsheviks took power by force, that is to say, "illegally." In 1918, the Bolshevik party dissolved a freely elected constituent assembly that had an anti-Bolshevik majority. In view of these historical facts, the Soviet regime has been plagued with the question of its legitimacy since its inception. One way to legitimize the regime and its monopoly of power, then, is to make people believe that the regime serves them; that is, it holds power by virtue of being the sole articulator of the interests of Soviet workers. By continually extolling the virtues of the democratic and egalitarian character of the Soviet system, and perpetuating the fiction that the whole nation is united in its support and approbation of the regime, the Soviet leaders succeed in making their regime appear legitimate.

Legitimacy may be gained through yet another channel. According to Zygmunt Bauman, one of the major characteristics of authoritarian socialist states is that they attempt to legitimize their practices by reference to what eventually might come out of these practices no matter how deficient they may appear at the present. The Soviet leaders justify their policy and conduct in the name of a better society that they alone know how to build. If the masses cannot agree with the leadership's policy, it only shows their immaturity and ignorance.[8]

In summary, the Soviet leaders allow the continued existence of the yawning chasm between the ideological goals of democracy, equality, and human rights and the reality of autocracy, unequal distribution of privileges, and repression because they find that (1) keeping these

[8]Zygmunt Bauman, "Officialdom and Class: Bases of Inequality in Socialist Society," in *The Social Analysis of Class Structure*, ed. Frank Parkin (London: Tavistock, 1974), pp. 136–37.

124936

goals provides them with convenient cover of respectability and legitimacy for their existence and practices, and (2) any actual discrepancies
can be explained away by reference to the ignorance and lack of understanding, on the part of the masses, of the rulers' true intentions.

The Legacy of Marxism

Our discussion of Soviet ideology has said little about the economic
aspects of Marxist ideology as it pertains to the present-day Soviet
economic system. There is a good reason for this omission. Marx advocated replacing capitalism by socialism, which would be based on
social ownership of productive means and accompanied by political and
economic democracy. Socialism, according to Marx, was to eradicate
all the evils of capitalism. The economic analysis contained in Marx's
Das Kapital was, however, related almost exclusively to capitalism. Marx
was rather Utopian in his belief that once socialism/communism was
established, things would work out smoothly in the way he predicted
they would. Consequently, he provided only a very crude sketch of a
postcapitalist society, and said virtually nothing about the economics
of socialism.

This is not to say that the present Soviet economic system is unrelated to Marxist economic ideology. The Soviet leaders since the Revolution have constructed their politico-economic system based on their
interpretation of Marx's economic theory. Specifically, the most important single legacy of Marx in shaping the character of the Soviet
economic system is his labor theory of value. As we shall see in Chapter
6, the Soviet price system still has a strong cost-basis (particularly,
labor-cost-basis) bias. And in spite of the openly admitted and widely
criticized deficiencies of the system in achieving efficient allocation of
resources, the Soviet leaders have thus far rejected the idea of a fundamental reform of the planning system that would necessitate an in-
corporation of users' demand in the pricing process. Not that they stubbornly resist implementing an economic reform out of a genuine respect
for and belief in the validity of Marx's economic theory. They have
modified, in the past, Marxist ideology very liberally whenever modifications and reinterpretations suited their purposes. Rather, their refusal to admit the importance of use-value in the pricing process is
rooted in their self-interest and fear of change. To admit that use-value
is important is to cast a shadow of doubt on the "correctness" of Marx's
analysis. This doubt would inevitably lead to the question of the legitimacy of the present regime. On a more mundane level, to allow the
influence of demand and let the prices be determined in the market
means losing control over the economy. Neither the party bosses nor

the entrenched economic bureaucracy can tolerate the loss of power, control, and privileges that such a genuine reform would bring about. The ghost of Marx is thus affecting the behavior of the Soviet leaders in this indirect manner and, ironically, preventing the Soviet economic system from moving toward a rational solution to the pressing problem of inefficiency.

QUESTIONS

1. Name several examples of *ideology.* Does each one of your examples conform to the definition of ideology given in the text? Specifically, does your example promote, advocate, justify, or legitimize something?
2. Can *liberty* or *loyalty* be considered ideologies? How about *rapid industrialization at all costs?* What is the difference between a *value* and an *ideology?*
3. Do you believe that your own personal value orientation is basically individualistic or collectivistic? Give a few concrete illustrations of your individualism or collectivism.
4. Under what circumstances, or for what reasons or causes, do you think individuals are willing to sacrifice their self-interests for the interest of a group or society?
5. Do you agree with the statement in the text that the United States is more ideological in its makeup than the Soviet Union or Japan? Isn't the Soviet Union a society built on the ideology of Marxism-Leninism? Isn't Japanism an ideology, too?
6. What are the sources of Japanese groupism? Describe the characteristics of familism. What would nonfamilistic groupism be like?
7. Do Americans have a sense of ethnohistorical continuum for their society? Can you name a few societies having such a sense?
8. Compare and contrast the relationships between nationalism and ideology in the United States and in Japan.
9. What is the nature of Japanism? Can Japanism exist outside Japan? Can Americanism exist outside the United States?
10. Compare and contrast Soviet collectivism and Japanese groupism.
11. What is the nature of the effective ruling ideology of the Soviet Union?
12. Compare and contrast the nature of nationalism in the Soviet Union, the United States, and Japan.
13. If Marxism-Leninism is no longer the effective ruling ideology of the Soviet Union, why is it still necessary for us to know something about it?
14. What is meant by *economic determinism?* Do you subscribe to it? How about technological determinism?
15. What is the real function of Marxism-Leninism in the Soviet Union today?

SELECTED READING

ARIELI, YEHOSHUA. *Individualism and Nationalism in American Ideology.* Cambridge, Mass.: Harvard University Press, 1964.

ARMSTRONG, JOHN A. *Ideology, Politics, and Government in the Soviet Union: An Introduction* (3rd ed.), chap. 2. New York: Praeger Publishers, 1974.

BLUHM, WILLIAM T. *Ideologies and Attitudes: Modern Political Culture,* chaps. 3, 4, and 8. Englewood Cliffs, N.J.: Prentice-Hall, Inc., 1974.

KAMENKA, EUGENE, Ed. *The Portable Karl Marx.* New York: The Viking Press and Penguin Books, 1983.

LANE, DAVID. *Politics and Society in the USSR,* chap. 1. London: Weidenfeld and Nicolson, 1970.

NOVE, ALEC. *The Economics of Feasible Socialism,* pt. 1. London: George Allen & Unwin, 1983.

SHERMAN, HOWARD J. *The Soviet Economy,* chap. 2. Boston: Little, Brown and Company, 1969.

SOLO, ROBERT A. *The Public Authority and the Market System,* chap. 1. Cincinnati, Ohio: South-Western Publishing Co., 1974.

CHAPTER 3

Social Relations and Social Stratification

In the preceding chapter we examined the values and ideologies of the three societies as they affect primarily the relationships between the individual and society. In this chapter, we shall continue our examination of sociocultural values, but shift our focus to the relationships among individuals and groups. Specifically, we shall examine the qualities of relationships among individuals and groups (social relations) and the relationships among social groups of different social status (social stratification).

DIMENSIONS OF SOCIAL RELATIONS

In Chapter 2 we defined *culture* as the sum total of society's learned behavior. Each society's cultural norms manifest themselves in a web of social relationships. The term *social relations* refers to the predictable and recurrent patterns of interaction among individuals and groups. The actions of individuals are determined appreciably by their concerns and expectations of others' actions toward them. Repeated often enough, a given pattern of interaction develops a high degree of expectability. The quality of social relations varies according to the situation or environment of the participants. Thus, in a crowd, social relations are weak and unstable. In a family, they are strong, permanent, informal, and personal. The relations among co-workers in a Japanese business firm are formal but personal, whereas those among American workers tend to be informal but impersonal.

In Chapter 1 the concept of *social organization* was introduced. Like social relations, social organization is an aspect of social relationships, and is related to the predictable and recurrent patterns of interaction. But whereas *social relations* refers to the *qualities* of social interactions among individuals and groups, *social organization* refers to the *functional structure* of social relationships having coordination and purpose. For example, the structure of decision-making authority between a superior and a subordinate in a corporation represents an aspect of social organization. By contrast, the relationships of emotional dependence of subordinates on their superiors in a Japanese firm and the adversarial relationships between managers and workers in an American corporation are examples of social relations.

Primary-Group and Secondary-Group Relations

Two types of social relations can be identified: one that exhibits primary-group characteristics and one that does not. A *primary group* is characterized by intimate face-to-face association and interaction. A family is a primary group par excellence. A close neighborhood group and a group of intimate friends at a school are other examples. Note that a blood relationship is not required for a primary group; what is needed is an intense, personal, and relatively permanent interaction among persons of similar values.

Relationships among members of a primary group are *diffuse*—that is, affecting the entire person—rather than *specific*—that is, focusing on specific roles. (I know my children as whole persons, but I know Mr. Jones only as the director of a local library. I know him only in that specific role; my relationship with him is specific.) Primary-group members are emotively tied together and share a community of interests. Self-interests of individual members normally take second place to the group's collective interest. Loyalty to the group is stressed.

Primary-group relations are *ascription* based (i.e., who or what a person is) rather than *achievement* based (i.e., what a person does, has done, or can do). For example, the status of each family member is ascribed by birth or marriage; achievements by the members cannot affect their interrelations.

Membership in a primary group is *particularistic* rather than *universalistic*. Membership is said to be particularistic when a person is accepted as a member because he or she is that particular person, and not because what he or she can do. Membership is universalistic when the position can be filled by anyone who happens to possess a set of qualifications.

In a *secondary group,* by contrast, members are related to one another as a means to some ends. Their relations are formal, and are built on contractual or legalistic grounds. Their relations are specific, achievement based, and universalistic. Their interactions lack an emotive content. Members' individual interests are paramount: the group's interests are pursued only as a means to serve individual members' ends.

Although the primary-secondary dichotomy represents two logical extremes in social relations, in reality the two sets of characteristics seldom exist in their pure forms. Most relations in a group show a mixture of some aspects of both.

Social Relations and Harmony of Interests

In Chapter 1 we introduced the concept of harmony of interests between the individual and the collective. One of the fundamental problems of social organization is that of reconciling the self-interest of the individual with the larger interest of a group or society. The feasibility of harmonizing the specific interest of the individual with the general interest of the group depends to a large extent on the quality of social relations in the group. Specifically, the stronger the primary-group characteristics of the group, the easier the task of harmonizing.

Since the individual is the basic unit of human action, the source of human motivation and behavior must be sought in the human psyche. At the physiological level, human beings have what are known as *primary motives,* that is, needs and urges related to food, shelter, sex, creature comfort, and so on. *Secondary motives* are those relating to psychological and sociological needs: freedom, security, love, prestige, approbation by peers, and so forth. Some motives are *instrumental motives* that serve as means of satisfying other (primary or secondary) needs. For example, money (economic power) or political power can be used to obtain food, security, prestige, creature comfort, and so on.

In Chapter 1, we discussed the motivation structure of social organization, and identified the following seven factors of human motivation: coercion, money, power, social obligation, social recognition, self-achievement, and group solidarity. For discussions of social relations and harmony of interests in modern industrial societies, perhaps it is better to use a more simplified paradigm consisting of four major motivational forces: money, power, group approbation, and group solidarity.

Money (i.e., economic power) and power (i.e., political power) are the two most powerful instrumental motives. They are powerful because they benefit the individual directly by satisfying his or her primary and secondary needs. In most industrial societies, economic power—or money—provides the most powerful motive of human behavior. It can buy what is necessary to fulfill all the primary needs and most of the secondary needs of human beings. This is particularly true in the United States where there is little that money cannot buy: it can be spent to acquire security, creature comfort, prestige, and even political power. Money is an important motive also in the Soviet Union and Japan, but its relative importance is less in the United States. In the Soviet Union, political power is relatively more important than money since there are many things that money cannot buy in that country because of their sheer unavailability. There, money cannot buy political power but political power can bring material privileges to the powerful. Even ordinary citizens without political power seek connections with the politically powerful because with connections they can have access to goods and services that money cannot buy. In Japan, as we shall see later in this chapter, group approbation is relatively more important than money or political power as a motivational force. *Group approbation* includes both *social obligation*, the fear of being ostracized by others, and *social recognition*, the desire to be accepted or respected by others.

Of the four major motivational factors identified above—money, power, group approbation, and group solidarity—the first two are egocentric or self-centered motives. The third—group approbation—is a self-centered but group-oriented motive. We want to be accepted, loved, and respected by others in the group to which we belong not because we place the interests and objectives of the group before our own, but because we, as individuals, are concerned about where we stand in the group. Group approbation, therefore, is basically a self-centered motive. Only the last of the four motives listed above—group solidarity—is a truly group-centered motive. Here, individuals are willing to sacrifice their self-interests and individual objectives in favor of the collective interests and objectives of their group.

Harmony of individual and group interests is easiest to achieve in a group having strong primary-group characteristics. In such a group, the feeling of "we" prevails over that of "I." There is a strong sense of shared purpose among the members, and the group solidarity motive can be as strong as, if not stronger than, the other motives. Strong primary-group characteristics in a group also means that group approbation motive can be a powerful motivational force. The fear of being rejected by one's peers, and the desire to be accepted and respected by them, induce individuals to behave in such a way as to promote the overall interests of the group even at the expense of their own private interests and objectives.

In a group in which secondary-group characteristics are predominant, harmony of individual and group interests is difficult, but not impossible, to achieve. In such a group, money and/or power is likely to be the most important motive. When money is the predominant motive, chances are that individual and group interests are at odds with each other, particularly if the group is large. If one group in a corporation, for example, wants a larger share of the firm's earnings, other groups will necessarily have to do with smaller shares. Here, we have a situation of a zero-sum game. As some members of a group get larger shares of the group's pie, others will end up with smaller shares unless the size of the pie itself can be increased. Acquisition of political power can also be a zero-sum game. If the Polish Solidarity movement succeeds in gaining increased political power, the power of the Polish government and Communist party is lessened accordingly.

It is possible to achieve harmony of individual and group interests in a group with strong secondary-group characteristics if the group is not very large. Some types of individual goals can be achieved only by cooperating with others in a group. If a minimum of three persons is necessary to build a rope bridge across a gorge, then, during the duration of the task of building the bridge, there exists a nearly perfect harmony of individual and group objectives. The three persons may not know, and may not care to know, each other as human beings on the personal level; but, as far as the objective of building the bridge is concerned, their individual interests and the group's interest are one and the same. Similarly, partners in a small business firm *may* find congruence between their individual interests and the firm's interests. Harmony of interests in a secondary-group situation, thus, is not an impossibility. It will be easier, of course, the smaller the group and the more primary-group characteristics there are in the group. As we shall see in the following section, Japanese society is characterized by strong primary-group characteristics in its social relations. This fact accounts for the much higher coincidence of interests in large Japanese social organizations such as modern corporations, as we shall see in later chapters.

SOCIAL RELATIONS IN JAPAN

Social relations in Japan exhibit strong communal and primary-group characteristics. Whereas the individual is central to Western societies, the *family* is the main framework of Japanese society. Many secondary groups in Japan such as business firms, government offices, and schools are organized on a familial principle, that is, with ascribed statuses and diffuse and particularistic interpersonal relations placed vertically in a hierarchical structure.

Familistic Groupism

Japan's traditional communalism is often explained by the pattern of traditional agriculture and the paucity of natural resources in Japan. Rice has been the main crop of most of Japanese farmers for centuries. Rice farming, it so happens, is not only highly labor intensive but also requires coordinated efforts by everyone in the village at critical moments for planting and harvesting. Weather conditions determine the time that is right for most of the steps in rice growing, and missing the right time may very well mean a disastrous crop failure. In such an environment, there is little room for a social maverick who wants to be independent and self-sufficient.

The need for mutual assistance and cooperation was institutionalized during the Tokugawa period (1600–1867). Each village was divided into groups of five peasant families (called *gonin-gumi*, or "group of five"), which were held collectively responsible for paying the rice tax to the local lord. Punishment for not meeting the tax quota was severe. Peasant families in each gonin-gumi, therefore, had to cooperate closely among themselves and depend on each other for survival. Ostracism by other members of the gonin-gumi or by other villagers often meant starvation. Because of the Tokugawa Shogun government's ban on peasants leaving their own village and moving to another, survival of peasants and their family members required that they stay in the villages of their birth and stick together with their relatives and neighbors. As a consequence, a strong sense of mutual dependency and obligations developed. The collective—the family, the gonin-gumi, and the village—became a community of shared destiny.

The traditional Japanese family has the following main characteristics. First, members' statuses are *ascribed*. One is either married, adopted, or born into a family. As new members enter a family, their positions relative to other members become fixed and cannot later be altered by their efforts or achievements. Second, the structure of social relations within a family is *hierarchical* with the father at the top and the youngest sibling at the bottom. The rank and authority of members are almost perfectly correlated with their age. Third, the relationships among the members are *diffuse*. They interact with each other as total persons, not as partners or associates in specific, instrumental functions. Members are emotionally tied together with a sense of shared goals, interests, and needs. Fourth, the membership in the family is *particularistic* rather than universalistic. Members are devoted to the interests of other members as particular persons, not because of what they can do. Fifth, particularism within a family leads to *exclusivism*, or an insider-outsider mentality. Family members treat the particular interests of other members (insiders) with special consideration and affection which they do not accord to strangers (outsiders). Family members are acutely aware of the boundary between the family and the outside world.

These familial traits are found, more or less, in families of most societies. What makes Japanese society unique is the fact that the foregoing attributes of a traditional family are found in nonprimary-group relations. Social groups, organizations, industries, and the nation as a whole are organized in the image of a traditional family. We shall use the term *familism* or *familistic groupism* to describe this unique primary-group character of Japanese society.

The Vertical Society and Rank Consciousness

A hallmark of Japan's hierarchical familism is its *vertical orientation* and *rank-and-status consciousness*. Persons as a rule do not interact with others as equals. Even among the persons of equal status (e.g., co-workers), there may exist subtle differences in age and seniority. Thus, almost any persons whom the Japanese encounter in their daily lives can be, and often must be, classified as their superiors or inferiors, and appropriate personal demeanor and language must be used.

There are only two types of relationship in which the Japanese feel completely equal to others in a group. One is the relationship among the classmates in a given class in a school or university. The other is a similar relationship among a group of new recruits in a given place of employment. Only in such groups can Japanese enjoy a sense of complete equality among persons. By way of contrast, it may be pointed out that relationships among the siblings in a family are clearly hierarchical. In fact, there are no words in the Japanese language that correspond to the English words *brother* and *sister;* the available words are *elder brother, younger brother,* and so on. In the case of twins, one twin must be designated *elder brother* or *elder sister* and the other *younger brother* or *younger sister* before their births can be recorded in the government's family registry. Even today, in traditional families, parents teach the younger of the twins to use appropriate deferential language and demeanor to the "elder" brother or sister.

In the Japanese language, the correct use of honorifics (*keigo*) is the most important consideration; it is much more elaborate and specific than the use of gender, tense, number, or case. Even a simple sentence, for example, "I ask him," can be said in a dozen or more different ways depending on the relative social rank of the speaker, the person spoken to, and the person who is referred to ("him" in this case). This elaborate superior-inferior consciousness in the use of the language is a reflection of the equally elaborate rank-and-status consciousness in Japanese social relations.

The rank consciousness of the Japanese extends even to nonpersonal relations. Sections within a firm are ranked according to their power and prestige. Corporations within an industry are ranked according to their capitalization and market share. Schools and universities are ranked according to their quality and reputation. Even nations are ranked according to their gross national product or by some other measure. As we shall see later, this vertical orientation and rank consciousness of the Japanese goes a long way toward explaining their competitive drive.

Dependency Needs

Another aspect of familism that shapes the character of social relations in Japan is the need to belong to a group. The Japanese as a rule have a strong desire to belong to a group that enables them to draw a sense of security and identity. Most adult Japanese feel insecure and out of place if they do not belong to a group or organization and totally accepted by it. This craving for dependence, the emotional need to belong to a group and be accepted by it, has its roots in the child-rearing practices and socialization process in the Japanese family.

Unlike the Western nuclear family, which revolves around the couple, the focus of the Japanese family is the mother-child relationship. The father normally has a place in the outside world, and does socializing with his co-workers or associates. Few wives participate in work-related socializing. Most young wives, therefore, are left alone at home. When the baby arrives, the new mother is prepared to devote herself totally to it. The baby becomes the focal point of her life. She surrounds the child with a warm blanket of protection, affection, and indulgence. This in turn generates within the child an addiction to such warmth and protection. When children who have been reared in this way become adults, they want to duplicate this sense of warmth and security in their adult social relations. This need is satisfied by their belonging to a group or organization that has the characteristics of a family. Since most members of secondary groups in Japan have such a need, those groups tend to develop strong primary-group characteristics.

The emotional submergence of Japanese workers in their work group explains the Japanese penchant for group harmony, or *wa*, and their emphasis on compromise and consensus. Their legendary hard work and cooperative spirit can be attributed to their desire to avoid the stigma of group contempt or rejection. They strive to live up to the role expected of them by the group. More positively, by their hard work they can improve their reputation in their group (be it a shop, section, or company), and the reputation of their group in a larger setting. The basic driving force of the Japanese people is here seen as emanating from their group orientation and dependency needs.

How can the Japanese derive emotional fulfillment from their group when it is organized hierarchically? Hierarchical organization implies authority and impersonality: Are these characteristics not obstacles to fulfillment of dependency needs? To answer these questions, we must first understand the special quality of the relationship between two individuals of upper and lower status (senior-junior, superior-subordinate) in a Japanese social organization. The Japanese subordinates (juniors) look to their superior (senior) much as children do to their parents: they seek emotional fulfillment from the relationship. The subordinates presume upon the personal affection and protection of the superior, which the latter provides, allowing a certain amount of indulgence. This emotional dependency relationship, known as *amae*, is observed to a degree in any situation involving vertical relationships among Japanese. Amae means indulging in one's senior's affection and protection. That there is no equivalent to this word in Western languages was pointed out by Takeo Doi, a noted Japanese psychologist, in his book *Amae no Kozo* (The Structure of Amae).[1]

The Insider-Outsider Mentality

One important manifestation of familism is the mentality of sharply distinguishing between the "insiders" (us, members of the group) and the "outsiders" (them, strangers).

To individualistic Westerners, the social boundary lies between the self and the rest of humanity; therefore, there is little need to distinguish "outsiders" from "insiders." By contrast, the Japanese start with a notion that human beings exist as a group, and the crucial social boundary lies between the group and the rest of the world. Within the basic group of a family, everyone is *miuchi* (inside the family). There is a strong sense of communal understanding among miuchi members and a great deal of indulgence and imposition is tolerated. People on the outside, however, belong to a separate category of human beings. They constitute a large, gray mass who may be treated with indifference or even with enmity.

The insider-outsider mentality of the Japanese extends beyond their

---

[1]Takeo Doi, *Amae no Kozo* (Tokyo: Kobundo, 1971). See also Takeo Doi, *"Amae:* A Key Concept for Understanding Japanese Personality Structure," in *Japanese Culture: Its Development and Characteristics,* ed. R. J. Smith and R. K. Beardsley (Chicago: Aldine Publishing, 1962; reprinted in Takie Sugiyama Lebra and William P. Lebra, eds., *Japanese Culture and Behavior: Selected Readings* (Honolulu: The University Press of Hawaii, 1974), pp. 145–54.

immediate family. Depending on the nature of the problem at hand, the "inside" may be a corporation, a section in a corporation, an industry, the business community as a whole, or even the nation as a whole. (As pointed out in the preceding chapter, the insider mentality does not extend beyond the national family.) Although the miuchi consciousness among the members of these organizations may not be as strong as that found among blood relatives, it nevertheless exists unmistakably and shapes the behavior of the Japanese toward both insiders and outsiders.

An example of miuchi mentality is found in the relationships among members of a Japanese corporation. All the employees of a corporation—whether management, white-collar, or blue-collar—belong to the same corporate family. The union members feel closer affinity with the management employees (the insiders) than with fellow industrial workers in other corporations (the outsiders). Worker solidarity in such a situation is naturally weak; what we find instead is a strong corporate solidarity.

Achievement Orientation

The nature of Japanese familism shapes the character of achievement orientation in Japan. Cultural psychologist George De Vos argues that while the Westerner's achievement orientation derives largely from the search for salvation or need for self-realization, the Japanese strive to achieve for the sake of the family or social group, and, by extension, the national family. De Vos points out that the Western ideal of self-realization has been totally alien to the Japanese way of thinking until very recently.[2]

Group Harmony
and Dispute Settlements

In Western societies, disputes are settled by resort to the power of either logic or number. Individuals clash in an adversarial relationship in debates, committee meetings, and in courts of law, and the winner is whoever has a better argument or evidence. In the political arena, decisions are made by a majority rule. Discussions are held and arguments are exchanged, but they are usually assertions of each side's positions made in attempt to convince the other side of its misinformation or faulty logic.

In Japan, disputes are settled in a totally different manner. In a family or group, conflicts must be avoided at all costs. Any disputes

[2]George A. De Vos, *Socialization for Achievement: Essays on the Cultural Psychology of the Japanese* (Berkeley, Calif.: University of California Press, 1973), p. 196.

arising within a group, therefore, must be settled amicably without resulting in a loss of face to any member. Laws and rules are of little help. They can be, and often are, bent to suit the nature of the problem at hand. Vote taking is avoided as much as possible since a majority vote means that somebody must lose unequivocally and therefore must lose face. The Japanese solution involves endless dialogues involving all the interested parties. The group strives to achieve a consensus with varying degree of compromise by all concerned. If a consensus cannot be achieved, the decision is likely to be postponed in the interest of maintaining group harmony. (The decision-making process in a large Japanese corporation will be discussed in Chapter 10.)

COLLECTIVISM IN SOVIET AND JAPANESE SOCIAL RELATIONS

In Chapter 2 we observed that the Soviet Union is characterized by authoritarian collectivism. In their social relations, the Russian people are known for their aversion to individualistic distinction and standing apart from the group. Hedrick Smith reports in *The Russians* that social relations in the Soviet Union are characterized by hierarchism, vertical orientation, rank consciousness, ready submission to authority, group conformism, and absence of the sense of the individual being of supreme moral value.[3] This characterization of Soviet social relations appears to be very much like that of the Japanese. What, if any, are the differences between the Soviet and Japanese varieties of collectivist social relations?

Despite their superficial similarities, there are fundamental differences between the authoritarian communalism in the Soviet Union and the familistic groupism in Japan. The differences center on the quality of the society's vertical orientation and the rank consciousness of the people.

In Japan's groupism, the consciousness of rank and status differences is part of society's cultural reflexes. Without knowing their vertical location, Japanese would have difficulties communicating with one another. They therefore try instinctively to place individuals on a vertical scale of statuses. This, however, is not the case with Russians. The vertical relations in the Soviet Union are basically a reflection of the *power relations* between individuals, or what Hedrick Smith describes as the question of what an individual Russian can do to another.[4] In

[3]Hedrick Smith, *The Russians* (New York: Quadrangle/The New York Times Book Co., 1976), chap. 10.

[4]Ibid., p. 260.

short, vertical relations to Russians means a pecking order; their rank consciousness is related to power consciousness.

The Russians realize that they cannot fight the power and authority of those who are above them, so they merely tolerate them just as they must tolerate a spell of bad weather.[5] Authority is accepted but is kept out of Russian consciousness. The Japanese, by contrast, accept authority by internalizing it. A Japanese social group is hierarchically structured and its members climb the scale as they grow in age and seniority. Virtually everyone is subjected to authority from above and exercises authority over those who are below. Authority flows naturally from top to bottom, as blood flows through the arteries of a body. Authority relations are an integral part of Japan's hierarchical familism.

Within a group, Russian communalism is basically horizontal and egalitarian. Russians exhibit a strong sense of egalitarianism among members of a small, personal group (whether a work collective or a friendship circle). Members are little conscious of their relative statuses, unless, of course, status differences involve power relationships. The group as a whole suffers and tolerates collectively the power exercised from above. The vertical relations, therefore, are external to a Russian group in the sense that such relations are not based on the values and norms of the members, but are imposed on the group from outside.

In a Japanese group, by contrast, vertical relations are internalized. Members are aware of each other as a superior or a subordinate. The ladder that takes a person upward in the group's hierarchy is an integral part of the group's organizational structure. Since one's group is vertically related to the larger society, finding one's place in the group is tantamount to finding one's place in society itself. This sense of having a place within a hierarchy gives the Japanese a much-needed sense of identity and security. As noted earlier, their dependency needs are satisfied through their amae relationships with their superiors and subordinates in a social group, particularly a work group. By contrast, the Russians draw their sense of belonging from the horizontal, egalitarian relationships with their co-workers and friends, and merely tolerate vertical power relationships with others as something over which they have no control.

SOCIAL RELATIONS
IN THE UNITED STATES

In sociocultural value orientation, the United States and Japan stand poles apart. Whereas groupism, vertical orientation, particularism, and diffuse personal relations characterize Japanese society, their diametric

[5]Ibid., p. 255.

opposites—individualism, horizontal orientation, universalism, and specific personal relations—constitute the basic principles of social relations in America.

Americans are instinctively averse to vertical social relations. This aversion can be attributed, of course, to the American belief in the moral equality of all human beings. (The persistence of racist and sexist attitudes in some segments of the American population is, of course, an exception to this generalization.) Individuals have a proclivity to relate to each other on a horizontal plane. In a modern, complex society, however, it is impossible to avoid all vertical relationships. Bureaucracies of corporate and government organizations, for example, must be organized on hierarchical principles. Americans awkwardly reconcile the conflict between their horizontal proclivity and the vertical requirements of complex society by stressing the universalistic and specific nature of positions in large social organizations. Vertically related individuals in these organizations are not related to each other diffusely, that is, as one total human being to another. Rather, their relationships are specific; that is, they are related to each other only in their occupational capacities (e.g., as manager and secretary, professor and student, or captain and sergeant). Moreover, the positions are filled by universalistic considerations; that is, the incumbents occupy the positions because of professional or technical qualifications, not because of who they are. The high degree of specificism and universalism in human roles in American society provides a cover of impersonality to these roles; individuals need not suffer the indignity of being subordinate to other individuals in a vertically structured social organization if they can believe that what are being vertically aligned are mere occupational roles, not the moral value of individual human beings.

One important corollary of American individualism is the value that is placed on individual achievement. Since the basic unit of society is the individual, successes or failures as well as rewards and penalties accrue to the individual. A collective is nothing more than a means to help the individual to achieve an end. The individual places his or her welfare above that of the collective, and draws much more satisfaction from his or her own success than that of the collective.

This emphasis on individual achievement, which has been the primary driving force of the American economy for over a century, has recently been undergoing a serious reappraisal. It has been argued that the excess of individualism is the root cause of the difficulties the American economy has experienced in recent decades in the productivity of its industries and the quality of its products. For instance, sociologist Amitai Etzioni argues in his recent book that the "decades of me-ism" have turned Americans into isolated individuals. He stresses the need to rebuild a new American community with a strong sense of mutuality among its citizens.[6] Similarly, Robert Reich, in his 1983 book *The Next American Frontier*, argues that America's industrial decline is attributable to the inability of Americans to work together, and suggests that America must make a difficult but necessary choice of restructuring its social relations and industrial organization with a view toward creating a less adversarial, and more participative and collaborative community.[7]

A study conducted in the 1950s by Inkeles, Hanfmann, and Beier clinically compared 51 Soviet emigrés with an American control group and found that the Russian personality was characterized by its affiliation and dependence needs, whereas the American control group showed strong needs for approval and autonomy. The study showed that the Americans wanted to remain at arm's length from the group, fearing that too close or intimate relations with other individuals might potentially limit their freedom of individual action. Nevertheless, the Americans were found to be afraid of being isolated from the group, and eager to be considered "all right" guys by others.[8]

The above finding is highly illuminating. Here, the achievement-oriented, individualistic Americans are portrayed as eagerly seeking approval of other individuals and groups. This observation appears to be consistent with the view that all human beings are social animals and need some forms of relationships with a group. Americans do not want to be too closely affiliated with a group, but they nevertheless fear isolation and want to be approved by others. This psychological and social need of the Americans will probably have an important bearing on the feasibility of rebuilding American society on a more communal foundation. To the extent that social relations in America have some primary-group characteristics, group approbation and even a degree of group solidarity may be built into America's social organization as powerful motivational forces.

SOCIAL STRATIFICATION

Inequality of income, wealth, power, and prestige among different social groups is found in every society. These groups constitute hierarchically structured *social strata*. A detailed examination of the theories of social

---

[6]Amitai Etzioni, *An Immodest Agenda: Rebuilding America before the Twenty-First Century* (New York: McGraw-Hill Book Company, New Press, 1983).

[7]Robert B. Reich, *The Next American Frontier* (New York: Penguin Books, 1983), chap. 12.

[8]Alex Inkeles and others, "Modal Personality and Adjustment to the Soviet Socio-Political System," in *Studying Personality Cross-Culturally*, ed. Bert Kaplan (Evanston, Ill.: Row, Peterson and Co., 1961), pp. 205–6.

stratification and the actual patterns of stratification in major industrial nations is beyond the scope of this book. In the remainder of this chapter we shall briefly examine the social stratification in Japan and the Soviet Union: what strata exist, how socially mobile the population is, and how the educational system affects social selection are the main foci of discussions that follow.

Social strata are social groupings that are marked off by differences in style of life, social outlook, and life chances. Crystalized social groups that are set apart by major cleavages are called *social classes.* Members of a social class share not only a common life-style but also common values and beliefs. They exhibit class consciousness, viewing themselves as a collectivity with common interests that are opposed to those of other classes.

Depending on how individuals and groups are assigned particular status, society may be characterized as either closed or open. In a *closed* society, social statuses are essentially *ascribed;* that is, they are either physically or socially inherited. For example, status may be based primarily on sex, ethnicity, family history, or wealth inherited from one's parents. In an *open* society, by contrast, status differences are largely *achieved* by individuals. Acquisition of skills and educational levels is by far the most important means of achieving status in modern industrial societies.

The closedness or openness of a society is closely related to the manner in which individuals and groups can move up or down within the society crossing stratum boundaries. In a completely closed society, mobility is limited to movement within the social class in which one is born. By contrast, in a completely open society, unimpeded upward or downward mobility between all status levels is allowed.

In a semiopen society, self-conscious and self-contained social classes are clearly visible, and people are generally aware of their own and others' "places." Although many people experience a considerable degree of social mobility, the occupational chances and choices of most people are highly influenced by both tradition and their parents' occupations. Among the major industrial nations that may be described as semiopen, we can name Britain and France.

In an open society, there is a great deal of social mobility made possible by mass higher education. An individual's affiliation with a given social stratum is nonpermanent, and is usually a matter of either personal choice or personal qualities and efforts. Among today's industrial countries, the United States, the Soviet Union, and Japan come close to being completely open societies. There nevertheless exists, in each of these three societies, a unique pattern of stratification that is characteristic of each society. As far as stratification goes, the United States is the most conventional of the three. There, *money* is the most important single factor determining social status. Inherited wealth, as well as high incomes from professional and entrepreneurial activities, are the main sources of social distinction. In the Soviet Union, it is *political power* that largely determines social status. The rank ordering of people into the ruling power elite, the intelligentsia, and the proletariat and peasantry is in proportion to the amount of raw political power that the members of each group can wield over those who are ranked below them. In Japan, the stratification that matters is based on *educational background*. What school one graduated from decisively determines one's occupational horizon and social status.

Japan and the Educational Escalator

There has been no agreement among scholars as to what social classes, if any, exist in Japan and what proportions of the population fall in different categories. Each year, the Prime Minister's Office conducts a survey in order to discover the people's subjective assessment of their level of living. The 1981 survey revealed the following percentage distribution: upper class, 0.6 percent; upper-middle class, 8.0 percent; middle-middle class, 54.5 percent; lower-middle class, 26.0 percent; lower class, 7.3 percent; and "don't know" and "not applicable," 3.7 percent.[9] The result of this survey shows that nine out of ten Japanese regard themselves as enjoying a middle-level living standard. Throughout the 1970s, the annual survey showed virtually the same result.

These survey results are not materially different from the various studies made of the social stratification of American society, in which it is typically found that somewhere between 80 and 95 percent of Americans are classified as belonging to the great middle class, including the "working class."[10] It thus seems safe to say that, notwithstanding the difficulty of defining social classes and estimating their relative sizes, both the United States and Japan can be described as overwhelmingly middle-class societies, or, alternatively, essentially classless, open societies. That eight or nine persons out of ten are identified with the large middle class seems to reflect the great leveling effect of economic democracy in the two countries.

To say that Japan is essentially a classless, open society is not to say that it is an egalitarian society or there is no social stratification in

---

[9]Keizai Koho Center, *Japan 1982: An International Comparison* (Tokyo: Keizai Koho Center, 1982), p. 73.

[10]See, for example, Daniel W. Rossides, *The American Class System* (Boston: Houghton Mifflin Company, 1976), p. 26; and Stanislaw Ossowski, "Non-Egalitarian Classlessness—Similarities in Interpreting Mutually Opposed Systems," in *Structured Social Inequality*, ed. Celia S. Heller (London: Macmillan Company, 1969), pp. 206–16.

Japan. There exists a strong rank-and-status consciousness in every aspect of Japanese social life. Every Japanese is acutely aware of finely graded status hierarchy and is mindful of using language and demeanor appropriate for each specific situation. The Japanese may not be class conscious, but they are extremely conscious of status differences based on education, occupation, rank, age, and gender. Particularly important in this respect is a person's educational background. The way in which one's occupational chances are affected by one's academic background—not necessarily the level of education but more importantly what school one graduated from—is unparalleled among the industrial nations, with the possible exception of France.

Present-day Japan, like the United States, is a mass higher education society. In the late 1970s, nearly 40 percent of Japanese in the college-level age group were attending colleges and universities. Comparable figures were 45 percent in the United States, 26 percent in France, and 23 percent in West Germany.[11] Unlike the United States, the most prestigious universities in Japan are *national* universities. The most able of the nation's youths vie for admission to the University of Tokyo, Kyoto University, and Hitotsubashi University. The two best private universities, Keio and Waseda, are rated in the public mind somewhat lower than the best national universities. Admission to the elite universities, both public and private, are based strictly on the results of entrance examinations. The relatively low cost of attending national universities and the fact that entrance is based strictly on merit combine to make these institutions effective conduits of upward social mobility of gifted children of low-income families.

Since the number of openings in good universities is far smaller than the number of eligible students seeking admission, competition for entrance to the most prestigious universities is extremely fierce. Ambitious students spend a great deal of time preparing for college entrance examinations, starting in some cases as early as their elementary school days. Many students who fail the examinations the first time may try again and again, thereby spending years before being admitted to a university of their choice. In the cases of the most prestigious universities such as Tokyo, Kyoto, or Hitotsubashi, typically fewer than half of a given year's entrants come straight from high schools. Thousands of *ronin* (a term that likens these students to the lordless, roaming samurai of the feudal age) spend countless hours learning examination materials by rote and taking mock examinations at hundreds of private cram schools located in major cities. A great deal of the Japanese youth's energy and emotion is wasted in this way in preparations for college entrance examinations. This pathological phenomenon known as the

---

[11]Keizai Koho Center, *Japan 1982*, various pages.

"examination hell" is one of the most serious social problems Japan faces today.

The obsession of many of Japan's youths with enrolling in elite universities has to do with the peculiarly Japanese pattern of social stratification, which is based on educational background. In a nutshell, one's educational background at the time one enters the labor force largely determines one's occupational horizon for the rest of one's life. In large bureaucratic organizations like government offices and large corporations (in which most youths seek to find their careers), the particular escalator on which a new recruit is placed depends almost exclusively on the recruit's educational qualifications—which school he or she graduated from—at the time of employment. High school graduates can, in rare cases, rise as high as section chief, in either blue-collar or white-collar work, by the time they retire at age 55 or 60. University graduates are hired as clerical or technical staff members with a possibility of promotion through the managerial ranks as high as company director or president. In the government bureaucracy and very large corporations, graduates of elite universities may form a special cadre of elite managerial staff whose members are promoted at a much faster rate than graduates of ordinary universities.

Thus, in today's Japan, there exists a stratification of people based on their educational backgrounds that only roughly parallels the traditional distinction of upper, middle, and lower classes. The whole working population is classified largely into three groups according to their educational levels: elite universities, ordinary universities, and high schools or less. Young men and women are pigeonholed into one of these "classes" at about age 18. Few people go back to schools in the middle of their career for further education. Taking time off for further education means loss of seniority in one's place of work. Moreover, acquiring an additional academic qualification will not do much good to an employee since government agencies and large corporations as a rule recruit their regular employees only at their "normal" school-leaving ages of 18 for high school graduates and 22 for university graduates.

It must be clear by now why the Japanese find it so important to enter right universities. The choice of going or not going to college, and the success or failure in getting into a "right" university, largely and irrevocably determines a person's occupational chances and hence his or her later station in life. The Japanese people's social statuses are *achieved* (in the sense that they are determined by competitive examinations) by age 18, after which they become *ascribed* statuses that cannot be changed for the rest of their lives. It is as though all Japanese have one, and only one, chance in their lifetime, at about age 18, to choose their social "class" affiliation. It is the irreversibility of this choice, more than anything else, that accounts for the frantic and desperate efforts of Japanese youths (abetted by their parents) to get into the university of their choice.

SOCIAL STRATIFICATION
IN THE SOVIET UNION

The absence of private ownership of productive means and the authoritarian nature of the political system in the Soviet Union make the social stratification there considerably different from that in the United States or Japan.

The Soviet Union is a "classless" society—so goes the official Soviet position—in the sense that there are no classes in Marx's sense of antagonistic social groups with opposing interests. Rather, socialist classes are nonantagonistic classes without class consciousness and hostility toward other groups. Official Soviet doctrine recognizes two classes— *workers* (the proletariat) and (collective-farm) *peasants*. The workers— in theory the most important and privileged class—are nonowners of productive properties. The peasants are distinguished from workers because of the difference in property relations. Whereas workers do not own the means of production, collective farmers are, technically at least, collective owners of the farms.

Official doctrine also recognizes a third group—the *intelligentsia*. This group consists of managers, professionals, technical specialists, and other nonmanual employees. This white-collar, nonmanual group of employees is distinguished from the two basic classes by virtue of education and occupation, not for reasons of property relations. Because of this difference, official doctrine insists that the intelligentsia does not constitute a class; rather, it forms a *stratum*. The members of this stratum are said to have roots in, or descend from, the two basic classes. Thus, a Soviet engineer or university student, for example, is regarded as a member of the working class (or the peasant class) who happens to be classified, for statistical purposes, in the intelligentsia stratum. Each and every member of the intelligentsia, therefore, is expected to be aware of his or her roots in one of the "mother" classes. By means of this rather circuitous logic, official Soviet doctrine attempts to reconcile the reality of technological complexity with the ideological fiction that in Soviet socialism no contradiction exists between mental and manual work.

Although official Soviet doctrine does not recognize it as such, there exists yet another distinct social stratum—the power elite group. Thus, the broad ·stratum of intelligentsia can be divided into three groups: the ruling elite, the professional and technical specialists, and the nonmanual white-collar "employees." Together with the industrial manual workers (the proletariat) and the collective-farm peasants, these five groups form a fairly well established hierarchy with a descending order of economic rewards and social prestige.

There is a considerable degree of intergenerational mobility between the five groups. The children of peasants join the ranks of the proletariat to escape the drudgery of collective-farm life, and the sons and daughters of industrial workers escape the monotony of manual work by becoming professional and technical specialists. The power elite forms a distinct stratum by itself; it enjoys an inordinate amount of political power and economic privilege that is not shared by the rest of society. In spite of the unequal distribution of power and privilege, however, class consciousness and snobbery are patently absent in the Soviet Union. In a nutshell, the country may be characterized by "non-egalitarian classlessness," and, in that sense, it is very much like the United States.[12]

The Ruling Elite

The exact size and composition of the Soviet elite is difficult to ascertain because there is no clear-cut and unequivocal definition of the term *elite* in the Soviet context. The elite is often equated with the intelligentsia, which consists of managers, professionals, and technical specialists, as well as white-collar, clerical workers. With their family members included, the elite in this broadest sense encompasses over 40 million persons. The other extreme—the narrowest use of the term *elite*— defines the Soviet elite as comprising some 20 or 25 aging men at the pinnacle of the party-government apparatus—that is, the members of the Politburo and/or the Secretariat of the Communist party. There is no doubt that this group of men represents the hard core of the Soviet elite; they are the true rulers of the nation.

It is unrealistic to assume, however, that a modern industrial society with the size and complexity of the Soviet Union can be effectively ruled by a handful of men. We must identify yet another group, larger than the ruling oligarchy but smaller than the intelligentsia, who collectively rule over the nation—the group of people to whom the term *ruling elite* most meaningfully applies.

The essential characteristic of the Soviet elite is that it is a *power elite*, consisting of those persons who are at, or very close to, the center of the country's power structure at all levels, from central to rural district. They hold posts of importance in the party apparatus and in governmental, economic, military, legal, scientific, journalistic, athletic,

[12]Stanislaw Ossowski, *Class Structure in the Social Consciousness* (New York: The Free Press of Glencoe, 1963), chap. 7.

and artistic activities. Their career advancement depends on their loyalty to the party and its ruling oligarchy. In exchange for this loyalty, they receive privileges that are beyond the dreams of ordinary citizens. Their loyalty to the party, and the power, status, and privileges they enjoy, clearly distinguish them from the rest of the population. The ordinary Soviet citizens regard those men and women of power, status, and privilege as "them"—the *vlasti*.

The *Nomenklatura* System

Perhaps the best way to define the scope of the Soviet power elite is to refer to the institution known as the *nomenklatura system*. The term *nomenklatura* simply means the list of positions that are under the jurisdiction of a Communist party committee. Party committees at all levels—from all-union to rural district—have authority to appoint (or nominate in cases of elective offices) individuals to the positions on their own nomenklatura. These positions include key executive positions in the party apparatus, government bureaucracy, the Soviets, the military, and such public organizations as trade unions, mass media, and unions of scientists and artists. In all, the nomenklatura system covers some 3 million positions.[13]

The number of *elite* nomenklatura positions must be considerably smaller than 3 million. This is necessarily so because many of the positions listed on the nomenklatury of lower-level party committees include such sensitive but nonelitist positions as the director of a state farm and the foreman in a plant of a strategic industry.[14] Michael Voslensky estimates the numerical strength of the most important nomenklatura positions to be about 750,000. Including their family members, roughly 3 million persons, or about 1.5 percent of the Soviet population, comprise the ruling class of the Soviet Union.[15]

The Privileges of the Soviet Elite

In the Western capitalist countries, privileges of all sorts—but particularly material advantages—that individuals can enjoy are roughly proportional to the amount of money they can command. Money is the source of power and privilege. In the Soviet Union, by contrast, it is the access to, or connection with, the core of state political power that gives

[13]Bohdan Harasymiw, "*Nomenklatura:* The Soviet Communist Party's Leadership Recruitment System," *Canadian Journal of Political Science,* 2, no. 4 (December 1969), 493–512.

[14]Ibid., pp. 497–98.

[15]Michael Voslensky, *Nomenklatura: The Soviet Ruling Class* (Garden City, N.Y.: Doubleday & Company, Inc., 1984), pp. 95–96.

persons power, status, and privileges. Money or income is of secondary importance.

Every member of the Soviet elite is carefully ranked within the respective sector of Soviet life. Those in the power elite group are naturally ranked according to the importance (power and authority) of the offices they hold. This situation is not materially different from one that exists within a military or civil service bureaucracy in a capitalist country. What appears odd to the Western observer is the Soviet practice of ranking individuals in the fields of activity that do not seem to necessitate formal and meticulous ranking. Academics, athletes, journalists, and artists of all sorts are ranked according to the quality of the contribution they make in enhancing the prestige and power of the Soviet system. Material advantages and other amenities—such as highly coveted overseas travel—are then parceled out according to the finely tuned ranking system.

Nowhere is the adage, "Rank has its privileges," more applicable than to Soviet society. The members of the ruling elite are virtually free of all material worries. Ample living quarters, good-quality food in abundance, and excellent medical services and recreational opportunities are provided by the state free or at very low prices. The members of the establishment and their families have privileges to shop at special stores unaccessible for the masses. In those stores, hard-to-find domestic and imported goods can be purchased at bargain prices. A nationwide network of such stores, hospitals, and recreational facilities is run by the government exclusively for the benefit of the elite members and their families.

The system of finely tuned allocation of material and other privileges to the citizens according to their political rank has an important functional significance from the point of view of the Soviet regime's control over the population. By parceling out privileges according to rank, the regime generates among the masses a desire to become part of the elite and to achieve high rank within it, very much as individuals in capitalist societies aspire to join the ranks of the rich. Soviet citizens who want to satisfy their materialistic and acquisitive instincts, or those who badly wish to escape the drabness of the life of ordinary citizens, can do so only by climbing up the sociopolitical ladder within the power structure of the establishment. Success in these endeavors, however, requires, above all, loyalty to the Communist party and its bosses. Thus, by permitting only a single-track outlet for people's energy, ambition, and desire for a better life, and by rewarding them primarily for their loyalty, the regime can be assured that its grip over the populace will remain strong and unchallenged.

The power and privileges acquired by members of the elite cannot be passed on to their heirs since they are merely perquisites of positions.

This fact differentiates the stratification of Soviet society from that of capitalist countries. Granted that offices cannot be inherited, can successful parents somehow pass on to their children conditions for success—for example, superior education or political connection? This is an important question since such intergenerational transmissions will give permanence and stability to occupational groups, so that they may eventually be transformed into true social classes. We now turn to a brief discussion of this question.

Social Mobility and Self-Recruitment

Various studies of the Soviet educational system have shown that the children of lower-status families are underrepresented in Soviet higher education.[16] In the Soviet Union, as elsewhere, there exists a degree of self-recruitment in each social stratum. The children of intelligentsia parents tend to be overrepresented in higher educational institutions, and consequently end up becoming intelligentsia themselves. The children of blue-collar and farm workers tend to have fewer years of schooling, and are likely to become manual workers. The direction of self-recruitment, however, may be assymetrical. Frank Parkin points out that the Soviet educational system tends to operate not so much to block upward mobility of lower-stratum youths as to restrict the downward mobility of the children of higher social strata.[17]

Those Soviet workers in the nonmanual strata naturally seek to preserve their privileged status for their offspring. Since the ownership and transmission of productive properties are not permitted, intergenerational transmission of privileges must rely almost exclusively on educational achievements. Parents in the nonmanual strata, therefore, tend to stress the importance of education to their children. Thus, the circle of self-recruitment of the nonmanual employees repeats itself.

Besides education, self-recruitment at higher social strata can be achieved by using connections or influence (*blat*). Members of the ruling elite can arrange admissions to schools and universities for their children through the network of well-developed personal connections. Hedrick Smith reports that certain schools and universities have become known as the spoils of the children of the ruling elite.[18]

Although the use of *blat* appears to be rampant in the Soviet Union,

---

[16]See, for example, Murray Yanowitch, "Schooling and Inequalities," in *The Soviet Worker: Illusions and Realities*, ed. Leonard Schapiro and Joseph Godson (New York: St. Martin's Press, 1981), pp. 145–46.

[17]Frank Parkin, "Class Stratification in Socialist Societies," *British Journal of Sociology*, 20, no. 4 (December 1969), 368.

[18]Smith, *The Russians*, p. 47.

the practice of nepotism does not appear to be as widespread as in many other countries. Perhaps the most obvious case of nepotism was Stalin's son Vasili, who was made a general in the air force at an early age. The present ruling oligarchs, however, seem to be restrained in exercising their influence in placing their relations in the positions of power in the party and government bureaucracies. There are examples of sons and sons-in-law of the members of the ruling elite occupying rather lofty positions, but they seem more like cases of competent individuals receiving all the benefits of high-quality blat, rather than cases of obvious nepotism. At the highest level of political struggle within the Kremlin, what matters the most is the patron-client relationships among the party leaders, not their blood relationships.

Yet another reason for the relative absence of the children of party bosses in the political elite has been suggested by Brzezinski and Huntington. The surest and fastest way to reach higher administrative posts within the party apparatus is to pursue the career of a party cadre, or an *apparatchik*. To do so, however, requires the ideological and personal commitment of a sort that is not usually found among the children of high-ranking party leaders. They are more likely to opt for careers in professional or technical fields. Full-time apparatchik careers, on the other hand, appeal greatly to the ambitious but less privileged youths of proletariat or peasant backgrounds.[19] Many of these youths are willing to endure years of hard work as party activists, climbing patiently each rung of the ladder of party hierarchy while remaining absolutely loyal to their superiors. The higher levels of the party bureaucracy are filled with career apparatchiki of this type. In this way, access to positions in the Soviet ruling elite remains relatively free to youths from all social strata.

Unlike the situation in Japan or France, the elite of Soviet society— the Communist party apparatchiki whose total numbers about half a million—are not recruited from the elite universities. The party's cadres of future leaders are trained at one of the two special schools affiliated with the party's Central Committee: the Higher Party School of the Central Committee, and the Academy of Social Sciences of the Central Committee. Students at these privileged schools are recruited from among the young rank-and-file party loyalists who are recommended by the party's regional committees. Successful candidates for admission to these schools must exhibit a correct Marxist-Leninist attitude. Their past work experience and their loyalty and devotion to the party are considered more important than their intellectual capacity. Candidates with working-class backgrounds are favored over those with intellectual

---

[19]Zbigniew Brzezinski and Samuel P. Huntington, *Political Power: USA/USSR* (New York: The Viking Press, 1964), pp. 139ff; discussed in Anthony Giddens, *The Class Structure of the Advanced Societies* (New York: Harper & Row, Publishers, Inc., 1973), p. 242.

family backgrounds, unless they are related to high-ranking party officials.[20]

Graduates of the special party schools do not return to their former occupations. Instead, they move up the hierarchy of key positions in the party apparatus. They may also be assigned to positions in the diplomatic service, security services, the mass media, and athletic and cultural organizations. These assignments are made at the discretion of the Central Committee's personnel department; the apparatchiki are deprived of freedom of occupational choice. As a compensation, they are given power and privileges commensurate with the importance of their positions. Most significantly, they are totally freed from everyday material worries that beset all ordinary Soviet mortals.[21]

Appendix: EDUCATION AND SOCIAL SELECTION IN WESTERN EUROPE, MAINLY FRANCE

The educational systems of the West European countries differ from those in the three countries discussed in this chapter in an important respect. In Western European countries there exists, in one form or another, a system of two-track education in which children are separated broadly into two groups—those who are encouraged or allowed to pursue advanced academic education and those who are channeled toward a vocational or technical track. As the selection usually takes place at about age 11 or 12, the system is commonly referred to as the *eleven-plus system.* By contrast, the educational systems of the United States, the Soviet Union, and Japan are, as a rule, comprehensive in the sense that the distinction between academic and vocational secondary education is an exception rather than a rule.

The opportunity-equalizing effect of education is somewhat limited in Western Europe because of the eleven-plus system of dual-track education. Education is not regarded primarily as a means of facilitating economic development of the country or improving social mobility of individuals. The tradition of separating academic education of the social elite and the vocational education of the working class is still alive and pervasive. Higher education is believed to be something that is to be pursued by a small group of intellectual elite, as learning for learning's sake, not as a means to increase the economic productivity of the individual. This intellectual elitism comes in direct conflict with the needs of a modern industrial state that demands human resources to be uti-

[20]Leonid Vladimirov, *The Russians* (New York: Frederick A. Praeger, Publishers, 1968), pp. 145–46.

[21]Ibid., pp. 151–54.

lized in the most efficient manner. Notwithstanding efforts made over the last decades to reform the systems, European education still retains a significant element of the eleven-plus selection system. As a consequence, the number of working-class youths attending academic secondary schools is still relatively small.

It is at the level of higher education that the difference between the comprehensive system and the two-track system becomes pronounced. While nearly one-half of the college-age youths in the United States and Japan attend colleges and universities, the comparable proportion in Western Europe is typically about one-fifth. Whereas college education is almost a necessity for a managerial career in the United States and Japan, in Europe a university degree is considered necessary only for a professional career. Many European youths begin their managerial career without a university degree.

Elitism in higher education is perhaps most pronounced in France where there exists a number of select institutions called *grandes écoles* outside the ordinary four-year university system. A small number of exceptionally capable students are admitted each year to the grandes écoles by nationwide competitive examinations called the *grands concours*. Customarily the examinations are taken by the holders of the *baccalauréat* (the diploma that qualifies the holder for admission to a university) who have spent a year or two preparing for the examinations. The grandes écoles offer high-quality education in professional and technological studies, and their diplomas have a higher prestige than most university degrees (or *licences*). The best known of the grandes écoles are the École Polytechnique (whose alumni are called *polytechniciens* or "X"), which is an engineering school run as a military academy under the jurisdiction of the Ministry of Defense; the École Normale Supérieure, which produces the elite of the teaching profession; the École des Sciences Politiques (known as "Sciences Po") under the Ministry of Education; the École Nationale Supérieure des Mines (the School of Mines); and the École Centrale, which is another engineering school.

Most of the graduates of the top grandes écoles pursue careers in the *grands corps:* the Conseil d'État (the elite civil service corps), the Inspectorat des Finance, the prefectorial administration, the national police, the mining corps, and so on. Many members of the grands corps later move to the private sector and assume top executive positions. Many graduates of the engineering grandes écoles—Polytechnique, des Mines, and Centrale—directly enter great French firms headquartered in Paris, and begin their careers in the upper management cadre (*cadre supérieures*).

The access to the top French bureaucratic order in both government and business is through grandes écoles, not through universities. The grandest of the grandes écoles is the Polytechnique. Some of the polytechniciens enter the elite civil service, while some others serve in government for ten years or so before they "parachute" into private firms. In the civil service, the Sciences Politiques is also very important.

Since 1945, all entrants into the higher civil service are trained and certified by the École Nationale d'Administration (ENA). Although this school is not considered a grande école proper, its importance in the French political life is overwhelming. It draws heavily upon the graduates of the Polytechnique, Sciences Po, and other top grandes écoles, and channels them toward the elite civil service. The alumni of the ENA, called the *énarques*, dominate the French higher civil service and politics, so much so that the government of France is nicknamed by its critics as being an *énarchie*, rather than a *monarchie* or *démocratie*.

QUESTIONS

1. List several social organizations that have predominantly (a) primary-group and (b) secondary-group characteristics. Consider the degree of organizational unity (i.e., harmony of interests) in each.
2. List the reasons why you, as an individual, might possibly be induced to serve the interests of a group at the expense of your own self-interests.
3. List the advantages and disadvantages of being a member of a primary group, in contrast to being a member of a secondary group.
4. As far as motivational forces in social relations go in your own society, what are the relative importance of the four motives—money, power, group approbation, and group solidarity? What factors account for your particular rank-ordering?
5. Both social organization and social relation may be described as a complex of predictable and recurrent patterns of social interactions. What, then, is the difference between the two concepts? Give a few examples each of social organization and social relation. Does one affect the other in a given society?
6. Suppose two middle-aged Japanese males, total strangers to each other, wearing the same business suit but having no other clues as to each other's social status, are thrown into a situation where they have to communicate and cooperate with each other for some length of time. How do you suppose they would handle the problem of using appropriate honorifics in the language?
7. How does the matriarchical orientation of Japanese society affect the quality of its social relations?
8. Explain the nature of *amae* in Japanese social relations. How does amae affect the nature of social organization in Japan? Specifically, does it make subordinates' acceptance of superiors' authority easier or harder?
9. What aspects of Japanese social relations explain the competitive drive of the Japanese people?

10. Given that the Russians are collectivist in their social relations, why don't such motives as group approbation and group solidarity contribute to high productivity and product quality of Soviet productive enterprises?

11. According to such critics as Etzioni and Reich, what are the fundamental deficiencies of American social organization that have given rise to America's industrial decline? How can they be corrected?

12. Do you think it is possible to rebuild America on a communal basis? Is there enough community-mindedness to rebuild America largely on the group solidarity motivation? If not, what other types of motives do you think can Americans draw on? What organizational changes are necessary?

13. What is the difference between ascribed social status and achieved social status? Is the United States a meritocratic society?

14. Do you think the Americans are class-conscious people? What factors militate against class consciousness in America?

15. Are the Japanese class-conscious people? Are they egalitarian in their social relations?

16. Is Japan a meritocratic society? Are social statuses in Japan basically ascribed or achieved?

17. What is the nature of the ruling elite of the Soviet Union? How large is it? How does one become a member of this group?

18. Describe the *nomenklatura* system. Do you agree with the statement that this system is one of the most important means by which the CPSU maintains its monopoly of power over the Soviet society?

19. What factors militate against a high degree of self-recruitment in the elite ruling class of the Soviet Union? What factors facilitate it?

SELECTED READING

AUSTIN, LEWIS. *Saints and Samurai: The Political Culture of the American and Japanese Elites.* New Haven, Conn.: Yale University Press, 1975.

GIDDENS, ANTHONY. *The Class Structure of the Advanced Societies.* New York: Harper & Row, Publishers, Inc., 1973.

NAKANE, CHIE. *Japanese Society.* Berkeley, Calif.: University of California Press, 1970.

REISCHAUER, EDWIN O. *The Japanese,* pts. 1, 2, and 3. Cambridge, Mass.: Harvard University Press, 1977.

SHIPLER, DAVID K. *Russia: Broken Idols, Solemn Dreams.* New York: Times Books, 1983.

SMITH, HEDRICK. *The Russians.* New York: Quadrangle/The New York Times Book Co., 1976.

VOSLENSKY, MICHAEL. *Nomenklatura: The Soviet Ruling Class.* Garden City, N.Y.: Doubleday & Company, Inc., 1984.

CHAPTER 4

The
Political
System

A *political system* may be defined as the complex of ideologies, institutions, and processes of government and politics in a given society. In this chapter we shall examine those aspects of the political systems of the three countries that have a direct bearing on the organization and management of their economic systems. Specifically, our attention will be focused on the structure of government organization and political power. In order to minimize confusion and misunderstanding, definitions of several key terms are presented below.

> *Government:* The organization that exercises political authority within a given geographic area
>
> *State:* An entity to which society ascribes supreme political authority
>
> *Power:* The ability to make others do what one wants
>
> *Authority:* Legitimate power
>
> *Legitimacy:* Acceptance on the part of those over whom power is exercized of the right of the power holders to exercise power on moral or legal grounds or by value consensus
>
> *Political authority:* The legitimate power of government
>
> *Politics:* The acquisition and exercise of political power

THE AMERICAN POLITICAL SYSTEM

The dominant ideology of the American political system is pluralism, which advocates that political power should be decentralized and diffused, with numerous power centers being able to check and veto each other's exercise of power, so that no single individual or group has monopoly of power. This aversion to concentrated power, of course, is rooted in the American ideology of individualism. In order to safeguard the freedom of the individual, government must be limited. In order to achieve limited government, Americans have written into their Constitution the systems of federalism and the separation of powers. Limited government can also be realized by allowing individuals and groups to form interest groups and compete among themselves in influencing public decision making. In this section we shall analyze the structure of limited government in the United States, and comment on the problem of special interest pluralism compromising the general interest of society.

Separation of Powers

Power is shared in the United States by the central and state governments, and, at the central government level, by the three branches of government. The idea of separating public power into legislative, executive, and judicial branches was first advocated by the French political scientist and philospher Baron de Montesquieu (1689–1755) in his celebrated treatise *L'Esprit des Lois* (The Spirit of the Laws) published in 1748. Montesquieu was concerned about the propensity of persons to abuse the power they acquire, and argued that the best safeguard against the abuse of power was to fragment the power into branches of government. Separation of political power was formally incorporated into the U.S. Constitution and has served as the guiding principle underlying the American political system.

    In Chapter 2 we observed that the basic ideology of American society centers on freedom of the individual. This ideology manifests itself in the form of the principle of the separation of powers and of the checks and balances that are built into the U.S. Constitution, thereby uniquely defining the character of the nation. Separation of powers and authority is so complete and pervasive that we can identify no *center* of either public or private power in America. Public power is fragmented between the federal and state governments, among the three branches of the federal government, and among professional politicians and government bureaucrats. Nor can we find concentrated power in the private sector. Big business does not present a unified front, business and labor are counterposed in adversary relations, and small business and agriculture are diffused and scattered all over the country.

Contrast the above situation with what we find in the Soviet Union where effective political and economic powers are concentrated in the Communist party leadership. Power emanates from that center, and authority relationships are vertical and downward, forming a pyramid with the masses at the bottom. By contrast, we can identify at least five major power subcenters in the United States: Congress, the executive and its bureaucracy, the courts, the states, and the big-business community. The relationships among these power subcenters are those of horizontal checks and balances, with little of vertical structure of authority relations.

The Supreme Court

Because of the Court's authority to rule on the constitutionality of any legislative, executive, or judicial act, and because the Constitution is vague or silent on many specific aspects of public policy, the Court has a wide discretion in its judicial decision making. The right of *judicial review* thus gives the Supreme Court enormous power in shaping the content and character of public policy of the United States. The Court is not a mere arbiter of constitutional disputes; it is an important political institution playing a vital role in both the making of law and the shaping of public policy.

Robert Solo makes a distinction between authoritative and composite choices made in an organization. An *authoritative choice,* according to Solo, is a decision made "by an individual in authority on the basis of that authority *for* an organization." A *composite choice,* on the other hand, is a decision made "through interactive processes that compound and reflect the diverse drives and interests of those who participate in the operations of the organization." Solo argues that choices made in Congress and by the executive are by their very nature composite choices, and consequently are susceptible to pressures from special interest groups. By contrast, decisions made by the Supreme Court are authoritative choices that are "the expression of a unitary purpose, a reasoning mind and an integral ideology."[1] This is an important point since, as we shall see later, one of the systemic weaknesses of the American politico-economic system is the fact that much of the decision making by its public authority is corroded by the lobbying activities of special interest groups. Being impervious to special interest pressures,

[1]Robert A. Solo, *The Positive State* (Cincinnati, Ohio: South-Western Publishing Co., 1982), pp. 36 and 38. Solo's italics.

the Supreme Court can serve as an important defender of the public interest.

In making a decision, each of the justices listens to his or her own conscience and is guided by his or her own ideology. There is thus a danger that the Court's judicial decisions may be at odds with society's dominant ideology. In some cases the Court may play a vanguard role in society by *leading* social conscience into a new era, as it did in the 1950s and 1960s in expanding the civil rights of the ethnic minorities. As a general rule and in the long run, however, the Court's decisions must be at least minimally congruent with the society's dominant ideology; otherwise, their enforcements would not be effective. Thus, although the justices may, in their individual choices, follow the dictates of their own ideological and moral convictions, their collective decisions, in the long run, must stay within the limits of the prevailing values and beliefs of American society.

Independent Federal Agencies

The 60-odd boards, commissions, and agencies of the federal government, which are known collectively as independent federal agencies or regulatory commissions, occupy a unique role in the structure of American government. Although they derive authority from acts of Congress, they are independent in the sense that they receive directives from neither the president nor Congress. By function, they are primarily administrative agencies. But they also exercise quasi-judicial and even quasi-legislative functions.

Members of the independent federal agencies are appointed by the president with the consent of the Senate. Congress exercises broad supervision over these commissions, but it as a rule refrains from interfering with their specific operations. Congress created these agencies as its "long arms"—agencies that perform needed regulatory and other functions for Congress without interference from the executive branch. Congress could have vested the White House with additional authorities, enabling it and the executive departments to perform these functions. Instead, Congress created independent agencies, authorizing them with specific functions. The motive, again, was the fear of concentrating too much power in the hands of the president.

Chief among the independent federal agencies that play important roles in the nation's economic activities are the following:

The Interstate Commerce Commission
The Federal Trade Commission
The Federal Power Commission
The Federal Communications Commission

The Securities and Exchange Commission
The National Labor Relations Board
The Board of Governors of the Federal Reserve System
The United States International Trade Commission

As we noted earlier, the members of these agencies and commissions are appointed by the president subject to confirmation by the Senate. The terms of office of commissioners are staggered so that no commission or agency can be exclusively staffed by the same president. The president, however, can, in many cases, designate one of the commissioners as chairperson of the commission. Congress exercises its power of supervision over these agencies through the appropriate Senate and House standing committees. All of these agencies with the exception of the Federal Reserve Board must rely on the appropriation of funds by Congress.

Many of these independent federal agencies are often referred to as *regulatory* commissions or agencies. In a strict sense, however, not all of these agencies have regulatory functions. (*Regulation* may be defined as "directing or controlling according to rules.") For example, the National Labor Relations Board does not direct the behavior of any business firms or labor unions; it merely adjudicates disputes in labor relations. For another example, the United States International Trade Commission is not a regulatory commission in the strict sense of the term. It is a fact-finding body with broad powers to study and investigate complaints about unfair practices in import trade, but it does not "regulate" any particular industries or firms.

The term *regulatory agencies* may be applied in the narrower, more strict sense to those agencies that truly regulate a particular industry or industries. These agencies issue regulations, establish rules, fix rates, and set standards for the industry or industries; they then enforce these rules and impose sanctions on violators. Examples of the truly regulatory agencies are the Federal Power Commission, the Interstate Commerce Commission, the Federal Communications Commission, and the Securities and Exchange Commission.

Special Interest Groups and the Public Interest

The nature of politics varies widely from society to society, depending on the nature of systems of law and government in each society. For example, in the Soviet Union the Communist party has a monopoly of political power so that politics there means largely the process of power struggle among the top leaders of the party. In a democratic society like the United States, by contrast, winning elections is the only way to gain control of the government. Politics in such an environment involves the activities of political parties, political campaigns and elections, and the activities of special interest lobbying groups attempting to influence the outcomes of elections and the decison-making pocesses of government.

Detailed analysis of the two-party system, political campaigns, national conventions, and elections in the United States political system is beyond the scope of this book. Suffice it to say that in the American political life, winning elections is the primary goal of politicians and political parties; political power is exercised primarily by gaining control of the government through elections. Elections are frequent: the president must be elected every four years, the members of the House every two years, and the U.S. senators every six years. To win elections and stay in office, therefore, most politicians must think about the next election the moment they are elected to office. Maximizing vote getting thus becomes the primary motivation of the behavior of American politicians.

Political campaigns are expensive. Campaign funds are needed to organize the campaign, to pay the staff and meet other costs, and—what is becoming increasingly more important and expensive in recent decades—to pay for campaign advertising in the mass media. To pay for these expenses, most politicians must turn to external sources of funds, including contributions from lobbying groups. In the 1980 elections, for example, various lobbying groups financed nearly half of the campaign spending of the typical House of Representative candidate who won the election.[2]

Members of Congress who are elected with the assistance of special interest contributions would naturally find it hard, in their voting behavior, to ignore pleas from the special interest groups to give favorable considerations to the bills that are being promoted by those groups. It is therefore only natural for most members of Congress to be biased, more or less, in favor of legislation that specifically benefits various special interest groups even if such legislation may not serve the broader, general interest of the entire nation. In fact, placing the public interest ahead of narrow, parochial interests of powerful pressure groups and of constituencies at home often spells political disaster for the legislator. In order to see how this unfortunate perversion comes about, let us examine a hypothetical case of a congressman facing proposed legislation designed to restrict imports.

Suppose the election district of a congressman named John Doe is an important steel-producing area and the prosperity of the district's

<hr />

[2]Brooks Jackson, "The Problem with PACs," *Wall Street Journal*, November 17, 1982, p. 28.

economy is closely tied to the prosperity of its steel industry. If foreign steel imports pose a serious threat to the viability of the area's steel industry, the industry—both management and labor in cooperation—will naturally argue for a public policy that will provide protection or relief from foreign imports. Of course there is nothing wrong with this position in itself since to do so is in the interest of the industry and the region; in a free-market economy like the United States, every individual or group is expected to seek to maximize its private gains. A difficulty arises, however, when there exists a conflict between the private interest and the public interest. Suppose that cheap imported steel benefits other U.S. industries that use imported steel as inputs. Suppose further that the sum total of the widespread and diffused benefits of low-priced steel to a large number of consumers throughout the United States is more than enough to offset the injury done to the domestic steel industry. Who would speak for the consumers and argue against restriction of imports? Certainly not the domestic steel industry. It is likely to argue, either sincerely out of conviction or insincerely with intent to mislead the public, that protecting the industry from imports *is* in the public interest ("What's good for the steel industry is good for America"). The consuming and voting public, being uninitiated in the intricacies of the technical arguments in international economics and not willing to invest time and effort to become fully informed about the issue, is likely to be swayed by the patriotic sloganeering by the domestic industry. What should Congressman John Doe do in a situation like this?

It would be a political suicide for the congressman to vote against protectionist measure in Congress. Regardless of his own ideological conviction or economic understanding, Congressman Doe must vote for the protectionist measure if he is to survive as a politician. He must behave to maximize the private or parochial interests of his own district in order to maximize his own vote-getting power, even if such a behavior may be injurious to the public interest. Unfortunately, public interests do not produce votes: the benefits of low-priced imported steel are widely diffused, and no single voting group takes them to their heart. Parochial interests, by contrast, do produce votes. Costs and benefits are immediate and clearly recognizable. Those who seek special interests are willing, therefore, to spend money and efforts for their favored politicians. (The economic theory of special interest groups and lobbying activities will be discussed in more detail in Chapter 7.)

Congressman Doe may vote for the protectionist bill, but there may not be enough votes in the House to assure the passage of the bill since not all members of the House come from steel-producing districts. But every district has some special interests. Congressman Doe therefore can engage in horsetrading (or logrolling). In exchange for a vote for a bill that allows a continuation of the federal subsidy to tobacco growers, for example, Congressman Doe may be able to gain a vote for his steel import restriction bill from a congressman from a tobacco-growing state. A network of such logrolling results in passages of a large number of special interest and pork-barrel legislation that benefits numerous interest groups. Public interest, often, is the loser in the process.

The bias against the public interest does not arise from regional and occupational interests alone. In general, voters, campaign workers, and fund donors are likely to support candidates whose legislative behavior helps maximize their short-term, private gains and minimize their short-term, private costs—often at the expense of more general, long-term interests of society as a whole. As a general rule, it is very difficult for legislators to vote for any measures that require an immediate sacrifice on the part of the public in the interest of a long-term benefit. If, for example, effective control of inflation requires a substantial increase in taxes, politicians vote for such a measure at a great risk to their political careers. Tax-cut measures, on the other hand, are much more popular, even if that might exacerbate the inflation problem in the long run.

We have noted above that legislators' voting behavior tends to be biased in favor of the narrow and parochial interests of minority groups at the expense of the broader, general interests of society as a whole. We approached the problem from the politicians' points of view with a focus on their overriding objective of securing reelection. But what about the behavior of the special interest groups? What types of interest tend to be promoted by special interest lobbies? These questions will be examined in some depth in Chapter 7.

THE JAPANESE POLITICAL SYSTEM

In Chapter 2 we observed that the dominant ideology of Japan is familistic groupism. The nation is regarded as a familylike organic unit, and its activities are not as sharply separated into the political (government) and the economic (business) as they are in the United States. The familistic nation-state-economy of Japan is managed collectively by the elites of the three loosely identifiable groups of people: the administrative bureaucracy, the big-business leadership, and the leadership of the ruling political party.

The Unitary System of Government

The Japanese system of government closely resembles that of the United Kingdom. Japan is a constitutional monarchy and parliamentary democracy. The National Diet (parliament) is composed of two houses.

The upper house, the House of Councillors (*sangi-in*), has 252 members who are popularly elected for a term of six years. The lower house, the House of Representatives (*shugi-in*), consists of 511 members who are elected by universal suffrage for a period of four years. The upper house may veto the legislation orginating in the lower house; the veto, however, can be overridden by a two-thirds majority in the lower house.

The executive organ of the government is headed by the prime minister who is elected by a majority vote in the House of Representatives. The prime minister appoints some 20 cabinet members. If the House of Representatives passes a motion of no-confidence, the cabinet must resign unless the prime minister dissolves the House and calls for a general election.

In 1981, there were the following 12 ministries: Justice; Foreign Affairs; Finance; Education; Health and Welfare; Agriculture, Forestry and Fisheries; International Trade and Industry; Transport; Posts and Telecommunications; Construction; Labor; and Home Affairs. In addition to these ministries, there were eight agencies and one commission headed by State Ministers, which included the Defense Agency, the Economic Planning Agency, and the Environment Agency.

Administratively, Japan is divided into 47 prefectures. Greater Tokyo is counted as a prefecture (*Tokyo-to*, or Tokyo Metropolis), so that the "city" of Tokyo does not exist as a political entity. Prefectural governors, mayors, and the members of prefectural and municipal assemblies are elected by local residents. Prefectures and municipalities are not enpowered to enact legislation. They carry out their functions through ordinances which must conform to national law. Although the Japanese Constitution (Article 92) and the Local Autonomy Law of 1947 declare the principle of local autonomy, in practice local autonomy is highly limited. For all practical purposes, prefectures and municipalities may be considered administrative subdivisions of the national government.

The Power Structure of Japan's Political System

The structure of power relations in the Japanese political system may be characterized as being somewhere in the middle of the broad spectrum ranging from the Soviet-style monopoly of political power at one extreme and the American-style separation of powers at the other. In Japan, there is a strong sense of communal unity; there is a feeling that the various constituent parts of society—public or private, national or local, big or small, legislative or executive, agriculture or industry— all belong to the same national community and share the same destiny. Unlike the Soviet Union, Japan does not have a single center of power. Neither is there found sharing of power by basically autonomous entities exercising checks and balances over each other, as in the United States. What is found, instead, is a pyramidlike power structure headed by a troika of major power centers—the leadership of the ruling political party, headed by the prime minister; the big-business leadership; and the administrative bureaucracy. The symbiotic relationships that exist among these groups, more than anything else, epitomize the nature of the Japanese economic system.

Prior to the democratization of Japan that took place after World War II, familistic statism prevailed in Japan. The whole nation was considered one big family, with the emperor as the father figure. Assisting the emperor in ruling the nation-family was *kanryo*, or the state bureaucracy. The imperial bureaucrats exercised authority of the state in the name of the emperor. For centuries, it had been taken for granted in Japan that *kan* (the imperial or state officialdom) was superordinate to *min* (the people). The imperial bureaucrats' attitude of self-importance and contempt of the people—*kanson minpi* (officialdom revered, people disdained)—was deeply ingrained and, even today, subtly affects the behavior and attitude of Japanese bureaucrats toward people.

With the postwar democratization of the Japanese government structure, certain major changes took place in the power relations. First, the emperor was removed from the position of authority; he became a "symbol of national unity." Second, the government became in effect two-headed. The cabinet headed by the prime minister, with its roots in the popularly elected National Diet, makes policy decisions, while the actual management of society is entrusted to the administative bureaucracy.

Although in theory the bureaucracy is subordinate to the cabinet, in reality the collective power of the bureaucrats is as great as, if not greater than, that of the cabinet. Politically appointed ministers come and go with each election and each cabinet reshuffling, but the bureaucrats—up to and including the administrative vice-minister (*jimu jikan*)—remain in the same ministry. Unlike the practices in the United States, in Japan there are no political appointments of bureaucrats. Ministerial chairs are allocated to major factions within the ruling party as part of the payoff in intraparty politics. Thus, a veteran politician who is appointed a minister knows, as a rule, very little about the day-to-day business of the ministry he or she heads. Actual running of the ministry is thus left up to the career bureaucrats headed by the vice-minister. Some ministers do try to interfere in ministerial matters, but they meet a strong organized resistance of the career bureaucrats, particularly if the inteference is in personnel affairs.

It is also worth noting that nine out of ten pieces of legislation in Japan's National Diet originate in the ministries; the bills are developed and drafted by assistant section chiefs and section chiefs in their 30s and 40s. Specialized knowledge of, and experience in, complex technologies of statecraft gives the bureaucrats a sense of self-importance and disdain for parliament and political parties. Asked to respond to the statement, "Basically speaking, it is the bureaucracy—not the political parties or parliament—that is adequately dealing with the nation's policies in general," 80 percent of the 149 high-ranking Japanese bureaucrats agreed with the statement, as compared to 21 percent of the British and 16 perent of the West German bureaucrats surveyed in similar studies.[3] These figures reflect in part the residual of the *kanson-minpi* attitude carried over from the prewar days, but are also partly a reflection of the elitist sense of mission of the Japanese higher civil servants. They see the political parties and the parliament basically representing the interests of various pressure groups, not the nation's public interests at large. Their sense of mission, then, is to promote and protect the long-run interests of the Japanese nation-family, as they define them.

It is worth noting that in the Japanese political system, the Diet (parliament) plays a rather insignificant role. Unlike the U.S. Congress, the Japanese Diet does not draft much law, nor does it make substantive decisions concerning the government budget. As we have noted earlier, most of the legislative bills are drafted by bureaucrats in the ministries. The all-important power to determine the national budget is deeply entrenched in the bureaucracy of the Ministry of Finance. The Diet's main function is to ratify the decisions made elsewhere, notably at the higher echelons of the administistative bureaucracy and the ruling-party machine.

We must hasten to add, however, that the Japanese parliament is not a rubber stamp like the Supreme Soviet of the USSR. It plays two important roles in Japan's *Realpolitik*. First, it legitimizes the power of the ruling coalition by providing the necessary number of votes. To stay in power, the ruling political party must have a majority of vote in the Diet. The Diet thus defines which political party (or coalition of parties and/or factions) is in power. Moreover, without the necessary number of votes, government bills cannot be enacted into law. In this sense, what matters is the party affiliation of the members of the Diet rather than what they do in the Diet. Second, the Diet plays a mediating role by serving as a forum for allowing the various off-mainstream groups in the country—farmers, small-business people, labor unions, public interest organizations, and so on—to air their minority views publicly. Not that their airings affect in a fundamental way the policies and legislative outcomes of the mainstream coalition of the bureaucracy,

---

[3]Akira Kubota and Nobuo Tomita, "Nippon Seifu Kokan no Ishiki Kozo," *Chuo Koron*, February 1977, pp. 190–96.

ruling party, and big business; but in a typically Japanese spirit of respecting minority positions, minimally necessary compromises are made by those in power to incorporate the minority interests into the country's public policy.

The self-importance of bureaucrats does not translate into their monopoly of power. Some activist ministers may assume a strong leadership position in the ministry in making strategic decisions. Although ministers as a rule refrain from interfering in the ministerial personnel matters, the selection of the vice-minister, because it is a highly political decision, at times hinges on the preference of the minister. Although it is customary for the retiring vice-minister to name his successor, a politically ambitious retiring vice-minister may yield to the political pressure from the minister or from the ruling-party leadership in his selection of the next vice-minister. Bureaucrats also need the support of their minister in the battles for their favorite legislation and policies which they must fight with powerful outside forces, namely, other ministries and hostile members of the Diet. In general, bureaucrats must rely, in trying to get what they want, on the support from the politicians in the minister's office, the cabinet, and the ruling-party leadership. Ambitious senior bureaucrats are also eager to accommodate the wishes of influential party bosses and big business leaders since the chances of landing lucrative postretirement positions in public or private corporations depend crucially on maintaining amicable relationships with the leaders in politics and industry. All in all, the higher the positions of senior officials, the more accommodating they tend to be to the wishes of powerful political figures and influential industrial leaders.

Politicians, in turn, find it useful to remain in friendly and accommodating terms with high-ranking officials in key economic ministries since such connections may bear fruit in bringing favorable official rulings on project approvals, loan applications, license acquisitions, and so on, which the politicians are eager to secure for their constituencies and support groups.

The Administrative Bureaucracy

The national government employs about 2 million persons, about two-thirds of whom are employees of various public corporations. Public employees are recruited, usually at their school leaving ages, through competitive entrance examinations. With the exception of the parliamentary vice-minister (*seimu jikan*) in each ministry and a few other positions in the Prime Minister's Office, there are no political appointments. Thus, unlike the situation in the United States, changes in the government (cabinet) in Japan leave the bureaucracy intact.

There are four levels of examinations for national government posts:

junior, middle, senior (class B), and senior (class A). High school graduates are recruited for the junior-level posts, which are primarily clerical. Junior college education is required for taking the middle-level civil service examinations. Although a university degree qualifies one to take either class B or class A of the senior-level examinations, class A examinations are attempted only by a small number of very able youths—mostly graduates of elite universities.

The class A examinations for senior national government posts are extremely selective, admitting only about 1,300 persons each year. Although both class A and class B careerists start with similar initial assignments, the class A elite bureaucrats are promoted much faster than their class B colleagues, being moved from one post to another within the same ministry (or sometimes outside the ministry) every one and one-half to two years. Class B officials, on the other hand, are likely to remain in the same area of service until their retirement, and their chances of advancement are highly limited. To be promoted to the all-important and prestigious rank of *section chief* in the Main (i.e., Tokyo) Office of a ministry or agency, one must have class A qualifications. Consequently, all the key posts in the Japanese government—those with the rank of section chief and above in the Tokyo office—are exclusively reserved for those officials who hold class A senior-level qualifications.

In the early years of their service, all the elite (i.e., class A) bureaucrats of the same year of entry are promoted at about the same rate. In their 30s, the difference between slow movers and high fliers become clearly recognizable. Even then, however, the distinction may be very subtle. Two officials with the same number of years of service behind them may have the same rank, say, subsection chief. Yet insiders can readily tell which one is advancing faster by the relative prestige of the section or subsection each is assigned to. In about 20 years after entering the service, the more successful of elite bureaucrats reach the position of section chief in the Main Office. About 1 in 6 reaches the level of bureau chief in about 30 years of service. Only 1 in 30, however, makes it to the highest post in the ministerial bureaucracy—the administrative vice-minister—before retirement.[4] In order to make room for their juniors (i.e., those belonging to later year-of-entry classes), administrative vice-ministers by custom resign in a year or two after their appointment.

This unique system of seniority-cum-merit-based promotion of Japan's elite bureaucrats deserves a close examination since the pattern is also observed, although in a less rigid form, in Japan's large corporations. The main features of the elite careerist system are as follows.

---

[4]Taro Kawamoto, "Sore demo Todai Hogaku-bu wa Nihon o Ugokasu," *Bungei Shunju*, September 1972, p. 173.

First, induction into the service is done, once a year, through competitive examinations. The only qualification, beside the citizenship requirement and age limits, is a university degree. As a rule, one can enter the national government service only at the lowest level of the bureaucratic hierarchy. Because of the extreme difficulty of the examinations, only the cream of the crop of Japan's higher education system tries the examinations. The overwhelming majority of those who succeed in the examinations are graduates of Japan's elite universities, especially the University of Tokyo. For example, in 1976, of nearly the 54,000 persons who took the class A Senior Civil Service Examinations, only 1,336 passed, of whom 35 percent were Tokyo graduates and 14 percent were from Kyoto University.[5]

Second, elite bureaucrats tend to be generalists. Career bureaucrats are divided into generalists (*jimukan*) and specialists (*gikan*), and the majority of those with the generalist designation have degrees in either law (i.e., political science) or economics. Once in the service, however, young generalist officials quickly master the technical aspects of their jobs in diverse fields thanks to frequent job rotations. Specialists with technical educational backgrounds, on the other hand, tend to remain in their specialized field throughout their careers, and their chances of promotion to the top ministerial positions, particularly that of vice-minister, are slim in the great majority of ministries.

Third, seniority-based promotion applies not only to individuals but to a group: those in the same year-of-entry class are promoted at the same rate of speed, except that, as noted earlier, distinctions between the high flyers and slow movers become clearly discernible to the trained eye after 10 or 15 years of service. The fact that a whole class of officials is moving up in ranks—with subtle but important differences in individual assignments—contributes to both a strong sense of camaraderie and competition among those in the same class.

Fourth, since the available positions necessarily decrease in number as the whole class moves up the hierarchy of positions, the class size must correspondingly become smaller over the years. Falling behind one's own class is of course possible, but lagging behind by more than a few years creates an intolerable situation. Members of junior classes are also moving up the hierarchy, and one would not serve under someone who is junior in terms of the year of entry. Thus, there is a strong presumption, almost a rule, that those who cannot remain within their own seniority group leave the office and are transferred to an equivalent post in a lesser office (e.g., a branch office in the country), or even leave the service for a position in the outside world. For example, elite officials in their early 50s who are not promoted to the rank of

---

[5]"Bureaucracy," *Kodansha Encyclopedia of Japan* (1983), Vol. 1, 219.

bureau chief and who have no prospect of being promoted within a year or two may choose to retire from the service and find a second career in a private corporation, or a public corporation affiliated with the ministry.

It must be noted that this "up or out" promotion practice applies only to elite bureaucrats. Nonelite bureaucrats must also enter the service at the lowest level after passing the entrance examinations. But once they are in the service, they can expect to remain there until the retirement age, except that the highest rank they can aspire to achieve, before retirement, is subsection chief in the Main Office or section chief in a local office.

The Roles of Former Bureaucrats

Since in a given ministry only 1 in 30 elite bureaucrats typically reaches the level of vice-minister, their retirement in their early or middle 50s is a rule rather than an exception. At the vice-minister level, it is customary that, every time a new vice-minister is appointed, all the contending bureau chiefs and agency directors resign. Because of this institutionalized pattern of early retirement, bureaucrats must cultivate, throughout their ministerial career, goodwill and personal connections that might lead to attractive second careers upon retirement. Considering the need for finding second careers, elite officials are naturally sensitive to the wishes of influential politicians and business leaders who might be able to help them later.

The practice of senior civil servants obtaining second careers in private and public corporations is known as *amakudari* (descent from heaven). The placement of these bureaucrats is highly institutionalized. One of the important functions of the minister's secretariat of each ministry is the placement of the retiring and former elite officials of the ministry. Each ministry and agency has under its jurisdiction a large number of public corporations and semipublic institutions whose top positions traditionally "belong" to the ministry as its "territory." It also has close ties with private corporations in the industry over which it has statutory authority to supervise. The vice-minister and the chief of the minister's secretariat determine the placement of retiring officials after carefully weighing the ranks, at the time of retirement, of the officials and the positions they are parachuting into. The ministry's control over postretirement assignments, moreover, is not limited to the initial appointments. In the public sector, the retired officials are promoted and transferred from post to post, all within the ministry's territory, by the ministry's secretariat.

Many of Japan's influential political figures are former bureaucrats. The most common pattern is that of high-ranking government officials running for election to a Diet seat from their home province after retirement from the civil service. Being a member of the National Diet is a necessary condition for playing a significant role in Japanese politics since, by custom, cabinet appointments are made from among the members of the Diet. The mainstream of the ruling Liberal Democratic party is controlled by the bureaucrats-turned-politicians, and most of the prime ministers in the postwar period have been former bureaucrats.

Thus, the system of bureaucrats "descending from heaven" plays an extremely important role in the Japanese political economy by providing an organic continuity, ease of communication, and ideological homogeneity between the members of the three power centers—the bureaucracy, the ruling political party, and big business. Of course not all politicians and busines leaders are former bureaucrats. But enough of them are, and the alumni of bureaucracy in politics and business form a powerful coalition (clique) with their juniors in the active service. Because of the uniquely Japanese character of the senior-junior relationships based on age and seniority, the vertical interpersonal relationships based on a common experience in a given ministry constitutes one of the most important channels of communication and accommodation between the three centers of power. This channel, along with the old-boy networks based on university affiliations, provides a powerful facility for the symbiotic relationships between government and business.

The Big-Business Leadership

One of the three major centers in contemporary Japan is the big-business leadership known as *zaikai* (literally, the financial or business circles). The *zaikai-jin* (zaikai persons), numbering perhaps fewer than 100, are not just ordinary corporate leaders. They are the leading members of the four major peak business associations in Japan, which are Keidanren, or the Federation of Economic Organizations; the Japan Committee for Economic Development; the Japanese Federation of Employers' Associations; and the Japan Chamber of Commerce and Industry. Some of the zaikai persons are officials of trade associations, while others are top executives of Japan's largest corporations. Zaikai persons are recognized as such because of their zaikai activities, whose purposes is to promote the interests of the business community through their close ties with key politicians. Zaikai members are well represented in the key advisory councils (see Chapter 9) attached to many ministries and agencies, and the political leaders seldom fail to consult zaikai leaders on key policy matters.

Zaikai's influence on politicians and higher civil servants has several sources. The most important is the ability of zaikai to raise campaign funds for politicians. Elections are expensive in Japan as elsewhere, and zaikai, being the biggest fund raiser for several political parties and factions within parties, naturally has easy access to the most influential of Japan's key politicians. Second, high-ranking government bureaucrats find it wise to curry favor with zaikai leaders since many lucrative postretirement positions are obtained through their connections with well-placed zaikai-jin. Third, many of the top leaders of zaikai are the alumni of elite universities and/or government bureaucracy. The common school or ministerial backgrounds they share with many politicians and bureaucrats enhance the symbiotic relationships they develop among them. These relationships are reinforced by the tendency of many young and promising elite bureaucrats to marry the daughters of influential polticians and business leaders. (Young career bureaucrats on the "elite course" are considered Japan's most eligible bachelors.) The kinship cliques that are developed through marriage bonds within Japan's elite stratum, although not as pervasive and influential as the university and bureaucratic cliques, further facilitate the symbiotic relationships among business, politics, and bureaucracy.

Political Party Leaders

Throughout most of the postwar period, and particularly since 1955, a coalition of conservative politicians known as the Liberal Democratic party (LDP) has held power in the National Diet. In recent elections, the LDP has managed to retain a slim majority, while other political parties—notably the Socialist, Komeito (The "Clean Government" party), Communist, and Democratic Socialist parties—have shared the remaining seats in parliament.

The LDP draws its support from farmers, small-business owners, big-business leaders, and corporate managers and white-collar employees. The largest opposition party—the Japan Socialist party (JSP)—has been unsuccessful in mounting an effective challenge to the LDP because of its ideological posture, which has cost heavily in small-business, rural, and middle-class votes. Support for the JSP comes mainly from urban, intellectual, white-collar public-employee groups.

The LDP is a coalition of a bewildering array of factions led by a dozen or so political bosses. A faction leader's power and influence in the party is roughly proportional to the number of followers he commands in his faction. This is so because the number of faction members translates into votes in the party's presidential elections. The LDP being the majority party in the Diet, the party president is automatically elected the prime minister in the Diet. The leaders of the larger factions vie for the president's office, while the bosses of smaller factions use the number of followers in their factions as bargaining chips in their maneuver to land an important position in the party or government. Ministerial chairs in the cabinet are allocated to these party bosses largely for political considerations.

The number of followers a party boss can command depends partly on how much money he can raise from various sources for his followers' campaign expenses. Elections are expensive, and for many candidates the cost of running a successful campaign far exceeds their personal means. Campaign funds can come from three different sources: the official party funds, contributions from the candidate's own *koenkai* (supporters' association), and the faction boss. An influential party boss who is well connected with high-quality money sources naturally attracts many followers. Former Prime Minister Kakuei Tanaka commanded a very large faction in the party chiefly because of his uncanny ability to raise and distribute huge sums of money to his followers.

Money—or more specifically, election campaign funds—is at the heart of the symbiotic relationships between the LDP and big business. Large sums of money flow from business to LDP politicians—individually, through faction bosses, and formally through the party machine. One of the main functions of the several peak business associations—for example, Keidanren—is to organize fund raising by allocating contribution quotas and assessing monthly dues and special fees on member corporations and associations. Politicians' power and influence in the party and in the government depends much on the quality of their money connections. Business firms and trade associations that contribute campaign funds naturally expect political favors in return. "Money-power politics" (*kinken seiji*) and business-government symbiosis are deeply entrenched in the system.

The internal politics of the Liberal Democratic party is extremely complex and defies simple description. Suffice it to say that the primary force at work is the *oyabun-kobun* (boss-follower or patron-client) relationships supplanted by considerations for money and votes. The psychological need to belong to a group, the charisma of faction leaders, the personal ambition of bosses and followers, the sense of interpersonal "loans" and "debts," the sense of loyalty and honor, the strategies for the Diet and party elections, the difference in career backgrounds (particularly between former bureaucrats and "pure" party politicians or *tojinha*)—all these factors and more combine to generate a bewildering complex of dynamics and inertia that is almost incomprehensible to an outside observer.

Special Interest Groups

We observed earlier that, in the United States, a large number of special interest groups try to influence public policy making and implementation primarily by lobbying Congress. America's big business, though powerful, does not enjoy an especially privileged position with lawmakers and public officials; their lobbying groups must compete with every other lobbying group. In Japan, the situation is considerably different. First, the Diet is not the central target of lobbying groups since it is merely a law-enacting body, not a law-drafting or policy-making body. As we have already noted, major policy decisions are made by the highest level of the ruling party (LDP) and the middle-to-top-level bureaucrats of the central government ministries. To be effective, therefore, special interest groups must have access to these centers of public power, either directly or indirectly through members of the Diet. Second, as already noted earlier in this chapter, Japan's big business through zaikai leadership has direct, easy, and frequent access to the ruling party leadership and the elite bureaucracy. In fact, the symbiotic relationship between the LDP, the higher civil service, and the big-business leadership is so intimate that it is more realistic to regard zaikai as an integral part of Japan's political power structure than to consider it an interest or pressure group. Third, because of the wide ideological gap between the conservative LDP and the largest of the opposition parties— the Marxist-oriented Japan Socialist party (JSP)—interest groups, too, are divided into two camps according to their ideologies. Labor union federations, particularly those representing public employees and teachers, lobby primarily the JSP members in the Diet. The effectiveness of this type of lobbying is limited since the JSP is effectively removed from the center of public power. The Socialists' role in Japan's public policy making is essentially passive and negative; that is to say, they influence the ruling party's policy formulation by making things difficult for it in the Diet.

The most powerful pressure group outside of the big business federations is the coalition of farmers represented by the Agricultural Cooperative Associations (Nokyo). With the membership of some 5 million farming households, Nokyo has a powerful influence over LDP since many of LDP Diet members come from rural election districts. Nokyo also has very close ties with the Ministry of Agriculture, Forestry and Fisheries. The payoffs of Nokyo's lobbying activities are primarily farming subsidies and restrictions on imports of foodstuffs.

Other interest groups include those of physicians, small businesses, local governments, and a host of citizens' and environmentalists' groups.

They lobby Diet members of various parties, as well as the ministry offices with which they are most closely associated.

THE SOVIET POLITICAL SYSTEM

In theory, the Soviet Union is a parliamentary democracy similar to those in the West. In reality, the Soviet government is a bureaucratic machine controlled by the leadership of the Communist party of the Soviet Union (CPSU). We have observed that in the United States, the three branches of government are separate and equal. In Japan, power is shared by the parliamentary government, the administrative bureaucracy, and the big-business leadership. A similar three-way structure exists in the Soviet Union: there we find that the troika consists of the party organs, the ministerial (administrative) organs, and the parliamentary organs. The uniqueness of the Soviet system, however, lies in the fact that the party organs predominate over the other two. It is this monopoly of political power by one political party that fundamentally distinguishes the Soviet system from that in the United States or Japan.

The de facto structure of the Soviet political system is depicted in Figure 4–1. Note that the direction of influence, as indicated by the direction of the arrows, point predominantly downward, emanating from the highest level of party organs and reaching people at the bottom.

The Organizational Structure
of the Soviet Political System

At the national level, power ostensibly rests with the Supreme Soviet of the USSR, the formal parliament, consisting of two houses with a combined membership of about 1,500 persons. The Presidium of the Supreme Soviet performs the functions of the Surpeme Soviet between sessions. The chairperson of this 39-member panel is the formal head of the Soviet state. The two houses of the Supreme Soviet—the Council of Nationalities and the Council of the Union—have the same number of deputies, each one representing one election district. Only one approved candidate runs from each district.

Although perhaps nearly half of the deputies of the Supreme Soviet are rank-and-file workers and peasants, the membership also includes important party and government officials. For example, in 1974, 84 percent of the voting members of the Party Central Committee were elected to the Supreme Soviet as deputies. These Party Central Com-

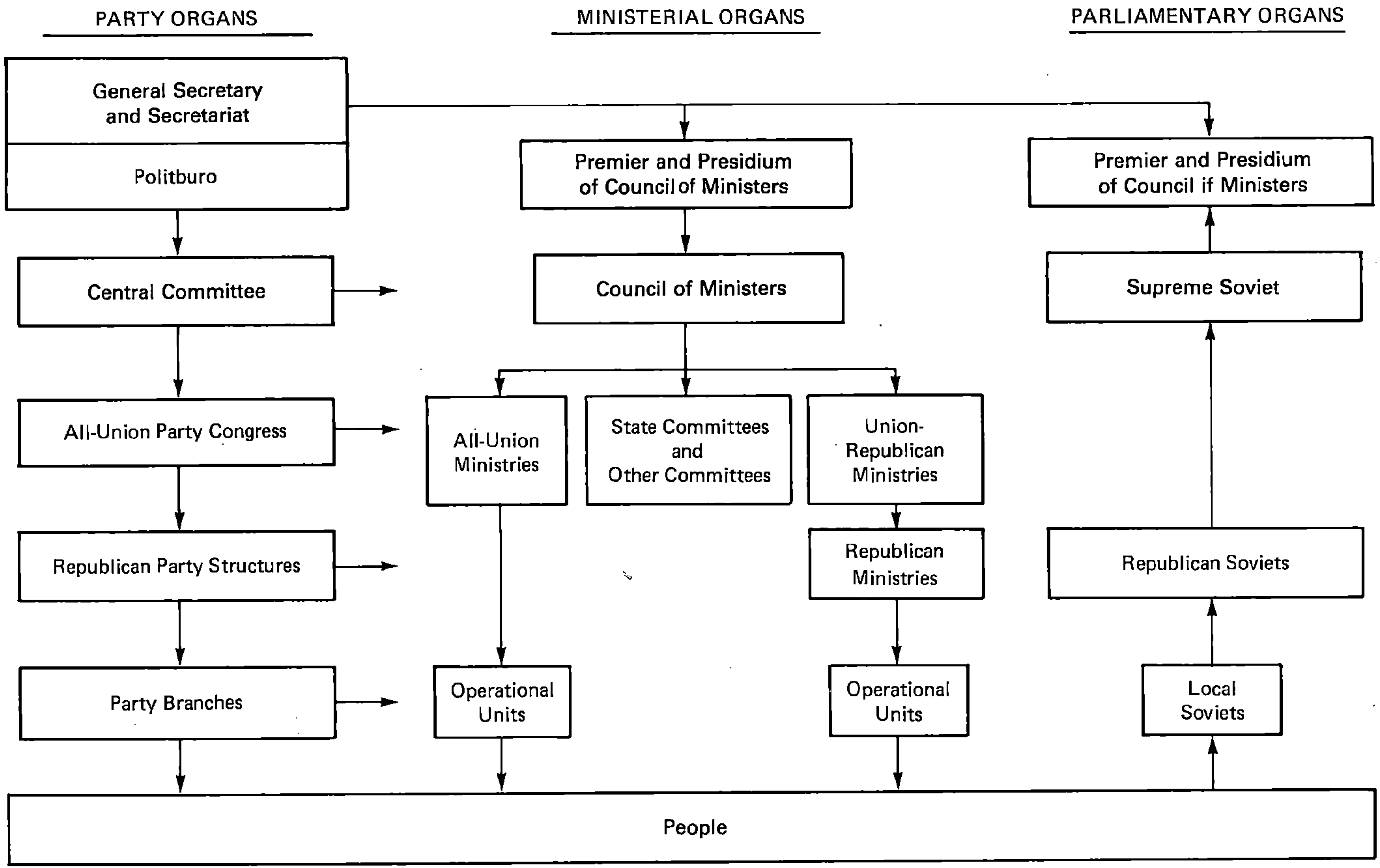

FIGURE 4–1 The organizational structure of the Soviet political system

PARTY ORGANS

MINISTERIAL ORGANS

PARLIAMENTARY ORGANS

General Secretary and Secretariat

Politburo

Central Committee

All-Union Party Congress

Republican Party Structures

Party Branches

Premier and Presidium of Council of Ministers

Council of Ministers

Union-Republican Ministries

Republican Ministries

Operational Units

State Committees and Other Committees

All-Union Ministries

Operational Units

Premier and Presidium of Council if Ministers

Supreme Soviet

Republican Soviets

Local Soviets

People

mittee members dominate the Supreme Soviet, occupying a disproportionately large number of chairs of the standing committees.[6]

At the apex of the administrative bureaucracy of the Soviet government is the Council of Ministers. With a membership roll of over
100, it is the "highest executive and administrative organ of state power
in the USSR" (Basic Law, Article 128). The chairman of the Council of
Ministers (or the premier) is the chief executive of the Soviet government. The Presidium of the Council of Ministers in 1982 consisted of
the chairman, two first deputy chairmen, and thirteen deputy chairmen.[7] Although one may be tempted to call this organ a de facto cabinet
of the Soviet government, such a designation is not warranted. The de
facto cabinet is the Politburo of the Part Central Committee. Only the
top two or three leaders of the Presidium of the Council of Ministers
(i.e., the chairman and the first deputy chairmen) are usually members
of the Politburo; other members of the Presidium are less influential
persons.

The Soviet Union is divided into 15 *union republics*, which are
organized along a fairly well-defined national or ethnic grouping. Each
of these republics has its own constitution, soviet, and council of ministers. (The Soviet terms that correspond to the American terms *federal*
and *state* are *all-union* and *republican*.) Below the level of the union
republic are the regions variously called *oblasts, krais*, or autonomous
republics. In 1977, the country was divided into 120 oblasts, 6 krais,
and 20 autonomous republics. The next lower level is the district, or
raion.

The All-Union Council of Ministers consists of the heads of all-
union ministries, union-republican ministries, state committees, and
other committees; and the 15 chairpersons of the union-republican
councils of ministers. All-union ministries, usually having jurisdiction
over heavy industries, control their operational units directly from Moscow. The union-republican ministries (which are the organs of the all-
union government) control the activities of the operational units of government and economy through their corresponding ministries in the
union republics.

State committees coordinate the activities of the various segments
of the polity and economy on the horizontal principle, as compared to
the ministries whose authority is over a single branch of activities. The
responsibilities of the state committees cut across ministerial lines. Examples of state committees are the State Planning Committee (Gosplan),
the State Construction Committee, the State Committee on Prices, and

---

[6]Jerry F. Hough and Merle Fainsod, *How the Soviet Union Is Governed* (Cambridge,
Mass.: Harvard University Press, 1982), p. 365.

[7]*USSR Facts and Figures Annual,* Vol. 7 (1983), 6.

the State Committee for Science and Technology. Other committees whose chairmen sit in the Council of Ministers include the State Security Committee (KGB) and the Board of the USSR State Bank (Gosbank).

The Structure
of the Communist Party

According to the 1977 Constitution (Basic Law) of the Soviet Union, "The Communist Party of the Soviet Union is the leading and guiding force of Soviet society, and the nucleus of its political system and of state and public organization" (Article 6). Although the Supreme Soviet is "the highest organ of state power" (Article 108) and the Council of Ministers is "the highest executive and administrative organ of state power" (Article 128), in reality the "leading and guiding force of Soviet society" takes precedence over the parliament, and the decisions made by the extraparliamentary party organs are faithfully implemented by the ministerial bureaucracy.

At the national level, the ultimate authority within the party lies theoretically in the All-Union Party Congress. Once every five years, approximately 5,000 delegates gather to hear speeches and "elect" a Central Committee to carry on the party's business until the next Party Congress. (In the early 1980s, the party had about 17 million members.) In reality, the selection of the Central Committee members takes place prior to the Party Congress and rests largely on the wishes of the general secretary and the members of the Politburo, except that the selection of many of the Central Committee memberships has an automatic character because they are ex officio posts representing institutions and regions.[8]

The Central Committee, whose membership numbers about 300, meets infrequently, often fewer than the required two meetings a year, and usually for only a day or two. The Central Committee ostensibly "elects" its executive arm, the Secretariat, and its policy-making body, the Politburo. (In reality, the members of the Secretariat and the Politburo are selected by cooptation by the existing members.) The Secretariat consists of 10 or 11 secretaries and a staff of about 1,000 appointed officials. The secretaries supervise the work of 21 or 22 departments of the Central Committee. These departments as a whole are called the party apparatus (*apparat*), and the full-time party functionaries, numbering about half a million, who staff the central and local party apparatus are called the *apparatchiki*.

Although the Secretariat and the departments are not technically executive organs of the party, they nevertheless exercise considerable

[8]Hough and Fainsod, *How the Soviet Union Is Governed*, pp. 452–53.

de facto decision-making power over the party and the government
through two channels. First, each department is responsible for supervising a group of ministries, state committees, or other public organizations. This lateral control of government organs by the party apparatus extends all the way down to the local level; government organs
at every level are subject to control by appropriate party committees.
Second, as we observed in Chapter 3, party committees at all levels
have authority to "confirm" the appointments or elections of important
government, party, and other public posts contained in their *nomenklatura* lists. The right of confirmation in reality often means the right
for a party committee to actually remove an official and select a successor.[9]

The Politburo is "the real cabinet of the Soviet system."[10] Although
the general secretary of the Central Committee in theory has only one
vote in the Politburo, in reality he is much more than the first among
equals. In the popular mind and in party practice, the general secretary
is treated as though he were the head of the Politburo. The actual power
relationship between the general secretary and the rest of the ruling
oligarchy is not well known, and can only be conjectured by those outside the Politburo.

The party structure at the national level is duplicated at the union-
republic, regional (*oblast*), city, and district (*raion*) levels. At all these
levels there are equivalents of the Party Congress, Central Committee,
and party secretaries. Party organs at all levels supervise the equivalent
level of government organs, and control the appointments and elections
of party and government officials through the nomenklatura system.
The rank-and-file party members are enrolled in party branches at places
of work, and are supervised by the district (raion) Party committee, or
raikom.

The Power Structure of the Soviet Political System

Hough and Fainsod state that "in functional terms the real cabinet
of the Soviet political system is the party Politburo, the real parliament
is the party Central Committee, and the real prime minister is the party
General Secretary."[11] This appears to be a valid description of the reality
of the power structure in the Soviet Union. But, as Hough and Fainsod
warn us, it would be a mistake to conclude that government institutions
are mere transmission belts of party policies.[12] We may safely exclude

[9]Ibid., p. 431.
[10]Ibid., p. 466.
[11]Ibid., p. 362.
[12]Ibid.

the hierarchy of soviets from the Soviet Union's *Realpolitik;* they merely serve the cosmetic function of giving the Soviet system an appearance of democracy. The formal government machinery, however, cannot be similarly dismissed as cosmetic or totally subordinate to the party. Rather, the party apparatus and the government machinery are functional divisions of the single bureaucratic hierarchy. At the top of this hierarchy, power is held by a handful of men who hold both party and govenment positions. Highest-level policy decisions are made, however, only by a collectivity of these men functioning as party, not government, leaders. Moving down the power structure, we find an increasing number of those who are *either* party leaders *or* government officials, but not both. And even though party organs at various levels supervise the activities of comparable-level government organs, lower-level party organs cannot control the activities of higher-level government organs. This is what Hough and Fainsod mean when they say that "party dominance of the government cannot be equated with party apparatus dominance of the government."[13]

The Maintenance of Power by the Party

The CPSU maintains a firm grip on the reins of power, primarily by manipulating the election system and by monopolizing the appointment system. The Soviet Constitution allows for democratic elections, but in practice only one nomination can be found on each ballot (i.e., the party's choice). Voters are allowed to strike this name out, and even to write in another candidate's name, but this is seldom done. Moreover, Soviet citizens are given the option of voting for the candidate out in the open, so that those entering the voting booths attract suspicion.[14] The appointment process centers on the nomenklatura system, as discussed earlier. To maintain power for long, an undemocratic government must maintain control over the population through appeasement, repression, or some combination of the two methods. The Soviet government uses various forms of persuasion and intimidation to "harness the masses."

The Soviet regime makes a great deal of effort to induce people to participate in the system, either by encouraging them to become party members, or by urging them to join one of the nonparty organizations that promote party aims. Indoctrination begins at an early age with the Octobrists (first to third grade) and the Pioneers (fourth to seventh grade). These organizations encourage their members to participate in public affairs, thereby serving a purpose roughly equivalent to the Boy Scouts

[13]Ibid., p. 449.

[14]John N. Hazard, *The Soviet System of Government,* 5th ed. (Chicago: University of Chicago Press, 1980), pp. 58–60.

and Girl Scouts in the United States. From the eighth grade on, children can join the Young Communist League (Komsomol) in preparation for becoming party members.

The Soviet leaders, of course, often find it necessary to use stronger methods of popular control. The party closely monitors or directly controls newspapers, radio and television, books, journals, plays, and other means of expression. The publishing industry is completely state owned and state controlled. The largest national newspaper, *Pravda*, is an organ of the CPSU Central Committee, and the other important newspaper, *Izvestiia*, is a government organ. The party assigns editors to various magazines and newspapers, and employs a large network of censors who engage in screening everything that is fed to the people.

Although no longer the instrument of *terror* that it once was under Stalin, the secret police (KGB, the State Security Committee) with an estimated force of 500,000 agents[15] and an untold number of secret informers, remains a very effective agent of *fear*. The KGB's methods are subtle but effective. It gives potentially dangerous dissidents a warning first, reminding them of their precarious positions. If the warnings are heeded and the dissidents correct their ways, nothing will happen. If they persist in the deviant ways, repressions will be applied and progressively tightened. These repressions in their early stages take the form of denials of privileges but later escalate to blacklisting and arrests.

"Interest Groups" in the Soviet Power Structure

Since the death of Stalin, it has become increasingly difficult to describe the Soviet society as totalitarian. Some Western scholars stress the importance of interest group activities in the Soviet Union, and argue that the subsidence of Stalinist terror tactics has allowed various elite groups to gain limited inputs into the system's policy-making processes.[16] Note that the term *interest groups* means something quite different when applied to the Soviet Union from when applied to the United States. Interest groups in the United States are extragovernmental associations that have often been developed from the grass roots. They direct their efforts to legislators, regulatory commissions, and executive agencies in an attempt to influence government policy, legislative and regulatory action, and public opinion. In the Soviet Union, by contrast, interest groups are informal groups *within* the establishment that have interests in influencing the decisions made by other groups and by the topmost leaders of the establishment. Three types of such informal groups

[15]Hedrick Smith, *The Russians* (New York: Quadrangle/The New York Times Book Co., 1976), p. 610.

[16]See H. Gordon Skilling and Franklyn Griffiths, *Interest Groups in Soviet Politics* (Princeton, N.J.: Princeton University Press, 1971).

may be identified: (1) the functional groups, which include party apparatchiki, economists, scientists, industrial managers, the police, the military, and so on; (2) the sectional groups, that is, government bureaucrats and party functionaries aligning vertically along industrial and ministerial lines; and (3) patron-client groups, which form strong personal ties of loyalty and protection around powerful party bosses.[17] Unfortunately, not much of the actual process and dynamics of intergroup influencing in the Soviet power structure is known to the outside world.

The interest group theory of Soviet society and polity has thus far failed to become the leading theory of Soviet society, perhaps largely because, as Hough and Fainsod note, it becomes "ambiguous in the treatment of the power of the interest groups."[18] Nevertheless, it has made enough of an impact to weaken substantially the validity of the totalitarian model of Soviet society, insofar as *total* control from the center is logically inconsistent with the power of the interest groups. Perhaps today's Soviet society can best be described as an authoritarian society effectively controlled by the ruling oligarchy and a loyal and dedicated power elite in which various informal subgroups jockey for positions of influence over each other.

INTERNATIONAL VARIATIONS IN THE CONCEPT OF LAW

Law means different things to different peoples. In the Western countries where the rule of law is viewed as an ideal, law is regarded by citizens primarily as a means for protecting their rights against those of other individuals and against the exercise of arbitrary power of government.

The *rule of law*, in its broadest sense as used in the Anglo-American societies, means that (1) individual freedoms and rights are guaranteed by the constitutional law of the land, (2) this constitutional law is superior to the power of the state and even to the majority will of the people, and (3) there exists an open and effective *judicial review* of the constitutionality of legislation and administrative action. The essence of the rule of law, then, is the rejection of control by arbitrary power. Exercise of all three types of government power—legislative, administrative, and judicial—must be limited by (constitutional) law.

The term *rule of law* is sometimes used in the much narrower sense of *government by law* (or *rule by law*.). In this sense, the rule of law means that the exercise of administrative power is limited by law that is en-

[17]Shugo Minagawa, "Soren Jinmyaku Seiji no Kozo," *Chuo Koron*, May 1982, pp. 225–26.

[18]Hough and Fainsod, *How the Soviet Union Is Governed*, p. 525.

acted by legislature and checked by judicial review of the legality of administrative action. What is missing in this narrower definition are the notion of judicial review of legislation and the guarantee of fundamental rights that even the will of the majority, through legislation, cannot violate. This definition of the rule of law, though it may appear rather restrictive to the Anglo-American mind, can be quite acceptable elsewhere. If fact, this is the old Germanic concept of law embraced by the Japanese. The old German notion of the principle of *Rechtsstaadt* (or the principle of legality of governmental action) requires only that the exercise of administrative power be limited by duly enacted laws. The Anglo-American notion of judicial review is alien to the Rechtsstaadt principle.

When legislative and/or judicial power is effectively subordinated to administrative power, government is in effect "above the law." Those who monopolize political power can be lawmakers, judges, and administrators all rolled into one. If, under these circumstances, laws are enforced consistently and impartially, we may speak of *government by decree* (or *rule by decree*). The situation in the Soviet Union today is best described by this concept of law. If, instead, laws are enforced arbitrarily, then there is *tyranny*.

Every modern society is governed by law; no government admits to presiding over a lawless society. In a comparative study of the legal systems of different countries, therefore, it is important to have a clear understanding of what *law*, or the *rule of law*, really means in each society.

Laws specify both the rights of individuals as well as their duties and obligations. In societies with well-developed legal culture, there exists a healthy balance between the rights and duties of citizens. In societies with less developed legal culture, however, laws are viewed primarily as prohibitions limiting the freedom of behavior. Thus, both in the Soviet Union and Japan, citizens do not normally turn to law as the primary means of safeguarding their rights. In the Soviet Union, ordinary citizens try to stay away from the law as much as possible. In Japan, resorting to legal recourses in the settlement of disputes is considered uncivil. Rather, people are guided by the principles of conciliation in the interest of group harmony. Thus, both in the Soviet Union and Japan, the notion of law is remote from the concept of the rule of law and individual rights.

The Japanese and the Law

Despite the overwhelming influence of the Western law and legal thought on the present legal system of Japan, the actual implementation of law in Japan is markedly different from that in the West. As we saw in Chapter 2, the predominant value orientation of the Japanese is one of hierarchy and group harmony. In such a social environment, the notion of individual rights does not flourish. Insistence on one's individual rights conflicts with the preservation of social hierarchy and therefore is disruptive of social harmony. To say that individuals have rights vis-à-vis other individuals is tantamount to saying that individuals are morally equal; such a notion is alien to traditional Japanese way of life and thought.

In Japan, law is generally perceived as an instrument of coercion in the hands of the state authority. To be involved with law is suspect, regardless of who is right or wrong, even in a civil matter. To insist on one's legal rights by going to court is regarded as uncivil, immature, and selfish. To have to settle a dispute in a court of law amounts to admitting to the public that the involved parties lack requisite social skills and reasonableness. The average Japanese would rather settle disputes amicably by mutual compromises so that everyone's face is saved. Litigations—confrontations over rights—must be avoided in order to maintain social harmony and protect one's face.

The average Japanese seldom has a need to deal with a lawyer. In 1977, there were only about 11,000 lawyers in Japan (i.e., roughly one in every 10,000 persons) as compared with half a million lawyers in the United States (about one in every 500 persons).[19] The roles played by Japanese lawyers are correspondingly smaller. There is no tradition of adversary procedure and grand oratory in Japanese courtrooms. Instead, judges play a much more active role than in the Anglo-American courts. Rather than serving merely as referees between the competing lawyers, the Japanese judges interview the litigants and witnesses, do legal researches for the case, and even suggest new avenues of exploration toward a conciliatory solution of the case.

Most disputes are resolved out of court by conciliation. A person who is respected by both sides serves as a go-between to work out a possible compromise solution. Parties to the dispute are expected to make certain concessions to each other; here again a legitimate legal claim takes a back seat to the consideration of social harmony. A requisite qualification for the go-between is not legal training or knowledge but a skill in interpersonal relations and, more importantly, social respectability and a reputation of reasonableness.

Although a contract, in terms of law, is just as binding in Japan as in the West, the Japanese do not attach as much importance to a contract as do the Westerners. The concept of a contract stating in detail the rights and duties of every party is basically repugnant to the Japanese way of thinking. The Japanese are apt to regard a contract as a

[19]"Lawyers," *Kodansha Encyclopedia of Japan* (1983), Vol. 4, 371.

memorandum of understanding that honorable persons are expected to abide by, but that may be reappraised as conditions change. What is far more important than what is written on a piece of paper is the quality of the relationships between the parties involved. If this quality is based on honor, trust, and reasonableness, conciliatory adjustments will be made relatively easily.

The Legality of Administrative Guidance

Primarily in the sphere of economic regulation, the Japanese administrative bureaucracy has developed a technique of influencing the behavior of private decision makers through informal and often extralegal means. This technique is known as *administrative guidance (gyosei shido)*, and its legality is often questioned by legal scholars.

The term *administrative guidance* is not a legal one. It is a "usage of government offices and the mass news media."[20] Administrative agencies try to influence the behavior of private parties, in matters pertaining to the agencies' statutory competence, by means of written or verbal communication and through voluntary compliance, with or without statutory authority to do so.

Certain statutes stipulate that the competent ministries can exercise authority over private parties through such written means as circulars, directives, requests, warnings, and suggestions. Private individuals and representatives of business firms and trade associations may be summoned to bureau offices and given oral instructions; at other times responsible officials may have meetings with private parties and deliver oral requests or recommendations.[21]

Certain types of administrative guidance are within the law. A statute may explicitly authorize an administistative organ to issue requests or directives to obtain necesary results. Then there is the somewhat questionable, but generally considered legal, practice of giving guidance backed up by the agency's authority to issue or revoke licenses and permits. Other types of administrative guidance are extralegal practices without a statutory basis and those administrative actions based on highly questionable statutory authority. In this category, the most frequently used technique is to invoke the broad mandate of the law that authortized the creation of the administrative organ. For example, the Ministry of International Trade and Industry (MITI) has exercised a wide range of administrative guidance in the areas of industrial production, distribution, and external trade on the basis of the authority

[20]Yoriaki Narita, "Administrative Guidance," in *The Japanese Legal System: Introductory Cases and Materials*, ed. Hideo Tanaka (Tokyo: University of Tokyo Press, 1976), p. 353.

[21]Ibid., pp. 355–56.

invested in the ministry by the Law Establishing the Ministry of International Trade and Industry (1952) that charged the ministry with the responsibilities of "promotion of external trade" and "promotion of the production, distribution, and consumption of mining and manufacturing products." MITI has used this blanket authority to justify its uses of various techniques of administrative guidance to promote corporate mergers, export cartels, production and export quotas, and joint research-and-development activities.

From a legal point of view, administrative guidance without statutory authority lacks force of compulsion, and compliance can be obtained only through voluntary action on the part of the recipients of the guidance. To assure compliance, various carrots and sticks are used by the administrative officials. A standard technique is to use the authority given to the administrative organ for purposes other than the issue at hand. For example, a recalcitrant business firm may be intimidated by a threat of losing a license or permit. (During the 1960s, MITI made effective uses of import licenses and foreign-exchange allocations in this manner.) A cooperative firm, on the other hand, may be rewarded by a special consideration for low-interest loans from government sources.

What makes extralegal administrative guidance effective in Japan is the subtle psychological pressure exerted on the recipients in an environment of the vertical, cliental relationships between administrative officials and private businesses. As discussed later (Chapter 9), each bureau of the key economic ministries has under its wing a certain number of industries to protect, nurture, and guide. There exist close personal relations between the bureau's key officials and the representatives of the industries and firms. These relationships are mutual and symbiotic in nature. The industry and corporate leaders accept guidance and suggestions from the ministry in exchange for the implied protection and promotion of their special interests. In this atmosphere, it is very difficult to flatly reject the requests and advices of the bureaucrats for fear that such a rejection may cause the offending firm to fall out of grace of the ministerial officials and may lead to subtly discriminatory and unfair treatment later. In the environment of overwhelming administrative power and the weak functioning of the nascent principle of the legality of administrative action, extralegal administrative guidance as a unique Japanese institution continues to thrive.

The Meaning of *Law* in the Soviet Union

Law in the Soviet Union means something quite different from what it means in democratic societies. While the Western nations including Japan are governed by variations of the *rule of law*, the Soviet Union is ruled under *government* (or *rule*) *by decree*. Neither the power of the state nor the authority of government is limited by some higher principles or values. In societies under the rule of law, law is a supreme force binding on every individual and organization, including the agencies of government. In the Soviet Union, law is politicized; it is merely a means by which the ruling power group (the Communist party) executes its policies. Although no individual Soviet citizen is above the law (at least since the death of Stalin), the Communist party as a group is. Since the Communist party *makes* the law, it cannot be said to be bound by it. A society in which the power of the state is not limited by law cannot be said to be governed by the rule of law.

Thus, in the Soviet Union, "laws" are mere instruments of state power, created and put to use by the party-government in its efforts to control the behavior of citizens. As such, Soviet laws can be, and are, changed frequently and easily to meet the needs of the socioeconomic policies at hand. Law does not, however, limit the behavior of those who make policy.

That the power of the Communist party is unlimited and unfettered becomes obvious when we find out the ways in which "laws" are made in the Soviet Union. Nominally, the Supreme Soviet (the legislature) is the sole lawgiver of the land. In practice, the Supreme Soviet merely rubber-stamps, in its annual meeting, what has been adopted by its Presidium. Besides the Presidium of the Supreme Soviet, the Council of Ministers (the executive) and the Central Committee of the Communist party are de facto lawmakers since their directives and resolutions are perfunctorily ratified later by the full sessions of the Supreme Soviet. We must also remember that the Presidium of the Supreme Soviet, the Council of Ministers, and the Plenum of the Supreme Court are all dominated by key party members and are naturally very sensitive to the expressed will of the party's Politburo. The de facto source of law in the Soviet Union, therefore, is the uppermost leadership of the Communist party.

The Soviet judical system—including the system of courts, the corps of public prosecutors, and the college of public defenders—is also highly politicized, and is under an effective control of the Communist party. Higher courts, including the Supreme Court, are elected by the Soviets of the corresponding level. The election, of course, is controlled by the party organs of the corresponding level through the system of nomenklatura. The Supreme Court does not have the right to declare a law unconstitutional. The Court's rulings, on the other hand, can be expected to faithfully reflect the will of the party leadership. Naturally, the concept of judicial precedent is meaningless in the Soviet context.

To say that the Soviet Union is not governed by the rule of law, however, does not mean that it is a lawless society where persons of power can exercise arbitrary authority. The general principles for criminal law and procedure enacted in 1958 stipulate that punishment can be ordered only by a court in conformity with the code of criminal procedure. Though Soviet citizens are not unequivocally guaranteed fundamental human rights, they are free from fear of unpredictable and capricious punishment. In a society governed by the rule of decrees, people can at least predict the consequences of their own behavior. And as long as they behave in accordance with the rules spelled out by the authority, they can stay out of trouble. This predictability of the authority's behavior makes the present-day Soviet Union a significantly more "lawful" society than Stalinist Russia of unpredictable terror.

Legal Provisions
Concerning Property

One substantive aspect of Soviet law that concerns us is its provisions concerning property relations. As we saw in Chapter 2, Marx attributed the evils of capitalism to the private ownership of productive property. His prescription for a better world, accordingly, was socialism, that is, collective ownership of productive properties. Although the present-day Soviet Union deviates in many ways from the prescriptions of Marx, it is still fairly faithful to the Marxist doctrine with respect to the prohibition against private ownership of properties. Thus, the Soviet Constitution of 1977 states, "Socialist ownership of the means of production in the form of state (belonging to the whole people) and collective farm-cooperative is the foundation of the economic system of the USSR" (Article 10).

Although all land is owned by the state (Article 11), "the land held by collective farms is allocated to them free of charge for an unlimited time" (Article 12). Collective farms' productive properties other than land (machinery, tools, farm buildings, and so on) are regarded as owned by the farms (Article 12). Ownership of *personal* property (as distinguished from income-generating *private* property) is permitted. "Personal property may include household objects, articles of personal need, of convenience and auxiliary household economy, a house and earned savings. Personal property of citizens and rights of its inheritance are protected by the state" (Article 13). Soviet citizens may use plots of land allocated to them by state or collective farms for growing vegetables, raising livestock and poultry, and building individual houses (Article 13).

In line with Marx's ideal of socialism where exploitation of an individual by another individual ceases to exist, the Soviet Constitution prohibits private individuals to employ labor of other individuals in productive enterprises. Thus Article 10 states, "Individual labor activity in handicrafts, agriculture and consumer services, and also other forms of labor activity based exclusively on the individual labor of citizens and members of their families, are permitted. . . ."

Whereas these constitutional provisions may sound overly restrictive, in practice, property relations in the Soviet Union are not much different from those in capitalist countries with one notable exception: no individuals are allowed to make a large sum of money using their own money or personal property. Except for this difference, economic life in the Soviet Union is not much different from that in the West. Some authors, athletes, and artists may earn huge incomes. Members of the power elite enjoy luxurious living in large state-owned homes and villas served by domestics who are state employees. Interest is earned on savings accounts and on state bonds. With various restrictions, individual citizens may own, buy or sell, and inherit dwellings and apartments, lease excess space, and buy or sell privately owned automobiles and motorcyles. Inheritance from abroad may be collected by heirs residing in the USSR. Medical doctors and other professional people may employ nurses and secretaries. Here again, the law, as well as the interpretation of Marxist doctrine, is what the Communist party leadership wants it to be.

QUESTIONS

1. What is the significance of the fact that the decisions made by the U.S. Supreme Court are *authoritative choices?* What are the merits and drawbacks of *composite choices?*

2. What are the unique characteristics of the independent U.S. federal agencies? What factors account for their proliferation? Do Japan and the Soviet Union have similar institutions? Why or why not?

3. Compare the difficulties the American and Japanese politicians and government bureaucrats encounter in trying to reconcile their private interests with the public interest. Which group in which country has the greatest difficulty? Which group in which country is the most public-interest minded? What factors account for these differences?

4. Compare and contrast the relative importance of the national parliament (the U.S. Congress, the Japanese Diet, and the Supreme Soviet) in the three countries' political power structure.

5. Describe the main differences between Japanese and American senior civil servants in terms of their educational backgrounds, selection or appointment processes, career patterns, and decision-making authority.

6. Discuss the roles played by the elite bureaucrats, both active and former, in Japan's political economy.

7. What is the exact nature of Japan's *zaikai?* What are the essential qualifications for being a zaikai person? Does the United States have a zaikai?

8. Judging from the descriptions in the text, in which country—Japan or the United States—do you think money (i.e., election campaign funds) play a relatively more important role in politics? How, do you think, does the manner in which the money is raised and distributed to politicians affect their legislative behavior? (Consider the effect on party discipline of the way the money is raised.)

9. All considered, in which country—Japan or the United States—do you think the public interest is relatively in greater jeopardy? That is to say, in which country are special interest groups relatively more successful in getting what they want through the political system?

10. What unique roles do the Communist party organs play in the de facto organizational structure of the Soviet political system? What is the de jure structure of decision-making authority in the Soviet system?

11. Identify both the de jure and de facto cabinet, parliament, and prime minister of the Soviet government.

12. What is the difference between the all-union ministries and the union-republican ministries in the Soviet Union? Are the latter organs of the re-publican governments?

13. What exactly is meant by the party *apparat*? Who are *apparatchiki* and how many of them are there?

14. Who are the real bosses of the Soviet system? What are relationships between government leaders and party leaders?

15. Is the Soviet Union a totalitarian state? What is the nature of *interest groups* in the Soviet context? What types of interest groups can be identified?

16. In what sense are the three countries ruled by law? What is the significance of the court's right of judicial review of the constitutionality of legislation and administrative action? Is the Communist party of the Soviet Union above the law?

17. Compare and contrast the concept of law in the United States, Japan, and the Soviet Union.

18. Under what legal authority does the Japanese government exercise administrative guidance? What factors contribute to the effectiveness of the extralegal administrative guidance?

19. What are the Soviet legal provisions concerning the ownership and use of *personal* property as contrasted to *private* property? Can Soviet citizens legally operate a small business? What types of incomes other than wages can be legally earned? What types of properties can be legally inherited?

SELECTED READING

BUNGE, FREDERICA M.   *Japan: A Country Study,* chap. 6. Washington, D.C.: Foreign Areas Studies, American University, 1982.

HAZARD, JOHN N.   *The Soviet System of Government* (5th ed.). Chicago: University of Chicago Press, 1980.

HOUGH, JERRY F., and MERLE FAINSOD.   *How the Soviet Union Is Governed.*
    Cambridge, Mass.: Harvard University Press, 1982.
IKE, NOBUTAKA.   *Japanese Politics: Patron-Client Democracy* (2nd ed.). New
    York: Alfred A. Knopf, 1972.
LANE, DAVID.   *Politics and Society in the USSR.* London: Weidenfeld and Ni-
    colson, 1970.
REISCHAUER, EDWIN O.   *The Japanese,* pt. 4. Cambridge, Mass.: Harvard
    University Press, 1977.

CHAPTER 5

The Soviet Economy: Organization and Management

In the preceding four chapters we reviewed some of the important aspects of the environment of an economic system with special references to the Soviet Union, Japan, and the United States. In that part of our study, we used a topic-by-topic approach. In Part 2, we shall examine the three major economic systems on a case-by-case basis.

This chapter and the next will examine the Soviet economy. After studying in this chapter the organization, planning, and management of both the overall economic system and the productive enterprise, we shall analyze in the next chapter the nature of what may be called the "Soviet disease," that is, the problem of inefficiency and waste in a complex industrial state that is administered from the center without much of the benefit of the market mechanism.

THE ECONOMY, INDUSTRY, AND ENTERPRISE

In the "socialist" economic system of the Soviet Union, virtually all of its productive assets (land and capital) are owned by the state. This fundamental fact decisively determines the basic character of the economic system: there is no private business sector, there are no factor markets other than the labor market, there are no producers' goods markets, and there are no individual incomes derived from private property.

The Two-Sector Economy

In market-oriented economies like those of the United States and Japan, productive activities take place predominantly in the private business sector. In the United States in the early 1980s, for example, the public (government) sector accounted for only a little over one-tenth of the total value added in the economy. Ignoring the foreign (rest-of-the-world) sector, we can identify three sectors in a market economy: government, business, and household. The business sector primarily produces, the household sector largely consumes, and the government sector does both. There are markets for both producers' and consumers' goods, as well as markets for factors of production. Factor incomes—wages, rent, interests, and profits—are paid by producers to households, and total factor payments are equal to the monetary value of the nation's total output.

The organizational structure of a socialist economy like that of the Soviet Union is quite different from that of a market economy. There, all the means of production are owned and controlled by the state. In other words, the state is the only producer; the "government sector" and the "business sector" are rolled into one. There are thus essentially two sectors in the economy: the state productive sector and the household sector. The two sectors interact through two markets: the consumer goods market and the labor market. In the consumer goods market, the state is the supplier (seller) and the households are demanders (buyers). In the labor market, households supply labor services, which the state producers purchase. There are neither producers' goods markets nor markets for factor services other than labor; producers' goods and non-labor factor services are merely *transferred*—not bought and sold—within the state productive sector.

There are virtually no property-based incomes accruing to households: the only types of household incomes are labor income (i.e., wages paid by the state sector) and transfer payments from the government and state enterprises (e.g., pensions and social welfare benefits) to households. (The state sector consists of the government and its operational units, i.e., state productive enterprises.) State enterprises—but not households—may earn "socialist profits" which accrue to the state, that is, the people as a whole. Socialist profits of state-owned enterprises constitute an important source of government revenues. Along with taxes and other government receipts, profits provide funds for government expenditures on capital investments, social services, defense, and other collective needs of society. As we shall see later in the chapter, profits are also used as a means to control the efficiency of operations of state enterprises.

Collective farms. For historical and ideological reasons, many writers in the West as well as the official Soviet doctrine treat the collective farms in the Soviet Union as constituting a separate sector outside the state productive sector.

There are two types of farm organization in the USSR—state farms and collective farms. A state farm (*sovkhoz*) is a "factory in the field"; it is organized and managed as a state productive enterprise. State farm directors are appointed by the government, and farmers are classified as workers and receive wages as do workers in any other enterprises. A collective farm (*kolkhoz*), by contrast, is regarded—in theory at least— as a cooperative owned and managed jointly by its members. Official statistics and ideology classify collective farmers as forming a separate social class—the peasantry—as distinct from the working class—the proletariat. Members of a collective farm's management committee are "elected" from among the peasants. As "owners" of the farm, collective farmers are presumably entitled to receive residual shares of the farm's income.

Although from the legal and ideological points of view collective and state farms may be treated differently, in their actual operations the two forms of agricultural organization are hardly distinguishable from each other. Both the *appointment* of state farm managers and the *elections* of collective farm managers are effectively controlled by the local Communist party apparatus. Both state farms and collective farms must fulfill production quotas specified in the government's agricultural plan. The only really significant difference between the two types of farm organization had been—before 1966—the ways in which the farmers were paid for their work. State farmers received wages, whereas collective farm peasants received residual shares of the farm's income. In 1966, however, the government decided to guarantee wage payments to collective farmers at state-farm wage rates. With this change, the only meaningful difference between collective and state farms disappeared. In this book, therefore, we treat both state and collective farms as "factories in the field."

Private plots. The Soviet state allows households in rural areas to cultivate small plots of land and raise some fowl and livestock. The usual size of these "auxiliary household plots" is approximately an acre or less. There are about 34 million such plots, of which 13 million are held by collective farm families, over 10 million belong to state farm households, and the rest (over 10 million) are cultivated by families of nonfarm workers living in rural areas. These plots occupy about 3 percent of the nation's total cultivated land area, and account for about one-fourth of the nation's agricultural output and roughly one-third of meat and milk output.[1]

The state-owned land is rented to the cultivators for a nominal fee. The size of the plots, as well as the types and quantities of livestock and fowl that can be reared on them, are strictly regulated by the government. The farming families are allowed to dispose of the output of their plots as they see fit. It is legal for them to sell produce in one of several thousand collective-farm markets found in towns and villages. The cultivating families, however, are not allowed to hire outsiders to work for them.

The backyard farming depends heavily on state and collective farms for forage; feed for animals raised on private plots comes largely from the socialized farms. Privately owned livestock is allowed access to part of state-owned land for pasturing. The state also provides free seeds, and often gives free chickens and pigs to be raised by backyard farmers. Also, farmers help themselves, often illegally, to feedstuffs and fertilizers that belong to state and collective farms. The relationship between the household plots and the socialized agricultural sector, thus, is a parasitic one. Backyard farms obtain much of their nourishment from state-owned lands and state and collective farms. Farming families, motivated by their self-interests, provide the other ingredient—hard work and intensive care.

Household farming on private plots is sometimes referred to in the literature on the Soviet economy as taking place in the "private agricultural sector." This description, however, seems somewhat of an overstatement. Private agriculture—and consumption and marketing of its product—is no different from the activities of industrial workers (say, electricians, plumbers, or automotive mechanics) providing services "on the side" to those who are willing to pay for them. Private farming is but one, albeit the largest, of the types of economic activities generally referred to as the *second economy*. To be sure private agriculture is extensive, its output constitutes a significant portion of total output of agricultural products, and its existence is explicitly recognized by law; but to say that it constitutes an economic *sector* seems a considerable overstatement. A Soviet official's reference to auxiliary household farming as "individual farming on state owned land" appears more descriptive of reality than calling it a "private agricultural sector."[2]

[1]Ann Lane, "USSR: Private Agriculture on Center Stage," in U.S. Congress, Joint Economic Committee, *Soviet Economy in the 1980's: Problems and Prospects*, pt. 2, 97th Cong., 2nd sess. (Washington, D.C.: U.S. Government Printing Office, 1983), pp. 24–26.

[2]David Brand, "Russia's Private Farms Show State-Run Ones How to Raise Output," *Wall Street Journal*, March 3, 1981, p. 1

The State Productive Enterprise

The state productive enterprise is an operational unit of the Soviet government. Its property (land, buildings, equipment, and other assets) is owned by the state and provided free of charge to the enterprise. The state-appointed director is a government official who is in full charge of the enterprise's operations. The director is selected by an appropriate Communist party committee having the *nomenklatura* jurisdiction over the position. (As we noted in earlier chapters, key executive and elective positions in the Soviet Union must be filled by persons who are on the party-approved list—nomenklatura—of eligible candidates.) The director is aided by a staff of several deputies including the chief engineer, chief accountant, and chief economist. These deputies are appointed and dismissed by higher government and party organs upon recommendation by the director. A director of a very important enterprise may be on the nomenklatura of the Central Committee of the CPSU. Its deputies, as well as directors and deputies of less important enterprises, are on the nomenklatury of lower-level party organs.

The primary task of an enterprise director is to fulfill the targets specified in the government's economic plans. In implementing the plans, the enterprise is expected to function on a *khozraschet* (profit-and-loss accountability) basis, which means that it is obligated to make extensive use of cost accounting with objectives of minimizing output costs and producing profits. The enterprise must do this while working under the constraints of prices of both inputs and outputs that are fixed by higher authorities and of delivery schedules of both inputs and outputs that are specified in the plans. The director is allowed a considerable degree of autonomy in deciding how to utilize the capital equipment assigned to the enterprise, the materials allocated to it, and the workers employed at the plant, as long as the operations do not deviate much from the framework laid down in the plans and by law.

The enterprise's annual operational plan (*tekhpromfinplan*) is expressed in both physical and financial terms, and contains the production and investment plans as well as the expected receipts of material supplies (the supply plan) for the year, broken down into quarters and months. As we shall see later, each enterprise is required to draw up such plans and have them approved by higher authorities. Once the plans are approved, their production and delivery targets must be observed since the approved plans are regarded as law.

The enterprise production plans contain a number of plan indicators by which the performance of the enterprise is measured. The most important of these "success indicators" include the following:

The volume of output in physical terms

Profitability (profits as percentage of the value of fixed and working capital)

Compliance with planned delivery contracts

Improvement in labor productivity

The share of highest-quality products in the total value of output

Planned payments of wages[3]

The organizational structure of the state enterprise sector is hierarchical and highly centralized. As we observed in Chapter 4 (see
Figure 4–1), state enterprises are controlled directly by the various layers of the Soviet government's ministerial hierarchy, and indirectly by
the corresponding echelons of the Communist party apparatus. The
government and the party exercise control over enterprise activities
through several channels. First, enterprise directors report directly to
the officials in the departments (*glavki*) of appropriate ministries. Second, local party organs exercise surveillance over the enterprise's management in order to promote the general interest of the party and to
guard against ministerial and regional sectionalism. Third, directors
must maintain good working relations with local officials of the state
planning and supply organs (Gosplan and Gossnab). Fourth, the enterprise has an account with the State Bank (Gosbank), and all the financial
transactions of the enterprise must be conducted through this account.
By this channel of control, known as "control by the ruble," the state
can monitor and supervise the behavior and performance of productive
enterprises.

What do the Soviet government and the party want out of enterprise management? The answer is, simply, production of high-quality
products at lowest possible costs, meeting of delivery schedules, and
introduction of new and improved methods of production. In order to
elicit these socially desirable outcomes from enterprises, the state provides both carrot and sticks. Managers who perform poorly are demoted,
transferred, or dismissed. In cases of serious malfeasance, managers
may be subject to criminal prosecution. (Remember that Soviet economic plans are *laws* that must be obeyed.) Neither these penalties nor
constant appeals to managers' and workers' "socialist consciousness"
have been very effective in themselves in extracting serious efforts from
them. This realization has led the Soviet leaders in recent years to rely
increasingly more heavily on what they call *financial leverages*, that is,
material incentives.

The incentive system within a Soviet enterprise works as follows.

---

[3]Gertrude E. Schroeder, "The Soviet Economy on a Treadmill of 'Reforms,' " in
U.S. Congress, Joint Economic Committee, *Soviet Economy in a Time of Change*, 96th
Cong., 1st sess. (Washington, D.C.: U.S. Government Printing Office, 1979), pp. 325–29.

Three types of *incentive funds* are established in each enterprise. These are (1) the material incentive fund, (2) the social-cultural and housing fund, and (3) the fund for the expansion of production. (Prior to the reforms of 1965, the incentive funds were known as the *enterprise fund.*) Part of the enterprise's realized profits are transferred into these funds in accordance with a set of complicated formulas that are designed to measure the enterprise's performance. In 1972, 60 percent of total profits of industrial enterprises was paid into the national budget. Of the remaining 40 percent, about two-fifths, or 16 percent, went into incentive funds.[4]

Bonuses are paid each month out of the material incentive fund to the three groups of employees—managerial personnel, white-collar employees, and production workers—according to different sets of rules.[5] Managerial personnel are paid bonuses of up to 50 percent of their base salary (60 percent in a small number of key industries) for fulfilling plans for labor productivity, product quality, and a few other plan indicators as determined by the ministry in charge of the particular industry.[6] In 1974, 88.4 percent of top managers received bonuses from all sources amounting to 38–65 percent of their earnings.[7] If the enterprise fails to fulfill its physical output plan for key products, however, managers are denied bonuses regardless of the performance in the above-listed areas. If the enterprise fails to fully live up to its planned delivery schedules, the managers again lose part or all of their bonuses. If the wage payments to all the workers exceed the planned wages fund, managerial bonuses are reduced by half.[8]

The Soviet manager.   The organizational structure and the style of management of a Soviet productive enterprise is—very much like those of the overall economic system—authoritarian, hierarchical, and centralist. The director exercises a great deal of administrative authority over other employees. There are several deputy directors, but the key deputy is almost always the chief engineer who heads the production department, which is divided into shops and sections. The director, the chief engineer, and the other deputy directors (the chief accountant, the chief economist, the chief technologist, and so on) make up the upper-level management of a Soviet productive enterprise. The middle-level

---

[4]Alec Nove, *The Soviet Economic System*, 2nd ed. (London: George Allen & Unwin, 1980), p. 94, table 5.

[5]Schroeder, "The Soviet Economy on a Treadmill of 'Reforms,' " pp. 325–29.

[6]Ibid.

[7]Jan Adam, "The Present Soviet Incentive System," *Soviet Studies*, 32, no. 3 (July 1980), 360.

[8]Schroeder, "The Soviet Economy on a Treadmill of 'Reforms,' " pp. 325–29.

managers consist of the assistant chief engineer and the heads of various line and staff departments. Shop and section chiefs, assistant chiefs, senior foremen, foremen, and assistant foremen constitute the lower-level management.

In the 1960s, at least 90 percent of enterprise directors were engineers. Economists and other technical specialists occupy most of the upper- and middle-level managerial positions. There are no specialists in management per se since management as such is not recognized as an independent field of study. Most of the upper- and middle-level managers have either higher or semiprofessional education, often acquired through part-time evening or correspondence study programs.[9]

Nine out of ten Soviet enterprise directors are Communist party members. Although party membership undoubtedly helps a manager to move up the managerial hierarchy, it is not a necessary condition for success. It is more likely that a person with outstanding technical abilities or leadership qualities is promoted to a key administrative post and simultaneously granted a party membership than that an unqualified party member is appointed to such a position.[10] What is necessary for a person to be appointed to a senior managerial position, however, is an approval by a party committee. Managerial positions are on the nomenklatura of one Communist party committee or another depending on the importance of the positions. Managers can be dismissed or transferred if they lose the support of the appropriate party committee. Note that when we refer to a party committee, we do not mean the enterprise's own party committee. The enterprise director is likely to be a party member, and, as such, is likely to wield greater influence in local party politics than the party committee's secretary within the enterprise. The director, however, must maintain good working relations with the leaders of the district party groups (i.e., *raion*, city, or *oblast* party committees).

As a group, enterprise managers are very well paid. They also enjoy a great deal of social prestige as well as various material benefits and privileges that are beyond the reach of ordinary employees and workers. For these reasons, management positions in state enterprises attract capable and aggressive individuals who are not averse to working hard and taking risks. As we shall see later, the Soviet economy with all its structural deficiencies has somehow managed thus far without major breakdowns, thanks largely to the ingenuity of enterprise managers who, often using quasi-legal or even illegal methods, obtain needed materials and fulfill plan targets.

[9]Barry M. Richman, *Management Development and Education in the Soviet Union* (East Lansing, Mich.: MSU International Business Studies, 1967), pp. 101–5.

[10]Ibid., p. 116.

The Soviet worker.   Every able-bodied adult citizen of the USSR has a constitutional duty and right to work. Exceptions to the rule of legal requirement to work are made only for women with small children and full-time students. Persons who try to avoid work are branded "parasites of Soviet society" and are compelled to work in exile or on farms or in plants in the offenders' own locality. The constitutional pronouncement of the Soviet citizens' right to work, on the other hand, has resulted in the redundancy (underemployment) of labor. In order to demonstrate the "superiority" of socialism, the Soviet leaders have a vested interest in maintaining a high rate of employment however it is achieved. There is thus a strong bias against dismissing workers even if they are redundant or incompetent. This implicit policy results in the absence of fear, on the part of workers, of unemployment and consequently in lax labor discipline.

Another source of the lax labor discipline in the Soviet Union is the shortage of labor. The decline in the birth rate combined with the catastrophic loss of lives in World War II have resulted in a sharp decline in the annual rate of increase in the able-bodied population—from 1.9 percent in the 1971–75 period to 0.3 percent in the 1981–90 period.[11] The labor shortage causes a high labor turnover; disgruntled workers simply quit their jobs, knowing that new jobs can be easily found. In the 1970s, the annual turnover rate was about 30 percent in industry and 62 percent in construction.[12]

Industrial labor force is paid either piecework-rate wages or hourly rate wages with a variety of bonus plans. The piecework wage system is the more common; more than 60 percent of industrial workers are paid in this manner. In the 1970s, the system of lump-sum wage payments also became widely used.[13] The basic wage rates for different job categories in different sectors of industry are determined by the Soviet government by agreement with the All-Union Central Council of Trade Unions. Most enterprises have wage-rate scales consisting of six grades. In 1975, the ratio of the highest-grade basic wage rate to the lowest-grade basic wage rate for the entire industry was 1.86.[14] In addition to the basic wages, the earnings of industrial workers include hardship allowances, regional supplements, overtime allowances, and awards

[11]Murray Feshback, "The Structure and Composition of the Industrial Labor Force," in *Industrial Labor in the U.S.S.R.*, ed. Arcadius Kahan and Blair A. Ruble (New York: Pergamon Press, 1979), p. 5.

[12]Ibid., p. 9.

[13]Constantin A. Krylov, *The Soviet Economy: How It Really Works* (Lexington, Mass.: Lexington Books, D. C. Heath and Company, 1979), p. 149.

[14]Janet C. Chapman, "Recent Trends in the Soviet Industrial Wage Structure," in *Industrial Labor in the U.S.S.R.*, ed. Arcadius Kahan and Blair A. Ruble (New York: Pergamon Press, 1979), p. 155.

and bonuses. When allowances for hardship conditions (e.g., hot, heavy, and hazardous work) were included, the ratio of the highest-grade to the lowest-grade wage rates in 1975 was 3.29.[15] Additionally, regional wage coefficients are used to increase the earnings of workers in unfavorable climatic conditions. For example, in 1972, workers on islands in the Arctic Ocean had their earnings multiplied by the coefficient of 2.0, while those in central regions of Siberia received 1.3 to 1.5 times the earnings of those in the temperate zones of European USSR, for which the coefficient was 1.0.[16]

Production workers receive bonuses from both the material incentive fund and the regular wages fund (see below). About half of the bonuses of production workers come from the wages fund.[17] Various types of incentive payments made to industrial workers are relatively lower than those paid to engineers and white-collar employees. In 1973, bonuses to manual workers including those that came from the wages fund amounted to 15.2 percent of their earnings. By contrast, the engineering and technical staff, including managers, received 22.1 percent of their earnings in the form of bonuses.[18] Some Soviet economists believe that for the incentive wages to be effective, their proportion of industrial workers' earnings must be at least 20 to 25 percent.[19]

The payments of wages to industrial workers are made out of the *wages fund*, which is a part of planned allocation of financial resources from the state to productive enterprises. From this fund are paid wages of workers; payments for workers' regular vacations, holidays, and leaves of absence; and bonuses to workers. As pointed out earlier, bonuses to workers also come from the material incentive fund of the enterprise. Bonuses are paid to production workers on the basis of increased productivity, improvement in product quality, and savings in the uses of materials.

The social-cultural and housing fund, which is established in each enterprise to take care of the social needs of employees, provides workers with yet another form of incentives to increase efficiency in production. The bulk of the money in this fund is used for building and repairing workers' housing, day-care facilities, and other facilities for social, cultural, and athletic activities. The fund is also used to finance athletic and public health programs within the enterprise. The uses of the fund are jointly determined by the enterprise's management and its trade union organization.

Where stimulative wage premia fail to create an incentive for hard

[15]Ibid.

[16]Ibid., p. 160.

[17]Adam, "The Present Soviet Incentive System," p. 357.

[18]Ibid., p. 360, table 3.

[19]Krylov, *The Soviet Economy*, p. 151.

work, the Soviet regime uses coercion to drive people to perform arduous tasks in logging, mining, construction, road building, farming, and manufacturing under hazardous conditions in harsh climates. According to a study made by the U.S. Central Intelligence Agency, no fewer than 4 million prisoners—or 3 percent of the nation's work force—are toiling in prisons and prisonlike labor camps scattered throughout the country.[20]

Trade unions.   Soviet trade unions are industrial unions in the sense that all employees—blue-collar, white-collar, and managerial—in a given branch of an industry belong to the same union. Though membership is voluntary, most employees join the union because of the social welfare benefits membership provides. The functions of a factory union committee include management of the social insurance fund, negotiation with the management over conditions of labor, provision of grievance services in settling disputes between the management and individual workers, and provision of recreational facilities for the members. The union, however, does not engage in collective bargaining over wage rates, or call a strike. Strikes are not allowed on the ground that, in a workers' state, there is no need for workers to strike against themselves.

The primary function of the Soviet trade union is to promote higher labor productivity. It is essentially a "transmission belt" of the policies of the party and the government to its members. Toward this objective, the union sponsors various forms of "socialist competition" in which individual workers and groups of workers compete for recognition, bonuses, and free vacations at public resort facilities. The Soviet trade union is thus an instrument of the Soviet state. Most of its officers are Communist party members, and their elections are effectively controlled by the party through the nomenklatura system.

The secondary function of the trade union is to represent and protect the members' interests. The factory trade union committee plays an important role in protecting workers against arbitrary dismissals by the management. Although workers can leave their jobs with two weeks' written notice, the management must secure the permission of the trade union committee before it can dismiss a worker. If the committee refuses to grant permission, the management may take the case to the people's court. The court, however, almost always supports the decision of the union committee.[21]

In cases of a conflict between the primary function of exhorting

[20]"A New Report: Soviets' Record on Slave Labor," *U.S. News and World Report,* November 22, 1982, p. 31.

[21]Blair A. Ruble, "Factory Unions and Workers' Rights," in *Industrial Labor in the U.S.S.R.,* ed. Arcadius Kahan and Blair A. Ruble (New York: Pergamon Press, 1979), p. 60.

workers to be productive and the secondary function of looking after workers' interests, there is no question about the union officials' position: they always side with the management. For example, if the management wants workers to work overtime to reach planned production targets, the factory trade union committee will almost certainly support the management. It is worth noting that, unlike American or British trade union officers, who are apt to assume an adversarial posture toward the management, the members of a factory trade union committee in the Soviet Union are likely to share a commonality of interests with the enterprise management. Some of the committee members are technicians, engineers, and even managers. The chairperson of the committee is likely to be a party member and have career ambitions to move up the union and party hierarchies. The chairperson's success in his career depends decisively on how his or her work is evaluated by the superiors in the union hierarchy. Thus, factory union chairpersons are predictably more sensitive to the values and wishes of their superiors than those of the rank-and-file workers.[22]

Here again, we see the hierarchical and centralist nature of Soviet society. Enterprise managers, union officials, and local party apparatchiki are all collaborating with each other to serve the interests of the party and the state. Individually, they are motivated by their career ambitions to move upward and toward the power center, gaining in power, authority, and privilege. Seen in this light, Soviet trade union officials as functionaries of the party-state are no different from functionaries in such other fields of state service as the education, the military, and athletics.

Organization of Industry

All state productive enterprises are organized administratively into a hierarchical whole and controlled from the center by the Council of Ministers of the USSR. Figure 5–1 depicts the organizational structure of Soviet industry.

Ministries, glavki, and enterprises. Each of the industrial ministries (about forty in all) is divided into a number of industrial departments (*glavki*) which are responsible for administering different branches of industry. All-union ministries and their glavki directly supervise their enterprises, whereas union-republican ministries and their glavki control enterprises under their jurisdiction indirectly through republican ministries and their glavki. In Figure 5–1, relationships of subordination between the Council of Ministers at the top of the pyramid and pro-

---

[22]Ibid., p. 73.

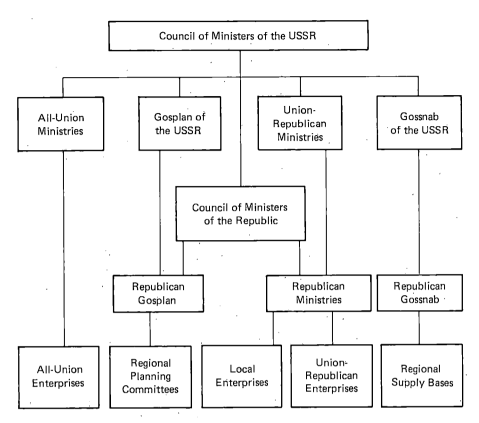

FIGURE 5-1   The organization of Soviet Industry

ductive enterprises at the bottom are indicated by vertical lines linking various organs.

Enterprises can be divided into three groups depending on which ministries have authority over them. The first group consists of enterprises that are under the jurisdiction of all-union ministries. These enterprises are directly subordinate to the industrial departments of the ministries no matter in which republic they are located. Industries that were under the jurisdiction of all-union ministries in February 1979 included automotive; aviation; chemical; communications equipment; defense; electrical equipment; electronics; gas; instrument making, automation equipment and control systems; machine building (in 11 ministries); medical; petroleum; pulp and paper; and shipbuilding.[23]

The second group of enterprises belong to the industries that are under the authority of union-republican ministries, which control en-

[23]Paul K. Cook, "The Political Setting," in U.S. Congress, Joint Economic Committee, *Soviet Economy in a Time of Change*, 96th Cong., 1st sess. (Washington, D.C.: U.S. Government Printing Office, 1979), p. 50.

terprises in republics through corresponding ministries on the republican level. In February 1979, industries in this category included agriculture, coal, construction materials, ferrous metallurgy, food, meat and dairy, nonferrous metallurgy, petroleum refining and petrochemical, timber and wood processing, and light industries.[24]

The third group of enterprises, about 3,000 in number, are subordinate only to the republican ministries; these enterprises provide for purely local needs. In 1971, 51 percent of industrial output was produced by enterprises that were directly subordinate to the all-union ministries, while the remaining 49 percent was provided by the other two groups of enterprises.[25]

It is important that the relationships between ministerial offices and enterprises are clearly understood. Ministries and their departments (glavki) are not merely organs supervising or regulating the enterprises under their wings. Rather, they *are* integral parts of the production establishments. Take the Soviet automotive industry, for example. The Ministry of Automotive Industry is responsible for producing automobiles, as well as providing necessary material and technical supplies to its operational units. Imagine if General Motors were the automotive industry in a socialized United States. GM's corporate headquarters is comparable to the Soviet Ministry of Automotive Industry, and its division offices can be likened to the Soviet glavki. Soviet enterprise directors are subordinate to the glavki officials in much the same way as GM's plant managers report to their respective division headquarters. GM's chairman of the board, naturally, is comparable to the Soviet minister of automotive industry.

In each of the Soviet industries, there exists a strong sense of "familyness" among the officials at all three levels—ministry, glavki, and enterprises. Instead of relying on undependable supplies of materials from other industries, ministries and glavki build their own factories and supply bases to take care of the needs of their own enterprises. Whenever there arise serious problems of supply shortage and delivery delays, ministries and glavki are apt to give allocation priorities to their own operational units. The entire Soviet industry is thus carved up vertically into self-sufficient and self-contained industrial empires, with little communication and cooperation between enterprises across the ministerial boundaries. Interindustrial coordination of efforts at the enterprise level can be affected only by enterprises sending communication up to the ministry, from the ministry to another ministry, then down to the enterprise level. This desire for industrial self-sufficiency and the absence of lateral cooperation across industrial boundaries are

[24]Ibid.

[25]Krylov, *The Soviet Economy*, p. 121.

major factors causing much waste and inefficiency in the Soviet planning system.

To overcome the weaknesses of the centralized system of ministerial administration, the Soviet government in 1957 instituted a sweeping organizational reform, changing the structure of administration from the ministerial to the territorial principle. Most of the industrial ministries were abolished. The entire nation was then divided into 105 regional economic councils (*sovnarkhozy*), which served as an intermediate tier of administration between the union republics and enterprises. The objective of the reform was to reap the benefits of integration of industrial activities within each region by eliminating the duplication of efforts by enterprises belonging to different ministries.

Soon after the new system was introduced, however, it became evident that the reform merely replaced ministerial departmentalism by regional sectionalism. Both the sovnarkhoz administration and the enterprises in the region gave preferential treatment to enterprises in the same region in the matter of materials delivery. Each sovnarkhoz attempted to become self-sufficient by producing its own materials needs and hoarding them within its boundaries. The sovnarkhoz system was abolished in 1964 and the ministerial system was reinstated.

State committees.   Paralleling and crisscrossing the direct, vertical structure of ministerial decision-making authority are the planning and supply channels of some state committees. Figure 5–1 shows the two most important of these committees—Gosplan and Gossnab. The chairpersons of these commissions have the rank of a cabinet minister. The importance of Gosplan and Gossnab is signified by the fact that, in 1982, the chairmen of both Gosplan and Gossnab were on the 15-member Presidium of the USSR Council of Ministers.

The State Planning Committee (Gosplan) coordinates the planning activities of ministries on both the all-union and republican levels. Gosplan has its own hierarchical structure paralleling that of the ministries and the party, and is divided into a number of departments that are responsible for supervising (without administrative authority) the planning activities of corresponding ministerial departments down to the enterprise level. Gosplan of the republic coordinates the planning activities of republican ministries, and, through local planning committees, the activities of locally subordinated enterprises.

The State Committee for Material and Technical Supply (Gossnab) also has a union-republican structure paralleling that of Gosplan. Gossnab is a wholesale supply organization. It handles the actual distribution of commodities, either through its nationwide network of warehouse facilities or by matching suppliers and users on a long-term contract basis. By contrast, Gosplan is a planning agency; as such, it controls planning of output and supply allocation, through the ministerial system, of about 2,000 key industrial materials that account for about 70 to 80 percent of the *value* of industrial output. Gosplan, however, does not engage itself in the actual (physical) distribution of materials. Instead, it issues "funds" or material allocation certificates to appropriate ministries, which in turn distribute them to lower-level units. Gossnab, through its regional supply offices and bases, allocates some 14,500 less important items, as well as the "funded" materials allocated by Gosplan.[26]

Besides Gosplan and Gossnab, several other state committees of ministerial rank are subordinate to the Council of Ministers of the USSR and are responsible for providing supportive services in plan formulation and execution. These economic commissions are the State Committee on Prices (Gosten), the State Committee for Science and Technology (Gostekhnika), the State Construction Committee (Gosstroy), and the Board of Governors of the USSR State Bank (Gosbank).

Production and industrial associations.   The administrative structure of Soviet industry is hierarchical; that is to say, production units, forming the base of a pyramid, are controlled from the top through several layers of administrative organs. Before the 1970s, most of the 50,000 or so industrial enterprises had been directly controlled by the lower-level organs of one administrative bureaucracy or another (either an all-union ministry, union-republican ministry, or a republican ministry) that had jurisdiction over the branch of industry. Excessive bureaucratization, duplication of efforts, ministerial sectionalism, obsession with self-sufficiency, and inability to take advantage of the economies of scale had been the major problems associated with the system of direct ministerial control of production units.

Beginning in the early 1970s, the Soviet government began promoting the formation of associations among enterprises. A party-government decree issued in April 1973 required the industrial ministries to formulate plans to merge enterprises that have similar characteristics—be they geographical location, types of inputs used, or the nature of production processes employed—into *production associations*. The objective of this reorganization program was to enable enterprises to gain from increased specialization, reap the benefits of large-scale operations, and effect saving in administrative costs.[27] Between 1970 and 1981, the number of production associations increased from 608 to about 4,000. In 1977, they accounted for about 40 percent of the total number

[26]Schroeder, "The Soviet Economy on a Treadmill of 'Reforms,' " p. 323.

[27]Ibid., pp. 315–16.

of plants and about 45 percent of the total number of workers and of industrial output.[28]

The party-government decree of April 1973 also called for conversion of some ministerial departments (glavki) into *industrial associations.* Unlike a glavk, which is merely a unit of ministerial bureaucracy, an industrial association is a semiautonomous producing unit. It operates with its own production and supply plans, and is supposed to function on a *khozraschet* (profit-and-loss accountability) basis. By 1978, more than 500 industrial associations had been formed.[29] There has not been, however, much of a change in the way business is conducted by these new organizations: "In many cases, their formation merely amounts once again to 'changing the names on doors'; most of them seem still to be located in Moscow, and even in the same buildings; . . . many of them manage the same enterprises as before, now amalgamated into associations, and their behavior continues as of old."[30]

Territorial production complexes. The July 1979 decree on planning reform assigned the task of managing what is known as *territorial production complexes* (TPKs) to USSR Gosplan. TPKs are defined as "major regional development projects that are planned and developed as integrated units, bringing together in one area all the related industries and associated infrastructure necessary for the production of important natural resources."[31] The Eleventh Five-Year Plan (1981–85) recognizes eight such complexes, most of which are located in Siberia. The assignment of the responsibility of managing the TPKs to USSR Gosplan has the purpose of maintaining a central control over the regional development projects while reducing the influence of central ministries, which tend to generate interministerial conflicts and attendant inefficiencies. The result of the TPK-based developmental strategies so far, however, does not appear very promising. The TPKs seem to be plagued by the same old problems of poor coordination, sectional conflicts, and managerial deficiencies that characterize the rest of the Soviet economy.[32]

[28]Raymond Hutchings, *Soviet Economic Development,* 2nd ed. (New York: New York University Press, 1982), pp. 87–88; Marshall I. Goldman, *U.S.S.R. in Crisis: The Failure of an Economic System* (New York: W. W. Norton & Company, 1983). p. 53.

[29]Schroeder, "The Soviet Economy on a Treadmill of 'Reforms,' " pp. 315–16.

[30]Ibid.; p. 317.

[31]David S. Kamerling, "The Role of Territorial Production Complexes in Soviet Economic Policy," in U.S. Congress, Joint Economic Committee, *Soviet Economy in the 1980's: Problems and Prospects,* pt. 1, 97th Cong., 2nd sess. (Washington, D.C.: U.S. Government Printing Office, 1983), pp. 242–43.

[32]Ibid.

CENTRAL ECONOMIC PLANNING
AND THE MATERIAL BALANCE

The primary function of any economic system is allocation of resources to alternative uses. Although consumption is the ultimate purpose of economic activities, goods and services must first be produced before they reach consumers. Production in a large, modern economy like the Soviet Union is a highly complex process; it involves tens of thousands of producing units (enterprises) producing goods primarily for other producing units. Outputs of producers become inputs of other producers. It is this matching of inputs and outputs within the state industrial sector that is the core of the problem of managing Soviet-type economies.

In market-oriented economies, resources are allocated to alternative uses primarily through the workings of the demand and supply forces. The system's organizational structure is predominantly horizontal in all three aspects—decision-making authority, information flows, and motivational systems. The market mechanism, and the prices that it generates, guide the behavior of economic decision makers at all levels. Pursuit of lower costs and higher sales revenues—in other words, higher profits—by microeconomic decision makers provides a basic motivating force that leads, as a general rule and on average, to reasonably efficient allocation of resources in the economy. Private decision making need be supplemented or constrained by a minimum of governmental decision making for such macroeconomic objectives as stability, equity, and environmental protection to be adequately met.

In the Soviet economic system, an entirely different approach is taken to the solution of the resource allocation problem. The market solution is rejected for ideological reasons. As discussed at some length in Chapter 2, the word *ideology* is used here in two distinctly different senses. First, the Soviets early on rejected market forces as arbitrary and irrational forces that respond blindly to the whims of the people. Scientific socialism should be built on objective facts (i.e., socially necessary labor), not on subjective evaluations(i.e., consumer demand). Such market phenomena as price, value, competition, and profit were viewed as products of the anarchy of an unorganized capitalist economy, and were regarded as tools used by capitalists to exploit the working class. By contrast, claimed earlier Soviet leaders, an organized socialist economy was to be managed by means of planning from the center. Central planning, it was argued, was capable of providing coherence, intelligence, and a sense of purpose, something that myriads of microeconomic decisions made blindly in uncontrolled markets could not provide.

Marxist doctrines thus gave the initial impetus to the rejection of market solutions in the Soviet economy. This historical fact, however, fails to explain adequately the continued refusal of the present Soviet leaders to embrace the market as either an alternative or supplement to the present system of authoritarian management which, by the leaders' own admission, is in serious trouble. In the past, the Soviets have not hesitated to drop any aspects of Marxism whenever such a riddance served their purposes. The fact that they stubbornly cling to the central administrative control of their economy, therefore, must be attributed to the real and effective ideology—the power ideology of the party-state control of society—not to the façade ideology of Marxism. The regime cannot abandon central planning since doing so will inevitably invite doubt as to its usefulness and lead to the question of its legitimacy. This point will be pursued further in Chapters 6 and 12.

Thus, for better or worse, today's Soviet economy is controlled from the center as though it were a single, gigantic industrial corporation. The enormous production machine forms a complex hierarchy, and its tens of thousands of operating units (enterprises) are managed from the central board (the Council of Ministers of the USSR) through several layers of line organs (ministries and departments) and staff offices (Gosplan and other state committees). No market relations exist inside this corporation, and transactions between its units are effected by administrative fiats in much the same way as transactions are conducted between divisions and plants within a capitalist corporation. In terms of the paradigm of organizational structure introduced in Chapter 1, the Soviet economic system has a totally centralized and hierarchical structure of decision-making authority. The structure of information flow is also predominantly vertical. Little horizontal relationship exists in decision making, information exchange, and coordination of efforts.

In Chapter 1 we observed that we could identify three levels of management: macromanagement, industrial management, and enterprise management. For the Soviet economic system, the lines of demarcation between these three types of management cannot be clearly drawn. The organizational structure of the USSR Incorporated is unitary, and the three levels of management form a continuum from top to bottom. Enterprise management is subsumed by industrial management, which in turn is subsumed by macromanagement. And the generic term used in the Soviet Union to refer to this integrated, continual management of the national economy is *planning*.

Plan Formulation

Preparing economic plans is primarily the responsibility of the State Committee for Planning (Gosplan). Gosplan prepares two types of plans: five-year plans and annual plans. The *five-year plans* are designed to provide general direction and strategy of national economic development. They are not, however, meant to be operational in the sense that specific production targets and delivery schedules are spelled out. The *annual plans* supply operational guidance to plant managers and ministerial officials.

Earlier in the chapter we noted that a Soviet industrial enterprise is guided by an output-input schedule known as the *tekhpromfinplan* (an abbreviation of *technical-industrial-financial plan*); this is an enterprise's operational plan for the year. The tekhpromfinplan spells out in great detail the output targets, materials supply schedules, investment plans, and financial flows of the enterprise, by department and shop, divided into quarters and months. The core of the tekhpromfinplan (hereafter, *plan* for short) consists of the planned output and planned input supplies of the enterprise. It also contains additional plan indicators including those on profitability, labor productivity, product quality, and wage payments.

In about May or June of the year preceding the plan year, enterprises are instructed to prepare a draft plan for the coming year. The instructions originate in Gosplan, which specifies broad targets in terms of the key plan indicators; these targets are based on the set of *control figures* that are issued earlier by the Communist party Central Committee, expressing the priorities the party places regarding the direction of the nation's economy.

There is an inherent difficulty in the enterprises' exercises of drafting their plans since they are told to prepare the following year's supply requisitions without the knowledge of their expected output goals, and to determine, at the same time, the output plans without knowing what and how much material inputs they can expect. A common practice is to base the projections for the plan year on the actual production levels of the preceding years using simple trend figures.

Enterprises' draft plans are submitted to their respective ministerial departments. The information is consolidated and synthesized before it is sent further up the channel. At each step of the way through the channel, specifics disappear as they become integrated into broader pictures. At each level, negotiations take place between the lower and higher echelons, the former trying hard to obtain as small output targets and as large supply allocations as possible with the latter trying the opposite. Ultimately, the plans prepared by the ministries for the respective branches of industry are fowarded to Gosplan.

Gosplan's first task is to see if the projected supply of each commodity is adequate for the projected total need for that commodity during the plan year. The method used by Gosplan to test the consistency of the projected magnitudes is that of material balances. A *material balance* is prepared for each commodity, listing estimated *sources* of supply on one side (domestic production, imports, and initial inventories) and estimated *uses* on the other side (production needs, investment needs, government and household consumption needs, exports, and end-of-year inventories). Gosplan prepares material balances for about 2,000 major products.

Gosplan's next task is to bring projected supply and demand into balance for each commodity. Imbalance between projected supply and demand is inevitable, and the imbalance is almost always on the shortage side. Gosplan officials negotiate with the officials of both producing and consuming ministries in an effort to achieve coherence of the overall plan. Balances are usually achieved (or approximated) either by increasing the planned output, if that is possible, or—and this is more likely the case—by decreasing the allocations of the commodities in question to the consuming industries (or to the households in cases of consumer goods), decreasing the size of inventories, and/or increasing imports. In any event, plans tend to become "taut" as many are told to do more with less. High-priority industries (heavy industries, defense, space programs) receive a preferential treatment, and low-priority areas (housing, consumer goods) must get by with what little is allowed to them.

At this stage in the plan formulation process, Gosplan tries to ensure balances not only between the current sources and uses of individual commodities but also between (1) the annual plan and the five-year plan, (2) development patterns of different industries and regions, (3) current consumption and investments for the future, (4) the effective purchasing power of the household sector and the available consumer goods and services, (5) demand for labor and the availability of labor, and (6) imports and exports. For these purposes, Gosplan prepares, in addition to material balances, other balances, notably labor-resource balances and financial balances. In this process of overall coordination, a large number of ministries and a number of state committees are brought into discussions. Through a great deal of mutual efforts, haggling, and arguments, a draft national economic plan finally takes shape. This plan is forwarded to the Council of Ministers, approved by it, and later confirmed by the Supreme Soviet upon which it becomes a law.

The plan-law is now sent downward through the channels of the administrative hierarchy, being disaggregated at each level. The pain of reduced material-supply allocations must be shared by all concerned, again through a series of hard and often acrimonious bargaining. At the enterprise level, the enterprise's share of the plan-law is translated back into a tekhpromfinplan, which now must be obeyed by the enterprise management.

Plan Execution

The primary actors in the plan execution stage are enterprise managers. They must meet monthly production and delivery quotas, make sure that adequate quantities of materials are supplied from outside or otherwise provided from within, and meet other plan targets such as net output, profitability, wage funds, and so on. They are guided in their actions, for better or worse, by the various incentive schemes built into the overall system of management.

In carrying out their assigned tasks, enterprise directors are supervised and supported by their superiors in the ministerial departments. Although departmental officials do not receive bonuses for fulfilling plan targets, their performance is measured nevertheless by how well the enterprises under their jurisdiction perform. They therefore try to get as much output as possible from enterprise managers, while helping them whenever necessary to secure materials that are in short supply.

In theory, executing the plans should be nothing more than plant managers following the plan instructions to the letter. In practice, however, things can get complicated. In the first place, seldom are plans internally consistent. We noted earlier that plant managers are asked to prepare draft plans without knowing either their exact output targets or expected availabilities of materials. Thus, there is a strong temptation for them to be "on the safe side" by understating their productive capacity and overstating their supply needs. Being thoroughly familiar with this defensive behavior of enterprise managers, higher authorities impose on enterprises ambitious output targets and tight supply allocations. In this hide-and-seek game, it is virtually impossible for the higher authorities to know who is hiding supplies, labor, and productive capacity and who is facing genuine difficulties. When Gosplan tries to reconcile the imbalances on material balances, it finds it very difficult to work out a plan that is totally consistent with the real conditions of the economy partly because of the absence of accurate information and partly because of the lack of needed time. Gosplan officials therefore find it necessary often to impose seemingly unachievable targets on enterprises and hope that somehow the job gets done. The upshot is that the plans for many enterprises are internally inconsistent: planned targets cannot be met with planned input allocations.

Because formally approved plans are often imperfect, they are revised frequently during the plan year. These changes generate their own cycles of confusion, misinformation, and imbalances. When planned deliveries of materials are suddenly transferred, during the plan year, from one enterprise to another, the deficit enterprise that has counted on the supplies must quickly find ways of dealing with the shortage. Because of the general tautness of the overall plan, any shortages developing in one corner of the economy tend to multiply and spread throughout the economy. Besides the shortages created by poor planning, there are other developments that generate their own ripples of shortages—for example, bad weather, botched production runs, and breakdown in transportation or communication. Since most enterprises and industries are operating with very small margins of inventories, shortages can quickly cause failures of other enterprises to meet their output and delivery targets, which, creating another round of shortages, spread to the rest of the economy. Given these circumstances, managers of most enterprises must assume that supply plans are unreliable and shortages are a normal state of affairs.

Since failure to receive materials as planned cannot be used as an excuse for inability to meet the production and delivery targets, plant managers and ministerial officials must resort to a series of unplanned corrective actions whenever they experience supply breakdowns. These actions, though often unlawful, are nevertheless an indispensable part of the Soviet planning system. The success of the execution phase of planning depends more on the initiative and ingenuity of the plan executors—plant managers and their superiors—than on the quality of the formal aspects of planning.

If prospects for finding deficit materials from outside sources are poor, the enterprise may choose to accommodate its operations to the shortage. The pattern of such an accommodation may take several forms, including production of goods that fall short of the plan requirements, substitution of the planned input by an unplanned material, and production of the needed material within the plant. In each case, quality and/or cost suffers. The widespread practice of trying to be self-sufficient in supplies is particularly wasteful because of the unavoidable diseconomies of producing in small batches.

Ministries may also try to produce important key materials in the plants under their jurisdiction in order to avoid supply disruptions. Sometimes even the party may become involved in expediting supply flows. The party group within an enterprise may appeal to the local party committee, through which appeals may be made to higher party organs; the latter may intercede for the enterprise in distress with the supply organs, bypassing some administrative and planning channels.

One method of improvising on materials acquisition is using the services of procurement specialists known as *tolkachi* (pushers or expediters). Tolkachi are usually employees of an enterprise occupying some innocuous positions, but their real job is to expedite movements of supplies using some highly questionable methods, including outright uses of bribes. Tolkachi's main talent lies in knowing where needed materials are located, and arranging their procurement, often through a barter deal.

The workability of the Soviet planning system, thus, depends to a large extent on the abilities of plan executors to improvise, that is, to adapt themselves to changing circumstances. Many of the adaptive measures are wasteful, corrupt, or even unlawful; but they are nevertheless indispensable for a tolerably coherent functioning of the system. For this reason, these adaptive measures are often denounced publicly but are tolerated in practice.

THE STATE BUDGET
AND THE FINANCIAL BALANCE

The Soviet economy is managed from the center by two distinctly separate but closely related means: the physical allocations of materials by Gosplan, and the control over financial flows ("control by the ruble") by Gosbank. The main instrument of the control by the ruble is the state budget.

The Soviet State Budget is a consolidated budget of the revenues and expenditures of the all-union, republican, and local governments. The budget is prepared by the all-union Ministry of Finance, and, along with the cash and credit plans prepared by the State Bank (Gosbank), constitute the *financial plans* of the Soviet government. The budget, like the production plan prepared by Gosplan, becomes a law when it is approved by the Council of Ministers and the Supreme Soviet.

The Soviet State Budget differs in many ways from the governmental budgets of Western nations. The most important difference is the role it plays in the management of the national economy. The budget occupies a pivotal nexus in the total financial network linking the state, the state productive sector, and the household sector. The financial flows that are regulated through the budget have counterparts in the real flows of goods, services, and labor resources. The real flows are controlled by means of the production, supply, and investment plans. The regulation of financial flows provides a useful complement to centralized control over real flows since output, supplies, and capital investments must be expressed in rubles and payments must be made in money whose flows can be closely monitored by Gosbank.

The official Soviet statistics on flows of financial resources are often incomplete and inconsistent, so that a certain amount of creative interpretation becomes necessary. The following description of the main features of the Soviet financial system and the major financial flows is unavoidably a crude and impressionistic approximation of the hidden reality.

Figure 5–2 represents a simplified model of financial flows in the Soviet economy. Information was obtained from different sources, some Soviet and some foreign, some actual and some planned, with a considerable amount of guesswork and approximations. Nevertheless, the picture is probably close enough to reality to be of some pedagogical value. In this diagram, nine major flows are recognized. Seven of them are taking place between the state (Gosbank and its agent), the state productive sector, and the household sector. The numerical values following the descriptions of the flows represent the approximate values of the 1977 flows expressed in billions of rubles.

The State Bank is at the hub of the two types of payment circuits that are found in the Soviet economy. (Although there are a variety of banks in the country, including tens of thousands of savings bank offices,

FIGURE 5–2   A simplified model of financial flows in the Soviet economy, 1977
Source: M. Elizabeth Denton, "Soviet Consumer Policy: Trends and Prospects," in U.S. Congress, Joint Economic Committee, *Soviet Economy in a Time of Change,* vol. 1, 96th Cong., 1st sess., 1979 (Washington, D. C.: U.S. Government Printing Office, 1979), pp. 766, 785, and 788; *USSR Facts and Figures Annual,* 2 (1978), 215.

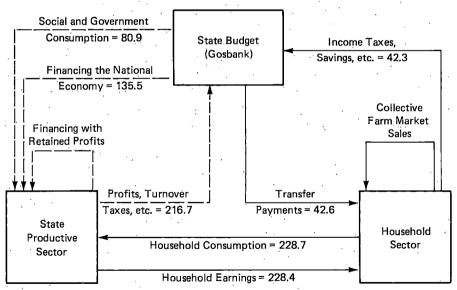

Figures in billions of rubles

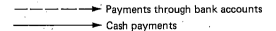 Payments through bank accounts

Cash payments

all of them may be regarded, for practical purposes, as divisions and branches of Gosbank.) The first payment circuit is the cashless circuit within the state sector, that is, between state productive enterprises and between the State Bank and the enterprises. In Figure 5–2, the payment flows in this sphere are shown by broken lines. All governmental units, including state productive enterprises, have accounts with Gosbank. Payments are made by transferring sums of money from one account to another. Between state enterprises, the normal means of transfer of funds is by bank drafts. The second payment circuit is between the state sector (Gosbank and state enterprises) and the household sector. Payments in this circuit are made by cash; they are indicated by unbroken lines in Figure 5–2. Although Gosplan regulates the flows of funds both within and between the cash and cashless spheres, its ability to control flows of funds is naturally greater in the noncash sphere where it can monitor changes in account balances to see if payments are being made in accord with the financial plans.

Revenues and Expenditures

The State Budget has two sources of revenue: the household sector and the state productive sector. From the household sector come personal income taxes, social insurance premiums, and household purchases of government bonds and savings bank deposits. These and other minor payments amounted to 42.3 billion rubles in 1977. From the state productive enterprises come payments out of profits (78.4 billion rubles in 1977), turnover taxes (73.3 billion rubles), and other payments including amortizations of capital assets; total payments from enterprises amounted to 216.7 billion rubles in 1977. On the expenditures side of the State Budget were social and government consumption (80.9 billion rubles), financing of the national economy (135.5 billion rubles), and transfer payments to the household sector (42.6 billion rubles).

From the above figures we can draw two conclusions: (1) the budgetary revenues from the household sector and payments to the same sector largely offset each other, and (2) deductions from profits and turnover taxes paid by state productive enterprises provide funds for social and government consumption and for financing the investments in the national economy.

Household incomes consist of state transfer payments (42.6 billion rubles in 1977) and earnings from the state productive sector (228.4 billion rubles). In 1977 the households spent 228.7 billion rubles on consumer goods and services purchased at state and cooperative retail stores. The remainder of the household sector's income, including transfer payments, is paid to the state in the forms of the personal income tax, insurance premiums, and savings.

The state productive sector has three categories of receipts: consumption spending by households, social and government consumption by the state, and the state's financing of the national economy. The sector's two payment flows are (1) payments for labor services rendered by households; and (2) payments out of profits, turnover taxes, and other payments made to the state. Additional financing of capital investments is made by state enterprises and paid out of their own retained profits.

The Nature of Financial Flows

We have noted above the directions and approximate sizes of the major financial flows between the state (Gosbank), the state productive sector, and the household sector. Below we make additional comments on the nature of some of the flows.[33]

Household earnings. Enterprises pay workers in cash withdrawn from Gosbank, and the size of their wage funds is predetermined in the economic plan. Managers are penalized in their bonus receipts if the actual disbursements of wages exceed the planned amount. Gosbank closely monitors the enterprises' withdrawals of cash for wage payments.

Personal income tax. Direct taxes on people's incomes are a relatively unimportant part of the Soviet government's revenues. In 1983, state taxes on the population accounted for only 8.25 percent of total revenues. Khrushchev had promised that personal income tax would be abolished by 1965, but this promise has not yet been fulfilled.

Household consumption. In 1977, about 47 percent of Soviet consumption spending was on food, whereas only 9 percent was on consumer durables. Comparable figures for the United States were 20 percent and 14 percent, respectively. Of the 228.7 billion rubles the Soviet households paid on goods and services purchased at state and cooperative retail stores in 1977, the turnover tax accounted for 73.3 billion rubles, or about 32 percent of the retail values. The turnover tax is paid to the state by state productive enterprises and by state sales organizations, but the burden of the tax ultimately falls on the Soviet consumer. The turnover tax, along with profit markups of state enterprises, constitute important sources of state funds for financing social consumption, capital investment, and defense spending.
The turnover tax also serves an important function by absorbing

---

[33]Figures for 1983 quoted in this section are from *USSR Facts and Figures Annual*, 7 (1983), 98.

the excess purchasing power of consumers, thereby achieving an equilibrium in the macroeconomy and preventing a buildup of inflationary pressures. (The mechanism of this function will be explained in the appendix at the end of this chapter.) The turnover tax is also used to achieve a microbalance in each of the consumer goods markets. If the quantity demanded at the officially fixed price exceeds the planned quantity supplied, the price can be raised by raising the turnover tax until the demanded quantity and the planned supply quantity are brought into balance.

Social and government consumption.   The turnover tax accounted for roughly one-third of the 228.7 billion rubles the Soviet consumers paid for personal consumption in 1977. If we add the profit markups of producers and wholesalers, we find that perhaps one-half of the total retail values represents hidden consumption taxes (the turnover tax plus the profit markups). These taxes provide major sources of funds for social and government consumption.

Collective consumption carried out by the Soviet government consists of social (or communal) consumption (in 1977, 34.8 billion rubles for education, science, and culture; and 12.0 billion rubles for health and physical culture, i.e., athletics), and government consumption (17.2 billion rubles for defense, 2.0 billion rubles for administration, and others). The government produces these services in the state productive sector, pays for them through the state budget, and consumes them for the benefit of the entire population.

Defense spending.   Defense-related expenditures, according to the official Soviet statistics, have remained at about 17 billion rubles for some years. Defense expenditures as percent of the state budget expenditures had declined from about 7 percent in 1977 to about 5 percent in 1983. The officially announced Soviet defense spending of 17 billion rubles per year had declined, as percent of gross national product, from over 3 percent in 1977 to less than 2 percent in 1983. By way of comparison, we may note that U.S. defense spending in the early 1980s was about 25 percent of the federal budget expenditures and about 5 percent of gross national product.

The official Soviet statistics on defense spending grossly understates the true burden of defense spending on the Soviet economy. The "prices" of armaments are substantially below their "costs," which means that a portion of the state expenditure for "financing the national economy" is subsidizing the production of arms. Furthermore, a great deal of "nonmilitary" activities—for example, education, scientific research, space programs, and highway construction—have a high military content. When the military content of the expenditures for social and government consumption and for capital investments are added to the officially reported expenditures for defense, the total defense burden on the economy is considerably greater than what the official statistics indicate. The U.S. Central Intelligence Agency estimates that the Soviet defense-related expenditures consume about 14 percent of gross national product in 1985.[34]

Financing the national economy.   A little over one-half (56 percent in 1983) of total budget outlay is for financing the national economy (FNE). These funds are allocated for capital investments (plant and equipment of enterprises, road and housing constructions, and capital repairs), increases in working capital of enterprises, and subsidies to enterprises where output prices are lower than input costs. Because of the incompleteness of the official Soviet statistics, it is difficult to es-timate how much of the capital financing of state productive enterprises is done through budgetary allocations, bank credits, or internal financ-ing through the use of retained profits and depreciation funds.[35]

Although accurate accounting of the composition of the FNE ex-penditures cannot be made, the sheer size of the flows of FNE funds leaves no question of its importance as means of redistributing incomes and allocating resources within the national economy. As we noted earlier, the major sources of state budget revenues are payments from enterprise profits and turnover taxes collected by enterprises. Perhaps one-half of national income is thus diverted from the household sector to the state, and returned to the state productive sector in the form of FNE expenditures. The FNE flow is important not only because of its function of redistributing incomes from the household sector to the state productive sector, but also because of the vital function it serves in reallocating resources *within* the state productive sector. Through the budget, funds are reallocated from low-priority industries to high-prior-ity industries.

Payments out of enterprise profits.   Payments out of profits in-clude capital charges on enterprises' fixed and working capital, differ-ential rent payments from some extractive industries and state farms, and deductions from profits, that is, that part of profits over and above what the enterprises are allowed to retain for specifically approved purposes.

Total profits of an enterprise are divided into two categories: profits

[34]Gregory G. Hilderbrandt, "The Dynamic Burden of Soviet Defense Spending," in U.S. Congress, Joint Economic Committee, *Soviet Economy in the 1980's: Problems and Prospects*, pt. 1, 97th Cong., 2nd sess. (Washington, D.C.: U.S. Government Printing Office, 1983), p. 333.

[35]Nove, *The Soviet Economic System*, pp. 242–43.

that the enterprise is allowed to retain, and profits that the enterprise must return to the state. The first category constitutes what is known as *incentive funds,* and can be used by the enterprise for such purposes as paying bonuses, making small investments in productive facilities, and building living quarters and recreational facilities for employees. The percentage of the enterprise's profits that can be transferred to its incentive funds is determined by a complex set of formulas.

The Functions of the State
Budget: Summary

In capitalist countries, resources are allocated primarily by the market, and governmental allocations through the budget merely supplement the market-guided patterns of allocation. In the Soviet Union, by contrast, resources are allocated by means of a pair of closely intertwined systems of planning and control: Gosplan's output and supply planning using material balances and Gosbank's "control by the ruble" using the State Budget.

The Soviet State Budget performs the following vital functions. First, it transfers resources from the household sector to the state productive sector by means of the turnover tax and enterprise profit markups. Second, in the process of allocating resources from household consumption to collective consumption and capital investment, it helps maintain an equilibrium between the household purchasing power and the ruble value of the available supply of consumer goods and services, thereby preventing an excessive buildup of inflationary pressures (see the appendix to this chapter). Third, the division of budgetary expenditures for different industries and regions determines not only the composition of total output but also the differential growth rates of the different parts of the national economy.

Appendix: MACROBALANCE BETWEEN
THE SECTORS

There are two types of balance to which Soviet planners must pay close attention. First, the quantities supplied and demanded of each product must equal at the state-determined price. Otherwise, there will develop either a surplus or shortage of the good. This is the *micro*balance. On a larger scale, there must be a *macro*balance between the household sector's effective purchasing power and the total ruble value of the available consumer goods and services. The size of consumer purchasing power must be regulated to prevent a buildup of inflationary pressures.

In this section we examine how a macrobalance is achieved in a socialist economy, using a simple numerical illustration.

Suppose that there are 100 million workers in a socialist economy, and that in a given year each worker, on average, earns 5,000 rubles. Since there is no property income under socialism, national income is 500 billion rubles (5,000 rubles × 100 million workers). To simplify the analysis, let us assume for the moment that households do not save and enterprises do not earn profits. The sum of 500 billion rubles represents both the household sector's purchasing power (national income) and the ruble values of total output (national product at factor cost).

What does the government do with the 500 billion rubles' worth of total output? The output must be allocated to the following three major categories of use: household consumption, collective consumption (health, education, defense, and so on), and investments in the national economy. Let us assume that 50 percent of the 500 billion ruble total output in our illustration is earmarked by state planners for household consumption. (In 1977, 50.3 percent of the Soviet gross national product was consumed by households.) We now have a potentially inflationary situation: 500 billion rubles of purchasing power can chase consumer goods that are valued, in terms of factor cost, at 250 billion rubles.

What if the government prices the consumer goods at factor (labor) cost and releases them with price tags adding up to 250 billion rubles? Since retail prices are officially fixed by the government, there will not be an *open* inflation. Instead, there will be a *repressed* inflation; shortages will develop, stores will be empty, and queues will be long. These conditions will result in widespread frustration and discontent among the population, leading to a decline in labor productivity and possibly to a rise in political instability.

In order to avoid the development of a serious repressed inflation, the state in our illustration must minimize the difference between total purchasing power (500 billion rubles) and the ruble values of available consumer goods (250 billion rubles). There are several ways of accomplishing this.

First, the government may impose an income tax of 250 billion rubles on the population. Consumers will then have just the right amount of purchasing power to absorb the available supplies of consumer goods. The Soviet government has chosen not to use this method since exploitation of working people by the state becomes too obvious under such a scheme. The Soviet government, instead, has opted for the second method—that of imposing the very high sales tax (called the turnover tax) on consumer goods. In our illustration, the government can add a sales tax of 250 billion rubles to the labor cost of 250 billion rubles, and charge 500 billion rubles on the consumer goods it sells to households.

In this way, the household purchasing power is equated to the value of consumer goods at 500 billion rubles each, leaving no inflationary pressure in the economy.

Of course the size of the turnover tax in the Soviet context need not be as high as 50 percent of retail values. The small income tax and savings by households help reduce consumers' effective purchasing power. Profit markups by enterprises help raise the ruble values of consumer goods. Thus, as we noted earlier, the turnover tax represents about one-third of the retail values of consumer goods.

One fact that complicates the Soviet planners' effort to achieve a macrobalance is the accumulation of past savings by households. Shortages of consumer goods over the past years have resulted in large accumulations of savings deposits which, when added to current wage earnings, help increase the inflationary pressures in the macroeconomy. That shortages of consumer goods remain a chronic problem in the Soviet Union clearly indicates that a macrobalance does not exist. To reduce the pressure of the repressed inflation, the Soviet government must either increase the turnover tax (thereby translating the repressed inflation into an open inflation), or else increase the supply quantities of consumer goods.

QUESTIONS

1. What kinds of market do not exist in the Soviet Union? What factors cause these types of market to be absent in a socialist economy?

2. If you were a member of a collective farm, would you rather be paid a guaranteed wage or receive a residual share of the farm's income? Why do you think the residual share method have such a negative effect on Soviet collective farmers' work incentives?

3. The auxiliary household plots occupy only about 3 percent of the Soviet Union's agricultural land area, and yet they contribute one quarter of total agricultural output. What factors account for the superior productivity of private plots?

4. Describe the structure of decision-making authority within the Soviet state enterprise sector. Who, or what group of people, have ultimate authority over enterprise directors?

5. What is khozraschet? Name a few U.S. government (or public) organizations which operate on a khozraschet basis.

6. What "success indicators" or performance criteria must Soviet enterprise directors observe? If you were the director of a Soviet enterprise, do you think you could work effectively under these criteria? Do you find conflicts

among the criteria? Which criterion (or criteria) do you think Soviet authorities stress more than others?

7. Describe the motivation structure of the Soviet state productive enterprise. Which types of motivation (see Chapter 1) are stressed? What accounts for this particular combination of motives? (Specifically, why is it that, in a socialist economy like the Soviet Union, group solidarity cannot be used more effectively?)

8. What are the most common educational and professional backgrounds of directors of Soviet enterprises? How does the situation compare with the backgrounds of American and Japanese corporate executives?

9. What are the relationships between enterprise directorship and Communist party membership? Does one help the other?

10. What is the nature of trade unions in the Soviet Union? How do union officials resolve possible conflicts between the major functions of a factory union committee? What is meant by a Soviet trade union being a "transmission belt"?

11. Describe the organizational structure of the Soviet industrial system using the paradigm introduced in Chapter 1 (decision-making, motivation, and information structures). What factors are responsible for the difficulty of horizontal communication and cooperation across industrial boundaries?

12. Explain the differences between the three types of enterprises classified according to their ministerial affiliation. What types of industry belong to each group?

13. Explain the roles played by Gosplan and Gossnab in allocations of industrial materials.

14. What does *plan* or *planning* mean in the Soviet economy? Is the emphasis more on the *time* aspect (i.e., control of future events) or on the *management* aspect (i.e., control of the economic system from the center)?

15. Describe the process of formulating annual economic plans. Soviet leaders maintain that the process is "democratic" since it involves negotiations between a large number of officials at all levels of the administrative hierarchy. Do you agree?

16. Suppose Gosplan finds that the projected demand for steel far exceeds the projected supply. Suggest several ways by which the imbalance can be reduced. Which method do you think is more manageable: reducing the *uses* side or increasing the *sources* side of the material balance?

17. Suppose that, in light of a projected shortage of steel on the material balance, Gosplan decides to increase the production of steel. What adjustments must be made to the material balances of other commodities? How would these additional changes affect, ultimately, the material balance of steel?

18. What factors contribute to the extreme tautness of Soviet plans? What are the effects of the tautness on the functioning of the Soviet material allocation system?

19. What is a *tolkach?* What vital services do tolkachi provide to an enterprise and to the economy? Why are such services necessary?

20. What is *repressed inflation?* What factors generate inflationary pressures in the Soviet economy? How can the Soviet government keep inflationary pressures in check?
21. Explain the budgetary mechanism by which resources are transferred from the household sector to the state productive sector.
22. What is meant by the "control by the ruble"? How is it supposed to work?
23. Overzealous or desperate Soviet managers often make larger wage payments than are planned in their efforts to reach or exceed planned output targets. What difficulties does such a practice create? How is this practice supposed to be prevented? Why do you think that this practice is often tolerated by higher authorities?

SELECTED READING

BORNSTEIN, MORRIS, Ed. *The Soviet Economy: Continuity and Change*, chaps. 1 and 2. Boulder, Colo.: Westview Press, 1981.
CAMPBELL, ROBERT W. *The Soviet-type Economies: Performance and Evolution*, chaps. 2 and 3. Boston: Houghton Mifflin Company, 1974.
HUTCHINGS, RAYMOND. *Soviet Economic Development* (2nd ed.), chaps. 10–14. New York: New York University Press, 1982.
KRYLOV, CONSTANTIN A. *The Soviet Economy: How It Really Works*, chaps. 4, 5, 10, 12–14, and 17. Lexington, Mass.: Lexington Books, D. C. Heath and Company, 1979.
NOVE, ALEC. *The Soviet Economic System* (2nd ed.), chaps. 2, 3, and 9. London: George Allen & Unwin, 1980.
U.S. CONGRESS, JOINT ECONOMIC COMMITTEE. *Soviet Economy in a Time of Change*, vols. 1 and 2, 96th Cong., 1st sess. Washington, D.C.: U.S. Government Printing Office, 1979.
U.S. CONGRESS, JOINT ECONOMIC COMMITTEE. *Soviet Economy in the 1980's: Problems and Prospects*, pts. 1 and 2, 97th Cong., 2nd sess. Washington, D.C.: U.S. Government Printing Office, 1983.

CHAPTER **6**

The Soviet Economy: Problems of Imbalance and Inefficiency

In the preceding chapter we examined the organization of the Soviet economy and the mechanism of central economic planning for material and financial balances. Our perspective there was primarily macroeconomic. In this chapter we shall take a closer look at the economy, focusing our attention on the problems of microbalance and efficiency in resource allocation.

We begin with an assessment of the performance of the Soviet economic system. Our conclusion that the system is experiencing problems of crisis proportions will lead us to a discussion of one of the systemic weaknesses of the system—the problem of irrational prices. We shall then proceed to examine some major problems that are plaguing the Soviet economic system. We shall conclude with discussions of the fundamental causes of these problems.

HOW WELL IS THE SYSTEM WORKING?

There is little doubt that the centralized system of administrative control worked sufficiently well in transforming the predominantly agrarian economy of Russia into a modern industrial state in a few decades after the Bolshevik Revolution of 1917. The logic of the system—centralized control of production and investments with preferential allocations of resources to high-priority sectors of the economy—is ideally suited to the task of crude and speedy foundation building. Until about the early 1950s the system had worked well in industrializing the Soviet economy—at least as well as other systems that relied more heavily on market forces.

As the Soviet economy entered an early maturity stage in the 1950s, the system's strengths became increasingly less relevant and its weaknesses became increasingly more apparent. By the early 1970s, it had become obvious that the system had very serious flaws.

The basic problem is the system's inherent inability to provide a balanced development of the economy with reasonable efficiency in its use of resources. Not only has this fact been widely observed by Western students of the Soviet economy, but it has been openly discussed by Soviet leaders. For example, Brezhnev in his 1970 speech stated, "Many problems are essentially connected with . . . the fact that we have entered a stage of development that no longer allows us to work in the old way but calls for new methods and new solutions."[1] Ten years later, the same leader, speaking at the Central Committee plenum, observed, "It should be frankly admitted that the mechanism of management and planning, the methods of management and the discipline in carrying out assignments have not yet been brought to the level meeting contemporary requirements."[2]

Since the middle of the 1950s, the Soviet government has introduced a series of rather ambitious economic reform measures to improve the "mechanism of management and planning." The fact that these reforms have not produced tangible results so far, and that "reforms of reforms" have been implemented without noticeably improving the declining health of the economy, suggests that the real cause of the problem is not poor management and planning, but is rooted deeply in the very nature of the Soviet system itself.

From the 11-year file of speeches made by Brezhnev and Kosygin during the 1970–80 period, research analyst M. Elizabeth Denton of the U.S. Central Intelligence Agency (CIA) distilled the following four problems as the foci of major concern by Soviet leaders:

. A chronic lag in the completion of investment projects

---

[1] M. Elizabeth Denton, "Soviet Perceptions of Economic Prospects," in U.S. Congress, Joint Economic Committee, *Soviet Economy in the 1980's: Problems and Prospects*, pt. 1, 97th Cong., 2nd sess. (Washington, D.C.: U.S. Government Printing Office, 1983), p. 32.

[2] Ibid., p. 38.

Weak incentives and poor management structure for the introduction of new technology

Weak incentives and poor management structure for the conservation of scarce resources, including manpower and materials

Consumer goods shortages, particularly food, that frustrate worker incentives[3]

Holland Hunter, observing that the economy now appears to face failure in the 1980s, identified the following four major problem areas in the Soviet economy: "declining output growth, serious inflationary pressure, slow technological progress, and accumulated deficiencies in housing and other public needs."[4] To these lists of the symptoms of the "Soviet disease," we may also add worker alienation, poor quality of products, declining labor productivity, and disguised unemployment.

The annual growth rate of the Soviet economy's real gross national product, as estimated by the CIA, was 5.0 percent in the 1960–65 period. The rate fell to 3.7 percent in 1970–75, and further down to 2.7 percent in the 1975–80 period. The average annual rates of growth of total factor productivity—that is, output per combined inputs of labor, capital, and land—for the Soviet economy fell from 1.1 percent in the 1965–70 period to −0.5 percent in 1970–75 and to −0.8 percent in 1975–80.[5] The slowdown in the growth rates of output and productivity is expected to continue into the 1980s. What is particularly alarming to Soviet leaders is the qualitative aspect of this slowdown; it is taking place within the context of increased worker alienation and continued inability to make significant technological progresses.

The long-run stability in the levels of official retail prices masks the very serious problem of repressed inflation. Very high turnover tax rates on consumer durables, long queues in front of government retail outlets, and large subsidies on some agricultural products (particularly meat) are symptoms of serious inflationary pressures. In order to absorb a portion of the sharp annual increases in consumer purchasing power, the Soviet government increased the prices of a number of luxury goods substantially in 1979 and again in 1981. These measures, however, were not strong enough to absorb the excessive consumer purchasing power.

[3]Ibid., p. 33.

[4]Holland Hunter, "Soviet Economic Problems and Alternative Policy Responses," in U.S. Congress, Joint Economic Committee, *Soviet Economy in a Time of Change*, vol. 1, 96th Cong., 1st sess. (Washington, D.C.: U.S. Government Printing Office, 1979), p. 23.

[5]Herbert S. Levine, "Possible Causes of the Deterioration of Soviet Productivity Growth in the Period 1976–80," in U.S. Congress, Joint Economic Committee, *Soviet Economy in the 1980's*, pt. 1, 97th Cong., 2nd sess. (Washington, D.C.: U.S. Government Printing Office, 1983), p. 154.

Throughout the 1970s and early 1980s, the increasing purchasing power helped push prices at collective farm markets. Between the end of 1970 and the end of 1980, the size of household savings deposits more than tripled.[6] Continued accumulations of unspendable purchasing power frustrate consumers and lead to a further decline in worker morale and productivity.

Closely related to the problem of repressed inflation is the problem of disguised unemployment. For both political and ideological reasons, workers are seldom allowed to remain idle for long. The Soviet authorities boast that all able-bodied citizens can find gainful employment. Workers are seldom laid off, even though they may be unproductive or incompetent. "We pretend to work, and they pretend to pay us," is a popular saying among cynical Soviet workers. Millions of workers are underemployed; that is, they are not contributing much to the output of the Soviet economy and therefore their removal from the work force would not reduce output much. This, of course, is a serious waste of human resources—another factor contributing to the overall inefficiency of resource use in the Soviet economy.

Technological progress is slow in the Soviet economy primarily because the system lacks incentives for innovative activities. Ambitious production targets and the excessive emphasis on meeting short-term output quotas discourage enterprise managers and ministerial officials from scrapping old machines and equipment and installing new ones, or trying new but untested production techniques; these efforts are time consuming and are more likely to reduce output in the short run. Soviet plant managers are not working with a long time horizon; they want to produce a quick result at a given assignment and, riding on the success, move on to greener pastures. Slow technological progress and the absence of innovative spirit among managers reduce the productivity of capital resources, contributing to the overall inefficiency in resource use.

VALUE AND PRICES

It is often observed that the waste and inefficiencies in the Soviet system of planning and management are in large part attributable to the irrationality of Soviet prices—prices that do not reflect relative scarcities of goods. It is further observed that the irrational Soviet price structure has its roots in the archaic Marxist theory of value, which attempted

---

[6]Ann Goodman and Geoffrey Schleifer, "The Soviet Labor Market in the 1980's," in U.S. Congress, Joint Economic Committee, *Soviet Economy in the 1980's*, pt. 1, 97th Cong., 2nd sess. (Washington, D.C.: U.S. Government Printing Office, 1983), p. 340.

to explain prices by reference to the labor content of production costs. Although these observations are valid, they are nevertheless misleading if they imply that the Soviet leaders' adherence to Marxist dogma is the fundamental cause of the failure of the Soviet economic system. To accept such an implication is tantamount to arguing that the present Soviet regime is incapable of instituting a genuine economic reform for fear of violating Marxist precepts. As we noted earlier, the real, effective ideology of Soviet society is not Marxism—which merely serves as a façade ideology whenever it is convenient to the regime—but the power ideology of the party-government elite. If the leadership genuinely desired to restructure the price system, nothing could prevent it from doing so. Irrational prices are preserved by the regime because a rationalizing attempt will threaten its monopoly of power. The fundamental cause of the "Soviet disease," therefore, is not Marxism or irrational prices, but the logic of Soviet power ideology—the obsession with the centralized, authoritarian control over economy and society.

Though irrational Soviet prices are not the ultimate cause of the failure of the Soviet economic system, they are nevertheless an important immediate cause of the variety of the problems besetting the Soviet economy today. For this reason it is important that we develop a good grasp of their structure and the ways in which they lead to resource misallocation.

The Meaning of Rational Prices

In any economic system, resources can be allocated by one (or both) of the following two methods: (1) physical allocation by administrative methods, and (2) market-oriented allocation by the price mechanism. The Soviet economy and many other so-called "socialist" economies in Eastern Europe and elsewhere rely primarily on the first method, whereas the rest of the industralized world are guided largely by the second method.

In a modern, complex economy like the Soviet Union, a sole reliance on the physical allocation method becomes impossible. As we noted in Chapter 1, the organizational structure of an economy has three dimensions: the decision-making authority, information flows, and motivational systems. For the decision-making structure to function efficiently, it must be supported by effective information and motivation structures. Because of the sheer size and complexity of the economy, however, the information and motivation structures must utilize a price mechanism. National output, enterprise production targets, managerial bonuses, workers' wages, and many more variables, must be expressed in monetary (i.e., ruble) values. Decisions must be made, and people must be motivated, on the basis of these ruble values. A refusal to use prices and price calculations would simply transform the system into a barter economy with an intolerably low productivity and income.

If allocative decisions are to be made on the basis of prices of inputs and outputs, then the prices must reflect relative scarcities of these inputs and outputs. *Scarcity* of a good is determined by the intensity of the demand (use value) for that good relative to the responsiveness of supply (cost) of that good. When the prices of goods A and B accurately reflect the relative scarcities of these goods, we say these prices are *scarcity prices* or *rational prices*. Specifically, prices of goods A and B are rational prices when:

$$\frac{MSC_A}{MSC_B} = \frac{P_A}{P_B} = \frac{MSU_A}{MSU_B}$$

where *MSC* stands for marginal social cost, *P* is price, and *MSU* stands for marginal social utility or use value. For example, if good A happens to be three times as expensive as good B (i.e., $P_A/P_B = 3$), then this price ratio of 3:1 is rational if and only if (1) the production cost of an additional unit of A, including all *social* costs (i.e., private *and* external costs), is three times that of B; *and* (2) good A has social use value, at the margin, three times that of good B. (Those readers who are not familiar with the concept of *social* costs and benefits are encouraged to consult any standard textbook in economic principles.) If either side (cost or use value) of the equation does not hold, then the prices are irrational. In market-oriented economies, the inequalities tend to be minimized by the working of market forces, provided certain conditions are met. Note that, to the extent prices are irrational, any decisions made on the basis of those prices are irrational; that is, they result in waste and inefficiencies in resource use.

It may be asked why a socialist economy based essentially on physical planning needs scarcity prices. Can it not get by with a set of *accounting prices* as a common denominator for all goods and services and satisfy the need for record keeping and information exchange without insisting that prices reflect relative scarcities? For example, can the planners arbitrarily decide that a kilogram of apples is worth 3 rubles and a kilogram of oranges is valued at 5 rubles, so that a total output of 200 kilograms of apples and 100 kilograms of oranges can be expressed as 1,100 rubles? In this way, returning to a barter system becomes unnecessary; all goods and services can be expressed by a common denominator, that is, by accounting prices.

It so happens that in the Soviet Union today, prices must play more important roles than merely serving as record keeping or accounting means. The need for scarcity prices arises from the fact that many decision makers are guided by prices in their decisions. First, consumers' decisions to buy or not to buy are affected by retail prices. If prices are not set properly, not only may surpluses or shortages develop, but wasteful uses of resources may also result. For example, if a loaf of bread is priced at a level that is insufficient to cover the cost (price) of grain that goes into that loaf, farmers may buy bread instead of grain as feed for their pigs. (This perversity actually happened in the Soviet Union.) Second, managers often have to choose between different inputs, and the prices of inputs affect their decisions since they are rewarded in part by the size of the profits their enterprise makes. (More on this point later.) Third, project makers—those planners and engineers who design projects such as dams and railroads—cannot make rational decisions unless they know accurately the real resource costs to society of the alternative designs of their projects. In all these cases, prices that accurately reflect the relative costs and use values of each product—that is, scarcity prices—are indispensable. And this need for rational prices becomes increasingly more acute as the economy matures and becomes more complex.

Marx and the Law of Value

As we noted in Chapter 2, Marx's law of value was based on the labor theory of value: things have value because of the amount of "socially necessary labor" embodied in them. Capital and land were not considered "productive," and therefore did not add to the value of a product. Note that Marx did include the contribution of physical capital to production. Tools and equipment were certainly needed, but they were considered reducible ultimately to past labor (or "dead" labor). What was not included was that part of capital cost that is now called *interest charges* or *return on capital.* Note that Marx's labor theory of value was essentially a cost-based (or supply-sided) theory of prices. A price was explained by the cost of production, which included current-labor costs and depreciation costs of productive assets (i.e., past-labor costs).

Later-day economists would argue that the Marxist labor theory of value had two serious flaws. For one thing, it neglected two very important types of opportunity cost involved in the production process. Marginal land may be free, but above-marginal land—because of its superior fertility or location—may have a positive opportunity cost. If one wishes to use this land, a premium—called *rent* by the English economist David Ricardo—will have to be paid for it; otherwise, the owners of the land would lease it to somebody else who would pay the premium.

More importantly, critics would argue, Marx failed to recognize the productivity of capital. There are two different types of capital cost:

(1) the wear and tear of the physical assets, and (2) a premium payment to the owners to compensate for the act of "abstinence" or "waiting." (The owner is "waiting" to consume the output sometime in the future, rather than now.) If the capital assets were not used in the production process of the good in question, they could be used elsewhere by someone else. Thus, capital in the "abstinence" or "waiting" sense does have an opportunity cost. The producers who benefit from the use of capital must charge both types of capital cost—depreciation and interest—against the price (value) of their product. Marx realized the significance of one type of capital cost (that of stored-up labor, or depreciation), but failed to see, or refused to see, the significance of the other type of capital cost (the opportunity cost of "waiting," or interest).

The second flaw of Marx's theory of value was even more serious than the first. Not only was his theory incomplete on the cost (supply) side, but it was also oblivious to the other side of the market forces that give rise to value—the demand side. Marx argued that demand was subjective, that it was something that existed only in the whims of people. Scientific socialism, argued Marx, had to be built on objective facts, like hours of labor embodied in a product. Modern economic theory rejects this view. Relative use values of products are as important as their costs in determining the price of a good. Suppose there are two types of fuel, one having twice as much calorific content as the other. If the two fuels can be produced at exactly the same cost per unit, should the two fuels be valued (priced) at the same level, or should one with a higher calorific content be priced higher than the other? The conclusion is obvious: we cannot determine relative values by cost considerations alone. Doing so would necessarily lead to misalloction of resources. The unfortunate omission of use value by Marx has made the price system based on Marxist doctrine practically useless and even damaging as a means of channeling economic resources to alternative uses.

The Structure of Soviet Prices

Five major types of prices are in existence in the Soviet economy today: the industrial wholesale price, the agricultural procurement price, the state retail price, the collective farm market price, and the price of labor.

Industrial wholesale prices. The prices at which goods are transferred between units of the state productive sector are known as industrial wholesale prices. This type of price was originally constructed on the basis of Marxist theory of value. It is based on the industrywide average cost of production which includes the cost of direct and indirect labor, materials cost, and depreciation allowances. The price that the producing enterprise receives is arrived at by adding a profit markup to the "average cost of production." The price that the buying enterprise pays is somewhat higher since it includes charges for transportation and the markup of sales organizations, and, in some cases, a turnover tax.

The use of profit markups in computing industrial wholesale prices needs an explanation. In a socialist economy, citizens collectively own the means of production; profits, therefore, are regarded as means by which the fruits of people's labor are returned to the people. As such, socialist profits do not carry a connotation of "exploitation" as do capitalist profits. Even so, why bother with profits? Why not formulate industrial wholesale prices strictly in proportion to the "average production cost"? The answer is, simply, that profit markups provide Soviet planners with a convenient way of promoting efficiency in enterprise operations. Whether or not the price system is rational, the size of the profit an enterprise generates can be regarded as a crude indicator of the efficiency of the enterprise's productive efforts. The larger the profits, *other things being equal*, the more efficient the enterprise probably is. At any rate, profit markups give Soviet planners one extra lever of control over industrial activities.

Prior to the reform of the industrial wholesale price of 1966–67, the wholesale prices were seriously flawed in that they reflected neither rent nor interest charges. As noted earlier, this omission resulted in a distortion of the structure of Soviet prices since it underpriced products whose production was land and/or capital intensive. The reform attempted to correct this anomaly by introducing (1) interest charges on bank loans, (2) a capital charge in the form of a tax on the enterprise's fixed and working capital, and (3) a differential rent (in some extractive industries) to be paid out of the enterprise's profits.[7] These reform measures represented a partial departure from the established Marxist dogma; "partial" because the Soviet wholesale prices are still basically cost-based prices. They do not reflect relative scarcities of goods since user demand is prevented from having an impact on the price formation process.

Agricultural procurement prices.   Prices at which farm products are *purchased* by state procurement agencies from collective and state farms are known as agricultural procurement prices. The prices at which

---

[7]A *differential rent* is a charge on a high-grade natural resource. For example, an iron-ore mine with high-grade ore deposits naturally has a cost advantage over other mines and therefore tends to enjoy higher profits. The reform required such a mine to pay to the state a differential rent to offset its cost advantage.

these products are subsequently *sold* to other state enterprises, however, are included in industrial wholesale prices.

For pricing purposes, farm products are treated differently from industrial products because the cost of production of the former varies more widely than that of the latter owing to great variations in geography, soil, weather, and length of growing season. In order to compensate for these variations, pronounced differences in procurement prices must be allowed.

The Soviet government uses a variety of methods designed to add flexibility in the procurement price structure. These methods include (1) differentiating the size of profit markup between products, (2) differentiating prices geographically by price zones (up to the price ratio of 1:2.5), (3) paying a temporary surcharge of up to 70 percent of the base price, and (4) paying premia of up to 100 percent for above-plan deliveries. A combination of these methods is used in order to stimulate output and increase sales to the state.[8]

The system of differentiated procurement prices is complex, cumbersome, and inconsistent, and often lags behind changing conditions. These prices, therefore, generate distortions of their own. For example, in the late 1960s and early 1970s, average rate of profitability of grain was substantially higher than that of livestock products, inducing farmers to "prefer to sell grain to the state rather than feed it to animals."[9] This practice had the inevitable result of perpetuating the meat shortage. In the mid-1970s, profitability was adequate on grain, sunflowers, cotton, pigs, and eggs; but for milk, cattle, sheep, potatoes, and vegetables it was "not sufficient to permit every 'normal operating' farm to cover costs and earn enough profits to pay bonuses and make scheduled investments."[10]

State retail prices.   State retail prices are charged by state retail outlets and service establishments on consumer goods and services. The major components of the retail price are the wholesale price and the turnover tax. On some agricultural products—notably meat and milk—subsidies are paid by the state, so that their retail prices are lower than wholesale prices. In the early 1980s, the retail price of beef in state stores was less than half of what it cost the state. In 1980 alone, agricultural subsidies cost the government 25 billion rubles.[11] Although no

[8]Morris Bornstein, "Soviet Price Policy in the 1970s," in U.S. Congress, Joint Economic Committee, *Soviet Economy in a New Perspective*, 94th Cong., 2nd sess. (Washington, D.C.: U.S. Government Printing Office, 1976), pp. 34–36.

[9]Ibid., p. 37.

[10]Ibid., pp. 38–39.

[11]David Brand, "Free Enterprise Helps to Keep Russians Fed but Creates Problems," *Wall Street Journal*, May 2, 1983, p. 1.

systematic statistics on turnover tax rates are available, it is estimated that the average rate is roughly one-half of the retail price.[12] In 1977, for example, the turnover tax on the Zhiguli automobile (model VAZ-2101) was 3,200 rubles, which was 58.2 percent of the retail price of 5,500 rubles.[13]

Collective farm market prices.   As discussed earlier, collective farm market prices are free-market prices determined by the forces of supply and demand. As such, these and other prices in the so-called second (or underground) economy are the only genuine scarcity prices in the Soviet economy.

In this market, both sellers and buyers belong to the household sector. Though important for many Soviet consumers, these prices are not part of the official Soviet price structure. Since state retail prices are kept stable by the planners, any fluctuations in consumer purchasing power are likely to cause similar fluctuations in collective farm market prices. Sharply rising free farm prices are sure signs of shortages of comparable items in the state retail outlets and a general state of repressed inflation.

A *Wall Street Journal* correspondent reported that in the spring of 1983, in a collective farm market in Leningrad, a kilogram (about 2.2 pounds) of beef commanded a price of 7 rubles, which was 3.5 times the official retail store price of 2 rubles per kilogram. The relative expensiveness of beef can be appreciated if we compare the price of 7 rubles per kilogram to the average monthly wage of 170 rubles of Soviet workers.[14]

The price of labor.   The labor market is the only factor market that exists in the Soviet economy. The households supply labor and the state demands it. In the product markets, the government can plan the supply but cannot plan the demand. Conversely, in the labor market, the government can plan only the demand, but not the supply. The demand for labor is derived from the state's need to produce the planned output. Between supply and demand, the prices of labor—or wage rates—are determined, subject to overall constraints placed by the planners.

Soviet officials may claim that labor supply is planned and wage rates are fixed by the government, just as output supply is planned and product prices are fixed by it. This claim is only partially true. The state

[12]Raymond Hutchings, *Soviet Economic Development*, 2nd ed. (New York: New York University Press, 1982), p. 163.

[13]Toli Welihozkiy, "Automobiles and the Soviet Consumer," in U.S. Congress, Joint Economic Committee, *Soviet Economy in a Time of Change*, vol. 1, 96th Cong., 1st sess. (Washington, D.C.: U.S. Government Printing Office, 1979), pp. 821–22.

[14]Brand, "Free Enterprise Helps to Keep Russians Fed," p. 1.

can affect the supply of labor only indirectly—that is, in an aggregative manner and in the long run. Educational policies affect the skill structure of the nation's labor force in the long run. The system of domestic passports that controls the movements of rural residents into cities also affects the aggregate supply of labor in a given metropolitan area. These policies, however, cannot determine the supplies of different occupational skills in the short run.

The basic fact of Soviet labor markets is that Soviet workers are free to choose occupation and place of work. To be sure wage *grades* and *rates* are officially fixed, but if there are not enough takers of a particular job at a given job grade and wage rate, the enterprise managers are prone to evade the system by offering needed workers de facto higher wages. This can be accomplished by upgrading the job or by offering easy piece-rate or bonus schemes. For example, if the official wage rates of clerk-typists are too low to attract applicants, the enterprise managers may ensure the services of secretaries by carrying them on the payroll as, say, skilled machine operators. Thus, although wage rates are officially fixed in a published national job-qualifications manual, the actual structure of relative wages is determined largely by the forces of supply and demand.

Although the relative structure of wages is determined largely by market forces, overall wage payments are controlled fairly closely by the government. Such control is necessary if inflationary pressure in the national economy is to be prevented from becoming excessive. Each enterprise has a planned wages fund, and authorization to exceed the limits of the fund is hard to obtain. Wages are paid in cash, which the enterprise withdraws from a branch of Gosbank, and this financial flow is closely monitored by Gosbank.

An Economic Analysis of State Retail Prices

Wholesale prices are used within the state industrial sector, and, as such, need to serve—in theory at least—only as accounting prices. Retail prices, however, must be more than mere accounting prices. For each commodity, the retail price must be set at the equilibrium (or market-clearing) level so that expected demand is brought in line with planned supply. If not, a shortage or surplus develops, disturbing the overall economic plan. This is the problem of microeconomic balance in consumer goods markets. In this section we analyze how the balance is achieved, what factors may cause imbalances to develop, and how the Soviet planners respond to the imbalances.

Figure 6–1 depicts supply and demand conditions in a consumer good market. The supply curves are drawn vertically to show that the

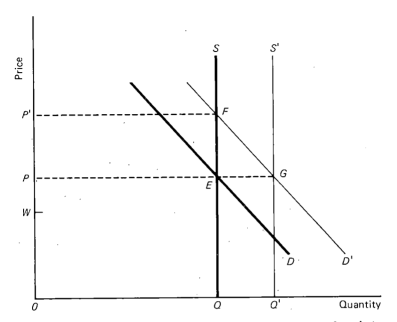

FIGURE 6-1   Microbalance and Imbalance In a consumer good market

quantities of the good supplied are determined by the planners and therefore are unresponsive to changes in the price. The initial supply curve, S, represents the planned output of the good, *OQ*, for the period. Consumer demand, which is shaped by the free choice of the households, is represented by the two downward sloping demand curves. The position and slope of demand curves must be *estimated* by the planners.

Suppose that the planners initially estimate the demand curve to be *D*. Assuming this estimate is accurate, we may now ask: At what level should the planners set the price if they wish to achieve a balance in this market? Basic economics textbooks tell us that equilibrium in a market is obtained when the quantity demanded is equal to the quantity supplied. Such a result is obtained at point *E* where the demand curve, *D*, and the supply curve, *S*, intersect. If the planners set the price of this good exactly at *P*, this market clears; in other words, there will be neither a shortage nor a surplus in this market. If we assume that the wholesale price of this good is *OW* (ignoring the profit markup), then we know that the Soviet planners must impose a turnover tax of *WP* on this product so that the retail price will be *OP*. Note that the size of the turnover tax is determined as a *residual*. Its size is determined by first determining the retail price and then subtracting from it the wholesale price.

Now, suppose that an expansion in the nation's economic activities has increased households' money income, which in turn has increased consumers' demand for the product in question. In Figure 6–1, the increase in the demand is shown by the rightward shift in the demand curve from D to D'. How should the planners react to this new situation? There are three alternative courses of action.

The first alternative is to raise the retail price from OP to OP' without increasing the planned supply. The quantity supplied remains unchanged at OQ, but this quantity is now sold at the higher price OP'. The new equilibrium point is F, where the new demand curve, D', intersects the old supply curve, S. The Soviet macromanagers generally refrain from using this alternative since it results in an *open* inflation. The Soviet leaders try to maintain price stability at all costs for both political and technical reasons. Politically, it is unwise to allow an open inflation since the regime has long boasted that price stability is inherent in a planned economy—one of the advantages that clearly demonstrates the superiority of socialism over capitalism. Technically, rising prices will complicate the problems of planning. Higher retail prices require "raising wages (and pensions, stipends, and other transfer payments), with subsequent pressure on production costs throughout the economy."[15]

In resisting retail price hikes, Soviet planners face a dilemma. Higher prices are politically unpopular and complicate the process of economic planning, but they are also useful since they absorb excessive purchasing power of consumers. The way out of this dilemma is to maintain price stability for such basic necessities as housing and food, but to try to absorb some purchasing power by sharply raising the prices of a few selected luxury goods. Substantial increases in the prices of such products as automobiles, vodka, jewelry, and imported furniture can be defended as a governmental policy of discouraging socially undesirable consumption.

The second alternative open to Soviet planners is to maintain the existing price, OP, and increase the planned supply of the commodity from S to S'. A new equilibrium is reached at point G, and OQ' of quantity is both supplied and demanded. This alternative assures price stability without generating shortages. One serious shortcoming of this method, at least from the point of view of the Soviet planners, is that it requires increasingly larger quantities of resources to be allocated to consumer goods industries. Such a change in allocational patterns may not be feasible because of the rising developmental and military demands on resources. More importantly, this alternative is faulted for ideological reasons. The Soviet regime cannot tolerate allowing con-

[15]Bornstein, "Soviet Price Policy in the 1970s," p. 48.

sumer demand to dictate the critical division of the nation's output between household use and governmental (investment, military, developmental, and so on) uses.

The third alternative method of coping with rising consumer purchasing power is to do nothing. The planners can keep the supply at the existing level, S, and keep the price at OP. The problem with this method, of course, is that the excess demand pressure will have to find its outlet one way or another. If neither supply nor price is allowed to change, then the increased demand inevitably produces a shortage of this good. The new demand curve, D', and the unchanged price, OP, result in a quantity demanded of $OQ' = PG$. Since the quantity supplied remains unchanged at $OQ = PE$, the excess of quantity demanded over quantity supplied, $QQ' = EG$, appears as a shortage. This much of consumer demand remains unsatisfied, and long queues and empty shelves lead to consumer frustration and resentment.

The moral of the preceding discussion of the third alternative method is that no government or authority can control *both* price *and* quantity of a given product *as long as demand itself is left free.* Here we find a *principle of economics* at work, a principle that has a universal applicability to any society, be it socialist or capitalist. If, in the Soviet context, the planners try to contain both price and quantity in the face of rising demand, the excess demand will merely manifest itself in the form of a shortage. Empty stores, long queues, arrogant sales clerks, and disgruntled customers—these are the symptoms of repressed inflation.

Which of the three alternative methods of coping with rising consumer income have Soviet planners used primarily? Consider the following set of records:

Between 1967 and 1977, total personal money income in the Soviet Union more than doubled (from 123 billion rubles to 277 billion rubles).[16]

Between 1965 and 1974, the state retail prices fell slightly.[17]

Between 1960 and 1978, total consumption as percent share of Soviet GNP decreased from 60.1 percent to 55.5 percent.[18]

Consumer-oriented investment as a share of total investment during 1971–77 was somewhat smaller than during 1966–77.[19]

Between the end of 1970 and the end of 1980, household savings deposits

[16]M. Elizabeth Denton, "Soviet Consumer Policy: Trends and Prospects," in U.S. Congress, Joint Economic Committee, *Soviet Economy in the 1980's*, pt. 1, 97th Cong., 2nd sess. (Washington, D.C.: U.S. Government Printing Office, 1983), p. 785, table 1.

[17]Bornstein, "Soviet Policy in the 1970s," p. 48, table 12.

[18]Denton, "Soviet Consumer Policy," p. 769, table 5.

[19]Ibid., p. 761.

increased from 46.6 billion rubles (30 percent of annual retail sales) to 156.5 billion rubles (58 percent of retail sales).[20]

Between 1975 and 1980, total household savings deposits increased by 72 percent while retail trade volume increased by only 29 percent.[21]

Putting all these pieces of evidence together and placing them in the analytical framework of Figure 6–1, we come to the following conclusion. Despite evidence indicating that there have been some selected price increases to discourage consumption of luxury goods (e.g., vodka and automobiles) and some rather substantial increases in the production of selected consumer goods, the basic pattern of response of Soviet economic planners to rising consumer purchasing power has been one of repressing the inflationary pressures. This conclusion is drawn from the observed fact that, in spite of the market increase in consumer's money income, retail prices remained stable and resources allocated to consumer goods remained about the same in proportion to total resources used in the economy. That portion of consumer purchasing power that could not be exercised because of the unavailability of consumer goods must have caused the sharp increase in the (presumably involuntary) savings deposits. It may also be safe to assume, too, that a large portion of the unsatisfied money income must have spilled over into various types of gray and black markets.

THE PROBLEMS OF THE SOVIET ECONOMIC SYSTEM

The centralized administrative system of managing the Soviet economy is essentially much like the ways in which large private corporations in Western countries are organized and managed. Lower-level operating units of a large corporation are directed by the company's top management to maximize or minimize some target variables (profits, output, sales, costs, or whatever) given a set of constraints (technology, physical plants, work force, prices, budget, and so on). Why is it so difficult for Soviet planners to manage their enterprises with a reasonable degree of efficiency? Why is it that, after heaping reforms upon reforms, the Soviet economic planners and managers find their economy still suffering from a seemingly hopeless case of anemia? Is the problem systemic, or is it something that can be corrected by a set of well-thought-out and smartly executed reform measures?

[20]Goodman and Schleifer, "The Soviet Labor Market in the 1980's," p. 340.

[21]Marshall I. Goldman, *U.S.S.R. in Crisis: The Failure of an Economic System* (New York: W. W. Norton & Company, 1983), p. 55.

In this section we shall examine the nature of some of the more serious problems that are plaguing Soviet economic managers. In the following section, we shall seek to identify the fundamental causes of these problems.

Macroeconomic Imbalances

In the preceding chapter we discussed how a macroeconomic financial balance is presumably achieved in the Soviet economy. Essentially, what is required is a balance between the effective purchasing power of households and the ruble value of available consumer goods and services. What is theoretically possible has not been achieved; for decades household personal incomes have grown more rapidly than the supply of consumer goods and services. Enterprises chronically overshoot their wage payment plans in their efforts to produce more. But the difficulties encountered in production and distribution of goods throughout the Soviet economy (to be discussed below) have resulted in shifting the burden of adjustment to consumer goods industries, so that output of consumer goods and services has chronically fallen short of planned targets. The result is the large and increasing accumulation of households' savings bank deposits, which represent a rising inflationary pressure. The widening disparity between household purchasing power and the available supplies of consumer goods has two serious implications. For one thing, Soviet workers' incentives to work are eroding as they ask themselves, What good does it do to work hard and earn all these rubles when we cannot spend them on things we really want? Reduced incentives to work lead to low productivity and the slower growth rate of the economy, which in turn reduces the supplies of consumer goods. Secondly, as we shall discuss in Chapter 12, the increasing inflationary pressure makes a genuine economic reform much more difficult to accomplish. The badly needed reform, which will necessarily involve easing up the government's tight control over supplies, may trigger an explosion of consumer demand for goods thus causing a serious actual inflation. The fear of an explosive open inflation is one of the reasons why Soviet leadership is averse to experimenting with a radical restructuring of the system.

Supply Shortages

Shortages of consumer goods are certainly frustrating to Soviet citizens and may become, in the long run, a serious political problem. Meanwhile, the system is burdened with the more immediate and pressing problem of widespread and chronic shortages of material supplies for productive enterprises. It is difficult for plant managers to meet the plan output and delivery targets when supplies are not available or arrive later than scheduled. Managers, however, must somehow find ways to meet the plan targets; unavailability of supplies is not accepted as an excuse for not meeting the plan targets. Hard-pressed managers are forced to engage in all sorts of unplanned practices and distortions. They overreport their material needs, underreport their productive capacities, hoard unnecessary materials with the hope of later bartering them for supplies they might need, produce their own supplies, carry expediters (*tolkachi*) fraudulently on their payrolls, and otherwise expend an inordinate amount of time and energy trying to ensure adequate and timely supplies of material inputs. These practices generate a great deal of waste and inefficiency throughout the system.

One of the most serious adverse effects of supply shortages is the practice known as *storming* and the related problem of underemployment of labor. Largely because of the lack of materials, enterprises cannot do much production work during the first two-thirds of each month. Materials tend to arrive late in the month, forcing the receiving plants to work at a hectic pace during the last third of the month. Alec Nove reports a Soviet economist's finding that during the last 9 days of each month 2.6 times more machine tools and 1.8 times more tractors and combines were produced than during the first 14 days of the month. These larger quantities were produced without much reported overtime work. As expected, workers were often underemployed during the earlier part of the month.[22] During the "storm" period, much illegal overtime payment is made by finagling the enterprise's wage and bonus funds, or by falsifying the payroll records.[23]

One other adverse effect of supply shortages may be noted. As we observed in the preceding chapter, many enterprises produce their own hardware and tools in their own workshops in order to avoid work stoppages caused by shortages of these items. Since these goods are not mass produced, their costs are at least two to four times higher—and labor productivity correspondingly lower—than costs of the same products made in specialized plants.[24]

Shortages and late arrivals of material inputs also cause many other types of distortions. Managers often substitute available (but not true to plan specifications) materials for the deficit materials, causing deterioration in the quality of the product. Shortages of materials at one plant may cause a delay in its deliveries to other plants, thus gen-

[22]Alec Nove, *The Soviet Economic System*, 2nd ed. (London: George Allen & Unwin, 1980), pp. 227–28.

[23]David A. Dyker, "Planning and the Worker," in *The Soviet Worker: Illusions and Realities*, ed. Leonard Schapiro and Joseph Godson (New York: St. Martin's Press, 1981), pp. 64–65.

[24]Ibid., p. 65.

erating a ripple effect of shortages and work stoppages throughout the economy. Extensive and intense *tolkach* activities practiced by most enterprises are naturally wasteful of time and energy.

The phenomenon of widespread and chronic shortages of industrial materials can be attributed to three factors. First, the overambitious growth targets of Soviet leaders create conditions of excess demand pressing against the productive capacity of the economy. As resources are preferentially allocated to such high-priority areas as defense and space programs, medium- and low-priority sectors must suffer the consequences of miscalculations and maladjustments that inevitably develop in the planning process. Second, shortages of specific materials for a specific user enterprise cannot be readily eliminated because the user has no freedom to turn to other suppliers. A supplier is specified in the plan, and if that particular supplier is unable to meet the delivery schedule, the user enterprise must patiently wait for the difficulties to be resolved. In the meantime, the user may not be able to meet its own supply schedules. Shortages thus tend to spread throughout the system with a ripple effect. Third, shortage situations are exacerbated by the fact that they do not trigger any spontaneous corrective actions on the part of the suppliers. In market economies, shortages result in higher prices, which in turn induce the producers to supply more. In the Soviet economy, not only are prices fixed, but suppliers are not guided by prices in their production and delivery decisions. Nor are they interested in maintaining the good will of the user enterprises since the suppliers, being monopolies, are not subject to the discipline of competition.

The 1965 Kosygin reforms introduced a new concept: direct contracting between user enterprises and supplier enterprises. The system of centralized supply allocation was to be gradually phased out in favor of a system of wholesale trade coupled with direct contracting under the aegis of the State Committee for Material and Technical Supply (Gossnab). Toward the end of the 1970s, however, the system of supply allocation remained essentially centralized. Direct contracting worked out by Gossnab was largely formalistic, and was subject to arbitrary changes by ministries.[25]

A 1979 decree issued by the USSR Council of Ministers attempted to speed up the transition to long-term direct contracting between supplier enterprises and customer enterprises. These contracts are scheduled to cover 80 percent of industrial production by 1990. The decree also provided for stiff penalties for contract violations, as well as for tying the contract failures to the delinquent enterprise's incentive funds

---

[25]Gertrude E. Schroeder, "The Soviet Economy on a Treadmill of 'Reforms,'" in U.S. Congress, Joint Economic Committee, *Soviet Economy in a Time of Change*, vol. 1, 96th Cong., 1st sess. (Washington, D.C.: U.S. Government Printing Office, 1979), pp. 323–24.

and managerial bonuses.[26] It may be noted that, although long-term direct contracting may improve the stability of supplier-user relations, it does nothing for the customer's right to choose a supplier. The supplier, therefore, continues to enjoy a monopoly position and the attendant freedom from the discipline of the marketplace.

The Question of Success Indicators

One aspect of the organizational structure of the Soviet economic system that has caused a great deal of headache to Soviet planners is the question of the motivation structure. How can enterprise managers be motivated so that they do what is right for society as a whole? Human beings everywhere are motivated primarily by their self-interest; they tend to do what is personally rewarding for them and to avoid what is unpleasant. Thus, simply telling enterprise managers to do the best they can, or to do what they think is good for the country or the party, is not good enough. Under such directives, most managers will put in a minimum amount of time and energy in their work, just enough to get by without being dismissed.

In Chapters 1 and 3 we discussed the question of motivation in industrial organizations, and identified coercion, material rewards (money), social approbation, power, and group solidarity as constituting basic motivational forces. Many of these motivations, however, are not directly applicable to the problem of ensuring that Soviet enterprise managers make right decisions in their day-to-day and month-to-month operations. In a technologically sophisticated and complex industrial state like the Soviet Union, coercion cannot be relied upon as a primary motive of managerial behavior. As we noted in Chapter 3, the Russians care little about what their colleagues think of their work performance. Social approbation, therefore, cannot be a powerful motive in the Soviet work environment. Power is admittedly a very important motive for politically ambitious Russians, but its effects are long run in nature. Managers may be strongly motivated by desire to acquire power over the long haul throughout their careers, but the desire for power cannot be expected to have an immediate effect on their month-to-month production decisions. Similarly, group solidarity must be ruled out as an effective incentive for eliciting correct managerial behavior. Soviet leaders have made strenuous efforts to use this leverage to motivate managers and workers. Appeals to socialist morality, patriotism, and the visions of greater things to come have largely failed to bring out self-

[26]Gertrude E. Schroeder, "Soviet Economic 'Reform' Decrees: More Steps on the Treadmill," in U.S. Congress, Joint Economic Committee, *Soviet Economy in the 1980's*, pt. 1, 97th Cong., 2nd sess. (Washington, D.C.: U.S. Government Printing Office, 1983), p. 75.

sacrificing behavior among the populace. This failure is to be expected in view of the self-serving behavior of the Soviet elite in monopolizing power and privilege, and the attendant widespread resentment and cynicism of the people. These considerations leave material rewards (money) as the only workable incentive for both managers and workers. Soviet leaders now openly speak of the need to improve the "financial leverage" for a better management of their economic system. This type of thinking has led to an extensive use of bonuses given to enterprise managers who successfully meet certain plan targets.

The task seems simple enough: what Soviet leaders must do is (1) define targets for enterprises (targets that are consistent with the planners' objectives), (2) establish performance criteria (or "success indicators") for measuring the quality of an enterprise's performance, and (3) evaluate actual performance according to the established criteria. In actual experience, a great deal of difficulty has been encountered in carrying out this task. As we shall see below, the cause of this difficulty lies chiefly in the self-serving behavior of enterprise managers. It is ironic that the only viable motivation system is the one rooted in managers' self-interest, and yet the effectiveness of that system is being compromised by the self-interest of managers.

What Soviet leaders want to see accomplished can be summarized as follows: a maximum rate of growth of output with reasonable efficiency in resource use and reasonable quality of products. This seemingly simple and straightforward requirement is often difficult to translate into an unequivocal guideline for successful performance of an enterprise manager. Consider a hypothetical example of a men's clothing factory. What kinds of indicator can be used to measure the performance of the plant's managers? The planners' emphasis on growth of output suggests that perhaps some measure of the quantity or volume of output may serve as a good performance indicator. But specifically what measure or measures should be used? The number of pieces of clothing produced? The weight (in tons) of clothing produced? Or the ruble value of output? What about the other dimensions or aspects of the product, such as style, variety, color, size, quality of materials, quality of work done to the products, and so on? Furthermore, there are other dimensions or aspects of production processes that need be considered: cost, labor productivity, research, technological innovation, after-sale services, customer satisfaction, and so forth. It would be impractical to require managers to mind all these dimensions and try to evaluate them on each of the dimensions. This is not only because there are too many dimensions, but, more importantly, because a multiple system of indicators will not work unless a priority or weight is assigned to each of the indicators. How else can a manager's performance be evaluated? Is a manager who has fulfilled plan target A but failed to meet target B a better or poorer performer than another manager who has succeeded in meeting target B but failed to meet A? A host of success indicators, therefore, must be arranged in a descending order, from the most important to the least important.

As soon as performance indicators are rank-ordered, shrewd managers learn how to play the game by concentrating their efforts on meeting the high-priority targets and neglecting or ignoring the low-priority requirements. In the past, the obsession of Soviet leaders with output growth has resulted in the physical quantity of output serving as the primary plan target. This requirement has created incentives for managers to focus on quantity at the expense of quality, cost, and product mix. Numerous examples of distortions have been widely reported both in the Soviet Union and in the West. A nail plant tends to produce, particularly when the "storm" is on during the last part of the month, too many small nails when the quota is given as the number of nails produced. When the quota is changed to total weight (in tons), the nails become too large. Metal roofing sheets become too heavy when the quota is in tons, too thin when the *norma* is in square meters. A motorcycle manufacturer whose quota is the ruble value of output deliberately chooses to use the most expensive materials available.

The problem of success indicators is not limited to manufacturing. An often quoted illustration, reported by Nove, goes as follows: in Soviet agriculture, success indicators for tractor drivers consist of (1) maximizing the area they plow, (2) economizing on fuel, and (3) avoiding mechanical breakdowns. Given this set of performance criteria, it naturally "pays" tractor drivers to plow shallow.[27] Since deeper plowing is necessary for a good harvest, the planners might be tempted to change the main success indicator to the depth of earth plowed. Of course it is easy to predict what the response of tractor drivers would be.

Whatever plan indicators the managers are given to work with, they manage to produce perverse results frustrating the intent of the planners, so long as such results serve the self-interest of the managers. The problem of success indicators, thus, is a fundamental problem every society faces; it revolves around the difficulty of reconciling individual self-interest with the general interest of society. We shall return to this point at the end of the chapter.

Prior to the reforms of 1965, the size of managerial bonuses was determined by reference to the fulfillment of the output plan. This method, as explained above, produced numerous perverse results as managers tried to maximize the quantity of output in the specified unit, neglecting other aspects of the product. Goods that could not be meaningfully measured in physical units were assessed in ruble values. The use of

---

[27]Nove, *The Soviet Economic System*, p. 143.

the gross ruble value as a success indicator, however, also produced undesirable results as managers preferred to use expensive inputs. Even after the volume of output was dropped as the *primary* plan indicator in the 1965 reforms, it was kept as one of the more important of the indicators (see Chapter 5), so that managerial bias for focusing on the quantity of output at the expense of other considerations has continued to inject an element of irrationality into the motivation structure of Soviet macromanagement.

Low Labor Productivity

The annual growth rate of labor productivity in the Soviet economy deteriorated steadily throughout the 1960s and 1970s. The average annual rate of productivity growth declined from 3.4 percent in the 1960–65 period to 1.3 percent in the 1975–80 period.[28] In 1981, the rate was 2.1 percent, which was only half of that year's target rate.[29]

There are widely reported cases of absenteeism, alcoholism, loafing on the job, and thefts by workers. Hedrick Smith reports that absenteeism among blue-collar workers, particularly around paydays, has reached disaster proportions. White-collar workers leave their positions during work hours to do personal shopping and take care of other personal business.[30]

There are many reasons for the low productivity of Soviet workers. Their wages are relatively much lower than the salaries of managerial employees. Even increases in money income may not provide incentives to work hard since supplies of consumer goods of reasonable quality and acceptable variety are always inadequate. Promises of better living conditions, long on words but short on delivery, have merely worsened the disillusionment of many a Soviet worker.

Workers do not have much say in the authoritarian environment of Soviet enterprise management, and local trade unions are more interested in organizing "socialist competition" and generally exhorting workers to produce more, than in promoting workers' interests and protecting them from managerial abuses. Workers are often resentful of the various manipulative methods that management uses to raise their production quotas. Workers' countermeasure is to work slowly and with many breaks to avoid the ratchet effect of output norms becoming too high.

[28]Levine, "Possible Causes of the Deterioration of Soviet Productivity Growth," p. 154.

[29]"Andropov Brings Back 'Labor Discipline,'" *Business Week*, February 7, 1983, p. 56.

[30]Hedrick Smith, *The Russians* (New York: Quadrangle/The New York Times Book Co., 1976), pp. 296–97.

The conditions of general labor shortage and the Soviet regime's commitment to full employment virtually guarantee that no one suffers from prolonged unemployment. As pointed out earlier, the Soviet leaders' commitment to full employment arises from their insecurity about their own legitimacy. Their monopoly of power is justified on the ground that they alone know how to promote the interests of the working class. Admitting that a significant level of unemployment may at times be necessary in the Soviet Union is tantamount to inviting a reassessment of the regime's raison d'être. Soviet leaders therefore try to protect their self-interests by ensuring full employment at all costs, and one way of doing this is by depriving enterprise directors of independent legal power to dismiss their workers. The unavoidable consequences of this policy are lessened work discipline and high labor turnover. Workers put in a minimum of effort, and generally just get by. Whenever they are dissatisfied with their wages or working conditions, they quit their jobs for better opportunities elsewhere.

One of the causes of low labor productivity of Soviet workers is undoubtedly the absence of genuine worker participation in enterprise management. In a Soviet enterprise, the management led by the director exercises authoritarian control over the rest of the work force. In 1958, provisions were made to form "production councils" in state enterprises as a means to promote association of workers and managers. As is the case with many other similar schemes, the idea of production councils seems to have been a propaganda stunt. Alec Nove concludes that, in view of the absence of any reports on production councils' activities, they must be of little practical significance.[31]

The emergence of the Solidarity movement in Poland in 1980, and the continued poor showing of labor productivity in the early 1980s, prompted Soviet leadership to experiment with the first reform in labor relations since World War II. The Law of Work Collectives, which went into effect in August 1983, stipulated that the enterprise management must consult with the smallest work unit—the brigade, with 10 to 50 members—on the enterprise draft plans before they are submitted to higher authorities. Brigade leaders are now elected by members, rather than appointed by management as in the past. Workers are no longer paid piecework wages; instead, wages and bonuses are distributed to brigades according to their collective output. Brigades are also held collectively responsible for meeting production targets, determining their staffing needs, and disciplining their own members.[32] These measures are designed to enhance workers' sense of participation in planning and

---

[31]Nove, *The Soviet Economic System*, p. 232.

[32]"Moscow Tries to Light a Fire under Its Workers," *Business Week*, August 1, 1983, p. 44.

management, as well as increasing labor productivity through collective incentives and group pressures. The reform measures, however, do not provide for active worker participation in the enterprise's management, nor do they give workers the right to strike.[33]

How successful the foregoing measures will be in improving Soviet workers' labor productivity is difficult to predict. One thing, however, is certain. Increased autonomy of workers may not improve workers' incentives and discipline as hoped for if management arbitrarily interferes with the brigades' autonomous decision making. Authoritarian management and meddlesome interference from above are the inherent and pervasive characteristics of the Soviet system. Participative management within an enterprise will certainly be in conflict with the authoritarian style of industrial and macroeconomic management.

Low Rates of Technical Change

The problem of slow technological innovation has several dimensions. At the macro level, there is the problem of inadequate research-and-development activities by governmental research organs. Then there is the question of the adequacy of the production and distribution of machinery and equipment embodying new technologies. There is also the problem of bringing the research organs and productive establishments closer together. And finally there is the very important question of how to provide managerial incentives for innovative activities. Let us examine the last question briefly.

Managers resist adopting new production techniques because, under the present system of plan indicators and bonuses, trying something new does not pay. Adopting new production techniques, using new machines, and introducing new products (1) require disruptions of familiar procedures, (2) involve investment of a considerable amount of time and energy, and (3) entail taking a certain amount of risk. It is virtually certain that fulfillment of current production targets will be placed in jeopardy, at least in the short run, with consequent losses in bonuses.

If an enterprise succeeds in improving its production techniques and quality of its products, the present planning system is more likely to penalize the enterprise than to reward it for taking the risk. The penalty comes in the form of an upward adjustment in the enterprise's various plan targets; fulfilling the plan, therefore, will become more difficult than before the innovations.

If innovations mean virtually certain short-run deterioration in the enterprise's performance and no assurance of a long-term payoff, we cannot fault Soviet managers for dragging their feet on technological

[33]Ibid.

innovations in spite of constant exhortations from above to be innovative. The managers' preoccupation with the short run, moreover, is
reinforced by the prevailing practice of rotating them from plant to
plant every three or four years. Obviously it makes little sense to them
to expend a considerable amount of time and energy on innovations if
their benefits are to accrue, if at all, to their successors.

Low Agricultural Output

Agriculture is the least productive part of the Soviet economy.
Although it ties down close to a quarter of the Soviet population (as
compared to 3 percent in the United States), it still cannot produce
enough to adequately feed the population.

When the Bolsheviks took power in 1917, they found the country
inundated by peasants, most of whom did not embrace the revolutionary
zeal of the new regime. During the 1920s, when the new government
badly needed a large quantity of agricultural output to feed the urban
workers and provide inputs for urban industries, the peasantry's selfish
response was to eat and hoard more food than before their liberation.
Stalin's solution to the "peasant problem" was the forced collectivization of agriculture. Many peasants and kulaks (rich farmers) bitterly
fought the collectivization drive, and altogether 5 million persons were
reportedly shot or exiled in Siberia. Thus, from the early days of the
present Soviet system, there has been no love lost between the regime
and the peasantry.

Until the mid-1960s, collective farms (*kolkhozy*) had been treated
as an ideological orphan of the Soviet system. Collective farms had been
technically considered cooperatives owned jointly by private farmers.
A corollary of this definition was that collective farm members' incomes
were residual shares of the farm's income; since the peasants were technically owners of the farm, they were entitled to receive a "profit" share
rather than fixed wages. A disadvantage of this arrangement from the
peasants' point of view was that they could not count on regular incomes. The government imposed heavy delivery quotas on the farms at
low procurement prices. In poor harvest years, there was little farm
product or money income left for the farm to share among its members.
Not knowing how much income they would receive at the end of the
harvest season, kolkhoz members naturally had little incentive to work
hard for the farm. Instead, they devoted most of their energy on cultivating their private plots.

As a means to improve agricultural productivity, measures were
taken in the 1950s and 1960s to raise farm incomes. Collective farm
delivery quotas were reduced, and procurement prices were raised by

stages. In 1966, minimum guaranteed incomes for kolkhoz members were introduced. With this move, the differences between the state farm and the collective farm disappeared for all practical purposes.

Both collective and state farms share, with all other industries, the same deficiencies of the Soviet system of planning and management, except that there are some problems that are unique to agriculture. Except for grain, agriculture is a highly labor-intensive industry that is not amenable to large economies of scale. Gigantic farms with heavy mechanization are productive only for limited types of crops, largely grains. Thus, small-size farms are generally more productive than large-size farms. Unfortunately, like everything else in the Soviet Union, most farms are huge. The average size of a collective farm is 6,200 hectares (15,320 acres) of agricultural land with 500–600 working members. State farms are much larger in acreage.[34]

There is another important factor that favors small size in agriculture. Unlike manufacturing industries where one can see the result of labor with a reasonable degree of specificity, in agriculture there exists the problem of "too wide a gap between the work of any individual and the final outcome."[35] In an automobile factory, for example, a group of workers operates in closed space turning out products whose dimensions can be measured and qualities assessed with relative ease. Thus, it is not difficult to evaluate the contribution (or its absence) of individual workers and reward them accordingly. In large-scale agriculture, this link between effort and outcome is too remote for an accurate assessment of individual contributions to be made. A peasant working in an open field may plow a little more (or less) deeply, and it is difficult for both the particular worker and others to evaluate exactly how much this extra (or insufficient) work contributes to (or diminishes) that year's total harvest. Since it is impossible to assess accurately the value of the marginal (i.e., extra) contribution, it cannot be properly rewarded. Knowing this, workers find no incentive to work any harder than the minimum required of them. This is one of the reasons why large-scale farming often suffers from low productivity.

The foregoing discussion suggests that the optimal form of farming may be one in which farms are managed (but not necessarily owned) by individual families or small groups of families. In family farming, the link between an individual family member's effort and the collective outcome is close and direct. A family member can put in a great deal of time and effort working on the family farm with a full knowledge that much of the benefit of that work will accrue directly to him or her.

[34]Nove, *The Soviet Economic System*, p. 142.

[35]Ibid., p. 143.

In such a situation, there exists a near-perfect harmony between the self-interest of an individual family member and the collective interest of the family.

Consumer Dissatisfaction

Soviet leaders in the past have been able to persuade the citizenry by maintaining that sacrifices and hardships are necessary in order to bring about a world of abundance in the future. As long as living conditions and material well-being were improving slowly but perceptibly, as in the 1950s and 1960s, the citizens could hope for a better future and could be persuaded to work hard under conditions of general scarcity. In the last decade or so, however, improvements in the Soviet standard of living have become less perceptible. Food shortages continue to be a very serious problem. The housing situation in urban areas is still appalling by Western standards. Consumer durables are still largely scarce and expensive. Lines at retail outlets are often long, and people must waste hours standing in queues trying to buy what little food, clothes, or other goods happen to be available on a given day. Working women frequently must leave their place of work to stand in lines for hours at a time. Sales personnel in retail outlets and service establishments are surly and arrogant. The quality of life in the Soviet Union, thus, has not improved much in the 1970s and 1980s.

The rising consumer dissatisfaction has resulted in poorer work morale, poorer work discipline, laziness at work, alcoholism, and increasing criminality of Soviet citizens. The police must maintain a tighter control over the people than before to curb expressions of discontent. The declining labor productivity caused by the rising consumer dissatisfaction further aggravates the shortages of consumer goods. More seriously, poor productivity threatens the viability of the producer and military goods industries, thereby directly threatening national security. Even more threatening is the possibility that the worsening consumer dissatisfaction may eventually transform into a political unrest. The problem of the unhappy Soviet consumer, therefore, presents a very serious headache to Soviet leaders. It is a problem that can threaten the very security of the Soviet system, both internally and externally. It has a potential of leading to an explosive situation.

THE UNDERLYING CAUSES
OF SOVIET PROBLEMS

Lest the reader receive a wrong impression of the imminent collapse of the Soviet economy from the list of problems enumerated in the preceding section, let us hasten to add that the economy, though suffering from a serious malaise, is not on the verge of collapse. Output is growing at an annual rate of between 2 and 3 percent, and the demands of such high-priority sectors as defense and space programs are quite adequately met. The problem, however, is one of balance and optimality. Low-priority areas are performing miserably. Products are shoddy. Workers are alienated. Consumers are frustrated. Technological innovations are slow. In all, waste and inefficiency throughout the system are reaching disaster proportions. What factors are responsible for these symptoms of malaise?

As is the case with any set of complex problems, the Soviet disease has a multiplicity of underlying causes. The most crucial among these causes are (1) the ideology of centralized control, (2) the complexity of large industrial economies, and (3) the inherent conflict between the private and public interests.

The Ideology of Centralized Control

The ruling ideology of the Soviet politicoeconomic system is authoritarian centralism. The Communist party leadership enjoys a monopoly of legitimate power and social purpose. The party is all-knowing and all-powerful; only the party is endowed with the requisite wisdom and ability to propel the society to socialism and communism. It is the duty of the party to lead the people in their social, political, and economic development. And this development must be planned by the central authority and carried out by its administrative apparatus with specific directives flowing from top to bottom. Important decisions cannot be left to the whims, biases, and ignorance of the masses.

Such is the logic of the Soviet ideology of authoritarian centralism. Administrative planning and management of the economy from the center, therefore, is not a mere technical arrangement that the regime has chosen for its efficacy; it is part and parcel the very essence of the Soviet system itself. Thus, no matter how serious the problems of inefficiency become, the party cannot abandon its control over the economy and allow consumers' demand or producers' convenience to dictate the direction and pattern of socialist development. To do so is tantamount to inviting the Soviet people to question the usefulness and legitimacy of the present party-government.

The Complexity of Modern
Industrial Economies

If the Soviet regime *must* control the nation's productive activities from the center, how can this control be exercised in practice? Note that we are not dealing with the economy of one of the ministates; we are discussing the problems of a modern, complex industrial economy of 270 million people scattered over an immense geographical area. Soviet planners must coordinate the input-output relations of tens of thousands of products and determine over 10 million prices. Products also vary in quality, grade, size, shape, weight, style, and so on in almost infinite ways.

The sheer size and complexity of the economy creates a very serious problem. The logic of central planning and management is such that detailed plan-instructions must be given to operating-level managers. Enterprises must be provided with specific instructions as to how much of each product is to be produced, in what product mix, using what specific inputs and production methods. In the process of disaggregating output plan targets and input allocation schedules, Gosplan and ministerial officials do the best they can to make the enterprise instructions as specific and detailed as possible; but there is definitely a practical limit to the degree of specificity that can be attained. Consequently, a great number of relatively unimportant decisions must of necessity be left to the discretion of operating-level managers. It is not that the planners *want* these decisions to be made at the enterprise level, but the sheer complexity of the task makes it impossible for them to provide detailed plan-instructions on every little aspect of plan execution. This is a technical constraint rather than a policy decision; planners have no choice in this matter.

The Question of Harmony of Interests

If enterprise managers cannot be given detailed plan-instructions, they must be provided, instead, with a set of operating principles or guidelines under which discretionary decisions are to be made. Soviet managers, being only human, are motivated by self-interest: they do what is personally rewarding to them and avoid what is unpleasant. Consequently, unless they are motivated to behave otherwise, their choice and action will always be to maximize their private gains even at the expense of public benefits. What is needed, therefore, is a set of rules of behavior, or rules for decision making, for enterprise managers that will ensure a congruence of private and public interests. The content of these rules must be such that, if managers observe them faithfully, both their private interests and social interests are served simultaneously.

As the discussions of the success indicator problem in the foregoing paragraphs demonstrate, the existing decision-making rules for Soviet managers do not yield congruence of private and public interests. This is because Soviet leaders, being prisoners of their own authoritarian-centralist ideology, cannot bring themselves to accept the use of the market mechanism and free prices as the primary means of allocating resources; such a decision would inevitably lead to a loss of their tight control over the economy. Instead, they insist on issuing a fairly large number of detailed and complex success indicators and expect enterprise managers to fulfill them simultaneously. The planners are fully aware that managers are motivated by material rewards (hence the use of bonuses). But they are either reluctant or unable to accept the fact that managers play games with the success indicators in order to maximize their private gains. As the planners make the decision-making rules more numerous and complex, more room for maneuver is found by enterprise managers.

The only viable alternative left open to Soviet planners is to reduce the number of success indicators to only one—one that accurately reflects the enterprise's performance, taking into account considerations of cost, quality, quantity, technical innovations, customer satisfaction, and so forth. Only one such success indicator is known to exist—profits. Profits based on rational (scarcity) prices of both inputs and outputs is an all-inclusive measure of the efficiency of an enterprise's operations. The use of profits, therefore, mandates that a system of free markets be introduced in the Soviet economy in which prices will be determined by spontaneous interactions of demand and supply forces. This, of course, means that the present system of centralized administrative allocations of materials must be scrapped in favor of free trading among state-owned enterprises. Profits, free prices, and free markets are the only means by which the Soviet economy can be freed from the present quagmire of inefficiency and decline. This radical departure from the traditional methods of planning and management, however, is not acceptable to the present Soviet leadership because it is diametrically opposed to its ideology of authoritarian control.

QUESTIONS

1. What is meant by *rational prices?* Are all prices found in the United States rational prices? Are rational prices synonymous with *scarcity prices?* With *market-clearing prices?* (Hint: What if the wholesale price *OW* in Figure 6-1 does not include all types of opportunity costs?)
2. Give a few examples of prices used in the American economic system that are accounting prices in nature and serve neither market-clearing nor resource-use optimizing functions.
3. To operate an enterprise on a *khozraschet* basis (see Chapter 5), is it necessary that input and output prices be scarcity prices or market-clearing prices?
4. Differentiate between the two types of capital cost. Explain why one is

readily acceptable by Marxists but the other is not. How is the second type of capital cost now handled in the Soviet industrial price structure?

5. Why do capital-intensive products tend to be underpriced relative to labor-intensive goods in the Soviet Union? What types of distortion in resource allocation are likely to be caused by this imperfection in the price structure?

6. Suppose the average production cost (including *all* opportunity costs) and the average expected length of usable service for two types of truck tires are found in the Soviet Union as follows: tire A, 50 rubles and 20,000 miles; tire B, 75 rubles and 40,000 miles. Should the relative wholesale prices of these two types of tires be 1:1.5 or 1:2? What do you think would happen if the planners price the two types at 100 rubles for tire A and 150 rubles for tire B? Explain why problems of this sort are not likely to be frequent or serious in capitalist countries.

7. Explain how it is possible in the Soviet Union that one enterprise making profits is less efficient in its operations than another running heavy losses.

8. List and explain the advantages Soviet planners find in incorporating profit markups in the structure of industrial wholesale prices.

9. In 1983, the official retail price of beef in the Soviet Union was one-half the state procurement price, and the collective farm free-market price was 3.5 times the official retail price. At the state procurement price, a "normally operating" farm could not cover costs and normal profits. If the official retail price was 2 rubles per kilogram, roughly how much, do you think, was the average production cost of a "normally operating" farm? Were those selling beef in collective farm markets at 7 rubles a kilogram making exhorbitant profits?

10. Suppose Soviet planners decide to keep the retail price of children's shoes artificially low, and find that an acute shortage of shoes develops. Describe the situation using a graph similar to Figure 6–1.

11. In the situation described in question 10, is the shortage likely to result in an increased supply of shoes? Why or why not? What is the difference between consumer choice and consumer sovereignty?

12. Why is it that Soviet planners cannot control *both* price *and* quantity of a given consumer good simultaneously? Explain using a graph similar to Figure 6–1.

13. What are the causes of the chronic shortages of industrial material supplies in the Soviet Union? What do you suggest as possible solutions?

14. What is *storming?* What factors are responsible for its widespread occurrence? How is it possible that much storming occurs without much reported overtime work?

15. What is the nature of the "success indicator" problem? What are its causes? What solutions do you suggest?

16. Suppose you are a member of a Soviet geological exploration team whose objective is to drill for oil. Assume that the team's bonuses are based on meeting the quota expressed in meters drilled. What would be the "rational" thing for the team to do?

17. List and explain the causes of low labor productivity in the Soviet economy. What solutions do you propose?

18. Describe the decision-making structure and the motivational structure of a Soviet state enterprise.

19. Discuss the factors that are responsible for the sluggish technological innovations in Soviet industrial enterprises. Do you think innovations and technological changes are more vigorous and rapid in American corporations? (See Chapter 8.)

20. Why, in the Soviet context, would family farming be more efficient than state or collective farming with several hundred families in each farm? Does it make a difference whether or not the family owns the farm? Can you argue that cooperative farming involving five or ten families may be even more efficient than single-family farming? Check outside sources to learn about predominant farm organization in Hungary, Yugoslavia, and China.

21. What differences does it make if Soviet consumers are dissatisfied with their living conditions? Have they not always been stoic and patient?

22. "If even *one* of the following three underlying causes of the Soviet disease were absent, the problem could be easily solved: (1) the ideology of centralized control, (2) the size and complexity of the Soviet economy, and (3) the pursuit of self-interests by Soviet managers." Do you agree with this statement? Why or why not?

SELECTED READING

GOLDMAN, MARSHALL I. *U.S.S.R. in Crisis: The Failure of an Economic System*, chaps. 2 and 3. New York: W. W. Norton & Company, 1983.

NOVE, ALEC, *The Economics of Feasible Socialism*, pts. 1, 2, and 3. London: George Allen & Unwin, 1983.

————, *The Soviet Economic System* (2nd ed.), chaps. 4, 7, and 8. London: George Allen & Unwin, 1980.

SCHAPIRO, LEONARD, and JOSEPH GODSON, Eds. *The Soviet Worker: Illusions and Realities*. New York: St. Martin's Press, 1981.

U.S. CONGRESS, JOINT ECONOMIC COMMITTEE. *Soviet Economy in a Time of Change*, vols. 1 and 2, 96th Cong., 1st sess. Washington, D.C.: U.S. Government Printing Office, 1979.

U.S. CONGRESS, JOINT ECONOMIC COMMITTEE. *Soviet Economy in the 1980's: Problems and Prospects*, pts. 1 and 2, 97th Cong., 2nd sess. Washington, D.C.: U.S. Government Printing Office, 1983.

CHAPTER 7

The American Economy: Macroeconomic Organization and Public Policy

The American economy is by far the most productive national economic unit the world has ever had, and its ways of doing economic things— the American economic system—is of interest to us partly because of its impressive accomplishments but also because of its unique characteristics, which are quite different from those of either the Soviet Union or Japan. Unfortunately, too many Americans take their economic system for granted, and familiarity breeds ignorance. As students of comparative economic systems, it is incumbent upon us to study this interesting economic system with the objectivity of an outsider, examining its strengths and weaknesses in contrast to those of other major systems. Only by such an objective examination can we develop a genuine understanding not only of the American system but also of the other systems studied in comparison.

The American economic system is a market-oriented (or capitalist) economic system. Saying that, however, adds little to our understanding of it since the major market-oriented systems—be they British, French, West German, or Japanese—are all quite different from each other and from the American system. In order to acquire a genuine understanding of the American system, therefore, we must examine both (1) the nature and characteristics of market-oriented industrial economic systems, and (2) the set of ideologies and institutions that uniquely shape the character of the American system.

THE OVERALL ORGANIZATION
OF THE AMERICAN ECONOMIC SYSTEM

The macroeconomic organizational and managerial structure of the American economic system is much more complex than the structure of the Soviet system, which we studied in the preceding chapter. In the first place, unlike the Soviet Union where politics overwhelms economics, the American national life takes place in two distinctly different but closely related spheres—economics and business on the one hand and politics and government on the other. The two spheres coexist, side by side, with their major actors maintaining an arm's length relationship with each other. There is a strong presumption that all economic activities are to take place in the market system; the public authority is permitted to interfere with market-oriented activities only to the extent that the market is incapable of producing optimum results. Secondly, in the United States, the economy, the industries, and the enterprises do not constitute a continuum, or an organized whole, as they do in the Soviet Union and in Japan. Firms are only loosely organized into an industry, and industrywide coordination in investment and production is implicit and often covert. More importantly, there exists in America a conspicuous absence of economywide organization of industries and firms. Organized business, as such, does not exist in the United States. Firms and industries, through their trade associations, deal directly with various government agencies without the benefit of powerful intermediation by economywide peak business organizations like Japan's Keidanren. Just as political authority is diffused and fragmented in the United States, so is its private economic power.

Figure 7–1 depicts the structure of organization and management of the American economic system. Unlike the Soviet economic system in which government is the single producer, in the American system there are a large number of autonomous, private producers functioning in various markets, and the relationships among them are coordinated partly by the spontaneous forces of the market and partly through trade associations and similar interest groups. Such societal concerns as equity, stability, and environmental health compel the public authority to inject collective preferences into the system by means of public policies, regulations, and rulings. Collective preferences are imposed on the market system not to replace private initiatives and preferences,

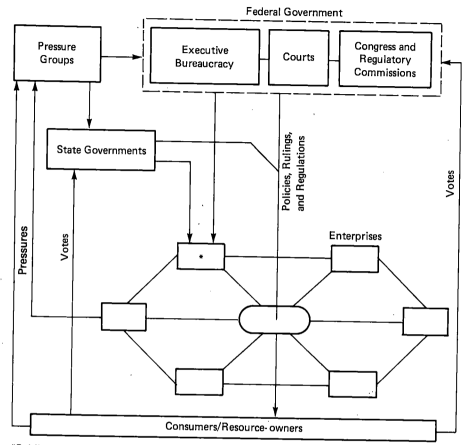

FIGURE 7–1   The organizational structure of the American economic system

but to modify the latter so that the outcomes of the nation's economic activities serve both the public and private interests in a reasonably satisfactory manner.

Public policies and regulations are the outputs of the American political system; in turn, the system receives, as inputs, votes and interest-group pressures. Two crucial characteristics of the American system are that both public and private powers are decentralized and fragmented, and the direction of influence between the two powers is horizontal and bilateral—*horizontal* in the sense that neither public nor private power is deemed superior to the other, and *bilateral* in that each exerts pressures and influence on the other. Characteristically, we do not find dominance of government over economy (as in the Soviet Union), or a symbiotic, collaborative relationship between the centers of public and private powers (as in Japan.) (Any symbiotic relationships that exist between business and government in the United States are found at the enterprise-agency level, not at the industry or economy level.)

Public policies and regulations in the United States are essentially limited to creating healthy conditions for the market and moderating its excesses. Characteristically absent is direct public intervention in production and investment decisions of firms and industries. It is uncharacteristic of the American public authority to engage in industrial management that has to do with public control of the direction and pattern of development of specific industries. In the Soviet Union, by contrast, industrial management is an integral part of its planning system; the government determines the patterns of development of the various sectors of the economy. In Japan, public officials actively and as a matter of right engage in the exercise of managing industrial development jointly with industrial leaders.

Since firms and industries in the United States are not integrated into a coherent whole, the largest autonomous economic unit is the modern corporation. In the Soviet Union, by contrast, a productive enterprise is merely the smallest unit of the state productive sector. In Japan, as we shall see later, most of the large corporations belong to larger industrial groups known as *keiretsu*. Such large American corporations as General Motors, Exxon, and International Business Machines are autonomous economic units of enormous size, wealth, and power. Most of the several hundred largest U.S. corporations are kingdoms unto themselves; their autonomous management groups make their own production and investment decisions with little interference from outside sources. Thus, in order to develop a good understanding of the organization and management of the American economic system as a whole, it is imperative that we examine in some depth the internal organization and management of the American corporation as well as the relationships between public authority and private initiative.

HISTORICAL DEVELOPMENT
OF REGULATED CAPITALISM IN AMERICA

Before turning to a discussion of the U.S. government's role in the contemporary American economic system, let us briefly review the historical development of capitalism in American over the last two centuries.

The Tradition of Laissez Faire

Capitalism—an economic system based on private property and free enterprise—emerged in its fully matured form for the first time in England toward the end of the eighteenth century. Its emergence was concurrent with the Industrial Revolution, and its development took the form of a reaction to the rigidity of the mercantilist regime. The transition from mercantilism to laissez-faire capitalism was accelerated by the ideas expounded by Adam Smith in *The Wealth of Nations* published in 1776. Smith argued that individuals, pursuing their own self-interests, were "led by an invisible hand" to promote the general interest of society. The less government interfered with private economic activities, the better the economic system worked to promote public interests. This new idea of economic liberalism spread quickly to parts of Europe and the New World. For about a century after the publication of *The Wealth of Nations*, laissez-faire capitalism saw its golden era in Western Europe, particularly England.

The spirit of liberalism that swept Western Europe, of course, did not appear suddenly in late eighteenth-century England. The Protestant Reformation of 1500–1550 succeeded in breaking up the monolithic power of the Roman Catholic Church, contributing to the demise of feudalism. During the mercantilist period of 1550–1775, various capitalist institutions developed slowly but inexorably. These emerging institutions included private property, freedom of contract, sales of land and labor as commodities, a free market system, a system of credit and finance, uniform monetary systems, and systems of courts and legal codes to enforce contracts. Increased commercialization gave rise to a prosperous merchant class (bourgeoisie) that began to exercise private initiatives and enjoy private economic power derived from private property. Individualism and demands for freedom grew out of these emerging institutions, which in turn reinforced individualism and freedom from arbitary interferences by political authority.

The individualism and liberalism that had emerged and developed in Western Europe since the sixteenth century blossomed in eighteenth-century America. The early settlers of America were those who had left the Old World in search of political, economic, and religious freedom. Thus, in 1776, in the year Smith's *The Wealth of Nations* was published, the American Declaration of Independence proclaimed that all persons had "certain unalienable Rights," among which were "Life, Liberty, and the Pursuit of Happiness."

In the U.S. Constitution adopted subsequently, the Founding Fathers of the new republic included *private property* as one of the unalienable rights of all persons. Thomas Jefferson, principal author of the

Declaration of Independence, believed that private property was one of the natural rights of human beings everywhere. Private property gave individual owners a measure of freedom—economic freedom—without which human beings could not be protected against the overwhelming political power of the state. Thus, in the United States, private property came to be protected by a written constitution, and, along with such other constitutional provisions as the separation of powers, has served to protect individuals from the power of the state.

Unencumbered by the oppressive interference by public authorites, the United States economy in the eighteenth and nineteenth centuries experienced a period of rapid growth and development. In the first half of the nineteenth century, the government provided private enterprises with developmental assistances in the forms of subsidies, tariff protections, and legal monopolies. In the second half of the century, however, the government began to pursue an increasingly purer form of laissez-faire policy.

The Growth of Big Business and the Emergence of the Regulatory State

During the last two decades of the nineteenth century, the American economy produced a burst of economic growth and technological advances that was reminiscent of the Industrial Revolution that had taken place in England about a century earlier. The booming railroad construction stimulated a rapid expansion of the steel industry. A host of new industries developed following such inventions as the electric light, telephone, typewriter, cash register, and automobile. The petroleum industry emerged as the major industry of the period serving the domestic heating and lighting needs as well as industrial demands. The corporate form of business helped raise huge sums of capital from both domestic and European investors. Economic power gradually became concentrated in large industrial firms under the leadership of such colorful entrepreneurs as John D. Rockefeller and Andrew Carnegie.

In the 1880s and 1890s, there was a surge of large firms forming monopolies through such devices as trusts, holding companies, and outright mergers. There emerged monopolies in oil, tobacco, railroad, steel, whiskey, and sugar, among others. Industrial combinations were followed by financial combinations: New York emerged as a major international financial center at the turn of the century. Gradually, the competitive free enterprise system of the nineteenth century gave way to the monopolistic financial capitalism of the early twentieth century.

Monopolization in industry and finance led, in the last decade of the nineteenth century, to a significant change in the institutional character of the American economy. First, the federal government began to assume a much more active role than before in regulating the behavior of private enterprises. This expansion in the central government's role in the nation's economic activities was brought about by the perceived need to control the abuse of economic power by the emerging big-business monopolies. Second, concurrent with the growth of big business was the development of various special interest groups in agriculture, industry and finance, and labor. Big business begot big government, as well as the countervailing developments of various private interest groups organizing themselves into powerful lobbying groups in order to mobilize support from political parties and key legislators.

Pressures from special interest groups representing agricultural and small businesses prompted the passage of the Sherman Antitrust Act of 1890. This landmark legislation heralded a fundamental transformation of the American economic system from laissez-faire capitalism to regulated capitalism that was to occur during the New Deal decade of the 1930s. The coercive power of the state could now be applied to the abuses of market power by big business, so that competition— one of the basic ingredients of the free-enterprise system—could be preserved. The role of the federal government in this new system, however, could still not be called *active*, since enforcement of antitrust laws gave government the role of a disinterested referee or judge, and not of an active economic policy maker. This situation, however, changed materially as a result of the Great Depression of the 1930s and the emergence of the New Deal socioeconomic policies.

The severity of the Great Depression produced a widespread demand that government do something about it. Both American farmers and industrial workers abandoned their traditional reliance on organized economic power and turned increasingly to political power, seeking relief. In retrospect, it appears that the U.S. government had no alternative but to respond affirmatively to the demands of farmers and workers that it take control of the situation. If the government had failed to do so, a revolutionary situation would very likely have arisen.[1]

Degrees of Government
Intervention in the Market

Our discussion has brought us to a stage in the history of American capitalism where the role of the government was to make an irreversible change to active participation. Let us digress here to discuss briefly the

---

[1]Calvin B. Hoover, *The Economy, Liberty and the State* (Garden City, N.Y.: Doubleday & Company, Inc., Anchor Books, 1961), pp. 188–89.

varying degrees of public participation or intervention in a market economy. We can identify four broad classes or degrees of governmental participation, ranging from purely passive to increasingly active. First, there is a market economy in which government performs only those functions that are minimally necessary for preserving market relations (e.g., enforcing contracts). This, of course, is the laissez-faire market economy. Second, the government may play the role of a referee or regulator. The government sets up basic rules of conduct, and supervises the overall behavior of private enterprises to see if they are observing the rules. Here, the role of government is primarily judiciary. The U.S. economy was in this stage prior to the New Deal of the 1930s. Third, in addition to playing the role of a regulator, the government accepts the responsibilities of maintaining macroeconomic stability and a minimum income security for its citizens. The major tools used by government in this stage are monetary, fiscal, and incomes policies. The U.S. economy in the postwar period has been in this stage. Fourth, the government may play a much more active role by accepting, additionally, the responsibilities of determining, often jointly with business, the pattern and direction of industrial development of the national economy. Industrial policy is the key instrument of activist government in modern capitalism. Many West European countries, notably France, and Japan are in this stage of capitalism.[2]

Keynes and the Legacy
of the New Deal

With the advent of the New Deal, the U.S. economic system was transformed from the second to the third stage of capitalism. The New Deal reforms left a legacy of government committed to the responsibility of maintaining macroeconomic stability and income security in a predominantly market-oriented economy. The ideological champion of this transformation was John Maynard Keynes. In his celebrated book *The General Theory of Employment, Interest and Money* published in 1936, Keynes argued that the basic cause of the Depression was the deficiency in the overall (aggregate) demand for goods and services. Output of goods and services did generate enough purchasing power to absorb (i.e., to purchase) the available supply of goods and services, but because of income inequality and the high propensity of the wealthy to save a large portion of their money income, there developed a growing deficiency in the *effective* purchasing power (or aggregate demand). Big

---

[2] The use of the word *stage* to refer to different types of the market economy does not necessarily imply that every capitalist economic system goes through these stages, or that higher stages are superior to lower ones.

business firms responded to weakening demand by cutting output and employment rather than lowering prices. Reduced output and employment spread throughout the economy, generating a ripple effect.

Keynes's prescription for the cure of the depression malaise was surprisingly simple. Since the culprit was the excess of private saving, he proposed that the government borrow this saving and spend it for public projects. Deficit financing would fill the gap between excessive private saving and inadequate private spending, raising the level of aggregate demand to a level compatible with aggregate supply. The program of deficit spending by the Roosevelt administration indeed produced the results that Keynes had predicted. Not only were national income and government spending increased substantially, but also private consumption and investment in real terms were raised to levels considerably above the Depression bottom.

The success of Keynesian deficit financing in producing an economic recovery had a lasting impact on the popular view toward the role of government in economic activity. Prior to the New Deal, the government could disclaim its responsibility for maintaining macroeconomic stability in income, price, output, and employment because conventional wisdom held that there was little government could do about these macroeconomic variables. This belief was now shattered. Similarly, such New Deal programs as Social Security and agricultural price supports demonstrated the government's capability in guaranteeing minimum income security and equality.

One surprising fact of the American economic system is that since the second transformation in its character that took place during the New Deal era, there has not been a major change in its basic character for nearly four decades. To be sure it has flirted with some interesting new ideas—French-type economic planning in the early 1960s, wage-and-price controls in the late 1960s, and supply-side economics in the 1980s—but its fundamental character has remained essentially intact. The system is characterized by a government that is content with its supervisory and regulatory role and is willing to interfere with the economy only in a general way in maintaining an overall stability in output, employment, and prices, and in safeguarding minimum economic security for its citizens. Production and investment decisions are made primarily by individual corporate managements, and the government maintains essentially a hands-off policy in this area. Unlike its counterpart in many other capitalist countries, big business in the United States does not actively participate in public authority's management of the overall economy. Rather, it operates as one—albeit a very important and powerful one—of the major special interest groups exerting pressures on the political process.

We have thus far identified the two major transformations the

American economic system has undergone since the late nineteenth century. These changes were macroeconomic in character, having to do with government-business relations. In the present century, the system has undergone yet another transformation of major importance. This third transformation—known as the Managerial Revolution—has to do with the organization and management of large corporations. Most of America's large corporations today are managed by a group of professionals who have no or little ownership interest in the firms they control. The professionalization of corporate management and the attendant separation of corporate control from ownership interests have had a profound impact on the character of the American economic system. This point will be discussed at some length in Chapter 8.

GOVERNMENT'S ROLE IN THE AMERICAN ECONOMIC SYSTEM

The American economic system is built on the principle of individual or corporate free enterprise. The price system, working through the market forces of supply and demand, is expected to solve society's basic economic problems of what, how, and for whom to produce, while assuring maximum freedom of choice for all concerned. While it is generally true that the market mechanism leads to allocative efficiency while permitting freedom of choice, it is also true that it has some intrinsic deficiencies that can be corrected only by some collective (i.e., governmental) action.

It is generally agreed that government in the U.S. economic system performs the following four broad functions: (1) maintenance of an institutional framework, (2) reallocation of resources, (3) redistribution of income, and (4) stabilization of economic activity. Each of these four functions will be discussed in turn in the following sections.

Government Regulation of Business

A price system cannot function in a vacuum; it requires a legal and social framework—a set of social, economic, and political institutions—that enables it to function effectively. The government's role in this function is that of rule maker, referee, and judge. Beyond the minimum requirements of enforcing contracts, defining and protecting property rights, settling disputes, providing standards of measurement, establishing a system of money and credit, and so forth, the U.S. government's role of establishing the "rules of the game" for its market economy encompasses a wide range of activities generally referred to as government regulation of private economic activities. The term *gov-*

ernment regulation in the broadest sense refers to three subcategories of regulatory activities.

One important area of government regulation is *antitrust* policies. Markets must remain reasonably competitive if the allocative efficiency of the price system is to be maximized. Thus, one of the first responsibilities of a government committed to a free-enterprise system is taking measures against monopolization and collusive restraints of trade.

Another important area of government regulation is public control over the prices, output, and profits of *public utilities*, that is, energy, communications, and transportation. Certain types of products—for example, electricity and telephone services—have such great economies of scale that competition by more than one producer in a given market area is wasteful of resources. Allowing a single firm to be a monopoly producer, however, may have undesirable effects unless its pricing and output decisions are regulated by public authority in the interest of society's general welfare.

Beyond antitrust and public utility regulation, the United States government engages in a variety of regulatory activities that may be collectively referred to as *socioeconomic regulation.* These activities include regulation of food and drug safety, consumer and environmental protection, occupational safety, employment of minorities, security exchanges, banking and insurance, and labor unions.

Regulation is applied usually by a specialized public agency—federal or state—to a particular industry or type of economic activity. In most of the Western democracies, regulation of business is the responsibility of the executive branch of government. In the United States, however, government regulation is exercised chiefly by a number of so-called independent federal agencies (and, at the state level, by state regulatory commissions). Some agencies in the executive branch also perform regulatory functions. For example, the two antitrust enforcement agencies in the United States are the Antitrust Division of the Department of Justice (an office within the executive) and the Federal Trade Commission (an independent federal agency).

Another source of confusion lies in the fact that not all of the so-called independent federal agencies are regulatory agencies. The Interstate Commerce Commission, the Federal Power Commission, the Federal Communications Commission, the Securities and Exchange Commission, and the like, are regulatory agencies in the true sense of the term. Under the statutory guidelines, these agencies generally formulate regulations for particular industries, and often determine their price structures. Some other agencies, however, do not "regulate" any specific industry or industries. The Federal Trade Commission, for example, polices the competitive market behavior and the fairness of business practices of any industry by serving as a prosecutor, jury, and judge. The National Labor Relations Board, on the other hand, issues no regulations of its own, regulates no particular industry, and brings no proceeding before itself or a court. The Board, therefore, is basically a judiciary agency; but is not a regulatory agency in the strict sense of the term.

Reallocation of Resources

It is generally accepted that the market system guided by free prices results in an efficient allocation of resources, provided, of course, monoploy and other anticompetitive practices are nonexistent. This is tantamount to saying that the pattern of resource allocation that takes place in response to the preferences of private producers and consumers is the most advantageous one for society as a whole. This presumption, however, is not totally valid. Under certain conditions, the market fails to produce optimum results. The sum of private interests being not always equal to the public interest, government must intervene with the market mechanism in order to inject collective preferences into the overall pattern of resource allocation basically determined by the market.

For optimum allocation of resources, government intervention with the market mechanism is justified on at least two grounds. First, government must provide *public goods*, which the price system characteristically cannot provide. Second, wherever there exist significant *externalities* in production or consumption, government must take measures to minimize their distortive effects.

Public goods. Most goods cannot be used or enjoyed by more than one person at a time. Such goods are called *private goods*. Goods that lack this attribute of exclusivity are called *public goods*. These goods, once produced, can be used or enjoyed simultaneously by anybody, and their consumption by one person does not diminish their use value to other persons. Examples of public goods are national defense, a lighthouse, a hurricane warning system, and public health. Since no one can be excluded from consuming a public good, it is impossible to charge anyone for its services. If you can use a public good without paying for it, why bother to pay for it? The provision of public goods, therefore, is always plagued by the free-rider problem. Since a price cannot be charged for a public good, no private enterprise is willing to produce it. If these goods are needed at all, they must be provided by the government. Note, however, that public goods need not be *produced* by government; they merely need be *paid for* by government.

Externalities.   In cases where production or consumption of a good has either a beneficial or adverse effect on people who are not directly involved in the production or consumption, an *externality* is said to exist. Environmental pollution, for example, is a problem involving a negative externality. Production or consumption of a good involves private costs to the producer or consumer, but there may be additional (i.e., external) costs to be borne by parties not directly involved in the production or consumption. For example, the consumption of a cigarette may give rise to external costs to those who are in the physical proximity of the smoker. A producer of soap may dump chemical waste in a nearby lake, thereby causing all people who use the lake to bear costs of having to deal with polluted water.

In a free-enterprise economy, decision makers are naturally guided by considerations of *private* benefits and *private* costs. The government must therefore intervene with the market mechanism, and impose an internalization of externalities on private decision makers. For example, if a soap producer is polluting lake water, the government by various means may compel the producer to absorb the pollution costs, so that the production cost of soap refects the true *social* costs (i.e., private costs plus external costs). By compelling private decision makers to consider *social* benefits and *social* costs in their production and consumption decisions, the government can eliminate the distortive effects of externalities on society's resource allocation. The methods of compelling private decision makers to internalize their external benefits and costs include paying subsidies to those who generate external benefits, taxing the polluter, charging the polluting firm a fee for a license to pollute, ordering the polluter to install an antipollution device, and prohibiting the offensive activities under the penalty of a civil fine or imprisonment. However it is done, the essential point is that some collective (i.e., governmental) action is unavoidable if the market system is to produce socially optimum results.

Methods of resource allocation.   If government *must* interfere with the market mechanism in order to reallocate resources, what methods should it use? A variety of ways are available. Government may promulgate laws, ordinances, and regulations to control the behavior of private enterprises. Or it may levy taxes on, or pay subsidies to, selected types of economic activities in order to influence private decision making. Yet another method is to levy general taxes on the populace, and spend the revenues from these taxes on goods and services that government finds necessary to consume collectively.

Of course the most direct way of allocating resources is by public ownership of productive enterprises. As we saw in earlier chapters, this is the method used in the Soviet Union; virtually all of the productive enterprises there are owned and managed by the state. In the industrial democracies of Western Europe and Japan, public enterprises account for a much higher percentage of national output than in the United States. In these countries, railroads, airlines, telephone and telegraph services, radio and television stations, electricity and gas services, and postal services are, as a rule, publicly owned and managed. Some large financial and industrial firms are also government-owed in many countries. Public and private interests often share in ownership and/or management.

Redistribution of Income

One of the shortcomings of the private-property, free-enterprise market system is the glaring inequities in income and wealth that are attributable not so much to interpersonal differences in intelligence and industry as to wide disparities in inherited advantages. In capitalist societies, it is generally accepted that maximum efficiency in resource use requires a degree of inequality in income and wealth. But it is also considered true that consideration of justice and fairness sets a limit to how much inequity society can tolerate. What constitutes an equitable and just distribution of income and wealth is a normative question, and, as such, cannot be resolved by a recourse to logic. Most people agree, however, that government in a capitalist society should make efforts to alleviate *excessive* hardships of poverty or to ameliorate *excessive* disparities in income and wealth, however the crucial term *excessive* is defined. In the final analysis, society must decide, through its political mechanism, how it wishes to define "fair and just" distribution of income and wealth, and modify income flows and wealth distribution by such governmental means as taxation, public expenditures, and transfer payments.

The classical economists, including David Ricardo and Karl Marx, were concerned about the distribution of society's product among the three major socioeconomic classes: landowners, capitalists, and workers. As we saw in the earlier chapters on the Soviet economy, this concern for income distribution among social classes formed the ideological and theoretical foundation of Marxist socialism. For our purposes, however, this approach to the problem of equality is too aggregative and simplistic. Since the beginning of the twentieth century, the relative shares of national income of labor and property in the United States have been remarkably stable at about 80 percent to labor and 20 percent to property. A statistic such as this conceals more than it reveals; it sheds no light on the dynamic and complex patterns of distributional changes and attendant conflicts taking place under conditions of rapid technological and socioeconomic changes.

Later in the chapter we shall examine in some depth the nature and problems of special interest groups as they function in American society. There we will observe that the various interest groups are more apt to promote narrow, parochial interests of their groups than to represent and promote broader interests of society as a whole. Special interest groups and their lobbies are likely to promote the interests of their members at the expense of other groups, particularly those large, unorganized groups as consumers, taxpayers, and the poor. For example, a public policy to restrict importation of foreign automobiles may benefit domestic automobile producers and workers at the expense of automobile importers and consumers. A governmental policy of restricting, or not restricting, automobile imports, therefore, has an effect of redistributing real income between these groups. And because of the very nature of special interest pressures, it is almost always the general interests of a large number of unorganized people that are sacrificed so that the parochial interests of some smaller groups are promoted. A few other examples of similar conflicts between narrower, parochial interests and broader, public interests may be noted. Should tobacco growers and dairy farmers continue to receive subsidies from the federal coffers? Should elderly and retired people be asked to forego part of the indexation of their Social Security benefits so that huge federal budget deficits can be reduced? If a financial disaster strikes a public utility company because of a failure of a nuclear power plant, who should be asked to bear the cost—the shareholders of the company, the consumers of electricity, or the general public? These are the pressing issues of distributional justice to which the American political system must address itself.

The nature of the special interest lobbies and their symbiotic relationships with politicians is such that America's political system is highly ineffective in solving the society's distributional problems from a position of the overall, public interest. Congress and many of federal executive and regulatory agencies are hostages to various pressure groups, and their redistributive activities are bound to be dictated by the relative powers and resources of the important self-interest groups. The resulting redistribution of income and advantages among the self-interest groups tends to reflect the power, effectiveness, and political skills of the various special interest lobbies. The upshot is that this system tends to favor the narrow interests of well-organized minority groups at the expense of larger, unorganized groups such as consumers, the unemployed, and the poor.

Stabilization of Economic Activity

Neoclassical economic theory, before the advent of the macroeconomics of John Maynard Keynes in the 1930s, assumed that competitive market-oriented economies automatically tended to full employment of resources. Price inflation was considered primarily a monetary phenomenon; it was believed that inflation could be controlled by reducing the quantity of money in circulation. Thus, economics before Keynes largely assumed away the problems of marcroeconomic instability—recession and inflation—and focused its interest on the problem of efficiency of resource use.

The complacency of the pre-1920s period was blown away by the Great Depression of the 1930s. It is now generally accepted in the United States and other capitalist industrial nations that government has the responsibility of maintaining reasonable levels of employment and price stability. In the United States, macroeconomic stabilization policy entails primarily the use of federal taxation and expenditure policies (i.e., fiscal policy) and the regulation of money and credit by the Federal Reserve System (i.e., monetary policy). The nature and the problems associated with fiscal and monetary policy will be discussed in the following section.

In many market-oriented democracies, notably France and Japan, the central government plays an active role in shaping the patterns of the nation's industrial development. The programs and strategies used for this purpose are collectively referred to as *industrial policy*. Whereas stabilization policies essentially entail short-run management of aggregate *demand*, industrial policy is aimed at affecting the long-run *supply* of different industries within the economy.

Primarily for ideological reasons, the U.S. government has traditionally shied away from this area of public policy. In recent years, however, there has been a growing interest in the feasibilty of introducing industrial policy in the United States as a possible solution to the problem of declining international competitiveness of U.S. industries. The industrial policy debate will be discussed later in this chapter.

STABILIZATION POLICIES

The basic approach to modern stabilization policy in capitalist countries is the management of aggregate demand, or total expenditures on goods and services. The theoretical foundation of this approach is Keynesian macroeconomics: the level of total spending is viewed as fundamentally determining the levels of output, employment, income, and prices. To affect the levels of various types of spending, the public authority may use a combination of *fiscal policy*—or governmental control of revenues and expenditures through the budgetary process—and *monetary policy*—or governmental management of the availability and cost of money and credit. In many Western industrial democracies, these two types of stabilization policy are closely integrated and implemented by a ministry of finance or a department of the treasury. In some countries, some forms of *incomes policy* involving direct governmental controls on wages and prices have been used in addition to conventional fiscal and monetary policy. The U.S. government, particularly under a Republican administration, has been reluctant to use incomes policy.

The basic theories and methods of fiscal and monetary policy are explained in detail in any standard economics textbook. Those readers who feel deficient in their understanding of this important subject are urged to consult their economics textbooks.

What is unique about the macroeconomic stabilization policy as practiced in the United States is that the two major policies—fiscal and monetary—are conducted by separate authorities. Fiscal policy is a joint responsibility of Congress and the executive. Basically, the president proposes a budget, the Congress authorizes and appropriates funds, and the president regulates the rate of spending. Monetary policy, on the other hand, is the responsibility of the Board of Governors of the Federal Reserve System. As an independent federal agency, the Federal Reserve Board (known as the Fed) does not report to the president of the United States; it maintains a considerable—if not total—degree of autonomy in regulating the nation's money supply, interest rates, and credit conditions. The Fed's monetary policy is aimed at private-sector spending; it affects public-sector spending only indirectly as the cost of borrowing in general is affected. The autonomy of the Fed in monetary policy matters is, of course, deliberate; true to their pluralist ideology, Americans try to keep the political power separate from the awesome economic power of creating and regulating money.

Fiscal Policy

The Keynesian macroeconomic theory on which fiscal policy is based is strikingly simple. It sees the federal government budget as a sort of reservoir of spending flows. A budgetary deficit supplies a needed purchasing power into the economy, raising income and output; a surplus works to remove excess purchasing power from the economy, reducing inflationary pressures. Unfortunately, this simple mechanism has not worked very well in many—if not all—industrial democracies largely because of the unacceptably high tradeoff between inflation and unemployment. This so-called Phillips curve tradeoff has resulted in an intractable coexistence of inflation and unemployment. An expansionary fiscal policy often aggravates inflationary problems without reducing unemployment much; a contractionary fiscal policy may lead to high unemployment without putting much of a dent on inflation.

In the United States, the problem of the relative ineffectiveness of fiscal policy is made worse by the effectiveness of special interest groups in influencing the policies of public authorities. Changes in federal government revenues and expenditures are made jointly by the president and the Congress. The Office of Management and Budget—one of the executive agencies of the Office of the President—prepares the budget in consultation with other government agencies. The budget is submitted by the president to Congress. The Congressional Budget Office assists the various House and Senate committees and subcommittees in studying and evaluating the specifics of the budget proposals for congressional authorization and appropriation. Thus, the budget process is highly politicized. Politicians in both the White House and the Congress are often guided more by parochial interests of their constituencies and supporting lobbies than the general interests of the entire population.

To assure a successful outcome of their pork-barrel legislation, members of Congress frequently engage in logrolling, that is, trading votes in order to get a majority on a bill one favors. The whole budgetary process, therefore, has a strong spending bias. Politicians vote for each other's pet programs. Voting for increases in tax rates or new taxes is unpopular back home, so this is done much less readily than voting for spending. The inevitable outcome of this spending bias is an accumulation of public debts, high interest rates, and inflationary pressures.

Unlike members of Congress who tend to place the interests of their back-home constituencies and special interest support groups ahead of the national interest, the president of the United States is presumably guided, in the main, by the overall interest of the nation in establishing policy priorities. This may very well be the case for the most part, but presidents are not by any means immune to pressures from special interest groups. The nature of the American electoral system is such that successful candidates must make innumerable promises and commitments to all sorts of regional, professional, vocational, and ideological interest groups during the long election campaign period. The general pattern is not that the president becomes a stepchild of a few self-interest groups but that so much is promised to so many interest groups during the campaign that the only way the promises can be delivered during the incumbency is by compromising more or less on the interest of the general public.

We may generalize the effectiveness of fiscal policy in the American economic system as follows. Politicians' interest in winning elections creates a bias toward steady increases in spending that minimizes the effectiveness of fiscal policy; fiscal policy thus has an inflationary bias. It can be used as an effective stabilization tool only when there exists a coincidence of its objectives with the self-interests of politicians and their support groups. Such a coincidence occurs only when the economy is depressed by an inadequacy of aggregate demand and there exist large unutilized productive capacities. The effectiveness of fiscal policy is highly limited in the 1980s when the basic problems are an excessive overall demand coupled with occasional supply bottlenecks.

If special interest lobbying and the resulting pork-barrel legislation are responsible for the underlying inflationary pressures in the U.S. economy, what accounts for the persistently high unemployment rate? According to the Keynesian theory, inflationary pressures (i.e., existence of excessive aggregate demand relative to productive capacity) should push employment to the full-employment level. How can we explain the persistence of high unemployment occurring in the face of high inflation? Conventional wisdom answers the question as follows: because of the mismatch between the patterns of demand for and supply of labor, there may exist extensive *structural unemployment* that cannot be reduced by increases in aggregate demand. For example, there may be a large number of carpenters unemployed while openings for computer programmers may go begging for takers because of a shortage of qualified programmers. A sharp rise in aggregate demand under such conditions will simply make the shortage of programmers more acute, and thereby generate an inflationary pressure, without reducing the number of unemployed carpenters. The more technologically complex the economy, and the faster the rate of technological changes, the higher, naturally, the rate of structural unemployment will be.

Other explanations of high unemployment in the face of high inflation—or the phenomenon of *stagflation*—relate the problem to institutional factors. For instance, stagflation is often attributed to restrictive practices of labor unions and minimum-wage laws that tend to exclude unskilled workers from employment. Mancur Olson, in his *The Rise and Decline of Nations*, provides an institutional explanation of stagflation incorporating his theory of special interest groups. He argues that the fundamental reason for the unnaturally high unemployment rate in such matured economies as Great Britain and the United States is the "distributional coalitions" of big business and organized labor effectively lobbying to prevent the masses of unemployed (and unorganized) workers from taking jobs at lower wages.[3]

Very briefly and in a highly simplified manner, Olson's argument

---

[3]Mancur Olson, *The Rise and Decline of Nations: Economic Growth, Stagflation, and Social Rigidities* (New Haven, Conn.: Yale University Press, 1982), chap. 7.

may be summarized as follows. In the labor market, organized labor has a monopoly power, and large corporations have a monopsony power. (*Monopsony* means a single *buyer*.) As a monopolist, the labor union faces a downward-sloping demand curve for labor. It can raise wages above the competitive level for its *employed* members by restricting employment, thereby causing unemployment. Conversely, the employer firm, having a monopsony power, faces an upward-sloping supply curve of labor. It can obtain labor at wages below the competitive level if it restricts employment. This practice, too, tends to generate unemployment. Although the actual wage rate is determined by the relative bargaining power of the two sides and therefore could conceivably settle at the competitive level, one inescapable byproduct of bilateral monopoly bargaining such as this is that the *quantity* of employment tends to be less than the competitive level. The special interest lobbies representing organized labor and big business push for legislation that effectively prevents unorganized workers from taking jobs at lower wages. High unemployment in matured economies, therefore, is a function of the institutional rigidity caused by a proliferation of powerful special interest groups.[4]

Monetary Policy

Because fiscal policy is often ineffective as a weapon of macroeconomic control, the burden of economic stabilization falls by default on monetary policy. It is particularly effective in combating inflation. If deemed necessary to fight a serious inflation, the Fed can engineer a massive slowdown of the economy using a very tight monetary policy, as it did in the fall of 1982. Although the backbone of the worst postwar inflation was successfully broken, the economy also had to endure the worst recession in the postwar decades. Thus monetary policy, even when successful, must contend with the problem of the Phillips curve tradeoff between inflation and unemployment. And this tradeoff can be worsened by irresponsible fiscal policy: the larger the federal budget deficit is, the tighter the monetary policy measures must be in order to achieve a given degree of inflation abatement. Notwithstanding these difficulties, one fact may be acknowledged: the Federal Reserve's monetary policy does work, and it works by forcing a bitter pill of recession on an unwilling public.

Because of the traditional fear of concentrated economic power, the American banking community had strongly resisted creation of a central bank for the United States prior to the passage of the Federal Reserve

[4]Ibid., pp. 201–2.

Act of 1913. With this act, the economy was provided with the *function* of a central bank without getting a central bank itself. Under the provisions of the act, the country was divided into 12 districts, headed by 12 Federal Reserve Banks. These banks are technically "private" banks whose shares are subscribed to by member banks. This "privateness," however, is in name only. For all practical purposes, these banks serve as "branch offices" of the phantom central bank of the United States—the Federal Reserve System. All nationally chartered banks have to be members of the system; state banks are given the option of joining the system.

Heading the Federal Reserve System—which consists of 12 district banks with 24 branches—is the seven-member Board of Governors. The board is an independent federal agency created by congressional legislation. Its members are appointed for staggered 14-year terms by the president and confirmed by the Senate. One of the board members is appointed by the president to serve as chairperson for a 4-year term. Being an independent federal agency, the board answers to Congress, not to the president. Barring an unlikely possibility of Congress deciding to make major changes in its relationship with the Fed, we can say that congressional authority over the Fed is minimum and that the Fed enjoys a high degree of autonomy in its policies. Board members cannot ordinarily be removed by Congress, and the board need not be concerned with appropriation of funds from Congress. (It is fiscally more than self-sufficient since it earns large sums in interests on securities in its portfolio; any excess incomes are returned to the U.S. Treasury.)

One significant fact about the Fed Board of Governors is its relative immunity to political pressures. The long and nonrenewable terms of appointment of its members and its fiscal self-sufficiency give the board virtually unassailable political autonomy. The choices made by the board members, therefore, are *authoritative choices* similar to those made by the Supreme Court justices, rather than *composite choices* made by politicians and bureaucrats.[5] To be sure, political pressures are frequently exerted on the board by Congress, the White House, and the business and financial communities seeking, almost invariably, relief from high interest rates; but the board *can* withstand these pressures, if it chooses to, and pursue an independent monetary policy in the public interest. Thus, during an election year, monetary policy often becomes "the only game in town" as fiscal policy becomes incapacitated by political considerations.

[5]See Chapter 4 for the meaning of these terms. See also Robert A. Solo, *The Positive State* (Cincinnati, Ohio: South-Western Publishing Co., 1982), pp. 36–38.

ECONOMIC PLANNING
AND INDUSTRIAL POLICY

Among the major industrial democracies of the West, only in the United States does there exist a widely accepted view of the natural superiority of private enterprise over public initiative in economic activities. The broadly held belief in the supportive role of public authority derives from an individualistic and pluralistic ideology that expresses a deep suspicion of authority, collectivism, and concentrated power. This ideological bias accounts for Americans' characteristic aversion to central economic planning.

As a generic term, *planning* simply means casting an objective within the framework of a timetable and taking appropriate measures to attain the objective. In other words, planning is an aspect of the function of management—management of resources over time. As such, planning requires an organization with a goal and coordinated action. Thus, corporations, families, and the Defense Department engage, respectively, in corporate planning, family planning, and defense planning. The American penchant for rejecting the notion of central economic planning manifests the underlying American view that a national economy does not in itself constitute an organized entity.

The United States is a classic example of what Chalmers Johnson calls the "market-rational" state; the government *regulates* business behavior without concerning itself with substantive developmental questions.[6] In the predominantly American view, the state should not try to orchestrate economic development of the nation. The economy is merely a conglomerate of private (and some public) enterprises, and coordination of their activities is best left to the workings of the market. Government should limit itself to the task of modifying the outcome of the nation's private economic activities by means of policies and programs that are generally applicable to the entire economy (e.g., monetary and fiscal policy). Interventions that are specific to firms and industries, in this view, should be limited to supervisory and regulatory activities. Specific strategic interventions in the production and investment decisons of firms and industries, as well as the economywide coordination of these interventions, are regarded as falling outside the purview of the legitimate functions of government.

In the industrial democracies of Europe and Japan, by contrast, government plays a positive and strategic role in planning and promoting economic development. Government is thought of as an instru-

---

[6]Chalmers Johnson, *MITI and the Japanese Miracle: The Growth of Industrial Policy, 1925–1975* (Stanford, Calif.: Stanford University Press, 1982), p. 19.

ment by which society remodels itself. Legitimate government involvement in the market economy includes not only regulation of business
behavior and short-run control of aggregate demand, but also long-term
management of the structure of the economy's productive capacity. This
additional function—variously referred to as industrial policy, industrial planning, or developmental policy—must of necessity involve specific government intervention in the investment and production plans
of individual firms and industries. Government accomplishes this aspect
of economic policy making by using laws, rules, and regulations as well
as subsidies, tax incentives, licenses, import controls, and moral suasion. Unlike central economic planning of the Soviet type, however,
modern capitalist economic or industrial planning does not involve the
state dictating every detail of investment, production, and materials
supply activities of firms and industries. Rather, the state plays the role
of an active partner of corporate and industrial leaders in making strategic investment and production decisions.

Federalism and the doctrine of separation of powers in the U.S.
political system assures that public power is fragmented and diffused.
Concentration of private power, on the other hand, is effectively held
in check by the strongest antitrust laws in the capitalist world. Moreover, as we saw earlier, the American business community is not organized in a hierarchy whose top leadership speaks in one voice for the
entire private sector. Even special interest groups "tend instinctively to
separate themselves off from the rest and to function as autonomous
entities."[7]

The fragmentation of both public and private power, according to
the late Andrew Shonfield, is the "real impediment to planning" in the
United States.[8] For national economic planning of the capitalist variety
to work well, argued Shonfield, there must exist an active, collaborative
relationship between government and business, working in pursuit of
common goals. His analysis of the development of capitalist planning
in France led him to conclude that the essential nature of modern capitalist economic planning is a symbiotic, even collusive, relationship
between the center of public power and the core of private power. In
France, it took the form of a close working relationship between the
elite civil servants and the top leadership of big business. In his words:

> In some ways, the development of French planning in the 1950s can
> be viewed as an act of voluntary collusion between senior civil ser-
> vants and the senior managers of big business. . . . The conspiracy
> in the public interest between big business and big officialdom worked,

[7]Andre Shonfield, *Modern Capitalism: The Changing Balance of Public and Private
Power* (New York and London: Oxford University Press, 1965), p. 335.

[8]Ibid., pp. 335–36.

> largely because both sides found it convenient. . . . Both sides had
> an interest in limiting the element of unpredictability and risk in
> their operations. Hence the conspiracy to plan. . . . It all depended,
> therefore, on a series of bargains between the main centres of public
> and private economic power.[9]

Shonfield concluded that modern capitalist planning of the French
type is not likely to be successfully adopted in the individualistic and
pluralistic United States. He asked, "Can a society, which is devoted to
this riot of pluralism in public as well as business affairs, plan itself?"[10]
The answer, obviously, is a definitive no. In subsequent chapters we
shall see how, in Japan, the close collaboration between government
and business leads to a finely tuned mechanism of joint decision making.
Although Japanese-style familistic collectivism differs significantly from
French-type bureaucratic corporatism, the two approaches are sufficiently similar to be clearly distinguished from the regulated but un-
managed captialism of the United States.[11]

Industrial Policy

In the early 1980s, there arose in the United States a surge of
interest in *industrial policy*. What triggered this interest was the perceived decline in the international competitiveness of U.S. industries
against the backdrop of Japan's remarkable success in expanding its
exports of such industrial products as steel, consumer electronics, and
automobiles. As proposed by the advocates of this new approach to
national economic management, American-style industrial policy would
require that the U.S. government identify which industries will be potential winners and losers in future worldwide competition, and give
firms in the winner industries financial, legal, regulatory, and technical
assistance, while providing the declining industries with adjustment
assistance in order to minimize the pain of downward adjustments.

Industrial policy is just another name for modern capitalist planning discussed in the preceding paragraphs. It requires the state to take
a strategic, goal-oriented approach to the task of promoting the nation's
industrial development. It necessitates selective interventions by the
central government with investment and production decisions of specific firms and industries. Furthermore, there must exist active collaboration between the centers of public and private power in pursuit of

[9]Ibid., pp. 128–29.

[10]Ibid., p. 336.

[11]French economic planning will be discussed further in Chapter 12.

common goals. These factors are characteristically absent in the United States.

Charles Schultze, former chairman of the Council of Economic Advisors (1977–80), argues that industrial policy would be unworkable in the United States. First, he seriously questions the ability of the government to determine which industries are winner industries any better than the market can. Second, he seriously doubts the ability of any U.S. government agency that is under the control of a partisan president and Congress to make sagacious decisions, with respect to the declining part of the economy, about which industries, firms, and regions are to be phased out and which are to be nurtured. Says Schultze:

> To be anything more than a universal protector of inefficiency, a systematic program of assistance to declining industries would have to call for some very hard-headed decisions among particular firms, cities, and group of workers—that the Youngstown plant can live but the Weirton one must close, for example, or that the cotton textile industry has a reasonable chance to rehabilitate itself but the wool textile industry is a hopeless case and must die.[12]

Because public authority in the United States is diffused and its various segments are captivated by a large number of powerful special interest lobbies, industrial policy, if attempted, would be hopelessly politicized. The outcome would be more likely to be provisions of public assistances to all types of industries—winners and losers alike—than strategic development of carefully selected industries.

As regards the potential dangers of politicizing industrial policy, Senator William Proxmire of the state of Wisconsin was quoted in a *Wall Street Journal* article as making the following observation:

> Money will go where the political power is. . . . It will go where union power is mobilized. It will go where the campaign contributors want it to go. It will go where the mayors and governors as well as congressmen and senators have the power to push it. Anyone who thinks government funds will be allocated to firms according to merit has not lived or served in Washington very long.[13]

Senator Proxmire put his finger right on the mark when he said "Money will go where the political power is." Power is unevenly distributed, tilting toward the declining industries and regions and away from the emerging high-technology industries as well as unorganized

---

[12]Charles L. Schultze, "Industrial Policy: A Dissent," *The Brookings Review*, 2, no. 1 (Fall 1983), 10.

[13]Bruce Bartlett, "The Old Politics of a New Industrial Policy," *Wall Street Journal*, April 19, 1983, p. 34. Reprinted by permission of The Wall Street Journal, © Dow Jones & Company, Inc. (1983). All Rights Reserved.

consumers and taxpayers. As our earlier discussions on the nature of special interest groups and their lobbying activities suggested, the benefit-cost ratios of lobbying activities are disproportionately more favorable for those groups whose investments and jobs are threatened by industrial changes than for those in the newly emerging high-technology industries or for unorganized consumers and taxpayers. Capitalists, managers, and workers in such large and well-established industries as textiles, steel, and automobiles have much more powerful and better-financed lobbies and better political connections than their counterparts in the emerging industries. Moreover, the emerging industries are less preoccupied with lobbying activities than the older industries. Since they are doing relatively well in the market, the newer industries' need for, and interest in, lobbying activities are less than those of the declining industries.

The implication of unbalanced political power to the workability of industrial policy is enormous. It is inevitable that the self-interest of various pressure groups distorts the pattern of industrial adjustments in such a way as to grossly favor the relatively inefficient, declining industries at the expense of the more efficient, emerging industries. A conclusion is inescapable: U.S. industrial policy, if implemented, is doomed to be counterproductive since it cannot help but preserve the inefficiency of declining industries.

Even though formal industrial policy is bound to be ineffective or counterproductive for reasons discussed above, there nevertheless remains a need in the United States for coordinating various government policies and regulations to minimize their distortive effects. Public policy decisions involving taxes, subsidies, import restrictions, interest rates, utility rates, government contracts, price supports, environmental regulations, corporate mergers, corporate bailouts, and so forth, benefit some sectors of the economy and hurt others. Whatever government does in the economic sphere inevitably interferes with the market and generates changes in the structure of the economy. Thus, the sum total of all the frequent and uncoordinated interventions amounts to an ad hoc "industrial policy" of a sort. What is missing is an effort to organize all the unavoidable public interventions into a coherent whole and imbue it with a sense of direction. But this is the sort of thing that the American system is ill-equipped to do.

INDUSTRIAL ORGANIZATION

At the heart of the question on the character of a capitalist economic system is the nature of the relationships between the public authority and private initiatives. In the old-style capitalism of decentralized markets and atomistic firms, the government-business relations were relatively simple and straightforward. In the contemporary U.S. economy, however, these relations are much more complex. In the first place, government is fragmented, decentralized, and professionalized. A central core of public authortity cannot be identified. And with the exception of the Supreme Court and some of the independent federal agencies, choices made in the American political system are what Robert Solo calls *composite choices*—that is, they tend to reflect the ideologies, biases, self-interests, and pressures of a wide variety of participants in decision making.[14] Secondly, the private sector is no longer characterized by a large number of individualized firms that are disciplined only by the forces of competition. The great bulk of private productive activities now takes place in the *organizational sector* consisting of several thousand large, complex corporations. The growth of the organizational sector has important implications to the government-business relationships in the United States. Large corporations themselves, and their allies, have acquired impressive economic and political power that rivals that of the fragmented public authority. Private power is often exercised to exert influence on public authorities' decision-making processes and outcomes. Thus, a study of the government-business relationships in the United States must focus on the dynamics and intricacies of the bilateral influences between the segmented and decentralized public authority and the coalitions of private power centers.

The large and complex corporation is a basic social institution and a major social force in contemporary America. We now turn to examine the extent to which individual corporations are organized into a larger whole. Do corporations exercise their influence and wield their power individually, in tacit but informal collusion among themselves, or in a formal and organized manner? Is private business power in America diffuse and fragmented, loosely organized, or tightly structured and centrally controlled? These are important questions, answers to which affect the quality of the government-business relationships, which in turn defines the nature and character of the total politico-economic system.

Before proceeding with our task, let us briefly examine the industrial organization in the Soviet Union and Japan. As we observed in Chapters 5 and 6, Soviet productive enterprises are organized into one gigantic state enterprise system. Thus, the middle-layer economic organizations in the Soviet economy—productive and industrial associations and ministerial departments—are administrative subdivisions of the state productive apparatus. And since that apparatus is an integral

[14]Robert A. Solo, *The Political Authority and the Market System* (Cincinnati, Ohio: South-Western Publishing Co., 1974), pp. 35–42; Solo, *The Positive State*, pp. 36–38.

part of the Soviet state, we find that Soviet enterprises, industries, and government bureaucracies constitute an organic unit so that the question of government-enterprise relationships is a moot one.

As we shall see in subsequent chapters, the private business sector in Japan is hierarchically organized. Japan's large corporations form enterprise groups, which, through trade associations and peak business organizations, establish close, symbiotic relationships with departments and agencies of the key industrial ministries of the Japanese government. Not only is the corporate sector (both private and public) highly organized internally, but organized business, the national government bureaucracy, and the ruling political party are so closely intertwined that the whole system must be viewed as an inseparable organic entity.

In sharp contrast to the high degree of organizational unity of the industrial sectors of both the Soviet Union and Japan, the private business sector of the United States economy is characterized by an almost total absence of effective overall organization. This is not to say the U.S. industries are atomistically competitive in the classical sense. Nor does it mean that there exists no intercorporate coordination in given industries, or no symbiotic relationship between a specific firm or industry and a government agency. What it means is this: there is no *overall,* unified organization of private corporations and industries, just as there is no overall, unified organization of the public authority. Firms and trade associations deal with executive departments, regulatory agencies, legislators, and political parties on an ad hoc basis. But these interrelationships are not systematically coordinated at a center. No dialogue takes place, and no bargain is struck, between a peak business organization and a center of public authority.

Intercorporate Coordination

Because of the antitrust rules against restrictive trade practices, U.S. corporations must compete in the marketplace *individually* without forming cooperative or collusive agreements with their competitors. Some intercorporate coordination and integration of activities do exist, but they are permitted or tolerated only to the extent that they do not violate the letter of the antitrust laws. The point is that there is not, and cannot legally be, a comprehensive design of an organic network of intercorporate coordination.

As profit-seeking entities, business corporations naturally try to increase their *market power,* which may be defined as an ability to control their output and price. A firm can increase its market power by either developing a large size (tending to monopoly), or by effectively colluding with others "in restraint of commerce." Naturally, this desire to increase market power is greatly curtailed by the actual or potential threat of antitrust prosecution. Within the framework of the antitrust constraints, American corporations try to expand and integrate their operations, thereby acquiring greater market power. Industrywide co-ordination and integration of efforts can take several forms.

Firms within the same industry can coordinate, to a considerable extent, their producing, pricing, marketing, and investing activities. As long as cooperation and coordination efforts are informal and involve no overt acts of collusion, the courts have allowed a wide latitude in anticompetitive behavior. In oligopolistic industries, for example, there often is a tendency for the prices to go up and down in parallel move-ments. Collusive agreements, though they may exist behind the price movements, are usually difficult to detect. It is more likely that the prices move in unison with a tacit understanding among the firms in the industry that competitive pricing is harmful to the industry since it can easily lead to a disastrous price war. Firms in the industry may follow the price changes announced by a price leader. Followers justify the coincidence of price movements by resorting to the logic that, since they all use the same markup formulae and face an identical pattern of cost increases, they are bound to experience the same pattern of price increases. This practice of *conscious parallelism* among oligopolists has not been declared unlawful by the courts, provided, of course, no col-lusion is demonstrable.

Firms in major industries form trade associations staffed with pub-lic relations specialists and professional lobbyists. In the early 1980s there were estimated 8,000 trade association offices staffed with 42,000 persons in the Washington D.C., area.[15] They compile and publish sta-tistical data for the industry, provide these data and industry "per-spectives" to government advisory boards and regulatory agencies, and engage in lobbying activities toward public officials and legislators. Trade associations also provide forums for intraindustry exchange of information and viewpoints that help enhance the quality of industry-wide coordination.[16]

Intraindustry communication and coordination can also be facil-itated by government regulation and joint membership on government advisory boards. Regulation often results in a creation of quasi-cartel setup. For example, in commercial aviation, the (now defunct) Civil Aeronautics Board controlled entry of firms into the industry, assigned routes to airlines, regulated air fares, and channeled subsidies to the airlines. It would be surprising if these regulatory practices had not

---

[15]Robert B. Reich, *The Next American Frontier* (New York: Times Books, 1983), p. 196.

[16]Ibid., p. 89.

created an atmosphere of shared goals and a sense of mutuality of interests among the airlines. The same result is obtained from joint membership on government advisory bodies, of which there were 820 with 18,742 members in December 1979.[17] These advisory boards provide ideal vehicles for exchanging information, not only between government and business but also among competitors within the same industry, without fear of antitrust prosecution.[18]

Another informal vehicle of intraindustry coordination involves control over several corporations by a family interest, institutional stock investors, and financial institutions. In none of these cases, however, does coordination amount to systematic, comprehensive, and compelling organization. First, the sheer size of major U.S. corporations, increased professionalization of corporate management, and the system of inheritance taxes have combined to make effective ownership and control of a major corporation by a family group almost a thing of the past. It is of course possible for a family group to have a minority ownership control in a number of corporations, but the antitrust rules effectively prevent these corporations from being related horizontally (i.e., as competitiors in the same industry) or vertically (i.e., as buyer from or seller to each other). Second, institutions do make huge stock investments in a number of major corportions, but their interest in the corporations is essentially as a portfolio of assets, not as an object of control. If institutional investors become disenchanted by corporations they own, they would rather sell off the stocks in them than try to assume management control. Third, financial control over corporations by banking institutions is limited in the United States where, unlike Japan, the typical corporation's debt-equity ratio is low and bank loans constitute only a small portion of its total debt structure. As a general rule, therefore, banks are interested more in the creditworthiness and earnings records of the corporations than in their management. Thus, in these three types of intercorporate linkages, coordination is sporadic and ad hoc at best. Such a coordination can be more adequately described as informal relationships of communication and community of interest among some firms in an industry than as a comprehensive and hierarchical organization of an entire industry.

In discussions of intercorporate coordination, one topic that has received particular attention is interlocking directorates among large corporations. This attention, however, is not justified by the actual significance of the practice. Director interlocks have been considered important by many because of the mistaken assumption that a board of

[17]Edward S. Herman, *Corporate Control, Corporate Power*, A Twentieth Century Fund Study (Cambridge: Cambridge University Press, 1981), p. 215.

[18]Ibid., p. 216.

directors wields effective power in corporate management. (See the next chapter on this point.) Moreover, the centralizing and anticompetitive effect of interlocking directorates within the same industry is almost nullified by a provision in the Clayton Antitrust Act prohibiting such an interlock. Thus, in 1975, among the 250 largest industrial and financial corporations in the United States, only 17 pairs of intraindustry interlocks were found, though indirect interlocks among these 250 firms, as well as direct interlocks crossing industrial lines, were extensive.[19] (A direct interlock exists when the same individual is on the boards of more than one firm. An indirect interlock is found when two or more directors from different firms serve on the board of a third company.)

Direct corporate interlocks crossing industrial lines may be an important element of corporate strategy. By accepting a board member from a key bank, for example, the management may hope to receive favorable considerations from the bank in its future loan applications. Other directors may be selected from among the directors and officers of other firms with expectations of improved business opportunities and favorable considerations. Seen in this light, director interlocks are used not so much as a means of intercorporate control, but rather as a means of improving communication with outside firms and thereby reducing uncertainty in the firm's environment.[20]

INTEREST GROUPS AND LOBBYING

The character of special interest groups in the United States differs from that in the Soviet Union and Japan in some important ways. In the Soviet Union, pressure groups as known in democratic societies do not exist. What may be called interest groups are various bureaucratic and occupational groups (e.g., the party apparatus, the military, the police, the scientific community, and so forth) that try to articulate their institutional interests in an effort to mobilize political support from the top party leadership. This articulation of group interests takes place within the confines of the authoritarian power complex; it in no way suggests emergence of pluralism in Soviet society.

In Japan, as in the United States, there exist numerous specialized interest groups (e.g., agricultural groups, small-business groups, labor unions, local communities, professional organizations, and public interest groups) that exert influence on political processes. But these groups differ from those in the United States in two important ways. First, unlike American interest groups, which target their activities primarily

[19]Ibid., pp. 200–202.

[20]Mark S. Mizruchi, *The American Corporate Network: 1904–1974* (Beverly Hills, Calif.: Sage Publications, 1982), p. 35.

on Congress and regulatory agencies, the groups in Japan tend to focus their lobbying activities on the highest levels of the national government bureaucracy and the top leaders of political parties. Second, big-business interests in Japan are so powerful and well organized that the label *pressure groups* can no longer be applied to them. Big business occupies a place of influence and power *inside* Japan's establishment; it is an integral part of the country's power structure. Big business in Japan need not "lobby" in Tokyo; it *is* part of the nation's public policy-making apparatus.

Interest-group activities in the United States are characteristically not focused on a center of public decision making. Since both public and private power is fragmented and diffused, it is not possible for a special interest group to form a coalition with the core of public authority. Consequently, alliances and symbiotic relationships that are formed between political and economic powers tend to be compartmentalized, developing as pockets of coalition among interest groups, executive and regulatory agencies, and congressional committees sharing a common interest. The best known alliance of this sort is the military-industrial complex, or the coalition of the Defense Department, the armed forces committees in Congress, congressional members from the regions having military bases and armament industries, and the corporations in defense-related industries. In the American environment, forming such a symbiotic alliance is much more effective than trying to influence the policy-making processes at the highest levels of the executive branch. Andrew Shonfield described the situation as follows: "The significant point is not, it seems, that organized business lacks ready access to the topmost level of the administrative apparatus; it is rather the doubt whether it would be able to settle the major practical issues which are of interest to the business community by penetrating there."[21]

The Theory
of Voluntary Association

In the United States there exists a strong ideological and legal basis for allowing various voluntary associations to exert pressures on the process of public policy making. The First Amendment to the U.S. Constitution guarantees freedom of assembly and the right to petition the government for redress of grievances. In the American ideology of participatory democracy, there is a persistent belief in political pluralism; mutual checks and balances among various conflicting groups within society are believed to produce a maximum welfare for all citizens.

---

[21] Shonfield, *Modern Capitalism*, p. 335.

The belief that the activities of special interest groups are all to the good and result in the promotion of the public interest has been seriously questioned in recent decades. Indeed, it has been argued that the activities of private self-interest groups—the most important and numerous type of pressure groups—is by their very nature detrimental to the collective interest of society. This argument is based on an economic theory of voluntary association developed by Mancur Olson in his *The Logic of Collective Action* published in 1965.[22]

Individuals are motivated to behave, both economically and politically, by comparing their private benefits and private costs of a given action. Thus, they would join a voluntary association, pay dues, do voluntary work, and contribute money to it only if the private benefits of such action exceeds private costs. The benefits of a given action, however, accrue not only to the individuals who initiate or participate in the action but also to the entire group. And in a large group, the individual's share of the benefit is infinitesimally small. Moreover, other members of the group who do not participate in the action also benefit, without paying the cost. Here, we have the free-rider problem commonly associated with the provision of public goods. Since every member of the group can reap the benefit without paying for it, nobody wants to pay voluntarily. This leads to what Olson calls the "paradox in the behavior of groups." Olson describes the paradox as follows:

> The very fact that the objective or interest is common to or shared by the group entails that the gain from any sacrifice an individual makes to serve this common purpose is shared with everyone in the group. . . . The individual in any large group with a common interest will reap only a minute share of the gains from whatever sacrifices the individual makes to achieve this common interest. Since any gain goes to everyone in the group, those who contribute nothing to the effort will get just as much as those who made a contribution . . . , so . . . there will be little, if any, group action. The paradox, then, is that . . . large groups, at least if they are composed of rational individuals, will *not* act in their group interest.[23]

This is an *economic* theory of individuals' behavior in a group: economic in the sense that individuals are seen as weighing their private benefits and costs in deciding to take a given action. If the group is large, the benefit-cost ratio is considerably less than one; the individuals consequently will not take the action. Olson argues that this theory explains why individuals ordinarily fail to behave in the collective in-

---

[22]Mancur Olson, Jr., *The Logic of Collective Action: Public Goods and the Theory of Groups* (Cambridge, Mass.: Harvard University Press, 1965). A very useful summary of Olson's thesis is given in Olson, *The Rise and Decline of Nations*, chap. 2.

[23]Olson, *The Rise and Decline of Nations*, p. 18. Olson's italics.

terest of a large group or society at large. He points out that in no major societies are masses of consumers, taxpayers, the poor, or the unemployed effectively organized.[24]

Under what circumstances, then, can a special interest group be successfully organized? What do the American Medical Association, the United Autoworkers, and the Associated Milk Producers have that consumers or taxpayers collectively do not have? Olson's answer to these questions is that "if the group that would benefit from collective action is sufficiently small and the cost-benefit ratio of collective action for the group sufficiently favorable, there may well be calculated action in the collective interest. . . ."[25]

A self-interest group can be successfully organized only if benefit from collective action accrues in a concentrated maner to a small number of individuals constituting the group, so that the share of the benefit accruing to the individual who sacrifices for the group's interest exceeds that individual's sacrifices. Here, the group's interest must of necessity be a narrow, parochial interest specific only to the group's members; and the benefits must not accrue to a large number of individuals outside the group. Nor can the interest of the group coincide with the interest of a larger group, because if such were the case, the benefit of collective action must be shared with members of the larger group, thereby making the benefit-cost ratio of the interest group unfavorable. The implications of this conclusion are momentous: special interest groups can exist and be viable only when their interest does not coincide with the public interest. A group can serve its members' interests only at the expense of those who are outside the group. Society cannot achieve either efficiency or equity through checks and balances among interest groups. Olson concludes:

> Some groups such as consumers, taxpayers, the unemployed, and the poor do not have either the selective incentives or the small numbers needed to organize, so they would be left out of the bargaining. It would be in the interest of those groups that are organized to increase their own gains by whatever means possible. This would include choosing policies that, though inefficient for the society as a whole, were advantageous for the organized groups because the costs of the policies fell disproportionately on the unorganized.[26]

The crucial fact of contemporary America (or any other democratic society for that matter) is that special interest groups gain economic and political advantages at the expense of society as a whole. Dairy

[24]Ibid., p. 34.

[25]Ibid., p. 29.

[26]Ibid., p. 37.

farmers receive subsidies for not producing milk, steel workers receive import restrictions that might save their jobs, and the elderly and the retired fight for greater Social Security and Medicare benefits regardless of their adverse effects on the federal budget. The important point is that not all of these special interest demands are necessarily antisocial; some of them may very well be highly justified and necessary in order to correct existing injustices. The point, however, is that the demands of these pressure groups are often accommodated without due considerations being paid to their social benefits and costs. In the lopsided political process of reacting to the pressures of self-interest groups, the general interest of society as a whole is often placed in jeopardy.

Lobbying

Lobbying is an activity aimed at influencing public policy making through personal contacts with legislators, bureaucrats, and their staff members. The most effective lobbyists are former lawmakers or those who are influential members of the target legislators' constituencies. Lobbyists may or may not be salaried. Many special interest groups engage the services of Washington law firms for their lobbying activities. Lobbyists monitor governmental activities that might affect their interests, attend hearings of congressional committees and regulatory commissions, testify before committee hearings, provide carefully researched background materials to targeted lawmakers, organize letter-writing campaigns, and in general try to influence decision making of legislators and other public officials by having conversations with them in their offices, in expensive restaurants (at the lobbyists' expense of course), and at private parties. The most valuable targets of lobbying activities are members of Congress, particularly those in key committees. Lobbying toward bureaucrats is much less common. Because of the general absence of party discipline in voting behavior, lobbying the machinery of political parties is of little use and therefore seldom attempted. In pleading their cases, lobbyists make subtle (and sometimes not so subtle) references to the past voting records of their constituents, campaign contributions, and potential future benefits in votes and money (or their possible withdrawals). The cases lobbyists make for their special interests are almost always presented as advancing the public interest.

The activities of lobbyists and lobbying groups are regulated under the Federal Regulation of Lobbying Act of 1946. The content of this act and its enforcement reflected the ambivalent attitude of the American public toward lobbying activities. On the one hand, the First Amendment's guarantees of freedom of speech and the right of redress of grievances had made it difficult to enact laws regulating lobbying activities.

On the other hand, widely observed uses of excessive group pressures on legislative processes and outright corruption of legislators and other public officials had led to public demands for measures to impose restriction on lobbying activities. The compromise solution, as embodied in the 1946 act, was to stress public disclosure of lobbying activities without substantially restricting lobbying activities themselves.

The Federal Regulation of Lobbying Act of 1946 requires lobbyists and their organizations to register with the Clerk of the House and the Secretary of the Senate if they engage in activities "for pay or for any consideration for the purpose of attempting to influence the passage or defeat of any legislation by the Congress of the United States. . . ." A 1954 Supreme Court ruling upheld the constitutionality of the 1946 act, but exempted individuals and groups from registration if their activities are aimed at stimulating grass-roots public pressures on Congress. There are several other important loopholes to this act, including the following: (1) groups or individuals who spend their own money are exempted from registration; (2) only the groups and individuals whose "principal purpose" is to influence legislation are required to register; (3) only direct lobbying with the members of Congress is covered by the act; contacts with congressional staff members are specifically not covered; (4) lobbying toward executive agencies and regulatory commissions is not covered.[27] Because of these loopholes, much lobbying activities that take place in Washington remains hidden from public scrutiny. Serious efforts have been made to produce new lobbying laws, but so far they have not resulted in new legislation primarily because of the effective opposition from the lobbying community.

Many corporations have their lobbying representation in Washington; some are represented indirectly through the services of Washington law firms. Trade associations like the National Association of Realtors and the American Petroleum Institute also lobby actively. The two most important umbrella organizations for business interest groups are the National Association of Manufacturers and the U.S. Chamber of Commerce. They lobby on a large number of selective issues on which they take positions. Corporations generally finance lobbying activities through their own revenues, which are regarded as legitimate business expenses for tax purposes. Organizational resources come from membership dues and assessments on member corporations.

The most effective of the U.S. business lobbying groups is the Business Roundtable whose membership consists of the chief executive officers (CEOs) of very large U.S. corporations. The Roundtable was formed in 1972 as a forum for presenting an effective voice of big business. Its

[27]Norman J. Ornstein and Shirley Elder, *Interest Groups, Lobbying and Policymaking* (Washington, D.C.: Congressional Quarterly Press, 1978), pp. 103–4.

membership roll, representing some 200 major corporations, includes CEOs of such towering corporations as General Motors, Du Pont, General Electric, IBM, Citibank, and U.S. Steel. The Roundtable's effectiveness in presenting big-business views to the White House and Congress arises from its ability to gain direct access to high-ranking government officials and key congressional members.

Other established business lobbying organizations include the American Business Conference and the National Federation of Independent Business. According to an interview-based opinion survey of 600 high-level U.S. corporate executives commissioned by *Business Week* magazine, only about a third of those interviewed expressed the belief that all these organizations were doing a satisfactory work in effectively communicating business's positions to government and the public.[28] Characteristically, American business lobbies are not organized into an integral and hierarchical whole, and therefore the American business community does not speak with one voice to government and the public. The lobbies vary in constituencies, ideologies, and modes of operation. Their effectiveness as mouthpieces and image makers for the business community is limited not only because they themselves are decentralized and unorganized, but also because their target—the public authority—is decentralized and fragmented.

The largest special interest group in the United States is the American Federation of Labor–Congress of Industrial Organizations (AFL-CIO). This is a federation of over 100 labor unions, with a total membership of nearly 14 million. Although in the popular mind the AFL-CIO is identified with "organized labor," there are several large unions that are not affiliated with it, the more important ones being the United Autoworkers (UAW), the United Mine Workers (UMW), and the Teamsters. Each of these unions, as well as the AFL-CIO and its member unions, has either lobbying offices or representatives in Washington. The strength of the AFL-CIO lies largely in numbers; its 14 million members are scattered throughout the country and form local pressure groups in virtually all the states and congressional districts. This is a powerful political force that few politicians can ignore. The political arm of the AFL-CIO—the Committee on Political Education, or COPE—engages aggressively in voter registration, fund raising, and election campaigns.

In many cases we find strange lobbying bedfellows fighting for a common cause. In the early 1980s, for example, the United Autoworkers and U.S. automobile industry lobbied forcefully for a law that would

    [28]"Executives Take a Dim View of Their Image-Makers," *Business Week*, March 8, 1984, p. 14.

require imported automobiles sold in the United States to contain as much as 90 percent U.S. labor and parts. This so-called domestic content bill was opposed by a coalition of the lobbyists representing the Japanese government, Japanese automobile industry, U.S. dealers of imported automobiles, and U.S agricultural interests that stood to lose from overall reductions in trade volume. Characteristically, the whole controversy over the domestic content bill was not so much the long-term interests of the American economy or American consumers as the short-run benefits and losses in profits, sales, and employment of the affected industries.

Whether lobbyists are merely monitoring political activities or trying to promote or oppose certain policy decisions, the most important ingredient in their activity is their *access* to governmental decision makers. This access is a two-way street; it depends not only on the ability of the lobbyists to reach the right politicians, but also on the receptivity of the politicians to the lobbyists' approaches. What factors affect this receptivity? According to Norman Ornstein and Shirley Elder, there are both positive and negative factors. On the positive side, politicians find lobbyists useful and important for the following reasons: (1) lobbyists can serve as an important source of information, often in an easily understandable form, for reaching policy decisions; (2) lobbyists can develop parliamentary strategies for legislators and coordinate their legislative efforts; (3) they can provide legislators with innovative legislative ideas; (4) lobbyists can be legislators' long-time friends and confidants; and (5) they can provide assistance, financial or otherwise, in legislators' reelection efforts. On the negative side, legislators may fear that lobbyists may take sanctions against them if they oppose or fail to assist the lobbyists' causes. The sanctions that can be used by pressure groups against unfriendly legislators include blacklisting, urging the groups' members to defeat them in the next election, providing campaign assistance to opponents, and otherwise making the lawmakers' work difficult both in Washington and in their home districts and states.[29]

Industry Influence in Federal Regulatory Agencies

Critics of the policies of various federal regulatory agencies have charged that agencies tend to serve the interests of regulated industries rather than the general interest of society. Paul Quirk classifies the

---

[29]Ornstein and Elder, *Interest Groups*, pp. 59–62.

source of industry influence on regulatory agencies into two broad categories: *policy incentives*, and *political environment*.[30]

Quirk identifies three policy incentives, or the incentives of the agencies to adopt certain kinds of policies over other types of policies:

> (1) the pro-industry appointments hypothesis, which states that appointees to high regulatory office generally have policy attitudes (and thus incentives) favorable to industry views; (2) the pro-industry budgetary incentives hypothesis, which states that regulatory agencies have budgetary incentives to avoid policies opposed by industry; and (3) the industry job incentives hypothesis, according to which regulatory officials have personal career incentives to favor industry viewpoints based on the possibility of future employment in regulated industries.[31]

Quirk's 1976 study based on interviews with high-level officials of the Federal Trade Commission (FTC), the Civil Aeronautics Board (CAB), the Food and Drug Administration (FDA), and the National Highway Traffic Safety Administration (NHTSA) arrived at the following conclusions.

Little evidence was found to support the proindustry appointments hypothesis. If anything, appointees overwhelmingly had held positions either opposing or neutral to industry policies. Quirk found some proindustry budgetary incentives in the FDA and NHTSA, but congressional budget support was considered in jeopardy only when the agencies took actions that were not only injurious to the industry but also to consumers. The FTC officials were found to have probusiness budgetary incentives in favoring the protection of small business, but they also perceived that vigorous attacks on the large and concentrated industries produced budgetary rewards to the agency. At the CAB, officials generally believed that the agency's budget was unaffected by its policies. With respect to perceived job prospects, proindustry policies were generally believed to lead to enhanced industry employment opportunities in the CAB and the NHTSA, antiindustry stance was perceived to be favorable to job prospects in the FTC, and the majority of respondents in the FDA believed that attitudes toward industry were irrelevant to their subsequent employment opportunities in industry. In sum, Quirk's study did not "provide an explanation of any overwhelming proindustry bias often attributed to regulatory agencies."[32]

---

[30]Paul J. Quirk, *Industry Influence in Federal Regulatory Agencies* (Princeton, N.J.: Princeton University Press, 1981), chaps. 1 and 6.

[31]Paul J. Quirk, *Industry Influence in Federal Regulatory Agencies.* Copyright © 1981 by Princeton University Press. (Princeton, N.J.: Princeton University Press, 1981), p. x.

[32]Ibid., pp. 175–77.

The phenomenon of industry protection by regulatory agencies could alternatively be explained by what Quirk calls the "nature of political environment" or the "configuration of groups and interests that are attentive to and seek to influence agency decision making."[33] Regulatory agencies must strike a balance between the particular interests of the regulated industry and the general interest of the nonindustry public. It is easy to say that agencies should aim at the general interests as a matter of principle, and concern themselves with the particular interests of the regulated industry only to the extent that the latter do not conflict with the former. Such a principle tends to be set aside in the concrete, face-to-face relationships between agency officials and industry lobbyists; these relationships tend to be, by the very nature of lobbying activities, close personally and/or professionally. Thus, it would not be surprising if there developed a frame of mind that affects the mental attitude of regulatory officials in such a way as to make them feel obligated to view the industry's particular interests as equally important as, if not more important than, those of the unseen and remote public. Since the nonindustry public whose general interest is compromised tends to be unorganized, agency officials find it possible to bend over backward and accommodate to the needs of the industry to a considerable extent without generating negative public reactions.[34]

Beyond the regulatory agencies' policy incentives and political environment, industry influence over regulatory agencies also derives from the appointment process of regulators. In the preliminary stages of identifying and selecting potential nominees, the regulated industry is almost always given opportunities to express its preferences on proposed commissioners, propose its own nominees, and reject unacceptable nominees. By contrast, views of consumers and public interest groups are seldom sought at this stage; their inputs are solicited only at the confirmation hearings at the Senate, at which point rejecting a given nominee is naturally very difficult. There thus exists a gross imbalance in participation between the regulated firms and the general public in the process of determining who, ostensibly, are to regulate the industry "in the public interest."[35]

QUESTIONS

1. What is meant by the statement, "Organized business, as such, does not exist in the United States"?

[33]Ibid., p. 13.

[34]Ibid.

[35]Herman, *Corporate Control*, p. 180.

2. Discuss the relationships between government and business in the United States today. Which dominates which? How are their respective decisions coordinated?

3. Where did the impetus for U.S. antitrust policy come from?

4. Discuss the four stages or degrees of the market economy in terms of the role of government in the economic sphere. Which stages has the U.S. economy gone through, and at which stage is it now? What are the prospects of it moving to the next phase?

5. Identify the stage(s) to which each of the following descriptions of government fits most appropriately: (a) silent partner, (b) active partner-collaborator, (c) referee-judge, (d) orchestrator, (e) interested bystander, and (f) stabilizer-promoter.

6. What was the nature of the transformation that took place in American capitalism as a consequence of the New Deal programs?

7. What role did Keynesian economics play in the transformation of American capitalism? Do you agree with the critics of Keynesian economics who argued that it was a presciption for socialism?

8. Explain the difference between the broader and the narrower definitions of the term *government regulation* as it is used in the United States.

9. List and explain the exceptions to the general rule that the market system produces optimal results. Do not limit your answer to the question of allocative efficiency.

10. Why is it not possible for the market mechanism to provide an adequate quantity of public goods? If the market cannot be relied on for provisions of public goods, how do we find out what and how much of public goods society needs?

11. Why must government be involved in society's allocative choices wherever significant externalities are present? Does this mean that problems of externalities would be nonexistent if government decision making totally replaced private decision making? Is there no pollution in the Soviet Union?

12. What are the main sources of economic inequalities in the United States and the Soviet Union? In which society do you think inequities are relatively greater?

13. What is the essential difference between fiscal and monetary policy, on the one hand, and industrial policy, on the other? Does the United States now have an industrial policy?

14. In this chapter the terms *industrial policy* and *economic planning* are used interchangeably. Do you think the two terms have different meanings.? If so, what exactly is the difference between the two as used within the context of a capitalist, market-oriented economy?

15. Discuss the difference between *fiscal policy* and *monetary policy* as they are practiced in the United States, by referring to the distinction made by Robert Solo between *composite choice* and *authoritative choice*.

16. Do you think it would be possible to minimize the degree of politicization of fiscal policy in the United States by entrusting it to a newly created

independent federal agency? What legal, political, and ideological problems do you foresee such a proposal would face?

17. What do you think would be the nature of fiscal, monetary, industrial, and antitrust policies in the Soviet Union? Does the Soviet Union have these policies?

18. What, according to Andrew Shonfield, is the "real impediment to planning" in the United States? What kind of planning did Shonfield have in mind? Are any other types of national economic planning feasible or conceivable for the United States?

19. Why would the Japanese-style industrial policy (of promoting sunshine industries and phasing out sunset industries) be unworkable in the United States? Do you agree with the points made by Charles Schultze and Senator William Proxmire?

20. What kind of industrial policy, if any, would be workable in the United States?

21. In Chapter 1 we defined an *organization* as a social system in which actions of the participants are coordinated with purpose. What is the nature of *industrial organization* in the United States? Is American industry "organized" in the above-mentioned sense? How does the organization of American industry differ from the ways in which Soviet industry is organized?

22. List and explain the ways in which American corporations can achieve intraindustry communication and coordination. What role does the federal government play in this process?

23. How prevalent is the practice of interlocking directorates among the major U.S. corporations? How does the practice affect the quality of intercorporate coordination?

24. Discuss the differences in the nature of American and Soviet interest groups.

25. Discuss the differences in the modus operandi of American and Japanese pressure groups. How does the role of big business interests differ in the two countries?

26. Summarize Mancur Olson's arguments leading to the conclusion that successfully organized interest groups are by their very nature antisocial. Under what circumstances can there be calculated individual action in the collective interest? Why can there not be successfully organized large voluntary groups serving the interests of consumers or taxpayers?

27. What are the implications of Olson's arguments to the desirability of allowing interest-group activities in a democratic society? More fundamentally, what are the implications of his arguments to the viability of parliamentary democracy combined with a free-market system?

28. How effectively are lobbying activities regulated in the United States? What loopholes exist in the present law regarding lobbying groups and their activities? Why can lobbying activities not be banned outright? Should they be?

29. What benefits do lobbyists and legislators derive from lobbying activities?

30.   What did Paul Quirk's study of industry influence over regulatory agencies find? In what ways does the appointment process of regulators create an additional element of proindustry bias?

SELECTED READING

DEWAR, MARGARET E., Ed. *Industrial Vitalization: Toward a National Industrial Policy*. Elmsford, N.Y.: Pergamon Press, 1982.

GALBRAITH, JOHN KENNETH. *The New Industrial State* (2nd ed.). Boston: Houghton Mifflin Company, 1971.

HERMAN, EDWARD S. *Corporate Control, Corporate Power*, A Twentieth Century Fund Study, chaps. 4, 5, and 6. Cambridge: Cambridge University Press, 1981.

OLSON, MANCUR. *The Rise and Decline of Nations: Economic Growth, Stagflation, and Social Rigidities*. New Haven, Conn.: Yale University Press, 1982.

ORNSTEIN, NORMAN J., and SHIRLEY ELDER. *Interest Groups, Lobbying and Policymaking*. Washington, D.C.: Congressional Quarterly Press, 1978.

QUIRK, PAUL J. *Industry Influence in Federal Regulatory Agencies*. Princeton, N.J.: Princeton University Press, 1981.

REICH, ROBERT B. *The Next American Frontier*. New York: Times Books, 1983.

SHEPHERD, WILLIAM G., and CLAIR WILCOX. *Public Policies toward Business* (6th ed.). Homeword, Ill.: Richard D. Irwin, Inc., 1979.

SHONFIELD, ANDREW. *Modern Capitalism: The Changing Balance of Public and Private Power*. New York and London: Oxford University Press, 1965.

SOLO, ROBERT A. *The Political Authority and the Market System*. Cincinnati, Ohio: South-Western Publishing Co., 1974.

CHAPTER **8**

The American Economy: Corporate Organization and Management

In the preceding chapter we saw how American industry is organized, how the U.S. government attempts to inject society's collective preferences into the nation's economic activities by means of public policies and regulations, and how private interest groups and wielders of public power join hands in promoting their shared interests. In this chapter we shall examine the other important aspect of the organizational nature of the American economic system: the question of internal organization and control of the large American corporation.

The goals and motivations of each of the constituent groups within a corporation, their relationships to each other, and how choices are made by key groups, are central to our understanding of the behavior of the corporate sector of the economy. Inquiries into these factors would not be necessary or fruitful if all private enterprises were small, individually owned firms. If that were the case, the firms' decisions would simply reflect the rational pursuit of profits by the individual entrepreneurs, and the profit motive would provide us with the clue to understanding the behavior of firms and industries. A large corporation, however, cannot be treated as a homogeneous unit with a single and common ideology and interest. It is a community consisting of diverse groups of people with different, and often conflicting, ideologies, interests, and expectations. Power relations that develop among these groups often resemble those found in groups in larger society. Thus, for a better understanding of the American economic system and how it differs from other systems, we must first examine the relationships among the various interest groups within a large American corporation and how these relationships are linked to those that exist among groups in the larger societal setting.

In this chapter our attention will first be focused on the question of who controls the large corporation and what purposes are being served by those who are in control. We shall then turn to the questions of the organizational structure and the styles of management in the American corporation.

CHARACTERISTICS OF THE AMERICAN CORPORATION

According to neoclassical economic theory, an economy is made up of a large number of individually owned and managed firms. Both the goals and motivations of these entrepreneurial firms are identical with those of the entrepreneur-owner. In today's American economy, this form of business ownership, though widespread, is relatively unimportant in terms of both output and employment. The bulk of the nation's productive activity has come under the control of several hundred large corporations that wield great economic and political power. In 1977, the largest 200 industrial corporations accounted for about 34 percent of value added by manufacturers and 44 percent of employment in manufacturing industries.[1] In 1982, the 500 largest industrial corporations had combined sales of $1,672 billion, which was roughly equal in size to a half of the gross national product of the country.[2]

A fundamental fact of modern capitalism is that these large corporations are not *firms* in the textbook sense of having the unified will, goal, motivation, and self-interest of an individual owner. Rather, they are communities of sorts with a large number of individual members who are related to each other in a complex pattern of organizational interactions. The corporate organizational sector in the United States has the following salient characteristics.

First, corporate property has lost much of its "privateness." Corporate assets that have been created out of steady accumulation of retained corporate earnings have acquired a semiprivate, semipublic

---

[1] U.S. Bureau of the Census, *Census of Manufactures, 1977, Concentration in Manufacturing,* MC77-SR-9.

[2] *Fortune,* May 2, 1983, p. 227.

character. Although shareholders have a legal title to shares of corporate assets and their earnings, they nevertheless have no actual power to make decisions concerning the utilization and/or disposition of the assets. If the shareholders do not approve the ways in which their assets are managed, their only recourse is to sell their shares—unless, of course, they could buy up a majority ownership share of the corporation and assume its control. In this sense, corporate property is much like public property in a modern democracy. Citizens have a collective "title" to all the public property in the country, but they have no rights, as individuals, to take possession of the "shares" of public assets. Public property is managed by government officials who do not own it, but are entrusted by the voting public with the task of managing it. In a similar manner, the "private" property of the corporation is controlled by a group of professional managers serving as trustees for the legal owners. This quasi-public nature of corporate property and its management by nonowner managers has resulted in the widely recognized phenomenon of *separation of ownership from control.*

Second, the large size of the corporation necessarily means that the number of individuals involved in all aspects of the firm's operations is large. There develop various groups within the corporate organization with diverse and often conflicting values, interests, and motivations. Actions and counteractions, pressures and counterpressures, and power struggles among the constituent groups in the organization shape the character of the corporation's behavior. Groups may be related to each other in a hierarchical manner, with some groups having power over others. Groups may engage in intrafirm politics and lobbying in an attempt to influence the decision-making processes of the controlling power group. Seen in this light, a large corporate organization as a community of interests is not much different from a nation-state in its organizational structure and behavioral patterns.

Third, in a large corporation there exists a sharp division of labor among its members. The modern technology involved in production, distribution, financing, marketing, and other functions of a large corporation is highly complex and specialized. To perform each of these functions adequately, the corporation must employ a large number of specialists working in groups and in cooperation with one another and with other groups. The crucial fact about the diversity and depth of these specialized skills and knowledge is that no individual person, however talented or experienced he or she may be, can comprehend all the important dimensions of all of the enterprise's activities. Most decisions in the corporate organization, therefore, must be made by groups of specialists who have the requisite information, skills, and experience in their narrow area of expertise. Other groups and individuals—including those at the highest echelon of management—must defer to the opinions and judgment of the specialists. The decision-making power in a large corporate organization is thus widely dispersed, and the power of top management is not absolute.

WHO CONTROLS THE AMERICAN CORPORATION?

The existence of diverse groups of individuals in a modern corporation raises the question of who, or what group, exercises effective power of decision making in the corporation. In the neoclassical world of atomistic competition, it was taken for granted that a business firm was controlled by its owner-entrepreneur. In the complex world of large, modern corporations, it is no longer possible to identify any single individual or group of individuals as the wielders of ultimate power. In a narrow, legal sense, effective control does, or should, reside with the board of directors, which is legally entrusted with the responsibility of safeguarding and promoting the shareholders' property and income interests in the corporation. Persuasive arguments have been made, however, that effective power of control lies in top management and/or the technical-professional staff. In this section we examine the relative power positions of the board, the top management, and the staff of subordinate managers.

Separation of Ownership from Control

In the landmark study *The Modern Corporation and Private Property* published in 1932, institutional economists Adolph Berle and Gardiner Means demonstrated, for the first time, that ownership of corporations had become divorced from control, and that large corporations were managed by professional managers who had insignificant stock holdings in the firms they managed.[3] Their findings spawned what has come to be known as the Managerial Revolution. This revolution represents a radical departure in our understanding of how business enterprises are controlled and to what ends. The managerial control thesis—often referred to as *managerialism*—in its most simplistic but widely accepted form, runs as follows.

As corporations raise large sums of funds by selling shares of stock, their ownership becomes widely dispersed. Very large corporations may have hundreds of thousands of shareholders. Thus, even though some

[3]Adolph Berle and Gardiner Means, *The Modern Corporation and Private Property* (New York: Macmillan Company, 1932).

large blocks of shares may be held by some individuals and institutions, these blocks are not likely to constitute more than a small fraction of the total shares of outstanding stocks. One effect of the wide dispersion of voting shares is to give effective control of the corporation to its management team. The managers solicit proxy votes from shareholders and cast them in annual meetings ostensibly for the absentee shareholders. The management almost always has enough proxies to override any proposals presented to the meetings by outside groups. This ability to control the outcomes of shareholders' meetings gives the management the right to appoint directors of its choice. Legally, the board of directors of a corporation represents the interests of the shareholders who elect it. The board hires professional managers whose duties are to manage the day-to-day operations of the corporation. In reality, however, directors are often handpicked by the management. Frequently, top managers appoint themselves as directors, and have the appointments approved at a shareholders' meeting. The upshot is that paid managers of corporations, particularly very large corporations with a large number of dispersed shareholders, come to enjoy almost complete autonomy, and perpetuate themselves through cooptation. They tend to regard the shareholders merely as one of the several constituencies of the corporation whose claims must be balanced against those of other constituent groups such as workers and customers. This, in a nutshell, is the managerial control thesis.

In the early stages of the development of managerial capitalism in the United States, ownership interests of large stockholders and the interests of bankers and other financiers were dominant at the highest level of corporate management. As firms grew larger, however, large stockholders representing family and financial interests receded into the background. Companies grew too large and complex for any owner family or creditor institution to retain effective control. Only professional managers had the requisite specialized knowledge for managing complex organizations. Many firms became large enough to generate huge sums of funds internally for capital expansion without much reliance on external sources. These developments resulted in a gradual but irreversible shift in the power of strategic decision making from large stockholders and financial institutions to a group of professional managers.[4]

In 1974, of the 200 largest nonfinancial corporations in the United States, some 81 percent were directly controlled by the management group having less than 5 percent ownership interest in the corporation. (In over three quarters of these corporations, the management group

[4]Alfred D. Chandler, Jr., and Herman Daems, eds., *Managerial Hierarchies: Comparative Perspectives on the Rise of Modern Industrial Enterprise* (Cambridge, Mass.: Harvard University Press, 1980), p. 13.

had less than 1 percent stock ownership.) Minority ownership control, including control by intercorporate owners, existed in 16.5 percent of the 200 firms, while majority ownership (50 percent or more) control was found in 1.5 percent of the corporations.[5] These statistics indicate a sharp upward trend in management control. Roughly comparable figures showing percentages of very large corporations under management control were 24 percent in 1900–1901 and 41 percent in 1929.[6]

What difference does it make whether a corporation is managed by owner-entrepreneur or professional managers? Presumably a great deal. Corporate objectives and behavior depend largely on who has effective control over key management decisions. Since the objectives, behavior, and performance of large corporations are the major determinants of the character of the nation's economic system, the question of how far managerial and corporate behavior departs from the traditional assumption of profit maximization becomes crucial in our understanding of the nature of the American economic system. Entrepreneur-managers, being themselves owners of the enterprise and hence direct beneficiaries of the firm's earnings, naturally are eager to maximize the earnings. Professional corporate managers without significant ownership interests, however, may not be primarily interested in maximum profits. According to the postulates of managerialism, hired corporate managers may pursue such goals as sales or growth maximization, job security, or the "quiet life," even at the expense of earnings. This important question of managerial objectives will be discussed further in the following sections.

Top Management versus the Board of Directors

We noted earlier that 81 percent of the 200 largest nonfinancial corporations in the United States in 1974 were controlled by management groups with limited ownership interests. How can this fact be reconciled with the legal stipulation that accords key decision-making power to the board of directors? We have already noted that through the effective use of the proxy mechanism, the management can establish managerial dominance over the dispersed ownership interests. Using this mechanism, the inside management can not only appoint its own members on the board but can also exercise a great deal of discretion and choice in selecting "outside" board members. Furthermore, beyond the power to select board members, the management has powers to

---

[5]Edward S. Herman, *Corporate Control, Corporate Power*, A Twentieth Century Fund Study (Cambridge: Cambridge University Press, 1981), pp. 56–57, table 3.1.

[6]Ibid., p. 66.

influence—often decisively—the decision-making processes of the board, as we shall see subsequently.

Concerning the relationship between the management and the board, it is worth noting that domination of the board is not necessary for an effective control of the corporation. A management group can exercise effective control, without representation on the board, merely by controlling the proxy mechanism. In such a case, the board is likely to be subordinate to the management. Thus, a board of directors that has both nominal and real power over the management is likely to exist only in rare cases where large (majority) shareholder(s) *choose* to be represented on the board without actively participating in management. In a great majority of corporations, whether controlled by the inside management or by the minority owners, dominance of the management over the board is the rule.

The spirit of the law designating directors as fiduciaries of shareholder interests is compromised by the practice of placing active managers on the board. Conversely, the intent of the law is better served by efforts to increase the proportion of outside directors on a given board. Perhaps as an answer to the mounting criticism of managerial domination of corporate boards, many corporations have in the past decades increased the number of outside directors on their boards. Between 1938 and 1976, the proportion of manufacturing firms having a majority of outside directors rose from 50 percent to 83 percent.[7] In 1975, 56 percent of the directors of the 100 largest industrial corporations in the United States were "outside" directors in the sense that they were not managers in the same corporation on whose board they served.[8] Does this rising proportion of outside directors reflect a weakening trend of managerial domination over the board? The answer is negative. According to Edward Herman, the following factors help preserve the power of the inside management relative to the board of directors.[9]

In the vast majority of corporations under managerial control, outside board members are normally chosen by the inside managers, often by the chief executive, on the basis of their potential usefulness to the management. Those whose attitude is considered to be friendly, helpful, and cooperative are sought. Outsiders are "invited" by the top management to serve on the board; thus "board criticism of the corporate leadership violates the laws of hospitality."[10] Troublemakers who do not observe the "rule of board of behavior" will be quickly eased out. "It is also considered bad form to ask questions that imply doubt about

[7]Ibid., p. 35.

[8]Ibid., p. 39, table 2.5.

[9]Ibid., pp. 23–48.

[10]Ibid., p. 31.

motives, competence, and honesty; or to ask serious questions and make challenges out of the blue. . . ."[11]

Another factor that tends to mitigate the effectiveness of outside board members as corporate watchdogs is the complexity of the problems they must deal with. The inside managers monopolize the pertinent information on the company's operations, and they are often secretive about it. Outsiders, therefore, are often compelled to refrain from poking their noses into the corporate affairs for fear of looking foolish or critical.

In 1975, 44 percent of the directors of the 100 largest industrial corporations were inside directors, and about a third of these firms had boards having an insider majority.[12] These relatively small proportions grossly understate the power of the insiders relative to that of outside directors. To protect their job security and enlarge their power of control over the corporation, inside (manager-) directors tend to stick together, protect each other, and generally "vote as a solid, unified block under the direction of top management."[13] This political advantage, combined with the advantage of technical knowledge about the company's operations, give the inside manager-directors overwhelming power relative to the outside directors.

We reported earlier that in 1975, 56 percent of the directors of the 100 largest industrial corporations in the United States were classified as "outside" directors. Edward Herman points out that the "outsideness" of many of these directors was questionable. The group included a large number of retired former insiders, relatives and personal friends of key insiders, and those who were affiliated with another firm having significant business relationships with the firm in question. Herman concludes that when these "outsiders" of questionable "outsideness" were subtracted, the proportion of outside directors of the 100 largest industrial corporations in 1975 was more likely to be "well below a quarter of the total."[14]

So what roles do outside directors play in large management-controlled corporations? Are they passive and compliant robots providing a cover of respectability and legitimacy to the exercise of real power by top management? Not exactly. A large proportion of outside directors represent important external constituencies of the corporation, often having business and financial relationships. For example, a major creditor bank or an important customer may be represented on the board. Even though these directors may be passive under normal circum-

[11]Ibid., pp. 47–48.

[12]Ibid., p. 36, table 2.2, and p. 39, table 2.5

[13]Ibid., p. 37.

[14]Ibid., p. 45.

stances, they may become active in response to financial or managerial crises with which the inside management group cannot cope effectively. Outside board members representing financial or creditor interests are particularly likely to assume active roles in corporate exigencies because the relative power of the insiders is weakened by the financial difficulties. As long as the inside management team is performing competently, however, the power of the outside directors remains latent, and "the board serves as the locus of some of the forces that influence managerial ideology and constrain management power."[15]

Top Management versus the Technostructure

In his 1967 book *The New Industrial State*, John Kenneth Galbraith coined the term *technostructure* to refer to professionals and specialists in large bureaucratic organizations.[16] That there are a number of power loci in a large management-controlled corporation is a well-established premise accepted by most observers of contemporary American capitalism. What is less widely accepted, however, is Galbraith's contention that the center of power tends to move down from top management to the technostructure.[17] The generally held view is that the power wielded by top management, although constrained, far surpasses that of any other groups in the organization.

It is true that most of the day-to-day operational decisions and even some of the long-range, strategic decisions cannot be made by top managers alone without the benefit of the highly specialized technical knowledge, skills, and experience of the technostructure. But the power wielded by specialists is by nature a specific and partial power relative only to some specific aspects of corporate activities. Only the top managers, by virtue of their strategic positions, are capable of making major decisions over a wide spectrum of corporate activities. The relative power positions of the top management and the technostructure, therefore, can be described as the difference between the general and strategic, on the one hand, and the specific and technical, on the other.

In virtually all of America's large corporations, the corporate office is separated, functionally and often geographically, from the corporation's operating divisions. Those senior executives who work in the corporate headquarters are seldom involved in the day-to-day operations

---

[15]Ibid., pp. 31–32.

[16]John Kenneth Galbraith, *The New Industrial State*, 2nd ed. (Boston: Houghton Mifflin Company, 1971), pp. 70–71.

[17]Ibid., p. 69.

of the company's business. (These are the responsibilities of division managers and their staffs.) Instead, the corporate managers' primary responsibilities center on making *strategic* decisions for the corporation. These decisions have to do with making choices about how to achieve the goals of the corporation. Specifically, strategic decisions entail "choices of products, major markets, volume and direction of investment, larger commercial and political strategies, and selection of top personnel."[18] In other words, top management's chief responsibility is to determine the direction of the company's development. Top management, not the technostructure, is the brain of the organization.

Top management's power relative to that of the technostructure is further enhanced by the fact that top managers have power to make personnel decisions (including hiring, firing, promotion, and compensation) of those in the subordinate managerial ranks. Middle managers are keenly aware that their job security, chances of promotion, and eventual cooptation into the ranks of top management depend largely on how well they internalize the ideology and expectations of top managers. There thus develops a structure of dependency of subordinate managers on top managers, which provides another source of power to the latter.

There is another important source of power of top management, a source that is normally beyond the reach of middle managers. As discussed earlier in this chapter, top management in a typical management-controlled company solidifies its power base by having effective control over the process of selecting members of the board of directors and over the board's decision-making processes. The power of top management that derives primarily from the authority and status of the officer positions of its members is reinforced by the legal power of stock ownership. Top managers almost always can, whereas middle managers cannot, claim that their power is legitimate not only because they are appointed to the positions of authority by the board, but also because they themselves, as members of the board, are legal protectors of ownership interests.

We may conclude that even though there may exist a number of power loci within a corporation, only the top management group may be called a true power center. Various specialist groups within the corporate organization, as well as other constituencies both inside and outside the organization, no doubt exert constraining influences on top management's decision-making processes. However, the goals of the organization, its developmental strategy, its behavior and performance, and its internal discipline and morale—all these are decisively determined largely by what top managers say and do. The ideology of an

---

[18]Herman, *Corporate Control*, p. 19.

American corporation is defined, by and large, by the ideology of the top management group. In short, "those at the top call the tune, [and] set the parameters within which choices are made."[19]

CORPORATE GOALS AND STRATEGY

In Chapter 1, we noted that the definition of an *organization* implies that its activities are *coordinated* with a *purpose*. What, then, is the purpose or objective of the American corporation? How are the goals of a corporation related to its strategy? How are the goals and strategy related to the corporate ideology? Who or what groups of people establish and develop strategy? These questions are crucial to our understanding of the behavior of the American corporation.

In Chapter 2 we defined an *ideology* as a complex of ideas, beliefs, and attitudes that guides choice and action. A corporation, being a social organization, is guided in its choice and action by its own ideology. In the literature on U.S. corporate organization and management, corporate ideology is also referred to as *corporate philosophy, corporate values*, and *corporate belief systems*. In this book, all these terms are used interchangeably.

Ideologies do not exist in isolation as abstract principles. Rather, they are embodied in, and reflected by, the thought processes, choices, and actions of the various constituent groups within the organization. There may exist numerous ideological configurations inside a corporate organization, but the dominant ideology of a given corporation, by definition, is that of the controlling power group.

A *strategy* is a grand design for implementing an organization's objective; it outlines a unified direction and often implies a competitive posture toward rival organizations. A strategy consists of a group of policies aimed at propelling the organization in a given direction that is in accord with its objectives. For example, an automobile manufacturing firm's strategy for achieving the objective of profitable growth may include such policies as producing only larger cars domestically, importing smaller cars from overseas subsidiaries, lobbying in Washington for import restrictions, introducing a participatory management style, and improving the quality of products by increased use of industrial robots.

Strategy, goals, and ideology are closely interwoven. Different goals call for different strategies. Goals are determined by ideologies, and choice of strategies is constrained by the ideological orientation of the organization. Even the questions of who sets the goals and chooses

[19]Ibid., p. 28.

strategy, and how the goals and strategy are determined, are the functions of ideology.

Strategies and goals are formed by the group within the corporate organization that wields effective power of control. As discussed earlier, effective decision-making power in the American corporation usually resides with the top management group, with a varying degree of identification with, and control over, the ownership interests. The question of the goals and strategy of the American corporation, therefore, is largely a question of the ideology and motivation of top management.

The Goals of the American Corporation

In the earlier chapters on the Soviet economy, we observed that the primary objective of the Soviet industrial enterprise is to maximize the quantity of output. By contrast, it is commonly accepted that the primary goal of a capitalist enterprise is to make money. Western neoclassical economics is based on the assumption that the ultimate goal of private enterprise is to maximize profits. However, the development of the theory of the autonomous management group that is divorced from ownership interests has produced a series of new hypotheses of management goals and motivations. Emphasized are such unconventional objectives as growth in sales volume or corporate size, maximization of executives' perquisites, and achieving a "satisficing" level of profits. Galbraith, for example argues that the technostructure regards growth in sales revenues as the primary goal of its organization. According to him, the members of the technostructure are more interested in improving their own chances of promotion and salary increases through the growth of their company than in maximizing profits for remote and faceless shareholders.[20]

The technostructure may very well be more interested in growth than in profits. But, as we saw in the preceding section, the effective power of strategic control in large U.S. corporations resides with top management, not with the technical and professional staff. And, as we shall see later, the primary objective of top management is more closely tied to the ownership interests in growth of earnings than to the organizational interests in growth per se.

Growth and profits are complementary goals. Growth means greater economies of scale and competitive strength, which lead to greater earnings, which in turn enable the firm to grow further. Maximum profits in reality mean maximum growth of earnings over time, and earnings are not likely to grow much unless the company's scale of operations

---

[20]Galbraith, *The New Industrial State,* pp. 171–72.

also grows. The most commonly used measure of corporate performance in America today is improvement in earnings per share. And in the highly competitive environment of product and technological innovations in the U.S. business today, firms cannot expect to experience steady growth in earnings per share unless they constantly expand and grow both qualitatively and quantitatively. Edward Herman sums up this widely held view by stating that *"profitable growth* is a reasonable summary of the primary objective of the large managerial corporation today."[21] *Profitable growth* is a more flexible concept than *profit maximization.* In Herman's words, "It does not assume that the quest for profits is always of constant, unremittingly high intensity but may vary from maximizing to satisficing or worse, depending on challenges, pressures, and individual or organizational special circumstances; and it stresses the expansive and nonstatic nature of the profit quest."[22]

Top management's interest in profits is heightened by the widespread practice of tying managerial compensations to earnings performance. Managerial bonuses are often tied to improvements in earnings per share and/or in stock prices. *Stock options* permit managers to exercise their options to purchase their own company's shares from the company at a predetermined price. Thus, rising stock prices bring handsome capital gains to successful managers.

Stock prices play an extremely important role in managerial motivation and behavior. Not only are they important in affecting the size of managerial incomes through bonuses and stock option plans, but they also influence the financial health of the company and thus ultimately affect the job security and mobility of the executives. Low and declining earnings adversely affect the company's stock prices, which in turn make external financing difficult and expensive. Healthy stock prices are regarded as a sign of the capital market's approval of the ways in which the company is managed. Higher stock prices also keep the stockholders happy and contented. Ownership interests, including outside directors, are less likely to challenge the autonomy of the inside management that is successful in keeping the shareholders happy by paying satisfactory dividends and assuring steadily rising share prices.

Furthermore, healthy stock prices are the best protection against takeover bids. When the share price is depressed below its asset value (i.e., the total market value of the outstanding stock falls below the total market value of the company's assets), an outside interest may be tempted to make a merger bid or a takeover bid in order to acquire the assets at a cost below their market value. A *takeover bid* is an offer to acquire the outstanding shares of the company's stock from the public at a price

[21]Herman, *Corporate Control,* p. 86. Herman's italics.

[22]Ibid., p. 353, note 37.

above the market price. If enough shareholders take advantage of the offer, the existing management may lose its control over the corporation. In both merger and takeover cases, but more assuredly in the latter, there is a high probability that the incumbent top management will suffer wholesale dismissal. Potential takeover raiders usually look for a company that is doing poorly in profits but has a good prospect of high earnings under a new and aggressive management with a radically different set of corporate strategies. The best defense against a takeover raid, therefore, is a record of high earnings—not only because it makes the cost of a takeover high (by making the stock price high), but also because it reduces the likelihood of a sharp profit increase after the takeover.

Yet another reason why managers tend to identify themselves with ownership interests and high earnings is suggested by Herman. In relative terms, the holdings by officers of the voting stock of their companies are rather small. In 1975, in 73.5 percent of the 200 largest nonfinancial companies, top officers on the board held less than 0.5 percent of their companies' voting stock.[23] In qualitative terms, however, these holdings may have been very significant to their owners. As Herman points out, "small percentages of ownership in very large companies can amount to large absolute values and possibly large fractions of the personal wealth of the officers."[24] In December 1974, individual officer-directors of the 100 largest industrial corporations had, on average, nearly $1 million in their company stock.[25] Few managers would be disinterested in the market value of a stock holding of this magnitude. They would naturally like to see the value of their stock appreciate, and the quickest and surest way of making that happen is to improve the earnings of the corporations they control.

Profitable growth is also pursued by managers for the sake of enhancing their reputation among professional colleagues and in the business community at large. Improved reputation also means improved marketability of their talent and enlarged future earnings potential. It is an undeniable fact that the performance of top-level U.S. corporate executives is measured, first and foremost, by their earnings record. Profitless growth and expensive policies and practices that lead to little earnings enhancement are frowned upon, and generally detract from the practitioners' performance record.

One aspect of corporate managers' motivation has to do with their game-playing instinct. Many top-level executives in large American cor-

[23]Ibid., p. 92.
[24]Ibid., p. 93.
[25]Ibid.

porations view their jobs primarily as contests of wits. Their native urge to compete, desire to excel, and desire to win drive them incessantly toward achieving bigger and better goals that are almost always measured in some numerical terms. Michael Maccoby in his 1976 book *The Gamesman* identified four character types of American corporate executives: the craftsman, the jungle fighter, the company man, and the gamesman. Maccoby found that at the highest level of corporate management, the gamesman is the most frequently found character type. The gamesman's main interest lies in organizing a successful campaign, making deals, taking calculated risks, and leading the corporate team to victory. In short, the gamesman practices management as though he were a quarterback in a football game. He loves to win, and detests being labeled a loser.[26] Profits in the context of corporate game playing become important for two reasons. First, they are the best measure of success, of winning. Second, they provide the game players with larger and better resources to play with. In this context, whether or not profits accrue individually to the managers is of lesser concern.

In summary, one can make a rather convincing a priori case for the proposition that top management has a relatively keener interest in profitable growth than in growth per se. Whereas Galbraith is undoubtedly right in his observation that the technostructure is primarily interested in growth per se, top management, because of its strategic position of power and control in the corporate organization, is of necessity more strongly attracted to the financial aspects of the corporation's performance. This relatively greater concern for profits is not attributable to the managers' interest in maximizing the wealth entrusted to them by the shareholders. Rather, it is traceable to a complex of motivations including enhanced personal earnings, increased job security and marketability, enhanced professional reputation among their peers, greater independence from interference by dissident stockholders, greater freedom from the threats of unfriendly takeovers, and greater freedom to play the corporate game as they like it.

The Preoccupation with Short-Term Earnings

The prevailing strategy of the great majority of large American corporations in the mid-1980s can be described by such terms as *bottom-line orientation, emphasis on the return on investment, management by the numbers,* and *obsession with short-term earnings.* The essential nature

---

[26]Michael Maccoby, *The Gamesman: The New Corporate Leaders* (New York: Simon & Schuster, 1976).

of this strategy is to regard a corporation not as a community of people but as a money-making machine or a portfolio of assets from which as much profit as possible is to be squeezed. Top management people are eager to show "results," which usually mean growth in earnings per share (the "bottom-line" figures) from one accounting period (a quarter or a fiscal year) to another.

In an article entitled "Managing Our Way to Economic Decline" published in 1980, Robert Hayes and William Abernathy strongly criticized what they called the "new principles of management." According to the authors, these principles encouraged a dependence on the theories of financial portfolio management as primary means of evaluating the performance of a corporation. Parts of a corporation—divisions, departments, plants, and product lines—are viewed not as clusters of human activities but merely as different types of assets—like bonds, stocks, and real estate—and, as such, their usefulness to the corporation is measured solely by their contributions to the firm's short-term earnings.[27]

What is wrong, one may ask, with trying to maximize returns on corporate assets? Is it not, after all, what the corporate business is all about—maximizing the returns on stockholders' equity? The answers to these questions hinge on the nature of control over assets. According to the "new management principles," corporate assets are viewed not as machines, equipment, buildings, and investments in human capital, but rather as *financial* assets—that is, as dollars and cents. This preoccupation with tight financial controls inevitably leads to a neglect of engineering and production—the factory floor and the assembly line. Emphasis tends to shift away from research and development, innovations in products and production processes, and development of better working relations among people, to short-term cost savings. Sacrificed in this process is the long-term competitive health and vigor of the enterprise.

Preoccupation with financial controls would not in itself be detrimental to corporate health if it were not combined with emphasis on the short run. According to one 1980 survey, 15 to 25 percent of American executives left their jobs, each year, over the preceding 6 years, and the average length of service of chief executive officers was fewer than five years.[28] If managers remained in the same company for 10 or 15 years or longer, and if their performance were evaluated over a long pull,

---

[27]Robert Hayes and William Abernathy, "Managing Our Way to Economic Decline," *Harvard Business Review*, 58, no. 4 (July-August 1980), 67–77.

[28]Robert B. Reich, *The Next American Frontier* (New York: Times Books, 1983), p. 161.

then it would be difficult to treat divisions, companies, and product lines as just other types of assets. It would then be imperative that nonfinancial aspects of the organization's operations be made integral parts of its strategic plans. The immediate cause of the widespread practice of the misguided "new management principles," thus, is the ' absence of corporate executives' long-term commitment to the companies they manage.

The preoccupation with short-term results has deep roots in American sociocultural values. Corporations are not thought of by their managers (and workers) as communities of people who work toward common goals and share common interests over a long time period. With some notable exceptions, corporate managers of many of America's large companies want to receive quick and handsome rewards for their performance, and then move on to greener pastures. There is ordinarily little sense of sharing one's destiny with one's colleagues or one's place of work. Not only the managers but also the shareholders often regard their corporation as a money-making machine to be milked for quick results. With increasingly larger numbers of institutions becoming major shareholders, the emphasis on short-term financial results—evaluated by the growth of reported earnings—is becoming even stronger. As we discussed in a previous section, many executive performance plans are designed to reward short-term results, and pay executives cash or stock bonuses for meeting targets in growth of earnings per share or in return on assets. Managers who fail to show favorable short-term results are likely to suffer reduced incomes or loss of their jobs. Companies that fail to show improved earnings are likely to experience falling stock prices, making them vulnerable to shareholder revolts and takeover raids.

The American corporate manager's preoccupation with short-term financial performance has an interesting counterpart in the Soviet Union. As we saw in an earlier chapter on the Soviet economy, the director of a Soviet productive enterprise is preoccupied with the task of meeting monthly production quotas that are normally expressed in quantity terms. Since typical Soviet enterprise directors are likely to be transferred to new assignments in three to four years, they have little incentive in devoting time, efforts, and resources to quality, product assortment, product improvement, or profitability. They are more interested in showing quick and assured results in the form of larger output quantities. We find here a curious parallelism: both American and Soviet managers are playing the "numbers game." Only the content of the "numbers" is different between the two countries. In both cases, there is a conflict between the self-interest of individual managers and the collective interest of either the enterprise or society at large.

Managerial Career Tracks
and Paper Entrepreneurialism

It has been noted above that the short-run time horizon of typical American corporate executives is related to their career patterns. Unlike typical Japanese senior executives who spend their entire career in the same company, most American senior executives as a rule have gone through three or four jobs in different companies before they reach the level of senior management. They advance in both position and salary with each job change, and their major qualification for advancement is their "performance record" in previous positions. The "fast tracks" in the American corporate circles are traveled by bottom-line oriented superplayers of the numbers game.

Another aspect of the career patterns of American managers is worth noting. In the Soviet Union and France, senior executive positions of large enterprises are occupied mostly by those with engineering backgrounds. Even in Japan where liberal arts graduates are the most numerous among corporate managers, persons with technical backgrounds are well represented. For example, one study shows that, in the early 1980s, two-thirds of the top three executives of 24 leading Japanese manufacturers had science or engineering degrees. The same study shows that over two-thirds of the top three executives of 20 leading American manufacturing firms had backgrounds in law, accounting, and finance.[29]

The large number of lawyers, accountants, and financial analysts being represented among America's corporate managers is a relatively recent phenomenon. Prior to World War II, key corporate decision makers were largely those in production, engineering, and marketing. During the 25-year period between the early 1950s and the mid-1970s, the professional origins of the presidents of the 100 largest U.S. corporations showed a marked compositional change. The percentage share of financial and legal specialists increased by nearly 50 percent, while that of technical specialists decreased by about 15 percent.[30]

Unlike Japanese managers who are moved from one functional assignment to another and thus become thoroughly familiar with all the key functional areas of the company's operations by the time they reach the senior ranks, American managers are promoted within their narrowly specialized areas until they reach the top, at which level they

[29]Yoshi Tsurumi, "U.S. Managers Often 'Technically Illiterate' and Out of Touch," *Pacific Basin Quarterly*, Summer-Fall 1983, p. 12.

[30]Hayes and Abernathy, "Managing Our Way to Economic Decline," p. 75, exhibit 6.

become responsible for all the aspects of the company's operations. This single-track promotion system and the bias in favor of financial and legal staff functions has produced a large number of senior corporate executives who have little "hands-on" experience in production, engineering, and marketing. Effective decision-making power has shifted decisively from those in the line jobs to those in staff positions. This shift has been blamed for the supercautious management strategy that has contributed to the recent slowdown in technological innovations in U.S. industries.

The misguided emphasis on law and finance has produced a perversion of corporate strategy, which Robert Reich called "paper entrepreneurialism" in his 1983 book *The Next American Frontier*. By *paper entrepreneurs* Reich means those corporate manipulators of financial rules and tax laws who generate large profits on paper without creating any new wealth. Their favorite tactics include tax avoidance, financial manipulations, corporate takeovers, and lawsuits.[31] Paper entrepreneurialism is an extremely misguided form of what Hayes and Abernathy called the "new management principles." Although the exact extent of the contamination of the managements of America's major corporations by this malady has not been ascertained, casual empiricism seems to suggest that it is widespread and is doing a serious harm to the long-run health of the American economy.

ORGANIZATIONAL STRUCTURE

The nineteenth-century market economic system was characterized by competitive interaction among a large number of small, owner-managed firms. Resources were allocated largely by the "invisible hand" working through the market mechanism. The dominant actors in the markets were individual owner-entrepreneur-managers who directly controlled the firm's assets and workers.

Starting in the late nineteenth century and largely completed by the early twentieth century was the process of transformation of the economic system from one comprised chiefly of a large number of atomistic firms to one consisting of large-scale business enterprises characterized by hierarchical bureaucratic organization with multiple levels of management. Chandler and Daems point out that in the middle of the nineteenth century middle managers did not exist in America, but by 1975 one of every five American industrial workers was employed by a large, hierarchically structured enterprise with at least 6 layers of

[31]Reich, *The Next American Frontier*, chap. 8.

management.[32] In 1981, Ford Motor Company was operating with 12 levels of management.[33] In this section we shall examine the basic characteristics of the organizational structure of the large American corporation and the nature of the recent changes in that structure.

The Basic Organizational Principles

In analyzing the structure of a given social organization, a distinction must be made between formal and informal aspects of organization. The formal organization of a corporation is what is described in its organizational chart: the interrelationships of authority and responsibility between a series of positions. The informal organization, by contrast, can be identified only by observing the interpersonal and intergroup behavior of the members of the corporation. Examples of informal organization are cliques, friendship groups, and status groups. In what follows, our attention is focused on the formal aspect of corporate organization.

In the earlier chapters on the Soviet economy we observed that the formal aspects of the organization and management of the Soviet productive enterprise are not radically different from those found in American government and business bureaucracies. We shall find in subsequent chapters that the organizational structure of large Japanese corporations is also similar to that found in the rest of the industrial world. Because of the complexity of modern technology, the formal aspects of large-scale organizations tend to be similar in that they contain a large number of positions organized hierarchically into multiple layers of functional divisions and departments. The structure is pyramid-shaped, with formal decision-making authority running through the chain of command that starts at the top and extends down through several layers to the lowest operational level. This much is common in the organizational structure of large productive enterprises in any industrialized society; it is dictated by the imperatives of modern, complex technology and the attendant need for specialization of tasks and coordination among the specialized tasks.

Notwithstanding the superficial similarity between countries in the organizational structure, we find that the ways in which corporate organizations function differ markedly from country to country. These differences are particularly pronounced between business systems having dissimilar sociocultural backgrounds—say, between the American and Japanese systems.

[32]Chandler and Daems, *Managerial Hierarchies*, pp. 1 and 11.

[33]"A New Target: Reducing Staff and Levels," *Business Week*, December 21, 1981, p. 69.

Top management and its constituencies.   At the heart of the U.S. corporate organization is a team of senior executives reporting directly to the chief executive officer (CEO). In an important sense, this group— the top management—*is* the corporation. Here, of course, we are looking at the corporation from the point of view of real power relations, and not in the legal sense. The top management must balance the conflicting demands and needs of the various interest groups or constituencies of the corporation, while taking care of their own collective and individual interests.

The most important of the corporation's constituencies is the *organizational constituency*. This group consists of the members of the technostructure, or those professional-technical specialists occupying middle- and lower-level managerial positions. As a rule, the top management and its organizational constituency form the "insider" group within the corporate organization, although the "insideness" of managers in some companies is rather questionable. Other constituencies— workers, customers, suppliers, creditors, and shareholders—are "outsider" groups providing some services to the corporation in exchange for payments of some kind. All these constituencies have claims, more or less direct, on the fruit of the corporation's activities.

The distinction between the insiders and outsiders of a corporation is not a clear-cut, unequivocal one. It does, however, point to the rather significant difference in the way corporate organization is perceived in different countries. For example, in Japan's large corporations, insiders generally include managers at all levels as well as clerical and blue-collar employees. In U.S. corporations, by contrast, nonmanagerial employees and even some of lower-level managers do not, as a rule, enjoy a sense of belonging to their corporate organization.

Specialization of functions.   Managers in American corporations are almost always specialists in certain functions—accounting, personnel, engineering, marketing, law, data processing, and so forth—and crossing the functional lines during one's career is uncommon. This tendency for life-long specialization may have its origin in the tradition of crafts and guilds in old European societies. Whatever its roots are, the practice is reinforced by the system of higher education in the United States that trains and graduates a large number of specialists. Even liberal arts graduates tend to choose a specialization early on in their professional career, and stick with it throughout the career. Thus, it is very rare to find a generalist corporate manager who is comfortable in several functional areas. This notion of specialized functions is closely tied to the relative absence of a community feeling in the American corporation. A manager does not become a member of the corporate family and grow with it, as new recruits into a Japanese company do.

Rather, a managerial employee of an American corporation is first and foremost an individual specialist selling the services of his or her skills to the corporation. Often, the individual identifies more closely with his or her profession (accounting, law, data processing, and so on) than with the company in which he or she happens to be working.

Separation of line from staff.   Yet another important principle of American corporate organization is the distinction made between line and staff. The positions in an organization are linked to one another by *lines* of decision-making authority. These lines flow from top to bottom forming a chain of command. *Staff* positions may develop around line relationships: their main function is to provide advice and service to the line component of the organization. Staff may consist of assistants to the line managers, or of staff departments—for example, personnel or accounting—which themselves may have elaborate line and staff components.

Although in principle staff has no formal authority over the line positions, it may exercise limited authority within its own authorized staff function. For example, a line manager may not be able to acquire a piece of equipment for his or her department without a formal authorization by the head of the accounting department. In the 1960s and 1970s, staff positions in large U.S. corporations, particularly in the functional departments in corporate headquarters, acquired considerable decision-making power over line officers. As we noted in the preceding section, the expanded power and influence of the staff over the line managers has been blamed for the unhealthy preoccupation with short-term financial performance.

The concept of the manager.   Closely associated with the concept of line and staff is the notion of the *manager*. The manager is a person who occupies a position having authority over at least one other position. Corporate organization consists of a pyramid-shaped hierarchy of the positions or offices of managers. Each manager is supported by a staff of assistants. The chief executive officer employs several managers—both line and staff—who assist the CEO in getting his or her work done. These managers in turn have authority over their own subordinate managers, and so on down the line to the lowest levels of management. All of the authority ultimately resides with the CEO, who, because of the impossibility of any one person being knowledgeable about all the aspects of the organization's operations, finds it necessary to delegate part of the authority down the line to successively lower-level managers. The origin of this type of top-down management organization was, of course, the entrepreneur-owner who, in a very small business, could carry out all the tasks of the firm with but a few assistants.

The organizational principles of the typical American corporation that have been described above may seem perfectly normal and ordinary to those who are accustomed to American corporate organization, but they are by no means universal. We shall see in later chapters that the principles of organization of the Japanese corporation are quite different from their counterparts in the American corporation. Japanese corporations are organized bottom-up, rather than top-down as in America. Japanese managers are generalists who see little use in the line-staff distinction. The concept of a specialist manager occupying an office is alien to the Japanese; instead, they see a manager as a head of a work team. From the perspectives of these Japanese organizational principles, the American practices appear rather odd.

Bureaucratization and the Flexible Organizational Structure

The severe recessions of the early 1980s and the intensity of the Japanese competitive challenge led to a serious reexamination in many large U.S. corporations of their oversized and costly bureaucratic organization. People came to realize that the bureaucratic organization and overgrown staff structure were detrimental to innovation, productivity improvement, and risk taking. In the 1970s and early 1980s, many new products—notably computers and associated paraphernalia—were developed and marketed by new, small startup firms financed with venture capital. Unencumbered by large corporate overhead and bureaucratic red tape, these startup firms exhibited a great deal of the entrepreneurial spirit that had been absent in many of America's largest companies for some years. To recapture the entrepreneurial spirit in their product development efforts, some large corporations—General Electric, Xerox, 3M, Texas Instruments, and IBM, among others—built very small engineering units with considerable autonomy for carrying out product development from the concept stage to the feasibility stage. Engineers and managers in these mock-startup teams receive compensation, over and above their contractual amounts, in proportion to their contribution to corporate earnings. This approach of creating semiautonomous and quasi-entrepreneurial teams and task forces appears to be spreading to an increasingly larger number of American firms.[34]

In early 1984, General Motors announced an ambitious reorgani-

---

[34]"Big Business Tries to Imitate the Entrepreneurial Spirit," *Business Week*, April 18, 1983, pp. 84–88.

zation plan that would divide the mammoth corporate structure into two automobile manufacturing groups, one for larger cars combining the Cadillac, Oldsmobile, and Buick divisions, and the other for smaller cars consolidating the Pontiac, Chevrolet, and GM of Canada divisions. The decision-making authority of operations-level managers was greatly increased, as well as the performance-based bonuses as percent of managerial compensation, particularly at the higher level of management. When the reorganization is complete, the company's lead time on introduction of a new car is expected to be reduced from four to three years.[35]

GM's reorganization plan may very well be a harbinger of a new era of the American economic system in which productive activities will become centered on what Robert Reich calls the "flexible system of production." This system, according to Reich, will be based not on the traditional, standardized, high-volume, low-technology goods but rather on technology-driven, custom-tailored, design-oriented, and precision-engineered products developed and produced by widely scattered, small productive units with a highly entrepreneurial and innovative spirit. Firms in this production system would not only be much smaller than the traditional manufacturing firms but would also have a highly integrated system of organization and management without clear-cut division between the traditional business functions of production, marketing, accounting, research, and so on. Because of their small size and integrated function, these firms would be able to respond much more quickly to changing conditions and new opportunities than the traditional giants. And again because of their small size and integrated functions, exercises of initiative, responsibility, and discretion would be more equally distributed among the firm's employees, and the relationships among them would be more conducive to active collaboration and cooperation than in the traditional firms.[36]

Firms in Reich's "flexible system of production" would have essentially the same characteristics as those that Alvin Toffler, author of the best sellers *Future Shock* and *The Third Wave*, calls "the third-wave companies." These firms would be smaller, more flexible, less standardized, more decentralized, more innovative, and more participative than the large, traditional firms of the second-wave era.[37] Although it is by no means certain that the American industrial system is actually going through a metamorphosis from the traditional system of mass production to a new system of miniproduction, there nevertheless seems little doubt that some of the best—old and large as well as new and

---

[35]Anne B. Fisher, "GM's Unlikely Revolutionist," *Fortune*, March 19, 1984, pp. 106–12.

[36]Reich, *The Next American Frontier*, pp. 127–33.

[37]Alvin Toffler, *The Third Wave* (New York: William Morrow & Co., 1980).

small—of America's corporations are trying to generate a high level of entrepreneurial and competitive spirit within their organization by adopting smaller, semiautonomous, and more flexible units for product development and manufacturing.

Paralleling the movement toward smaller and more flexible production units is an equally significant change in the relative size and influence of middle management. This change takes the form of a shift in decision-making power away from the staff (analysts and advisors) to those in operations (designers, makers, and sellers), and an accompanying dimunition in the size and influence of the middle-layer, professional staff.

During the 1960s and 1970s, many companies hired professional managers—many of them new MBAs trained in financial analysis and strategic planning—who came to swell the ranks of middle management. These specialists began to exercise control over operations managers through the use of financial analysis and complex systems of control replete with rules and regulations. Since top management also relied heavily on financial analyses, and since huge quantities of information had to move upward, there was a pressing need for the services of a large professional staff that compiled data, sorted them out, and analyzed and interpreted them for top managers. Staff work and red tape multiplied, as entrenched staff bureaucrats created work for each other.

In the early 1980s, with a deemphasis of financial analysis and a rediscovered emphasis on engineering, production, and marketing, top managers began communicating more directly than before with first-line operating managers while giving them greater decision-making power. This direct communication, of course, was made easier and less expensive by the rapid development of electronic communications technology. Professional staff and middle management came to be increasingly viewed as redundant and wasteful by top managers, who began to restructure, in company after company, their corporate organization into a leaner and more fluid form.[38]

The American industrial system appears to be going through a process of quiet transformation from a period of excessive centralization and bureaucratization to an era of decentralized, leaner, and more flexible organization. Consequently, American industry may in the end be spared the trial of the Soviet-type bureaucratic quagmire filled with rigidity, inefficiency, and spiritlessness. Thanks to their ideological penchant for individuality and creativity in thought and action, the Americans seem much more amenable than the Russians to the logic of a flexible production system. There remains, however, one crucial issue:

---

[38]"A New Era for Management," *Business Week*, April 25, 1983, pp. 50–83.

a flexible system of organization requires collaborative and participative working relationships among employees. Can such relationships be successfully created in the workplaces of individualistic American society?

PHILOSOPHY AND STYLE OF MANAGEMENT

Corporate goals, strategy, and organizational structure do not exist in a vacuum; they are a function of the complex of values, beliefs, and attitudes—that is, ideologies—that pervade a given business community and society. Because of the nature of modern production technology, which is based largely on principles of physical sciences, international variations in the methods of production on the factory floor are small. By contrast, there exists a much wider variation in the methods of managing human activities in factories and offices because they are deeply rooted in the cultural and ideological orientations of different societies. In this section we shall examine some of the more conspicuous ways in which America's predominant management philosophy and style is influenced by the values and ideologies of American society.

Mechanistic and Organic Concepts of Corporate Organization

One attribute of social organization that accounts for international differences in the philosophy and style of corporate management is that which concerns the difference between the mechanistic and organic interpretation of organization. A *mechanistic* structure consists of components whose interrelationships can be explained by the laws of physics and chemistry. For example, an automobile has a mechanistic structure. If all the component parts of a car are replaced by identical parts, the resultant car is no different from the original car. By analogy, a "mechanistic" social organization is one that consists of participants any number of whom can be replaced by others with similar qualifications without noticeably affecting the character of the organization. For example, the group of brokers on the floor of the New York Stock Exchange comprises a mechanistic organization; any number of brokers can be replaced by others with similar qualifications and experience, and the quality and the character of the organization remain virtually the same. The relationships between participants in such an organization are mechanistic because the members are related to each other solely on the basis of job qualifications. It does not matter *who* they are as long as they can meet certain specific qualifications. In other words, their membership is *universalistic* and their relations are *specific*. (Review Chapter 3 for the meaning of these terms.)

An *organic* social organization, by contrast, is made up of participants who interact with one another as whole persons. That is, the qualities of their interactions are *particularistic* and *diffuse*. *Who* these participants are to each other does matter, so that the character of the organization changes if the existing members are replaced by others. A family is an organic social organization par excellence. If, for example, the father were replaced by another man, the new family would not be the same as the original one. There would be a completely new pattern of interaction among the family members. In a sense, the old family is dead and a new family is born.

In an organically constituted social organization, members interact with one another as whole human beings, and the sum total of the complex pattern of interaction among them encompassing all the intricacies of their personality assumes a life of its own. Consequently, there emerges a reality that is different from and greater than the sum of the constituent members. This phenomenon is analogous to what we find in a living organism, for example, a human body, in which there exists a reality—life—that is other than and greater than the sum of its constituent parts. Such a social organization can be called an *organic* or *holistic* organization.

Of course no social organization is completely like a living organism, just as no society can be completely machinelike. In a social organization, individual members are easily separable from it and are independently mobile; in a living organism, by contrast, cells and organs are rigidly fixed in their relative positions and are totally dependent on the organism. What matters for our study, however, is the predominant orientation of the individuals and groups in a social organization. In the traditional corporate work environment in America, for example, the organization tends to be structured mechanistically, or is *perceived* to be so structured by all concerned. By contrast, the Japanese tend to view the social organization in their corporate work environment as essentially organic. This difference in the orientation or perception of the relationships between the individual and the collective—whether mechanistic or organic—arises from the fundamental differences in the sociocultural orientations of different societies.

The holistic orientation of social organization has an important bearing on the question of harmony of interests between the individual and the group. In an organic social environment, individuals do not regard themselves as distinctly separate and autonomous entities. Rather, they tend to view their group as a basic frame of reference within which they exist and function. Their individual self-interests and their group self-interests are often hard to distinguish from each other. When a mother willingly and gladly sacrifices her personal welfare for the sake of her children, it is difficult to tell whether she is sacrificing her personal self-interest or trying to maximize her group (family) self-interest. In larger social organizations, such a close identification of individual and group interests is rare. Nonetheless, we cannot deny that there are many cases where individuals see their group's interests as nearly as important as, if not equally or more important than, their individual self-interests. If this observation is valid, then we can safely conclude that *group solidarity,* or the individual's desire and willingness to serve the interest of the group, *can* be an important motivating force in human social behavior.

In a previous section on corporate strategy, we identified maximization of short-term earnings as the primary goal of a great majority of American corporate managements. In this strategy, corporations are viewed essentially as a bundle of assets whose returns are to be maximized in the short run. In other words, a corporation is regarded as a money-making *machine,* and its managers play the numbers game of squeezing as many profit dollars from it as possible. A corporation is merely a shell, so to speak, consisting of positions connected by lines of authority and communication. To be sure, human beings occupy these positions, but *they* are not the corporation. Technically, any outsiders who have requisite qualifications for the positions can fill them, and perform the required tasks. Such is the mechanistic concept of the corporation. This, essentially, is how a modern corporation is perceived in the United States.

The organic view of the corporation, by contrast, defines a corporation as a community of human beings having shared interests and a common destiny. In this view, a corporation is not regarded as a bundle of financial and physical assets or a series of empty positions to be filled by qualified outsiders, but rather as a sum total of social relations existing among the members of the community. A corporation is like a hippie commune; the human bonding among its members is what defines the organization. The group has work to do, so work is assigned to various members of the group, not as individuals' responsibilities, but as individuals' *shares* of the *group's* responsibilities. All members of a corporation, in this view, are insiders; top managers are merely leaders among the members of the community. Those who hold this organic view of the firm are likely to have a strong aversion to the idea of selling a part of the firm, say a branch office or a plant, because that would mean severing ties with a group of fellow members of the community. To those who see a corporation merely as a bundle of assets, the same decision is perceived as being no different from one of parting with some stocks or bonds in the company's portfolio.

Individualism
and the Mechanistic Concept

The American corporate world is characterized by a coexistence of the mechanistic concept of social organization and the individualistic value orientation. It has been popular in the United States in recent years to blame what is perceived as an excess of individualism for many of the country's economic problems. Certainly there is an element of truth in this belief. A selfish insistence on the rights of an individual at the expense of the welfare of a larger community can create many serious problems. This does not mean, however, that individualism in its totality should be rejected. Individualism in the sense of independence of spirit, creativity, and self-reliance is the primary source of the vitality and strength of American society. In many cases where individualism is blamed for problems, it is not individualism per se that is at fault, but rather the mechanistic concept of social organization that comes hand in hand with individualism.

As an example of how individualism can lead to the mechanistic view of organization, examine the relationship between the American firm and its individual employees. This relationship is essentially *contractual*. Individuals provide their labor services to the firm in exchange for money wages under the terms of their service contract, whether they are explicitly stated or not. Sovereign individuals are, in theory at least, free agents and, as such, enter into the contract with the corporation on an equal footing. This much of the "fiction" of employment contract does little harm. What is harmful is its byproduct, the mechanistic interpretation of the relationships among individuals in the corporate organization. Since individual workers in the firm are viewed as vendors of a commodity called labor, their interactions are perceived merely as exchanges of commodities—that is, a mechanistic process—and the humanity of the vendors recedes into the background. What matters is the quantity and quality of the commodity, labor, that is traded, not the human actors involved in the transaction.

A corollary of this mechanistic view of interpersonal relations in a U.S. corporation is the idea of the separation of professional managers from workers. Earlier we noted that American top management tends to view the cadre of professional managers as quasi-insiders of the corporation. By contrast, the operations-level employees—both white-collar and blue-collar—are regarded as outsiders, like customers and creditors. The management communicates with the worker constituency primarily through formal channels of worker representation, which in most cases is the labor union. Within a given corporation, the management (top management and the technostructural staff) and labor form two distinctly separate status groups. They dress differently, get paid in different ways (salaries as compared to hourly or weekly wages), and often use different dining halls, rest rooms, and parking lots. Whereas the management group tends to identify its collective interest with that of the corporation, the workers are apt to regard themselves as playing a zero-sum game with the company—that is, their gain is the company's loss and vice versa. In many corporations, particularly in those traditional industries with a large number of unionized blue-collar workers, the relationship between management and labor is fundamentally adversarial. This situation is in sharp contrast to that which prevails in most of Japan's large companies, where all employees—including top managers—share a common culture and community of interests.

The mechanistic concept of corporate organization in U.S. corporations has another important byproduct—the autocratic management style. Since employer-employee relations are viewed essentially as commercial transactions, and since the humanity of the sellers of the labor commodity is hidden in the background, the buyer (the firm) sees little need to pay attention to more than the quality and quantity of the commodity it purchases. The buyer merely insists on getting its money's worth out of the transaction. Thus, notwithstanding the prevalence of democratic ideals in American society at large, management practices of the typical American corporation are basically autocratic. Since company-employee or management-labor relations are deemed commercial and contractual, there is little need to be concerned about whether or not the relations are democratic, participative, or humanistic.

In a company with autocratic management philosophy, all the important decisions are made at the top, and subordinate managers and workers are given specific orders to be carried out under close supervision. Standards of performance are determined unilaterally at the top, and subordinates are rewarded or penalized by their superiors according to a set of rigid rules. The amount of authority that superiors delegate to their subordinates is kept to a necessary minimum. Top management has little trust or confidence in the employees' willingness or motivation to work for the best interest of the company. It is presumed that employees at all levels are motivated by their private, individual self-interests rather than by a common desire to promote the interest of the company as a whole. Layers of management are created to check on the activities and performance of employees. In general, there prevails in the corporate hierarchy an indifferent or condescending attitude toward subordinates and an absence of respect for their human needs and concerns.

Conclusion

The characterization of American management philosophy and practices presented in this section is naturally an oversimplification of complex reality. Although it is safe to say that the predominant management philosophy of a great majority of large U.S. corporations is autocratic, mechanistic, and individualistic, and that management and labor are separated into two adversarial groups, it is nevertheless also true that many large U.S. corporations have successfully tempered their traditional autocratic management methods with some employee participation in decision making, and have in general created a sense of corporate community and common cause embracing all types of employees. For example, Thomas Peters and Robert Waterman reported in *In Search of Excellence* that many of America's best-managed companies are characterized by respect for and a caring attitude toward their employees.[39]

A crucial challenge to the American corporate system, then, is that it must find ways to reconcile the strengths of America's native individualism with the technological requirements for less autocratic and mechanistic management methods. In seeking answers to the question of how this reconciliation can be achieved, it is well to remember that it has been done quite satisfactorily by many athletic teams of excellence. There seems to exist a near-perfect harmony of individualism and team spirit in America's most successful sport teams. Indeed, teamwork has long been a key ingredient of American culture. That viable and successful teamwork is possible in a corporate setting has been amply demonstrated by the experiences of America's best-run companies. Whether or not a similar convergence is possible between private self-interests and the public interest of American society, however, is a different question altogether.

QUESTIONS

1. In what sense are America's largest corporations semipublic institutions?
2. Check out a recent issue of the U.S. Bureau of the Census, *Statistical Abstract of the United States* to find out the changes, since 1963, in the percentage share of total employment in manufacturing for the 50 and 200 largest U.S. manufacturing corporations. Interpret the result.
3. Describe the main features of the Managerial Revolution as reported by Berle and Means.

[39]Thomas J. Peters and Robert H. Waterman, Jr., *In Search of Excellence: Lessons from America's Best-Run Companies* (New York: Harper & Row, Publishers, Inc., 1982), pp. 13–16.

4.   Compare and contrast (a) the legal fiction, and (b) the reality of how a large U.S. corporation is controlled.

5.   What difference does it make whether a corporation is controlled by an owner-entrepreneur or a group of professional managers with limited ownership interests?

6.   How can a top management group effectively control a corporation without having a majority representation on the board of directors?

7.   What factors mitigate the effectiveness of outside board members as corporate watchdogs? Do you believe a new law requiring large corporations to accept several outside directors representing the public interest will improve the performance of the corporations? Why or why not?

8.   What is the real function of the board of directors of a large U.S. corporation? Under what circumstances does the board assume an active role toward the management team or the CEO?

9.   Describe the relative power positions of top management and the technostructure.

10.   Both criticize and defend (a) the profit-maximization thesis, and (b) the growth-maximization thesis of the objective of the large U.S. corporation. Then, describe the profitable growth thesis.

11.   List and explain the reasons why top corporate managers pay so much attention to the price of their company's stock.

12.   How does a takeover raid work? If you were a shareholder of a large U.S. corporation, would you welcome or object to your board's proposal to amend the company's bylaws to make an outsider takeover more difficult?

13.   How do you account for U.S. corporate managers' preoccupation with maximizing short-term earnings? What would be wrong with trying to maximize earnings for the shareholders? What factors are conducive to the obsession with the short run?

14.   What is meant by *paper entrepreneurialism?* What are its undesirable effects? What accounts for the predominance of senior manufacturing executives with backgrounds in law, accounting, and finance?

15.   What is *top management?* What major constituencies of the corporation does top management deal with? Which groups are insiders and which are outsiders of the corporate organization?

16.   What is the difference between *line* and *staff* in corporate organization? Which group of managers yield greater power in corporate headquarters of major U.S. corporations?

17.   What factors do you think are responsible for the recent trend in U.S. industries to favor smaller, more flexible research and production units with a leaner staff? What does Robert Reich mean by *flexible system of production?* What implications does this development have for the changing character of the American economic system?

18.   List a few each of predominantly (a) *mechanistic,* and (b) *organic* social organizations with which you are familiar. For the mechanistic organizations, give examples of universalistic membership and specific social rela-

tions. For the organic organizations, give examples of particularistic membership and diffuse social relations.

19. Describe the goal, strategy, and structure of the U.S. corporation from (a) the mechanistic, and (b) the organic points of view.

20. Is there a conflict between the organic view of a social organization and the individualistic value orientation? In other words, do you think it is possible for individualism to coexist in harmony with an organic view of social organization?

21. In the 1984 Los Angeles Olympics, the U.S. gymnastics teams achieved impressive results in both the individual and team events. Which of the following descriptions do you think best characterize the quality of social organization of the U.S. teams: (a) mechanistic individualism, (b) organic individualism, (c) mechanistic collectivism, or (d) organic collectivism?

22. Which of the four descriptions in question 21 above best describe the quality of social organization of each of the following groups: (a) a large Japanese corporation, (b) a Soviet productive enterprise, (c) the Politburo of the Communist party of the Soviet Union, and (d) the United States Supreme Court?

23. How do you explain the paradox that individualism in America leads to political democracy but to autocracy in corporate management?

24. What do the changing technological and competitive conditions of the global economy require of the management philosophy and practices of U.S. corporations?

25. If harmony of interests between individuals and a social organization like the business corporation appears at least achievable with some serious efforts, why is it that similar harmony between individuals and the American society as a whole appears so much more difficult to achieve?

SELECTED READING

BERLE, ADOLPH, and GARDINER MEANS. *The Modern Corporation and Private Property*. New York: Macmillan Company, 1932.

CHANDLER, ALFRED D., Jr. *The Visible Hand: The Managerial Revolution in American Business*. Cambridge, Mass.: Harvard University Press, 1977.

DONALDSON, GORDON, and JAY W. LORSCH. *Decision Making at the Top: The Shaping of Strategic Direction*. New York: Basic Books, Inc., Publishers, 1983.

GORDON, ROBERT AARON. *Business Leadership in the Large Corporation*. Berkeley, Calif.: University of California Press, 1961.

HERMAN, EDWARD S. *Corporate Control, Corporate Power*, A Twentieth Century Fund Study. Cambridge: Cambridge University Press, 1981.

MARRIS, ROBIN. *The Economic Theory of "Managerial" Capitalism*. New York: Basic Books, Inc., Publishers, 1968.

REICH, ROBERT B. *The Next American Frontier*. New York: Times Books, 1983.

TOFFLER, ALVIN. *The Third Wave*. New York: William Morrow & Co., 1980.

CHAPTER **9**

The Japanese Economy: Industrial Organization and Economic Policy

In Chapter 4 we discussed in some detail the complex power relations among the three major power centers of Japanese society: the administrative bureaucracy, the ruling-party leadership headed by the prime minister, and the big business leadership called *zaikai*. We noted that there are circular and symbiotic relationships among these power centers. It is difficult to say which of the three is supreme; their relative power relations vary from situation to situation. In this chapter we shall examine the ways in which (1) corporations are organized into enterprise groups and supraindustry business organization, (2) the economic bureaucracy is organized and related to business organizations, and (3) various economic policies are formulated and implemented by the administrative bureaucracy.

INDUSTRIAL ORGANIZATION

The term *industrial organization* refers to the ways in which, or extent to which, firms in a given industry or economy are organized into a coherent and purposeful whole. In the preceding chapters on the Soviet economy we found that economic power is totally concentrated in the state productive enterprise, which is one gigantic monopoly embracing the entire economy. In such a situation, industrial organization is synonymous with the organization of the state administrative apparatus for economic planning. In the United States, by contrast, firms are autonomous decision-making units whose activites are coordinated horizontally through market relations. Overt acts of collaboration among firms are prohibited by the antitrust laws. Of course the U.S. economy is not perfectly competitive in the textbook sense; there are a variety of forms of interfirm coordination, as we saw in Chapter 7. Nonetheless, we find that the U.S. economy is workably competitive, and that there is practically no formal organization of firms either within or across industries.

The character of Japan's industrial organization lies somewhere between the two extremes of the Soviet Union and the United States. Business firms in Japan are organized into larger groups forming a pyramid-shaped hierarchy. At the apex of this hierarchy are the powerful federations of business organizations that collaborate closely with the public authority in managing the economy. As noted earlier, industrial organization in the Soviet Union is essentially a public phenomenon, whereas in the United States the public authority plays the role of a meddlesome outsider to whatever organization exists among private corporations. In Japan's industrial organization, by contrast, the distinction between public and private is blurred. Active participants include private corporations, business associations, public enterprises, and administrative bureaucracies.

Public Enterprises

Japan's *public enterprises (ko-kigyo)* are government-owned business organizations whose capital is either totally or partially subscribed by the government. They differ from *government enterprises (seifu kigyo)*, which are administered directly by the government. The five government enterprises are the postal service, the forest service, the printing bureau, the mint, and the alcohol monopoly. Our concern in this book is the former—the *public* enterprises that are operated on a commercial basis—and run by the *national* government. (Besides the 100-odd national public enterprises of various types, there are several thousand *local* public enterprises running such public service facilities as waterworks, hospitals, and local transport systems.)

National public enterprises are created by special laws. Having been created by an act of the legislature, these companies enjoy special privileges but are also obligated to pursue the specific national policy objectives spelled out in the statutes. Although these companies are run on an independent profit-and-loss basis, making profits for the shareholders (primarily the government) is not an objective. Because of their strategic roles in the national economy, their activities can and do have a significant impact on the behavior and performance of private enterprises. Therefore, their production, purchasing, investment, and loan activities are closely controlled by the government. These activities naturally provide ample opportunities for close government-business cooperation and for symbiotic relationships among bureaucrats, politicians, and industrial leaders. As we noted in Chapter 4, public enterprises provide numerous postretirement jobs for government officials who "descend from heaven." Each ministry and agency jealously defends its public-enterprise "territories" for its postretirement bureaucrats, and remote-controls their assignment, promotions and transfers.

In February 1982, there were 106 national public enterprises. They varied a great deal in size and function. The largest public enterprises are the three public service corporations *(kosha)*—the Japanese National Railways (JNR), the Nippon Telegraph and Telephone Public Corporation (NTTPC), and the Japan Tobacco and Salt Public Corporation. These three public corporations combined employed 84 percent of the total 930,470 employees of all the public enterprises in 1982.[1] The JNR and the NTTPC were two of Japan's largest employers outside the national government. The next three largest public enterprises were Japan Air Lines Co., Ltd., the Japan Broadcasting Corporation (NHK), and the Metropolitan Tokyo Rapid Transit Authority.

Other important public enterprises include the following: Japan Highway Corporation, Housing and Urban Development Corporation, National Space Development Agency, People's Finance Corporation, Housing Loan Corporation, Japan Development Bank, Export-Import Bank of Japan, Central Cooperative Bank for Agriculture and Forestry, and Japan External Trade Organization (JETRO).

Each of the public enterprises is affiliated with a ministry that has jurisdiction over the operational, budgetary, and personnel matters of the enterprise. As of January 1975, the four ministries that had the largest number of enterprises assigned to them were the Ministry of International Trade and Industry (27 enterprises); the Ministry of Agriculture, Forestry and Fisheries (19); the Ministry of Finance (16); and the Ministry of Transport (14).[2] The competent ministries of some of the major public enterprises are listed below.[3]

---

[1]"Public Corporations," *Kodansha Encyclopedia of Japan* (1983), vol. 4, 263–64. On April 1, 1985, NTT became a private corporation.

[2]Japan, Gyosei Kanri-cho, *Tokushu Hojin Soran, Showa 50-nen ban* (Tokyo: Ministry of Finance, Printing Bureau, 1975).

[3]Ibid.

PUBLIC ENTERPRISE	COMPETENT MINISTRY
Japanese National Railways	Transport
Japan Tobacco and Salt Public Corporation	Finance
Japan Air Lines Co., Ltd.	Transport
Japan Broadcasting Corporation	Posts and Telecommunications
Japan Highway Corporation	Construction
Japan Development Bank	Finance
Japan External Trade Organization	International Trade and Industry

The so-called credit-and-loan public corporations such as the Japan Development Bank, the Export-Import Bank of Japan, and the People's Finance Corporation are under the administrative jurisdiction of the Finance Ministry. This jurisdiction, however, does not mean that the ministry has total control over the allocations of funds by these institutions. As we shall see later in the chapter, other ministries and agencies have authority to approve specific credit (who gets how much money at what interest rates for what purposes) for the programs and projects under their jurisdiction. For example, the Ministry of International Trade and Industry (MITI) exercises considerable control over the allocations of low-interest financing to various projects under its jurisdiction (e.g., urban renewal, improvement of the distribution systems, energy source development, merchant marine development, research and development in electronics industries, and so on) provided by such public credit-and-loan corporations as the Japan Development Bank, the Export-Import Bank of Japan, the Small Business Finance Corporation, the People's Finance Corporation, and the Central Cooperative Bank for Commerce and Industry. MITI's ability to approve these loans is one of the main sources of its power and influence over the industries and firms for which it is responsible.

Enterprise Groups

In the prewar years, Japanese industry was controlled by several of the huge industrial and financial conglomerates known as *zaibatsu* (literally, "financial cliques"). These groups were hierarchically organized combines controlled at the top by family-owned holding companies. Ten zaibatsu groups were predominant, the largest four of which were Mitsui, Mitsubishi, Sumitomo, and Yasuda. Mitsui and Sumitomo had roots in merchant houses of the Tokugawa period (1600–1867). In all but one (the Nissan Zaibatsu, one of the lesser six) of the ten major zaibatsu groups, the top holding company was dominated by a family.

The holding company in turn held controlling interests in the key zaibatsu firms in each group—a bank, a trading company, and several large companies in manufacturing, mining, and finance. (The Yasuda Zaibatsu was a financial complex; it had no industrial base.) These large zaibatsu firms in the modern industrial sector held stocks in the second-line subsidiaries, which in turn controlled lesser firms, many of which were smaller firms in the traditional sector. The controlling family also held shares in some of the larger firms in the conglomerate, and larger firms in the group held shares in other firms. Firms in the group borrowed funds from the group bank, and engaged in buying and selling among themselves largely through the group's trading company.

In every major industry, most of the zaibatsu groups were represented by a firm. Thus, each industry was oligopolistic, with the market share of the largest firm seldom exceeding 20 percent. In each industry, competition among the rival zaibatsu firms was fierce. Within each zaibatsu group, however, affiliated firms enjoyed cooperative relationships. The highest-echelon leaders of the various zaibatsu groups formed close, collaborative, and symbiotic relationships with influential political bosses and military chieftains.

During the Allied occupation following the end of the Pacific War, the Japanese government, under the directives from the occupation authorities, dissolved the zaibatsu holding companies and purged some 1,500 top zaibatsu managers from public and corporate offices. The stocks that had previously been held by the zaibatsu families and holding companies were sold to the employees of the dissolved firms and to the general public. As a consequence of the zaibatsu dissolution measure, Japanese industry became completely freed from the centralized, hierarchical control by family-dominated holding companies; and the ownership of Japan's largest corporations became widely diffused among the public.

During the 1950s, after the ban on the use of old zaibatsu names and logos was lifted, the former zaibatsu firms that had escaped the dissolution began to reassemble themselves. By the early 1960s, three enterprise groups having roots in the former Mitsui, Mitsubishi, and Sumitomo zaibatsu became clearly identifiable as significant enterprise groups. Most of the firms in these groups restored their old zaibatsu names and logos. Each of these three groups has its own bank and trading company. For example, the new Mitsubishi group consisting of about 30 firms coalesces around the Mitsubishi Bank, Mitsubishi Corporation (the trading company), Mitsubishi Heavy Industries, and Mitsubishi Electric. In part prompted by the reassembly of the former-zaibatsu groups, other large corporations that had no previous zaibatsu ties developed their own enterprise groups around three major national banks—the Fuji Bank (the former Yasuda Bank), the Sanwa Bank, and the Dai-ichi Kangyo Bank. These enterprise groups are commonly referred to as *keiretsu* (literally, "alignment" or "affiliation"). The three former-zaibatsu groups—often called the *zaibatsu-keiretsu*—form stronger ties among member firms than the three new banking keiretsu.

Although there exist some similarities between the prewar zaibatsu organizations and the postwar keiretsu groupings, they are more of form than substance. The most important difference is the absence of a central command (holding company) in the postwar keiretsu structure, with an attendant absence of vertical control. Although affiliated firms in a group differ in size and influence, their relationship is not one of superior-subordinate decision-making authority. The relationships among the top half dozen firms in each group—typically a bank, a trading company, an insurance company and/or a trust bank, and a few larger manufacturing firms—are those of equal partners. To be sure there exist intra-group buying and selling, mutual shareholding, interlocking directorates, and borrowing from the group bank; but these relationships exist also across group boundaries. Member banks often borrow funds from outside sources and use the facilities of nongroup trading companies. It is worth noting, too, that Japan's Antimonopoly Law prohibits any bank from holding more than 5 percent of the equity share of a nonfinancial corporation; this prohibition places an effective limit on a group bank's ability to control member firms through shareholding. All in all, managements of the firms affiliated with a keiretsu group can be said to exercise autonomous self-control.

As was the case with the prewar zaibatsu groups, each of the postwar keiretsu groups has sought to be represented in every major industry. This tendency is known in Japan as the *one-set principle (wan setto shugi)*; each group wants to have one complete set of major product lines. For example, if one group starts producing a new product, say optical fibers, all the other groups want to follow suit and try to supply their own optical fibers. Each group's bank funds the project and its trading firm handles purchases of inputs and marketing of the output. If this were not done, then the group would have to turn to "outsiders" for purchases of optical fibers. Besides, a group that does not supply this new product, when others do, is perceived by all concerned as less than complete. In rank-conscious Japanese society, this is an anathema. Although this one-set principle often results in unnecessary duplication of investments and production deplored by many in Japan as *excessive competition (kato kyoso)*, it nevertheless has undoubtedly contributed significantly to the technological progress and product innovation in the postwar Japanese economy.

The keiretsu phenomenon is a manifestation of the familistic groupism of the Japanese people that we discussed in Chapter 2. Of particular importance is the role of a group bank as the lender of last resort. Even though member firms do not limit sources of their credit to the group bank, it is always reassuring to have a major national bank as a *miuchi* (insider). As we shall see later in the chapter, banks play a much more important role in the Japanese economy as a provider of financial resources than commercial banks in the United States do. When credit is cheap and abundant, banks compete intensely for borrowers. But when money gets tight and a condition of sellers' market develops, long-established goodwill between the bank and the potential borrower becomes an important determinant of who gets the credit and who does not. Because of the strong insider-outsider mentality of the Japanese, banks naturally show a tendency to take care of the needs of their group members before they extend credit to outside applicants. Thus, any firm that needs a loan for an out-of-the-ordinary purpose— say for a risky new venture into an unproven product line—finds that its group bank is more sympathetic to its application for a loan than other banks. This is particularly so if there exists a consensus among the keiretsu firms regarding the desirability of developing the new product line.

We thus find that most of Japan's major corporations in diverse fields of activities belong to one keiretsu group or another. There are exceptions to this rule, but they are few and far between. For instance, Sony and Honda have avoided affiliation with any one particular group. Also, truly large and powerful firms like Toyota, Nippon Steel, and Matsushita Electric have only loose affiliation with many banks either because no single bank can supply major portions of their huge borrowing needs or because their internal funds are so ample that they have little need for borrowing from banks.

Capital grouping. The former-zaibatsu and the new banking keiretsu groups discussed in the preceding paragraphs are loose, *horizontal* associations of large firms. Many of these firms, as well as the large independents like Toyota and Matsushita Electric, have a *vertical* grouping of their own based on equity interest and supplanted by interlocking directorates. The holding company (*oya-gaisha*, or "parent" company) is usually a large manufacturing firm, and the subsidiaries (*ko-gaisha* and *mago-gaisha*, or "child" and "grandchild" companies) are smaller firms supplying component parts or special services to the parent company. In 1971, the largest 100 of these holding companies had 5,881 subsidiaries in which their equity interest exceeded 25 percent, and in nearly half of these subsidiaries the parent company's equity exceeded 50 percent.[4] This type of vertical integration is called *capital grouping (shihon keiretsu).*

---

[4]"Industrial Organization," *Kodansha Encyclopedia of Japan* (1983), vol. 3, 295.

The use of the words *parent, child,* and *grandchild* to describe the relationships between the operating-holding company and its subsidiaries is highly suggestive of the familistic group relations among the firms in a vertical capital keiretsu. The parent company is not only the purchaser of the products of the subsidiaries, but is also a provider of much needed capital and technology. The parent company also dispatches some of its less competent employees and retiring managers to its subsidiaries on an *amakudari* (descent from heaven) basis. The relationship between the parent company and its subsidiaries is one of control and dependency; control is exercised through the managerial personnel dispatched from the top, as well as through the parent's judicious allocations of financial and technical resources to its children. Many of the subsidiaries are so dependent on their parent company that their bargaining power relative to the latter is minimum. (More on this point in the next chapter.)

Notwithstanding the various types of grouping that crisscross Japanese industry, its overall organization cannot be characterized as forming a cartel. The vertical capital keiretsu organization certainly enhances the market power of the operating-holding company at the top of the pyramid. Many of these parent companies are affiliated horizontally with other large corporations in a former-zaibatsu or new banking keiretsu. The vertical linkages that exist in a capital group, however, do not connect with other vertical groups because there exists little control-dependency relationship among the large firms in a horizontal keiretsu group. Moreover, as we noted earlier, the horizontal keiretsu setup generates intense rivalry in each industry among the oligopolistic firms representing different groups. To sum up: The organizaton of Japan's industry is characterized by the coexistence of (1) strong ties of control-dependency relationship among larger and smaller firms in vertical capital grouping, (2) loose affiliation among large firms in horizontal keiretsu grouping revolving around a major bank; and (3) fierce rivalry in each industry among oligopolistic firms, some of which are independents but most of which represent a horizontal keiretsu group.

The Antimonopoly Law
and the Fair Trade Commission

In 1947, under the directives of the Allied occupation authorities, the Japanese Diet enacted an antimonopoly law modeled after the U.S. antitrust laws. The law prohibited private monopolization, unreasonable restraint of trade, and unfair busines practices, and it created the Fair Trade Commission (FTC) as its enforcement agency. The Antimonopoly Law, which was based on the guiding principle of individualized competition, was alien to the Japanese way of thinking, which essentially equated competition with rivalry with outsiders and regarded cooperation with insiders as a norm. The FTC was also an anomaly; a quasi-judicial agency that is independent of the authority of the government is unprecedented in Japan. The incongruity of the law and its enforcement agency with the traditional values of the country has caused a considerable amount of confusion, and generated friction between the FTC and the Ministry of International Trade and Industry (MITI), which has made strenuous efforts to promote interfirm coordination in order to strengthen the international competitiveness of Japanese industries.

Soon after the end of the Allied occupation in 1952, the Japanese amended the Antimonopoly Law and eased some of its provisions. Specifically, the 1953 amendment eliminated the *per se* illegality of cartels and legalized certain types of cartels. Cartels were allowed for the purposes of (1) overcoming temporary hardships caused by a recession (the *recesson cartels*), (2) improving production technology and quality of products (the *rationalization cartels*), or (3) meeting the requirements of special legislation (the *special-law cartels*). The law was amended further in 1977; this time the provisions of the law were tightened somewhat. The FTC was given, for the first time, a limited power to break up a monopoly; provisions against cartels were also tightened.

Business Associations and Pressure Groups

In each industry there exists a trade association organized ostensibly for the purposes of exchanging information, standardizing products, controlling quality, and generally promoting amicable relations among the members. There are over 100 such organizations. In the prewar period, many of these associations served as vehicles for cartelizing the industry. The Antimonopoly Law prohibits anticompetitive practices of trade associations. These associations provide a convenient nexus for communication between government bureaus and industries. Trade association officers provide important information about their industries to the bureau officials and lobby them for the special interests of their industries. Many trade association officers also serve on the advisory councils attached to the ministry.

The 100-odd trade associations of all major industries, together with over 800 major corporations and several public corporations, form the very powerful peak business organization, the Federation of Economic Organizations (Keizai Dantai Rengo Kai, or Keidanren for short). Outside the government, it is the most powerful organization in Japan. As we noted in Chapter 4, it forms, along with three other peak business organizations (the Japan Federation of Employers' Association, or Nikkeiren; the Japan Chamber of Commerce and Industry, or Nissho; and the Japan Committee for Economic Development, or Keizai Doyukai) the core of Japan's *zaikai,* or big-business leadership. Its political power derives from its ability to raise large sums of campaign funds for the ruling political party and its factions, as well as the direct and regular access its leaders enjoy with influential politicians and bureaucrats. No major economic or political decisions, including the selection of key economic ministers and drafting of the national budget, are made without consultation with the president of Keidanren and other zaikai leaders. It is widely believed that under certain circumstances, Keidanren has power to influence even the selection of the prime minister. Keidanren's primary function is to speak with one voice to the political and bureaucratic leaders conveying the desires and preferences of the business community for the purpose of influencing the content and direction of public policy decisions.

Although Keidanren and the other peak business organizations forming zaikai are often referred to as *pressure groups,* the designation is not quite appropriate. As we noted in Chapter 4, zaikai is an integral element of Japan's power establishment. Along with the ruling party high command and the topmost level of the administrative bureaucracy, zaikai shapes the pattern and direction of the nation's economic and social change. It therefore cannot be called a mere pressure group. Nor is it appropriate to label zaikai a *special interest group.* Zaikai's membership roll is so comprehensive that its ideology must necessarily be that of the entire big-business community. It cannot, and does not, represent the parochial interests of specific industries or regions. Zaikai leaders regard themselves as defenders of the general interests of the Japanese business community, which they equate to the general interests of the Japanese economy and society.

In Chapters 3 and 7 we discussed the problems of special interest lobbies in the United States, and observed that the coalition of various special interests tend to undermine the overall interest of society. To a certain extent this problem is also found in Japan. Various interest groups in such diverse fields as small business, agriculture, organized medicine, public employees, citizens' groups, trade unions, teachers, local communities, and religious groups try to influence public policy primarily by lobbying political party leaders, Diet members, and senior bureaucrats. As in the United States, the special interests of these groups are often in conflict with the public interest. But there exists one important difference between Japan and the United States in this regard. As we have noted above, the big-business leadership as it interfaces with the political and bureaucratic leadership tends to promote the general interest of the Japanese economy. And, as we noted in Chapter 4, Japan's elite bureaucrats are pursuing their own version of national interest. Most of them sincerely believe that their mission is to protect the overall national interest of Japan against the encroachment of special interest lobbies and their politician allies. Thus, although the behavior of politicians—members of both the ruling and opposition parties—is strongly influenced, as in the United States, by special interest pressures, the collaboration between elite bureaucrats and zaikai leaders creates a condition that is not highly susceptible to special interest pressures. Their choice and action are more likely to be guided by what they regard as the best interest of the national economy as a whole than by parochial interests of some special interest groups.

Ministerial Advisory Councils

The business community's access to public officials and political leaders has several channels. We have already noted that trade association officers have regular contacts with the responsible officials in the related ministries. Top leaders of zaikai have direct and regular access to the high-ranking bureaucrats and the influential leaders of the ruling political party. In Chapter 4 we also noted other informal channels such as the old-boy networks based on common university and bureaucratic backgrounds, and kinship cliques based on marriage bonds. We now add another channel of communication between business and government: ministerial advisory councils.

About 250 advisory councils, commissions, and committees are attached to various government agencies and ministries. The best known of these councils include the Tax System Study Council attached to the Prime Minister's Office, the Economic Council belonging to the Economic Planning Agency, and the most influential of them all, the Industrial Structure Council (ISC) affiliated with MITI. The size of council membership ranges anywhere from 3 to that of the largest council, ISC, which is authorized to have 130 members. Membership of most of the councils consists mainly of "persons of learning and experience," including academics, other specialists in the field, and nonexperts representing the general public. There may also be members representing important constituencies involved in a given issue.

Advisory councils are created by law. Typically, the law authorizing the creation of a given ministry or agency has a provision for establishing an affiliated advisory council. The statutory purpose of the advisory council is to study the question raised by the minister and prepare a report on the question including policy recommendations. Since the initial question posed to an advisory council as well as the final report to the minister are almost invariably drafted by ministerial officials, it is likely that the recommendations made by the council are not far removed from the position held by the ministerial officials. Besides, the selection of the members of a given council is almost always made by the officials of the associated ministry and recommended to the minister for appointment. Persons whose views are known to be opposed to the government's or the ministry's positions are deliberately ruled out. Within the limits of this basic framework, advisory councils function to provide a forum for communication and collaboration between bureaucrats, business leaders, and academics who share a common interest in an issue.

The roles played by advisory councils, and the extent of ministerial influence on the quality of councils' deliberations, vary from council to council. In a great majority of cases, councils' recommendations are not much more than window dressing for the predetermined positions of the ministry. This does not mean, however, that councils' meetings and deliberations are dominated by the members representing the ministry. Particularly in larger councils, the social status and political influence of some of the key members, especially those representing zaikai, are far greater than those of ministerial officials. What it means is that important and strategic decisions are made outside the council in close consultations among the top leaders in politics, business, and bureaucracy; the real purpose of council deliberations is to articulate the predetermined positions while incorporating, as much as practicable, the views of academics, experts, and other minority members.

THE EPA AND ECONOMIC PLANNING

Of the 12 ministries and several agencies of the Japanese government that we listed in Chapter 4, several are known as economic ministries, the most important ones of which are the Ministry of Finance (MOF), the Ministry of International Trade and Industry (MITI), and the Economic Planning Agency (EPA). The Ministry of Finance regulates the banking system, controls the budget, and engages in monetary and fiscal policy. MITI, of course, is the general headquarters of Japan's industrial strategy. Both of these powerful ministries control and guide the industries and firms under their wings through various statutory and extrastatutory means. What these two ministries do largely determines the pattern and direction of Japan's economic development. The Finance Ministry and MITI will be studied in some detail in the following two sections. In this secton, we take a brief look at the EPA and its economic planning activities.

In discussing Japan's economic "planning," it must be emphasized at the outset that Japan is not a planned economy and that any plan that is developed by the government is nonoperational. The series of national economic plans that are developed by the Economic Planning Agency in consultation with the Economic Advisory Council are essentially public statements concerning the government's strategic policy objectives and a set of forecasting and projections of key macroeconomic variables. As such, targets and projections are not binding on any party, and no attempt is made by the EPA, or by any other ministries or agencies, to guide the activities of private business in the direction of the plan targets. The EPA has neither the authority, staff, nor connections with the business community necessary to implement what is stated in the national economic plan. Besides, the plan targets are too aggregative to be applied to any single industry or firm. In other words, Japan's EPA is not a Gosplan.

The real significance of the EPA's economic planning lies in its announcement effect: it provides information to the public as to what the government perceives as the desirable direction of the development of the national economy. Japanese officialdom uses the English word *vision* to describe the government's picture of the future structure of the Japanese economy. The EPA's planning activities provide a long-range vision of the Japanese economy, thereby enabling both public and private decision makers to shape a consensus concerning the requisite developmental strategies. In contrast to the EPA's vision making, the substantive aspect of the Japanese government's developmental strategy is carried out by MITI's industrial policy, as we shall see subsequently.

THE FINANCE MINISTRY AND FISCAL POLICY

The Finance Ministry is the most powerful and prestigious of Japanese government agencies. It supervises the Bank of Japan and, through it, the entire banking and financial system of the country, drafts the national budget, administers taxation, and regulates the availability and cost of money and credit. In this section we shall examine the organization and functions of the Ministry of Finance as they relate to the fiscal system. In the next section, we shall study Japan's banking system and the monetary policy undertaken by the Bank of Japan under the supervision of the Finance Ministry.

The Finance Ministry: Organization and Functions

In Chapter 7 we noted that in the United States the twin monetary and fiscal policies are used primarily as tools for short-run management of aggregate demand for the purpose of stabilizing output, employment, and prices. Neither policy is used as an instrument of developmental strategy, that is, as a means of shaping the long-run supply of the economy. In Japan, the situation is quite different. Monetary policy conducted by the Bank of Japan is used almost exclusively for short-run stability control of the economy. The Ministry of Finance has the responsibility of managing the overall fiscal system (the budget, taxation, national debt, and public expenditures). But this fiscal policy is not regarded primarily as a means for short-run demand management. Rather, it is viewed essentially as a means of achieving broader social goals such as balanced growth of the economy, technological advancement, international competitiveness, and higher quality of national life. In other words, the term *fiscal policy* is used in Japan to refer to government policy of using tax revenues, borrowing, and expenditures for economic development and social welfare; and its short-run stabilization effect is considered secondary.

The ministry's Main Office *(honsho)* has the following seven bureaus: Budget, Tax, Customs and Tariff, Financial, Securities, Banking, and International Finance. Attached to the Main Office are the three ancillary bureaus (Mint, Printing, and Customs) and the large, semiautonomous National Tax Administration Agency with nearly 500 tax offices located throughout the country.

The Budget Bureau is responsible for drafting the various types of national government budget (see below). Based on the budget requests from other ministries and agencies, the Budget Bureau officials, after consultation with appropriate officials of the ministries and agencies, prepare a preliminary budget. After further negotiations with the ministries, the draft budget is approved by the cabinet and submitted to the Diet for approval. Throughout this process of budget drafting, various interest groups as well as officials of other ministries and agencies lobby the bureau's budget officers, the finance minister, the majority party leaders, and members of the Diet. Frequently, members of the Diet, representing their constituencies, lobby the budget officers. The strongest pressure is exerted by the ruling party and zaikai leaders on the finance minister, who has a final say on the ministerial draft submitted to the cabinet.

The Tax Bureau is responsible for formulating the country's tax policy and procedures. Drafting new tax laws and amendments to the existing laws are the bureau's main tasks. The Financial Bureau's major responsibilities are management of government bonds, the Trust Fund Special Account, and the Fiscal Investment and Loan Program (see below). The Banking Bureau formulates monetary policy, supervises the activities of the Bank of Japan, and regulates the entire financial and banking system.

The Finance Ministry prepares, for submission to the Diet for its approval, three types of budget. The most important is the General

Account Budget, which shows the most of the national tax revenues as well as proceeds from the sales of government bonds on the revenue side, and all the government expenses for the fiscal year on the expenditure side. Until 1965, the general account revenues and expenditures were in balance. Since then, public bonds have been issued to finance public construction projects and generally to fill the gap between revenues and expenditures. By 1980, bond proceeds had come to occupy nearly a third of the general account revenues.

In addition to the General Account Budget, the government draws up two types of budget: the Special Account Budget and the Public Corporation Budget. The special accounts are used for matching revenues and expenditures for a specific project or enterprise, or earmarking tax revenues for specific purposes. For example, the government's foreign exchange receipts and payments are kept in the foreign exchange fund, and gasoline tax receipts are earmarked for road improvements. The government also prepares a set of budgets for 15 major public corporations.

The Fiscal Investment and Loan Program

The Financial Bureau of the Finance Ministry manages a special type of financial program called the Fiscal Investment and Loan Program (FILP, *zaisei toyushi keikaku*). Among the special accounts discussed in the preceding paragraph, there are several accounts whose annual revenues far exceed their expenditures. The major sources of surplus funds are postal savings, postal life insurance and annuity programs, and government-run pension and annuity programs. The surpluses in these funds are pooled into the Trust Fund, and are made available to local governments and public corporations as low-interest, long-term loans. A significant portion of these loaned funds is channeled back to the private sector as some of the recipient public corporations make loans to private borrowers. The credit-and-loan public corporations that serve as intermediaries of FILP funds include the Housing Loan Public Corporation, the Japan Housing Loan Public Corporation, the People's Finance Corporation, the Export-Import Bank of Japan, the Small Business Finance Corporation, and the Japan Development Bank. The FILP is the Finance Ministry's plan for allocating the Trust Fund's surplus funds to the primary borrowers (local governments and credit-and-loan public corporations). As we shall see below, allocations of the FILP funds by the credit-and-loan public corporations to secondary (i.e., private) borrowers are jointly determined by the corporations and appropriate ministries.

The FILP serves two important functions in Japan's public economic policy. First, as we noted earlier, ministries other than Finance have a considerable degree of control over the lending activities of the public credit-and-loan corporations. For example, MITI has authority to determine the maximum amount of loans that the Japan Development Bank can make to the types of projects for which the ministry is responsible, and also to determine the rate of interest the bank can charge. Moreover, MITI makes recommendations to the bank as to who should get loans, and these recommendations are invariably accepted. In all, MITI has considerable power to mediate FILP funds channeled through several public credit-and-loan corporations to specific industries and firms. This power of mediating loans in turn enhances the ministry's power of control over the industries under its jurisdiction. Furthermore, since FILP funds are provided to specific industries and firms at a low interest rate, their judicious use greatly enhances the effectiveness of MITI's industrial policy. In fact, FILP funds have been allocated in large scale to what the government has designated as strategic industries and to projects for development of social overhead capital. This use of FILP funds as an instrument of industrial policy is the primary function of the FILP.

The second function of the FILP is to serve as a complement to monetary policy. As the Bank of Japan tightens or eases the money supply and credit availability by using its conventional monetary policy measures, the Finance Ministry's Financial Bureau slows down or steps up FILP loan activities to reinforce the effect of the monetary policy. More importantly, FILP loans can be used selectively to mitigate the restrictive effects of a tight monetary policy. The effect of monetary policy is *general* in that it affects all industries and firms without discrimination. A needed degree of selectivity can be achieved by a judicious use of FILP loans. Thus, during a period of tight money, the Finance Ministry in cooperation with MITI can increase low-interest loans to selected industries and firms that, from the point of view of industrial policy, need to be treated favorably. This flexible use of the Trust Fund money as an instrument of public economic policy is not available to the policy makers of the United States.

It may be noted that the FILP has both fiscal *and* financial characters. We can identify three main flows of funds in the Japanese economy outside the main income-consumption flow. First, there is the flow of taxes and bond proceeds moving from the public to the government and back to the public. This is the *fiscal flow*, and its management by the government is fiscal policy. The second is the *financial flow* of household and business savings deposited in private financial institutions, and made available as loans to the public by banks and other financial institutions. As we shall see shortly, the Bank of Japan plays an important role as a major intermediary in this flow. The management of this financial flow is monetary policy. The third flow is the *hybrid fiscal-financial flow* of the FILP. Private savings in the forms of postal savings and contributions to government-managed social security and pension programs are channeled through the Finance Ministry's Trust Fund Account (hence a fiscal flow) and loaned back to the public by way of public credit-and-loan corporations (hence a financial flow). The regulation of this flow by the Finance Ministry and other ministries has important effects of reinforcing the effectiveness of monetary and industrial policies.

THE BANKING SYSTEM
AND MONETARY POLICY

In the United States, corporate financing is done primarily through the capital (i.e., stocks and bonds) market, and loans from commercial banks are limited largely to short-term borrowing for working capital. In Japan, capital markets are relatively underdeveloped; there, borrowing from financial institutions, primarily commercial banks, provides the largest source of funds for corporations. Typically, the ratio of all types of *debts* to shareholders' *equity* is about 4 to 1, as compared to about 1 to 1 in the United States. Of external debts, bank loans are the largest source, and corporate bonds provide only a small fracton of external financing. The very high debt-to-equity ratio has two important consequences. First, Japanese corporate managers are less sensitive to the wishes and preferences of the shareholders than their American counterparts; conversely, commercial banks play a relatively much more important role in the Japanese business community than in the United States. (This point will be discussed further in the next chapter.) Second, because of the overwhelming importance of bank borrowing in Japanese corporate financing, the availability and cost of money and credit is relatively more important in corporate decision making in Japan; consequently, monetary policy is relatively more effective in Japan than in the United States.

The Banking System

Besides the credit-and-loan public corporations we discussed earlier (e.g., the Japan Development Bank and the Export-Import Bank of Japan), there are several other types of banking institutions that are legally authorized to engage in banking business. These institutions include trust banks, long-term credit banks, mutual savings-and-loan banks, credit associations, credit cooperatives, and agricultural cooperatives. In what follows, we limit our discussion to the most important type of banking institution, the commercial banks (*futsu ginko*, or "ordinary banks").

There are two types of commercial banks: city banks and regional banks. In 1979, there were 13 city banks (including the Bank of Tokyo, which is technically a specialized foreign exchange bank) and 63 regional banks. Both types of commercial banks combined had about 8,000 branches throughout the country. Additionally, there were 63 foreign banks operating 84 branches in Japan; these banks were licensed as commercial banks.[5] City banks cater primarily to large corporations, while regional banks serve other types of businesses and their operations are limited to their respective regions.

Because of heavy demands by large corporate borrowers for funds needed for their plant and equipment investments, city banks are perpetually short of funds. By contrast, regional banks and other financial institutions like agricultural cooperatives and mutual savings-and-loan banks tend to have an excess of deposits over loans. Therefore, city banks borrow heavily the surplus funds of regional banks and other banking institutions. City banks also borrow from the Bank of Japan by discounting commercial bills or on promissory notes backed by government bonds as collateral. (Huge quantities of low-interest yielding government bonds are "allocated" to city banks by the Finance Ministry in an almost compulsive manner. When city banks use these bonds as collateral for borrowing funds from the Bank of Japan, the national debt becomes "monetized." The net effect is virtually the same as the Bank of Japan printing new money to finance the government deficit.) Because the primary source of investment funds of large corporations is city banks, and because city banks rely heavily on borrowings from other financial institutions and the Bank of Japan, the central bank's monetary policy measures affecting interest rates have sharp and immediate effects on the level of the nation's economic activities.

The Bank of Japan and Monetary Policy

The Bank of Japan is the central bank of Japan. It issues bank notes, serves as the lender of last resort to commercial banks, and conducts monetary policy. The Bank is under a broad supervision of the Finance Ministry in its execution of monetary policy. Although the technical aspects of the monetary policy measures are left to the Bank's discretion, major policy decisions are made by higher levels of the government including the Finance Ministry and the cabinet. The Bank's governor and vice-governor are appointed by the cabinet. Its policy-making organ, the Policy Board, consists of seven members including the governor of the Bank, one representative each of the Finance Ministry and the Economic Planning Agency, and four members representing the banking community. The members of the board are appointed by the cabinet with the approval of the Diet.

Standard monetary policy measures available to the central banks of mature capitalist countries are changes in reserve requirements, changes in lending rates, and open-market operations. The reserve requirement policy is not used in Japan (nor in the United States) as a major policy instrument because its effects, if used, would be too drastic. Open-market operations, the primary policy weapon of the U.S. Federal Reserve monetary policy, have limited effectiveness in Japan because of the small size of the government securities market.

The main monetary policy measure of the Bank of Japan is its discount and loan policy. The Bank periodically announces changes in its basic lending rate known as the *basic rate*. Changes in the bank rate per se, however, are not expected to produce direct and immediate effects on the quantities of funds demanded by commercial banks. Rather, their usefulness is limited to their announcement effects. The Bank regulates money supply largely by means of *quantitative* adjustments of its loans and discounts.

As part of the Japanese government's aggressive developmental strategy, the Bank of Japan has traditionally followed a cheap money (i.e., low interest rate) policy. Given generally low interest rates, private demands for bank loans, and consequently banks' demands for the central bank loans and discounts, have been strong. If the Bank wishes to follow a tight money policy, it merely has to be less generous than usual in granting loans and discounts to banks. Increases in the bank rate put the banking community on notice that the Bank is getting stricter in loan and discount approvals.

The Bank of Japan has supplemented its own lending policy by a method of direct control over commercial banks' lending policies. Known as *window guidance (madoguchi shido)*, the method involves the Bank's issuing, during periods of monetary tightness, quotas on maximum lending each bank can make. Although ostensibly presented to the banks as suggestions for voluntary action, the banks find it difficult to ignore the "guidance." It must be remembered that the Bank's discounting and loan facilities available to commercial banks are not rights but *privileges*, and any banks that are uncooperative with the Bank of Japan's window guidance will find the Bank becoming less generous in granting loans and discounts. For this reson, the window guidance method has been very effective as a means of regulating the volume of commercial banks' lending to their customers.

In the Japanese financial system, the dozen or so city banks play an extremely important role. They raise large sums of loanable funds by borrowing from the public (deposits), other financial institutions, and the Bank of Japan. They supply the money thus raised to their customers, which are mainly large industrial corporations needing funds for capital investment purposes. Because of this strategic role of city banks as the primary conduits of investment funds, the Bank of Japan's monetary policy is focused on the regulation of lending activities of these banks. Major industrial corporations have well-established business connections with some city banks, often through their horizontal keiretsu affiliation. During a tight-money period, city banks give preferential treatments to larger borrowers, particularly those in their keiretsu groups. Smaller firms that have no vertical keiretsu affiliation experience a great deal of difficulty in obtaining needed funds. This is the main reason why smaller firms in Japan have a strong incentive to seek affiliation with a keiretsu group. Seen in this light, industrial organization in Japan can be understood primarily as a pyramid-shaped structure of relationships of dependency on loanable funds, with the Bank of Japan situated at the top of the pyramid.

MITI AND INDUSTRIAL POLICY

Chalmers Johnson makes a distinction between two types of state according to the nature of their government-business relationship. The United States, says Johnson, is a *regulatory state*, a state that "concerns itself with the forms and procedures of economic competition," but that "does not concern itself with substantive matters." By contrast, Japan is a *developmental state*, a state that *leads* the industrialization drive.[6] Whereas the priority in economic policy of the regulatory state is antitrust policy, the developmental state's chief concern is *industrial policy*, that is, policy for improving the industrial structure of the country for greater international competitiveness and faster economic growth. In Japan, the government agency that is most closely identified with industrial policy is the Ministry of International Trade and Industry (MITI).

MITI: Organization and Functions

Under the provisions of the law establishing the ministry, MITI is responsible for promoting, regulating, and guiding almost all of Japan's industries. (The only industries that are not under MITI's jurisdiction

---

[6]Chalmers Johnson, *MITI and the Japanese Miracle: The Growth of Industrial Policy, 1925–1975* (Stanford, Calif.: Stanford University Press, 1982), p. 19.

are transportation, communication, finance, food and drugs, and some wooden products.) MITI's implicit authority to conduct industrial policy is based on this broad statutory requirement. Specifically, the major functions of MITI are promotion and regulation of Japan's international trade; promotion and regulation of industrial activities in manufacturing, mining, and distribution; regulation and maintenance of adequate supplies of industrial raw materials and energy resources for the national economy; and promotion and guidance of small businesses.

The MITI Main Office *(honsho)* is divided into the Ministerial Secretariat and seven bureaus. Four of the bureaus are known as general or "horizontal" bureaus, which are International Trade Policy, International Trade Administration, Industrial Policy, and Industrial Location and Environmental Protection. The functions of these bureaus is to provide a general policy direction for the national economy; these bureaus do not have specific industries under their jurisdiction. By contrast, the remaining three bureaus, known as the industrial or "vertical" bureaus, serve as "bureaus of primary jurisdiction" *(genkyoku)* for the industries under their wings. The three industrial bureaus and their sections are given below:

> *Basic Industries Bureau:* General Affairs, Iron and Steel Administration, Iron and Steel Production, Nonferrous Metals, Basic Chemicals, Chemical Products, and Chemical Fertilizers
>
> *Machinery and Information Industries Bureau:* General Affairs, International Trade, Industrial Machinery, Cast and Forged Products, Electronics Policy, Data Processing Promotion, Electronics and Electrical Machinery, Automobile, Weights and Measures, Aircraft and Ordnance, Bicycles and Motor Cycles, and Machinery Credit Insurance
>
> *Consumer Goods Industries Bureau:* General Affairs, International Trade, Fiber and Spinning, Textile Products, Paper and Pulp Industries, Household and Sundry Goods, Recreational Goods, Ceramics and Construction Materials, and Housing Industry.[7]

Affiliated with the ministry's Main Office are the three semiautonomous external agencies, which are the Agency of Natural Resources and Energy, the Small and Medium Enterprise Agency, and the Patent Agency. The Natural Resources and Energy Agency serves as the bureau of primary jurisdiction for the following industries: petroleum refining, petroleum products, nonferrous metal mining, coal mining, coal products, electricity and natural gas, and atomic energy.[8]

---

[7]Japan, Gyosei Kanri-cho, *Gyosei Kiko-zu, Showa 48-nen ban* (Tokyo: Ministry of Finance, Printing Bureau, 1973), pp. 71–72.

[8]Ibid.

Industrial Policy

Historically, the centerpiece of MITI's industrial policy has been promotion of strategic industries at each stage of the country's economic development. During the immediate postwar years, MITI orchestrated the development of the four basic industries: coal, steel, electric power, and shipbuilding. Beginning in the mid-1960s and throughout the decade, the ministry forged ahead with what came to be known as "heavy and chemical industrialization." Material and technological resources were allocated preferentially toward the machinery and chemical industries. Tax incentives and subsidies were provided to the favored industries, accompanied by effective protection from imports and foreign investments. In the 1970s, the ministry's focus shifted to the so-called knowledge-intensive industries: computers, industrial automation, biogenetics, optical fibers, and so on.

Promotion of strategic industries is but one, albeit very important, aspect of Japan's industrial policy. The other aspects are industrial rationalization and industrial reorganization. *Industrial rationalization* refers to the improvement of the micro aspects of the economy, that is, the upgrading of industrial technology, productive facilities, and corporate management. *Industrial reorganization* refers to the streamlining of existing industrial organizations by eliminating overcapacity, reducing excessive competition, promoting specialization, and improving the vertical alignment among firms within an industry. For these two aspects of industrial policy, MITI's favorite prescription has been to limit competition by cartels (*rationalization cartels* and *reorganization cartels*) and promote bigness by mergers. This strategy clashes head on with the goals of the Antimonopoly Law and of the Fair Trade Commission (FTC); consequently, MITI's attempts to gain expanded statutory authority as a promoter of cartels and mergers have often been frustrated by strong opposition by the FTC and other government agencies.

The cornerstone of MITI's industrial policy is the cliental relationship that each industry maintains with its bureau of primary jurisdiction. Trade association officers and senior executives of the leading firms of the industry are in close working relationships with the key officials of the appropriate section and bureau of the ministry. These relationships are unavoidable because many business policy decisions require governmental approval and/or support. We have already noted, for instance, that the ministry has a large say in the allocation of low-interest loans made by public credit-and-loan corporations. In the general atmosphere of statism prevailing in the Japanese society and economy, few business decisions of importance can be made by private firms without touching bases with appropriate public officials. These contacts can also take place through formal mechanisms of consultation such as the various advisory councils affiliated with the ministry. Trade associations and advisory councils provide the ministerial officials with vital information concerning the industry's activities and plans. Between the business leaders and the bureau officials, therefore, there are constant exchanges of information. Officials' views and ideas are conveyed to the industry; and industry wishes, requests, and complaints are registered with the appropriate officials.

Based on the information provided by the industry, MITI officials develop their own industry forecasts, analyses, strategies, and "visions" of the future. The high quality of economic analysis and strategic thinking generated by MITI officials is one of the reasons why MITI's industrial policy is taken seriously by all concerned. MITI is not always right, and industries do not always cooperate; but few doubt that MITI's proposed policies, particularly those concerning growth industries, are good for the country. With respect to proposed strategies for declining industries, consensus is harder to obtain. We have already noted the objections raised by the FTC to MITI's penchant for using cartels. Specific firms may refuse to participate in a cartel, or to be merged with a bigger firm, when such measures are called for by MITI strategists.

In the 1950s and 1960s, MITI carried a big stick to be used on firms that refused to go along with its policies. This weapon was the ministry's authority to issue licenses for foreign exchanges needed to pay for imported machinery, raw materials, and technologies. In the famous 1965 case involving Sumitomo Metal, MITI withheld Sumitomo's licenses for importation of coal when the firm refused to participate in a cartel arrangement sponsored by the ministry. A similar sanction had been imposed on cotton spinners in the 1950s. The mere knowledge on the part of industries that the ministry could use such a stick was enough to induce most of the firms to conform to MITI's administrative guidance whenever it was applied to them.

With the gradual liberalization of foreign exchange and import controls in the 1960s and 1970s, MITI has steadily lost its power to control the behavior of industries and firms by withholding import licenses. Today, this power is virtually nonexistent. Having lost the big stick, the ministry must now rely on lesser permit-issuing and approval-granting authorities as well as various types of carrot to back up its administrative guidance. We noted earlier in our discussion of the Finance Ministry's Fiscal Investment and Loan Program that MITI has authority to mediate with credit-and-loan public corporations as to who get loans at what rates of interest. Although these loans are not large in size, they have been frequently used to provide financial supports to MITI-sponsored developmental projects. Perhaps more importantly, firms find it easier to borrow funds from commercial and other banks when they have FILP loans because of the widespread practice of banks granting "cooperative loans" *(kyocho yushi)* to firms that are receiving FILP funds. Frequently, a combination of FILP loans and commercial bank loans is arranged as a package deal by MITI in cooperation with the Finance Ministry and the Japan Development Bank (JDB). In a sense, MITI-mediated FILP loans are used as seed money for firms to obtain commercial bank loans.

We may summarize MITI's role in promoting structural changes in the Japanese economy as follows. Mobilizing all of its brain power and administrative authority, the ministry tries to induce changes in industrial structure in a direction that it perceives as good for the country. Business firms, working in close cooperation with the bureaucracy and generally acknowledging that its ideas are usually sound, nevertheless would not comply with the ministry's guidance unless they were convinced that to follow it is in their best interest. The interest of business firms, of course, lies in taking advantage of available market opportunities and increasing their profits and/or market shares. There thus exists a symbiotic relationship between MITI and industry: each side needs the other side's cooperation in order to get what it wants. In the otherwise confused, uncertain, and ad hoc processes of the country's economic development, the superagency and think tank MITI injects some sense of intelligence, coherence, and direction, thereby accelerating, perhaps, the inexorable process of structural changes in this dynamic economy by a perceptible degree. Does this mean, then, that MITI has created the "Japanese miracle"? Is the industrial policy of the Japanese government, with MITI playing the leading role, the major cause of Japan's spectacular economic performance over the last decades? We now turn to a discussion of this important question.

THE SOURCE OF THE JAPANESE MIRACLE

The strengths and advantages of the Japanese economic system have been manifested by what has come to be known as the Japanese miracle of the last few decades. Japan's gross national product as a percentage of that of the United States grew from less than 5 percent in the early 1950s to about 40 percent in the early 1980s. In terms of GNP per capita, Japan's is about four-fifths of that of the United States. These are impressive figures considering the facts that the population of Japan, which is about half that of the United States, lives in an area half the size of the State of Montana, that less than one-fifth of the country's land is arable, and that the country has few natural resources to speak of.

Japan's economic performance centers on its modern industrial sector, particularly manufacturing of consumer products and industrial products of relatively high technological sophistication. Japan's industrial forte lies in high-volume production of goods whose production techniques are standardized and whose production requires application of a well-organized and disciplined labor force of relatively high skill levels. In these industries (e.g., steel, ships, cameras, motorcycles, automobiles, and consumer electronics), Japanese firms hold positions of worldwide supremacy. Their record of productivity, growth, and international competitiveness has been impressive indeed.

In his book *MITI and the Japanese Miracle*, political scientist Chalmers Johnson asks the question, How do we explain the Japanese miracle? He presents five broad categories of plausible explanations. First, there is a sociocultural explanation. Japan's success is attributed largely to the uniquely Japanese character, rooted in the traditional sociocultural values, of being able to cooperate with each other and create a consensus among all the major participants in the economy. Second, there is the economic explanation. There was no miracle; the Japanese simply have taken advantage of the available market forces and opportunities. The recent rapid growth of the Japanese economy and impressive international competitiveness of some of its products can be explained largely by the stages of growth the Japanese economy has gone through. The third plausible explanation attributes the Japanese miracle to some of the uniquely Japanese institutions such as the "lifetime" employment system, the seniority-based system of wages and promotion, and the enterprise-union system. To this list of institutions, Johnson adds others, including the high rate of personal savings, the *amakudari* (descent from heaven) system of postretirement careers, and the *keiretsu* grouping of enterprises. Fourth, some would argue that Japan's high growth rate can be explained primarily by the "free ride" Japan has enjoyed in defense expenditures, market opportunities, and technology transfers. As the fifth category of explanation of the Japanese miracle, Johnson adds his own: the developmental state thesis. According to this view, to which we alluded earlier in the chapter, the high rate of growth of the Japanese economy is attributable primarily to the high quality of the leadership role played by the state. Specifically, Johnson credits MITI's industrial policy.[9]

All of these explanations, of course, are valid inasmuch as they touch upon some important aspects of the intriguing and complex question of the secret of Japan's success. They all provide valuable partial insights into the nature of the Japanese miracle. In the opinion of this writer, however, they fail to zero in on the most important cause—the very source—of the Japanese drive.

[9]Johnson, *MITI and the Japanese Miracle*, pp. 7–19

The basic driving force of the Japanese economic engine is the Japanese people's ability and willingness to work very hard as a group toward a common goal while extracting necessary sacrifices from individual members. The process by which Japan's familistic groupism manifests itself in orientation toward hard work and goal achievement is more complex than what is generally understood as the Japanese people's penchant for cooperation, consensus, and harmony. The basic scenario goes as follows.

Perhaps because of the paucity of natural resources and the pressure of population against the niggardliness of nature, the Japanese have developed a complex—bordering on paranoia—that their external environment is harsh. Therefore, in order to survive, individuals must stick together as a group; their survival and prosperity depend largely on their group's survival and prosperity. The group in this context may be a family, a village, a corporation, or the nation. A group, then, must establish priorities and channel resources and members' efforts into high-priority tasks, or else the whole group may fail to survive. The setting of priorities, choice of objectives, and their implementation are naturally carried out in the vertical organization of the Japanese group. Those persons or groups at the top of the organization make strategic decisions in behalf of all the members of the group. The authority of those higher up must be respected by those below them, and everyone must sacrifice his or her personal interests for the sake of the group.

This "village survival mentality" of the Japanese people nurtured over centuries of struggles against the paucity of natural resources is still very much alive in today's Japan. To be sure, the unprecedented prosperity of the Japanese economy in the recent years has helped to reduce its urgency, but the survivalist mentality still manifests itself in a variety of rivalrous behavior (e.g., a family's efforts to place a son in an elite university, a corporation's fight to increase its market share, and the government's efforts to develop a fifth-generation computer). In the energy crises of the 1970s, the whole nation was gripped literally by a fear of ruin. The relentless Japanese drive to economic overachievement must be understood in relationship to this deeply ingrained sense of economic insecurity. Overachievement is merely added insurance against a possible catastrophe. This Japanese complex of economic insecurity is somewhat analogous to the Russians' paranoia of military and political insecurity. Whereas the Americans are frustrated by the possibility of losing the position of Number One, the Japanese and the Soviets are harboring a deep fear of not being able to survive.

If groupism is the main source of Japanese drive, how does it specifically translate into achievement orientation? What aspects of groupism motivate the Japanese to press forward to ever higher grounds? In trying to answer these questions, it may be useful to examine the relationships between a group and its members at both micro and macro levels. At the micro level, we may ask questions about the relationships between a corporation and its employees. At the macro level, the relationships among business firms, as well as those between the nation state and corporations, may be examined. Since groupism is essentially a phenomenon of social psychology, it can be expected that its effects on human behavior are more direct and pronounced at the micro than at the macro level. We shall see, however, that even at the macro level, the behavior of the actors (corporations) is strongly influenced, although in a somewhat muted form, by the group orientation of Japanese society.

For the purpose of our discussion of Japanese groupism at the micro level, the relevant group is a business corporation (or a government office). Individual employees draw emotional nourishment and a sense of security from belonging to the corporate family and its various subgroups, and experience a sense of achievement and realizaton by making contributions to the group's welfare. Individuals' sense of self-worth comes primarily from their perception of how they are accepted, appreciated, or respected by others in their groups—superiors, equals, and subordinates. The desire for group approbation and the fear of group rejection is the basic motivation of Japanese employees—workers, managers, and executives alike. Group rejection is particularly painful in the environment of the Japanese corporate world where employment relations may last for one's entire working life.

Within a corporation, interpersonal relationships are vertically organized, and there exists a strong consciousness of rank and status derived primarily from one's educational background, seniority, age, and gender. There is a high degree of respect for, and even submissiveness to, authority. Also strong is a sense of duty and obligation to other members of the group—superiors, equals, and subordinates alike. Those in the higher ranks demand, as a matter of right, obedience and hard work from their subordinates. The subordinates' hard work is motivated by their respect for the superiors' authority, their sense of obligation to other workers, and their desire to increase peer approbation and to avoid loss of face. Employees are willing to sacrifice their self-gratification for the welfare of the company, but in return expect the company (and superiors) to look after their long-term personal and emotional needs. Superiors reciprocate the subordinates' desire for security by making sure that the distribution of the fruits of the group efforts is reasonably fair and that the decisions they make do not ignore the interests of the minorities and the powerless in the group. Subordinates are often unhappy about the demand for hard work and the stifling atmosphere of group conformity, but these are usually tolerated as the price one must pay for being a participant in collective work life. Younger workers are equally tolerant of their relatively low status and income because of the prospect of their rising slowly but steadily through the ranks over the years. In an overall social and institutional framework such as this, an intense demand for hard work by superiors tends to produce the intended results.

Corporations must demand hard work relentlessly from their employees because intergroup rivalry is fierce. As noted earlier, competition for market shares is extremely keen in Japan since most firms operate in only one industry. The strong interfirm rivalry contributes to the cohesion, cooperation, and camaraderie among employees within a corporation and among firms within a keiretsu group. Just as there exist relationships of dependency and obligation between superior and subordinate employees within a firm, there exist similar relationships between larger and smaller firms within a vertically organized capital keiretsu group of firms. For the survival and prosperity of larger firms, smaller firms must often sacrifice their profits or accept amakudari managers from their parent firms. This is the price the smaller firms must pay for the privilege of being members of an industrial group. Many smaller firms cannot survive alone; their health depends largely on the health of their parent company.

Unlike the tenured employees of Japan's large corporations (who account for about a quarter of Japan's labor force), most employees of smaller firms, in both manufacturing and services, work with low pay, few fringe benefits, and little job security. A large proportion of them are women and older workers. (More on small businesses in the next chapter.) The outstanding performance of Japan's large manufacturing firms is made possible, to a large extent, by the sacrifices of smaller firms and their employees. The superior-subordinate relationships between big and small firms, and the sacrifices of the firms and workers at the bottom of the industrial hierarchy, are integral parts of the industrial system that has produced the Japanese miracle.

At the national economy level, a similar group orientation is observed. A unique characteristic of Japan's familistic groupism is that it enables a group's efforts to be concentrated in a chosen high-priority area through self-sacrifices of members in the low-priority areas. To begin with, in Japanese society all the major institutions—educational, governmental, industrial, and financial—are vertically aligned and converge at the top. The top siphons off the best and most of the human and financial resources from all over the country, and these resources trickle down to lower levels of the hierarchy. Next, at the top level of this hierarchy, the troika of the leaderships of the ruling party, elite bureaucracy, and big business jointly determine the pattern and direction of the economy's development, and channel resources preferentially to the chosen strategic industries. Although strategic choices of private corporations are made primarily by commercial considerations and in response to market forces fueled by desires for greater profits and/or expanded market shares, they are nevertheless constrained to a remarkable degree by the considerations for the national interest championed by elite bureaucrats. The willingness of business leaders to accommodate the expressed wishes (and some arm twisting) of ministerial officials may be attributed in part to the traditional respect for the authority of state officials and in part to the business leadership's belief that the bureaucrats have the overall interests of the national economy at heart. Unlike American corporate executives who would instinctively reject government intervention in their decision-making processes, Japanese big-business leaders, for sociocultural reasons, are willing to work jointly with government officials in setting business goals and priorities.

In short, Japan's native groupism is capable of generating remarkable human drive and energy by essentially harmonizing, to a considerable degree, the self-interests of individuals and collective interests of larger groups up to and including the nation state. This congruence of interests is not achieved by an imposition of collective preferences by the state over the populace (as is done in the Soviet Union), or by the workings of an invisible hand of the market (as is presumably the case in the United States). Rather, it is a derivative of the emotive content and vertical orientation of Japanese groupism. The congruence is by no means perfect, and self-interests of individuals and groups are manifest at all levels of Japan's socioeconomic hierarchy. The essential point, however, is that Japanese individuals and groups realize their self-interest primarily by working through larger groups. Put differently, individuals find it difficult to realize their own interests unless they work for and with a group. Herein lies the source of both strengths and weaknesses of the Japanese system. The inherent weaknesses of Japan's familistic groupism will be discussed at the end of the following chapter.

QUESTIONS

1. What is the difference between the United States and Japan in the nature of industrial organization? Specifically, what differences do you find in the roles played by the public authority in industrial organization?

2. Name several public enterprises affiliated with the U.S. federal government. What major differences do you find between Japanese and U.S. public corporations?

3. Explain the nature of Japan's public credit-and-loan corporations. How do they differ from the public service corporations?

4. Discuss the differences and similarities between the following types of industrial grouping in Japan: (a) prewar zaibatsu, (b) postwar former-zaibatsu grouping, (c) new banking keiretsu, and (d) capital keiretsu.

5. Decribe the market structure of Japan's major industries. Are they collusive or competitive? How do you reconcile keiretsu grouping and government-sponsored cartels, on the one hand, and fierce rivalry among oligopolistic firms in an industry, on the other? How does the one-set principle fit into the picture? How does the market structure of Japan's industrial organization relate to Japan's familistic groupism?

6. What do you think are the motivations of Japanese corporations seeking affiliation with an enterprise group? Why can companies like Toyota or Nippon Steel do without affiliation? Why, do you think, do Sony and Honda deliberately avoid industrial affiliation?

7. In what sense is the Fair Trade Commission an anomaly in Japan's politico-economic system? How did such an anomaly come about?

8. Decribe the roles played by Keidanren in the Japanese economic system.

9. Discuss the problem of reconciling the special, parochial interests of different groups and the general, national interest of society as they are championed by different groups in Japan. What roles do politicians, elite bureaucrats, and zaikai leaders play in the process of reconciliation? Why is this reconciliation relatively easier in Japan than in the United States?

10. What channels of communication are open between Japan's business leaders, on the one hand, and public officials and political leaders, on the other? Compare them with similar channels open to U.S. business leaders.

11. What roles do ministerial advisory councils play in policy-making processes?

12. What is the nature of economic planning as practiced by the Economic Planning Agency? Is Japan a planned economy? Compare and contrast EPA's planning with Soviet central economic planning.

13. Discuss the differences between the United States and Japan in the nature and practices of fiscal policy.

14. Describe the main functions of the Ministry of Finance. What public agencies in the United States perform comparable functions?

15. Describe the nature and functions of the Fiscal Investment and Loan Program (FILP). In what ways does the program complement Japan's monetary and industrial policies?

16. Discuss the differences between the United States and Japan in the nature and practices of monetary policy.

17. Explain why monetary policy as a means of controlling the level of the nation's economic activities is relatively more effective in Japan than in the United States.

18. Explain why the Bank of Japan uses quantitative adjustments of the volume of its loans and discounts, rather than the price (i.e., interest rate) adjustments, as the primary instrument of monetary control.

19. Explain the special roles played by city banks in Japan's financial system. Why is it that the Bank of Japan regards city banks' lending activities as the primary target of its monetary policy?

20. Discuss the roles played by MITI in Japan's industrial development. Does the United States have a similar public agency? Does the Soviet Union?

21. Describe the main channels of the flows of loanable funds in Japan. What public agencies regulate the flows in what manners?
22. What is meant by *industrial policy* as it is practiced by MITI? What are its major aspects? How have the ministry's policy targets shifted since the immediate postwar years? What instruments or methods does MITI use in implementing its industrial policy?
23. Describe the nature of the cliental relationships that exist between MITI bureaus and private industrialists. Do similar relationships exist in the United States? (Hint: What about the relationships between the U.S. Defense Department and the defense-related industries?)
24. Conduct a brief research in a library to find out what strategic industries MITI is bent on developing now.
25. What motives do private corporations have in cooperating with MITI in its industrial policy? Under what circumstances would they refuse to go along?
26. Do you think the United States would benefit from a MITI-type industrial policy? Do you think it would be feasible for the United States to adopt such a policy? Why or why not?
27. Is MITI's industrial policy chiefly responsible for Japan's impressive economic growth record?
28. Critically evaluate the "village survival mentality" explanation of Japan's economic drive presented in the last section of this chapter.

SELECTED READING

CAVES, RICHARD E., and MASU UEKUSA. *Industrial Organization in Japan.* Washington, D.C.: The Brookings Institution, 1976.
HADLEY, ELEANOR M. *Antitrust in Japan.* Princeton, N.J.: Princeton University Press, 1970.
HAITANI, KANJI. *The Japanese Economic System: An Institutional Overview,* chaps. 4, 5, 8, 9, and 10. Lexington, Mass.: Lexington Books, D. C. Heath and Company, 1976.
JOHNSON, CHALMERS. *MITI and the Japanese Miracle: The Growth of Industrial Policy, 1925–1975.* Stanford, Calif.: Stanford University Press, 1982.
PATRICK, HUGH, and HENRY ROSOVSKY, Eds. *Asia's New Giant: How the Japanese System Works.* Washington, D.C.: The Brookings Institution, 1976.

CHAPTER 10

The Japanese Economy: Corporate Organization and Management

As elsewhere in the industrialized capitalist world, the basic units of productive activities in Japan are large private corporations. In Chapter 8 we discussed the organization and management of the American corporation. Many of the characteristics of large corporations are similar in both countries. In this chapter, our attention will be focused on those aspects of the American and Japanese corporate life that are markedly different. These differences, along with the differences in the government-business relationships that we discussed in the foregoing chapter, portray in sharp relief the systemic differences that exist between these two economic systems of global importance.

As we noted briefly in Chapter 1, one of the basic difficulties of comparing diverse economic systems is the virtual impossibility of placing them in a conceptual framework of universal applicability. For instance, we can logically divide our analysis of the U.S. economic system into macroeconomic and corporate organization since there exists no organic integration of private corporations into the national economy. Thus, in Chapter 8, we could discuss the organization and management of the American corporation as a sufficiently self-contained topic. In the chapters on the Soviet economy, it may be recalled, such a treatment would have been meaningless since enterprise organization and national economic organization constitute a continuum. Enterprise organization and management, therefore, could not have been discussed separately from macroeconomic organization and management. In the Japanese case, we find a situation somewhere between the American and Soviet cases. The Japanese corporation is technically a distinct and autonomous legal entity whose organization and management is not formally linked to the organization and management of the national economy. However, as we shall see, Japanese corporations are in practice closely tied to, and organically integrated into, the hierarchical order of the Japanese politico-economic system. Therefore, even though we have here a separate chapter on the Japanese corporation, the reader is well advised to regard it as a continuation of the discussion on Japan's industrial organization presented in the preceding chapter.

CORPORATE IDEOLOGY
AND BASIC PRACTICES

It is in the realm of corporate ideology that the differences between the American and Japanese styles of management are most notable. Corporate ideology defines the nature of the organization and its goals, and explains the relationships between the organization and its component parts as well as those between the organization and the larger society.

The ideology of the Japanese corporation is rooted in Japan's familistic groupism. A corporation is, first of all, a familylike community, which is organically integrated into the larger familylike community of the national economy. Individuals are integrated into the societal whole through memberships in successively larger groups organized into a hierarchy (individual, family, school, enterprise, industry, and economy), and the individuals and groups in this hierarchy are related to each other in a complex network of interdependency and reciprocity. Both a social organization like the business corporation and the entire society are regarded as organically, rather than mechanistically, constituted. Individuals and parts must fulfill their assigned roles; if they did not, the survival of the whole would be threatened. Individuals and parts, in return, draw their sustenance from the fruits of the collective effort of the whole and share in its prosperity.

The ideology of familistic groupism, although not always articulated as such, underlies the value and belief systems of all social organizations in Japan. In many corporations, the metaphor of the firm being "one great family" is often used, and is accepted by its members quite naturally with little psychological resistance. The ease with which this metaphor is embraced attests to the intensity and depth of the group orientation of the Japanese psyche.

The following paragraphs describe the basic organizational philosophy and practices of the typical large Japanese corporation, which are rooted in the ideology of familistic groupism.

Unlike the typical American corporation, where top management is the controlling insider group and employees are regarded essentially as hired hands, the typical large Japanese enterprise makes no formal distinction between managers (insiders) and employees (outsiders). Everyone who works in the organization, from the board chairman down to the most junior recruit, is considered a member of the corporate community. (Only temporary workers are considered outsiders.) As a rule, members are recruited only at the lowest level of the hierarchy, preferably fresh from schools and universities. They grow in the corporate family in age and seniority, and their relationships to the organization, as a rule, are on a long-term basis. (Female employees' status, however, does not follow this rule.) Members are usually hired as generalists, and are trained to become familiar with almost all the aspects of the company's operations. Various positions within the Japanese firm's hierarchy are not mechanistic and function-specific as in the U.S. corporation; rather, they are merely way stations for the corporate members to fill in turn as they grow in age, seniority, and experience.

Ranks in Japanese corporations are standardized as in the military and civil services, and the hierarchical relations among persons of progressively higher ranks are strictly observed. Age and seniority are the basic criteria for promotion and salary increases. These criteria are modified more or less—depending on the firm and the nature of the task—by considerations of merit. Since promotion is largely a function of age and seniority, and since salaries are closely tied to the rank progression, there is a high correlation within a given job classification between employees' age, rank, and salary.

The interests of the members of the corporate family (i.e., managers and employees) must be served before those of the other constituents (i.e., shareholders, banks, related firms, and the local community) can be considered. Dividend payments to shareholders and interest payments to the banks are the two financial obligations the corporation cannot afford to neglect. But the concerns for profits and other financial outcomes of the firm's activities are important only as the means by which the corporate family pursues its primary goal, which is the survival and growth of the organization. A typical Japanese corporation is most likely to sacrifice shareholders' dividends before it dismisses its workers, whereas in the United States the sequence is likely to be reversed.

A Japanese corporation is a social group as well as an economic unit. As such, the quality of interpersonal relations is very important.

Harmonious and emotionally satisfying human relationships must prevail if the community can function effectively as such. It is important that readers be reminded that *harmony (wa)* has a distinctive meaning in the context of Japan's familistic groupism. It does not mean a happy and pleasant agreement in feeling, interest, or action among participants of equal rank or status. Rather, it means absence of dissonant and adversarial relationships observed among persons who are vertically positioned to each other. Harmony exists largely because everyone is willing, or feels compelled, to accommodate his or her position to the emerging group consensus. Naturally, greater sacrifices are made by those who are lower in rank and status in the group. As explained in Chapter 3, those in subordinate positions gain, in return, in emotional gratification that helps satisfy their dependency needs. Harmony in a Japanese social organization, thus, is not a simple state of accord, but is rather a complex set of dynamic social forces maintaining a precarious equilibrium.

The basic unit of work in a Japanese corporation is not an individual position, but a work team. For the team members, peer evaluation and pressures are the primary motivation for hard work and achievement. As noted in Chapter 3, individuals work not so much for their self-realization or self-worth as for the sense of satisfaction of being able to contribute to their group's welfare, being fully aware that what is good for the group is good for its members in the long run.

Since the relationships between managerial and lower-echelon workers are not viewed as those between employers and employees, but rather as those between employees (or corporate members) of greater and lesser seniority, the superior-subordinate relationships in a Japanese corporation are typically much more "democratic" than those found in the typical American corporation. The participative management style enables those at the middle-management level to exercise a considerable degree of meaningful decision-making power. Top-level managers in the typical Japanese corporation are more likely to be facilitators, harmonizers, and motivators than the autocratic, take-charge kind of decision makers found in many U.S. corporations.

Since corporate members are not segregated into occupational or status groups, and since all the members including future top managers at first join the labor union, a union organized on the company basis (enterprise union) makes much better sense in Japan than the Western-style unions based on occupational categories or industrial grouping. The enterprise union is the only type of unionism that is compatible with Japan's corporate familism. The commonality of interests among the members of a corporation is much greater than that existing among "outsiders" belonging to different corporate families. A Japanese enterprise union is conterminous with the corporate family; its membership is identical with that of the corporation, except that the law requires that those who attain senior managerial ranks must leave the union.

In the foregoing paragraphs we have made a cursory survey of the basic philosophy and practices of the typical large Japanese corporation. These observations are generalized descriptions of the basic tendencies and pervasive patterns found in the great majority of Japan's large companies. Naturally, these generalizations do not apply to all cases. In the next four sections, we shall discuss some of the major aspects of Japanese corporate organization and management. In the last section of this chapter, we shall comment on the weaknesses of Japan's groupism in general and corporate familism in particular.

ORGANIZATIONAL STRUCTURE

In this section we shall examine the following three aspects of the organizational structure of Japanese corporations: (1) the internal structure of decision-making authority, (2) the external structure of intercorporate relationships, and (3) the structure of work organization.

Corporate Control

The outward appearance of the organizational structure of a large Japanese corporation is very much like that of a large American corporation. A corporation (joint-stock company) is organized by a group of shareholders who, in the general shareholders' meeting, elect a board of directors. The shareholders, with whom the ultimate power of control technically lies, entrust the responsibility of managing the company to the board. A company must have one or more *representative directors*, elected from among the directors, to legally represent the company to third parties. The law also requires that a joint-stock company has at least one statutory auditor. The auditor is elected by the general shareholders' meeting; a director or an employee of the company is not eligible to be the auditor.

In an American corporation, the board of directors and the management team are usually two separate groups, although some managers may also sit on the board. In Chapter 8 we reported that, in 1975, more than half of the directors of the 100 largest industrial corporations in the United States were outside directors. In Japan, the situation is quite different. In the typical large Japanese enterprise, the board and the management team are virtually the same. In 1977, 91 percent of the directors of 134 large Japanese corporations were inside directors in the sense that they were employees of the companies who had been pro-moted from within.[1] A few outside directors may be on a board, but they are likely to be representing the interests of important outside groups such as a parent company or a bank, *and* they almost always serve as active executives with full-time responsibilities. For all prac-tical purposes, therefore, directorship in a large Japanese corporation constitutes a special category of corporate *rank* to which employees of seniority and merit are promoted. For example, a department head may receive, as a promotion, the title of director. Although he may keep the previous title and responsibilities as the sales manager, legally he ceases to be an employee (*shain*) of the company and becomes an officer (*yakuin*). He now attends the directors' meetings, and is exempt from mandatory retirement at the age stipulated in the company's bylaws. A large Japanese corporation may have anywhere from 20 to 30 direc-tors, an overwhelming majority of whom are senior executives. A meet-ing of the board, therefore, is a de facto meeting of the senior staff of the corporation, although it is de jure a meeting of the representatives of shareholder interests. Little discussion of substance takes place in a board meeting; important decisions are made by top management out-side the board meeting. Operating-level managers with the added rank of director are called ordinary directors. The top management team of a typical large Japanese corporation consists of those officers with the rank of managing director or above. The top management team of a large company may consist of the following positions:

> Board chairman/(representative) director
> President/(representative) director
> Vice-president/director
> Executive managing director(s)
> Managing director(s)

A managing director may have two or three ordinary directors reporting to him. In a smaller firm, there may be only one executive managing director reporting directly to the president. The *executive committee* of the board of directors (*jomukai*) consists of those officers holding the rank of managing director or above. This group, numbering between five and ten persons, is the locus of effective power of control in a Japanese corporation.

In a typical large corporation, the power of the president is nearly total. (The position of board chairman is honorary as a rule, being

---

[1]Taishiro Shirai, "A Supplement: Characteristics of Japanese Managements and Their Personnel Policies," in *Contemporary Industrial Relations in Japan*, ed. Taishiro Shirai (Madison, Wisc.: University of Wisconsin Press, 1983), pp. 373–74.

reserved for a retired president. In some cases, however, the board chairman either wields real power or serves as "the power behind the throne.") The president's power arises from his ability to determine the outcome of both directors' and shareholders' meetings. We have already noted that the directors' meetings are, de facto, meetings of senior managers. In the Japanese environment of respect for authority of one's seniors, few junior directors dare challenge the decisions taken in the executive committee. Within the top management team, the president is likely to have a great deal of influence over the managing directors since the president by tradition has the right to recommend his successor to the shareholders' meeting.

The relative unimportance of outside directors on a typical corporate board also contributes to the near dictatorial power of the president. Because of the underdeveloped state of the equity market in Japan, most corporations rely more heavily, for sources of funds, on borrowing from banks and other financial institutions than on sales of stock. Of the outstanding shares, on average over two-thirds are owned by financial institutions and related firms, and less than one-third is owned by the general public. And, unlike the situation in the United States, those financial institutions (largely commercial banks) and related companies hold shares in the company in question not as financial investments but as a means of maintaining close business relationships with the firm. As long as their relationships with the company's top management are satisfactory and as long as interest is paid on bank loans, these outside parties do not interfere with the internal management of the firm. Thus, as long as the firm's performance is generally satisfactory, the president's power remains unchallenged. The absence of the practice of corporate takeovers contributes to the entrenchment of the president and his close associates as a controlling power group.

In the United States, shareholders' meetings in large corporations are basically rituals, and few decisions of substance are made there. Important matters are decided ahead of time among the directors and/or the top managers, and are submitted to the shareholders' meeting for formal approval. The management seldom fails to secure such approval because it controls the proxy votes. In Japan, the situation is much the same with some minor differences. Important decisions are made by the top managers in consultation with the major outside interests such as the main bank and the key related firms. Since these outside interests typically hold about two-thirds of the voting shares, collecting proxy votes from small shareholders is not really necessary. In the great majority of cases, shareholders' meetings are pro forma rituals to approve the slate of "proposals" submitted by the board of directors. As a rule, meetings do not last more than an hour; often they end in less than 20 minutes. Small shareholders who dare demand the floor and raise questions about the company's policies and practices are outshouted or intimidated by professional troublemakers called *sokaiya* (shareholders' meeting specialists) who receive payoffs from the company for their services. Although it is illegal for companies to make payments to these professional silencers, many companies somehow find ways to make under-the-table payments as insurance against prolonged and disruptive meetings in which many sokaiya ask embarrassing questions and raise havoc. Several hundred sokaiya, many with organized crime connections, are active in the Tokyo area alone; their surface occupations are business consultants or business journalists.[2]

To sum up: The president of a typical large corporation in Japan has relatively much greater freedom of action than his counterparts in the United States. He is nearly totally free of constitutional limitations to his exercise of power within the corporation. Virtually all of the other directors are his juniors whom he has had a hand in promoting, and some of the senior directors need his support to eventually succeed him as president. Shareholders' meetings are under total control of the management. Provided that the president does not fail to maintain a good working relationship with the leaderships of the key banks and related firms, his position and power in the company are assured.

The Industrial Context

The question of who controls the typical Japanese corporation cannot be answered adequately unless we know something about the nature and extent of the control over corporate management exercised by outside interests. In the preceding chapter we analyzed two types of enterprise grouping: horizontal enterprise groups and vertical enterprise affiliations. In what follows our interest will focus on the control-dependency relationships between vertical affiliates. Many of Japan's largest corporations have a large number, often hundreds, of subsidiaries and other affiliated firms under them. The managements of these "child" and "grandchild" companies are effectively controlled by the parent company through stock ownership and dispatched personnel. The subsidiaries and affiliated firms are also frequently under the influence of the group bank.

When a parent company owns more than 50 percent of the stock of the smaller company, the latter is called a *subsidiary* of the former. The term *related firm* or *affiliated firm* is used to describe a subcontracting firm in which the parent company's stock ownership is 50 percent or less. The parent company's stock ownership, whether or not it exceeds

---

[2]Bradley K. Martin, "Japan's Gadflies, Down but Not Out," *Wall Street Journal*, July 5, 1983, p. 23.

50 percent, is almost always accompanied by concurrent appointments of officers and employees of the parent company as executives of the subordinate companies.[3] Although it is possible that these dispatched executives divide their time between the two firms, it is more likely that these officers serve in the subordinate firm on a temporary leave from the parent company.

Of the 34 first-line subsidiaries and other affiliated firms of Nippon Steel Corporation in 1970, 13 had presidents who were from Nippon Steel, and 28 had directors coming from Nippon, ranging in number from 1 to 8. (The number of directors in these companies ranged from 7 to 26.) The percentage of the stocks of these firms owned by Nippon Steel ranged from 0.6 percent to 100 percent, with the average being 29.4 percent.[4] These figures indicate that there was a considerable degree of vertical integration between Nippon Steel and its child companies. In fact, business policies of subordinate firms are in general so effectively controlled by the parent company through the dispatched executives that transactions between the two can be viewed as de facto intrafirm transactions.[5]

The larger company within a capital keiretsu group often takes advantage of its greater bargaining power relative to its subordinate firms by "squeezing" the latter in intragroup dealings. For example, during periods of economic downturn, a parent company may impose on the subordinate firms prices and loan terms that help protect the profitability of the former at the expense of the latter. During a recession, a parent firm may even force the weaker firms to absorb some of its surplus workers on a temporary basis. This hierarchical relationship is one of dependency and reciprocity. The larger firms may "squeeze" the smaller ones, but they also recognize that they have a responsibility to look after the welfare of their dependent firms. The benefits to smaller firms from affiliation with the larger firm include a stable volume of business, technical and managerial assistance from the parent company, and provision of loans. As a rule, a small firm that belongs to a large capital keiretsu group is less likely to fail than others that have no vertical affiliation.

Another source of vertical coordination and external control over a corporation's management is the practice of accepting a director from the group bank. Many firms find it useful or necessary to have a former

---

[3]Hiroshi Okumura, "Interfirm Relations in an Enterprise Group: The Case of Mitsubishi," in *The Anatomy of Japanese Business*, ed. Kazuo Sato and Yasuo Hoshino (Armonk, N.Y.: M. E. Sharpe, Inc., 1984), pp. 177–78.

[4]Naoto Sasaki, *Management and Industrial Structure in Japan* (Oxford: Pergamon Press, 1981), p. 83.

[5]Okumura, "Interfirm Relations," pp. 177–78.

bank official on its board. A bank manager at the retirement age may be sent to one of the bank's related firms on the *amakudari* (descent from heaven) basis. Note that these bankers are not merely placed on the board as an outside member with no managerial duties, although such an arrangement is not totally unheard of. Rather, they are employed as full-time senior directors with active managerial duties, with a potential of later succeeding the president. Firms naturally prefer not to accept these amakudari directors from banks, but considerations of cementing a tie with important banks often overrides the internal resistance. A similar situation exists with respect to amakudari executives from the parent company.

The Organization of Work

In Chapter 8 we noted that in American companies the basic unit of work is a manager's office, and that managerial positions are organized hierarchically along the lines of authority and responsibility. In contrast to the *linear* organizational principle of American corporations, the Japanese corporate organization is built on the *modular* principle of piling up blocks or modules of work teams. The basic unit of work in a Japanese bureaucratic organization is a section (*ka*), which may consist of up to 20 persons, including a section chief (*kacho*), a few subsection chiefs, and section members who are either university graduate careerists or clerical workers with high school education, mostly young women. A section is large enough for specialized function(s) to be assigned to, but small enough to allow face-to-face working relationships among its members.

In a typical corporate office, the desks of section members are placed in double rows, facing each other, with the section chief's desk placed at the end of the row a few feet away facing the rectangular block. Work is assigned collectively to a section; there are no job descriptions for individual employees. Secretarial work is handled collectively by the clerical workers in each section; few Japanese senior executives have a private secretary. Secretarial work for top managers is handled collectively by the personnel in the secretarial section.

Three or four sections may comprise a department (*bu*), which is led by a department head (*bucho*). A large corporation is likely to be divided into divisions, each division being a branch office or a plant. As noted earlier, department and division heads may have an added rank of director. Although organization charts may show vertical lines of authority relationships running from the president down to the section chief through the executive managing director, the managing director, the division head, and the department head, this vertical linear relationship is not taken as seriously as its counterpart in an American corporation.

In contrast to the linear organizational structure of a typical U.S. corporation, what we find in Japan is a much more flexible organizational structure with little emphasis on the staff-line distinction, the "one man, one boss" principle, or the proportionality of individual authority and responsibility. Accompanying the flexibility of organization is an emphasis on coordination of efforts by all concerned, regardless of their functional responsibilities, toward achieving the company's goals. Communication and coordination take place by osmosis, following an elaborate network of both formal and informal interpersonal relationships, rather than linearly along the formal line-staff chains of command, as they do in the United States.

In a Japanese corporation and also in the larger social setting, such designations as section chief and department head are not merely for convenience of organizing a company's work. They have a considerable social significance, and the rank a person holds within a corporate (and government) organization is directly comparable to the ranks other individuals hold in other organizations. This situation is very much like the military or academic ranks in the United States. If a college teacher has a rank of associate professor, or a military officer has a rank of colonel, their relative standing in their respective organizations, and in the larger society, is immediately apparent to everyone. The Japanese corporate (and governmental) ranks have a similar social significance. In rank-conscious Japanese society, people take corporate ranks very seriously; to be promoted to the position of a section chief in a large corporation (or in the government bureaucracy) is a sure sign of one's success in life.

In the United States, authority and responsibility are delegated downward through successive levels of offices, and the incumbent of each office is held responsible *as an individual* for the execution of the tasks assigned to the office. In Japan, work is assigned to a group, and the group is collectively held responsible for performance of the assigned task. The American notion of authority being commensurate with responsibility is alien to the Japanese. Each group has a responsibility to do its best in performing the tasks given from above. The authority of the group leader (e.g., the section chief) is the function of the leader's formal rank in the organization as well as that leader's ability, personality, and attitude toward the subordinates. Thomas Rohlen points out that the concept of authority (*ken'i*) is not commonly used among Japanese in discussing group dynamics. Good Japanese leaders are those who, rather than relying on the authority of their rank or status, make efforts to earn the willing acceptance and participation of their subordinates. Says Rohlen, ". . . the leader's virtue, his concern for others, and the general esprit within the group are the most effective means to individual acceptance and participation."[6]

CORPORATE GOALS AND STRATEGY

In Chapter 8 we observed that the primary goal of the typical American corporation is growth in earnings as measured in such financial indices as earnings per share of the company's stock or returns on the company's assets. The strategy used by U.S. corporations to attain their goals centers on the use of sophisticated techniques of financial analysis designed to produce attractive short-term results. In this section we shall describe the goals and strategy of a typical large Japanese company. We shall find that Japanese firms value growth more highly than profits, and that they are less concerned about short-term financial performance than their American counterparts.

Corporate Goals

We noted earlier that the separation of ownership and control in a typical large Japanese corporation is even more advanced than that in an American counterpart. We also noted that top managers of large Japanese companies tend to view their companies as communities and all the regular employees as members of the corporate family without a clear status distinction between managers and employees. Also observed was the fact that corporations, as members of the national family, are held responsible for contributing to the welfare of society by producing useful products. These ideological convictions tend to generate a preference for growth in production and an increase in market shares as the primary goal of the corporate organization.

It is of course recognized that no corporation can survive long without producing a reasonable amount of profits. A company that is losing money is considered to be sick and is viewed with alarm by banks, government bureaucrats, and the public at large primarily because such a company is deprived of financial resources with which to grow (i.e., to develop new products and expand market shares). But beyond a certain minimum or reasonable amount of profits—reasonable in the sense that the level of profitability is favorably comparable with that

[6]Thomas P. Rohlen, *For Harmony and Strength: Japanese White-Collar Organization in Anthropological Perspective* (Berkeley, Calif.: University of California Press, 1974), p. 119.

of other firms in the same industry—pursuing profits solely for profits' sake is regarded as selfish or even unethical.

In an interview survey of 64 presidents of large Japanese electric equipment manufacturing firms conducted in 1970, the presidents were asked to choose, from among seven business goals listed, the three they considered the most important. Since each president chose three items, there were 192 items chosen in all. The four most frequently chosen items were growth (50), profits (49), market shares (30), and the ratio of new product sales to total sales volume (30).[7] These results show that (1) *both* growth *and* profits are important business goals for a great majority of Japanese firms; but (2) when the other two growth-related objectives (market shares and new product ratio) are considered, growth as a corporate goal appears more highly valued than profits.

In this connection, it must be remembered that most Japanese corporations depend largely on borrowings from banks rather than the equity markets as sources of their investable funds. And the large share-holders—banks and related firms—hold shares in the company, as a rule, for the purpose of maintaining good business relations with the company, not as a source of investment income. Since the small investors who tend to benefit from high profitability are relatively less important to the management than the large investors, and since the large investors are not much concerned about the dividend rate, the management has little reason to be preoccupied with high profitability. The total absence of fear of corporate takeovers that could be triggered by falling stock prices contributes to the lower degree of importance Japanese corporate managers attach to high profitability.

By contrast, growth of sales volume and market share is considered very important by every Japanese management. As noted earlier, Japanese corporations (as well as individuals and other groups) are extremely rank conscious. The reputation that a firm enjoys in a given industry depends almost exclusively on the firm's share in the market. Because of Japanese companies' penchant for specializing production in one industry, the market share becomes doubly important; a firm cannot compensate for the decline in its market share in one industry by the increase in another. Thus, the market share becomes one of the most important indicators of success of a Japanese firm.

Growth in sales and expanded market shares are important also for reasons of better employee morale. Because of the traditional system of long-term employment and seniority-based promotion, a large number of employees tend to bunch up at the middle and higher levels of

[7]Ryuhei Shimizu, "The Growth of Firms in Japan: An Empirical Study of Chief Executives," in *The Anatomy of Japanese Business*, ed. Kazuo Sato and Yasuo Hoshino (Armonk, N.Y.: M. E. Sharpe, Inc., 1984), pp. 95–97.

management as they grow in age and seniority. Since the number of positions are smaller at higher levels of management, promotion of older employees becomes increasingly more difficult unless the company is steadily growing. People are very sensitive about this aspect of corporate performance; the average number of years for new recruits fresh from schools to be promoted to, say, section chief are compared from company to company and are even published in national magazines. Companies in which promotion is known to be slow will naturally have a harder time in attracting high-quality graduates as new recruits than those that are expanding steadily.

Corporate Strategy

To achieve the goals of growth and expanded market share, what strategy does the Japanese corporation follow? Three major practices characterize the typical Japanese strategy: (1) long-term outlook, (2) emphasis on manufacturing excellence and product quality, and (3) productivity through people.

The long-term outlook. Japanese top corporate managers use a long time horizon to evaluate their companies' performance. There is nothing out of the ordinary about this practice. It has received attention in recent years merely because American corporate managers are singularly concerned about short-term performance.

The long-term outlook of Japanese corporations is a concomitant of the long-term employment of Japanese managers. Since almost all managers are expected to stay in the same company and promoted slowly as a group, there is no need to evaluate and reward their performance in the short run. The corporation has a long memory, and it rewards individual achievements subtly but assuredly over years or even decades. In such an environment, every decision maker can afford to take a long-term outlook. Even though an investment project or a new product may not produce immediate profits, decision makers can afford to sit it out if they are convinced that it is good for the company in the long run. Similarly, even during a business downturn and deteriorating earnings, they may make necessary investments in new plants, equipment, or research and development activities if they deem them necessary for the long-run health of the company.

Emphasis on product quality. Whereas many American managers are apt to use cost cutting as a primary weapon for improving their company's financial performance, Japanese managers tend to stress better product quality as a primary means of increasing their company's market share. This quality consciousness has a root in the traditional Japanese respect for craftsmanship and perfection. People take great pride in making, having, and using objects of quality. Shoddy and poor products are causes of shame; they bring shame not only to people who buy and own them but also to people who make and sell them. Against this background of quality consciousness of the populace, Japanese producers have little choice but to stress product quality. Any company that fails to produce quality products not only loses out in rivalry for market share, but also suffers a loss of reputation in the public eye. Such a company would have difficulty in maintaining high worker morale and in attracting good people to work for it. In Japan, therefore, it pays to stress quality.

Productivity through people.   Perhaps the most important single quality of the Japanese management system is its unfaltering belief in the importance of the human factor in the production process. That *people*—not machines, techniques, or theories—make products, and that good products can be made only by people pulling in the same direction is deeply ingrained in the Japanese management psyche. Unlike the American management philosophy that treats workers as suppliers of labor services that the buyer (i.e., the firm) may choose to buy by the hour, week, or year, or not to buy at all, the Japanese philosophy starts with the premise that by some karma (*en*) all the members of the corporate family are brought together to work with and for each other. They are not strangers to each other, but are *miuchi* (all in the family). As such, they must work in harmony, toward a common goal, without calculations of short-term gains and losses.

The emphasis on harmony and cooperation among individuals and groups within a corporation does not mean, however, that the management respects the rights, dignity, creativity, and privacy of individuals. Rather, individuals are expected to behave as though they were in a traditional Japanese family, that is, to know their places, to respect the authority of the seniors, and in general to sacrifice self-gratification for the sake of the family. In other words, the Japanese strategy of "productivity through people" does not mean an attempt to enhance productivity by encouraging individual initiative and creativity. Nor does it mean an effort to keep employees particularly "happy." Management demands, as a matter of right, very hard work out of each and every employee. For all employees to work together smoothly, much sacrifice of individual freedom is required. Most Japanese do not consider this too high a price to pay, since their need to belong to a group and feel secure in its warmth is far more pressing than their desire to feel free and independent as individuals.

THE EMPLOYMENT SYSTEM

In the American management system, strategic planning and financial control are the centerpieces; dealings with employees are but one of the aspects of managing various types of resources available to the management. By contrast, in the Japanese system of management, *human relations* (*ningen kankei*) are the central concern of managers at all levels. Here, human relations refers to the structure and processes of organization of both formal and informal interpersonal relations involving both the outsiders (bankers, bureaucrats, clients, suppliers, and persons in related firms) and insiders (employees) of the corporation. The bulk of the time and effort of Japanese managers, even those in technical fields, is devoted to solving problems in human relations. In this section, our discussion will focus on the structure and process of human relations inside large Japanese corporations.

Categories of Employee Status

Earlier in this chapter we observed that members of a Japanese corporation are divided into officers (i.e., those with the designation of *director*) and employees. Although this distinction is significant from a legal point of view, in practice it is considered unimportant; the directorship is just another rank to which middle managers can aspire. In a great majority of large Japanese companies today, all the members are *employees* of the corporation, whether or not they perform managerial functions. Salaried executives are often referred to as *managerial workers*.

In a Japanese company, neither the distinction between managerial and ordinary employees nor the difference between blue- and white-collar workers is registered in people's minds as sharply as in an American firm. There is a tendency to avoid uses of ostentatious symbols of rank and status. Parking lots, rest rooms, cafeterias, and gyms are not segregated according to occupational category or status. In most Japanese plants, everyone—from the plant manager down to the apprentices fresh from schools—wears the same plant uniform with a name badge on it. Visiting corporate VIPs, when touring the plant, don the same uniform. Japanese managers need not fear that an egalitarian atmosphere of this sort might lead to a diminution of respect for authority. The respect for authority of office, rank, status, and age is deeply ingrained in employees' psyche and remains unaffected by a mere outwardly display of workplace egalitarianism.

Employees of a large Japanese corporation are classified into different categories by criteria that are uniquely Japanese. The most important distinction is made between regular employees and nonregular employees. *Regular employees* are the full members of the corporate community. They are the ones who enjoy all the amenities of the so-called Japanese Employment System: lifetime employment, seniority-based promotion and wages, and a variety of corporate welfare benefits. They are accepted into the corporate family membership by a rigorous selection process and only after a probational training period. *Nonregular employees* are temporary workers, who are mostly seasonal workers and part-time women workers. These employees have no guarantee of steady employment, receive substantially lower wages than regular workers, and enjoy few fringe benefits. They are hired without a rigorous screening process, and fired just as easily. They are not regarded as members of the corporate community. (As we shall see later, the employment situation of Japan's myriads of very small firms is essentially the same as that of the nonregular employees of large corporations.)

Among regular employees, three major categories can be commonly identified. First, university graduates (predominantly male) are managerial and technical employees and have a status similar to that of commissioned officers in the military. They start with the lowest level of staff work as ordinary members of a section, but can rise to the highest position in the company. Second, male high school graduates may start as apprentice production workers and may rise as high as the section chief in a production department by their retirement age. Third, there are female high school graduates who start either as production workers or clerical workers but who by custom leave the company at marriage or with the arrival of the first baby. Although the courts have ruled that the compulsory retirement age for young women (say at age 30) is unconstitutional, and therefore no firm can legally force its young women workers to leave the company, it is still customary that almost all women do leave. Many of these women come back in their middle age as temporary workers. Thus, young women in this third category are regular employees but are not "permanent" workers. They work for a few years between schooling and marriage "to see the world." They work with little concern for promotion since their tenure with the company is very short. A very small minority of female workers in this category do try to make careers out of their jobs, but they must suffer the humiliation of being a nuisance or oddity in their workplace.

Lifetime Employment

The so-called lifetime employment of Japanese workers is really a system of tenured employment of regular employees practiced in large corporations. Only one in every four Japanese employees works under some system of tenured employment. It is not a legally binding rule, nor does the moral obligation to provide steady employment extend beyond the compulsory retirement age, which is typically between 55 and 60. Companies as a rule do not dismiss regular workers or managers unless the employee is disabled or has committed a grave criminal offense. Incompetent workers and misfits are assigned to positions where they can do a minimum amount of harm to the company. During the worst of a business adversity, some regular production workers may be temporarily laid off, but these laid-off workers almost always receive partial wage payments. Before such a step is taken, however, the firm is likely to arrange a work slowdown, and to have workers do such nonproductive works as holding discussion sessions on productivity improvements and doing maintenance and repair work around the plant. When the management of a large Japanese firm has to discuss permanent dismissals of its regular employees, one can be sure that it is on the verge of bankruptcy.

Lifetime employment is a social norm that both management and employees regard as natural and morally correct. Their efforts to live up to this norm, however, are not without calculation of self-interest. Most of the managers of large Japanese companies justify the system by reference to the familistic nature of Japanese corporations, and many of them are genuinely proud of their policies of not dismissing their regular employees. In exchange for guaranteeing career-long employment, however, top executives expect regular employees to be wholeheartedly committed and loyal to the firm. Job security, high wages, and various ancillary benefits provided to regular employees are often regarded by management as the necessary price the company must pay in order to assure employee commitment and loyalty. Employees, on the other hand, are willing to make personal sacrifices for the company so long as they know they have secure jobs with steadily rising status and income. Should this expectation be betrayed, the employees' devotion to the company's goals deteriorates rapidly. Thus, lifetime employment as a social norm can be best understood as an implicit social contract based on reciprocity of obligations.

During a business downturn, American firms reduce costs of operations by laying off workers. This option is not readily available to large Japanese firms, which carry a permanent work force drawing fixed salaries and wages. They try to maintain operational flexibility by a combination of the following practices. In the first place, firms keep the size of their regular work force at a level that is just adequate for the amount of work during a period of weak demand. During periods of strong demand, management pressures regular workers to do overtime work and hires an increased number of temporary workers. Thus, a redundancy of the regular work force occurs only when a business slowdown is much worse than expected. Second, after the number of temporary workers and the amount of subcontracting is reduced, if the amount of work is still inadequate to keep regular workers fully occupied, the pace of work is slowed and regular workers may be given special assignments, as noted earlier. Third, the firm may pressure its dependent firms (subsidiaries and subcontractors) to use some of its redundant workers on a temporary basis, or accept some of its retirees on a permanent basis. Naturally, special efforts are made to encourage early retirement under especially favorable terms. Fourth, as noted earlier, in a deep recession the management may have to lay off some of its regular employees for several months, often at 50 percent or more of regular wages. (In a severe recession, government subsidies under special legislation may become available to help firms pay their layoff wages. For example, in the recession of 1975, the government subsidized one-half of large firms', and two-thirds of smaller firms', layoff wages for up to nine months.) Finally, severance of regular employees may have to be considered. Such a drastic measure will be taken only as the last resort, after all the steps discussed above have been taken.

Dismissal of permanent employees is a serious matter precisely because the prevailing system of lifelong employment makes it difficult for those who are dismissed to make a fresh start elsewhere. As midcareer transfers, dismissed workers almost invariably must move to a lesser firm. In the new environment, the midcareer recruits may find themselves seriously handicapped in promotion and other matters for years to come. Perhaps more importantly, they may have to suffer the stigma of not being genuine insiders for the rest of their careers.

Since regular employees cannot be dismissed easily, companies take great care in selecting them. Firms naturally seek intelligence and industry in their recruits, but these qualities alone are not enough. Acceptable candidates must also have the right family background as well as the right personality and attitude to fit well into the corporate family.

As a rule, firms recruit their regular employees only from schools and universities. Midcareer applicants are considered only when shortages of certain skills make it impractical to insist on virgin labor. New graduates are considered desirable because (1) they are more malleable than older workers and therefore can be more easily molded into the firm's ways, and (2) they fit into the seniority system better than midcareer job-changers. Each firm recruits from schools and universities that have a reputation comparable to the company's reputation in the industry. Thus, the largest and most prestigious firms recruit only from the "best" schools and universities.

Having passed written examinations and personal interviews, successful candidates are subjected to investigations into their personal and family backgrounds conducted by either the company's personnel section or private investigators. Many of the questions raised in these investigations (e.g., the history of mental illness in the candidate's family and the social reputation of the candidate's father) are not directly relevant to the candidate's ability to work. Their significance can be understood only when we realize that the firm is not merely trying to locate "hired hands" but is engaged in a serious process of finding right children to be adopted into its corporate family.

Seniority-Based Promotion and Wages

In order to understand the Japanese system of promotion and reward based on seniority, it is necessary first to understand exactly what is meant by *seniority* in the Japanese context. In large companies, salaries (paid monthly for both white- and blue-collar workers) and promotion are not based on individuals' performance or labor-market conditions, but are calculated under a complex formula for *nenko*. Nenko literally means "merit of years of service": it is based on the employee's education, age, and years of service within the company. All the employees who enter the company in the same year upon graduation from school or university have exactly the same nenko. They are promoted according to their nenko at about the same rate for the first several years; afterwards, subtle differences in both rank and assignment will appear. By the time all the members of the same year of entry reach the retirement age, differences among them in rank (but not in salary) may be substantial. As we observed in our discussion in the career pattern of Japanese government bureaucrats, one major difficulty with a nenko promotion system is that as employees advance through the ranks, increasingly fewer positions become available. The company tries to weed out slow movers by finding them lower-paid jobs with subsidiaries and subcontractors. The problem of an increasingly larger number of older employees vying for available positions at higher levels of management has become especially acute with the slowing down of the growth rate of the Japanese economy in the 1970s and 1980s.[8]

Under the nenko wage system, older employees approaching the retirement age may receive salaries and benefits that are considerably higher than those of younger workers. For example, in 1980, male production workers in the 50-to-54 age group received wages that were 57 percent higher than those of male workers in the 21-to-24 age group. Comparable statistics for West Germany for 1972 showed that the highest wage group was the 35–39 age group whose wages were 8.2 percent

---

[8]For a discussion of the problem of the rising ages of workers within an environment of slower economic growth, see Kanji Haitani, "Changing Characteristics of the Japanese Employment System," *Asian Survey*, 18, no. 10 (October 1978), 1029–45.

above the 21–24 age group. Above the 35–39 age group, wages fell steadily so that the 50–54 age group received only 3 percent more than those in the 21–24 age group.[9] Wage differentials are even greater in the largest Japanese firms. In 1978, for example, male production workers in the 50–54 age group in firms employing over 1,000 persons received wages that were 122 percent higher than those of the 20–24 age group.[10]

Paying older workers so much more than younger workers may appear irrational since the productivity of production workers is generally believed to peak in their 30s. Therefore, if production workers are paid in proportion to their productivity, those in their 30s should be receiving the highest wages, which was the case in West Germany in 1972.

But when we consider nenko wages in combination with the nenko promotion system, we find that the Japanese wage system is not as irrational as it first appears. If employees are to stay with the same company until they retire, it is not necessasry for the firm to match workers' productivity and wages every month or every year. Younger workers can usually get along with relatively small incomes since most of them live either with their parents or in company-subsidized housing. Older workers, by contrast, need much larger incomes because of their increased social and family responsibilities. Moreover, firms incur large expenses in training young workers; these expenses are recovered over the career of the workers by underpaying them when they are young, and increasing wage payments as workers become better trained and more experienced. It must also be remembered that under the nenko promotion system older workers do have higher ranks, status, and responsibility than younger ones. They are also expected to be more mature and experienced in human relations skills, which are considered a key factor in the Japanese management system. Steadily rising wages based on employees' age and length of service within the company also make it profitable for them to stay in one firm rather than change jobs in the middle of a career. Employees who are thus locked into a career in one company are likely to be more committed and devoted to their firm than those who have other options.

In most firms, wages and salaries are not based strictly on nenko; serious efforts are being made to have individuals' wages to reflect their merit (i.e., abilities, performance, and attitudes). Various types of supplements and allowances are added to the base pay to reward meritorious services. But these supplements and allowances tend to be so

[9]Keizai Koho Center, *Japan 1982: An International Comparison* (Tokyo: Keizai Koho Center, 1982), p. 60.

[10]Japan, Keizai Kikaku-cho, *Keizai Hakusho, Showa 54-nen ban* (Tokyo: Ministry of Finance, Printing Bureau, 1979), p. 182.

closely related to the base pay that the overall wage structure is essentially based on nenko.

There are two reasons why an adoption of truly merit-based wage system would be next to impossible in Japan. First, there still exists a widely held view that people's incomes should be commensurate with their family and social responsibilities. It is feared that merit-based wages may undermine the financial security and social positions of older employees. Second, and perhaps more importantly, paying individuals according to their individual merit is deemed both difficult and undesirable. It would be difficult because each individual's contribution to the firm's performance is difficult to measure in an environment where efforts are made collectively as a group. It is considered undesirable because singling out and rewarding specific individuals may have an adverse effect on the group's morale. The Japanese solution to this dilemma between group harmony and individual merit is to pay employees largely according to their nenko but to recognize individual merit by subtle differentiations in the assigned position and the speed of promotion.

The Enterprise Union

Earlier in this chapter we observed that Japan's corporate system has rejected the Western-style craft or industrial unionism and instead has developed its own variety known as *enterprise unionism*. Whereas in the West a union is regarded as an entity existing outside the corporate organization, the Japanese union is coextensive with it. In this sense the Japanese enterprise union is much like the labor union in the Soviet Union. Its membership consists of all the regular employees of the company—including managerial, clerical, and blue-collar workers—except for managers with ranks of section chief and above who are by law prohibited from belonging to a union.

All regular employees automatically become union members upon joining the corporate organization. The union in most corporations has an office within the company compound. Clerical work of the union may be handled by the personnel of the company's labor section. Elected officers regard themselves as being on a temporary leave of absence from the regular jobs in the company; they ordinarily keep their tenure and seniority in the firm, but are paid by the union. Most unions are loosely affiliated with some federations of national industrial unions, but each local enterprise union enjoys almost complete autonomy in making decisions. Collective bargaining takes place between an enterprise union and a firm or a plant.

For ambitious junior managers, a successful tenure as a union officer is one of the ways to attract recognition by top management.

Thomas Rohlen reports that in the bank that he studied, there was a definite pattern of top union officers being promoted to the rank of section chief after completing their three to four years of service in the union.[11] Among blue-collar workers, there exists a close parallel between supervisory positions and union positions. More likely than not, union officers at a plant are also foremen or supervisors.[12]

The Japanese enterprise union serves two major functions. First, as a voluntary association of employees, it serves to represent the employees' rights and protect them against abuses of managerial power. It engages in collective bargaining, and calls a strike. In this role, the Japanese union is much like the trade union in the United States. Second, the enterprise union serves as a channel of communication between management and employees for their mutual benefit. Management consults the union about conditions and problems of employment and working. Through this channel, management also provides information to the employees concerning the current conditions of the industry and the enterprise, and their future prospects. In this role, the Japanese union is much like the works council in some Western European countries.[13] (See Chapter 13.) Management is willing to provide information to the union, and pay the necessary expenses of supporting union activities, in order to cultivate and nurture cooperative relationships with the employees and to secure their commitment to the firm's goals. "The aim is," concludes Rohlen, "to build morale, and energetic union leadership is encouraged and rewarded as long as this is the result. Cooperation in these matters earns for the union's leaders a degree of reciprocal cooperation from management."[14]

In the familistic atmosphere of the Japanese corporation, enterprise unionism is perhaps the only sensible form. Top managers generally detest and resist having to deal with union officials who are not their own employees. Employees feel closer to other members of the corporate family, including the management personnel, than to their fellow workers in other firms or industries. Substantial differences in wages and benefits existing between larger and smaller firms are another reason why a sense of camaraderie and shared interests do not develop between unions of different corporations.

[11]Rohlen, *For Harmony and Strength*, p. 184.

[12]Ronald Dore, *British Factory, Japanese Factory: The Origins of National Diversity in Industrial Relations* (Berkeley, Calif.: University of California Press, 1973), p. 169; Satoshi Kamata, *Japan in the Passing Lane: An Insider's Account of Life in a Japanese Auto Factory* (New York: Pantheon Books, 1982), p. 145.

[13]Taishiro Shirai, "A Theory of Enterprise Unionism," in *Contemporary Industrial Relations in Japan*, ed. Taishiro Shirai (Madison, Wisc.: University of Wisconsin Press, 1983), pp. 120–21.

[14]Rohlen, *For Harmony and Strength*, p. 189.

THE DECISION-MAKING PROCESS

In the preceding chapter we observed that, in Japan's government bureaucracy, middle-level bureaucrats in their 30s and 40s (primarily section chiefs) participate extensively in strategic decision making in public policy. The same situation exists in corporate bureaucracy: section chiefs and department heads in their 40s are the kingpins of Japanese corporations' decision-making processes.

In the traditional decision-making process in the West, the flow of information is mainly vertical between senior managers in a given functional area and his or her line and staff subordinates at the middle-management level. Lateral communication and coordination take place, as a rule, primarily at the higher levels of corporate hierarchy. In the Japanese organization, lateral communication and coordination at middle levels of responsibility are extensive. In the first place, management personnel are not specialized in any particular function. Because of extensive job rotation in their 20s and 30s, Japanese managers become well versed in most of the major operational areas of their firm's activities, and are well acquainted with a large number of people in a variety of functional departments. Secondly, communication and coordination cutting across departmental lines are facilitated by the close and intimate relationships that exist among members of the same year-of-entry groups, university cliques, and various other informal patron-client cliques. Thirdly, lateral communication also takes place on an organized basis. In most corporations, there exists a practice of holding regular meetings among middle-level managers of a given rank. For example, there may be monthly meetings of section chiefs, deputy department heads, or department heads, usually without the presence of their superiors. Ideas are exchanged and issues of common concern are discussed in these meetings.

The major difference in the decision-making process as practiced in Japan and in the United States lies in the role played by senior executives. In the United States, senior executives *are* the key decision makers; they are the ones who set objectives and issue orders. Their subordinates, the middle managers, are in the main functional specialists whose responsibility lies in faithfully executing their superiors' directives. The locus of corporate decision making thus lies in top management. In a typical Japanese corporation, by contrast, senior managers characteristically sit back and wait for their subordinates to come up with ideas. In other words, they practice participative, bottom-up decision making. They expect their front-line managers (section chiefs and department heads) to understand the company's philosophy and strategy, and to be able to decide what courses of action are good for the company. Specifically, the bosses want middle managers to develop policies and shape solutions. In this process, the senior managers by no means act as passive ratifiers of their subordinates' decisions. They perceive their roles as facilitators and motivators: they ask questions, make suggestions, and provide both moral and material supports to promising ideas and projects. This philosophy of encouraging bottom-up initiatives does not exist only at the top: successive managers down the corporate hierarchy deal with their subordinates with the same "show me what you can do; tell me what you think" attitude.

The collective and participative decision-making process in a Japanese bureaucracy, both governmental and corporate, centers in a formal procedure known as the *ringi* system. Ringi means submitting and circulating proposals for collective deliberation and final approval at the top. The section originating a proposal draws up an interdepartmental memorandum and circulates it first among the related sections and departments, collecting seals of approval of appropriate section chiefs and department heads. Concurrently, a great deal of informal spadework and buttonholing (called *nemawashi*) is done by the members of the initiating section and department, with the key members of the sections and departments that have vested interests in the proposal. The head of the initiating department may also discuss the proposal informally with his immediate superior. When the time is ripe, a meeting of heads and chiefs of affected departments and sections is called, perhaps with an appropriate managing director participating in the discussion. Meanwhile, the memorandum may have accumulated 20 or 30 seals and be ready for submission through the channel to the executive committee of the board of directors. When approved by the committee and the president, the proposal becomes a company policy.

While the memorandum is circulating throughout the corporate organization, it may meet with resistance or be objected to by an affected section or department. If a necessary seal cannot be obtained because of the objection, the initiating section or department must try to reach some kind of accommodation with the objecting section or department. If an accommodation cannot be reached, the proposal may die. Also, the proposal may be returned by a superior to his or her subordinate for improvement.

In this type of participative decision-making method, the responsibility for making the decision is collective; that is, no single individual is solely responsible for it. For the corporate organization to reach a decision, there must be a consensus of all involved parties. No single individual, even the president, can make a major decision without first obtaining a general consensus in support of it. One advantage of this system is that it allows a great deal of initiative to flow from bottom up. Another advantage is that, once a decision is reached, implementation is swift because everyone is familiar with the proposal. The disadvantages of this method are that it is time consuming and often in-decisive. A decision-making process can get bogged down if there is a substantial opposition to the proposal.

Effective leaders in a Japanese organization know that they must work through people. The group does the work. The leaders' responsi-bility is to provide an environment in which the subordinates can work in harmony and pull in the same direction. In the end, the leaders themselves are credited with the group's achievements. Because of Jap-anese employees' respect for authority of rank and status, senior exec-utives need not fear that their preferences and wishes will be slighted or ignored by their subordinates. They need not feel threatened by their subordinates' superior performance since they are protected by the sys-tem of seniority-based promotion.

THE WEAKNESSES OF JAPAN'S GROUPISM

If the native groupism of Japanese society has contributed to the unique strengths of the Japanese economic system, it has also been responsible for one of the most serious problems of the Japanese system, namely, the wasteful use of its human resources. According to one estimate, the labor productivity in the United States in 1978, as compared to Japan's 100, was 115 in manufacturing, 156 in distribution and services, 277 in agriculture, and 160 in all industries. Productivity of American white-collar workers was estimated to be 30 to 50 percent higher than that of their Japanese counterparts.[15] Although the relatively low productivity of Japanese workers may be explained by the differences in technology and the quality and quantity of other resources used in combination with labor (particularly in agriculture), it cannot be denied that a large part of it is attributable to the wasteful ways human resources are utilized in Japan.

In Japanese social organization, human beings are conceived es-sentially as integral components of an organization; their individuality receives little attention. Herein lies the basic cause of the failure of the system to make a full and complete utilization of its human resources. Whereas collective efforts and teamwork are conducive to high pro-ductivity in large-scale production of standardized products, they are not necessarily the best approach to some other types of human activ-ities. For example, revolutionary new ideas and truly creative work of

---

[15]Japan Productivity Center, *Rodo Seisansei no Kokusai Hikaku ni Kansuru Kenkyu* (Tokyo: Industrial Research Institute, 1981); cited in Jon Woronoff, *Japan's Wasted Workers* (Totowa, N.J.: Allanheld, Osmun Publishers, 1983), pp. 17–18.

all kinds are more likely the fruits of individual labor than the products of group endeavors. Cooperative group efforts can work wonders, but there is a definite limit to what they can do since such essential qualities as ambition, inspiration, imagination, and insight are more closely associated with the self-contained individual than with a group of individuals.

The Japanese are inclined not only to subordinate their personal preferences to the collective interest of their group, but also to make every effort to blend into the group to avoid standing out as individuals. The old adage, "A nail that sticks out gets hammered down," is as applicable to today's corporate managers and government officials as to the merchants and samurai of the Tokugawa era. Individualized ambition and achievements are often frowned upon by superiors as being disruptive of group harmony, and are met with jealousy and even enmity by colleagues. A Japanese group, therefore, is quite capable of effectively stifling spontaneous expressions of individuality.

The excessive emphasis on group harmony and conformity has other drawbacks. As we observed earlier, the decision-making process in a typical Japanese organization is not only time consuming and often indecisive, but also runs the risk of prematurely suppressing critical viewpoints. As soon as it appears that a majority position is beginning to take shape, individuals often hurry to embrace that position, often uncritically, just to avoid "missing the bus."

Perhaps the most damaging aspect of Japan's familistic groupism is its adverse effects on rational utilization of human resources. In the environment of seniority-based promotion and wages, it is often very difficult to make a full use of individual talents. For example, exceptionally competent young employees cannot be promoted rapidly bypassing their seniors, nor given disproportionally large salary and bonus adjustments, for fear that such measures will be disruptive of group harmony. Conversely, deadwoods and misfits cannot be easily demoted, transferred, or dismissed for exactly the same reasons. This inability to value and reward labor services according to their relative merits, so that fullest use can be made of them, is the most serious source of inefficiency in the Japanese economic system.

One disturbing aspect of Japan's groupism is its elitist chauvinism. As we saw earlier, the benefits of the so-called Japanese employment system with lifetime employment, seniority-based wages and promotion, and extensive fringe benefits are enjoyed by only one out of every four Japanese workers. The great majority of employees of small businesses and temporary workers of large companies work under conditions of little job security, low pay, little chance of advancement, and few fringe benefits. Most of these workers do not have unions. In 1974, only 3.4 percent of the employees of firms with fewer than 30 workers, and 9 percent of those in firms with 30 to 90 workers, were unionized.[16] Many of these workers are older retired workers, women who have returned to work after their children left home, and those who did not graduate from the best schools and universities. Japan's industrial system has failed to bring millions of these workers into its mainstream. The Japanese developmental strategy of channeling the best of the country's human resources into the big business sector has created a huge pool of disfranchised workers who harbor a deep sense of frustration and resentment. The outstanding performance of Japan's internationally competitive corporations has been made possible by the sacrifices of these workers. Meanwhile, the economy as a whole has suffered a great deal inasmuch as these alienated workers are not as productive as those privileged and well-motivated male employees of large corporations.

Particularly unbecoming to a major industrial power of Japan's status is its treatment of female workers who consitutue 40 percent of the labor force. The overwhelming majority of women work at dead-end jobs with little chance of advancement. Between 1978 and 1985, Japanese women's average wages fell from 56 percent to 52 percent of men's wages.[17] Professional career opportunities are largely closed to Japanese women. The proper place for women is said to be home; women are expected to stay home, marry, and have children. Most Japanese men find taking orders from women very difficult, if not unthinkable. This chauvinistic attitude of Japanese men toward women is deeply rooted in Japan's familistic groupism that must place everything and everyone on a vertical scale of superiority and inferiority.

The Japanese have embraced the market system and its rationality in all aspects of their lives having to do with physical and tangible things. By contrast, in all aspects of their lives having anything to do with human relations, they have thus far been unable to apply the universal principles of economic calculus.

Of course Japan need not totally abandon its groupism; emphasis on community, consensus, and teamwork will continue to be the source of Japan's strength. What is needed, however, is a greater balance between groupism and individualism. The Japanese should be able, as *individuals*, to find satisfaction and reward in their contribution to groups' efforts. There should be much easier movements of individuals in and out of groups, and a more spontaneous and immediate acceptance of new members by the existing members, than under the present situation. Individuals should be promoted and rewarded in an organization

---

[16]"Labor," *Kodansha Encyclopedia of Japan* (1983), vol. 4, 343.

[17]"Japan's Secret Economic Weapon: Exploited Women," *Business Week*, March 4, 1985, pp. 54–55.

primarily by the quality of their work and their contribution to the group's work, regardless of their age, gender, or educational backgrounds. Individuals should be encouraged to be different, original, creative, and openly critical of the majority viewpoint for the sake of contributing diversity and critical objectivity to the group's decision-making processes. Group leaders should become freer to make their own decisions based on their own convictions, for the group, without feeling compelled to seek a near unanimous consensus of the entire group. Above all, individuals must come to be respected, appreciated, and rewarded for what they can do *as individuals*. Considering the depth and intensity of Japan's familistic groupism, however, we may have to conclude that these badly needed changes will occur only very slowly.

QUESTIONS

1. Describe the main features of the basic organizational philosophy and practices of a large Japanese corporation.
2. Describe the differences between the United States and Japan in the relationships between the board of directors and the management team of a large corporation.
3. What groups are insiders and what groups are outside constituents of a large Japanese corporation?
4. What is *top management* of a large Japanese corporation? Why is it that the power of this group is relatively more secure than its counterpart in the United States?
5. Describe the control-dependency relationships between the "parent" and "child" companies in a vertical keiretsu group.
6. Describe the modular organizational principle of Japanese corporations. What is the role of a manager in this context? How does it differ from that of an American manager?
7. Suppose a large American company builds a library in its corporate headquarters and assigns one of its employees to manage it without direct supervision. Do you think an American employee would welcome or object to such an assignment? How do you think a Japanese employee would react to a similar situation? (See Thomas Rohlen, *For Harmony and Strength*, p. 30.)
8. Hiroshi Yamada, age 40, is the chief of the accounting section of a large Japanese electric equipment manufacturing firm. Why do you think he takes a greater pride in being a section *chief* than in being the company's chief *accountant?*
9. Explain why large Japanese corporations tend to value growth and market shares more highly than profits as key business goals.
10. In Chapter 8 we noted that American corporate executives have a keen interest in rising prices of their company's stocks. Why do Japanese senior executives not exhibit a similar interest?

11. Why do Japanese corporate executives use a much longer time horizon than their American counterparts?
12. What factors account for Japanese corporate management's emphasis on product quality?
13. What exactly is meant by achieving high productivity "through people"? Does it mean efforts to keep employees happy? Does it mean driving employees to work very hard? What is the essential nature of this strategy?
14. In the text it was noted that in a Japanese corporation there are few ostentatious displays of rank and status differences. How can this statement be reconciled with the fact that the Japanese are highly sensitive to rank and status differences?
15. Explain the differences between regular and nonregular employees, and between permanent regular and nonpermanent regular employees in a large Japanese corporation. In which category are the following groups of employees included: (a) top managers, (b) managerial employees with university degrees, (c) male high school graduates in blue-collar jobs, (d) female high school graduates in white- and blue-collar jobs?
16. What do you think are the reasons why most Japanese women do not make long-term commitments to corporate careers? Who do you think are the culprits and victims—management or the women? (See Jon Woronoff, *Japan's Wasted Workers,* chap. 4.)
17. Explain the nature of lifetime employment practiced in large Japanese corporations. What are the advantages and disadvantages of this system to the employer and the employees?
18. Describe the ways in which a Japanese corporation carrying a permanent work force maintains operational flexibility.
19. Describe the process of selecting new employees used by large Japanese corporations. Why is it necessary to use such an elaborate system?
20. What is meant by *seniority* (*nenko*) in the Japanese context? Explain the rationality of the seniority-based system of promotion and wages.
21. Explain why it would be difficult to adopt a truly merit-based system of promotion and wages in Japan.
22. Describe the main features of enterprise unionism. What are the advantages of this system from the management's viewpoint? Why do you think Japanese workers prefer this type of unionism to the American-type industrial or craft unionism?
23. Describe the differences between the American and Japanese styles of corporate decision making with special references to (a) the flow of information, and (b) the role of senior executives.
24. Describe how the *ringi* system of decision making works. Which is at the heart of this method: the use of a formal memorandum or the extensive informal discussions behind the scenes (*nemawashi*) by the interested parties?
25. Discuss the advantages and disadvantages of the Japanese-style participative and bottom-up decision making process.

26.   Critically evaluate the discussion of the weaknesses of Japan's groupism presented in the last section of this chapter.

SELECTED READING

CLARK, RODNEY.   *The Japanese Company.* New Haven, Conn.: Yale University Press, 1979.

DORE, RONALD.   *British Factory, Japanese Factory: The Origins of National Diversity in Industrial Relations.* Berkeley, Calif.: University of California Press, 1973.

HAITANI, KANJI.   *The Japanese Economic System: An Institutional Overview,* chaps. 3, 6, and 7. Lexington, Mass.: Lexington Books, D. C. Heath and Company, 1976.

LEE, SANG M., and GARY SCHWENDIMAN, Eds.   *Management by Japanese Systems.* New York: Praeger Publishers, 1982.

ROHLEN, THOMAS P.   *For Harmony and Strength: Japanese White-Collar Organization in Anthropological Perspective.* Berkeley, Calif.: University of California Press, 1974.

SHIRAI, TAISHIRO, Ed.   *Contemporary Industrial Relations in Japan.* Madison, Wisc.: University of Wisconsin Press, 1983.

WORONOFF, JON.   *Japan's Wasted Workers.* Totowa, N.J.: Allanheld, Osmun Publishers, 1983.

YOSHINO, M. Y.   *Japan's Managerial System: Tradition and Innovation.* Cambridge, Mass.: The MIT Press, 1968.

CHAPTER 11

The Chinese Economy

INTRODUCTION

With a population of over 1 billion, the People's Republic of China is the world's most populous country. It is the third largest in terms of land area, but less than 15 percent of its land is arable. In 1949, when the Chinese Communist party (CCP) under the leadership of Mao Zedong unified the country, it had a population of over 500 million, nearly 90 percent of whom were peasants living in rural areas. The country was characterized by stagnant agriculture using traditional production methods, large rural unemployment, a very small and underdeveloped socioeconomic infrastructure, and small enclaves of modern industrial and commercial enterprises in port cities along the seacoast and great rivers. In the mid-1980s, China is still a poor country, but its people are no longer destitute. They are fed, clothed, and nearly fully employed. Their level of living, though still very low by Western standards, is rising slowly but perceptibly.

In recent years there has been a surge of interest in the economic system of the People's Republic of China. This surge is attributed in large part to the sheer size of the country and its potential importance as a major economic, political, and military power in the decades to

come. At the beginning of this book we stated that the criteria for selecting countries for an in-depth analysis in this study were (1) the size
and importance of their economies relative to the industrialized world,
and (2) the degree to which the characteristics of their economic systems
are fundamentally different from those of other countries. On the basis
of both criteria, the economic system of China may appear to deserve
a full treatment in this study along with those of the United States, the
Soviet Union, and Japan. Upon careful reflection, however, we find that
the Chinese system at its present stage of development fully satisfies
neither of the two criteria.

In the first place, China's economy at the present time comes nowhere near those of the other three countries in terms of importance.
Because of its sheer size in population and land area, China may appear
to the uninitiated as a world-class economic power. The reality is, however, that it is a very poor country. In terms of gross national product
(GNP) per capita, which is probably the best indicator of the relative
level of economic development of a country, China's level in the early
1980s was roughly one-tenth of that of the Soviet Union and one-twen-
tieth of that of the United States. Of course GNP figures are notorious
for their crudeness as a measure of relative levels of living of different
societies. These figures particularly understate the living standard of a
largely agrarian society since in such an economy much production is
consumed directly by the producers without entering the national income accounting system. But the difference by the factor of 10 or 20
does indicate that there is a considerable gap. According to estimates
by the U.S. Central Intelligence Agency, GNP per capita in 1979 was
$510 for China, $5,200 for the Soviet Union, $8,890 for Japan, and $10,740
for the United States.[1] Assuming that China's GNP per capita of $510
was to grow at an annual rate of 6 percent (i.e., doubling in every 12
years), we find that it would take the country 40 years to catch up with
the Soviet Union's 1979 level of development. To reach the Japanese
and U.S. levels, it would take 49 and 52 years, respectively. Following
this type of reasoning, we are led to conclude that China's decades of
economic takeoff and drive to maturity will probably not start until the
early part of the next century. In the meantime, the nation will be
preoccupied with the task of coping with the problems of underdevel-
opment. Comparison of China's economic system with those of the in-
dustrially advanced countries, therefore, will remain a relatively unproductive exercise for some time to come.

The second reason why China is not included in the main body of
this study has to do with the very close similarity between the Chinese

---

[1]U.S. Central Intelligence Agency, *Handbook of Economic Statistics, 1980* (Washington, D.C.: U.S. Government Printing Office, 1980).

and the Soviet forms of organizing and managing the economy. During the early 1950s, the Chinese adopted Soviet-type socialist institutions in virtually all aspects of their social life. In spite of the rift that later developed between the two socialist countries, China has not been able to rid itself of much of the Soviet influence. Thus, descriptions and analyses of Chinese politico-economic institutions and their problems often sound like those of the Soviet Union. Detailed discussions of the Chinese economic system in the main body of this study, therefore, would mean an unnecessary duplication.

There is yet another reason why inclusion of China in the earlier parts of this book is not warranted. During the decades since the creation of the People's Republic in 1949, China's economic system has undergone some drastic changes. In recent years the Chinese leaders have been experimenting seriously with the market system and material incentives (see Chapter 12). There is no assurance, however, that these reforms will remain intact or be developed further in the years to come. It is plausible that today's reforms may be rejected tomorrow, and the system will go back to the old methods of tight administrative control. This absence of stability in economic structures and policies is attributable partly to the immaturity and backwardness of the Chinese economy, but also and more importantly, to the chronic factionalism of the Chinese Communist party's leadersip. The deep schism that exists within the party has manifested itself in the past in the form of wide policy gyrations in both economic and noneconomic matters.[2] Consequently, the Chinese system of economic organization and management does not exhibit the degree of stability and relative permanence that is found in the American, Soviet, and Japanese systems. This fact alone makes an integration of the discussions of the Chinese system into the main body of this study extremely difficult.

Partly because of China's potential importance in the global economy in the coming decades, and partly because of the worldwide attention the country is receiving on its recent reforms, we devote a chapter here to discussions of the organization and management of the Chinese economy as they have developed since 1949. For the economic history of China before 1949, readers are referred to some of the introductory books on the Chinese economy.[3] Descriptions and analysis of the Chinese economic system included in this chapter relate mainly to China's administrative-command economy of the late 1970s, or the system that was in existence after Mao's death in 1976 and before the gradual in-

[2]John E. Elliott, *Comparative Economic Systems*, 2nd ed. (Belmont, Calif.: Wadsworth Publishing Company, 1985), p. 432.

[3]See, for example, Ramon H. Myers, *The Chinese Economy: Past and Present* (Belmont, Calif.: Wadsworth, Inc., 1980).

troduction of the various economic reform measures that started around 1980. Discussions of the recent reform measures will be included in the following chapter.

PHASES OF DEVELOPMENT, 1949–79

During the period 1949 through 1979, the Chinese economic system went through several phases of development marked by wide gyrations in policies and ideological manifestations. The characteristics of each of these phases will be briefly described below.[4]

The People's Republic of China was established in October 1949. The first task of the leaders of the new republic was to rebuild the economy, which had been debilitated by decades of civil war, foreign invasions, and hyperinflation. Not only did physical facilities have to be reconstructed, but more importantly, an entirely new society had to be built on the basis of a totally new set of social values and politico-economic principles. To this end, the new regime set out to implement a series of social, political, and economic reforms. By far the most important of these reforms involved a radical transformation of the property relations in the countryside—the land reform. "Surplus" land of landlords and rich peasants was confiscated from them and redistributed to poor peasants and landless laborers. Landlords were collectively and individually humiliated in public, and were effectively eliminated as a social class. The land reform program, which had been essentially completed by 1952, paved the way for complete collectivization of agriculture, which was to be accomplished by 1957. Socialization in property relations in nonagricultural sectors proceeded parallel to the land reform. The percentage of gross output value of Chinese industry attributable to privately owned firms declined from 56 percent in 1949 to 17 percent in 1952.[5]

The First Five-Year Plan, 1953–57

China's entry into the Korean War in 1950 greatly increased the country's dependence on the Soviet Union. China's First Five-Year Plan was patterned after Soviet economic plans, and in its implementation China relied heavily on Soviet technical and financial assistance. During this period, China's economic institutions underwent thorough Sovieti-

---

[4]The demarcation of the earlier phases closely follows that used in Jan S. Prybyla, *The Political Economy of Communist China* (Scranton, Pa.: International Textbook Company, 1970).

[5]Ibid., p. 67, table 3–8.

zation. The planning mechanism, the ministerial system of control over the nation's economic activities, the price and wage systems, the financial system and the state budget, and the methods of enterprise management were all closely patterned after the Soviet model.

Following the pattern of Soviet development in the 1930s, the Chinese adopted a policy of rapid industrial development with a primary emphasis on heavy and capital-intensive industries. Light and consumer goods industries were largely ignored. The resources needed for these superindustrialization efforts, with the exception of those provided by the Soviet Union, had to come mainly from the rural sector. Like the new Bolshevik regime in the Soviet Union in the 1920s and 1930s, the new Chinese regime had to find quickly the most efficient way of squeezing surplus from agriculture and transferring it to industry. In 1953, the Chinese government introduced a system of compulsory grain quotas under which rural households were required to sell grain to the state at prices considerably below market prices. Furthermore, just as Stalin had opted for collectivization of agriculture in 1928, Mao Zedong, overruling the majority view within the Communist party, acted in favor of collectivization of Chinese agriculture. During the 1955–56 period, household farming was eliminated, and rural households were organized into agricultural cooperatives. By 1957, rural collectivization had been completed. Nationalization of private enterprises in industry and commerce, too, had been completed by this time.

The Great Leap Forward, 1958–60

During the period of the First Five-Year Plan, the Chinese became increasingly unsure about their Soviet-type strategy of concentrating on heavy industries at the expense of agriculture. The unsatisfactory performance of Chinese agriculture during this period was the primary source of this uncertainty. The Chinese Communists also became uneasy about what they considered the increasingly revisionist stance of Soviet leaders. The agrarian roots of the leaders of the Chinese Communist party, their ideological zeal bordering on fanaticism, and their belief in the superiority of human-wave tactics over mechanistic methods, convinced them that China should try a totally new road to socialist industrialization.

In mid-1958 the Chinese made a radical departure from the Soviet pattern of development and launched a new strategy called the *Great Leap Forward*. In industry, this strategy meant a heavy reliance on the use of highly labor-intensive techniques applied to small and primitive industrial plants and workshops scattered all over the country but particularly in rural areas. This approach came to be known as the "iron and steel foundry in every backyard" strategy. Huge masses of unskilled workers were expected to produce incredible quantities of industrial goods motivated primarily by revolutionary zeal and guided by Mao thought.

In agriculture, collectivization was pushed to its extreme form. Member families of cooperatives lost their private plots, livestock, and farming implements to the newly organized people's communes, each of which consisted of several thousand households. Peasants were to work together in farming and public works, and have meals in communal dining halls. As in industry, material incentives were deemphasized. People were to receive income (mostly in kind) according to their needs, and work for the common good driven by their ideological zeal.

The Great Leap Forward turned out to be a great fall downward. After an initial surge, industrial output suffered a very serious setback. The drop in output was particularly serious in heavy industry. Gross output value rose sharply between 1958 and 1960, but fell afterwards to the 1958 level and below, and did not return to the pre-Leap level until the mid-1960s. Poor quality of products and irrational output mix posed a serious threat to the country's industrialization efforts. Food shortages developed, and by 1969 China faced a threat of famine. The disastrous effects of the Great Leap Forward were aggravated by the decision of the Soviet Union to withdraw, in mid-1960, its economic, technical, and military assistance to China. Jan Prybyla describes the reaction of the Russians to China's big push strategy as follows:

> As the ideological and practical wrangling went on behind the scenes, occasionally bursting into the open, the Chinese leadership launched the Great Leap Forward, in one respect a declaration of economic independence from the Soviet Union. At first the Soviets were taken aback. They were shortly to be dumbfounded by the rural people's communes and the ideological rider attached to them. By late 1959 they had sorted out the evidence, gathered their wits about them, and drawn pessimistic conclusions regarding the Leap's meaning and future.[6]

Angered and frustrated by the Chinese refusal to heed their advice, the Russians decided to sever ties with China with the intention, mainly, to teach the Chinese a lesson. The Soviet withdrawal inflicted a severe blow to the Chinese economy. By the summer of 1960, the Great Leap Forward had been completely abandoned. The left-wing radicals of the CCP, including Chairman Mao, experienced a serious setback in their position of dominant power within the party.

[6]Ibid., p. 315.

The Period of Economic
Readjustment, 1961–65

During the period 1961–65, a new economic policy was implemented with an emphasis on agriculture as a foundation of economic development. Industry was now viewed primarily as serving the needs of agricultural development. Communes were kept as administrative units, but were greatly reduced in size and operational significance. Communal dining halls were abolished, private plots of farming households were restored, and sideline productive activities of commune members were encouraged. During this period, the political power was in the hands of the pragmatic moderates of the CCP under the leadership of President Liu Shaoqi.

The Great Proletarian Cultural
Revolution, 1966–69

The Cultural Revolution was a political-ideological campaign mounted by the left-wing faction of the Communist party, led by Chairman Mao. The Mao faction incited Chinese youths to attack China's establishments in the name of preserving the purity of Marxism-Leninism-Maoism. It was largely an urban phenomenon, bypassing the large rural hinterland of China. Consequently, damage to agricultural development was minimal. Industrial production fell in 1967, but recovered by 1969. By contrast, the Cultural Revolution had long-lasting adverse effects on the authority, intellectualism, elitism, and professionalism of the establishments in the party, government, military, arts, sciences, and education.

The greatest damage was done to higher education. All universities in China were closed between 1966 and 1972. Classes were resumed slowly starting in 1972, but only after radical changes had been made in the universities' admission criteria and curricula. For admission, political activism and proletarian work experience were stressed at the expense of academic qualifications. In the classroom, the study of Mao thought became the centerpiece of instruction. Thus, for a period of ten years between 1966 and 1976, college education in the traditional sense (i.e., academic, scientific, and technical training) was virtually nonexistent in China. The void of higher education lasting for a decade seriously disrupted the development of human capital in China, adverse effects of which on the country's socioeconomic development would certainly be felt over the decades to come.

The primary targets of the Cultural Revolution were the party moderates, intellectuals, professionals, and other persons of authority in all branches of China's establishment. Mao saw a danger of Chinese communism being corrupted by the Soviet-type mentality of using material incentives to motivate workers and by the bureaucratic and professional elitism that was deeply rooted in the thought and behavior of the members of China's establishments. By means of the Cultural Revolution, Mao tried to cleanse China of all these bad influences once and for all, and create a new breed of human beings who were motivated solely by a desire to serve the needs of their fellow citizens. Cleansing the party leadership of the "bad" elements, of course, meant restoration of the Mao's group to the position of predominance within the party.

The Period of Transition, 1970–76

The widespread social and economic disruptions and the atmosphere of escalating crisis caused by the Cultural Revolution worked as a brake on the revolutionary fervor of the Mao faction, and the fury of the revolution began to subside in 1969. The prerevolution conditions slowly returned to Chinese society. With Mao's health failing, the party moderates, who had a numerical majority, regained control. The radical leftists, however, were still a power to be reckoned with since they had a direct access to the chairman through his wife Jiang Qing, who was a major leftist leader in her own right. The leftist leaders continued to agitate against intellectualism, professionalism, material incentives, and the Soviet-inspired methods of economic planning and control. When Mao died in September 1976, there existed a precarious balance of power between the moderates and the radicals.

Restoration of Political and Economic Order, 1977–79

After Mao's death in 1976, the pragmatic moderates headed by Deng Xiaoping succeeded in eliminating the remnants of the Maoist radical faction (the Gang of Four, including Mao's widow) and began reestablishing much needed political and economic order. Liberal economic policies were reintroduced with strong emphasis on material incentives. In 1978, the program of modernizing China known as Four Modernizations was announced. In 1979, formal diplomatic relations between the People's Republic of China and the United States of America were established.

The Record of Development, 1952–79

Between 1952 and 1979, the population of China nearly doubled, from 570 million to 1,018 million. During the same period, the country's gross national product in 1978 U.S. dollars rose from $99 billion to $468 billion, and its GNP per capita increased from $174 to $460. Agricultural

production nearly doubled; but, because of the near doubling of population, agricultural output per capita increased only slightly. By contrast, industrial output increased by nearly 15 times in total terms and
by more than 8 times in per capita terms.[7]

The primary objective of the Chinese economic system is rapid
industrial development. By this criterion, we are obliged to conclude
that China's performance is commendable. Considering the backwardness of the economy and the destitute conditions of the overwhelming
majority of its people prior to the 1950s, and the enormous size of China's
population and its annual increases, we must conclude that the Chinese
record is highly creditable. More than a billion people are fed, clothed,
and housed. Most of them are employed, educated, and are receiving
rudimentary health care. We can appreciate the significance of the Chinese
record when we realize that the same cannot be said about most of the
developing nations today. The system could probably have done considerably better, however, if it had not experienced those frequent and
sharp changes in its economic policies.

POLITICAL INSTITUTIONS

The political institutions of the People's Republic of China (PRC) are
nearly exact duplication of those in the Soviet Union. The only significant difference lies in the fact that the Chinese government is based on
the unitary principle, whereas the Soviet Union is a federation of republics. The effective power of control in China resides with the leading
members of the Chinese Communist party who occupy key posts in the
party's Political Bureau and the government's State Council. The National People's Congress, although nominally designated as "the highest
organ of state authority" by the Chinese Constitution of 1978 (Article
20), does not exercise independent political power. The relative power
relations in China among the party's Political Bureau, the State Council,
and the National People's Congress are essentially the same as those
existing in the Soviet Union among the party's Politburo, the USSR
Council of Ministers, and the Supreme Soviet. At all levels of the state
administrative hierarchy, there exists a corresponding level of the party
hierarchy. At each level, those who occupy influential positions in the
state administrative hierarchy are also key party members. Important
state policies and programs are either published jointly by the State
Council and the party Central Committee, or announced unilaterally by
the party.

Towering over the bureaucracy of the entire administrative hier-

[7]Elliott, *Comparative Economic Systems*, p. 446, table 20–1.

archy of the state and economy is the State Council chaired by the premier. It has broad executive power, and has under its jurisdiction some 30-odd ministries organized on the industrial branch basis (e.g., agriculture, commerce, finance, electric power, light industry, metallurgy, coal, and so on) and various state commissions and committees (e.g., the State Planning Commission, the People's Bank of China, and the State Scientific and Technological Commission).

Administratively, China is divided into 21 provinces and 5 autonomous regions. Three large cities (Beijing, Shanghai, and Tianjin) are under direct control of the central government. Provinces are divided into municipalities and counties. The counties, numbering about 2,100, are further divided into over 50,000 communes.

THE MANAGEMENT OF THE ECONOMY

The Chinese economy is organized hierarchically and managed from the center in much the same way as the Soviet economy is. In this section we shall first discuss the overall organization of China's politico-economic system, economic planning as a means of managing the physical side of the nation's economic activities, and the state budget as a means of regulating the financial aspect of the economy. In the following two sections, the organization and management of industry and agriculture will be discussed in somewhat greater detail.

Overall Organization
of the Economy

In the Chinese economy there is no private business sector. Private productive activities do exist, but they are either unorganized, peripheral activities of households or a small number of widely scattered activities (largely in services) that are either tolerated by the authorities or allowed to exist on an experimental basis.[8] Virtually all of the nation's economic activities take place in the state productive sector. This sector, as contrasted to the household consumption sector, can be divided into the state economy sector and the commune economy sector. The former (the state economy) consists of enterprises and other organizations in industry, commerce, agriculture (i.e., state farms), services, construction, and transportation. Also included in this subsector are urban collectives that are nominally owned by their workers but effectively controlled by the state. The latter (the commune economy) consists of rural

---

[8]The various economic reform measures currently being undertaken, however, may some day lead to an emergence of a full-fledged private sector. See Chapter 12.

farming households organized into production teams, production brigades, and rural people's communes.

The only type of productive factor that the state does not own is labor service. In our discussion of the Soviet economy we noted that the government does not regulate the supply of labor directly, and therefore there exists a de facto free market in labor in the Soviet Union. By contrast, labor supply is closely regulated by the government in China. Workers and employees are assigned to particular enterprises or organizations by government labor bureaus. An annual labor plan specifies the allocation of new school-leavers to different enterprises and organizations, as well as permitted migration of workers. Once assigned to a specific organization or enterprise, transfer to another is very difficult. Enterprises and organizations cannot refuse allocated labor. Thus, it is safe to say that in China there is no labor market, and that labor service is allocated by administrative command like all other types of economic resources.

Operational units of the state productive sector—that is, enterprises, organizations, and collectives—are controlled from the center through a hierarchical channel of command. Decision-making authority flows from the top down, and information flows mainly upward. Administrative command rather than horizontal market relations is the primary controlling mechanism. Physical quantities rather than prices serve as the primary information carriers. The ruling organizations at the top—the Political Bureau of the CCP and the State Council—exercise their authority through three separate, vertical channels of command: (1) the administrative hierarchy of the government (i.e., provinces, municipalities, counties, and communes), (2) the hierarchy of the industrial ministries (i.e., ministries, bureaus, and departments), and (3) the hierarchy of state committees and commissions having responsibilities in planning and material supply (e.g., the State Planning Commission and its provincial bureaus and county offices). Additionally, the Communist party apparatus, through its hierarchy of party committees and branches in enterprises, organizations, and communes, exercises its own surveillance and control.

Economic Planning

The flows of goods between sectors, regions, and enterprises within the Chinese economy are subject to administrative decisions made within the framework of central economic planning. The formulation and implementation of economic planning in China are essentially the same as in the Soviet Union. The State Planning Commission formulates various economic plans (both annual and long-term) for such important aspects as output of key products, investment, construction, and labor supply. As in Soviet planning, the formulation process is "democratic" in that it involves consultation with lower-level planning bureaus and individual enterprises. The aggregated plans are approved by the State Council.

Whereas five-and ten-year plans provide an overall planning framework, the operational plans are annual plans. The State Economic Commission supervises the implementation of annual plans for industry and transportation. The State Capital Construction Commission supervises large-scale capital construction projects, and the State Agriculture Commission regulates the implementation of the agricultural plan. All these commissions maintain their bureaus at the provincial level and offices at the county level.

The core of the annual planning process concerns allocations and distributions of industrial materials among industrial enterprises. The production and distribution of approximately 1,000 key commodities are controlled from the center.[9] The technique used for allocating these goods is the rather crude "material balance" method developed in the Soviet Union (see Chapter 5). For each of the 1,000 commodities, planned sources (production, imports, and inventory depletion) and planned uses (production, investment, consumption, exports, and inventory accumulation) are specified. Changes made in the material balance of one product require a series of iterative changes in related material balances. Less important commodities are allocated within provinces and communes by the lower-level planning bureaus and offices in collaboration with the provincial bureaus and county departments of relevant industrial ministries.

The State Budget

The nature and functions of the state budget in China are virtually the same as in the Soviet Union. By controlling the flows of money through the state budget, the Chinese government can maintain a tight surveillance and control over the financial aspects of the nation's economic activities. Although the three levels of the state government—national, provincial, and county—prepare their own budgets, in reality the budgets of the three levels constitute a single state budget since the budgetary control by the center is very strong.

Government revenues.   The two most important sources of the state's revenues are profits of state enterprises (including depreciation reserves of enterprises) and the industrial and commercial tax. In 1979,

[9]World Bank, *China: Socialist Economic Development* (Washington, D.C.: The World Bank, 1983), vol. 1, 49.

these two sources accounted for 44.7 percent and 42.9 percent, respectively, of total budget revenues. The agricultural tax yielded an additional 2.7 percent.[10]

The industrial and commercial tax includes the tax levied on the output of state enterprises and the tax levied on incomes of those establishments that do not remit profits to the state (e.g., urban collectives). As in the Soviet Union, transers of industrial and agricultural goods between state enterprises are conducted on the basis of wholesale prices. Turnover taxes are added to wholesale prices to form retail prices. The tax rates are zero or very low on essential goods, and are high for nonessentials. As discussed in Chapter 5, the primary purposes of the turnover tax in socialist countries are (1) to redistribute income from the household sector to the state sector, (2) to influence the pattern of consumer purchase decisions, and (3) to achieve a financial macrobalance, that is, to equate the total money value of consumer goods with the total disposable income of consumers.

The agricultural tax is a tax levied on the output and land value of agricultural communes. The grain tax is the kernel of this tax. In the late 1970s, the rate of this tax was 9 percent on grain and 5 percent on other products. Often this tax is collected in kind.[11]

Prices of both inputs and outputs of state enterprises are set by the government in such a way as to allow most enterprises to earn profits. Enterprises, however, are required to remit most of the profits to the state. This requirement is tantamount to imposing a de facto profit tax on state enterprise. If, for example, enterprises are allowed to retain 10 percent of their profits, they are in fact paying a 90-percent profit tax.

Government expenditures.   Since the state owns virtually all productive facilities in China, the government must make allowances, in its budget outlays, for large sums of money for financing the national economy. This type of expenditure accounts for more than half of total budgetary expenditures. The money is spent on building up the economy's infrastructure (transportation, communications, housing, and so on), providing investment and working capital to productive enterprises, and subsidzing enterprises that incur losses in their operations. In 1979, 59.9 percent of total budgetary expenditures was in this category.[12] Other expenditures in 1979 were health, education, and social

---

[10]Ibid., p. 51, table 2.1.

[11]Gregory C. Chow, *The Chinese Economy* (New York: Harper & Row, Publishers, Inc., 1985), p. 10.

[12]World Bank, *China* p. 52, table 2.2.

programs (13.7 percent); defense (17.4 percent); administration (4.9 percent); and others (4.0 percent).[13]

The Chinese government can shape the pattern of economic development of its economy and effect redistribution of income among its citizens by exercising centralized financial control using the state budget. The main conduit of the financial flows is the People's Bank of China and its nationwide network of branch offices. The Bank's surveillance of financial flows is particularly effective since all the state productive enterprises and other organizations maintain their accounts with the Bank and make payments to each other through these accounts. Appropriations of capital construction funds go through a separate conduit—the Captial Construction Bank. The responsibilities of controlling these funds are shared by the Ministry of Finance and the State Planning Commission.[14]

The Price System

The Chinese government exercises its control over the national economy largely by regulating the flows of goods between enterprises, sectors, and regions. Prices are used mainly for accounting purposes; their roles as regulators of autonomous production and investment decisions are rather limited. This does not mean, however, that prices have a neutral impact on the Chinese economy. The pattern of relative prices and the general level of prices do play an important macroeconomic role of allocating resources and distributing income between the household sector and the state sector, and among different subsectors within the state productive sector. For example, high rates of industrial and commercial tax—and hence high retail prices relative to wholesale prices—serve an important function of generating revenues that the state can spend to finance the activities of the state economy. Similarly, by maintaining relatively low agricultural procurement prices and relatively high industrial goods prices, the state can transfer a large portion of agricultural communes' surplus to the state industrial sector. The general level of consumer goods prices are set in such a way as to assure at least a rough equality (i.e., macrobalance) between the monetary value of available consumer goods and the total purchasing power (disposable income) available to consumers.

Almost all prices in China are set by the government. The prices of commodities of national importance—those whose production and distribution are centrally controlled—are set by the Price Bureau of the

[13]Ibid.
[14]Ibid., pp. 51–53.

central government. The price bureaus of provincial and county governments are responsible for establishing prices for those goods that are controlled locally.

As noted earlier, the structure of prices in China is based on the cost-plus principle of the Soviet prototype. Industrial wholesale prices—the prices that enterprises use for accounting purposes—are basically made up of industry-average labor costs, depreciation allowances, and profit markups; neither the productivity of capital nor relative use values are taken into account in their formation. In other words, Chinese wholesale prices, like their Soviet counterparts, are "irrational" prices that fail to reflect relative scarcities of the commodities within the system. As such, they cannot be used as autonomous guides to rational microeconomic decision making. Any microeconomic decisions made on the basis of these prices may be rational from the point of view of the decision maker (i.e., the enterprise), but may be totally irrational from the macroeconomic (i.e., societal) point of view. Also, if prices are irrational, profits calculated on the basis of those prices are also irrational. Profits, therefore, cannot be used as indicators of successful performance of enterprises. The irrationality of industrial prices thus lies at the heart of the problem of allocative inefficiency of the Chinese (and in general, Soviet-type) economic systems.

The retail price of a good may exceed its wholesale price, the difference being the turnover tax. Prices of "nonessential" goods are kept especially high in order to discourage consumption. Prices of some "necessities" (e.g., staple foods and medicines), are kept low in order to make them affordable to the masses. In such cases, the government may have to subsidize the difference between the retail price and the wholesale price (or the procurement price in the case of agricultural commodities). If the quantity of a consumer good demanded exceeds its supplied quantity, the available supply quantity must be physically rationed (for example, by means of coupons) or else left unsatisfied. Thus in China, as in the Soviet Union, a combination of the pattern of relative prices of consumer goods and physical rationing is used to influence consumer purchasing decisions.

ORGANIZATION AND MANAGEMENT IN INDUSTRY

In this section we look at the organization and management of the state productive enterprise. Although the discussion relates primarily to industrial enterprises, essentially the same can be said about the organization and management of state-owned enterprises and organizations in commerce, services, construction, and transportation.

The Enterprise and the Manager

Each enterprise is managed by a hierarchy of government-appointed managers including a director, a chief engineer, and a chief accountant. As in the Soviet Union, the management principle is highly authoritarian; there is little participation in management by workers and staff. Since 1978, managers below the factory director level in some enterprises have been elected by workers.[15]

The managerial authority of the Chinese factory director is considerably less than that of the Soviet director. We noted in Chapter 5 that the typical Soviet director is likely to be more powerful than the secretary of the party committee within the enterprise. There, the party control over the enterprise is exercised through the subordinate relationship of the factory director to the bosses of the party apparatus in the local community rather than through the party committee in the factory. The Chinese first copied the Soviet system of authoritative enterprise director, but soon found that there was a shortage of managers who had sufficient experience and training in management. In 1960 they modified the Soviet system of enterprise management by requiring the director to manage "under the leadership of the Party committee."[16] Industrial enterprises operated under this management principle for nearly two decades until the late 1970s.

The system of placing the enterprise manager under the leadership of the factory party committee created two very serious problems. First, the party secretary, confusing the party's political leadership role with the manager's responsibility for administrative decision making, interfered with administrative matters. Second, as a result of the blurring of the chain of administrative command, there developed an atmosphere and practice of shared irresponsibility. The enterprise managers developed a habit of looking to the party secretary to make important administrative decisions and assume responsibility for them. This situation began to improve in 1979 when enterprise managers were given more authority than before.[17]

The primary responsibility of an enterprise director is to fulfill the targets of the annual plan, which consist of (1) output value, (2) output mix and quality, (3) input quantities and costs (including those of labor), (4) use of working capital, (5) investment and innovation, and (6) profits.[18]

[15]Stephan Feuchtwang and Athar Hussain, eds., *The Chinese Economic Reforms* (New York: St. Martin's Press, 1983), pp. 234–39.

[16]Lin Wei and Arnold Chao, eds., *China's Economic Reforms* (Philadelphia: University of Pennsylvania Press, 1982), p. 148.

[17]Ibid., p. 149; Chow, *The Chinese Economy*, p. 137.

[18]World Bank, *China*, p. 59.

As noted earlier, the prices of both inputs and outputs of enterprises are set by the government in such a way as to enable most enterprises to earn profits. Enterprises are allowed to keep a portion of these profits and place it in the three *enterprise funds,* which are (1) the development fund for localized investments, (2) the bonus fund for paying bonuses to workers and staff (and, more recently, to managers), and (3) the social welfare fund for financing workers' social welfare programs and facilities. Additionally, a sizable portion of the enterprise's depreciation reserves is now allowed to go into the development fund.[19]

The Worker and Wages

Earlier we noted that workers are assigned to their jobs by the government labor bureau. This, however, is not an iron-clad rule. Workers have the right to refuse job assignments, but few do so because there is no assurance that a more suitable job will be found later. (The enterprises, however, cannot refuse workers allocated to them.) Collective enterprises are allowed to recruit their workers freely. Since 1979, recruitment of employees in trades and professions through examination was started on an experimental basis. Since 1980, seeking employment outside the channels of the government labor bureau has been permitted.[20]

All workers of state enterprises other than those who are employed explicitly as temporary workers can expect lifetime employment. This practice of implicitly guaranteeing lifetime employment and income is known as the system of "iron rice bowl" (*tie fanwan*). Such a practice naturally generates rigidity in enterprises' labor utilization policies, and creates inefficiency in the economy's use of resources. Recently adopted reform measures allowing enterprises a greater freedom to dismiss workers is putting a crack in the iron rice bowl.

The nature and functions of trade unions in China closely parallel those in the Soviet Union. Chinese trade unions are organized on an enterprise basis, and all employees—managerial, staff, and manual—can belong to the enterprise union. Union activities are controlled by the enterprise union committee. The primary function of the union is to transmit the aims of the party to the workers. In this role, unions engage in political education, promote socialist labor emulation campaigns, and cooperate with the management in enforcing labor discipline. The secondary function of unions is to provide social welfare services. They administer labor insurance and pension programs, or-

[19]Feuchtwang and Hussain, *The Chinese Economic Reforms,* pp. 204–5.

[20]Rosalie L. Tung, *Chinese Industrial Society after Mao* (Lexington, Mass.: Lexington Books, D. C. Heath and Company, 1982), pp. 216–17.

ganize social activities, provide social and welfare facilities, and watch over industrial safety. Their national federation—the All-China Federation of Trade Unions—is in theory consulted on governmental policies on wage rates, but in practice this role is purely nominal. Unions do not engage in collective bargaining, nor call a strike.

The wage rates in China are set by the central government. The wage scales of industrial workers have eight grades, with the highest (class 8) being about three times that of the lowest (class 1). Class 1 is for unskilled workers who have completed their apprenticeship; class 8 is for highly skilled workers with specialized knowledge and long experience. These scales vary among occupation, branches of industry, and regions. The wage scales for technicians and engineers have 16 grades, and those for government administrators have 26.[21] About 10 to 12 percent of the total wage bill of state industrial enterprises is paid as bonuses to workers.[22] The incentive effects of these bonus payments, however, are highly limited for two reasons. First, these payments are made not to individuals but to a group of workers (workshops and work teams) for fulfilling some plan targets. Second, enterprise managements tend to regard these payments as simple wage supplements to be shared equally by all workers.[23]

ORGANIZATION AND MANAGEMENT IN AGRICULTURE

Chinese agricultural output comes from three sources: people's communes, state farms, and private plots of rural families. *State farms* are "factories in the fields." They are owned and operated by the state just as any other state enterprises are; their directors are appointed by the government, and their workers receive wages. They are mostly single-crop farms located in border provinces, and occupy only 4.5 percent of the country's total cultivated area.[24] *Private plots* of farm families account for about 8 percent of total cultivated land, and produce about 30 percent of China's total agricultural income.[25] These plots are "private" only in the sense that farming households are allowed to make free decisions as to their use and the disposition of the income arising

[21]World Bank, *China*, p. 60.

[22]Ibid., p. 61.

[23]Jan S. Prybyla, *The Chinese Economy: Problems and Policies*, 2nd ed. (Columbia, S.C.: University of South Carolina Press, 1981), pp. 164–67.

[24]World Bank, *China*, p. 55.

[25]Ibid., pp.55–56.

from it; the land is owned collectively by the production team and the production brigade (see below).

By far the most important source of China's agricultural output is the economy of *rural people's communes*. In 1980, there were some 53,000 people's communes with an average of 15,000 persons in each.[26] This means that nearly 800 milion people, or nearly four-fifths of the entire population of China, belonged to these units.

One unique characteristic of Chinese communes that distinguishes them from the Soviet collective farms is the fact that communes are both economic and political units. A commune is an amalgamation of agricultural cooperatives, but it is also an administrative subdivision of the county, or the lowest level of the hierarchy of the government bureaucracy. In fact the present form of the people's commune was created in 1958 by merging county districts (*xiang*) with agricultural cooperatives. The people's commune now serves as the nexus of contact between China's state economy and its rural agricultural economy.

According to Stephan Feuchtwang and Athar Hussain, the advantage and drawback of combining rural administration and agricultural production were as follows. The advantage was that peasant agriculture could be brought into the framework of China's planned economy without having to take the Soviet route of forced collectivization. One serious problem, however, was the fact that the merging had to compromise the ideal of collective farming. One of the original purposes of forming the agricultural cooperative was to create a community of self-governing farmers. This ideal was compromised by the inevitable intrusion of the state bureaucracy into the governance of the farm collective; this intrusion took the form of the county and provincial authorities appointing commune officials.[27]

The basic unit of the commune economy is the family. As noted earlier, each family cultivates a small private plot, and engages in a variety of sideline activities associated with it. Each household is free to dispose of the incomes arising from private plot activities as it sees fit. The basic responsibility of cooperative farming resides with the *production team*, which consists of an average of 30 to 40 families. The families belonging to a production team collectively own the land they cultivate and farming implements. A team is formed of all the families in a small village, or a neighborhood of families within a larger village.[28]

Several (7 or 8) teams form a *production brigade*. A brigade may correspond to one large village, or a group of small villages. Brigades own large machinery (e.g., tractors) and rent them to production teams.

[26]Ibid., p. 55.

[27]Feuchtwang and Hussain, *The Chinese Economic Reforms*, p. 43

[28]World Bank, *China*, pp. 55–56.

They also operate primary schools, cooperative health services, and small-scale industries.[29] Rental fees for tractors and other farm machinery, and sales of output of brigade-operated small-scale industries, constitute important sources of brigades' revenues.

A *rural people's commune* consists of 13 to 15 brigades. In geographic terms, a commune covers a rural area consisting of a number of villages and perhaps a few market towns. Besides providing an umbrella of civil administration, the commune operates secondary schools, health clinics, and capital-intensive industries. It also organizes large-scale construction projects for the area, and provides marketing and technical services for the area's farmers. As the lowest level of the state administrative bureaucracy, the commune also serves as a tax collection and food procurement agency for the state.[30]

The production team is the basic unit of collective farming with responsibilities for making both production and income-distribution decisions. The collective income of a production team is distributed as follows. During a productive season, each household accumulates *work points* for the types and lengths of different tasks its members perform for the team. The net income of the team is distributed to each household according to the number of work points accumulated. In 1979, of total output of production teams, an average of 32 percent was production costs, and 18 percent represented collective withholdings used for paying taxes, building up cash and grain reserves, and a small welfare fund. Investments by the team and the team's contributions to investments by the brigade and the commune were to be made out of the cash and grain reserves. The remaining 50 percent of the gross output of the team was distributed to individual households according to the number of work points.[31]

The primary purpose of the state's control over the commune economy is to effect an orderly and assured transfer of agricultural surplus to the state economy. This transfer is realized by the systems of agricultural planning and procurement. In 1979, for example, about 50 million tons of grain, representing about 15 to 20 percent of total grain output of the country and about 90 percent of total marketed output, were procured by the state in the following three ways: (1) 10 million tons of grain were paid to the state as agricultural tax in kind, (2) 25 million tons were procured at a low delivery-quota price, and (3) the remaining 15 million tons were procured at prices that were above the quota procurement price.[32]

[29]Ibid.

[30]Ibid.

[31]Ibid., pp. 56–57.

[32]Ibid., p. 58.

QUESTIONS

1. What were the purposes of Mao's Cultural Revolution? What are its legacies?
2. Assess the record of economic performance of the Communist regime in China since the creation of the People's Republic in 1949.
3. Discuss the differences between the Soviet Union and China in the ways labor service is allocated.
4. What is the nature of the industrial and commercial tax?
5. Discuss the nature and dispositions of state enterprises' profits. Do they reflect the efficiency of enterprises' operations? Why or why not?
6. In 1979, 60 percent of China's state budget expenditures was spent for financing the national economy. How can the government do this without imposing income taxes on its population? Where do the funds come from?
7. Discuss both the macroeconomic and microeconomic functions of Chinese wholesale and consumer goods prices.
8. What are the similarities and differences between China and the Soviet Union in the authority of the enterprise manager?
9. What are the similarities and differences between China and the Soviet Union in the organization and management of the agricultural system?
10. What are the differences between the production team, the production brigade, and the people's commune? Which has the basic responsibility for collective production and income distribution?
11. Describe the ways in which agricultural surplus is transferred from the communes to the state sector.

SELECTED READING

CHOW, GREGORY C.   *The Chinese Economy.* New York: Harper & Row, Publishers, Inc., 1985.
HOWE, CHRISTOPHER.   *China's Economy: A Basic Guide.* New York: Basic Books, Inc., Publishers, 1978.
MYERS, RAMON H.   *The Chinese Economy: Past and Present.* Belmont, Calif.: Wadsworth, Inc., 1980.
PRYBYLA, JAN S.   *The Chinese Economy: Problems and Policies* (2nd ed.). Columbia, S.C.: University of South Carolina Press, 1981.
WORLD BANK.   *China: Socialist Economic Development.* Washington, D.C.: The World Bank, 1983, vols. 1–3.

CHAPTER 12

Market
and
Planning

Market (or *exchange*) and *planning* (or *command*) are two alternative ways of organizing an economic system. Of the basically market-oriented systems, the United States comes closest to a pure market economy. At the other end of the spectrum, the Soviet Union is closest to a pure command economy. Japan and France are examples of market economies having significant degrees of planning. Hungary and Yugoslavia are examples of basically command-based economies utilizing many aspects of a self-regulating market mechanism. China, a Soviet-type command economy until recently, is making serious efforts to incorporate market relations into its economic organization.

MARKET AND PLANNING: IDEAL FORMS

In order for us to be able to compare and contrast market- and plan-oriented economic systems, it is helpful if we first understand exactly what *market* and *plan* mean in their "pure" or "ideal" forms. Major features of the two alternative systems of economic organization are contrasted in Table 12–1. It is important to note that these two alter-

TABLE 12-1   Major Characteristics of Ideal Market and Planned Systems

THE MARKET SYSTEM	THE PLANNED SYSTEM
Resource allocation is guided by consumers' preferences (consumers' sovereignty).	Resource allocation is guided by preferences of the system's ruling organization (planners' sovereignty).
Decision-making structure is horizontal and decentralized.	Decision-making structure is vertical and centralized.
Information flow is primarily horizontal.	Information flow is primarily vertical.
Autonomous decision-making agents are motivated solely by self-interest, and motivate each other by offering material incentives.	Superior decision-making agents motivate subordinates by utilizing a combination of compulsion, self-interest incentives, and appeal to group solidarity.
Exchanges of goods and services are regulated by automatic and impersonal forces of demand and supply, with free prices serving as regulators.	Goods and services are merely transferred between units within the system, with or without monetary accounting.
Competition among buyers and sellers tends to produce overall balance and efficiency.	Cooperation among the system's participants tends to generate coordination of efforts, which in turn helps achieve the system's goals.

native approaches to economic organization are not mutually exclusive. All the actual economic systems exhibit characteristics of the pure forms of both market and planning. The pure form of the market system is the perfect competition model described in economics textbooks. A large number of atomistically small buyers and sellers compete in the market to produce a result that serves the best interests of consumers, whose preferences are not manipulated by producers. At the other extreme, we find the model of pure central planning. The omnipotent and omniscient rulers make all the economic calculations and decisions needed to produce a result that best serves their objectives. Perfect information flows from top to bottom, and all lower-level agents faithfully perform what they are told. Obviously, these pure models of perfect market and perfect planning do not mix; we would have either one or the other, assuming that were possible, but not both at the same time. More specifically, consumers' sovereignty and rulers' sovereignty are mutually exclusive; and so are perfect decentralization and perfect centralization in decision-making structure.

In reality, however, all the actual economic systems are mixed, dual-preference systems. Resource allocation in one system may be guided primarily by the rulers' preferences, but certain accommodations may be made to consumers' preferences. Or we may find a system in which most decisions are made horizontally and in a decentralized manner, except that some vertical and centralized decision making may be allowed. Thus we can characterize most economic systems in today's industrial world as primarily either market-oriented or command-based economies.

PLANNING IN BASICALLY MARKET-ORIENTED SYSTEMS

In the market-oriented economic system of the United States, the government participates in the market economy merely as a referee and supervisor; it does not assume the role of an economic planner. Almost all transactions within the economic system are essentially guided by the market, and the role of government is limited to modifying the results of the market by regulation and short-term management of aggregate demand. Central economic planning, or active government intervention with the market in order to affect the direction and pattern of the nation's economic development, is totally alien to the country's ideological makeup.

Unlike the United States, Japan does have a formal system of long-range economic planning. The Economic Planning Agency (EPA) prepares medium- and long-term economic plans in close cooperation with the other economic ministries (notably with MITI and Finance), the political leadership of the ruling party, and the Economic Council whose membership comprises the topmost leaders of Japanese business. As we noted in Chapter 9, this planning activity of the Japanese government is devoid of much substance; it is essentially an econometric exercise in forecasting mixed with wishful thinking. The real substance of economic planning in Japan, instead, lies in the industrial policies of MITI and other economic ministries.

Most Western capitalist countries practice economic planning of one sort or another. Because of the ideological and legal constraints imposed on public authority, however, national economic planning in democratic capitalist countries cannot be *imperative* planning of the Soviet type. Government can merely *indicate* the direction in which it wishes the economy to develop. The main focus of *indicative* planning is likely to be decisions on investment in both public and private sectors, and a coordination between the two. By minimizing long-term risks of private investment activities, the public authority can reduce uncertainty in private business decisions and minimize waste arising from long-term structural imbalances in the economy. The best-known variety of indicative national economic planning is that of France.

French Economic Planning

In its general and idealized form, French indicative planning brings government officials and business leaders into a large-scale joint exercise in industrywide forecasting by utilizing investment and production plans of nationalized and private firms. The picture of generalized market that emerges from this forecasting exercise is the French plan. Presumably it is free of inconsistencies and duplications because it is drawn up by consolidating and synthesizing the microeconomic plans of individual firms. The government injects its own preferences into the plan by active participation of its representatives in the process of plan formulation. Although industry-by-industry plan targets are not specified for individual firms, they nevertheless are presumed to be helpful to private decision makers to the extent that they minimize their uncertainty as to the future course of their respective industry and of the economy. In trying to implement the plan, the government uses such positive incentives as tax advantages, subsidies, and low-interest loans to those firms that cooperate with plan objectives. By this method, the French government is said to be able to generate coherence in economic activities while injecting its collective preferences into them.

Formal economic planning in France began in 1946 with the creation of the Planning Commission (Commissariat Général du Plan, or CGP). The objective of the first Plan of Modernization (the Monnet Plan) was to facilitate the postwar reconstruction of the French economy with a particular emphasis on the six heavy industry areas of coal, electric power, steel, cement, transportation, and farm equipment.

Jean Monnet, the first postwar commissioner, and the members of the Planning Commission developed a unique style of planning that was suited to the special circumstances of postwar France. Representatives from industry and interested government agencies were brought into consultation with the planners. Investment and production targets were discussed and proposals were reviewed in joint meetings of industrial leaders, ministerial officials, and the CGP staff members. Although no targets were fixed for individual firms and they were left free to do as they wished, their cooperation was actively sought in exchange for offers of regulatory favors and preferential access to low-cost financing. The First Plan, which covered the period from 1947 to 1953, achieved its goals; the French economy broke away from stagnation and moved into the era of sustained growth.

Since the First Plan was completed in 1953, there has been continual evolution in the importance of planning and the Planning Commission. Specifically, under the conservative governments during the period from 1966 to 1981, French planning lost much of its weight and dynamism. The task of modernization and reconstruction of the French economy having been completed, the planning system lost much of its relevance under conditions of increasingly freer international trade. Starting in the 1970s and continuing into the 1980s, comprehensive indicative planning has become overshadowed by industrial planning for export growth.

Prior to the 1981 elections in which the Socialist government was brought into power, the commissioner of planning had reported to the prime minister. Since 1981, under the Socialist government, the commission has been under the jurisdiction of the Ministry of Planning and Regional Policy.[1] In terms of power and influence, the CGP is now eclipsed by the powerful Ministry of Finance and Ministry of Industry. Between 1966 and 1981, the commissioner of planning was turned into a minor government functionary having little authority and influence.[2]

The CGP is a permanent administrative organ staffed by a small number (about 140 in 1979)[3] of planning specialists and clerical employees. The commission has no executive power or resources of its own. Its functions are to coordinate the planning effort and submit the end product to the government for approval. Actual work of drawing up a five-year plan is done by working commissions that are made up of representatives of private and public enterprises, industrial associations, labor unions, and government ministries and agencies whose interests are involved. For the Ninth Plan for Economic and Social Development (1984–88), there were the following seven working commissions: (1) scientific, technological, and cultural conditions of development; (2) economic development; (3) financing the economy; (4) employment, income, and solidarity; (5) decentralized development and regional balance; (6) international relations; and (7) social education and cultural development.[4] In the 1970s, the working commissions ceased to be the nexus of contact between the government and industry, as the Ministry of Industry assumed the role of chief coordinator of industrial policy with authority to approve funding.[5]

Ever since the golden age of French indicative planning in the 1950s and 1960s, the real significance of working commissions has never been that they symbolize the formal and open consultative planning process;

[1]Saul Estrin and Peter Holmes, *French Planning in Theory and Practice* (London: George Allen & Unwin, 1983), p. 91.

[2]Ibid., p. 92.

[3]Ibid., p. 91.

[4]Robert Eisner, "Which Way for France?" *Challenge*, 26, no. 3 (July-Aug. 1983), 37.

[5]Estrin and Holmes, *French Planning*, p. 93.

rather, they have provided a convenient legitimizing cover for what Shonfield called the "clandestine affair," or the secretive bilateral bargaining between the higher civil servants and the leaders of big business. French government officials have long known that indirect and formal dealings with the mass of firms through their trade and employer associations does not achieve much in the way of securing the specific changes in the industry that the government wants; such changes can be much more easily obtained through direct contacts with large firms that have the real power of making strategic changes. The informal negotiations between the large firms and the government take place, in the main, outside the formal consultative processes of the working commissions.

In Chapter 7 we quoted Andrew Shonfield's apt description of French planning process as "conspiracy in the public interest between big business and big officialdom." If the real essence of French planning is a "clandestine affair" between big business and big government, it does not really matter where it takes place, as long as it is hidden from public scrutiny. The opportunities for contacts may be provided by working commissions, as they used to be, or by the relationships of tutelage and accommodations that now exist between the powerful economic ministries and big business firms.

A close, symbiotic relationship between business and government leaders is easily established in France since in that country, as in Japan, graduates of the top elite schools of higher education—the *grandes écoles*—form a tight and exclusive elitist group that dominates the top echelons of both the civil service and industry. Thus, in Shonfield's words, the "very elitist conspiracy . . . relied essentially on the close contacts established between a number of like-minded men in the civil service and in big business."[6]

There are some interesting similarities between economic planning as practiced in France and Japan. In both countries, the formal aspect of national economic planning essentially amounts to an exercise in econometric forecasting. Both France's CGP and Japan's EPA are relatively powerless, small agencies whose primary function is to formulate the plan in close collaboration with leaders of big business. In both countries, the primary emphasis of economic planning is economic development and long-term supply management. Selective allocations of low-interest loans are the primary instrument of plan implementation. In the implementation stage, the powerful economic ministries play a much more important role than the planning agency. The elitist ties between senior civil servants and leaders of big business arising from

---

[6]Andrew Shonfield, *Modern Capitalism: The Changing Balance of Public and Private Power* (New York and London: Oxford University Press, 1965), pp. 130–31.

their shared school backgrounds are important factors in facilitating the "conspiracy in the public interest."

There are also some important differences between the French and Japanese styles of planning. In Japan, the forecasting aspect of planning is primarily the responsibility of the Economic Planning Agency, while MITI is the chief architect of industrial policy. By contrast, planning in France is less well organized; the Planning Commission and the economic ministries all want to play the game in their own ways. In Japan, MITI is the single command center of industrial policy; its various bureaus and agencies have well-organized, systematic, and long-lasting relationships with their counterparts in the private sector. MITI deals with both large and small firms, and it has a great deal of influence over the flows of industrial loan funds. By contrast, there is little central guidance and coordination of industrial policy in France. Both the Finance Ministry and the Industry Ministry go their own separate ways developing their own industrial schemes and funding programs. Measures taken by the government bureaucracy are often guided by considerations of political and administrative expediency or are ad hoc responses to crisis situations. Thus, the whole French planning system, according to Estrin and Holmes, is "something of a mess."[7]

MARKET IN BASICALLY
PLAN-ORIENTED SYSTEMS

As we saw in Part 2, the Soviet economy is completely centralized in strategic decision making. Because of the complexity of the large, technologically complex industrial economy, effective implementation of the decisions made at the top requires a considerable amount of downward delegation of decision-making authority. Nor is it possible to design a completely centralized information structure. Accordingly, there exists a great deal of upward and downward flow of information in both formulation and implementation stages of planning.

A fundamental and inherent weakness of the Soviet-type centralized planning system is its inability to develop a motivation structure that works in harmony with the decentralized decision-making and information structures. Appeals to socialist morality and nationalism have failed to produce a strong solidarity motivation. Effective uses of egocentric motivation and material incentives have been hampered by the ambivalent ideological attitude of Soviet leadership toward such methods. The leaders find distasteful the use of prices or profits as a

[7]Saul Estrin and Peter Holmes, "How Far Is Mitterrand from Barre?" *Challenge*, 26, no. 5 (November–December 1983), 46–50.

means of providing incentives to lower-echelon decision makers. Thus, they use a combination of compulsion and material incentives—both half-hearted—as primary motivational forces. Such a strategy naturally results in a high level of alienation of lower-level managers and workers. In the meantime, lower-level decision makers, not being effectively motivated by a sense of loyalty and commitment to the collective, take every opportunity to maximize their private benefits at the expense of the interests of larger groups and society as a whole.

The market and the price system *are* being utilized in some areas of the Soviet economy, notably in consumer goods markets. Prices in these markets, however, do not affect strategic decisions concerning allocation of resources. The market mechanism is utilized merely as a subsidiary means of clearing the available supply whose quantities are predetermined by the planners. Consumers are allowed *free choice*, but they do not enjoy *sovereignty*. Strategic decisions in resource allocation are made in response to the planners' objectives and preferences; in other words, rulers' sovereignty prevails in the Soviet system. The one truly free market in the Soviet economy—the collective farm market— is limited in its impact on the rest of the system because of its size and the nature of its products. In qualitative terms, however, this market is very important for Soviet citizens' daily lives because it gives them room to breathe some fresh air in the otherwise suffocating environment of bureaucratic rigidity of the command economy.

The collective farm market is part of the Soviet Union's huge *second economy*, as the term is broadly defined. The second economy is that part of production and exchange activity that lies outside the *first economy* of centralized planning and supply. It includes all activities that are undertaken for private gain. Such activities may be legal (e.g., collective farm market), semilegal (i.e., illegal but tolerated or not strictly enforced), or strictly illegal.[8] Some writers define the term *second economy* narrowly, including only the semilegal and illegal activities. In this sense, *second economy*, *underground economy*, and *black market* are synonymous.[9]

The prevalence and intensity of second-economy activities in socialist countries go to show that self-interest and material incentives are inherent in all human societies. The latent spirit of private initiative, now suppressed by the rigidity of the planning system, could very well prove to be a source of powerful energy needed for vitalization of the

---

[8]Gregory Grossman, "The 'Second Economy' of the USSR," in *The Soviet Economy: Continuity and Change*, ed. Morris Bornstein (Boulder, Colo.: Westview Press, 1981), pp. 71–72.

[9]See, for example, Marshall I. Goldman, *U.S.S.R in Crisis: The Failure of an Economic System* (New York: W. W. Norton & Company, 1983), pp. 55 and 98.

Soviet economy. The recent economic reforms in China and some of the East European countries entail some degree of legalization of the second economy. Similarly, we can expect that a genuine economic reform in the Soviet Union, if and when it is undertaken, will start by building on the collective farm market and legalizing much of the heretofore illegal production and exchange activities.

Prospects for a Genuine Economic Reform in the Soviet Union

Analysis of the so-called Soviet disease has led most Western (and some Soviet) observers to conclude that the malady can be cured only by a fundamental restructuring of the economic system involving a wholesale introduction of market methods and principles—competition between producers to serve the needs of consumers, prices determined primarily by market forces of supply and demand, and success indicators based on profits. Producers' performance will have to be measured by *profits* that are computed under a regime of *rational prices*, that is, prices that reflect both the opportunity costs of resources to producers and the relative use values of users/consumers. Only if producers' success indicators are expressed in terms of profits based on rational prices, can fulfillment of specific targets given to producers lead to the maximum well-being of the country as a whole.

Although Soviet leaders habitually complain about the waste in their economic system, they have thus far failed to replace the time-honored system of centralized supply allocation. As we saw in Chapter 6, the "reforms" that have been introduced in the past amounted to nothing more than cosmetic changes in the old system of centralized control. No radical changes have been made where they are sorely needed: rationalization of the price system and decentralization of managerial decision making. Managerial success indicators continue to be primarily based on the physical quantity or ruble value of output. To be sure the latest reform measures have introduced increasingly greater uses of "profits," but profits made under the existing system of administrative (hence irrational) prices fail to reflect accurately the relative efficiency of managerial decisions. Decisions made using irrational prices can only lead to irrational results. While the superficial and half-hearted reforms of the past failed to produce tangible results, and debates over "reform of reforms" continue to thrive, a fundamental reform is put off further into the future. Why the delay? What are obstacles to a genuine reform?

The Soviet leadership's desire for political stability is an immediate impediment to reforms. Proposals for radical structural changes are often fiercely attacked by the party *apparatchiki* who have vested interests in preserving the tight control over the economy and society.

A powerful coalition of the apparatchiki, economic bureaucrats, and military leaders—all those who would lose power, prestige, and privileges if the center's control is lost to the free play of the market—is certain to go to great lengths to silence any cry for genuine reforms. The older leadership before Gorbachev opted for accommodating the collective self-interests of the powerful antireform coalition than for listening to the voices of the politically weak and fragmented group of reform advocates.

Marshall Goldman argues that one of the reasons for the Soviet leadership's reluctance to change the status quo lies in its fear of the potentially explosive effect of a drastic reform. Because of the past neglect of consumer needs, there now exists an enormous amount of consumer purchasing power locked up in the form of savings bank deposits. Under such a circumstance, a sudden change from a tightly controlled supply to production geared to consumer demands could set off an explosive situation generating enormous inflationary pressures. Supply bottlenecks, shortages of some types of capital goods, and pressures for imports would be accompanied by unemployment of certain types of labor and surpluses of outmoded plants and equipment. Inflation, unemployment, chaos, and shortages of much-desired goods would lead to a prolonged period of political instability that might produce mass upheavals. Fearing that such an explosion could threaten the survival of the present Soviet system, the politically conservative Soviet leadership clings to the status quo under the illusion that a series of piecemeal cosmetic "reforms" would somehow keep things from getting worse. The tragedy is that the longer the Soviet leaders put off the badly needed reform, the more explosive it will be when it finally arrives.[10]

The fundamental impediment to a radical reform in the Soviet economy lies in the Soviet leadership's fear of losing control to the "vagaries of the market." Authoritarian control of society is the central ideology of the Soviet system, a fundamental value that defines the very essence of the system itself. The whole system is built and maintained on the premise that control of society and its direction of change is so important that it cannot be entrusted to chaotic and irrational forces of the marketplace; it must be held by the center, which is all-knowing and all-capable. This control, therefore, cannot be abandoned merely because the economy happens to be functioning inefficiently. Giving up control is tantamount to renouncing the system's legitimacy. A genuine, comprehensive economic reform involving free markets and rational prices, therefore, will not be seriously considered until and unless the Soviet regime's control over Soviet society is in a serious and imminent

[10]Goldman, *U.S.S.R. in Crisis*, pp. 54–56 and 182.

danger. A more likely course of action is a policy of gradualism. The new Soviet regime headed by Gorbachev may very well begin its agricultural reforms by expanding the land area devoted to private plots and generally liberalizing private, family-based productive activities in agriculture along the Hungarian and Chinese lines (see below).

THE MARKET-ORIENTED PLANNED ECONOMY

In this section we shall consider the theoretical feasibility and actual experiences of the centrally controlled economy that relies significantly on the market mechanism for the purpose of allocating resources. The market economy is represented by its abstract model, that of perfect competition. It is also possible to conceive of a model of perfect planning (or "perfect computation"), a system that is controlled and coordinated from a center that has perfect monopoly of decision-making authority and needed information. Similarly, a theoretical model of a sort exists for the market-oriented planned economy where all the means of production are socially owned and managed. This is Oskar Lange's model of *competitive* (or *market*) *socialism*. In this section we first examine briefly the main features of the Lange model. We shall then discuss the experiences of Hungary and China in their efforts to move toward genuinely market-oriented socialist economies.

The Lange Model of Market Socialism

In Chapter 6 we discussed the meaning of rational prices, and found that prices are rational if they reflect both relative marginal social costs and relative marginal social utilities (or use values). The Soviet-type planned economy is not capable of generating rational prices, partly because "costs" do not include all the opportunity costs involved in production, and partly because relative use values are not allowed to affect the price formation process. Incorporating relative use values is particularly difficult with respect to wholesale prices since the state owns the entire productive sector, and, therefore, there exists no *market* to test (or measure) the relative strength of demands for goods transferred among the productive units within the state sector. This point was raised in the early 1920s in the famous "socialist controversy." Ludwig von Mises challenged socialists by arguing that *rational* resource allocation under socialism was a contradiction in terms since the absence of markets for capital, land, and producer goods in a socialist economy prevented formation of rational prices.[11]

In a famous article published in 1936–37, Polish economist Oskar Lange argued that rational socialism is not only logically feasible but also operationally workable.[12] Without getting into technical details, we present the bare essentials of the Lange model as follows. In a socialist economy, all the means of production are collectively owned and managed. Both the labor market and consumer goods market are completely free. The managers of socialized enterprises are given the prices of both inputs and outputs by the Central Planning Board (CPB), and are told to observe the following two rules: (1) to produce at the level of output where the price equals the marginal cost of output, and (2) to produce that output level by achieving the lowest-cost combination of inputs. These two rules simulate the rules of the perfectly competitive model, thereby assuring efficient use of resources.

How would the CPB know at what levels to set the prices of outputs and inputs? What could it do if there developed shortages or surpluses? Lange's answers to these questions were simple. The CPB sets all prices at first by trial and error. If shortages of some goods develop, the CPB simply raises their prices until supplied and demanded quantities are brought into balance. Conversely, for surpluses, price decreases would be used to restore equilibrium in the market. Lange argued that this is how the free market works anyway. The CPB, by passively reacting to changes in the forces of demand and supply, simulates the result of the market system in which the preferences of users/consumers ultimately determine the pattern of resource allocation. Since prices are determined by the interaction of demand and supply forces, they are rational.

The CPB, however, is not to be totally passive in all aspects of economic decision making. Among other things, it sets the economywide rate of saving that is to be used for the formation of society's capital stock. Socialist ownership of the means of production means that the state owns land and capital goods. Since socialist enterprises pay the state for the use of these inputs, the state realizes a large inflow of socialist income. The CPB may choose to pay out part of this state income to citizens as "socialist dividends," or retain part of it for capital accumulation. Just as a private business corporation can determine its growth rate by deciding what proportion of its business income to pay

[11]Ludwig von Mises, "Economic Calculation in the Socialist Commonwealth," in *Collectivist Economic Planning*, ed. F. A. Hayek (London: Routledge and Kegan Paul, Ltd., 1935), pp. 87–130.

[12]Oskar Lange, "On the Economic Theory of Socialism," *Review of Economic Studies*, 4, no. 1 (October 1936), 53–71, and no. 2 (February 1937), 123–142; reprinted in Oskar Lange and Fred M. Taylor, *On the Economic Theory of Socialism* (New York: McGraw-Hill Book Company, 1964), pp. 57–142.

out to shareholders as dividends and what proportion to retain for capital investment purposes, so can a socialist state determine the division of national income between social dividends and social accumulation. The higher the rate of accumulation, the faster the growth rate of the economy but the lower the level of current consumption by citizens. Lange argued that the CPB's ability to *arbitrarily* determine these proportions, and thereby to positively determine the rate of growth of the national economy, is one of the greatest advantages of socialism over capitalism. By contrast, in a decentralized market system, consumers individually make their decisions concerning the division of income into current consumption and investment in future earnings. Their propensity to favor current consumption at the expense of savings tends to lead, in many societies, to underinvestment and a slow rate of growth.

The preceding is by no means a comprehensive summary of the main features of the Lange model, but it touches upon the heart of the model and is quite sufficient for our purposes. The model has been found to contain some serious weaknesses, but its most serious drawback has to do with its assumption concerning managerial motivation. As Neuberger and Duffy point out, Lange's model "is based on the implicit assumption of complete organizational unity."[13] Lange naively assumed, it seems, that the CPB has merely to tell the managers of socialized enterprises to follow certain rules, and the managers will faithfully follow them. In other words, Lange assumed that the CPB and the managers share identical objectives and preferences. In our terms, Lange saw a complete harmony between managers' self-interests and the collective interest of society as perceived by the CPB. But what if this congruence of interests does not exist in reality? What if enterprise managers pursue their own individual self-interests even if doing so would be at the expense of society as a whole? This is not an idle speculation; we saw in Part 2 numerous examples of antisocial and self-serving behavior of Soviet enterprise managers. If the CPB cannot expect managers to blindly obey the rules, then it must provide incentives—positive and negative—to managers to induce or compel them to observe the rules. The experience of the success indicator problem in the Soviet economy tells us that this is not an easy task. Suppose that the CPB were to tell managers that they would receive bonuses for maximizing profits. It does not take much imagination to predict what most managers would do. They would simply reduce output, create shortages, and induce the CPB to raise the price. At a higher price, their profits would also be higher. Managers are now simulating the profit-maxi-

[13]Egon Neuberger and William J. Duffy, *Comparative Economic Systems: A Decision-Making Approach* (Boston: Allyn and Bacon, Inc., 1976), p. 93.

mizing behavior of capitalist monopolists described in economics textbooks!

Thus we are once again reminded of the crucial importance of a harmony of interests (or organizational unity). The Lange model may be theoretically feasible, but its operational workability depends critically on the degree of harmony of interests. The past experience of the Soviet economy shows that it is extremely difficult to achieve a harmony of individual self-interests and the collective interest within a hierarchical framework of authoritarian centralism. One way of escaping this predicament is to abandon the centralized control in many areas of national economic life, and let the forces of the market do the coordination work. The self-interest of individuals and groups, and competition among them, can be expected to produce, hopefully, a result that approximates the collective interest of the larger group.

While the Soviet Union remains hesitant and indecisive about instituting a fundamental reform of its economic system, other "socialist" countries, which after World War II adopted the Soviet-type centralized administrative control and planning, have in recent years made rather dramatic changes in their economic organization and institutions. Whereas their political systems have remained basically autocratic under one-party control, their economic systems have acquired many features of the market system. Market forces, rather than administrative fiats, are largely relied upon in many of these countries as the primary means of guiding and coordinating production and investment decisions. In some cases, prices are allowed to change freely in response to changes in the demand and supply conditions. A limited degree of private ownership or productive means is allowed in some sectors of the economy in some countries. In the following two subsections, we shall examine the recent experience in two socialist countries, Hungary and China, that have made a decisive departure from the centralized system of planning and control, and are moving toward an extensive reliance on the market mechanism.

The Hungarian Reforms

In analyzing the Hungarian economic system, it is important to bear in mind that the system is definitely not an applied Lange model. The Hungarians have developed their present system of market-oriented planned economy largely through trial and error, aided by the knowledge of many of its citizens of how the market system worked before the system was converted to the Soviet-type planned central control. It is difficult to say whether the Lange model of market socialism is any less descriptive, relatively speaking, of the present Hungarian system than the theory of perfect competition is of the American system or the model of perfect computation is of the Soviet system. In all three cases, the theoretical models are so far removed and abstracted from the actual cases that their analytical usefulness is highly limited.

After a few years of careful study and preparation, the Hungarian government in January 1968 launched a major program of economic reforms. The program, called the New Economic Mechanism (NEM), was designed to integrate the market mechanism in the overall framework of strategic central planning. Enterprise managers were freed from compulsory production quotas and product mixes, and the government-administered system of materials allocation was abolished. Managers were also given nearly complete freedom to make their own decisions concerning investment, production, employment of labor, and purchasing of inputs. Prices of most producers' good were decontrolled. Efforts were made to make domestic prices compatible with world prices, so that goods could be traded readily across national borders. Managers' bonuses were based on their enterprises' profits. Enterprises were to raise funds for necessary investments by loans from banks, and to pay interest on them.

The government retained its direct control over the strategic sectors of the economy including banking, transportation, communication, and public utilities. The government's central planning was now limited mainly to (1) investment and production decisions in the key sectors, (2) specification of nonobligatory production targets for all industries, and (3) determination of the macroeconomic parameters for the national economy, for example, social investments, consumer prices and other controlled prices, and wage scales. The government also continued to appoint and dismiss enterprise managers, and to influence their decision making through its authority to issue or deny various permits and licenses. The authoritarian management of the enterprise by the state-appointed manager remained unchanged. In other words, the Hungarian leaders chose not to give workers the right to participate in enterprise management.

Hungarian agriculture had been fully collectivized by 1958–59, and agricultural cooperatives had been placed under the management of the most able of former private farmers. As in the Soviet Union, members of agricultural cooperatives had been allowed to work on their private plots and dispose of the produce as they saw fit. Under the reform of 1968, compulsory delivery quotas for cooperatives were abolished. Farms were given freedom to decide what to produce, how to produce, and what inputs to purchase from where. Prices of food delivered to the state were to be negotiated between the state and the farm. Members of cooperatives entered into contracts with their cooperative or with the state to fatten livestock on their private plots. A great deal of freedom was allowed for peasants to use the facilities, land, equipment, and tools of their cooperative in raising their own livestock and growing their own vegetables.

Although the 1968 reform did not legalize large private enterprises, a new form of semiprivate enterprise began to blossom in the late 1960s as a result of the changes in government regulation associated with the reform measures. Various types of private entepreneurs (skilled workers, technicians, engineers) entered into contract with agricultural cooperatives to establish auxiliary plants and shops within the cooperative. These individuals ran the plants and shops as autonomous units independent of the cooperative's management, and paid the latter 60 percent of the venture's income after taxes. These plants engaged in various types of repair, construction, and small-scale industrial activities. In return, the cooperatives provided administrative protection to the entrepreneurs.[14]

These were the main features of Hungary's New Economic Mechanism (NEM) inaugurated in 1968. The new mechanism of economic management was characterized by two types of liberalization. The first was the liberalization of the state's control over state-owned productive enterprises. Perhaps more importantly, the NEM entailed significant liberalization of many of the practices in the second economy. Secondary occupations—or moonlighting—of industrial and agricultural workers and of government employees are commonplace throughout the Soviet-bloc countries. These activities, though illegal in many cases, serve important functions by not only providing badly needed secondary incomes to workers, but also lessening the extent of large-scale disequilibria in consumer goods markets. Thanks to the ubiquitous and lively second economy, daily lives of ordinary citizens in the Soviet-bloc "socialist" countries have been made less unbearable than otherwise. The second economy, in short, serves as an important lubricant for centrally planned economies. A greater tolerance or legalization of the heretofore illegal aspects of the second economy signifies a move toward an increasingly more market-oriented economic system.

Hungary's road to market socialsm met, in the early 1970s, some stiff resistance from the old-school hard-liners who persisted in their belief in the superiority of centralized allocation methods and who feared loss of their control over the economy, lessening of their privileged positions, and widening inequality of incomes. The reformers prevailed, however, when it was realized that Hungary, a country with only scant natural resources, must improve its export competitiveness and that,

---

[14]Kalman Rupp, *Entrepreneurs in Red: Structure and Organizational Innovation in the Centrally Planned Economy* (Albany, N.Y.: State University of New York Press, 1983), pp. 2–3.

for that purpose, liberalization of the economic institutions was the only viable alternative.

The scope of private enterprise was further expanded in 1981. State enterprises were permitted to lease, to private operators, stores employing not more than 5 workers and restaurants employing up to 12 persons. Multiyear leases were sold to private entrepreneurs by auction. The managers of these stores or restaurants could hire employees of their choice, and were free to spend the net profit (after wages, taxes, and other expenses) in any way they liked.[15] In 1982, a further liberalization was put into effect. Individuals were allowed to set up private industrial or service establishments in association with larger cooperatives, or to form a small cooperative employing not more than 100 persons.[16] With these changes in place, Hungarian small businesses in retailing, personal services, arts and crafts, and small-scale manufacturing became virtually indistinguishable from those in the West. A significant consequence of these reform measures is that in Hungary today all sorts of consumer goods are in ample supply, and Hungarian consumers can easily buy them without having to waste much time in long lines. Ample supplies of food contribute appreciably to the country's economic vitality and political stability.

In the Soviet Union, retail prices of some agricultural goods are lower than the government's procurement prices paid to agricultural producers. In many of the Soviet-bloc countries, retail food prices are maintained at stable levels while subsidies are paid to producers. The desire to maintain political stability is the main motivation behind this pricing policy. Increases in consumer prices are unpopular with consumers, whereas agricultural productivity suffers if procurement prices do not cover costs of production. Thus, the government is tempted to keep retail prices low, and subsidizes the producers by paying them high procurement prices. In Hungary, however, the government has been able to raise food prices repeatedly without causing a political upheaval. Goldman points out that the Hungarians have been remarkably successful in creating a consensus among themselves that everyone must accept some serious belt-tightening if their economy was to be freed from the Soviet-type rigidity and stagnation. He attributes this political consensus to the high quality of political leadership under Janos Kadar, coupled with the Hungarian people's resolve that the tragedy of the 1956 uprising must never be repeated.[17]

---

[15]K. F. Cviic, "Hungary's Reforming Road," *The World Today*, 37, no. 10 (October 1981), 385.

[16]Ibid.

[17]Goldman, *U.S.S.R. in Crisis*, p. 175.

By raising consumer prices to the levels that permit payments of attractive prices to agricultural cooperatives, the government has been able to assure that the consumers' demands are adequately met. As noted earlier, this abundance of food supplies is one of the basic reasons for Hungary's economic vitality and political stability. It in turn has driven the people to work hard—largely by moonlighting—to earn enough money with which to buy the available supplies of consumer goods. Thus, in the small-enterprise sector of the Hungarian economy, a beneficial circle of a sort is at work: supply creates demand, which, in turn, leads to more supply. On the supply side, people work hard, raise productivity, and improve product quality—all in order to earn more money. Larger money incomes enable people to buy more consumer goods, which, in turn, induces more individual entrepreneurs to supply a larger quantity and a greater variety of consumer goods. Driving this beneficial circle, of course, is the desire of Hungarian workers and consumers to improve their material well-being.

Allowing one part of the economy to be driven by self-interest but managing the rest of it on the socialist principle is bound to generate some serious distortions and conflicts. Four problem areas may be identified. First, there is the inevitable conflict between the self-interest and the public interest. Workers tend to neglect work in their regular workplaces (cooperatives and factories) and concentrate their efforts on money-making activities in the second economy. Tools, supplies, and equipment in the first economy are siphoned off to the second economy. (Borrowing public equipment after work is now allowed by law.) Managers of enterprises become more interested in showing improvements in short-term profits and obtaining subsidies from the government than in improving the long-term viability of their operations. Second, the *efficiency* of free markets can be obtained only at the price of *inequality*. Emergence of socialist millionaires, however, may be offensive to the basic socialist morality, which stresses the equality of outcome. Third, a similar conflict exists between considerations of efficiency and *security*. In a socialist society, full employment of labor must be assured regardless of cost; it is the ideological cornerstone and the main source of legitimacy of a socialist regime. Thus, in order to maintain virtually full employment, workers must be kept whether or not they are justified by considerations of efficiency. This means that large industrial firms often have to be supported by large government subsidies, and bankruptcies of unprofitable enterprises have to be avoided. Finally, the goal of efficiency may also conflict with that of *stability*. Allowing enterprise managers to set their own prices may lead to a price inflation, and freedom to purchase inputs may lead to balance-of-payments difficulties.

In pressing forward with further liberalization of their economy, the Hungarian leaders must pay close attention to two very important constraints. First, the hard-line government and party leaders who still carry a torch for central planning may become sufficiently annoyed by widening inequalities and threatened by the steady diminution of their power of control over the economy that they may mount a concerted counterattack on the present policy of liberalization. Second, an even more serious threat to the present course of action is the possibility of a Soviet intervention. The Soviet Union has tolerated Hungary's economic reforms because they have not affected the monopoly of political power of the Hungarian Communist party. But there is no reason to believe that greater economic freedom will not lead to a demand for greater political freedom. If and when that happens, the Hungarian experiment will face a major test of its long-term survivability.

The Chinese Reforms

The Hungarian economic reforms are studied intensively by the leaders of other socialist countries and are used as a model when reforms are attempted in those countries. One important socialist country that has recently launched itself on the road to a market-aided planning system is China. After the fiasco of the Cultural Revolution (1966–69), the post-Mao government under the new chairman Hua Guofeng (now demoted) and Deng Xiaoping launched an ambitious investment program in industry and agriculture with a heavy reliance on foreign loans and imported technology. It was soon realized, however, that the overzealous undertakings had caused serious distortions in the economy. The distortions took the forms of serious imbalances in industrial supplies, deterioration in household consumptions, deficits in the state budget, and an inflation of consumer prices. After a considerable debate, a new policy of economic *readjustment* was announced in 1979.

As the Chinese use it, the word *readjustment* means a change in the emphasis in the strategy of economic development. The word *reform* is used, by contrast, to refer to a fundamental restructuring of the economic system. The Chinese maintain that a basic reform must be implemented slowly and carefully, after the necessary readjustment is completed under the existing system.[18] However, since readjustments must be made in the direction of, and in harmony with, the coming reforms, the line of demarcation between the two is often blurred.

China's economic readjustments and reforms started with an attempt at improving the system of incentives in agriculture. In place of the former method of distributing farm incomes to a production team

---

[18]Lin Wei and Arnold Chao, eds., *China's Economic Reforms* (Philadelphia: University of Pennsylvania Press, 1982), pp. 40–43.

of peasant families, the new system of "household production responsibility," adopted in 1979, assigns part of the farmland collectively owned by the production team to a family, an individual, or a group of team members on a long-term basis. The family or group of individuals signs a contract for farm jobs and output quotas with the production team. After making the delivery of the contracted quota to the team, the household or group can dispose of the surplus in any way it chooses, including selling it on the open market at free-market prices.

Industrial enterprises, too, are given a much greater freedom and responsibility in their production and marketing decisions. Instead of the former method of linking their accounting directly with the state budget, managers of enterprises are made responsible for their firms' profits and losses. They are given the right to retain part of their profits to be used as bonuses for themselves and for their workers and as funds for providing housing and other facilities for workers. Enterprises are also allowed, after meeting their production targets, to sell or barter away their surplus products. Enterprises can also borrow funds from banks at various rates of interest, depending on the purpose of the loans.

Starting in 1981, individual businesses have been allowed in urban areas in the fields of retailing, repairing, restaurant trade, and handicrafts. Each individual business must be approved by the government. The owner-manager(s) can hire one or two helpers, not counting their family members. Skilled craftspeople may hire up to five apprentices.

In 1984, the government allowed, for the first time since the revolution, a large private enterprise to resume operations outside the state planning sector. Minsheng Shipping Co. was the largest conglomerate in China before the revolution. It is based in the industrial city of Chongqing (also known as Chungking), and provides freight shipping services along the Yangtze River. The shareholders of this new company, most of whom are employees, share both the firm's profits and losses. The company pays taxes to the state on its profits, instead of turning over most of the profits to the state as other large enterprises do. The company, run by the son of the founder of the prerevolution conglomerate, has freedom to hire and fire workers, and sets its business targets independent of state planning. The government expects the former capitalists who now run the company to contribute their managerial skills and experience and the overseas business connections to the success of the enterprise. If this experiment should prove successful, the government intends to allow similar operations throughout the rest of the country.[19]

---

[19]Vigor Fung, "China Allows the Rebirth of Some Private Corporations," *Wall Street Journal,* August 10, 1984, p. 22.

The Chinese reform measures have a great deal in common with the Hungarian reforms. Three differences between the two systems may be noted, however. First, because of the large size and greater complexity of the Chinese economy, reforms there seem to take much longer than in Hungary. Often, a new measure is started as an experiment in one part of the country and, if successful, is then allowed to spread to the other parts of the economy over a period of years. For this reason, it is very difficult to state what set of measures constitutes *the* Chinese reforms at a given point in time. Second, the Chinese have not been able to be as bold as the Hungarians are in allowing the flexibility in the price system. Only the prices in agricultural free markets are allowed to fluctuate according to demand and supply. On certain nonessential consumer products, prices are allowed to fluctuate within limits prescribed by the state. Most other prices are rigidly fixed by the state. The existence of the irrational price system thus constitutes one of the major contradictions in the Chinese experiment with the market mechanism. (This situation, however, is expected to change in due course. See below.) Third, although the Chinese leaders may have to be concerned with the reemergence of hard-line politicians who favor a tight, centralized control of the economy, they need not, as the Hungarians do, worry about the negative reactions from the Russians. The absence of this external constraint gives the Chinese leadership a greater degree of freedom in experimenting with reforms than the Hungarian leadership has.

In October 1984, the Central Committee of the Chinese Communist party under the leadership of chairman Deng Xiaoping approved a plan for a major economic reform which was to be gradually implemented over a period of several years. The approved plan merely stated the policy objectives, with specific plans yet to be drawn up. The plan objectives called for (1) freeing state enterprises—except for those in such key areas as steel, energy, and banking—from the administrative control of the state, (2) eliminating state subsidies to enterprises and workers, (3) allowing prices and wages to be determined freely by the market, and (4) regulating the economy with a greater reliance on such economic levers as taxes and interest rates.[20]

In pressing forward with their economic reforms, the Chinese and the Hungarians experience the same contradictions that are inherent in any attempt to harmonize the two opposing principles of economic organization. Specifically, the efficiency and flexibility of the market system can be obtained only at the expense of some sacrifices in stability, security, and equality, which are fundamental goals of socialism. These

---

[20]"Deng's Tune: Peking Turns Sharply Down Capitalist Road in New Economic Plan," *Wall Street Journal*, October 25, 1984, p. 1.

contradictions are succinctly described in the *Business Week* article entitled "China Walks the Edge of the Capitalist Road," which is reproduced as an appendix that follows this section.

The main theme of the *Business Week* article concerns the difficulty which Chinese leadership experiences in finding ways to reconcile "the two mutually incompatible systems." Particularly troublesome seems to be the conflict between the "centrally planned prices and the profit incentive." In more general terms, the contradiction is in the motivation structure: the state wants to continue to rely on national solidarity as the basic motivating force, whereas the people seem to be more responsive to the various incentives appealing to their egocentric, materialistic interests. Because of the inordinate difficulty of organically integrating the market system with the central planning structure, the Chinese leadership expects the process of gradual economic reforms to extend into the Seventh Five-Year Plan (1986–90) period. Even then, however, there will be no assurance of a successful integration of the two fundamentally incompatible systems of economic coordination.

Appendix: CHINA WALKS THE EDGE
OF THE CAPITALIST ROAD[21]

Western-style economic reforms are proving to be a heady brew for socialist China. So readily are its citizens taking to free enterprise, market-oriented prices, profits, and cash bonuses that Beijing's political leaders are beginning to worry that things are getting out of hand. "If planned production and [distribution] do not cover the main body of China's economy," warns a recent editorial in *People's Daily*, "the state-owned economy will disintegrate . . . and the socialist economy will become controlled by the unbridled, spontaneous force of the market economy."

But China's leaders are well aware that they have uncaged a dragon. The new economic policies cannot be rolled back easily. And the careers of some top officials—including the secretary general of the Communist Party, Hu Yaobang, and his counterpart in the civil government, State Council Premier Zhao Ziyang—are staked on the reforms.

Beijing now appears dedicated to continuing the search, however difficult, for meeting points between the two mutually incompatible systems. The sense of security and order China gets from state planning is as indispensable as the motivation and entrepreneurial spirit engen-

[21]*Business Week*, October 18, 1982, pp. 80–86. Reprinted from the October 18, 1982, issue of *Business Week* by special permission, © 1982 by McGraw-Hill, Inc.

dered by the reforms. Material incentives will continue to be fostered in China's mammoth economy, adding to, but not replacing, ideological exhortations to hard work.

No backtracking.   In his speech to the 12th Communist Party Congress in early September, Hu Yaobang underscored the leadership's growing nervousness by going out of his way to assert the primacy of the state sector, cental planning, and ideological rather than material incentives. "In the past few years, we have initiated a number of reforms in the economic system. . . . This orientation is correct, and its gains are apparent," Hu reported. "However . . . cases of weakening and hampering the state's unified planning have been on the increase. . . . Hereafter, while continuing to give play to the role of market regulation, we must on no account neglect or relax unified leadership through state planning."

Even while promising that there would be no backtracking on the reforms, the message was clear that there would be no immediate forward movement either. Hu described the Sixth Five-Year Plan (1981–85) as a time of "consolidation" and planning for further gradual economic reforms to take place in the next planning period (1986–90).

The party's vociferous comments on the need for centralized planning reflect the extent of the decentralization of China's economy in recent years. Only four years ago, the current economic reforms were launched. The impetus for them came from Zhao Ziyang, then first secretary of the Communist Party in Sichuan Province. Zhao compared China's centralized management to a "silkworm which wraps itself up in a cocoon" and, seeking a less stifling alternative, gave six industrial enterprises in his province the authority to run their own affairs.

In Zhao's experiment, the six factories were permitted to keep a portion of profits for reinvestment in new capital equipment or distribution to the workers. Once they had fulfilled their quota for the state plan, they could market directly any surplus production, diversify into new products, and even seek out export markets. Managers could also reward productive workers with generous bonuses and punish lazy workers.

Within two years, the experiment was expanded to 6,600 enterprises across the country, producing 45% of the nation's industrial output. Today, nearly half of China's industrial base is operating outside strict centralized planning. At the same time, other sectors of the economy are beginning to break free of rigid planning. Farmers are allowed to plant what they choose on small private plots and sell surplus produce in local markets at prices set by supply and demand. Any profits belong to the farmers.

In addition, a market in capital equipment—long considered state property—has sprung up. And on the city streets, thousands of outdoor stands and small repair shops are run by individual entrepreneurs, who now have the party's protection against the charge of "following the capitalist road." In an economy plagued by massive hidden unemployment, these roadside stands are mopping up several million of China's estimated 20 million unemployed.

Pricing traps.   Yet these free-enterprise, free-market, profit-oriented policies are facing troubling times. They are being grafted onto a slow-moving, deliberately controlled system of bureaucratic management and central planning. In many cases, the two systems do not mesh.

Nowhere are the contradictions more apparent than in the destructive interplay between centrally planned prices and the profit incentive. For example, the state deliberately keeps prices of coal and other raw materials low while pricing certain types of consumer durables well above their true market value. State pricing policies can trap the factory between artificially high prices for its material inputs and artificially low prices for its product—a no-win scenario for even the most adept of managers. Reverse the situation, and a poorly managed factory with less productive workers can end up with a hefty profit to distribute at bonus time.

Pricing distortions encourage some factories to keep producing high-priced goods, even though consumers find them too costly, and warehouses already bulge with them. At the same time, other factories are dropping the manufacture of inexpensive, everyday items because they have a low profit margin. In one province, according to *People's Daily,* 40 new factories were recently set up to produce washing machines even though warehouses are stuffed with them. Consumers cannot afford the machines, but the factories are still making profits because of the artificial state-directed pricing mechanism.

Ungainly hybrids.   Beijing has tried to offset the effect of fixed prices by introducing new taxes on resources and fixed assets. This year it required successful enterprises to purchase government bonds as a type of "windfall profits" tax. In the long run, Chinese economists realize, China needs a major realignment of prices to reflect real shortages and surpluses. But because of bureaucratic turf-protection and a deep fear of inflation, reform will be politically difficult and can be accomplished only gradually, at best.

Pricing is not the only area where the merging of capitalism and socialism has produced ungainly hybrids. Paradoxes abound:

- The "right to hire" is allowing some entrepreneurs to be too successful. In one case, a farmer in Guangdong province made a fortune for himself, according to *China Daily*, by setting up a fishpond business, hiring several assistants—permitted in the cities but taboo in the countryside—and paying them high wages. While some criticized the farmer as a capitalist, a leading party official conceded that there was much to be learned from his methods.

- The "right to fire" is meeting strong resistance and has the potential to be a major drain on the nation's treasury. Foreign companies in joint-venture arrangements have been given the legal right to fire lazy or incompetent workers, and the government is considering extending this right to some domestic enterprises. But firing goes against the grain in China's socialist system. "A worker can be fired from a workshop but not from society," notes one Beijing official. Before a worker is fired, he is given many chances to reform, and if he is fired, he is guaranteed a new job. He is also guaranteed nearly all of his working income while he "waits for employment." Together with unemployed youths who receive much smaller welfare stipends, fired workers could create an enormous drain on state funds. So far, resistance to the concept is so strong that very few workers are likely ever to be fired.

- Managers are finding that rewards do not necessarily go to the most efficient. Because factories have been rewarded according to their percentage increase in profits, backward enterprises—which can grow faster than advanced enterprises—get disproportionate rewards.

- Workers are increasingly interested in big bonuses and less interested in hard work. In the Shoudu (Capital) Brewery in Beijing, for example, workers refused to work overtime to overhaul the fermentation tanks unless they were given exorbitant bonuses. Ultimately, the brewery resorted to ideological pressure coupled with moderate bonuses.

- Egalitarian ideals are robbing bonuses of their stimulative effect. In many factories, managers are distributing bonuses equally, regardless of performance. In 1981, when production fell off in heavy industry, bonuses actually rose while labor productivity in state enterprises fell an estimated 3.2% from the previous year.

- Success can be very threatening to entrenched managers. In one case, a public utility bureau in Chongqing (Chungking) advertised for managers for its taxi company subsidiary, according to an article in *China Youth News*. Six were selected from 216 applicants, and they helped increase the taxi company's income by 144% in six months. But some of the other employees—including the previous manager—made things difficult for the newcomers, and the new managers were allowed to keep their jobs only after a "leading comrade" on the party Central Committee in Beijing intervened.

The paradoxes arising out of conflicting economic policies are increasingly disturbing to China's leadership. Beijing today is taking a far more pragmatic approach to its mistakes than in the past, publicly acknowledging them and proposing specific solutions rather than seeking scapegoats for its errors. Yet the leadership is still very concerned about recent trends. In his September speech to the party congress, Secretary General Hu criticized some state-owned factories for hoarding materials, withholding profits, evading taxes, and raising prices. In rural areas, he said, there have been cases where farmers damaged irrigation works, cut down trees wantonly, and depleted collective funds—all in pursuit of individual profit.

Fatter purses. Even more important, disparities in income are worrying the leaders. "In some low-yield rural areas, or those hit by natural disasters, the peasants are still impoverished," Hu reported. "Urban people, too, still have many problems." Because of this, he called a halt to further rises in farmers' income and to any expansion of the rural free markets.

Beijing's current preoccupation with ideology reflects just how seriously the leadership is taking the problems—and how badly it wants the reforms to succeed. The task has now become to find a new "socialist road"—somewhere between the state-enforced planning and egalitarianism of China's previous economic system and the no-holds-barred, get-rich-quick type of capitalism it sees in the West and across the border in Hong Kong. According to the new rhetoric, economic reforms are not capitalist, since they do not allow individuals to own the means of production or to hire large numbers of laborers. Similarly, paying each individual according to his work—rather than his investment—is seen as a socialist principle.

In the end, the current Chinese leadership is far too committed to improving living standards to abandon the economic reforms. Too many people have already gotten used to the extra pocket money and the higher-priced goods they now can afford. If they are to achieve their goal of quadrupling output by the end of the century, the Chinese leaders need a policy that will truly motivate people to work harder. However high their socialist ideals, they know the power of the promise of a fatter purse and a more comfortable lifestyle.

QUESTIONS

1. Compare and contrast the major features of a market-oriented economic system and a centrally planned economic system.
2. Compare and contrast the major advantages (strengths) and disadvantages (weaknesses) of a market-oriented economic system and a centrally planned economic system.
3. Compare and contrast the fundamental nature and character of the two systems in terms of the organizational structure of decision making, information, and motivation.

4. Are market and planning "two mutually incompatible systems"? Or can they be organically combined with varying degrees of mix?
5. Would it be more (or less) difficult to incorporate some planning mechanism into a basically market-oriented system than to graft some market mechanism onto a fundamentally planned system? If so, what accounts for the asymmetry?
6. Is the problem of the harmony of individual and collective interests inherently more serious with a market or a planning system?
7. Discuss the differences between imperative planning and indicative planning. How can indicative planning be implemented?
8. What do the French mean when they say that the objective of their planning system is to bring about *cohérence* in their national economy?
9. What did Shonfield mean when he described the French planning process as a "clandestine affair," and a "conspiracy in the public interest"?
10. Discuss the similarities and differences between the French and Japanese styles of indicative planning.
11. Define *second economy*. Is there a second economy in the United States? What are the functions of the second economy in the Soviet Union?
12. Why do you think the second economy is so widespread and prosperous in the Soviet Union? Would a severe crackdown on second-economy activities be productive? Desirable? Possible?
13. Describe the nature of a genuine economic reform that is badly needed in the Soviet Union. Why has a fundamental restructuring of the Soviet economic system not been attempted? What obstacles to a genuine reform are there?
14. Briefly describe the main features of Lange's market socialism model. What are its drawbacks?
15. Describe the main features of Hungary's New Economic Mechanism. Do you believe that Hungary is moving in a right direction? Do you foresee any difficulties ahead?
16. What similarities and differences do you find between the Hungarian and the Chinese approaches to market socialism?
17. What difficulties are China's leaders finding in their efforts to restructure their economic system? Do you think they are moving in a right direction? Do you foresee any difficulties ahead?

SELECTED READING

ESTRIN, SAUL, and PETER HOLMES.   *French Planning in Theory and Practice.* London: George Allen & Unwin, 1983.

FEUCHTWANG, STEPHAN, and ATHAR HUSSAIN, Eds.   *The Chinese Economic Reforms.* New York: St. Martin's Press, 1983.

GOLDMAN, MARSHALL I.   *U.S.S.R. in Crisis: The Failure of an Economic System,* chap. 7. New York: W. W. Norton & Company, 1983.

HARE, PAUL, HUGO RADICE, and NIGEL SWAIN, Eds. *Hungary: A Decade of Economic Reform.* London: George Allen & Unwin, 1981.

NOVE, ALEC. *The Economics of Feasible Socialism.* London: George Allen & Unwin, 1983.

RUPP, KALMAN. *Entrepreneurs in Red: Structure and Organizational Innovation in the Centrally Planned Economy.* Albany, N.Y.: State University of New York Press, 1983.

TUNG, ROSALIE L. *Chinese Industrial Society after Mao.* Lexington, Mass.: Lexington Books, D. C. Heath and Company, 1982.

WEI, LIN, and ARNOLD CHAO, Eds. *China's Economic Reforms.* Philadelphia: University of Pennsylvania Press, 1982.

CHAPTER **13**

Managers and Workers

Paralleling the dichotomy of market and planning in macroeconomic organization and management is the dichotomy of adversarial and participative management-labor relations in enterprise organization and management. In Part 2, our discussions of enterprise organization and management were concerned mainly with the relationships between management and employees in general; the problems and issues of labor conflict between management and industrial labor was not specifically dealt with. In this chapter we shall contrast the adversarial industrial relations, primarily those in the United States, with more integrated patterns of management-labor organization and relations found in other industrial countries. Specifically, we shall examine Japanese-style management as it is practiced in the United States and in Great Britain, management-worker codetermination in West Germany, and workers' self-management in Yugoslavia. We shall conclude the chapter by speculating on the prospects for improved industrial relations in the United States.

MANAGEMENT-LABOR RELATIONS
IN THE UNITED STATES

The adversarial and polarized relationships between management and labor in American industries are legendary; they are pervasive and deeply entrenched. Since the heydey of the Knights of Labor in the 1880s, employers and workers have confronted each other with deep-seated suspicion and hostility. The origin of these antagonistic relations can probably be traced to America's native ideology of individualism. The captains of American industry in the 1800s and the early 1900s were mostly self-made men who had little tolerance of employees who would dare to challenge the authority and prerogatives of property owners. Workers, on the other hand, were mostly people of independent spirit who resented having to serve at the pleasure of those who had no higher moral value as individuals than workers themselves except that they owned property. In other words, it may be that the passionately independent and individualistic American workers were, and to this day have been, unaccustomed to being placed in a position of collective inferiority vis-à-vis managers and supervisors. Workers' resentment of their subordinate positions manifests itself as hostility toward their superiors, and stands in the way of developing harmonious and integrated relationships with them. Such is not the case with European and Japanese (and even Russian) workers who have had a long tradition of living and working in hierarchical social organization.

Whatever their roots are, the adversarial relationships between employers and workers in the United States have had a long and troubled history laden with a high incidence of industrial conflict. These relationships became institutionalized in the early decades of this century with the advent of "scientific management" and its byproducts, rigid job classifications and inflexible work rules.

Continuing problems of conflict between employers (managers and supervisors) and workers led, in the early 1900s, to the advocacy of scientific management by Frederick W. Taylor. He believed that much of the antagonism between management and labor could be eliminated by rationalization of work organization, greater efficiency in production methods, and increased material incentives for workers. Taylor argued that the higher productivity that was made possible by better organization and work methods would enable employers to maximize earnings of both employers and workers, thereby contributing to minimization of industrial conflict. To this end, he prescribed increased specialization of tasks, precise measurement of the time-and-motion aspects of each task, and better coordination among the tasks by strict work rules. Taylor believed that management-worker antagonism could be minimized if arbitrary and despotic applications of rules of thumb by employers and supervisors were replaced by a set of scientific rules of management by which both bosses and workers must abide. His ultimate goal was to create a work environment in which employers and workers could work in harmony toward a shared goal of greater output benefiting all concerned.[1]

Unfortunately, however, the methods of scientific management were used by employers primarily as a convenient means of increasing their control over workers and raising their productivity, not as a way of securing greater harmony in the workplace. Ironically, America's emerging industrial unions of the 1930s also embraced Taylorism as they saw in it a safeguard against arbitrary exercises of managerial power over workers. They believed that they could maximize worker rights in the shop by carefully defining each work task and clearly defining the work rules governing the relationships between the tasks. The rigid system of job classifications and work rules has since become an integral part of American industrial unionism. This system has given unions at the shop level a great deal of control over job assignments and work practices. Michael J. Piore reports that the constraints that this job control by unions impose on management's ability to organize production, design jobs, and assign workers are, in management's view, a much more serious problem than the high wages that have been attributed to union pressures.[2]

Narrow job classifications and rigid work rules are generally regarded as the most irrational and counterproductive aspect of American industrial unionism. They prevent management from developing a flexible production strategy, and stand in the way of generating harmony of group action in America's workplaces. Often heard are such anecdotes as assembly workers having to wait for an electrician to change a burned-out light bulb, and toolmakers being prohibited by work rules to clean their own tools. The inefficiency of these practices is well recognized even by union leaders. According to a calculation by United Auto Workers insiders, elimination of inefficient work rules could result in a one-time increase of labor productivity of perhaps 10 percent.[3]

[1]Frederick W. Taylor, *Scientific Management* (New York: Harper & Brothers, 1947).

[2]Michael J. Piore "American Labor and the Industrial Crisis," *Challenge*, 25, no. 1 (March-April 1982), 8.

[3]"Can GM Change Its Work Rules?" *Business Week*, April 26, 1982, pp. 116–19.

JAPANESE-STYLE MANAGEMENT
IN THE UNITED STATES

The polarized pattern of management-labor relations has existed in the United States for decades, but has come to be recognized as a serious problem only recently. The weaknesses of the American system of industrial management have become increasingly more evident in contrast to the more integrative pattern of industrial relations in other countries. The contrast has become particularly pronounced during the 1970s and 1980s as the substance of the Japanese management system has become widely known. Many American business and labor leaders have come to realize that in an environment of increasingly keener global competition and more complex technology, management and labor must cooperate much more closely than in the past, each pulling in the same direction in the interest of mutual prosperity. The continued threat of keen competition from Japanese manufacturers in labor productivity and product quality has sharpened the sense of urgency about the need for a fundamental restructuring of American industrial relations. Specifically, it is recognized that ways must be found to bring American industrial workers into the corporate community, and to give them a sense of belonging to that community. Out of this sense of belonging, it is hoped, will come a sense of workers' pride in, and commitment to, their work and company.

This quest for the organically integrated, cooperative, and communitylike business organization is a search for an optimal form of voluntary association of individuals where they can have a sense of belonging without having to give up their individuality. In other words, it is a search for the best way of harmonizing employees' self-interests with the overall interest of the corporate community.

It must be emphasized that the cooperative American corporation cannot be the embodiment of the Japanese (or any other) style of management. American workers are, as a rule, more individualistic, independent, and unsubmissive to authority than their Japanese counterparts so that purely Japanese-style management cannot be a viable alternative for them. We must assume that they are basically interested in working for material rewards, not willing to make a long-term commitment to the company (as most Japanese workers are), and resentful of measures that might compromise their individual dignity and privacy. It is also safe to assume, too, that they are less disciplined but perhaps more creative than Japanese workers. On the other hand, American workers can be assumed to be just as responsive to thoughtful and sensitive treatment by management as Japanese workers are. Given a proper motivation, American workers will be quite capable of cooperating with their co-workers and turning out high-quality work. The key to successful labor management in the United States, thus, is to make employees feel that they genuinely belong to their company and that they benefit from its successes.

One way to discover how American workers respond to an organic and integrative management philosophy is to examine the experience of Japanese-owned companies operating in the United States. In 1984, there were 309 such firms employing 73,000 workers at 479 plants in the United States.[4] In many of these plants, product quality is presumed to be equal to, if not better than, that found in plants located in Japan. Productivity, too, is approaching the Japanese level. It is important to note, however, that these plants are *not* operated under the Japanese management system. *Management* is Japanese, but management *practices* are hybrid Japanese-American. More importantly, the ingredients—workers, suppliers, government regulations, unions, local communities, and the sociocultural milieu—are American. In such an environment, it is impossible to practice purely Japanese-style management. The Japanese companies must give up much of their traditional methods and adapt to the foreign environment. In such a hybrid system, it is likely that the best of the two approaches are synthesized and retained, and the excesses of each system (e.g., the excesses of rank consciousness and group indecision of the Japanese system and the obsession with short-term financial performance of the American system) are rejected by mutual agreement. This outcome of retaining the best and rejecting the worst of both systems is very likely since both sides tend to veto each other's irrational features but agree to try those features that, although they may appear strange at first, make some sense in terms of reason or human nature. The end product, therefore, often turns out to be a valuable learning experience to both American and Japanese managers who are involved in the joint enterprise.

A study conducted by Tony Hain involving interviews with over 100 Japanese and American managers at 20 different U.S. facilities of Japanese-owned firms revealed the following set of characteristics of these hybrid management systems.[5]

In terms of management strategy, these firms tend to have longer time horizons (five to ten years) than typical U.S. corporations, stress quality as the most important strategic variable, avoid unions if at all

---

[4]"The Japanese Management Meets the American Worker," *Business Week*, August 20, 1984, pp. 128–29.

[5]Tony Hain, "Japanese Management in the United States," in *Management by Japanese Systems*, ed. Sang M. Lee and Gary Schwendiman (New York: Praeger Publishers, 1982), pp. 433–49.

possible, prefer building small plants in rural locations, and emphasize doing simple things well in their manufacturing operations. As for management organization, these Japanese-owned companies use a lean and flexible (but often ambiguous) organizational structure with a strong emphasis on crisscrossing coordination.[6]

In terms of managerial practices concerning employee relations, these firms show the following characteristics. The status distinction between managers and workers is consciously minimized by the use of common parking lots, common canteens, and company uniforms. Managers' offices tend to be spartan and to be located close to the production area. Companies sponsor social and athletic events for the employees and their families at a considerable expense. Although employment stability is not guaranteed, management makes serious efforts to let employees know that they can count on secure jobs. Firms may reduce wages, assign surplus employees to special projects, or just keep them on payrolls temporarily, before they consider layoffs. Management provides, to operating-level workers, a great volume of information on production, product quality, and financial conditions of both the firm and the industry. Employee selection is much more careful and thorough than that of indigenous American firms. High educational levels and positive attitude are valued employee attributes. Applicants may be required to attend classes or appear before a panel of employees before they are accepted. Both promotion and decision-making processes tend to be slow. Above all, harmonious and cooperative relations among individuals and work units are emphasized by management.[7]

The above-listed characteristics of Japanese-managed plants in the United States as reported by Hain strongly remind us of management practices employed in Japan. None of them separately, however, are uniquely Japanese. In fact, many of these characteristics are found in the management practices of the best-managed companies in the United States.[8] Here we find no lifetime employment, seniority-based wages and promotion, or enterprise union—the so-called three pillars of the Japanese employment system. Instead, we find long time horizons, efforts to give workers a sense of belonging, lean and flexible organization, and emphasis on product quality and manufacturing excellence. All of these are the basic ingredients of America's best-run companies.

In applying the Japanese-style management philosophy and meth-

[6]Ibid.

[7]Ibid.

[8]See, for example, Gene Bylinsky, "America's Best-Managed Factories," *Fortune,* May 28, 1984, pp. 16–24; and Thomas J. Peters and Robert H. Waterman, Jr., *In Search of Excellence: Lessons from America's Best-Run Companies* (New York: Harper & Row, Publishers, Inc., 1982), pp. 13–16.

ods to an American environment, the most crucial factor appears to be the relationship with the union. It is not always possible, or even desirable, to keep unions out of the plant. Trying to create a Japanese-style enterprise union, of course, is out of the question. The most sensible strategy is to accept the union as a fact of industrial life, and try to work out a relationship with the union that is consonant with the Japanese management philosophy. If management first succeeds in creating an atmosphere of cooperation and in reducing the functional differences and status distinction between management and labor, it may very well be possible to negotiate with the union a contract that includes few of the traditional features that are damaging to group harmony and worker productivity. We shall return to this question at the end of the chapter.

BRITISH WORKERS UNDER JAPANESE MANAGEMENT

Industrial relations in the United Kingdom are generally believed to be even more stressful and strained than in the United States. All the elements of adversarial relations found in the United States are also found in the United Kingdom, particularly the strong trade union traditions and their insistence on "restrictive working practices." Additionally, management-labor relations in Britain have an overtone of a class conflict. The status distinction between the manager and technician, on the one hand, and the worker, on the other, is much more than a mere manifestation of functional specialization of labor. In Britain, as in some other parts of Europe, the two groups differ in life-styles, language, demeanor, and educational backgrounds. At work, they wear different uniforms; use segregated eating places, parking lots, and rest rooms; and in general have little personal or social contact with each other. In short, the two groups of people belong to two different worlds. Naturally there exists a strong sense of resentment among workers toward managers and engineers. This sense of apartness and alienation between the two groups contributes to the deeply entrenched antagonism between the manager and the worker.

In recent years many Japanese firms began manufacturing operations in Britain. Questions have been naturally raised concerning the compatibility of Japanese management practices with individualistic, working-class conscious, and alienated British workers whose traditional work ethic is presumably on the wane. Would British workers who resent the authority of their own managers accept the authority of Japanese managers? How would they react to demands by Japanese managers for discipline and hard work? The answers to these questions have immense implications for the universality of the perceived advantages of Japanese management methods. For if it can be demonstrated that the methods can work in such an alien environment as blue-collar Britain, it becomes difficult to support the argument that the Japanese management system works only with group-oriented and submissive Japanese workers.

In a pioneering book entitled *Under Japanese Management,* two British researchers, Michael White and Malcolm Trevor, reported the result of their 1980 case studies involving six Japanese subsidiaries in Britain, three in manufacturing and three in financial services. Their findings are significant in that they largely confirm what we observed in the United States, with one notable exception. British blue-collar workers seem more impressed than their American counterparts by the egalitarian, "classless" outlook and behavior of Japanese managers (e.g., wearing the same uniform, using the same canteen, and getting their hands dirty on the shop floor). This difference is probably attributable to the greater class consciousness of British blue-collar workers. In what follows we report the salient points of White and Trevor's observations about management-labor relations in the three manufacturing subsidiaries.[9]

As in the cases of Japanese firms operating in the United States, the Japanese-managed firms in Britain do not use the traditional Japanese employment practices. There is no explicit system of lifetime employment, no seniority-based promotion and rewards, no enterprise unions, no elaborate programs of welfare or fringe benefits, and no participatory decision-making processes involving local employees. As far as the employment practices go, the only unusual feature is the extremely careful and systematic methods of selecting and training workers.[10]

The major differences from the traditional British practices are found in working practices and operational methods on the shop floor. What distinguishes the Japanese production methods used in Britain is the extraordinary degree to which management emphasizes detail, quality, and discipline. As is the case with Japanese manufacturing plants everywhere, quality is built into the production process with production workers serving as quality-control engineers. Quality consciousness is instilled into workers by the managers' emphasis on "checking and double checking" and allowing no defective products to leave the plant. Managers themselves frequently get involved in production processes, showing interest in details and quickly picking up and investigating any quality problems the workers may experience on the production

[9]Michael White and Malcolm Trevor, *Under Japanese Management: The Experience of British Workers* (London: Heinemann Educational Books, 1983).

[10]Ibid., p. 124.

line. In brief daily meetings between shifts, the supervisor discusses production problems with workers and even criticizes the deficiencies of some workers. In this way, each worker becomes personally responsible for the quality of his or her products.[11]

White and Trevor report that the satisfaction and contentment of workers in these firms is at a "good average" level; workers are not particularly happier or more satisfied than those in good British firms.[12] The workers' response to the working practices that stress discipline and responsibility, on the other hand, is predominantly positive, although there are inevitably some who complain about the fast and disciplined pace of work. There seems to be a widespread recognition among workers that work is a serious business, that everyone must work and help each other, that goofing off or carrying on is not tolerated, but that good work is appreciated and rewarded. There is also an appreciation that management cares for employees as individual human beings, and that managers work just as hard as (and Japanese managers much harder than) workers.[13] The authors of the study report that there is among the workers "often some pride at being part of such an exceptional effort."[14] On the basis of these findings, White and Trevor suggest that the long-assumed demise of the work ethic in Britain perhaps has little substance, and that the latent work ethic can easily be rekindled by proper management methods.[15]

White and Trevor also find that British workers, contrary to the popular belief, readily accept managerial authority when such authority is based not on a mere status distinction but on technical competence and dedication to high-quality work.[16] The managers' caring and respectful attitude toward workers, their personal touch like giving birthday presents, and their willingness to share a great deal of information with workers on the company's operations—all these factors, though subsidiary, do contribute to the esprit de corps of the employees. It is interesting to note that British workers in these Japanese subsidiaries are often more critical of their British managers than of Japanese managers. Reaction to the company's mixed managerial group are "more favorable the greater the Japanese influence and presence."[17]

What can we conclude from these findings? Again, as in the cases

[11]Ibid., p. 128.
[12]Ibid., pp. 126–27.
[13]Ibid., pp. 44–45.
[14]Ibid., p. 130.
[15]Ibid., p. 132.
[16]Ibid., p. 131.
[17]Ibid.

of Japanese-managed firms in the United States as well as America's best-run companies, the secret of good management seems to lie in the basic philosophy and attitude of managers. It seems to have little to do with the traditional Japanese employment practices; rather, it seems to be a function of management's commitment to hard work and high-quality products, and its respectful attitude toward workers. We shall return to this question at the end of the chapter.

MANAGEMENT-LABOR CODETERMINATION IN WEST GERMANY

One way to enhance workers' sense of belonging to the corporate community is to invite them to participate in managerial decision making. Management-labor *codetermination* has had a long history in Western Europe, and is now written into the laws of many Western European countries. The best known form of codetermination is that of the Federal Republic of Germany, the main features of which are discussed below.

The Works Constitution Act of 1952 introduced the *works council* (*Betriebsrat*) into firms and plants. Members of the works council of an enterprise are elected from among *all* of its employees—managerial, clerical, and blue-collar. Whereas the labor union exists *outside* the corporate organization, the works council is legally an integral part of the corporate structure. It is required by law to cooperate with the management in *codetermining* the firm's policies relating to working conditions, work rules, hiring and firing, job assignments, and overtime. It also negotiates with the management over *local* formulas for wage-rate determination, bonuses, and fringe benefits. The works council, however, cannot negotiate or call strikes; it is prohibited by law to take a position on political or union matters.

In order to understand the relationship between the works council and the labor union, it is necessary for us to briefly survey the characteristics of labor organization in West Germany. West German unions are traditionally more active at the national level than at the plant level. Unions bargain collectively with associations of employers on an industrywide basis. Basic wage scales and fringe benefits are determined in these negotiations, and the union's major weapon in collective bargaining is the threat of a strike. At the firm and plant levels, the works council, rather than the union, is the forum for joint management-labor consultation and collaboration. Although the union has the right to nominate candidates to positions on the works council, and many of works council members are thus union members, the union's role on the works council is minimal.

The works council system has worked well in West Germany. It has enabled German workers to have a meaningful participation in plant management in areas that directly pertain to their welfare. Management has also benefited from the security and certainty that the council has provided in dealing with workers. Peter Lawrence reports that there exists a near total and matter-of-fact acceptance of the works council by top German managers, and concludes that it is "the central institution of the co-determination system."[18]

The other aspect of West German codetermination has been less productive and more controversial. Under the Codetermination Law of 1976, West Germany's largest corporations employing more than 2,000 persons (about 500 companies in all) must have employee representatives on their *supervisory board* (*Aufsichtsrat*). Unlike the American or Japanese board of directors, the West German supervisory board has no representation by top corporate managers. The board's main function is to hire the top managers who comprise the *management executive committee* (*Vorstand*), and supervise its performance. The supervisory board meets infrequently, and does not get involved in day-to-day operations of the corporation. Members of the management executive committee are appointed by a two-thirds majority vote of the supervisory board. The 1976 law requires that 50 percent of the board members must be elected representatives of the employees and unions, and the remaining 50 percent are elected from among the company's shareholders. One of the employee board members must be elected from among the managers who are not on the management executive committee. The chairperson of the board must be a shareholders' representative. In case of a tie vote at a board meeting, the chairperson has an additional vote to break the tie. Thus, in spite of the numerical parity between the shareholders and the employee and union representatives, the shareholders enjoy a superiority in voting power.

The worker representation on corporate boards has been unpopular with both management and labor. Management dislikes it because it makes running the corporation more complicated than otherwise. Labor is frustrated, on the other hand, because it does not have a decisive voting power. Labor representatives naturally favor giving higher wages and larger bonuses to workers, but because of their lack of the majority vote, their proposals are voted down in board meetings. Labor complains that management uses devious tactics to lessen labor's influence on corporate policies, while management complains that labor representatives leak company secrets to outsiders.[19]

---

[18]Peter Lawrence, *Managers and Management in West Germany* (New York: St. Martin's Press, 1980), p. 49.

[19]"Germany's Requiring of Workers on Boards Causes Many Problems," *Wall Street Journal*, December 10, 1979, p. 1.

The basic lesson that can be learned from the West German experience with labor representation on the corporate board is that having
workers on the board in and of itself does not help to create a sense of
common purpose if such a sense does not exist in the first place. Allowing a numerical shareholder-labor parity while giving a de facto veto
power to the shareholder-management coalition can only help to increase the tension between management and labor. The relative success
of the works council and the relative failure of board representation can
be explained in the following way. In the works council arrangement,
both management and labor stand to gain by cooperating with the other.
It is not a zero-sum game; cooperation is likely to increase the size of
the pie. Moreover, the potential conflict over the distributional issue is
deliberately minimized by making the works council politically and
ideologically neutral and also by keeping negotiations over the important part of wage-rate determination out of the council's business. At
the board level, by contrast, the distributional issue looms large. Union
representatives on the board are likely to assume an ideological posture,
demanding that a large portion of the company's earnings be given to
workers rather than paid to shareholders or spent for debt services and
capital investment. They are also likely to object to any proposals that
are necessary for the long-run health and prosperity of the company
but are harmful to the short-run benefits of workers. In other words,
union representatives on the board constitute a special interest group
whose main objective is to obtain a larger share of the company's earnings in what it perceives as a zero-sum game. This is definitely not the
case with the workings of the works council.

What are the implications of West Germany's experience with codetermination to the task of improving management-labor relations in
the United States? Would having labor representatives on a corporate
board improve workers' morale and efficiency? A *Business Week* article
entitled "Labor's Voice on Corporate Boards: Good or Bad?" concluded
that worker involvement in the corporate board's decision making, when
combined with partial or total ownership of the firm by the workers,
can improve worker efficiency and product quality.[20] It must be stressed,
however, that this conclusion applies to U.S. firms that are *worker-owned*
(most of them partially), in which worker representation on the board
is a consequence of the ownership. The conclusion, therefore, does not
necessarily apply to the (very few) U.S. firms having labor directors but
no workers' ownership in the company. The *Business Week* article points

[20]"Labor's Voice on Corporate Boards: Good or Bad?" *Business Week*, May 7, 1984,
pp. 151–53.

out that there remain several problems with labor representation on the board, including the following:

> *Ideological opposition to the concept.* While many executives and directors of large U.S. corporations would feel uncomfortable or even hostile to the idea of surrendering their monopoly of decision-making power, unions may fear that their representatives on the board may be co-opted by management.
>
> *Conflict of interest.* If union officers sit on the board, they experience a conflict of interest. As union officers, their loyalty is to the union. As board members, however, their responsibility under U.S. laws lies in promoting shareholders' interests. (By contrast, worker representatives on a German supervisory board are responsible to their fellow workers.)
>
> *Clashes of constituent interests.* Union representatives on the board naturally tend to favor larger distributions of corporate earnings in the forms of higher wages, bonuses, and benefits to workers, whereas considerations of the firm's long-term viability may dictate the use of earnings for other purposes. Unreasonably large wages and benefits would damage the company's credit rating and competitiveness.[21]

The idea of worker representation on the U.S. corporate board, however, is not totally without merit. A small minority representation by labor may have a positive effect of facilitating exchanges of information between management and labor; at least it would keep the board open and "honest." Of course the whole exercise would be fruitless unless there exists, in the first place, a sense of shared *interest* (not necessarily a sense of trust or goodwill) in the long-term prosperity of the company. If such a relationship does not exist, labor representation could make a bad situation worse.

WORKERS' SELF-MANAGEMENT IN YUGOSLAVIA

For over a third of a century, the economy of the Socialist Federal Republic of Yugoslavia has been operating under a unique brand of socialism that is more radical a departure from the Soviet model than the reformed Hungarian or Chinese varieties. Whereas in Hungary and China the market mechanism is merely to supplement, but not to replace, the centralized direction of the economy by the government, in Yugoslavia the government plays the role of a partner in the process of making economic decisions jointly with socialized enterprises. Workers

[21]Ibid.

are collectively responsible for the internal management of an enterprise.

The Background

Following the end of World War II and until 1949, the Yugoslav economy had been managed under a Soviet-type system of centralized administrative planning and control. After the country broke away from the Soviet bloc in 1948, it began to develop its own brand of decentralized socialism, which combined the elements of both central planning and market solution. The centerpiece of Yugoslav market socialism was to be the rejection of centralized administrative management of the economy in favor of self-management of economic activities by workers. Under the law of June 1949, the management (but not the ownership) of state enterprises—in industry, agriculture, mining, trading, transport, and communication—was formally handed over to the collectivity of workers. The enterprises were to be managed by workers' councils that were elected by workers.

During the next two and a half decades, the Yugoslav system underwent slow but continuous evolutionary changes. Numerous changes were made in the legal and administrative structures of government as well as in rules pertaining to workers' self-management. The basic thrust of these changes was to generate greater independence and increased autonomy of workers' collectives, progressive lessening of governmental tutelege over enterprises and their workers' councils, and increased reliance on the market mechanism in economic decision making. The present system of workers' self-management in the Yugoslav economy is based on the new Constitution of 1974 and the Associated Labor Law of 1976.[22]

Administratively, Yugoslavia is a federal republic comprising six socialist republics. The largest of the six republics, Serbia, contains two autonomous provinces of Kosovo and Vojvodina. The organizational structure of the state of Yugoslavia has three layers of governmental units, called *sociopolitical communities,* which are the federation, the republics and autonomous provinces, and the communes. The basic sociopolitical community—the communes—of which there are 510, range in population from fewer than 10,000 to more than 100,000 persons.[23]

---

[22]For a detailed account of the evolutionary changes of Yugoslavia's system of workers' self-management between 1949 and 1974, see Najdan Pasic, Stanislav Grozdanic, and Milorad Radevic, eds., *Workers' Management in Yugoslavia: Recent Developments and Trends* (Geneva: International Labour Office, 1982), pp. 1–14.

[23]Martin Schrenk, Cyrus Ardalan, and Nawal A. El Tatawy, *Yugoslavia: Self-Management Socialism and the Challenge of Development* (Baltimore, Md.: Johns Hopkins University Press, 1979), p. 45.

Each level of the state organ has its own assembly in which resides both legislative and executive power. The executive council of each assembly exercises the executive power. For an authoritarian state, there exists a considerable degree of downward delegation of authority, with the communes playing important roles in social and public services.

The Communist party of Yugoslavia, now called the League of Communists of Yugoslavia (LCY), has a membership of about 1 million persons, or about 15 percent of the country's adult population. Although the Yugoslav Communists play a rather low-keyed role in the country's political system, they are nevertheless the guiding intelligence and prime movers of the Yugoslav society. The LCY members are well represented in the key sociopolitical and economic organizations at all levels, and influence their decisions along the party lines.

The Basic Principles

According to the official Yugoslav position, workers' self-management is more than workers' participation in management. It is a revolutionary principle governing the new status of individual citizens as they relate to each other in their places of work and in the community at large. The principle is articulated as follows: "The essence of the idea of workers' management in Yugoslavia is the creation of a system of relations in which individual workers, in association with their fellows, directly manage the means, conditions and results of their labour and thus achieve control over the totality of social relations in the community."[24]

What the Yugoslavs have been trying to do away with are (1) the subordination of workers to their employers under the system of wage labor (i.e., labor being bought and sold as a commodity), and (2) the monopolization of managerial functions by the bureaucratic and technocratic elite. Both of these "evils" of production relations are found equally in the capitalist economies in the West and in the Soviet-bloc economies, and presumably have contributed to the dehumanization of working conditions and the alienation of the working people. The Yugoslav leaders propose to eliminate these evils of subordinated labor by moving workers directly to the center of the process of enterprise management, and by integrating productive enterprises with local sociopolitical communities. Workers in every Yugoslav productive enterprise are said to have rights and responsibilities to "use, manage and dispose of the social resources entrusted to them and the product of their labour" for themselves and for other workers "on the basis of equality."[25] Spe-

[24]Pasic, et al., *Workers' Management,* p. 15.

[25]Ibid., p. 19.

cifically this means that workers, through the mechanism of workers' councils, have the power to determine what and how to produce, in what to invest, whom to hire, what prices to charge, what wages to pay, and how to distribute the enterprise's profits between various uses including their shares of earnings.

It is assumed, perhaps naively, that giving the workers' collective a nominal power to make strategic decisions on production, investment, and income distribution results in (1) workers in fact exercising the power, and (2) harmony of workers' self-interests and the collective interests of both the enterprise and society as a whole. Hence a pronouncement:

> Since decisions on the distribution of income between personal earnings, joint consumption and investment are taken by the workers themselves, and not by some higher authority or outside centre of economic power, they are motivated to strike a balance between their immediate interests and the long-term interests of organisation. The principle that workers' earnings depend on their own good judgement in managing the affairs of the organisation is one of the basic driving forces behind the whole system of workers' management.[26]

The Basic Institutions

The workers' collective (i.e., all workers in an enterprise including managers) not only in productive enterprises but also in public and social service institutions is organized into a Basic Organization of Associated Labor (BOAL). One BOAL is formed for each group of workers jointly producing a marketable good or service. Most enterprises have at least several BOALs. BOAL members participate in managerial decisions both directly, by expressing their views at meetings, and indirectly, through their representatives on workers' councils. Each BOAL has a workers' council, and a larger enterprise with more than one BOAL also has a central workers' council separate from the BOAL councils. Members of workers' councils are elected by secret ballot from among the members of the BOALs and the enterprise for a term of two years, with a maximum of two consecutive terms. Persons who hold managerial positions in the enterprise are not eligible to be elected to the workers' council.

The authority of the workers' council includes establishing bylaws and other rules of self-management for the organization, drafting the organization's plan, deciding on the organization's policy and its day-to-day implementations proposed by the management, deciding on credit

[26]Ibid., p. 21.

transactions, appointing the organization's managing board or director, hiring and firing of other personnel, and—most importantly—determining the division of the organization's net income into investment, collective consumption, and personal income for the organization's members. (Here, the term *organization* refers to either a work organization—i.e., an enterprise—or a BOAL within the organization.)

Each organization, whether an enterprise or a BOAL, is headed by either an individual director or a management board. Notices of openings for managerial positions must be published nationally. Final selection of candidates is made by the workers' council. Managerial officers are appointed for a four-year renewable term. Managers (director or members of the managing board) are responsible for carrying out the day-to-day operations of the organization and making proposals to the workers' council concerning the organization's business policy and its implementation. Managers, however, do not have authority to decide matters concerning hiring or firing of personnel, or determining the disposition of the organization's net earnings.

The major constraints on managers' discharging of their duties include the following:

> First, they must succeed in generating income over and above production costs, for if they do not, the workers will not be entitled to any personal income above the guaranteed minimum and the managers will be completely discredited. Secondly, they have to gain the confidence of the workers' council, to which they are always accountable and which may recall them at any time during their term of office. Thirdly, they have to carry out the decisions and conclusions adopted by workers in meetings and by referendums, as well as the decisions of the workers' council, which may occasionally run counter to a manager's own policies and views on the subjects in question. Fourthly, they are subject to close scrutiny by the socio-political organisations, which, while pursuing the same objectives of efficiency and development, may see them from a different point of view.[27]

The socially owned resources of the enterprise generate revenues. Total revenues from all sources *less* production costs (exclusive of wages and salaries) and taxes yield net income of the organization. Net income is divided into three main categories at the discretion of the organization "taking into account the social character of income and planned development goals."[28] The three categories of income disposition are (1) reserves for investment and working capital, (2) collective consumption by the organization (e.g., housing, welfare, and cultural and recreational

[27]Ibid., p. 54.
[28]Ibid., p. 110.

activities), and (3) personal income. Workers' individual incomes are determined by subtracting contributions to social insurance, bonus funds, and other purposes from the organization's personal income. Workers are paid wages and bonuses according to the amount and quality of their work, except that a statutory minimum income is guaranteed for all workers. Distribution of net income of an enterprise to its component BOALs and individual workers is the responsibility of the workers' councils at different levels of the organization.

The Problems In Workers' Self-Management

The realities of power relations within Yugoslav enterprises are substantially different from what the various laws and rules governing workers' self-management suggest. There are two broad areas of difficulty with the concept and practice of workers' self-management. First, the effective power of managerial decision making does not, and cannot, belong to rank-and-file workers. Second, to the extent that workers' councils participate in the enterprise's decision making, they are likely to be more interested in seeking immediate material gains for their members than promoting the long-term interests of the enterprise or of society at large.

The problem of organizational power. As Galbraith pointed out in *The New Industrial State,* the effective decision-making power in any large organization utilizing modern, complex technology belongs to the technostructure, or the group of professionals having monopoly on specialized knowledge. The real power of making managerial decisions in a Yugoslav enterprise, regardless of ideological imageries or statutory provisions, resides with the cadre of professional managers. This decision-making power based on information may be reinforced by political power if the managers enjoy a backing of the local political elite. (The LCY and its members play a decisive role in selection, retention, and dismissal of enterprise managers, both directly through the local party organs and indirectly as members of the workers' councils.)

Just as it is impossible or impractical for all the shareholders or all the workers of a Western capitalist corporation to participate in the enterprise's management, so it is not feasible for all the rank-and-file workers of a Yugoslav enterprise to actively participate in its management in any meaningful way. Even if such participation were technically feasible, most workers would probably choose not to participate. Sociological studies done in Yugoslavia tend to show that average workers have little interest in self-management. Workers rank their interests, in the order of preference, as follows: (1) high earnings, (2) nice co-workers, (3) capable supervisors, (4) possibility of advancement, and (5) self-management. Moreover, workers' interest in participation is limited primarily to those decisions concerning their shop floor and their incomes; specifically, few rank-and-file workers show interest in such technical questions as investment decisions.[29]

The problem of workers' self-interests. If Yugoslav workers truly identified themselves with their enterprises, and were convinced that what is good for their firm is good for them, then they would insist that their enterprise organization adopt measures that would benefit it in the long run even at the expense of their own short-run rewards. Since this is not the case, the Yugoslav workers' behavior is like the behavior of hired wage earners elsewhere: they tend to demand maximum short-term incomes for themselves, even if that means smaller investments in the enterprise's productive facilities. This conflict between the goals of the workers and of the collective is inherent in any economic system. It is unavoidable as long as the system operates as a zero-sum game. The contradiction is reduced in proportion to the extent to which the organization succeeds in harmonizing the collective and individual interests.

Workers' self-interests conflict with the goal of self-management in yet another way. As we saw in our discussion of the theory of collective action and interest-group behavior (Chapter 7), individuals have little incentive to participate in collective action unless their immediate private gains exceed their immediate private costs. Individual workers in Yugoslavia have no motivation to expend time and effort in self-management activities when they know that they can enjoy the fruits of these activities as long as others participate in them. Activist workers in workers' councils are likely to be those who are trying to use the opportunity to their personal advantage—for example, advancing their personal careers. The activists and others who happen to be drawn into involvement with managerial decision making are most probably inclined to expend only enough time and effort to protect and promote their immediate interests in money incomes and working conditions on the shop floor. It is naive to believe that merely enacting laws to give workers self-management rights will automatically induce all workers to actively participate in enterprise management in the best interest of the enterprise and society at large.

[29]Ljubo Sirc, *The Yugoslav Economy under Self-Management* (New York: St. Martin's Press, 1979), pp. 174–76.

PROSPECTS FOR IMPROVED INDUSTRIAL RELATIONS IN THE UNITED STATES

Thus far in this chapter we have observed that the basic flaws of industrial relations in the United States are the adversarial relations between management and labor in which management treats labor mechanistically as an expendable cost item and labor tries to defend workers' rights by insisting on rigid job classifications and inflexible work rules. There is a widespread consensus of opinion among both business and labor leaders that greater worker participation in corporate decision-making process, particularly at the shop floor level, is indispensable if product quality and labor productivity in U.S. industries are to be raised to a more acceptable level. We have also noted that Japanese-style management cannot be transplanted directly to American soil because of its incompatibility with the American environment. Neither is legislation of large-scale worker participation in management, whether in the form of West German codetermination or a capitalist variety of Yugoslav self-management, likely to produce a marked improvement in the quality of industrial relations in the United States. The fundamental flaw of these approaches is that we cannot legislate spontaneous behavior and organizational unity when none exists in the first place.

The most promising direction in which U.S. industries can move toward improving their management-labor relations seems to be indicated by the experience of American firms under Japanese management. The performance in terms of product quality and worker productivity in these firms appears to be much better than the U.S. average, if not better than that of some of the best-run plants of domestic U.S. corporations. The question of whether or not the Japanese-style management philosophy and practices will have a moderating effect on the traditional adversarial relationships has not been fully answered, but the available evidence thus far appears quite promising. In what follows we shall briefly examine the experience of the new GM-Toyota joint venture in Fremont, California, and the highly successful Employee Involvement (EI) program at Ford Motor Company's Edison, New Jersey, plant.

The New GM-Toyota Venture

The New United Motor Manufacturing, Inc. (NUMMI) is jointly owned by Toyota and General Motors, and produces Toyota-designed subcompact cars in its former GM assembly plant at Fremont, California, under Toyota management. Toyota at first balked at the idea of having to rehire the laid-off Fremont workers and to deal with the United Auto Workers (UAW), but later changed its mind. The interim agreement reached in 1983, according to a *Fortune* article, was "one of the most innovative labor agreements in U.S. industry."[30] Toyota agreed to recognize the UAW as the bargaining agent, and to pay wages and benefits that are "generally prevailing" in the U.S. automobile industry. The UAW, in return, agreed to do away with the traditional work rules and rigid job classifications. There is only one job classification for assembly-line workers and three job classifications for skilled-trades workers. Workers are trained to do a variety of jobs in the same general work area, and are reassigned to different jobs as needs change. This flexible use of labor—a standard Japanese practice—is expected to enhance productivity and lead to cost savings.[31]

Other aspects of the GM-Toyota venture are also suggestive of the changing character of management-labor relations in U.S. industries. The traditional distinction between management and labor is becoming blurred at Fremont. Union leaders interview and test job applicants. The UAW representative and the plant's labor relations manager cooperate in developing mutually beneficial contract provisions and finding ways of reducing the costs of fringe benefits such as pension plans and health insurance programs.[32] It appears that a new type of hybrid Japanese-American industrial relations based on cooperation rather than confrontation is beginning to take shape.

Ford's Employee Involvement Program

A *Business Week* article entitled "What's Creating an 'Industrial Miracle' at Ford" is reproduced as an appendix following this section. What the article calls an "industrial miracle" is the success of the employee participation program called Employee Involvement (EI) at the Edison, New Jersey, plant of Ford Motor Company. The centerpiece of this program is the "stop button" system, in which workers can stop the assembly line whenever they spot a defective product. This "radical step" has been in use in major Japanese manufacturing plants for years. It is surprising that such a simple change in production methods can result in such a big drop in the rate of defective products; the article reports that within four months after the stop-button system was introduced, defects dropped from 17 per car to 1 per car. More importantly, the change seems to have been received enthusiastically by the workers. Rank-and-file workers appear to be thrilled by their newly

---

[30]Michael Brody, "Toyota Meets U.S. Auto Workers," *Fortune*, July 9, 1984, pp. 54–64.

[31]Ibid.

[32]Ibid.

given roles as front-line quality controllers. It is even more surprising, however, that these relatively minor changes are producing such a marked improvement in product quality and worker morale. The statement that workers had been "walking around like zombies" before the EI program was started reveals the extent and depth of America's industrial malady.

Although the article makes no mention of Japanese management, most of the reported changes in people's attitudes and production methods seem to have been decisively influenced by the discussions of the last decade over the deficiencies of the American industrial system and the relative merits of the Japanese ways of organizing and managing industrial production. Whatever their origins may be, the recent changes in the management-labor relations in the U.S. automobile industry will have very important implications for the future of industrial relations in the United States. If these experiments at GM-Toyota and Ford prove successful, they will inevitably produce profound changes in labor climate in the rest of the American economic system.

Appendix: WHAT'S CREATING AN "INDUSTRIAL MIRACLE" AT FORD[33]

At Ford Motor Co.'s Edison (N.J.) plant, the high-pitched whir of power tools rings out along the assembly line where workers install fenders and hoods. They have 55 seconds to fit, bolt, and drill as each car hull glides by, and they move with a rote-like rhythm. It is easy to let defects slip by when the job is so monotonous and the line keeps moving. U.S. auto makers have always emphasized uninterrupted production over quality, and only rarely would even a foreman dare shut down a line to catch a mistake. But the Edison plant has reversed those priorities. Each work station is equipped with a "stop button," and the workers themselves often halt the line 10 to 20 times a day when a problem prevents them from doing their jobs. A foreman hurries to the trouble area, helps the worker correct a malfunctioning machine or a defect in the car, and usually within 30 seconds the line is moving again.

The innovation at Edison—other Ford plants are now installing the stop concept—is only the most visible symbol of a near-revolution in labor-management relations that started five years ago and has since become entrenched. Ford and the United Auto Workers have established what may be the most extensive and successful worker participation

[33]*Business Week*, July 30, 1984, pp. 80–81. Reprinted from the July 30, 1984 issue of *Business Week* by special permission, © 1984 by McGraw-Hill, Inc.

process in a major, unionized company. Thousands of teams of workers and supervisors at 86 of Ford's 91 plants and depots meet weekly to deal with production, quality, and work-environment problems. Employee Involvement (EI), as the process is called, has reduced production costs and absenteeism and played a major role in what one outside expert calls "an industrial miracle" in improving product quality.

It was to improve quality that the Edison plant took the radical step of allowing hourly workers to stop the line. The idea would have shocked Henry Ford, who once remarked that "the assembly line is a haven for those who haven't got the brains to do anything else." But Edison management and UAW Local 980 decided that if assemblers were "treated like adults," as Foreman Frank Cunningham puts it, permitting them to stop the line to correct defects would pay off. "For the first time in their lives they had the authority to control quality at the source, and their response was fantastic," says Philip I. Staley, the plant manager. Within four months after the stop buttons were installed in 1982, defects had dropped to less than one per car, down from 17.

"Zombies before."   As many as 20,000 to 34,000 hourly employees—20% to 30% of Ford's work force—have some direct involvement in an EI project during the course of a year, Ford estimates. This is an extraordinary level of participation for a voluntary process. "It's been like a firestorm," says W. Patrick Dolan, a consultant who has helped set up EI at some 25 Ford plants. He adds: "We can see now that rank-and-file workers were walking around like zombies before we started EI."

Participation still has opponents, particularly among first-line supervisors and UAW committeemen, and EI efforts simply collapsed at a few plants. But at many other plants, union and management roles are being stretched far beyond the traditional "management decides, union reacts" relationship. Managers are consulting union officials and workers on a wide range of issues, such as work scheduling and technology changes, before making decisions. And while many UAW officials still worry that EI reduces members' dependence on the union, participating leaders contend otherwise. "It's democracy in the workplace," says David A. Curson, chairman of UAW Local 898 at Ford's Rawsonville (Mich.) plant. "It makes the people more aware of their own self-worth and intelligence, and it makes them better union members."

Neither Ford nor the UAW make any effort to measure the economic results of EI, believing that "playing the numbers game," says Peter J. Pestillo, Ford's vice-president for labor relations, would kill the process. Plant managers think that EI has had the most impact on quality and cite improvements in warranty repairs above 40% for many products. An independent research firm reported that a survey of 6,500 buyers of 1984 Ford cars showed that "things gone wrong" had declined 55%, compared with a 1980 survey.

EI's impact on productivity is less clear. Hours worked per vehicle at Ford declined 27% from 1980 to 1983, largely because of new technology. To prevent EI from undermining the union's role as the bargaining agent, the teams are prohibited from discussing collective bargaining issues, such as wages and work rules, that most affect productivity. The teams, however, often reduce production costs, by suggesting changes in equipment or production flow, which in turn increases efficiency.

Staying competitive. The more cooperative relationships fostered by EI have enabled local unions to negotiate work-rule changes with a direct impact on efficiency. At Edison, Local 980 in 1983 agreed to eliminate 220 jobs, saving $8 million, to keep the plant competitive. Says Local 980 Chairman Earl D. Nail: "We're learning to accept automation, and we're working toward a goal of no layoffs except by attrition."

Ford was a latecomer to worker participation compared with General Motors Corp., which started its quality-of-worklife (QWL) process with the UAW in 1973. Some GM plants today are just as innovative in labor relations as any Ford plant. But participation is not as pervasive in GM, knowledgeable observers say. The union charges that some GM managers have used QWL in manipulative ways. Last year, Ford changed practices at about 10 plants where abuses had been reported by the UAW.

Worker participation is only one of several mechanisms by which Ford and the UAW have changed their labor climate. EI was established in 1979 negotiations. Japanese competition and the 1980 and 1981–82 recessions then brought large job losses that forced both sides to reassess their relationship. In late 1981, Pestillo says, "we made the corporate policy decision that a trained work force is an asset to the company and that labor would no longer be treated as our most variable cost." This led to major job-security and training provisions in the 1982 contract. Also in that year, Ford and the UAW initiated Mutual Growth Forums, quarterly meetings at which managers brief UAW officials on business developments.

The combination of these elements makes a powerful lever for changes to increase Ford's competitiveness. In 1979, for example, the Rawsonville plant began losing products, such as brakes and fuel pumps, to companies that could supply them to Ford assembly plants at lower prices. Some 3,000 jobs disappeared. In 1980, Local 898 at Rawsonville and plant management began an EI process and now have 90 teams at work.

EI "opened up lines of communications," Curson says, enabling the two sides to collaborate on cutting costs and outbidding competitors. Last March the members of Local 898 ratified a precedent-setting agreement that calls for experimentation with new forms of work organization, such as production teams, and, in a major cost-cutting move, consolidates 24 skilled trades into 14. In return, all 2,582 full-time, hourly workers at Rawsonville are guaranteed 32 hours of work per week for three years—the most comprehensive job guarantee in the auto industry.

Minor maintenance. Plant management can no longer use temporary layoffs to balance production needs with employment. Instead, it will use part-time workers to fill in during production surges. But the 100% job-security protection gives management flexibility to make the plant competitive, says Dennis J. Cirbes, the plant's industrial-relations manager. "People had a strong reluctance to make changes that would allow us to be more efficient and competitive when they feared losing their jobs," he says.

Collaboration has also saved jobs at the Indianapolis steering gear plant, the site of Ford's first participation program. Productivity has increased by 8.5% annually since 1980, and a year ago the plant underbid its old competitor, TRW Inc., to supply the steering gear mechanism for the Taurus, a midsize car that Ford will introduce in 1985. Among other things, UAW Local 1111 agreed to let machine operators perform minor maintenance chores that had always been the job of skilled tradesmen. This and other changes in work practices, says Plant Manager Arland E. Phelps, reduce the labor cost of producing the Taurus gear by 15%, or $4 million.

Winning the Taurus bid will save roughly 300 jobs at the Indianapolis plant and add about 200 new ones, depending on production volumes. "We have a common objective of wanting to stay in business," Phelps says, "and so we've been making the union more a partner in what we're doing. We share data with them, instead of doing things [unilaterally] and making them react." He adds: "We're not to the point of jointly running the organization, but we're moving in that direction."

At Ford's Chesterfield trim plant in Mt. Clemens, Mich., 35% of the 1,500 hourly workers belong to EI "circles," as they are called—a particularly high level of involvement. Moreover, 70% to 75% of workers in a department typically turn out when Plant Manager William R. Brooks calls meetings for ideas about reorganizing the workplace to produce a new product. A visitor can sense participation in the plant's atmosphere. Not confined to team meetings, it is becoming a way of life. This is Pestillo's goal for the entire company.

Willed into being. UAW officials and managers at Chesterfield informally settle a wide range of issues that previously would wind up in the grievance system. This eliminates the legalistic climate that exists in plants where the union and management spend much time defending their "rights" under the contract. Brooks no longer insists on asserting management's right to make various decisions instead of consulting with the union. "That right doesn't mean anything if you've got a bunch of unhappy people who aren't going to give you 100% on the job," Brooks says. "We bend the rules all the time."

The future of EI, however, is not entirely settled. Negotiations for a new national contract, which begin on July 24, will create strong tensions that could hurt the process in some plants. Moreover, leadership changes in the union and the company could weaken the commitment to participation. EI started fast and matured quickly at Ford, largely because Pestillo and Donald F. Ephlin, a UAW vice-president and former director of its Ford Dept., personally promoted and willed it into being. Last year, Ephlin became the UAW's chief negotiator at GM and was replaced at Ford by Stephen P. Yokich, a more conventional unionist. Company and union sources say Yokich has come to accept EI because the members want it, but he is not a crusader as Ephlin was.

On the company side, Chairman Philip Caldwell and possibly other top managers who are partisans of EI may retire next year. Dolan, the management consultant, worries that their successors might be less committed. "There's a question whether some of Ford's financial management people have been involved in EI at all or even understand it," Dolan says.

"Some fear is always warranted when there is a change in leadership," Pestillo says. "But it would be hard for the new guys to go back to the old ways and give up everything we've gained." At the Indianapolis plant, UAW member Gilbert Lynch expresses what many rank and filers feel: "EI might be called something different in the future, but I can assure you it's here to stay."

QUESTIONS

1. What was the objective of Frederick W. Taylor's scientific management movement? How were Taylor's methods of scientific management to help reach the objective? How did scientific management lead to the rigid job classifications and work rules on the American shop floor?

2. Critically evaluate the scientific management approach in terms of our discussions of mechanistic and organic concepts of corporate organization (see Chapter 8).

3. What are the basic flaws of industrial unionism in the United States? What is the nature of the needed reform?

4. Discuss the similarities and differences in the management practices of Japanese-owned firms as they are found in Japan, the United States, and the United Kingdom. How do British blue-collar workers' reactions to Japanese management methods differ from those of their American counterparts?

5. What conclusions may be drawn regarding the applicability of Japanese-style management to a non-Japanese environment?

6. Describe the main features of West German management-labor codetermination. How does the works council differ from the labor union? Why is it that the works council aspect of codetermination has been more productive and popular than that of worker representation on the corporate supervisory board?

7. Do you believe that worker representation on the board of directors will help improve the quality of management-labor relations in the United States? Discuss the pros and cons of this proposal.

8. Explain the nature of the Yugoslav workers' council. How does it differ from the West German works council?

9. What are the basic principles of workers' self-management in Yugoslavia?

10. List and explain the problems that are encountered in the actual application of the principles of workers' self-management in Yugoslavia.

11. What is the significance of the GM-Toyota venture to the changing characteristics of industrial relations in the United States?

12. The Ford Motor Company's Employee Improvement program contains many changes or innovations that seem to have been inspired by Japanese labor management practices. List as many of these changes as you can find. (You should be able to find at least half a dozen.)

13. Speculate on the future prospects of the changing characteristics of management-labor relations in U.S. industries. Defend your optimistic or pessimistic conclusions, as the case may be.

SELECTED READING

DORE, RONALD. *British Factory, Japanese Factory: The Origins of National Diversity in Industrial Relations.* Berkeley, Calif.: University of California Press, 1973.

KÜHNE, ROBERT J. *Co-determination in Business: Workers' Representatives in the Boardroom.* New York: Praeger Publishers, 1980.

LEE, SANG M., and GARY SCHWENDIMAN, Eds. *Management by Japanese Systems.* New York: Praeger Publishers, 1982.

MARTIN, BENJAMIN, and EVERETT M. KASSALOW, Eds. *Labor Relations in Advanced Industrial Societies.* Washington, D. C.: Carnegie Endowment for International Peace, 1980.

PASIC, NAJDAN, STANISLAV GROZDANIC, and MILORAD RADEVIC, Eds. *Workers' Management in Yugoslavia: Recent Developments and Trends.* Geneva: International Labour Office, 1982.

SCHRENK, MARTIN, CYRUS ARDALAN, and NAWAL A. EL TATAWY. *Yugoslavia: Self-Management Socialism and the Challenge of Development.* Baltimore, Md.: Johns Hopkins University Press, 1979.

SHIRAI, TASHIRO, Ed. *Contemporary Industrial Relations in Japan.* Madison, Wisc.: University of Wisconsin Press, 1983.

WHITE, MICHAEL, and MALCOLM TREVOR. *Under Japanese Management: The Experience of British Workers.* London: Heinemann Educational Books, 1983.

CHAPTER 14

Concluding
Assessments

THE QUESTION OF THE PART
AND THE WHOLE

In the preceding chapters we analyzed in some depth the organization
and management of the three major economic systems and some selected aspects of a few other systems. Cutting across these apparently
diverse systems is the common thread of a philosophical and technical
issue, that of the relationship between the part and the whole. Specifically, the problem manifests itself as the question of the relationship
between the individual and the collective, or that of individual self-
interests and a group (collective or societal) interest. Paralleling this
question of holism is the question of the nature of social organization,
that is, the dichotomy of organic and mechanistic relationships among
constituent parts of a social organization.

   At a risk of oversimplification, we may characterize the three economic systems under study as follows. As for value and ideology orientation, both Japan and the Soviet Union are collectivist, whereas the
United States is individualist. There is, however, a decided difference
between the familistic collectivism of Japan and the autocratic collectivism of the Soviet Union. As for organizational unity (or harmony of

interests), Japan's familistic groupism is fairly successful in harmonizing the individual (or specific) interests and the collective (or general)
interests, whereas both the Soviet Union and the United States experience considerable difficulties in doing so. As for the quality of social
organization—that is, the relationships between the individuals and the
group—we find that it is essentially organic in familistic Japan and
mechanistic in the individualistic United States. The Soviet Union, and
perhaps most other societies in the industrialized world, fall somewhere
between the Japanese and American extremes.

The United States

Primarily money, and secondarily power, are the most important
motivational forces in the U.S. economic system. These egocentric motivators are rooted in the dominant individualistic value orientation of
American society. On the other hand, the Americans are less significantly
affected by considerations of social obligation, social recognition, and
group solidarity than many other peoples. The individualistic quest for
material privileges and political power, while it is the source of nearly
limitless energy of America's economic activities, nonetheless presents
a serious problem of organizational disunity. Specifically, the zero-sum-
game mentality of egocentric pursuits of self-interests creates such problems as the adversarial management-labor relations in productive enterprises and the "public-be-damned" demands for advantages by special interest groups. The inherent weakness of the American system,
thus, is the difficulty of inducing individuals and groups to work, under
normal circumstances, toward the common goal of a larger group. Individuals and groups tend to compete for larger shares of the economic
pie, often hindering in the process the growth of the pie itself.
    Given the individualistic value orientation of American society, an
attempt to create organizational unity will not succeed if it requires a
significant curtailment of individualism. Organizational unity among
individualistic members of a group is possible, however, if it can be
demonstrated that cooperation will yield benefits to the individual
members with a minimum of sacrifice of individual freedoms and rights.
As the discussions of the theory of collective action of Chapter 7 showed,
such harmonizing of interests is easier the smaller the group is. It is for
this reason that we are beginning to see the signs of the development
of the cooperative and integrative American corporation, whereas no
such sign is visible in the larger societal scene. The problem of harmonizing the interests of various special interest groups with those of
the country as a whole, therefore, remains as the most serious systemic
problem of the American economic system.

The Soviet Union

The Soviet Union also suffers from a serious problem of organizational disunity, but its cause is diametrically opposed to that in the United States. In the United States, conflicts arise between private interests and the public interest because the former are allowed a free play while there is no ideologically acceptable mechanism for orchestrating the national consensus. In the Soviet Union, by contrast, the collective interest, as defined by the Communist party leadership, is imposed on the populace, while there exists no formal mechanism of channeling individual preferences to societal decision-making processes. Individual objectives and preferences work through the interstices of the central planning mechanism (e.g., in the second economy), but their overall impact on the patterns of resource allocation and economic development is minimal. The authoritarian imposition of collective preferences upon the population has its advantages, but it also contributes to the notorious inefficiency and rigidity of the Soviet economic system.

In order to coordinate decision-making activities at all levels of the administrative hierarchy of the national economy, the Soviet leadership must rely on a motivation system. It makes efforts to appeal to the people's patriotic sentiments or "socialist morality," but their effect is highly limited. In the main, the leadership tries to manipulate people's motivation by offering incentives involving coercion, access to political power, and material rewards. Their effectiveness, too, is very much limited. The problem of "success indicators" attests to the difficulty of achieving a minimum degree of organizational unity in the present Soviet system. The problem is so serious as to justify the use of the words *crisis* and *failure* in describing the present Soviet economic system.

Two alternative ways are open to Soviet leaders if they genuinely desire to achieve a measure of organizational unity in their economic system. First, group solidarity can be made to work as a major motivational force, particularly in the workplace. For this approach to be successful, however, the leadership will have to make serious efforts to reduce the degree of alienation of Soviet workers and consumers. Empty sloganeering of the past years will not do. Soviet leaders must begin to show a genuine respect for individual human rights, and take effective steps to tear down the wall separating the privileged *nomenklatura* class and the common people. Second, the present half-hearted and irrational system of material incentives can be restructured into a comprehensive and truly effective system of financial leverages with a heavy emphasis on bonuses and incentive wages that accurately reflect the recipients' contributions to production. Such a restructuring of the motivation system naturally requires a fundamental reform of the Soviet price system, as well as substantial increases in the quantity, quality, and variety of consumer goods.

Both of the above-mentioned approaches for reducing organizational disunity in the Soviet system require a measure of liberalization—democratization in the political system and a wider use of the market mechanism in the economic system. It is highly unlikely, however, that either political or economic liberalization will be seriously contemplated by Soviet leaders since it is fundamentally at odds with the very essence of the Soviet system.

Japan

Social recognition, social obligation, and group solidarity are relatively more important as motivational forces in Japan than in the United States or the Soviet Union. Consequently, there is a greater degree of harmony between the interests of the parts and the whole in the Japanese economic system than in others. Organizationally, there is a fairly smooth and progressive integration of the parts into the whole. Not only are individuals related to groups in a vertical structure, but groups are also integrated into the larger social whole, forming a familylike hierarchy. Within the entire politico-economic system of the country there exists a considerable degree of integration of individual self-interests into larger interests of social organizations and ultimately of the national family. This integration is by no means perfect, but is significant enough to give the Japanese economic system an organic and holistic quality that is not found in either the individualistic United States or the centralist Soviet Union.

Organizational unity in Japanese society is by no means a happy congruence of individual preferences. It is often imposed on individuals and groups, particularly those at lower echelons of a hierarchical organization. If the Soviet state imposes collective preferences on the populace by means of political pressure, Japanese groups impose their preferences on their members by means of social pressure. If the underprivileged millions who are not allowed to swim in the mainstream of the Japanese industrial system do not cry out for better opportunities and greater equality, that is because they are conditioned by tradition and upbringing not to challenge the authority of a group, whether it is a work team, a corporation, or the state. If a young factory worker does not dare object to her supervisor's demand for overtime on a weekend, that is because she may be afraid of being ostracized by the supervisor and other workers. If a junior corporate manager takes only three or four paid holidays a year, that is perhaps because he believes that anyone who dares take two full weeks of legally allowed vacation is considered selfish and disloyal to the company, and therefore harms his chances for promotion and a good bonus. The legendary capacity of the Japanese people for harmony, consensus, and cooperation is thus built on a great deal of sacrifice by those persons and groups in subordinate positions. The price the Japanese pay for harmony is the loss of individual freedom, dignity, and creativity. It is for them to determine whether this loss is justified by the superior performance of their economy known as the Japanese miracle.

THE CONVERGENCE OF ECONOMIC SYSTEMS

As the Hungarian, Chinese, and other socialist economic systems make progressively greater uses of the self-regulating forces of the market, and as the management-labor relations in large U.S. corporations begin to acquire some of the integrative characteristics of Japanese-style management, the age-old question of the "convergence" of economic systems is raised again. Do diverse economic systems learn from each other, adopt each other's useful institutions and methods, and through this process of mutual adaptation eventually become similar to each other?

Economic systems may become *similar* in superficial characteristics and modes of behavior, but their essential characteristics—the very nature and character of the system—are not likely to change much over time. This conclusion is based on the premise that an economic system does not exist in a vacuum, and that it is so closely intertwined with the political and social aspects of a given society that it can be meaningfully studied and compared with others only if it is understood as a "socio-politico-economic complex." In other words, the question of the convergence of economic systems is tantamount to asking whether or not different societies—with their diverse values, ideologies, and institutions—are becoming alike. All human societies may well become very much like each other—in the same way as the societies of the 50 U.S. States are now—in, say, a few hundred years. Thus, all of us who are alive today can safely assume that societies will remain different from each other in the foreseeable future. Only the technical aspects of the purely economic dimensions of the social system (e.g., organization of production and consumption, industrial policy, and management-labor relations) may become very much alike from society to society; but such a tendency toward superficial resemblance can hardly be described as a "convergence."

What is not likely to change for a long time is the very essence of each social system. In the Soviet Union, it is the authoritarian, centralized direction of the economy by the political power elite. In the United States, it is the ideology of individual liberty and fragmented power. In Japan, it is familistic groupism. These characteristics *define* the three systems, and thus are not susceptible to radical transformation in the short run. Changes in these characteristics are slow to occur because they are closely and tightly intertwined with the historical, sociocultural, ideological, and political elements of each society. Because the economic institutions of a society must be compatible with other social institutions, they all must change simultaneously in the same direction if any significant changes are to occur at all. For example, the Soviet system of economic organization and management cannot be made freer without a simultaneous liberalization of the Soviet political institutions and practices. The Japanese style of enterprise management is not likely to undergo a metamorphosis unless there occur simultaneous changes in the Japanese people's need to belong to a group, and in their rank consciousness, acceptance of authority and aversion to individualized responsibilities and achievements. The idea of industrial policy will not be readily acceptable by the majority of Americans unless their ideology relating to the role of government in economic activities, and their aversion to concentrated power, go through a radical transformation and become compatible with the methods of industrial policy of the French or Japanese variety.

The fundamental point that is being made here is that no radical change in any aspect of a social system—be it economic, political, legal, educational, and so on—can take place unless there first occur accommodating changes in the society's values and ideologies. These values and ideologies are, however, the quintessential qualities of any society, and, as such, are the hardest and slowest to change.

That the fundamental nature and character of a given economic system are not likely to undergo radical changes in our lifetime—barring catastrophic or revolutionary events—does not mean that societies cannot correct the excesses of their ways by learning from others. Thus, the Americans can learn, and indeed are learning, from the Japanese that, in the era of complex technology and large organizations, an excess of adversarial relationships among socioeconomic groups is counterproductive, and that a little cooperation toward mutually shared objectives goes a long way toward benefiting everyone. The Chinese are learning, as the Hungarians have learned, that the market mechanism can be effectively utilized to improve the efficiency of socialist resource allocation. That these societies are able and willing to admit their shortcomings, adopt the strong points of other systems, and make necessary adjustments in their own systems is a tribute to their viability and flexibility. By contrast, other societies are less able or willing to make fundamental changes. For example, the collectivist Soviet Union is still unable to integrate the market mechanism into their economic system and harness the energies of individual citizens. Similarly, the group-oriented Japanese have yet to discover the ways to minimize the stifling effects of their groupism on the energy, initiative, and creativity of individual Japanese.

It is extremely difficult to predict the future patterns of adaptive modifications and responses of various socioeconomic systems. Will the United States be able to find ways to harmonize the conflicting interests of special interest groups toward a common good? Will the Soviet Union be able to implement a genuine economic reform without producing a social unrest and political instability? Will the Chinese be able to successfully integrate market and planning? Will the Japanese discover the individual? These are profoundly complex questions, and we dare not try to make attempts to provide even tentative answers in this book. It is hoped that the readers, aided by the descriptive information and the partial insights provided in this book, find it worth their while to pursue these questions for further contemplation and discussion.

QUESTIONS

1. Do you think it is possible to compare the *performance* of the three major economic systems we studied in this book? If so, which system do you think shows superior performance? If not, why not?
2. List and describe the *similarities* between each pair of the three economic systems we studied in this book. Then, identify the *commonality* that runs through the three systems.

Index

THE PERFECT
KITTEN

THE PERFECT

KITTEN

PETER NEVILLE &

CLAIRE BESSANT

SPECIAL PHOTOGRAPHY BY JANE BURTON

THE READER'S DIGEST ASSOCIATION, INC.
Pleasantville, New York/Montreal

A Reader's Digest Book
Edited and designed by
Hamlyn

Text copyright © Peter Neville 1997
Design copyright © Reed International Books 1997
Special photography © Reed International Books 1997
Illustrations © Reed International Books 1997

Executive Editor: Simon Tuite
Project Editor: Katie Cowan
Copy Editor: Jane Royston

Art Director: Keith Martin
Executive Art Editor: Mark Stevens
. Designer: Ginny Zeal
Photographer: Jane Burton
Picture Researcher: Wendy Gay

Production: Dawn Mitchell

First published in Great Britain in 1997

Library of Congress Cataloging in Publication Data

Neville, Peter (Peter M.)
     The perfect kitten/Peter Neville and Claire Bessant.
          p. cm.
     Includes bibliographical references (p.) and index.
     ISBN 0-7621-0038-9
     1. Kittens. 2. Cats. I. Bessant. Claire. II. Reader's Digest
Association. III. Title.
SF447.N48 1998
636.8'07–dc21   97-17994

Printed in China

CONTENTS

INTRODUCTION

Kittens are wonderful creatures. Tiny and vulnerable, yet already equipped with the innate skills and strength of design befitting a top-of-the-food-chain predator, a new kitten will occupy hours of your time but leave you all the richer for it. That beauty of feline athletic power and grace is legendary, but the cat's adaptability in so many varied environments and social circumstances has also made it arguably the most successful predatory mammal yet to evolve on earth. Make no mistake, as a species the cat moved in on us – not the other way around – over 4,000 years ago purely for its own advantage, and each and every pet cat still only remains with us for all those things that it enjoys – warmth, company, shelter, and food. Having said this, however, it is also true that if a cat expects a great deal it gives an enormous amount in return, as you will discover from the day your kitten first arrives in your home.

From that day onward, you will be a parent figure to your cat and, although it will grow up to be independent of mind and unique in personality, the first days and weeks are when it will need you most to help it to adapt to living in your human den. You will need to provide the best opportunity possible for your kitten to learn your ways and a few house rules, as well as how to enjoy your love, care, and protection. At the same time, you must also be willing to learn, as this is the time when your kitten will be teaching you how to respond to its every request – and most young kittens are remarkably successful at producing well-trained owners!

Vets and pet therapists agree that the vast majority of medical and behavioral problems arising in cats could be prevented by owners choosing cats that are suitable for them, by understanding them and looking after them properly, and by responding early to signs of distress. This book is intended to help you to see life from your kitten's point of view – how it perceives and relates to you, your other pets, and your home. By understanding these things more clearly you will be able to care for your kitten in the best way possible, and you will know what to do and whom to turn to for advice if you are concerned in any way about its welfare.

As well as giving detailed advice on the practical aspects of caring for your kitten, from feeding to basic training and health care, part of the aim of this book is to address a growing concern of feline behaviorists about the way cats are being kept more and more in urban environments. Behavioral problems are increasingly arising from the restricted lifestyle that many owners impose on their cats, and also from a lack of understanding of their needs. While there is no shortage of love, or of concern when things go wrong, many people fail to realize just how specialized their pet cats are as predators, and to appreciate that they need more than love to lead a happy life. Every cat requires mental stimulation and the opportunity at least to practice what it is, and what has shaped its every sense, bone, muscle, and whisker – and that is to be a hunter, even if only of moving toys.

Your pet kitten is not just an appealing bundle of fur but a highly sensitive and emotional creature that will all too easily be upset or even made ill, and certainly made dull, by a lonely, unstimulating lifestyle as a pet kept in a city apartment if you do not understand and fulfill its needs – social, environmental, and predatory. Subjugate its needs to yours and it will suffer; fulfill them and you will have the joy of sharing a friendship, and of appreciating to the full one of nature's finest products. From kitten to cat – the responsibility and the enjoyment are yours, and we hope that this book helps you take enormous pleasure in both.

Acknowledgments

We would like to thank Sarah Whitehead for her enormous help in the research and preparation of this book, and Jane Burton, both for her stunning photography and for raising and organizing her kitten models so beautifully.

Simon Tuite and Katie Cowan at Hamlyn deserve much more than the customary authors' thanks for their editorial skills and encouragement. Their consideration and understanding throughout this production have gone well beyond the call of duty, and we are extremely grateful.

Special thanks also go to Gwen Bailey for writing the sister volume to this book, *The Perfect Puppy*, so well and so successfully that *The Perfect Kitten* was called for. We would also like to acknowledge the remarkable insights into feline and canine behavior of Peter's colleagues at the Centre of Applied Pet Ethology (COAPE: PO Box 18, Tisbury, Wiltshire, SP3 6LZ, England), especially Robin Walker MRCVS, and the late and sadly missed John Fisher.

Finally, our thanks to all our cats past and present, especially to the calm, collected Bullet, a London feral kitten who turned into the world's best country cat – may your hunting grounds be forever full and your place by the hearth ever warm!

CHAPTER ONE

THE RAW MATERIAL

Some people have owned cats all their lives – childhood memories are punctuated by cats of character, and they feel that home is incomplete without a resident feline. To others, owning a cat is a pleasure discovered later in life, perhaps because they are unable to keep a dog or simply because they have become late converts to ailurophilia (the love of cats). Ironically, it is often those people who profess not to like cats who are "adopted" by a stray cat or kitten, and who subsequently become the most ardent of cat enthusiasts.

In most of the Western world, more cats than dogs are now kept as pets, taking over the latter's traditional role of man's best friend. All around the globe cats have adapted incredibly well to a variety of environments and lifestyles, surviving and even thriving in extremes of temperature and harsh conditions, while as domesticated animals they have managed to combine their independent nature with an ability to share affection and live happily within our homes.

The pleasure of getting to know a new kitten – playing with it, feeding and training it, and watching it grow and develop – can be shared by all members of the family.

Whenever you enter the world of cat companionship (most people feel that they are "owned" by their cats rather than the other way around, and would hesitate in labeling such free spirits as possessions), bear in mind that the kitten you choose is likely to spend at least 14 years living with you – possibly even more. This makes choosing the right type of kitten for you and your family a vital first step, which will need to be given careful thought. The following information should help you to make some key decisions.

PEDIGREE OR NOT?

Mention that you have a cat, and most people will envisage a non-pedigree individual – in fact, only about 10 percent of all cats kept as pets are pedigree (purebred) animals. In general, even though many people are easily able to name a wide variety of dog breeds, they remain unaware of the extensive range of cat breeds that is now available.

Cats are naturally independent creatures, and are a delight to watch – both indoors and out – as they explore and learn about their environment.

There are probably several reasons for this, the first being that cats are very personal pets – they are not taken out for walks or for trips in the car like dogs, so we may not even see very many breeds unless they belong to family or friends; indeed, some cat breeds have only recently been discovered or developed. Even when we come across new breeds, we may not notice the more subtle differences between them, as most are about the same size and have the same general shape. In this, cats are also unlike their canine cousins, which vary from being smaller than a cat to the size of some breeds of pony – a fact we cannot fail to notice!

Perhaps another reason for our lack of knowledge about cat breeds is the way we often acquire our kittens, many of which come via a friend whose queen has "accidentally" given birth to a litter, through advertisements in newspapers and magazines, or from animal welfare societies. This has been the traditional method of obtaining a kitten, and there is still some resistance to actually paying for a kitten when many are given free "to good homes."

Types of kitten

There are three basic types of kitten available, as follows:

• A pedigree – or purebred – kitten is the offspring of pedigree parents of the same breed. The advantage of choosing a purebred kitten is that you will have a good idea of how it will look as an adult, and of the typical temperament characteristics of the breed.

• A kitten is described as cross-bred if both its parents were pedigree cats, but of different breeds. In this case, the kitten could grow up to resemble either or both of its parents.

• A kitten is known as a non-pedigree if one or both of its parents were crossbreeds themselves. Indeed, different breeds may have been mixed over several generations, making the appearance of kittens in a litter difficult to predict before they are born.

Whichever type of kitten you choose, your main priorities should be that it is healthy and has been well cared for by its breeder. The bright eyes and glossy coat of this non-pedigree kitten are good indicators that it is fit and well.

The terminology used to describe these three categories may vary in different countries – for instance, a non-pedigree kitten is often called a "mixed breed" in the United States, but a "moggie" in the United Kingdom. However, for the purposes of this book, two basic terms are used: pedigree (purebred kittens) and non-pedigree (all other kittens).

Types of coat

Whether you choose a pedigree or non-pedigree kitten (and many people happily keep both together), the care you need to give it will be similar. One of the major decisions you must make is whether you would like a short- or a longer-haired cat. For instance, you may love the look of the Persian, but will you have the time for plenty of grooming, and would you be prepared for the amount of hair it may shed around your home?

Cats vary in their type and length of hair, and in their ability to look after their own coats. Breeds of cat are classified according to their coat type as follows:

• **Longhair:** These impressive-looking cats have long, very full coats that require a great deal of attention to keep them in good condition. Some individuals – such as Persians with very flattened faces – may find it difficult to groom themselves thoroughly, and, if they are not groomed every day, will end up with seriously matted coats.

• **Semi-longhair:** These cats have long but less full, or thick, coats. They will be able to tend to their fur very efficiently themselves, but they will appreciate a little extra help from their owners.

• **Shorthair:** These cats can of course look after their own coats perfectly well, and need very little in the way of grooming. However, regular brushing will help to keep both the skin and the coat in top condition, and many cats also enjoy the attention.

Owner involvement

Another decision that you should make at the start concerns how much interaction you wish to have with your future kitten. We all like to have a cuddle and a game, but this can become mandatory rather than a matter of choice if you choose one of the more attention-demanding breeds such as the Siamese. If your preference lies with a somewhat quieter cat and you are happy to carry out a thorough daily brushing routine, you may decide to opt for an elegant Persian. An American or British Shorthair is also likely to be the choice of many – these popular cats are independent and self-reliant, thereby combining ease of maintenance with companionship and feline friendship.

WHICH BREED?

Although the physical variations between cats are quite small when compared with the huge range of body size and shape in the canine world, there are differences between the breeds in body conformation and head shape, coat length and color, and between various colors and patterns of coats occurring within particular breeds, so there are plenty of options. Non-pedigree cats also come in a beautiful array of different coat colors and patterns, and nature designs some extremely unusual and pretty "one-offs" as well as the very common colors such as black-and-white or tabby.

Coat-color variations in non-pedigree kittens are almost limitless. Common bicolor mixtures such as black and white are always popular.

Breeds are maintained by only allowing cats with certain characteristics to mate with other, similar cats, or by bringing change through controlled mating so that the origin of any variation is known. Genetics is a highly complex subject, and the range even within coat colors in the breeds is constantly changing. This means that, while some breeds have one coat color, such as the "blue" Korat (the coat is actually gray, with a light silver tipping), others may have many colors (such as the Persian).

There is a good chance too that, because we select certain cats to mate, and so control which genes are put into the melting pot, the disposition for certain behaviors may be passed onto the kittens along with their physical characteristics. Thus, when you hear that Siamese cats are vocal or that Ragdoll cats are loving, these are generalizations that may give an indication of the temperament of your chosen kitten. However, scientists agree that the differences between individual cats are still greater than the general variation between breeds.

There are currently over 40 breeds of cat in the United States. These have arisen in different ways: some came about naturally in geographically isolated areas, while others have been "man-made" by further manipulating the breeding of the originals or by using one-off mutations to develop new types. For example, the Siamese developed in isolation from other groups of cats to form the basis of the individuals we know today, yet we have introduced additional changes through selective breeding to produce color varieties and alterations in body shape that we like. Breeds such as the Somali have arisen by crossbreeding (in this case, by introducing a gene for long hair into the Abyssinian), while the Maine Coon and Norwegian Forest breeds developed from a mixture of cats which, by various means, reached the United States and Norway – now their home countries.

Some breeds have come about by breeding from one or two kittens born as mutations – in other words, kittens different from the norm thrown up naturally from time to time in nature. Examples are the Devon and Cornish Rex with their sparse, curly coats, the hairless Sphynx, the American Curl, and the Scottish Fold. Some people have even tried to breed a miniature cat, although the closest that we have come naturally to this is the Singapura, a small- to medium-sized cat familiarly known as the Singapore drain cat, which – as legend has it – originated in the back alleys and drains of Singapore. However, an important ethical consideration here is that, as buyers of such breeds, we must ask ourselves whether we really wish to create a demand for cats with no hair, short legs, or other mutations, or whether we would prefer the cat to remain as nature intended: a tough, independent, agile creature that is able to hunt and to live a long, healthy life.

Cat shows

Most people are aware of a handful of breeds – notably the Persian, Burmese, and Siamese – because of their distinctive looks and great popularity. However, there are many more feline breeds available and, if you are contemplating a pedigree kitten, the subject is worth some investigation. One of the best ways of deciding what you may like is to visit a cat show. In some countries, large shows and many smaller or specialized breeds shows are held throughout the year (look in cat magazines for details – see page 158). When you visit a show, have a good look around and talk to the breeders and other enthusiasts there.

It is even more important to start off with knowledge of the show world if you intend to show and breed with your own kitten – every enthusiasm has its own rules and regulations, and its likes and dislikes, so you should get in on the ground floor and start asking questions before you obtain your kitten, not afterward.

For additional information on some of the most common cat breeds, and their appearance and characteristics, see Chapter Two.

HOW MANY KITTENS?

Many people who are thinking of acquiring their first feline companion only consider having a single kitten, but there are many advantages to obtaining two kittens together. Although this may at first seem to mean twice the cost of feeding, neutering, vaccinations, medical expenses, and so on, there are also many non-cost-related benefits, not to mention the fun to be had with two inquisitive kittens learning about the world around them.

Students of animal behavior know that the dog is a pack animal and needs to be part of a group, whereas the cat is a solitary hunter, which explains much of their differing behavior. However, this fact does not preclude a cat from enjoying social interaction with its own species, as owners with more than one feline can testify.

Unlike their feral counterparts, pet cats have the need – if not the desire – to hunt removed by a ready supply of food at home, and, with the time and effort of territory patrol and reproduction no longer on the agenda if they are neutered, they have even more "spare time" to fill. Cats normally sleep for up to 60 percent of their lives and spend about one-third of their waking hours grooming themselves, but this still leaves time for social interaction – whether this be with other cats or with their human owners.

By bringing what is still essentially a wild animal into the home, and removing many of the dangers it would normally face by feeding and tending to it, we provide the pet cat with what would seem to be a very easy lifestyle – albeit one that attempts to curb its independence to fit into our way of living. This can be successfully achieved because the cat is an extremely adaptable species and, as is

Having two kittens can be double the fun. You will be treated to great displays of feline behavior as they play, but taking on two kittens is something to consider carefully.

evident in millions of homes, provides us with companionship and entertainment while still maintaining much of its instinctive wild behavior outdoors. However, it can also mean that cats come to rely heavily on human owners for their social behavior, a responsibility that we must be sure to fulfill.

Advantages of two kittens

It is a great deal of fun to have two kittens, and you will see much more of the feline behavioral repertoire as they play. Kittens enact the whole gamut of body language in their daily frolics, and this provides a wonderful opportunity to see just how much they can contort themselves or erect the fur on various parts of their bodies in their play-fights. It does mean that the kittens will often shoot around the house and, yes, sometimes up the curtains together, but this phase will soon pass as they grow and become heavier.

Of course, the personality of every cat is highly individual, and not all kittens are as boisterous as others. In fact, if one kitten is a little nervous and quiet, another less-inhibited kitten may help it to interact and to tackle some situations it would otherwise have avoided. Companionship will be of particular help in those first few days on entering a new home, when all is strange and very frightening. Obtaining two kittens together also removes many of the problems of introducing a companion to the household at a later date, since, once one cat has acquired territorial attachments to both its house and its owners, and when maturity – even if neutered maturity – has introduced the additional sexual-competition factor (see opposite), it is that much harder to get two cats to share happily together.

Many cat lovers already know the value of getting two kittens – sometimes it is twice the trouble, but usually the fun factor is squared!

Disadvantages of two kittens

Obtaining two kittens certainly relieves much of the "guilt factor" of leaving a single kitten alone all day, and makes going to work much easier on the conscience, as the kittens race around the house or curl up together, oblivious of your departure. However, this cat companionship does raise the question in some owners' minds as to whether the two kittens will bond to each other instead of to them. This is a valid concern, perhaps more so for people who hope for a type of dog-like devotion from their cats. However, cats do seem to be able to switch from feline to human interaction fairly happily, and do not spurn our attention simply because they have been curled up with their feline partners all day. As ever, they usually make the best of both worlds and will still seek out a warm lap whenever it becomes available.

One other practical consideration for anyone wishing to buy two long-haired kittens is the extra effort required to groom two cats instead of one – a time-consuming process that should not be underestimated!

Kittens from different sources

Obtaining two kittens from the same litter makes life fairly simple but, if you would like to own one of the pedigree breeds yet cannot afford twice the cost, you could consider getting a non-pedigree cat to go with it. Make sure, however, that you are fully aware of the medical implications – both kittens must be healthy and not a potential disease risk for each other (you should discuss their ages and vaccination status with your vet to minimize any risk).

MALE OR FEMALE?

Having decided to obtain a kitten – or even two – what about its sex? If you are buying from an experienced breeder, there should be no problem in ensuring that you are given a kitten of the sex you desire, but veterinary clinics probably have a daily intake of Sams who come in to be castrated and leave as Samanthas (or vice versa), much to their owners' embarrassment. While it can be difficult to tell the sexes apart when kittens are tiny, it does become easier as they grow up.

Many of the differences between the sexes are shaped by hormones that dominate cats' reproductive lives. In general in the animal kingdom, it can be said that males tend to be rather more difficult to control than females and are more prone to aggression, especially during the breeding season. However, with most of our kittens we remove the influence of these hormones by having them neutered before they become sexually mature (neutering is generally carried out at or before six months of age – see pages 150–3).

There is actually very little difference between the sexes once they are neutered, and their behaviors are very similar, but what may affect your choice is whether you are introducing your kitten into a household where there is already a resident cat. In this case, it is usually better to choose a kitten of the opposite sex to the older cat in order to remove any element of sexual competition. They will therefore be less of a threat to each other, as this competitive drive can still have some influence even if both cats are neutered.

Similarly, if you plan to obtain two kittens together, it is probably best to choose one of each sex – or two females – to avoid the risks of potential competition that would normally develop later between males, especially

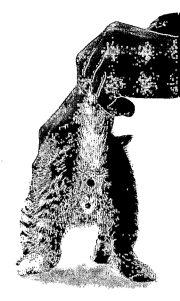

In a male kitten, the tip of the penis is hidden in an opening ½ in (1cm) below the anus, with the scrotal sacs in between.

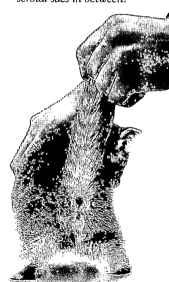

In a female kitten, the vulva is a vertical slit almost joined to the anus like a letter "i."

as they approach sexual maturity. Neutering will, of course, remove much of the difference in behavior between males and females, so this may not be a vital consideration, but it could be an issue with some types and some Oriental breeds that may become more competitive with members of their own sex.

WHAT IS THE BEST AGE?

Eight weeks is the optimum age for a non-pedigree kitten to be transferred from its breeder's house to its new home. All kittens must by this time have encountered a broad range of experiences, people, and animals, to ensure that they will develop into confident and sociable family pets (see pages 41–4). Many pedigree kittens also go to their new homes at eight weeks, though some may remain with their breeders until they are a few weeks older, when they will have completed their primary vaccinations (see page 87) and be litter-trained (see pages 82–5).

If you already have an older cat (or if you plan to obtain two kittens), you must think carefully about the sex of the new kitten. Introductions to an older cat will also need careful planning (see pages 64–8).

If you decide to obtain a kitten from an animal welfare society, you may have less control over its age. If the kitten is more than eight weeks old, you should be very cautious if nothing is known about its previous history – it may not have been properly socialized (see pages 42–3), which could lead to great problems later on.

WHEN TO GET YOUR KITTEN?

It is often in the winter with the fire roaring and the family snuggled beside it that we feel the need for an addition to our homes, in the form of a kitten to curl up on our laps or to snooze in the chair. However, this may not be the easiest time of year actually to find a young kitten.

Breeding times

Most cats have their kittens in the spring or summer, when there is an abundance of wildlife on which to feed their offspring. Pet cats, of course, will be fed by their owners and could have a litter at any time of year, but nature has adapted them for survival in the wild, not for the human household. If you would like a non-pedigree kitten, you should therefore bear in mind that starting your search in the spring or summer will give you the greatest chance of finding one.

Having said this, it is also true that nature can sometimes be "fooled" by breeders in order to produce pedigree kittens at other times of the year. This is done by keeping a female intended for breeding (known as a queen) indoors in artificial light to create a constant "day length," since it is the shortening of daylight hours that will bring a queen out of the fertile phases of her reproductive cycle and depress her ability to mate (see also pages 150–1). Some pedigree cat breeds seem to have more unusual breeding patterns, so you will need to check with a breeder as to the availability of kittens.

The best time for you

Not only will you need to find out when kittens are most likely to be available, but you must also be able to set aside time to look after the new addition to your family. Many owners of recently acquired kittens and puppies can be heard to remark that they had forgotten what hard work it was to have a baby in the house! You should be prepared to spend at least a weekend with your new kitten, settling it in, learning about its needs and its character, and helping it with litter training if this has not already been done at the breeder's house (see pages 82–5). If you can have a few days at home, then so much the better.

It is obviously inadvisable to collect your kitten just before you go away on vacation, as this would mean a stay at a boarding kennel (see pages 106–8) before the kitten has even had the opportunity to become used to your home. While there is nothing wrong in familiarizing a kitten with a kennel at which it is likely to stay in the future, it will need time to settle in and to decide where home is first.

Similarly, avoid obtaining a kitten just before Christmastime, or when there may be many strangers in the house. A kitten needs consistency and care, and does not deserve to be forgotten during a period of festivity when there is likely to be considerable disruption and perhaps the challenge of excited, noisy children in the home. The baubles on a Christmas tree and other decorations around the house can also prove irresistible to an inquisitive pet so, if you do have a new kitten at this time of year, take care that it cannot reach them.

It is also unwise to obtain a kitten just before a baby is due. Even though the risks are very small, a pregnant woman should wear gloves as a precaution when cleaning out a litter box because of the risk of toxoplasmosis (see page 70). When the baby arrives, disruptions to the household can also be huge, and there may simply not be enough time to give both baby and kitten attention. A first-time mother in particular naturally tends to worry about the health of a new baby and, in the early days, may be concerned about hygiene, or the kitten accidentally jumping on the baby, and so on. To avoid these worries, it is best to let the baby grow up a little, and then introduce a kitten. To the kitten, the child will then be a normal part of the household, and it will learn to enjoy or avoid as it prefers!

CHAPTER TWO

CAT BREEDS

This chapter outlines the size, shape, coat type, and color of some of the more common breeds of cat, as well as a few of those less often seen. It also attempts to give a general idea of the breeds' behavioral characteristics, although it should be remembered that variation between individual cats can still be greater than between breeds.

There are three different coat types in the cat: longhair, semi-longhair and shorthair. If you decide to take on a longhair, you must be prepared to carry out a thorough daily grooming regime (see pages 96–9).

Unlike pack-oriented dogs, where humans have shaped the different breeds to do a job of work – be it herding, guarding, hunting, or acting as companions – cats have developed as solitary hunters. They may have lived alongside us for thousands of years (see pages 110–13), but they have not been expected to perform particular tasks, or to do as they are told. The excellent hunting skills of the cat have made it useful as a rodent controller, but we have done nothing to shape those predatory skills as we have done in the canine world.

However, there are some general characteristics that can give us something to go on when we are trying to decide just which type of cat ·we would like, and how it may be likely to behave. Although very little scientific research has been carried out on the behavioral characteristics of the different breeds, owners and breeders have noted specific breed tendencies, some of which do seem to be fairly clear-cut.

Neither the details of any particular breed "standard" – those of shape, size, and form set down by the feline authorities (such as the American Cat Association and the American Cat Fanciers' Association – see page 158) – nor the variations between breed standards in different countries are discussed here. If you wish to buy a kitten for breeding and showing, you may wish to contact the society or club of your preferred breed, from which you will be able to obtain much more detailed information. If you would simply like a pedigree kitten as a pet, the following information may help you to decide on the look and general characteristics that you like, and therefore on the breed of cat that will best suit your lifestyle.

LONGHAIR

Persian

The Persian is one of the most popular cat breeds, although its looks have changed somewhat over the years. The modern Persian is medium-sized and sturdy (or "cobby") in build, but has a much longer and thicker coat, a flatter face, and smaller ears than when it was first shown in the late 19th century. The eyes are large, round, and usually copper-colored, but can vary from orange to green and blue.

The Persian's coat is long and luxuriant with a soft undercoat, and requires regular grooming to keep it from matting. The coat can range from "self" (solid) colors from black through chocolate, cream, lilac, and blue to white. White Persians may be copper-eyed or blue-eyed, or may have one eye of each color. The white coat and blue eye color can be associated with deafness, so take care when choosing this type of kitten, and seek veterinary advice if necessary.

Persian cats can also be bicolored (a mixture of white with one of the self colors), blue-cream, cameo (a white undercoat with darker shading toward the tips of the hair), chinchilla (a white coat and emerald-green eyes that look rather as though they have been outlined with a dark eye pencil), Himalayan (a coat pattern similar to that seen in the Siamese, with a range of different-colored "points" at the mask, ears, stockings, and tail, which are darker than the paler body; this is because these areas are at a cooler temperature than the core of the body, and the hair is pigmented differently as a result), shaded silver (a white undercoat with black tipping), golden, smoke (a pale undercoat with darker tips; this cat looks solid colored until it moves), tabby (with the tabby markings in a variety of colors), tortoiseshell, and calico.

In temperament, the Persian is a gentle, friendly, and generally undemanding cat.

SEMI-LONGHAIRS

Balinese
The Balinese is a semi-longhaired Siamese with a silky coat. Its body shape is long and slender, and it has a typical wedge-shaped Siamese head. The ears may be tufted. The darker color points may be seal, blue, chocolate, lilac, red, cream, tortie, or tabby (in the United States the last four of these varieties are known as Javanese).

By nature the Balinese is a little less demanding than the Siamese, but it is similarly lively and intelligent.

Birman
The Birman is a long-bodied cat with a rounded head and blue eyes. Its coat is long and silky in texture, with darker points on a pale body color. The darker legs end in white paws, and these give the breed a most attractive and distinctive look. The coat colors are seal, blue, chocolate, and lilac.

The Birman is said to have been a sacred temple cat in Burma, its country of origin, and this perhaps gives rise to its intelligent, often reflective personality and quiet disposition.

Maine Coon
The Maine Coon is regularly described as the biggest of the feline breeds. However, males of up to 18 lbs (8.2 kg) are at the extreme, and most are simply sturdy cats with long legs, a long body and head, and a squarish muzzle. This breed has a very friendly and playful nature.

The coat of the Maine Coon is everything that it should be to protect the cat outside in a harsh winter – heavy, thick, and waterproof.

The fur is thicker around the neck, giving the cat a distinctive ruff, and its ears and paws may be tufted. The "Coon" part of the name is thought to come from its large size and bushy tail (early American settlers thought that the animal was a cross between a cat and a raccoon). The coat may be of any color or pattern.

Norwegian Forest

The Norwegian Forest cat developed to survive in the cold temperatures of Norway, and is renowned for its great proficiency at climbing. It is strong and long in shape with a thick, waterproof coat – which may be any color or pattern – and a woolly undercoat.

This is probably not a cat to be kept indoors, as it is a great hunter with an independent but friendly personality.

Ragdoll

The Ragdoll is surrounded by tall tales – such as the story that the mother of the first litter was run over by a car and so produced "floppy" kittens, or the myth that cats of this breed cannot protect themselves because they are too docile – but in fact it is simply a good-tempered, gentle cat that will often "flop" in a person's arms like a rag doll.

This cat is fairly big, with a strong body and a flat-skulled head, large tufted paws, a beautiful bushy tail, and blue eyes that are large and oval in shape. The coat is silky and medium in length, and the fur is fairly dense. The coat comes in seal, blue, chocolate, and lilac, and in three patterns: color-pointed, mitted (with paw tips of a different color), and bicolored (white combined with any of the self, or solid, colors).

Somali

The Somali is a semi-longhaired version of the Abyssinian, its double coat being dense, fine, and very soft to the touch with treble-banded ticking (each hair bears three dark bands). The coat colors of this breed are ruddy red, blue, lilac, fawn, and silver.

The Somali is an intelligent cat and has an extrovert's temperament.

Turkish Van

The Turkish Van is a cat that seems to break the feline rules – we all know that cats hate water, but not this one. Named after the Lake Van region of Turkey, where it was first seen, this breed loves water and enjoys a swim – it will even take to the bath if a natural water source is not available.

The Turkish Van has a long, sturdy body, a strong wedge-shaped head and straight nose, and orange, blue, or odd-colored eyes. Its long, silky coat is described as auburn and cream, with the auburn often only at the head and ears. It is a friendly and intelligent cat.

SHORTHAIRS

Abyssinian

The Abyssinian still looks much as it did in the 1800s, when it arrived with traders visiting from Africa, with its close-lying, double-ticked coat (each hair bears two dark bands) giving a similar appearance to that of a wild rabbit or hare. Four further colors – blue, ruddy red, lilac, and fawn – have since been added to its repertoire.

The Abyssinian needs human company to share its intelligent and outgoing personality.

British and American Shorthairs

The British Shorthair (right) is a large cat with a sturdy body, heavy feet, and a large, round head with small, neat ears and large eyes. The American Shorthair (opposite page, top) is similar in appearance but has a longer head and a medium-sized, sturdy body.

The short coat of both breeds is dense and shiny. Self (solid) coat colors range from black, chocolate, blue, cream, red, lilac, and white to mixed combinations of bicolor (white combined with any of the self colors), blue-cream, smoke, tabby (either classic or mackerel, in a variety of

colors; the latter has a series of lines that run vertically down the body), spotted (this is similar to the pattern visible in some types of wild cat), tipped (a white undercoat, with various darker shades at the hair tips), and tortoiseshell.

Both Shorthairs have a very friendly, affectionate temperament.

Burmese

Among the pedigrees, the Burmese is now almost as popular as the Siamese with cat owners, and this is true even in the United Kingdom, where the breed arrived only as recently as 1948. Almost all of the Burmese cats in existence today can be traced back to a single walnut-brown queen called Wong Mau, who was brought from Rangoon (the capital of Burma) to the United States in 1930.

The Burmese has a short, shiny, dense, and very soft coat that feels wonderful to stroke and requires little in the way of grooming, which is an advantage for many owners. This cat's body is medium-sized and often muscular and sturdy, and it has a rounded head and wide-set ears. In profile it has a firm chin and a distinct nose "break" (in this characteristic it is unlike the Siamese, which has a straight profile). The four recognized coat colors of the breed are sable, champagne, blue, and platinum.

The Burmese is an outgoing cat and will always let you know when it is around, although it may not be quite as talkative as the Siamese. It is intelligent and enjoys human attention, liking to be involved in whatever is going on. It usually has plenty of energy, and has been described as brave, athletic, humorous, and capable of showing great ingenuity. Many members of the breed enjoy retrieving thrown balls of paper or other objects, often keeping their owners playing for hours at a time, and take well to being walked on a harness and lead (see page 78).

The Burmese is thought to be one of the longer lived of the cat breeds, with individuals commonly reaching their late teens.

Exotic Shorthair

Just when you thought you were coming to grips with all the breeds and their various colors, the Exotic Shorthair pops up. This is really a short-haired Longhair: in other words, it has the same body shape and form standards as the Persian cat, but with less

of the very thick undercoat to deal with. So if you like the look of the Persian but think that you could not cope with all the grooming, the Exotic Shorthair may be the cat for you. This breed is available in all the colors and color points of the Persian. It has the same affectionate and undemanding temperament, making it a good indoor cat.

Korat

The Korat is a breed whose coat comes in just one color – blue (actually a dark gray). It originated in Thailand, and is one of the oldest-known cat breeds. It has become popular because of its quiet, friendly temperament and its pretty, pear-shaped face and very large eyes, which give it a very appealing expression.

Manx

The Manx cat is another easily recognizable breed, in this case because of its tail – or lack of one. In fact, there are three types of Manx cat, each characterized by the length of tail: the completely tailless Rumpy, the Stumpy, and the Tailed.

If the Manx cat were presented as a new breed today, it would probably not be accepted by the cat-breed authorities because of the problems associated with breeding these cats (the lack of a tail is actually the result of a spinal deformity). Indeed, two completely tailless individuals cannot

be bred together because of this deformity, so the Stumpy and Tailed cats are used for breeding, with the resulting Rumpy kittens then being sold as pets.

The Manx is a well-rounded cat, whose short, thick fur – which can come in any color and pattern – needs regular grooming to keep it in good condition. Cats of this breed are generally docile and outgoing.

Oriental Shorthair

This breed has a long, slender body shape like that of the Siamese, but has a solid coat pattern instead of the colored points. It comes in a variety of colors, from self (solid) colors such as ebony, blue, cream, chestnut, red, white, caramel, fawn, cinnamon, and apricot, to non-self colors such as tabby (classic), tabby (spotted), tabby (ticked – each hair has two to three dark bands), tortoiseshell, and torbie (tortoiseshell and tabby). The blue-eyed white form of the Oriental Shorthair, which is called the Oriental White, does not suffer from the congenital deafness that is common among other blue-eyed, pure-white cats – this is probably because the blue of the Siamese eye is genetically different from that of non-Siamese breeds.

The Oriental Shorthair is among the most intelligent and energetic of cat breeds, and makes a very lively and rewarding pet for the right owner. Like the Siamese, members of this breed are typically vocal – with a distinctive voice that ensures they will not be ignored for long – and enjoy human attention. Individuals tend to become very attached to their owners.

Russian Blue

The Russian Blue (which really did originate in Russia) is a medium-sized to large cat with a beautifully soft double coat – the fur is like thick velvet and feels silky to the touch. This cat has a straight profile and whisker pads that stand out a little, giving it a very strong face. The almond-shaped eyes are a vivid green. In temperament, the Russian Blue is quiet, gentle, and affectionate.

Siamese

The Siamese is probably the best known of the pedigree breeds, and the beauty of its long, elegant body, fine legs and tail, and wedge-shaped head is accentuated by the darker color points. However, when the Siamese first appeared in an exhibition of cats in London in 1871, it was described as "an unnatural nightmare kind of a cat" – probably because of its striking coat and bright blue eyes (which may have been squinting), along with a kinked tail. These defects of a kink and a squint were common in the breed at that time, but have since been greatly reduced through selective breeding. Its combination of grace, beauty, and strong personality has made the Siamese sought after around the world.

The breed comes in a range of color points, from the most commonly known seal point to chocolate, lilac, red, cream, tortie, tabby, and torbie (tortoiseshell and tabby) points.

The Siamese character is well known: these cats are intelligent and talkative, playful and outgoing, and are often referred to as "dog-like" because of their willingness to retrieve items, to walk on a harness and lead, and even to learn tricks. However, their best trick is to train their owners to do as they are told – Siamese are not cats to be ignored.

Like the Burmese, Siamese cats are generally long-lived, happily reaching their teens with no apparent signs of aging and gracefully moving into old age.

Tonkinese

The Tonkinese is a cross between a Siamese and a Burmese, and was first developed in the United States in the 1960s. As both of these breeds are beautiful individually, it is no surprise that the Tonkinese is also a very attractive cat. In looks, it lies about midway between the two, and may be the ideal choice for cat lovers who prefer the "chunkier" look of the more traditional-type Siamese.

As you would expect from a combination of two breeds not renowned for their reticent personalities, the Tonkinese is intelligent and interactive, and enjoys joining in with whatever is going on. It has a fine, close-lying, short coat that comes in brown, blue, chocolate, lilac, red, and cream, as well as in the various torties, tabbies, and torbies (tortoiseshell and tabby).

OTHER COATS

Cornish and Devon Rex

In the 1950s and '60s, two cat breeds originated from the southwest of England. Both are natural mutations – in other words, they come from kittens that were born into normal litters and were then developed into specific breeds. The Rexes have a curly, rather sparse coat, in which the hair is fine and has a rippled appearance. It may be any color or pattern. The coat seems to molt less than that of other breeds, and some people who are allergic to cat hair have found that they can live with the Rexes without problems.

The Cornish Rex (above) has a slender, muscular body and long legs, and a long, tapering tail; the head is wedge-shaped with large, high-set ears.

The Devon Rex (right) has a shorter coat than its Cornish cousin. The ears are large and low-set, giving the breed a pixie-like appearance.

The Rexes are intelligent, playful, and friendly, and appreciate plenty of human attention.

Sphynx

Most cats are recognized because of their coat type or color, but the Sphynx is an exception. Its claim to fame is that it appears to be hairless (it does in fact have a fine down of fur), so that the skin's pigmentation and pattern are clearly visible.
This breed is now accepted by many cat associations in the United States.
The Sphynx is a medium-sized cat with slender legs and large ears, and is gentle and good-natured.

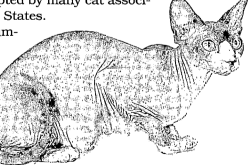

CHAPTER THREE

FINDING THE RIGHT KITTEN

Wherever you go for your kitten – be it a purebred kitten from a breeder or a non-pedigree individual from an animal welfare society – you need to know exactly what you are looking for in order to take home a healthy, friendly kitten that will be a rewarding and much-loved companion for many years to come.

FINDING A NON-PEDIGREE KITTEN

An old theory was that all female cats should be allowed to have one litter before they were neutered – to "settle" them, or simply because it was considered a pity not to give them this opportunity. This is now thought totally unnecessary, and most owners have every intention of neutering their cats – female or male – to avoid unwanted pregnancies. However, cats grow up very fast – they can be sexually mature by five or six months of age (see page 150) – and sometimes a "baby" female kitten finds a tom earlier than its owner had anticipated.

Picking from a litter

The unexpected arrival of many non-pedigree litters means that people often do not actually go looking for a kitten, but are asked by a friend or a neighbor to give a beautiful and irresistible little ball of fluff a good home. Kittens are also often advertised, "free to good homes," in newspapers and at veterinary clinics.

If you select a kitten from a litter such as this, be sure to follow the guidelines outlined on pages 33–6 on how to pick out the best kitten for you, and how to check its health and general condition.

Pet-store kittens

It is best to avoid buying a kitten from a pet store, and there are many reasons for this. Firstly, you will probably not know the age of the kitten, which is an important consideration (see pages 42–3). If it is on its own, you will not be able to establish the health status or character of its mother and littermates, or the character of its father (this may have a strong influence on that of the kitten – see page 37).

Another drawback is that you will not know how well the kitten is being looked after. Many pet-store kittens are taken from their mothers

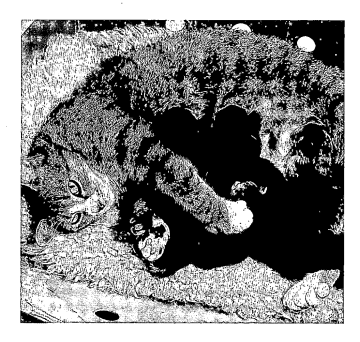

All young kittens – such as this non-pedigree litter – are very appealing, but you need to choose carefully in order to end up with the right kitten for you and your family.

too early; their normal diet is suddenly changed, and they are placed in a strange environment where they do not receive the care and attention they need, and this can cause great stress and illness.

A kitten in a store may also be housed with other individuals that are carrying disease. The cats are unlikely to be vaccinated (see page 87), and you could buy a kitten that not only succumbs to disease very quickly but also brings it into your home – an important consideration if you have other cats. If you must buy from a pet store, check all these aspects very carefully, and ask for a certificate of vaccination if the owner claims that this has been carried out.

Animal welfare societies

The number of welfare societies that care for cats is vast, and they range from large national organizations to kind people who simply take unwanted cats into their homes. Although there are many cats needing good homes, do not be overcome by sentiment when choosing a "rescued" kitten. Remember that you will become attached to it very quickly, and, if you have picked out a kitten because it looks unwell and you feel sorry for it, you may well be on the road to grief. Young kittens that are sick die very easily, so take care.

If you would like to obtain a kitten from a welfare society, find one that is well run, clean, and orderly. Bear in mind that the more cats that are kept together in a small space, the greater the risk of spreading

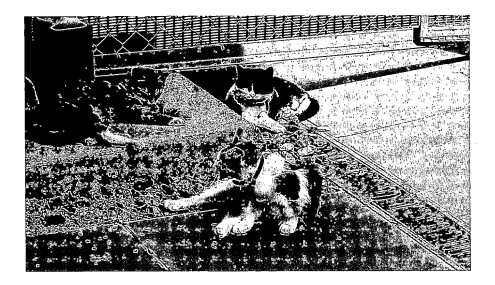

disease (see pages 89–91). Kittens in this environment may be protected by antibodies from their mothers' milk for a few weeks, but will subsequently stand a high risk of catching a feline disease in the period before they can be vaccinated. Many responsible and knowledgeable individuals who rescue cats will take on only a litter or two at a time – or will find new homes for kittens individually – and ensure that both their hygiene precautions and the management of the cats' environment is extremely strict.

Many people obtain kittens from animal welfare societies. This can be a good option, but you should be cautious when taking on an older kitten with no knowledge of its background.

If you do decide to take on a kitten from a welfare society, you will be asked questions about yourself, your home, and how you will care for the kitten. A member of the staff could even visit your home. You may have to agree to neuter the kitten when it is older, to prevent more unwanted litters (see pages 150–3). You may be asked to pay for the kitten, or to give a donation toward the work of the society.

Ferals

There is a chance that you will be offered a feral kitten to take in. This type of kitten will have been born "in the wild" and lived without human interference, so it is really a wild animal. Some pet cats that have become lost or were abandoned by their owners (these would be classified as strays rather than ferals) may live a feral lifestyle of scavenging and hunting for a period, but will usually reintegrate into a human home if it is offered.

However, kittens born feral will remain wild if they are not introduced to humans by the age of seven or eight weeks, and even then they may be very spitty, nervous, and prone to hiding. This is because there is only a very short period in a kitten's life when it can form bonds with other species (see pages 41–4). A kitten that is brought up from birth in an environment with numerous people, dogs, and other cats will take this as normal and accept the presence of different species in its new home, whereas a feral kitten will follow its natural instincts to run, hide, and protect itself from them.

For these reasons, if you hope to obtain a kitten that will grow up confident and relaxed in your home with people, other animals, and a normal busy lifestyle, you need to be sure that it has met all these situations before you take it on, or that you obtain it young enough to have an influence on it. Some people do have the talent and patience to work with older ferals, and gradually succeed in "domesticating" them, but, if you are offered a feral kitten of more than seven or eight weeks old, you may never have the friendly cat that you envisage.

FINDING A PEDIGREE KITTEN

When you go to a breeder for a pedigree kitten, you will obviously have already decided on the breed you would like. Most good breeders are very well informed about their particular breed – and about cats in general – and will give you excellent advice about your kitten.

Choosing a breeder
As with most specialist interests, there is a wealth of information available on cat breeders if you know where to look for it, such as in specialist cat magazines or from cat societies. There are a number of cat associations in the United States that will help you locate a good

Some breeders keep cats in outdoor quarters. Wherever they are, the quarters should be clean and provide the cats with a stimulating environment.

As a litter grows older, their breeder may keep them out of harm's way in a special pen or crate (see also page 49).

breeder and will provide useful additional information about cats, including lists of breed clubs, advisory groups, and shows (see page 158).

Once you have selected one or more breeders, telephone them to find out if and when they will have kittens available. You will probably need to make an appointment to see the kittens and make your choice when they are fairly young, and then need to wait until they are the correct age to be sent to their new homes – this is usually at eight weeks.

Tell the breeder whether you plan to breed from your kitten, or whether you simply wish to keep it as a pet. Breeders sometimes have kittens available that are not quite right for showing – for example, with a small marking or color in the wrong place (this is known as a "fault" in breeding circles) – and these are described as pets rather than breeding-quality kittens. If this does not worry you, you may be offered a kitten at a considerably cheaper price than one destined for the show ring. You may have to agree in writing to have the kitten neutered when it is old enough (see pages 150–3), in order to prevent the fault from being passed on.

One other cheaper option is to buy a kitten on what are known as "breeding terms." With this arrangement, the breeder has the right to decide which stud the kitten will mate with once it is grown, and can then choose a number of the offspring.

Visiting the breeder

This will give you a chance to see the kittens with their mother (and, ideally, their father, if he is kept there, as his personality will affect that of the kittens – see page 37). You will also be able to evaluate the environment in which the cats are kept, by checking whether it is warm and clean, and whether the breeder is aware of the need to keep infectious diseases at bay. If there are many cats and the surroundings are dirty, it may be wise to choose another breeder.

Equally, you should not be overimpressed by sparse, ultra-clinical surroundings, as producing healthy and sociable kittens requires good attention to hygiene combined with knowledge of a kitten's social development (see below and pages 41–4). Kittens brought up in an unstimulating environment with little human contact are less active and interactive, and may remain wary of new sights, sounds, or people.

A good breeder should also ask you a number of questions about your house, garden, lifestyle, and knowledge of cats, to ensure that you will be able to provide a suitable and caring environment for the kitten.

THE RIGHT KITTEN FOR YOU

Whether you have opted for a pedigree or a non-pedigree, choose a kitten in the litter that seems to want to interact both with you and with its littermates. It is very difficult to sum up personalities in the brief period when you are introduced to a litter – looks and color often take preference. However, research carried out on cat personalities indicates that there seem to be different types of kittens: those that enjoy social interaction both with people and with other cats, and those that prefer their own company. The more owners attempt to interact with them, the more this second type will distance themselves.

Try to imagine for a moment that you are very small kitten. So far, your only experiences of the world have been living with your mother and littermates in a cozy, quiet nest. Your human owners, a quiet couple, have been kind and considerate. They have fed you well and cared for you, stroking you gently and making gentle cooing noises. Now they have found you a new home. That new home could not be more different from your past experience. It is full of strange smells, noisy children, barking dogs, and an adult cat that is clearly not pleased to see you – in other words, completely overwhelming. No wonder a new kitten sometimes prefers the underside of the spare room bed to the chaos of the living room carpet!

By trying to take the kitten's perspective (see also pages 117–21), it becomes easy to appreciate why the experiences and environment of a young kitten during the "sensitive" socialization period are so influential. A kitten that has never before set eyes on a dog or a young child, for instance, will find the transition to its new home much more difficult than one already familiar with them. This means that, if you have a busy family, with a hectic social life, children, dogs, or any other pets, it will make sense to buy your kitten from somewhere with a similar environmental profile.

Most potential owners would like a loving and interactive kitten with an outgoing personality that is happy to be shown off to friends and family, and is not nervous of everything around it. Choosing an active, interactive, healthy kitten from the litter is therefore the obvious first step. Remember that, while a cat's character may change over time, a timid cat is unlikely suddenly to become an extrovert.

Carefully open the jaws and look inside the mouth: a young kitten's milk teeth should be clean and white, the gums pale pink and healthy, and the breath should not smell.

The coat should be clean and glossy, and the skin pale and smooth. Part the fur in places with your fingers to check for the presence of parasites such as fleas (see pages 92–4).

The eyes should be bright and clean, with no discharge. The third eyelid should not be showing in the lower part of either eye – if it is, the kitten may not be entirely well.

The ears should be clean and free from discharge or wax. The presence of dark-colored wax – particularly if the kitten is scratching – may indicate ear mites (see pages 94–5).

GETTING A HEALTH CHECK

The health of your kitten is vital. Just because you have traveled all the way to a breeder's house, or because you are desperate to take a kitten home from an animal welfare society, it is very important that you do not rush into a decision; instead, having picked out a kitten that you like, stand back and check it over very carefully and objectively. You want to avoid taking home a sick kitten, having to pay for expensive veterinary treatment, becoming deeply attached to the kitten, and then losing it suddenly through illness.

No matter how good the breeder or animal welfare society, check the kitten over yourself for your own peace of mind. This is often a question of following your instincts – some kittens simply look "not quite right," or are very quiet. Tell your vet what symptoms you have seen and ask for advice; alternatively, once you have collected your kitten, take it for a checkup with your vet to ensure that there are no health problems that you may have missed (see pages 86–8). If your vet does come across a problem during this examination, he or she will help you decide what to do (most breeders of pedigree kittens will sell them subject to veterinary approval).

What to look for

The kittens and mother should all look healthy and bright, and the kittens should be lively and inquisitive. If there are any ill kittens within the litter, it is very likely that – even if you choose a healthy one – it may have been infected but that the disease has not yet shown itself, so be tough. Do not let yourself be tempted by the runt of the litter or the little sick kitten sitting in the corner – this will only bring you problems and a lot of heartache.

Gently pick up the kitten that you like and check it over from top to toe. The coat should be clean and glossy, with no dry patches or dandruff. There should be no signs of fleas or other parasites (see pages 92–5) – part the fur and have a look. Check inside the mouth for healthy, pale pink gums and clean white milk teeth; the kitten's breath should not smell. There should be no discharge from the eyes or nose. The nose itself should feel cool, velvety, and slightly damp, and the kitten should not be sneezing or sniffing. Its breathing should be even and not "rattled" or wheezy.

Ensure that the kitten's third eyelid is not showing in either eye (you will see this as a white membrane covering the lower part of the eye), as this is a sign that the kitten may not be entirely well. The ears should be clean and free from discharge. If there is dark-colored wax in the ear and the kitten is scratching, it may be suffering from an infestation of ear mites (see pages 94–5). The area around the base of the tail should be clean – any sign of reddening or fur-soiling should be investigated, as the kitten may have diarrhea. It should not be pot-bellied (this may indicate a heavy worm infestation – see pages 91–2), and should walk without stumbling or limping. If you are in doubt about anything at all, ask the breeder or a vet.

If you are happy that your chosen kitten looks healthy in all these respects, let the breeder know your final choice. If the kitten is a pedigree, you will probably need to pay a deposit of at least part of the price. Finally, unless you are taking the kitten home the same day (in which case you will need to have made all the appropriate arrangements at home in advance – see Chapter Five), arrange the date when you will return to collect it.

CHAPTER FOUR

YOUR KITTEN'S DEVELOPMENT

Your kitten's appearance, personality, and behavior are unique – no other kitten in the world will be the same. How this individuality and these characteristics are formed is a magical combination of nature and nurture: the effect of genetics, development in the womb, and the kitten's experience of the world around it after birth.

PARENTAL INFLUENCES

Studies have shown that the personality of a kitten's father has a direct effect on that of the kitten – an interesting point when one considers that most kittens have no contact at all with their fathers, and that most owners do not even know the identity of the father! This means that a kitten born of a sociable, affectionate, and outgoing father is more likely to have those qualities, whereas a kitten fathered by a nervous, antisocial cat may well reveal those characteristics as an adult itself. Of course, the mother's genetic influences will be equally important, but study of these is complicated by the fact that the mother's behavior also influences the kittens after they are born.

   Such research does not discount the added effects of the environment and the vital role of good socialization on cat behavior (see pages 43–4), but it does indicate that a kitten's genetic blueprint is highly relevant.

BEYOND GENETICS

Your kitten is also subject to physiological influences. Even while cocooned in the womb, it is developing and is affected by various factors. The normal gestation period for a domestic cat is 63 to 66 days. At only 24 days after conception, it is likely that the kitten has an awareness of touch; by day 54 in the womb, it already has the basic "righting" reflex, which becomes refined after birth (see page 42).

   During the pregnancy, the kitten is continually bombarded by the effects of hormones, nutrition, and even the chemical changes caused by any stress in the mother. A nutritionally well-balanced, calm, and contented mother is therefore more likely to produce kittens that reflect this state of health – mentally and physically. Kittens born of a severely undernourished mother may well have poorer learning aptitude, show less tolerance of other cats, and reveal higher levels of reactivity (for example, running away or showing aggression) in stressful situations.

However, these influences are likely to be uncontrollable by you as a potential owner: you may not even know about the state of the mother before she gave birth, and the father's identity may be lost in the annals of time. A kitten is rarely conceived, born, and brought up in the most ideal of situations – yet the majority of kittens become happy, much-loved family pets. How is this possible? The answer is that the environment into which a kitten is born, the mother's behavior after birth, and human influences all have a huge impact on its behavior.

THE DEVELOPMENTAL STAGES

The development of a kitten is divided into four main stages – neonatal, transitional, socialization, and juvenile – before adulthood is reached at the age of about one year. These divisions are not distinct or rigid, but depend on an individual's growth rates as well as on factors such as the mother's health and welfare, and the influences of the environment.

Neonatal period
The neonatal phase lasts from birth to about 10 days of age.

Physical development At this first stage of the kitten's life, eating and sleeping are the only vital functions for staying alive. The kitten is totally dependent on its mother, and relies on her to feed it, to keep it warm, and to stimulate its bowel and bladder movements by licking the area under its tail.

A newborn kitten cannot regulate its own body temperature and has very little control over its limbs or body movements – it will not be able to walk for at least three weeks.

If very young kittens are left by their mother for a brief period, they will huddle together for shared body warmth.

However, the kitten will cry out if it becomes separated from its mother, and by four days old can "paddle" short distances (for example, if it becomes separated from the warmth of the litter), using a simple "rowing" action of the forelegs to drag itself along.

Sensory development The kitten's eyes are closed at birth. Although the ears are also covered by folds of skin, even a very young kitten will respond to loud noises by raising its head. It probably locates the teat area through a combination of warmth, touch, and also the sense of smell (it is thought that a kitten follows a saliva trail, left by the mother after giving birth, to the nipples).

Feeding Once at the teats, the kitten learns to latch onto a nipple through small, innate bobbing movements of the head, known as the "rooting reflex." It is also born with a sucking reflex, which causes it to turn its head toward any object – such as a finger – that touches the area of its mouth. This reflex gradually becomes more sophisticated and, after a few days, only the feel of a teat will provoke this response.

At this stage suckling will take place for up to eight hours per day. A kitten usually weighs about 3½–4 oz (100–120 g) at birth, but this can double in the first week alone.

Behavior Soon after birth some coordination in the forelegs allows the kitten to make treading movements around the teats to stimulate the mother's milk flow. This "kneading" behavior is sometimes also seen in adult cats at moments of great contentment. Interestingly, a little later the kitten will begin to purr as it suckles. This also seems to stimulate the mother's milk flow, and soon becomes a signal to all the other kittens that food is about to arrive.

A queen may decide to move her litter after only about two days in a nest site – perhaps to a safer place, but perhaps also to offer her kittens the stimulation of a more diverse environment than the safe comfort she needed for giving birth. To move the kittens, the queen grasps each in turn by the scruff of the neck before carrying it to the new spot she has chosen. Being picked up by the scruff in this way causes a reflex action in a kitten – its forelegs become limp, while its hindlegs and tail curl up out of the way. During the transportation in its mother's mouth, the kitten will appear to be temporarily immobilized, and will not attempt to struggle or make any noise.

Presumably of great adaptive value in avoiding predators, this reflex action (known as flexor dominance of the vertebral musculature) continues into adulthood in many cats, making it very useful for restraint in an emergency. Some vets have even been known to grasp the skin on the back of a cat's neck with a clothespin, creating the instant trance-like, immobile state in the cat and leaving both hands free for administering first aid.

If the queen wishes to move her kittens for any reason, she will do so by picking up each in turn by the scruff of the neck.

Transitional period

This phase lasts from approximately 10 days to three weeks of age.

Physical development In this phase the crawling movements that were possible at the end of the first week have become more developed, and by about 17 days the kitten will make attempts to stand up, although it will remain wobbly for some time to come. The milk teeth begin to appear at about 14 days of age.

Sensory development The eyes usually open at about 10 days, although a kitten cannot see with clarity or accuracy until the age of approximately four weeks. At 15 days the ears are open and fully functional.

Feeding In the third week, the kitten starts to experiment with eating solid food, and will spend up to one minute a day attempting to do so. It will try any food it sees its mother eating, and this imitative behavior has a very strong impact later (an adult cat's taste preferences often originate from the food eaten as a kitten).

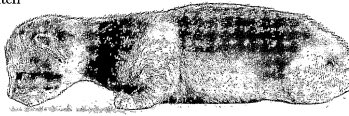

A kitten's eyes normally open at about 10 days old, but this may happen as early as the middle of the first week.

Behavior The weaning period marks a huge behavioral step for the kitten. This is the time when the mother starts to withdraw her milk supply by spending more time away from the litter and by lying in positions in which her teats are inaccessible. In the wild this behavior is vital for the queen's survival, as providing the litter with enough milk would now be severely depleting her body reserves. However, it creates frustration in her kittens, which try harder to get to the milk.

Eventually the conflict between mother and offspring is resolved, as the queen redirects her kittens' attention to solid food (or prey, in the wild). Weaning therefore encourages nutritional independence as well as being a kitten's first experience of learning to resolve frustration and conflict (see also pages 128–30).

During weaning the mother begins to deny her kittens continuous access when they attempt to feed from her.

Studies indicate that the process of weaning also influences the development of play behavior. Before weaning takes place, a kitten is primarily engaged in social play with its littermates and mother. However, the onset of weaning coincides with a reduction in social play and a marked increase in play with objects. This would appear to be in preparation for the predatory skills needed to hunt and kill prey, yet studies also show that such play is not necessarily an indicator of a cat's hunting proficiency as an adult. Hunting skills are instinctive, but practice makes perfect, and having a good teacher – in the form of the mother – seems to make the difference.

Socialization phase

This lasts from about three weeks to between 9 and 14 weeks of age. The end of the socialization phase varies greatly between litters, and seems to depend on the richness of the environment: a kitten born into complex and stimulating surroundings will start exploring them earlier, concentrating less on social play, while a kitten in a poor environment may continue to engage in social play until it is 14 weeks old.

The "sensitive" period for socialization to humans and other animals is between two and seven/eight weeks of age.

Physical development Between the age of three and four weeks a kitten begins to gain self-control over urination and defecation, and will start to move away from the nest to relieve itself. A kitten of this age will also start to toilet in loose, rakeable litter in a litter box. Imitation of the mother may play an important role in this behavior.

By the fourth week the kitten will move around quite confidently, and can often run and balance well by the fifth week. However, it will be another five or six weeks until it can run, jump, and leap with accuracy, balance, and coordination.

A five-week-old kitten can groom itself – and its littermates – effectively, and this natural behavior is vital for coat health, temperature regulation, and social contact. Grooming also acts as a "displacement" activity in cats: it seems to reduce tension and anxiety as an individual goes through a familiar, comforting, and physically pleasurable routine. This may also be one of the reasons why most cats love to be stroked or petted by humans.

Kittens engage in a great deal of social play; this teaches them social skills and is vital for the development of prey-handling abilities.

The so-called "righting reflex" – which ensures that a cat lands on its feet after a fall – is fully functional after six weeks. This reflex works by orienting the head and upper body first (by twisting in the air), so that the cat faces the ground. The rest of the body is then turned in line with the upper half, and the cat literally falls on its feet. While this means that cats can often survive fairly serious accidents, it does not always prevent injuries. A fall from a great height – such as from an upstairs window – may result in broken hindlegs and/or other severe injuries.

Sensory development The kitten's hearing is fully developed at about four weeks, which allows it to orientate itself and to move toward noises. Its vision will also have improved considerably by this time. The kitten is now able to judge distance and depth accurately, and so can follow moving objects by sight alone. Visual development will continue until 16 weeks.

Feeding By the fourth week, the kitten will spend approximately 25 minutes per day eating solids; this increases to about 50 minutes per day by the age of six weeks.

Behavior The socialization phase is the time when a young kitten forms relationships with members of its own species, learning to communicate with them through body language and social signals (see pages 121–6), and also discovers how to cope with other species such as humans and dogs. This important period could be regarded as the "make-or-break" stage in a kitten's life as, to a great extent, it determines how well the kitten will cope with life as a domestic pet in the years to come.

Social play teaches the kitten how to react and respond to the actions of other kittens, and the increased time spent on this activity tends to correlate with the mother spending less time with her offspring. Kittens tend to play differently from adult cats. Adult play is usually centered around a predatory-style pounce and chase, while kittens prefer "belly-up" games, leaping, and "stand-offs." This play between littermates is often fairly rough, and a kitten will soon learn that it must inhibit the scale of its "attacks" on other kittens if the violence is not to be reciprocated. Such "attacks" therefore gradually tend to be moderated, and become play in the form of rushing toward another kitten, and then veering away or rearing up at the last minute instead of actually making contact.

Social play with the kitten's littermates is usually overtaken by play with inanimate objects – known as object play – at about 14 weeks of age (female kittens become particularly intolerant of their male siblings' attempts to play with them as they enter the juvenile stage). Research has shown that object play – such as chasing, pouncing, batting, and scooping – stimulates cats in a very similar way to that of their natural hunting activities.

The socialization phase is also the time when a kitten needs to meet and be handled by as many people as possible if it is to grow into a suitable pet. Behavioral studies have demonstrated that a kitten must be handled by a bare minimum of four different people during this phase, in order to be friendly with everyone whom it encounters later in life. In addition, it needs to be individually handled for a minimum of 40 minutes every day if it is to cope well with close human contact as an adult cat.

43

Of course, the timing of the socialization phase – and in particular the "sensitive" period from the age of two to seven/eight weeks – puts the responsibility for adequate, pleasant exposure to people firmly on the kitten's first owner, or breeder. A kitten must experience as much as possible of domestic life during this period in order to be able to take everything in its stride.

What this means is that the kitten needs to meet plenty of different types of people – those with beards, glasses, or wearing hats. It has to understand that people with loud voices or sudden movements – such as children – are not threatening, but pleasurable to be with. It must learn that car rides are not frightening, that to be sniffed by a friendly dog is strange but bearable, and that other, adult cats exist, but are not a danger. It needs to have seen and heard sights and sounds as diverse as the washing machine on a spin cycle to people sneezing – and everything in between. There is so much to learn about life, so much that a kitten can regard as either terrifying or tolerable, and only five or six weeks in which to learn how to react for the rest of its life. This is a heavy burden indeed, and it explains why choosing the right breeder is so important.

Juvenile phase

This is the period between the end of the socialization phase and the onset of sexual maturity. Its timing can vary a great deal not only from breed to breed, but also between pedigree and non-pedigree kittens (see page 150).

Physical development By now the kitten's motor coordination and skills have improved; muscle development and balance reach a peak.

Sensory development All the senses of the adult cat – sight, the sense of smell, hearing, balance, and touch sensitivity – are now fully developed in the kitten.

With the onset of sexual maturity, the vomeronasal organ (sometimes called the Jacobson's organ) may come into play. This structure – a pair of fluid-filled sacs situated directly above the upper incisor teeth – is connected through fine ducts to the nasal cavity. Its function is to provide the cat with an extremely specialized third chemical sense that is a kind of cross between smell and taste. Most often using it in connection with sexual behavior, an adult cat can sometimes be seen drawing scents – particularly the smell of other cats' urine – in through the nose, into the vomeronasal organ, to be "analyzed." This action is accompanied by a distinctive gape, where the upper lip is drawn back and the mouth held open for several seconds. The "Flehmen response," as this gape is known, is thought to be an important part of the courtship ritual, perhaps as a means of judging the receptiveness (or otherwise) of a prospective mate.

Feeding By this stage the kitten will be able to live entirely on solids provided by its owner (if it is leading a domesticated life), and no longer requires any milk in its diet. It is also now able to hunt effectively. Research shows that the efficiency of the cat as a hunter does not appear to be determined by the amount of object play in which it has previously engaged, but the teaching abilities of the mother do seem to have an impact. A mother who provides a lot of injured prey for her kittens to kill, or who allows them to accompany her when out hunting, is likely to pass on her particular hunting skills to the kittens through their observation and imitation.

Behavior A kitten in the juvenile phase can perform almost every behavior of an adult cat. In a natural environment, this would be the time that the kittens in a litter would normally disperse, either of their own volition or because they are ousted by their mother, who may have had enough of sharing her home and food with so many hungry mouths and must conserve her strength for her next litter.

Although cats are often regarded as being solitary creatures, it is in fact quite possible – and indeed common – for them to live together in social groups. However, they are unlike dogs in that they have no strict social "rules" or cooperative hierarchies to unite or structure a group. Instead, group living and cohesion are more likely to depend on the amount of space and resources – particularly food – that are available, and also on individual character and tolerance. This may perhaps account for the differences between a home in which several cats live in harmony, and another where just two cats cannot tolerate living together. Personality types, previous experience as a kitten, socialization, and the

During the juvenile phase a kitten continues to learn the full repertoire of adult behavior – especially prey-handling skills and how to interact with other cats.

success of introductions to people, other cats, and a range of animals (see Chapter Six) are also likely to influence whether a kitten will get along well with other felines in the same household. For instance, a kitten that is hand-reared from birth and isolated from other cats will never fully learn that it *is* a cat, and will react aggressively or defensively with others of its own species.

CHAPTER FIVE

PREPARING FOR YOUR NEW KITTEN

If you choose a pedigree kitten from a litter, there may well be an interval of several weeks before the kitten is old enough to come home with you, and you can use this period to make the necessary preparations for its arrival. Even if you plan to choose and collect your kitten on the same day, you will need to have bought some essential items and ensured that your home is as safe and secure as possible.

BASIC EQUIPMENT

A kitten does not require vast or expensive arrays of accessories. It is also worth remembering that, although there are huge numbers of products on the market – from toys to luxury beds – their cost does not necessarily reflect their value. The following is a list of the basic items you should obtain before your new kitten arrives; you can of course add to these later on as you wish.

A carrier

You will need a secure carrier for bringing your kitten home. There are many types of cat carrier available, from cardboard and wicker to solid plastic and plastic-coated wire mesh. Whichever type you choose, you are likely to keep the carrier for the duration of your kitten's life. If it is to be a show cat, it will travel in the carrier regularly; otherwise you may only need it for trips to the vet or boarding kennel.

The carrier that you choose needs to be safe, secure, and cleanable. Make sure that the lid fits tightly, as kittens have very supple bodies and can squeeze through unbelievably tiny spaces. It is best to avoid a cardboard carrier, which may break if it becomes damp with urine and may be scratched through by a very persistent cat. You will also have to buy a new carrier every time it is soiled, as you will not be able to disinfect it.

The easiest carriers to use are the plastic-coated mesh, top-opening variety. Not only are these secure and washable, but you will be able to lift out your kitten easily. With a front-opening carrier – especially one with plenty of "foot holds" – if the occupant decides not to come out, it can scratch at the hand coming through the opening, or brace itself on either side of the exit so that getting it out becomes a challenge.

Feeding bowls and food

Whether ceramic, stainless steel, or plastic, all feeding bowls should be sturdy and have nonslip bases. Saucers are not ideal, as kittens often try to climb onto them, with messy results. As a minimum, you will need one bowl for food and another for water. Many owners like to leave dry food out so that their cats can help themselves as they wish during the day; if you also decide to provide canned (moist) or other fresh food such as fish, you should put it in a separate bowl. Keep all bowls scrupulously clean, and wash them separately from your own dishes for hygienic reasons.

Feeding bowls are available in various materials, and must be sturdy with nonslip bases. Shown here (clockwise from top) are stainless steel, plastic, and ceramic bowls.

You will also need a supply of suitable food for your kitten. Changing a cat's diet – particularly at times of stress, such as when moving to a new home – is often responsible for causing stomach upsets and diarrhea, so it is best to keep to the food with which the kitten is familiar for at least a week or so until it has settled in with you (ask the previous owner for a diet sheet and perhaps also a little of the kitten's food to tide you over when you first bring the kitten home). If you wish to change subsequently to a food of your own choice, you will need to do so gradually. If you have any worries about feeding, talk to your vet (see also pages 79–82 for further information on feeding).

A stable plastic bowl will be ideal for your kitten's drinking water; you should clean and refill this every day.

A litter box and litter

Many different designs of litter box are now available. Some kittens prefer open boxes, while others seem to like the security of the hooded variety, particularly if they feel vulnerable to disturbances such as assaults from other pets while using the box.

The type of litter you choose will also depend on your own kitten's preference to some extent – for example, the majority of cats seem to prefer fine-grade, loose material to clumps or pellets. How easy the litter is to dispose of, as well as its weight when you carry it home from the store, may also influence your choice (see pages 82–5 for further details on litter boxes and types of litter). At first you should use the same litter used by your kitten's breeder, as this will be familiar and therefore help the kitten feel more at home. If you wish to change to another type of litter, do so gradually.

A bed

It is essential to provide your new kitten with a bed of its own. This can be as rudimentary as a cut-down cardboard box with a warm blanket or soft cushion inside, or a more luxurious commercially made model, but its main purpose will be to provide a much-needed sense of security on your kitten's first nights away from its old home.

A comfortable bed will provide your kitten with warmth and security. It should be placed in a quiet position, away from the general bustle of the house, so that your kitten can rest in peace and without disruption.

The bed should be as warm and draft-free as possible if it is to win favor in your kitten's eyes: fake-fur or "sheepskin"-type fabric placed in the bottom of the bed will make it warm and inviting. It should also be a sanctuary away from other pets, children, and the general hustle and bustle of the household. Your kitten will need to sleep a great deal in its early weeks, and must be able to rest securely and without disruptions. Encouraging your kitten to sleep in its own bed will also help prevent a takeover of your furniture or beds.

A contented cat will often "knead" the area in which it is about to curl up, and this pummelling can be hard on more delicate or easily caught fabrics. They also need to be easy to clean, as bedding can be a breeding ground for fleas (see pages 92–4). A plastic bed will be easy to wipe clean with a damp cloth, but remember that the blanket or cushion in the base still needs to be fully washable. Wicker has a tendency to attract dust and is also more difficult to clean, so should be avoided if possible. Most cushioned fabric beds can be machine-washed, and some are made with a hood to make them feel very "safe." Bean-bag beds are also available, but beware the inquisitive kitten that chews a hole in the cover – all the polystyrene beads inside the bag may make an entertaining night for the kitten, but will give you a lot of work in the morning.

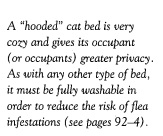

A "hooded" cat bed is very cozy and gives its occupant (or occupants) greater privacy. As with any other type of bed, it must be fully washable in order to reduce the risk of flea infestations (see pages 92–4).

Finally, a hammock designed to hang in a window or on a radiator is often a favorite. This type of bed may be useful if your kitten is a little nervous or in a busy household, as it will feel more secure resting above ground level. When the hammock is hung on a radiator, the warmth from beneath will be a magnetic attraction for most discerning cats.

A crate or pen

Using a kittening pen or indoor crate for your kitten's first few weeks will be a great time- and stress-saver for you, and will also serve as a nice secure den for the new arrival. It will be impossible for you to watch your kitten's every move throughout the day, or to be sure of its whereabouts all the time, and – however thorough your safety precautions (see pages 53–7) – a kitten can chew electric wires, escape from the house or even drown in the few moments it takes to answer the telephone or to open the front door. A crate or pen will also make introductions to other cats and dogs much easier and less traumatic for all concerned (see pages 64–9).

Ideally, the crate or pen you use should be large enough to allow your kitten to move about freely inside – the kittening pens used by many breeders to raise young kittens are perfect, and you may even be able to borrow one of these for a few weeks. A dog-transit cage (often also known as an indoor kennel, or crate) will also be suitable for your kitten's first weeks with you, and will probably be large enough to accommodate the kitten, its bed, a litter box, and a bowl of water if you need to leave the kitten inside for longer spells. A cage of this type will be fairly costly to buy, but you may be able to rent one from your vet or a breeder.

A kittening pen or crate provides a secure den for a kitten's first few weeks in its new home. The pen should be sufficiently large to allow the kitten to move about freely; a few toys placed inside will provide entertainment.

A collar

It is essential that your new kitten becomes used to wearing a collar, with identification attached, right from the start. Even if the kitten is to live an indoor existence, accidents can and do happen – a kitten can slip out through the smallest opening, and identification becomes even more important if an escapee is unused to being outside and fending for itself. A collar and identification will also mark your kitten as a well-cared-for pet, while cats that go roaming without collars are often taken in by unwitting neighbors who believe that they are looking after stray animals.

Should your kitten become lost, a safe, elasticized collar will help identify it. When fitting a new collar, make sure that you can slip at least one finger underneath it.

The collar you choose must be of the safety type, incorporating a piece of elastic that will allow the kitten to wriggle free should it become caught. Identification can be either an engraved disc, a barrel with the details inside, or a plastic label holder. Make sure that this is not too heavy for your kitten to carry, that the collar is not too tight (you should be able to slide one finger underneath it), and that the skin does not become irritated. Your kitten may scratch at the collar at first, but should soon become used to it. Some collars have a reflective strip or are fluorescent, for extra safety on roads in low-light conditions.

Some owners attach a bell to their cats' collars to warn birds of their approach. However, the efficacy of these collars is questionable. Some cats simply learn to keep their heads very still while stalking prey and then pounce at the last minute to avoid sounding the bell; others seem highly irritated by the noise of the bell, which is very understandable for an animal with such sensitive hearing.

Permanent identification As an alternative to a collar, it may be possible to have your kitten permanently identified with a microchip. This tiny device – the size of a grain of rice – is painlessly injected under the skin using a special needle, and the kitten's identity is then logged onto a national computer database. Should the kitten become lost, a scanner can be used to read the unique identity with which the microchip is programmed. The disadvantages are that there is no way of telling – just by looking at a cat – whether it has a chip implanted, and no guarantee that the person who finds the cat will know to take it to be scanned. However, many animal welfare societies now check for implants on "lost" cats, and a general awareness of the technique is slowly growing. If you would like to have your kitten identified with a microchip, ask your vet for further information.

Identification tattoos for cats are also available, although this method is less popular, and the marks can become blurred over the years.

A scratching post

This is a piece of problem-prevention equipment for the home. It is a natural part of a cat's behavioral repertoire to scratch on trees, wooden fence posts, or other surfaces – generally wooden – while it is outdoors. Scratching has several very important functions. It removes the outer surface layer of the claw, revealing a sharp new point underneath (which is vital for a perfected predator); it also spreads secretions from glands between the footpads, signaling to all other cats that the area has been used by this particular cat. A cat scratching in front of another cat seems, too, to be a rather assertive gesture, used to demonstrate that the cat is marking out its territory.

A sisal post (available from pet stores) is a source of fun for young kittens, as well as providing a scratching facility. Ensure that the post is properly mounted on a secure base.

As this is such a natural behavior, it is sensible to provide a practical outlet for it, rather than sacrificing the end of the sofa or the Chippendale furniture. A scratching post can be a log or bark from the garden, or a store-bought post wound with sisal. Posts impregnated with catnip (see page 52) are also available. It is best to avoid a carpet-covered post, which will look, feel, and smell just like the carpet in your home, unless you are quite happy for your living-room to turn into one giant scratching post. This type of post may also harbor fleas (see pages 92–4).

If you watch a cat scratching outdoors, you will see that part of the ritual is to stretch up high and pull down, to achieve a really good pull on the claws. For this

Scratching is a natural part of the cat's behavioral repertoire. Even if you plan to give your kitten access outdoors, you must provide a scratching post indoors – a log like this is ideal.

reason, you should ensure that your kitten's indoor scratching post is sufficiently tall – approximately 20 in (50 cm) high – to allow the kitten to stretch up to it, even when it is fully grown. The post must also be stable so that it cannot topple over when in use.

Declawing The claws are sometimes surgically removed from kittens' forepaws to prevent them from scratching in the home. However, this practice is totally unacceptable to the governing bodies of vets and to cat-behavior specialists in Europe.

You may want to consider very carefully the implications of declawing for your kitten – the pain that will be caused by the procedure, the use of an unnecessary anesthetic, and the loss of its claws for climbing, hunting, and so on – before you decide to go ahead with declawing. Remember, too, that simply providing a suitable and specially designated scratching post in the home will usually remove the necessity to curb the kitten's natural behavior in this way.

Cats will play less as they grow older, but still enjoy a game – and play is essential for an indoor cat (see pages 72–3).

Toys

You should have ready a selection of safe toys for your kitten, to exercise both its body and its mind. Many different toys are now available for cats, but the simplest types are often the most enjoyable, and you will only need one or two at first. Even a crumpled-up piece of paper or a length of string to drag around the floor will provide cheap and fun entertainment for your kitten.

Catnip Many of the toys available for cats are stuffed or impregnated with dried catnip. This herb has an interesting effect on many cats (although about 50 percent of cats do not respond, and kittens under eight weeks old are unlikely to do so). Catnip (*Nepeta cataria*) – also known as catmint – contains a chemical called nepetalactone, which has mild hallucinogenic effects on the cat's brain. Its soporific or excitatory effects are shortlived, nonaddictive, and harmless. A cat's typical response to a toy stuffed with catnip is to rub, chew, and roll over it, and to meow. Those cats that do respond to it can go into a "trance-like" state for up to 15 minutes, and certainly seem to enjoy the experience.

Grooming equipment

No matter what its coat type, it is essential that your kitten becomes accustomed to being groomed from an early age. While short-coated breeds or types are likely to be able to groom themselves thoroughly, some of the flat-faced, long-coated breeds will require help in the form of careful, regular grooming.

However, a grooming routine is not only about the health of the coat – it is about establishing a relationship between you and your kitten. Friendly cats groom each other to maintain social bonds, and we can do the same. Grooming will also accustom your kitten to being touched with an object, and to associate pleasant connotations with it. This will make visits to the vet less traumatic, as the use of equipment such as a stethoscope on its body will seem much less frightening.

A range of grooming equipment is available for use on cats (see pages 96–9). If you are unsure of which tools are suitable for your kitten's coat, ask your vet or a professional cat groomer for advice.

HOME SAFETY

As with many traditional sayings, "curiosity killed the cat" is probably based on some truth – cats are naturally curious creatures, and kittens even more so. They are full of mischief and, like the young of any animal, are inquisitive and adventurous because that is how they learn about the world. However, this can mean that they get themselves into trouble in numerous ways, from climbing onto dangerous machinery or chewing poisonous plants to falling from high places or simply getting stuck in inaccessible places.

Try to distract your kitten if it shows particular interest in a houseplant, and encourage your children to do the same. If the kitten persists, you may need to move the plant out of reach – you should certainly do so if you suspect it could be poisonous (see page 56).

While you may not be able to prevent all accidents of this kind – and your kitten will inevitably manage to do the one thing you have not thought about – you will be able to remove, lock, or make safe many of the obvious potential dangers.

Household hazards

When you first bring your kitten home, you should try to think from its perspective (see pages 117–21). Not only do you then have to look up from kitten height (and it is amazing what you see from that angle), but you also need to have thought about those high places that an agile little kitten can reach. Small, dark holes seem to attract kittens, so check chimneys, holes in the floor, gaps in skirting boards, and even under the bath before your kitten arrives.

Even if you plan to allow your kitten outdoors, you will need to keep it in for two to three weeks until it is used to your home and has had its primary vaccinations (see page 87), so ensure that everyone in the house knows that things have to be kept shut. Washing machines and clothes dryers feature regularly in terrifying tales about kittens rescued halfway through the first wash or just before they overheat. Close

Some plants in the garden – such as the Laburnum *shown here – are poisonous to cats. Most cats do not eat much plant material, and cases of poisoning by this means are extremely rare, but it would be wise to prevent access to such plants if possible.*

all windows or other obvious escape routes, and block off access to awkward areas such as behind the oven and freezer.

Kittens can also easily become shut in cupboards, refrigerators, clothes dryers, and freezers, having just "popped in" to investigate the contents while your back was briefly turned. Always discourage your kitten from jumping onto the stove or near the kettle, for obvious reasons. If you have a "cable chewer" – and some cats do seem to enjoy getting to grips with plastic covers on cables – make sure that you turn all electric appliances off at the wall at night or before you leave the house.

Some cats' toys can even be dangerous to a kitten, which could chew off and swallow eyes, loose squeakers, or the whole toy if it is small. Make sure that any toys you buy are strong, well made, and suitable for a young kitten.

A tiny mouth can pick up, chew, and swallow all sorts of small items you may not have noticed. Sewing thread with a needle attached, and elastic bands, are high on the list of reasons for visits to the vet (backward-pointing barbs on a cat's tongue mean that, once taken into the mouth, an item such as a length of sewing thread can be extremely difficult for it to spit out).

Climbing is of course a favorite pastime for a young kitten, and there is probably a great deal of truth in the much-quoted stories of Siamese cats and shredded curtains. However, it is not only the Siamese kitten that will climb anything at hand, and most kittens will persevere with this activity until they become too heavy or until the curtains fall down – whichever comes first!

A number of our common household plants – such as this umbrella plant – are poisonous to cats. Your kitten is unlikely to show any interest in plants, but you should remove them to be on the safe side.

Of course, your kitten needs to learn about its own abilities and limits, and most falls do not cause any damage. However, having said this, a fall from a kitchen dresser onto a hard tiled floor could cause injury, and you should take your kitten for a checkup right away if it seems sick or to have hurt itself. Cats are fairly good at righting themselves during falls from a reasonable height (see page 42), but you must remember that a cat *is* just a cat, not a mythical animal able to drop from an indefinite height without coming to any harm. Indeed, vets now recognize what has been labeled "high-rise syndrome" in cats – injuries commonly sustained by falling from a few stories – so make absolutely sure that any high windows are secure, covering them over with wire mesh if necessary (see page 72).

Digitalis, *better known as foxglove, is another potentially poisonous plant. Your kitten may encounter this growing in the wild, but fence off any plants in your own garden.*

Poisonous plants

Many of our household and garden plants are poisonous to cats, with consequences varying from a mild stomach upset or burning of the skin to instant death. Cases of serious poisoning by plants are actually very uncommon, since cats do not usually eat much plant material except some grass and herbs (see page 74). However, an inquisitive or bored kitten may play with and chew at a harmful plant, so never leave your kitten unattended in a room with a plant that you know to be poisonous – put the plant somewhere else until the kitten is older and wiser. Take care, too, if you buy a bunch of flowers from the florist. Some of the prettiest ones – such as the cornflower, delphinium, iris, hyacinth, and monkshood – are poisonous, so keep your kitten away. You should be able to get a list of poisonous plants from your vet.

Other poisons

Some human medicines such as aspirin and paracetamol are highly toxic to cats, so always keep them stored safely, and never give your kitten human medication except on the advice of your vet. Some foods – such as onion, cocoa, and an excess of liver or fish – can also be poisonous to cats.

You must be sure to control your kitten's access to any poisons kept in your garage or greenhouse – such as herbicides (sodium chlorate and paraquat), fungicides (pentachlorophenols, or PCPs), insecticides (pyrethrins, pyrethroids, organophosphates, carbamates, and organochlorides) – by keeping them safely locked away when they are not in use. You should also be very careful not to allow your kitten access to lawns or flowers treated with chemicals for 48 hours – the risk of poisoning is small, but it is best to be on the safe side.

Slug pellets containing methaldehyde can easily be eaten by a kitten if they are scattered on the garden, so you may wish to let the slugs have a feast while your kitten is small, or to choose an alternative method of controlling them.

It really goes without saying that any rat- or mouse-baited food or pellets (these include rodenticides such as warfarin, and the related substances colciferol, strychnine, and bromethalin) should not be left anywhere within reach of your kitten – or indeed of children or any other animals – at any time.

Always keep car antifreeze in a safe place – preferably on a high shelf in the garage – as its sweet taste seems to be attractive to some animals. Make quite sure, too, that fuels and wood preservatives are not able to leak out where your kitten could perhaps stand in them or contaminate its coat (coat contamination is a common source of poisoning, as the affected cat is very likely to lick at its coat in an attempt to rid it of the substance).

If, at any time, you think that your kitten may have ingested a poison, or has a poisonous substance contaminating its coat or skin, you will need to take prompt action and consult your vet immediately for advice (see page 95 for further information).

Outdoor hazards

Once your kitten has completed its primary vaccinations (see page 87) and can safely go outdoors, it will face a multitude of dangers that you will obviously have less chance of controlling than inside your house. Roads can be a major problem, and, although you can reduce the risk somewhat by keeping your kitten in at night, you will have to hope that the kitten learns how to cope with potential dangers for itself to a great extent (see also pages 75–6).

Another possible problem can arise when an inquisitive kitten that is learning to hunt tries to catch wasps and bees, especially if the insects are trapped against a windowpane. The kitten may be stung as a result of these attempts, but this does not usually cause any long-term damage, and the kitten will certainly learn by its mistakes. A kitten that enjoys hunting frogs may also occasionally pick up a toad instead and be treated to a mouthful of a vile-tasting slime, causing it to salivate and shake its head to try to get rid of the taste. However, this is not usually dangerous, and the kitten will soon learn to tell a toad from a frog – or, better still, to avoid them both.

CHAPTER SIX

BRINGING YOUR KITTEN HOME

When you first bring your new kitten home, you will need to decide how to organize its equipment, how to settle it in, and how and when you are going to introduce it to other members of the household – human or animal. Just how you manage all these aspects can have a major influence on your kitten's confidence and future harmonious relationships, so it is very important to get them right from the start.

COMING HOME

The day you bring your kitten home will be one of the biggest challenges of its life. It is unlikely ever to have been in a carrier, let alone in a car, so you must ensure that it is safe, warm, and secure. Line the carrier with newspaper to absorb urine, then add some washable bedding or (ideally) a piece of bedding from the kitten's old home to make everything seem less strange. Lift the kitten into the carrier, and secure the lid.

A secure carrier (see page 46) is a vital piece of equipment for transporting kittens. Sturdy plastic ones are also available.

Ask the breeder, owner, or animal welfare society to give you a diet sheet containing details of the kitten's current diet and mealtimes. You should also find out what type of litter has been used, and where the kitten has been accustomed to sleeping. Ask whether the kitten has been wormed and vaccinated (see pages 87 and 91–2); if so, ask for the vaccination record card so that you can give it to your vet.

If you have bought a pedigree kitten, make sure before you leave that you have its pedigree certificate, and that the kitten has been registered with the appropriate organization. If you wish to show your cat, you will also need to arrange for a transfer certificate or registration document to show the change of ownership.

Traveling home

Do not feed the kitten just before the journey, in case it turns out not to be a good traveler. If the journey is to be a long one, you should provide a litter box.

If you are traveling by car and the weather is warm, offer some water at regular intervals and NEVER leave the kitten without adequate ventilation. The temperature inside a car can build up rapidly, and overheating can be fatal. Place the kitten's carrier in a footwell, or on the back seat secured with a seat belt, so that it cannot be catapulted forward should you have to brake suddenly. The kitten may well urinate on the way home because of the whole new frightening experience, so place something waterproof under the carrier. If you are traveling a long distance, it may be useful to pack some wet wipes in case the kitten makes a mess. If you are prepared for the worst, you are bound to have a trouble-free journey!

The kitten may make an awful noise and cry pitifully on the way home. However, try not to worry: if it is warm and secure, it can come to no harm, so concentrate on getting home safely and quickly. Covering the carrier to darken the interior may help to calm some kittens. When you get home, ensure that all doors and windows are shut tightly before you let the kitten out of the carrier.

YOUR KITTEN'S FIRST NIGHT

Kittens vary in their responses to spending the first night in their new homes. A few simply saunter in with a street-wise swagger and take over the dog's quarters, but most need time to familiarize themselves with the unfamiliar surroundings. Cats feel most secure in a small, warm environment, and your kitten may feel somewhat afraid if simply placed on the floor and expected to take everything in – do not forget how gigantic furniture and people must seem to a tiny kitten.

Ideally, you will have prepared a small, warm, and cozy place containing your kitten's bed, where the kitten will spend its first night with you. This could be a crate or pen (see page 49), or simply a special area that

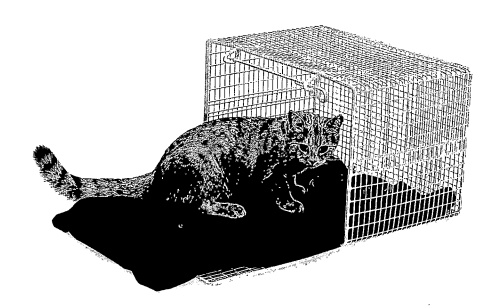

If your kitten dislikes being put in its carrier, try leaving the carrier open on its side, lining it with some soft bedding, and feeding the kitten inside from time to time so that it becomes accustomed to it.

the kitten can call its own. Allocating a small area in this way has several advantages. Your kitten will be out of the way, and so not overly disturbed by the hustle and bustle of people going to bed or getting up in the morning. It also means that you will have a good night's rest, knowing that the kitten is secure.

If you have brought a piece of bedding from the kitten's old home, place this in the bed to offer an olfactory reminder of its mother and littermates in this strange environment. Offer your kitten a little of the food to which it is accustomed, and fill up its water bowl. Your kitten should also become used to wearing its collar from the start, so gently put this on, ensuring that it is sufficiently loose for you to slip one finger beneath it.

Remember that your kitten will need a chance to relieve itself. Gently lifting it into the litter box every few hours before bed will help it to learn where the box is and remind it to go to the toilet. (If your kitten has an "accident" elsewhere, you must be sure to clean it up very thoroughly – see page 85.) Place the box where the kitten can reach it during the night, but a good distance from its bed and food.

Most kittens are only too happy to fall into an exhausted sleep on this first night, but a few do cry or become restless. Offer a little vocal comfort if necessary, but try to avoid smuggling the kitten under your blanket unless you want to continue this practice for the rest of its life.

Encouraging the kitten to adapt to your waking and sleeping hours is a sensible routine to establish from day one. Felines are naturally crepuscular – they are usually most active at dawn and dusk – but this does not mean that they cannot adapt to a different regime. Cats are perhaps more at risk of being hit by a car if they go out at night, and are also more likely to be involved in fights with other cats during evening and night-time periods. Keeping your kitten in at night but allowing it out during the day may be a good compromise between safety and stimulation in many circumstances (see also Chapter Seven).

After a long night's rest, most kittens wake refreshed and ready for the new day. This may be early, particularly if the kitten has not eaten for some time. Try to encourage use of the litter box immediately after waking, and also after eating. Your kitten will now be ready to explore its new environment.

VISITING YOUR VET

It is a good idea to make an appointment for your kitten to see your vet at an early stage. You could arrange this for the day you collect your kitten, but, with all the new experiences the kitten is already having to face, it may be more sensible to wait until the following day.

This visit will allow your vet to examine your kitten thoroughly to ensure that it is not suffering from any developmental problems, and to vaccinate it and give an initial worming dose if necessary (if your kitten is a pedigree, it may already have been vaccinated – see page 87).

If your kitten does need vaccinating, it will not be fully protected for seven to 10 days (although it may still have some natural immunity to disease, passed on by its mother) so, if you have other cats in the house, you may want to keep them separated from the kitten for this period. In any case, the introductions between them should only take place very gradually, as described on pages 64–8.

SETTLING IN

Your kitten will probably be keen to explore its new surroundings, but take things slowly. Your supervision of this process should be not only practical but enjoyable, as it will help to strengthen the bond that is already starting to form between you and the kitten. Introduce your kitten to one new room at a time. Talk reassuringly, and allow the kitten to investigate new objects, sights, and smells at its own pace – the smaller the space to be explored, the braver it is likely to be.

Try not to panic if your kitten jumps down behind the sofa or wants to explore under the sideboard – the worst thing you can do is to chase it around the room or drag it from under an object where it was resting briefly. If you do need to retrieve the kitten quickly, try luring it out by pulling along a piece of string in front of its nose or calling it for some food. Again, this creates good habits for the future. Provided that you have closed all windows, blocked off any escape routes, and taken other sensible precautions, the kitten should not come to any harm.

HANDLING

Kittens tend to fall into two distinct groups: those that like to be stroked, petted, and given tactile affection from people, and those that like to play. This generally means that kittens in the first group also take to being picked up and handled with no problem, while those in the second group are more play-oriented and will need a little more experience of being handled.

All cats and kittens are well equipped to demonstrate that they are unhappy about being picked up, and may employ their claws and teeth to defend themselves before attempting to run away. Even cats that like to be picked up and gently held tend to want to be there

To pick up your kitten, gently scoop it up under the chest with one hand while supporting its hindquarters with the other.

just for brief periods (and then only if they know and trust the person concerned), so you should aim to build up your kitten's confidence gradually.

The correct method for picking up your kitten is to scoop it up under the chest area with one hand, while supporting its hindquarters with the other. If you need to carry the kitten, keep your hand under its chest with your fingers between its forelegs, then close your arm into your side so that the kitten's weight is supported by your body. This will leave your other hand free to hold the kitten's head gently, or to restrain it gently by the scruff in an emergency.

Some cats discover that an excellent way to gain attention is by leaping onto their owners from a height, or by jumping onto their

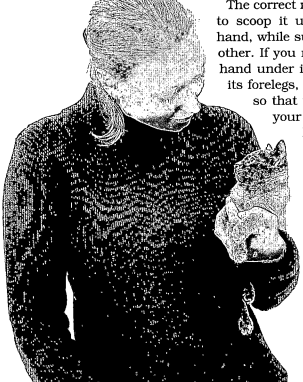

Carry the kitten by keeping your hand underneath its chest and your fingers between its forelegs, and support its weight next to your body.

laps with all claws extended. It may be difficult, but the only way to extinguish this sort of obnoxious behavior is simply to get up immediately and walk away without looking at, talking to, or touching the kitten. It must learn that only initiating attention gently will achieve what it wants.

When introducing children to the kitten, sit them on the floor and then allow the kitten to investigate them in its own time. Encourage the children to stroke the kitten gently.

FAMILY INTRODUCTIONS

The next important step is to introduce your kitten to all the other residents in the house. Even if the kitten has already been used to living with another dog, or with an adult cat, do not assume that it will immediately accept your pets as well. Nor, indeed, should you take it for granted that your pets will welcome a new kitten wholeheartedly. A little time spent preparing the animals for a harmonious life together at the start of the relationship really will be worth the time and effort.

Introducing children

As we all know, children are not the same as adults – they move, talk, sound, and even smell different. Caring for pets and learning about their needs, likes, and dislikes fills a vital and educational niche in many children's lives, but they do need to be taught how to care for their pets, and how to handle them gently and in a non-threatening way. If your kitten has been brought up in a household full of children, it is unlikely to react fearfully when it meets the younger members of your family. However, if it has come from a quiet, adult-only household, meeting children for the first time may be quite a shock.

Introductions should always be gradual, gentle, and very quiet, as any sudden movements or unexpected loud noises are likely to scare the kitten. It is often better to ask a child to sit down on the floor and wait for the kitten to approach him or her to investigate. Ask the child to offer a small food treat and then to stroke the kitten very gently in areas where you know it likes being touched, such as on its back.

Discourage children from picking up the kitten, since, especially if it is wriggling, they may easily squeeze it too hard around the abdomen and put it off being carried for life. Instead, encourage the kitten to climb onto a child's lap and to remain there briefly to be petted or given a morsel of tasty food. The kitten should not be restrained during these encounters, and children need to be taught to allow the kitten to walk away freely if and when it wishes.

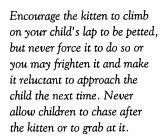

Encourage the kitten to climb on your child's lap to be petted, but never force it to do so or you may frighten it and make it reluctant to approach the child the next time. Never allow children to chase after the kitten or to grab at it.

Similarly, you must prevent all children – particularly toddlers – from chasing your kitten. The sight of a fleeing tail seems too much for some children to resist, but is a sure way to put the kitten off a child for some time to come. Equally, the kitten should be able to rest in its favorite spot or in its bed without being pestered, as nervousness and fearful behavior are fueled by lack of sleep and unpredictable attacks from others. Naturally, children want to explore their new pet and to establish a relationship, but poking it in the ear or trying to examine its teeth while it is asleep is not the best way to do so.

Having said all this, if the introductions are carried out carefully, most children and cats become the best of friends. Many kittens bond quickly with the youngsters in a household, and seem happy to play with them, curl up with them, and "help" them with their homework!

Introducing an older cat

You may decide to get a new kitten when a previous cat has died, leaving another by itself, or when your present cat is getting on in years. Alternatively, you may simply want to provide an adult cat with some feline company – typically, owners of one loving pet cat who decide to get another do so not for themselves, but as a companion for their pet. It is therefore somewhat ironic that an adult cat may have different ideas about a new kitten, and may not be at all pleased at its arrival.

Think about meeting someone new yourself. Would you rush into his or her home, sit on the furniture, lie on the beds, and eat his or her food without even being asked? If you did, you would be unlikely to be invited back. Meeting another person for the first time requires social rules to be observed. We shake hands, smile, and keep our distance, and such conventions give us time to sum each other up before forming any kind of relationship.

The same principle is true for a domestic cat, which needs time, space, and social rules to discover that the other party is not a threat to itself or to its resources. These elements need to be controlled – simply bringing a new kitten into the house, placing it on the floor, and expecting the cats to get along may result in hissing, growling, spitting, or a dust-up behind the television set, and will not bode well for a good future relationship.

So what is the best way to shake hands and smile in cat language? Carefully, is the answer. Not many cats will instantly welcome a feline "intruder" into their territory, so it is up to you to make both kitten and adult cat feel as secure and comfortable as possible. It is also essential that you prevent the kitten from being chased, cornered, or otherwise assaulted. The ideal way to achieve this is to use a kittening pen or indoor crate (see page 49). Such protection works to the benefit of both cats. With the kitten confined in a pen, the adult cat has the opportunity to investigate, to take in the kitten's scent, and to assimilate the fact that it is here to stay without feeling that its food, resting places, or territory may be threatened. Equally, the kitten remains secure. It is also prevented from running away – which could well trigger an attack by the adult cat – and from disappearing under the guest room bed for a week or two while it regains its confidence.

Introducing a kitten to an older cat must be carried out very carefully, or it may lead to conflict. Using a crate or pen (see pages 66–7) will prevent the cat from chasing the kitten, and allow calm investigation.

Keeping the kitten in a pen or crate at first also means that both cats have a chance to see and smell each other, but with a tangible barrier between them. This means that they are not forced into unnatural social contact with each other, but can sum each other up at a distance. Of course, the protective bars also mean that the kitten will be safe if the adult cat does decide to launch an attack. In turn, you will not become injured while trying to separate the warring factions, but will be able to intervene without confrontation. If a pen or crate is not available, a plastic-coated wire-mesh carrier (see page 46) makes a good alternative, and will allow all-around vision.

Always supervise both cats during the introductions. Watch the body language of each closely, and try to spot the danger signs that one may be about to attack. Generally, flattened ears, a low body posture, and wide, staring eyes with dilated pupils indicate fear. A stiff body, a "pounce" posture, a fixed stare with narrowed pupils, and a lashing tail all show tension and the threat of aggression. Cats often "freeze" in this way in novel or frightening situations, and it usually precedes a "fight or flight" response. If it becomes necessary to interrupt the cats' behavior, use a remote interruption – such as a sudden noise – but pretend that it has not come from you. The aim is to make the cats think that their own behavior caused the interruption, making them less likely to repeat it.

The step-by-step instructions given below should help you to introduce your new kitten and cat with the minimum of fuss. However, only time will tell whether these careful preparations have really paid off. Despite the best intentions and great care, some cats never learn to curl up together, wash each other behind the ears, or become great friends. Personality types play a great part in all social interactions – human and feline – and it is impossible to ensure that all people, or all cats, will love each other. Sadly, friendship can never be guaranteed.

Stress-free introductions, step-by-step

Remember that all cats are different. Some may require only a brief period of introduction; others may take longer to accept each other.

1 Accustom the kitten to spending short periods in the pen, crate, or carrier. Initially, you should place this somewhere above ground level – such as on a table – so that, when the time comes, both cats can see each other but are not forced into direct eye contact on the floor.

2 Bring your adult cat into the room. Make sure that it feels secure by talking to it and giving it your affection all the time that it is being non-confrontational. Ignore the kitten for the time being, as this will help to ease any "jealousies" over the new arrival. Give your kitten affection and contact when the other cat is not around to see it. In the cat's presence, your kitten will probably prefer to be ignored rather than be forced into a jealous confrontation by your attention.

3 Allow the adult cat to investigate the kitten more closely. If it decides to depart to the nearest shelf to examine the newcomer from a distance, accept that this is your cat's way of coping. Never try to force a meeting

between cats, because they will need to establish a relationship in their own time. Introductions like this should be both brief and positive. A few minutes of controlled, gentle introduction, several times a day, will be far better than long, tense periods of confrontation.

4 If possible, employ a "remote" distraction to interrupt any signs of aggression between the two cats. Making a loud noise by dropping a bunch of keys is usually enough to achieve this, provided that you intervene before a full-scale attack occurs.

Once you have carried out the initial introductions with the kitten in the pen, reverse the situation by placing the older cat inside. The body postures of this pair show that they are still unsure of each other, and will need more time to adjust.

5 With the kitten still confined, feed both cats – at opposite ends of the room – with some extra-special food (cats are more likely to eat when relaxed, so this will be a useful indicator as to their emotional states).

6 Gradually move the adult cat's food bowl closer and closer to the kitten's pen or crate. Watch for nonchalant body postures in both cats – a willingness to eat in close proximity will indicate calmness in one another's company.

7 Move the pen around the room, and then around the rest of the house. Place it on floor level and feed the cats close together again.

8 In between these short, sweet introductions, keep the two cats apart. Play with your kitten in the other rooms of the house to ensure that its scent is as widespread as possible in the older cat's territory. In a natural situation a new cat wanting to join a group would "visit" intermittently when the other cats were absent, to leave its smell for the others to detect; this allows gradual familiarity without confrontation.

9 Do not be in too much of a hurry to allow the cats a face-to-face meeting. As part of the process, it can be helpful to place the existing cat in the pen or crate while the newcomer is free to wander in the same room.

10 When you feel that they are ready, allow the cats to meet in one room, with the door closed. Prepare for this first "free" meeting carefully. Delaying both cats' mealtimes so they can be fed together with some extra-tasty food often helps to defuse the situation. Place the bowls some distance apart, and stand by with a means of interrupting any antagonistic behavior, just in case. Make sure that the established cat has a place of safety to jump up to if it feels threatened.

11 Graduate to supervised meetings between the cats in other parts of the house, allowing the kitten greater freedom (if you have a pet door, remember to shut it first).

12 Once you are confident that the cats are happy with each other, leave them alone for short and then longer periods, until you no longer need to supervise them.

Introducing a dog

Contrary to popular myth, dogs and cats can become great companions, greeting each other, resting, and even playing together. This kind of positive relationship is usually the outcome of broad early experience and good socialization for both species, but can also be achieved by careful and patient introductions.

If you are unsure as to how your dog will react to a kitten in the household, it will be a very good idea – and may save you a great deal of potential worry in the long run – if you carry out a little research beforehand. For example, some breeds or types of dog – such as some greyhounds – may never cope

A pen or crate also comes in very useful when introducing a dog. You may need to confine the kitten for the first few days or even weeks when the dog is about, until you are sure that they are used to each other.

with the temptation of small quarry in the house. In such a case, it may be sensible to let your dog spend some time with an older cat that is quite used to being around dogs, before deciding to bring home your own kitten.

Even a Corgi can look big to a kitten. This situation should be avoided: the kitten has arched its back and is hissing, which could provoke an attack.

Think, too, about your dog's character. In possibly stressful or unfamiliar situations, does it tend to exhibit high excitement, intense frustration, or even fear? Consider the reality of having a kitten, confined to the house for the first two or three weeks, being trailed around by your panting, ever-hopeful pooch. Think about how tolerant the dog will be of a newcomer investigating its food, its toys, and its bed – your kitten will get everywhere once it feels secure in its new environment. If your dog is likely to be upset by the kitten's activities, you will need to take the introduction very gradually in order to build up confidence on both sides.

Most dogs chase cats because they are excited by the thrill of the hunt, rather than because they actually intend to cause real bodily harm. Keeping the kitten secure and unable to run away is therefore the best policy in the early stages of introduction. Confine the kitten to a large pen or crate (see page 49) for the first few days or even weeks while the dog is about, to allow each animal to sum the other up and to cope with the new smells, sights, and sounds with the protection of bars between them.

Once you are happy that the dog and kitten are used to one another's presence, short and frequent meetings carried out under your close supervision – just as when introducing another cat – are required. Only allow the animals access to each other once they appear to be completely relaxed in one another's company. For these first meetings, keep the dog on a lead and make sure that the kitten always has a clear escape route available.

Your kitten and a new baby

Cats and babies together seem to have created more urban myths than any other combination of animal and human. Some visiting nurses and even a few doctors seem keen to perpetuate tales of woe surrounding pets and the new addition to the family but, as with so many issues in life, common sense is all that is actually required. Indeed, there are so many health issues to worry about with pregnancy that it is important to keep them in perspective. Domestic cats offer no more potential risks than any other pet in the average household, and basic, sensible precautions will eliminate those risks altogether.

Expectant mothers are warned about health risks, particularly from infection. *Toxoplasma gondii* is a protozoan parasite that can be passed to humans (a cat may carry the parasite, having eaten infected wildlife, and pass it via its feces). This means that it is sensible for a pregnant woman to wear gloves when gardening and when emptying or cleaning litter boxes – or, of course, to ask someone else to do it.

However, cats are not the sole source of toxoplasmosis: it can also be transmitted via undercooked meat or vegetables grown in contaminated soil. If you are concerned about the risks, it may be sensible to ask your doctor to run a blood test to show whether you are immune to the infection (immunity means that there is no danger of passing the infection to a fetus; lack of immunity simply means that you have not been infected previously, making sensible hygiene precautions a priority).

Keeping your kitten away from work surfaces on which food or bottles are to be prepared, as well as regular hand-washing after handling the kitten, are basic necessities in any household.

Once the baby is born, common sense is again the order of the day. Parents are often concerned by stories suggesting that a kitten may climb into the crib or carriage and suffocate the child by lying on it, but this is very unlikely. Cats do like to snuggle into small, warm areas, and a human-oriented cat may want to curl up with the new member of the family, but basic precautions mean that for the very short time that a baby is unable to turn over or move itself, there should be no need to worry. Ensuring that the kitten is not left alone in the same room as a very young baby, or fitting a cat net (available from baby-care stores) over the baby's crib or carriage will offer peace of mind.

Your kitten may cope with the arrival of a new baby in a number of ways. Some cats seem to want to be involved, sniffing the baby and its clothing and equipment. Others seem to disappear and want nothing to do with the strange creature. Whichever option your kitten chooses, prepare it for the baby's arrival by thinking ahead. If you have developed a close bond with your kitten, cool the relationship slightly before the baby's birth, so that it will not be such a shock to the kitten when it is suddenly demoted by the amount of time that a new baby demands. Learning to cope without constant contact also means that your kitten is less likely to associate the new arrival with a reduction in attention.

CHAPTER SEVEN

YOUR KITTEN'S LIFESTYLE

The idea of keeping a cat indoors throughout its life may seem very unnatural to many people. However, if you live in a large town or city, the dangers of allowing your kitten to go outside will be fairly high. Even on country roads with little traffic, cats seem to manage to get run over and are injured or killed, and it is thought that about 40 percent of feline deaths are caused by such accidents. Many of these cats are young – often under one year old – and not quite "street-wise."

Some cats – particularly of the quieter and less active breeds (see Chapter Two) – take to indoor life quite happily, but they need plenty of mental and physical stimulation.

You may feel that your kitten simply has to live as nature intended and to take its chances outdoors, but some people, having already suffered several losses, decide to keep their cats indoors. Alternatively, as a compromise between stimulation and safety, you could take the kitten out on a harness and lead.

The following information discusses the practicalities of all these different options, and gives tips on how to tackle some of the possible problems that may arise.

KEEPING YOUR KITTEN IN

Many cats – particularly breeds with a placid temperament, such as the Persian – will take to indoor life quite happily. However, just as some humans are very much the outdoor type while others are happy to stay in, if you keep your kitten indoors, you will have to judge over a period of time how well it is coping with the restriction. If you decide to take

the indoor option, you should do so from day one. While a cat kept indoors from kitten-hood can learn to go outside, it would be very unfair to make an outdoor cat stay in and would be likely to cause great frustration. You must therefore be clear in your own mind as to how you wish to keep your kitten before you bring it home, bearing in mind the following potential problems:

If you live in an apartment above ground level, or if you wish to keep your kitten indoors for any other reason, you may need to make your home "cat-proof." Bars or screens are another option, but remember that a small kitten will be able to squeeze through the tiniest of gaps.

• The cat is a natural hunter, and has great energies and abilities to be used in this pursuit (see pages 113–16). If your kitten is not allowed to venture outdoors, it could become frustrated and develop behavioral problems such as scratching the furniture or indulging in wild bouts of running around the house.

• The lack of exercise may cause your kitten to become overweight if you do not pay very careful attention to its diet.

• The kitten may become bored, and also lonely if you are out all day.

• It may become overreactive to changes within its small territory (your house), and therefore unable to cope with novelty – whether in the form of people or of objects brought in.

• There will be a much greater dependence on you for stimulation and activity, and a risk of overattachment.

• If your kitten does get out, it may be disoriented and will not have any "street" skills. If you keep the kitten in a high-rise apartment, the dangers of a fall resulting from an attempt to escape are obvious.
• If you have only one cat, it may be very difficult to introduce another at a later stage into your first cat's restricted territory, as there will be no neutral ground to which either party can retire.

Minimizing problems

You can take active steps to reduce or eliminate many of the above problems, by the following means:
• Keep your kitten entertained. A solitary cat kept entirely indoors will often center its waking and active time around the comings and goings of its owners, so you will have to spend time interacting with it and catering to its hunting and social needs. This is especially important with some of the more doglike, socially demanding breeds such as the Siamese and Burmese, which form very strong attachments to their owners. Indeed, some individuals may even begin to overgroom or self-mutilate due to the stress of being left alone with insufficient stimulation. You must therefore be continually creative and produce new toys and games to keep your kitten exercised – both physically and mentally. Kittens and cats love newspaper "tents," cardboard boxes, and paper bags, not to mention the various play centers and climbing frames that are now commercially available.
• Monitor your kitten's food intake to ensure that it does not put on excess weight, either through lack of exercise or due to overeating because of boredom. Make the kitten "work" and forage for food by placing dried cat tidbits in, under, or behind objects to encourage it to be active and to simulate "hunting."
• Try to ensure that you have regular visitors and that life is not too quiet – especially when your kitten is small – because this is what it will come to see as normal. As the kitten's whole world may consist of two or three rooms in an apartment, it is important to avoid hypersensitivity to change, and human or animal visitors can potentially introduce huge novelty in the day-to-day environment.
• Your kitten will need to act out its normal behavioral repertoire within your home. One of these natural and important activities is scratching. Even an outdoor kitten – which may well choose a tree in the garden or a special post for this – should have a scratching post in the house, and this is essential for an indoor kitten unless you are willing to let your carpets and furniture suffer. (For detailed information on scratching posts, refer to pages 51–2.) Let your kitten play around the post, and drape toys over it for the kitten to swat at so that it becomes used to the post and to climbing around it. Then gently lift the kitten's front paws and rub them against the post to introduce the idea of what to do. This will also deposit some scent from the glands between the kitten's footpads on the post, and so encourage it to use the post again.

• Try to accept that your house may not always stay looking at its best, especially when your kitten is at the "running around the walls and up the curtains" stage. Put away any precious ornaments, even if they are fairly high up – you need to imagine that you have a toddler who can fly! Choose a litter box big enough for the kitten to scratch about in and become used to – the hooded type may be better than an open box, as this will prevent spillage. These boxes also often contain air fresheners, to help keep smells at bay.

• Have two kittens instead of one right from the start. Another cat will bring change and interaction, and is highly preferable if cats are kept permanently indoors. It will also help to reduce your sense of guilt at leaving one kitten on its own when you go out. Having two kittens will relieve you of some of the burden of providing stimulation and exercise, as they will happily wear each other out playing and then collapse together in a heap (see also pages 13–14).

• An outdoor cat will nibble on grass and herbs as part of its diet (one reason for this may be that it assists in the regurgitation of hairballs). You should provide grass indoors (seed kits are available from pet stores), and perhaps catnip (see page 52), thyme, sage, or parsley. You can even grow cereal grasses such as wheat and oats in a potting mixture. Sow every two to three weeks so that there is always a fresh supply for your kitten.

• Invest in some good claw clippers designed specifically for cats (see page 100). Your kitten's claws may not wear down as quickly as they would if it walked on hard surfaces outdoors, and long claws also have a tendency to become snagged in carpets and upholstery. If you are not confi-dent about cutting your kitten's claws, ask your vet or a professional groomer for a demonstration of how to restrain your kitten and use the clippers correctly.

Grass and herbs form a small but important part of the cat's natural diet outdoors, so you should provide a regular supply indoors for your kitten. Seed kits are available from pet stores and garden centers.

• Ensure that your home is "cat-proof," especially if you live several stories up. Put wire mesh over the windows, and train everyone in the family to keep all external doors shut. An inquisitive and bored kitten will be able to get through a very small hole, or may work persistently at an edge until it gives way.

LETTING YOUR KITTEN OUT

Giving cats the freedom to roam outdoors is to many people the natural course of action, and will allow them to lead active and stimulating lives. The cat is one of the most successfully adapted hunters in the animal kingdom today, and its shape, size, and personality have developed accordingly. Most cats will continue to hunt – and sometimes to eat their prey – even when plenty of food is offered to them at home (see pages 113–16), and many owners feel that this natural activity must be respected.

A safe open window is one way to provide outdoor access for your kitten whenever you wish; alternatively, a pet door fitted in a suitable door or window (see page 78) will be a very good option.

However, the following are just some of the potential dangers that an outdoor cat may face on its daily excursions.

• Traffic on the roads – the risk of your kitten becoming involved in an accident will obviously be greater the nearer you live to a road and the busier it is, especially at night, when the kitten may be "blinded" by car headlights.

• Your kitten may be injured in an encounter with a dog, with a wild predator (such as a fox), or even with a person.

• It faces the risk of infection with a number of serious feline diseases when meeting other (mainly feral or uncared-for) cats (see pages 89–91); the risk involved here will depend to some extent on where you live.

• There will be a risk of catching disease (such as toxoplasmosis – see page 70) and worms (see pages 91–2) from eating infested prey.

• The kitten could be affected by eating poisoned prey.

• Fights with other cats could lead to injury.

• The kitten could become shut in someone's outbuilding or garage, or stranded in a tree or on top of a roof.

• On its travels, the kitten could be regularly taken in and fed by another well-meaning person or cat lover, and could eventually make the decision to move in with them instead.

The "natural" cat, allowed unlimited access outdoors in a safe rural environment, has perhaps the best life of all, and is happy to sunbathe during the day and to hunt at night.

Minimizing the risks

You will reduce the risks of allowing your kitten outdoors by taking the following steps.

• Let your kitten out during the day but perhaps keep it in at night, which is a more dangerous time for cats to be outdoors because of the presence of other, wild animals and traffic on the roads (see page 75). A reflective or fluorescent collar (available from pet stores) will be a good idea, especially in the dark winter months. Dawn and dusk are the most common times for cat fights to take place, so make sure that your kitten is indoors at these times.

• Encourage your kitten to come inside during the busiest times on the road – such as the rush hour in the morning and evening – perhaps by making these its regular feeding times.

• Ensure that your kitten is protected against all the infectious diseases for which vaccines are available (your vet will advise you on this; see also page 87).

• Worm your kitten regularly. This is especially important if it is a prolific hunter, as roundworm eggs eaten by earthworms, beetles, rodents or birds may in turn infest the kitten (see also pages 91–2).

• Ensure that your kitten is wearing a collar with identification details, or has had a microchip inserted or a tattoo made (see pages 50–1). If someone finds the kitten simply wandering, injured, or trapped in an outbuilding, he or she can then contact you more easily.

• Have your kitten neutered, as the risks to intact animals are much greater than to neutered ones. An unneutered tom may wander for long distances and will be much more likely to fight other cats over territorial rights, causing greater risk of disease; an unspayed queen may become pregnant (see also pages 150–3).

Letting your kitten out for the first time

All kittens must stay indoors for a period when they first move to their new homes. Even if you have decided to allow your kitten outdoors, you will need to wait until it has completed its course of primary vaccinations (see page 87). If your kitten has already been fully vaccinated by the time you bring it home, you must still keep it in for a minimum of two to three weeks so that it can become accustomed and bonded to its new home.

The day of "freedom" in the outside world can be nerve-wracking for owners. Cats can jump or climb over most garden fences, and even the best-laid plans can go awry when a kitten finds a tiny hole and decides to squeeze through it. If you do not have a garden, or fencing, it may be sensible only to allow your kitten out on a harness and lead at first (see pages 78 and 138–9).

Prior planning of the first excursion into the garden will help to ease your anxiety and help to direct your kitten's behavior in the correct way. Firstly, make the excursion early in the day so that if your kitten does decide to go on a wander, it will have plenty of time to return before dark. Next, make sure that the kitten is hungry. If you plan to allow it out first thing in the morning, get up and encourage it to use the litter box, but do not feed it. Cooking some food that has a strong and alluring odor – such as fish – may help to whet the kitten's appetite so that it will be keen to come back inside to eat.

When you are ready, open the door (or pet door), step outside, and encourage your kitten to follow by calling it to you and crouching down. Wait with the kitten all the time it is taking in the new surroundings. Walk with it around the garden, talking gently and encouragingly all the time. Spend a few minutes sitting with your kitten, playing with it or watching it explore. It is sometimes suggested that a new kitten should be carried out into the garden and then placed on the ground, rather than walking outside itself. However, cats have scent glands between their footpads, and it is important that they have the opportunity to make an immediate and essential scent trail back to the door.

After some time, encourage your kitten to follow you indoors again, using the same strategy as before. Once the kitten is inside, feed it immediately with the delicious food you have prepared, then play a game together or allow it to rest.

Over a period of days your kitten's confidence about venturing outdoors will increase, and this is when basic "recall" training will be extremely useful. If your kitten has learned to come when called (see pages 133–5), it will be willing and happy to come back indoors for a tasty food treat or a meal, even if out of sight.

Do not panic if the kitten decides to broaden its horizons at some time in the future. Feline territories sometimes spread over quite an extensive area, and your kitten will merely be joining the ranks of adult cats out and about. While this means exposure to some risks outside the home, your kitten's enjoyment of the sights, smells, and sounds of the real world remains a substantial reason why so many of us keep this enigmatic and fiercely independent creature.

Fitting a pet door

If you decide that you will allow your kitten outdoors, you may well opt for the convenience of a pet door. This could simply be a hole in a door or window, covered with a piece of plastic to keep out drafts, or a custom-made hinged pet door that swings in both directions. A two-way locking device will give you some control over your kitten's movements – for instance, so that it can come in but not go out at night.

If other cats in the neighborhood are likely to come into your house and cause havoc, a magnetic pet door is a good idea. Your kitten will

then wear a magnet on its collar, which acts as a "key" for the door when the kitten comes within range. However, a great many cat owners now use these magnets, so, if you live in a very cat-dense area, you may wish to invest in an electronic pet door that will open solely in response to your kitten's personalized electronic key, again kept attached to its collar.

If you cannot offer your kitten free access outdoors but would like to give it some fresh air, walking it on a harness and lead may be one possibility; this can be a good compromise between allowing your kitten to roam outdoors and keeping it indoors full time. However, accustoming a cat to wearing a harness outdoors requires slow and careful training, and some individuals – such as the Burmese (shown here) and the Siamese, which show more doglike characteristics – may take to the experience more readily than others.

Using a harness and lead

One possible compromise between allowing your kitten to roam outdoors at will and keeping it confined indoors all the time, and an option that is chosen by some owners, is to train your kitten to walk on a harness and lead, so that you can take safe walks into your garden or in a park together. However, while cats of some breeds – most notably the Siamese and Burmese – will take well to this experience, others will not.

If you decide to take this option, you will need to train your kitten very carefully to accept the use of a harness and lead (see pages 138–9). Even if you feel that your kitten is completely happy in a harness, it is really only advisable either to walk in your garden, or perhaps in a quiet park. If the kitten were suddenly frightened, you might be badly scratched in your efforts to keep control.

CHAPTER EIGHT

FEEDING AND LITTER TRAINING

Some owners firmly believe that feeding a kitten involves no more than simply opening a can or a bag of dry food, but when, where, and what you feed your kitten can actually make a vital difference to its general health and well-being. Before you consider exactly what you would like to feed, it is therefore worth taking a moment or two to learn about your kitten's very special nutritional requirements. Your kitten's toileting habits are also important, and providing a suitable litter box and teaching the kitten how to use it correctly are two of the most basic necessities of good cat care and ownership.

A young kitten grows rapidly, and needs specially formulated, good-quality kitten food if it is to turn into a well-developed, healthy adult cat.

FEEDING YOUR KITTEN

Cats have evolved to become highly efficient hunters, and, because of their success in feeding themselves on prey, they have not needed to rely on vegetable matter as a source of nutrition. They do, however, require very specific forms of nutrients found only in animal tissue (examples are vitamin A and niacin). They also need high levels of dietary protein with the correct balance of amino acids. For instance, the animo-acid derivative taurine is vital for a cat's eyesight, and this must come directly from an animal source – it cannot be manufactured from other materials.

Like humans and most mammals, cats use protein in food to build body tissue and carry out "repairs," and for other biological actions such as making hormones. However, they also use protein in the way that we use carbohydrates – as a source of daily calories, or energy – so the type, quality, and proportion of protein in their diets, which can only be obtained from animal tissue, are very important. Certain fats must also be provided directly in the diet from animal fat in milk, meat, or fish. In short, cats are what are known as "obligate carnivores" – they must eat meat and cannot live on a vegetarian diet.

When to feed

When a pet cat feeds itself by hunting, it is unlikely to kill prey large enough to allow it to eat only once or twice a day, as most catches will be small rodents or birds. Cats are more naturally "snackers," and will eat 10 to 20 small meals a day.

If you give your kitten dry food on a "free-choice" basis, you will notice it returning to the bowl many times during the day for a quick snack, rather than working its way through the food at one sitting. Cats fed on moist food do tend to eat bigger meals (this type of food becomes unpalatable and dry fairly quickly if left uneaten, so your kitten may choose to eat more when the can is freshly opened and the flavor, taste, and smell of the food are at their most potent), but most would probably prefer small and frequent meals to one large bowlful given at the end of the day. In fact, cats often do not let us get away with infrequent feeding and demand more every time we go into the kitchen.

A kitten needs small, frequent meals in order to be able to ingest and digest enough nutrients to grow rapidly, and must therefore be fed much more frequently than an adult cat. When you first get your kitten at eight to 12 weeks of age, it will need about five meals a day. If you are out during the daytime, one way to manage this is to provide dry food, which can be left for the kitten to help itself as it likes. If you prefer to use moist canned food, you may want to

Give your kitten small meals at frequent intervals, rather than larger amounts once or twice a day. With time, the number of meals can be reduced.

invest in an automatic feeder – this is a dish in which the food will remain covered until a pre-set time, when the lid will open and allow the kitten access to it.

By the time your kitten is six months old – and about 75 percent of its full size – you can reduce mealtimes to twice a day. (If you are feeding dry food on a "free-choice" basis, your kitten will obviously continue to decide how many meals it wishes to eat every day.)

Where to feed

You should feed your kitten in a quiet spot where there will be no competition from other cats and no likelihood of the food being stolen by a dog, and where there will be no other interruptions. Be sure to place your kitten's feeding bowl well away from its litter box (see pages 83–4).

Commercially produced kitten and cat foods are available in three forms: moist (above), semi-moist (below left, top), and dry (below left, bottom).

What to feed

Making any sudden dietary alteration can cause a stomach upset, so, for the first few days, keep to the food to which your kitten is accustomed, before changing gradually to another food if you wish.

It is important to feed a diet that has been formulated specifically for the rapid growth period of a kitten's first few months of life. Most of the major food manufacturers make a kitten food designed for the first six months of life. Choose a good-quality one that suits your kitten – in other words, the kitten should enjoy eating the food, thrive on it, and not suffer from stomach upsets.

If you dislike the idea of feeding a commercially prepared food and would like to feed your own diet, bear in mind that it can be very difficult to get right the vital balance of nutrients and energy content, and that putting together a homemade diet for your kitten will be very time-consuming. Cat nutrition is a complex science – you will need to feed a wide range of meat and fish, supplemented with all the necessary vitamins and minerals – and the results can be haphazard, especially at a time when your kitten's body is demanding very specific nutrients for healthy growth and development.

If you are worried about any aspect of feeding, or you are concerned that your kitten is not growing and putting on weight as it should, ask your vet for further advice.

Drinking water

The ancestors of our domesticated cats were semi-desert-dwellers, and this has given our pets the ability to conserve water efficiently. If you feed your kitten on a canned moist food, it may not drink a great deal because most of the water it requires will be provided by the food (moist foods usually contain between 60 and 85 percent water, compared with five to 12 percent water in a dry food).

An average adult cat requires a minimum of about 5 fl oz (150 ml) of water per day. As you cannot know exactly how much your kitten is taking in with its food, you must always keep a supply of clean, fresh water available so that the kitten can adjust its intake to suit itself.

Milk

Cats and weaned kittens do not require milk as part of their diet, and certainly not as a substitute for water. Indeed, soon after a kitten is weaned, it loses the ability to digest lactose, a sugar found in milk. This is why some cats cannot tolerate cows' milk, and may suffer from stomach upsets if they are allowed to drink it. Even if your kitten can tolerate milk, it is inadvisable to give it if the kitten is prone to suffering from digestive problems.

LITTER TRAINING

Whether or not you intend to allow your kitten outside once its primary vaccinations are complete (see page 87), you will need to keep it indoors for at least two to three weeks so that it gets to know your house as home and as the place to return to when it eventually does explore the great outdoors (for information on allowing your kitten out for the first time, see pages 77–8).

You will therefore need a litter box for the interim period, or on a longer-term basis if your kitten is to live indoors, so what type of box and litter should you choose, and how should you teach your kitten to use them?

A simple open litter box is the type chosen by most owners. It should be fairly deep and large enough for a grown cat to turn around in easily.

Types of litter box

Litter boxes for cats range from the simple open variety made of plastic to a covered box with an air freshener in the hood. Your kitten may be quite content with the open type – especially if it is only for a few weeks – but many prefer the privacy of a closed box in the longer term (for advice on preventing problems associated with litter boxes, see pages 143–4).

Some boxes are very shallow, but cats like to have quite a deep litter – at least 1 in (2.5 cm) – to scratch up, so one of the deeper types of box will ensure that the litter does not end up all over the floor. The box should also be big enough for your kitten to turn around in easily.

Types of litter

When your kitten first comes home with you, try to use the cat litter with which it is familiar, as the kitten will associate that substrate with toileting. You can then gradually change to a new variety if you wish. The three most popular types are clay-based, sand-based, and wood-based litters (the latter is made of highly absorbent sawdust or paper pellets).

Three widely used cat litters (clockwise from top): clay-based litter, fine-grain litter with a sand-like consistency, and wood-based litter made of sawdust or paper pellets.

Some of the litters come with added deodorizing chemicals or air fresheners to reduce the smell that may escape if a litter box has become a little too well used. However, it is much better to clean a box more frequently than to try to mask the smell. In addition, the footpads of some cats – particularly those living permanently indoors – can be fairly soft and sensitive, and the deodorizing chemicals have sometimes been known to irritate their feet, so keep an eye on your kitten if you decide to use this type of litter. Another possible problem is that some cats may dislike the strong smell of the chemicals, and so be dissuaded from using the box.

The finer litters may stick to your kitten's feet, so it is a good idea to put a mat by the exit of the box to catch the pieces. Likewise, the contents of an open box are much more likely to land on the surround-ing floor if the kitten is a little overenthusiastic when covering up its urine or feces, so you may want to put down some sheets of newspaper around the box.

It is possible to use newspaper as "litter," although this will not be particularly absorbent, and the ink may come off onto your kitten's feet (where it may cause harm) and be spread around your home. Another potential problem is that your kitten may well come to regard any newspaper lying around the house as fair game for toileting purposes.

Positioning the box

It is important that you place the litter box in a quiet part of your house. Cats often feel quite vulnerable when going to the toilet, so you must help your kitten to feel secure and not in danger of being unexpectedly disturbed. Do not place the box near the kitten's food and water bowls, or near its bed, as cats would naturally move away from such areas to use a latrine.

If you have a dog or a toddler in the house, be warned that both are likely to find the litter box irresistible, which may well affect its positioning. Wherever the box is, your kitten must be able to gain access to it 24 hours a day.

Cleaning the box

Do not change the litter too often at first – perhaps once every two or three days – as the smell will help your kitten to learn that this is its latrine area. (If more than one cat is using the box, you will obviously need to clean it out more frequently.) A litter scoop is a useful tool for removing solid waste without having to tip out the whole box contents on each occasion, thus allowing you to get a little more mileage from the litter.

A covered litter box helps to prevent spillage; some types also have an odor absorber or air freshener in the hood.

When you empty the litter box, you should wash it out thoroughly with hot water and disinfect it. However, be very careful here, as disinfectants are designed to kill certain bacteria, viruses, and fungi, and can also be dangerous to other organisms. Cats in particular are highly sensitive to certain chemicals found in disinfectants. Some of the most dangerous are those containing phenol (found in some disinfectants), cresols (found in Lysol and similar disinfectants), and chloroxylenols (found in other disinfectants). Other chemicals that you should steer clear of include hexachlorophone, iodine, and iodophors. Always refer to the disinfectant container for details of the chemicals used, and ask your vet's advice if you are in any doubt.

Whatever disinfectant you choose for cleaning the litter box, do not be tempted to use a higher-strength solution than is recommended on the label "just to be sure," as this can considerably increase the danger of a low-toxicity product.

Teaching your kitten to use the box

Kittens are fast learners when it comes to litter training, and must discover how to do so for themselves when very young. In fact, most of any additional work required will usually have been done by the kitten's mother before you bring the kitten home – if she used a litter box, her kittens will have learned what to do by watching and copying her. As a result, all that you should need to do is to show and then regularly remind the kitten where its new litter box is over the first few days. If the kitten needs a little encouragement, show it what to do by placing it on the litter box and, holding its paws, gently scratching and digging the litter – it will soon get the idea.

When you first arrive home with the kitten, lift it onto the box so that it can relieve itself. If nothing happens at first, repeat the procedure at regular intervals until you have success. If the kitten has an "accident" elsewhere, put it onto the box again, along with the tissue or cloth you have used to mop up urine or any feces deposited in the wrong place. The smell will help the kitten to associate the box with the functions that you wish it to perform there.

Clean up the area of the "accident" thoroughly with a solution of a biological washing powder, rinse it, and leave it to dry before you allow the kitten to return there, or it may be attracted to use the spot again. Never "rub the kitten's nose in it," as this will only make it nervous and more likely to perform in the wrong place. It will also make the kitten fearful of you. (For further information on problems associated with litter training, see page 144.)

To encourage use of the box, place the kitten onto the litter after feeding and on waking from sleep, as these are the most likely times when it will need to empty its bladder or bowels.

Toileting outdoors

If you intend to allow your kitten to go to the toilet outdoors, you may wish to encourage it to stop using the indoor litter box and to switch to the soil. (If you keep your kitten indoors at night or any other time, you must of course continue to provide a litter box inside the house during these periods.) If you have fitted a pet door, you can assist this learning process by moving the box closer and closer to the door, at the same time adding some soil to the litter so that the kitten begins to associate soil with toileting.

At first, tip the contents of the litter box out onto the garden near the kitten's usual exit, instead of disposing of them, so that again the kitten associates the appropriate smells and substrates, and gets the message that it can use the soil (however, do not do this if you have dogs or children who could get at the dirty litter). The last step is to move the litter box so that it is outside the door, leaving it there until the kitten no longer uses it.

Finally, on an important hygienic note, be sure to cover over any children's sand boxes in your yard when they are not in use. If you do not do this, it is highly likely that your kitten – as well as any other cats that happen to be roaming about in the vicinity – may look on them as ideal large litter boxes.

CHAPTER NINE

HEALTH CARE

K eeping your kitten fit and healthy does not simply mean taking it to the vet if it becomes ill or is injured. One of your first considerations will be vaccination, but

A vet will discover a great deal about your kitten's well-being through physical examination.

whether you buy your kitten from a breeder who has completed the kitten's primary-vaccination regime or you obtain it from an owner who has left vaccinations up to you, you need to find yourself a vet.

When you first bring your kitten home, it is also wise to go along and register the kitten as a patient and have it checked over by your vet, who may notice something that you have missed in your initial health check (see pages 34–6). In addition, the vet will be able to advise you on diet, vaccinations, worming, and health matters in general.

FINDING A VET

Most people use their local veterinary clinic for convenience, and are very pleased with the service it provides. If you live in an urban area, the majority of patients here are likely to be dogs and cats, along with some parakeets, hamsters, rabbits, and a few exotic pets such as lizards and snakes. A clinic of this kind will be well equipped for feline work, and is likely to be knowledgeable about the most up-to-date developments in feline medicine. There are also an increasing number of vets who limit their work solely to cats.

If you live in a very rural area, it may be worthwhile looking at all the veterinary clinics in your vicinity and finding out whether any have a special interest in cats, as many of the vets working at the clinics may concentrate on large animals and leave the small-animal or pet work to one person within the practice. You could also ask other cat owners in the area if they can recommend a good "cat vet."

If you have several choices available, decide whether you would prefer a large clinic with numerous vets and probably (but not always) more specialized equipment for treating small animals; or a smaller practice where you are likely to see the same vet on each visit and build up more of a relationship with him or her.

Vets also vary in how much they charge for their services, which may be a consideration for you, but bear in mind that the cheapest option may not be the best one for your kitten.

VACCINATIONS

A vaccination works by exposing the body's immune system to a harmless quantity of a particular infectious agent. The white blood cells in the body then produce antibodies that attack the infectious agent. By remembering the exact design of these antibodies, the body can mount a rapid and strong immune response if it comes into contact with the disease again, making the cat immune to that virus or bacteria for as long as the vaccination lasts.

A kitten is usually vaccinated for the first time between eight and 10 weeks of age, with a second dose given at 12 weeks. Full protection will not be achieved until seven to 10 days after the second vaccination, so a kitten must not be allowed outdoors – where it could meet other cats – during this period. Your kitten will need annual "booster" vaccinations to maintain immunity.

Keeping up-to-date with a routine vaccination program is vital to protect your kitten against a number of serious feline infectious diseases (see pages 89–91).

A full veterinary examination of your kitten, which should be carried out soon after you bring the kitten home (see page 61), will involve a number of basic tests, including listening to its heartbeat with the aid of a stethoscope.

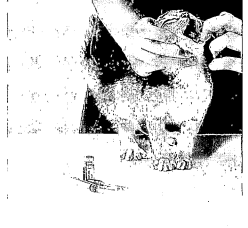

Your kitten's initial checkup is likely to include taking its body temperature rectally with a thermometer; the vet will also do this if at any time the kitten appears to be sick in the future.

Your vet will check inside the kitten's mouth to see that the gums are healthy and that there are no problems with the teeth. Brushing your kitten's teeth regularly will help prevent problems (see pages 100–1).

Feline diseases

Your kitten will be vulnerable to a number of diseases, although those to which it may be exposed will vary according to where you live (for instance, the rabies virus – see below – is found in all continents except Australasia and Antarctica). Your kitten's chances of encountering the organisms responsible for disease will depend to some extent on its lifestyle – a kitten that goes outside and regularly meets other cats will obviously be at greater risk than one confined indoors.

Vaccinations are available against the following infectious diseases: feline panleukopenia infection (also known as feline infectious enteritis), feline upper-respiratory-tract disease (caused by one of two viruses: feline herpesvirus type 1 [FHV-1] and feline calicivirus [FCV]), feline chlamydial infection, feline leukemia virus infection (FeLV), and rabies. The names of the diseases alone are enough to make you rush to the vet to protect your new kitten!

A vaccine against feline infectious peritonitis (FIP) is available, but at present is rather ineffective and not recommended. There is no vaccine as yet against feline immunodeficiency virus (FIV).

Feline panleukopenia infection This highly infectious disease causes a severe and often fatal gastroenteritis. Any cat may suffer from panleukopenia, but it mainly affects young kittens. The disease is generally transmitted through direct contact with an infected cat, or through exposure to contaminated objects (the virus is very hardy, and can survive for months in the environment).

Vaccination against feline panleukopenia infection provides a high level of long-lasting protection.

Feline upper-respiratory-tract disease The FHV-1 or FCV virus infects the cat's respiratory system, causing a disease that is commonly termed "cat flu." It is common in situations in which many cats are kept together, such as at boarding kennels. The disease is not normally life-threatening, but can cause long-term problems such as persistent coughing and "sniffles."

The vaccines available against cat flu may not actually prevent a cat from infection, but will significantly reduce the severity of the disease.

Feline chlamydial infection This is a particular problem in colonies of cats. Chlamydia is a bacterium that can cause swelling and painful inflammation of the conjunctiva (the membrane around the eye) in a condition known as conjunctivitis. The infection is most prevalent in kittens of five weeks to nine months old, and a whole litter may be affected at once. The disease is generally transmitted through direct contact with an infected cat.

Vaccination is recommended particularly for cats exposed to environments in which the infection is (or has been in the past) a problem.

89

Feline leukemia virus infection This disease is a relatively new discovery, for which vaccines have only been available for a few years. While most cats are able to combat this disease themselves, some 30 percent of those that come into contact with the virus will become what is called "persistently affected" and unable to rid their bodies of it. Infection suppresses the immune system, and an infected cat can develop tumors or other diseases associated with its inability to fight off infection. Saliva is the most common source of infection with FeLV, and the virus is generally transmitted via cat bites sustained during fights or by regular close contact.

The current vaccines against FeLV provide a good level of protection. However, because the virus can take many months before it actually causes disease, an infected cat may appear normal or simply a little off-color. Your vet may therefore suggest carrying out a blood test on your kitten prior to vaccination, to ensure that it is not already infected with the virus. FeLV vaccination can pose a risk to breeding queens, and so is not usually recommended for them.

Rabies This virus affects a cat's central nervous system. In almost all cases it is transmitted by bite, as the virus is present in the saliva of infected animals. A slight change in temperament and excessive licking at the bite wound may be followed by the "furious" stage of increasing nervousness, irritability, and lack of coordination, or the cat may go straight from the initial symptoms to fits, paralysis, coma, and death.

Vets and the humane societies in the United States believe that all cats – even those kept indoors – should be vaccinated against rabies. When you take your cat in for a checkup, your cat will receive a rabies vaccination or booster shot.

Feline infectious peritonitis This virus is transmitted through contact with the feces or saliva of an infected cat, usually before that cat shows symptoms itself. The result of infection will depend on factors such as the cat's age and the state of its immune system.

If the immune system cannot fight off the infection, it will spread around the body in one of two forms – "wet" FIP (symptoms such as abdominal swelling, fever, anemia, and depression develop in just a few weeks), or "dry" FIP (symptoms associated with the development of inflammatory growths take longer to appear and include depression, weight loss, and fever). Most cats die as a result of infection with FIP.

Feline immunodeficiency virus infection Infection with this disease results in immunosuppression, in which a cat is unable to fight off infections. FIV belongs to a specific group of viruses that includes FeLV (see above) and HIV (the virus responsible for humans AIDS). Transmission is thought to occur mainly through saliva, making cat bites a common cause. About five weeks after infection a cat may appear to be a little off-color, but may then suffer no further symptoms for months or even years. When symptoms do develop, they generally result from other recurrent infections because FIV has suppressed the cat's normal immune response.

Many of the antiviral drugs used to combat HIV have been shown to be effective against FIV, but further investigation and tests are needed in the long term. FIV infection is diagnosed by a blood test. If a cat becomes infected, diligent health care and routine vaccinations are especially important. The cat may be kept safely with other, uninfected individuals, provided that they do not fight, but the cats should be fed separately as a precaution.

Does vaccination carry risks?

Some owners worry about the risks associated with vaccination, but these are generally low, and severe reactions are very rare. Your kitten may have a small lump at the injection site, or may be quiet and not eat much for 24 hours, but will soon recover. However, if you are worried by your kitten's behavior or health after vaccination, you should contact your vet as soon as possible for further advice.

WORMING

All cats are at risk of intestinal worms. When you obtain your kitten, you should ask the breeder, owner, or animal welfare society whether worming has been carried out and, if so, what type of wormer was used and when it was last given.

Roundworms and tapeworms commonly infest cats, but, depending on where you live, your kitten may also be vulnerable to other types of worm. Heartworm, for example, is prevalent in warm, humid parts of the United States and Australia. Another parasite, usually known as lungworm, is thought to be fairly common in cats in the United Kingdom, but is rarely a cause of disease. Ask your vet for specific advice on the worming treatment required to protect your kitten.

Roundworms

These worms have pointed, cream-colored bodies. They are very common in kittens, which can be infested by ingesting worm eggs present in the feces of another cat or small rodent, or by eating an infested rodent. A queen can also pass on the worm eggs to the kittens through her milk. It is best to assume that your kitten has roundworms, and to administer worming doses on a regular basis.

Tapeworms

Tapeworms consist of many individual segments. They are less common than roundworms in kittens, but can be passed on by fleas or picked up by eating infested prey.

Worming products

There are many different wormers available, and you should check with your vet as to which are most appropriate for your kitten. A typical regime is to treat a kitten from four to 16 weeks old for roundworms every two weeks; when the kitten is six months old, it will require treatment every two to six months against both roundworms and tapeworms. This regime may vary slightly according to the particular products used and to the prevalence of worms where you live – your vet will be able to give you specific advice.

FLEAS

If your kitten has a freely roaming outdoor lifestyle or mixes frequently with other animals, it is almost certain at some time to come into contact with fleas. The most common type of flea is the well-known cat flea, although rabbit fleas will also feed from a cat.

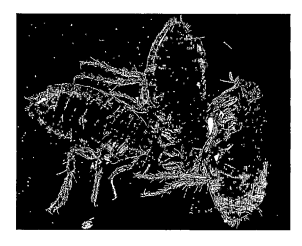

Any fleas that are brought in by your kitten will also infest your home. This is because, although adult fleas live and feed on a cat, the females lay eggs that fall off into carpets or bedding. These first develop into larvae and subsequently into pupae, which lie dormant until a suitable meal – animal or human – comes along.

Flea larvae like warm, moist environments, the ideal place being at the base of the carpet pile in a centrally heated house. They feed on debris in the carpet – especially the feces from adult fleas that fall from the kitten along with the eggs. This is a very clever ploy for survival that ensures you can have fleas in your home all year round, not just in the summer months, when they are more common outdoors.

The ubiquitous cat flea lives mainly in the environment, jumping onto a passing cat to feed. Treating your kitten and cleaning its bedding regularly are vital to prevent infestations.

Checking for fleas

Even if your kitten has an infestation of fleas, you may not be able to see them, as they can scuttle through the fur at great speed. However, you can easily check your kitten for fleas by brushing through its coat with a comb or your fingers onto a piece of damp white blotting paper. Any flea feces – consisting mainly of digested blood – will show up as black dots surrounded by pink on the white paper.

Some cats do not scratch or show any reaction to the presence of fleas; others develop an allergy to flea saliva, and may groom themselves excessively and develop skin disease. Some kittens rescued from poor environments have heavy flea infestations, which can cause anemia (a lack of red blood cells).

Treating your kitten

There are many flea products available, including sprays, foams, shampoos, powders, spot-on products (one drop is put on the skin at the back of the neck about once a month), tablets, flea collars, and even strange ultrasonic devices said to repel fleas.

Sprays are quick and easy to apply, but some cats dislike the sound and feel of them. As an alternative, foams (similar to hair mousses) and other medications may be brushed or stroked into the coat. Shampoos and powders have limited effectiveness because they only work for a short while after application; similarly, flea collars may not work well enough to cope with an environment containing great numbers of fleas.

Ask your vet for advice on which products to choose: this is very important, as certain products must not be used on young kittens. Always read the label and follow dosage instructions carefully, as some flea products can cause problems if used too frequently or in too great a quantity. Do not mix different products unless on the advice of your vet, as you could overdose your kitten.

Treating the environment

Simply treating your kitten for fleas will not solve the problem – you must also tackle them in the environment and on any other animals in the house. Remember, too, that fleas are very likely to be brought in on subsequent occasions by animals that have regular access to the outdoors, so it is a constant battle.

Various products are available to tackle fleas in the home. Some are insecticides and kill the fleas on contact; others contain chemicals to inhibit their growth. Alternatively, if you can interrupt the life cycle, you will prevent new fleas from emerging, and several products aim to do this (for example, one product is given to a cat in its food, and renders flea eggs on the cat incapable of hatching).

Another recently available option is a special whole-house treatment done by professional concerns, which will dry out eggs and larvae in the carpets, flooring, and upholstery for a year. This can be expensive, but is much less time-consuming than other methods and is also non-toxic to all inhabitants of the house (except, of course, the fleas). Ask your vet about the treatments available where you live, and for advice on which will be best for you.

Whichever flea product you use, you will need to treat all the areas within the house to which your kitten has access. Take special notice of areas in which the kitten lies, or where it jumps down from a chair or bed, as eggs and larvae are most likely to fall off here. Move furniture and cushions to treat areas under and behind them, as well as the cracks in wooden floors.

You should also wash your kitten's bedding regularly at a high temperature. When you vacuum the house, throw away the dust bag afterward, as it is likely to contain flea eggs and larvae that will hatch out inside it and reinfest the house.

OTHER PARASITES

If your kitten goes outdoors, it may also come into contact with the following parasites. If you are not confident about removing a tick using the method described, or you are unsure of the identity of a parasite, always take your kitten to the vet for a diagnosis and treatment.

Ticks

Ticks are leathery creatures that are visible to the naked eye but become most obvious when their bodies enlarge after feeding. They spend most of their lives in the environment, only visiting cats or other animals to feed for a few days during spring and fall. Your kitten may pick up ticks by brushing against plants infested with them. Certain ticks can spread serious infections, such as Lyme disease, and may cause skin irritation or even anemia in a heavy infestation.

To remove a tick, dab it with cotton wool soaked in an appropriate insecticide (ask your vet's advice on this). Leave it for a few minutes to die, then use a pair of tweezers to grasp the tick, rotate it, and pull it from the skin. Do this very carefully or you may leave the tick's head embedded in your kitten's skin, which could cause an infection.

Lice

Lice are wingless insects that are spread between cats either through close contact, or by sharing bedding and/or grooming tools. They are visible to the naked eye, but a magnifying glass will help identify them and their eggs, or nits, which will be attached to individual hairs. If your kitten has an infestation of lice, there may be a "mousey" smell to the coat and/or signs of skin irritation.

Routine insecticidal treatments used to kill fleas (see above) will kill any lice on your kitten.

Mites

Mites are tiny creatures related to spiders, and various types may affect your kitten (ask your vet's advice on those that are likely to be a problem in your area). One common example is the ear mite, which spends its entire life inside an animal's external ear canal; this causes irritation and an excessive production of dark brown wax. Ear mites are passed on by direct contact between cats.

If your kitten is showing signs of ear irritation – such as shaking or scratching its head – take it to your vet, who will prescribe medication to kill the mites and relieve the irritation.

POISONS

Cats are far more fastidious in their eating habits than scavenging dogs, but there are several other ways in which a poison can get into a cat's system. A cat may actually ingest a poison in its efforts to get rid of it: for example, by licking and trying to groom away a toxic substance contaminating the coat; another route of poisoning is by eating prey – usually rodents – that have themselves been poisoned. Some toxins can even be absorbed through the skin, especially through the paws: for example, if a cat has walked through a poison such as creosote (wood preserver).

Although cats are poisoned less frequently than dogs, they may not be able to deal with the poison in their bodies as well as their canine cousins because they are small and lack certain enzymes in their bodies that would help render the toxin harmless.

If you suspect poisoning

There are many signs of poisoning, depending on the actual poison and on the amount taken into the body. Signs can range from vomiting or diarrhea to neurological indications such as lack of coordination or depression. Your kitten's breathing pattern may also change, or it may start drinking water excessively.

If you think that your kitten may have been poisoned, go to your vet immediately. Take the suspected poison – or a note of what was on the label – with you, as identification may make the treatment both more rapid and more effective.

If you suspect that your kitten has been licking something from its coat, wrap the kitten in a towel to prevent further ingestion of the poison (this method is also useful for restraint if the kitten is being aggressive or difficult to control). Remove a flea collar if worn (cats are very sensitive to chemicals, and there could possibly be an interaction between those in the collar and a chemical contaminating the skin).

If a contamination of the coat is obvious, very carefully cut away the affected fur before washing the kitten in warm, soapy water (keeping its head above water). It is important to try to remove most of the poison before washing, as the washing process can sometimes enhance a poison's absorption through the skin.

Do not try to make your kitten sick but, if it is vomiting spontaneously, note anything unusual about the vomit so that you can inform your vet (for example, a blue color may indicate consumption of slug pellets or rodent killer). If your kitten will drink, offer milk or water to help dilute the poison and wash through the toxins.

GROOMING

A shiny cat moving gracefully in that dignified manner unique to the feline species is one of nature's wonders. Both wild and domestic cats have some of the most beautiful coats in the animal kingdom, and you can help keep your kitten's coat in tip-top condition by providing a good diet, proper health care and regular grooming.

A soft toothbrush will be very useful for gently brushing your kitten's face and the sensitive area around its eyes.

Whatever type of kitten you have, regular grooming is not only necessary for coat health but will also enable you to examine the kitten in detail on a frequent basis. You can check for the presence of fleas and other parasites such as ticks or lice, and will feel any unusual lumps and bumps that should be checked by your vet.

As with any sort of handling and routine, the younger your kitten is when you start grooming, the more quickly it will accept the procedure. Accustom the kitten to having its coat brushed, its ears and eyes checked, and its claws trimmed. You may even wish to clean your kitten's teeth (see pages 100–1), in which case you need to start as soon as possible.

It is no good deciding that you want to give a semigrown cat its first grooming session because its coat is looking very matted, and then to expect it simply to sit there and accept the pulling and cutting without complaint. If you groom regularly, the need for drastic action will be less, and your kitten may even enjoy these sessions if they cause no discomfort. You will then avoid the surprisingly common situation in which an owner has to take a fractious cat to the vet for a general anesthetic simply to have its matted, dirty coat shorn off. Start early, kindly and firmly, and you may both enjoy the experience and form closer bonds because of it.

Grooming equipment

The extent of your grooming kit will vary according to the type of kitten you own. For instance, if you have a Persian with a long coat and thick undercoat, you will need a number of tools; if you have a short-coated kitten that goes outdoors and looks after itself to a great extent, you will really need very little in the way of grooming equipment to keep its coat in top condition.

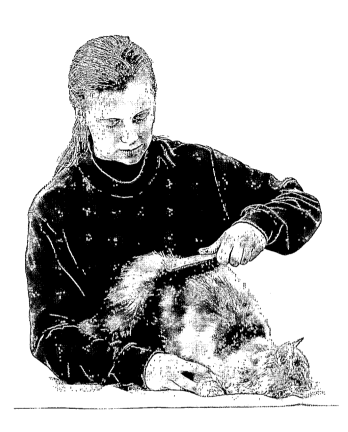

Many cats – and owners – enjoy the grooming process, and this is an ideal time to strengthen the bond with your kitten. All the members of the family should be shown how to groom and encouraged to take their turn. Most cats are easy to handle during grooming, particularly if they become accustomed to the routine from an early age.

A metal comb is useful for removing loose hair, but never attempt to "drag" it through the coat as you will hurt your cat – instead, remove tangles gently.

Longhairs and semi-longhairs need particular attention in areas that tend to be prone to matting, such as under the belly and around the tail area.

A cat's tail is very sensitive, so brush or comb the hair here very gently. Hold your kitten gently but firmly – never try to restrain it forcibly.

Finish off the grooming session by gently wiping around your kitten's eyes with a cotton ball dipped in clean water (use a new piece for each eye).

For a long-haired kitten, you will need several types of brushes: one with wider teeth to remove any tangles gently from the coat, and perhaps another, finer wire-and-bristle brush, or a comb, to get into the detail of the undercoat. In addition, a fine-toothed comb (also known as a "flea" comb) may be very useful. If you do need to cut out a tangle, use a pair of scissors with blunt (rounded) ends to avoid any chance of injuring your kitten should it move suddenly. An unused toothbrush is ideal for brushing the hair around the ears and eyes.

For a short-haired kitten, a bristle brush is ideal for removing dirt and loose hairs. A chamois leather, velvet mitt, or piece of silk, used after brushing, will bring a shine to the coat.

The soft, sparse coat of the Devon and Cornish Rexes (see page 27) may need more gentle attention with a soft-bristled brush.

When and how to groom

Ideally, you should give your kitten – whatever its type of coat – a thorough groom at least once a week, with an additional touch-up as necessary. Always start with the least sensitive parts of the kitten's body (such as its back), and finish with the more sensitive areas (such as under its tail and between the hindlegs).

With a long-haired kitten, check the fur under the base of the tail and at the backs of the hindlegs to ensure that it has not become soiled (particularly if your kitten has suffered at any time from a bout of diarrhea); if so, gently remove any soiling with damp cotton balls. You must also check the hair between the toes, as this can become choked with damp litter and contents from the litter box.

Almost all cats molt or shed hair in the spring – and to some extent in the fall – and you may need to groom your kitten more frequently during this period. This will help remove excess hair and prevent it from being ingested and forming hairballs in the stomach. Grooming it out will also help prevent the spread of hair around your house!

Eyes Cats with very flat faces may have constantly moist eyes because the fluid is not able to drain away properly through the tear ducts, causing tear staining on the fur at the inner corners of the eyes. Gently wipe this away with a cotton ball dampened with clean water or a little baby oil. Use a separate piece of cotton for each eye, and dry with more cotton or a soft tissue, making sure you do not touch the sensitive eyeball at any time.

If your kitten needs eye drops, you must administer them very carefully. Keep the kitten's head still, and do not position the bottle too close to the eye in case the kitten moves suddenly.

Ears If you feel that you should clean your kitten's ears because they look a little grubby inside, take great care. Most vets would advise you not to tamper with ears at all, as the tissues lining the ear canals are very delicate and easily damaged. However, if you do need to clean the ears, use a cotton ball moistened with baby oil and just wipe the outer part of the ears with a very light motion. NEVER poke the cotton into your kitten's inner ear.

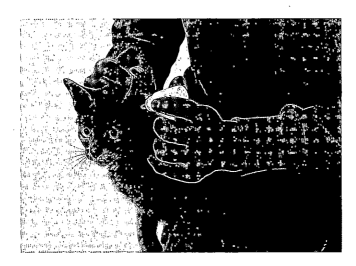

If your kitten suffers from an infestation of ear mites (see pages 94–5), your vet is likely to prescribe ear drops to kill the mites and relieve the irritation. Holding the kitten's head and ear, gently administer the drops and then massage around the outside of the base of the ear to spread the liquid evenly and thoroughly.

A good pair of "guillotine" clippers, specifically designed for the purpose, will make claw trimming easy. An indoor cat in particular may need its claws attended to regularly, as it will not wear them down naturally as an outdoor cat will do.

If there are large deposits of wax in the ears, or the ears look red, take your kitten for a checkup with your vet in case it is suffering from ear mites or an infection.

Claws If your kitten does not go outside and wear down its claws naturally, you may want to invest in a pair of good-quality "guillotine" clippers to clip them neatly and safely. If left untrimmed over a long period, claws can actually grow around into the footpads, causing great

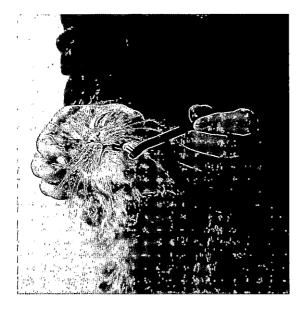

(Above) Tooth-brushing is a process that needs to be carried out gradually and gently. At first, simply allow your kitten to become used to the brush.

(Left) Always brush gently, using special feline toothpaste.

discomfort. Look carefully at each of your kitten's claws, and be sure to clip below the little blood vessel in the claw (this is visible as a thin red line that gradually disappears). Work quickly and calmly so that your kitten does not become agitated.

Teeth A regular check in and around your kitten's mouth will reveal any lurking problems, from sore gums or a buildup of tartar on the teeth to broken teeth or lumps that should not be there. There are now kits available containing brushes or little fabric pads designed to slip onto a finger to clean a cat's teeth, along with feline toothpastes (these are similar to human toothpastes, but are more palatable to cats and do not foam) and cleaners. Just as human teeth benefit from brushing to prevent the buildup of tartar, a regular clean will do the same for your kitten's teeth.

Your kitten will lose most of its milk (baby) teeth by the age of about five months, so do not panic if you see a tiny tooth coming out. Check that this has not been caused by an injury of any kind and that the mouth looks normal, and then don't worry – another tooth will soon come through in its place.

GIVING YOUR KITTEN MEDICINE

If your kitten has to take medication for any reason – be it a regular worming dose or a drug prescribed by your vet – you need to know how best to get the medicine into the kitten so that it receives the correct dose. Kittens are very small and can easily be overdosed – they are also very wriggly and capable of spitting out most of what has been put in their mouths.

You must be accurate in your dosing, so weigh your kitten and check the dose that you need to give (if your vet has not already done so for you). Cut up large tablets or measure out powder accurately. Check whether the medicine needs to be given on an empty stomach or with food, as this can affect how efficiently it works, and also at what time of day you should administer it.

Always complete a course of treatment – never alter the medicine dosage or stop it unless your vet tells you to do so. If you are worried about your kitten's lack of response – or seemingly strange response – to a medicine, consult your vet.

Giving a medicine with food

Provided that it is acceptable to give the medication with your kitten's food (always check with your vet first), you can hide small tablets in a little tasty food such as cheese, butter, or a piece of meat, or crush them and mix them with the kitten's usual food. Powders and syrups may also be given in this way.

However, kittens are very adept at detecting "doctored" food and, if your kitten refuses to eat it, you will have to try the conventional method of administering a tablet by mouth (see below). Similarly, if you have several cats in your house, or any other animals that may eat the kitten's food, you will need to feed the kitten alone or to try alternative tactics. If the kitten only eats a part of the food, it may also be difficult for you to gauge how much of the medicine has gone down.

Giving a tablet

If you really want to be sure that your kitten has taken all the medication required, you may need to give it by mouth. In this case, having an assistant to restrain the kitten for you will make the process much easier (when the kitten is small, you may be able to manage on your own, but kittens can be extremely wriggly, and the following two-person method works well as they grow and become less easy to control). If no assistant is available, you can restrain your kitten if necessary by wrapping its body firmly in a towel.

With your kitten properly restrained by a helper and the tablet ready in your fingers, gently open the kitten's mouth.

1 Sit the kitten on a table or other suitable surface, in front of and facing away from your helper, and ask him or her to clasp both palms around the kitten's chest. It is likely to try to prevent you from dosing it by using its front paws, so your helper should hold its forelegs between his third and fourth fingers, and use his arm and upper body to hold the kitten firmly to his side.

Drop the tablet as far back into the mouth as possible, on the center of the tongue, so that the kitten cannot spit it out.

2 Stand at the side or in front of the kitten. Place the palm of your hand over the kitten's head with your thumb and third finger on either side of the angle of the jaw, so that you are in effect holding the upper jaw and head.

3 Take the tablet between the thumb and second finger of your other hand, and place your forefinger on the lower teeth at the front of the mouth.

4 Tilt back the kitten's head and press on the corners of the mouth to ease it open. Gently but firmly, press down on the lower jaw and then drop the tablet as far back into the throat as possible so that the kitten cannot spit it out.

Still holding the kitten's head tilting upward, gently stroke down the throat with a finger: this will encourage swallowing.

5 Close the kitten's mouth and, with the head still tilted back, stroke down the throat with a finger to encourage swallowing.

Pill dispensers or "guns" These simple devices – available from many vets – can make the whole process of giving tablets easier and reduce the chances of having a finger bitten by a particularly fractious feline. You will have to discover the best method for giving tablets to your kitten – some are easy and calm, and others will fight to the bitter end!

A pill dispenser, or "gun," can make giving a tablet easier – this may be useful if your kitten dislikes the procedure.

Administering a liquid

If you need to give a medicine in liquid form, restrain your kitten (as described opposite) and use a syringe to introduce the medication. To do this, gently push the nozzle of the syringe between the kitten's teeth at the side of its mouth and then squeeze in the fluid very slowly – aiming diagonally across the mouth rather than down the throat – so that the kitten has a chance to swallow.

Giving eye drops or ointment

If you need to treat your kitten's eye with drops or ointment, as prescribed by your vet, first ensure that the eye is clean by gently removing any discharge with a cotton ball dampened in clean water. Restrain the kitten (as described on page 102), and carefully open the upper eyelid with the thumb and finger of one hand. Hold the dropper or tube slightly away from the surface of the eye in case your kitten makes a sudden movement, and then administer the drops or ointment directly into the eye.

Giving ear drops

To give ear drops, restrain your kitten (as described on page 102), turn its head to one side, and then carefully drop in the required dose of the medicine. Gently massage the outside of the ear at the base to spread the medication around the whole area.

COPING WITH AN EMERGENCY

If your kitten suddenly becomes ill, collapses, or is involved in a traffic accident, you must contact your vet as soon as possible. Always keep the telephone number handy, and make sure that everyone in the household knows where it is.

If you make your emergency call at night or during a vacation period, leave a message on the answering machine (someone will call you back as soon as they can) or wait to be transferred to the vet on call. All veterinary clinics have a duty to provide 24-hour cover for animals in their care, so you will always be able to contact a vet in an emergency.

Try not to panic, as you will be much better able to reassure your kitten if you remain calm yourself. If the kitten is in imminent danger, such as on a road, gently place it on a towel or blanket, or on a makeshift stretcher such as a road atlas, and move it to safety.

In an emergency situation you will usually be asked to bring your kitten to the clinic, so that the vet has access to the full range of equipment and drugs. If it seems appropriate to put your kitten in its carrier, do so; if not, wrap it in a towel or blanket and hold it firmly but gently so that it cannot try to escape.

Chapter Ten

GOING ON VACATION

Many owners do not fully enjoy their annual vacations because they are worried about the welfare of their cats or kittens while they are away. However, with a little organization and research you should find a good solution and will be able to go for a well-deserved rest, knowing that your kitten is in good hands.

LEAVING YOUR KITTEN WITH A NEIGHBOR

Leaving a young kitten alone in the house, with a neighbor coming in to feed and check on it – even just for two or three days – is not a very good idea, no matter how dependable the neighbor. Kittens get up to all sorts of mischief, especially if they are bored, so if you could arrange for a friend to stay in your house and provide more constant care, this would be preferable to someone popping in once or even twice a day.

If you do choose the neighbor option, remember that, while you are away, your kitten should not be allowed outdoors, in case it feels confused and wanders off. Caring for another person's pet is a great responsibility, and even a temporary disappearance by your kitten would be very upsetting both for you and the person left in charge. Instead, provide an indoor litter box for the kitten to use, and be sure to leave full instructions regarding food, water, play, medications, and so on for your care person to follow.

When your kitten is a little older, you may be able to trust its care to a neighbor who will visit several times a day to put down fresh food and give it some attention. You will have to decide whether to let the kitten out over this period or keep it in, where you know it will be safe. This very much depends on the kitten – for instance, an older kitten or cat that is used to being alone (and that is likely to sleep most of the day away) will probably be quite safe for a day or two. The younger the cat, the more advisable it is to keep it indoors for the short period you are going to be away.

Before you leave, give the person looking after your kitten details of where to contact you in an emergency, as well as the address and telephone number of your veterinary clinic. Drawing a map of how to get to the clinic will be helpful if the person is not familiar with the area. It is also a good idea to inform your vet that you will be away.

CAT-SITTERS

Another option is to pay for the services of a house- or cat-sitter. A house-sitter will actually stay in your home to look after your kitten and possessions; a cat-sitter will visit once or twice a day to tend to the kitten. Provided that the sitter is reliable, and that you will not be away for a very lengthy period (this is important if you have a young kitten, and are using the cat-sitter option, rather than a resident house-sitter), this can work very well. If you have a number of animals, it may also be the most cost-effective solution.

If house- or cat-sitters are available in your area, check that they have good references and plenty of experience, and, if possible, talk to other cat owners who have used them on previous occasions.

CHOOSING A BOARDING KENNEL

If you are going away for more than a few days and do not have someone to "cat-sit," the best way to ensure your kitten's health and safety is to choose a good boarding kennel – ask your vet for recommendations of any in your area. Sadly, there are many poorly run boarding kennels, so what are the criteria for a good one?

You obviously need to know that your kitten will be safe and properly fed, but you also want a kennel to be run by staff who will spend time with the kitten and make it feel at home – in other words, to care for it as you do. The premises must also be clean and hygienic. Below are some pointers to help you choose the best kennel for your kitten.

Minimizing infections

Despite recent advances in our understanding and knowledge of cats, and of the diseases from which they suffer, many kennels are still run by apparently well-meaning people who offer living conditions hazardous to the cat. High on this list are kennels offering communal runs or exercise areas, or in which contact between cats in their enclosures is possible.

Nowadays, more cats are being exposed to feline chlamydial infection, FeLV, rabies, and FIV, to name but a few diseases (see pages 89–91). It is therefore imperative that kennels are built to specifications that preclude any form of contact between the boarders, while still allowing them the pleasure of viewing each other and communicating across barriers. These barriers should be either 20-in (50-cm) gaps or full-height solid partitions – so-called "sneeze barriers" – between runs, to prevent the airborne transmission of infectious diseases. Each cat (or cats from the same household) should be provided with a separate unit, containing both a sleeping area and an outdoor run, and any kennel housing all cats indoors with a shared air supply should be avoided. There should also be isolation facilities available for sick cats.

Choosing a good boarding kennel means that both you and your kitten will enjoy the holiday. Taking your kitten's bed, bowls, and some favorite toys will make it feel at home.

The kennel should insist that your kitten has been fully vaccinated against feline panleukopenia infection and cat flu, and that the vaccinations – whether primary or "booster" injections – have been carried out far enough in advance to allow maximum protection (see page 87). This should be a fundamental requirement for any boarding kennel. Many cats carry latent health problems that may manifest themselves under stress and can be transmitted to other cats, and a stay in a kennel – especially a poorly run one – can be just such a trigger.

Clean, pleasant premises

If the kennel proprietor will not give you a tour, look elsewhere. The owner of a good kennel will be pleased to let you see how it is run and where your kitten will be kept. It is better to search further afield, and to be prepared for a slightly longer journey to reach the kennel, than to subject your kitten to a period of privation in a poor establishment.

Look for clean, well-kept premises in tidy and well-tended surroundings. The buildings should be well maintained, and the enclosures and their concrete bases free of algae stains. The accommodation for each cat should include a comfortable sleeping and an individual open-air exercise area of reasonable size.

Many of the best kennels make a great deal of effort to ensure not only that cats in their care are kept in both clean and safe conditions, but also that they have something interesting to look at and keep them occupied. For instance, the kennel may be in sight of a nearby house so that the cats can watch people coming and going, or the area around the runs may be planted with flowers that attract butterflies, providing something for the cats to watch.

The cats themselves should appear contented, and there should be no obvious smell in their environment, either of feces and urine or of strong disinfectant that has been used to disguise inadequate cleaning. Water bowls should be clean and filled with fresh water; food bowls should also be clean or (preferably) disposable, and the food provided fresh and suitable to each individual.

Look at the state of the litter boxes – are they clean and sufficiently large for the cats, and what type of litter is used? Check the provision of heating or of a cooling system for hot weather – is it individually controlled for each unit, and will there be an additional charge for electricity? Some cats – depending on their age, coat, and what they are used to at home – feel the cold much more than others, and their special needs should be met.

Caring proprietors

A good guide to assessing the caring nature of a proprietor is whether he or she asks you about your kitten's history – particularly its medical history – and checks that its vaccinations are up to date (he or she should ask to see a vaccination certificate when you bring your kitten for a stay at the kennel). You should also find out whether the kennel would be prepared to continue with any ongoing medication prescribed for the kitten by your vet. The proprietor should ask you about your kitten's diet, its likes and dislikes, and about any particular foibles such as not liking to be picked up by strangers.

Instances have occurred in which owners have been given the wrong cat to take home, or have returned to collect their beloved cat only to find that it has disappeared or – even worse – has died (this does not take account of very elderly cats that occasionally have to be boarded, in which case the owner and kennel proprietor should already have discussed this possible outcome and what should be done in the event that the cat does not survive until the owner's return). However, escape through negligence and death through accident should never be allowed to happen. In a good, professionally run kennel, the care of each of its occupants should be paramount.

Find out what would happen if your kitten were sick while you are away on vacation, or if you were unable for any reason to collect it on the pre-arranged date. When you leave your kitten at the kennel, be sure that the owner knows how to contact you in an emergency, and has the details for your veterinary clinic.

CHAPTER ELEVEN

CAT BEHAVIOR

Cats are an exception among all our domesticated animals in that they are obligate predators and have retained many of their wild outdoor instincts. Some owners become distressed by the hunting activity of their cats – which will continue regardless of whether plenty of food is provided for them at home – but this is entirely natural behavior. Indeed, it is this aspect of the feline character, combined with its very loving and loyal nature, that makes cats such intriguing and rewarding companions.

The general appearance and body shape of today's Domestic Shorthair have not changed significantly from those of its ancestor, the African wildcat (see below and page 110).

With the help of new DNA technology, scientists have now proved beyond doubt that the domestic cat is the true descendant of just one species, Felis sylvestris lybica, or the African wildcat. This animal, with its strong, agile physique and beautifully marked coat, is fairly tolerant of human beings and can still be found living in and around villages in various parts of Africa, scavenging for food as well as hunting.

To understand our relationship with the domestic cat of today, it is first necessary to look back at how that relationship has developed over many thousands of years and in different parts of the world.

THE HISTORY OF MAN AND CAT

Evidence has been found of cats living in association with humans from about 1500 BC in ancient Egypt, and archeological studies in the region point to the African wildcat (*Felis sylvestris lybica*) as the main ancestor of our modern pet cat. Indeed, recent studies in South Africa

have been unable to distinguish the DNA of the domestic cat from that of the African wildcat, while the European wildcat – which is often assumed to have contributed to the development of the pet cat – is clearly distinguishable from both.

The implication is that the pet cat is still genetically almost identical to the African wildcat. To explain this, the local population of the African wildcat in the Nile Delta must have become less reactive to the usually threatening presence and activity of man, enabling it to remain close to human settlements. African wildcats with this decreased sensitivity would then have been able to exploit the resources of higher concentrations of rodents living around man's grain stores, edible waste in dumps, and better shelter. They would have bred with much-improved chances of success,

The relationship between man and cat is an ancient one, and cats have exploited the presence of humans to the full in their search for food and shelter.

and, because small cats can reproduce relatively frequently (with two or even three litters per year), populations of "friendly" African wildcats living alongside humans would have developed quickly in ancient Egypt.

The beginnings of domestication

The kittens of these wildcats would soon have had physical contact with sympathetic people, being taken into their homes for care and coming to view them as substitute parents. Their infantile dependency would have been maintained by early handling and perhaps feeding during the "sensitive" period of socialization from two to seven/eight weeks (see pages 43–4). Indeed, it is remarkable that in and around the human den in this more urban habitat, the cat has become much more sociable with its own kind and other species – such as humans and dogs – compared with its previous highly territorial behavior in the wild.

This localized decreased sensitivity in the reactivity of the African wildcat perhaps explains why a close companion-animal relationship became uniquely established between this species and man, yet without affecting the cat's predatory behavior (see pages 113–16), which is dictated by other parts of its brain.

Additional evidence of this is that feral kittens, born to free-living queens anywhere in the world, can be easily tamed and will become friendly adult pet cats for life if they are handled to establish the substitute-parent relationship and are "stress-immunized" to human activity within the "sensitive" socialization period. Kittens of other species of small cat – such as the European wildcat – even if they are initially infantile and accepting of human contact up to the age of weaning, then cease to regard their human surrogates as parental figures. They become increasingly reactive to approach and socially independent as they reach sexual maturity, and cannot be kept as friendly, cuddly pets at all.

Further developments

Cats were latecomers on the domestic scene compared with dogs and other animals domesticated for food purposes such as sheep, chickens, and ducks. These are all known to have been living with humans in the Mesolithic Age, at least 8,000 to 10,000 years earlier than when the first cats are recorded as living in association with man.

However, once this unique relationship had begun, there is great evidence of cats being kept as companions in an area radiating out from ancient Egypt via known trade routes throughout the world. For example, a terracotta head of a cat and a fresco depicting the cat dating from 1500–1100 BC (the late Minoan period) have been discovered in Crete, a nearby civilization with which the maritime Egyptians are most likely to have traded. By 500 BC the cat appears to have become a regular feature of folklore and civilized life in mainland Greece and elsewhere in southern Europe.

The cat was also depicted in Roman religion – in many art forms – at the feet of Diana, Goddess of Light. Pliny mentioned the hunting of the cat in his *Natural History*, written in AD 77, and, in the third century, Palladius recommended using cats to catch moles. It is probable that cats were still kept and transported during this period

The domestic cat, while giving great affection and loyalty to its owner, still retains much of the independence of spirit and natural hunting instincts of an animal living in the wild.

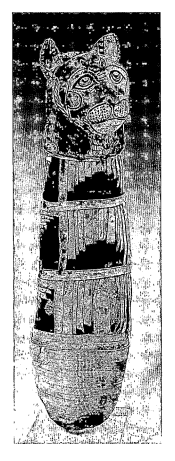

(Left) Cats were revered as sacred creatures in ancient Egypt, and thousands of them were mummified and placed in lavishly decorated sarcophagi.

(Above) A representation of the cat-headed fertility goddess Bast. A temple at Bubastis was devoted to her, with a yearly festival held there in her honor.

(Above and left) Cats featured regularly in the paintings of the ancient Egyptians.

(predominantly to keep down rats and mice on board ship, and then in newly settled towns around the world), and that they were sold and bartered for the same purpose.

The other indigenous small wildcats around the world, such as the European wildcat, were – and still are – extremely shy and fearful of humans, compared with the mutated African wildcats brought by traders. By virtue of their innate adaptability to new environments and their continuing tolerance of humans, the immigrant cats quickly and firmly established themselves in and around their settlements. They then out-competed their wild relatives, and their populations expanded along with man's urbanization of the countryside. Many of these cats then adopted more of a free-living lifestyle, being at least partially dependent on their own hunting skills and not solely on man's direct or indirect provision of food.

The pet cat

The cat's entry to our homes as a pet – as opposed to living "free" around our farms and towns – became established in Europe perhaps over 2,000 years after it had done so in the homes of the ancient Egyptians. In more recent times this has paved the way for a much greater selection of the cat for human standards of beauty, in breeds determined solely by their physical appearance at cat shows. Only about 10 percent of pet cats are of recognized breeds, usually defined by the length and color of coat and physical shape; the vast majority of our pets are non-pedigree cats and come in a huge variety of colors.

The African wildcat that we now recognize as "domestic" has been subjected to far less selective breeding for type (and none for task) than our pet dogs, and over a much shorter timescale. Unlike the domestic dog when compared with its ancestor, the wolf, the cat's physical and behavioral characteristics are virtually unchanged from those of its wild ancestor. For example, most cats naturally still carry out the complete sequence of predatory behavior: stalking, chasing, catching, and killing their prey of birds and small rodents, while few types of domestic dog can complete such a hunting sequence to feed themselves.

PREDATORY BEHAVIOR

The ultimate sheltered biological niche in the world must be as a pet in a human's den. It is warm in winter, cool in summer, draftproof, and full of comfortable resting places, not to mention the food that miraculously appears to replenish empty dishes. So it is often a source of great frustration for owners of valuable pedigree and non-pedigree cats alike that our pampered pets still hunt, especially during the springtime. However, undoing 13 million years of perfected evolutionary process is impossible, and, apart from keeping your kitten indoors, you can do little to prevent it from hunting.

Although the cat uses its teeth and its claws in hunting, predatory attacks tend to be silent and straightforward, and composed of a fairly rigid sequence of behavior: "eye-stalk-pounce-grasp-bite-kill." The object is not to communicate with prey, but to capture, kill, and eat it, so it is futile for a mouse, for example, to try to appease a cat by rolling on its back to avoid being eaten.

Why do pet cats need to kill?

Few owners complain when their cats catch an occasional mouse or kill a rat, but the first damp-feathered songbird fledglings brought in during the spring are very upsetting. But why should a well-fed cat need to kill anything at all?

Not all the prey killed by a cat is required for food, but mice and birds are used for the purposes of practice for the hunter. Research has shown that prey hunting and killing occur independently of hunger in the cat, so your kitten – given the opportunity – will not be able to help hunting, and will simply be performing its natural behavior.

Why do cats play with their victims?

Many owners are distressed by the way that cats appear to play with their prey, apparently torturing it to death rather than ending its days quickly with a rapid, fatal bite to the nape of the neck.

When such play is prolonged, it can be indicative of an incomplete learning program when the cat was young – particularly in one brought up indoors by a mother who did not bring home half-dead mice on which her kittens could practice and develop their killing skills. Hence the cat will "bat" and play with its victim only as far as it used to bat and play with toys, its littermates, and its mother's tail when it was a kitten exploring the capacity of its physical abilities.

The cat may also use the half-dead prey to practice its hunting abilities for the next occasion, safe in the knowledge that this particular victim has already been taken and can be killed and consumed at any time. Another factor is that the well-fed pet has never had to learn to kill its prey quickly to relieve great hunger. A cat may see its owner as a friend or perhaps even as a kitten in the shared den, and may bring its quarry in for the owner to play with and learn how to kill, or to ensure that he or she maintains the ability to do so.

When you are the prey

A cat possesses innate hunting skills, but it cannot become an efficient predator and hunter without practicing and refining these skills. It must frequently exercise its hunting reflexes and practice its agility, coordination of senses, and muscular control in play with objects or with anyone it can persuade to play the role of "victim," such as another friendly cat, the family dog, or its owner. Indeed, all play in adult cats is now regarded mainly as hunting practice for the predator.

As with true predatory behavior, the cat seldom makes any sound during these play "attacks." Young cats are most likely to attack their owners in this way as they seek to develop into expert predators, but mature cats will also play like this. Such attacks are almost always triggered by a movement of the "victim," and some cats learn to lie in wait to ambush their owners from a favorite vantage point behind a door or chair as they pass. A "victim" may be stalked and pounced on in this way, but the force of the final "killing" bite – although often painful – is usually inhibited, and the claws may be kept retracted.

To avoid injury, carry small toys with you around your house, or leave them lying near known sites of attack to throw ahead of yourself as you pass or to divert your kitten's attention if it becomes over-excited when playing with other toys. You should never respond to being pounced on with a counterattack of hitting or pushing your kitten away, as this may be interpreted as reciprocal play. If your kitten feels threatened by such physical reactions, it may run away and give you the impression that your response has reformed its behavior, or it may fight back in self-defense. Either way, the problem of attacking you will then become much worse and also more difficult to treat effectively, because the kitten will be even more strongly motivated in future due to the added element of threat.

The importance of play

If your kitten lives indoors, it is essential that you play with it frequently and provide outlets for its predatory behavior every day by offering moving safe targets to stalk, chase, and pounce on, even if the final "kill" is restricted to inanimate toys. A playful kitten needs to be played with, using suitable, safe toys moved erratically to elicit and sustain interest. This is especially important if your kitten has learned to focus its predatory practice behavior (play) solely on you, or is forced to do so by being kept in an unchanging home environment without suitable stimulating prey substitutes.

Do make sure that you invest the necessary time and effort to join in these play sessions, especially if your kitten is to spend its life either predominantly or totally indoors.

Time spent playing not only helps to strengthen the bond between kitten and owner, but also enables the kitten to sharpen the skills it will use for hunting, such as scooping, batting, and pouncing.

The environmental impact of pet cats

The detrimental effect that pet cats can have on the wildlife in their local environments is similar to that of feral cats or of the receding wildcat species in the world. In the United States, one estimate put the carnage of rodents at 5.5 billion per year by 10 million cats in the countryside and suggested that, because cats were removing the main prey of hawks and kestrels, these raptors were in decline as a direct result of a high pet cat population.

In contrast, we have also valued the efforts of pet and factory cats at controlling rodents. Some highly successful cases are noted in British record books. One impressive example is that of Towser, a female cat born in a whisky distillery in Scotland, who caught an average of three mice per day in her 23-year lifetime – a working total of over 25,000! However, even this feat is perhaps outweighed by the great ratting cats. In the six years between 1927 and 1933, another female called Minnie

earned her keep by catching 12,500 rats at the White City Stadium in west London. Bearing statistics such as these in mind, you may yet come to appreciate your kitten's developing predatory skills, if you would prefer not to have rodents in the vicinity of your home!

However, if you find the spectacle of dead birds very upsetting, you may be able to reduce the carnage a little by not allowing your kitten out at dawn, dusk, or night during the birds' nesting season. In some parts of Australia, all cat owners are legally required to take their cats indoors at dusk and to keep them there until dawn, in an attempt to reduce the threat that the cats pose to wildlife such as possums and the rare lyrebird. The owners could face substantial fines if they fail to adhere to this law.

Although the predation is distressing to birds, bird lovers, and cat owners, there is no evidence to suggest that the occasional high mortality of birds due to pet cats has had any damaging effect on even one species of bird. You will simply have to learn to live with the fact that your cuddly kitten will one day be a fully grown and lethal predator.

The cat is a highly athletic creature, confident at leaping and climbing – sometimes to considerable heights. This agility enables it to view its environment from many different perspectives.

YOUR KITTEN'S EYE VIEW

Have you ever gotten down to the eye level of a toddler and wondered at how different the world looks – at how feet look so huge and adult heads so far away? Take this a little further down to ankle level and look afresh at your home and garden, as this is the angle from which your kitten (unless, of course, it is halfway up the curtains) will see.

However, although a kitten lives in the same physical environment as we do, it may perceive things in a very different way because of its heightened senses of hearing, smell, and touch, and may be influenced by factors of which we are only vaguely aware. Remember that your small bundle of fur is, in fact, a developing predator, and that its senses are highly tuned to ensure frequent success on hunting missions. Below is a brief outline of how the cat sees, hears, smells, and feels the world around it – interpreted to the best of our limited understanding.

Confidence of movement

Although your kitten may dash about and bump into objects during a skittish five minutes, or may drop to the floor during a frantic rush to the top of the curtains, its athletic abilities give it a poise and balance way beyond the abilities of our own bodies: even the most clumsy cat can make our top human gymnasts look slow and cumbersome.

To an inquisitive young kitten, everything it sees is fascinating and worthy of investigation. Its highly developed senses allow it to perceive the world and be influenced by it in a very different way from a human.

A fully grown cat can leap to five times its height from a standing start with very little effort, climb a tree, walk without a wobble along the slimmest of fences, and bend and stretch to the envy of any yoga expert. A young kitten will not yet have mastered every trick to perfection, but all that dashing around, jumping in the air and climbing are practice for the time when the grace and speed of its actions will make it one of the most successful hunters in the animal kingdom.

Through feline eyes

The feline eye, although basically similar to that of other mammalian species, does have unique specialities of its own. It is thought that cats can see some color, although their vision is mainly adapted to see well in very poor light and to be very sensitive to movement (because cats hunt mainly at twilight, when most of their rodent prey is on the move, they do not actually need to see in color). Special nerve cells located in the cat's brain respond to the very smallest movement, and the cat is then able to pinpoint this movement very quickly and accurately.

Meeting other species is all part of the learning process, and needs to begin during the all-important socialization phase (see pages 41–4) if a kitten is to grow up confident in any situation that it encounters.

Behind the splendid color of your kitten's eye (the iris) lies the dark pupil, with its light-sensitive layer of cells (the retina). A special layer of cells situated behind the retina (the tapetum) reflects back any light that has not been absorbed on its way through, so that the eye is given a second chance to intercept the image. It is this layer of cells – acting in the same way as a mirror – that is reponsible for the remarkable gold or green shine that we can see in a cat's eyes when they happen to be caught for a moment in the glare of a passing car's headlights.

These special adaptations of the eye, along with the ability to open the pupil very wide, allow your kitten to see perfectly well in what we would term "darkness" – cats cannot in fact see in total darkness, but they can see in light approximately six times dimmer than we ourselves need to find our way about, and in light that sophisticated scientific instruments can barely detect.

The twitch of an ear

Your kitten has very mobile ears – they can swivel 180 degrees, lie flat against the head, or be extremely "pricked," and even move in opposite directions at once. Although we tend to think of dogs as our keen-eared friends, the cat is sensitive to sounds of even higher frequency than the dog (a dog hears up to about 35 kHz, a cat to about 65 kHz).

Our ears are sensitive up to about 20kHz, so we miss many of the high-pitched squeaks and sounds made by small rodents, to which the cat is very attuned. Locating prey very accurately by sound means that a cat can move in swiftly, directly, and silently, and not have to rely solely on sight to pinpoint its prey's position until it is close up. There are therefore probably all sorts of high-pitched sounds in your home of which you will be blissfully unaware, but which your kitten is registering all the time.

The importance of touch

Watch your kitten investigating a new object, learning to play with prey, or sneaking up on something strange. It will first touch the object rather timidly with its paw, then touch it again with a little more determination, and finally move in closer to investigate with its nose. The pads of the paw and the nose – both covered in soft skin and usually still pink in many kittens – are very sensitive to stimulation.

The pads are also very sensitive to vibration – indeed, deaf cats are thought to "hear" with their feet, feeling vibrations and interpreting them in order to perceive what is going on around them. Strangely enough, although they are sensitive to touch, the pads are not very responsive to the sensations of hot or cold, and this is probably the reason why some cats jump up on top of a stove, seemingly oblivious to the heat radiating from it.

The nose and upper lip are the only parts of the cat's body that are very sensitive to temperature. Even a tiny newborn kitten will use its temperature-sensitive nose to "home in" on the warmth of its mother, and will follow the temperature gradient to the warmest spot. A cat also uses its nose and lips to estimate the temperature of food, preferring to eat it at body temperature (as freshly killed prey would be) rather than chilled from a refrigerator.

If you look at your kitten with the light behind it, you will notice whiskers on its upper lip, above the eyes, and on the chin and elbows. These coarse hairs, called vibrissae, form a type of "force field" of sensitivity that may be switched on by the tiniest touch or even by a slight breeze. The vibrissae sprout from a deeper layer of the skin than other hairs, and

The learning experience is a mutual one. Given time, even the most unlikely of animals can become friends.

119

they act as levers, magnifying any slight movement when they bend. By stimulating nerve endings, they can provide detailed information on the kitten's surroundings, enabling it to "feel" the presence of objects simply because of the air currents circulating around them. The nerve impulses travel along the same route to the brain as information received from the eyes, and the brain uses the two systems to build a three-dimensional picture of the environment.

Whiskers are not static on the face, but are actually very mobile. For instance, if your kitten is frightened by something, it may hold the whiskers near its face to make itself appear smaller; when hunting, it may splay the whiskers farther forward, using them as a "third paw" to feel the prey in its mouth and ensure that it has the correct positioning for the killing nape bite.

The senses of smell and taste

A kitten may entertain itself for long periods with simple toys – over 10 types of object-play behavior have been identified.

If you are starting to get a feel for the world of your kitten, with its view of fairly drab colors but amazing night vision, its sensitive "hearing" feet and "seeing" whiskers, you are ready to enter the strange realm of scents. A cat can detect smells to the same intensity that we can see – in detail and in the smell equivalent of glorious technicolor – and relies on this sense as much as we do on our sight. Our own dull sense of smell makes it very hard to imagine a world of smells so intense that it must be like swimming through numerous different colors, textures, and tastes of fluids, receiving important information from them about the surroundings and even about who or what has passed that way.

Having investigated a new toy, a kitten may grasp, poke, bat, or toss it into the air.

Unlike the dog – which hunts by scent – your kitten will use its eyes and ears for hunting, and its sense of smell more for the purposes of communication. The sense of smell functions to help the kitten meet or avoid other cats and, inadvertently, humans and other members of the household such as dogs. Just how its sense of smell helps it communicate is outlined on pages 121–3.

Your kitten's tongue – which is also an essential implement for self-grooming – is very sensitive to temperature and taste. In fact, the cat is said even to be able to taste plain water (but perhaps not to experience the taste sensation of "sweet"). This could be the reason why many cats do not like to drink water straight from the tap – with its added chlorine, fluorine, and other chemicals – but will happily drink from a muddy puddle. Similarly, most cats are unexcited by the prospect of sweet items such as chocolate, which is understandable as there are very few sweet-tasting rodents about.

Objects that can be pulled along on a length of string are great favorites, and help to sharpen the kitten's reactions.

You may already be feeling a little overwhelmed by the feline senses, but another one to consider – which we cannot fully understand because it is lacking from our own physiology – is the vomeronasal organ (see page 44). This seems to enable a cat to concentrate smells and taste them at the same time, and therefore to extract much more information than would be possible by smell alone.

FELINE COMMUNICATION

Cats communicate via scent and body language, and sometimes vocally. With a little observation you can learn to gain an insight into what your kitten is feeling and what message it is trying to convey.

Talking smells

When you stroke your kitten, you are not only giving it a physical message but also adding your own smell to a complex mixture of scents that give the kitten a sense of social grouping and home. A cat has areas of skin on its

Kittens are most actively involved in so-called "social play" between the ages of nine and 14 weeks. The games may look at times more like fights, but will usually end amicably.

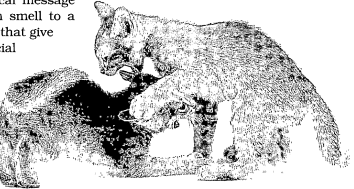

chin, lips, temples, and at the base of its tail where some special subcutaneous glands produce an oily secretion specific to that individual (like a human fingerprint). It will use this scent to mark areas around it, as well as other cats, animals, and people in its group. By stroking your kitten, you are spreading its scent and mixing it with your own, thus helping to create a communal smell comprising members of the household and the environment in which the kitten lives. In other words, your home will have a certain smell profile.

This is the reason why many cats become very upset when something new comes into the home. For instance, the smell of a new carpet is fairly strong even to us, so imagine what it does to the smell profile of your home, and how the extremely sensitive nose of your kitten will perceive it. Some cats resort to urine-spraying indoors when they are upset, to add their own scent in more concentrated form to the den in an attempt to overcome the insecurity brought on by the strange smell (see below and pages 144–5).

Even young kittens make use of the entire adult behavioral repertoire during their play activity: here, one kitten is rolling over in order to invite the other kitten to play.

As your kitten grows up, you may see it experimenting with marking by rubbing its face and lips against twigs in the garden, or on corners of items in the house. The purpose of this is to deposit scent from glands on its face. When the kitten rubs around your legs and head-butts you with delight when you are stroking it, it is also brushing you with scent. Another method of leaving a scent is by scratching. Glands situated between the pads of an adult cat's feet secrete a fluid that adds information to the visual mark left behind by scratching. Kittens often become very excited when they scratch, and will follow this with a mad dash around.

All the movements that will be used for hunting are used in play: the kitten on the left has crouched down and pounced forward, surprising the other kitten into a retreat.

While rubbing and scratching are more subtle and intimate forms of communication between cats, the spraying of urine is more potent – the pungent smell of a tom cat's spray in particular is not easily ignored. Your kitten will not start to mark by spraying until it is sexually mature (usually at about six months of age – see page 150). Both male and female cats spray, but their desire to use this form of communication is reduced by neutering.

Cats employ all these means to inform other cats of their movements; this allows them to "time-share" their hunting territory, and to meet up to reproduce if and when the time comes.

Body language

Kittens are very good teachers when it comes to body language. In their play and hunting practice they often exaggerate the movements and the body language that are visible in a more subtle form in adult cats, and some of the most appealing of all aspects of a cat's behavioral repertoire are displayed during play. Young kittens will put on a lively pantomime of hunting, fighting, and courtship that may not be shown by older cats living in a peaceful household.

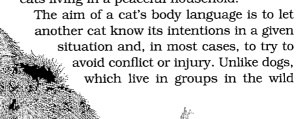

Boxing and ducking, the kittens' turned-back ears show that neither is quite sure what is going to happen next, but after a brief pause the rough and tumble will start again.

The roles are reversed every few seconds during the game, as first one and then the other kitten gains the advantage. Such games often only come to an end through exhaustion!

The aim of a cat's body language is to let another cat know its intentions in a given situation and, in most cases, to try to avoid conflict or injury. Unlike dogs, which live in groups in the wild

and have to learn to cooperate and signal their appeasement in certain circumstances – the cat is a solitary creature that can choose to be social or not if it wishes. It does not have the behavioral repertoire or facial language of the dog, and will usually either flee or freeze in the face of danger. Only rarely, when it has no other option, will it actually fight.

The cat uses its whole body to signal its feelings, although the main areas of communication are its eyes and ears, as well as the position and size of its body. These are examined individually below, but the combination must be taken into account to try to read the whole story.

Eye contact This is essential to us, and also has an important role in feline communication. However, prolonged eye contact or staring is an assertive act in the cat world, and is often used by rival toms – for example, in an attempt to intimidate one another.

This kitten is frightened: it has erected the fur along its back and tail, and stands sideways to look bigger to its opponent.

Your kitten's eyes will also be good indicators of its mood. A narrowing or widening of the eye is able to display interest, anger, or fear, and the size of the pupil is not only governed by the amount of available light but also reacts to the kitten's emotions. A dilated pupil may be a sign of fear or of arousal (you will also need to look at the

This kitten is feeling very defensive: note its flattened ears, raised fur, hissing reaction, and body posture.

ears and the body to decide which). When your kitten is relaxed, it will probably not have its eyes wide open, but the eyelids may appear heavy, and it may blink slowly as a sign of contentment. Blinking is also a reassuring signal between cats. If your kitten is frightened, its pupils may be extremely dilated, with the eyes appearing almost black, giving a "boggle-eyed" effect.

Ear movements Your kitten's ears are one of its most important instruments of communication. Flattened ears, for instance, are normally a sign of fear – the kitten will usually also be trying to make its body appear smaller so that it is not seen as a threat, or simply to make itself less noticeable.

You will often notice that your kitten's ears twitch if it is a little unsure of something, as though it is thinking about what to do. Licking the lips may also be a sign of anxiety, although a cat that sits with the tip of its tongue sticking out is usually relaxed and contented.

Use of the tail As well as being an important tool for balance, your kitten's tail is an excellent flag for communication, and its position and movement can tell you a great deal. Unlike a dog with a wagging tail, we all know that a cat with a swishing tail is not happy – in fact, quite the opposite. A swishing tail means that a cat is agitated and in emotional conflict, and is best left alone. When your kitten is happy to see you, it will greet you with its tail up – this is really so that you can investigate the scent produced under its tail, but fortunately we are oblivious to this.

If a cat feels seriously theatened by an attacker, it may become so defensive that the hairs on its tail become erect, making it bristle like a bottle brush. This is not often seen in an adult cat, but, when your kitten meets next door's dog for the first time, it may exhibit this use of the tail beautifully.

Cats in conflict with one another may hold their tails at a strange angle (rather like an inverted "L"). This can be seen in kittens when they are at play, as can an inverted "U" tail position – usually when they are indulging in a fast and furious game.

Body postures The whole body position will give you an indication of your kitten's mood. By erecting the hair along its back and tail, the kitten can make itself look significantly bigger than it actually is, which is useful both when on the attack and when trying to frighten off an animal that is trying to attack. The kitten may also stand sideways – again, to appear bigger – and then move sideways, keeping the whole body facing its opponent until it is safely out of harm's way. This crab-like motion can often be seen during kitten play.

In contrast, if your kitten is frightened by something, it may try to shrink down and look as small and unthreatening as possible, so as not to provoke an attack or draw any attention to itself. Alternatively, it may arch its back in an attempt to make itself look bigger, and begin to edge away slowly with a sideways movement.

This kitten has been frightened by something and has raised the hair along its arched back. If the threat does not disappear, the kitten will start to edge away using a crablike motion.

Cat talk

Your kitten will soon learn to meow for attention, and will do it even more if you leap into action – cats train us very well. They have a range of "meow" sounds, ranging from the pitiful and despondent (when they want something) to the extremely cross (if they do not get it). Experts are still studying feline sounds to try to establish how many there are and what each of them signifies, but, in the meantime, it is up to you to assess your own kitten's repertoire.

A kitten will hiss, spit, and growl when it is frightened of something, but the sound that we enjoy best is the purr. All cats purr at the same frequency – 25 cycles per second – but exactly how they produce the sound still puzzles scientists, although

During conflict a kitten may hold its tail at a strange angle, as here – this is known as the "inverted L" tail position.

many believe that it arises in the cardiovascular system rather than in the lungs or throat. Kittens purr when they are very tiny, and, as purring does not interfere with nursing, it can continue as a message between mother and kitten that all is well. The queen may also purr as she enters the nest to reassure her kittens.

Kittens purr when they play together, and when they are trying to encourage other kittens or even people to join in – perhaps to ingratiate themselves or to convey the idea of enjoyment. However and whenever they do it, we humans certainly have a soft spot for the contented purr, and hearing and feeling it must be one of the most rewarding of all the aspects of owning a kitten or cat.

This kitten is demonstrating a beautiful tail-up greeting: it is obviously delighted to see the approaching cat or person. The ears are pricked, showing interest, and the whiskers are held pointing forward.

CHAPTER TWELVE

LEARNING AND TRAINING

A kitten starts learning about its environ-ment from the moment it is born. Initially it may only discover what feels warm and where to feed, but this soon progresses to learning about its mother, its littermates, and the world around it – including human beings.

As kittens grow older, they must learn about the world for themselves. The kittens in this litter are starting to become a real handful, and weaning needs to begin in earnest.

Life is a complex, sometimes difficult series of events and challenges. Animals that learn to cope well with these challenges, and to face them in a non-confrontational yet adaptable way, are usually life's winners. Such individuals will survive and thrive in the environment in which they are placed, and this, surely, is what makes the cat such a unique and successful creature. It has managed to populate almost every part of the world, made itself comfortable, found food to eat, and, very often, found its way into our hearts and homes as well.

However, the adaptability of the cat has to be learned, and each and every kitten needs to discover how to be flexible in an ever-changing environment, how to cope with life's demands, and, most important of all, how to compromise.

127

LEARNING THE FIRST LESSON – WEANING

Studies of weaning in mammals have traditionally concentrated on the physical changes and nutritional demands of moving from milk to solid foods, but research recently carried out suggests that there may be more significance to weaning than simply what is on the menu.

A kitten learns all its social skills from its mother and siblings. For the first few weeks of life, it depends entirely on its mother for survival, and she provides food and warmth on demand. However, because the cat is a largely solitary species, a kitten must learn as quickly as it can to be independent of its mother and litter-mates, so that it can also learn to hunt, kill, and feed itself.

This transition – from total dependence to independence – needs to take place before the age of 18 to 20 weeks, when kittens in a wild environment would usually leave their mother and start fending entirely for themselves. This means that, during this period, the mother must teach her offspring to accept solid food and become less dependent on her by withdrawing her milk supply. From a behavioral perspective, weaning occurs in four stages.

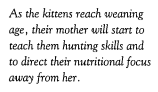

As the kittens reach weaning age, their mother will start to teach them hunting skills and to direct their nutritional focus away from her.

Stage one

This consists of "continuous reinforcement:" that is, the mother allows the kittens to feed – or to be rewarded – each and every time they approach her and root for milk.

Stage two

At three to four weeks old, the kittens are much more capable and active, and will approach their mother and demand food in no uncertain terms. She now needs to leave the nest more frequently to feed herself, in order to be able to produce the increased quantity of milk that the rapidly growing kittens require.

However, on her return, despite the kittens' active demands, the queen may not always allow them to feed. Even if they do so, she may get up and walk away after a brief period, letting the kittens simply fall off her teats. Really persistent kittens may even have to be nosed away, or may be dragged out of the nest as they desperately cling to the teats. For the first time the kittens learn to experience rejection by their mother. This creates frustration, as they can clearly see the object of their desire, yet may not be permitted to have it.

Stage three

As we know, frustration increases vigor – in other words, we try harder to get what we want. Having failed in their attempts to get to their mother's milk, yet motivated by their frustration, the kittens start to experiment with different ways of getting food. It is at this stage that the mother starts to initiate an interest in prey by bringing stunned rodents back to the nest for the kittens to investigate.

Stage four

This allows the kittens to relearn that their mother's approach no longer means milk, but signals food of a different kind. Not only has the process of weaning been completed, but the kittens have experienced the effect of frustration and learned to adapt their behavior to obtain rewards as a result.

Coping with frustration through weaning is one of the first of many challenges that a kitten will face in its life. It is not always possible for any living being to have exactly what it wants, whenever it wants it, and learning this early on encourages cats to be adaptable and able to compromise – and, ultimately, to fit into family life more easily.

The kittens learn about their environment by making forays farther and farther away from their mother, but will soon dash back to her if alarmed.

New ideas on the role of weaning perhaps explain why hand-reared kittens can be so difficult later on in life. Hand-reared cats do not usually experience the same pattern of redirected frustration that other kittens learn naturally from their mother, and this can sometimes make them more reactive or even spiteful during adolescence and adulthood.

If you ever face the prospect of hand-rearing kittens, you should seek help on how to instigate a weaning process that will gradually expose the kittens to behavioral experiences such as frustration. Your vet or a trusted breeder may be able to give you more information on this specialized subject.

LEARNING FROM LIFE

Like the vast majority of living creatures, cats will behave in certain ways because it benefits them to do so. A good rule of thumb to bear in mind when you are starting to train your kitten is therefore: "If it gets rewarded, it gets repeated." However, rewards come in many shapes and forms, and what is a "good thing" to one kitten may not be so to another, which is worth remembering at all times during your kitten's upbringing. This is important because owners often unwittingly reinforce unwanted or undesirable behaviors in their cats, simply by rewarding them inadvertently. For instance, most cats regard pleasurable physical contact as rewarding, but many also view vocal contact or even eye contact – being looked at by a person – as something worth working for.

Providing food is one of the best ways for a kitten's "new mother" to form bonds with it. The kitten is now weaned and independent from the queen, and has learned to adapt its behavior accordingly.

On the other hand, behaviors that go unrewarded will gradually extinguish, diminishing in frequency and intensity over time; this is because there is little point in the cat investing energy in any action if it brings no benefit. Having said this, however, do not forget the effects of frustration, and do use them to your advantage when training by delaying the provision of anticipated rewards. If you are trying to stop your kitten from doing something, and you take away the expected reward (such as food, or attention), remember that the behavior may increase before it decreases as the kitten tries harder to get the reward.

TRAINING YOUR KITTEN

Cats are not small dogs – an obvious point, but one that is particularly relevant when talking about training. Dogs allow some humans to get away with thoughtless, compulsive, and even punitive techniques to train them to do what they want. This is not necessarily because they want to "please" us, as has been traditionally thought, but more probably because they simply cannot escape.

Most cats, on the other hand, are unlikely to put up with any training technique that does not fit their view of life by simply walking or running away. Cats do not have to put up with humans attempting to force them to perform specific actions, and do not have to put a brave face on the indignities of being trained by a clumsy owner. If they don't like it, they leave.

This characteristic will make training your kitten both challenging and enormously rewarding. If you can train a cat, you can train almost anything (even members of your family) because you will have learned how to work with the animal, how to motivate it, and how to hone your timing skills so that your rewards are meaningful and effective.

Why train your kitten?

Teaching your kitten to do specific things when asked is valuable for many reasons. Some owners are reluctant to train their cats in any way, believing that it is demeaning to make them perform "tricks." When dealing with such an independent and dignified animal, this is understandable, but sensitive, fun training should never be demeaning.

Training your kitten to respond to you has a practical purpose. For instance, teaching it to come when called can be a lifesaver, and will be vital if you ever need to locate it in a dangerous situation. In order for your kitten to become an accepted and much-loved member of the household, you also need to instill some guidelines about what is appropriate behavior and what is not.

However, more than any other reason, training is important because it will strengthen the bond and enhance the relationship between you and your kitten. Training time for most cats means interaction. It is quality time that you are spending to stimulate your kitten's mental abilities and to build on your relationship. Training that is fun also increases the confidence of many animals.

Success breeds success, and the more enjoyable activities that your kitten takes part in with you, the more reinforcing – or rewarding – they will become. Good relationships, and good training, are built on mutual respect and communication between individuals. For many owners, training their new kittens to perform simple actions through kind, gentle, and effective methods is a true meeting of minds – you really do need to be open to the feline view of the world in order to communicate effectively (see also pages 117–26).

Motivating your kitten to learn

As has already been mentioned, cats rarely do something for nothing. If you are aiming to teach your kitten a new exercise – even something as simple as coming when called or using the pet door – the kitten will have to work at learning something new, and the motivation for this effort needs to be apparent.

This "salary" that you offer in return for your kitten's "work" also needs to be attractive – it is no good offering a piece of uninteresting dry cat food and expecting your kitten to turn back flips, unless of course it really loves dry cat food. In most instances, the rewards offered for a new behavior need to be special – the equivalent of the salary plus company car, in human terms.

Many cats will work hard for a small piece of fish or chicken, or even a tiny piece of cheese. Many different cat treats are available from pet shops and supermarkets, and your kitten may love one of these. Novelty value also counts for a great deal. Offering your kitten a small piece of what it usually gets to eat for dinner is not likely to have the desired effect – after all, the kitten can simply wait until dinnertime and have 10 times as much for nothing.

If your kitten is not particularly motivated by food and is not tempted even by a special treat, a game with you, or a particular toy may have the desired effect. The general rule is to find something that your kitten really likes to provide motivation in the initial stages of training. It is also vital that you give the reward the moment your kitten performs the desired behavior, as a delay of even a second will weaken its effect.

Taking things slowly

Any training, of any description, must be done at your kitten's pace. It is almost impossible to try to rush training a cat, and impatience could result in your kitten being put off the experience altogether.

Always break down the task into as many small stages as possible, and work toward each goal in a quiet and methodical way. Teaching your new kitten should be done without any distractions and in a relatively quiet place. Other cats or dogs will almost always attempt to muscle in on the fun if they are aware that the kitten is receiving some extra attention, particularly if you are using food as a lure. It is therefore best to practice training on a one-to-one basis, which will also give your relationship with your kitten an opportunity to mature away from the other pets.

Like us, cats can have off days. Your kitten may have been keen to play with you or to come to you quickly when you practiced the day before, but may seem sluggish or bored the next time you try. Equally, you may not always be in the best of moods to begin a training session. If you have been stuck in traffic on the way home, or your kitten seems restless or disinterested, stop, have a break, and resume at another time. This so-called latent learning – the experience of having a break from learning a new behavior, and then returning to it with a greater understanding the next time – often helps in training, usually when least expected. This makes taking rests between very short, very sweet training sessions vitally important.

What about punishment?

NEVER use physical punishment of any kind when interacting with your kitten. Punishment is counterproductive, will break down your relationship, and will lead to resentment, fear, and stress on both sides.

An owner sometimes claims that a cat "knows it has done wrong" after behaving inappropriately. Sadly, this is a misinterpretation of the cat's body language, as no animal is able to understand the complexity of our human values. A cat cannot be expected to comprehend the difference between scratching the curtains or the sofa if its scratching post is made of similar material, nor that the best potted plant in the corner was not put there for indoor toileting.

A cat that behaves in inappropriate ways often learns to associate its owner's presence – particularly a stern face or tone of voice, or an aggressive approach – as threatening. It may cower or run away, but this does not indicate "guilt" as we might experience it, as the link between the cat's own behavior and the person's anger is rarely made. Instead, the cat is simply showing fear at the owner's attitude.

If your kitten does scratch the sofa, an angry reaction on your part – shouting or smacking, for instance – might stop the problem on that occasion, but the kitten is likely to do it again when you are not there. Instead, you need to interrupt the unwanted behavior in some way. A sharp hissing sound will quickly distract most cats, as will a sudden noise such as clapping your hands. Try to avoid your kitten associating the interruption with you, so that it imagines the interruption to be a direct result of its actions.

Coming when called

One of the most vital lessons you need to teach your kitten is to come when you call its name. This can save endless hours of worry and energy in the long term: a kitten that responds quickly and willingly when you call will be far easier to locate than one that ignores you, and you will always be able to discover its whereabouts (provided of course that it is within earshot). You should teach this lesson at an early stage, as it will be very useful if and when you let your kitten outdoors for the first time (see pages 77–8).

In an emergency, a cat that comes when called can also be removed from danger, or "rescued." Cats are notorious for wandering into sheds, garages, or other inviting places, only to become trapped when someone unwittingly closes the door on them. In this situation, you will at least have some chance of locating your kitten if it knows its name when you call, and responds by calling back or trying to get to you.

Last but not least, it is also enormously satisfying to call your kitten's name out of the back door, to hear a faint call in response from somewhere in the distance, and then to see the kitten bounding through the hedge in anticipation of reaching you.

1 The way to most cats' hearts is through their stomachs. This means that the easiest way to start teaching your kitten to come when called – in other words, to provide the motivation for the kitten to do so – is to make a strong association with its name and food.

When your kitten is close by, call its name, then immediately offer something delicious, such as a sumptuous tidbit or a tasty meal. Call the kitten's name every time you are going to do this, and keep your tone of voice light and pleasant. Tests have shown that words or sounds of two syllables seem to have more of an activating impact on many animals, while single, flat-sounding tones appear to have a slowing or calming effect. If your kitten's name has two syllables, simply use that; if not, it may be helpful to add another sound to it. For example, "Tig-ger" is easy to call out of the back door, while "Blue" naturally becomes "Blue-y"!

Initially, only call your kitten when it is in view, just to build the association. Watch for your kitten turning its head toward you in anticipation of something pleasant happening, and remember to give the reward the moment you get a response.

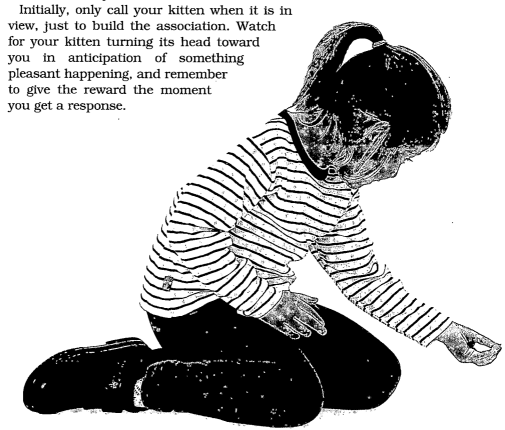

2 Start to move farther away before calling, until your kitten will come running even when you are out of sight. Intersperse rewarding with food, games, or affection at this stage. Many kittens will come simply for company or affection, and this makes training them easy at an early age; others are more independent and will need to be offered a bigger inducement. Whatever your kitten's personality, always make coming to you a pleasurable experience.

3 If you wish to sharpen your kitten's recall even further, start to reward only the fastest or best responses. You can even put your kitten on a random reward schedule as a final stage of training.

One word of warning. NEVER call your kitten to you and then "punish" it in any way. As has already been discussed (see pages 117–21), cats perceive the world in different ways from us, making some experiences appear to be punishing from a feline point of view, even if not from ours. Errors to avoid are calling your kitten in order to put it in a carrier before going to the vet, or to carry out a procedure that the kitten dislikes, such as giving medicine.

One poor owner who had worked extremely hard for about five weeks to establish and maintain her kitten's recall on command was forced to start all over again after calling the kitten to her, putting it on a table, and spraying it with flea spray. Cats have long memories, and the association to your kitten of its name and an unpleasant experience can remain firmly fixed for a long time.

Much like dogs, the way to most cats' hearts is through their stomachs. Use a treat or a morsel of favorite food to encourage your kitten to come when you call, and to increase its interactions with you and the other members of your family.

135

By your propping open the pet door with a pencil or securing it with a piece of tape, the kitten will gain in confidence and see that it may enter and leave as it wishes. Encourage your kitten with morsels of food and plenty of praise initially, as the first step can be a little daunting.

Using the pet door

Once your kitten has completed its primary vaccinations (see page 87), you may decide to allow it in and out of the house as it pleases, and many people find that a pet door works well. However, to many kittens the sight of a strange, swinging door – heralding a route to a daunting new world outside – is a terrifying experience. Always build your kitten's confidence about going outdoors (see pages 77–8) before training it to use the door. After all, it will not be very rewarding for your kitten to learn to use the door, only to find that the result of pushing it open is becoming lost or being attacked by another cat waiting on the doorstep.

Some confident kittens learn the knack of pushing a pet door open very quickly, as their desire to come in or go out motivates them to do so. Other, more anxious individuals take a long time to discover that the movement, noise, and sight of the door are not dangerous and that they will not come to any harm by pushing it.

As with all training exercises, you should work on one stage at a time, and only continue at your kitten's pace. Never try to push the kitten through the door, or to push its paws or head against the door in an attempt to show it what to do. You could put your kitten off for life by frightening it in this way.

1 Your kitten needs to understand that the door is now an entrance and exit to the home. This can be a strange concept for some cats to cope with, particularly if they have not already seen other animals using the door. At first, prop the door open with a pencil or piece of tape so that your kitten can look out through the hole. Allow as much

time as it takes for the kitten to become comfortable with this idea –
if you sit down nearby, you will give it extra confidence.

2 Most kittens find the first experience of going through a pet door less
frightening if they are entering their area of security rather than leaving
it, so gently placing your kitten at the entrance to the open door from
the outside is usually the best option at first. Ask someone to help you
with this by holding the kitten carefully outside the door, while you
encourage it to come through the hole by luring with a food treat and
calling its name. Remember to give your kitten the food the instant it
comes through the door.

*Once the kitten seems happy
and confident about going
through the pet door when it
is propped open, take away the
pencil or tape and encourage
it to push the door open itself.
Dangling a toy invitingly on the
other side of the door should
help to tempt the kitten through
if it is a little reluctant at first.*

3 Once the kitten has mastered coming in through the hole, squat
outside the door and call the kitten through from inside the house.
Praise and reward any attempts to walk through initially, then give the
food and plenty of praise for a confident walk through the open door.

4 Prop the door so that it is only half-open. This will show the kitten
that, although it is still an entrance/exit hole, a hint of an obstruction
needs to be overcome to get the reward. Encourage your kitten to push
gently against the door to gain access to the food.

5 Once the kitten is confident about pushing the door like this – from
both sides – lower it a little more and then let the kitten experiment
again. In no time at all, the kitten will be popping in and out of the flap
just for the fun of it.

"No-exit" signs If you plan to keep your kitten in at night – or at any other time (see Chapter Seven) – it is a good idea to signal the times when the pet door cannot be used as an exit. If you think about it, although you may be able to see quite well that the door is locked in place, your kitten will simply not understand why it cannot push the door open when only minutes before a single shove with its front paws worked beautifully.

Placing a "signal" next to or across the door is a useful strategy, as your kitten will learn to associate the signal with an inability to open the door, and so will give up excessive attempts to break out. The signal can be anything that is convenient – such as a towel hanging nearby or a piece of board placed across the door – but must be consistent right from the start. As your kitten starts to get the idea, the "no-exit" signal can gradually be reduced in size or moved farther away.

Walking on a harness and lead

If you do not plan to allow your kitten free access to the outside world, training it to walk on a harness and lead can provide a reasonable compromise between freedom and safety (see also page 78). You may, for example, decide that you wish to exercise your kitten on a harness solely in the comparative safety of your garden, so that it can explore the outside world but is protected from other cats, dogs, and traffic.

Some owners manage to train their cats to go for walks farther afield without becoming at all fearful, but this takes a great deal of gradual, patient practice and training from an early age. In contrast to what some people may think, walking a cat on a harness is not the same as exercising a dog on a collar and lead. In fact, more often than not, it is the cat that decides where it wishes to walk and the owner who follows behind.

If you would like to accustom your kitten to wearing a harness for outdoor exercise, you must start early. Make the experience rewarding and soothing for the kitten, using food and plenty of praise.

Cats can easily become panic-stricken if they are frightened and find that they cannot run away. For this reason it is essential to accustom your kitten to wearing a harness, and to the feeling of the lead being attached, very gradually.

1 The process of training must be carried out extremely carefully, and you must always stop immediately if your kitten appears to become at all distressed by the restriction of the harness. The first step is to accustom your kitten to the sensation of wearing the harness without the lead attached. Put on the harness very gently and then leave it in place for a few seconds while you play together; or feed the kitten in the harness.

2 Gradually extend the periods that the harness is worn in the house, taking things entirely at your kitten's pace. It should remain completely relaxed throughout, and this may take some time to achieve. As when you first began the training, if the kitten at any point seems to become distressed by the restriction of the harness, remove it and try again at another time.

3 Attach a fairly short, very lightweight length of cord or string to the harness (the use of cord or string instead of a lead at this stage is so that the kitten – and, even more important, you – can become accustomed to the feel of having some-thing attached to the harness). Holding the end of the cord very gently, allow your kitten to wander at will for a few seconds – preferably lured by a food treat held in your other hand. If the kitten starts to move away from you, either drop the cord or follow the kitten calmly. Never attempt to jerk or pull on the cord as a means of restraint, or allow the kitten to begin playing with the end of the cord (or later the lead). In doing so, it could easily pull on the cord, tightening the harness around itself and panicking at such a sudden, self-inflicted restriction.

Once your kitten is completely accustomed to wearing the harness without the lead attached, you can progress to using a very lightweight length of cord or string, and then to using a proper lead. Practice around the house, and only venture out of doors once you are quite sure that the kitten is relaxed with the feel of this restriction on its movement.

4 When your kitten is happy to walk on the harness and cord, swap the cord for a light lead. Practice in short, fun sessions, walking around the house, and always reward your kitten for good and confident behavior. Once the kitten is truly relaxed about the harness and lead, venture out into the garden to allow your kitten some of the benefits of outdoor stimulation, without the perils. Going out beyond the boundaries of the garden – unless perhaps to a very quiet park – is not advisable, as something unexpected could occur and frighten your kitten.

Training your kitten to retrieve

This exercise is very easy to teach some cats, but more challenging with others. Carrying prey is a natural behavior, and many breeds are adept at chasing, picking up, and carrying toys, and then bringing them back to their owners to be thrown again. This provides wonderful stimulation for an active cat – particularly one living indoors – as it exercises hunting skills that may not have many other outlets.

1 As always, time and patience are the key. Select a toy in which your kitten is especially interested, and begin an exciting chase game with it. (If your kitten shows no initial interest in any item, no matter how small or "rodentlike" you have made it, try smearing the toy with a little of the kitten's favorite food to make it more attractive.)

Toys are loved by children and kittens alike, and they will play happily for long periods. First get the kitten interested in the toy, then throw it – the kitten will follow the movement.

2 As soon as your kitten runs after the toy and picks it up, call the kitten to you. Offer a food lure, or an identical toy to the one that you have already thrown, as a "swap" for the retrieved item. Do not ever be tempted to engage your kitten in a tug of war with any item in an effort to get it back. Your kitten is the one with the claws and may win the struggle, which will simply encourage it to run off more quickly with the article the next time, or not to return with it at all.

Once your kitten seizes the toy, call it to you, offering a piece of food or another toy. Many kittens love this game, and learn to retrieve very well.

CHAPTER THIRTEEN

PREVENTING BEHAVIORAL PROBLEMS

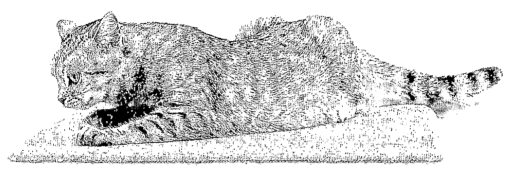

Your kitten will make new discoveries every waking minute of every day. In the same way that it learns about its surroundings by trial and error, and by watching others, it will be constantly discovering what feels good and what does not, what actions will result in getting delicious things to eat, and what will make you reward it with your undivided attention.

Although cats usually scratch to sharpen their claws, or leave a scent mark using a branch or post, they will happily scratch indoors too – the carpet can be a great favorite if a designated scratching post is not provided.

Cats are themselves exceptional teachers, and many have their owners trained and reliable within only a few days of arriving in their new homes. Most of us are more than happy to be "owned," loved, and trained by our cats – it is part of what makes them such fascinating and independent personalities – but some tasks that our cats set us to do may be less enjoyable than others.

For instance, most cats have their owners trained to give them affection when they ask for it. The deliberate and distinctive approach – tail up, possibly a meow along the way, and a quick rub – all ensure that any human with a heart is stroking, cooing, and talking to the cat within seconds. Many cats also ask their owners for food, or games, by communicating in a way that the owner understands. If your kitten rubs against your legs, gives plaintive chirps, and looks pleadingly at the food dish at five o'clock in the afternoon, you may consider it very cute and clever. However, if it leaps onto your head at three o'clock in the morning, meows so loudly that you cannot possibly sleep, or deliberately knocks ornaments off the mantelpiece in order to be fed or petted, it is quite another matter.

PREVENTION IS BETTER THAN CURE

As a general rule, it will be much easier to train your kitten positively – in other words, to do certain things – rather than to teach it not to do something once it has learned an undesirable habit. As has already been discussed (see page 133), punishment is never a solution to any problem. Whether physical or vocal, it will almost always be associated with the last event that occurred – often your appearance – and rarely with the kitten's own behavior. It is highly likely to lead to conflict in the kitten's mind about your presence, causing more stress and therefore an exacerbation of the original problem.

Unwanted behaviors in cats are nearly always natural behaviors that simply seem inappropriate to us. Many are also learned behaviors that have often been inadvertently taught by owners. The following are therefore two vital ways to prevent the occurrence of problems.

Be consistent from the start

Try not to allow your kitten to do things you may not appreciate later on. For example, if you habitually place its feeding bowl on a specific work surface, the kitten will build an association that the work surface is a good place to be. From its point of view, one work surface looks very much like the rest, so it is then hardly fair to blame the kitten if it decides to find out what the other work surfaces, stove top, and kitchen shelves have to offer. Of course, if the kitten finds these "forbidden" surfaces unrewarding, it may decide to stick to the only one associated with food. On the other hand, a kitten that explores a different work surface for the first time and finds the Sunday roast there for the taking is extremely likely to repeat that behavior.

Kittens will be kittens

Equally important in preventing problems is to anticipate your kitten's natural – and often essential – behaviors, and to provide a practical and appropriate outlet for them.

All cats need to be able to perform certain basic functions in order to maintain their physical health. These include the following:
• Eating
• Drinking
• Toileting (including territory marking with urine and/or feces)
• Scratching
• Self-grooming
• Resting

Some of these behaviors may seem almost too obvious to be examined, but thinking about them in some detail can be very enlightening.

Eating Of course your kitten needs to eat, but have you ever thought about what it might be like to eat too little, too much, the wrong type of food, or to eat in a frightening place? One behavioral horror story told of an owner who placed her kitten's food dish next to that of the family's eight-month-old Labrador. She told the vet that she simply could not understand why her kitten would not eat and was so thin, despite the fact that she kept putting food down for it.

Prevent behavioral problems by feeding appropriate food, at set times during the day, in a place in which your kitten will feel secure and comfortable. Give the kitten its own food dish and monitor its eating patterns. Stay in the vicinity and talk to your kitten, and let food help build the bond between you.

Try to be firm, and not to give in to your kitten's demands for food at all times of the day and night, or the demands will soon become a habit. If the kitten always appears to be hungry, ask your vet's advice – it could be that you are not feeding it enough or even that the kitten is suffering from intestinal worms (see page 91).

Drinking Cats are highly individual in their need and taste for water. Some love to drink running water straight from a tap or hosepipe, and will not drink from a bowl. Others seem to need very little water and may fulfill all their needs by licking dew from leaves in the garden, or from their food.

Some cats are extremely fussy about the freshness of their drink, as well as their food. If you allow water to stand in a bowl for more than about 24 hours, do not be surprised if your kitten decides that water in a glass, or even out of the toilet bowl, looks more appetizing.

Keep an eye on your kitten's daily water intake. A sudden increase could indicate a health problem, so contact your vet if you are concerned.

Always provide fresh, clean drinking water for your kitten, especially during periods when it has no access to outdoor and other sources of water.

Toileting However obvious it may seem, a kitten that has not yet been vaccinated, and therefore cannot go outside, will need a toilet somewhere indoors. Do not place a litter box somewhere so inappropriate, or inaccessible, that the kitten learns to go to the toilet elsewhere.

143

Common sense is your best guide here. You would not like to eat your dinner in the toilet, and neither do cats, so placing your kitten's food a respectful distance from the litter box is an essential requirement. Equally, your kitten needs to feel secure while in the box, and must be protected while in this vulnerable position from the advances of children, dogs, and other cats.

Another factor almost guaranteed to put your kitten off toileting on the box is being grabbed while there in order to be given some medicine. Even though this may be the only time in the day when your kitten keeps still long enough for you to hold onto it, resist the temptation and administer medicine or other treatment well away from the box.

Your kitten could decide that the soil in a potted plant looks more inviting than using the litter box, or, if it is allowed outdoors, venturing outside on a cold winter morning. Once again, avoiding the occurrence of the problem at the start will be better than trying to solve it after the event, so try covering over the soil in plant pots with a handful of gravel, or small stones, as a temporary measure.

Scent-marking with urine from a squatting position. The cat squirts a small volume of urine onto a horizontal surface, thus leaving a message about itself for other passing cats.

Territory marking If a cat feels under threat in its territory and needs to feel more secure, it may begin to "mark" in and around the home, using urine and/or feces, once it approaches the onset of sexual maturity (see also page 150). Both male and female cats, whether neutered or not, may do this. The marks that are left may be urine patches deposited from a squatting position on flat surfaces, or sprayed urine (generally on vertical surfaces); or they may be feces left in open places (middening).

As the marking is often carried out by cats in an effort to make themselves feel more secure, punishment will be especially counter-productive. It also means that cats frequently attempt to link their

144

own smell with that of their "protectors" – in other words, with their owners. It is therefore not uncommon for cats to mark with urine, feces, or both, on areas that we find particularly disconcerting. Clothing (or other items that smell of us), furnishings, and even the middle of the bedspread are relatively common targets.

In all cases of indoor toileting, the scent of the cat's own urine is likely to lead it back to the same place to mark again, so removing all traces is essential. Cleaning the area with any product that smells good to you, but simply masks the smell to your kitten, may make it think that another cat has marked over the top. Cleaning all areas with a solution of biological detergent or bicarbonate of soda is the most effective way to break down the proteinaceous compounds that are present in urine, and you should follow this by light agitation with a brush and low-grade alcohol – such as a solution of rubbing alcohol – to remove any further fatty deposits (check for colorfastness of furniture or fabric dyes by cleaning a hidden corner first).

There are many reasons why cats engage in inappropriate indoor soiling. Some of these include the fear of their core territory being invaded from external sources – either by another cat, such as a local tom, or by other animals. Some cases involve stress from a source from within the home – such as direct competition for sleeping areas, food, or even the owner's attention – between two or more cats.

In almost every case, the cause of the anxiety or frustration needs to be explored and removed. This may be as simple as blocking up the pet door so that next door's adult cat cannot chase your kitten indoors, but marking generally has a number of causative factors, and finding the root of these is essential. Success in treating problems nearly always lies in getting help early. Take the kitten to your vet to ensure that it is not suffering from any medical problem that could be causing the behavior. If all is well physically, ask your vet for a referral to a qualified cat-behavior expert as soon as possible.

Scratching All cats have a need to scratch, and the action is a very deliberate and necessary one. Scratching helps to manicure the claws, is a fundamental method of scent communication between felines, and makes a cat feel more secure in that environment. In order to preserve your best furniture, and also to ensure that your kitten has an outlet for this natural behavior, you must provide a suitable scratching post for it to use (see pages 51–2).

Although some scratching is essential for all domestic felines, if a cat is anxious or stressed, it will feel the need to scratch other objects as well as its designated post, and may do so in several locations around the home. If your kitten is insistent on using many different areas and items of furniture for scratching, there may be an anxiety problem. This should be investigated as soon as possible, so ask your vet for a referral to a cat-behavior expert.

Self-grooming It is estimated that a healthy adult cat may spend up to 30 percent of its time engaged in grooming its own coat. This is mainly a kind of "combing" with the tongue, rather than washing, but cats can also cool themselves by smearing their coats with saliva and allowing it to evaporate.

If your kitten is not grooming itself regularly, it may be suffering from an illness of some kind or from severe stress. Equally, overgrooming, in which a cat may groom itself so excessively that it pulls its own coat out, may well be a sign of illness or anxiety. Always have your kitten checked by your vet in such a case and referred on to a cat-behavior expert if necessary.

Resting Your kitten needs a designated place in the home – or several places – in which to rest peacefully. One of the major causes of stress in cats, particularly those that live an entirely indoor existence, is being unable to remove themselves from the hubbub of daily life to find somewhere safe to sleep.

Cats love high places – they feel secure in being able to watch the world go by from above, and providing such a sanctuary for your kitten is essential if you have young children, dogs, or other cats. Even where comfortable resting areas are available, some cats will perceive that there are not enough to go around and may refuse to share with another cat in the household. Disputes may occur over specially favored spots, such as by the fire, but confrontations of this kind can often be avoided by providing enough prime sites to keep all the members of the household happy.

Providing stimulation

In addition to the basic natural behaviors that have been described above, the following activities will all be fundamental to your kitten's behavioral repertoire:
• Acting out predatory sequences
• Exploring
• Exercising (including climbing, jumping, and running)
• Social contact
These behavioral needs must all be catered to, in order to help prevent the development of behavioral problems.

Cats need to play, to act out predatory sequences, and to explore. Each of these activities provides all-important mental stimulation, as well as physical exercise. If you do not provide your kitten with an adequate outlet for its hunting skills, chasing behaviors, and pouncing abilities, it will continue to practice them – but perhaps on you instead (see pages 114–15). Many of the aggression cases presented to behavior experts are linked to lack of stimulation in the cats' environment. Of course, cats that are given the freedom to go outside will tend to find their own stimulation and gain plenty of exercise by performing natural activities – including climbing trees, running, and jumping – even if they are not proficient hunters.

One study has suggested that the minimum area used by a semiferal urban cat is 240 sq yds (200 sq m). However, more important than space is the complexity of the environment. Your kitten needs to be able to explore and to find its home full of interesting objects and areas that stimulate its three-dimensional perception (see pages 117–21).

This means that you must provide the opportunity for your kitten to climb up and run along high surfaces, and produce stimulating and novel objects for investigation and play. Even an object as simple as a safe cardboard box is new and different. "Puzzle feeders" of various descriptions are also available, and mean that the kitten has to "work" in order to get its food.

Introducing a wide variety of toys will help enrich your kitten's lifestyle if it is kept indoors, although many cats also like their owners to interact with them as they play. Cats need contact with people, or another cat, and "quality time" spent with your kitten is vital. You will probably feel better for it too!

Getting expert help

If you are experiencing any behavioral problem with your kitten, ask your vet to refer you to a qualified cat-behavior expert. If you need help with your kitten, try to arrange it as soon as possible – this is because early treatment is always likely to be more successful than attempting to correct a well-established problem.

CHAPTER FOURTEEN

GROWING UP

K ittens grow up fast. Within a few weeks of birth they are fully mobile and beginning to take solid food; by eight weeks they should be completely weaned and ready to go to their new homes.

Unlike a puppy within a dog pack in the wild, which will be helped, looked after, and fed by other members of the group until it can join in the hunt, a kitten must learn very quickly to look after itself and to catch its own prey. It needs to be an independent and successful hunter by the age of about 18–20 weeks, so it has little time for kittenhood.

MILESTONES OF DEVELOPMENT

Comparing the age of a kitten with the equivalent stage of a child's development will give you an idea of just how rapidly your kitten is growing up. During its first six to eight weeks, a kitten must develop from a tiny creature – unable to walk and with poor senses of hearing and sight – to an agile animal that can eat solid food and is learning how to hunt, using precision hearing and eyesight (see pages 117–8). Within eight weeks a kitten has developed as much as a one- to two-year-old child; by the time it is four months old, it has mastered the basis of adult communication, equivalent to that of a four- to five-year-old child.

A kitten must develop rapidly – from complete dependence at birth to being able to move, feed, and comprehend like an adult cat in just a few months. This two-week-old kitten is barely mobile, and will call to its mother for help if it falls out of the nest.

The next major stage in kitten development is sexual maturity, which occurs at approximately six months of age (see page 150), and represents the equivalent development of a 12- or 13-year-old child. Indeed, a six-month-old kitten is said to be 75 percent grown, so the comparison seems a fairly accurate one. This may also explain all those adolescent frolics and games that kittens play, and all the trouble they can get into at this particularly demanding age.

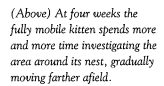

By the time a kitten is one year old, scientists consider it to be the equivalent of a 15-year-old person. At 14 months it is like an 18-year-old person – fully grown physically, but with quite a lot still to learn. By the time it is two years old, it is thought to be rather grown up – the equivalent of a 24-year-old person. From that stage onward, if you add four years for every year that your cat lives, you will be able to calculate its rough equivalent in human years.

On average, cats live to about 14 years of age, which is the equivalent of 72 of our human years. However, thanks to the expert veterinary care that is now available – combined with good nutrition and dedicated owner care – many cats are now surviving for considerably longer than this, and even 20-year-old felines (equivalent to 96-year-old people) are not uncommon.

Cats are in fact unusual in that they live a long time for their size – longer than any other of our small domestic pets.

(Above) At four weeks the fully mobile kitten spends more and more time investigating the area around its nest, gradually moving farther afield.

(Below) By nine weeks the kitten is already able to jump and move like an adult, and is starting to put basic hunting sequences together during play.

At six months old, the cat is the equivalent of an adolescent human. If you do not plan to breed from your kitten, you must have it neutered before it becomes sexually mature.

NEUTERING YOUR KITTEN

Your kitten will reach the stage of sexual maturity (in other words, will be capable of producing kittens itself) from the age of approximately six to seven months, although exactly when this occurs can vary considerably. The onset of sexual maturity in a non-pedigree kitten is thought to be weight-related, so that females first come into season when they weigh 5–5½ lbs (2.3–2.5 kg) at about seven months of age, while males begin the change when they are 2¼ lbs (1 kg) heavier and sometimes a month or two older.

In pedigree cats the timing is much more variable. For example, a Siamese queen may come into season at five months, whereas a Persian may not do so in the first year. The timing also depends on when a queen was born. A cat born in early spring may come into season that fall, but one born later in the year may not do so until the next spring.

Well before your kitten is likely to reach sexual maturity, you must decide whether or not you would like it to parent a litter of kittens. If you do think that you would like to breed from the kitten later, when it is old enough, consult your vet before going ahead – breeding is a great responsibility and not a decision to be made lightly. If you do not wish to breed from your kitten, you will need to have it neutered (or "spayed" in the case of a female kitten; "castrated" in the case of a male).

Spaying

Until fairly recently it was suggested that all female cats should be allowed to have one litter before being spayed (the reasons for this were never clear, and were probably based on human needs rather than those of the cat – see page 28), but this is now considered unnecessary.

A female cat will only have the desire to mate when she comes into season (also called being "in heat"), at which time she will begin to "call." The meaning of the word call will be obvious once you have heard a female cat making it known that she is looking for a tom. Owners of the vocal Siamese in particular will get the message – again and again!

A cat will keep coming into season every three weeks or so during the breeding season unless she becomes pregnant, so simply keeping your kitten indoors to avoid pregnancy will be a noisy business. One option is to ask your vet to administer hormone treatment in order to prevent the kitten from coming into season, but doing so could cause fertility problems if you wish to breed from her later, and is not recommended as a long-term solution.

If you do not wish to breed from your female kitten, the best option is spaying. Most people do not want the responsibility of a litter of kittens, not just because of the work involved, but because of the difficulty in finding good homes for them – there are already far too many unwanted cats looking for loving homes. Once spayed, your kitten will not come into season, and will be spared any of the diseases associated with the uterus or ovaries that may occur in later life, as well as the risks associated with pregnancy and birth.

Spaying means surgically removing the uterus and ovaries under a general anesthetic (your vet will ask you to withhold all food from your kitten after its dinner on the evening prior to the day of the anesthetic). The fur at the operation site will be shaved, and an incision made through the skin, muscle, and peritoneum (the lining membrane of the abdomen). The ovaries and uterus will then be removed and the incision closed. Your kitten should be able to return home the same day, and will need to return to have the skin stitches removed after about a week (unless soluble suture material is used, in which case the stitches will gradually dissolve on their own).

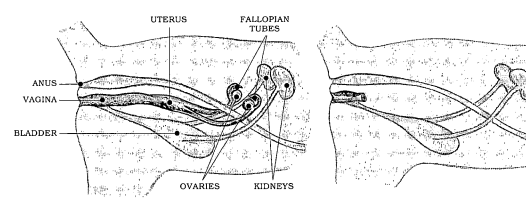

The female reproductive tract comprises the ovaries, fallopian tubes, and uterus; the uterus is Y-shaped, with two "horns."

During spaying, the ovaries, fallopian tubes, and uterus are removed through an incision made along the midline of the abdomen or in the flank.

151

Castration

As a male kitten matures, it will start to behave like a tom. An intact (uncastrated) tom cat has a very different lifestyle from that of his neutered counterpart: while he may be extremely affectionate to human companions, his priorities lie elsewhere, and he may spend a great deal of time patrolling his territory – which can stretch over a considerable area – fighting off rivals and looking for females.

The life of an intact tom is often somewhat rugged and likely to be considerably shorter than the life of a castrated male. Not only is the intact tom likely to become injured in fights with other cats in his territory, but he will be at much greater risk of infectious diseases such as feline leukemia virus infection and feline immunodeficiency virus (see pages 89–91), which can be passed on via bites.

Although all cats – neutered or not – will usually spray around their territory (see pages 144–5), an intact tom may be more likely to do so indoors. The urine produced will also be extremely pungent and cannot be ignored – inside or out.

If you have never seen a cat spray, watch from your window when one passes through your yard. Notice how he sniffs posts and places where other cats may have been – you may see him lift his head and seem to draw back his lips as he smells and tastes the air, using the vomeronasal organ to identify which cat passed by and when (see page 44). When the cat comes across such a scent – for instance, on a wooden post – he may turn around with his tail next to the post, and you will see his hind feet paddle up and down a little and his tail quiver slightly. In that moment the cat has squirted a small volume of urine, mixed with a combination of hormones and odors, onto the post at cat-nose level, so that the next passing cat will know that he has been there. In other words, spraying is an extremely effective method of feline communication.

Urine-spraying may not be a problem in the garden, but it can be very offensive when it happens inside the house. Most people prefer to neuter their toms to help prevent this, as well as to ensure that the cats do not roam too far or become injured in fights. This is also the decision of responsible owners who do not wish their cats to sire unwanted litters of kittens.

Ideally, you should have your kitten castrated at an early age (between six and nine months), before urine-spraying and the other behavioral changes start to occur (castration stops the production of testosterone – the primary motivating hormone for these behaviors). If you leave this until too late, your kitten may continue to exhibit some of the behaviors – such as spraying indoors – because they have become learned as well as instinctive.

Castration involves surgically removing part of the vas deferens and both testicles under a general anesthetic. It does not usually require the use of stitches, and the cat will have recovered well by the following day.

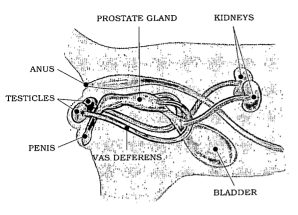

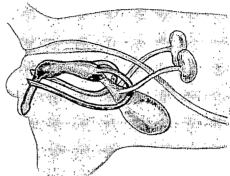

PROSTATE GLAND KIDNEYS

ANUS

TESTICLES

PENIS

VAS DEFERENS

BLADDER

The male reproductive tract:
the two testicles lie in a skin
sac called the scrotum, and are
connected to the penis via the
vas deferens (spermatic cord).

Castration removes part of the vas
deferens and both testicles. This is
done though a tiny incision made
at the base of the scrotal sac, and
stitches are seldom necessary.

Post-operative care

When your kitten comes home after being spayed or castrated, keep it warm and comfortable in a soft, clean bed in a quiet area, with a litter box available. Offer a drink of fresh water and, after a few hours, a small meal of white fish or chicken. Your vet will advise you whether you need to keep the kitten indoors overnight or longer.

Discourage your kitten from jumping or playing wildly for the first few days. Most male cats recover from castration extremely quickly, as it is not a major operation. Even though spaying is a major internal surgical procedure, a female kitten is also likely to be up and about almost immediately, seemingly none the worse for the experience. She may be drowsy for a few hours because of the anesthetic, but should be back to normal by the next morning. Some cats try to remove their stitches, so keep a close eye on your kitten. If you have any worries at all, contact your vet for advice.

Will neutering affect your kitten's weight?

All neutered animals have a tendency to gain surplus fat and could put on a little weight. This occurs partly because their priorities change – they expend less energy out and about, patrolling territory (in the case of a tom) and looking for mates, and activities such as eating become more interesting.

However, cats are very good at limiting their food intake to suit their needs, and, provided that you check regularly that your kitten is not becoming fat, there should be no problem. In any event, the risks of putting on weight are certainly less significant than those of an intact tom's lifestyle, the risks of pregnancy and birth for a female, and, of course, the possibility of unwanted kittens.

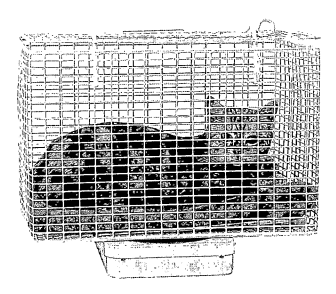

Dark fur patches

In some female cats, such as the Siamese, the fur that grows back over the operation site can be much darker than on the rest of the body. This is because the exposed area of skin will be at a lower temperature – as are the color points of a Siamese (see page 26) – making the fur grow back darker.

Neutered cats tend to gain surplus fat, so weigh your cat regularly as shown above, and keep a record. If you are at all concerned about your cat's weight, ask your vet for advice.

This darker fur will eventually grow out as the kitten loses and regrows hair naturally. However, if you intend to show your kitten in neuter classes and wish to avoid a dark patch, bandage a piece of padding over the operation site and keep the cat in a heated room (approximately 75°F, or 24°C) until the hair has regrown.

THE MATURE CAT

Your cat will reach its full physical size by one year to 18 months (depending on its breed or type, and on other health factors). Its coat may develop further, and the color may change a little, depending again on its breed or type. The cat will also have passed the most hazardous period of its life – when accidents were most likely to happen – and, having done so, is likely to be with you for many years to come.

It is a good idea to weigh your cat regularly at this point. Up until now, it is unlikely to have put on excessive fat because it has been growing rapidly, but growth will now stop, and the cat will be at its mature weight. Keeping a record of this will help you to calculate later on whether it has put on too much weight or has lost weight for any reason, and to take the appropriate action.

The way your cat looks at this age will change very little for at least the next 10 years, if not more. The rate of aging and the way in which individuals show their age vary from cat to cat, and also to some extent from breed to breed.

On average, cats now live to about 14 years of age, thanks to better nutrition, preventive vaccinations, and health care, and good veterinary care. However, many can and do go on until their late teens, or even longer. Siamese and Burmese cats are said to be fairly long-lived and regularly reach their late teens, although – just like humans – some look ancient by the age of nine (the human equivalent of 50), while others look positively youthful at 16 (the human equivalent of 80).

It is very difficult to age a mature cat accurately, since it could be anything from three to 13 years old, and yet still look fit and move with agility and speed. Most 20-year-old cats do look a little unkempt, but in general cats age extremely gracefully – much more so than their canine counterparts.

CARE INTO OLD AGE

As the years go by, your older cat may begin to suffer the ravages of time, but some fairly simple actions on your part should ensure that its life remains carefree and comfortable.

Your cat will reach physical maturity between one year and 18 months of age; at this stage it will be the equivalent of a 15-year-old person.

Regular veterinary checkups

While "old age" is not in itself a disease, it does cause the body's systems to become less efficient in a number of ways. This means that, while in its youth a cat may have suffered from one disease at a time, as an older cat it is likely to be troubled by a combination of problems that may interact with one another.

The key to good health care for your older cat lies in vigilance. Take your cat to the vet for a thorough physical checkup twice a year (rather than just once a year when vaccination boosters were due, as you did when it was younger), so that the vet can pick up any signs of kidney, heart, or other problems as early as possible. You may like to begin these checkups when your cat reaches the age of nine or 10. If there is nothing wrong, your mind will be set at rest; if a problem does arise, early treatment will be much more effective.

Some vets now even run special clinics for older pets, recognizing the need for spending a little extra time on these much-cherished companions and dealing with problems quickly.

Monitoring your cat at home

Regular veterinary checkups are very important in later years, but you should also keep a watchful eye on your older cat on a day-to-day basis. Continue with your own regular health checks, and take note of the cat's general well-being. If you monitor the basics and notice anything unusual – for example, if your cat is not eating well, is drinking water excessively, or seems to have trouble passing urine or feces – you can report these observations to your vet so that he or she can investigate the cause and treat it as necessary. Veterinary medicine is continually advancing, and a great deal can now be done to help, so never write off an aged cat too early.

Your cat's environment

Look afresh at your cat's environment as the years roll on. Does the cat have difficulty in making the leap up to its favorite perch on the windowsill, and does the jump down seem to jolt its whole body? If so, make things easier with a repositioned chair or stool, so that the steps up are smaller and the descent more gentle.

Similarly, is that stiff old pet door proving a struggle to operate or snapping shut on your cat's tail, or is the step on either side too high? Is the cat feeling the cold a little more because it is less active, and because its coat is not quite so oily and well kept? Perhaps a bed on or near a radiator, or a hot-water bottle wrapped in a towel on very cold nights, will provide additional comfort.

Your cat may also appreciate a gentle wipe with a cotton ball or a soft cloth dampened with warm water to clean any discharge from the eyes. A long-haired cat may need extra attention to keep its coat free from mats, especially under the tail.

Keep an eye on claws, too, which may become overgrown. Older cats also seem less able to retract their more brittle claws as fully as when they were young, perhaps because the elasticity of the muscles and tendons holding them in place has decreased. As a result, the claws tend to remain slightly unsheathed and may catch in upholstery or carpets, causing pain and distress.

Changes in behavior

Your cat's behavior may alter with age. While most cats sleep more and generally get on with life without causing a fuss, some seem to feel more vulnerable, and demand reassurance and attention. Some of the more vocal breeds such as the Siamese or Burmese can become very chatty, and will certainly let you know when they need something – be it food or a cuddle, or simply to find out where you are in the house.

The need for reassurance can often manifest itself in "night calling," where a cat waits until the house is quiet and everyone is cosily asleep, and then cries as if on its last legs. As soon as its panicking owner appears and shows concern, the cat yawns deeply and drops off to sleep, reassured that it has not been abandoned. If your cat shows a need for security in its later years, you could perhaps move its bed into your bedroom, provide a radio for company, or even set up a baby intercom so that you can voice reassurance without having to get out of bed on each occasion. Otherwise, make sure that the area in which the cat sleeps is warm and cosy, and try to be patient – it is a small price to pay for many years of love and companionship.

As your cat grows older, taking it for regular physical checkups is even more important, so that your vet can detect any signs of poor health at an early stage. Older individuals can tend to put on too much weight – as this 10-year-old cat has done – so continue to weigh your cat regularly, and adjust its food intake as necessary.

157

USEFUL ADDRESSES

American Cat Association, Inc.
8101 Katherine Avenue
Panorama City, CA 91402
Tel: 818-781-5656

American Cat Fanciers'
Association
Post Office Box 203
Point Lookout, MO 65726
Tel: 417-334-5430

Cat Fanciers' Association
Post Office Box 1005
Manasquan, NJ 08736
Tel: 908-528-9797

Cat Fanciers' Federation
9509 Montgomery Road
Cincinnati, OH 45242
Tel: 513-787-9009

TICA (The Independent Cat
Association)
P.O. Box 2684
Harlingen, TX 78551
Tel: 210-428-8046

Magazines

Cats Magazine
P.O. Box 56886
Boulder, CO 80322

Cat Fancy
P.O. Box 6050
Mission Viejo, CA 92690

PICTURE CREDITS

The Publishers would like to thank the following sources for their kind permission to reproduce the photographs in this book:

Key: b=bottom, c=center, l=left, r=right, t=top

Animal Photography/Sally Anne Thompson 75;
Animals Unlimited 78;
Ardea 9t/Jean-Paul Ferrero 72;
Bridgeman Art Library/Louvre, Paris 112tl/Oriental Museum, Durham University 112tr;
Bruce Coleman Ltd/Kim Taylor 92;
Corbis UK Ltd/Yann Arthus-Bertrand 23t, 26t;
Cyril Laubscher 22b, 31;
Elizabeth Whiting Associates 71;
Frank Lane Picture Agency/ K Delport 110/Foto Natura 27t/Foto Natura 9b;
Philip Perry 109b;
Marc Henrie 18, 20c, 20b, 20t, 21b, 21t, 21c, 22c, 23c, 24c, 25b, 25t, 27c, 27b, 30, 76;
Peter Clayton 112br;
Reed International Books Ltd/Michael Boys 56/Nick Goodall 107/Ray Moller 19, 24b, 24t/Guy Ryecart 55/George Wright 54;
Warren Photographic/Jane Burton 2, 10, 11, 13, 22t, 144, 157;
Werner Forman Archive/British Museum, London 112bl;
Your Cat Magazine 26b.

Special photography by Jane Burton

INDEX

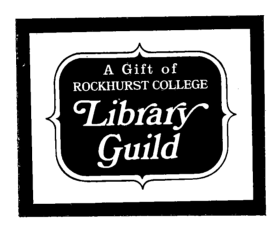

PROGRAM

EVALUATION

Methods and Case Studies

EMIL J. POSAVAC, *Loyola University of Chicago*

RAYMOND G. CAREY, *Lutheran General Hospital*

PRENTICE-HALL, INC., ENGLEWOOD CLIFFS, NEW JERSEY 07632

Library of Congress Cataloging in Publication Data

POSAVAC, EMIL J.
    Program evaluation.

    Bibliography: pp. 332–42
    Includes index.
    1. Evaluation research (Social action programs)
—United States.   I. Carey, Raymond G., joint
author.   II. Title.
H62.5.U5P62   309.1'73'092   79-26344
ISBN 0-13-729665-7

Editorial supervision and interior design by Serena Hoffman
Cover design by RL Communications
Manufacturing buyer: Ed Leone

Printed in the United States of America

10 9 8 7 6 5 4 3 2 1

PRENTICE-HALL INTERNATIONAL, INC., *London*
PRENTICE-HALL OF AUSTRALIA PTY. LIMITED, *Sydney*
PRENTICE-HALL OF CANADA, LTD., *Toronto*
PRENTICE-HALL OF INDIA PRIVATE LIMITED, *New Delhi*
PRENTICE-HALL OF JAPAN, INC., *Tokyo*
PRENTICE-HALL OF SOUTHEAST ASIA PTE. LTD., *Singapore*
WHITEHALL BOOKS LIMITED, *Wellington, New Zealand*

**To the people of two organizations
in which we both have been pleased to participate:
Loyola University of Chicago
and
Lutheran General Hospital, Park Ridge, Illinois**

Contents

Preface

In recent years, several trends have converged that have made the work of program directors and managers in human service facilities more challenging, but possibly more productive. These trends include the demand for accountability, the need to document goal attainment, and the application of modern management procedures to social service agencies. No longer can well-meaning human service personnel institute a program meant to help people without including some means of demonstrating that the costs of the program are justified by the improved state of the clientele. Although Congress initiated the requirement of including program evaluation in human service grants, the source of funding of a program now has little consequence on whether programs must be evaluated. They must.

Program evaluation has been called a new social science developing out of several social and administrative science fields (Lund and Kiresuk 1979). The increasing use of social science methods to improve the effectiveness of human service programs and institutions has made evaluation a "growth industry" in the 1970s according to Guttentag (1976). She estimated that $600 million was spent in 1976 for evaluation of human service programs. Writers in the health care field have suggested that two to five cents of every dollar spent for health care will be spent on the evaluation of its quality (Egdahl and Gertman 1976).

These are several reasons for this growth. Expensive attempts to relieve the effects of disadvantaged backgrounds during the middle and late 1960s were by and large ineffective; at least the impact of these efforts did not measure up to the overly optimistic expectations held by many program developers, government officials, and the general public. During the 1970s, considerable hesitation was shown in beginning programs whose effectiveness had not been demonstrated.

Over and above the limitations on the development of new programs, there are persistent and increasingly strong pressures on existing programs. Traditionally, government programs often are not explicitly terminated. Instead, new approaches to problems are tried by implementing new programs alongside of the old ones. Proposed Sunset Laws would put an end to this practice (Chelimsky 1978); Sunset Laws would require that a limitation be placed on the length of time a program could be authorized. After that time period expired, the program would automatically go out of existence unless its success could be documented. If a program achieved its goals, it could be authorized to continue for an additional, but limited, period of time. The methods of program evaluation would be necessary in such documentation of success.

It is true that the requirement to evaluate programs does not necessarily mean (1) that evaluations are uniformly good (they are not); (2) that evaluations are always utilized (they are not); or (3) that ineffective programs no longer exist (they do). However, many social scientists believe that the widespread requirement for evaluation, if coupled with increased sophistication in evaluation methods, will contribute to the achievement of the desirable goals of improving the effectiveness of social programs and making the introduction of new programs more sensitive to the needs of the people to be served (Guttentag 1977; Triandis 1978; Wertheimer 1978).

Types of Programs Requiring Evaluations

The preceding paragraphs have been very general, and the reader may have had some difficulty in knowing just what sort of programs are begin discussed. The following is a brief discussion of the types of human services that can and ought to be evaluated.

Health Care Facilities. Hospitals, clinics, extended care facilities, nursing homes, mental health centers, and similar organizations sponsor many services for their patients and clients. Such facilities expend much money on services whose effectiveness has never been fully documented. Educational services for patients, some forms of psychotherapy, certain novel medical treatments, recreational programs, and innovative ways of treating medical/behavioral problems are among the types of programs that should be evaluated in some fashion. Common sense and good management practices concur that the effectiveness of such programs should be documented in order to justify the continued expenditure of funds. Peer review and examination of records (such as, hospital charts) are among the methods of program evaluation specifically developed within the health care field, although other methods also apply.

Criminal Justice Systems. Police departments, court systems, and prisons all sponsor programs to encourage respect for law enforcement, to develop citizen–law enforcement officer rapport, to intervene in the lives of potential and convicted criminals, as well as many other programs to achieve varied goals. According to the Department of Justice, the federal government alone sponsors programs costing hundreds of millions of dollars to reduce juvenile delinquency. The effectiveness of these and other criminal justice programs is often questioned. Carefully done evaluations can aid in the selection of which programs to implement and in the improvement of existing programs.

Educational Systems. Schools and colleges should evaluate the effectiveness of their teaching staffs as well as specific programs that they offer (such as enrichment and remedial programs). The effectiveness of new curricula should be assessed before their introduction. Evaluation of such a wide variety of educational programs requires many different approaches.

Industry and Business. Training programs are widely used in all types of business. The effectiveness of such training programs should be evaluated periodically. Newly designed training programs are especially in need of evaluation. A new company-sponsored safety training program, for example, would be an ideal program to evaluate using cost-benefit techniques, because both the cost of the program and the cost of accidents can be calculated.

Public Administration. Local communities support a variety of service programs. Preventive medicine (for example, blood pressure checks), park district programs, and fire safety inspections are among the varied service programs that are sponsored by local communities. These programs need evaluation. Are they reaching the population for which they were planned? Are the recommendations of safety inspectors followed? Are people in need of medical care detected?

The Orientation of this Text

Implied at various points above is a recognition of the *need for different kinds of evaluations,* depending on the needs of the decision makers and community representatives, the expense of the program, and the goals of the program. There are two major types of services that evaluators offer to programs and administrators: feedback and the documentation of effectiveness.

Feedback refers to providing descriptive material about the program and its participants. Surprisingly little systematic material is typically provided for feedback purposes in most settings. Teachers do not know how students react to the courses they have taught. Directors of mental health centers do not know what improvement is felt by the clients of the center. Physical therapists seldom know whether patients follow the exercise regimens taught to arthritic and other patients. Valid information on performance is critical in all learning situations. However, gathering and summarizing such information is not easy in human services because systematic and convenient evaluation procedures may not be available. Evaluators can make contributions to the growth of skills and psychological satisfaction of staff members if they develop easy-to-use and informative procedures to describe the services offered and to assess the program participants' reactions to these services.

The second major thrust of the evaluator's job is to provide information that links participation in the program to the improved condition of the recipients of the program. In other words, was the human service program actually responsible for the improved status of the people served? Would a less expensive program have been as good, or would participants have improved even without any help? The process of isolating the causes of a change is difficult in real-life settings. To isolate causes requires gathering information from individuals not receiving the services in question.

The Purpose of this Book

Our purpose in writing this book was to provide a basic text for students preparing for careers in human service fields and in applied social science. Social science methodology has much to offer in the society-wide movement toward accountability in human service facilities and among human service providers. With appropriate training, social science students can find rewarding and challenging careers in program evaluation. A second purpose of this book is to meet the needs of currently employed social workers, psychologists, educators, sociologists, public health professionals, government employees, and others who are increasingly involved in some form of program evaluation.

Most important, we hope that this text imparts some of the excitement of participating in the growing, developing field of program evaluation. The field is not fully defined, its techniques are varied, and its application is challenging. But we believe it promises to have a positive influence on our society.

It is assumed that readers have taken several courses in social science and some undergraduate work in statistics; we do not assume any particular concentration in the courses taken. Because we do not assume that the readers have a great deal of confidence in their statistical capabilities, we have illustrated several useful statistical procedures in the Appendix.

This text emphasizes the nontechnical aspects of evaluation. To plan, conduct, and report on an evaluation requires personal skills not always possessed by people trained only in technical methods. Discussions of these skills and the typical interpersonal problems encountered when working in service organizations are intended to help the less-experienced evaluator become sensitive to the needs of the program staffs whose programs are being evaluated.

Several chapters include examples of edited evaluation reports. Our decision to use case studies was based on the reader's need to see the types of evaluation reports prepared for use within institutions or for publication.

How this Book Is Organized

The chapters of this book are arranged in a systematic fashion that reflects the steps in conducting a program evaluation. The flowchart that follows provides a preview of what is to come. The reader can keep track of how each chapter fits into the organization of the text and can identify the major aspects of the program evaluator's responsibilities by referring to this figure now and also as the course progresses.

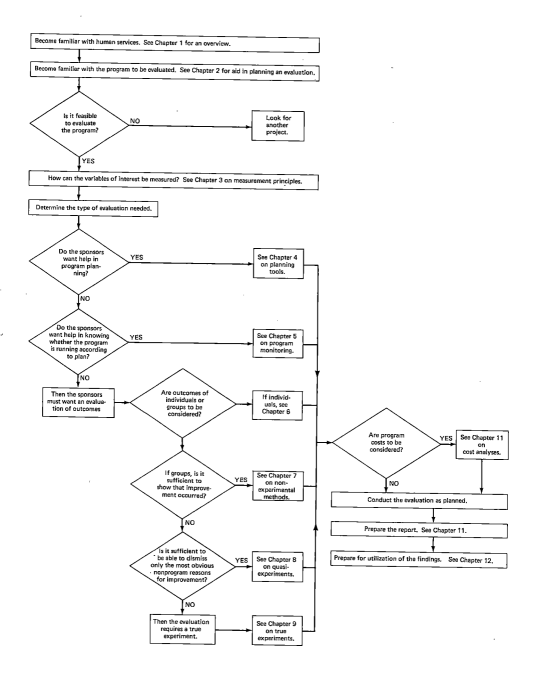

Become familiar with human services. See Chapter 1 for an overview.

Become familiar with the program to be evaluated. See Chapter 2 for aid in planning an evaluation.

Is it feasible to evaluate the program? — NO → Look for another project.

YES

How can the variables of interest be measured? See Chapter 3 on measurement principles.

Determine the type of evaluation needed.

Do the sponsors want help in program planning? — YES → See Chapter 4 on planning tools.

NO

Do the sponsors want help in knowing whether the program is running according to plan? — YES → See Chapter 5 on program monitoring.

NO

Then the sponsors must want an evaluation of outcomes → Are outcomes of individuals or groups to be considered? → If individuals, see Chapter 6

If groups, is it sufficient to show that improvement occurred? — YES → See Chapter 7 on non-experimental methods.

NO

Is it sufficient to be able to dismiss only the most obvious nonprogram reasons for improvement? — YES → See Chapter 8 on quasi-experiments.

NO

Then the evaluation requires a true experiment. → See Chapter 9 on true experiments.

Are program costs to be considered? — YES → See Chapter 11 on cost analyses.

NO

Conduct the evaluation as planned.

Prepare the report. See Chapter 11.

Prepare for utilization of the findings. See Chapter 12.

xvi

Acknowledgments

The following organizations and journals are thanked for permission to reprint or adapt material for this text: Institute for Program Evaluation, Inc., Roanoke, Virginia; *Hospital and Community Psychiatry; The American Journal of Public Health; British Journal of Addiction; Evaluation; Behavior Research and Therapy; Journal of Applied Behavior Analysis; Evaluation Quarterly;* Illinois Health Care Research Symposium; American Psychological Association; and Insurance Institute for Highway Safety.

A number of secretaries and assistants have helped us in the preparation of the manscript. At various times, the following people have given much-appreciated help: Carolyn Foraker, Karen Giafortune, Bernadette Jaroch-Hagerman, and Susan Borkowski Lueger.

The authors are grateful to their respective institutions for encouragement during the writing of this text. The first author's contribution was greatly facilitated by a sabbatical leave awarded by Loyola University of Chicago. The second author acknowledges with thanks the explicit support of his contribution by Lutheran General Hospital.

The authors also wish to express their appreciation for the helpful comments of the following reviewers: Amado M. Padilla, University of California at Los Angeles; Alan Siman, School of Social Work, San Diego State University; Ross F. Conner, University of California at Irvine; Brian T. Yates, American University; Myron Mast, School of Public Service, Grand Valley State Colleges; Clara Mayo, Boston University; Richard M. Wolf, Teachers College of Columbia University; Robert J. Calsyn, University of Missouri at St. Louis; and Francis G. Caro, Institute for Social Welfare Research of the Community Service Society of New York.

The first author thanks his wife, Wendy Cook Posavac, for reading and commenting on the manuscript and for providing unfailing encouragement through all stages of this text's preparation, and his son, Steve, for accepting his father's apparent obsession, in spite of being somewhat surprised by how long it takes to write a book. The second author acknowledges with gratitude the contributions to his personal and professional development made by his parents, Elizabeth Carey and the late Raymond G. Carey.

part

I

AN OVERVIEW OF

PROGRAM

EVALUATION

What do marriage counseling, blood pressure screening, school hot lunch programs, education at Harvard, job training at Leavenworth Prison, and day care for children of working mothers all have in common?

All these activities are human services designed and administered to help people. Of a myriad of services and products available in modern industrial societies, the greater proportion of workers and professionals are involved in meeting human needs for health care, education, training, counseling, emotional support, rehabilitation, and so on. The field of human services includes programs and facilities to help people lead more satisfying, healthier, safer, and more productive lives. Many of these needs have traditionally been met through the extended family or through voluntary charity; however, increasingly, such needs are being met through organized, publicly funded efforts. The federal government has increasingly become involved in providing or supporting human service programs and organizations. These services do not always achieve their goals, and they usually can be improved. The field of program evaluation provides methods that can be used to meet the demand for accountability and to isolate aspects of reasonably effective programs needing improvement.

The first three chapters of this book provide an orientation to the field and an overview of the methods and goals of program evaluations. In Chapter 1, we describe human service organizations and the types of programs and services offered. The people responsible for these organizations have many questions about how to plan the programs and to judge their effectiveness. The contributions of program evaluation to the various stages of program development and implementation are illustrated.

An overview of the approach evaluators take in preparing to conduct program evaluations is provided in Chapter 2. Often, program evaluations succeed or fail due to decisions, oversights, and misunderstandings made during the initial contacts with the program managers or sponsors. The principles described apply to all the types of evaluations discussed and illustrated in later chapters.

Because program evaluation is essentially a science of information and its utilization, evaluators must be prepared to assess the quality of the information forming the basis of their work. In Chapter 3, the reader is guided to the major ways to gather information on human service programs and the ways to judge the quality of information obtained. This presentation reflects the need for multiple sources of information in evaluation work because various sources have different strengths and weaknesses. The chapter should expand the reader's appreciation of measurement principles in applied settings.

1

Program Evaluation

and

Human Services

Program evaluation is a new and exciting applied social science, and its proponents hold high expectations for its usefulness. However, because the field has only a short history, the terminology of program evaluation has not been standardized. Before discussing specific applications of program evaluation methods, we shall attempt to define the field as a whole and illustrate its uses.

DEFINING PROGRAM EVALUATION

Program evaluations are usually conducted in not-for-profit human service organizations or in government offices. In order to understand what program evaluation is and the reasons the field is growing rapidly, it is necessary to describe briefly the type of organization that employs most program evaluators.

Human Service Organizations

Human service organizations are quite different from profit-making, product-oriented organizations that develop around production needs. These two types of organizations differ in two general ways: the way the task is defined, and the degree to which people identify with the organization (Demone and Harshbarger 1973). Profit-oriented organizations have specific, concrete objectives, such as making doorknobs or selling groceries. The specific tasks of the employees are defined by these objectives. For example, doorknobs are made of metal, so some workers will be engaged in a variety of metalworking activities, such as heating, casting, mold-construction, and so forth. In contrast, think of the courses that are offered in high schools. The specific offerings are dictated not by specific goals of the organization but by what educators and school boards think should be taught. Since human service organizations are developed to provide services rather than to seek a profit, they are shaped more thoroughly by culture than are profit-oriented organizations.

The second major difference concerns the way workers identify themselves. Counselors, teachers, doctors, among others, have professional identities that go beyond the organization for which they may be working at the particular time. Membership in professional societies is important to them. Typically, college professors in different departments of a college, although doing the same kind of work (lecturing, grading papers, advising students), will belong to totally different professional societies. On the other hand, if employees of production-oriented organizations belong to any job-related group, it is a union local representing many different jobs at a given plant. In general, human service employees identify with a discipline (psychology, medicine, social work), but the employees of profit-making organizations identify with the organization itself. The result of these differences is that human service providers will expect to play a bigger part in planning than would those working in commercial organizations. They perceive themselves to be more independent of the specific organization because the way they do their job depends on the discipline, not the given organization in which they work. In later chapters, this characteristic of human service professionals will be seen as important in the work of an evaluator. Not recognizing the style of human service providers would make the evaluator's work more difficult and at times ineffectual.

Not only are the form of the organization and the commitment of the individuals working in human services different from those of profit-oriented groups, but the products of these organizations are different. It is much more difficult to describe the intended outcomes of human services than those of product-oriented organizations. Whenever the intended outcome is hard to define, assessments of success will be very complicated. Industrial firms make things that can be seen, weighed, and counted. Department stores, supermarkets, and bakeries sell merchandise. To evaluate the success of such organizations is easy—at least in theory. To judge success, it is necessary to determine whether the products were in fact made and sold, and whether the amount collected for the products exceeded the cost of making and selling them. In practice, these questions are complex due to the nature of large businesses; however, the approach to judging the success of such an organization is easy to define and widely accepted.

In contrast, the methods of measuring the success of human services are neither straightforward nor widely accepted. For some human services, the nature of the "products" is as difficult to describe as are the methods of assessing their quality. What are the goals of a remedial education program? How do we know that a child has obtained what the program was designed to offer? When is an injured person rehabilitated? What level of rehabilitation should be hoped for? If the state provides hot lunches to a school, but the children throw out the vegetables, is the program a failure? Should we change the menu or teach nutrition to the parents? If, after marriage counseling, a couple gets a divorce, was the counseling inadequate?

If human services were available only on a fee-for-service basis, evaluating them might be left to free-market forces. The services that were purchased would, by definition, be successful; unwanted services would fail because there would be few if any buyers. The free-market approach has not been permitted to govern the field of human services. There are two major reasons why this is so. First, many human service providers are licensed by state agencies. Licensing has been instituted under the assumption that the public cannot easily differentiate poor from good human service providers. Who, for example, can really tell when a physician is competent? Traditionally, qualifications for offering services were based on training; however, a trend is developing that will require a demonstration of skill before relicensing. Thus, we now see physicians attending in-service training programs and taking examinations in order to remain in practice. Developing rational criteria necessary for relicensing requires the preparation of definitions of good medical care—a formidable task, given the complexity of medical care.

A second reason why free-market forces do not control human services is that the recipient usually pays for the service indirectly. Private insurance companies, large charitable organizations, local governments, and, increasingly, the federal government cover the costs of many human services. Once a service program is covered, the intended recipients have little to say about how it is administered or what is provided. However, it is important that insurance and public funds be used wisely and productively. The need to demonstrate the effectiveness of human services is critical.

Because of the differences between commercial businesses and human service organizations, a new discipline is developing to provide human services with the information to serve the same function as the information that accounting and business economics have provided for commercial firms. That new discipline is program evaluation, or simply, evaluation. The mission of this new social science is to improve the quality of services offered to people in need of human services. More specifically, *evaluation is a collection of methods, skills, and sensitivities necessary to determine whether a human service is needed and likely to be used, whether it is conducted as planned, and whether the human service actually does help people in need.* While doing these tasks evaluators also seek ways to improve programs. Evaluation is developing from concepts in psychology, sociology, administrative and policy sciences, economics, and education. The nature of the field is changing and is not identical to any of its forebears.

Evaluators fill a position between, on one hand, the role of the research social scientist concerned about theory, the design of experiments, and the analysis of data but for the most part uninvolved in the delivery of human services, and, on the other hand, the role of the practitioner dealing with people in need and seldom interested in or trained in the methods of data collection and analysis. Evaluators are able to read the language and to use the tools of the research social scientist. Research design, validation, reliability, statistical significance, and so forth, are familiar to evaluators. In addition, the effective evaluator will be sensitive to the concerns and style of the service delivery staff. Finally, evaluators interact with administrators who are ultimately responsible for the effectiveness and cost of the program. Because the field is so new and the tasks assigned to the evaluator are so varied, the role of the evaluator is not widely understood.

Participating in such a new field has advantages and disadvantages. The advantages include the intellectual stimulation provided by exposure to people serving various roles in human service programs and the satisfaction of seeing research methods used in ways that can be of potential benefit. The disadvantages include being viewed as intrusive and unnecessary by some service delivery personnel. As will be seen in the chapters that follow, the most effective evaluators show that they are allies of service providers, while at the same time asking searching questions and requiring documentation of answers.

Various Kinds of Programs

Some human service programs are developed to help individuals with acute but temporary needs; others seek to intervene to correct or alleviate long-standing problems; yet others help to prevent future problems.

Acute needs include the need for health care for injuries and for illnesses, the need for emotional and financial support after accidents or criminal attack, and the need for housing after a home or apartment fire. Such needs are pressing and must be met without delay if lives are to be saved or if worse emotional harm is to be averted. We are all aware of hospital care and emergency rooms, which alleviate physical needs. Acute needs of an emotional nature are sometimes met through community mental health crisis services. Some police departments try to help victims of crimes handle their emotional reactions. The help these programs offer is short term and must be quickly mobilized for maximum effectiveness.

Alcoholism counseling, drug abuse treatment programs, psychotherapy, physical rehabilitation, and training services in correctional facilities seek to help people with long-standing problems. There is a very high failure rate within such programs. Often, neither the cause nor the actual nature of the problem is easy to define. Thus, the programs are difficult to design, hard to deliver, and confusing to evaluate. Accountability in these fields has traditionally been minimal. However, because the amount of money and human resources devoted to mental health and criminal justice programs are staggering, evaluation work in these fields is being strongly encouraged, if not required.

Some human services are of a preventive nature. Preventive programs include law enforcement agencies suggesting ways to make a home or a store less inviting to criminals, health education programs providing nutritional information to enable people to avoid certain health problems, and health screening programs to detect illness or weakness that, if unchecked, could lead to serious disorders or even early death.

Educational programs constitute a major part of the human services industry. The products and goals of these programs are difficult to describe fully. Americans sponsor education at a variety of levels from kindergarten through postgraduate work for a variety of purposes. Among the purposes of educational programs are accreditation or licensing for various occupations or professions, teaching specific skills, enjoyment, self-help, enhancing social standing, and intellectual and psychological growth. Accounting for the funds spent on education must take into account the specific purposes of the program being studied.

Programs developed to reduce the effects of economic disadvantages

7

make up another large area. Welfare, job-training programs, Medicaid, Medicare, and Social Security are large-scale programs; their major function is to help people maintain life despite limited financial resources. The extent of such programs is illustrated by the amount—over $11 billion—that was budgeted in 1979 for programs to help the unemployed find work (*Time* October 9, 1978).

Human services are delivered by a variety of agencies with very different characteristics. Human services can be administered as regional or national projects involving millions or even billions of dollars. At the other extreme, a human service can be directed to a small group of people in a given institution over a very short time period.

We have purposely concentrated our discussions throughout this text on evaluations of the smaller programs likely to be encountered by evaluators working in human service facilities or agencies. Although some national programs are described, the focus on smaller programs is useful in an introductory text because most readers are more familiar with local government or agency-level programs than they are with national programs. We do not intend to imply that the methods used to evaluate national projects are totally different from the methods used by the evaluator in a particular agency. However, it is likely that the complexity of the statistical analyses increases as the scale of the evaluation increases because the more participants providing data, the more complex the analysis can be. Although complex analytical tools are useful, the use of simpler techniques is sufficient for most evaluators and may produce greater utilization by administrators who find statistics to be an incomprehensible if not an intimidating topic.

Reasons To Evaluate Programs

There are many reasons for conducting program evaluations. Among these reasons are:

1. Fulfillment of accreditation requirements.
2. Accounting for funds.
3. Answering requests for information.
4. Making administrative decisions.
5. Assisting staff in program development.
6. Learning about unintended effects.

The uses of evaluation will be described in more detail in the chapters on methods. At this point, these major reasons are discussed only briefly.

First, many facilities are required to evaluate their programs for accreditation purposes. Administrators usually seek accreditation for their facilities. Colleges, hospitals and mental health centers need accreditation to maintain viable facilities. Although many accreditation evaluations are nonempirical and may not require a high level of effectiveness to maintain accreditation, the threat of the loss of accreditation serves to maintain a certain quality of service.

Second, the vast majority of grant applications to government and philanthropic agencies require a discussion of the techniques to be used to evaluate the effectiveness of the activities supported by the grant. If a program to teach elderly people about nutrition is supported, the program administrators will be required to gather empirical evidence that the elderly are being reached and that the program increased their nutritional knowledge and practices. If programs are to be accountable to government or charitable agencies (and, indirectly, to the public), it should be possible to show some results for the expenditure of funds.

A third reason to gather evaluative information is to facilitate the completion of the vast number of surveys that government bureaus require for the continuation of funds. If an agency does not keep systematic records, each request for information will require a time-consuming manual search through files. If evaluation purposes are recognized and records are kept up in ways that are easily accessible, the evaluator will be a valuable member of the facility's staff.

Fourth, there are a variety of administrative decisions that can be enhanced by evaluative data. Any agency will be requested to expand its programs. However, budgets cannot be stretched to cover all the services that community residents or an enthusiastic staff suggest. Administrators are ultimately responsible for allocating resources. They must face questions such as: If job counseling is begun, what current service is to be eliminated or deemphasized? Is the proposed program suited to the needs of the local community? If evaluation activity has been a routine aspect of the facility, some material will already be at hand to help in the decision. In addition, if the principles of objective evaluation are accepted, an empirical approach to making decisions would be more likely to be followed. An objective approach to decision making would be an improvement over the typical strategy of selecting programs on the basis of impressionistic and anecdotal evidence or political pressures.

A fifth purpose of evaluation is to obtain information to improve practices. Without feedback concerning effectiveness, people cannot improve their skills. Providers of human services need information concerning how well they do their work. Also, evaluators can provide feedback on how well human service providers are viewed by those receiving the service. Good interpersonal relations are more important to human service providers than to people whose jobs require only superficial contact with people.

Sixth, a program has various effects on the facility and the community, as well as on the program's participants. Some of these effects are intended, some are unintended. Just as useful medicines can have negative side effects, so can useful and successful programs. This issue was addressed by Scriven (1967) when he coined the term *goal-free* evaluation. Goal-free evaluations seek to learn about all program effects. For example, the introduction of Western, mechanized farming methods has led to increased unemployment in some third-world nations because tractors do the work of many laborers. A focused evaluation that assessed only whether food output increased might overlook this all-important negative, unintended effect.

What Program Evaluation Is Not

In seeking to define an area, it is helpful to describe what it does not include. Program evaluation is not to be confused with basic research or with individual assessment.

Basic research concerns questions of *theoretical* interest, without regard to immediate needs of people or organizations. In contrast, program evaluation is directed at helping people improve their effectiveness, assisting administrators to make program-level decisions, and making it possible for programs to be accountable to the public. If evaluators do not provide information that is relevant to decisions, they are not fulfilling their major purpose as practitioners. Furthermore, evaluation, but usually not basic research, is often done under a time pressure and in settings (hospitals, courts, schools) that are designed for the delivery of a service, not for research.

If program evaluation is indeed a new social science with unique methods, it will require basic research on new evaluation methods and new procedures to encourage implementation of findings. Individuals creating such advances are essential to the practice of program evaluation; however, they do not fill the role of a program evaluator. Readers who have taken social science courses in which the role of basic research is held up as an ideal may be surprised to find that the role of practitioner is so central in the presentation of this text.

The second professional activity often confused with program evaluation is individual assessment. Educational psychologists, personnel workers, counseling psychologists, and others have traditionally provided diagnostic information for human service organizations. These people have served by administering intelligence, aptitude, interest, achievement, personality, and other tests for the purpose of "evaluating" an individual's need for a service or his/her qualifications for a job or for advancement. These activities are not involved in the program evaluator's role. Some of the material in the following chapters refers to ways of providing information about individuals. However, information describing people will be derived from measures of performance in their jobs or from measures thought to be sensitive to changes caused by a human service program. For example, program evaluators might measure depression to find an effect of counseling or other service, but *not* to assess a person's mental state.

Common Types of Evaluations

An evaluation of a program can be conducted from a number of points of view. This text divides evaluations in two ways: (1) according to the type of question asked about the program; and (2) according to the purpose of the evaluation.

The questions asked of programs can be classified into four general types: *need, process, outcome,* and *efficiency.* Each type of question leads to a particular focus and will be involved in our presentation. Process and outcome, however, will receive the bulk of the attention in later chapters.

The Evaluation of Need. An assessment of need seeks to answer questions such as:

What is the socioeconomic profile of the community?
What are the particular needs of this community with respect to the type of program being considered (for example, health, mental health, employment, education, crime prevention)?
What forms of service are likely to be attractive to this particular community?

The measurement of needs is a prerequisite to effective program planning. Today, more evaluators than in the recent past view planning as closely related to evaluation. Planning is, in fact, a form of evaluation, a form of evaluation that occurs before the program is implemented. In the late 1970s, the close association of planning and evaluation became evident in a number of ways. A journal titled *Evaluation and Program Planning* was founded. *Evaluation,* a journal especially directed toward mental health program evaluation, broadened its emphasis to include the principles and practices of the advocacy of change.

In order to be a good advocate and a good planner, one must have correct information about need. There are techniques that are useful for measuring or estimating need. Although some of these techniques are less quantitative than are other aspects of evaluation, the accumulation and synthesis of information is a necessary aspect of need assessment. This text includes a brief discussion of the evaluation of need. Those readers who become involved in the evaluation of need will find references to some key works on this subject at the end of Chapter 4.

The Evaluation of Process. Once a program has been developed and begun, evaluators will turn to documenting the extent to which the program was implemented *as designed* and is serving the *target* population. One might think of process evaluation as an examination of the effort put into the program. The kinds of questions that a process evaluation seeks to answer are:

Is the program attracting a sufficient number of clients?
Are clients representative of the target population?
How much does the staff actually contact the clients?
Does the work load of the staff match that planned?
Are there differences among staff members in the effort expended?

Answering these questions does not indicate whether the program is successful. However, the answers to these questions are important. Anyone responsible for directing, funding, or expanding the program wants answers to these kinds of questions. It is conceivable that a good plan has been inadequately implemented or that a successful program is not serving the population it was commissioned and funded to serve. Early warnings about such problems provided by a process evaluation would give the directors opportunity to redirect the program to give it a chance to be successful.

The information necessary for a process evaluation is often gathered by an agency; however, the information is typically not in a usable form. Material describing the clients is on application or intake forms but seldom summarized. Details of services received are part of prose notes made by care givers and added to the files. To retrieve filed information requires a special effort and considerable expense. Process evaluations are best conducted when a system of reporting is designed to facilitate gathering and summarizing useful information. In Chapter 5, we illustrate the use of simple information systems for human service settings. References are provided for descriptions of more ambitious systems.

The Evaluation of Outcome. The assessment of the outcome achieved by the people in a program has been the major focus of evaluators. For example:

Do the people who take a speed reading course read fast?
Do they read faster than those not taking the course?
Can evidence be found that taking the course *causes* increased reading speeds?

Although it is reasonable to ask these questions, it will be clear just by the length of our treatment of outcome evaluation that it is difficult to identify the causes of behavioral changes observed in people. For example, many people begin psychotherapy during a life crisis. If, several months later, they feel better and seem better adjusted, the change may be due to therapy, to the natural resolution of the crisis, to a combination of both, or to something else entirely. If a change in on-the-job requirements is followed by better morale, can we say that the program change caused the better morale, or should we conclude that it was simply the attention of management that led to improved morale? Perhaps, a better national economic outlook was the actual cause.

The presentation of methods will range from the very simple through the very complex. There are situations in which a research plan with many technical weaknesses will be quite appropriate for answering the questions facing the administrators and public representatives at certain times. Other more demanding questions will require more complicated research plans. In fact, evaluators might work with more complicated research designs than do laboratory research scientists. This is true because laboratory social scientists can control some of the experiences of the people in the research. In contrast, evaluators gather data from people participating in actual ongoing programs. Although these people are very interested in the benefits they can obtain from the program, their interest in the needs of the evaluators is marginal at best. The evaluators will be seen by some as requiring their energy and time without providing any service in return.

When designing and conducting outcome evaluations, the most basic task for evaluators is the need to define the ways to measure success. The evaluators of the national Head Start preschool program chose improved cognitive skills as the outcome of most interest. They were criticized as having defined the goals too narrowly because health examinations and improved nutrition were also included in the program (Datta 1976b). The definitions of successful outcome may well vary if we compare the opinions of various interested groups, such as the agency funding the program, the program staff, and the participants. A job-training program may be funded to provide job skills so that the long-term unemployed may obtain jobs with private companies. The staff may view the training as a reward for participation in local elections. The trainees may view the program as a good, albeit temporary, job. Whose definition of outcome is to be used?

At times, the outcome sought by one or more of the groups will be purposely hidden from evaluators. In politically sensitive settings, careful evaluators will be in an uncomfortable position if publicly stated goals conflict with privately held goals. Developing methods to measure success is difficult when goals are clear; when they are hidden, evaluators' jobs are all the more difficult. We will discuss ethical concerns that are relevant when evaluators believe that a program is using resources for purposes other than that intended. For example, in Dade County, Florida, an investigator charged that some funds for unemployed workers were used to hire relatives of politicians *(Time* July 24, 1978). If the outcomes of programs are regularly evaluated, such misuse of money should be more readily discovered than in the past.

Another problem centers on the issue of how long after participation the outcome is supposed to be maintained. People leaving a program typically return to the same environment that was partially responsible for their problems to begin with. The good intentions of an alcoholic may not withstand the social pressures of his or her peers. Cigarettes are smoked by habit in a number of situations, such as after meals, when worried, or when bored. Breaking down longstanding habits is very difficult. Although changes may be caused by an intensive program, the changes may only be superficial and dissolve in a matter of months, weeks, or days. If so, was the program a failure, or are the initial positive changes achieved while still in the program enough to label the program a success? These questions about outcomes are treated in Chapters 6 through 9.

The Evaluation of Efficiency. A program may successfully help the participants; however, cost is an additional issue that administrators and legislators must address. Evaluations of efficiency raise the following questions:

>   Does the program achieve its success at a reasonable cost?
>   Can dollar values be assigned to the outcomes achieved?
>   Does the program achieve a better level of success than other programs costing the same or less to administer?

There are often competing suggestions for the best ways to help people in need. Are people who are convicted of crime in need of psychological counseling for emotional conflicts, moral instruction on values, vocational training for holding a job, or academic instruction to help them complete school? Institutions cannot do everything. Choices must be made among possible services. To make choices, the criteria on which to base the choice must be defined.

Two important criteria used to compare programs are effectiveness and cost. If two programs appear equally effective, then the less expensive program is getting more results per dollar. If the more expensive program is more effective, the problem becomes more difficult. Is the additional improvement worth the additional cost? Another complication is added because most programs seek to cause changes on more than one characteristic. One program may spur improvement on several characteristics, and another on different characteristics. The weighing of the relative effectiveness of two such programs is very difficult if the decision maker wishes to be objective. An introduction to cost-benefit and cost-effectiveness analyses is given in Chapter 10.

PURPOSE OF PROGRAM EVALUATION

There really is only one major purpose for program evaluation activities, although this purpose is often broken down into several subpurposes. Human behavior is adaptive only when people obtain feedback from the environment. Our physical existence literally depends on the feedback within our bodies to regulate breathing and heart rates, levels of hormones and chemicals, eating and drinking, and so forth. Social behavior also requires feedback, but such feedback is not as dependable as that of our bodily systems. Delayed feedback, not clearly associated with the behavior causing it, is not very informative. Some writers have said that environmental problems are hard to solve because of the long delay between environmentally destructive policies and the feedback indicating a weakening of natural systems (Meadows and Perelman 1973). Program evaluation seeks to provide feedback in social systems.

What effect do social interventions such as jail sentences, nutrition counseling, community hotlines, crime prevention measures, or job-training programs have on the people expected to have needs for these interventions? Figure 1.1 illustrates the place of program evaluation as the feedback loop in human services and delivery activities.

This general feedback principle is often divided into two purposes. Evaluations can be done to improve the plans for services or their delivery, to raise the outcomes of programs, or to increase the efficiency of services; such evaluations are called *formative evaluations* (Scriven 1967) because they are designed to help form the programs themselves. The second general purpose is to decide whether a program should be started, continued, or chosen from among two or more alternatives; such evaluations are called *summative evaluations* (Scriven 1967). There is a finality to summative evaluations because, once the value of the program is assessed, it is possible that the program might be ended.

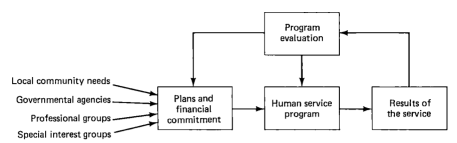

FIGURE 1.1: Schematic diagram of the place of evaluation as a feedback loop for a human service program.

In actuality, few evaluations really determine whether or not a program will be terminated (Hansen 1978; Weiss 1972a). There are many sources of information about programs available to administrators, legislators, and community leaders. Because program evaluations are only one of these sources, evaluators are not surprised when clear evaluation reports are not followed by definitive decisions. Thus, nearly all evaluations are formative, hopefully serving to improve the program evaluated.

Evaluations are also done for less than noble purposes, some of which are discussed in the next chapter.

TRENDS MAKING EVALUATION NECESSARY

The growing interest in program evaluation is the result of several trends in American society. *Accountability* has become a word often heard in human service settings. The call for accountability seems to have resulted from the consumer movement, from professionals' own desires to improve services, from an awareness of good management practices, from a recognition of the limits of society's ability to support human services, and from legislation.

The Consumer Movement

In recent years, a number of groups have been organized to make the needs of the consumer known to large corporations. This movement has had repercussions in human service fields. The philosophy behind this approach is summarized in the following comment: "The assumption that *operating* a service is equivalent to *rendering* service, and that both are equivalent to rendering *quality* service are no longer being honored as inherently valid" (Speer and Trapp 1976, p. 217). The right of professionals to make unchallenged judgments has been

16

curtailed. Physicians must practice with the knowledge that a Professional Standards Review Organization (PSRO) may be looking over their shoulders. A form of medical care evaluation, malpractice suits and the threat of malpractice suits, has already altered the practice of medicine. Although the change in working style may be greatest for physicians because they had attained a great amount of respect and freedom, no professional is above being held accountable. Government administrators, teachers, nurses, military officers, and even priests are among those whose performance is being more closely analyzed than in the past. Increasingly, respect and acceptance have to be earned by performance, not by certification or status.

Professional Concern

The service providers themselves have often cooperated and led in the movement toward the evaluation of human services. In the early part of the twentieth century, American medical care received initial evaluation from the medical societies themselves. There were three major thrusts to the evaluation of medical care: the structural approach, the process approach, and the outcome approach. Standards were developed for the organization of hospitals, the training of health care personnel, equipment, record systems, and so on. Most of the variables included in this approach to evaluation were objective and easily quantified. The process approach, however, did not have the advantage of such ready quantification because its focus was on the processes of rendering medical care. The care rendered was evaluated on the degree to which it conformed to the best practice or to the typical level of care available. The outcome approach focused less on the way care was given than on the results of care. An outcome evaluation conducted by the American College of Surgeons in the early decades of this century revealed such a poor level of outcome that the reports of this particular evaluation were destroyed (*National Standards for Community Mental Health Centers* 1977). Medical outcome evaluation on a national scale was not attempted for six more decades, or until the 1970s. The evaluation activity of hospital and medical groups was further encouraged in 1965, when Congress mandated that a form of national health care review program be implemented by hospitals participating in Medicare (Egdahl and Gertman 1976).

Managerial Effectiveness

Good management procedures have become more widely used in human service fields. McConkey (1975), while serving as a state-wide United Fund chairperson, was distressed to learn that some organizations requested funds but provided neither a description of what services they gave nor evidence that the services produced positive outcomes. Human service administrators are now much more aware of the necessity of effective management than they were in the past. The Crusade of Mercy (United Fund) of Chicago, Illinois, ran full-page ads picturing their "priorities committee." The caption under their picture stated that the ". . . hardest noses of Chicago run the Crusade of Mercy." The caption went on to describe the auditing procedure used and how some agencies are dropped from support.

The reasons for tardy development of careful management procedures in human services may lie in two major areas: (1) the difficulty of specifying what the outcome of an effective human service should be; and (2) the origins of many human services in small charitable settings. Commercial firms can be clearer than human service agencies can be about the goals they seek to attain. In addition, commercial managers did not have the "God-will-provide" attitude of the sincere but unsophisticated people who traditionally ran charity services. This is not to say that human service settings do or should act on the same values as business firms. Nevertheless, there is much to be learned from modern management methods.

Program evaluation in human services received impetus from the development of several data-oriented tools for managers. Tools for studying and improving the ways in which organizations function in accomplishing their purposes, such as operations research (Johnson 1967) and systems analysis (FitzGerald 1973), have helped evaluators with their work in human service organizations. Program evaluation can help managers learn which programs are successful and which programs are serving target populations. Such information can make some of the administrator's decisions more objective.

Limitations on Resources

The recognition that society cannot fulfill every possible need that people may have requires that priorities be set. Which is more valuable, treatment of alcoholics in the work force or park programs for potentially delinquent children? Seldom are questions phrased so simply; however, the point to be made is important—devoting resources to one program means that these resources cannot be devoted to another program. Each program has its own supporters and beneficiaries. The conflicting wishes of these groups can make decision makers feel pulled in two, three, or more directions. Programs, of course, can be ranked on the basis of the power of the backers of the various programs. Hopefully, the availability of objective information will help rank programs on the basis of their potential effectiveness rather than on the power of their supporters. In this way, the resources of society may be expended in a more fair and more useful manner than has traditionally been the case.

Legislative Mandates

The federal government has increasingly insisted on the evaluation of programs. The social programs of the federal government have grown considerably during the 1960s and 1970s. Health, Education, and Welfare (HEW) programs required approximately $2 billion in 1953, which was 3 percent of the federal budget. By 1975, HEW programs made up 14 percent of the federal budget, not counting Social Security costs (*U.S. News & World Report* 1975). Social programs have a reputation of costing more than they were expected to cost when initially planned. Medicare and Medicaid, for example, cost $39 billion in 1977 but only $6 billion in 1967 (*Newsweek* 1977). An important effect for our purposes was the result of the Congressional reaction to rapid cost escalation. Congress sought to contain Medicare costs by monitoring the time required for treatment and by examining the quality of treatment given (Gosfield 1975).

In addition to monitoring health care, the federal government has sought to limit the expansion of health care facilities. The belief that health care facilities are used whenever they are provided has often been voiced. It seems that more disease conditions "require" hospitalization when more inpatient facilities become available (Ball 1978). If that is so, then careful planning, taking into consideration existing facilities and community need, must precede hospital expansion. Congress has required more thorough planning through the National Health Planning and Resources Development Act (Public Law 93–641).

The government's role in evaluation is also evident in the requirement that all educational or service grants are directed to include evaluations of the project. Do people learn? How well do they learn in one program compared to some other possible program? These requirements are often met with less than adequate research methods. However, we believe that thinking in evaluative terms is a step forward.

Although the federal government alone has the power to require steps to be taken to evaluate programs, other groups are becoming increasingly active. For example, Blue Cross and Blue Shield, administered by people in health care professions, have traditionally paid whatever bills were submitted by hospitals and doctors. Recently, these groups have become more strict about what charges will be honored. In 1977, some twenty medical/surgical procedures were listed by Blue Cross as ineffective and not to be paid for because research has shown that these procedures provide no relief for patients or have been superseded by better diagnostic procedures *(Blue Shield News* 1977). The Aetna Life and Casualty Company has run a series of magazine advertisements on the need for greater efficiency in health care facilities.

Because of these trends, the field of evaluation is expanding. This text is an introduction to program evaluation for people who may want to consider entering the field as a career or who need to understand the methods and concepts of the field.

THE ROLE OF EVALUATORS

Before actually describing the specifics of program evaluation, it would be worthwhile to describe where evaluators work. There are three major roles for evaluators. Some evaluators work for the organization, usually a human service organization, that desires certain programs to be evaluated. Such people are called in-house evaluators. Because of the trends discussed in the previous section, program evaluation is necessary if administrators want their services to survive the competition for funds within their agency or within the city, state, or federal budget.

A second role is employment with governmental or regulatory agencies. The Government Accounting Office, for example, is responsible to Congress for reports on how legislative programs are working out. The GAO's reports can influence legislation on welfare, health, education, and so forth. Some government agencies and private firms conduct evaluations for regulatory or accreditation needs. Especially in government, the evaluator may synthesize and organize evaluation reports prepared by members of the third major type of organization employing evaluators.

This third area includes those people working for private research firms or universities who perform specific evaluations desired by government agencies. The announcements of government needs are called Requests for Proposals, or RFPs for short. The social science research firms bid on jobs in a fashion similar to that used by businesses seeking a job, such as building a garage or a bridge. The proposal with the most promising methods at an acceptable cost is then selected, and that firm signs a contract to do the research.

There are many other roles filled by evaluators, and the types of work they do is increasing; however, these three types of positions—in-house, government/regulatory, and private research firm/university—cover most of the positions filled by program evaluators.

Consultants Compared to In-house Evaluators

There are only two general ways that an evaluator can relate to the organization needing the evaluation: (1) evaluators can work for the organization and do a variety of evaluations; or (2) they can come to the organization from a research firm or a university to work on a specific program only. For the purposes of discussion, the terms *in-house evaluator* and *consultant* are used to summarize these two different roles. The particular role filled has implications for the size of the evaluation project attempted and for some of the characteristics of the research itself.

Factors Related to Competence. In terms of *knowledge about a program,* in-house evaluators have the advantage because they have better access to program directors and to the organization's administration. A person who is physically present forty hours a week is likely to see the program in action, to know the staff, and to learn about its reputation from other people in the organization. The information gained informally by a secretary in the cafeteria would be unavailable to a consultant not based in the organization. The more that is known about the actual workings of the program, the easier it is to ask the relevant questions in an evaluation.

The *technical expertise* of the evaluator is important. An in-house evaluator often works with a small group of two or three. Some evaluators work alone. However, working alone provides limited opportunity for helpful feedback. In contrast, the consultant may have the resources of a larger organization to draw upon.

A different facet of the question of technical expertise is suggested by the necessity of performing evaluation work in many different areas of an organization. During one period of two years, the authors of this text performed work on psychosomatic illness, stroke disability, a dietary supplement, patient satisfaction, medical education programs, and employee satisfaction, among other topics. It is challenging and stimulating to work in new areas; however, there is also a risk that inexperience with a given area may lead to oversimplifications. By selecting a consultant with experience in a specific program area, an organization may avoid the errors possible when an in-house evaluator faces a problem in a new area of the organization.

Personal Qualities. There are personal qualities unrelated to technical competence that are important to evaluators. Evaluators can do more effective work if they are objective, trusted by administrators, and interested in improving the program being evaluated.

In terms of *trust,* in-house evaluators are most likely to have the edge. Being well-known and, hopefully, having been found worthy of trust, in-house evaluators usually find program directors and staff more willing to devote time to the evaluation, to admit problems, and to share confidences than they would to a consultant not previously known.

An in-house evaluator can also be expected to have a *desire to improve the organization* sponsoring the program and paying the evaluator's salary. Although intentions are sometimes misunderstood, it is always in the best interests of evaluators to find ways to improve the organizations in which they work. Consultants might not have the same motivations because they are less dependent for continuing support on the organization sponsoring the program.

On the other hand, being or not being dependent on the organization for a job may affect one's *objectivity,* which is important if reports are to be creditable. The objectivity of in-house evaluators may be questioned because they may know the program designer and the staff delivering the service. It is not easy to criticize the work of a friend. The consultant, on the other hand, is unlikely to have developed personal relationships within the organization and thus may be more objective. An in-house evaluator may also hesitate to report critical findings because future work may be jeopardized. Research in an applied setting depends on the cooperation of many people. If they believe that negative results will come out of the project, the needed cooperation may be hard to obtain.

There is another side to the question, however. Nonobjective evaluators will lose their credibility and, thus, their effectiveness. In the short run, it might be quite easy to ignore sensitive issues. The authors prepared a report that showed positive outcomes to the patients in a medical/psychological program (Carey and Posavac 1977b). If the report had stopped there, it would have been welcomed. However, it went on to show that other patients obtained the same degree of positive benefit at less cost in a different program. This observation was not welcome. It is important to emphasize, though, that this short-run loss should be weighed against the likelihood that willingness to report negative or ambivalent findings will increase one's credibility in the long run.

The Purpose of Evaluation Required. Earlier in this chapter, two purposes of evaluative studies were described—formative evaluations and summative evaluations. In-house and consultant evaluators can and do perform both types of evaluations. However, there are certain situations that are better served by one or the other type of evaluator. The in-house evaluator is likely to be more effective than a consultant in implementing procedures to follow for formative evaluations. Such evaluators will be available and committed enough to see the project through, and, because formative evaluations cannot lead to a traumatic decision to end a program, negative results will not destroy the evaluator's role in the organization. If, in contrast, a summative evaluation is wanted because there is a strong suspicion that a program is failing and a negative evaluation will end the program, an outside evaluator will probably be more helpful than in-house personnel. A school board, knowing that it had to close one of the three grade schools because enrollments had dropped, decided to select a consultant with no ties to the school district to recommend which school be closed. The consultant performed an evaluation of efficiency for each school and recommended that the least efficient school be closed. Although there were some hard feelings and a number of verbal attacks were leveled at the consultant and his report, the selection of the school to be closed was made and implemented with fewer difficulties than was the case in neighboring school districts making similar decisions.

There are advantages and disadvantages to both an in-house evaluator and a consultant evaluator. The in-house evaluator is likely to be more sensitive to the needs of the program and to be treated as part of the team. The consultant evaluator may be more objective and have greater technical skill if experienced in the specific type of program being evaluated. Both types of evaluators do all kinds of evaluations. However, the in-house evaluator is most suited to evaluate ongoing programs in need of improvement. On the other hand, a consultant, being more insulated from the pressures of the organization, is better suited to recommend curtailment of a program.

Evaluation and Other Activities of an Organization

Professional interaction among people with similar interests is often beneficial to all concerned. An evaluator working alone will find it hard to grow and to develop professionally. If an organization is too small to employ more than one full-time evaluator, it may be wise to attach evaluation to another function of the organization. Three functions that are sometimes joined with evaluation are research, records, and education.

Research and Evaluation. Some human service organizations routinely sponsor research directly with operating funds or indirectly with grant funds. Evaluation can become one function of the research team. For example, a police department was awarded a grant to study the effect of providing emotional support to the victims of crime. The social scientists responsible for that research would be excellent colleagues of an evaluator. University-affiliated hospitals carry on research. Individuals conducting research into psychiatric problems or emotional issues related to serious illness have interests similar enough to those of evaluators to serve as colleagues.

Records and Evaluation. Some hospitals have joined the functions of evaluation and medical records into one office. With current emphasis on medical care evaluations, the medical records staff is responsible for providing and summarizing information necessary for these evaluations. Although the responsibility for medical care evaluation ultimately rests with physicians, the medical records staff have some interests in common with program evaluators. Careful planning in selecting forms can make records more useful to program evaluations than is typically the case.

Education and Evaluation. Some organizations have joined the functions of education and evaluation. There is a long tradition for this marriage in educational psychology. New study materials and curricula are evaluated before being widely used by schools. Universities are combining faculty development and evaluation into one office. Many organizations besides schools sponsor educational programs. For example, industries have safety education programs, apprenticeship programs, job-training programs for minorities, and so on. Sponsoring firms want to know if the programs are achieving their goals.

Other Activities. Planning is an activity in which evaluators can assist. It is common for service providers to serve as a planning group. This choice is wise; however, many direct-service providers are not data oriented, feel uncomfortable constructing need surveys, and may be unable to analyze the information obtained. Usually, planning groups are set up for a specific purpose and then are dissolved. Thus, an evaluator can seldom be attached permanently to a planning group.

Consumer relations may be another area in which evaluators in human service facilities can assist. It is important to know what programs are effective, but it is also important to know how providers are viewed by those utilizing the service. Hospitals have patient relations departments with some interests that overlap with program evaluation.

SUMMARY

National trends, such as the consumer movement, professional concern, increased managerial effectiveness, limitations on resources, and specific Congressional mandates, have converged to create a need for methods to use in making rational managerial and legislative decisions in human services. The social science methods of program evaluation include planning, program monitoring, outcome assessment, and benefit/cost considerations. Evaluators are quantitative social scientists working to improve the delivery of human services. Their efforts to effect such improvements are on a program level, not on the individual person/client/patient level frequently associated with human service organizations.

STUDY QUESTIONS

1. From newspaper and magazine articles, gather examples of the trend toward increased accountability and examples of the use of program evaluations in the formation of public policy. You might find articles dealing with medical care (malpractice, peer review, costs), education (children reading well or not reading well), program planning (need assessment), relative costs of programs with similar goals, as well as others.

2. What aspects of program evaluation could be used in organizational settings with which you are familiar? Illustrate.

3. List the advantages and disadvantages of making program evaluation a part of American human services delivery systems. Save your list, and, when you have finished the text, consider how you might change the list.

FURTHER READING

DEMONE, H. W., and HARSHBARGER, D. 1973. The planning and administration of human services. *Developments in human services,* vol. 1, ed. H. C. Schulberg, F. Baker, and S. R. Roen. New York: Behavioral Publications.

WEISS, C. H. 1974. Evaluation research in the political context. In *Handbook of Evaluation Research,* vol. 1, ed. E. L. Struening and M. Guttentag, chap. 2. Beverly Hills, Calif.: Sage.

2

Planning

an

Evaluation

The initiation of a program evaluation may arise in several different ways. The program personnel themselves may initiate the request. The program sponsors (such as the funding agency or the head of the institution in which the program functions) might order an evaluation as a condition for beginning or continuing a program. The evaluation team might sense the opportunity for a productive project and submit a preliminary proposal to either the program sponsors or the program director.

Whatever the source of the proposal, evaluators need to address a number of issues and make certain decisions before the collection of data begins. Before committing their efforts, they need to learn about the goals and mechanics of the program, about the people who sponsor the program, about the program personnel, and about groups that may resist the evaluation of the program. After obtaining this information, evaluators must then decide whether the evaluation should be done immediately, whether it should be done in the way in which it is proposed, or whether it should be done at all.

In the first part of this chapter, we provide an overview of the order and manner in which the above issues can be approached by identifying the steps to be taken between the time of the initial proposal and the beginning of data collection. The time and effort that are devoted to each step will vary, depending on the complexity of the program, the relationship of the evaluator to the program sponsors and personnel, and the urgency of time constraints. Some steps, such as selecting or developing measures, are very complex, and Chapter 3 is devoted to explaining them in detail. In the second part of this chapter, we deal with potential sources of resistance to program evaluation that should be considered in the planning stage.

SIX STEPS IN PLANNING AN EVALUATION

Step 1: Identify relevant people.

The first thing effective evaluators do is to identify relevant people; that is, those who have a serious interest in the program and whose lives may potentially be affected by the evaluation. Relevant people are those who are heavily personally involved in the program, who derive a portion or all of their income from the program, whose future status or career might be affected by the success or failure of the program, or who are the clients or potential recipients of the program services.

Program personnel are the first to be considered. They will usually be more personally involved in the program than either the sponsors or the clients. The program director will be the key person to whom evaluators will relate during the entire project. It will help to learn as much about the background, interest, attitudes, and reputation of the program director as is possible. In addition, other people involved in the delivery of program services must not be overlooked. It is also important to involve them in the planning stage so that they will assume ownership of the project and provide maximum support during the data collection stage. If possible, it helps to learn about the relationship between the director and other program personnel so that they can be dealt with more effectively during the planning meetings to be described below. For example, if the director tends to be a dictatorial person, it will be more difficult for evaluators to draw out the ideas of other personnel and determine when a consensus exists or when a power decision has been made by the director.

Program sponsors are next to be considered. At times program personnel are the sponsors. In other cases they will be funding agencies or the head of the institution in which the program exists. Often enough, there will be a single person to whom the evaluators are to relate. The funding agency may delegate one or two representatives to handle the commissioning and supervising of an evaluation project. In an institution such as a hospital, the program sponsor might be the vice president or administrator to whom the program director reports and who is ultimately responsible for the management of the program. Contact with the program sponsor will be especially important during the initial stages of planning and at the end of the evaluation. At the beginning, it is important that the sponsor fully supports the proposed evaluation and that all the program personnel are aware of that support. At the end of the evaluation, it is important that the report be presented to sponsors in such a way that it will be fully utilized in decision making. The presentation of the report and effective utilization of findings will be discussed more fully in Chapters 11 and 12.

Finally, the clients or recipients of the program services need to be identified. The amount and type of contact with the clients will depend on the nature of the program and of the evaluation. For example, if a cancer care unit is to be evaluated, are the program recipients the cancer patients only or are the relatives of the patients also included in the program goals? Are all cancer patients included, or only those with an established diagnosis of cancer or with certain types of cancer?

Step 2: Arrange preliminary meetings.

Before a final decision is made to undertake an evaluation and before the writing of a detailed proposal, it is advisable to meet with relevant people to gather background information on five questions: (1) Who wants the evaluation? (2) What type of evaluation is desired? (3) Why do they want it? (4) When do they want it? and (5) What resources are available?

Who Wants the Evaluation? The ideal situation occurs when both the program sponsor and the program personnel desire to have the program evaluated. In this instance, the evaluators will usually be interacting with competent people who are secure in their professional expertise, who are open to suggestions for improvement, and who welcome the opportunity to have documentation for what they feel is a successful program.

If the program sponsors initiate the evaluation proposal, either without the knowledge of, or against the desires of, the program personnel, the evaluators are faced with making the program personnel comfortable with the goals and methodology of the evaluation before data collection begins. If evaluators do not succeed in doing this, they face the possibility of open opposition or a lack of essential cooperation on the part of the program personnel. On the other hand, when the program personnel see the evaluators as "allies," rather than "the enemy," they are more likely to give the evaluators much needed assistance in the difficult job of data collection as well as valuable insights into the interpretation of the data.

If the program personnel initiate the evaluation proposal, either without the knowledge of, or against the desires of, the program sponsors, the evaluators need to convince the sponsors of the usefulness of the evaluation, or it will be very difficult to have any worthwhile changes effected. Sponsors who do not assume ownership of the evaluation project during the planning stage are more inclined to allow the finished report to gather dust in a corner of their office.

What Type of Evaluation Is Desired? Early in the evaluators' meetings with program sponsors and personnel, it will be clear that the term *program evaluation* does not have the same meaning for everyone. More often than not, program personnel will be thinking in terms of a formative evaluation that will help them modify and improve the program. On the other hand, program sponsors may desire a summative evaluation because they may be under pressure to divert resources to an alternate program and must decide whether or not to continue the present program. Finally, some program personnel and sponsors will have little awareness of the whole concept of *program* evaluation and will therefore be expecting *individual* performance appraisal.

The task of evaluators at this point is to clarify the pertinent concepts for those who do not understand them and to help the relevant people decide what type of evaluation best meets their desires, their needs, and their resources. The decision is seldom to choose between one type of evaluation or another. Often it is possible to incorporate some elements of various types into the total scope of the project, depending on the complexity of the program goals and the resources available for the project. For example, in the evaluation of "Sesame Street" conducted by Cook (1975), various types of assessment were included in the overall evaluation. He assessed: (1) whether the program reached its target audience; (2) effectiveness by analysis of learning scores; (3) the magnitude of effects relative to the magnitude of the need that gave rise to the problem; (4) the ratio of benefits to cost; (5) the aspects of the complex viewing treatment that led to learning and the conditions of viewing that most promote learning; and (6) the value of program objectives, that is, the importance of stimulating the growth of all social

groups of preschool children and of narrowing the academic achievement
gap.

Why Is the Evaluation Desired? Closely tied to the previous question
of what type of evaluation is desired is the question of why evaluation
is desired. The commissioning of an evaluation is rarely the product of
an inquiring scientific spirit. More often it meets the needs of political
forces. Evaluation furnishes ammunition for institutional combatants in
fluid lines of battle and in transient alliances. Program sponsors often
need to satisfy constituents and want to keep politically advantageous
programs alive. Effective evaluators will put a high priority on identifying the reasons why the evaluation is desired. Were there some groups
in the organization who objected to the evaluation? What were their
motives? Is there real commitment among the program personnel and
program sponsors to using the results of the evaluation to improve decision making? Ideally, program personnel are seeking answers to pressing
questions about the program's future: Should it be continued? Should
it be expanded? Should it be modified?

One aspect of the evaluators' role is to assist both the sponsors and
program personnel to arrive at a consensus on the precise decision(s) to
be made. For example, in the evaluation of a physical medicine and
rehabilitation program (Carey and Posavac 1978), the decision under
consideration was not whether or not the program should be continued,
because the program was generally recognized as useful and had abundant referrals both from physicians on the hospital staff and from physicians at other hospitals. However, the program personnel were concerned
about patients who were discharged to their homes as apparent successes. They did not really know whether or not these patients maintained their levels of rehabilitation. After extended discussion, it became
clear that the primary focus of the evaluation was whether or not a
follow-up program was needed for those patients who were discharged as
successfully rehabilitated.

In other instances, evaluations are conducted to determine how much
of an impact a program has on other areas of the sponsoring institution.
In such a case, the program personnel are not decision oriented, but are
seeking to assure themselves that no serious side effects arise from the
introduction of a new program. For example, the authors evaluated
the impact of a physician residency program at a teaching hospital on
other areas within the hospital. The study uncovered certain tensions
and conflicts that might develop into serious problems unless they were
attended to immediately. The evaluators concluded the report with
suggested corrective actions to be considered by the medical education
committee.

Some evaluations done for public relations or political purposes are acceptable. For example, administrators may be reasonably certain that they have an effective program and wish to generate greater support for that program. In other words, they desire greater visibility for the program with influential people who can provide increased political or financial support.

Evaluation may also be done solely to fulfill grant requirements. Many grants from government and private sources include an evaluation requirement. In this situation, the decision to evaluate originates from pressure external to the program itself. For example, all projects for disadvantaged pupils funded under Title I of the Elementary Secondary Education Act are required to be evaluated. These two motives are not without merit. When the need to ask evaluative questions is forced on people, they are forced to become more self-critical than they would be otherwise. There is a need to gather support for a good program and to justify a program to the people who fund it.

There are some reasons for program evaluation that are unacceptable. For example, an administrator may use program evaluation as a ploy to avoid making a decision. Administrators who are pressured about the viability of a given program can buy time by saying that the program is being evaluated; by giving as little support as possible to the evaluators, they insure that the evaluation can take a long time to be completed. If there is still a need to buy more time when the evaluation is completed, administrators may appoint a committee to study the evaluation report. Evaluation is also inappropriate when administrators know what decisions they will make, but wish to go through the charade of program evaluation to give their decision legitimacy. These are illustrations of program evaluation being used for blatantly political purposes.

When Is the Evaluation Desired? The scope of an evaluation project can be limited by situational factors. If the evaluators are given a deadline, they may be forced to make choices that are not ideal. For example, operational measures specifically designed for a program may have to be forgone in favor of existing questionnaires or instruments, although these existing instruments may not have the desired reliability, validity, or applicability. The number of respondents or participants in the study may have to be curtailed, thereby increasing the probability of not detecting the true effect of the program. Adequate control groups may not be immediately available, although they might be available at a later date. Evaluators must decide whether they should proceed under less than ideal circumstances, delay the evaluation, or refuse to do the evaluation in order to avoid the possibility of generating misleading results. For example, Carey and Posavac (1979) were invited to evaluate a new cancer care center five months before it was to be introduced within an acute care hospital. The brief forewarning did not affect the

evaluation design. However, there was inadequate time to develop measures for all the program goals, and it was not possible to collect data
on as large a sample of cancer patients as was needed for a good comparison group before the institution of the center. The problem was
approached in two ways. First, to measure patient moods the evaluators
chose an instrument used by other cancer researchers. This choice ob-
viated the need to develop a new instrument to measure the psychological distress of patients. Second, two in-house comparison groups
were used: (1) a sample of cancer patients before the unit was inaugurated; and (2) a sample of cancer patients after the center was opened,
but who were treated in other medical units in the hospital.

Even when there is no deadline, program personnel may be eager for
results and push evaluators for an estimated date when the report will
be finished. It is usually better not to commit oneself to a deadline that
can be met only if everything occurs on schedule. Murphy's law ("If
anything can go wrong, it will") is especially applicable in program
evaluation: data collectors become ill; respondents are unavailable; the
mail is slow; computers break down when they are most needed.

When an estimated date for the completion of the report is required,
extra time should be allotted. If evaluators finish behind schedule, they
are suspected of being disorganized at best, or incompetent at worst. On
the other hand, when they finish ahead of schedule, they build a reputation for speed and efficiency. Nevertheless, it is important to remember
that evaluators work in settings in which time is important—more important than in the setting in which university-based research is usually
conducted.

What Resources Are Available? Besides time, another situational
factor that can limit an evaluation is available resources. For example,
if in-house evaluators are working within a budget, how much can they
spend on a given project? Will they have the assistance of program
personnel or volunteers to hold down the expense of data collection?
Will involvement in a new project delay or eliminate another evaluation project of greater importance?

If no formal contract was signed, it is also advisable for outside
evaluators to put into writing an exact list of what is covered and not
covered in a cost estimate, and name the time when payment should be
made. The agreement should be signed by a responsible officer of the
contracting institution or the program sponsor. Verbal agreements pave
the way to hard feelings. This does not imply a lack of good faith on the
part of either party. Honest misunderstandings occur because busy
people can be distracted and fail to remember the details of an agreement.

Step 3: Decide whether the evaluation should be done.

After identifying relevant people and meeting with them to gather information on basic background issues, a conscious decision should be made on whether or not to do the evaluation.

The decision is not always difficult. In-house evaluators may be told by their superior to conduct the evaluation. Outside consultants may need the job because they need contracts to maintain their staff.

At other times, options are available. An evaluation could be delayed because circumstances are not opportune. For example, program personnel might be so threatened that cooperation will be difficult to obtain until they are given a greater feeling of job security. In one hospital, an employee survey was delayed because a labor union made an attempt to organize nurses, and there was fear that the National Labor Relations Board might view the survey as an illegal attempt to thwart the union's effort to organize.

Finally, there are situations in which it is best not to evaluate a program. For example, evaluation is best delayed or omitted in those instances in which the program is not clearly defined and the staff is operating under crisis management; that is, they improvise their goals and procedures from day to day. It would also be inadvisable to undertake evaluation when there are not enough resources (money, people) to do the job effectively.

Horst and others (1974) discuss some underlying causes of why those in charge of programs and those who evaluate them have not joined their efforts in a manner that more frequently results in program improvements. They suggest three underlying causes that they say are not the responsibility of the evaluator: (1) a failure to define the problem addressed or the program intervention being made; (2) a lack of clear logic, that is, the connection between the program intervention and the immediate outcome is not understood clearly enough to permit testing it; and (3) a lack of management, that is, those in charge of the program lack the authority or ability to follow through on evaluation results. When any of these three causes are operative, evaluators might do well to hold off on an evaluation or turn to another project.

In conclusion, evaluators ought not to accept a project for which they are not enthusiastic or in which they do not believe. Their attitude will make it difficult to do professional work. On the other hand, they might accept a job in which they have marginal interest in the hope of winning good will and securing a more meaningful and challenging evaluation project at a later date. The main consideration is to make a conscious decision and not merely to drift into the project because it is there.

Step 4: Examine the literature.

Evaluators often work on a wide variety of projects. An independent evaluator, for example, may evaluate a school system, then a community program for alcoholics, and then organizational climate in a bank. Such a researcher has the need to become familiar with an enormous amount of literature. Although this is difficult, some evaluators prefer this because they enjoy the variety and do not like to restrict their efforts to a single area of interest.

Evaluators who specialize in limited areas have a less formidable task in drawing up a proposal. If they have been exclusively evaluating educational systems, mental health programs, or personnel problems in organizations, they develop an extensive knowledge of evaluation in their specialty area. They also can more easily build on their own past research and contribute to the development of theory in that area.

However, when evaluators work in an area that is new for them, it is important to make a careful search of the literature before designing or developing new instruments. They should learn from the successes and failures of others and get a picture of the methodological, political, and practical difficulties that must be overcome.

Depending on the type of evaluation, computerized search services might be a good place to begin a search. Data on Program Evaluation (DOPE), MED-LINE, Psychological Abstracts Search and Retrieval (PASAR), and Educational Resource Information Center (ERIC) are four such useful systems. A search of professional journals recommended by program personnel is also helpful. After a few useful articles have been identified, the bibliographies of these articles will provide additional references.

While reading the articles, evaluators should keep these key questions in mind: Has any evaluation been done on this type of program? What designs were used? Were new measures developed? How reliable and valid were the measures? What type of statistical analysis was used? Was it appropriate? Is there a consensus among the findings of various studies? If there is conflict, is this due to sampling procedures, design, or interpretation of findings? What issues were not addressed or investigated?

Step 5: Determine the methodology.

After the review of literature has been made, the evaluators are ready to make some methodological decisions regarding the strategy and design, the population and sampling procedures, the control or comparison groups, operational measures, data collection, and statistical analysis.

Separate chapters are devoted to some of these issues, but it is helpful to examine the main issues at this point so that the reader can better understand their interrelationships and how they fit into the planning stage of an evaluation.

Strategy and Design. Strategy and design will largely be determined by the type of evaluation needed. Will the project be a need evaluation? A process evaluation? An outcome evaluation? An evaluation of cost effectiveness? Perhaps the project will include more than one kind of evaluation.

Strategy and design will also be influenced by whether the program is already in operation or whether it is still in the planning stage. If a new program is to be initiated, its effectiveness can be evaluated by gathering data on one or more occasions prior to the introduction of the program and comparing these data to information collected after its introduction. If the program can be introduced in some segments of a target population on a staggered basis, this is more desirable than introducing the program in the entire population at the same time. With this strategy, evaluators can make multiple comparisons of the same group over time, and between groups.

Population and Sampling. Once the target population (participants, respondents) has been identified, evaluators need to decide whether to include the entire population or take a sample from that population.

There are at least two arguments for including the entire population. The first is political or psychological; namely, people may be offended if they are not included. For example, the organizational attitude of nurses at a given hospital could be accurately measured by taking a stratified random sample from the various nursing services. However, experience has shown that the hospital climate survey itself has a more positive impact on nurses' job satisfaction when all nurses are given the opportunity to express their views through the survey.

The second reason for including the entire population is methodological. If a sample is too small, there is some danger of finding program effects that do not really exist (Type I error), but even greater danger of disregarding true program effects as statistically insignificant (Type II error). For example, if a random sample of ten program participants is compared to a sample of ten who did not participate in the program, the program would have to have quite sizable effects before the results would be statistically significant.

There are two main arguments for using a random sample of participants rather than the entire population when the populations are large, namely, time and money. Program evaluation must be done within a budget, and usually there are some time restraints. When Andrew

Greeley (1972) studied the effects of the Vatican Council on Catholic priests in the United States, he quite properly used a 10 percent stratified random sample of the 55,000 Catholic priests. Diocesan and religious order priests, priests of different age groups, priests from different geographical areas, and priests with different job categories (pastors, associate pastors, and those in special work) were represented in the sample. Greeley was able to get over an 80 percent return from his sample and had sufficient numbers for studying subsets of the population. Because he chose to work with a sample rather than the entire population, he kept within his budget and had the project completed in a reasonable time.

Whether one chooses to include the entire population in the evaluation or to do a random sampling, a very important factor must be kept in mind, namely, the probability that subjects will drop out of the study. It is important to identify the characteristics of nonparticipants and those who drop out at various points of time. Both the rate of dropouts and the reasons for dropouts have a bearing on the conclusions to be made from the data collected.

If more than 50 percent of the target population or random sample are lost, the extrapolation of the findings to the entire population cannot be done with any confidence. Therefore, with a population of 1,000 respondents, evaluators will generally be able to make more valid interpretations if they take a 10 percent sample and obtain a 75 percent response rate (N = 75) than if they try to reach the entire population and obtain only a 30 percent response rate (N = 300).

The composition of the participant group will have an effect on subject drop-out rates. For example, in a hospital setting it is more difficult to obtain a high percentage of returns from housekeeping personnel than from nursing personnel on a written employee questionnaire because many housekeeping personnel have a problem with reading or with reading English. In contacting patients on the aforementioned Cancer Care Center study, it was difficult to obtain an adequate response rate because of the serious physical conditions of the target population. Therefore, the questionnaires had to be as short and simple as possible in order to obtain a response rate of 50 percent or better.

Control and Comparison Groups. When participants can be randomly assigned to a group where they do not receive the services of the program being evaluated, they constitute a true *control group.* When a basis of comparison for the evaluated program is a group of people who do not receive the services of the program but were not randomly assigned to that group, this group is referred to as a *comparison group* (or by some authors as a *nonequivalent control group*). The ideal situation involves random assignment of participants to the treatment and control groups. It is then easier to establish the existence of causal relationships and attribute differential effects to a program rather than to other factors.

Random assignment is frequently impossible in program evaluation but should not be dismissed too quickly. There may be a way to achieve random assignment, even when the evaluators do not have total control of the situation. For example, in an evaluation of primary nursing in a hospital,[1] the evaluators did not have control over which patients were assigned to the units with primary nursing or the units with team nursing. However, investigation showed that all physicians allowed their patients to be assigned to medical units on the basis of bed availability. This meant that although the evaluators had no control over the assignment of patients, situational factors resulted in random assignment. Demographic records of the patients in each group demonstrated that this system of random assignment resulted in two groups that were reasonably comparable.

One way of strengthening the interpretation of findings when one cannot have true control groups is to have more than one comparison group. For example, this was of great value in the Cancer Care Center evaluation previously mentioned. On some criteria, patients in the special cancer unit reported attitudes significantly more favorable than did one comparison group and significantly less favorable than did the other comparison group. On other criteria, the patients in the special unit scored higher than both comparison groups. Therefore, with the use of two comparison groups the evaluators were able to identify the advantages of the program with greater precision.

Nevertheless, one can question whether meaningful evaluation must always be comparative. Are there not some *absolute* standards of performance or quality against which results can be compared? For example, if one is evaluating a newly introduced drive-in banking service and 80 percent of banking customers are pleased, does one need a control or comparison group? It would not seem to be necessary if the program sponsors (the bank) set an 80 percent satisfaction rate as their goal. Nevertheless, it would be of value to know what level of customer satisfaction had been attained before the new service was made available.

Selection of Measures. The key idea with respect to measurement is to plan for multiple measures from multiple sources. Obviously, one of the main sources for data in program evaluation is the client. However,

---

[1] Primary nursing refers to a situation in which an individual nurse is assigned to give complete care to a few patients in a unit. It is distinguished from team nursing, in which a group of nurses works under a head nurse to provide care as needed to an entire unit of patients, perhaps alternating their responsibilities from day to day. Primary nurses work more closely with physicians in developing care plans and in discharge planning.

clients can provide data in more than one way. Clients can provide self-report measures by responding to direct questions about their perceptions and satisfaction with the program. They can also take tests designed to measure attitudes or moods that might have been affected by the program. Some such tests are described in the next chapter.

The behavior of clients can also be a source for data. For example, satisfaction with a new job-training program might be measured by the percentage of applicants who drop out of the new program as compared to other programs. Or, the emotional adjustment of various groups of widows might be measured by the percentage of each group who remarried.

Another important source of data is significant others; that is, those people who are in close contact with the clients, for example, spouses, relatives, or close friends. Under some circumstances, their perceptions may have less danger of bias than those of the clients themselves. For example, Ellsworth (1979) developed a multiple-scale measure of the progress of mental health patients to be taken by the spouse or main relative with whom the patient lived after discharge from the hospital.

Finally, program personnel are a source of data. Because program people are often skilled professionals, their perceptions in some ways can have greater validity than the perceptions of either the clients or significant others. On the other hand, they may tend to be biased by their personal involvement in the program.

In addition to collecting data from various sources, evaluators should consider whether multiple measures from each source are necessary or desirable. For example, instead of using an instrument that measures only anxiety, it might be preferable to use an instrument that also provides a measure of depression, fatigue, or confusion (moods sometimes closely associated with anxiety). Or, if evaluators were measuring the effectiveness of a program for the rehabilitation of stroke patients, it would be important to have separate measures for activities of daily living (such as walking, feeding oneself, dressing oneself, and so forth) and for speech skills. Right and left hemiplegics experience qualitatively different damage and can be expected to respond differently to speech therapy than they each do to physical therapy. In the evaluation of the rehabilitation program mentioned above, Carey and Posavac (1978) used two scales to measure progress within the hospital and three additional scales to measure progress at home after discharge from the hospital.

Data Collection. Who will handle the day-to-day mechanics of data collection? This will usually involve an on-site coordinator who will keep the program evaluators abreast of the whereabouts of the program clients, personnel, and other sources of data, so that they can be contacted at appropriate times by the evaluation team. This is ordinarily a thankless and tedious task, and yet the evaluators need a reliable person to handle it.

Data collectors need to be sensitive to the issue of confidentiality. First, confidential information must be kept confidential. If information was obtained with a previous understanding of confidentiality, it should not be released until explicit approval is obtained. Second, the obligation of others to keep information confidential must be respected. Evaluators do not have a right to all information, even when it might have a bearing on the evaluation. Other values may at times conflict with the rights of evaluators. Care must be taken not to ask information from people in a manner that they find to be an invasion of privacy.

Choice of Statistics. In any type of evaluation, appropriate statistics that will demonstrate both the level of statistical significance and the magnitude of effects are needed. It is preferable to use statistical procedures that are simple because the findings will be presented to program sponsors and personnel who often do not have a great deal of mathematical expertise. Nonevaluators should ideally be able to understand and be convinced by the interpretation of the results, not merely impressed with statistical sophistication. At times, multiple-regression analysis and analysis of covariance will be the statistics of choice. However, it is good to keep in mind that nonevaluators will usually be more comfortable with less complicated statistics.

One aspect of statistical planning that is often overlooked is the power of the test. Power is even a more important consideration in program evaluation than it is in laboratory investigations because negative findings for an existing program cause anxiety to both program personnel and sponsors. Therefore, it is useful and desirable for the evaluators to state the probability of Type II error; that is, the probability that the true program effects went undetected. For example, suppose that an existing program was obtaining a favorable response from 75 percent of respondents on a given measure, and a new program was designed to raise the favorable response to 80 percent. If .05 is chosen as a level of statistical significance (Type I error), 1,272 respondents are needed to keep the probability of Type II error to .10 or less. The power of tests is often unreported in evaluation reports.

Final Report. Finally, some thought should be given during the planning stage to the format of the final report. Graphs and bar charts are usually preferable to tables of statistics. Where tables of statistics are necessary, they should be kept to a minimum and put in an appendix. It is advisable to rough out a few tables or charts and use some estimated figures to see whether or not the type and amount of data are appropriate for the planned layout. Often, a consideration of the style of the report will suggest changes in the plans for data collection and analysis. Chapter 11 is devoted to more complete discussion of evaluation reports.

Step 6: Present a written proposal.

After having completed the search of the literature and having thought through the various methodological considerations outlined in Step 5, the evaluators are ready to prepare a written proposal for presentation to program personnel. The overall purpose is to be certain that the evaluators and program personnel agree on the nature and goals of the program, the type of the desired evaluation, the operational measures of the program goals, and on the readiness of the program for evaluation. It is psychologically important for the program personnel to fully understand the evaluation process, feel comfortable with it, and if possible be enthusiastic about it.

Some issues that were previously discussed during the initial meetings may have to be worked through once again. Program personnel may now see procedural problems that were not previously apparent. It may be necessary to delay the beginning of data collection either because they feel the program is not sufficiently operational to undergo evaluation or because the temporary presence of extraneous factors might interfere with the interpretation of data. For example, if the proposal called for the collection of data from hospital patients on their reactions to resident physicians who made rounds with attending physicians, it would be advisable to collect this at a time when medical students were not also making rounds with the resident and attending physicians. Otherwise, the patients might confuse the residents with medical students who have not graduated from medical school and are not providing care to patients. The problem can be handled by delaying data collection until the months when the medical students are not present on the floor.

POTENTIAL SOURCES OF RESISTANCE
TO PROGRAM EVALUATION

Political and psychological factors can undermine an evaluation project. Some factors are based on genuine concerns, while others are based on misunderstanding of an evaluation. Effective evaluators will identify these factors during the planning stage, bring them to the surface promptly, and resolve them gently and directly.

Expectations of a "Slam-Bang" Effect

Program personnel are generally enthusiastic and confident about the potential effects of their program. Because they are enthusiastic and put forth a maximum effort, they expect their new program to have dramatic results—a "slam-bang" effect. They will have a tendency to feel betrayed if evaluators are able to demonstrate only a moderate improvement over the old program. The difficulty can arise when the program that was replaced was already achieving its goals reasonably well, and the new program is expected to improve on the replaced program.

One way to handle the high level of expectation is to help program personnel arrive at some rule of thumb for improvement that can reasonably be expected. For example, if a previous system for admitting patients to a hospital received a favorable or satisfactory response from 75 percent of patients admitted, the sponsors of a new program for admitting patients should be satisfied if they raise the percentage of satisfied patients to 80 or 85 percent. Anything beyond that is unrealistic.

There are other reasons why the expected "slam-bang" effect may not occur. Whenever a group of participants is chosen for comparison with a group of participants in a new program, the comparison group will almost always be receiving some kind of service. It is rare when participants in a new program can be compared to a group that receives no service at all. When evaluators are comparing two modalities of service, both of which are considered good, it is unlikely that they will find great differences between the treatment group and the comparison group. For example, if a group of psychosomatic patients admitted to a special program in a hospital are compared to psychosomatic patients treated privately by physicians but without the benefit of the special program, both groups should improve because both groups are receiving professional treatment. Often the value of such a program is better demonstrated by showing that the type of patient treated in the special program is more in need of the services offered and that improvement of equal magnitude is more difficult to attain with severely distressed patients. When this approach is explained to the staff, it may help to lower "slam-bang" expectations.

Self-Styled Experts in Evaluation

Frequently, program personnel have had some experience working on a research project. Because of this experience, they may feel attached to a specific evaluation design. For example, they may insist on testing subjects prior to a treatment or new program, when the evaluators feel

41

that a pretest may artificially sensitize the subjects to the treatment to be evaluated.

Self-styled experts may also want to use their own favorite measurement instrument, even when the professional evaluators feel that it will needlessly lengthen a questionnaire that they judge to be adequate for measuring the goals of the program. Evaluators are advised to take the time to listen to such suggestions carefully and with an open mind because they may have some merit. If the suggestions seem counterproductive or not feasible, they are well-advised to be gentle but firm in adhering to the design and measures that they feel are appropriate. If evaluators give in to pressure against their better judgment, they will have no one to blame but themselves if the project is poorly executed.

Fear That Evaluation Will Inhibit Innovation

Personnel in human service organizations may worry that evaluation will interfere with innovation by inhibiting them from experimenting with new techniques. In both process and outcome evaluations, the staff may feel that evaluation permits absolutely no variation in the program during the period of data collection. This is partially true insofar as there cannot be major structural changes in the program that would alter the essential goals or nature of the program. However, the need for retaining program identity does not mean that clinicians or program personnel cannot be flexible in the day-to-day operations of the program within broad structural boundaries. Every program will have variability built into it. Evaluation will not limit this.

Fear That the Program Will Be Terminated

It is true that an evaluation could result in the curtailment or elimination of a program in those instances in which results demonstrate that a given approach is not working out as expected. In fact, cost-effectiveness evaluation is specifically concerned with cutting losses in time, effort, and money. However, before sponsors can completely eliminate a program designed to meet a specific problem, they are ordinarily under some pressure to decide what to put in place of the terminated program. Therefore, it is more likely that an evaluation will result in the reassessment of a program rather than its elimination.

Early in the planning stage, effective evaluators will try to have program personnel view them as valuable and needed associates. Evaluators can often achieve this goal by describing their work in terms of "documenting success." Program sponsors are inclined to demand accountability from program personnel as a condition for funding. Evaluators are there to assist program personnel in fulfilling this obligation to the sponsors.

It is not always possible to dispel the threat of evaluation completely. The reputation of the evaluators for trust and competence is a valuable asset. One practice that will allay some anxiety is to promise the program personnel that they will see the final draft of a report for their suggestions and clarifications before it is sent to the sponsors. Nevertheless, evaluators will not be able to eliminate anxiety completely in people who are basically insecure or who have doubts about their own competence. In a good program, these persons will be in the minority.

Fear That Information Will Be Abused

In addition to the fear that a program may be terminated, there may exist some concern that information gained about the performance of staff may be abused. Even competent clinicians are rightly concerned about merit reviews, future promotion, and career advancement. Past experience may have taught them to be wary of evaluators who have overstepped the boundaries of program evaluation or who have been careless about maintaining confidences. Once again, being trusted is critical in allaying these suspicions. The reputation of evaluators for integrity and for being responsible is the most valuable asset for defusing this suspicion. The reputation for trust is very fragile and hard to regain, once it has been lost. Effective evaluators will not only explicitly try to convey the idea that program evaluation is distinct from individual performance appraisal, but they will carefully avoid speaking or acting in such a way that might even give the appearance that they are engaged in individual performance appraisal.

Fear That Qualitative Methods May Be Supplanted

Clinicians rightly feel that their day-to-day observations are a valuable source of input both for improving the functioning of a program and for evaluating its effect. They may feel that the evaluators' questionnaires, complicated research designs, and statistical techniques are less sensitive than are their own personal observations and evaluations. At times, they are right.

However, the point to be made with clinicians is that their input is one very valuable source of evaluation data. Nevertheless, their subjective evaluations can be biased and can be strengthened by both quantitative and qualitative data gathered from other sources. Their subjective observations will be of greatest importance when the data are being interpreted. The ideal is not to eliminate either the quantitative or qualitative approaches, but to integrate and blend the findings from both methodologies.

Accusations That Evaluation Methods Are Insensitive

Closely allied to the objection that quantitative evaluation methodology devalues subjective observations is the accusation that evaluation designs are insensitive to the intricacies of human services. Program objectives are often varied and complex. Progress is often slow and irregular. For example, a hospital program for psychiatric patients presents a very difficult evaluation project. This is true because it is very difficult to find many persons with exactly the same diagnosis. The severity of the problem often varies widely. Individual goals differ greatly from patient to patient. Behavior considered to be progress for one patient cannot be rated as progress for another. Similar comments could be made about children in educational programs and adults in job-training programs.

There is a good deal of merit in the charge of insensitivity. Evaluators will gain the confidence of managers and staff not only by being aware of this problem but also by articulating this awareness in such a manner that program staff members are reassured that the intricacies of human services have been appropriately addressed. Early in the planning stage, the program personnel can be assured that the evaluation will not begin until they have had the opportunity to carefully review the evaluation proposal and feel comfortable that their concerns in this area have been addressed properly.

Evaluation Drains Program Money

The seven sources of resistance described thus far are focused on various aspects of evaluation, but not on the concept of evaluation itself. Two objections to evaluation strike at the very concept of program evaluation. The first objection is that program evaluation drains money that could be spent on direct service. As the statement stands, it is true. However, the main question is whether or not it can improve clinical service. The alternative to spending money on evaluation is to risk spending money on services that are of doubtful value. Those who present this objection fail to face the reality that the day of accountability has arrived. Today, it is hard to find a program funded either by government agencies or private foundations that does not carry the stipulation that a certain amount of money in the grant be spent on evaluation.

Those who are not convinced by the accountability argument may be convinced by a more pragmatic one, namely, that evaluation research, if done well, may help spread a good idea and may result in attracting more money and resources to a program.

Evaluation Has Little Impact

A second argument of those who are totally opposed to the concept of evaluation is that evaluation has had very little impact on programs. There is a good deal of validity to this objection. Evaluators have often been frustrated by seeing their reports set aside and disregarded.

However, the frustration of evaluators should be eased when they reflect on the hard reality that evaluation research is not a benign social science activity, but rather a political decision-making tool. The prosperity of evaluation research does not stem primarily from dedicated social researchers undertaking technically sophisticated studies. Rather, the major thrusts for rational policy making and program development are political and pragmatic, and it is the politician, the planner, and the foundation executive who exercise the leadership in the evaluation research field. Because evaluation researchers work in a political context, the results of their work must be timely and appropriate for decision making. Well-designed and carefully executed studies are worthless if they do not contribute to the decision-making process. In some instances, evaluators cannot put all the blame on policy makers if reports are not used.

In spite of the apparent validity of complaints about lack of impact, there is also some evidence that these complaints are overstated. First, evaluation studies have had an accumulative effect in certain areas. For example, the common finding that class size has marginal effects on learning may at first incline one to set aside class size as being of minimal importance. However, as more research was done on schools in other countries, it became clear that the marginal effect of class size was true only within the range of class sizes customarily found in American schools (Berk and Rossi 1976). Therefore, it sometimes takes time before the significance of evaluation research can be put into perspective.

Second, evaluation research has some long-term value insofar as it challenges conventional wisdom. For example, those who sanctioned and conducted the New Jersey negative income tax experiment boldly tested one of the oldest, most central economic assumptions. Most economists and politicians predicted that even a limited amount of guaranteed income would lead to massive malingering and a loss of motivation to work. The study yielded mixed results, some significantly at odds with expectations. To the extent that the results of the experiment can be generalized to the national low-income population, they indicate that a national program of guaranteed income at the benefit levels considered in this experiment would have only relatively small effects on the labor supply of male family heads (Haveman and Watts 1976). The potential of evaluation research for challenging conventional wisdom is also illustrated by the Coleman Report,[2] which showed that schools made smaller contributions to the learning of children than did family background.

An unexpected benefit of the apparent lack of impact of evaluation on programs has been the shift from summative evaluation to a greater emphasis on formative evaluation. This shift helped to increase the involvement of evaluators in the planning stages of programs. This new emphasis and orientation of evaluation research is reflected in the subject matter and style of this text. Chapter 4 develops the role of the evaluator in program planning at greater length.

STUDY QUESTIONS

1. As an outside consultant, you are invited by a large manufacturing plant to evaluate a new training program for managers called "Management Contact," which you are told applies the principles of "Transactional Analysis" to employer-employee relations. Explain the steps you would take and what you would need to know in approaching this job. What would be the major difficulties you would see?

2. You are part of an evaluation team retained by a major university. The chairman of the Department of Psychology instructs you to evaluate a new section to be established called "Community Psychology." How would you approach this task? What would be the major pitfalls to avoid?

FURTHER READING

RIECKEN, H. W. and BORUCH, R. F., eds. 1974. Social experimentation: A method for planning and evaluating social intervention, chs. 6 and 7. New York: Academic Press.

[2] James Coleman is the chief author of the highly publicized study, *Equality of Educational Opportunity*, published in 1966 and popularly called "the Coleman Report."

3

Measurement

Principles

and Tools

The selection of measurement instruments is of critical importance in designing an evaluation. Specific instruments must be selected to measure the achievement of goals and to answer the questions posed to the evaluator. The authors decided to present this subject at this point because these principles apply to all forms of evaluation to be described in later chapters. The selection of measures is not easy, and a poor choice could reduce an otherwise well-planned evaluation to a futile endeavor. Each approach has advantages and disadvantages; therefore, a measurement approach useful in one evaluation may be inappropriate in another.

SOURCES OF DATA FOR EVALUATIONS

There are six major sources of data relevant to evaluations: (1) the program records; (2) the program participants; (3) the staff delivering the program; (4) family members or other people with significant relationships to the participants; (5) special evaluation teams; and (6) community-level indexes. Some types of programs will be better studied using some sources rather than others.

The Program Records

A search of the program's records and files, its archives, can provide reliable and inexpensive data for the evaluator. Archival data are most useful when the evaluation includes an examination of client characteristics, types of service provided, and work load of the staff members. When archival data are objective (for example, number of visits, type of service, or identity of the care giver), the data will be very valid. On the other hand, diagnoses and other subjective entries may not be very valid. Two of the most important advantages of archival data are: (1) the measurement process does not affect the program participant; and (2) there can be no participant loss due to refusal or inability to participate. Some aspects of archival searches used as feedback material are discussed at greater length in Chapter 5.

Maintaining confidentiality is a problem that can become acute when using the program's records. Some evaluations using public documents need not be concerned with limiting access to the data. However, many evaluations utilize hospital and counselor records that are clearly confidential. Some information in files may even be damaging to the person's social and financial affairs. The inadvertent release of such data could open evaluators to legal suits in extreme cases. In less sensitive situations, evaluators would look unprofessional, and the loss of credibility might result in their being denied access to records the next time it is requested. Evaluators cannot function without access to data.

There are a number of ways in which evaluators can protect the confidentiality of the data used in the evaluation. For example, it is not always necessary to identify data by the person's name. At times, researchers have used information to identify records that only the clients or patients themselves would recognize. For example, the first name and birthdate of the respondent's mother would provide a code for gathering all of a person's data together without using the person's name. If it might be necessary to contact the respondent in the future, the project director alone should keep a master list of the respondents' names and addresses and the associated code information. Some workers using very sensitive material have stored the names and code information in a different country. Most readers of this text will not be dealing with data this sensitive. For those who find themselves in sensitive positions, more sophisticated methods for guaranteeing confidentiality are discussed by Riecken and Boruch (1974) and by Campbell et al. (1977).

The Program Participants

There are several reasons to look to the program participants for evaluative information. First, the person who actually receives a service is often in an excellent position to evaluate many aspects of the program. The direct contact the clients have with the staff provides them with important knowledge about the program that no one else has. Second, only the clients have access to their own feelings about the program and staff. Third, for many criteria the clients will be the most knowledgeable about their current state, especially at follow-up intervals. Further, they might well be the only available source for the use they make of additional follow-up services. A fourth advantage is that the information they provide is often relatively inexpensive.

On the other side of the coin, however, certain participants may be too incapacitated to be valid sources of evaluation information. In planning an evaluation of a physical medicine and rehabilitation unit, one will quickly discover that few recent stroke victims can validly describe their own capabilities. Some are unable to talk, others have poor judgment, and others are so crushed emotionally by their impairments that it seems cruel to discuss their problems with them. Certain types of patients seeking psychotherapy cannot provide valid data; however, many others can.

Perhaps participants can provide good data for some aspects of the program but not others. General hospital patients usually know if rooms are clean, whether nurses and resident physicians treat them politely, and how long they have to wait outside the X-ray room. However, they cannot evaluate the choice of medication or the competence of their surgeons.

Evaluators are faced with the task of motivating the program participants to provide personal information about their attitudes and judgments. Fear of public disclosure of personal information is a reason to refuse to cooperate. Routinely, anonymity in the final report is offered. Many people do not understand the social scientist's disinterest in the personal facts about individuals. Nor do they understand the necessity of using overall group averages and proportions in the final report. They are familiar with the case study approach often used in popular newspaper and magazine reports of medical treatment, counseling, and educational programs. It is not surprising then that some respondents do not believe promises of anonymity. One respondent to a survey administered in a group setting without a way to identify the respondents wrote the following: "I have tried to be honest. I hope I don't lose my job." American society is going through a litigatious and suspicious period. Evaluators cannot afford to give respondents cause to question their motives for requesting personal information.

Even when people are not afraid of public disclosure, they must still be motivated to contribute their time to completing the forms and surveys. One approach is to appeal to the person's interest in improving the program being evaluated. Many people are sufficiently altruistic to be willing to share their feelings if they realize that their time can contribute to the improvement of services for others. However, they are not so altruistic that they will spend a long time or struggle with a poorly written survey.

Which program participants are most likely to cooperate? The experience of survey users is that those with the most favorable impressions of a program or facility are the most likely to respond. The 86 percent who responded to a lengthy survey on a chaplaincy internship were independently evaluated by their supervisors as having performed better during the internship year compared to the 14 percent who did not return the survey (Posavac 1975).

The Staff

Program staff people are important sources of data for evaluations. Staff members are trained to assess the degree of the participants' impairments and are in a good position to assess improvement. Also, they are the most likely to know how well a program is managed and how well the program runs on a day-to-day basis. On the negative side, staff members can be expected to be biased toward seeing improvement. After committing their efforts to helping people improve their skills or adjustment, it may be hard to accept failure.

Over and above these concerns, the evaluators need to recognize that evaluating a program is in some ways an evaluation of the staff's performance. Few people unhesitatingly welcome an evaluation of the effectiveness of the services they provide. Most people will be concerned about the use to which an evaluation will be put. If they are worried, they will resist the evaluation. Some college professors refuse to permit students conducting course evaluations to enter the classrooms. Some psychotherapists argue that checklists of symptoms and rating forms are blind to the crucial but subtle changes in a client that the therapist alone can sense. Because evaluation is not a developed science with unquestioned techniques (see Cronbach 1977), it is easy to find weaknesses in the most carefully planned program evaluation. One way to reduce staff resistance is to provide some benefit for the staff as a byproduct of the evaluation of their program. Opportunities for improvement, workshops, and individual guidance, for example, should be tied in with an evaluation so that it is a learning experience. One must recognize that some evaluations have not been learning experiences. At times, evaluators have even neglected to make a presentation to the staff of the program evaluated. Making a presentation to the staff is the least evaluators can do in return for the staff's cooperation.

Significant Others

Family members are the people most affected by a person's behavioral changes. They must adjust their own behaviors as patients or clients change. Significant others see the recipients of human services (except for inpatients and prisoners) more frequently than the staff does, and they see the participants in natural settings, not merely in the short-term, artificial setting created by the program. Family members may have biases just as staff may have; however, the direction of these biases may be hard to predict. In a comparison of nurses' ratings with spouses' ratings of the capabilities of stroke patients, we learned that nurses rated the patients as more proficient in performing daily activities (dressing, eating, grooming) than the spouses did. On the other hand, spouses rated the patients as being more proficient in cognitive tasks (speaking, reading, memory) than the nurses did.[1] In any program, some family members will report more improvement than actually occurred while others will report less. Because the focus is on program-level outcomes, not *individual* assessments, these idiosyncratic biases are less important than systematic biases such as were found with the stroke patients.

When requesting information about program participants from significant others, it is necessary to have the participants' permission beforehand. People will vary in how willing they are to have spouses or others provide personal information to the evaluation staff. In evaluations of hospitalized psychiatric inpatients, Ellsworth (1979) reports that 21 percent were too incapacitated to give or withhold permission, 19 percent refused to give permission, and 7 percent could not name a significant other to complete the evaluation forms. Therefore, a smaller proportion of the population can be assessed using the ratings of significant others compared to the proportion who can provide self-ratings. Motivation to cooperate must follow the lines previously mentioned—

---

[1] For the interested reader, this finding was explained in the following fashion: spouses, being familiar with the stroke patient, needed fewer cues for effective communication; like all people, stroke patients tend to perform grooming and self-care types of behaviors at a higher level for strangers than for family members.

long-term improvement of the program for others. In seeking permission
to contact a patient's or client's significant other, care should be taken
so that the request does not imply that good treatment in the program
is contingent on the person's giving permission for such contact. Further,
it is important that permission forms be written at a level that is com-
prehensible to the program participant. Often these forms are written
at a level more suitable for a professional researcher (Gray, Cooke, and
Tannenbaum 1978).

Special Evaluation Teams

A specially trained team knowledgeable in both research techniques
and the service skills of the program staff can provide the best evaluation of a program if cost is no object and if the goal is to obtain the
least biased evaluation possible (Endicott and Spitzer 1975). Certainly,
professionals trained in the disciplines most closely related to the type
of program being evaluated will be better able to evaluate a program
than will evaluators trained primarily in research methods. Also, such
appropriately trained but independent evaluators are less likely to "see"
improvements than emotionally involved staff members. However, it is
seldom true that money is no object, and usually evaluators would
rather produce a useful evaluation with a likelihood of improving the
program than the most valid, detailed evaluation theoretically possible.
Therefore, less threatening sources of evaluative data gathered by people
who have earned the trust of staff may well lead to evaluations having
more potential positive impact on the program and its staff than that
obtainable by outside evaluators.

Community Indexes

Some programs are planned to improve community-level variables.
Examples of programs designed to influence the community would be a
crime-reporting program that is supposed to increase citizen participation in criminal surveillance and to change community-level indexes,
such as arrest rates and crime rates; a reading program that is to raise
the achievement levels of the children in a school district; and a citizen-
developed project to monitor housing code violations that is designed to
increase or maintain the quality of the housing in a neighborhood.

The major difficulty with using community-level indexes is that there
are many causal links between the program and the hoped-for end result.
There are so many variables that may influence arrest rate, quality of
housing, or reading level that an effective program may not be detect-
able. In addition, there are many things that can interfere with the

implementation of the program before the community level is reached. An evaluator who uses only community-level indexes in an outcome study may be left quite in the dark about the causes of apparent failure or success.

Which Source Should Be Used?

The choice of sources of data depends on the cost of obtaining data, the type of decision to be made on the basis of the evaluation, the size of the program, and the time available to conduct the evaluation. If a program needs feedback information, it is likely that records, participant attitudes, and family reports may be very helpful. If a decision is planned to expand (or to eliminate) an expensive, controversial program, the judgments and observations of outside experts may be the only source of data that will suffice. Such decisions must be made carefully on the basis of a widely accepted evaluation.

Regardless of the type of program or anticipated decision, evaluators should strive to use multiple measures from more than one source. In choosing multiple measures, it is especially important to select measures that are not likely to share the same biases. For example, a subjective assessment of the success of a program by a client may be mirrored by the subjective feelings of the client's spouse. If, on the other hand, a measure of subjective feelings is used with ratings of ability to function in specific settings or with objective achievement, evaluators are less likely to obtain sets of data with the same biases. When the same implication is drawn from a variety of sources, the evaluation will be received with greater credibility.

However, it also is possible that the multiple approaches will not agree. Shipley (1976) conducted an evaluation of a companion program for mentally ill patients. College students served as volunteer companions to discharged psychiatric patients. The volunteers, patients, and hospital staff all subjectively evaluated the program in quite glowing terms. However, more objective measures of the patients' behavior (by staff ratings and by frequency and duration of rehospitalizations) revealed quite *variable* reactions; some patients apparently benefited, and others did not. Shipley suggested that a more thorough understanding of the patients' reactions to companion programs be obtained before instituting them more widely. His use of multiple measures led him to a different conclusion from previous studies using only subjective attitude measures. Evaluators should be sensitive to the possibility that their selection of sources of data and of specific measures can lead to misleading conclusions.

The fact that evaluators frequently work with people trained in service delivery techniques, not in research methods, means that evaluators have considerable discretion in choosing the criteria of effectiveness and the analyses of those criteria. Berk (1977), Berk and Rossi (1976), and Zigler and Trickett (1978) go so far as to say that evaluators can determine the results of an evaluation before it is conducted by means of their choice of variables and methods of analyses. Thus, to be fair to programs and to the consumers of program evaluations, evaluators must examine their own attitudes as they design an evaluation, or their own biases may determine their findings. In the following section, the most important issues to consider when choosing assessment procedures are discussed.

PRINCIPLES IN CHOOSING ASSESSMENT PROCEDURES

There are several criteria that evaluators use in selecting methods of gathering the data required in an evaluation. Keeping these principles in mind while planning a study will save evaluators time and inconvenience later.

Multiple Variables

In the beginning of this chapter, we recommended the use of multiple sources of information. It is also recommended that evaluators use multiple variables from a single source because the elevation of a single variable to be *the* criterion of success will probably corrupt it. A grisly example is the variable "body count" used in daily reports on the Vietnam War. The nature of the war made it hard to claim territorial gains. Thus, dead enemy soldiers were to be counted as a measure of the success of friendly forces. It became apparent that focusing on this variable led to its being inflated by counting every death as that of an enemy, even when those killed were civilians not taking part in the fighting. Barbour and Wolfson (1973) describe the difficulty of defining productivity of police officers. Concentrating on arrests may unintentionally encourage poor practices in gathering evidence necessary for convictions, or police officers may make arrests when the interests of justice would be better served without an arrest, such as in domestic quarrels. Turner (1977) described the effect of a poorly defined criterion for mental health workers who refer clients to other public agencies. The criterion of successful referrals was defined as "90 percent of referred clients actually make contact with the new agency." The evaluator quickly learned that the mental health workers were escorting the individuals to the other agencies. Although the workers were scoring well on the criterion of successful referral—those referred to other agencies did make contact—other work was being ignored.

One way to avoid corrupting the criteria chosen and to avoid distorting the operation of a human service system is to use multiple variables. It would be especially important that the variables serve as a check on one another. Thus, *both* arrest rate and conviction rate should be used as the measures of police productivity. Percentage of successful referrals *and* number of clients served should be used as criteria for a mental health worker screening people in need of various services.

Important Variables

Because program evaluation is an applied social science, the variables to be measured must be relevant to the specific informational needs of facility management, community representatives, those responsible for budgets, and others. Thus, in planning an evaluation, evaluators must learn what questions are pressing and are yet unanswered. Then, the variables to be measured are chosen on the basis of their importance to the questions facing administrators and program staff.

The time at which a variable is measured may determine whether it provides appropriate information. The impact of educational services can often be assessed at the end of a program. Other human services are provided with the goal of altering the course of a person's life. Thus, the success of a program for juvenile delinquents can be better judged by the degree to which participants stay out of trouble with the law over a period of time. The participant's status at the end of a program is less informative than his/her status three or six months later. Still other programs should be evaluated on the basis of their success over a period of years.

The major way to approach selecting important and relevant variables is through discussions with staff and managers. If there is no decision to be affected by the variable regardless of its value, or if no program standards mention the variable, then it probably is not important or relevant to the evaluation. If the location of the program participants' homes is not at all important to administrators, evaluators probably will not record it. However, at times evaluators may feel that a variable *should* be important and would be seen as important once summarized. Evaluators should not feel completely restricted to just what information their clients (program managers and staff) recognize as important. In other chapters, we point out specific instances in which information that was not requested came as a surprise to the program staff. Further-more, unintended negative side effects, which will certainly not be men-tioned in program goals, should not be ignored.

Sensitive to Change

There are two general types of measures of psychological and intel-lectual variables. One type seeks to assess an individual's general, typical level on some variable, and the other type seeks to assess current mood or achievement. An intelligence test is an example of the first type of measuring instrument. Although intelligence is certainly not fixed and does change in response to many environmental influences, the developers of intelligence tests sought to find test items that were minimally influenced by the individual's mood and immediate situation. Some writers have called such an instrument a *measure of trait* (Spiel-berger 1972). The other type of measure has been developed to assess effects that trait instruments seek to minimize. Such an instrument is called a *measure of state*. A measure of state seeks to assess the indi-vidual's current level on a variable. The extent that a measure of state is influenced by the individual's typical way of being is defined as a weakness of such a measure.

The distinction between intelligence tests and classroom tests may help to illustrate this point. Before a course, few class members are expected to score well on a test covering the course material. However, after the course students are expected to do well if they have mastered the course material. The classroom test should be sensitive to the changes that have occurred in the abilities of the students. Fairly stable charac-teristics of the students (such as intelligence) should not be primary factors leading to differences among the students' classroom test scores. In contrast, stable characteristics are expected to lie behind the differ-ences obtained using standard personality and ability tests. It is not possible for a test to be completely unaffected by the person's condition prior to entering the program; however, when measuring program out-come, the goal is to use instruments least affected by prior condition and, thus, most likely to detect real changes in participants.

Evaluators usually choose measures of program output that are maxi-mally sensitive to change because change is what evaluators are trying to detect. This point is especially important in the evaluation of various forms of psychotherapy because therapists, who are so familiar with standardized personality tests, often approach program evaluation in the same manner as they approach individual client assessment. Individual assessment instruments are designed to measure personality and intelli-gence traits. Tests that show marked sensitivity to situational differences are not desirable for personality and intelligence measurement. In contrast, evaluators want a measurement instrument that is sensitive to the respondents' current (hopefully improved) state. Using a trait measure to detect change puts the program at a considerable disadvantage by needlessly raising the probability of overlooking the change that did in fact occur.

A final point about sensitivity to change was alluded to in the previous chapter—very good performance is hard to improve. Just as it is harder to go from an A to a perfect paper than it is to go from a C to a $C+$, it is hard to improve a program participant's condition or level of satisfaction if the program is already fairly effective and well received. Measures of such criteria cannot change much. Evaluations dependent on detecting such small changes will usually conclude that the innovative program is no better than the old one, even when the innovative program is indeed better. There are statistical approaches to dealing with such situations; however, they are beyond the scope of this text (see Posavac and Carey 1978).

Valid Measures

In an evaluation, the instruments must validly measure the behaviors that the program is designed to change. These behaviors may be the ultimate criteria behaviors (such as long life, better adjustment, employment) or more immediate behaviors that are believed to be useful in achieving the planned long-term outcomes.

In order to assure themselves of the validity of chosen measures, evaluators should share the measures with the program staff. If staff members have not approved the measures, they may later disown a negative evaluation as being based on invalid tools. Implementation of suggestions for program change may be strongly resisted if staff members did not share in the choice of instruments. However, evaluators must not depend totally on the staff members to suggest the measures because they are often inexperienced in social science methodology.

In general, any measurement tool will be more likely to have acceptable validity if the tool focuses on objective behavior rather than on undefined or vague terms. Objective behaviors (such as "late to work less than one day out of the week" or "speaks in groups") are more likely to be measured validly than less precise phrases (such as "is punctual" or "is assertive"), regardless of what specific measurement approach is chosen. Mager (1972) presents an informal but thorough discussion of the usefulness of behavioral criteria rather than personality trait words in specifying the achievement of a goal.

Some variables may appear to be valid when in fact they are very misleading. Campbell (1969) presented several measures of the frequencies of types of crime in Chicago plotted over time. In 1957 a liberal, highly regarded person was installed as chief of police. The year after his term began, official statistics on the number of thefts under $50 increased dramatically. Did the new chief cause a crime wave? Not likely. Instead, his reforms led to a more thorough reporting of crime and perhaps some reclassification of crimes. A check on the interpretation that the chief caused a crime wave was provided by the homicide rate. Homicides seldom go unreported and cannot be reclassified into a different crime category. When frequency of homicides was plotted over time, there was no noticeable change after the chief began. Evaluators try to select and interpret variables carefully in order to avoid a misleading conclusion based on a poor choice of performance criteria.

Reliable Measures

Social behaviors cannot be measured perfectly because such measurements are affected by the respondent's mood, attitude, and understanding of directions—things that are extraneous to the behavior of interest. The degree that people who are theoretically equivalent on a social variable such as depression actually score the same on a test is the test's reliability. In somewhat oversimplified terms, a reliable test will yield much the same values if administered twice within a short period of time. Reliability, like validity, is higher if the scores are minimally influenced by the passing mood of the person completing the instrument, whether that person is a program participant, staff member, or evaluator.

Variables referring to objective information and behavior are likely to be more reliable than are subjective ratings or opinions. This does not mean to imply that ratings should never be used. We simply want to stress that it is harder to judge whether people are, for example, ambitious, than to record whether they have found jobs or have been promoted at work. Subjective ratings are usually less reliable because they are influenced not only by the behavior of the person being rated but also by the person doing the ratings.

Evaluators must appreciate the differences between the use of measures to estimate the general level of a *group* on some variable and their use to assess an *individual* on the variable. The greater the number of individuals whose responses are combined to estimate the level of the group, the more stable the estimate is. Thus, surveys and other forms of measurement that would be rejected as insufficiently reliable to assess the views or behaviors of individuals may be very useful as measures of a group's views or behaviors. The following paragraphs illustrate the importance of the difference between estimating an individual's score and a group's score.

By using the standard deviation of a test and its reliability, it is possible to calculate a range of values that is likely to include the individual's true score. For example, assume that a person scored 105 on an IQ test with a standard deviation of 15 and a reliability of .95. The true scores of 68 percent of the people getting 105 will be between $105 \pm 15 \sqrt{1 - .95}$, or between 101.6 and 108.4. The standard deviation times the square root of one minus the reliability is called the *standard error of estimate* and is applied when an *individual's* score is the question of interest (see Brown 1976).

On the other hand, when a *group's* mean score is to be estimated, the standard error of the mean is the statistic to be used, instead of the standard deviation as in the calculation given above. If a group of 100 people scored an average of 105 on the IQ test, the standard error of the mean is $15/\sqrt{100}$, or 1.5. We can conclude that 68 percent of such *groups* have true mean scores of between $105 \pm 1.5 \sqrt{1 - .95}$, or between 104.7 and 105.3. With the reliability assumed, this is a very precise estimate. Even a measure with a reliability of only .40 would yield a sufficiently precise group estimate, although a test with such a low reliability would be inappropriate for use with individuals.[2]

There are a variety of reliability indexes that are reported in test manuals. Some are very relevant to evaluation work, and others are not useful for evaluators. The classic test-retest approach to reliability is not as important to evaluation as to the area of psychological assessment. The reason it is less important to evaluators was alluded to in the section on sensitivity to change. Tests that are developed to be stable over time measure well-entrenched, habitual behaviors and are precisely the sort of tests evaluators do not want. Evaluators require measures of behaviors that are subject to change.

Split-half reliability, which is found by correlating the scores that respondents earned on the odd-numbered test items with the scores earned on the even-numbered test items, is quite important to evaluators. Split-half reliability is a measure of the extent a psychological measure is homogeneous, that is, sensitive to one concept or characteristic rather than a mixture of things. If a reading program is to be evaluated, the instrument to measure reading achievement should not include items requiring a broad general knowledge or quantitative skills.

Evaluators must also look for *interrater reliability,* that is, agreement between independent raters. Often, the criteria of success of a program

---

[2] Readers wishing more details on these points should examine an introductory statistics text, such as McCall (1975), and a testing text, such as Brown (1976).

include ratings made by professionals or relatives. An instrument that yields similar ratings when used by different observers is usually better than one that yields quite different values. Obviously, if the observers view the rated individuals in very different situations—at home versus in school—low interrater reliability may tell us more about the differences in situations than about the reliabilities of the ratings.

Nonreactive Measures

The mere act of requesting information from people or observing people can influence the behavior being studied. Measurement instruments will create questions that some people had never considered before. Raising the issue may make people more aware of things they previously ignored. The test itself will bore some respondents, offend some, and please others. The greater the behavioral change created by the measurement instrument, the greater its *reactivity*. Measuring the effect of human services is not at all similar to making physical measurements of inanimate objects.

Usually evaluators do not want to select measurement procedures that influence the people studied. If the instruments have an impact, the evaluation loses some of its usefulness, because the outcomes may be different once the instruments are no longer used. Completely nonreactive measurement is an ideal seldom actually achieved. An extended discussion of reactivity has been prepared by Webb et al. (1966).

At times, a tool becomes part of the program because it not only provides data, but because it influences the person to follow correct procedures or raises questions that need to be answered if the program is to be a success. Figure 6.3 is an example of an evaluation tool designed to cause staff members to do certain things that were previously overlooked. If the staff members serving alcoholics responsibly complete the form, they will not only provide evaluation data for the state board but will also be fulfilling crucial steps in the ideal treatment of alcoholics.

Cost-Effective Measures

In planning a program evaluation, the cost of the test materials and the costs of gathering data must not be forgotten. It is necessary to select instruments that will measure the required variables within acceptable cost limits. Several principles are usually true. First, time and money invested in making test materials attractive and easy to use will be repaid in higher response rates. Second, money spent on published forms will be small relative to the costs of the evaluation staff in collecting and analyzing the data. Third, because interviews cost far more than do other measurement approaches, they should not be used unless the potential respondents are unable to use written material, need prompting or encouragement to respond, will not respond to written surveys, or may be expected to be defensive or misleading in answering written surveys. Interviews are also useful because the interviewer can rephrase questions and select questions depending on the respondents' answers; however, this flexibility raises the cost of the evaluation.

Fourth, the effect of the instruments on participant loss must be considered. No participant would be lost to the research in a study of the program's records. Many participants, on the other hand, will be lost if a lengthy survey is mailed to people after they have left the program. Thus, an instrument that is itself inexpensive may not be cost effective if the only way to get people to complete it requires evaluators to spend a considerable amount of time following up on many tardy respondents, or if so few respond that the results are not representative of any group.

TYPES OF MEASURES

There are several general types of measures that evaluations employ. The major distinction among the approaches is the degree to which they depend on self-reported impressions versus objective observations. The principles just introduced will be used to describe the strengths and weaknesses of the approaches presented.

Written Surveys Completed by Program Participants

Probably the most widely used technique for evaluating programs is the written survey. The survey technique provides the most information per dollar or hour investment by the evaluation staff. Surveys are not expensive to reproduce or to buy. If they are complex and especially constructed for a particular evaluation, their cost will be higher. (Guidelines for writing survey items will be discussed later in this chapter.)

Surveys vary greatly in their reliability and validity because the topics of the surveys are so different. A survey asking former clients to give a global, subjective evaluation of their experience in therapy will not be highly reliable because responses will vary with the moods of the people responding. Similarly, students' evaluations of teachers may be influenced by whether a difficult assignment is due soon or whether test results have just been returned. On the other hand, a survey may yield quite reliable judgments if it focuses on current behavior, such as jobs held, further treatment sought, source of referral, and so on. Many of these same remarks apply to the validity of surveys as well. The more objective the material evaluators request, the more likely the responses will be valid estimates of the issue in question.

The loss of participants to the evaluation may be large if the samples are mobile, if the survey is long, or if the participants feel ambivalent toward the program. Evaluators must be prepared to follow up a mailed survey with reminder letters or phone calls to those who do not return the survey within ten days to two weeks (Anderson and Berdie 1975). If only a minority of the sample returns a survey, the responses of the whole sample cannot be estimated. Certainly, receiving returns from fewer than 50 percent of the sample makes the survey useless for many purposes but not all purposes, as will be mentioned later.

Regardless of how the survey is to be used, those who do not respond will still be different from those who return the survey. In one study, the 66 percent who returned a survey about their experience in outpatient counseling participated in an average of 20.2 counseling sessions, and those who did not respond participated in an average of only 9.5 sessions (Posavac and Hartung 1977). Experienced survey users expect to find such differences and recognize the limitations such differences impose on the certainty with which conclusions may be drawn.

Ratings of the Program Participants by Others

Ratings by people important in the program participants' lives can be used as measures of program success. As with surveys, ratings made by significant others may be very reliable if they focus on relatively objective behavior, such as absenteeism, participation in discussions, or physical health. On the other hand, they may be unreliable if they focus on undefined and vague variables, such as adjustment or success in the program. Our experience with forms mailed to spouses indicates that the return rate for forms mailed to significant others is similar to that of mailed self-report surveys.

The cost of ratings may be high if professional staff members are expected to perform numerous or detailed ratings. If ratings are done by nonprofessionals and are kept brief, the cost may be acceptably low. Who is expected to do the ratings will be related to how complete the data will be. Members of the evaluation team will probably complete nearly all the ratings planned; however, significant others may resent the intrusion of the team, and professional staff members may feel that the ratings are an affront to their professional judgment or performance. The best that evaluators can do is to keep the ratings

lives in the client's family. A spouse would be the most knowledgeable rater, but an adult son or daughter or a parent would certainly be quite acceptable. Pretreatment and posttreatment forms for both males and females are available. Ellsworth has recently developed a children's form of the PARS. A sample of items from the PARS is given in Figure 3.1. The items are oriented behaviorally, not diagnostically.

One unique feature of the PARS is the development of change norms. Ellsworth has obtained PARS ratings of inpatients and out-patients at the beginning and ninety days after the end of psycho-therapy. For people with a specific pretherapy PARS rating, the change norms indicate how much change can be expected on the average. Using change norms, an evaluator can determine the extent of improve-ment without testing comparison groups. In essence, the norms provide information about a comparison group for users without access to people not in the program. The change norms also permit the compari-son of types of treatment, therapists, or facilities, using the degree of improvement achieved by the clients receiving different forms of treatment.

Depression Check List. An example of a self-report measure that has many desirable features is the Adjective Depression Check List (Lubin 1967). There are actually seven forms of this check list. Normative data is provided for each list, and tables are available for converting raw scores into standard scores, thus making the forms comparable. Having various forms is useful for repeated testing because the evaluator may not want to ask the respondent to complete the same form over again. A number of people take offense at being asked to complete the same measure after treatment that they had completed before. Even if the instructions emphasize that the survey should be completed in the light of the person's current state, program participants often feel that once a survey is completed, there is little use in doing it again. The availability of different but parallel forms permits the evaluator to avoid this problem.

Global Level-of-Functioning Scales. There has been a need for gen-eral rating scales for assessing degree of overall psychological health with behavioral definitions of the various levels. Endicott and associates (1976) have recently described the Global Assessment Scale, which is useful for obtaining ratings from a busy staff without requiring a great deal of time. The Global Assessment Scale is presented in Figure 3.2; it may be duplicated without the authors' permission. The scale could be used by staff or relatives; however, it clearly cannot be used by clients themselves. The scale has acceptable interrater reliability and is both valid and sensitive to change.

An unnamed measure of function has been recommended by Carter

INSTRUCTIONS:

A. Please describe the person's community adjustment <u>during the past month</u> by answering each question below.

B. Please answer <u>every</u> question even though you might feel unsure of your answer.

C. Mark your answer to each question by making an X in the box under your answer choice, like this:

| X |

	Answer choices			
<u>DURING LAST MONTH, HAS SHE</u> . . .	1 Rarely	2 Some- times	3 Usually	4 Always
1 . . . Shown consideration for you. <u>Mark one answer for each question</u>	☐	☐	☐	☐
2 . . . Shown interest in what you say (mark one answer)	☐	☐	☐	☐
3 . . . Been able to talk it through when angry	☐	☐	☐	☐
4 . . . Shown affection toward you	☐	☐	☐	☐
5 . . . Gotten along with family members	☐	☐	☐	☐

	Answer choices			
<u>DURING LAST MONTH, HAS SHE</u> . . .	1 Almost Never	2 Some- times	3 Often	4 Almost Always
6 . . . Acted restless and tense	☐	☐	☐	☐
7 . . . Said things looked discouraging or hopeless	☐	☐	☐	☐
8 . . . Had difficulty falling or remaining asleep	☐	☐	☐	☐
9 . . . Been nervous	☐	☐	☐	☐
10 . . . Talked about being afraid	☐	☐	☐	☐

FIGURE 3.1: Selected items from the Personal Adjustment and Role Skills Scale, Female Pretreatment Form. (Reproduced by permission of IPEV, Inc., Box 4654, Roanoke, VA 24105. Copyright 1974 by IPEV, Inc.)

66

Rate the subject's lowest level of functioning in the last week by selecting the lowest range that describes his functioning on a hypothetical continuum of mental health-illness. For example, a subject whose "behavior is considerably influenced by delusions" (range 21–30) should be given a rating in that range even though he has "major impairment in several areas" (range 31–40). Use intermediate levels when appropriate (e.g., 35, 58, 63). Rate actual functioning independent of whether or not subject is receiving and may be helped by medication or some other form of treatment.

91–100   No symptoms, superior functioning in a wide range of activities, life's problems never seem to get out of hand, is sought out by others because of his warmth and integrity.

81–90   Transient symptoms may occur, but good functioning in all areas, interested and involved in a wide range of activities, socially effective, generally satisfied with life, "everyday" worries that only occasionally get out of hand.

71–80   Minimal symptoms may be present, but no more than slight impairment in functioning, varying degrees of "everyday" worries, and problems that sometimes get out of hand.

61–70   Some mild symptoms (e.g., depressive mood and mild insomnia) OR some difficulty in several areas of functioning, but generally functioning well, has some meaningful interpersonal relationships, and most untrained people would not consider him "sick."

51–60   Moderate symptoms or generally functioning with some difficulty (e.g., few friends and flat affect, depressed mood and pathological self-doubt, euphoric mood and pressure of speech, moderately severe antisocial behavior).

41–50   Any serious symptomatology or impairment in functioning that most clinicians would think obviously requires treatment or attention (e.g., suicidal preoccupation or gesture, severe obsessional rituals, frequent anxiety attacks, serious antisocial behavior, compulsive drinking).

31–40   Major impairment in several areas, such as work, family relations, judgment, thinking, or mood (e.g., depressed woman avoids friends, neglects family and housework), OR some impairment in reality testing or communication (e.g., speech is at times obscure, illogical, or irrelevant), OR single serious suicide attempt.

21–30   Unable to function in almost all areas (e.g., stays in bed all day) OR behavior is considerably influenced by either delusions or hallucinations OR serious impairment in communication (e.g., sometimes incoherent or unresponsive) or judgment (e.g., acts grossly inappropriately).

11–20   Needs supervision to prevent hurting self or others, or to maintain minimal personal hygiene (e.g., repeated suicide attempts, frequently violent, manic excitement, smears feces), OR gross impairment in communication (e.g., largely incoherent or mute).

1–10   Needs constant supervision for several days to prevent hurting self or others, or makes no attempt to maintain personal hygiene.

FIGURE 3.2: The Global Assessment Scale. (Reproduced from Hargreaves, Attkisson, and Sorenson 1977)

and Newman (1976) for routine use in counseling or mental health centers. The scale provides nine levels of function, as shown in Figure 3.3. Instructions for using the scale are given by Carter and Newman (1976). The advantage of this simple nine-level scale is that once a clinician is familiar with the scale, it can be completed very quickly. Such a single-rating measure would not be sufficiently reliable for use as an individual assessment tool; however, for a program evaluation in which the ratings of many clients made by many clinicians are to be averaged, the instrument is quite adequate.

Preparing Special Measures

The major disadvantages of published measures are easy to imagine. The program being studied may have goals and purposes not related to any currently published material. For example, there are relatively few special hospital units specifically for nonterminal cancer patients; when the authors were asked to design materials to measure patient reaction to such a new unit, we found little in the literature to help. Once the evaluators have decided that no existing measure is appropriate, then a new instrument must be prepared. However, evaluators must be realistic about how much time they can afford to put into the construction of new instruments. The time pressure of work in service settings precludes the routine development of innovative research instruments.

The Format of a Survey. The format of a survey will be important in gaining the cooperation of respondents, in analyzing the data, and in interpreting the results. If the survey is to be self-administered, the layout must be attractive, uncluttered, and easy to use. One aid to achieving these standards is use of a structured format rather than the open-ended question approach. Open-ended questions are hard to summarize because each respondent will approach each question somewhat differently. Although much information can be obtained from open-ended questions, it may be hard to draw recommendations from the survey because the answers are unique.

If a structured survey format is adopted, the survey might still be cluttered if the questions each have different response alternatives. For example, mixing "Yes" and "No" questions, "Agree-Neutral-Disagree" attitude statements, and "Frequently-Seldom-Never" reports of past behavior will make the survey harder to complete. The greater the proportion of questions that can be answered in the same answer format, the better. Figure 3.4 contains an example of a specially prepared survey that violated good practices. The respondents must constantly figure out what type of answer is required of them. People inexperienced in preparing surveys often construct surveys that are difficult to use. Figure 3.5, in contrast, would be easy to complete. The degree of difficulty experienced in completing a survey will affect the proportion of respondents who will complete it. A standard response format not only encourages a greater response rate, but it also increases the ease with which the results can be presented and interpreted; since the results can be summarized on one table, comparisons can easily be made among survey items. The use of an unnecessary variety of response formats can cause as much confusion for readers of a report as it does for the respondents to a survey.

Preparing Survey Items. There are a number of useful guidelines to the preparation of survey items. The most important principle is to remember who is going to respond to the items. A statement that is clear to an evaluator may not be clear to someone reading it from a very different vantage point. Questions that have the best chance of being understood will be written clearly, simply, and briefly. Such statements cannot be prepared in one sitting. On the contrary, they must be written, scrutinized, criticized, rewritten, pretested, and rewritten. Items written one week will not seem as acceptable the following week. If the first draft cannot be improved, either evaluators have not learned to criticize their own work or they are geniuses at item writing.

There are several characteristics of clear, simple survey items. The items should avoid negatives. Negatively worded sentences take more effort to read and are misunderstood more frequently than positively worded sentences. Double negatives are especially difficult to read. Well-written items use short, common words rather than less common or longer words. Good survey items focus on one issue. An item such as, "My physical therapist was polite and competent" combines two issues. In this case, it is possible to interpret an affirmative answer but not possible to interpret a negative answer. What should the director of the unit do if many people answer negatively—have a workshop on charm or on the latest physical therapy practices? Finally, we urge that survey items be grammatically correct.

Several practices can help to detect survey items that need improving. First, the sentence should be read aloud. Often, awkward phrasing is more obvious when read aloud than when simply silently reviewed. Second, someone on the program staff should read the draft items. Third, evaluators should think critically of how to interpret each possible answer to the item. As mentioned above, sometimes one answer can

I. Overview of Scale

The scale is used to describe a client's overall ability to function autonomously in the community. A scale rating is assigned *at the time of every clinical encounter* by balancing the relative contributions of four criteria as they affect a person's overall ability to function autonomously:

1. Personal self-care
2. Social functioning in ordinary social unit and in the general community
3. Vocational and/or educational productivity
4. Evidence of emotional stability and stress tolerance

Dysfunctioning in any one or more of the four areas could affect a person's overall ability to function autonomously.

II. Some Details Describing the Four Criteria

The criteria should always be translated to fit the age bracket and circumstances of the individual. Special notes are indicated below where such considerations may be necessary.

1. Personal Self-Care (for children, adjust to age level)
   a. Personal maintenance of washing, dressing, eating, elimination chores
   b. Ability to recognize and avoid common dangers
   c. Taking responsibility for own maintenance, e.g., caring for own room, personal belongings, daily schedule, personal finances, selecting own clothing and accessories

2. Social Functioning (adjust by age, living conditions, and possibly by community)
   a. *Familiar*—the degree to which those familiar with the person, particularly those in the ordinary social unit (family, roommate, boarding house residents) can tolerate and interact with the person, i.e., jointly socialize and/or participate in recreational activities with the person
   b. *Impersonal*—the degree to which relative strangers can interact with the person and vice versa, e.g., store clerks, policemen, or others encountered in ordinary vocational or recreational activities

3. Vocational and/or Educational Functioning
   a. *Working Adults*
      (1) The ability to support one's self and one's dependents
      (2) The ability to meet the demands and pressures of one's chosen (or present) vocation, be it lawyer or janitor
   b. *Homemakers and/or Parents and/or Elderly Persons*
      (1) The ability to organize and/or monitor the daily routines of the household, e.g., meals, child care, washing, etc.
      (2) The ability to organize, maintain and/or monitor family budgeting, shopping, social and/or recreational activities
   c. *Children*
      (1) Should be considered by general age categories of 0–5, 6–11, 12–14, 15–18
      (2) Play and social activities such that constructive and productive social learning can occur
      (3) Educational activities and performance such as would be expected of that age

FIGURE 3.3: A global rating scale of psychological functioning developed by the Central Montgomery Mental Health and Mental Retardation Center, Norristown, Pennsylvania. (Reproduced from Carter and Newman 1976)

4. Evidence of Emotional Stability and Stress Tolerance
   a. The degree to which the symptom(s) reflects personality disorganization of such degree that the symptoms and the accompanying disorganization cause discomfort to whomever the person ordinarily interacts with.
   b. The degree to which the person can tolerate the amount of expected daily variation in *present* social, vocational and/or educational realms.

III. Definition of the Nine Scale Levels of Functioning

With regard to the balance of the four criteria (personal self-care, social, vocational/educational, and emotional symptoms/stress tolerance), the person's ability to function autonomously in the community is at Level X, where X can assume one of the following nine (9) levels:

LEVEL 1: Dysfunctional in all four areas and is almost totally dependent upon others to provide a supportive protective environment.

LEVEL 2: Not working; ordinary social unit cannot or will not tolerate the person; can perform minimal self-care functions but cannot assume most responsibilities or tolerate social encounters beyond restrictive settings (e.g., in group, play, or occupational therapy).

LEVEL 3: Not working; probably living in ordinary social unit but not without considerable strain on the person and/or on others in the household. Symptoms are such that movement in the community should be restricted or supervised.

LEVEL 4: Probably not working, although may be capable of working in a very protective setting; able to live in ordinary social unit and contribute to the daily routine of the household; can assume responsibility for all personal self-care matters; stressful social encounters ought to be avoided or carefully supervised.

LEVEL 5: Emotional stability and stress tolerance are sufficiently low that successful functioning in the social and/or vocational/educational realms is marginal. The person is barely able to hold on to either job or social unit, or both, without direct therapeutic intervention and a diminution of conflicts in either or both realms.

LEVEL 6: The person's vocational and/or social areas of functioning are stabilized, but only because of direct therapeutic intervention. Symptom presence and severity are probably sufficient to be both noticeable and somewhat disconcerting to the client and/or to those around the client in daily contact.

LEVEL 7: The person is functioning and coping well socially and vocationally (educationally); however, symptom reoccurrences are sufficiently frequent to necessitate some sort of regular therapeutic intervention.

LEVEL 8: Functioning well in all areas with little evidence of distress present. However, a history of symptom reoccurrence suggests periodic correspondence with the Center; e.g., a client may receive a medication check from a family physician, who then contacts the Center monthly, or the client returns for bi-monthly social activities.

LEVEL 9: The person is functioning well in all areas and no contact with the MH/MR services is recommended.

NOTE: Levels 5 through 8 describe persons who are usually functioning satisfactorily in the community, but for whom problems in one or more of the criteria areas force some degree of dependency on a form of therapeutic intervention.

High School Evaluation Form

1.   How do you like attending your high school? (Circle one.)

Very Much   Much   OK   Little   Not at all
     1   2   3   4   5

2.   How would you describe your teachers? (Check one)

   ____ 1. Mostly excellent   ____ 4. Mostly marginal
   ____ 2. Mostly good   ____ 5. Mostly Poor
   ____ 3. Half good/half marginal

3. To what extent would you agree with the following statement: The physical facilities of my high school (classrooms, halls, gym, lunchroom, etc.) are good.

Strongly   Disagree   Neutral   Agree   Strongly
disagree   agree

4. Are your teachers good teachers and willing to talk with students after regular classes?   Yes _____   No _____

5. What is the place of interscholastic team competition in your school?

   _____ Not at all important
   _____ Very important
   _____ Not sure

FIGURE 3.4: Example of survey items violating many of the principles of easy-to-use, self-administered surveys.

be interpreted but another cannot. Fourth, if ambiguities remain, they will probably be detected if the revised draft is administered as an interview with several people from the population to be sampled.

SUMMARY

The most important concept in this chapter concerns the use of multiple measures from multiple sources. The use of multiple sources of information is one of the basic characteristics of valid and useful evaluations. When choosing measures of variables, evaluators should use the criteria of a good measurement instrument to evaluate the specific instruments selected. Is something *important* being measured? Is the measure *sensitive to change,* even small changes? Does the measure seem *valid, reliable,* and *cost effective*? Is *reactivity* to the instrument a problem?

After leaving the hospital, some coronary patients have questions about their physical condition, recovery, recommended changes in diet, exercise, and/or smoking habits.

Please indicate if you feel you would like *more information* on any of the following topics. Circle your answers.

How much additional information do you want about these topics?	Does not apply	None	A little more	Some more	Much more
1. Cholestrol restrictions	DNA	N	L	S	M
2. Salt restrictions	DNA	N	L	S	M
3. Recommended weight loss	DNA	N	L	S	M
4. My medications	DNA	N	L	S	M
5. Restrictions on alcohol use	DNA	N	L	S	M
6. Sexual activity	DNA	N	L	S	M
7. Smoking	DNA	N	L	S	M
8. A good exercise program	DNA	N	L	S	M
9. Excessive emotional stress	DNA	N	L	S	M
10. Handling stress	DNA	N	L	S	M
11. Understanding of my heart attack	DNA	N	L	S	M
12. Anxiety	DNA	N	L	S	M
13. Depression	DNA	N	L	S	M
14. Other _____			L	S	M
(Please specify)					

A coronary patient faces many potential problems during the period of convalescence. Which issues did you encounter and how difficult was your adjustment? Circle your answers.

How much difficulty did (or do) you experience over these potential problems?	Does not apply	None	Little	Some	Much
1. Going back to work	DNA	N	L	S	M
2. Sexual activity	DNA	N	L	S	M
3. Smoking	DNA	N	L	S	M
4. Diet	DNA	N	L	S	M
5. Anxiety	DNA	N	L	S	M
6. Depression	DNA	N	L	S	M
7. Activity restrictions	DNA	N	L	S	M
8. Understanding my doctor	DNA	N	L	S	M
9. My spouse's reaction to my health	DNA	N	L	S	M
10. My family's reaction to my health	DNA	N	L	S	M
11. Other _____			L	S	M
(Please specify)					

FIGURE 3.5: A section of a self-administered needs-assessment survey that is easy to use because standard alternatives are provided for each item.

STUDY QUESTIONS

1. Improve the wording or the structured options of the following questions that could be suggested for use in various evaluations.

   a. Would you like to continue receiving counseling at the ABC Mental Health Center? ____Yes ____No

   b. Is the warmth of the staff an important reason for your continued participation in the XYZ Center? ____Yes ____No

   c. Please rate the quality of the care you received in the recovery room after your recent surgery.

   ____Excellent ____Good ____Fair ____Poor

   d. Police officers do not really care about the feelings of the victims of a crime.

   ____Strongly Agree ____Agree ____Disagree ____Strongly Disagree

   e. The times that services are available during the day should be extended because people are waiting too long for appointments. ____Yes ____No

2. Rewrite the items in Figure 3.4 so that they have a common response format.

3. In planning an evaluation of the ALPHA County Community Mental Health Center, the Freudian counselors insist that the Rorschach Inkblot Test be administered at one-month intervals to current clients. What would your reaction be to this proposal?

4. When an evaluation of clinical services was planned, the evaluator introduced the level-of-functioning scale given in Figure 3.3. Some clinicians resisted this suggestion by saying that the scale merely refers to coping behaviors, NOT to intrapsychic growth. What would you respond?

5. Suppose someone looks up the reliability of the Global Assessment Scale (Figure 3.2) and correctly reports that it is .76. The conclusion is then drawn that because .76 is too low for reliable individual psychological assessment, the scale should not be used for program evaluation purposes. Does this conclusion logically follow?

FURTHER READING

NUNNALLY, J. C., and DURHAM, R. L. 1975. Validity, reliability, and special problems of measurement in evaluation research. In *Handbook of evaluation research*, vol. 1., ed. E. L. Struening and M. Guttentag, chap. 10. Beverly Hills, Calif.: Sage.

NUNNALLY, J. C., and WILSON, W. H. 1975. Method and theory for developing measures in evaluation research. In *Handbook of evaluation research*, vol. 1, ed. E. L. Struening and M. Guttentag, chap. 9. Beverly Hills, Calif.: Sage.

WEISS, C. H. 1975. Interviewing in evaluation research. In *Handbook of evaluation research*, vol. 1., ed. E. L. Struening and M. Guttentag, chap. 11. Beverly Hills, Calif.: Sage.

The single best source of measures useful in educational settings is:

BUROS, O. K. 1972. *Seventh mental measurements yearbook*. Highland Park, N.J.: Gryphon Press.

There are many recent sources of variables and scales for someone who is developing an evaluation plan for a mental health facility. A few of the best are:

CARTER, D. E., and NEWMAN, F. L. 1976. *A client-oriented system of mental health service delivery and program management: A workbook and guide*. Rockville, Md.: National Institute of Mental Health. DHEW Pub. No. (ADM) 76–307. U.S. Government Printing Office Stock No. 017-024-00523-1.

HAGEDORN, H. J.; BECK, K. J.; NEUBERT, S. F.; and WERLIN, S. H. 1976. *A working manual of simple program evaluation techniques for community mental health centers*. Rockville, Md.: National Institute of Mental Health. DHEW Pub. No. (ADM) 76–404. U.S. Government Printing Office Stock No. 017-024-00539-8.

HARGREAVES, W. A.; ATTKISSON, C. C.; and SORENSEN, J. D., eds. 1977. *Resource materials for community mental health program evaluation*. 2nd ed. Rockville, Md.: National Institute of Mental Health. DHEW Pub. No. (ADM) 77–328. U.S. Government Printing Office Stock No. 017-024-00554-1.

WASKOW, I. E., and PERLOFF, M. B., eds. 1975. *Psychotherapy change measures*. Rockville, Md.: National Institute of Mental Health. DHEW Pub. No. (ADM) 74–120. U.S. Government Printing Office Stock No. 1724-00397.

Sources for measures of attitudes on a variety of topics include the following collections:

ROBINSON, J. P.; ATHANASIOU, R.; and HEAD, K. B. 1969. *Measures of occupational attitudes and occupational characteristics*. Ann Arbor, Mich.: Institute for Social Research.

ROBINSON, J. P.; RUSK, J. G.; and HEAD, K. B. 1968. *Measures of political attitudes*. Ann Arbor, Mich.: Institute for Social Research.

ROBINSON, J. P., and SHAVER, P. R. 1973. *Measures of social psychological attitudes*. Ann Arbor, Mich.: Institute for Social Research.

The U.S. Government Printing Office also makes available evaluation guides useful for evaluators in criminal justice areas.

ADAMS, S. 1975. *Evaluative research in corrections*. Washington, D.C.: Law Enforcement Assistance Administration, U.S. Department of Justice.

ALBRIGHT, E.; BAUM, M. A.; and FORMAN, B. 1973. *Evaluation in criminal justice programs*. Washington, D.C.: Law Enforcement Assistance Administration, U.S. Department of Justice.

part

II

EVALUATION

OF

NEED AND PROCESS

In Chapter 1, readers learned of the need for program evaluation and the growing trend to use evaluation methods to improve and to justify the offering of human service programs. An overview of the evaluator's role vis-à-vis the human service provider and the administration of human service organizations was given in Chapter 2. Measurement principles were discussed in Chapter 3 to emphasize that evaluators are research professionals who know how to approach the quantification of variables important to human services.

In Part II, the discussion of the specific tasks of evaluators is initiated. Evaluators can make contributions to the administration of programs without actually examining the effectiveness of human services in achieving goals. First, Chapter 4 shows how evaluators can participate in the planning of programs by using their social science skills to help planners find indicators of need and to quantify and summarize these indicators. Second, evaluators can assist in monitoring a program to learn the extent to which it has been implemented as planned. Administrators and representatives of the public want to know: "Who gets what services from whom?" Program evaluation methods, as illustrated in Chapter 5, can be applied to answer such a question.

4

Evaluation

in

Program Planning

What sort of service can a person trained in social science methods provide to planners of human services? How can a program evaluator do anything *before* there is a program? There are two general types of contributions to be made: one, to specify the needs a program should meet; and, two, to select from among various possible programs.

Planning is required before any human service program is begun. Long before the doors of a service agency swing open, some people must shape the service according to their perceptions of the need for it and the best ways to meet those needs. A surprisingly number of programs have been planned on the basis of little more than an influential person's impression of what a group needs. Whether the program is for alcoholics, malnourished children, or unemployed blue-collar workers, subjective impressions often guide the planning of the program. Before we illustrate the methods that an evaluator might use to help the planners of human services, a brief discussion of the problems faced by planning committees may be helpful. These comments are based on observations of meetings of planning committees made up of such human service providers as teachers, social workers, or nurses. Since individuals working in such positions are seldom trained in social science research techniques, evaluators have made valuable contributions to such planning groups.

THE EVALUATOR
AND THE PLANNING COMMITTEE

What Planning Committees Want to Accomplish

There are two important general goals: to produce the best possible practical plan, and to find a plan with broad-based support. Many planning sessions, however, follow the less than ideal patterns of planning by administrative fiat or of dilatory, boring planning sessions. Some similar reasons lie behind both patterns, which include the lack of definitive information and the difficulty for any individual to grasp the total set of needs and program possibilities.

Unambiguous information is hard to obtain and in fact may not exist. Even experts in an area cannot know what policy is the most likely to succeed. Evidence for following a given path can usually be found; however, often there is other evidence supporting a different course. After hearing experts use the expressions, "on one hand . . . but on the other hand," a Senate committee chairman expressed a desire for "one-armed scientists" (David 1975). His desire was obviously facetious; however, it illustrates a crucial point—even when information is available, it will seldom point to a single plan to solve a problem.

Planning committees may have difficulty selecting the best plan because human beings are limited in how much information they can use at one time. To consider simultaneously all the variables involved in selecting a "best" plan is impossible. Fortunately, methods are available to break a decision down into parts or steps. The jargon word for this process is to *disaggregate* a decision. Actually, the suggestion to disaggregate is good advice for making any decision; however, planning committees may persist in grappling with the whole problem without seeing that aspects of the problem can be approached one at a time. The last section of this chapter describes a system to use in disaggregating a decision.

The frustration of not seeing a clearly best approach to solve a problem sometimes inhibits planning. When a committee tackles a complex problem, often no one structures the task for the committee. This lack of structure leads various individuals to either engage in small talk or push their own views. Once it becomes clear that the planning committee is not getting anywhere, an administrator may decide what the plans should be. This action may be much to the relief of the committee.

To be fair, some planning groups do not function well because they have access only to funds earmarked for certain purposes. These planning groups work within a rather narrow range of options. However, the planning group still has a critical task because a human service program can take many specific forms, even within a narrow range of options.

Evaluators Can Help Program Planners

It is unfortunate that evaluators are so often consulted only after a program is already in place. Doubly unfortunate is the situation in which the evaluator is consulted after a program is suspected of being ineffective. Well-managed human service organizations are directed by managers who recognize the need for evaluation. Such managers may encourage evaluators to sit in on planning sessions because planning is much like evaluation. The planner merely uses a future tense (for example, *Will* the program help?), and the evaluator typically uses the past tense (for example, *Did* the program help?). If evaluators are involved early, planners have the advantage of convenient access to knowledge about what can be evaluated objectively and at what cost. Such collaboration is likely to be helpful because in many human services the innovators are not trained in research or program evaluation methods. In addition, most human service administrators and planners do not have experience in phrasing evaluative questions in ways that can be answered using social science techniques. For example, the goals of many service programs are written in such general terms that it is impossible to know when the goal was attained and when it was not. For example, "giving quality medical care," "reducing crime," or "opening meetings to the community" could all be goals; however, none can be evaluated as phrased. When do you know "crime" has been "reduced"? What crimes? How much of a reduction would count? One percent? Ten percent? For how long must a reduction last? All these questions (and others) must be answered before a plan can be made and before an evaluation can be initiated.

The next section of this chapter concerns some general issues that evaluators should bring to the planning sessions. Next, methods of carrying out an assessment of need are described. Last, a method to help planners to divide a complex decision into manageable parts is presented.

GENERAL ISSUES TO ADDRESS IN PLANNING

Identifying the Intended Participants

Clearly identifying the population(s) to be served by a program is the most advisable first step in program planning. It is easy to evade the hard task of clearly specifying who is to be served by a particular program. Some people talk about serving the needs of the "community." As long as a vague term is used, the various people involved in the planning may comfortably continue to "plan" while each holds a different view of the community to be served. Even worse, each person not having a clear idea of the community assumes the others know who the community is. The evaluators can help the planning group to address the question of who really is to be served. Evaluators can expect foot dragging because the task is both hard and anxiety arousing. This is so because once a choice is made among the possibilities a commitment is involved, and it will be difficult to hide weak plans in a veil of vague descriptions of the "needs of the community."

Carefully identifying those to be served is crucial because the needs of one group are different from the needs of another group. Alternately, an approach possibly effective with one group may not be effective with a different one. Examples of the importance of identifying the target population include the following: junior high school students have different social and academic needs from senior high school students; repeat offenders are less likely to benefit from a program that may benefit teenagers who have been convicted of one crime, although both may be correctly identified as "juvenile delinquents"; people from more privileged economic backgrounds probably expect human services to be housed in more attractive settings than do people used to less plush housing; and an elderly population needs different services from a mental health center than do teenage runaways.

One way to force oneself to be specific and clear is to put ideas down on paper and permit someone else to react to them. A chart summarizing the characteristics of the target population may be useful. A hospital planning an ambulatory care center may define the following groups as the target populations: the elderly; indigent or near-indigent families; children of all families requiring immunizations and other routine care; and newcomers to the local community. It is possible to obtain estimates of the sizes of these groups from local governments. A more difficult task is to estimate the numbers of these groups who will make use of the new facilities. For the present example, the proportion of private physicians on the hospital staff not accepting new patients would be useful information. If only a few local physicians will accept new patients, one can expect greater acceptance of the planned center. Also, if the community contains many relatively mobile families, many families will not have established relationships with physicians.

Knowing where people currently obtain a service is helpful in planning a new service. How attached are people to the facility or agency they now use? Medical outpatient centers are often initially overstaffed, even though other medical care in the area is hard to obtain. People develop loyalties to locations and to care givers and are often slow to seek services at new locations, even if these new facilities are more convenient and, at least in some ways, better than the facilities they currently use. Knowing where people obtain service provides information about the possibility of duplication of facilities. Such duplication is a frequent target of criticism. Hospital administrators are accused of seeking status for their hospitals through the acquisition of the latest treatment and diagnostic equipment. If equivalent equipment is available at a nearby hospital, government agencies and insurance companies question plans to expand or upgrade facilities and capacity. Similarly, universities are under great pressure not to add new programs or departments that merely duplicate existing programs elsewhere.

Identifying the Needs to be Met

Successful programs seek to meet real needs that are felt by the population to be served. Certainly, planners of human service programs are likely to do a better job if they know what the needs of the target population are. There is a critical difference between the needs felt by a population and the needs professionals attribute to the population. The program planners will be most effective if they understand the population as it really is. If the target population does not recognize a need, the program will have to include an educational aspect. The staffs of screening and treatment programs for high blood pressure deal daily with people who do not recognize a need for care. When the disease first develops, elevated blood pressure usually does not produce felt symptoms; in addition, the treatment does have undesirable side effects (*Medical World News* 1977). Because people expect to feel better after taking medicine, many reject the treatment. A rejected treatment means a program failure, even though the medication is effective in prolonging the lives of the hypertensive patients because it reduces the likelihood of strokes and other cardiovascular diseases.

A university English professor provides a second example of the disappointing results of not realizing that a target population may not construe a problem in the same way as a professional offering a service. She reasoned as follows: (1) many college students do not write very well, and professors in many fields agree that improvement would be desirable; (2) English professors have only limited contact with students, compared to professors in the students' major fields; therefore (3) a way to improve student writing is to improve the ability of non-English faculty to grade, evaluate, and improve the writing done for non-English courses. She developed a series of workshops for non-English department faculty members involving a number of her departmental colleagues and obtained funds from the college dean for a guest speaker. The flaw in her plans was very basic. It was wrong to assume people who complain want to act upon their complaints. Although many college professors complain about student writing ability, relatively few may be ready to involve themselves actively in the grading and counseling required to encourage improvement. Consequently, the attendance at the workshops and the lecture was primarily from the English department; non-English department faculty could be counted on the fingers of one hand. As a matter of fact, there were more graduate student evaluators present to observe the first workshop than there were faculty members from departments other than English. Other workshops were then cancelled. The point should be clear: Programs will be effective only when they meet real needs and when the target population agrees that it has those needs.

In assessing the need for a human service, it is very important to be objective because the extent of need is easy to overestimate. Nurses were concerned about the large number of stroke patients in a medium-sized hospital. They felt they were unable to meet these patients' needs without a special stroke unit. Because of these concerns, the administrators cooperated in a study of the severity of stroke patients in their hospital. It quickly became clear that there were actually very few stroke patients in the hospital. Those few admitted with possible strokes were usually discharged with much less severe diagnoses. In spite of the subjective feelings of many of the people on the staff of that hospital, there was no way to justify the added expense of a special stroke unit. The administration needed to deal with the concern of the staff, but in ways other than the institution of a new unit.

Another reason for objectivity is that the no-nonsense people who are responsible for funding human service projects will be more likely to respond to clear plans designed to meet objectively determined needs. If the project just described had found that a large number of stroke patients were being treated at the hospital and that many of these patients were being discharged with greater disabilities than were the patients of other hospitals, then the response of the hospital's administrators would have been more favorable to plans for a new service unit.

The Program's Resources

An evaluation of a proposed program will include an evaluation of the type of staff required. What training and experience should the staff members have? Will their training fit the actual needs of the people to be served? Is their work planned to use their talents effectively? We will point out here only that effective people may not be effective if placed in situations for which they were not trained or if the situation restricts the use of their skills.

The staff must be housed in adequate facilities. If they lack appropriate areas in which to meet program participants as individuals or as groups, the program may be impossible to deliver. Work-training programs must have up-to-date equipment, or the training will not be useful to the trainees. The location of the facilities is important; public transportation may be a necessity for the people to be served. Access for physically handicapped people will be a federal requirement in the future for all public facilities (*Time* December 5, 1977).

In addition to the human and physical resources of a program, the actual plan for the human service should be examined to determine whether it is sufficient to meet the identified needs of the target population. At various points in this text we show where programs are developed that are found to be grossly inadequate for the program that they were designed to meet. Can a summer in a preschool program such as Head Start realistically be expected to overcome the handicaps of living in a setting that has not taught the basic skills needed to begin formal education? Can inmate counseling really affect a prisoner's ability to get and hold a job after release?

When it appears that a program will be insufficient to meet the needs it is designed to serve, one of two paths are open. On one hand, the program's goals could be scaled down. It may be better to strive to meet realistic goals than to fail to meet overly optimistic ones. On the other hand, the program could be strengthened. Both paths may require that the entire program be reconsidered. Program sponsors might not be satisfied with scaling down their expectations, but strengthening the program may require the expenditure of more funds than the sponsors wish to provide. The evaluator's contribution to a better program is important in the long run; however, in the short run, the suggestion that a program might not be sufficient for its purposes will not be joyfully received.

TOOLS FOR THE ASSESSMENT OF NEED

People who have participated in planning committees have complained that so much is unknown that their job is close to impossible. No one can make the planning committee's job easy; however, there are a number of techniques of gathering information that can reduce some of the planners' confusion. Sources of information that have proved useful include census data relevant to need for human services, surveys of residents of the community to be served, existing community agencies serving similar problems, and knowledgeable people in the community, often called *key informants.*

Census Data

Census data are available for many years. Some of the items in the census surveys are relevant to program planning. This source has much to recommend it for use in program planning: it is usually considered reliable and valid; it is public when in summary form; and it is relatively inexpensive, compared to other types of data. The indexes in Figure 4.1 were derived from census information. This information was part of a needs assessment study utilized in a plan to expand mental health facilities in a group of rural counties. By comparing these indexes with similar variables for the whole state and for the nation, the extent of needs could be estimated. Census data will not be useful when planning a program in a rapidly expanding locality. In such communities, census data will be out of date soon after the census is conducted.

Similar or Related Existing Services

Before launching a new facility for human services, the planning group should make an inventory of existing agencies in the area that offer similar or related services. Such a survey will help to avoid the duplication of services and to locate key informants who can provide good estimates of certain community needs. For example, there are a variety of sources where people seek the emotional support that could be provided by a mental health center. Clergy and physicians probably deal with more such people than do psychologists and psychiatrists (see

FIGURE 4.1: Census data used in the needs assessment study prepared for the Spoon River Community Mental Health Center (Source: *Community Mental Health Plan, Spoon River, Illinois;* Spoon River Community Mental Health Center, Inc., 1977)

Age distribution of population
Percentage of teenagers not in school
Percentage of black teenagers not in school
Percentage of working mothers of children under 18
Percentage of working mothers of preschool children
Percentage of aged persons living alone
Percentage of aged persons in poverty[a]
Percentage of extremely crowded housing units[b] without
   plumbing facilities
Percentage of large households[c] with low income
Percentage of female-headed families with children
Percentage of disabled persons not in institutions
Percentage of disabled persons not in institutions and unable to work

[a] *Based on local income levels*

[b] *More than one person per room*

[c] *Six or more persons*

Posavac and Hartung 1977). There is a wide range of estimates of the percentage of people seeing physicians who basically are not physically ill. The estimates range as high as two-thirds of all patients. The clergy of certain religious denominations spend much time with parish members experiencing crises. Thus, members of the clergy and physicians would be good key informants in plans for the development of new mental health services.

Number of People Under Treatment

Once the facilities and personnel currently offering a service are identified, an empirical study of the number of people who are being treated or served is often conducted. There are at least two approaches to the number under treatment. The most direct approach to use in estimating the number of people receiving related services would be to survey the appropriate individuals in the area. Physicians and clergy could be asked how many people they have served during the last month(s) who may require attention for certain mental health problems. The problem list would be kept short because classifying people into a few categories would be less subject to error than asking informants to use finely discriminated categories. One need survey presented only three categories: mental illness (defined very broadly to include "problems in living"), drug abuse, and alcohol problems. Specific services to children and to elderly adults are being stressed more than in the past. A persons-under-treatment survey may include a gross age categorization such as: seventeen and under, eighteen to sixty-four, and sixty-five and over.

The number of people actually in programs can be ascertained from the existing programs. These values will often be more accurate than estimated values. Medical and mental health programs must keep accurate records, although such records will not be flawless. Programs filling social and recreational needs, such as park programs or centers for senior citizens, probably will have far less accurate records.

Since additional services are being planned, the number of people who were referred to other agencies would be of interest. Also, perhaps of most interest would be estimates of the numbers of people that the current care giver would have liked to have referred to another service or agency but could not because the service did not exist in or near the community. Such information is important because some individuals are already in appropriate programs but others receive care that may not be closely related to their needs.

Simply documenting a need is not sufficient to show that people will leave the care giver from whom they currently obtain services. People do not view care givers as readily interchangeable because trust develops slowly. Offering a service for which there is an objective need is not the same as offering a service that people would prefer over what they currently use. The continued use of native healers by some Spanish-American residents of cities in the United States is an example of a preference for what is known over services offered by public agencies (Adler and Stone 1979).

It is important to repeat a word of caution: informants, even quite knowledgeable ones, often overestimate need. Therefore, estimated needs must not be considered as actual needs without collaborative evidence. Estimated needs are not worthless values; however, they should be treated as estimates.

Community Resident Survey

The residents of the community have attitudes toward the development of human services and toward the particular services needed. Their attitudes can be part of the planning. If the service is relevant to all citizens, the community should ideally be surveyed systematically to obtain a representative sample of the opinions of the residents. Obtaining a truly representative sample is extremely difficult and thus expensive. Avoiding clearly biased samples, however, is possible if the planner is careful in the selection of community respondents. Interviewing only professionals, only low-income residents, or only elderly people would render the results quite useless. A compromise might be possible by using intact groups that are likely to be fairly representative of the community. Such a course would not be expensive because intact groups completing a survey do not require much time from a survey administrator. Public schools and church groups are two sources of respondents that may be available to a planning group. Depending on the nature of the program being planned, special groups of likely users could be sought. For example, medical planners would want to contact emergency rooms and outpatient clinics. Because parenting programs are more likely to be used by new parents, the names of families with babies might be obtained from hospitals or churches. (Some facilities may not be willing to provide names in order to protect the privacy of their members or patients.)

The form of the community survey requires some care in construction. It is important to remember the purpose of the survey when constructing it. The purpose is to assess the need for a service, the acceptability of a particular service, and the willingness of people to use the program or facility. Some surveys, however, have been set up in a way that guaranteed a very high response in favor of the proposed facility. In attitude measurement, this bias is called *acquiescence*. Acquiescence refers to the tendency of people to say "yes" to questions if the questions at all encourage it. Some needs surveys have essentially listed various services and asked if such a service "should" be available to people in the community who needed it. Imagine being asked:

Do you think that (your hometown) should have an emergency service that provides immediate counseling any time of the day or night for people who are having a crisis with personal or family problems?

Do you think it would be helpful to you to learn more about mental illness and where to get mental health services, or to be able to handle a specific situation?

Wouldn't you answer "yes" to these questions? Most people would. There is nothing terribly wrong about these questions in themselves, but there are some additional approaches that should be added to this type of question.

The lack of a measure of intended behavior and the silence about costs of the services are among the reasons that the sample questions above are not sufficient for a needs assessment. People can agree that a service *should* exist but feel that the need for it is so small that they are unwilling to devote more than a token amount of money to it.

If this were the case, a marked degree of assent to a question of need would be quite misleading. If few want to pay for a service, the fact that many think it should be available is irrelevant.

Another useful approach to an assessment of need is to estimate what use people intend to make of a service. If the assessment of need concerned mental health programs, the survey constructor would be careful not to ask personal questions respondents would be unwilling to answer honestly. The survey should seek to estimate whether individuals have looked for a similar service for themselves or for someone they know.

For some services, the community survey would be especially helpful. For example, many burglaries and acts of vandalism go unreported because the victims feel there is little hope of regaining the stolen goods or that it is too much trouble to report the problem. If the community survey revealed that such hopelessness was widespread, the need for programs of help might be even more compelling than the crime statistics themselves.

Whether a planned program is large or small, the principles described above can be used in assessments of need. The need for programs within large organizations, such as faculty development, student counseling, worker safety programs, and special hospital programs are among the kinds of small-scale programs for which needs should be documented before beginning the program. For each of these programs, a survey of those currently offering similar services, estimates of the number of those receiving similar services, and a survey of potential users would be valuable approaches to gathering information about need.

A DECISION THEORY APPROACH TO PLANNING: THE MULTI-ATTRIBUTE UTILITY (MAUT) METHOD

Having identified the general issues to be addressed in planning and having described some of the tools for the assessment of need, we can now consider a practical approach by which evaluators can assist planners in choosing among possible programs. The method described in the remainder of this chapter is the Multi-Attribute Utility (MAUT) Method (Edwards, Guttentag, and Snapper 1975). This method is a technique derived from decision theory, which has been used for program planning, especially for allocating resources to competing human service programs. The method can also be adapted to making decisions of any kind, for example, the purchase of new equipment, the choice of a new career, or personnel selection. However, in this book attention is focused on the use of the MAUT method for program planning. After first examining the basic purpose and design of the MAUT method, we shall outline and illustrate the method itself.

Basic Purpose and Design of the MAUT Method

The basic purpose of the MAUT method is to disaggregate a decision, that is, to separate the elements of a complicated decision and evaluate each element separately. Instead of approaching a decision from a global viewpoint and beginning with a debate about the merits of competing programs, decision makers begin by reaching agreement on what they are trying to accomplish through the available programs. Having agreed on their overall goals, they then develop a consensus on the criteria to be used in judging the desirability of the competing programs. After having established this common ground, they can debate the merits of the programs in the light of the criteria established. This approach will in many cases narrow the focus to the exact area of disagreement and highlight the basic agreement among the planners.

A simplified version of decision disaggregation might be described as follows:

1. Decide on the appropriate criteria on which to base a decision. These criteria are values that the decision maker(s) wish to maximize through the program. These criteria will guide their choice among available programs.

2. Weight the criteria to reflect their subjective importance to the decision maker(s). This procedure determines the relative importance of the values of the decision makers.

3. Evaluate each possible program on the basis of each criterion. This step enables the decision makers to pinpoint the strengths and weaknesses of each alternative program.

4. Combine the evaluations made on the basis of individual criteria into an overall judgment. This step shows the overall desirability or utility of each program.

Consider the example of a high-school graduate choosing between attending College A and College B. A college experience may be viewed as a program to facilitate personal growth. Rather than trying to make the decision by stepping back and choosing a college on the basis of overall feelings, the student might choose to disaggregate the decision in the manner outlined in Figure 4.2. The student first identifies the criteria that reflect his or her values with respect to a college. In this instance, the student identified acceptable cost, good academic reputation, attractive location, and good social opportunities.

FIGURE 4.2: Disaggregation of the selection of a college

Criteria in choosing a college (values)	Weight of criteria (importance)	Rating of options	
		College A	College B
Attending a college with:			
An acceptable cost	3	8	6
A good academic reputation	2	7	8
An attractive location	2	4	5
Good social opportunities	1	9	5

Computing desirability

College A's desirability: 3(8) + 2(7) + 2(4) + 1(9) = 55
College B's desirability: 3(6) + 2(8) + 2(5) + 1(5) = 49

Decision: Choose College A

Second, the student weighted the criteria to reflect their relative importance. As is seen in Figure 4.2, the item called social opportunities was ranked last and given a weight of 1. Location and academic reputation of the college were considered of equal importance, and both were thought to be twice as important as social opportunities. Therefore, they were given a weight of 2. Finally, cost was judged to be the most important item and given a weight of 3, which indicates that it is three times as important as social opportunities and half again as important as both location and academic reputation.

Third, each college was rated on a scale from 1 to 10 on each of the four criteria. The table shows that College A was judged more desirable on cost and social opportunities, while College B was judged more desirable on academic reputation and location.

Finally, the overall desirability (utility) of each college is determined in a quantitative manner by multiplying the rating on each criterion by its weight and adding the products for each college. The sum of the products equals 55 for College A and 49 for College B. The decision is to choose College A.

When more than one decision maker is involved in a decision, the decision disaggregation method provides a system for combining their input in a manner that minimizes conflict. The decision makers begin by establishing common ground by agreeing on the criteria and the relative value of each before debating the merits of the available options. This procedure disciplines the discussion by identifying the areas of potential disagreement; that is, whether there is a difference in priority of values, in the estimate of how much each option will maximize the values, or in both areas.

For example, suppose that in the above illustration the student's mother and father were to share in the selection of a college with their son or daughter. Rather than beginning the discussion with the parents declaring their preference for College B and the student opting for College A, they would begin by discussing their values and trying to agree on priorities before discussing the merits of either school. It would then become clear whether there was a conflict of values or rather a conflict on how well each college was judged to fulfill a common set of values.

The decision disaggregation method of decision making is really not a new concept, but rather an old idea with new terminology and extended application. Benjamin Franklin may have been among the earliest people to use a simplified MAUT approach in decision making (Dawes and Corrigan 1974). In a letter to his friend Joseph Priestly dated September 19, 1772, Franklin suggested the following procedure for arriving at decisions:

> My way is to divide half a sheet of paper by a line into two columns; writing over the one *Pro,* and over the other *Con.* Then, during three or four days consideration, I put down under the different heads short hints of the different motives that at different times occur to me *for* and *against* the measure. When I have thus got them all together in one view, I endeavor to estimate the respective weights . . . [to] find at length where the balance lies. . . . And, though the weight of reasons cannot be taken with the precision of algebraic quantities, yet, when each is thus considered, separately and comparatively, and the whole matter lies before me, I think I can judge better, and am less liable to make a rash step; and in fact, I have found great advantage for this kind of equation, in what may be called *moral* or *prudential algebra* (Dawes and Corrigan 1974, p. 95).

What Franklin called "prudential algebra" is a simplified MAUT approach, although he places less stress on the quantitative analysis and more on the qualitative analysis of various arguments for and against a given measure.

Ten Steps of the MAUT Method

There are ten steps to the MAUT approach to measuring the relative usefulness of action alternatives. In an article, "Social Utilities" (1971), Edwards described the steps in detail. The steps are briefly summarized and explained below.

Step 1: Identify the organization whose utilities are to be maximized.

In other words, what is the organization or person for whom the evaluation is being conducted? In the example above, the person for whom the evaluation was being conducted would be the student planning to attend college.

Step 2: Identify the issue or issues to which the utilities needed are relevant.

That is, what is the purpose of the evaluation? What decision is the organization or individual addressing? In the above example, the decision to be addressed is which college to attend.

Step 3: Identify the entities to be evaluated.

The "entities to be evaluated" are the options or choices that the organization or individual has at hand. The options may be action alternatives or programs designed to meet an organizational need. For example, should the high-school graduate attend College A or College B?

Step 4: Identify the relevant dimensions of value.

The "relevant dimensions of value" are the criteria on which the organization or individual will focus in order to make a choice between competing options or courses of action. They reflect organizational values as they are applied to the decision at hand. The dimensions should be clear and specific enough so that all the planners will understand them in the same way. In our example, the cost of college might be further defined as tuition plus transportation and room and board, so that the statistics gathered on Colleges A and B would be comparable.

Finally, the criteria should be concrete enough to allow for accurate measurement. In our example, "an acceptable cost" is the criterion that can be most objectively measured, and "good social opportunities" is a poorer criterion from the standpoint that it must be measured in a more vague and subjective manner.

Step 5: Rank the dimensions in the order of importance.

After the dimensions have been selected in Step 4, the organizational representatives rank the dimensions in the order of importance. Disagreement between representatives is almost certain at this step, and this disagreement should be resolved through discussion and consensus. It should be made clear that the order can, and probably will, be altered later on during the discussions that take place during Step 6. In the

94

example, "an acceptable cost" was rated first, "good academic reputation" second, "an attractive location" third, and "good social opportunities" fourth.

Step 6: Rate dimensions in importance, preserving ratios.

The process begins by assigning the least important dimension a rating of 10. (The figure *10* is arbitrary, but allows for fine grading of subsequent dimensions while still retaining integer numbers.) Then the next least-important dimension is considered. If this dimension is considered to be twice as important as the previous one, it is given a rating of 20. If it is only half again as important, it is assigned a rating of 15. In fact, the representatives may decide that the second dimension rated is really no more important than the first dimension rated and give it a rating of 10 also, or even reverse the order of importance in light of further discussion. As the process continues, many changes are likely to be made both in ranking and rating of dimensions. Such changes are acceptable and often desirable. Because the college-choice example was deliberately simplified, the refinements of this sixth and the following steps were not used in the manner described.

Step 7: Sum the importance weights, divide each by the sum, and multiply by 100.

This is purely a computational step so that the ratings of all the dimensions will add up to 100. Edwards refers to this process as "normalizing" the weights. This process provides a clearer picture of the relative values of the weights given to each dimension and makes subsequent calculation easier to manage.

During Step 7, the representatives will be able to recognize the reason for not including too many dimensions under Step 4. If there are too many dimensions, some will end up with trivially small weights that will, in effect, eliminate them from having any real impact on the decision. About six dimensions are ordinarily adequate and manageable. Lower-ranked dimensions can also end up with trivial weights if more highly ranked dimensions are carelessly judged to be 5 or 6 times more important than the lower-ranked ones.

Step 8: Measure the location of the entity being evaluated on each dimension.

These "measurements" are judgments and usually very subjective estimates. At times, objective data may be available. Edwards suggests asking each representative to estimate the probability on a 0-to-100 scale that a given option will maximize each dimension. In other words, if a program is judged to have a high probability of fostering the value represented on a certain dimension, it might be assigned a .70 probability. If the program has a low probability of fostering the same value, it might be given a .20 probability. It is likely that all available options will be thought to have merit on each dimension of value. Therefore, it will be seldom appropriate to use a weight of *0*.

Once again, there will probably be divergence of estimates by different representatives. However, through the MAUT, process common ground has previously been established through agreement on the dimensions and their relative weights. As a result, disagreement is now narrowed to the estimate of each option's probability of maximizing a given dimension of value.

Step 9: Calculate utilities for entities.

The equation is

$$U_i = \sum_j w_j u_{ij}$$

Remember that $\sum_j w_j = 100$. U_i is the aggregate utility for the ith entity; w_j is the normalized importance weight of the jth dimension; and u_{ij} is the rescaled position of the ith entity on the jth dimension (Guttentag and Snapper 1974, p. 58).

Stated simply, the utility of each program or action alternative is obtained by multiplying the weight for each dimension (from Step 7) by the rating of an option on that dimension (from Step 8) and summing the products.

Step 10: Decide.

If a single act is to be chosen, the rule is simple: maximize U_i. If a subset of i is to be chosen, then the subset for which $\sum_j U_i$ is a maximum is best (Guttentag and Snapper 1974, p. 59).

U_i (aggregate utility) is the final score for each program. If the decision makers want only one program and are indifferent to cost, the best decision will be the program with the highest aggregate utility.

However, the question of cost can be handled in more than one manner. In the college-choice example, cost was a value dimension. If cost is not introduced as a value dimension, then the utility of each option is considered in light of the budget available. It may be possible to fund the two best options or programs. If the cost of the program with the highest utility exceeded the budget, then the next program in line would be chosen.

An Application of the MAUT Method

To understand more fully the ten steps of the MAUT method as described above, consider the example of a large manufacturing firm that is concerned with high turnover among its employees. The firm would like to build loyalty and trust among its employees so that there would be greater stability in the work force. The president of the firm invites the firm's four vice presidents to meet and to suggest what steps should be taken. The vice presidents decide to use the MAUT method to approach the problem.

Step 1. The organization whose utilities are to be maximized is the manufacturing firm. The firm will be represented by the vice presidents.

Step 2. The issue to which the utilities are relevant is how the firm will best build the loyalty and trust of its employees.

Step 3. When the vice presidents meet for the first time, they identify the available options or action alternatives. Let us suppose that they identify four possible courses of action:

1. Presidential visits to employees in their work areas.
2. "Skip-one" contact sessions (where employees have the chance to discuss their work life with their own supervisor's supervisor).
3. Training of the supervisors and all management personnel to develop better supervisory skills.
4. Career-planning sessions for all employees.

Step 4. Next, the vice presidents identify the following six dimensions of value that would guide their choice and then rank them (*Step 5*) in the following order:

1. Personalization of relationships.
2. Increased input by employees into the decision-making process.
3. Removal of fear of retribution from the communication network.
4. Increased job self-determination.
5. Assurance to employees that the company followed through on previous employee recommendations.
6. Clarification of company goals.

Step 6. Next, the vice presidents proceed to assign weights to each dimension. First, they give dimension 6 a value of 10 and then decide that dimension 5 is of equal importance; therefore, dimension 5 is also given a value of 10. Then, dimension 4 is considered and judged to be twice as important as either dimension 5 or 6; dimension 4, therefore, is given a weight of 20. In like manner, dimensions 3, 2, and 1 are assigned weights of 30, 45, and 55, respectively.

Step 7. The weights are normalized by dividing each by the sum of the six weights and then multiplying by 100. This process results in the following normalized weights:

Dimension	Raw Weight	Normalized Weight
1	55	32
2	45	26
3	30	18
4	20	12
5	10	6
6	10	6
	170	100

Step 8. The group discusses the probability of each value dimension being maximized by each option. For example, option 1 (presidential visits) is given a .25 probability of maximizing dimension 1 (personalization of relationships); option 2 (skip-one contact sessions) is given a .50 probability; option 3 (training of supervisors), a .65 probability; and option 4 (career-planning sessions), a .50 probability. The process is repeated for the remaining five dimensions. The probabilities are all given in Figure 4.3.

Step 9. Utilities are calculated for each option by multiplying the weight of each dimension by its probability estimate. For example, option 3 receives the highest utility score: $32(.65) + 26(.85) + 18(.80) + 12(.50) + 6(.40) + 6(.80) = 70.50$. Option 2 ranks second with a utility score of 59; option 1 ranks third with a utility score of 38. Finally, option 4 is last with a score of 35. These calculations are summarized in Figure 4.3.

Step 10. Decide. In the supposition that a training program for supervisors (option 3) would consume all the available money and resources, the vice presidents would probably recommend to the president that only option 3 be implemented. However, if enough resources are available to implement option 2 (skip-one contact sessions) as well, then option 2 might be recommended along with option 3. The skip-one contact sessions received a utility score (59) that was not too far behind the score for a training program for supervisors (70).

In the supposition that there are not enough resources available

Options (specific action proposals)		1	2	Dimensions (Values) to be maximized 3	4	5	6	Utility	Final rank
Weights =		32	26	18	12	6	6		
1. Presidential visits to employees in their work area	Probabilities =	.25	.30	.75	.00	.70	.70	37.70	3
	Wts. × Probabilities =	8.00	7.80	13.50	0	4.20	4.20		
2. Skip-one contact sessions	Probabilities =	.50	.60	.75	.50	.50	.70	58.30	2
	Wts. × Probabilities =	16.00	15.60	13.50	6.00	3.00	4.20		
3. Training of supervisors and management personnel to develop better supervisory skills	Probabilities =	.65	.85	.80	.50	.40	.80	70.50	1
	Wts. × Probabilities =	20.80	22.10	14.40	6.00	2.40	4.80		
4. Career-planning sessions for all employees	Probabilities =	.50	.15	.20	.75	.10	.10	33.70	4
	Wts. × Probabilities =	16.00	3.90	3.60	9.00	.60	.60		

FIGURE 4.3: Multi-attribute utility (MAUT) worksheet.

for option 3 (training for supervisors), then option 2 would be recommended as the best choice within the firm's budget. The remaining
two options (presidential visits and career planning) received utility
scores of 37.70 and 33.70, respectively, and are clearly judged to be less
effective than either options 3 or 2.

Rather than rely solely on the recommendation of the vice presidents,
the president might be well advised to seek input from other groups
within the plant who would be affected by the decision. For example,
the president might have a group representing first-line management
and another group representing nonmanagerial employees meet separately and address the question of building employee trust and loyalty
using the MAUT method. If both groups arrive at the same conclusion
as did the vice presidents, the president would have greater certainty
that a supervisory training program would be accepted. Even more
important, both management and nonmanagement employees should
react positively to the fact that the president wishes to learn of their
ideas about earning employee loyalty and trust. The president might
even openly declare his/her desire to see that the employees are
treated fairly and have opportunities for growth on the job.

If there is no consensus among the recommendations of the vice
presidents, the management group, and nonmanagement group, then
the president might ask that a joint committee be formed to iron out the
differences. If there is need for immediate action, then the president
would choose the option that seemed most closely to fit the value
systems of all three groups.

Use of the MAUT Model to Guide Evaluation

The MAUT model not only is a guide to decision making; it also
provides a means of focusing evaluation on the area where it most
needs to be done. Suppose that in the example just given, the president
decides to proceed with a program to train supervisors and management
personnel. However, the president questions how correct the vice
presidents were in the high probability (80 percent) they assigned to
the effectiveness of the training of supervisors in removing fear of
retribution from the communication network. Therefore, the evaluation team can focus its efforts on clarifying the degree to which fear of
retribution is removed through supervisor training.

Subsequent evaluation will be needed to estimate the probability
that the program did achieve its goal on one or more value dimensions.
This could either confirm the wisdom of the choice of a given option,
or make the decision makers review their commitment to that option.
One method of taking into account both prior probabilities and those

yielded by the evaluation is to use Bayesian statistics, as recommended by Guttentag and Snapper (1974). An explanation of Bayesian statistics is beyond the scope of this discussion; however, a brief introduction can be found in Morgan (1968).

SUMMARY

After discussing general issues in planning and the tools for assessment of need, this chapter presented an example of the decision theory approach to planning. Evaluators who have the opportunity to cooperate with planning committees in selecting programs in this manner will have gained valuable background information and will develop personal rapport that will facilitate subsequent program evaluation.

STUDY QUESTIONS

1. Assume that the following questions appeared in a community survey. Discuss the strong and weak points of each.
   a. Is it important that (your town) have a program for gifted children in the public schools?
   b. Would you use a nutrition information service if it were available in (your town)?
   c. Have you ever sought counseling help for yourself or for someone else?
2. A key informant survey on the nutritional needs of the children of a particular community included the individuals listed below. Describe the degree to which each is a good or a poor source for information on the nutritional level of children of the community.
   a. The mayor
   b. The members of the
   city council
   c. A private-practice physician
   d. The school nurse
   e. A restaurant owner
   f. The truant officer
   g. Day-care center teachers
   h. Elementary-school teachers
   i. Senior-high school teachers
3. Assume that your college has a $50,000 grant to reduce crime on campus. What might a MAUT decision matrix look like when completed by a representative group of students?
4. Assume that you are chairperson of the local school board. Because a recent tax referendum has failed, the board must choose

between discontinuing a remedial reading program or an advanced program for gifted children. As board chairperson, how would you approach the decision using the MAUT method?
5. Prepare an illustrative MAUT decision matrix as in Figure 4.3. Use the method to disaggregate a choice you must make or have recently made.

FURTHER READING

Additional information on need assessment is available in:

BELL, R. A.; NGUYEN, T. D.; WARHEIT, G. J.; & BUHL, J. M. Service utilization, social
       indicator, and citizen survey approaches to human service need assessment.
SIEGAL, L. M.; ATTKISSON, C. C.; and CARSON, L. G. Need identification and planning
       in the community context.
Both of these chapters appear in ATTKISSON, C. C.; HARGREAVES, W. A.; HOROWITZ,
       M. J.; & SORENSEN, J. E., eds. 1978. *Evaluation of human service programs.*
       New York: Academic Press.

The Multi-Attribute Utility Model is described by its originators in this chapter.

EDWARDS, W.; GUTTENTAG, M.; & SNAPPER, K. 1975. A decision-theoretic approach to
       evaluation research. In *Handbook of evaluation research,* vol. 1., ed. E. L.
       Struening and M. Guttentag. Beverley Hills, Calif.: Sage.

Carey has adapted the MAUT method to the selection of chief executive officers in hospitals. The method is called the Weighted Value Assessment System.

CAREY, R. G. *In press.* Selecting hospital leaders through shared decision making.
       Hospital Progress.

5

Monitoring the Operation of Programs

The most basic form of program evaluation is an examination of the program itself—its conception, the population it serves, and how it functions. Process evaluation includes an assessment of how much effort in the form of human and physical resources is invested in the program and whether the effort is expended as planned. The evaluation of effort is important because a program without sufficient resources cannot be expected to influence the participants in the program, and a program planned to meet one problem will be less useful when applied to a different problem.

An evaluation of the plan and the resources available to implement a program cannot reveal whether the clients actually benefited from the program. Evaluation of the degree of successful outcome ultimately achieved requires an approach different from the methods described in this chapter. Outcome evaluation can be done more easily, however, when process evaluations are conducted as the program is being planned and implemented. People unfamiliar with program evaluation some-times confuse process evaluation with the process of change or with interpersonal interaction during psychotherapy. However, process evaluation should be thought of as a way to monitor the degree to which a human service program is implemented as planned.

A well-planned, well-staffed, and well-housed program may not function effectively. Evaluators commissioned to assess the quality of a program will also inquire into its day-to-day performance. Businesses evaluate their performance by counting cash receipts at the end of the day and by performing inventories of stock at regular intervals. Human service managers need measures of activity similar to those available to commercial firms. The problem, of course, is that the ultimate products of human service programs, well-functioning people, are not nearly as objectively measured or as concrete as store inventories.

The place to begin is to ask whether the human service program has been implemented as planned. If well-designed advertisements encouraging seat belt use are not actually published or broadcast, there is no reason to evaluate the impact of the material. If drug abusers do not attend a drug abuse program, there is little need to ask whether the program reduced drug abuse. Systematic methods have only recently been developed to monitor medical care, counseling and psychotherapy, training, and other forms of human services. Some of these methods assess the degree to which previously specified optimal procedures are followed. In this chapter, we do not address the question of following optimal procedures; that question is pursued in Chapter 6. At this point, evaluation is limited to a description of the services that are actually delivered.

Managers need such information to facilitate their planning and decision making, to anticipate problems, and to justify the existence of the program. For example, if it is discovered that a population receiving assistance is not the one targeted, then the program is not serving the need it was designed to meet and may have to be altered. Striking differences in the contributions of different staff members or an unusually heavy client drop-out rate would be other problems important to detect. Managers can act to correct problems only if they have adequate information. Without accurate information, problems may become apparent too late to be corrected.

THE PROGRAM AUDIT AS A MEANS OF PROGRAM EVALUATION

Some evaluators have come to use the term *audit,* taken from accounting terminology, to describe the process of quantifying the amount of services rendered and the identity of program participants (Sells 1975). Others simply refer to this activity as monitoring the input of a program (Mechanic 1975). To keep the term separate from the functions of accountants, the term *audit of services* is used to refer to a systematic examination of program inputs, the effort put into a program.

Evaluators who conduct an audit of services gather information so that they can describe the program. A description of the program includes a profile of the clients coming into the program, a summary of the services given, work loads of the staff members, and sometimes the evaluations the clients have of the program. Program directors and staff often believe that they do not need quantified information to summarize the type and amount of services they provide and to whom these services are given. However, it is common knowledge among evaluators that the subjective feelings of the staff members are often in error.

In several studies in which the authors have participated, program staffs have been very wrong in describing the population that was served by the program. In an evaluation of an innovative organization of nursing on a hospital unit (Carey 1979), the staff said that 90 percent of the patients would have one of three major problems: respiratory illnesses; diabetes; or hypertension. As part of the evaluation, the diagnoses of the patients on the unit were recorded. It turned out that only 20 percent of the patients were diagnosed as having one of these three ailments. Is it possible that service could be improved if the nurses realized that they were actually serving a very heterogeneous patient population? An educational program designed for a relatively homogeneous patient population cannot be very effective when given to a group containing individuals with many unique needs.

The description of the population served and the services rendered by a program fills several needs. The immediate needs of management may be most obvious. In order to manage a human service program effectively, it is necessary to know who receives what service from whom and when the service is given. Managers fill their roles better the more they avoid a management-by-crisis style.

There are additional purposes, however. An audit of services is a necessary prelude to rigorous study of the outcome of services. Planning for future growth or redistribution of resources is a third reason for an audit of services because knowing what is currently done provides a way to plan rationally.

Information suitable for planning or for use as a baseline before a rigorous evaluation may be gathered through a modest audit of services conducted between two specific dates. In contrast, management needs require an ongoing information system and may well require the development of a system to obtain information routinely. The limited approach provides a snapshot of the program; the ongoing method provides a motion picture of the program. An examination of the program's records for a limited time period is undertaken to answer some particular questions about the level and types of services given; such information can give the planner and manager some directions to follow in program planning. On the other hand, repeated descriptions of a program over fairly short time periods such as one month permit closer monitoring and allow adjustments to be made in the way the program is run.

As with most dichotomies, this contrast of special, limited audits and extended, routinized audits may break down in practice. However, the distinction is useful because programs have different needs at different times. If a manager needs information that is gathered repeatedly over short time intervals, an approach requiring hand retrieval of data would be overly expensive and slow. On the other hand, a small program may not be sophisticated enough to require a complex information system; in such cases, a simpler, less ambitious procedure would be used. Both forms of process evaluation will be illustrated at the end of the chapter. One case study illustrates an audit of a state's alcoholism services at a particular time, and the second illustrates the repeated monitoring of services of a drug abuse hot line. Some writers in program evaluation view the development of management information systems as a major part of the role of in-house program evaluators (for example, see Attkisson et al. 1978).

WHAT SHOULD BE SUMMARIZED
IN AN AUDIT OF SERVICES

There is no formula for selecting and gathering the information required to describe a program. Programs differ in the types of people served, in the services given, and in the type of institution offering the services. Evaluators bear in mind several points as they prepare an audit of services. These points are not explicit guides to which information to gather or which procedures to use. Rather, these points should help to focus on the issues that need to be addressed.

Relevant Information

The information gathered must be central to the purpose of the audit. Effective evaluators attempt to gather only information that is relevant to describing the program and how it functions. Many characteristics of clients and programs are not central to program decisions. Evaluators may find many potentially interesting hypotheses to explore while doing an evaluation, such as, "Is birth order related to the probability of becoming a juvenile delinquent?" This question could have import for theories of social development. If evaluators have the time to study issues of basic research, they may seek to explore some of these hypotheses. However, every bit of additional information recorded in an audit increases the cost of data collection and analysis.

Actual State of Program

A second point important to an audit is that it must describe the actual state of the current program. Evaluators are careful to distinguish between the program as described and the program as administered. Many programs that look very good on paper fail, not because they were designed poorly, but because the staff or the participants did not actually follow the design or the procedure as planned. In a large university with many commuting students, an attempt was made to help freshmen become part of university life. One approach to achieve this early identification was a program for inviting groups of eight to twelve freshmen into faculty homes for social evenings. There were a number of enthusiastic faculty members who volunteered to take part in the program. One of the major findings of the evaluation was that, in spite of this early enthusiasm on the part of the faculty, 40 percent of the faculty did not actually invite the students whose names they were given. Second, among the students who did receive invitations, 60 percent declined to attend. One particular faculty member, who did not request that students respond to the invitation, prepared a fairly generous buffet dinner only to discover as the evening passed that not one student was going to come. This program to involve students in the life of the campus did not need to be evaluated with an experimental design as planned. A simple report of the number of faculty who did not invite the students whose names they were given and the proportion of students who did not accept the invitations that were made was enough to show that the program was not being carried out. The actual program was very unlikely to reduce the rate of freshman dropout or to improve student morale. Without a careful study of the implementation of the program, administrative officers concerned with freshmen drop-out problems would have been at a loss to understand just what went wrong with the program.

The information necessary to describe the services rendered include: (1) the type of service offered by the program (such as job training, group therapy, immunizations); (2) the extensiveness of the program (such as hours of training or therapy, skills to be learned, location of the program, facilities); and (3) the number of people participating in the service, especially the proportion of people completing the program.

The Providers of Services

The preparation of an audit of services should include a description of who gives the services. In large hospital settings, many care givers, such as physicians, nurses, and physical therapists, are state licensed for the particular job. In other human service settings, especially where pay is low, people with limited training are involved in giving the service. Counseling programs for drug addicts or former addicts are sometimes staffed by people who are neither trained nor psychologically equipped for the positions they are filling. It is also possible for the staff to be overqualified. An evaluation of a project staffed by volunteer lawyers to help ex-convicts readjust to community life found mixed results because the released prisoners looked to the volunteers for legal aid, not for general readjustment help. Thus, the identity of the volunteers stood in the way of a truly effective program, in spite of sincere efforts (Berman 1978).

Program Participants

A fourth major part of an audit includes a description of those who receive the services. If a program was well planned, the population to be served would have been specified carefully and the program tailored to meet the needs of that group. An audit should document the identity and the needs of the people using the service and compare these findings to the program plans. In other words, the fit between the program and the needs of those using it can be examined. If the fit is not good, changes or redirections for the program can be considered. If the agency never actually defined the group to be served, a description of the people using the agency may be especially enlightening.

The people using the program are routinely described by gender and age. The choice of additional information to be presented depends on the specific nature of the program: where the people live; the major problems they seek help to resolve or adjust to; the source of referral; ethnic background; and so forth.

The ease or difficulty people have in obtaining the service is an aspect of the description of those receiving the service. Unfortunately, this information is seldom in agency files. It would ·be necessary to prepare a short survey to be administered to people using the service. Questions asked should cover how much time elapsed between initial contact and first appointment; what mode of transportation was used; parking availability (if required); and time necessary to wait for care. In preparing such a survey, one must be aware of differences in ease of access that are related to variables such as time of day (morning versus afternoon versus evening), day of the week (workdays versus weekends), type of service, and welfare status of the individual. It would be unlikely that a facility would need to gather all this information routinely. Obtaining it soon after beginning the program and at later time periods as the facility changes or expands would be sufficient.

When audits are reported, evaluators have come to expect to be told that the results of the audit (and this is true of any evaluation for that matter) were already known. It is a common human tendency to assimilate new information without realizing that it does conflict with what was previously expected. An accomplished evaluator will not reveal the findings of evaluations before obtaining some information on what the staff and director expect the audit to show. Only in this way will an evaluator actually know whether the audit produced "nothing new" or whether the results did indeed yield new material. After all, evaluators must be concerned about their own egos once in a while. (Case Study 5.1 illustrates a retrospective audit of the services to a select population—alcoholic native Alaskans.)

AN APPROACH TO PROVIDING REPEATED AUDITS

When setting out to prepare a method of providing periodic reports describing the way an agency functions, the evaluator needs to have a hand in designing the agency's records. Instead of using existing files, the evaluator can help the agency design recording and filing procedures that will be useful for evaluation and for routine agency needs. When records are designed for use in evaluations, it becomes quite economical to prepare the type of reports to be described in this chapter.

The Existing Records of a Program

It would be impossible to perform an empirical evaluation of effort without adequate records. However, it is no secret that the records of human service agencies are often in abysmal condition. Inadequate records are frequent even in hospitals, where sloppy handwriting has resulted in fatal drug overdoses and the amputation of a healthy leg instead of the diseased one (Dixon 1977). Why are charts and records in such poor condition? Record keeping is a dull and time-consuming task. Individuals attracted to human service occupations often view record keeping as time taken away from clients, students, or patients. In the very short run, that view may be correct. Furthermore, records were less important in the recent past because impressionistic evaluations of success and effort were sufficient evaluations in many settings. The existence of this and other books on evaluation methods shows that impressionistic evaluations are no longer accepted as sufficient by regulatory and accrediting agencies. We hope that the reader will also see that in the long run well-kept records (and evaluation, in general) will result in more effective attention to human service program participants.

Evaluators helping an agency to develop an ongoing plan for documenting the provision of services will probably first ask what material is available in the records as currently maintained. However, even agencies with highly detailed and carefully maintained records may not have all the information useful for program evaluation purposes. Such records often contain long narrative accounts of progress or disability. The reason narrative records are not useful is that they lack a common frame of reference.

The lack of a common frame of reference is caused in part by the different points of view people adopt in evaluating success in human services. For example, the care giver, the program participant, and the community tend to evaluate success in quite different terms. In the area of mental health, these different perspectives are often quite evident. People in the local community are distressed by public acting-out behavior. Communities do not want individuals around who act disturbed in public, such as wearing unusual clothing, arguing frequently with neighbors or shopkeepers, or telling passersby about hallucinations. The larger society wants individuals to keep up their living quarters, hold jobs, and, in general, behave responsibly. If mental health counseling or tranquilizer medication can keep people looking and acting relatively normal, society will evaluate the service as successful and effective.

Therapists, on the other hand, have traditionally been less interested in day-to-day responsible behavior than in personality structure or emotional health. They would not view therapy as effective if it only assisted people to cope better or to conform passively to social norms. Instead, they would desire to detect greater autonomy, greater self-actualization, less guilt, and more frequent assertiveness. These are behaviors that are largely not observable by the community and not relevant to its evaluation of a mental health center.

Individuals receiving therapy may have an altogether different set of standards. They may evaluate therapy on the basis of whether they feel better about themselves. It is quite possible for clients to find a mode of adjustment that is acceptable to themselves but that would not satisfy the therapist or many members of the community.

Strupp and Handley (1977) have discussed these three points of view in more detail, especially with regard to negative outcomes in therapy. When individuals differ in their relative emphasis on these three points of view, free narrative reports will not be very useful to the evaluator. If the therapists also differ in theoretical orientations (such as Freudian versus behavioristic versus medical), the narratives will be even more difficult to compare and to summarize.

Increasing the Usefulness of Records

It is first necessary for the program director and other information users to develop a list of essential information useful in the managing and evaluating of the program. A point repeatedly stressed in this book is that information is gathered only when it is useful. If there are legal requirements to obtain certain information or if decisions are to be made on the basis of the information, then it should be gathered. Otherwise, the material need not be recorded, unless negative side effects are suspected to be occurring.

The information thought useful should not be gathered simply to fill folders in file cabinets. Methods of summarizing the information will be developed in the process of increasing the usefulness of files. In different contexts, staff or managers have confidently assured evaluators that certain information is "in the files." Unfortunately, many files are incomplete; however, the major point is that in-the-files information is not useful information. Retrieving material from client folders is a time-consuming task, and it is a sensitive task because the privacy of the clients must be maintained. It is more efficient to develop a system that permits the routine summary of participant descriptors (that is, age, sex, disability) and service provided without manually going through file folders that often contain personal material important to the client and the care giver but irrelevant to the evaluator.

How Records Can Be Used in Process Evaluations

One approach to the use of these records would be in the preparation of monthly summaries of all new clients. Figure 5.1 is a form that could be used when people initially request counseling at a center offering outpatient counseling. It contains some of the same information that many counselors request. Regardless of the size of the facility, a sheet such as this one would become the first entry in the individual's file. Notice that the center personnel add some information them-

PLEASE COMPLETE THIS FORM AND RETURN IT TO THE SECRETARY IN THE ENVELOPE PROVIDED. THE INFORMATION YOU GIVE US IS CONFIDENTIAL AND WILL BE CAREFULLY SECURED.

Name _____   Please do not write in boxes below:

Address _____   ☐ ☐ ☐ ☐ ☐ ☐ ☐

_____ zip _____   ☐ ☐ — ☐ ☐ — ☐ ☐

Telephone _____

Marital Status: (Circle one)
  1. Never married 2. Married now 3. Widowed 4. Divorced/Annulled 5. Separated

Sex:
  1. Female   2. Male   3. Couple application

Age: _____   Age of spouse if married now: _____

Who referred you to the center? (Circle one)
  1. Myself, friend, family   4. Hospital   7. Another agency
  2. Another client   5. Physician   8. Other _____
  3. Clergyman   6. Psychiatrist   _____

What problem(s) has prompted you to consider counseling at this center?   ☐ ☐
_____   ☐ ☐
_____   ☐ ☐
_____   ☐ ☐

What form of counseling are you most interested in at this time? (Circle one)
  1. Individual   2. Family   3. Marital   4. Group

Who lives in your immediate family?
  Adults (give their relationship to you) _____   ☐ ☐
  _____   ☐ ☐
  Children (give ages)   _____   ☐ ☐
  _____   ☐ ☐

Have you previously received counseling from some other agency or counselor?
  1. Yes
  2. No

If "Yes" and if you do enter therapy with a counselor from the center, may we contact this person or agency about you?
  1. No
  2. Yes (Give name of counselor) _____

  Please sign _____

Where are you employed? _____

Please give the name and address of any insurance company that will meet part of your expenses at the center.

Name _____   Address _____   Ident. No. _____

FIGURE 5.1: An application form for potential clients of an outpatient counseling center.

selves, such as an identification number[1] and a problem code. Otherwise, the form could be self-administered.

To use this information most easily, it is necessary to have the material keypunched and summarized using computer facilities. In order to maintain the client's privacy, it is necessary to have some of the material in Figure 5.1 on a second copy in a form that is not easily identifiable. A second copy can be obtained using two printed forms with carbon paper bound between the pages. Confidentiality can be maintained by making it impossible for the client's name, street address, telephone number, and other traceable material to print through. The information would be identified by the number added by the intake worker or secretary before the copies are sent to a keypuncher. Figure 5.1 includes spaces to code type of problem(s) leading to a request for counseling.

The specific information to be gathered will depend on the needs of the particular human service agency preparing the system. Figure 5.2 contains a list of items that agencies would want to consider in preparing forms for gathering information about new clients.

Simply having some of the information in Figures 5.1 and 5.2 summarized each month or quarter would yield a more complete description of new clients than many agencies traditionally have available. For each calendar or fiscal year, the individual reports could be combined into a yearly profile of new clients.

Figure 5.3 is an illustrative new client report for a given month. The report includes information important to a particular center. For example, one counseling center with which we are familiar seeks to be a service to community clergy when they are faced with parish members who have emotional problems that cannot be handled by brief supportive counseling. A variable included in a hypothetical report of new clients for this center would be source of referral. This center can document that it is fulfilling one of its goals by showing that a large proportion of its referrals do indeed come from clergy. Age, sex, apparent problem, type of therapy desired, and location of residence are useful types of information that can be used to judge whether an agency is serving the population it was designed to serve.

The value of having summaries such as that shown in Figure 5.3 would be apparent to anyone who has worked in a large organization—it is necessary to let people know what you are doing. Program managers can more easily justify the continued existence of their programs if they

[1] Recently colleges and social service agencies, among other groups, have begun using social security numbers for identification purposes. Using social security numbers, however, means that unscrupulous people can more easily match up an agency's records with other information about an individual (*Time* July 18, 1977).

Initial Information
Name
Address
Sex
Age
Educational level
Marital status
Family description
Ethnic background
Referral source
Problem(s) leading to request for services
Previous participation in similar human services programs
Insurance coverage
Veteran's benefits
Welfare status
Dates: Of initial application
         When formal participation begun

Some information will be unique to the type of agency involved. For example:

Mental health services:	Previous hospitalizations
	Type and extent of therapy
	Current medication
	Previous diagnoses
	Alcoholism/Drug user
	Functional life status
	Identity of previous therapist
Criminal justice programs:	Status with court system
	Type of previous programs
	Location of programs
	Voluntary or forced participation
Job-training programs:	Jobs held, length of previous employment
	Income
	Reason for unemployment
	Types of previous job-training programs
	Location of programs
Educational programs:	School attending
	Grade level
	IQ or other standardized tests
	Location of previous programs

Ongoing information
Amount of service rendered (hours of therapy, courses completed, skills mastered)
When service given
Identity of care giver(s)
Functional status or adjustment during and at termination of service
Reason for termination
Degree of self-support
Fees charged
Referral made

FIGURE 5.2: Types of information that an agency might include in the basic descriptive information gathered about those seeking service and the type of information added as the service is given.

NEW CLIFNT APPLICATIONS FOR MAY. 1980

GENDER AND AGE OF NEW CLIENTS

INDIVIDUAL CLIENTS

		N	%	AGE
	FEMALE	98	65	34
	MALE	30	20	27
COUPLES (2 PEOPLE)		11	15	32
		---	---	--
TOTAL NEW CLIENTS		139	100	32

MARITAL STATUS AND GENDER

	FEMALE	MALE
NEVER MARRIED	28	12
MARRIED NOW	48	15
WIDOWED	3	0
DIVORCED/ANNULLED	15	3
SEPARATED	4	0

SOURCES OF REFERRAL

	N	%
SELF.FRIEND.FAMILY	27	19
ANOTHER CLIENT	5	4
CLERGY	67	48
HOSPITAL	15	17
PSYCHIATRIST	2	1
ANOTHER SOURCE	3	2

PROBLEM CODE

	N	%
MARITAL PROBLEMS	80	58
INDIVIDUAL ADJUSTMENT	128	92
PROBLEMS AT WORK	30	22
PROBLEMS AT SCHOOL	8	6
PROBLEMS WITH CHILDREN	62	45
ALCOHOLISM/DRUG USE	28	20
UNDIAGNOSED PHYSICAL SYMPTOMS	16	12

SERVICF SOUGHT

	N	%
INDIVIDUAL	82	59
FAMILY	15	11
MARITAL	32	23
GROUP	10	7

NUMBER (%) HAVING PREVIOUS PSYCHOTHERAPY   45 (32%)

NUMBER (%) EMPLOYED   92 (66%)

FIGURE 5.3: An illustrative monthly report describing applicants for outpatient counseling.

are able to provide documentation of the number of people served, as well as brief demographic descriptions and the reasons they give for seeking the service. Having information available also facilitates responding to requests for information. Frequently, government agencies request material that may be available only by searching through the files. Chapman (1976) reported that the need to quickly prepare an extensive survey precipitated a crisis in a mental health center because much necessary information was not easily available. The crisis ultimately led the center to prepare an information system capable of routinely summarizing client characteristics as well as much additional information.

Following the Course of Service

The course of a service can be followed by preparing standard forms with spaces for therapists to record certain information after each client contact. This short contact report does not take the place of the therapists' process notes, which are normally for the personal use of the therapist. Figure 5.4 is an example of such a contact report. The identification number would be used to match this report with other information about a particular client, such as information gathered at the beginning of therapy and from previous contact reports. The therapist number and therapy type are useful for documenting workload. The functional status ratings could be based on the procedure described in Chapter 3 (see Figure 3.3). Including the charges on this form would

Client name *Mabel Smith* Date [10] [15] [79] (month--day--year)

Client ID No. [1] [9] [1] [5] [3] [3]

Type of service [1] 1.Individual 2.Group 3.Family 4.Marital 5.Diagnostic 6.Special ______ 7.No show

Client's functional status [7]

Charge [ ] [2] [5] [0] [0]

Next appointment *2:30* AM (PM) M (T) W TH F SA [10] [23] [79] (month--day--year)

Referral made? [ ] To whom? ______________________

Termination? [ ] If so, was it by: Mutual agreement? ☐ Client decision? ☐ Therapist decision? ☐

Therapist signature *M. J. Hahn* __________ and ID No. [1] [2]

FIGURE 5.4: An illustrative form for a therapist to use after each therapy session with a client. This copy would be kept by the center.

facilitate an automated billing system. A record of referral is to be made on this form as well as notification that a formal end of therapy has occurred.

To make more efficient use of the contact report in Figure 5.4, there should be copies for the therapist, the client, and the keypuncher. All three copies could be made simultaneously. The client's copy and the data center's copy would not include all the information included in the therapist's copy. The copy for data processing would not include any of the printed labels included in Figure 5.4; it would not even indicate that the report referred to a therapy session. Figure 5.5 includes just the numbers and instructions to the keypuncher. The name of the client is not included; however, the identification number is. The client's version of the form is shown in Figure 5.6. It includes the client's name and center number (to facilitate access to records if a question should occur), charge, the name of a referral (if any), the time of next appointment (if any), and the therapist's signature. These contact reports provide information useful for the management of a program.

A monthly report of clients who have ended their association with the center could follow a format similar to that in Figure 5.7. Informa-

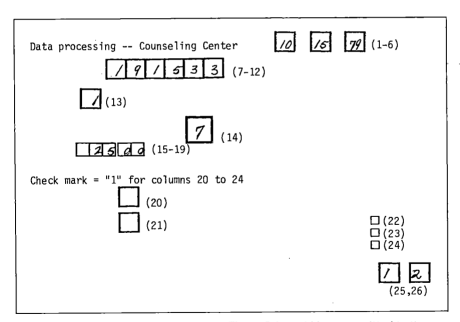

FIGURE 5.5: The way the information in Figure 5.4 would be transmitted to the person responsible for key-punching the information for future use.

```
Client ____Mabel Smith____  Date  10 - 15 - 79

Your center no./  9  /  5  3  3

In case a question or a need to change your next appointment
arises, our number is 887-7325.  Please mention your center
number when calling.

The charge for today's session is
     $   25.00
                    AM
Next appointment 2:30 PM   M  (T)  W   TH  F  SA   10 - 23 - 79

Referral, if any, is to:




Therapist        M. J. Hahn
```

FIGURE 5.6: The client's copy of the therapist's form illustrated in Figure 5.4 would contain the information shown above.

tion about the amount and type of service received,[2] mean functional status at the beginning and the end of the therapy, amount of charges, number of referrals and the type of termination occurring could be summarized and related to the demographic information previously obtained. Examining just the information in Figure 5.7, the director and staff can learn that about one quarter of the clients apparently reject the services offered. This conclusion can be drawn from the fact that 24 percent of the clients accept two or less units of counseling and that 29 percent of the clients leave without the therapist's agreement. A director would probably seek to lower these proportions. The illustrative reports offers some clues about how to approach such a goal. The lower part of the report shows that older clients rejected therapy more frequently than did the younger clients. Approaches to older clients could become a topic for in-service training at this center. Material presented later in this chapter will provide further suggestions for the director who seeks to lower the proportion of clients who receive little care at this center.

A monthly report can also be prepared for each therapist. Such reports would provide the therapists with information about their work

[2] A unit of service can be considered as one 50-minute period of individual psychotherapy or two 50-minute periods of group therapy.

118

```
REPORT OF TERMINATED CLIENTS IN MAY 1980

CASES TERMINATED IN MAY:  84

  TYPE OF TERMINATION          N     X
                              ---   ---
    MUTUAL CONSENT             57    68
    CLIENT DECISION            24    29
    THERAPIST DECISION          3     4

  UNITS OF SERVICE RENDERED    N     X
                              ---   ---
    2 OR LESS                  20    24
    3 TO 6                     14    17
    7 TO 15                    36    43
    16 TO 30                   13    15
    OVER 30                     1     1

  RATINGS OF FUNCTIONAL STATUS

                                  CLIENTS AT EACH FUNCTIONAL LEVEL
                                  WHEN THERAPY           AT
          LEVEL                      BEGAN           TERMINATION
                                  ------------      ------------
      DYSFUNCTIONAL:  1             0(  0%)           0(  0%)
      DYSFUNCTIONAL:  2             0(  0%)           1(  1%)
      DYSFUNCTIONAL:  3             2(  2%)           0(  0%)
      DYSFUNCTIONAL:  4            25( 30%)           3(  4%)
    ------------------------------------------------------------------
      FUNCTIONAL:     5            41( 49%)           2(  2%)
      FUNCTIONAL:     6             8( 10%)           7(  8%)
      FUNCTIONAL:     7             6(  7%)           4(  5%)
      FUNCTIONAL:     8             2(  2%)          21( 25%)
      FUNCTIONAL:     9             0(  0%)          46( 55%)

      MEAN FUNCTIONAL STATUS        5.00              8.05


  TYPE OF TERMINATION AND AGE OF CLIENT

                                  UNDER 29          30 AND OVER
                                  --------          -----------
    MUTUAL CONSENT                25( 76%)           32( 63%)
    CLIENT DECISION                6( 18%)           18( 35%)
    THERAPIST DECISION             2(  6%)            1(  2%)
                                  --------          -----------
    ALL                           33(100%)           51(100%)


  UNITS OF SERVICE AND AGE OF CLIENT

                                  UNDER 29          30 AND OVER
                                  --------          -----------
    2 OR LESS                      5( 15%)           15( 29%)
    3 TO 6                         7( 21%)            7( 14%)
    7 TO 15                       14( 42%)           22( 43%)
    16 TO 30                       6( 18%)            7( 14%)
    OVER 30                        1(  3%)            0(  0%)
                                  --------          --------
    ALL                           33(100%)           51(100%)
```

FIGURE 5.7: A report on the clients terminated during one month, including characteristics of services rendered to these clients.

compared to that of the other therapists as a group. People working in human services seldom have quantified information on how their work compares to the work of others in their own field or institution. However, the value of feedback in improving one's performance has repeatedly been demonstrated. Seligman and Darley (1977), for example, showed that residential use of electricity could be reduced over 10 percent simply by providing consumers, on a weekly basis, with information on how much electricity was used. Other examples of the value of feedback were given in Chapter 1.

A report format that could provide information for the individual therapist is given in Figure 5.8. This example describes the therapist's caseload and the amount of service rendered during the month in question. Note that therapist Helper has some problems. He had a higher proportion of clients terminate during the previous month than did the other therapists in the center. Of more importance, this hypothetical report shows that those who quit had received less service than was given to other clients before termination. This therapist also has a relatively large number of inactive clients, that is, clients who have not received any service for ninety days or more. The report politely requests that therapist Helper terminate these clients or see if they are still interested in continuing therapy. Last, there is a frequency table of ratings of psychological function of Helper's clients who officially ended their contract with the center during the last month.

Program changes or procedural changes can be planned to remedy deficiencies found. What sorts of questions might therapist Helper want to discuss with his director? It seems that he is losing many clients after only one or two counseling sessions. Everyone has a string of bad luck once in a while. If Helper's record does not improve and he continues to lose clients prematurely, he should seek some assistance in improving his manner of relating to clients. Perhaps he is too judgmental; perhaps new clients need more direction during the first sessions. Ideally, noting undesirable characteristics early in a therapist's career should permit improvements in techniques before poor practices are deeply ingrained. Also, it is to a therapist's advantage to learn of problems before hearsay and rumor define his/her therapy as below average in quality (House 1976).

A Threatening Use of Process Evaluation

Gathering the type of information requested in Figures 5.1 and 5.4 permits the presentation of information in a way that can be very controversial. No one enjoys being evaluated. Nevertheless, so long as the process evaluation is only on a facility-wide basis, staff members

```
REPORT FOR THERAPIST: HELPER

                                        HELPER          OTHER THERAPISTS
                                        --------        ----------------
TOTAL CASE LOAD ON JUNE 1, 1980         64                433

  ACTIVE CASES                          49( 76%)         364( 84%)
  INACTIVE CASES                        15( 24%)          69( 16%)
  (NOT SERVED IN 90 DAYS)

  THE NAMES OF YOUR INACTIVE CLIENTS ARE:

    ARCHIBALD, J          NORRIS, M/M
    BEST, F               OVERMAN, S
    BOULDER, M/M          PAKOWSKI, M/M
    ERNEST, G             RASMUSSEN, P
    GRAND, K              THOMAS, A
    HANSEN, M/M           TRAVERSE, P
    MORRISON, S           WILSON, G
    NARWELL, B

  PLEASE FILE A TERMINATION NOTICE OR A REFERRAL NOTICE, OR HAVE AN
  APPOINTMENT WITH EACH OF THESE INACTIVE CLIENTS BY JULY 31, 1980

                                        HELPER          OTHER THERAPISTS
TERMINATED CASES IN MAY                 --------        ----------------
    TERMINATED BY MUTUAL CONSENT        10( 48%)         47( 75%)
    TERMINATED BY CLIENT DECISION        9( 43%)         15( 24%)
    TERMINATED BY THERAPIST              2( 10%)          1(  1%)

    NUMBER OF THERAPY SESSIONS
    WITH CLIENTS TERMINATED IN          4                 7.5
    MAY 1980 (MEDIAN)


  RATINGS OF THE FUNCTIONAL STATUS OF TERMINATED CLIENTS WAS AS FOLLOWS:

                                    CLIENTS AT EACH FUNCTIONAL LEVEL
        LEVEL                           HELPER         OTHER THERAPISTS
                                        --------       ----------------
          DYSFUNCTIONAL: 1              0(  0%)          0(  0%)
          DYSFUNCTIONAL: 2              0(  0%)          1(  1%)
          DYSFUNCTIONAL: 3              0(  0%)          0(  0%)
          DYSFUNCTIONAL: 4              2( 10%)          1(  1%)
        -------------------------------------------------------------
          FUNCTIONAL:    5             1(  5%)          1(  1%)
          FUNCTIONAL:    6             1(  5%)          6( 10%)
          FUNCTIONAL:    7             2( 10%)          2(  3%)
          FUNCTIONAL:    8             4( 20%)         17( 27%)
          FUNCTIONAL:    9            11( 52%)         35( 56%)
```

FIGURE 5.8: A possible format for feedback to individual therapists.

may "grin and bear it." If the information available about an individual care giver is released only to that person, the controversy may
concern merely the time and expense of the information system.
However, the information generated by the methods just described
permits numerical comparisons to be made among individual therapists.
Most staff members dislike having their work compared to others in
this way. Although the evaluation of the effort of individuals will be
resisted, a manager needs objective comparative information. If staff
members offer quite different services, obviously such comparative re-

| THERAPIST | CURRENT CASES AS OF JUNE 1, 1980 | | | | | | TERMINATED CASES IN MAY 1980 | | | |
| | ACTIVE CASES | | | INACTIVE CASES | | | | | | |
	N	% OF CENTER CASES	FUNCTIONAL STATUS (MEAN)	N	% OF CENTER CASES	FUNCTIONAL STATUS (MEAN)	N	FUNCTIONAL STATUS % ABOVE 7	% SEEN LESS THAN 3 TIMES	MEDIAN NUMBER OF VISITS
ABRAMS	39	11	6.5	4	7	6.3	6	100	33	6
COULDER	29	8	7.2	0	0	DNA	9	89	22	7
GREGORY	43	12	6.8	9	15	5.9	4	75	25	8
HELPER	49	13	6.7	15	25	6.7	21	71	48	4
MATTHEWS	28	8	6.5	1	2	6.0	6	50	17	9
NELSON	29	8	7.0	6	10	7.2	5	90	0	8
NICOLET	36	10	6.6	8	13	6.2	8	75	12	6
PETROVICH	38	10	6.2	10	17	5.9	5	80	0	7
RUDOV	19	5	7.1	1	2	5.0	4	100	0	9
VINCENT	35	10	6.5	4	7	6.3	10	80	20	7
WILLIAMS	20	5	5.9	2	3	6.5	6	100	17	8
ALL	365	100	6.6	60	100	5.4	84	90	24	7

FIGURE 5.9: A report permitting the center director to spot problems and to suggest ways to improve services given.

ports are more difficult to prepare. For example, crisis counselors, outpatient therapists, and inpatient group leaders cannot easily be compared to each other. However, when many individuals perform much the same tasks, contrasts among individuals become possible. In general, information on individual staff members should never be released in a general report. Individuals can be given their own data, which they can compare to summary data from the whole facility; however, only the director has a right to information on each individual staff member.

In Figure 5.9, the work of each therapist is summarized in one line. Contrasts among the therapists are invited. Those with very low or very high caseloads and those with many inactive clients can be easily noted. If there are particular therapists who lose a disproportionate number of clients early in the course of counseling (and thus often deliver only a minimal service to these clients), they can be readily identified. See, for example, the information on Helper.

Therapist Helper has the largest proportion of inactive clients and loses more than anyone else before three counseling sessions. However, Helper rates his clients as functioning higher than all other therapists except Nelson. There are at least two interpretations of these findings. One, Helper has been assigned clients who do not really need counseling. He correctly sees them as generally functioning well and does not provide unnecessary counseling. Two, Helper is not providing counseling that is seen as helpful by the clients. Although they drop out, Helper rates their functioning "good" as a way of justifying his high rate of client loss. The first interpretation is tenable if the pattern does not continue. However, if clients are assigned at random or to whomever has an opening and the pattern continues, the second interpretation appears more likely. Such a negative evaluation does not mean that Helper should be dismissed. It may mean that Helper should have some in-service training; perhaps his approach in setting the stage for counseling is not appropriate to the population utilizing this center. Such possibilities should be explored and may resolve the situation. If so, Helper will be a better counselor and his clients will be better served.

Even though initial objections to process evaluation as presented in Figure 5.9 are likely to be numerous and intense, there are important advantages to preparing such materials. We believe that accurate information is better than impressionistic information of unknown accuracy. What is to be gained by giving the program director the sort of information in Figure 5.9? The director's chief responsibility is to facilitate the delivery of quality human services—psychotherapy in this example. If a therapist is performing markedly less well than others, clients are being shortchanged when they are assigned to that therapist. It would be best if therapists took the initiative in approaching the director for help in improving their work. However, if the individual does not approach the director, the director's job requires approaching the individual. The reason for providing this information frequently—once a month or once a quarter—is to encourage improvement before a situation becomes intolerable.

Figure 5.9 should be supplemented with an accounting of time spent on various activities. For example, if therapists Rudov and Williams are devoting much time to community work, to administration, or to inservice training, their rather low caseloads are readily understandable. As an exercise, readers may wish to try to prepare a form for therapists to use in accounting for their time. Categories of activities would include individual therapy, group therapy, administration, education, and community service. How might such report forms be designed? How might Figure 5.9 be extended to include this new information?

As with any type of information, a report such as Figure 5.9 can be misused. A criticism of providing summaries of information usually hidden in files is that they can be used in a vindictive manner. Most evaluators believe that providing more information will reduce the opportunities for directors to behave tyrannically. Most unfair managers restrict information, just as despotic rulers control the media in the nations they govern. Nevertheless, certain precautions can be built into the system to circumvent some possible misuses of the information. For example, the system should be designed to minimize the possibilities of acceptable variations in personal style appearing as deficiencies. Some therapists may encourage clients to leave therapy sooner than other therapists do. They may do this because of personal and theoretical convictions, not because of inadequate therapeutic skills. An information system should be planned in a way that does not confuse therapy designed to be short term with rejected therapy. In Figure 5.9, we sought to avoid this confusion by separately reporting the number of clients terminating after one or two counseling sessions because even those who plan on short-term therapy expect to retain clients beyond two sessions.

Implementing an Information System

Chapman (1976) states that a computer-based information system is not cost effective in agencies or programs with ten or fewer care givers serving one thousand or fewer people in a year. Once an organization includes fifty care givers, such as in a large community mental health center, computerization is imperative. The system described in this chapter is relatively simple. An even simpler one for a telephone hotline service is described in Case Study 5.2. Examples of more complex information systems can be found in Chapman (1976).

Evaluators seldom have sufficient programming skills to develop an information system alone. An experienced systems analyst will be required to write programs that can produce reports ready to be copied and distributed; bypassing special file searches, hand calculations, and typing will repay the cost of the consultant's work. Complete and timely reports will then be available with only a small additional investment of the time of the director, the professional staff, or clerical workers.

If done poorly, process evaluations can be an expensive, disruptive, and unpleasant experience for all involved. If done well, such evaluations of effort can provide feedback on performance that often enhances growth. Kreitner (1977) has called such feedback *informational feedback*. There are other forms of feedback, such as *corrective feedback,* that are also useful in helping people to improve their performance. Although automated systems such as those described in this chapter provide very valuable sources of feedback, managers should not permit these and similar systems to be the only source of feedback given to staff members.

AVOIDING MAJOR PROBLEMS IN IMPLEMENTING AN INFORMATION SYSTEM

There are problems in implementing an information system because of the natural hesitancy of people to try something new and their suspicion of the motives of anyone gathering information. In addition, the evaluator can fall into some traps that will make the task all the harder.

Avoid the Duplication of Records

Human service staffs will not happily cooperate with an information system that duplicates information already reported and stored elsewhere (Stull 1977). Few agencies exist without any records. When introducing an information system, it would be undesirable to simply impose the system as an addition to the existing recording procedures. Instead, integrating the information required by the old system with the automation of the new system would be preferable.

It is likely that staff members may question the accuracy of an automated system. The fact that staff cannot describe the population they serve in quantitative terms may mean that they will at times be surprised at the content of summaries of the information gathered. Kivens and Bolins (1977) report that such surprises led some service providers to keep their own records for a time as a check on a new information system. If staff want to duplicate records for their own satisfaction, that is no problem. However, the evaluator should avoid requesting program staff to provide information for overlapping record systems.

Avoid Narrow-minded Technology

Once a computerized system is considered, there is a temptation to concentrate on the technology of the system and to overlook the needs of the users. Lucas (1975) writes that information systems fail when user needs take a back seat to the technology of an information system. To avoid this problem, the users must be involved in the design of the system. The information that is needed, the manner of summarizing it, the frequency of reports, and other issues should all be determined with the people who will use the information. The systems analyst may be enthusiastic about getting the system operating and experienced in producing elegant work. However, learning what will be useful requires patient work with the staff and administrators. Although a completed information system is not chiseled in granite, it is very expensive to change if someone thinks of a new bit of information after the system is operational. Involving users early and thoroughly will minimize the possibility of producing an expensive product that no one really wants.

Avoid Serving the Needs of Only One Group

Different people fill different roles in an organization. They have different informational needs because their responsibilities are different (Patton 1978). Hawkins, Roffman, and Osborne (1978) describe the different informational needs of judges, probation officers, and program planners in reference to drug user programs. In other settings, systems analysts should know that the needs of the accounting department will be different from those of the billing department, which in turn will be different from the needs of service delivery staff. By working closely with only one or two of such groups, the evaluator runs the risk of providing information useful only to some groups. When that happens, the information system will be seen as irrelevant by those whose needs remain unmet. Furthermore, the contribution of information by these people will be grudging. The quality of information supplied can only be eroded when the system is not respected and valued. There is no substitute for an understanding of the organizational roles of all potential users.

SUMMARY

Human service agencies can begin an evaluation with a systematic description of their programs, the amount of service given, and the identity of those receiving the services. Such a process evaluation permits an accounting of how the agency's funds were expended and a comparison between the program as designed and the program as implemented. This sort of evaluation can be invaluable for learning what aspect of a program needs additional effort or why a program never had the impact intended. Also, the need to complete accrediting agency and government surveys can be met more easily if process evaluations are planned before the requests for information are made.

The two general approaches to process evaluation were illustrated: a summary of effort over a given time period and a systematized information system to permit repeated summaries of effort on a monthly or quarterly basis. The former requires a manual search through existing files that are often not designed with evaluation procedures in mind. If problems are found, even this kind of evaluation can lead to plans for improvement. When records are designed to facilitate evaluations, ongoing or repeated evaluations of effort are possible whether a computer-based system or a manual data-gathering approach is used.

STUDY QUESTIONS

1. College education is a human service that is seldom evaluated as thoroughly as mental health programs are coming to be evaluated. What variables should be measured and recorded in order to do an evaluation of the effort expended by your college department? How would you summarize and present the information gathered? Make up illustrative tables and graphs. To do this assignment, you will need to know more about the activities of college faculty members than you probably know now. Evaluators often begin projects by gathering basic information about the program they are to evaluate. Interviews with faculty members will help you get started.

2. Readers who are not full-time students should develop a plan for a process evaluation of the facilities in which they work.

3. People sometimes object to an evaluation of effort on the grounds that it reveals nothing about the quality of the service rendered. This statement is true. Why does this criticism not negate the reasons for doing the types of evaluations described in this chapter?

4. Design reporting forms for gathering data on the way professionals spend their time as mentioned on page 124 of this chapter. How would this information be presented in a way that will be informative but not misleading?

5. Improve the form given in Case Study 5.2 for keypunching and ease of use.

FURTHER READING

In the late 1970s, several major publications appeared that are useful to mental health systems employees who wish to initiate and use thorough process evaluations. Although the content of many of these manuals is taken from mental health settings, the principles in these texts are applicable regardless of the setting in which an evaluator works. These materials also provide considerable help in organizing information into meaningful presentation formats.

CARTER, D. E., and NEWMAN, F. L. 1976. *A client-oriented system of mental health service delivery and program management.* DHEW Publication No. (ADM) 76–307. Rockville, Md.: U.S. Department of Health, Education, and Welfare.

CHAPMAN, R. L. 1976. *The design of management information systems for mental health organizations: A primer.* Rockville, Md.: National Institute of Mental Health.

HARGREAVES, W. A.; ATTKISSON, C. C.; and SORENSON, J. D., eds. 1977. *Resource materials for community mental health program evaluation.* 2nd ed. DHEW Publication No. (ADM) 77–328. Rockville, Md.: U.S. Department of Health, Education, and Welfare. See Part III for materials on management information systems.

HAGEDORN, H. J.; BECK, K. J.; NEUBERT, S. F.; and WERLIN, S. H. 1976. *A working manual of simple evaluation techniques for community mental health centers.* DHEW Publication No. (ADM) 76–404. Rockville, Md.: U.S. Department of Health, Education, and Welfare.

LASKA, E. M., and BANK, R., eds. 1975. *Safeguarding psychiatric privacy: Computer systems and their use.* New York: Wiley.

For further information of needs assessment, the following works may be useful.

HARGREAVES et al. (cited above) includes a section on the assessment of need.

WARHEIT, G. J.; BELL, R. A.; and SCHWAB, J. J. 1974. *Planning for change: Needs assessment approaches.* Gainesville, Fla.: University of Florida.

CASE STUDY 5.1

An Audit of Current Quality of Services

Understanding the current state of a service program is important for several reasons. Chief among these reasons are to meet management and planning needs. Managers must know what services are being offered. Without such information, it is impossible to plan in an intelligent manner. This audit study using existing records revealed clear inadequacies in the practices of alcoholism treatment programs and, by implication, suggested concrete ways in which services could be improved.

AN EVALUATION OF
ALCOHOLISM TREATMENT SERVICES
FOR ALASKAN NATIVES *

Sheldon I. Miller, M.D.
Associate Director, Department of Psychiatry
Cuyahoga County Hospital, Cleveland, Ohio

Edward Helmick, M.P.H.
Project Director, Alaskan Native Board of Health
Anchorage, Alaska

Lawrence Berg, B.A.
Associate Director

Paul Nutting, M.D.
Program Development Officer

Gregory Shorr, M.D.
Program Development Officer
Office of Research and Development
Indian Health Service
Tucson, Arizona

Alcoholism and alcohol-associated delinquency and violence are increasing problems in Alaska, particularly in the urban centers and the transitional native communities. The purpose of the study was to describe services available to Alaskan natives and to assess the degree to which the health system was responding to clients with drinking problems.

The evaluation was an assessment and analysis of the degree to which the service agencies were responding to clients with drinking problems.

* Condensed with permission from *Hospital and Community Psychiatry* 23 (1975); 829–31. Copyright 1975 by the American Psychiatric Association.

The study focused on the delivery system rather than on treatment outcome. This methodology differs from the traditional evaluation approach, which is outcome oriented and focuses on the results of treatment.

Our basic plan was to examine the management of clients or patients with a recognized alcohol problem in both medical facilities and alcoholism programs throughout the state to determine if problems of alcohol abuse were being solved or prevented in a logical manner. The problem-solving process was defined as including information gathering, or assessment of severity and review of related problems; development of a treatment plan based on information gathered; and a follow-up and evaluation of treatment. These elements of the problem-solving process were used as standards of care in evaluating alcoholism services.

The review instrument was a flow sheet, which presented a logical sequence for evaluating the problem-solving process. In addition, the review instrument attempted to gather some information on the types of treatment in use and the severity of the problems seen in each treatment category. For the latter, alcoholism was defined along a continuum, with the well individual at the beginning and death secondary to alcoholism at the end. The intermediate stages were drawn, in part, from the American Psychiatric Association's Diagnostic and Statistical Manual.

Members of the Alaskan Native Health Board selected twelve medical facilities and twenty alcoholism programs to be studied. The medical facilities included all of the U.S. Public Health Service's Alaska Area Native Health Service Hospitals, three of their clinics, and two locally managed hospitals that provide health care to Alaskan natives under contract and serve areas with a high prevalence of drinking problems among natives. There were twenty alcoholism programs in the state at the time the evaluation was planned.

A one-year study period, from July 1, 1971, to June 30, 1972, was chosen. A six-month period was added for follow-up of those cases occurring during the last six months of the study year. Charts of patients or clients over ten years old were reviewed. The audit at each agency ended after twenty-five charts were found in which the care provider recognized that the patient had a drinking problem.

A total of 4,435 charts were reviewed at the twelve medical facilities, and 637 were reviewed at the twenty alcoholism programs, bringing the total number of charts reviewed to 5,072. The data from the medical facilities and the alcoholism programs were kept separate since the medical facilities are charged with treating a variety of diseases including alcoholism, and alcoholism programs are expected to treat alcoholism only.

Medical Facility Data

The review of charts for all individuals over ten years old (4,435) revealed that 291 patients were recognized by the care provider as having a drinking problem. In many instances, the medical system's response to 291 problem users of alcohol left a great deal to be desired; in other cases it adequately answered certain needs. One area of deficiency was information gathering. For only 97 of the 291 charts was there enough information for the investigator to assess the severity of the problem, and for only 89 charts did the chart keeper make such an assessment. That indicates that in 2 percent of the charts reviewed, information was gathered but was not assimilated and used by the care provider.

Although alcoholism is a complex medical and social problem, in only 56 of the 291 charts reviewed was there any attempt made to outline related problems—social, economic, or psychological—influencing the comprehensive care of an alcoholic. The medical system did treat the presenting physical complaint, both alcohol-related and nonalcohol-related, in 94 percent, or 274, of the patients. It should be pointed out, however, that for 6 percent, or 17 of the patients who were recognized as needing physical treatment, no such treatment was given.

Although the system responded to a high percentage of the needs for treatment of presenting medical complaints, it did not do so well in relation to the basic problems of alcoholism. The maximum estimate of problem drinkers in medical facilities for whom a treatment plan for problems other than the presenting physical problem was developed was 148. It should be pointed out here that many of these individuals for whom a treatment plan was developed entered into the plan without having first been evaluated either as to the severity of their drinking problem or for alcohol-related problems. A minimum estimate of the percentage of patients for whom there was no assessment of severity and related problems, but for whom a treatment plan was developed, was 57 percent of the 148 patients.

A crucial factor in the continuing treatment of the patient is an evaluation of that treatment, and the first step in evaluation is a follow-up of the patient. For only 40 of the 274 patients with a treatment plan was there a documentation of follow-up. And for only 22 was there an attempt at follow-up to evaluate the outcome of the treatment plan. Of the 22 who were evaluated, a negative result was noted for nine. In none of those cases, however, was an alternative treatment plan developed. Thus it can be estimated from the medical facility data that a treatment plan will be developed, followed up, and its impact evaluated for only 8 percent of the recognized problem drinkers.

In the process of evaluating the function of the system, we noted the types of treatment used as well as the frequency with which information that would permit the assessment of the stage of severity was gathered. Unfortunately, even when severity was noted, the data were often insufficient to allow placement of the patient into one of the stages.

The treatment methods for the 274 patients were clearly noted. The most common form of treatment was the direct care of alcohol-related medical complications, which occurred for 76 percent of all identified problem drinkers. The second most common form of treatment was individual counseling, which was used for 22 percent of all the identified problem drinkers. Thirteen percent of the patients were referred to a detoxification unit, and 11 percent were given tranquilizers. (Percentages total more than 100 because some patients received more than one treatment at a time.)

Alcoholism Program Data

The data from the alcoholism programs are based on 484 patients recognized by the care provider as having a drinking problem. The assessment of severity of the alcohol problem was audited on two parameters. First, a maximum estimate was made of the percent of charts in which some degree of assessment of severity could be made by the investigator. In 55.2 percent of the charts that was possible. However, on the other parameter—whether the care provider himself made an assessment of severity—a maximum level was calculated to be 40.5 percent.

A comprehensive evaluation of the patient should involve a review of related problems, and a maximum estimate of the number of charts in which that occurred was 275, or 56.8 percent. For 433 patients, or 88.4 percent, a treatment plan was developed. As with the medical facilities, however, we found that treatment was often formulated without sufficient assessment. For 234 of the patients with a treatment plan, there had been no assessment of severity or of related alcoholism problems.

Follow-up occurred with only 124, or 29 percent, of the patients with a treatment plan. Of those patients who were followed up, the evaluation of 82 was documented. Thirty-nine of those evaluated had negative results, and for only eight was an alternative plan initiated. Thus in the alcoholism programs it can be estimated that a treatment plan will be developed, followed up, and its impact evaluated for only 16.7 percent of the recognized problem drinkers.

During the review of clients of the alcoholism agencies, efforts were made to determine the most common forms of treatment. They were somewhat different from those used by the medical facilities. Sixty-two percent of the clients received individual counseling, 32 percent went to halfway houses, 29 percent received group counseling, and 15 percent were referred to Alcoholics Anonymous. In addition, several other treatments were used, including detoxification, inpatient psychiatric hospitalization, and sleep-off centers. (Again the figures total more than 100 percent because more than one treatment modality was used for some patients.)

Conclusions and Observations

Although this study was conducted by chart review and therefore may not fully reflect actual practice in all cases, serious deficits in the health systems' response to alcoholism and problem drinking were found.

The fact that the records might not reflect actual practice is in itself a serious deficit. Since any individual care provider could, for a variety of reasons, become unavailable to the client, the record becomes an important factor in providing continuity of care. Use of an accurate record is also the only way to audit the health system and to determine whether a system is functioning for a given client.

The absence of even an attempt at a record system is, therefore, a further indictment of the quality of the care offered by the provider. When records are written, information must be organized, processed, and understood by the therapist. Absence of a record raises the question of whether the provider was unable to understand and interpret the information gained from the patient. It might be said that inferior or missing records, rather than raising a question about the validity of a quality-of-care study based on chart review, are in themselves one of the more serious deficits that such a study could find.

The records reviewed indicate a failure to provide the basic components of care that are routinely expected in the treatment of other health problems. Alcoholism seems to be viewed as a single entity rather than as a chronic illness with various levels of severity. The complex nonmedical problems so important in the development of alcoholism and the treatment given the alcoholic are identified only on occasion. While clients and patients are treated for the problem, they frequently are not evaluated, and the treatment method may be determined by program needs, not by client needs.

It must be emphasized that the results of this study are presented in summary form. Some programs did quite well, but for the individual with a drinking probem seeking any help available, that is of little benefit. Generally the quality of the delivery system is poor. The presence of alcoholism seems to put an individual not only at high risk for the development of a variety of problems, but also at high risk of entering a treatment setting that will fail to systematically deliver the service needed to either prevent progression or find and treat current problems.

CASE STUDY 5.2

A System for Routinely Describing and Reporting Services Given

In this case study, the authors describe a simple system for evaluating the services provided by a telephone crisis intervention service. Note the reasons the authors list for developing the system and the criteria of a good reporting system.

A PRACTICAL REPORTING AND EVALUATION SYSTEM FOR INTERVENTION PROGRAMS: GUIDING PRINCIPLES AND POTENTIAL USES *

David Zalkind, PH.D.
Harvey Zelon, M.P.H.
Mary Moore, DR.P.H.
Arnold Kaluzny, PH.D.
Department of Health Administration
University of North Carolina School of Public Health

Local government officials and directors of local human service agencies such as the United Fund are increasingly being asked to recognize the importance of and provide funding for crisis intervention programs. Often called "telephone hotlines," "suicide prevention centers," or "emergency aid services," crisis intervention programs are becoming one of the most prevalent types of human services programs across the country. While funding is currently available from the federal government through the National Institute of Mental Health, the National Institute of Drug Abuse, and the National Institute of Alcohol Abuse and Alcoholism, most of these small crisis intervention programs are faced with the reality of requesting additional support from local government authorities or United Fund agencies.

To justify their request for funds, a viable record and reporting system is needed. The purpose of this paper is to outline a series of general principles critical to the design of a recording and reporting system and then describe a system based on these principles that can be developed and/or modified for intervention programs. In addition, the paper briefly describes a simple evaluation approach, essentially based on data generated by the reporting system, supplemented by a minimal amount of program operations data. The system discussed here was developed for intervention-level drug abuse programs by the Department of Health Administration, School of Public Health at the University of North Carolina at Chapel Hill under contract to the North Carolina Drug Commission.

The Basic Principles

The basic principles of developing a recording and reporting system for intervention programs are presented below:

1. Determine what decisions program directors are likely to have to make.
2. Determine what information program directors feel would aid

* Condensed with permission from the *American Journal of Public Health* 67 (1977); 370–73. Copyright 1977 by the *American Journal of Public Health*.

them in decision making, and in what format(s) that information would be most useful. (Mock-up tables displaying such information should be developed to help ensure that the desired information will appear in a useful form.)

3. Determine specifically what data need to be collected for use in the tables.
4. Determine what information is either mandatory or prudent to report to other agencies.
5. Develop a simple reporting format. Considerable time should be spent at this stage to ensure that the format is complete and functional. Most intervention programs need a form that can be filled out at the time of contact between the program staff member or volunteer and the client. A form that is too complicated or time-consuming would be dysfunctional, as would one that left out valuable information. Recognize that early drafts of the form will need revision as experience with the system is gained.
6. If there is to be computerization of the system, design the recording forms to be self-coding. If data tabulation is to be done by hand, do not be too ambitious with regard to data that will need to be cross-tabulated.
7. Let the recording form for a client contact serve a dual purpose. When the recording form is done in duplicate, using a carbon, one copy can become part of the client record system. The other copy (minus any client identifiers or other confidential information) may be used for constructing program reports.

Using these principles, the program director should take time to carefully consider his/her decision-making patterns before establishing a reporting and recording system. Determining what decisions need to be made and the information needed to make them increases the survival potential of the agency as well as potentially minimizing funding problems.

A Simple System

A reduced copy of the second page of the client contact form that was developed is given in Figure 5.10. Each form consists of two pages joined at the bottom. The form is self-carboned so information recorded on the top page is automatically reproduced on the second page. However, the bottom page is longer than the top page (8½" by 14" as opposed to 8½") to permit the inclusion of additional information. In Figure 5.10, the sections for client and caller identifier, and problem notes will appear only on the longer sheet. This sheet is retained within the agency while the top sheet is sent to the central office to be key punched and processed. The central office collects such sheets from participating programs once each month and sends back reports compiled at program, regional, and state levels.

INTERVENTION PROGRAM CONTACT REPORTING FORM

Caller Identifier: _____ Client Identifier: _____

Problem Notes: (Four inches of space was provided here.)
. . . .

Staff Identifier _____
                                    Name   Number

PROGRAM CODAP# _____

_____ Staff Type: 1. Paid   2. Volunteer
_____ Date (Month, Day, Year)
_____ Time (Hour, Minute)
_____ Time: AM   PM
_____ Time Spent (minutes)
_____ Contact by: 1. Phone   2. Walk-in   3. Offsite
_____ Contact Status   1. First Contact
                               2. Prior Contact

Presenting Problem(s) and Service(s) Provided:

Problems	Services Into 1	Refer 2	Counsel 3	Other 4	Crisis (YN)
_____	_____	_____	_____	_____	_____
_____	_____	_____	_____	_____	_____
_____	_____	_____	_____	_____	_____
_____	_____	_____	_____	_____	_____
_____	_____	_____	_____	_____	_____
_____	_____	_____	_____	_____	_____

Caller Relationship to client   _____
1. Self   2. Spouse   3. Friend   4. Relative

Client: Age   _____

Client: Sex (M or F)   _____

Client: Race B. W. O-Other. U-Unknown.   _____

Referred to program by: _____
1. Self   2. Individual   3. Agency   4. Other   5. Unknown

If self, learned of program from: _____
1. Media ads   2. Word of mouth   3. Prior client   4. Other

FIGURE 5.10: Client contact reporting form.

FIGURE 5.10 continued

Problem List:

Medical Health Problems	Psycho-Social Problems
10 Veneral Disease	20 Family
11 Pregnancy, Abortion	21 Sex
12 Hepatitis	22 Suicide
13 Drugs	23 School
14 Other	24 Job
15 Other	25 Housing
16 Other	26 Financial
17 Other	27 Legal
18 Other	28 Interpersonal
19 Other	29 Other
	30 Other
	31 Other
	32 Other

_____ If referred, to: 1. Hospital   2. Private _____
                        Professional   3. Inhouse   Name (for your records)
                        4. MHC   5. Other Agency   6. Other Drug Program

_____ If counseling, type: 1. Individual   2. Family   3. Group

_____ If DRUG related, type(s):

40 HEROIN	48 Anti-depressants	56 Cough and
_____ 41 ILLEGAL	49 Sedatives–Hypnotics	cold
METHADONE	(nonbarbiturates)	remedies (in-
42 Opiod Analgesics	50 AMPHETAMINES (in-	cluding anti-
43 Non-Opiod	cluding combination	histimines)
_____ Analgesics (in-	diet pills)	57 Sedatives
cluding OTC)	51 COCAINE	(i.e., Somi-
44 ALCOHOL	52 MARIJUANA, HASHISH	nex, Nytol)
45 BARBITURATES	53 Hallucinogens	58 Anti-
_____ 46 Major Tran-	54 Delinents (i.e., phen-	infectives
quilizers	cycledine and atropine	59 Cardiovas-
47 Minor Tran-	55 INHALANTS	cular and
quilizers and		Diuretics
Muscle Relaxants		60 Unknown
		61 Other

Sequence Number _____

There are fourteen tables that appear in each report. They include: a compilation of contacts made by day of the week and hour (useful for scheduling staff), demographic characteristics of clients (for comparison with target population), and self-referral information source (for estimating effectiveness of different publicity efforts).

However, the information in the report tables is not sufficient to answer all questions, particularly those related to evaluation of the intervention program. Additional information is required.

Summary

The continued existence of intervention programs is contingent on the ability to answer basic questions such as "What is your program doing?" and "Why should we fund your program?" This paper outlines basic principles and describes a practical reporting and supplemental evaluation system that can be used by administrators of even the smallest intervention program.

part

III

EVALUATION

OF

OUTCOME

Descriptions and illustrations of outcome evaluations make up a large portion of this book. A major purpose of these presentations is to encourage an understanding of the variety of forms an outcome evaluation can take. The selection among these methods is determined by the decisions evaluators and program managers make about the primary purpose of the evaluation.

The first decision is whether the evaluation would be better focused on the degree each individual achieves the outcome desired, or whether summary information on groups of participants is more useful. Individualized assessments of outcomes are well suited to evaluations of medical and mental health care and managerial effectiveness. In Chapter 6, several widely used individual goal attainment evaluation methods are introduced.

Drawing up individualized goals is often expensive. Further, such goals are often not required, because many programs are offered to fairly homogeneous groups of people who seek to gain quite similar benefits. Evaluators will probably work with group-based data far more frequently than with individual-based information. Such evaluations are described and illustrated in Chapters 7, 8, and 9. These chapters have been organized so that the simplest form of outcome evaluation is presented first.

A simple examination of the state of program participants after receiving a service will tell program managers and sponsors whether the participants leave a program with acceptable levels of achievement or health. If there are objective program goals that are widely accepted as valid, the simple evaluation designs described in Chapter 7 may be quite satisfactory.

When simple evaluation designs will not suffice, additional information must be gathered to improve the interpretability of the evaluation. Chapter 8 includes three approaches to improving the clarity of the interpretation of an evaluation: observing the program participants more than twice; observing additional groups; and measuring additional dependent variables. Of course, these approaches can be combined to produce even better evaluation designs.

When the purpose of an evaluation is to ascertain beyond any doubt whether a program did or did not cause an observed change in the program participants, the methods of Chapter 7 will not be adequate. If the evaluation is carefully planned, the methods of Chapter 8 will often be quite satisfactory. All doubts about causality, however, are most easily eliminated if a true experiment is used to assess the outcome of a program. The advantages of true experiments and the precautions to follow to guarantee that an evaluation designed as an experiment remains an experiment when implemented are the topics of Chapter 9.

Once the outcome of a service program is known, it is possible to ask whether the outcome is worth the cost. In other words, is the program an efficient use of resources? The basic principles of cost-benefit and cost-effectiveness analyses are described in Chapter 10. Since support for social programs has been eroding since the late 1960s, it is likely that cost concerns will become more important in evaluations of human services than they have been in the recent past.

6

Assessing the Achievement of Individualized Goals

Implicit in Chapter 5 on process evaluation was the necessity of developing goals or standards for programs. The most effective use of the information gathered in a process evaluation requires a comparison with some standard of quality for the particular type of services rendered. Without standards, a process evaluation can find only, for example, that X units of care were given, or that one staff member sees more clients than another member. Therefore, the question of whether the amount of care given or whether the effort of any staff member is satisfactory cannot be answered using the methods described to this point.

Society sets many standards. There are fairly clear and objective fire safety standards, such as: the halls of public buildings must be so many feet wide, exit doors must open out, and furniture must not be placed in exit routes. In schools, a specified number of square feet must be provided for children of various grade levels. In counseling settings, there may be standards about how many hours of direct service each counselor must offer per week.

More important than standards describing physical structures or effort expended, however, are standards of quality of outcome. Within limits, it is usually more important to achieve good outcomes from a human service than to follow particular procedures. The end does justify the means, so long as the means are ethical and responsible. This would be especially true in human service settings because professionals seldom really know what does and what does not reliably work to help people learn, to improve emotional health, to hold a job, and so on. This chapter focuses on methods that assess the achievement of individualized goals, that is, goals that are prepared for specific individuals or for a specific category of people.

The task of evaluating success in meeting a goal would be relatively easy if the parties involved could agree on objective goals. There are programs that have widely accepted goals. When such agreement exists, a program can be evaluated simply by observing the group of people experiencing the program. Foxx and Azrin (1973) have described a method of toilet training based on the behavioristic principles of shaping and reward. They evaluated the procedure with one group of children who were not toilet trained. The goal or criterion of success was the time required to train the child to use a child-sized toilet. Because the standard of time to successful outcome that they set for the program was so much shorter than the time most parents require, there was ready agreement with the goals of the program. Specifically, Foxx and Azrin promised to have the children toilet trained in less than a day. For parents who have worked for months to achieve that goal, there is no need to ask whether such an outcome would indicate that the program was successful.[1] A program that far exceeds typical levels of outcome is not difficult to evaluate, especially if a wide consensus endorses the level of outcome achieved.

The problem for evaluation is that few outcomes are so striking as that in Foxx and Azrin's work, and seldom is consensus so easily achieved. Outcomes are not striking because longstanding behavior is hard to change; change is usually small, even after an effective program (Rossi 1972). Consensus on ideal outcomes is not likely, because people with different viewpoints desire different outcomes. In Chapter 3, the different expectations of the client, the therapist, and the community were described for the case of psychotherapy. Also, ideal outcomes are hard to specify because people enter programs with different

[1] For those new parents among the readers, Foxx and Azrin did succeed. The mean time required to toilet train the children was 3.9 hours. See Case Study 7.2 for further information on this program.

levels of abilities and, therefore, are likely to complete programs at different levels.

In order to assess the degree to which programs achieve their goals, methods are needed that aid the evaluator to develop standards and to assess whether those standards or objectives were achieved.

This chapter focuses on several techniques used when there is a need to evaluate the degree to which the service approaches predetermined standards of effective work. There are three general methods illustrated: medical care outcome audit, management by objectives, and peer review in mental health. These techniques have been found useful in a variety of settings, and they illustrate a number of principles important to evaluation.

DEVELOPING OUTCOME GOALS

It is extremely important to have specified goals for every human service facility for a number of reasons. In the first place, specifying a goal forces people to become more realistic in their goals. It is very easy to set very ambitious but vague goals that are seldom achieved by anyone (House et al. 1978). Often, in perhaps a sincere attempt to persuade decision makers, people describe the possibilities that *could* be achieved by someone accepting counseling, therapy, job training, or some other human service. When the therapy or treatment is over and these very optimistic goals have not been achieved, it is fairly easy to rationalize why these goals were not achieved. It is important to be optimistic, but it is also important to be realistic. Spelling out the specific goals to achieve is a discipline that helps human service professionals look very carefully and critically at their plans.

A second reason why specified goals are important is that it is hard to know just when a human service should stop. When helping a person to learn social skills, to write more effectively, or to develop marketable job skills, it is possible to see additional room for further improvement, regardless of positive changes that have occurred. By having specific goals prepared ahead of time, it is easier to decide when the service can end.

A third reason why it is important to have specified goals is related to the second. When goals are specified, the client, other staff members, and third parties such as insurance companies or employers can participate in setting and evaluating the achievement of goals of human services. Psychotherapists, for example, often have been criticized for having private goals and for being the only judge of whether those goals were achieved. Frequently these criticisms are valid. By preparing specific goals, discussing them with the client, with other staff members, and at certain times with employers, many individuals participate in setting the goals and in evaluating whether (or hopefully when) the goals have been achieved.

A fourth reason to set specific goals is that clear goals are in themselves motivating. People work more efficiently when they know what is expected of them. Industrial psychologists have found that difficult but specific goals lead to better performance than do nonspecific goals (such as, "Do the best you can"), easy goals, or no goals at all (Locke 1968; Yukl and Latham 1978). McCarthy (1978) used goals to reduce carelessness in a textile plant. Dicken (1978), a nurse, writes that goal setting is a motivator for patients recovering from serious illnesses. Burns (1977) found that setting goals was effective in improving the performance of school principals. Most workers and students are happier, more productive, and more satisfied when they know what is expected of them. Realistic but challenging goals can provide human service care givers considerable help in their work.

Problems in Setting Goals

There are certainly many problems in setting goals for any human service facility. One of the major problems that students raise when goal setting is first described to them is: what is to keep people from setting very low goals, therefore guaranteeing that they will always achieve and often exceed those goals? If the mere achievement of goals was all that was important, then this would be a damning criticism of this approach to program evaluation. However, just as athletes cannot set unrealistic goals that they can easily achieve, neither can human services care givers set unrealistic goals because other people are involved in evaluating the validity of the goals. A counselor whose only goal is to prevent clients from committing suicide would probably achieve that goal with more than 99.9 percent of his clients; if, however, the therapist must share these goals with other staff members and with the client, then this very minimal goal will be challenged and rejected as meaningless for the vast majority of clients seeking counseling. It is likely that if clients and other staff members share in the development of human service goals, a balance will be found between the ambition to achieve overly challenging goals and the temptation to set easy-to-achieve goals.

A second problem that people raise when they first consider explicit goal setting is that the care giver's job is harder to do. Very often in health care settings, if therapists or nurses are asked what their goals are, they usually say to provide good medical care so that people can get better. Colleges set goals such as training educated and cultured men and women. Such goals cannot be challenged. However, they are so general that it is impossible to know to what extent the goal is ever achieved. Setting explicit goals will make the care giver's job somewhat harder. However, if human services are necessary and helpful to people in need, and if human service care givers expect to be paid for their efforts, they will have to show that they are planning services for every individual client, that they usually achieve what they expect, and finally that what they expect is accepted as worthwhile by patients or clients and institutions or individuals paying for the service.

The Approaches to Be Presented

This text will explicitly discuss two approaches to goal construction. One of these approaches is that developed by Kiresuk, called Goal Attainment Scaling (Lund and Kiresuk 1979; Kiresuk and Sherman 1968). This second approach discussed is called management by objectives (McConkey 1975). Goal Attainment Scaling (GAS) and management by objectives (MBO) are actually quite similar; however, the person whose behavior is described in the goals is different for the two approaches. MBO concentrates on the manager's behavior, whereas GAS concentrates on the behavior of a client of a human service facility. There are other forms of goal setting for clients, patients, or managers. GAS and MBO, however, are widely used and well-known and are good illustrations of the value of individualized goal-setting approach to evaluation.

INDIVIDUAL TREATMENT GOALS

Constructing individual treatment goals is important as a discipline, as an evaluation strategy, and as a means of encouraging communication between client and therapist. Explicitly recording goals requires much more discipline and thought from the therapist than is required by simply saying, "We'll do the best we can." As an evaluation strategy, the preparation of explicit goals is important because the quality of intended care and actual care can be compared among various approaches or organizations. Finally, sensitive care givers realize that their goals may not be the same goals that the client has. For example, a couple seeking marital counseling may, by chance, select a counselor who concludes that divorce is the only option and directs the counseling toward having the couple accept divorce and carry it out as smoothly as possible; another couple with the same level of difficulties may select a counselor, just by chance, whose goal will be to avoid a divorce at all costs. It seems important that clients and therapists discuss goals ahead of time to minimize this chance aspect from the counseling relationship. Communication is also to be encouraged between client and therapist as a means of avoiding the waste of time on minor problems or by repeatedly following the whims of client or therapist while forgetting the major problems.

What is required in the construction of individual outcome goals? First, goals must be explicit, and they must be recorded. Second, they must be realistic yet ambitious. The balance between realism and ambition is likely to be achieved when the goals are constructed in cooperation with the client and in consultation with other staff members. Third, the goals must be reviewed. They must be reviewed because as therapy progresses the client may become dissatisfied with the original goals and wish to revise them. On the other hand, the client may become satisfied in having achieved the goals and desire to end therapy. Or, the client may realize that those goals have been achieved and may wish to construct new goals that would have seemed overly ambitious when therapy began.

Goal Attainment Scaling

Goal Attainment Scaling goes beyond what has been discussed in the preceding paragraphs because it permits measurement of the *degree* of attainment of the outcomes desired, regardless of the unique needs of an individual client. Such measurement takes some ingenuity because human service goals are often difficult to quantify. However, obtaining a quantified index of success is an advantage in that comparisons among treatments and institutions will become possible.

In selecting the goals for a therapy relationship, the initial discussion with clients must center.on the reasons they have requested therapy and what they would like to get out of it. Therapists will at the same time discuss what they feel can be expected and, if all goes well, what might be possible. In the initial one or two interviews, clients and therapists should be able to agree on some outcome goals for the therapy.

It is possible that the therapist may have some additional goals that would be important for a client to achieve but that the client would not be prepared to accept as legitimate goals during the early stages of counseling. One can easily imagine a psychotherapist being struck by the abrasiveness or the manipulating manner of a new client. Few people enter therapy because they are dissatisfied with their abrasiveness or their manipulative approach to social relations. It may be possible as counseling progresses that they would begin to sense that one of their own characteristics is involved in the problems that brought them to counseling. At that time, they may wish to include it as a goal in their therapy. Thus, there is a place for goals that the therapist may not wish to share immediately with the client. However, having made this point, the reader considering the use of GAS should remember that GAS goals must be shared to obtain the method's full usefulness.

After the goals have been stated and recorded, GAS requires that each goal be weighted by its relative importance. In general, the client is to cooperate with the therapist in rating the importance of these goals. One of the easier procedures to use in rating the importance is to assign some arbitrary value to the least important goal. A value of 10 is easy to work with. Then, the therapist and client must decide how much more important the next goal is. Perhaps that goal would have a weight or value of 20 because they agreed it was twice as important as the least important goal. In this way, numerical values can be applied to the goals that therapist and client agree are central to this therapeutic relationship. (This weighting process is identical to the method of assigning weights described for use with the MAUT model in Chapter 4.)

An Example of the Use of GAS

If a school counselor was going to begin a counseling relationship with a student in academic and disciplinary trouble, several school-related goals might be set up to guide the counseling. Perhaps the student wants to achieve higher grades, to be sent less frequently to the principal's office for discipline, and to improve his/her reading speed.

Once the dimensions have been specified, the next step is to describe the state the student is expected to be in by the end of some time period, if counseling goes normally. Then, the most unfavorable and the most favorable outcomes are described. The dimensions and the descriptions are the basis of the GAS grid. For example, a D student may be expected to improve to a C level: the worst outcome would be to fail; the most favorable outcome would be to obtain B's and A's. In terms of improving reading speed, the worst outcome would be to stay the same, since it seems unlikely that reading speed would drop during the following several months. On the basis of standard test scores, the counselor feels that the student could double his/her reading speed if real effort were expended. Finally, suppose that the student was being sent to the principal's office an average of six times a month when counseling began; the worst outcome would be even more dis-

FIGURE 6.1: Example of a goal attainment grid using objective individualized levels of goal attainment (Adapted from Garwick 1973.)

Level of outcome	Value of outcome	Scale 1: school grades Weight: 15	Scale 2: reading speed Weight: 10	Scale 3: trips to principal Weight: 20
Most unfavorable	−2	D− or F	75 wpm ✔	7+
Less than expected	−1	D✔	100 wpm	4–7✔
Expected level	0	C− or C*	150 wpm*	2–3
More than expected	+1	C+ or B−	200 wpm	1*
Most favorable	+2	B or A	250+ wpm	0

Check marks refer to levels at the beginning of counseling. T = 33.53

Asterisks refer to levels at the end of counseling. T = 52.99

cipline problems; the most favorable would be no discipline problems. These scales and descriptions are shown in Figure 6.1.

The values recorded to the right of the various outcome levels are equivalent to z-scores.[2] The expected outcome is valued at 0 because the mean of a set of numbers has a z-score of 0. The most favorable outcome is expected to occur only 5 times out of 100, so it has a z-score of 2. Finally, the least favorable outcome, also expected 5 times out of 100, is valued at −2. The two less extreme outcomes are assigned z-scores of +1 and −1.

To take full advantage of the method would require the assignment of importance weights to the three scales. If we assume that the student was in danger of being expelled for behavioral problems, scale 3 would be weighted most heavily, and reading speed would be least important. The counselor assigned reading speed a weight of 10. Grades were felt to be 50 percent more important, so scale 2 was weighted 15. Finally, fewer trips to the principal was weighted 20. These weights do not sum to any set value since only their relative values are important.

The beginning level of the student is checked on the grid. After counseling, an asterisk was added to record what the student achieved during counseling. Numerical values can be calculated using the weights and the scale attainment levels associated with each level of outcome.

[2] Standard scores such as z-scores are described in the statistical appendix.

The formula given by Kiresuk to calculate a standard (T) score analogous to the standard scores on personality tests is:

$$T = 50 + \frac{10 \Sigma \, w_j x_j}{\sqrt{(1 - \rho)\Sigma w_j^2 + \rho(\Sigma w_j)^2}}$$

In the formula, w_j is the weight assigned to the scales, x_j is the attainment level on the scales, and ρ refers to the average scale intercorrelation, which is assumed to be .30. For our hypothetical student, the initial value of T was found by substituting the attainment levels before counseling as follows:

$$T = 50 + \frac{10[15(-1) + 10(-2) + 20(-1)]}{\sqrt{(1 - .30)(15^2 + 10^2 + 20^2) + .30(15 + 10 + 20)^2}}$$

Carrying out the calculations, we find that the student began at a level of 33.53.

If the student remains in counseling and tries to adjust better to school, the student is expected to improve to 50. Any better achievement will result in a score above 50. Assume that the asterisks in Figure 6.1 indicate the level of the student at the end of the school year. If the counselor calculates the goal attainment level after counseling, a value of 52.99 would be found. Thus, the student did a bit better than was expected and is functioning quite a bit better than at the start of counseling.

The use of GAS is a valuable discipline for counselors. Although calculating the T-values for a single client provides little useful information not already available from the grid itself, comparisons of outcomes among programs or types of approaches to counseling can be made if GAS is used routinely. Often individual therapists receive their GAS results plus a summary of the overall average attainment levels of the rest of the staff. In this way, therapists learn how effective they are in comparison with other therapists without the possible embarrassment caused by general release of each therapist's average attainment level.

The question of who does the final outcome rating is critical. In the example of a junior-high school student, the outcomes are objective and very easy to assess. The question of outcome assessment is far more difficult for counseling when outcomes are stated in terms of less dependence or less manipulativeness. An example grid for counseling requiring such scales is given in Figure 6.2. In such situations, periodic follow-up by

Check whether or not the scale has been mutually negotiated between patient and CIC interviewer.

SCALE ATTAINMENT LEVELS	SCALE 1: Education (w₁=20) Yes X No	SCALE 2: Suicide (w₂=30) Yes __ No X	SCALE 3: Manipulation (w₃=25) Yes __ No X	SCALE 4: Drug Abuse (w₄=30) Yes X No	SCALE 5: Dependency on CIC (w₅=10) Yes X No
a. most unfavorable treatment outcome thought likely (-2)	Patient has made no attempt to enroll in high school. ✓	Patient has committed suicide.	Patient makes rounds of community service agencies demanding medication, and refuses other forms of treatment. ✓	Patient reports addiction to "hard narcotics" (heroin, morphine).	Patient has contacted CIC by telephone or in person at least seven times since his first visit.
b. less than expected success with treatment (-1)	Patient has enrolled in high school, but at time of follow-up has dropped out.	Patient has acted on at least one suicidal impulse since her first contact with the CIC, but has not succeeded. ✓	Patient no longer visits CIC with demands for medication but continues with other community agencies and still refuses other forms of treatment.	Patient has used "hard narcotics," but is not addicted, and/or uses hallucinogens (LSD, Pot) more than four times a month. ✓	Patient has contacted CIC 5-6 times since intake.
c. expected level of treatment success (0)	Patient has enrolled, and is in school at follow-up, but is attending class sporadically (misses an average of more than a third of her classes during a week).	Patient reports she has had at least four suicidal impulses since her first contact with the CIC but has not acted on any of them.	Patient no longer attempts to manipulate for drugs at community service agencies, but will not accept another form of treatment.	Patient has not used "hard narcotics" during follow-up period, and uses hallucinogens between 1-4 times a month. *	Patient has contacted CIC 3-4 times since intake.
d. more than expected success with treatment (+1)	Patient has enrolled, is in school at follow-up, and is attending classes consistently, but has no vocational goals. *		Patient accepts non-medication treatment at some community agency. *	Patient uses hallucinogens less than once a month.	
e. best anticipated success with treatment (+2)	Patient has enrolled, is in school at follow-up, is attending classes consistently, and has some vocational goal.	Patient reports she has had no suicidal impulses since her first contact with the CIC.	Patient accepts non-medication treatment, and by own report shows signs of improvement.	At time of follow-up, patient is not using any illegal drugs.	Patient has not contacted CIC since intake. *

FIGURE 6.2: An example of goal attainment scaling when outcomes are hard to quantify. The level at intake is marked with a check and yields a value of 29.4. The level at follow-up is marked with an asterisk and yields a value of 62.2. The difference between these values is the Goal Attainment Change Score of 32.8. (Reprinted with permission from T. J. Kiresuk, "Goal Attainment Scaling at a County Mental Health Service," *Evaluation*, Monograph No. 1, 1973, p. 15. Copyright 1973, The Program Evaluation Project.)

independent raters is probably required to use GAS to contrast treatment types or to evaluate the competence of individual therapists.

MANAGEMENT BY OBJECTIVES

One of the current approaches to management that is achieving a great deal of attention and is being applied in many human service facilities is management by objectives (often abbreviated MBO) (Gerstenfeld 1977). The approach used in MBO was first suggested in the mid-fifties by Drucker (1954) and McGregor (1960). Their approaches to management stressed the following three points: (1) organizational goals must be clearly established and communicated to all managers in the organization; (2) the managers of the organization are to set individual goals that conform to the intent of the organization's goals; and (3) periodic review of the degree to which managers are achieving their objectives is necessary.

The present book is not a book on management; therefore, we cannot go into management procedures in great detail. However, the program evaluator should have some familiarity with this well-known and widely used management technique.

The initiation of MBO requires commitment of the whole organization to the MBO approach. Top levels of management set their own goals; however, it is important to notice that in the MBO approach, all managers are involved in some way in the goal setting. Goals are not imposed on anyone, but are developed jointly by managers and their supervisors.

Performance must be reviewed or, in our terms, evaluated. Managers must receive feedback and evaluation on the degree to which they are meeting their goals. Such evaluation assumes that all managers have some freedom in developing their approaches to achieving the goals of their units. If the managers had no freedom to choose how to approach meeting the goals, then one could hardly hold them accountable for the success or failure of their own unit.

Sloan and Schrieber (1971) asked managers to discuss the advantages and disadvantages of the MBO approach. The most important advantage of MBO was said to be the improved planning of their work and the fact that they could organize their work better. The second most important advantage for these managers was the help they were given in understanding the goals of the organization and their own responsibilities in meeting those goals.

Like all management and all evaluation procedures, MBO has some disadvantages as well. A repeated objection to MBO is the amount of time consumed in completing the paperwork and in developing the goals themselves. It is likely, however, with any systematic procedure of keeping records and developing goals that the time commitments will decrease as people become familiar with the system.

Preparing MBO Goals

The central step in developing a workable MBO plan is the statement of goals, or objectives. Such objectives must refer to observable organizational behavior and be compatible with the organization's overall objectives, regardless of the level of management preparing them. To illustrate objectives, some examples based on the case study of alcoholism treatment for Alaskan native citizens (Case Study 5.1) can be written.

The reader may remember that there were a number of problems with the assessment of severity of alcoholism, with treatment planning, and with follow-up procedures. For example, in only 283 out of 775 cases of alcoholism did the therapist make an assessment of the severity of the problem.

Objectives that could be written in response to the conclusions of the search of records are:

1. The severity of the alcohol problem of every client is to be assessed by the care giver before a treatment plan is developed.
2. A review of the client's related problems must be made during intake procedures.
3. Assessment of treatment effectiveness must be attempted.
4. When follow-up proves that the treatment did not result in improvement, alternative treatment plans should be used.

Achievement of these goals should be facilitated for the care givers. Every staff member must be aware of and understand these goals and needs to know that management will be directed by these goals. A casual presentation of goals would be insufficient to assure a wide understanding of the goals. Perhaps each care giver could have the importance of these goals discussed with him or her. A minimal requirement would be that each manager discuss the importance of these goals with the staff.

Institutionalizing MBO Goals

A way to institutionalize these goals would be to develop some formal procedures that incorporate them. If these goals were incorporated into a record form that was used at all institutions, the communication of these goals would be carried out. Although it may seem that a new form is a minimal response to these clear needs, using a form that requests information about the client's condition, the planned treatment, and the timing of follow-up may be sufficient to change the care giver's behavior to meet the goals we have suggested above.

Figure 6.3 is the form that was developed by the Alaskan Native Health Board as a first step in improving care for people needing alcoholism treatment. Persons gathering intake data from new clients would be required to assess the severity of the problem by completing the form. Because the form requires a description of the plan for treatment, one cannot complete the form unless there is a plan for treatment. There is also a section of the intake form that is filled in after treatment when follow-up is attempted. One cannot require therapists to contact all clients after treatment; however, one can require documentation of an attempt to contact the client. If care givers fill in this form completely and accurately, they will have achieved the objectives described above.

The Native Health Board also had a long-range goal in mind in developing this form. They discovered in their process evaluation that it was impossible to compare the effectiveness of any one institution with another because records of the clients' needs for treatment and the outcome of treatment were not available, or else the records were so different from one another that comparisons were impossible. The use of this standard form in all alcoholism treatment facilities in the state made possible comparisons among facilities. In addition, the use of a common form made it easier for a client to move from one facility to another. A common problem that human service givers face is the number of clients who are lost to the program. Many clients change homes or for personal reasons wish to seek service at a different facility. The use of a common form permits the facilities to keep track of transient clients. Such long-range goals may conceivably become the subject of future MBO goals the health board would develop for the whole state.

PEER REVIEW

The methods described so far have focused on monitoring the procedures used in offering care (Chapter 5) and on the outcome of the care (GAS and MBO). However, neither approach is primarily designed to examine the skill or judgment of the care giver in achieving desired outcomes for human services. Neither approach can directly isolate inadequate care nor provide clues to guide the improvement of care. In

FACTORS WHICH MAY INDICATE SEVERITY OF DRINKING PROBLEM		SYMPTOMS – DISABILITY INDEX			INSTRUCTIONS: STAGES REFER TO FACTORS PRESENT IN LAST THREE MONTHS ONLY. CHECK APPROPRIATE BOXES. WRITE ADDITIONAL INFORMATION ON REVERSE SIDE.		
		STAGE 0	STAGE 1	STAGE 2	STAGE 3	STAGE 4	STAGE 5
PHYSICAL	APPARENT INTOXICATION & ADDICTION	None	Alcohol abuse averages less than once per month	Alcohol abuse averages more than once per month	Evidence of addiction Can't go more than one day without drinking and/or DT's		
	INJURIES DUE TO INTOXICATION	None	Only one alcohol related injury in the past 3 months that required medical att'n.	More than one injury in the past 3 months that required medical attention.			
	PATHOLOGIC CHANGES (This section may be completed by a physician)	None	None	Preclinical target organ damage	Symptomatic target organ damage	Irreversible liver damage	Irreversible brain damage
SOCIAL	FAMILY RELATIONSHIPS	No problems related to alcohol abuse	Some quarrels related to alcohol abuse (with spouse, parents, etc.)		Breakage of family ties because of alcohol abuse (divorce, drinker leaves home, etc.)		
	NON-FAMILY RELATIONSHIPS	Usually does not associate with alcohol abusers		Usually associates with alcohol abusers	Only associates with alcohol abusers		
ECON.	EDUCATIONAL/ VOCATIONAL	No problems with school, job, or employability related to alcohol abuse	Some problems with school, job or employ-ability related to alcohol abuse.	Threatened with expulsion from school or loss of job because of alcohol abuse.	Out of school or unem-ployed because of alcohol abuse.		

PERSONAL DATA

NAME ____________________
Last First Initial

Individual's Agency Number ____________________

Social Security Number ____________________

Birthdate ____ / ____ / ____ (month, day, year) Sex: Male ____ Female ____

Race: White ____ Black ____ Indian ____ Oriental ____ Other ____ Unknown ____

Marital Status: Married ____ Single ____ Widowed ____ Separated ____ Divorced ____ Unknown ____

INFORMATION ABOUT THIS CONTACT

Ambulatory care ☐ or Institutional care ☐

First contact ____ Recontact ____

Appointment ____ Walk-in ____ Home Visit ____

Referral from ____________________

Who is seen

Individual with drinking problem ____________

Family members or others (name-relationships) ·

____

PROBLEMS WHICH MAY CONTRIBUTE TO ALCOHOL ABUSE

	Yes	No	Plan For: Past Three Months	Plan For: Today and/or Future
1. Physical Disabilities	__	__	____	____
2. Psychiatric Problems	__	__	____	____
Social Problems				
3. Vocational/Educational	__	__	____	____
4. Family	__	__	____	____
5. Housing	__	__	____	____
6. Legal.	__	__	____	____
7. Financial	__	__	____	____
8. Other (specify)	__	__	____	____

Physical / Psychiatric Diagnoses

____

____

____

____

TREATMENT PLAN FOR ALCOHOL ABUSE

Counseling

		Plan For: Past Three Months	Plan For: Today and/or Future
20. Individual	· Insight	____	____
	Supportive	____	____
21. Group	Insight	____	____
	Supportive	____	____
22. Family Therapy		____	____
23. Behavior Therapy		____	____
24. Alcoholics Anonymous		____	____
25. Counseling for family members		____	____
26. Other (specify)		____	____

Institutional Admission

	Plan For: Past Three Months	Plan For: Today and/or Future
9. Sleep-off Ctr.	____	____
10. Halfway House	____	____
11. Jail	____	____
12. Med. Hospital	____	____
13. Psych. Hosp.	____	____
14. Nursing Home	____	____
15. Other (specify)	____	____
Medical Treatment of Alcohol Abuse		
16. Antabuse	____	____
17. Tranquilizer	____	____
18. Detoxification	____	____
19. Other (specify)	____	____

FUTURE CARE

Follow-up at this Agency
1. None ____ ____
2. or ____________ visits a month here

Referred to other Agencies
Names of Agencies ____________________

____

Agency ____________________

____
Signature of Therapist and Job Description

Today's date ____ / ____ / ____ (month, day, year)

NO TREATMENT PLANNED

27. Individual refuses care ____
28. Individuals' family refuses care for themselves ____
29. Care deferred until next visit ____
30. Other (specify) ____

CASE CLOSED ON THIS VISIT

31. Planned ____________ or Unplanned ____________

Closure by:

32. Individual ____________

33. Therapist ____________ 34. Both ____________

FIGURE 6.3: A form to promote better treatment for alcoholism. (Reprinted with permission from E. Helmick, et al., "A Monitoring and Evaluation plan for Alcoholism Programs," *British Journal of Addictions* 70 (1975); 371. Copyright 1975 Longman Group, LTD.

both medical and psychotherapeutic settings, the trend is toward requiring some sort of outcome review that can document patterns of good and poor care (Jacobs, Christoffel, and Dixon 1976; Markson and Allen 1976).

Peer review refers to any system whereby peers of care givers (physicians or psychotherapists) examine the techniques used and outcome produced in treating patients or clients. Sometimes these systems are called *quality assurance, quality control,* or *utilization reviews.* Without acceptable peer reviews, hospitals risk the loss of their accreditation.

Peer reviews can serve different purposes and can vary in their thoroughness and the degree to which they intrude into the care giver's behavior. The least thorough and least intrusive peer reviews may simply consist of a staff meeting at which therapists voluntarily describe cases and their plans for treatment. The comments of other staff members fill an educational function and serve as a way to help the care giver obtain new points of view. If the procedure is voluntary and if the advice does not have to be followed, the reviews may be done only infrequently and they may have limited impact on the behavior of the care giver.

Low Threat Peer Review

Newman and Luft (1974) described how a community mental health center met the problem of unacceptably high costs for psychotherapy through a peer review process. The center's administrators did not want to develop a harsh, conflict-prone system to control costs, but they did feel costs were out of control. The most direct cause of high costs was the amount of therapy hours provided. It was decided to introduce peer review panels whose approval was necessary if therapists intended to provide tax-supported counseling for more than six sessions. To obtain such approval, the therapist was required to make a case presentation to a three-member panel justifying the longer therapy. In order to minimize hostility and the perception of coercion, the reviews were organized in a way to increase the potential educational benefits of the review. Note that this approach is not threatening to the therapists because the only information that the panel obtains is from the therapists themselves.

How well does the system seem to work and how well are the reviews received by the therapists? Luft (1979) reports that the review system resulted in fewer treatment sessions per patient and that clients spent fewer months as active patients of the center. The most striking effect was the reduction in the number of very long-term patients.

Many therapists report that they have come to value the assistance they receive from the review panels. The therapists believe that only a few patients required more therapy than they received, and a survey of patients revealed a high level of agreement between therapists and patients about improvement and whether there was a need for additional therapy. Most patients and therapists agreed that sufficient therapy had been obtained.

Luft found that that system has been received far more favorably than the administration had expected. Overall, the therapists feel that the review procedure has been an aid to their professional growth. Those who most frequently utilize the panels seem to be influenced in their nonreviewed cases as well. Only a small proportion of therapists felt that the review procedure had interfered with their work.

A more thorough review procedure would require an examination of the actual content of the therapy sessions or the medical care given. Psychotherapy peer review can be based on tape recordings of counseling sessions. Experienced clinicians report that most clients do not appear to be disturbed by the tape or cassette recorder. A major difficulty with reviewing tapes is the time involved. A less desirable alternative would be to review the counselor's notes on a case. Unfortunately, a counselor's notes are subjective, and reviewing them would also require much time. There probably is no good *and* practical way to review the content of more than a small proportion of counseling sessions.

Peer Review with Potentially More Threat

Medical care, however, is more objective than psychotherapy, and medical peer review is highly developed (Jacobs, Christoffel, and Dixon 1976). The initial approach to peer review was for several experienced physicians to leaf through patient charts. The time-consuming nature of this approach reduced its usefulness. Recently, several relatively automated approaches have been developed and widely adopted. Evaluators working in hospitals should have some familiarity with these methods because they are likely to become involved at some level with such reviews. Also, reviews modeled on medical methods are being prepared for mental health use (Blom and Moore 1979).

The Joint Commission on Accreditation of Hospitals (JCAH) has prepared a quality review system called Performance Evaluation Procedure, or PEP (Jacobs and Jacobs 1974). In order to use PEP it is necessary that a disease (for example, pneumonia) or a procedure (for example, appendectomy) be selected for audit. Next, a committee of local physicians on the staff of the hospital sponsoring the audit prepares objective criteria for determining whether patients have been diagnosed correctly and have experienced good outcomes of treatment. In addition, indicators of quality care are defined, including the care to be given when a patient develops a complication. For example, all patients admitted with a tentative diagnosis of heart attack must have an electrocardiogram (ECG) taken within twenty-four hours. To be correctly diagnosed, the ECG must be accompanied by other symptoms of a heart attack. Exceptions to all criteria are possible. An exception to the requirement that an ECG must be taken within twenty-four hours is made if the patient does not live for twenty-four hours after admission. In other words, if a patient dies within twenty-four hours of admission of a suspected heart attack, quality of care is not questioned even when the patient did not have an ECG.

Because PEP is outcome oriented, the expected outcomes of quality care are listed by the committee of physicians. For heart attack patients, the discharge criteria may include being able to walk, being pain-free, having a stable ECG, and demonstrating knowledge of risk factors and other topics important to recovering heart attack patients. A preexisting disability would constitute a valid exception to the outcome criteria of walking.

The committee also prepares what PEP terms *indicators of quality care*. In this section are criteria not covered by diagnostic or outcome criteria. A range of days hospitalized for patients with the diagnosis being audited is given. Possible complications and the correct critical management procedures are also included in this section of the audit.

An important advantage of this approach is that a nonphysician, a medical records analyst, can evaluate the patients' charts using the criteria listed because the criteria are objective. If a patient's chart does not include documentation of the procedures required to make the diagnosis given, or if a less than desirable outcome occurs that is not included in the exceptions, the chart goes to a committee for peer review. The same process is followed when a chart is found that does not meet the outcome criteria or that shows care not conforming to the indicators of quality care. For example, hospitalizing a heart attack patient without complications for five weeks is seldom necessary; diagnosing a heart attack without administering an ECG is poor practice; or discharging a patient who still cannot describe the symptoms of heart attacks is unwise. Incidents that indicate poor treatment or failures to demonstrate good practices are labeled "variations," that is, they are at variance with the criteria of good care. The medical records analyst passes the charts containing variations on to the review committee made up of physicians.

The peer review committee selects between two general options when evaluating a variation. The committee can decide that: (1) the variation was justified because of an unusual situation described in the chart or because the original criteria were not complete; or (2) the variation was unjustified. Patterns of inadequate care can be detected, and remedial work required of physicians who have not been following proper procedures or whose patients have not been meeting the discharge outcome criteria. This method of peer review goes beyond the voluntary, educational approach sometimes practiced in psychotherapy settings.[3]

When should peer review be used? If staff education is an important concern, evaluators should consider a peer review approach. The approach described by Luft (1979) was found to be educationally helpful. Peer review should also be considered when evaluation is to focus on the quality of care given, not just on the outcome of therapy (as in GAS) or on the completeness of diagnostic and treatment activity performed by the care giver (as in the Alaskan audit). When seeking to evaluate the quality of care, the peer review committee must have direct access to records, not just therapist's description of care given.

SUMMARY

The common thread tying together the methods in this chapter is that criteria describing good outcomes of human services can be developed. Services can be evaluated by comparing the actual outcome observed with standards of good outcome. The outcome-oriented methods in this chapter differ from those in the following chapters in two ways: (1) specific criteria of success are given, in contrast to programs that attempt only to lead to some (unspecified level of) improvement; and (2) the methods in this chapter can be applied only when outcome is assessed on an individual basis, but those in the following chapters utilize statistical procedures requiring data based on groups. Because of this individual emphasis, these methods are applicable in settings in which an individual's ideal behavior can be described. Thus, these methods are useful in counseling, rehabilitation, and medical facilities in which the client's or patient's outcome is assessed, as well as in all management settings in which the manager's achievement is of interest.

STUDY QUESTIONS

1. Suppose that a peer review panel was formed to monitor length of psychotherapy as described in this chapter. Further suppose that

---

[3] Some have criticized the JCAH's methods as not sufficiently problem-focused and without an effective procedure to guarantee improved performance. In order to meet these criticisms, the JCAH has recently adopted an optional, alternative approach to peer review which is different from the method above (Fifer 1979).

the review panel concluded that some psychotherapists were incompetent. What ethical problems confront the facility's managers upon learning about the panel's conclusions?

2. Discuss the problem of maintaining confidentiality of records when peer review procedures are used in mental health settings.

3. Improve the following objectives as if they were written for a manager of a human services program. Explain your suggested changes.

    a. Improve the level of community mental health.

    b. Conduct in-service training workshops.

    c. Reduce the waiting time for new clients seeking care.

    d. Have all people referred to a second agency actually make contact with that second agency.

4. What is to keep a psychotherapist from setting GAS goals that will be easy to meet?

5. Answer this objection to GAS: "The method forces me to harden my treatment plans, but I think I should remain flexible. In fact, my clinical experience indicates that the flexible clinician is far more helpful than one that makes hard-and-fast plans or sets inflexible goals for therapy."

6. Among the goals that a university wished its graduates to achieve were:

    a. Reflection and critical judgment

    b. Passion for justice

    c. Enjoyment of life in its highest forms

On the basis of what was presented in this chapter, what would a program evaluator say about these goals? How could an evaluator go about learning whether these goals were achieved?

FURTHER READING

Evaluators considering the use of GAS should obtain materials from:

Program Evaluation Resource Center
501 Park Avenue South
Minneapolis, MN 55415

The center provides guides, conducts workshops, publishes a journal, and even has produced videotapes about the use of GAS.

For further information on MBO the following materials are helpful:

McConkey, D. D. 1975. *MBO for Nonprofit Organizations*. New York: AMACON.
Morrissey, G. L. 1970. *Management by Objectives and Results*. Reading, Mass.: Addison-Wesley.

The following book contains one of the best treatments of peer review in medical care.

JACOBS, C. M.; CHRISTOFFEL, T. H.; and DIXON, N. 1976. *Measuring the quality of patient care.* Cambridge, Mass.: Ballinger.

Other materials are available from JCAH at:

875 North Michigan Avenue
Chicago, IL 60611

A helpful book for preparing objective goal statements whether GAS, MBO, or another system is chosen would be:

MAGER, R. F. 1972. *Goal analysis.* Belmont, Calif.: Fearon.

)

7

Nonexperimental Approaches to Outcome Evaluation

Chapter 6 was focused on the achievement of outcomes for individuals. Medical care, psychotherapy, and managerial achievement can often be evaluated using that approach. However, the measurement of individual outcomes and a comparison to individualized goals may not be a feasible approach to evaluation in many settings. A neighborhood crime prevention program, a new way of admitting patients to a hospital, and a class for diabetic senior citizens can be better evaluated using information describing group performance rather than measures of the degree to which specific individuals achieve goals. This chapter is the beginning of a major section of this text focused on the analysis of data gathered from groups for the purpose of the evaluation of the outcome of human service programs. The chapters begin with the simplest approaches and progress to the more complex and more scientifically rigorous. Each approach, regardless of its scientific rigor, has its place in program evaluation. However, the usefulness of a particular approach depends on the questions the evaluator is seeking to answer. As is indicated in the chapter titles, evaluators, when commissioned to learn *why* an outcome occurred, must use a more rigorous research design than when commissioned to show merely that clients leave a program at a certain level of competency or health.

As these chapters progress, the questions that each approach can address will be described and illustrated, as well as the misuses of each approach. The reader should develop a sense of the purpose of careful experimental design and see how each level of control is introduced to increase the clarity of the interpretation of the data.

SINGLE-GROUP DESIGNS

One Set of Observations

When teachers, nurses, administrators, or judges inquire into the success of some social service program, they frequently use the simplest form of outcome evaluation. Basically, they want to know how the program participants are faring after the service has been provided. Do the members of a job-training group have jobs three months after receiving job skills training? What percentage of smoking clinic participants are in fact not smoking one month after the program? The first step in deciding if a program seems useful is to learn if the participants finish the program with a level of achievement that matches the program's implicit or explicit goals. This simple form of evaluation requires that a set of systematic observations be made of one group at some specified time after completion of the program. This simple posttest-only assessment of outcome will show the staff and the evaluators whether the participants finish the program at a low, medium, or high level of achievement. For example, the rearrest rate for released first-time felons may be 5 percent, 15 percent, 30 percent, or 75 percent. If the program is to help ex-convicts avoid further trouble with the law but nearly all fail to do so, then there may be no need to evaluate outcome any further. Improvements should precede any further outcome evaluation. On the other hand, if program "graduates" do have a low rate of recidivism, the staff *may* have an effective program which should be studied more thoroughly. As a matter of fact, evaluators would not even know whether the program participants improved during the program. To learn whether people improved requires a more complex design.

One Group—Two Sets of Observations

If the question the evaluators are seeking to answer cannot be addressed through one set of observations made some time after the completion of the program, then the next more complex research design should be considered. The pretest-posttest design is used when the evaluators want to ascertain that the participants improved or at least did not deteriorate while being served by a program designed to help them. One cannot conclude that the program caused the improvement. The program might have caused the improvement; however, the pretest-posttest approach to data collection is not sufficient to permit such a conclusion.

The reasons why causal interpretations may not be permitted have been labeled "threats to internal validity" in the classic work by Campbell and Stanley (1963). *Internal validity* refers to the interpretability of the data in light of the way the observations were made. For example, showing that people who complete a reading program do indeed read well or, for that matter, better than a month before does not mean that the program itself led to the improvement. This caution is especially serious when only a small portion of those who began the program actually complete it. A plausible alternative interpretation is that the most motivated learned, but the program is unsuccessful for most people. In order to evaluate the adequacy of various approaches to outcome evaluation, a detailed understanding of the threats to internal validity is critical. As the reader will see, the posttest-only and the pretest-posttest approaches are very deficient in terms of internal validity. As more complex designs are presented, various plausible alternative interpretations will be eliminated until finally the only plausible cause of change is the human service program itself.

The questions that can be answered by simple, nonexperimental approaches to outcome evaluations are summarized in Figure 7.1. The bulk of this chapter is devoted to the appropriate uses of the pretest-posttest design and the reasons why care must be exercised when interpreting the results of pretest-posttest evaluations.

USES OF THE PRETEST-POSTTEST DESIGN

Did the Program Participants Change?

Before describing the various reasons unrelated to the program that may explain why participants change, the statistical tests necessary to show that they did change are presented. Statistical tests distinguish

FIGURE 7.1: Single-group evaluation designs and the questions that they can answer

Name and symbolization[a] of the evaluation design	Questions that can be answered
Posttest Only X O	How well are the participants functioning at the end of the program? Are minimum standards of outcome being achieved?
Pretest-Posttest O X O	Both of the above questions. How much do participants change during their participation in the program?

[a] *Throughout this text, the notation adopted by Campbell and Stanley (1963) will be used. The program is symbolized as X and an observation by O.*

between random variation and systematic variation. In other words, statistical methods permit us to decide whether the observed improvement between pretest and posttest is large enough to indicate that some real change occurred in the participants or whether the change is so small that it cannot be distinguished from such chance influences as the participants' health, mood, care in completing the forms, transient level of motivation, or liking for the interviewer. If unexplained chance variation is so large that one cannot be certain that participants did change, for whatever reason, there is no point to examine the data any further to learn whether the program could have affected the participants (Winch and Campbell 1969).

A Statistical Test for Continuous Variables. The required analysis depends on the nature of the measures of program success used. Frequently, evaluations employ measures yielding continuous scales. For example, measures of psychological or physical function (such as depression, academic achievement, or minutes of unassisted walking) are treated as continuous variables with equal intervals. Income level, length of employment, and credits for good prison behavior are further examples of variables that can be treated as continuous. For such variables, program success is indicated by the mean value attained by a group of participants.

The correct statistical test for the pretest-posttest evaluation design using continuous variables is the correlated-groups *t*-test (McCall 1975). This test is also called the matched-group *t*-test. This analysis is correct whenever the data from the pretest and the posttest are not independent, that is, each pretest value is associated with a posttest value. The most frequent use of this method occurs when the same people are tested before and after a program. No person makes a closer match with anyone than with him/herself. The Statistical Appendix at the end of this text includes a worked example of this statistical tool.

The major advantage of the correlated-groups t-test is a recognition that a person with a low pretest score can hardly be expected to achieve at the same level or to do as well as another person with a relatively high pretest. In a sense, this analysis tests whether the *changes* that were observed are reliably greater than zero. Such changes may occur when a person goes from a low pretest to a moderate posttest or from a moderate pretest to a high posttest, among other possibilities. The standard form of the t-test for randomly assigned independent groups is less likely to detect changes than the correlated-groups analysis.

Much more will be presented about statistical analysis in later chapters; however, the presentations are not a substitute for a statistics text. The statistical procedures are presented as a way to remind the reader about previous course work and as a way to help the reader apply statistical methods to program evaluation.

A Statistical Test for Categorical Variables. In some evaluations, program participants are classified into categories, such as employed or not, at home or in a nursing home, or rearrested or not. For categorization data, the measures of program success are best expressed as a proportion or a percentage. For example, program success could be expressed as: 57 percent are able to live independently; 68 percent are employed after job training; or 15 percent are back in jail after twelve months.

If the measure of success is a percentage or a proportion of the participants achieving some goal, then nonparametric tests are to be used. Suppose a program was designed to assist ex-convicts recently released from prison to obtain and retain employment. One measure of success of such a program would be an increase in the number of participants holding jobs. If 19 had jobs when the program began and 41 after two months in the program, the evaluators may wish to learn whether these numbers are reliably different. (Remember, finding a significant difference is only the first step in analysis. It means that the program *might* have caused a change, not that it did. A significant difference should be followed up with a more rigorous evaluation if a question of the cause of the change needs to be answered.)

Because these values refer to the same individuals, a nonparametric test applicable to a test-retest situation is needed. The McNemar test for the significance of changes (Siegel 1956) was designed for this purpose. To conduct this test, it is necessary to know the number of ex-convicts who had jobs before the program but lost them and the number who did not have jobs before but had jobs afterward. These are the people who changed, and clearly the program staff wants more participants to move from unemployed to employed rather than the reverse. Suppose that the program served 125 people and that the pre- and post-program employment status is as indicated in Figure 7.2. The 19 employed before the training (14 + 5) appear in the upper half of the table. The 41 employed after the program appear on the left half of the table (14 + 27). To test if more people gained jobs than lost them, the number of people in the lower left cell, 27, should reliably exceed the number in the upper right cell, 5. The McNemar test contrasts 27 with 5 using a χ^2 ($df = 1$) as follows:

$$\chi^2 = \frac{(27 - 5)^2}{(27 + 5)} = 15.12$$

Because this value exceeds the tabled χ^2 value (2.71), the evaluators may conclude that the increased number of employed program partici- pants was large enough to be reliable—more ex-convicts are indeed employed after the program than before. If there are three, four, or five levels of program success, there are other nonparametric tests that would be appropriate. Readers are directed to discussions of gamma and Spearman's rank-order correlation in Davis (1971) and McCall (1975), respectively.

Did the Participants Change Enough?

If the change from pretest to posttest is statistically significant, evalu- ators face another issue. That issue is whether the participants changed *enough* to demonstrate a real effect in their daily lives. Singh, Greer, and Hammond (1977) found that the outcome of a classroom program

FIGURE 7.2: Numbers of employed and unemployed before and after a job-training program for 125 ex-convicts[a]

	Employed after the program (N = 41)	Unemployed after the program (N = 84)
Employed before the program (N = 19)	14	5
Unemployed before the program (N = 106)	27	79

[a] *Illustrative data*

on civic responsibility was an increase of three points on a ninety-two-point attitude test. The authors concluded that the amount of change, although statistically significant, was not large enough to have a practical impact on the children's behavior.

If evaluators want program evaluation findings to have an impact on decisions, they will be sensitive to the issue of meaningful change, not just statistically significant change. Many texts on statistics do not devote much attention to the question of the actual size of the differences between two values. Consequently, many students feel their job is complete after they have performed a statistical test and found a statistically significant difference. Applied social scientists, however, cannot stop at the point of reporting a "significant" finding. The sponsors of human services want to know if the participants are in any *practical* way better for having participated in the program. It is true that these questions are easier to raise than to answer. However, these are important questions, and they will be answered by someone, perhaps by an administrator, a funding agency, or a newspaper reporter.

For in-house evaluators performing a simple evaluation, the best approach to use in addressing the question of importance of the findings is through consultation with the program staff *before* the evaluation is begun. After measures have been chosen, the staff can examine the variables and describe what minimum amount of success would please them. For example, would a job-training program staff be pleased if only 10 percent of trainees found employment after three months? Or would 25 percent be sufficient? Or 75 percent? Would a mental health program be satisfied if depressed clients improved five percentile points relative to norm values? Or would a fifteen-point improvement be required to feel that the improvement was satisfactory? In addition to the program staff, there are other groups who have an interest in the achievement of a program—community groups, funding agencies, and program participants are three important groups. The minimum amount of change necessary to define the outcome of a program as a success cannot be fully specified without a consideration of costs necessary to achieve that outcome. The relationship between the outcome and the costs of a program can be analyzed using the simple forms of cost-benefit and cost-effectiveness analyses discussed in Chapter 10.

Relating Change to Services
and Participant Characteristics

The discussion of the pretest-posttest design to this point has concentrated on methods to use in documenting the possible improvement of program participants. Another approach to evaluation is to relate the amount of service received to the degree of improvement observed.

Although such research may be open to the criticism that the results can be interpreted in various ways, it can be very useful in certain situations. For example, a very important study in the history of medical research followed the strategy of relating the patient's condition to amount of treatment received. In 1835, Pierre Louis (Eisenburg 1977) reported his study comparing the amount of blood let from patients with their progress in recovering from "inflammation" (pneumonia). Early nineteenth century medical theory led to the expectation that the more blood let, the better the treatment and the more likely a recovery. Louis measured the volume of blood drawn from the patients. He then compared these values to the course of their illnesses. He found that a patient's prognosis was not related to volume of blood taken. This finding was an important influence on medical practice of that time and contributed to the eventual discreditation of bloodletting as a form of medical treatment. Louis was unable to conclude anything about the cause of or the proper treatment of pneumonia, but he did identify a useless treatment.

Another reason to do an evaluation even if it is unable to identify the cause of change is to search for characteristics of the participants that might be related to achieving program goals. Do men experience better outcomes than women? Do members of minority groups complete the program as frequently as majority-group clients? Is age related to outcome? These questions can be explored, tentatively to be sure, using a simple research design. If policy-relevant relationships are found between outcome and a characteristic of participants, that variable would be involved in any future studies. The findings may even have immediate impact if a program appears to have a good effect on some segments of the target population but little effect on other segments.

Although it is quite easy to discuss the idea that personal and service characteristics may be related to success in a program, the statistical method of relating improvement to other variables is often misunderstood. The most intuitive approach is to subtract pretest scores from posttest scores, label the difference "improvement," and correlate the improvement scores with age, number of units of service received, and any other variables of interest. This "obvious" method is not desirable, and evaluators who use it have given themselves a handicap. When change between pretest and posttest is used as a variable, one is using a variable with a very large proportion of error. Change scores contain so much error because they are numerically small and are obtained from values that themselves include error. The greater the proportion of error, the less the likelihood of finding variables that reliably correlate with each other.

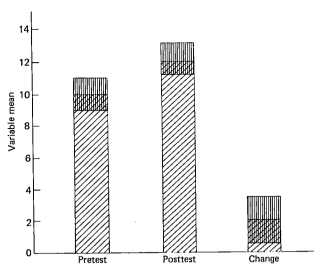

FIGURE 7.3: A graphic illustration of the large proportion of error in a change score compared to that found in the pretest and posttest scores. Note that although the mean change is quite small (diagonally shaded), the error in the change score (vertically shaded) is larger than the errors of the pretest or the posttest. (See Figure 7.4 for a numerical demonstration of these relationships.)

To illustrate the large proportion of error in change scores, assume that a pretest score is measured precisely and that all scores on the pretest equal ten. In a totally random fashion, add a plus or minus one to the values of that variable. Call this random addition "error." Now assume a posttest on which all people score twelve. Again, randomly add or subtract one from that variable. You can visualize the mean and the ±1 unit of variability around it as pictured in Figure 7.3.

Now subtract pretest from posttest. The mean of the difference, the change score, will equal two. However, the error will be even greater than the ±1 we added to each test score. The precise value of the random error is calculated in Figure 7.4. The essential point, however, can be appreciated by examining the size of error compared to the mean value of the change score. The variation of change scores (either defined as the variance or as the range between the mean change plus and minus the standard deviation) is larger than the mean change score. The reliability of such a change score is very low. Evaluators know that their instruments are not error-free and that they usually work with rather small levels of improvement. Using raw change scores with so much relative error will reduce the evaluator's effectiveness. Since dealing with change is important to the evaluator, it is fortunate that there is a better way.

	Error-free pretest	Error ±1	Pretest	Error-free posttest	Error ±1	Posttest	Raw change score
	10	+1	11	12	−1	11	0
	10	−1	9	12	+1	13	+4
	10	−1	9	12	−1	11	+2
	10	+1	11	12	+1	13	+2
	10	−1	9	12	+1	13	+4
	10	−1	9	12	−1	11	+2
	10	+1	11	12	−1	11	0
	10	+1	11	12	+1	13	+2
Means	10	0	10	12	0	12	2
Standard Deviations[a]	—	1.069	1.069	—	1.069	1.069	1.512

[a] *Using the unbiased formula, S.D.* $= \sqrt{\Sigma (X_i - \bar{X})^2/(N - 1)}$

The better way is to use *regressed change scores,* also called *residual change* (Nunnally 1975). That term sounds very complicated, but in practice it is not that difficult to apply. Recall the regression procedure presented in introductory statistics textbooks. One variable, X, is used to "predict" a second variable, Y. The word *predict* is in quotation marks to indicate that when the regression formula is being calculated, X and Y are *both* available for a sample of people. Thus, nothing is really being predicted; however, when regression techniques are used to relate X and Y, the term *predicted Y* is used. The general formula is written:

$$\hat{Y}_i = A + BX_i$$

The meaning of the terms is illustrated in Figure 7.5. For example, the equation of the regression line in the figure is: $\hat{Y}_i = 20 + 10X_i$. This means that for the hypothetical X and Y variables, the best[1] way to "predict" a person's Y score (for example, school grade point average) from X score (for example, ability test) is to multiply 10 times the X value and add 20 to it. The most likely Y score for a person with 6 on X is 20 plus the product of 10 times 6. $\hat{Y}$ equals 80. Not all people

[1] "Best" in this context means that the difference between $\hat{Y}_i$ and Y_i when squared and added up for every person is smaller than any other set of predicted Y_i scores derived from a linear (straight line) regression equation.

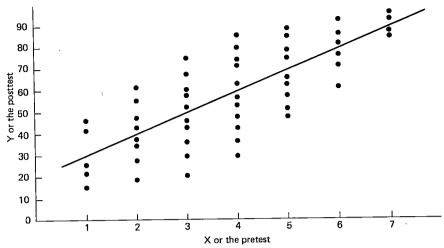

FIGURE 7.5: The solid line represents a regression line relating X to Y. The equation of the line as drawn is $\hat{Y}_i = 20 + 10X_i$.

scoring 6 on X will have actual Y values of 80. But 80 will be closer to the typical Y score for people whose X score equals 6 than the mean of Y. (If this presentation of regression includes ideas that are not familiar, the reader should go over regression in a statistics text.)

Regression equations can help in handling change scores. Treat the X variable as a pretest and the Y variable as a posttest. The pretest scores can be used to predict each person's posttest. The amount that each actual posttest differs from the predicted posttest (that is, those calculated from the regression equation) is an indication of the degree people benefit from the program. Those whose actual posttest scores, Y, are greater than their predicted scores, $\hat{Y}$, benefited more than the average, and those whose actual scores are lower benefited less than the average. The difference between Y_i and $\hat{Y}_i$ is a regressed change score. An example is given in Figure 7.6. This change score reflects the degree participants improved more than expected or less than expected on the basis of the pretest. For example, persons 2 and 5 benefited quite a bit while person 6 benefited least within this group.

The best way to search for characteristics of participants that led to better outcomes is to correlate[2] regressed change with whatever variables are suspected to facilitate improvements. For example, age could be correlated with regressed change to learn if older or younger people benefit more. Or, the mean regressed change score for men could be

[2] An example of the calculation of a correlation coefficient is contained in the Statistical Appendix at the end of this text.

compared to that for women to learn if gender is related to amount of change. To do this, regressed change scores would be calculated as in Figure 7.6, and the mean change score for men would be compared to the mean for women using a standard *t*-test.

To reiterate, sometimes analyses of change with one group of participants are conducted to learn whether change equaled or exceeded some predetermined goal. However, these analyses are usually conducted to learn if there was enough improvement to merit further investigation using the methods of Chapters 8 and 9. The reasons for caution in interpreting the meaning of change are described in the balance of this chapter.

THREATS TO INTERNAL VALIDITY

Once a statistically significant improvement has been found that is large enough to be nontrivial, evaluators need to eliminate explanations of the change that are not due to the program. For example, sixth-grade children will do better on a task requiring precise eye-hand coordina-

FIGURE 7.6: An example of pretest and posttest scores and the calculation of regressed change scores

Person (Number)	Pretest (X)	Posttest (Y)	Predicted posttest[a] ($\hat{Y}$)	Regressed change $(Y - \hat{Y})$
1	95	99	103.9	−4.9
2	90	106	100.4	+5.6
3	63	84	81.9	+2.1
4	69	85	86.0	−1.0
5	79	97	92.9	+4.1
6	68	77	85.3	−8.3
7	79	96	92.9	+3.1
8	70	87	86.7	+ .3
9	88	102	99.1	+2.9
10	98	102	105.9	−3.9
Means	79.9	93.5	93.5	.0[b]
Standard Deviations	12.3	9.6	8.5	4.5

[a] *Regression equation:* $\hat{Y}_i = 38.60 + .69X_i$

[b] *In the long run, the mean of regressed change scores should be zero. Therefore, the mean of a regressed change score has no meaning. The mean impact of the program is posttest mean minus pretest mean.*

tion than they did as second graders. Is this a result of primary school (the "program") or the result of maturation? Maturation is an alternative explanation that cannot be eliminated in this situation and one that forbids attributing the cause of the change solely to the effect of grade school education. Such alternative explanations of research results were labeled "threats to internal validity" by Campbell and Stanley (1963). As mentioned above, the reasons why participants achieve a certain level of outcome cannot be unambiguously attributed to the program when either a posttest-only or a pretest-posttest approach is used. However, it is important to know why these single-group approaches fail internal validity considerations. As this and the next two chapters progress, different methods will be described to eliminate plausible nonprogram explanations of change. When the nonprogram explanations are eliminated, then the cause of change can be attributed to the program.

Actual but Non-Program-Related Changes in the Participants

Two threats to internal validity refer to *real* changes that occur in program participants due to influences not related to the program. *Maturation* refers to natural changes in people that can be expected solely due to the passage of time. The most obvious example is a child growing older. *History* refers to events happening in the community, society, or even worldwide that will change the behavior of the participants of a program. Such events as an election, a recession, or a war may all influence the measures of program success.

Maturation. Children can perform more complex tasks simply because they get older, people get more tired the longer they have gone without sleep, and there are predictable general patterns to the developmental processes of adults and elderly people. If an evaluation utilizes variables that can be expected to change merely with the passage of time, maturation could be a plausible explanation for the changes that occur between the time of the pretest and the time of the posttest. In other words, the evaluator may well have found that real change occurred during the course of a program; however, the reason for the change is that the program lasted *x* number of months and thus the participants are *x* months older and *x* months more experienced, not that the participants gained anything from the program.

The existence of maturation-based changes does not mean that maturation is the *only* explanation of the changes observed. Nor do plausible, alternative hypotheses mean that the program had no effect.

Interpretations would be .easier if the evaluator could learn how much of the change was due to maturation and how much due to the program. Using the pretest-posttest design, this separation cannot be made. Methods to estimate the change due to maturation involve testing other groups of participants or potential participants and testing over a greater number of time periods.

History. History refers to any specific event that occurs between the pretest and the posttest that affects the people in the program. For example, a recession may make even the most well-designed program to help people find jobs look like a dud. On the other hand, an economic recovery would make a similar ·but poorly run program look like a winner. These concurrent national economic changes are plausible alternate interpretations of any changes found among the participants of employment programs. All nonprogram events or series of events that affect the participants would provide plausible alternative explanations.

Some of the same approaches used to account for maturational effects can help isolate historical effects: test additional groups and test at additional times. However, maturation is more predictable and stable than is history. Unexpected events can occur at any time or may not occur at all during a given evaluation. Evaluators should be sensitive to societal or organizational changes that may affect an evaluation. In addition, Cook and Campbell (1976) discuss the influence of events occurring in a particular group under the term *local history*. Events such as a member being involved in a staff feud, the presence of a particularly influential individual in a program group, or a local community disaster cannot be accounted for by any evaluation research design unless the evaluation is replicated a number of times in different settings.

Who Was Observed

Three threats to internal validity must be considered when the participants in a program are not a random or representative sample of the people who might benefit. These three threats are called *selection, mortality,* and *regression.*

Selection. Participation in a human service program is voluntary. Even when prisoners or parolees are forced to participate, the level of meaningful participation is voluntary. Thus, the people obtaining a service are different from those not obtaining it. In the posttest-only form of evaluation, the process of self-selection may mean that the participants were already quite healthy when they began the program.

The fact that the posttest detects a desirable state tells the staff nothing about the effectiveness of the program. It is true that sometimes an evaluation of a program is based only on the end result of the people completing the program. Clearly, these individuals chose to complete the program and do not represent the effect of the program on all for whom the program was designed.

The pretest-posttest approach to evaluation is much stronger in controlling the unwanted effects of self-selection. By measuring the participants before the program, the possible change can be documented. Centra (1977) has reported that the college teachers most likely to be involved in faculty development programs are "good teachers who want to be better." After a faculty development program, most of these teachers, the program participants, will be quite good teachers. Their competence will tell us nothing about the quality of the program because these teachers were good to start with. However, observations of their achievements before the program will permit an estimation of the amount of improvement.

Mortality. The posttest-only design is also inadequate when participant drop out is a problem. People differ in whether they will begin a program (selection), and they differ in whether they will complete a program (drop out). Campbell and Stanley (1963) use the term *mortality* to refer to dropping out of a program for whatever reason. Students drop courses they do not like or find too challenging, people in therapy quit when they learn that personal growth is hard, and in medical settings some patients in programs do actually die.

The level of achievement observed at the end of a program may indicate how well the program functioned, how good the people were when they started, or how motivated the people were who stayed until the end. As a general rule, those who stay are more prepared for the program than are those who drop out. Failing students are more likely to drop a course than are those earning B's and A's. Patients who die were probably the least likely to benefit from a health care program. Without a pretest, the evaluator will not know how much dropping out there was nor what sort of individuals dropped out. A director of a small drug user program informally mentioned that his program had a 90 percent success rate. Upon inquiry, however, it was learned that only about 10 percent of those who start the program are there at the end. Having success with 9 out of the 100 people who begin the program gives a markedly different impression from saying the program has a 90 percent success rate.

As with selection, the pretest-posttest design handles participant mortality fairly well. By pretesting, the evaluators know who has dropped out and how they compared to those who remained. The pretest-posttest design enables evaluators to know when high preprogram achievement and participant drop out are not plausible explanations of the good level of outcome observed at the end of the program.

Regression. The threat to internal validity labeled *regression to the mean* is one of the hardest threats to understand. This is true probably because some statistical thinking is required to understand this threat. However, like most basic statistics many people already understand regression to the mean at a conceptual level even though they may not apply it consistently.

Kahneman and Tversky (1974) report that airplane pilot trainers have a practice that illustrates how people can be misled by the effects of regression. If you think carefully about the example, you will see what regression means and why its effects are often undetected. It is said that after a particularly good landing, the trainers do not compliment the trainee because when such a compliment is given the next landing is usually done less well. On the other hand, after a poor landing the trainers severely reprimand the trainee in order to elicit a better landing on the next try. It is clear that the empirical observations are true—complimented exceptionally good landings are often followed by less good ones, and reprimanded bad landings are often followed by better ones. However, let us see why the compliments and the reprimands have nothing to do with the quality of the following landing.

Imagine learning a complex task. Initially, performance level fluctuates—sometimes better, sometimes worse. What goes into the better performances? At least two things: the degree of skill achieved, and luck or chance. Flight trainees know they should touch the plane down with the nose up but they do not yet sense the precise moment to lower the wing flaps and at the same time adjust the elevators to achieve the proper touch–down angle (Caidin 1960). Sometimes they do it too soon, and sometimes too late. Because these errors are largely chance, the likelihood of doing everything correctly at the precise second for two consecutive landings is low. Similarly, the likelihood of badly estimating the precise instant two times in a row is also low. Therefore, the likelihood of two consecutive good landings is low for pilot trainees. In other words, an observer (or a trainer) should *not* expect two consecutive good landings by a novice trainee, regardless of what is said or not said by the trainer.

The essentials of the effects of regression to the mean can be further illustrated with a rather silly but instructive example. Choose twenty pennies and flip each six times, recording the number of heads out of the six flips for each penny. Select the penny that produced the most "excessive" heads (five or six heads can be considered excessive). Reprimand the penny for producing too many heads. Then flip that penny six more times to see if the reprimand had the desired effect. If the penny yields fewer heads than it did during the first set of six flips, the penny is behaving in the way it was urged to behave. On the average, the reprimand will appear to have been effective 98 percent of the time if the penny originally produced six out of six heads and 89 percent of the time if the first result had been five out of six heads. Knowledge of the binomial distribution permits the calculation of these percentages (Hays 1963).

In summary, regression to the mean warns that whenever a performance level is extreme, the next performance is likely to be less extreme. This principle applies to emotional adjustment just as well as to learning to fly airplanes and flipping pennies. If the people who currently are the most depressed are included in a therapy group, it is very likely that in three months they will be as a group less depressed. This does not mean they will be at a healthy level of adjustment. Most likely, they will still be more depressed than the general population. However, some of the transient random events that caused the worst depression will have passed, and as a group the most depressed people will be less depressed than they were before.

Is regression a threat to the internal validity of the pretest-posttest evaluation design? Not necessarily, but it often is. If individuals who are representative of some intact group are tested before and after a program, then regression is not a problem for evaluations following this evaluation design. For example, if all children in a school are given a special reading curriculum, regression will not be a threat to internal validity. However, if only the children reading at the lowest levels on the pretest are included, regression will be a threat to the correct interpretation of a pretest-posttest change. The reasons children are low in a single test include poor reading skills, but the reasons also include such chance things as poor guessing, breaking a pencil point, having a cold, misunderstanding directions, worrying about a sick sister, or planning recess games. A day, a week, or a semester later on a second test, these events will not be experienced by exactly the same individuals. On the average, these retest scores will be higher than those on the first test for the children who previously had scored the worst. Also, these retest scores will be lower for those who previously scored the best.

Regression is often a plausible alternate hypothesis for pretest-posttest change when human service programs are aimed at those people who are in need of help. Remedial programs are not prepared for everyone, but rather for those who have fallen behind: reading very poorly, earning a low income, feeling emotional distress, and so forth. Sometimes, a screening test to select people for the program is also used as the pretest in an evaluation plan. For example, students reading the most poorly on a test are placed in a reading-improvement program, and a second administration of the same test or a parallel form is compared to the preprogram test scores. This is a poor practice because regression is a very plausible alternate explanation for at least part of the improvement. Improvement in such an evaluation cannot be interpreted. On the other hand, if poor readers or troubled clients get worse (that is, go downhill when regression effects were likely to improve their level), then the evaluation can be interpreted. The correct interpretation is that the program has failed.

The Methods of Obtaining Observations

There are two additional plausible hypotheses discussed by Campbell and Stanley: *testing* and *instrumentation* effects. At times, these can make the interpretations of outcome evaluations ambiguous. These threats to interpretation are generated by the evaluators themselves and their observation methods.

Testing. The effect of testing refers to changes in behavior due to the observation techniques. First, two administrations of a test or survey may differ simply as a function of the respondent's increased familiarity with the tool at the second administration. Ability scores increase reliably on the second administration for people unfamiliar with the test (Anastasi 1976). People interviewing for jobs gain from the experience and can present themselves better on subsequent interviews.

A second aspect of the effects of testing is called *reactivity*. People behave differently when they know they are being observed, compared to when there is no observer or when people are not aware of an observer. This concept was discussed previously in Chapter 3; however, it is worth recalling the principle. Clients, patients, prisoners, school children, and so on, will be affected when they know someone is recording their behavior, opinions, or feelings. Observation techniques vary in how reactive they are.

The pretest-posttest design is clearly weak in the control of testing effects. If program participants were unfamiliar with the observation procedures, they could change by the second test. The direction of change that should be expected due to repeated testing does not seem clear except for ability and achievement tests, on which improvement is usually expected. The research design itself does not create reactivity if both pretest and posttest can be done in an equivalent and non-reactive fashion.

Instrumentation. The last threat to internal validity to be discussed refers to the use of measurement procedures themselves. Most college instructors know they are not totally consistent when grading essay examinations. There is a real potential for standards to change as the instructor becomes familiar with written examinations. The standards may become higher or lower.[3] If a pretest-posttest design uses measures that are not thoroughly objective, it would be wise not to score the pretest until after the posttest is administered. Then shuffle the tests together and have them scored by someone who does not know which are pretests and which are posttests.

If the measures require observations that must be made before and after the program, the examiners may become more and more skilled as they gain experience. Thus, the posttests may go much more smoothly than the pretests. If so, a change in instrumentation becomes a viable alternative to concluding that the program had an effect. In such situations, the examiner will be most effective if highly experienced before the pretest is administered.

The Interactions of These Threats

Over and above the influences of these seven threats to internal validity, it is possible for our interpretations to be confused by the joint influence of two of these threats. For example, the parents who seek out special educational opportunities for their children (self-selection) may have children who are developing more rapidly than those of parents who do not seek special help for their children (different rates of maturation). This situation would be called a selection-by-maturation interaction. More will be said about this threat when more complex evaluation designs are discussed in later chapters.

. *Summary.* The threats to internal validity refer to reasons why an observed change may not be caused by the program or human service that the group obtained between the pretest and the posttest. Internal validity is thus the most basic concern of evaluators who are examining

---

[3] A way to minimize these changes is to read all answers before assigning any grades. Only then are grades assigned. When there are a number of questions, there is a way to minimize the effect of the instrumentation change. Grade all answers to the first question, shuffle the papers and grade all answers to the second question, and so on. Even if standards change, the likelihood of individual total test scores being systematically affected is very low.

whether a program was responsible for the observed improvement.[4] As noted above, obtaining strong evidence of causal relationships is not the sole reason for conducting an evaluation. However, if evidence for causality is needed and if there are plausible explanations based on the types of influences just described, the evaluator may well avoid conducting an evaluation using these basic designs.

CHANCE AND CREATIVITY
IN SINGLE-GROUP DESIGNS

Threats to internal validity summarize why some data collection procedures forbid interpretations of a causal connection between the program and the observed condition of those who received the program. The ways the data are analyzed can also create misinterpretations. Taking advantage of chance and developing creative interpretations can make an evaluation appear insightful when it is not. Because evaluators want to conduct valid research, being aware of these misleading practices is important.

Students and professionals not experienced in research methodology often engage in a practice that fosters inaccurate conclusions. This is the practice of "fishing" for statistically significant relationships among a large number of outcome variables and variables describing the people (such as sex, age, ethnic background). Fishing is often done by repeatedly subdividing the sample of program participants and comparing the ad hoc groups on the outcome measures. For example, if participants are divided by gender and the means of the outcome measures of the two groups are compared, then divided on the basis of age, then ethnic background, and so forth, some of the comparisons will reveal differences that may indeed be significant but just by chance. Finding significant differences just by chance is what is meant by *Type I error*. If a large number of relationships are studied, some will appear to be strong, just as flipping a large number of coins six times each will reveal that certain coins appear to be biased toward heads or tails. The same coins, if retested by flipping them six more times each, will be found to be unbiased. Unfortunately, when performing evaluations, new observations cannot be obtained as easily as flipping coins several additional times.

The second reason erroneous, chance relationships are not discovered is that *once the data are examined* the evaluator or the program

---

[4] If there is no "improvement," there usually is nothing to explain, except in rare circumstances where a loss of function is expected without intervention. A program for arthritic patients is an example of a service in which the goal is to avoid deterioration. Such programs hope at best to maintain abilities, not to cure.

staff can usually make sense out of the results. Once a young graduate student presented a senior professor with findings that seemed markedly at variance with the professor's own research.[5] The professor quickly interpreted the results in a way that coincided nicely with the professor's work. A week later, the student discovered that the computer program was malfunctioning and the initial results were meaningless. This anecdote has a happy ending because when the results were correctly analyzed they were as originally expected, quite compatible with previous work. The point to remember is that reasonably creative people can make sense out of nearly any finding *once the information is presented.* This ability, coupled with the practice of gathering many variables and "fishing" for results, can lead to erroneous findings that appear to be well thought out.

A nearly foolproof manner of discovering which results are simply Type I errors is to repeat the research. In controlled laboratory social science research, replication is not that difficult. However, because program evaluation often disrupts the service setting, it is seldom replicated. A more practical approach involves collecting only the information that can be used and having rational or theoretical reasons for the planned analyses. In addition, unexpected findings are best treated as very tentative, especially if they are embedded in a large number of analyses that are statistically nonsignificant. Finally, be very suspicious of surprising findings that require a number of assumptions or elaborate theorizing to understand. The professor mentioned above was only able to interpret the computer-generated nonsense results by making elaborate and novel, although plausible, assumptions.

USEFULNESS OF SINGLE-GROUP DESIGNS

When there are minimum standards for the outcome of a human service program and when the participants do not drop out, the pretest-posttest design may serve the needs of the program's manager to document the program's success. However, even when standards are not available, the reader should not gain the impression that these approaches do not have any legitimate uses. These single-group designs are less intrusive and less expensive than more ambitious designs and require far less effort to complete than the methods described in later chapters. Thus, these designs can serve a very important function in the evaluator's toolbox as first steps in planning rigorous program evaluations. There are at least three purposes that single-group evaluations serve: (1) to

[5] The first author of this book was the student, but the senior professor must remain anonymous.

assess the likely usefulness of more rigorous evaluations; (2) to search for promising variables related to success in the program; and (3) to "soften up" the facility for more rigorous evaluation in the future.

Assessing the Usefulness of Further Evaluations

Before embarking on a rigorous plan that will control for all the plausible alternate interpretations, a single-group design would serve to show whether there is any improvement to interpret. If no program participants have jobs for which they were trained, it is likely that no further research is needed to evaluate a job-training program. The program failed, period. No statistical analyses are necessary. If participants finished at a good level, the pretest-posttest design may show that the people improved during the program. This finding may well satisfy some users of program evaluation reports. Also, the finding of reliable improvement may justify a more complex evaluation. Lenihan (1977) used a simple design as a first step in learning whether the use of the phone helped pretrial defendents to raise bond. Showing that 22 percent of the defendents who used a phone that was available on an experimental basis did raise bail suggested that a more rigorous evaluation could be worth the expense. Had only 2 or 3 percent been able to raise bail, the possible effect of the phone would have been very small and no further study would have been done.

Correlating Improvement with Other Variables

The use of the pretest-posttest design and the calculation of regressed change scores permits change to be related to the amount of service obtained and to characteristics of the program participants. It may be that a program offered to a very needy population primarily benefits people who are relatively well-off. Thus, the good achievement found by a posttest design was due to the already-competent people who selected themselves for the program. If so, further work is unnecessary. On the other hand, the good level at the end of the program may really indicate a general improvement in most participants. Perhaps the improvement is due to the impact of the program. Further work would be merited.

Preparing the Facility for Further Evaluation

A third reason for conducting an evaluation using only the program participants as respondents is to help staff accept the idea of evaluation. As described in earlier chapters, human service providers, from para-

professional counselors to teachers to physicians, are only now beginning to recognize that their work can and will be evaluated. This
realization does not come easily because the quality of human services
is hard to quantify. However, if evaluators begin their work with less
threatening approaches, they have better chances of leading service
providers to see the usefulness of evaluation and to value the contribution of evaluators.

The methods described in this chapter and the previous one are
among the least threatening. There is no possibility that the research
could show that unserved people do as well as people who got the
service—a very frightening possibility to staff members. There are studies
indicating that in some situations people who receive counseling are
not much better off than similar people not counseled (see Ellsworth
1975, p. 242). However, evaluators who suggest that counseling does
not work are not going to find that the counseling staff readily welcomes
their services. Less threatening but still an unwelcome possibility is the
finding that an alternative service is just as beneficial to program participants. If the alternative service is less expensive, a comparison of
people in the two groups could create anxiety for the staff of the more
expensive program. This anxiety will be manifested in roadblocks to
the study, hostility, and general uncooperativeness.

Just this type of response occurred during an in-house evaluation of
a hospital program. The director of the program was very cooperative
in initiating and implementing a study of the patients in his program.
He displayed considerable openness to evaluation saying such things as,
"Maybe we don't help people as much as we think we do—we should
know that," and, "If a patient is institutionalized after leaving here, we
have failed." However, when the evaluators proposed increasing the
rigor of the evaluation by gathering data from a neighboring hospital
without a similar program, the director seemed to change his position.
Such a comparison could conceivably have shown that similar patients
regained as much ability as those in the director's expensive program.
He now said, "The additional data was unnecessary since the value
of these programs was well-known and fully documented." The expanded
study went on anyway. His negative attitudes dissolved when it became
clear that the neighboring hospital had surprisingly few patients of the
necessary diagnosis and those who were available were much milder
than those served in the program. Because the two groups of patients
were not compatible, the study could not threaten the program. Co-
operativeness and cordial relations returned.

Rational resource use requires that ultimately such comparative
studies be done. But they should not be done in a way that leaves the
staff demoralized or bitter. In-house evaluators who try to force

methodologically rigorous evaluations on staff and who are unable to
see the value of approaches with less-than-precise experimental control
will find their work undervalued and their influence on the program
diminished. Beginning in a nonthreatening way permits evaluators to
gain the confidence of staff members. We do not intend to devalue the
more rigorous approaches. The point stressed here is that less rigorous
studies can serve several purposes and are useful.

SUMMARY

There are two major emphases presented in this chapter. First, a careful
understanding of the needs of the users of an evaluation may indicate
that a simple research design is able to serve quite well to answer these
needs at a particular time. Evaluators perform unnecessary work when
they insist on giving users more than they want or can use. The second
major emphasis concerns the conceptual tools useful to understand why
simple single-group evaluation designs cannot answer certain questions
often important to administrators and those responsible for financial
support of a program. These conceptual tools have been called "threats
to internal validity" and have become part of the vocabulary of social
scientists in the past decade. Evaluators are able to analyze their work
using this conceptual scheme to select the research design most appropriate to answer the questions put to them by those needing services
and programs evaluated.

STUDY QUESTIONS

1. Not many years ago when a child had frequent bouts of sore
throat, family doctors recommended removing the child's tonsils.
Typically, the child's health improved afterwards. If parents and
doctors attributed the improved health to the effects of the operation, what threats to internal validity are ignored?

2. Some fifty elementary school children witnessed a brutal murder
on the way to school in a suburb of a large city. The school officials
worked with a social worker, a school psychologist, and others in an
attempt to help the children deal with their emotions, to avoid
long-term ill effects, and to help parents with their children. A year
after the tragedy, there appeared to be no serious aftereffects. Was
the program a success? What reasons support your answer?

3. Watch newspapers and news programs for instances in which the
reporter's approach to drawing conclusions is, in essence, a posttest-
only research design. For example, find reports similar to the one

described in question number 2. What threats to internal validity were ignored in the reports you found?

4. Politicians are notorious for attributing any improvements in government affairs to their own efforts and any deteriorating affairs to the policies of others. Find or recall examples. What threats to internal validity are most typically operating in government affairs?

5. Why can a smoking control clinic be evaluated using a one-group pretest-posttest study? It is also possible to gather useful post-treatment data to evaluate the program. What index of success could be used to summarize effectiveness if participants can be observed only after the program?

FURTHER READING

Internal validity is discussed more fully in the following works.

CAMPBELL, D. T., and STANLEY, J. C. 1963. *Experimental and quasi-experimental designs for research.* Chicago: Rand-McNally.

COOK, T. D., and CAMPBELL, D. T. 1976. The design and conduct of quasi-experiments and true experiments in field settings. In *Handbook of industrial and organizational research,* ed. M. D. Dunnett. Chicago: Rand-McNally.

For a review of Type I errors that often occur when "fishing" randomly for relationships and a review of regression principles, see any statistics textbook. The book listed below is a well-received introductory text.

McCALL, R. B. 1975. *Fundamental statistics for psychology.* 2nd ed. New York: Harcourt Brace Jovanovich.

Regressed change scores are discussed thoroughly in this chapter by Nunnally.

NUNNALLY, J. C. 1975. The study of change in evaluation research: Principles concerning measurement, experimental design, and analysis. In *Handbook of evaluation research,* vol. 1, ed. E. L. Struening and M. Guttentag. Beverly Hills, Calif.: Sage.

CASE STUDY 7.1

A Program for Psychosomatics

To avoid appearing overly critical of the work of others, the first case study is from the authors' own research. The report is excerpted from an evaluation of an inpatient program for psychosomatic individuals in acute need of medical treatment. The essence of the pretest-posttest design is illustrated. Readers ought to be able to find numerous weaknesses in this case study related to uncontrolled threats to internal validity. The original evaluation controlled for some of these weaknesses because it included more variables, a comparison group, an additional testing time, and a consideration of costs. Nevertheless, even this simplified version of the study could have provided unit managers and hospital administrators with some basic information; the unit was well-received by many patients, and they as well as their spouses felt improvement was experienced.

EVALUATION OF THE MEDICAL ECOLOGY PROGRAM

Raymond G. Carey and Emil J. Posavac

Summary and Conclusion

The major issue of the evaluation concerned whether the patients in the Medical Ecology Program (MEP) improved in their psychological functioning. Multiple measures were used, and all indicated improvement. In answer to direct questions about the benefit they received, about 80 percent of the patients who completed the program said they received much benefit and were glad they participated in the program. All self-descriptive measures by the patients (such as anxiety, depression, fatigue) indicated substantial improvement between admission and the ninety-day follow-up. Physicians and program counselors agreed that there was substantial improvement in the level of psychological functioning. Significant others (usually spouses) reported some improvement from admission to follow-up, although not as much improvement as the patients reported.

A second issue dealt with how much program patients improved as compared to similar patients who received other modes of treatment. Normative data were available for the rating scales used by the significant others describing the changes that occurred in outpatients receiving psychotherapy. The patients who completed the program changed on the average as much as the patients represented in these change norms.

On the basis of this limited study, the MEP appears to serve a population of patients who respond favorably to the program and who show improvement to the same extent as patients receiving psychotherapy only.

Background

The ecology program. The Medical Ecology Program was developed to serve the needs of people with physical dysfunctions whose medical treatment is "impeded or complicated by emotional factors." In addition, the unit serves psychiatric patients with somatopsychic illnesses who need acute medical treatment and other patients who have emotional difficulty in accepting or adjusting to their illnesses provided they require acute medical care.

Patients in the program receive medical care as other hospital medical patients, and they participate in the three-week program. The program consists of: (1) twice-weekly lecture/discussions on the relationships between emotions and health; (2) twice-weekly medical lectures; (3) weekly religious discussion/lecture sessions; (4) weekly movie/discussions; (5) twice-weekly group counseling/psychotherapy; (6) thrice-weekly individual counseling/psychotherapy; and (7) therapeutic recreation and occupational therapy three to five times per week. There are additional services available as needed. Spouses and family members are included in a weekly orientation program.

Every patient is assigned to one of several program counselors who is responsible for the patient's participation in and understanding of the program. Program counselors provide the inpatient counseling/psychotherapy sessions and plan for outpatient follow-up services.

The purpose of the study. The JCAH medical audit system[6] used at the hospital selects patient charts for peer review on the basis of a disease entity or the type of procedure used. Special programs serving a wide variety of diagnoses, such as the MEP does, are not compatible with the JCAH audit system. Therefore, a specially prepared evaluation was requested for the MEP. Because the major thrust of the program focused on improved psychological functioning, the evaluation focused on those goals. Quality of medical care was not examined.

Method

The authors met with the director and the staff of the MEP during the late summer and fall of 1975. These meetings familiarized the authors with the goals of the program, which are largely reflected in the Outpatient Progress Report sent to the physicians of participants in the Outpatient Program. These goals include: reductions in anxiety, relief from depression, improved self-image, increased sense of responsibility, improved family life, and decreased concern with medical condition.

[6] The JCAH approach is described in Chapter 6 of this volume.

Selection of measures. The discussion of goals resulted in agreement on the selection of research instruments to measure success in achieving program goals. The measures included:

The Profile of Mood States (POMS) for use at admission and follow-up.
A specially constructed Patient Survey for use at discharge and follow-up.
The Global Assessment Rating Scale (GARS) for use at admission and discharge.
The Personal Adjustment and Role Skill (PARS) for use at admission and follow-up.

As can be seen, multiple measures were used to gather data from a variety of sources—the patient, relatives, and professionals. These instruments and the times at which they were administered are described in the following paragraphs. [The original report described the measures at this point.]

Collection of data. Patients were asked to provide data at admission, discharge, and ninety days after discharge. Within a day or two after admission, the unit secretary gave the admission surveys to the program counselor, who asked the patient to complete the surveys. All of the measures listed above except GARS and PARS were included in this packet. A blank GARS form for the physician was placed in the patient's chart, and the program counselors completed GARS forms as soon as they became acquainted with their patients. The spouse or other appropriate relative was asked by the program counselor to complete the pretreatment PARS scales. If the relative could not be contacted personally, the PARS form was mailed.

At discharge, the MEP patients responded to a number of direct questions about their experiences on the unit. The physician and program counselor were again each asked to complete the GARS.

Ninety days after discharge, the former patients were mailed the same set of measures completed at admission and the direct questions about their participation in the program. The person completing the pretreatment PARS was mailed the post-treatment form. Follow-up telephone calls were made by the Office of Evaluation and Research to those patients and relatives who did not return the material within ten days.

Description of the patients. Patients admitted to MEP between June 1 and November 30, 1976 were eligible for the study. During these months there were 112 program patients and 92 nonprogram patients on the unit. Of the 69 patients who agreed to participate, 63 completed the admission materials, 58 completed the discharge survey, and 38 the follow-up materials. Of the 69 patients who provided at least some information, most were women (84 percent) and middle-aged (median age $=$ thirty-eight years). A large minority (42 percent) were taking anti-anxiety medication, 23 percent were prescribed major tranquilizers, and 29 percent were prescribed anti-depressants. The length of stay ranged from three to sixty-six days. The median stay equaled the program's planned length, twenty-one days.

The sixty-nine MEP patients in the study were 62 percent of the program patients during the period of the study. The forty-three program patients not represented either refused to participate or were discharged soon after admission. These forty-three unrepresented program patients and the ninety-two nonprogram patients averaged approximately seven days on the unit.

Results: Do the Patients Improve?

Direct questions about the MEP. Figure 7.7 contains the percentage of patients who responded favorably when asked about their experiences in the MEP. Nearly nine out of ten patients reported they were glad they participated in the program. The patients also believed they learned much about their physical symptoms and emotional lives (79 percent). The table shows that the positive feelings about the program held up over the three-month period between discharge and follow-up.

Patient self-descriptions. Figure 7.8 contains the various self reports of the patients. Substantial improvement in mood including anxiety and depression can be seen when admission and follow-up levels are compared. This improvement is not an artifact caused by the drop out of respondents from admission to discharge because the correlated-groups *t*-tests were used. This analysis used only the data from those who

FIGURE 7.7: Percentage of patients responding favorably about their experiences in the Medical Ecology Program (MEP)

	Time of report	
Survey item	Discharge (N = 58)	Three-month follow-up (N = 37)
GLAD they participated in the program	88%	86%
Reporting MUCH benefit from the program	78%	70%
Reporting MUCH relief from presenting medical symptoms	50%	47%
Reporting having learned MUCH about physical symptoms and emotions	79%	73%
Reporting the ultimate causes of their physical problems were half or more emotional	86%	81%

FIGURE 7.8: Means of the self-report and relative-completed measures

	Time of rating	
	Admission	*Follow-up*
Self-report using POMS		
Tension-anxiety	18.6	10.9**
Depression	23.3	10.5**
Anger-hostility	12.0	8.0*
Vigor	11.0	14.7**
Fatigue	14.4	8.5**
Confusion	12.3	7.7**
Evaluation by relatives using the PARS scales		
Interpersonal relations	13.6	14.2
Anxiety-depression	13.9	9.7*
Confusion	11.8	9.3*
Alcohol/drugs	5.5	4.9
Household management	12.0	13.7
Relationship to children	12.1	10.0
Outside social	6.2	8.1*
Employment	6.9	5.9

Note: Means showing better adjustment are underlined. Sixty–three patients filled out the POMS at admission, 38 at the follow-up. Fifty–three spouses completed the PARS at admission, 26 at the follow-up; however, scales that are gender-specific were answered by fewer spouses.

* $p < .05$

** $p < .01$

completed both the admission and follow-up ratings. If at all misleading, Figure 7.8 may slightly underestimate the amount of improvement reported by the patients.

Evaluation of improvement by others. The evaluation of the patients' psychological improvement as made by others is not as consistent as that indicated by the direct questions or the self-descriptions. Figure 7.8 contains the mean ratings from the PARS scales at admission and at follow-up. On all but one PARS scale, the change is toward better adjustment; however, there are only few changes that are large enough to achieve statistical significance. The anxiety-depression scale shows a sizable drop, and the confusion and the outside (of home) social scales also show some improvement. Relationship to children indicated a slight worsening. The other differences were not large enough to be viewed as reliable. Overall, the relatives did report less anxiety and depression, but they did not report the thorough improvement that was shown in the self-report measures.

The global psychological functioning rating by the physicians and the program counselors showed substantial and highly significant improvement. At admission patients were rated at about fifty, indicating that approximately half were viewed as having moderate symptoms causing some difficulty in functioning and about half as having serious symptomatology requiring treatment. The GARS discharge ratings in the sixties described patients with "mild symptoms" who are generally functioning well and who would not be considered sick by untrained people.

How Much Do MEP Patients Improve Compared to Similar Patients?

It seems clear that MEP patients improve. A further question concerns the amount of improvement relative to other patients who are treated differently. One approach to answering this question was available. The manual for the PARS scales provides change norms. "Change norms" give the follow-up PARS ratings that can be expected for all possible admission ratings. Using the change norms, one can determine if the amount of change reported by the relatives of the MEP patients is more or less than that observed in other populations. Without going into detail, the improvements observed for the MEP patients are quite similar to that found among either outpatient psychiatric clinic patients or hospitalized psychiatric patients.

CASE STUDY 7.2

Toilet Training Children

When the behavior of people who do not receive a program is well-known, an evaluator need not conduct an evaluation of any more complexity than a pretest-posttest design. In this case study, the common frustration of parents seeking to toilet-train their children was evidence that a rapid method of training children would be an improvement over standard practices.

DRY PANTS: A RAPID METHOD OF TOILET TRAINING CHILDREN *

R. M. Foxx and N. H. Azrin

Although all normal children seem to learn eventually to toilet train themselves, parental "common sense" procedures have resulted in no more benefit than has occurred without training. For example, Madsen et al. (1969) found that parental training for one month reduced accidents by only 5 percent, which is about the same insignificant decrease that they obtained without any toilet training. In view of this failure of training efforts, the common attitude of permissiveness regarding toileting (Spock 1968) is understandable and justified. One can understand why this permissive view of toilet training as an exercise in futility has recurred about every decade for the past sixty years.

Recently, a method has been developed for rapidly training the retarded to toilet train themselves without prompting (Azrin, Sneed, and Foxx 1973). The success of those efforts indicated that similar and even more rapid training might be achieved with normal children by use of that general method. The present study evaluated a modification of that method with a group of nonretarded children.

Method

Children. Thirty-four children were selected for training, twenty-two boys and twelve girls. Because the training procedure required the child to be capable of responding to verbal instructions, a screening test was devised for ascertaining a potential trainee's instructional responsiveness.

General rationale. The general method was to provide an intensive learning experience that maximized the factors known to be important for learning; then to fade out these factors once learning had occurred. The learning factors maximized were a distraction-free environment, a large number of trials, consideration of the component responses, operant reinforcement for correct responses, a variety of reinforcers, quality of the reinforcers, frequency of reinforcement, manual guidance, verbal instruction, immediacy of reinforcement, immediacy of detection of incorrect responses, and negative reinforcement for the incorrect response.[7]

* Condensed with permission from *Behavior Research and Therapy,* 11 (1973); 435–42. Copyright 1973, Pergamon Press, Ltd.
[7] A lengthy discussion of the program has been omitted in this condensation.

Results

Reduction of accidents. Figure 7.9 shows the number of accidents before and after training for the 34 children. The mothers had recorded the number of accidents by counting the number of times the child had to be changed each day during the week preceding and following training. Following training, the parents were contacted every month for four months by telephone or by a personal visit from one of the trainers. Prior to training, the children averaged about six accidents per day per child. Within the first post-training week, accidents had decreased by 97 percent to 0.2 accidents per day per child, or about one per week. This near-zero level of accidents endured during the entire four-month follow-up period and applied to bowel movements as well as urinations. A within-subject comparison of the children's pre- and post-training accidents by the Wilcoxin Matched-Pairs Signed Ranks Test showed a significant ($p < 0.01$) reduction of accidents for the very first day after training and for each month of the post-training period.

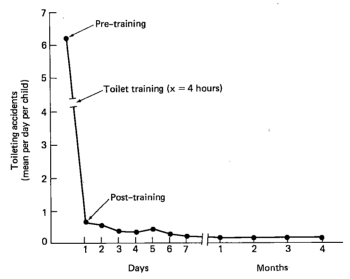

FIGURE 7.9: The effect of the Dry Pants toilet training procedure on the frequency of toileting accidents, both bladder and bowel, of 34 normal children. The toilet training period is shown as an interruption in the curve and required an average of 4 hours per child. The Pre-Training data point represents the children's accident rate per day during the week prior to training. Data points are given for the first 7 days after training and monthly thereafter. Each datum point is the average number of accidents per day per child.

Training time. The mean training time was 3.9 hours; the median time was 3.5 hours, and the range was one-half hour to 14 hours. Training was considered complete when the child toileted himself completely and with no prompts. The older children, aged twenty-six to thirty-six months, were trained in a training time of about 2.25 hours. The twenty to twenty-five-month old group had a mean training time of about 5 hours.

Parent reaction. The parents characteristically expressed disbelieving pleasure.

Reaction of the children. Most of the children reacted to the training program as if it were a very pleasant experience, hugging and kissing the trainer.

Bedwetting. None of the children was given specific training for bed-wetting (enuresis). Yet, the mothers of ten children (about 30 percent) reported that their child stopped wetting at night during the entire first week immediately following the daytime training. Follow-up checks showed that all ten of these children continued to stay dry at night during the four-month follow-up period.

Discussion

The results showed that the training program was an effective method of training normal children to toilet themselves without any prompting. All thirty-four children were trained. Training was accomplished rapidly, requiring an average of only 4 hours per child and only about 2 hours for children older than twenty-six months. The accidents quickly decreased to a near-zero level and remained near zero during the four-month follow-up. Bowel training and bladder training were accomplished concurrently with no need for a differential training procedure. An incidental benefit was that bedwetting (enuresis) was also eliminated for about one-third of the children. Successful training was achieved even for children as young as twenty months, for problem children who resisted any type of training, and for children who did not speak. The training program appeared to be a pleasant experience for the children.

The present results demonstrate that toilet training is not a futile exercise; training can be achieved by intensive learning procedures, as was also indicated by recent reinforcement studies (Madsen et al. 1969). Consequently, one can no longer defend an attitude of fatalistic permissiveness on the grounds that bladder and bowel control cannot be hastened. A permissive attitude would still be justified if the training effort produced an enduring negative emotional attitude. The results showed the converse: the children who were negative prior to training were described as more pleasant and cooperative after training. Overall, we suggest that training be deferred until a child is twenty months of age because the training effort for the average child below that age might counterbalance the convenience of having him trained.

REFERENCES

Azrin, N. H.; Sneed, T. J.; and Foxx, R. M. 1973. Dry bed: A rapid method of eliminating bedwetting (enuresis) of the retarded. *Behavior Research and Therapy* 11; 427–34.

Madsen, C. H.; Hoffman, M.; Thomas, D. R.; Koropsak, E.; and Madsen, C. K. 1969. Comparisons of toilet training techniques. In *Social learning in childhood,* ed. D. M. Gelfand. Belmont, Calif.: Brooks/Cole.

Spock, B. 1968. *Baby and child care.* Rev. ed. New York: Pocket Books.

8

Quasi-Experimental

Approaches

to

Outcome Evaluation

The previous chapter demonstrated how very simple research designs can answer important questions for the evaluator and for users of evaluations. However, early in that chapter it was stressed that these designs can seldom help evaluators identify the cause of changes in program participants. Whenever program administrators and governmental agencies commission evaluators to discover the cause of changes in the program participants, evaluations of greater complexity must be designed. In order to show that something causes something else, it is necessary to demonstrate that: (1) the cause precedes the supposed effect in time; (2) the cause covaries with the effect; and (3) no other alternative explanations of the effect exist except the assumed cause. It is easy to satisfy the first criterion by showing that a program preceded an improvement. The second criterion is not that difficult to test either. Both can be demonstrated using the methods described in Chapter 7. The third, however, is much more difficult and is the focus of this and the following chapters.

In this chapter, various methods are presented that possess greater internal validity than the simple methods described in Chapter 7. The validity of outcome evaluations seeking to demonstrate causal relationships can be increased by (1) observing the participants at additional times before and after the program; (2) observing additional people who have not received the program; and (3) using a variety of variables, some expected to be influenced by the program and others not expected to be affected. These methods have been labeled "quasi-experiments" by Campbell and Stanley (1963) because although these methods do not achieve the airtight control of true experiments, quasi-experiments control for many biases and, thus, can yield highly interpretable evaluations if carefully planned.

DISTINGUISHING CHANGE FROM RANDOM FLUCTUATIONS

Increasing the number of observations across time is one approach to reducing the chances that an observed change was due to a nonprogram source. All behaviors show random variation over time. The number of crimes on a given day or week is not a constant, nor is it a uniformly decreasing or increasing variable. Although there are some predictable influences on the number of crimes committed (for example, cold weather inhibits crime, warmer weather seems to encourage it), the causes of most changes in the day-to-day crime rate are unknown. Nevertheless, the popular media often act as though such causes were known, and effective remedial action well understood.

In July 1975, a few days after several thousand police officers were laid off in New York City, there were two days in which an abnormally high number of murders occurred. There were nine and eight murders on July 8 and 9, respectively. These two high-crime days were contrasted with the average for the year—four per day. Were newspapers (see Egelhof 1975) correct in attributing the cause of these additional murders to the reductions in the size of the police force?

The first criterion necessary for a causal conclusion was met: the police were laid off before the murders. However, it is not known if murder covaries with size of police force, and alternative interpretations of the observed number of murders were not even considered. Without some information about the normal variation from day to day, it is hard to know whether eight or nine murders is unusual on a summer day. No information was provided about the weather. It may have been unusually hot. Did the murder rate stay that high after July 9? Without this additional information, it is impossible even to draw the most tentative conclusions about the effect, if any, of the reduction in number of police officers on murder rate. Ignoring these threats to internal validity can lead to quite erroneous interpretations of the causal relations between two events. As was mentioned before and will be stressed again, it is even possible that an effective program will look ineffective if possible explanations of change are ignored.

A second and frequently cited example of the possibility of misunderstanding a phenomenon given limited information occurred in Connecticut during the 1950s (Campbell 1969). In 1955 there were approximately 14.2 automobile accident fatalities per 100,000 residents. This was a record rate and was especially high compared to the 1954 rate. The governor initiated a speeding crackdown during 1956. The fatality rate in 1956 dropped to about 12.2 per 100,000. Could the governor justifiably claim that the measures he took were responsible for the reduction in fatalities? Readers might stop for a moment to develop an answer to that question.

The way to decide if the governor could take credit for the drop requires information about fatalities before the crackdown year as well as after the crucial year. The fatalities before the record in 1955 may show that fatalities per year were systematically rising in response to the number of autos per resident on Connecticut roads and the number of miles driven per auto. Because accidents increase when the number of cars increase, a steady increase in fatalities, while undesirable, may be unavoidable in this situation. A program to reduce fatalities would be up against strong forces and could be expected to yield few results.

A second alternative would be that the record rate in 1955 was simply a statistical artifact. Perhaps a few very tragic but fortunately infrequent multi-fatality accidents occurred during the same year. Or perhaps especially bad weather occurred just before or just after holidays when many drivers were on the road. Because consecutive years of such coincidents are unlikely, a remedy for the high fatality rate is quite likely to appear to succeed regardless of how well or poorly conceived.

The actual fatality rates for the years before and after the Connecticut speed crackdown were reported by Campbell (1969) and are given in Figure 8.1. The reader can see that the 1955 rate does appear to be a discrepant value, even though the magnitude of fluctuations from year to year is markedly large. This example will be discussed in more detail later in this chapter. The point of interest at this time is to note

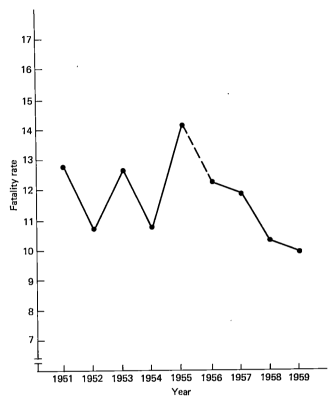

FIGURE 8.1: Automobile accident fatality rate for Connecticut by year before and after the beginning of a crackdown on speeding drivers. (Adapted from D. T. Campbell, "Reforms as Experiments," *American Psychologist* 24, 1969: 419. Copyright 1969 American Psychological Association.)

that looking at accident rates over a number of time periods permits a much better-informed conclusion, compared to that possible from an examination of only the rates just before and just after the introduction of the treatment.

A third example of the usefulness of examining information over a number of time intervals is provided by Rheinstein (1959), who examined the effects of tightening of divorce laws in Germany in 1900. The divorce rate dropped dramatically after the change and even dropped slightly the following year. A complex analysis revealed that the law had an impact; however, examining the divorce rate over a longer period (from 1902 to 1914) revealed that within four years the rate was equal to that in 1899, and by 1914 the rate was nearly double that of 1899.

Time-Series Design

In recent years, considerable attention has been given to the use of information across many time intervals. These approaches have come to be called *time-series analyses*. Influences fostering this interest have come from economics at a macro level and from behavior analysis at a micro level. Economists have used information over long time periods, seeking to learn the effects of policy changes on such variables as income level, industrial output, and employment. Economists are usually concerned about aggregate information referring to units (such as nations) much larger than those of interest to most program evaluators; nevertheless, the methods economists have developed have found increasing application in program evaluation.

On a very different scale, behavior analysis research has utilized objective measurement of a single individual over many time periods during which various interventions were begun and stopped. Once again, the unit of analysis, in this case, a single person, is not appropriate for most evaluations; however, the importance that the behavior analyst places on obtaining stable base line measurement before an intervention and on documenting both change and the maintenance of change have become part of the concerns of program evaluators. A study done in this tradition will later illustrate the behavior analysis approach to program evaluation (see Case Study 8.1).

It is worth noting that the data of the economist and the behavior analyst are more similar to each other than might be supposed on the basis of a consideration of the units of analysis used. Whether referring to a country or a single child, the researcher obtains one value per variable for each time period. For example, for the economist there is only one unemployment level in the nation per time period, one GNP, and one inflation rate. For the behavior analyst, there is only one index of a specific abnormal behavior per time period. Thus, writers can refer to "single subject" research in both cases.

Time-series designs as applied to program evaluation received strong encouragement through the work of Campbell and Stanley (1963), who gave them an important place among their quasi-experimental designs. Collecting data over many time periods is a way of satisfying some of the internal validity tests described in the previous chapter. Because maturation effects can be traced during the time periods before and after the intervention, the likelihood of confusing the program's effect with maturation effects is greatly reduced when using a time-series design rather than a pretest-posttest design. Similarly, the effects of history will be more easily detected using a time-series design than when an evaluation is performed using observations at only one or two time periods. By examining the reaction of the dependent variables to historical events, it is possible, at least at a qualitative level, to distinguish the effects of the program from the impact of major nonprogram influences.

A time-series approach to program evaluation minimally includes the following characteristics: (1) a single unit is defined, and (2) quantitative observations are made (3) over a number of time intervals (4) that precede and follow some controlled or natural intervention (Knapp 1977). In the language of experimental design, the unit observed (person, group, or nation) serves as its own control.

Program evaluators, unlike economists, use time-series designs almost exclusively when a definite intervention has occurred at a specific time. The design is often called an *interrupted time series* (Caporaso 1973) and the evaluator's job is to learn whether the interruption—that is, the human service intervention—had an impact. Figure 8.2 illustrates this design in symbols.

There are a number of possible outcomes observable in a graph of a program's outcome plotted over time intervals. Figure 8.3 illustrates some of these possibilities. Each part of the figure is plotted with time intervals along the abscissa, and magnitude of the outcome dependent variable on the ordinate. Figure 8.3*a* illustrates no effect of the intervention. There appears to be no out-of-the-ordinary change in the observations after the program compared to those before it. In contrast, Figure 8.3*b* illustrates what is usually the most hoped for result of an interrupted time-series analysis. The graph shows a marked increase from a fairly stable level before the intervention, and the criterion remains fairly stable afterwards. One might expect this sort of result from an effective training program that increased the skills of employees or from

FIGURE 8.2: Simple quasi-experimental designs for program evaluation

Name and symbolization	Questions that can be answered using this design for a program evaluation
Interrupted time series O – O – ...O – X – O – ... – O – O	All the questions in Figure 7.1 Are there maturational trends that might explain an improvement? Do historical events cause the dependent variable to change?
Pretest-posttest with a nonequivalent control group O – X – O O – – O	All the questions in Figure 7.1 Is improvement more than the effect of history, maturation, testing, selection, or mortality?

the introduction of labor-saving devices. Clearly, the method can be
used when the intervention is designed to lower variables as well as to
raise them. Accident rates and failure rates are examples of variables
one would like to see drop.

Figures 8.3*c* to 8.3*f* all show some sort of an increase after the intervention, but their interpretations are much less clear. Figure 8.3*c* shows
an increase in slope after the intervention. The variable being measured
began to increase over time after the intervention; however, there was no
immediate impact as in 8.3*b*. An influence, such as television viewing or
improved nutrition, whose impact is diffuse and cumulative might produce the result in Figure 8.3*c*. In 8.3*d*, there is a general trend for the
variable to increase that is superimposed on a localized increase ap-

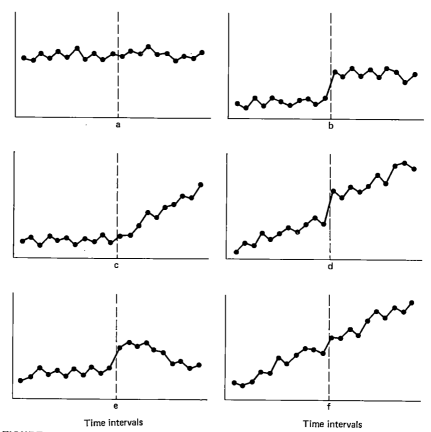

FIGURE 8.3: Some illustrative possible patterns of a criterion of program success
plotted over time. Time of the program or intervention is indicated by
the dashed vertical line.

parently due to the intervention. This pattern was observed in an analysis of the number of laboratory tests ordered for inpatients before and after a hospital became a teaching hospital for medical residents. Over the months preceding the change and after the change, the monthly totals increased quite regularly in response to societal factors, advances in medical technology, and probably gradual changes in the type of patients treated. However, the very month the number of residents was increased the number of laboratory tests increased by approximately ten thousand.

In Figure 8.3e, there appears to be an effect due to the intervention; however, it seems to be temporary. Many new programs are introduced with much publicity, and the deeply involved staff members want the program to work. Perhaps extra staff effort is responsible for the immediate impact. However, once the program is part of the regular procedure and the extra effort is no longer extended, the outcome achieved returns to its former levels. Schnelle and colleagues (1978) showed that a helicopter patrol decreased crime in a high-crime area. However, the authors questioned whether the effect would hold up if the experiment had been continued beyond the initial trial period. It is possible that although the *novelty* of the helicopter patrol served to frighten potential thieves and thus to lower crime for a short period, the airborne patrol's inherent effectiveness is not strong.

A possible pitfall for an evaluator could exist when a situation occurs such as that illustrated in Figure 8.3f. Here, a steady increase over time is observed. A naive approach to the analysis would be to contrast the mean of the time periods before the intervention with the mean of the time periods after. This contrast may be statistically significant, but it has no relevance to understanding the effect of the intervention.

Analysis of Time-Series Design

Rigorous analysis of interrupted time-series design is beyond the scope of this book. The methods now accepted are described by Gottman and Glass (1978); however, advanced statistical sophistication is required to understand and use these methods. For readers of this book, some steps that fall short of the most correct and complete analysis may be taken that will help in the interpretation of time series data.

First, when the effects of the intervention are striking, statistical analyses may be unnecessary. Case Study 8.1, concerning the safety of sanitation workers, illustrates a situation in which the change in the dependent measure, the criterion of success, is so strong and so closely related to the intervention that one can conclude that the program had a positive effect. Similarly, McCarthy (1978) found a strong effect from a daily posting of the number of high bobbins in a textile plant. High bobbins lead to tangles and lost production time, but their incidence can be greatly reduced by additional employee care. The feedback and the workers' attempts to meet the posted goals resulted in a dramatically reduced rate of malfunction. A graph of the number of high bobbins showed a dramatic drop after feedback was initiated. Furthermore, when McCarthy temporarily removed the feedback procedure, the number of high bobbins began to climb. Reinstatement of the feedback brought the number back down again. It is hard to argue with the interpretation that the feedback caused the results when they produce such a pattern over time intervals.

There are other examples of time-series records that are not as easy to interpret. The literature on medical education shows that resident physicians on the average order more laboratory tests for hospital patients than do community physicians who have more experience (for example, Dixon and Laszlo 1974). To learn whether this finding held for a specific community hospital, a plot of the number of laboratory tests per month was made beginning three years before a major expansion of the hospital's residency programs and one year after, as mentioned above. Because neither the hospital's size nor its utilization rate changed systematically during the four-year period, the influence of these variables was ignored. The most striking observation was a steady increase in the average number of laboratory tests compared to the previous month. This increase of an additional five hundred tests per month was observed throughout the time period. However, the increase that occurred between the month before the program was expanded and the first month of the expanded program was about ten thousand. Because the steady monthly increase resumed after this big jump, that is, the graph resembled Figure 8.3d, the evaluators felt safe in attributing the cause of the increase to the fact that young residents were ordering the bulk of the laboratory tests rather than more experienced physicians, as had been the case previously.[1] The effect of the residents on laboratory tests seemed clear, and the interpretation fit published reports on the topic. However, the interpretation was not as compelling as the effect of feedback on high bobbins described above. The residency program could not be introduced, removed, and then reintroduced as McCarthy did in manipulating the high bobbin feedback.

Finally, there are situations in which there is a valid question of the interpretation of the results of time-series design. Figure 8.1, showing the results of the speed crackdown, cannot be validly interpreted using

[1] Partially on the basis of this sudden jump, the program director instituted procedures to reduce the excessive use of laboratory tests by residents.

the informal examination methods described here. Cook and Campbell (1976) report that recent analyses support the belief that the program had a reliable (that is, statistically significant) effect. The methods necessary to make that interpretation require mathematical skills beyond those assumed for readers of this text and beyond those possessed by most active evaluators. It is likely, however, that program evaluators will use these methods (for example, Gottman & Glass 1978) to a greater extent in the future.

OBSERVING OTHER GROUPS

Nonequivalent Control-Group Design

The simple time-series design increases the interpretability of an evaluation by extending the periods of observations over time. Another approach is to increase the number of groups observed. If the pretest-posttest design could be duplicated with another group that did not receive the program, a potentially good research design would result. So long as the groups are comparable, nearly all the internal validity tests are satisfied by this design, called *nonequivalent control group design* (diagrammed in Figure 8.2). Nonequivalent control groups will also be called *comparison groups*.

The evaluator expects to observe a larger improvement between pre-test and posttest for the program group than for the comparison group, as illustrated in Figure 8.4. The correct statistical tool to analyze the

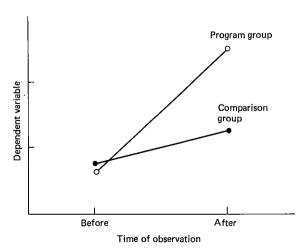

FIGURE 8.4: Hypothetical results of a nonequivalent control (comparison) group design.

data from such a design is the two groups by two time periods analysis of variance with repeated measures over time periods (Kirk 1968).[2] If the program was successful and the group means followed the pattern in Figure 8.4, the analysis of variance would reveal a significant interaction between group and testing period.

Including the comparison group permits a distinction to be made between the effects of the program and the several alternate plausible interpretations of change. Because the comparison group has been tested at the same time periods as the program group, both groups have had the same amount of time to mature. Historical forces have presumably affected the groups equally. Because both groups would have been tested twice, testing effects should be equivalent. Finally, the rates of participant loss between pretest and posttest can be examined to be sure they are similar.

Weakness of the Design

Clearly, the major weakness in all nonequivalent control group designs is in selecting a comparison group not sufficiently similar to the program group to permit drawing valid interpretations. For example, it is possible that those who choose to be in the program may be maturing at a different rate from those in the comparison group. Parents who seek out special programs for their children may also be devoting more attention to the children at home than are parents who do not seek out special programs. Campbell and Stanley (1963) called this threat to internal validity a "selection-by-maturity interaction." Another problem will arise if the program participants are chosen because of extreme scores on the pretest, and the comparison group is selected from others with less extreme scores. If so, as mentioned in Chapter 7, the results may be distorted by regression effects.

A way out of the problems caused by using a nonequivalent control-group research design is often sought by matching the comparison groups with the program group. That is, the people forming the comparison group are chosen because they are in some ways like the program participants on income level, objective test score, rated adjustment, locality of residence, and so forth. While matching is often used to select comparison groups for quasi-experiments, matching is a controversial way to form such groups.

The widely cited evaluation of Head Start (Cicarelli, Cooper, and Granger 1969) has been criticized for its use of matching (Campbell and Erlebacher 1970). Head Start is a program for disadvantaged chil-

---

[2] Other names for this design include the *split-plot factorial* or *mixed* designs.

dren offered in the summer or during the year prior to beginning first grade. The program was designed for the preschool children most lacking in school-relevant skills and attitudes. In addition, nutritional and medical goals were involved in the program.

When Head Start was selected for evaluation, it was already widely accepted and offered in many communities (Datta 1976b); therefore, the program could not be withheld from any group of children. The evaluation utilized a posttest-only design with national samples of children, some in Head Start programs and some matched samples not in Head Start. The evaluation compared achievement on standard tests of Head Start children in first, second, and third grades with similar non-Head Start children, and concluded that Head Start was largely a failure. Critics have attacked the methodology utilized in this evaluation on a number of grounds; however, the focus of the present discussion is on regression effects that likely lie behind the conclusions of the Head Start evaluation.

Because the population of children available for the non-Head Start comparison group was less disadvantaged than the children in the Head Start group, those children selected as matches could not be equivalent to the children in Head Start. In order to find children qualifying for Head Start who had cognitive achievement scores similar to those of children not qualifying, either or both of the following points must have been true: (1) the comparison group was selected from among the less able children not qualified for Head Start; or (2) the experimental group was selected from among the more able children who attended Head Start.

To understand the effects of regression toward the mean, it is important to understand why the previous statement is true whenever matching is used to select a comparison group for an evaluation of a program aimed at people in need. Once a group is selected on the basis of need for a national program, there is no other group that can be found that is just like the people in the program. Thus, no perfect comparison group exists. However, on some variables (for example, family income, school grades, test scores) there will be overlap among the members of the two groups. Who will overlap? The people in the "needy" group who overlap with the "not-needy" group *must* be among the relatively better off among the "needy" people. Those in the "not-needy" group who overlap with the "needy" children *must* be among the least well-off among the "not needy" people.

Consider an artificial, but illustrative example. Suppose a teacher wanted to provide a special spelling program for all the second graders. If the teacher wanted a comparison group, he or she could find some third graders who scored as low as the second graders. Are these groups equivalent? Probably not. These third graders would have been selected from the lower portion of a population that, in general, is more capable than the second-grade experimental group. What will happen upon retesting the groups of the program? Because no spelling test is completely reliable, the low-scoring third graders in the comparison group will look as though they improved, not only because they learned some new words but also because they are regressing toward the mean of third graders. This regression will make the second graders' improvement due to the program appear smaller and less impressive than it may actually have been.

To put this into other words, the groups of children have different influences raising their scores. The program children will probably show an improvement because the new program has affected them and because they matured a bit. The comparison children will improve because of exposure to the regular spelling classes, their added maturity, *and* regression. Campbell and Erlebacher (1970) assert that the Head Start evaluation was biased in just the way that this hypothetical teacher's evaluation would be biased. Because human service programs typically produce small improvements, the size of the regression effects might even exceed the program's effect. In fact, Campbell and Erlebacher (1970) argue that regression artifacts may make compensatory education look harmful when, in fact, the programs may have had a small positive influence.[3]

The moral of this section is simply the following: the nonequivalent control-group design is especially sensitive to regression effects when the groups are systematically different on some dimensions. In compensatory education evaluations, a systematic preprogram difference between experimental and comparison groups is likely to be found. It should be noted that if the program effect was massive and the program children improved markedly, the evaluation may reveal that the program was effective. Nonetheless, the size of the effect will still be underestimated. On the other hand, when similar groups do exist, the nonequivalent comparison-group design is quite powerful and very useful.

OBSERVING OTHER DEPENDENT VARIABLES

At this point, the methods described in Chapter 7 have been expanded to include observations of the program participants at many times and to include observations of groups other than the program participants.

[3] There is no controversy over whether regression occurred in this evaluation; however, the size of the likely regression effects is hotly disputed (see Cicirelli 1970; Evans and Schiller 1970).

It is possible to increase the validity of interpretations by observing additional dependent variables that are not expected to be changed by the program, or at least expected to be changed only marginally. Consider a remedial reading program offered during the summer vacation for children reading below their grade level. A pretest-posttest design would be markedly strengthened by testing the children before and after on arithmetic as well as vocabulary, grammar, and reading speed. All extraneous influences such as self-esteem, history and testing effects that may affect reading scores will also affect arithmetic scores. Thus, if scores on reading increase but those on arithmetic do not, the conclusion that the program is effective is fairly safe. As long as the children were not selected for the program on the basis of the pretest, regression is not a viable alternative interpretation of the cause of the change either.

There is a problem with this approach. The added dependent measures must be similar to the major dependent measure without being strongly influenced by the program. In the example above, if the children did read better, it might be expected that they will do better on a written, standardized arithmetic test than they did before the program. It is hard to imagine additional dependent measures that (1) would be affected by the same threats to internal validity as the outcome measure but (2) would not be affected by the program. Cook, Cook, and Mark (1977) suggest that these difficulties mean that this "nonequivalent dependent variable" design is best used as an adjunct to other methods, not as the major evaluation design.

COMBINING METHODS TO INCREASE INTERNAL VALIDITY

Time-Series and Nonequivalent Comparison Groups

The most interpretable quasi-experimental designs are those that combine the approaches mentioned above into one evaluation. If a group similar to the program participants can be found, the simple time-series design is considerably strengthened. The analysis of the Connecticut speed crackdown mentioned earlier was made possible by examining the fatality rates of four neighboring states. Figure 8.5 contrasts the average of these four states with Connecticut's fatality rate. As can be seen in the figure, there seems to be a general trend towards a lower fatality rate in all five states; however, Connecticut's 1957–1959 rates are increasingly divergent from those of the neighboring states. Although regression towards the mean is a plausible alternative interpretation of the drop from 1955 to 1956, the continued favorable trend is hard to

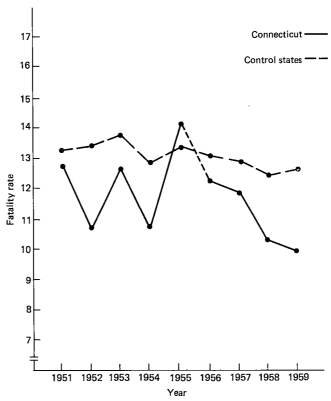

FIGURE 8.5: Automobile accident fatality rate for Connecticut and for comparable
states. (Reprinted with permission from D. T. Campbell, "Reforms as
experiments," *American Psychologist* 24, 1969: 419. Copyright 1969
American Psychological Association.)

explain if the crackdown, which was kept in force during the following
years, did not have an effect. Riecken and Boruch (1974) state that tests
of significance are less important than a qualitative understanding of the
various threats to the validity of causal conclusions about the impact
of the intervention. However, methods to be used for precise analyses
are being developed (see Gottman and Glass 1978).

A key to drawing valid interpretations from observations lies in
being able to repeat the observations. If a study can be replicated,
one can be much more sure of conclusions than if it cannot be. The
time-series design with a comparison group that receives the same intervention as the experimental group but at a later time provides additional
safeguards against validity threats. Figure 8.6 illustrates the ideal pattern
of results from such a study. Cook and Campbell (1976) call this design
an "interrupted time series with switching replications." If the observations fit the pattern in Figure 8.6, little in the way of statistical

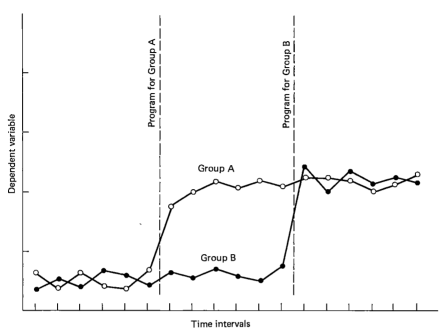

FIGURE 8.6: Hypothetical results of an interrupted time-series design with switching replications.

analysis needs to be done. Unfortunately, many societal changes are also occurring during the time of the observations, so that the dependent variables do not fall into an easily interpreted pattern. Case Study 8.1 is a successful example of a time-series design with switching replications in an evaluation of a solution to a municipal problem.

Time-Series and Nonequivalent Dependent Variables

Another improvement in the time-series design involves the use of nonequivalent dependent variables. Ross (1973) provided information on a 1967 crackdown on drinking drivers in Britain. Because the intervention was nationwide and because comparable information from other countries might not be comparable, relevant, or available, a nonequivalent dependent measure was sought. A feature of the laws introduced in 1967 was that pubs may be open only certain hours. Because people drinking at home are less likely to be driving than are those drinking in pubs, one way to evaluate the impact of the program is to divide the traffic fatalities into those that occurred during pub hours and those that occurred when the pubs were closed. These variables satisfy the requirements of the nonequivalent dependent measures approach because historical trends that would affect drivers during pub

211

hours should also affect drivers at other times. Severe weather, in-creased police vigilance, and improved record keeping, for example, would affect both accident rates equally. The data followed the pattern presented in Figure 8.7. A dramatic drop in casualities was observed during pub hours after the introduction of the breathalyzer, but no drop was found during other hours.

The Patch-Up Design

Cook and Campbell (1976) use the term *patch-up design* to describe an approach that illustrates the essence of the quasi-experimental ap-proach. Being aware of the threats to internal validity that are most likely to affect an evaluation, evaluators may decide to add comparison groups specifically designed to control for certain influences until the most plausible competing interpretations are eliminated.

The dean of a college of arts and sciences in a medium-sized uni-versity requested an evaluation of a junior year abroad program spon-sored and supervised by his college. The report was needed for a board of trustees meeting scheduled in six weeks. Clearly, there was no opportunity for a time-series design. (As mentioned in earlier chapters, it is not unusual for evaluators to work under considerable time pressure.) The research was planned around the obvious comparison—college seniors who studied abroad versus seniors who studied at the

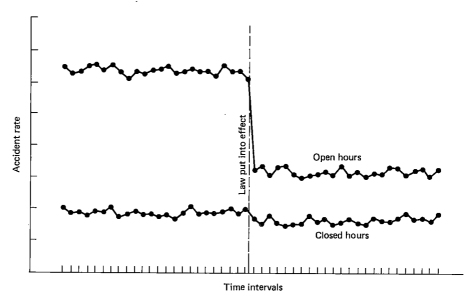

FIGURE 8.7: Illustrative outcome from a time-series analysis using two dependent variables, one likely to be more affected by the program than the other.

parent campus. In this comparison, selection is one threat to internal validity that cannot be ignored. Students who decide to go abroad for a year are clearly different from those who remain at home. An approach to estimating the preexisting differences between these two groups is to test individuals before they leave. A pretest-posttest design was impossible due to the short time allotted for the study. Because the decision to study abroad is costly and requires much planning, sophomore students sign up rather early for the program. By comparing seniors who have been abroad with sophomores arranging to go abroad, the self-selection threat is negated because both groups have selected themselves to go abroad. However, now a second threat to internal validity becomes a problem. Sophomores are less mature than seniors are. Two years in age may not be that critical for middle-age or elderly people, but two years may make quite a difference in an evaluation of a program for college students. By adding one more group, sophomores who did not intend to study abroad, the major threats to the internal validity of this evaluation were covered.

The design is summarized in Figure 8.8. If self-selection was related to higher scores on the dependent measures, one would expect the groups in the upper row to have higher scores. If maturation leads to higher scores, those in the right column should have higher scores. If the program had an impact, then the upper right group, the self-selected seniors, should have especially high scores as illustrated. Unfortunately, the sophomores planning to spend the year abroad were very hard to find, and only three were tested. Therefore, the means in Figure 8.8 are hypothetical.

A more complicated patch-up design was described by Lawler and Hackman (1969). They wished to evaluate the success of having custodial employees design their own incentive plan to reduce absen-

FIGURE 8.8: Hypothetical mean scores on a measure of international understanding for the students in the junior year abroad evaluation. A program effect is indicated by these means.

| | | Maturation Level | |
		Sophomores	Seniors
Self-selection	Students who will study or have studied abroad	50	65 (Experimental group)
	Students who have not studied and will not study abroad	40	45

teeism. The authors believed that an incentive plan would work only if the employees designed it themselves. The authors had to use intact, existing work groups; therefore, some form of the nonequivalent control-group design had to be used. Three intact work teams making up the experimental group developed their plans in consultation with the experimenters. The first comparison group had an incentive plan similar to that developed by the experimental group, but it was imposed upon them by management. Including this group enabled the evaluators to distinguish between the effect of an *employee*-designed incentive plan and the incentive itself. A second comparison group simply met with the experimenters to talk about the work and absenteeism. This group was necessary to show that any reduction in absenteeism would have been due more to the incentive plan than to the discussions with industrial psychologists. Finally, a comparison group with no incentive plan and no discussion was added.

The data were analyzed using a time-series analysis because the rate of absenteeism may change slowly and because absenteeism is a very natural variable to be calculated on a weekly basis, whether or not there is a program. Comparing the rate of absenteeism for the twelve weeks before the intervention with the rate during the twelve weeks afterwards showed that the participant employees improved from 12 percent absent to 6 percent, while the rates for the other groups did not change. Note that without each of the control groups (just as in the junior year abroad study) some alternative interpretation would have been plausible. The comparison groups were selected to counter specific, plausible interpretations of any improvement in the absenteeism of the experimental group.

There are other threats to internal validity with which the design does not deal because they were not plausible in this study. For example, instrumentation refers to possible changes in measures of outcome or success such as those that occur when staff become more vigilant or experienced because of the interest in the evaluation. Because job absenteeism is a critical variable in work settings, the development of a program is unlikely to make any changes in the measurement of absenteeism.

SUMMARY

The use of quasi-experimental research designs in program evaluation is widespread. These approaches are often compatible with the need to minimize disruption in organizations and the need of evaluators to obtain sufficient information to permit the isolation of probable causes of changes in program participants. However, the use of quasi-experimental research designs is not straightforward because the evaluator needs to consider which specific threats to internal validity must be accounted for in each evaluation. Anticipating just which threats are likely to be problems can cause headaches for evaluators because there are no standard approaches to designing quasi-experimental evaluations. Often, the correct statistical methods to use in analyzing a quasi-experimental evaluation are controversial. One of the most promising quasi-experimental methods, the interrupted time-series design, is receiving considerable theoretical study. New analytical methods are likely to become widely known in future years.

STUDY QUESTIONS

1. Explain which threats to internal validity are not covered by an evaluation of a parole program in which male parolees are tested before and after the program and compared to a sample of men living in the same neighborhoods as the parolees.

2. Assume that reading levels in a school district were steadily declining over the recent years and that a new reading program was implemented to counter this trend. After two years, the reading levels continued to decline but the superintendent announced that the program was a success because reading levels would have declined even more without the program. What would be necessary to evaluate the validity of such an announcement? Think of the minimum amount and the least expensive sources of such information.

3. Suppose a new medical treatment were offered to residents of an upper-middle-class suburb. As a comparison group, similarly aged patients with the same diagnosis were found in a county hospital providing free care to welfare families. Evaluate this nonequivalent control-group evaluation design.

4. A problem with quasi-experimental evaluations is that often a particular set of results can be interpreted but a different set cannot. For example, assume a service to a disadvantaged group resulted in improved performance on some variable. If the post-program performance of this disadvantaged group is better than that observed in the middle-class comparison group, the interpretation of the evaluation is clear. However, if post-program performance of the disadvantaged group is lower than that of the middle-class comparison group, then there are many more possible interpretations. Explain these statements.

FURTHER READING

Cook, T. D. and Campbell, D. T. 1979. *Quasi-experimentation*. Chicago: Rand McNally.

CASE STUDY 8.1

A Program to Increase the Job-Related Safety of Sanitation Workers

The use of an interrupted time-series design is illustrated in this evaluation. An intervention was introduced to one group while a second served as a comparison group. Later when the intervention was introduced to the second group, the first was used as the comparison group. This design, called the *interrupted time-series design with switching replications,* is one of the most powerful quasi-experimental research designs. It is useful when an intervention or a human service must be given to all members of an already formed group or not at all, and there is at least one other group that can be given the service at a later date. This case study also illustrates some aspects of the responsibilities of program evaluators to report their findings to all concerned (see Chapter 11) and to encourage the use of the results of program evaluations (see Chapter 12).

EVALUATING MUNICIPAL POLICY: AN ANALYSIS OF A REFUSE PACKAGING PROGRAM *

Trevor F. Stokes and Stephen B. Fawcett

Proposed changes in city service operations are often not subjected to formal pilot testing prior to their implementation. The present study examined the effectiveness of one proposed change in the operation of a city sanitation service, that is, the modification of refuse packaging requirements. This research resulted from consultation with officials of the Sanitation Worker's Association on various problems within the sanitation department. Issues of concern to the workers and city management included the packaging of refuse by city residents, the quality of sanitation services, the safety of equipment and work procedures, job security, and worker morale. The inadequate packaging of refuse by city residents was a matter of particular concern to the workers.

Method

The study examined the refuse packaging behavior of persons living in 183 residences in Lawrence, Kansas, a community of fifty thousand. These residences were arbitrarily divided into two experimental areas, one on either side of a major city street. There were ninety-four private residences in the West, and eighty-nine in the East.

* Condensed with permission from the *Journal of Applied Behavior Analysis* 10 (1977); 391–98. Copyright 1977 by the *Journal of Applied Behavior Analysis.*

Observation. Before the sanitation crew collected refuse, packaging violations were counted each collection day in the experimental areas. Observations occurred at the same time each day. An observer was driven by car through each section according to a predetermined route. The car stopped at each residence to allow counting of violations. Observation of individual residences was always concluded prior to the arrival of the crew.

The presence or absence of refuse to be collected was recorded for each residence. Furthermore, if refuse was out, that residence was scored for adherence to the packaging standards. The type and number of violations were scored for residences violating the regulations.

Violation types were predetermined by the city ordinance covering sanitation service. However, the precise wording of the violations [largely omitted in this condensation] adopted for the present study incorporated the concerns of the workers and city management personnel and were defined so as to facilitate reliable observation. These ordinances were designed to ensure the safety of sanitation workers and reduce the likelihood of spilling refuse during collection.

There were six categories of packaging violations:

1. Edge of container (can or bag) more than six feet from the collection point.
2. Refuse extending more than nine inches above the top rim of can.
3. Untied or torn plastic refuse bags.
4. Unacceptable refuse containers (cardboard boxes, paper bags, pasteboard or fiberboard barrels, and wicker baskets).
5. Yard trimmings not tied in bundles less than eighteen inches in diameter and less than four feet long.
6. Loose litter, trash, or garbage greater than two inches in diameter and within six feet of refuse container.

The reliability of observation was assessed on four days (3, 5, 9, and 13) by having the driver of the observation car independently score each residence at the same time as the regular observer. An agreement was scored if both observers agreed to the categorization of a residence. These comparisons yielded the following percentages of interobserver agreement: scoring of violating residences, 98.3 percent; nonviolating residences, 96.9 percent; residences without refuse, 98.6 percent.

Municipal enforcement program. The enforcement program involved instructions and feedback about packaging and contingent collection of refuse appropriately packaged. Instructions consisted of a letter signed by the City Manager and the Superintendent of Sanitation mailed to each resident following the last day of baseline. The letter emphasized the intent of the city to enforce the packaging standards. Attached to the letter was a copy of the standards for packaging garbage and trash that detailed the violation types and provided reasons why these violations reduced the safety and efficiency of the sanitation service. In addition, each letter contained a copy of a violation tag that would be left as a courtesy to residents if part of their refuse was not collected. Feedback consisted of violation notices distributed by the sanitation crewman riding on the back of the truck. These notices, checklists specifying the relevant violation type, were usually attached to the handle of the refuse can. Fifteen to thirty seconds was required to fill in and leave a notice at a violating residence. Nonviolating residences did not receive written feedback. Contingent collection involved collection only of adequately packaged refuse. All refuse failing to meet the minimum standards was not collected until the packaging met the standards.

Experimental Conditions

The effect of the enforcement program was analyzed in a multiple-baseline design across the West and East neighborhoods.

Baseline. Baseline observation in both sections commenced shortly after the City Commission formally gave approval for the study to proceed and directed that the enforcement procedures be implemented in the two test neighborhoods. Additional public notification of the particular neighborhoods involved and the details of the enforcement procedures to be followed (noncollection of inappropriately packaged refuse) appeared in the local newspaper's report of the commission meeting, which also occurred prior to baseline. During baseline, the sanitation crew followed their normal procedures, collecting refuse packaged correctly or incorrectly.

Enforcement program in the west. Following the fifth collection day, a notification letter was mailed to each resident in the West section. The enforcement program was instituted beginning the next collection day and remained in effect through day 15. Baseline conditions remained in effect for the East section.

Enforcement program in the east. Following the tenth collection day, similar notification was provided to residents in the East section. The enforcement program was implemented as of day 11, and remained in effect through day 15.

Follow-up. Following day 15, a letter was sent by the city to each of the 183 residences in the experimental area. This letter thanked the residents for their cooperation in the testing of procedural changes in the Sanitation Department and informed them of the successful conclusion of the study. The sanitation crew was instructed to discontinue the enforcement procedures after day 15 and resume the "normal" baseline conditions. Four weeks later, on day 23, a follow-up observation of packaging violations was made.

Results

Figure 8.9 shows the daily number of violations in the West and East sections. Before enforcement, there were means of 59.4 and 79.9 violations per day in the West and East, respectively. After enforcement, the number of violations was markedly reduced to means of 9.7 and 23.2 per day in the West and East, respectively. These lowered numbers of violations were maintained at a follow-up observation four weeks after completion of the study.

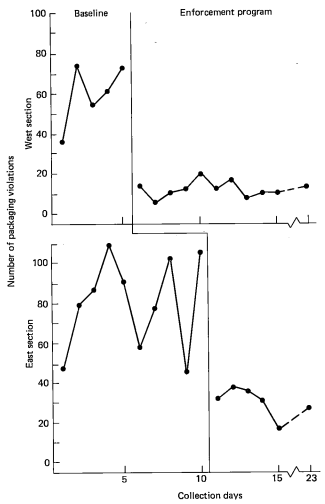

FIGURE 8.9: Daily number of packaging violations in the West and East neighborhoods.

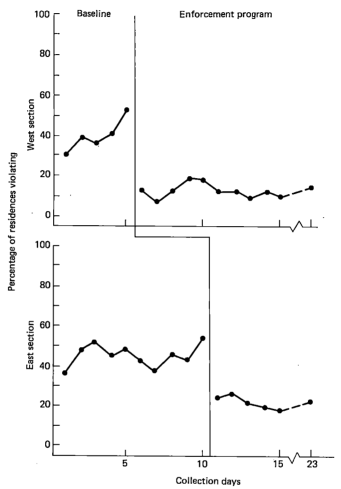

FIGURE 8.10: Daily percentages of residences violating the packaging regulations in the West and East neighborhoods, based on those residences with refuse out.

Figure 8.10 shows the daily percentages of residences violating at least once. During the study, a mean of 45 of the 183 residences did not have their refuse out when violations were counted. In the West, a mean of 39.9 percent of residences with refuse out committed at least one violation per day before enforcement, whereas a mean of 12.5 percent of residences violated per day during the enforcement program. Similarly, in the East, the mean percentage of residences violating decreased from 45.4 percent to 22.6 percent. Lowered rates were maintained at the follow-up observation.

Of the 183 residences studied, 27 (14 percent) never committed a violation during the fifteen collection days (eight weeks) of the study. Of the other 156 residences, which committed at least one violation, 88 percent averaged fewer violations per day during the enforcement period than they had averaged per day during baseline; 6 percent showed no change; and 6 percent showed increased violations. Seventy-four of the 183 residences met the noncollection contingency: 45 residences experienced the contingency on one day, 17 on two days, 7 on three days, 4 on four days, and one residence had refuse not collected on 6 different days. Of course, many residents observed the application of the enforcement contingency to their neighbors.

Discussion

The enforcement program, which consisted of instruction, feedback, and contingent refuse collection, was effective in markedly reducing the number of violations of packaging regulations and the percentage of residences violating. Correlated with these objective data changes, the ratings by the sanitation crew established the social validity of the effects of the enforcement program. The differences between sections in baseline and enforcement levels of violations were mirrored by the men's ratings: refuse was rated as better packaged, safer, and easier to collect. The workers' ratings suggest that these procedures might be a valuable component in a comprehensive safety and efficiency program for sanitation workers.

Fewer than 19 percent of the test neighborhoods' residents complained to the sanitation workers or city officials about the requirements of the enforcement program when part of their refuse was not collected. This type of program will probably always be met with some dissatisfaction, especially when first implemented. In this context, it should be noted that the number of complaints in the study areas did not differ significantly from the rest of the city.

The conduct of policy research is not a simple activity. As with many other research endeavors, the researchers cannot enter the experimental setting, collect their data, and depart cheerfully without regard to the political realities of that setting. Policy research, necessarily, involves close cooperation with both the policy makers and those persons involved in the procedural testing of proposed changes. The Sanitation Workers' Association initiated the present research through their identification of the packaging problem and request for assistance from the authors. The city of Lawrence (through the office of the City Manager) and the workers' association provided the support and political insulation essential for the conduct of the research. The authors formulated the details of the municipal enforcement program in consultation with local residents, the sanitation workers, and city management personnel. They also developed the experimental procedure, design, and measurement system. Through the City Manager, a request to conduct a pilot testing of the possible policy changes was submitted to the city commission. Such approval was given, and the research was then conducted.

Following the completion of the study, the research findings were discussed with sanitation workers and city management personnel with the aim of formulating a proposal for city-wide implementation of the test procedures. The research data and an implementation plan that were similar to the procedures of this study were then submitted to the policy-making body, the elected city commission. After considering the authors' report, the commission adopted the recommendations: a new refuse packaging ordinance was passed. This new ordinance incorporated the old specifications for refuse packaging, but also included the new enforcement provisions tested in the present study. The city management personnel were then instructed to implement the new policy.

In summary, the municipal enforcement program decreased the number of refuse packaging violations in the test neighborhoods. The data formed the nucleus of a recommendation of change in one area of public policy. Thus, the present study described an inexpensive and effective application of contingencies to ameliorate a municipal problem, and provided an example of the contribution of applied behavior analysis to the data-based determination of public policy.

CASE STUDY 8.2

Helmets and Motorcycle Accident Fatalities

The effects of legislation are very hard to evaluate because the laws apply to large units (states), and seldom are perfect comparison states available. This case study utilized the records of sixteen states in a study of the effectiveness of laws requiring motorcyclists to wear crash helmets. Because the states did not adopt laws simultaneously, the study compared fatality rates before and after the laws were passed, regardless of the actual date of passage. There are a number of possible explanations of the results. Readers should exercise their critical skills to find the threats to internal validity that may not be covered by the research design.

HELMET LAWS REDUCE FATALITIES *

Motorcyclist helmet use laws are reducing fatalities in motorcycle crashes, according to a recent study of the effectiveness of these laws. The study, which was conducted by Leon Robertson, senior behavioral

* Condensed from Insurance Institute for Highway Safety, *Status Report* 10 (November 5, 1975); 1–3.

scientist for the Insurance Institute for Highway Safety, examined the effects of helmet use in terms of compliance with the laws and their effects on fatalities.

The highway safety program standards adopted by the National Highway Traffic Safety Administration include a requirement that states implement all standards, including motorcycle helmet use laws, or face loss of all federal highway safety program funds and a portion of federal highway construction funds. Only three states had motorcycle use laws prior to 1967; during 1967–1969 an additional thirty-seven states enacted such laws in accordance with the federal requirement. Currently all but two states, California and Illinois, have such laws. Utah's law, however, applies only at speeds above 35 miles per hour.

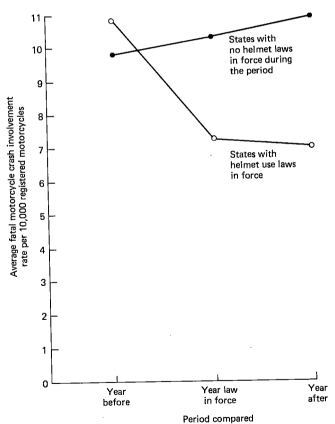

FIGURE 8.11: Average fatal motorcycle crash involvement rates per 10,000 registered motorcycles of 8 states that have helmet use laws and 8 matched comparison states that did not have helmet use laws during the same periods.

To determine the effect of helmet use laws on motorcyclist fatalities, the Institute's study compared the fatal crash involvement rates in eight states (Arizona, Colorado, Idaho, Kansas, Kentucky, Louisiana, Maryland, and Minnesota) that adopted helmet laws with those of similar states (California, New Mexico, Montana, Iowa, Virginia, Mississippi, West Virginia, and Iowa) that had no such laws during a comparable period.

The study found that the "average fatal involvement rate for the eight states that enacted helmet use laws declined from more than 10 per 10,000 registered motorcycles the year before the laws' enactments to about 7 per 10,000 registered motorcycles, both in the years of enactments and the following years. In contrast, the average fatal involvement rate in the eight matched states that enacted no helmet laws at the time that their comparison state did so remained at about 10 per 10,000 registered motorcycles throughout the period studied" (see Figure 8.11).

During the study, observations of helmet use were conducted along heavily traveled roadways in Atlanta and Baltimore, where helmet use laws are in effect, and in Chicago and Los Angeles, where there are no such laws. In Atlanta and Baltimore, "virtually all of the riders . . . were using helmets." In Los Angeles, more than 60 percent of the riders were using helmets, "but only 25 percent of Illinois riders were using them." The study noted that these findings do "not necessarily mean that these states had high use immediately upon enactment of their laws, nor that all states with such laws have the same experience."

9

Analysis
of
Causes of Change

The previous chapter described various approaches to reducing the number of plausible interpretations of change observed in program participants. The plausible interpretations of change include many possible sources of bias as well as the actual effect of the program itself. The biases refer to the ideas summarized in the threats to internal validity—self-selection into the program by those who would benefit, general community or societal changes that overshadow all effects of the program, and the reactive effects of making observations, among others. The ways of separating these biases from program effects involved observing the participants at a number of time intervals and observing both the relevant dependent measures and dependent measures not likely to change due to the program. In addition, observations of intact groups not experiencing the program could improve interpretability if they were similar to the program participants. Even when carefully designed quasi-experimental evaluations are conducted, there usually remains a lingering doubt that some influence other than the program led to the improvement observed. Perhaps the people forming the non-equivalent control group were different from the experimental group in some way that was not considered in planning the evaluation. Perhaps the people in the nonequivalent control group were less motivated or reacted to the observations differently than the program participants did.

The only way to put these doubts to rest is to adopt a research strategy that accounts for all the possible threats to internal validity. The only method that will do this is the classic experimental design utilizing random assignment of participants to the program or to a control group. This chapter reviews the need for experimentation as a tool in program evaluation, describes the most opportune times to introduce experimentation, and makes practical suggestions for meeting the problems of conducting experimental research in organizational settings.

EXPERIMENTATION IN PROGRAM EVALUATION

The Logic of Experimentation

Before discussing details of experimentation, a brief review of the logic of randomized experimental design may be useful. A true experiment refers to an evaluation based on observations made of people who are randomly assigned to be in the program group or in some control group. In the previous chapter, quasi-experimental methods were presented that are useful when evaluators do not have the administrative power to assign people to particular experiences. In such settings, evaluators utilize preexisting intact groups; however, such intact groups were formed for reasons other than the need for an unambiguously interpreted evaluation. Because such groups exist of their own accord, it is very likely that the groups will be different on many variables.

Deniston and Rosenstock (1973) showed that neither a nonexperimental nor a quasi-experimental design validly estimated program effectiveness of a treatment program for rheumatoid arthritics. The cyclical nature of the severity of this illness creates large biases in any design other than an experimental one. In other words, threats to internal validity (particularly regression to the mean) could not be handled by a quasi-experiment when studying this population. No group can be used effectively as a non-equivalent control group for a study of the value of treatment for rheumatoid arthritis. Although this is an unusual population, Deniston and Rosenstock make the general point that even when evaluators recognize a potential source of bias, they may be unable to control for it, short of forming the groups themselves through random assignment. When done on a completely random basis, the treatment and control groups are comparable because they do not differ systematically before the program begins.

Setting up truly equivalent experimental and control groups requires a nonbiased method of assigning the participants to the groups. Often evaluators believe that random assignment is impossible, when in fact it is a possibility, even within the strictures of functioning organizations. Carey (1979) evaluated the reorganization of a nursing service, taking advantage of a natural random assignment procedure. One of two medical floors of a large hospital was redesigned around a more personalized nursing concept. Assignment of new patients to rooms (and consequently to floors) was made on the basis of bed availability by admitting personnel unaware of the research and uninvolved in nursing organization. Because severity of illness and physician practice determine length of stay, the floor on which a bed is available in a hospital operating near capacity is a random occurrence. Thus, with no disruption of hospital routine, randomly assigned equivalent groups were obtained. Because the groups were not formed in some biased fashion (for example, physician preference for a floor or assignment of the more severely ill to one of the floors), the results could be interpreted without concern for the various threats to internal validity.

Boruch and Rindskopf (1977) liken a randomized experiment to an aspirin for evaluators because the evaluator is relieved of the headaches involved in trying to identify and estimate the sizes of the biases that are present in nonrandomized evaluations such as the nonequivalent-group design. The discussion of the patch-up design suggested that the evaluator introduce control groups to measure the impact of the identified biases. Although this is a good approach, there are times when the biases are recognized too late in the course of the evaluation. Further, there will be times when a comparison group needed to eliminate a particular threat to internal validity will be unavailable. There are statistical methods that are used to remove the biases when randomization is not possible. However, the use of these methods is controversial and can lead to incorrect conclusions. Campbell and Erlebacher (1970) point out that evaluations using these statistical corrections might make a program look successful when it is not or unsuccessful when it is successful. Boruch (1975) and others have shown that the statistical methods cannot correct for biases in basic evaluation designs whenever the variables describing group differences are imperfectly measured. Because measurements of academic achievement, emotional adjustment, criminal recidivism, productivity, and so forth, are never perfectly reliable, the statistical adjustments fail to remove all biases.

Experimental Designs

Figure 9.1 includes diagrams of several experimental designs. Each of the groups in the research designs is formed by randomly assigning possible participants to receive the program (the experimental group) or not to receive it (the control group). The most simple form of the true experiment, diagrammed in the top section of the figure, employs observations after the program is delivered but uses no pretests. Because the groups are formed randomly, there is no necessity to use a pretest to show that the groups were equivalent before receiving the program. Such pretests are advisable, if not essential, when preexisting groups are used for an evaluation as in the quasi-experimental, nonequivalent control-group design. As pointed out in Chapter 8, without pretests, the evaluator and the information users would never know if the program and the nonequivalent comparison groups were indeed comparable before the program group was influenced by the program. This is not an issue when true control groups are used.

At times, a program can be divided into two parts that might be provided separately or together as a unit. In such a case, the posttest

FIGURE 9.1: Evaluation designs utilizing random assignment to groups and the questions that these designs can answer

Experimental design	Symbolic representation*	Questions that can be answered
Posttest-only control group	X O O	Did the program cause a change in the program participants?
Two-by-two factorial	O X O Y O X Y O	Did either or both of the aspects of the program cause a change in the program participants? Is there something about having the two aspects of the program given together that creates an especially favorable climate for change? Or, do X and Y interfere with each other?
Solomon four group	O X O O O O X O	Did the program cause a change in the program participants?
Time series with random assignment to groups	X O O O O O O X O O O O O O X O O O	Did the program cause a change in the program participants? Did the effect of the program hold up over time?

The program is represented by X or Y; observations are represented by O.

228

design can be enlarged, as the second entry of Figure 9.1 shows. An evaluation using this design and the best method analyzing it will be discussed later in this chapter.

A brief review of the threats to internal validity can illustrate the power of random assignment to distinguish between the effect of the program and nonprogram causes of participant change. There is no reason to believe that the groups differ in maturation rates or levels or that they experience different historical influences. The groups have not selected themselves into the program being evaluated. Since participants did not begin at different levels of health, adjustment, achievement, and so forth, regression to the mean is not a viable threat. Both groups have equivalent testing experiences. The possibility of instrumentation changes exist in evaluation projects especially when observations are made over an extended period of time. The possibility of the meaning of scores changing as observers gain more experience with the research instruments or get tired of the project exists, regardless of the research design used. Similarly, the potential problems caused by participant drop-out after the evaluation has begun are no worst than with other designs.

In spite of the power of randomization to assure that the control and experimental groups will not be systematically different, some evaluators may feel more comfortable with pretests for both groups. Also, having pretests for experimental and control groups might help in communicat-ing the findings to others who do not understand the advantages of randomization. For these reasons, the third design is given in the figure. The four-group design is not in any theoretical way better than the two-group design with posttests only. The apparent compromise of using a two-group design with pretests is not advisable.

Often, the act of observation is reactive, especially in social settings. It is possible that the pretest would sensitize the program participants to the influences of the program, and thus the program will really only work when the pretest is given. If this is true, then the pretest becomes part of the program. There is nothing at all wrong with including a pretest as part of any program; however, it is easy to forget that the pre-test may cause the participants to react differently than they would have had the pretest not been given. In Campbell and Stanley's termi-nology (1963), adding pretests to the first design weakens its external validity because the pretest may have interacted with the program to cause the observed change. If testing is expensive, it is unlikely that pro-gram designers will want to incorporate the testing procedure into the program, even though the evaluation only showed that the pretest *and* the program lead to change—not that the program alone leads to change.

The advantages of time-series designs can be added to the experimental method by making repeated observations at regular intervals. In this way, evaluators can learn whether the program's impact held up across time. The last design in Figure 9.1 would be especially useful if follow-up assessments are desired and if the program is implemented on a staggered basis. The built-in replication provided by this design is a very attractive feature.

This discussion is not meant to imply that there are only four experimental designs. Many options are possible depending on the needs of the evaluations. These four designs are described in order to illustrate the type of possibilities that are available to the evaluator.

OBJECTIONS TO EXPERIMENTATION

When evaluators fail to use experimental methods, the reasons may be related to frequently voiced objections to experimental methodology. It is important for evaluators to be familiar with these objections, lest they encounter them for the first time while planning an evaluation or, even worse, after random assignment to programs has already begun.

Don't Experiment on Me!

People rightly are not anxious to have someone use them in a poorly thought out experiment. Unfortunately, experimentation has sometimes been unjustly associated with CIA and Army "experiments" on the effects of hallucinogenic drugs (*Time* August 4, 1975). The media does not use the word "experiment" in the careful way that experimental design textbooks do. Consequently, it is not surprising when people not trained in social science methodology equate experiments to evaluate the effects of a social program or a medical treatment with the covert administration of dangerous drugs to unsuspecting people. Evaluators planning an experiment will be careful to treat the question of experimentation with respect. The advantages of experimentation should be stressed. Furthermore, the fact that the program or service has been carefully planned by competent personnel should be clear to possible volunteers and committees overseeing the research.

Clinical Prerogatives

Often people are hesitant to become involved in experimentation because they want the best service available for their problem, be it a health, emotional, educational, or any other problem. They feel that because human service providers are trained and paid to choose the service most likely to help a person, random assignment to a control group means they are missing out on what they really need. In a similar fashion, service providers usually feel able to select the best care for a person in need or to select the people most likely to benefit from a service program. When they feel this way, the service provider is not likely to endorse an evaluation requiring random assignment to groups.

The fact of the matter is that in many ways people in need get a particular form of service on a fairly random basis. Different counselors follow various theories of counseling that an individual will not know about when seeking counseling. Physicians do not follow set treatment patterns. Different cities draw up quite different welfare programs. Judges do not assign identical sentences to people convicted of the same crimes. The reasons why a particular person experiences a particular form of counseling, medical treatment, or job training, are often unrelated to clinical insight.

It is quite natural for service staff to believe that they know best about the selection of treatments. The literature on clinical judgment and decision making also suggests that it is not unusual for a staff to believe that the selection of a particular treatment is appropriate, when in fact it is worthless or even harmful to people (Gilbert, Light, and Mosteller 1975). These misperceptions occur because we remember successes and fulfilled expectations; we often explain away and forget observations that do not fit our expectations (Chapman and Chapman 1967, 1969). Highly prejudiced individuals remember incidents in which a minority member commits a social gaffe but quickly forget or sympathize with a person from a higher status group committing a similar misstep (see Allport 1954). Partisan fans see more rule infractions by the opposing team than by their own team (Hastorf and Cantril 1954).

It takes a considerable amount of tact to convince service providers that their clinical judgment may not always be valid. Providing examples of nonrandomized studies that were later invalidated by randomized research may help service providers to see the possibility of misperceptions and the advantages of unambiguous documentation of service effectiveness. In Chapter 2, we described the necessity of encouraging the development of an experimental orientation among program managers and staff. Campbell (1969) suggested that society should approach new human service programs as if they were experiments, treating a failure of a well-conceived program as an indication of our incomplete understanding of human nature, not as an indication of the low motivation or the incompetence of the staff. Admittedly, this philosophy is not practiced as often as it could be. Human service providers act as though a negative evaluation means that they are incompetent and therefore they develop rationalizations whenever particular individuals do not seem to benefit from the human service provided. Few teachers examine their own performance when a student does not pass an examination. By explaining away all failures, the program staff avoids the opportunity for growth that is provided by unfulfilled expectations. At these times, evaluators feel the full force of the conflict between their skeptical role toward service programs and the providers' confidence in the effectiveness of care offered.

Time and Effort Involved

Anyone who has conducted research in an applied organization knows that research requires a commitment of time and effort. Evaluators should not agree to conduct a research project if they do not have the resources to carry it through promptly. Nevertheless, it takes only a little additional work to conduct an experiment compared to a noncontrolled evaluation. Planning and obtaining approval for an experiment requires more time and perseverance than a pretest-posttest single-group evaluation. However, once approval has been obtained, data collection, analysis, and presentation require the same time, regardless of the quality of the evaluation design. Some care is required of the evaluator to be sure the experiment is not corrupted. These concerns will be discussed in the last section of the chapter.

THE COSTS OF *NOT* DOING AN EXPERIMENT

Performing a randomized experiment in a service delivery setting requires a lot of effort and tenacity on the part of the evaluator. In addition, the staff is inconvenienced because, at a minimum, additional forms must be completed. At worst, the staff may feel threatened and treat the evaluator with hostility. Is it worth it? Gilbert, Light, and Mosteller (1975) point out that too often the cost of experimentation is not evaluated properly. Instead of considering the cost in absolute terms, planners should compare it with the cost of *not* doing an experiment. Gilbert, Light, and Mosteller describe several medical procedures that became widely accepted on the basis of observational, nonexperimental studies. For example, in 1964 there were approximately one thousand treatment units being used to freeze duodenal ulcers in the United States for ten thousand patients. After a careful randomized experiment, the treatment was discarded. Although the study that finally showed the treatment to be worthless was expensive, the cost of the worthless treatment was expensive as well. The cost of bloodletting, previously mentioned, was high as well. Patients in this latter case did not receive a worthless treatment, they received a harmful one. The cost of a small-scale experiment would have been miniscule, compared to the cost of the mistreatment.

If a quasi-experimental study cannot be clearly interpreted, its cost is largely wasted. A number of writers have found that published, poorly controlled studies often favor a novel treatment. Although these poorly controlled studies may be a little less expensive than a well- controlled study, they actually cost more because of misinformation provided to readers who may seek to duplicate the results with their own clients, students, or patients. The proliferation of misinformation supporting an ineffective program means that people seeking help, who expect to receive the "best treatment" for them, may actually be served quite poorly. Even those who would have refused to be part of an experiment on the assumption that they would not be treated in the best way possible may end up with something worse than a recognized experimental program. They may actually end up with what is, in fact, an experimental program that is only assumed to be effective.

Gilbert, Light, and Mosteller (1975) say that the alternative to careful clinical trials is "fooling around." A service provider trying an approach supported only by uncontrolled studies often does not inform the client/patient/trainee that the treatment is new and not thoroughly understood. Nor does the service provider seek to obtain informed consent from a client/patient/trainee as an evaluator would when conducting an experiment.

The costs of not doing an experiment, then, are many. Evaluations that seek to identify causes but cannot are totally wasteful. Evaluations that purport to have found an effective program when the program is ineffective may encourage the use of ineffective programs. There are many reasons to initiate program evaluation. When the reason is to identify causal relationships between a human service (the independent variable) and outcome (the dependent variable), the cost of an experiment is surprisingly low when compared to not doing it.

THE MOST DESIRABLE TIMES TO CONDUCT EXPERIMENTS

It is the contention of this text that evaluation should be built into the daily operation of human service organizations as well as other organizations. Usually, such evaluation procedures will not be experiments but program-monitoring approaches described in Chapters 5 and 6. There are, however, circumstances that are especially well-suited to conducting experiments, as the following sections will illustrate.

When a New Program Is Introduced

When a new program is introduced, there are several conditions that are likely to make staff and administrators interested in an experimental evaluation: (1) responsible people are thinking about change; (2) if the control group receives the old program, it is hard to argue that its participants are being unfairly treated; (3) the program may take some time to implement, thus providing time for an evaluation; and (4) there is need to document the program's success for internal requirements, as well as to show that it might work elsewhere.

One of the obstacles to good program evaluation is the fear people often have of change. It is only natural to become comfortable in continuing to do things in the same way year after year. Thus, an important variable that needs to be considered in planning evaluations is the staff's and administration's openness or readiness to change. Salasin and Davis (1979) have developed a scale to measure the beliefs of the staff about the likelihood that an evaluation (as well as other innovations) will be accepted and will have a positive effect on the organization. When the impetus for change comes from within the program in the form of a plan for a new service, the staff does not require prodding to consider change. Of course, the staff may need to be cautioned that most innovations, even when well planned, are not successful (Gilbert, Light, and Mosteller 1975).

When beginning a new program, the current form of service can be given to the control group. Whatever needs a group may have, its members receive help somewhere. It may be from a previous program, from another agency, from family members, or elsewhere. Because the service to be evaluated is new, it is hard to argue that randomly assigning people to continue receiving the service that they have been getting is a deprivation. (People who believe deeply in the new program will raise the argument nonetheless.) The evaluator seeking to assign participants randomly will have an easier time defending the random assignment when a new program is introduced than when the program has been running for several years and is considered standard policy.

The fact that most new programs do not go into effect in all parts of the organization simultaneously is an advantage to evaluators. Human relations seminars for managers, for example, will not be given to all managers at one time. All that is necessary to conduct an experimental evaluation is to develop a random procedure to schedule the managers for the training sessions. This evaluation design will be very powerful if there are several groups, each receiving the program at a different time. The essential aspects of this design were diagramed in the fourth entry of Figure 9.1. The delivery of the program at different times permits the formation of multiple control groups and the repeated replication of the experimental evaluation at times one through four. Furthermore, the possibility of follow-up assessment of success is possible. The most desirable outcome of the evaluation would be for the dependent variables to follow the pattern shown in Figure 9.2. If all five groups were to improve a similar amount after receiving the program and if the groups maintained their post-training level, alternative, non-program explanations of the results would be very hard to support.

In order to conduct this sort of an evaluation, it is important for evaluators to have access to organizational plans. All too often, evaluators' services are requested after the program is in place or after its implementation is planned. People untrained in social science methods seldom understand the evaluator's request for changes in implementation plans to accommodate the design needs of the evaluation. Because service personnel will have worked hard to gain approval for a new program, they will resist the idea of postponing implementation for the evaluator's sake. Whenever possible, it is far better to be involved in the planning stages than to ask for a change in plans.

A fourth reason why new programs may be evaluated is that there may be less anxiety over the possibility of failure, compared to a program widely accepted in the organization. Less is at stake if the program

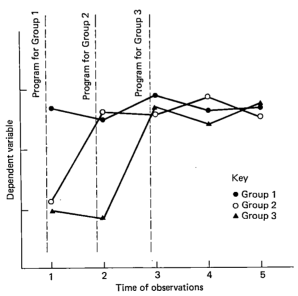

FIGURE 9.2: The most desirable outcome for a three-group design with delayed program participation for Groups 2 and 3. Group 1 received the program before the first observations; Group 2, between the first and second observations; and Group 3, between the second and third observations.

does not look perfect because fewer people have become committed to it.

A fifth reason to document the success of a new program concerns the favorable publicity generated among the general public and organizations. Employees are likely to feel pride in being associated with an organization that has a reputation as an innovator. Referrals are more likely to be provided if human service personnel in other organizations have respect for an innovating agency. Of course, there are many ways of increasing employee pride and of increasing the perceived success of an agency; however, documentation of the success of innovations in human services can certainly help.

When Resources are Scarce

A second circumstance in which experimentation may be accepted is when resources are scarce. If the program cannot be offered to everyone who could possibly use it, some way must be found to decide who will get the program and who will not. The most desirable, from the evaluator's point of view, is to use random selection to determine who can obtain the service. Riecken and Boruch (1947) report that the general public is remarkably willing to accept the idea of a lottery to determine who does and does not obtain a valuable service. In a real sense, a lottery is more fair than a first-come, first-served policy because often those with "connections" are the ones who hear about the program first. Teenagers whose relatives are involved in city government will probably hear about a summer job program before those who must depend on newspapers or other sources for the announcement of application dates and eligibility criteria.

When resources are scarce, many service providers strive to give the program to those most in need. There is no question that such a strategy is in some ways just; however, it is also true that the ways of determining eligibility are not perfectly reliable. In fact, the way in which eligibility is determined is often quite unreliable, with different service providers coming to different conclusions. In cases where the most needy are to get the program, perhaps an agreement can be reached defining a category of uncertain eligibility. From this group, program participants and controls could be selected randomly and an experiment performed utilizing just the people whose eligibility is uncertain (Crano and Brewer 1973).

When There Is Controversy About Program Effectiveness

Evaluators who work with a program of uncertain worth enjoy some advantages and must adapt to some disadvantages. This section stresses the advantages, but first a word about the disadvantages.

If service providers disagree about a program, evaluation research will be viewed very critically; contending factions might each seek to recruit the evaluators to their side. The evaluators' behavior may be scrutinized for signs of favoritism. In such situations, evaluators would do well to keep everyone informed of plans and to carry out plans with care and evenhanded policies. Although such scrutiny may make program evaluation somewhat more stressful for the evaluator, the final products may actually be of higher quality unless evaluators refuse to draw any conclusions from the research. More will be said about handling controversial conclusions in Chapters 11 and 12.

Controversy provides an advantage to evaluators because controversy over programs can be directed to support an experiment. If some influential people in an organization do not believe in the program, they will not be moved by arguments that it is unjust to deprive a control group of a particular service. If there are others who strongly support the program, it is possible that there will be an institutional battle. In such a case, the question of offering the program may be decided on political grounds. If, on the other hand, both sides could agree on what they would accept as evidence of the program's success, the setting for an experiment could well be excellent.

For example, various forms of welfare reform have proponents and detractors. A number of experiments have been conducted to test whether income supplements would enhance or reduce the willingness of people to seek employment (Kershaw 1972). Some welfare recipients were randomly assigned to participate in various forms of income maintenance programs or to remain in current programs. Liberal legislators may argue that the people in the control group were being treated unfairly, while conservative legislators might argue that the new program was a giveaway. If program evaluation can supply social science observations to both groups, evaluation will fill a useful role in society. Whether or not welfare is ever designed on the basis of the findings of this research, the level of debate will be raised and the validity of arguments used will be increased on the basis of good research on controversial topics (Abt 1977).

Program evaluation is useful in controversial areas in order to convince possible adopters of the program of its effectiveness. In education, a standard policy is to experiment with new teaching materials before trying to market them to school districts using other texts. The most unassailable evidence that one can provide to show that an educational program is effective is evidence from an experimental evaluation that shows the program group did better on some commonly accepted outcome measure than did a randomly selected control group learning from a standard program.

There has been controversy over the question of whether nutritional supplements to malnourished children in tropical areas would have long-term effects on cognitive development (McKay et al. 1978). McKay and his colleagues randomly assigned low socioeconomic, malnourished children of Cali, Columbia, to receive food supplements beginning at four different times before they reached school age. The four groups received the supplement for periods of forty-five, thirty-four, twenty-six, or ten months before starting school. The authors found that the sooner a nutritional supplement was begun, the more impact there was on cognitive development. However, for all groups there was a positive impact lasting at least one year after the supplements were no longer given. By use of an experiment, the cause of improvement was shown to be due to the nutrition, not to self-selection, regression to the mean, testing effects, or any other nonprogram effects. (This particular experiment was strengthened through the use of two additional untreated groups, one high and one low in socioeconomic status, that were not made up of randomly assigned children.)

When Change Is Desired

Program evaluation utilizing experimental methodology is useful when there is widespread dissatisfaction with current conditions but no consensus about what changes should be instituted. Income maintenance evaluations (Kershaw 1972) are examples of experiments conducted in response to a desire for change in welfare policies accompanied by uncertainty about what to do. In the 1960s, the desire to prevent, or at least to reduce, the rate of school failure of disadvantaged rural and urban children led to a series of experiments with Head Start, a preschool program aimed at teaching cognitive skills and providing medical care and nutritional assistance (Datta 1976b). On a facility level, Carey (1976) took advantage of dissatisfaction with a mandatory counseling requirement for couples seeking sterilization to conduct a randomized experiment in a general hospital. Experimentation as a conscious, rational approach to selecting among alternatives is the prime example of Campbell's concept of the "experimenting society" (1969), in which government and public alike agree to submit proposed changes in human services to experimentation, recognizing that although most innovations do not live up to expectations, the best way to choose among various possibilities is through careful program evaluation.

PRESERVING AN EXPERIMENTAL DESIGN

Up to this point, the emphases of this chapter have been on (1) the advantages of experiments over other approaches as methods to infer that a program caused a change in behavior; and (2) the situations that are likely to lead to the acceptance of random assignment to experimental and control groups. As unfortunate as it seems, evaluators cannot rest after planning and getting approval for an experimental design. Once begun, experiments have a way of breaking down without careful sheparding. There are some precautions that can be taken to maximize the likelihood that the evaluation will remain an interpretable experiment.

Precautions Before Data Collection Begins

One of the problems with evaluations is that participants drop out of various groups. If the experimental group is receiving a service, its members are likely to be more easily followed than the control people, who have nothing to gain by staying in contact with the evaluator. It is also possible that participants will drop out of the experimental group if the program makes rigorous demands on participants. Harris and Bruner (1971) sought to measure the impact of a contract weight reduction program involving a cash deposit that would be refunded at a rate of so many dollars ($1.00 or $.50) per pound lost in a given week. In the first experiment, 58 percent of the program participants dropped out after random assignment. In the second experiment, *all* participants dropped out after random assignment to the program. The evaluation was not without any utility; the drop-out rate clearly showed that a program requiring a cash deposit was not acceptable to these overweight people! If the drop-out rate is high and if dropout is different from group to group, the best planned experiment will become uninterpretable.

Perhaps one of the most thorough attempts to minimize treatment-related dropout was carried out in the selection of participants for the New Jersey Income Maintenance Study. Riecken and Boruch (1974) report that in order to minimize treatment-related dropout, the evaluators explained to possible participants all the levels of income supplement involved in the study and described the information that would be needed from them. Only those people who agreed to provide the information regardless of the group to which they were assigned were retained and randomly assigned to groups.

Few advantages are gained without some accompanying cost. Postponing randomization until some dropout has occurred introduces the possibility that the participants no longer represent the population for whom the program was designed. The people who dropped out because they would not agree to provide information regardless of the group they were in are likely to be different from the people who agreed to all the conditions. It is most likely that those who dropped out included some irresponsible or transient people. It is also possible that some of the most motivated obtained jobs during the initial negotiations and thus were no longer interested in the program. Income maintenance programs, if incorporated into the welfare system, would be provided to all who qualified through low incomes—not only to those who would agree to cooperate in an experiment on income maintenance. If a large proportion of possible participants refused to cooperate with the research, those who refused may have been quite different from those who agreed to cooperate. If so, then conclusions drawn from the experiment may not apply to more than a fraction of the population. What appears to be a successful program may only be successful with some. Sound experiments whose results cannot be applied to other locations or populations are said to lack external validity (Campbell and Stanley 1963).

A way to counter this threat to generalization is to compare those who refuse to participate with those who do participate. When evaluating a welfare program, a considerable amount of information is available about those who do and do not cooperate. If such variables as age, income, or education do indeed differ between the groups, the usefulness of the evaluation is reduced. If, on the other hand, the groups do not differ on such variables and if the proportion of dropouts is small, the conclusions drawn from the experiment can be trusted.

Precautions While the Experiment Is Occurring

Even after the experiment has begun, evaluators must remain close to the data-gathering procedure in order to be sure that agreed-upon procedures are being followed. Cook and Campbell (1976) describe four additional threats to internal validity not presented in Chapter 7 that can occur after an experiment has been designed and begun; each of the four serves to reduce the interpretability of an experiment.

First, *diffusion or imitation of the program* can occur when the controls learn about the program and, in effect, administer it to themselves. Straw (1978) described a weight reduction program in general terms to all volunteers before random assignment. One member of the control group (randomly assigned to receive the program at a later time) used the brief verbal description to design her own weight reduction program. By imitating the program, she achieved a greater weight reduction than any of the people in the experimental group.

Second, *attempts to compensate the control group* occur when staff or managers seek to give the members of the control group some special service to make up for their not being in the experimental group receiving the program. Posavac (1974) was evaluating an information/counseling program for postcoronary inpatients. Part way through the evaluation, he learned that nurses were distributing a short book to control patients who were the most insistent about getting more information. The nurses had difficulty accepting the requirement that controls not be given the program textbook until after the predischarge assessment of knowledge and attitudes. Successful compensation will result in a negative evaluation because compensation will tend to make the experimental and control groups equivalent on the outcome measures. A way to discourage such compensation is to point out that compensating the controls can serve to reduce the likelihood of finding support for the program and, consequently, reduce the probability of the program being offered in the future. Thus, if the program is actually effective, compensation of the controls could result in the loss of a worthwhile service for people who need it.

Third, control groups sometimes feel a *rivalry with the experimental group*. Rahe (1978) experienced this problem in an evaluation of an exercise program for Navy fliers. The program was designed to increase the fitness of the fliers in an attempt to lower physiological stress reactions when landing on an aircraft carrier. Because the groups were all aboard a single ship, some of the controls heard about the program and were observed working out on the exercycles in order to "score" as well on the physiological outcome measures as the pilots in the experimental group.

Each of the above three threats serve to make the experimental and control groups similar. The fourth, *local history,* is a threat that could also do this or the reverse. *Local history* refers to events that occur to members of one group in an experiment. This may be a threat when participants are tested in groups although randomly assigned individually to control or experimental conditions. The possibility exists that one member of the group may affect the others in a way that will enhance the group differences or reduce them. One member of an elementary-school class may act out during testing and affect the scores of the other children. If the class is part of the experimental group, group differences could be reduced. If the class belongs to the control group, the controls might appear even less accomplished due to this one student. Thus, local history could bias the evaluation to favor the control group or the experimental group. The way to avoid the effect of local history is to deliver the program and assess its effectiveness to many small groups (or even to individuals), not just to a small number of large groups.

There is no substitute for an evaluator keeping close track of the data-gathering process. Although close personal attention is time-consuming, the delegation of duties to program staff or to people not really involved with the evaluation process may lead to situations that destroy the usefulness of the evaluation. The insidiousness of these four threats is that they can destroy a sophisticated experiment that was designed and implemented with great care without the evaluator even being aware that the experiment cannot be validly interpreted. By analogy, if we consider the original threats to internal validity as structural defects in the design of a house, then these four threats are like termites negating the advantages of the well-designed structure from within.

METHODS OF ANALYZING EXPERIMENTS

T-Test

Because random assignment to groups removes the reasons for administering a pretest, the standard form of the *t*-test is the most appropriate statistical test of a simple two-group evaluation. The pretest was introduced only when random assignment was impossible and it was necessary to demonstrate that the control and experimental groups were indeed reasonably equivalent. Any standard elementary statistics text will present an example of the use of this analysis (for example, McCall 1975).

Simple Analysis of Variance

If the evaluation employs three or more groups, such as would occur when a control group is contrasted with two versions of a program, simple (one-way) analysis of variance is the best statistical test to use. Analysis of variance simultaneously compares the means of three or more groups to learn whether at least one of them is different from the other means.

For example, a school system may want to learn whether a tutoring program helps poor readers. In addition, it may be of interest to learn if the value of the tutoring is increased when a short programmed study guide is provided along with the tutoring. If three groups are randomly formed and reading scores obtained at the end of a semester, both program groups would be expected to read better than the control group. Analysis of variance will show whether one or more of the groups produced a mean reliably above the control group.

Of course, evaluators want to know more than that "the group means differed." They want to know whether program group A was reliably better than group B, or whether the program groups were equally effective and both better than the control group. To do these analyses requires statistical techniques usually not covered in introductory statistics courses. Planned comparisons using the Newman-Keuls or the Tukey procedures are discussed in Kirk (1968). The beginning evaluator might simply use a t-test to compare pairs of means but only *after* finding a statistically significant result from an analysis of variance.

Complex Analysis of Variance

Sometimes, the evaluator wants to determine if two approaches to a problem are each effective, and in addition, whether using both approaches simultaneously is even more effective. Landes (1973) studied the effects of two approaches to reduce the anxiety of children hospitalized for tonsilectomies. The important dependent measures were physiological and behavioral signs of anxiety. Two approaches to reduce anxiety were available; one focused on the children, and the second on the mother. Four random groups were formed. The control group was provided no service other than the normal efforts of the surgeon, pediatrician, and nurse to reduce the child's or the mother's anxiety. One program group of children watched a puppet show about tonsils and hospital stays. The mothers of a second program group attended a group session to explain procedures to them on the hypothesis that well-informed, less tense mothers would have less anxious children. The third program group watched the puppet show and their mothers attended the group session to learn about procedures.

The results of this experiment were examined using a complex analysis of variance analysis. Instead of treating the experiment as a four-group design, it can be considered a two-by-two design as illustrated in Figure 9.3. There is a distinct advantage to analyzing the results as a two-by-two design rather than using a simple analysis of variance. First, one can examine the effect of the puppet show and the effect of the mothers' group separately. In essence, the analysis combines the control group and program group B and compares the overall mean of those two groups to the overall mean of program groups A and C. This compari-

FIGURE 9.3: A two-by-two factorial evaluation design best analyzed using complex analysis of variance

	Did not attend mothers' group	Attended mothers' group
No puppet show	Control group	Program group B
Puppet show	Program group A	Program group C

son reveals whether the puppet show had an effect. Then, the means of the columns of the matrix in Figure 9.3 are found. If these means differ, the efforts with the mothers was effective.

Over and above these comparisons, complex analysis of variance permits one to examine the interaction of the two approaches to the reduction of anxiety. (*Interaction* refers to the joint effect of the two approaches to anxiety reduction.) To illustrate, see the graphs of several possible outcomes of a two-by-two factorial design given in Figure 9.4. The upper left graph shows no effect; anxiety is the same

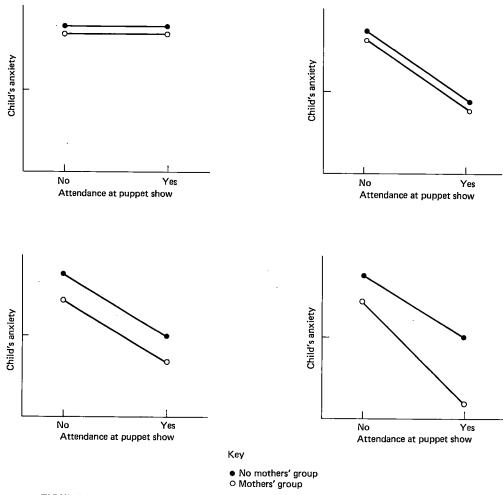

Key

● No mothers' group
○ Mothers' group

FIGURE 9.4: Four possible outcomes of a two-by-two factorial design. When the lines in the graph are not parallel, the possibility of a significant interaction exists.

whether the children see the puppet show or not, and the same level of anxiety is observed, whether the mothers participate or not. In the upper right, the graph illustrates a reduction for the puppet show but not for the mothers' group. In the lower left, both approaches have an effect, and the group with both is the best off. In the lower right, however, there is an interaction between the approaches. In this graph, the group with both services is especially calm. In fact, if the means followed this pattern, the children would be more calm than would have been predicted by knowing that both approaches were individually effective.

The reader may recall that the concept of interaction was utilized to isolate the effect of the junior year abroad study in Chapter 8. Readers for whom the idea of interaction is new would do well to compare the example in Figure 9.3 with that in Figure 8.8 in order to be sure that the idea is thoroughly understood.

SUMMARY

Whenever program evaluations are designed to determine whether or not a human service program caused any change in the people served, an experimental research design should be considered. It should not, however, be forced on a program or facility that does not support the requirements of experimental research. When implemented, program evaluations based on experimental research designs are easier to interpret and to analyze than are the less well-controlled evaluations described in Chapter 8. Recall the comment that experimental designs are like aspirins; they reduce the number of headaches experienced by evaluators—Reduce, but not eliminate. The best-designed evaluations will not be interpretable if they are not carried out as planned. Evaluators recognize that many human service professionals will not fully understand the advantages of the experimental approach and could in all innocence nullify the evaluator's plans. As with all forms of evaluation, someone will need to maintain close contact with the way the data are collected and the way individuals are assigned to research groups.

STUDY QUESTIONS

1. Why was testing not a viable threat to internal validity in the evaluation of the program to reduce the anxiety of children before surgery?

2. If more program participants than members of the control group drop out of an experimental evaluation, what can be concluded from the evaluation? (Note: the answer "Nothing" is incorrect.)

3. List the advantages and disadvantages of experimental and quasi-experimental evaluation designs. Use parallel columns so that when you are finished with the list you have a concise way to compare these two approaches.

4. Using language that can be understood by someone without training in statistics and research methods, explain the advantages of experimentation, including random assignment to groups. Imagine you are addressing an elementary-school teacher, a nurse, a police officer, or similar human service staff person. The adequacy of your answer depends both on its technical correctness and its appropriateness to the intended audience.

5. Suppose that after an experiment is described (as in question 4 above), someone asks, "If the new program is worth experimenting on and if the staff feels that the program is good, how can you justify not letting the controls reap the benefit of the program?" What would be an appropriate answer?

FURTHER READING

There are many good sources of material on experimental evaluations. The first reading is a lengthy and compelling argument for experimental evaluations.

GILBERT, J. P., LIGHT, R. J., and MOSTELLER, F. 1975. Assessing social innovations: An empirical base for policy. In *Evaluation and experiment,* ed. A. R. Lumsdaine and C. A. Bennett. New York: Academic Press.

The previously cited materials by Donald Campbell and colleagues are useful for this chapter as well.

CAMPBELL, D. T., and STANLEY, J. C. 1963. *Experimental and quasi-experimental designs for research.* Chicago: Rand-McNally.

COOK, T. D., and CAMPBELL, D. T. 1976. The design and conduct of quasi-experiments and true experiments in field settings. In *Handbook of industrial and organizational research,* ed. M. D. Dunnette. Chicago: Rand-McNally.

CASE STUDY 9.1

Telephones and Raising Bail

The author of this case study took advantage of the introduction of a new program to conduct a true experiment in a criminal justice setting. Note that the evaluator utilized qualitative information obtained from interviews to aid in the interpretation of the quantitative measures. The complete report of this evaluation was cited in Chapter 7 as an example of the use of a nonexperimental design to investigate whether a rigorous evaluation would be useful. You may recall that the introduction of a telephone was associated with an increase in the proportion of detainees released on bond. However, that nonexperimental finding did not constitute proof that the telephone led to the increased rate of releases on bond. The experiment summarized in this case study followed up on the lead provided by the nonexperimental design.

TELEPHONES AND RAISING BAIL *

Kenneth J. Lenihan
Center for Policy Research

Bail is set for many defendants, who are often unable to raise even small amounts—sometimes only $50 or $100 cash, or bonds of $500 to $1,000—and are held in detention until final disposition of their case, which might not come until sixty to ninety days later. Usually, they cannot raise bail because they lack financial resources, but some observers have noted other reasons—in particular, that defendants in custody are cut off from the outside world, so that it is difficult for them to mobilize friends and relatives to raise money on their behalf (Foote 1955; Suffet 1965).

With the cooperation of the New York City Department of Corrections, we installed a telephone in The Tombs, a detention prison in lower Manhattan. The telephone was manned by a staff member of The Vera Institute, and Vera paid for its installation and service out of federal funds granted to help solve problems of criminal justice.

Defendants requesting the use of the phone were classified according to the length of time they had already spent in detention and the amount of bail that had been set. Only defendants with bail set at $2,000 or less who had been detained ten days or less were admitted to the experiment. Defendants who qualified were then classified into one of eight cate-

* Condensed with permission from *Evaluation Quarterly* 1 (1977); 569–86. Copyright 1977 Sage Publications, Inc.

gories, according to the amount of bail and the length of time they had been detained so far. Within each classification, defendants were then randomly assigned to either the treatment or control group.

The treatment group was given the opportunity to call the next day; the control group was not allowed to make calls until seven days later. If the telephone were instrumental in raising bail money, it would be reflected in the rates of release and detainment of the two groups. And the treatment group did indeed benefit: 25.4 percent were released on bail within seven days, while only 13.1 percent of the control group were released during the same period ($Z = 1.712$; $p < .05$).

This finding was reinforced by what happened to the control group. When, after seven days, the controls were finally given the opportunity to use the phone, their rate of release rose sharply to 24 percent—roughly equivalent to the 25 percent release rate of the treatment group during its first seven days.

After the fourteenth day, three more defendants in the treatment group were released on bail, but no more in the control group.

Although the control group began to close the gap after they started using the phone, they never quite caught up with the treatment group: 33 percent of the treatment group obtained pretrial release on bail, compared with only 28 percent of the control group.

The telephone was installed on the assumption that if a defendant could reach family or friends, he had a better chance to raise bail. The question remained, were defendants really cut off from the outside? To find out, we interviewed the fifty-nine defendants in the treatment group to find out how much contact they had with friends and family after they had been taken into custody. Their responses suggest why the telephone call turned out to be so important.

When an accused man is taken into custody, his first opportunity to reach someone may be by telephone while he is being booked at the police station. Only six of the fifty-nine defendants reported having used the telephone at the station house, and one of these stated that his call did not go through. Moreover, at the station house the accused person does not yet know if the charge will be sustained at arraignment court, if bail will be set and, if so, for how much. So the station house call is not likely to deal with bail, since the facts are unknown, and first offenders may not even be aware that bail is a potential problem.

The next opportunity for contact with outsiders is at arraignment, and only four out of fifty-nine defendants reported that a friend or family member was present in court when they were arraigned.

After arraignment, if bail is not posted immediately, defendants are confined to a detention prison. Here there are three ways in which they may communicate with people on the outside: they may send a letter; they may send a message through a corrections officer; or they may be visited.

Nineteen of fifty-nine defendants reported having written a letter, the most common way of trying to contact someone outside. (Four other defendants said they did not know how to write, six that they were unable to get writing materials.) Only four defendants reported having had a visitor—a number that is understandably low, since a visit to the jail requires prior communication.

Finally, every defendant has the legal right to send a message through a corrections officer. A statement of this right is usually mumbled in a perfunctory manner as the defendant passes through arraignment—whether it is heard or understood is doubtful in many cases. Of the fifty-nine defendants, sixteen tried to send a message through the corrections officer. An officer usually has more requests than he can handle, so some messages simply are not sent. Many others do not get through. Unfortunately, the defendant is never told whether the message was received or what the reply was, if any.

To sum up, almost half of this sample (44 percent) had had no contact at all with the outside, even though they had been in custody for at least four days. One could assume—and many corrections officers did—that this relative failure to make contact with people outside reflected a lack of motivation—yet *every one* of the fifty-nine defendants in the experimental group filled out a request to use the telephone.

Why did the telephone succeed where other forms of contact—notably letters and messages through corrections officers—failed? Perhaps because the telephone more closely approximates direct contact. A message or letter goes in only one direction, but the telephone permits a dialogue, persuasion, a discussion of alternatives—especially about where money might be obtained.

CASE STUDY 9.2

A Preventive Health Program

The authors of this evaluation took advantage of the high demand for a desirable service to conduct a randomized experimental evaluation. As with other case studies, this is a condensed report. It omits references to another control group and a comparison group. As so simplified, the design does not control for a threat to the validity of generalizations drawn from the results of this evaluation. What is that threat and what can be added to the design that would control for it? Note the authors' comments on the use of randomly selected groups and their decision not to test their hypotheses at the conventional .05 level.

EVALUATION OF A POSITIVE HEALTH CARE PROGRAM *

Jack McKillip and Linda Kamens

Department of Psychology
Southern Illinois University at Carbondale

In this report, we describe one aspect of a comprehensive positive health care program developed by the Student Health Services of Southern Illinois University at Carbondale and directed toward changing students' lifestyles. The project was based on the work of and was organized in consultation with Dr. John C. McCamy (McCamy and Presley 1975). The importance of lifestyle for health is underscored by the statistics on degenerative diseases; that is, the three top killers of adult Americans are heart attacks, strokes, and cancer. All of these diseases are strongly related to lifestyle, are predictable, and (at least theoretically) are preventable.

The primary assumption underlying the lifestyling program is that health is not a gift or an accident but rather a creative act. The program seeks to lessen susceptibility factors that increase the likelihood of disease and to strengthen resistance factors that lower the possibility of disease by influencing lifestyle in the areas of diet, exercise, stress reduction, and ecological awareness.

Program Description

The lifestyling program consisted of a cultivation session, a weekend workshop, and weekly support/follow-up groups. The cultivation session consisted of a short presentation on the history of the program, a description of the workshop and support/follow-up groups, and an explanation of the time commitment and the purpose of the program's structure. The workshop was a three-day live-in experience involving both cognitive and experiential presentations. The former included presentations on: (1) differences between traditional and preventive models of health; (2) differences between average and normal conceptions of health; (3) the concept of risk factors; and (4) the four areas of health: nutrition, stress, exercise, and environment. The experiential aspects of the program included: (1) techniques to increase awareness of environment in eating and to reduce stress; (2) aerobic and stretching exercises; and (3) a detailed individual disease risk factor analysis.

At the end of the workshop, participants set goals for themselves and arranged to meet with their support groups. All participants were given Dr. McCamy's book *Human Life Styling,* a set of log sheets to be filled out daily for the duration of the program, and a feedback questionnaire concerning their reaction to the workshop. Support groups of eight to

* Condensed with permission from R. V. Robertson, ed., *Health Care Research in Illinois,* vol. 2, pp. 352–357. (Springfield, Ill.: Southern Illinois School of Medicine, 1977).

ten participants met with two staff members weekly for the reinforcement of progress and the sharing of experiences and group problem solving.

Evaluation Design

Since the lifestyling program was a treatment in short supply—there were over two hundred eligible applicants for fifty workshop openings— volunteers were randomly assigned either to the full program group described above or to a no-treatment control group. Prior to randomization, volunteers were grouped on age, sex, and race. Fifty volunteers were assigned to the full program, and sixty-one to the control group. The randomization is, of course, the crucial component of the design, guaranteeing that the groups did not differ systematically prior to the lifestyling program.

Outcome measures. The evaluation included indicators of both process and impact, but only the latter will be discussed in this paper. Outcome measures were obtained twice, before the program began (prior to randomization) and six months later. These measures included: (1) physiological indicators; (2) attitudinal scales; (3) behavioral scales; and (4) institutional records, for example, incidence of use of the student health service. This report will be concerned exclusively with the self-reported behavior scales.

Procedure. The actual evaluation was conducted by a team (the authors) who were independent of the Student Health Service staff. The measurement activities were presented as a study of the Student Health Service and not associated with the lifestyle program. All correspondence was handled out of the Department of Psychology, and every attempt was made to keep the lifestyling project and the evaluation separate.

Analysis. The method of analysis was analysis of covariance[1] of post-test scores with group and sex of respondent as independent variables and age and pretest score as covariates (Huck and McLean 1975). The analysis compares post-program scores after statistically adjusting for differences due to age and preprogram status. In addition, because of conservative biases built into the full-program group versus the control group comparison, and because the authors generally feel that when testing a new program Type II errors are a greater problem than Type I errors, the alpha level was set at .20.

[1] Analysis of covariance is useful when program participants are randomly assigned to groups, and something about the individuals is known to correlate with the outcome measure. For example, in this case study, preprogram attitudes correlated with post-program attitudes; that is, those students relatively more predisposed to following good nutritional habits tended to still be relatively more inclined after the program, even though as a group program participants improved. Analysis of covariance enables the evaluator to perform a more powerful statistical test than is otherwise available. The analysis is complex and cannot be further discussed in this text (see Kirk 1968).

Results

The first concern for analysis was the comparability of groups at the time of posttest. Attrition, that is, failure to complete posttest measurements, was 28 percent for full-program participants and 29 percent for control-group members. Comparisons of demographic characteristics revealed no significant differences between those who did and did not complete the posttest measurements, for either group. In addition, analysis of characteristics of the random sample showed the same distribution on age and sex as the experimental groups.

Figure 9.5 presents the pre- and posttest means for the experimental groups and the outcome measures for the random sample for various behavioral measures. Each will be discussed in turn.

The diet scale indicated frequency of eating each of fourteen non-nutritious foods (for example, sweet between-meal snacks) during an average week. Analysis revealed a significant difference between full program and control group on this measure in the direction of a positive program impact ($p < .001$). In addition, a comparison was made between members of the experimental groups (program volunteers) and the random sample.

The exercise scale indicates frequency of involvement in twelve physical activities, for example, jogging, swimming. Although the trend in

FIGURE 9.5: Behavioral outcome measures

Measure	Range	Test	Full program (N = 36)	Control group (N = 45)
Diet[a]	0–14	Pre	4.4	4.5
		Post	3.4	4.9
Exercise[b]	0–12	Pre	1.7	1.7
		Post	2.0	1.8
Stress[a]	13–65	Pre	32.7	33.8
		Post	34.7	37.3
Environmental awareness[b]	0–12	Pre	3.6	3.7
		Post	4.6	4.2
Alcohol use[a]	1–6	Pre	3.4	3.6
		Post	3.1	3.5
Other drug use[a]	0–4	Pre	.5	.5
		Post	.5	.9
Symptoms[a]	0–71	Pre	12.8	14.5
		Post	6.4	13.2

[a] The lower the mean, the healthier the behavior.

[b] The higher the mean, the healthier the behavior.

Figure 9.5 is in the direction of a positive program effect, the differences are not significant.

The stress scale indicates the frequency of engaging in thirteen stress-related activities (for example, making lists of things to do). Analysis revealed significantly less stress for the program group compared to the control group ($p < .13$).

The environmental awareness scale indicates the frequency of involvement in twelve positive environment-improving activities (for example, pick up litter around the house, join an environmental group). Although the trend was in the direction of a positive program effect, this difference was not statistically significant.

Two drug-use questions were asked, one indicating the frequency of use of alcohol and the other the use of four other drugs: uppers, downers, hallucinogens, and cocaine. Both alcohol use ($p < .06$) and other drug use ($p < .09$) was lower for the full program than for the control group. The last analysis revealed significantly fewer symptoms for the full program as compared to the control group ($p < .001$).

Conclusions

It is our opinion that the data presented are persuasive evidence of the effectiveness of a positive health care program. While qualifications are in order due to the liberated uses of significance levels, the data suggest that a more detailed examination of the lifestyling model for the design of positive health programs would be worthwhile.

REFERENCE

McCamy, J. C., and Presley, J. 1975. *Human life styling: Keeping whole in the 20th century.* New York: Harper & Row.

10

Analysis

of

Costs and Outcomes

The outcomes of human service programs can be fully evaluated only when their costs are considered. Most service providers do not have training in cost accounting and thus often begin work remarkably naive about costs. However, Demone and Harshbarger (1973) state that recommendations for programs whose costs are not estimated are simply statements of philosophy that will not be taken very seriously. Similarly, conclusions about the outcome of a program are not really complete unless the evaluator has discussed the costs of obtaining the outcome. Even an evaluation design that accounts for all threats to internal validity and finds a highly significant amount of improvement may receive a negative evaluation if the costs of obtaining the outcome are prohibitive or if the outcome could be achieved less expensively using a different program (Levin 1975).

Cost analysis is not a new idea to commercial people and industrial analysts. The local hardware store manager counts receipts every evening and periodically records costs. By converting transactions into dollars, business people can compare input costs (salaries, inventory, and building costs) with cash receipts. A comparison of these two values tells managers whether they are going into debt or making money. Bookkeeping, of course, is not this simple in practice; however, the principle is straightforward and the unit of analysis (a dollar) is widely accepted. In human service settings, the principles are less clear, and the benefits are usually hard to convert into dollars.

COST ANALYSES

The first step in a cost analysis, whether the program is already functioning or planned, is to divide the program's costs into categories. It is impossible to estimate the costs of a program as a whole without this breakdown. Popham (1975) presents several ways of conceptualizing costs. His categories of costs include: variable versus fixed, incremental versus sunk, recurring versus nonrecurring, and hidden versus obvious.

Variable versus Fixed Costs

All human service facilities must be housed somewhere. If the service requires special equipment, the facility cannot easily be used for any other purposes. Medical and dental care and vocational training require extensive, specialized equipment that make it impossible to use the rooms for any other purpose. Also, it is necessary to have a complete set of equipment before treating the first patient or training the first student. Thus, the costs of the facilities and equipment are fixed costs. Because of the fixed costs of getting started, there probably is some optimal number of people to serve in order to minimize the fixed costs per person served.

Variable costs are those that will change with the size of the program. The supplies used by the individuals served clearly vary with the size of the program. The costs of maintenance, postage, custodial services, and secretarial assistance are examples of costs that will grow as the program grows to its optimal size.

Incremental versus Sunk Costs

Incremental costs are those that occur as the program continues, and *sunk costs* are those that have already been expended. Thus, the distinction is useful only for decisions about continuing or terminating a program because there are no sunk costs for a planned program.

In 1978, the General Accounting Office suggested that it might make financial sense for the Postal Service to abandon a billion-dollar automated system for sorting packages (*Chicago Tribune* June 14, 1978). It may seem foolish to abandon a billion-dollar system after two years. However, the decision to continue or abandon it should be made on the basis of the costs to run the system compared to alternative systems. The money already invested (a sunk cost) is irrelevant to the new decision. Writing off the expensive system may be a big waste; however, it is cheaper than continuing to lose even more money. The GAO concluded that the incremental costs of the automated package system exceeded the benefits received; the sunk costs were not considered. Such a decision reflects the popular wisdom that there comes a point at which people seek to "cut their losses" because the losses may simply grow in the future.

Recurring versus Nonrecurring Costs

Recurring costs are, as the name suggests, those that will be due at regular intervals, such as salaries, rents, and utilities. The costs of purchasing equipment is a nonrecurring cost if the equipment is expected to last a number of years before wearing out.

Hidden versus Obvious Costs

In estimating the costs of a new building, no one will forget to include the costs of construction; less obvious costs include furniture, custodial service, lighting, heating, and maintenance. In estimating the costs of expanding staff, salaries will certainly be considered; somewhat hidden but just as real are fringe benefits and other costs, such as the employer's insurance for injured employees or for the careless behavior of employees toward others.

An Example

Figure 10.1 gives the budget of a small Equal Opportunity Program for minority college students. The proposal writers assumed a small office could be found with furniture in an existing building. The writers did not include maintenance, custodial services, or insurance costs because these would be the same, regardless of what program the university decided to adopt and house in that space. Thus, the budget is for the cost of this program operating in the space available. Note that some costs are recurring (salaries and phone), and others are nonrecurring (typewriter). To make a decision on this proposal, the college

FIGURE 10.1: Proposed first-year budget for an Equal Opportunity Program serving 25 college students

Director (half-time)	$ 8,000*
Tutors (graduate student teaching assistants) 3 @ $2,500	7,500
Secretary (half-time)	4,000*
Work-study tutors 3 @ $800 (University contribution, 20%; state contribution, 80%)	2,400
	$21,900
Supplies	$ 1,000
Typewriter	750
File cabinets	300
Copying	500
Phone	500
	$ 3,050
* Fringe benefits @ 15%	$ 1,800
	$26,750[a]

[a] *All costs are in 1978 dollars.*

administrators must compare this budget with a similar budget from an alternative program in light of the college's values, goals, and expected benefit from the program.

Direct versus Indirect Costs

Although the terms above adapted from Popham (1975) are very helpful for conceptualizing the cost involved in programs, another set of terms is also frequently employed. The distinction between direct and indirect costs is important in understanding the costs of human services (Carter and Newman 1976). *Direct costs* are those that are incurred in providing services for specific clients. *Indirect costs* are those that cannot be associated with specific clients. For example, the time a social worker spends helping a family obtain assistance from city agencies is a factor in direct costs. The wages (including all fringe benefits) make up the direct cost of the service. The salary of the secretary in the social welfare office who makes the social workers' appointments cannot be related to specific clients. Thus, the cost of secretarial assistance, as crucial as it is in maintaining a service, is not a direct cost but an indirect cost. The facility administrator's salary, telephone bills, amount paid for custodial service, and so forth are all indirect costs. In providing a service program, both direct and indirect costs (also called *overhead*) are incurred, and both must be considered. These costs are then to be related to the amount of service given.

The Necessity of Finding Costs

At times agencies supported by public funds have ignored the task of calculating costs per unit of service. Mitlying (1975–76) participated in a cost analysis of a publicly funded alcoholism treatment facility. The agency discovered that the cost (including direct and indirect costs) for each hour of service was $60. This figure, which was more than anyone in the agency expected, was unacceptably high. Regardless of a facility's source of funding, costs should be found and should be divided into direct and indirect costs.

The exact way specific costs are labeled direct and indirect is not standard (Carter and Newman 1976); however, the distinction is necessary to permit rational decisions about the amount of charges that should be allotted to given clients. Although the college students in the minority program (see Figure 10.1) will not be billed over and above their tuition, the budget items can be divided into direct and indirect costs. Direct costs include all the tutors' time and probably part of the director's time because he/she will certainly also be directly involved with the students. Part of the director's time, however, will be spent for indirect services, such as handling correspondence, organizing and supervising the tutors, and finding space for the tutors. All the cost of the secretary and the office expenses will be indirect costs.

At this point you should have begun to appreciate the basic fact that costs must be considered. Administrators cannot make decisions without an understanding of the costs required to implement a program. The discussion should not suggest that estimating costs is easy. Many estimates have been grossly in error. Congress passed a bill to support kidney dialysis for people suffering kidney failure and unable to obtain a kidney transplant (Culliton 1978). When the bill was approved in 1973, the costs were estimated to be in the low millions. By 1978, the cost was $1 billion, which was half the entire budget for the National Institute of Health. The failure to provide an accurate estimate of costs led to an unexpectedly large cost to the taxpayer and made it impossible to implement other programs also dealing with pressing health problems.

Further, more detailed presentations of cost analysis can be found in Hagedorn et al. (1976) and Carter and Newman (1976). Although the work by Hagedorn and his colleagues is directed to community mental health center evaluators, the methods presented apply to all human service settings. In addition, this work includes estimates of the time required to carry out the analyses described. Evaluators with limited training in accounting procedures can benefit from this material.

COMPARING BENEFITS TO COSTS

Once costs are calculated or estimated, the next step in a cost-benefit analysis is to develop an approach to estimating the benefits of a program. Benefits occur when goals are achieved. Surgeons save lives when they remove diseased appendixes. Because their patients lead normally productive lives afterward, there are considerable benefits to this and many other surgical procedures. Another example of a cost-effective program is the federal attempt to reduce the number of government forms. The commission set up to do this is reported to have saved 350 times as much money as the cost of the commission (Abelson 1977). A number of cost-benefit analyses have shown the worth of education after high school. Sussna and Heinemann (1972) concluded that the benefits of two-year training in health services were such that the increased earnings were equivalent to putting the cost of education into a bank and obtaining 34 percent interest per year for nursing students and 21 percent interest for laboratory technician students. Clearly, education was a better investment for these students because no savings account can rival such rates of return.

The Essence of Cost-Benefit Analysis

The essential characteristics of cost-benefit analyses can be illustrated with a study conducted by Schnelle and colleagues (1978). They sought to evaluate the effectiveness of a helicopter patrol in reducing burglary in a high crime area. Increasing the number of patrol cars seems to do little to reduce crime (Kelling et al. 1976; Schnelle et al. 1977). However, there was some speculation that a helicopter patrol with its inherently better surveillance ability might reduce burglary. In the city in which the project was done, most burglaries occur during daylight hours and are perpetrated by local youths. Because helicopters can repeatedly observe large areas (in daylight hours), the patrol was expected to frighten off potential burglars.

Schnelle and co-workers used an approach developed in the field of behavior modification to test the effectiveness of the helicopter. The experiment was divided into five parts. First, a baseline rate of burglaries in the target area was obtained during twenty-one days. Second, the helicopter was introduced for twelve days. The pilot was shown the area and asked to fly low enough to be able to observe suspicious activity. Third, for sixteen days the helicopter did not patrol. Fourth, the helicopter was used again for twelve days, Last, eighteen days without helicopter patrol ended the experiment. Regular car patrol continued during all phases of the experiment.

The burglary rate during the 9 A.M. to 5 P.M. shift was the outcome measure of interest. The experiment was a success in the sense that an average of 1.02 burglaries per day were committed during the periods of regular car patrols (baseline) in contrast to an average of only .33 burglaries per day when the helicopter patrol was on duty. However, these data alone did not form a complete evaluation because the helicopter patrol added to the police department's costs.

Because the helicopter pilot and hanger were already part of the police department, these costs were not considered. However, the costs of additional fuel and maintenance were calculated. These costs were compared to the benefits of lowered amount of goods stolen. Figure 10.2 summarizes the calculation of the benefit-to-cost ratio. The cost of using the helicopter was easy to calculate. The cost of the burglaries was estimated from insurance company material. The fact that the benefit-to-cost ratio was 2.6 indicates that the program was a success. The helicopter patrol did lower crime in an efficient manner.

Several costs and benefits were not considered. Citizen feelings of security may have increased (a benefit), but feelings of decreased privacy and irritation at the increased noise may also have occurred (costs). Opportunity costs were not considered because the pilot continued traffic surveillance as before. The benefit of lowered court costs, which occurred because it was necessary to try fewer burglars, was ignored. Also ignored was the fact that fewer burglaries permitted police officers to devote more time to other crime-preventive and investigative work (an additional benefit). Ignoring these benefits and the psychic costs of loss of privacy and of increased noise illustrates an important prin-

FIGURE 10.2: The calculation of the benefit-to-cost ratio of the helicopter patrol*

	Total	Per day
Cost of the program (24 days)	$ 3,032	$126
Cost of the burglaries during no-helicopter patrol periods (55 days)	$27,171	$494
Cost of burglaries during helicopter patrol periods (24 days)	$ 3,853	$161
Benefits (for 24 day program)	$ 8,004	$333
Benefit/cost ratio	--------	$333/$126 = 2.6

* The burglary cost figures were not supplied by Schnelle et al. (1978); however, these costs could be approximated from their report.

ciple for applied social scientists. Evaluators seek to address the questions directed to them in an efficient manner; once the essential question can be answered, they collect no more data. For Schnelle and his colleagues, the essential question could be answered using costs and benefits that were fairly easy to estimate. Therefore, the evaluators did not concern themselves with the very difficult task of pricing additional benefits. If they had, the benefit-to-cost ratio would have simply increased above 2.6. If the ratio had been less, say 1.1, then the additional benefits of reduction of court use and freeing police time might have been priced. Because it was not necessary, it was not done. A theoretical social scientist may want to estimate the "real" benefit-to-cost ratio. An applied social scientist requires only enough information on which to base a practical decision.

Although Schnelle chose to use costs and benefits that were fairly easy to convert into dollars, many cost-benefit studies have found it necessary to quantify costs and benefits that are hard to price. The Army Corps of Engineers has routinely used the recreational value of water projects to help justify construction plans. The dollar benefits of human services are even harder to estimate. If a service prolongs the working life of an employee, some benefits can be calculated. If a job-training program permits some to leave welfare rolls, certain savings can be quantified. But what is the dollar value of better mental health? Of reduced anxiety among cancer patients? Of a 5 percent gain on a standardized reading achievement test for sixth graders? Of increased levels of art and music appreciation? Clearly, these outcomes are worthwhile. But how much they are worth would be subject to considerable disagreement.

Military planning provides an even more striking example of the limitations of cost-benefit analysis. How are the "benefits" of a bomb to be calculated? Clearly, the bomb destroys. Benefits, if there are any, would occur to the nation if the war were later won. However, the net outcome of a war is negative, not positive, even for the victor. Instead of calculating cost-benefit ratios, one can ask how *effective* the bomb is in fulfilling its purpose. In oversimplified terms, the bigger the hole, the more effective the bomb. Thus, the concept of *cost effectiveness* was developed to use in situations in which the dollar values of benefits were very difficult to quantify.

The Essence of Cost-Effectiveness Analysis

A bomb could be rated in terms of the size of the hole it made (expressed in cubic yards) divided by the dollar cost of the bomb. There is no way of deciding if the yard^3/\$ figure is good or bad until compared to the effectiveness-to-cost ratio of a second bomb. By comparing the two ratios, military planners can choose the bomb providing the bigger bang per buck. This same approach can be utilized in human service agencies whenever improvement can be quantified. If two or more programs effect an improvement on some variable, the amount of improvement per dollar can be found for each program and a cost-effectiveness evaluation can be made.

When Outcome Cannot Be Quantified

The size of a bomb crater can be measured directly. Quantification of improved mental health is hard, but measuring improvements in perceived environmental quality is harder. Measuring increased art appreciation may be impossible. In these instances, another approach can be used. Methods that incorporate the subjective value of the decision maker, funders, and the consumers of a program are called *cost-utility analyses* (Levin 1975). In this case, the subjective values and the costs of two or more programs are compared, and the one offering the most apparent (subjective) utility per dollar is chosen. The proposed Equal Opportunity Program (Figure 10.1) would be compared to other proposals in terms of subjective utility, not in terms of quantified effectiveness or benefits.

SOME DETAILS OF COST ANALYSIS

There are a number of issues to examine when conducting an analysis of costs that can affect the conclusions of cost-benefit and cost-effectiveness analyses. Although some of these points are details subordinate to the major ideas presented above, these issues are extremely important, both when preparing these analyses and when evaluating them. We present these points as "issues of concern" because there are no widely accepted formulas for a cost analysis in the human services.

Units of Analysis

The units of the cost analysis should be compatible with the goals of the program. Binner (1977) illustrated how use of two different units can make quite a difference in a cost analysis of inpatient psychiatric treatment. What is the most obvious approach? If there are an average of one hundred patients in a facility and the cost for the year is $912,500, then the cost per patient per day would be $25. Is cost per patient-day a reasonable unit? The way to answer that question is to reflect on the reasons for institutionalizing a person. The goal is to aid patients to function in society, not simply to house them. A better unit than cost per patient-day would be cost per healthy, discharged patient. (For the moment, assume that each patient discharged is able to adjust to society and to earn a living.) The use of cost per patient-day actually encourages a departure from the true goals of institutionalization. Whatever can be done to lower the cost per patient-day will be encouraged, using this unit of analysis. The term *warehouse for people* was coined to describe the practice of developing the cheapest means of keeping people alive. On the other hand, the unit cost per patient discharged alive encourages a return to the real reason for institutionalization.

Note how the unit chosen affects the conclusion drawn from the cost-effectiveness analysis in the following example. Binner cites a state hospital that could house and feed a patient in 1901 for $2.38 per day (corrected to 1974 dollars). The cost per discharged patient in 1901 was $10,309 (1974 dollars). Comparing this hospital to 1974 averages, we find evidence for a 1300 percent increase and evidence for a 50 percent decrease in costs since 1901. Can both figures be true? Yes, they can. In 1974, the average cost per patient-day was $30.86 (the 1300 percent increase), and the average cost per alive discharged patient was $5,513 (the 50 percent decrease). Should we be heartened by the decrease or alarmed at the increase? If the goals of the treatment focus on restoring patients to the community, then we should be heartened by the decrease. This does not mean that treatment in the contemporary hospital is as effective as possible or that it is provided as efficiently as possible. A comparison of these figures does reflect the fact that restoring the ability to live in society requires therapy, community contacts, and medical treatment, among other things. Providing these services raises cost per day but lowers cost per discharged patient because patients are now more likely to return to the community than they were in 1901.

In recent years, some nursing homes for disabled elderly people have been the subject of intense criticism for inadequate treatment—poor food, little medical care, few recreational opportunities, limited privacy. Such conditions would be encouraged by the cost per patient-day approach. Although it would not be easy to implement, relating a cost analysis of such facilities to measures of the patients' level of function could encourage the facility to help the patients stay healthy and alert (see Kane and Kane 1978).

There is another complication related to the units of analysis used. At times, the meaning of improvement on the variable of interest may change, depending on what level of the variable is involved. For example, it is not necessarily true that an improvement of work skills that leads to an increase in income from $0 to $3,000 is equivalent to an increase of $2,000 to $5,000. The amount of change of motivation and upgrading of skills related to these numerically equal benefits are probably markedly unequal. This is so because changing a person from being unable to hold a job to being able to hold one is probably harder than simply improving a person's skills.

Alternative Uses of Investments

A mistake often made by people informally considering costs is to ignore the component of costs called *opportunity costs*. The most expensive aspect of college education is not the tuition, even at the most exclusive private schools. The cost of tuition is less than the income students could have earned had they been employed rather than attending college. This lost opportunity is a cost of college and should be considered by potential students. Ignoring the cultural, intellectual, and social growth available to college students, people evaluating a college education on the basis of cost alone will ask whether the salaries available to college graduates sufficiently exceed those to high school graduates to allow the college student to make up for this initial deficit of four years' wages. Economists interested in education report that college education in simple dollar terms is more cost effective than simply going to work after high school, although the advantage has eroded in recent years (Freeman and Hollomon 1975). Further, if people value the conceptual, intellectual, and cultural values of college, these hard-to-quantify benefits add to the advantage of a college education over forgoing it.

A person's time is part of the cost of all human services. However, the time that an individual spends waiting for a human service is often not considered a cost of the service, although it should be. Medical care that is ostensibly free is not free if waits of three or more hours are required to obtain it. If people in need of medical care do not have any employment, perhaps the oversight is permissible. However, even then, time spent waiting cannot be devoted to rearing children, preparing meals, or looking for work.

An everyday example of failing to consider alternative uses of resources occurs when people arrange financing of purchases. Often people only evaluate whether they think they can afford the monthly payment. They fail to note how much they will pay over the length of the contract. They also do not ask themselves what alternative uses exist for the money, and they fail to evaluate the cost of making the purchasing immediately versus postponing the purchase.

Long-Term Outcomes

A sophisticated cost analysis will include benefits occurring at times in the future. Successful rehabilitation or therapy will enable a person to live with less need of special services in future years. Improvements in work skills, psychological adjustment, and physical health may well have benefits for the children of people served or cared for. The worth of these long-term benefits is, not surprisingly, hard to estimate. Viewing the human services recipient as a member of a family system and a community system is a way to become sensitive to possible secondary benefits of human services. What are some of these secondary benefits? Drug rehabilitation should lead to less crime because addicts frequently support their habit through theft. If crime is reduced, commercial activity may be encouraged because people might be more willing to venture into the central business district. Also, the lower the crime rate, the lower the amount that the community needs to spend on detection, prosecution, and punishment of criminals.

Who Bears the Costs and Who Reaps the Benefits?

There are many human service programs sponsored and paid for by people who do not obtain the benefits. Clearly, the costs of primary education are borne by the whole community, but only the teachers and the children (and their parents) benefit. The community indirectly benefits by gaining a reputation for good schools that attract and hold residents. The value of homes remains high, and good employees are not likely to move away. A tax increase referendum is more likely to pass if residents believe they benefit at least indirectly by having good schools in their community.

The impact of the evaluation of the helicopter patrol cited above (Schnelle et al. 1978) was weakened by the fact that the program would be supported by the taxes of local residents, but the insurance companies would be the ones to benefit from the program. Ultimately, a lower crime rate should result in lower charges for insurance policies to cover burglary. However, the benefits would probably be spread across all policy holders, whether they lived in areas patrolled by the helicopter or not. Whenever the benefits are enjoyed by someone other than those paying for the program, special problems may exist in mobilizing political action to initiate and to maintain the program. Public transit systems are often criticized by people who are required to support the systems through taxes, but who never expect to benefit personally from them.

This discussion should serve to sensitize evaluators to the issue of who benefits from programs. However, it is important to note that people voluntarily enter into many contracts from which they hope to receive no dollar benefits. All insurance policies—home, life, health, and car—are designed to provide fairly large amounts of money to those in need after an illness or accident. Clearly, the costs are borne by the majority, who benefit little in terms of dollars. The year-to-year benefit is primarily the peace of mind created by knowing that large expenses will be covered if a misfortune occurs. Most policy holders are satisfied with such assurance and would be delighted to never experience the need to receive a tangible financial benefit from their insurance.

Multiple Outcomes

A complication in seeking to draw clear, definitive conclusions from evaluations is created by the fact that programs often have multiple outcomes. Thus, a comparison of the benefits of two different possible programs with overlapping but not identical types of outcomes becomes quite complicated. If the benefits can be priced in dollars and a cost-benefit analysis done, one approach is simply to select the program producing the largest benefit-to-cost ratio. In a cost-effectiveness analysis, the existence of different levels of effectiveness for different outcomes creates confusion. Is the success of an educational program in improving mathematics achievement as worthwhile as the improvement in English grammar created by an alternate program? Because some people will support each program, evaluators may find themselves in the middle of a dispute that they cannot resolve on the basis of the evaluation itself.

Future Costs and Benefits

The noneconomist faces a problem in comparing programs requiring funds but providing benefits at different times in the lives of the program. This is true because the money needed and the benefits available in the future are worth less than if the same amount of money were needed now or if the benefits were available now. This principle makes perfectly good sense if you ask yourself whether you would rather have $100 now or in twelve months. Ignoring for the moment our normal preference for instant gratification, it makes economic sense to have the money now, because if it is put into a savings account it will be worth $106 in twelve months. On the basis of this observation, some have criticized state lotteries that spread out $1 million grand prizes over twenty years. The state has the use of some of the money during those years, not the prize winner, so, in a real sense, the prize is not worth as much as the promotions promise. The present value of the twentieth $50,000 payment of the million-dollar grand prize is only $10,730, because that sum invested in a readily available 8 percent savings account will yield $50,000 after twenty years. There are some tax advantages in spreading out the awards; however, the basic point remains true.

This text cannot go into the methods used to calculate the current worth of a benefit projected to occur in twenty years. The point to remember is that the cost of programs should include what could be obtained by an alternate use of the costs. For example, is it worth spending $100 now in order to receive a benefit of $200 ten years from now? The answer depends entirely on the assumed rate of return for an alternative use of the $100. The amount one could obtain from the alternative use is the *opportunity cost*. If the rate of return for the alternate use were 3 percent, the answer to the question above is "Yes" because $100 invested at 3 percent will be worth only $134 in ten years. The opportunity cost is less than the benefit. If the rate of return were 8 percent or more, the answer is "No" because $100 invested for ten years at 8 percent will equal $216. It would be better to put the money into an 8 percent savings account than to seek the $200 future benefit.

The interest rate assumed should be realistic. Critics of the cost-benefit analyses provided by the proponents of large-scale water re-source projects have asserted that the rates of interest selected are unrealistically low (for example, Hanke and Walker 1974). If so, the cost of the project would appear lower and the benefit-to-cost ratio would appear higher than they really are. For example, the oppor-tunity cost of a $200 benefit that is ten years away would be $134 if an interest rate of 3 percent is chosen, but it would be $179 if a more realistic figure, 6 percent is used. It is probably obvious to the reader that a high rate of inflation greatly complicates these analyses.

Major Criticisms of Cost Analyses

There are a number of major criticisms of cost-benefit and cost-effectiveness analyses. Users of these approaches will profit by being aware of these criticisms because they point up limitations of these useful methods.

Psychic Benefits. As mentioned above, improved emotional health is hard enough to price. But what about clean air? Clean streams? An unlittered park? Access to quiet places to walk? One approach would be to study what people are willing to pay to escape environmental deterioration. Another approach is to calculate what must be paid to induce workers to accept employment in dirty, dusty, noisy, or dangerous occupations. These approaches are indirect and probably will never be completely satisfactory.

The Value of Lives. A second major criticism concerns the approach to valuing lives. Strictly economic analyses based on current or projected earning power place low values on the lives of children and the aged. The present economic value of young children is very low because they cannot earn anything until ten to fifteen years into the future. However, people clearly do not act as though children are to be evaluated on the basis of economic value. Considerable resources are expended on all children and especially on sick children. Very ill, premature babies may be hospitalized for months at a cost in the tens of thousands of dollars. In a somewhat similar way, economic analysis fails as an approach to determine the value of the elderly. Those who are unlikely to have a job in the future would have a negative dollar value. Because elderly people also have emotional value to others, this economic value does not reflect the feelings or predict the behavior of others toward the elderly.

An alternate approach to estimating the value of lives is an indirect way similar to the approaches suggested for pricing the benefits of clean air. An examination of court settlements involving accidental deaths and the amount of money the community will spend to save lives will suggest the dollar values of lives. Abt (1977) reported that in spite of widely discussed large damage awards, American society placed a $10,000 to $20,000 price tag on a year of human life.

Degrades Life. Critics respond to an observation such as Abt's by saying that cost-benefit analysis degrades life by putting a price tag on the priceless. No amount of money can correctly describe life, and attempts to do so are inhumane, the critics charge. Social scientists often respond, as Abt did, that reporting what people do does not imply that the reporter (in this case, a social scientist) endorses what is reported. At times social scientists are indeed similar to newspaper reporters describing, for example, a legislative decision. Some people will approve of what they hear; others will disapprove. Some may seek to change the situation. The reporter's views, whatever they are, did not cause the legislative decision. If people believe that society's actions are wrong and that lives should be worth more, then those feelings will become part of the political process.

Not Complete. Sometimes cost analyses are criticized for being incomplete. This criticism was implied in material already discussed. All benefits cannot be properly priced. Those that cannot be properly priced should not be assigned an arbitrary or purely speculative price (Levin 1975). Meaninglessness values lead to disguised error. Such errors are bigger problems than those caused by incomplete pricing. This incompleteness need not be viewed as a failure of the approach. Cost-benefit analyses are but an aspect of the evaluation of programs and only a portion of the information evaluated by managers and community representatives. Those who criticize the approach as being incomplete are attacking a false issue.

Costs must be considered because, regardless of our values, there are limitations on our resources. Communities must make choices among the various human services that could be offered. Some services will be offered regardless of what a cost-benefit analysis would show. Children will not starve in contemporary American communities because of values unrelated to the dollar worth of the child. The value assigned to the life of the child transcends the child's economic value. However, many other decisions and choices may be more closely related to dollar benefits. For these decisions and choices, cost analyses will take on more importance, but they still will not be the only inputs considered. And this is as it should be.

Note: There are no case studies in this chapter because readers of this book are unlikely to conduct cost-benefit or cost-effectiveness analyses without considerable further study. These approaches require skills that few social science or professional school students (other than economics or business majors) possess. If readers have become sensitized to the need to consider costs and have developed some conceptual tools for analyzing costs, this chapter has been a success.

STUDY QUESTIONS

1. Form an answer for a person on a human service staff who suggests a new program but who ends the proposal saying that he/she does not know what it would cost but is sure it would not be too much. Remember, successful evaluators are tactful and avoid specialized jargon in their dealing with program managers and staff.
2. Pretend you are involved in planning a storefront legal aid program. Draw up a budget for the first year. Take educated guesses at costs of salaries, rent, supplies, and so on. Label each entry as to whether it is a recurring, fixed, hidden, or other type of cost. (Some costs will have more than one label.) Then group the costs into two categories—one for direct costs and one for indirect costs.
3. The state of medical technology is such that ill or injured

people can be unable to do anything—see, hear, talk, read, walk, groom, or dress—but yet be considered alive because their hearts are still beating. The families of such patients face very large bills yet do not have a loved one, either. This problem has ethical, legal, and cost implications (see Fox 1976). What would a cost-benefit approach have to say about this problem? Think about psychic costs and benefits, opportunity costs, and alternative services to other ill patients before beginning your answer.

FURTHER READING

There are two valuable chapters in a major work on evaluation that has often been cited in this text.

LEVIN, H. M. 1975. Cost-effectiveness analysis in evaluation research. In *Handbook of evaluation research,* vol. 2, ed. M. Guttentag and E. L. Struening, pp. 89–124. Beverly Hills, Calif.: Sage.

ROTHENBERG, J. 1975. Cost-benefit analysis: A methodological exposition. In *Handbook of evaluation research,* vol 2, ed. M. Guttentag and E. L. Struening, pp. 55–88. Beverly Hills, Calif.: Sage.

Step-by-step procedures specifically directed to the staff and managers of community mental health centers are included in these books.

CARTER, D. E., and NEWMAN, F. L. 1976. *A client-oriented system of mental health service delivery and program management.* Rockville, Md.: National Institute of Mental Health. DHEW Publication No. (ADM) 76–307.

HAGEDORN, H. J.; BECK, K. J.; NEUBERT, S. F.; and WERLIN, S. H. 1976. *A working manual of simple evaluation techniques for community mental health centers.* Rockville, Md.: U.S. Department of Health, Education, and Welfare. DHEW Publication No. (ADM) 76–404.

part

IV

EFFECTIVE

APPLICATION OF

FINDINGS

"They never read the report! Those who did read it did nothing about the recommendations!" This is the frequent complaint of evaluators who feel that they conducted a sound evaluation of a program and made concrete and useful suggestions but find that decision makers ignore the report and recommendations. At least one young evaluator quit her job in order to call public attention to her findings and her recommendations concerning prison conditions (Solomon 1975). The question of utilization has received considerable attention by writers in the field of program evaluation. Material spanning over a decade is included in the following sources: Suchman (1967), Weiss and Rein (1970), National Institute of Mental Health (1971), Rossi and Williams (1972), Weiss (1972b, 1973), Davis and Salasin (1975), and Posavac (1979).

Although devising an effective and appropriate design and writing a clear and meaningful report give evaluators satisfaction, nothing fosters the feeling of psychological success as much as seeing the report effectively utilized. On the other hand, it is disheartening and deflating when a report with substantial and meaningful findings remains in a file drawer, neglected and unused. The final payoff for the professional evaluator is not receiving the check for services rendered, but rather knowing that the evaluation will have an effect on policy and program improvement. The skills involved in bringing about effective application are partly technical, partly psychological, and partly political.

The final two chapters in this book deal with the effective application of findings. When findings are not effectively utilized, it is often difficult to pinpoint the precise reason. The problem could lie with the manner in which the report was written, the way in which the report was presented, the climate in which the report was presented, or any combination of the above.

Chapter 11 contains a discussion of how to write and present an evaluation report in such a manner that it gets read. Methods that will contribute to a climate conducive to the effective use of evaluation findings are presented in Chapter 12.

11

The Evaluation Report:

How to Get it Read

A clear, concise, and attractive report enhances the possibilities of effective impact and represents the first step in having findings effectively utilized. After the data have been collected and analyzed, the results must be communicated to multiple audiences, such as program sponsors, program managers, program personnel, program recipients, other researchers, and the public at large. Because all groups do not have equivalent needs or equal rights to know all the results, a single version of the report will ordinarily not be appropriate for all readers. Therefore, the quality and quantity of material, as well as the style of presentation, is best tailored to the group addressed. In this chapter, suggestions are made about effective writing and presentation of an evaluation report as we discuss the content and style of a report, pitfalls to avoid in reporting, and the manner of report distribution.

THE CONTENT OF A REPORT

The introduction of an evaluation report should describe the setting and nature of the evaluation project. First, the author should describe the program being evaluated, answering such questions as: What is the nature of the program? Who is supervising or delivering program services? How long has the program been in operation? What are the major characteristics of the physical setting in which the intervention takes place?

Second, reports should describe the type(s) of evaluation(s) undertaken. Have the evaluators conducted a need, process, outcome, or cost-effectiveness study? If the evaluation has a primary and secondary focus, what are these? For example, is the primary focus on outcome evaluation, with secondary attention to cost-effectiveness? If the program has a number of aspects, which aspect of the program is being evaluated?

Third, why was the evaluation commissioned? The general purposes can be described. The evaluation may have been undertaken to maintain accreditation, to improve participant satisfaction, to justify funding, to choose between educational organizations, or to improve public relations.

Fourth, have similar evaluations been undertaken? If so, how does the present evaluation project fit into the literature? What inadequacies (if any) does the evaluator see in previous attempts to evaluate similar programs?

Consider how the above principles are observed in the following excerpt from an in-house report entitled, "Cancer Care Center—An Evaluation of Support to Patients and Relatives," conducted for a large metropolitan teaching hospital (Carey and Posavac 1977a). The introduction reads as follows:

> On September 1, 1976, the Cancer Care Center of Lutheran General Hospital began accepting patients. The Center is a 20-bed unit designed to treat advanced cancer patients utilizing a team approach. Patients are actively treated with the hope of arresting the illness. However, regardless of whether the illness is arrested, the Center's overall goal is to help patients cope with their condition and thus to live more effectively than they could otherwise.
>
> The specialized unit was developed because it is believed that cancer patients have needs unlike those of patients with illnesses that are less frightening and less serious than cancer. Further, it is believed that medical care personnel who are particularly interested in the needs of such patients would be better able to help them compared to personnel with no particular interest in cancer care.

In order to help patients retain an effective and satisfying life style, the Center staff includes a social worker, a chaplain, a nutritionist, and other personnel in addition to physicians and specially selected nurses.

Although most observers would agree that the Center's goals are laudable, it is necessary to document the success of the Center in meeting its goals. The project described in this report was designed to assess the success of the Center in meeting the emotional and personal needs of patients and their relatives. To assess the Center's success in improving the various aspects of physical care requires Quality Assurance studies. Quality of medical care is not discussed in this report.

The above introduction contains a brief description of the cancer care program, when it began, various personnel included on the staff, the type of evaluation, and the focus of the study. The review of literature was not mentioned because at the time of the evaluation, medical and nursing journals contained no reports similar to this study. As will be mentioned in the next section on the style of the report, an effort is made to keep the introduction brief for an in-house report because readers are fairly familiar with the program. However, for the article that was later submitted for journal publication, the introduction was considerably expanded. A more extended description of the cancer care program and the need for such a program were provided for journal readers.

Who Were the Participants?

The section of an evaluation report following the introduction should deal with methodology. This section should contain both information on program participants and details about the procedure employed. The part dealing with participants should include a description of the target population, the nature of the sampling method used, pertinent demographic material on the sample, and the degree of cooperation obtained from the target population. If the percentages of participants who failed to return surveys or who dropped out of the program are fairly large, some effort should be made to explain their lack of participation.

Consider the following paragraphs from the methods section of the above-mentioned study:

Patients studied. There were three groups of patients studied in preparing this report. A pre-unit comparison group $(N = 67)$ was surveyed before the Center was opened. After the Center was opened two more groups were surveyed. A sample of patients ($N = 52$) who were treated on the specialized Center and a group of patients ($N = 53$) with similar diagnoses but treated on regular medical units of the hospital were studied.

Not all cancer patients in the hospital were candidates for the research; however, the same selection procedures were used with all three groups. An experienced nurse examined the chart of every patient discharged with a diagnosis of cancer. Only those patients who were admitted with a diagnosis of cancer could be part of the study. Those admitted without a diagnosis of cancer were eliminated because they could not have been part of the Center's program. The following criteria were used to eliminate patients who would have difficulty responding to a survey because they were too sick:

1. the chart indicated the patient was close to death,
2. the patient was described as disoriented (i.e., suffering metastasis to brain),
3. the patient was discharged to a nursing home.

In addition, patients over 70 were eliminated because it was expected that many of these patients would find the surveys difficult to complete and may also be suffering from other physical ailments. [Figure 11.1] includes a demographic description of the patients who responded to the surveys in the three groups. Overall, the

FIGURE 11.1: Descriptions of the patients in the three cancer treatment groups

	Patient group		
Variable	Center	Pre-unit comparison	Post-unit comparison
Number of surveys mailed	52	67	53
Number of usable surveys returned (% return rate)	29 (56%)	38 (57%)	31 (58%)
Age (means)	54.4	54.4	60.2
Sex: Males	31%	45%	36%
Females	69%	55%	64%
Marital status (% married)	62%	84%	81%
Self-reported diagnosis:			
Cancer	90%	90%	67%
Other	10%	10%	33%
Median stay (days)	12	10	13
Number of patients who died before follow-up telephone calls (%)	7 (13%)	9 (13%)	2 (4%)

groups were quite comparable in terms of age, sexual composition, marital status, etc. The one possible difference is found in the different death rates among the patients who were telephoned to inquire about nonreturned surveys. The rate (4%) for the post-unit comparison patients contrasts with the higher values (13%) found for both the Center patients and the pre-unit comparison patients.

Notice that the program patients are carefully described, along with the patients in the two comparison groups. No sampling method was used in this study. However, certain types of patients were eliminated from the study for methodological and humanitarian reasons. Although mention of the two comparison groups introduces the question of evaluation design before the procedure section, this was done to establish the comparability of the groups on the same table that described the Cancer Care Center patients.

How Was the Evaluation Conducted?

The procedure part of the methodology section appropriately contains material on the evaluation design, methods of data collection, and the operational measures of the dependent variables under investigation. In this section, discussion can focus on the details of the experimental or quasi-experimental design chosen, possible biases in data collection and how they were controlled, and the validity and reliability of measures that were designed specifically for an evaluation. A description of the plan for statistical analysis can either be included in the procedure section or in the beginning of the results section. If a fairly complicated analysis has been selected, then it is advisable to explain the details either in a footnote or in an appendix, especially for in-house presentation. Comments may be made about the tests for significance or the degree of association and about the power of the tests chosen. The amount of detail on these items will depend on whether the author is writing a journal article or an in-house report. More will be said about this in the section on the style of the report.

In the Cancer Care Center evaluation we have been describing, the authors chose to place a description of statistical analysis in an appendix so the flow of the report would not be broken for in-house readers. Read the following paragraph taken from the appendix and see whether or not you agree with that decision.

Without very sizable numbers of patients in each group it is not possible to detect small differences among the answers of the three groups tested. With sizes of the groups available differences among groups would have to have been at least 20 percentage points to be "significant" using standard statistical procedures. For example, if pre-unit care was rated at 72% favorable, the Center's care would have to be rated at least at 92% for the statistical test to detect the improvement. Clearly, an improvement of 20% over an already high 72% may be too much to hope for. Because of the problems with such an item-by-item analysis, the data in this study are analyzed on a *set*-of-items basis. The statistical tests used answer the question of whether a set of items has shown *overall* improvement, not whether any given item has shown improvement. The result of this form of analysis is that the reader should *not* view the results of any single item as worthy of particular attention. This is true whether the individual comparison is favorable to the Center or unfavorable.

What Was Observed?

In the results section, the data should be presented without lengthy interpretation or discussion. The author should be answering the questions: "What happened? What findings appeared?" Editorial comments should be saved until the discussion part of the report.

Tables and figures should be brief and simple. All the results for the Cancer Care Center evaluation were presented in three easy-to-read tables (Figures 11.2, 11.3, and 11.4). Notice that in the report's second table (Figure 11.2) containing questions relevant to the evaluation of process, the appropriate comparisons were percentages. In the third table (Figure 11.3), the three groups of patients were compared on the basis of mean scores; percentages were again used to evaluate the attitude of relatives in the fourth table (Figure 11.4). In all three tables, the most favorable value among the three groups was underlined to facilitate reading.

The text describing the results can be presented very succinctly, as the following example from the Cancer Care Center report illustrates:

Patients' reactions to hospital care. Before closely examining the results, a few points must be noted. Whenever patients make generally favorable comments about their treatment, innovations of any sort are not likely to greatly improve the patients' ratings of the care received. This fact, called the "ceiling effect," should be borne in mind whenever innovative programs are introduced into a setting that is already well-received. The ceiling effect is often a problem in detecting the positive impact of an innovation here because most patients already view the hospital quite favorably.

The percentages of patients in the three groups who responded favorably to the survey items are summarized in [Figure 11.2]. In no

FIGURE 11.2: Percentage of patients answering YES to the questions concerning hospital care

		Patients' unit	
Questionnaire items	Center	Pre-unit comparison	Post-unit comparison
1. Were you admitted to your hospital nursing unit in a respectful manner?	96[a]	95	93
2. Were diagnostic tests clearly explained?	82	74	80
3. Were questions about your illness answered to your satisfaction?	82	74	90
4. Were possible side effects of treatments explained before you received the treatments?	92	71	75
5. When you had pain, was something done to relieve it?	96	90	96
6. Did you know why you were given medication?	96	95	90
7. Were you able to sleep at night?	75	58	70
8. Did you receive assistance with your diet?	87	75	68
9. Was someone available when you wanted to talk?	92	88	85
10. Did you share in the planning of your care?	68	50	50
11. Were your family members encouraged to be involved with your day-to-day care?	91	72	68
12. Did you feel the staff was interested in helping you?	100	90	90
13. Was there adequate planning for your needs after discharge? (If not, please explain on the other side.)	92	81	88
14. Because of your stay in the hospital, are you better able to cope emotionally with your illness at home? (If not, please explain what you would have liked done.)	70	81	78

Figure 11.2 (continued)

15. Was the ministry of the chaplain of value to you?	<u>88</u>	61	64
16. In your opinion did the hospital staff communicate well with each other?	89	89	<u>90</u>
17. Was the general atmosphere of your nursing unit depressing?	7	10	<u>3</u>

[a] *The most favorable percentage among the three groups is underlined.*

unit did patients evaluate their care in unfavorable terms. In spite of the problem of the ceiling effect, the Center's patients described their care in more favorable terms compared to the patients in the other two groups. The Center's care was evaluated more favorably than the care given the pre-unit group on 15 characteristics while the reverse occurred only once. The Center's care thus was reliably evaluated as better than that obtained before the unit was opened $(x^2 = 12.25, df = 1, p < .001)$. In comparing the Center's patients with those treated at the same time but on different units, the Center's care is again evaluated more favorably on 12 out of 16 characteristics $(x^2 = 4.00, df = 1, p < .0025)$. A note about the method of analysis is in the Appendix.

The patients' moods. The mean values for the patients' moods are presented in [Figure 11.3]. On this set of measures Center patients were better off than the pre-unit group; however, the post-

FIGURE 11.3: Means of the patients' self-described psychological moods (mean scores)

	Patients' unit		
Profile of mood states (POMS) scale	Center	Pre-unit comparison	Post-unit comparison
Tension-anxiety	11.08	11.76	<u>8.84</u>[a]
Depression	<u>7.80</u>	10.03	7.84
Anger-hostility	3.40	6.24	<u>3.24</u>
Vigor	12.80	12.47	<u>14.00</u>
Fatigue	10.60	11.65	<u>8.60</u>
Confusion	6.68	7.18	<u>5.68</u>

[a] *The most favorable value among the three groups is underlined.*

FIGURE 11.4: Responses about medical care personnel by the relatives of the cancer treatment patients

	Patients' unit		
	Center	Pre-unit comparison	Post-unit comparison
Description of relatives			
Sex of relative: % Male	48	43	56
% Female	52	57	44
Relationship: % Spouse	55	79	68
How much help did you receive from the following personnel?	% reporting having received GREAT help		
Physicians	50	65[a]	58
Nurses	74	51	56
Social workers	39	24	31
Chaplains	38	29	19
Nutritionists (diet counselor)	35	10	27
Physical therapists	44	13	27
Were you disappointed in any of the same hospital personnel?	% reporting disappointment (% YES)		
Physicians	4	6	0
Nurses	0	8	4
Social workers	0	6	4
Chaplains	0	12	4
Nutritionists (diet counselor)	0	10	4
Physical therapists	0	0	0

[a] *The most favorable value among the three groups is underlined.*

unit group described themselves as the best off of all. Finding the post-unit group to be the best off was a surprising finding. It may be that this finding is related to the death rate found as a result of calling discharged patients to ask them about the nonreturn of surveys. If the proportion of patients dying within four weeks of going home is an index of seriousness of illness, then it may be that the post-unit group is the most healthy. If so, then their higher values on the POMS may be due to their generally better state of health. This reasoning is supported by the Center's staff belief that they treat patients who are in more advanced stages of cancer than other units in the hospital.

Relatives' views of medical care personnel. The relatives' reports of
how much help various medical care personnel gave them personally are summarized in [Figure 11.4]. Also in this table are the
proportions of relatives who reported disappointment in various
medical care personnel. As in [Figure 11.2], no group of relatives
contained a large proportion of disappointed people. The most
favorable ratings were given by relatives of the Center's patients on
nine out of the 11 items ($\chi^2 = 4.45, df = 1, p < .0025$).

A description of treatment effects should include the standard devia-
tions as well as the mean scores of each group. Merely to report that a
treatment group differed from the comparison group at a given level
of statistical significance does not provide the reader with any idea of
how clinically important the difference was. For example, if a report
states that the mean scores were 8 and 6 for the treatment and comparison groups, respectively, and that the standard deviation was 3 for
both groups, the reader can conclude that effects were not clinically
important even though they may have been statistically significant. On
the other hand, if the mean scores were 15 and 6, then the difference
was clearly important.

Other statistics that are useful and helpful are various measures to
describe the strength of association, for example, the gamma statistic
(Davis 1971; Mueller et al. 1970) or the eta or omega statistics (Hays
1963). Some comment about the power of the statistical test used is
also very helpful, although this is rarely mentioned in most evaluation
reports being done at the present time.

What Action Should Be Considered?

The discussion section should interpret and comment on the results.
In the case of a need evaluation, how strong are the arguments for
saying that the given program should be established? In a summative
evaluation, what are the arguments for and against continuing the
given program? In a formative evaluation, what steps should be taken
to improve the program? Is further evaluation indicated? What recommendations are appropriate in light of the results? It is not always easy
to say whether or not the benefits of a given program justify the cost,
although the fixed and variable costs of a program can be enumerated.
In a cost-effectiveness evaluation, the author should indicate whether
or not the findings suggest that the same results could be obtained
more economically by an alternate program.

Consider excerpts from the discussion section of the Cancer Care
Center evaluation:

The overall impact of the Cancer Care Center is positive. Patients and relatives alike view the program in more favorable terms than the care provided on other units of the hospital. The results of the study are unambiguous except for the POMS variables. Previous research has shown that the more discomfort and pain people suffer, the more depressed and, in general, less well-adjusted they seem (Carey, 1974). If the Center's patients are indeed in more advanced stages of cancer, the less pleasant moods can be readily understood. To evaluate the impact of the Center on patient's moods requires a group of patients just as ill. If the death rates in [Figure 11.1] do reflect the health of patients, then the Center patients ought to be compared with the pre-unit group only. If that comparison is made, then the Center was successful on all three sets of variables used in this study.

This study has shown that the emotional and educational needs of cancer patients are better met by the program in the Cancer Care Center compared to other nonspecialized units. The study does not address the question of whether medical care is better on the Center than on other units. Such a question can be addressed by a Quality Assurance study done before the Center's organization contrasted to one with patients only from the Center.

Notice that a long discussion section is unnecessary. A cost-benefit analysis was not included because it was not requested by the decision-makers. The discussion section also makes it clear what is not evaluated, namely, the quality of the medical care offered to patients on the Cancer Care Center.

THE STYLE OF REPORT

In-house Reports versus Journal Articles

As was mentioned in several places in the previous section, in-house reports and journal articles differ to some extent on style and emphasis. An in-house report deemphasizes the introduction and methodology sections and emphasizes the discussion and results sections. The reason for this is that in-house readers are more familiar with the situational elements of the program and have no need for elaborate details of methodology that would enable them to replicate the study. Therefore, they have less interest in the review of the literature, program design, and methodology. In-house readers are most anxious to obtain a general overview of the results of the evaluation and to learn what recommendations were made. For these reasons, the authors of this text suggest putting a 200- to 500-word summary of the salient findings and recommendations at the beginning of an in-house report of ten to twenty pages. The needs of many readers will be met by this summary immediately preceding the introduction. Clearly, the summary will be longer for evaluations of wider scope and greater length.

In journal articles, on the other hand, it is appropriate to put considerable emphasis on the introduction and methodology sections. Journal readers, and especially other researchers, are likely to be interested in theoretical issues, the value of the present evaluation to the particular field of study, and the possibility of replicating the study. These readers would be less interested in the implications for the specific institution where the evaluation was conducted. For these reasons, more details on the experimental design and the statistical analysis of results are appropriate.

In a case in which evaluators have undertaken an ambitious and well-funded evaluation for some large institution, it may be necessary to write a single report for multiple audiences. In this case, the report may take the form of two volumes, the first volume being a short, easy-to-read text listing the main findings and explaining the conclusions and suggestions for action. This volume would be intended for executive use in decision making. The second and more lengthy volume would contain copies of the correspondence that set up the goals, conditions, and financial agreements of the study, as well as extensive methodological details and specialized charts that would have interest only for those needing more detailed information. An example of such a report is the need and planning evaluation conducted with the help of Arthur D. Little company for the Catholic Hospital Association (1977). Another example is the report of the evaluation of New York State's drug law. There were actually three published reports of this evaluation: (1) a 33-page conclusion section that would be read by those interested in the overall findings; (2) a 115-page section providing the supporting data for the conclusions; and (3) a 322-page report providing more detailed backup analyses (*The Nation's Toughest Drug Law: Evaluating the New York Experience* 1978; *Staff Working Papers of the Drug Law Evaluation Project* 1978).

Quantitative versus Qualitative Style

A *quantitative style* of evaluation puts heavy emphasis on the collection of "hard" data that can be analyzed statistically; a *qualitative style* emphasizes observations either by participants or outside observers. Both the quantitative and qualitative approaches have their

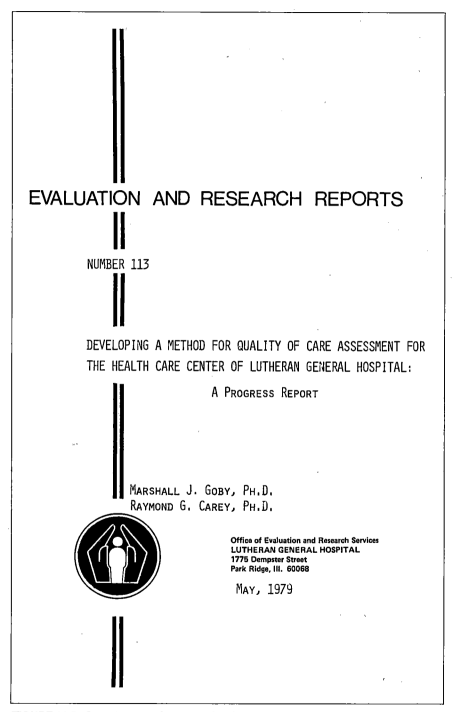

EVALUATION AND RESEARCH REPORTS

NUMBER 113

DEVELOPING A METHOD FOR QUALITY OF CARE ASSESSMENT FOR
THE HEALTH CARE CENTER OF LUTHERAN GENERAL HOSPITAL:

A PROGRESS REPORT

MARSHALL J. GOBY, PH.D.
RAYMOND G. CAREY, PH.D.

Office of Evaluation and Research Services
LUTHERAN GENERAL HOSPITAL
1775 Dempster Street
Park Ridge, Ill. 60068

MAY, 1979

FIGURE 11.5: Sample cover for an evaluation report.

PITFALLS IN REPORTING

Overgeneralization From Inadequate Sampling or Return Rate

The first pitfall to avoid in reporting findings is overgeneralization based on inadequate sampling of the total population or inadequate return rate on a survey. For example, if evaluators chose to take a 10 percent sample of a population, some evidence should be presented that this was done in a manner adequate to test the hypotheses or answer the questions posed by the evaluation. Stratified random sampling (that is, sampling that assures various subgroups of the population will be proportionately represented) is a stronger procedure than a mere random sample. However, let us suppose that only approximately one-third of a 10 percent random sample completed a program being evaluated. This situation represents a sizable dropout of participants. If the data show that the participants who actually did complete the program are much improved compared to a control group who did not receive the program, the evaluator has to be very careful about interpreting the results. It is not legitimate to conclude that the dropouts would have profited as much as those who actually did complete the program.

Consider the example of a survey sent to bank customers to assess their satisfaction with a newly instituted drive-in banking service. Suppose that the bank had ten thousand customers and that questionnaires were sent to all of them. Three thousand customers (30 percent) responded. Of those responding, 60 percent said they were pleased with the new drive-in service. Is it possible to generalize from the results and say that the majority of bank customers are pleased with the service? Very clearly, this generalization cannot be made because there are a large number of possible respondents about whom it is not possible to make any definite statement. In fact, it is more likely that there is a larger percentage of indifferent feelings or negative feelings among nonresponders than among responders. In this instance, the evaluators would have done better to take a random sample of 10 percent (one thousand customers) and follow-up the first questionnaire either with a second mailing or personal phone call. If they were able to obtain responses from 750 customers (75 percent of the sample), they would have been in a much stronger position to generalize from the findings that 60 percent of the customers were satisfied.

Finally, consider the results of a national poll of United States priests conducted by an organization called CORPUS on the issue of optional celibacy for Catholic priests. CORPUS sent questionnaires to 39,097 priests, including all priests assigned to parish work. They were asked their opinions on four statements on priesthood changes. As a result, 6,414 priests (16.3 percent) responded, and there was no effort to make a follow-up contact. The findings showed: (1) 53 percent of respondents favored the resumption of ministry by resigned priests; (2) 55 percent favored optional celibacy for priests; (3) 53 percent favored ordination of married men; and (4) 31 percent favored the ordination of women. The newspaper article reporting the results of the survey carried the following headline: "U.S. priests want celibacy option, active ministry for married clergy." The article further quoted the study director as saying, "The survey results are extremely valid in view of the number of respondents and the general consistency of respondents across the country."

On the supposition that the newspaper article accurately quoted the study director, the study director would have to be accused of over-generalizing on the basis of an inadequate rate of return on his survey. A response rate of 16.3 percent is completely inadequate to justify the conclusion that priests in the United States want optional celibacy and an active ministry for married clergy. As pointed out in Chapter 2, the important issue is the representativeness of a sample, not its size. The evaluators would have been better off to have sampled 4,000 priests (10 percent of the target population) and put more time and effort into obtaining a favorable rate of response.

Conclusions That Are Too Strong for Modest Differences

When evaluators have received a sizable grant for a project or have put a great deal of time and effort into an evaluation, there is a strong desire to demonstrate that their time and money were well spent. This results in pressure on evaluators to read more into their findings than is actually there. In the long run, the reputation of evaluators will be enhanced by interpreting findings cautiously. Modest differences between program and control groups should be interpreted as "some evidence" in support of the program and should not be seen as "demonstrating" or "strongly suggesting" that a program is a success or that a hypothesis has been supported.

Consider for example the very interesting study on the relationship between nutrition and cognitive development in rural Guatemala (Freeman and others 1977). The evaluators found the nutritional status of three- and four-year-old children in four rural Guatemalan villages, as measured by height and head circumference, to be related to cognitive performance. In the final section of the report the authors stated: "The findings presented *strongly suggest* [italics added] that calorie intake affects cognitive development as well as physical growth

and general health status" (p. 239). This is a surprisingly strong statement after they admitted in the previous section of the report that there
was some unreliability in both the social and psychological measures,
that many of the measures were metrically inelegant, that they did not
meet all the statistical assumptions required for some of the analyses
performed, and that the amount of variance explained by the nutrition
measures was not always substantial. The last comment is actually an
understatement because the highest amount of variance explained was
16 percent (with three-year-old females), but in the other three groups
the amount of variance explained averaged less than 7 percent. However,
much to their credit, the evaluators interpreted the strength of their
findings more realistically in the abstract of their article, where they
stated: "Although the longitudinal study still is ongoing, there is
some evidence [italics added] that the children who receive higher
calorie supplement . . . are most likely to score high in cognitive
performance" (p. 233).

Ignoring the Possibility of Type II Errors

Some evaluators feel that if results do not reach the level of statistical
significance, they should be ignored (Nunnally 1975). However, the
authors of this text take the position that evaluators cannot afford to
throw costly data out the window whenever effects "fail to reach significance." Other authors, such as Cronbach (1975), support this position.
This caution applies particularly when one is looking at samples where
numbers may be too small to produce statistically significant differences.
This is not to say that one should be careless about admitting the
possibility of Type I error, but rather that evaluators have to be
equally cautious about Type II errors. When an existing program has
absorbed a great deal of money, time, and effort, evaluators should
be reluctant to tell program personnel that their efforts have been
largely unsuccessful when there is a good possibility of Type II error.
Being cautious about Type II errors is not the same as saying that
every nonsignificant interaction must be seen as a "trend." However,
when one is guided by strong prior knowledge, or sample size is small,
nonsignificant findings can at times be considered as a trend with
justification. For example, when a sizable but statistically insignificant
relationship was predicted on the basis of solid theory or previous
evaluations, then the evaluators are more justified in giving serious
attention to trends supporting those relationships. Trends without such
strong a priori support should not be given serious attention until
replicated.

Analyzing Specific Rather Than Total Effects
of a Program

When an index of the success of a human service program approaches the maximum possible, detecting a statistically significant improvement on individual criteria is a difficult task. For example, this problem would be experienced by evaluators working in a well-run bank. In such a bank, customer satisfaction measures would be highly skewed with the bulk of responses toward the favorable end of the satisfaction continuum. With respondents answering 80 to 90 percent favorable on individual items, innovative programs designed to give customers better hours, more convenient service, and so on, can seldom raise the level of satisfaction by more than a few percentage points.

In instances such as this, the personnel in an innovative program are usually more concerned with answering the question of whether or not their new program has an overall positive effect, rather than knowing whether or not it was successful on every single criterion. If, indeed, a single criterion was so important that the program would not be a success if it were not achieved, then the researchers must evaluate that program on this single criterion. However, this is often not the case.

The problem of observing significant findings in a well-run organization might be restated by saying that when statistical methods are unlikely to detect differences between groups, the methods are said to have *low power*. One solution is to survey a larger number of participants. If this can be done, it is the solution of choice. However, to detect a 5 percent increase in a premeasure with an 80 percent favorable rating, with a power of 90 percent, and using a one-tailed proportion test with a significance level of .05, would require 1,066 participants in each of the comparison and innovative program groups. If the evaluator was satisfied with the power of only 50 percent, the required sample sizes drop to 388 (Fleiss 1973). Obtaining this many respondents is obviously a formidable task for evaluators.

Another approach would be to evaluate the program *as a whole*, rather than on a goal-by-goal basis. In this case, rather than evaluating the success of a program by examining each individual standard of success, the evaluators look at the total effect of the program. For example, this was the approach that Carey and Posavac (1979) used in evaluating the Cancer Care Center. (A description of the statistical approach was put in the appendix of the report and was included earlier in this chapter.) Analysis revealed that patients reported better results on thirteen of the proposed seventeen specific goals than either of the two comparison groups. Although the program was not significantly

superior to the comparison groups on any individual criterion, the program taken as a whole was demonstrated to be successful. In effect,
the evaluators traded evaluative specificity for statistical power. A more
detailed explanation of this approach can be found in an article by
Posavac and Carey (1978).

Being Honest to the Point of Being Tactless

The final pitfall in reporting is to present the findings in such a
blunt fashion that the feelings of the program personnel are injured.
It is possible to be honest to the point of being tactless. Negative findings
must be presented in a manner that demonstrates a humane concern
for the dignity and feeling of people connected with a given program.

For example, in an evaluation of presterilization interviewing conducted by chaplains at a religiously oriented hospital, the findings clearly
showed that mandatory pastoral interviewing before sterilization operations did not have great value for most couples in the study (Carey 1976).
However, for many years the chaplains had put a great deal of time
and effort into this service. It was important to couch the findings in
language that would convey the message, but still not place the entire
blame for the lack of effect on their skills or efforts. Indeed, lack of
effort or skill was not responsible for the negative finding. The evaluator
tried to put the findings and focus in a tactful way, as the following
excerpt from the discussion section demonstrates:

> Follow-up interviews suggested that the failure to find value in the
> interviews may have been due to the manner in which they were
> structured and conducted. First, some couples quoted their physi-
> cian as telling them, "The interview is only a formality," in a tone
> and manner that indicated that it was a waste of time. The inter-
> views might have been viewed differently if the physician had set
> the stage for the interview by recommending it as worthwhile and
> outlining its purpose and nature. Second, some chaplains dislike
> mandatory interviews. They feel that couples have made up their
> minds and that nothing is gained in the interview. Chaplains who
> feel they are conducting a useless interview are likely to communi-
> cate this feeling. Finally, the time assigned (15 to 30 minutes) seems
> inadequate to cover the issues involved.
>
> However, a few couples were clearly in need of help. One of the
> original 100 couples cancelled the operation because they obtained
> a divorce. Another woman admitted to extreme guilt that she was
> not handling well. Five spouses said their marriages were unhappy
> and their sexual relationships were dissatisfying.
>
> In addition, nearly half of the wives reported some degree of

anxiety, although this was not necessarily connected with the operation. There is no indication that adequate counseling will be provided by physicians. Only 13 percent of the responding couples
saw a physician for counseling, and less than half of these found
his counseling of great value. Therefore, in spite of the findings
of this study, one should not hastily conclude that mandatory interviews should be dropped without providing an adequate substitute
(Carey 1976, p. 494).

Notice that in this example the evaluator considered the role of the
physician in making presterilization interviewing a success, as well as
the attitudes of the patients who came for interviewing. The evaluator
also pointed out that some patients, indeed, were in need of counseling,
and that the interviews should not be hastily dropped without providing
some substitute. As it turned out, this report was well-received by the
Division of Pastoral Care in the hospital, and hospital policy was
modified to make counseling mandatory only for those couples under
thirty years of age. This change in policy seemed to concentrate the
efforts of the chaplains on the age group where most difficulties were
likely to arise. Also, the physicians were urged to make greater effort
to prepare the patient for a more meaningful interview.

MANNER OF DISTRIBUTION

Respecting Both Sponsors and Program Personnel

The manner in which a report is released is almost as important as
the quality of the research design and the composition of the report
itself. If evaluators wish to see action taken on the basis of their report
findings, it is critical to maintain the good will and support of decision
makers and of those who wield power in an organization. Consider a
situation in which several people feel they have the right to obtain the
evaluation report first. Program personnel, the program director, and
program sponsors (administration or the funding agency) may be eager
to see the results and may be somewhat anxious about the effects the
report could have on their work situation. The problem the evaluator
faces is how to be sure that none of these groups feels slighted because
it was not the first to see the report.
    The authors of this text have found it helpful to distinguish between
the *final draft* and the *final report*. It seems best to give those who are
in immediate operational control of a program the first peek at the
findings. This is done by letting them know that they are going to see
the final draft on a confidential basis and that their suggestions for clarify-

ing or elaborating on points that are made in the report will be accepted. This preview, however, should not result in the censorship of valid interpretations. This look at the final draft usually has the effect of allaying the anxiety of program directors who are often hoping for the best but expecting the worst. It also gives them a chance to reflect on any surprises that might be in the report.

After meeting with the operational directors of the program and obtaining their comments, the evaluators can incorporate whatever modifications are necessary in assembling the final report. The final report, then, is presented first to the top administration of the organization or institution, who may have funded or at least sponsored the program and the evaluation research. It is important that they are made to feel that they are special people and the first to see what is potentially sensitive information. The failure to do this may mean that the evaluators will lose the administration's support, which is necessary for future evaluation projects, or perhaps not even be invited to conduct further evaluations in the organization.

After presenting the report to the top administration, the order of further release depends largely on the importance of the report and the sensitivity of its contents. Evaluators must be guided by administration with respect to the order and time sequence of distribution. It is possible that administrators can abuse this authority and try to keep the report from being distributed any further, but this is not the ordinary situation in a well-run organization.

Personal Presentation to Key Persons

In presenting both the final draft and final report, it is strongly suggested that evaluators resist the temptation to simply mail a copy of the report to program personnel or administration. It is recommended that evaluators set up a personal appointment with the key people who will be seeing the draft or report and distribute a copy to them marked "CONFIDENTIAL" soon enough for them to have the opportunity to read it before the meeting, but not so far ahead that there is danger of the report being leaked to other people within the organization. The purpose of the personal presentation is to give the evaluator first-hand knowledge of which sections of the report need further clarification, of the specific reactions of key persons, and of the likelihood that they will take some concrete actions in light of the recommendations. This information, which can be obtained only in a face-to-face meeting, will guide the evaluators in the manner in which they will release the information to other people in the organization and also to those outside the organization. They will know which parts of their report can be shortened, strengthened, or clarified.

Interim Reports

Interim reports are those that are given in the course of an evaluation project before the final report is ready to be released. They are usually unofficial communications about the progress of the evaluation project, the problems being experienced, and, when appropriate, the findings that are beginning to emerge. Interim reports are especially useful in evaluation projects that last a year or more. They help to maintain the interest and enthusiasm of program personnel who focus their attention on the delivery of program services, not on the evaluation. Program personnel can also be informed of how helpful their assistance has been in the project to date and can be advised about how they might further help data collection.

Distribution Outside an Organization

Neither program personnel nor sponsors are always enthusiastic about having an evaluation report published outside the confines of their organization or institution. Few evaluations will be entirely positive, and program personnel are as anxious to have outsiders believe only the best about their programs, as mothers are to have others see only the good aspects of their children. On occasion, program personnel want to be the first ones to write about their program and resent being up-staged by a researcher who publishes before they do.

Evaluators can also be faced with the sensitive situation of balancing their obligation of confidentiality against the obligation to share findings with those who have a need or right to know. In the case of evaluations that are funded by government, this will rarely be a difficulty because part of the grant money will be earmarked for publication of results. However, in privately funded evaluations it would be helpful to agree beforehand on ownership of the data and rights of publication. Many private institutions have a research and publication committee or its equivalent that claims the right of censorship over articles published on institutional operations. It is good to clarify the limitations on the rights of the evaluator before the evaluation begins.

If the evaluation is of such a nature that local community or civic groups might be interested in the results, the public relations department of an organization can often be of great help to the evaluators. Public relations personnel can usually give expert advice on which local newspapers would be most interested, on the type of release that would be most appropriate, and on the names of people to contact.

Evaluators will also wish to share their work with the professional community. This involves choosing an appropriate journal for the evaluation report. In writing a journal article, it is important to keep the audience in mind. Some journals are read mainly by clinicians and practitioners; others are read mainly by university teachers and researchers; still other journals appeal to a mixed audience. In any event, it is helpful for evaluators to know the editorial policies, type of audience, and level of professional acceptance of the journals relevant to the field in which they are working.

In addition to the printed media, evaluators may wish to contact others through a presentation to their professional organization. There is a good deal of value in doing this. First, evaluators can keep in touch with professionals of similar interests and promote the sharing of their work. These presentations help others to keep current, because it usually takes over a year before journal articles are published. Second, some evaluators are in the position of having their expenses paid to a meeting only on the condition that they make a presentation. Finally, it may help evaluators to have an additional item on their resumés indicating that they have made a presentation to a society in their field to demonstrate that they are active and productive in their chosen field of expertise.

On the other hand, presentations to professional organizations have some drawbacks, compared to writing for appropriate journals. First of all, the audience is more limited in scope. A journal article will reach more people over a wider area and over a longer period of time. Second, the atmosphere at many professional meetings may not be conducive to a thoughtful presentation of complicated material. At times, there is a good deal of noise and distraction, even when papers are presented, and schedules are so crowded that the attention span of the audience becomes shorter as the day wears on.

Feedback to Participants

In addition to distributing the evaluation report to key personnel within the institution and also to those who have a right or interest in knowing about the findings outside the institution, it is important to keep in mind the obligation of providing feedback to participants. The program would not have existed, nor would the evaluation have been conducted, without the help and cooperation of those people who received the program. In many cases, they have a desire to know something about the results of the evaluation, and at times they have a right to know. If evaluators promised participants that they would obtain some information on the results of the program, then evaluators should fulfill their pledges. This does not mean the evaluators have to send a complete report to everybody who took part in the program. However, they can give a brief summary of the findings with information on where more details can be obtained.

The manner and time of release of this information to program participants should be approved by the administration or program sponsors. Once again, depending on the nature and sensitivity of the findings, administrators may see potential political problems that have to be addressed in light of the findings. They need time to prepare to address these potential problems before information is released on a wide scale. Releasing the report in a proper fashion provides them with the opportunity and time needed to prepare themselves.

Providing summarized feedback to participants does not have to be an expensive undertaking. Also, it is possible in the course of data collection to sort out the participants who wish to receive some information on the final study from those who do not. For example, in doing survey research the evaluators might request respondents to include a stamped self-addressed envelope together with their return questionnaire if they wish to receive a copy of the results. In this manner, the evaluators can respond to the interest of the participants without unduly increasing the cost of disseminating the report.

SUMMARY

A report will be read when the contents include pertinent information but are not ponderous; when the style is attractive and thought-provoking, but not tactless; and when it is distributed in a manner that respects the authority and sensitivities of the organization and its personnel. A well-written report will not necessarily be utilized, but unless it is well written, it has no possibility of having an impact on policy. Creating a climate conducive to effective utilization is the subject of the next chapter.

STUDY QUESTIONS

1. In Figure 11.3, the mean scores of the Cancer Care Center patients are compared to the mean scores of the comparison groups without including the standard deviation scores. Why is it ordinarily useful to include standard deviation scores along with mean

scores? Why is it appropriate to omit the standard deviation scores in this particular comparison?

2. Under what circumstances do results that fail to reach the level of statistical significance deserve serious attention? When should they be ignored? What is the danger involved in being too permissive toward Type II errors?

3. Explain why the representativeness of a sample is more important than its size.

4. Discuss the merits of the quantitative and qualitative style in reporting evaluation findings. How can these two approaches be integrated in the same report?

FURTHER READING

EWING, D. 1974. *Writing for results: In business, government, or the professions.* New York: Wiley-Interscience.

12

A Favorable

Evaluation Climate:

How to Get Results

Used

The first step in having findings utilized effectively was discussed in the last chapter, namely, writing and presenting a report in a manner that will get it read. In this chapter, attention is given to fostering a climate that is conducive to having the report implemented aggressively. This subject is discussed under five headings: (1) encouraging the proper attitude in practitioners and policy-makers; (2) dealing with negative findings in a constructive fashion; (3) dealing with mixed results; (4) overcoming the obstacles to effective utilization of findings; and (5) improving evaluations.

ENCOURAGING PROPER ATTITUDE IN
PRACTITIONERS AND POLICY MAKERS

The realization that not every innovation or creative idea will be a success is the first element of a productive attitude that will contribute to the effective utilization of evaluation findings. Program directors and practitioners must feel free to innovate, recognize failure, and learn from failures. Accepting the possibility of failure enables individuals to read an evaluation report with a relaxed and open mind, rather than a defensive attitude that prompts them to reject an entire report at the first sign of criticism. It also enables practitioners to set aside less productive ideas and procedures when the evidence in the evaluation report is not sufficiently strong to support a certain approach to a problem. Freedom to fail also enables staff to experiment with other approaches to achieve program goals.

An example of the effect of the fear of failure is provided in a book of essays on organizational development (OD) edited by Mirvis and Berg (1977). Organizational development is a relatively new and developing behavioral science that aims at assisting organizations in their efforts at self-improvement. Sometimes this involves introducing complex programs designed to change the structure of an organization, its social climate, or the day-to-day behaviors of specific individuals within the organization. Because of the complexity of the situations addressed by OD programs, mistakes are unavoidable. However, because of pressure to succeed, many failures in OD efforts are ignored, denied, and remain unrecognized. When failures are covered up, it becomes impossible to learn from them. Problems common to OD efforts in many organizations are considered unique because they have not been publicly described. As a result, some prevailing OD practices go unquestioned and are not improved. In the final essay of the volume, it is pointed out that errors in nonroutine situations such as those faced frequently in complex and rapidly changing organizations are neither shameful nor completely avoidable, and that patience and persistence may eventually be viewed as the only "right" answers in organizational development. The more fruitful approach is to measure competence, not by skill in avoiding errors, but by skill in detecting them and acting on the information openly. The authors further state that we must learn to reward those who recognize the risks involved in creating change, and yet still choose to risk, persist, and learn from their errors in OD.

While an atmosphere that respects the freedom to fail is essential for the effective use of findings, it will often be beyond the power of evaluators to foster such an atmosphere where it does not already exist. The attitude of top administration will usually determine whether an organization or program is characterized by a desperate need to make a program work or whether there is a relaxed attitude toward the possibility of failure. In healthy organizations administrators understand that innovation entails the possibility that even well-designed and implemented programs may fail. Where a healthy attitude toward failure already exists, evaluators can make the most of it and use every opportunity to underscore and publicize the enlightened attitude of the administration. Where the atmosphere is somewhat clouded and undetermined, evaluators may be able to foster a healthy attitude towards failure by requesting top administration to make some explicit statement to allay the anxiety of timid or insecure program personnel. In those organizations where the need of success is paramount and the fear of failure is rampant, evaluators will very likely be able to do little to bring about a change in attitude that will enable a research report to be received in a productive manner. However, evaluators will rarely be faced with this situation because organizations with a strong fear of failure will not be very inclined to sponsor evaluation research in the first place.

A second element of an attitude conducive to the effective application of evaluation findings is that personnel are not led to expect "good" or "bad" news, but rather suggestions for new ways of developing and improving existing programs. It is a relatively rare situation where an existing program will be terminated or continued solely on the basis of an evaluation report. In fact, evaluators are pleased when their report produces any noticeable modification in policy and procedures. However, program personnel tend to be highly involved in their program and are occasionally unduly worried about the continuation of the program in the face of a bad report. As a result, they are often looking for a one-line answer to the question: "Does the evaluation support our program or not?" In other words, does the evaluation bring good news or bad news? Evaluators will have a better opportunity of seeing their findings utilized effectively in those instances in which program personnel understand that every evaluation report brings some good news and some bad news, and that the more important question is: "What concrete improvements are suggested by the evaluation report that are feasible for implementation?" Evaluators will encourage program personnel to see evaluation as a way to help them improve and modify their program, not as a means to enshrine it or to destroy it.

For example, in conducting the evaluation of the physical medicine and rehabilitation unit in a community hospital, the health care delivery team understood from the beginning that the rehabilitation unit was going to stay intact regardless of the outcome of the evaluation. However, they were interested in finding out just how much progress the stroke patients were making during their stay in the unit, and also whether or not those who had improved during their hospitalization continued to improve, or at least maintained their improvement, after they left the hospital. The results of the study showed that during their hospitalization the stroke patients improved their physical skills (walking, eating, dressing) more than their cognitive skills (speaking, remembering). This information focused the attention of the health care delivery team on improving their efforts to restore cognitive skills. The results also showed that the majority of patients who made progress during their hospitalization maintained their improvement after they left the hospital. The information gave the rehabilitation team a more exact picture of the percentage of those who did not maintain their improvement and enabled them to evaluate whether or not a follow-up program geared to these patients would be worth the time and effort.

The third way evaluators can promote healthy attitudes is to assist program managers to be aware of the connection between the findings of the report and their own specific needs. On some occasions, program managers fail to see the full value and implications of the report. For example, the chairman of a large department of pastoral care at a religiously oriented hospital commissioned an evaluation of the department in the hope of learning what the patients, nurses, and physicians expected from chaplains and the extent to which patient and staff needs were being met by the chaplains (Carey 1972). The immediate value of the research was to enable the chaplains to get a clear picture of the differences in expectation among patients of different religious denominations, ages, and marital situations. It also revealed that physicians and nurses had slightly different role expectations for the chaplains than did the patients. Furthermore, many chaplains were surprised to find that the physicians and nurses placed a higher value on the assistance chaplains gave them in their work than the patients did on the more traditional role of the chaplains. This latter finding was largely due to the very active role the chaplains play at this hospital in assisting the staff to care for patients and family in a time of serious illness and death.

These secondary findings with respect to physicians and nurses turned out to be more valuable than originally expected later that year when representatives from Medicare and certain insurance companies refused to reimburse the hospital for the one dollar a day per patient that is set aside to pay for the care from chaplains. The representatives took the position that these expenses should be disallowed, and the cost of the chaplaincy should be underwritten by the religious organization sponsoring the hospital. They took this position because they assumed that the role of the chaplains was primarily to provide emotional support to a minority of patients who had religious needs. However, the president of the hospital was alert enough to see the application of the evaluation to defend the financing of the chaplaincy program out of patient room costs. The evaluation found that 87 percent of the nurses and 76 percent of the physicians said they found chaplains to be of great help to them personally in their work with patients. Because this was true, it could not be argued that chaplains were assigned primarily to serve a minority of the patient population. The hospital's viewpoint prevailed, largely on the force of the evaluation report. In this instance, hospital administrators saw implications of the evaluation report not recognized by the director of the pastoral care program. The most effective evaluators will be alert to practical issues that may be peripheral to the original intent of the evaluation. If they fail to do so, the full implications may go unappreciated because even program managers cannot always be relied upon to see all the values of the evaluation findings.

A final aspect of engendering a proper attitude for a productive use of findings is to phrase conclusions as working hypotheses, rather than as definitive generalizations. It would be very satisfying to be able to summarize a report with a clear, succinct statement that settles a question or solves a problem once and for all. When much time, effort, and money are spent on a report, one would like to have something solid to show for the results. However, those who look to an evaluation report to provide definitive conclusions are almost certainly bound to be disappointed.

One of the reasons why conclusions must be seen as working hypotheses is that local conditions do not allow for a generalization that can be applied to every situation. For example, Cronbach (1975) explains that those using personnel tests have long known of the danger in generalizing about how widely specific personnel tests can predict job success. This is true because test validity varies with the particular applicants taking the tests, the conditions of the specific job, and the criteria of job success. To select sales people on the basis of a test found valid in *other* firms is unacceptable in the absence of solid knowledge about how aptitudes interact with the dimensions along which sales jobs vary. For the same reasons, positive results obtained with a new educational program in one community warrant another community trying it, but instead of trusting that those results apply, the next community needs its own local evaluation. Of course, there comes a point when a generalization can be made, and the focus of evaluation can turn from documenting successful outcomes to documenting adequate implementation of the program.

Definitive conclusions are equally hard to arrive at, even in those instances in which a strict experimental design is used. Even with true experiments, program personnel should not be allowed to entertain unrealistically high hopes for a critical experiment. For example, Sloane and his colleagues (1975) conducted one of the best evaluations of psychotherapy ever designed. Groups who received behavior therapy and psychoanalytically oriented psychotherapy were compared with each other and a control group. The results showed that the target symptoms of all three groups improved significantly, but the two treated groups improved equally well and significantly more than those on a waiting list. However, one year and two years after the initial assessment, all groups were found to be equally and significantly improved. These researchers tried to move beyond the basic question of whether or not psychotherapy is effective to the question of what type of therapy would be most productive with what kind of patients. Even with an excellent experimental design, the study fell short of giving definitive answers to this question. Nevertheless, the study is a model for future work. More important, it has provided new hypotheses for future investigations that will enable researchers to fine tune their research designs.

DEALING WITH NEGATIVE FINDINGS CONSTRUCTIVELY

Negative findings are disappointing. The temptation is to equate them with failure and to try to rationalize one's way out of the situation by saying, for example, ". . . the program was never fully implemented . . ." or "a number of special and unusual cases in the sample affected the outcome. . . ." Unless evaluators take firm control of the situation, they run the risk of allowing program personnel to rationalize negative findings in a way similar to Linus (from the "Peanuts" cartoon) explaining to Lucy why he failed to buy her a birthday present. He explained that he saw a bottle of cologne in the store and wanted to buy it for her, but instead did something that would make her even happier. He knew how concerned she was for the sick in the world and how happy she would be if he became a famous doctor. To do this, he would need good grades. To get good grades, he would need to be healthy, which in turn meant he should eat properly. So, instead of buying her the bottle of cologne, he bought himself a sandwich!

There are more productive ways of dealing with negative findings than rationalizing apparent failures. One such productive approach is to focus on the arguments for continuing a human service program, even if the findings are not supportive, when there are good reasons for continuing the program other than those originally proposed. For example, Waldo and Chiricos (1977) caused some consternation for policy makers who supported growth of a work-release program for prisoners. An analysis to determine whether or not members of work-release programs and those in a control group differed in recidivism showed that the programs had no advantage on measures of rehabilitative success. In analyzing and discussing the results, the authors speculated that the work-release program had become an established policy in the absence of empirical justification because it saved money and because it appealed to the common sense of legislators and policy makers. The research, in fact, showed that the program led to no harm. The authors did not argue for the elimination of work-release programs because they might be justified on humanitarian and economic grounds. However, they concluded that policy makers should not attempt to "sell" work release on the basis of its rehabilitative merits but should be prepared to discard it when better programs are demonstrated. The researchers concluded that in the long run legislators (and consequently correctional administrators) are most concerned with economic utility—even in those fields where "changing people" is the presumed mission of the organization.

Common-sense plausibility is another reason for continuing a program in the face of negative findings. When there is considerable agreement on the plausibility of a hypothesis, nonsupportive findings argue for an intensification of research rather than an abandonment of it. Ross (1975) argued in this manner after the evaluation of the Scandinavian laws on drinking and driving failed to support the deterence hypothesis of the severe punishment for drunken driving. According to the deterence hypothesis, an interrupted time-series analysis of motor vehicles casualty data from Sweden and Norway should have showed change as a result of the initiation of the legal reforms in question. The expectations were not fulfilled. Ross concluded:

> Failure to find support for the deterence hypothesis does not disprove the hypothesis, which has the merit of common-sense plausibility, but it indicates that the current widespread faith is without firm grounding. From the practical standpoint, it is suggested that the continuation of current policy in Sweden and Norway, and its adoption elsewhere, should be more tentative and subject to more scrutiny and critical evaluation than has been the case to date (p. 286).

Another approach to dealing constructively with negative findings is to use no-difference findings to eliminate costly elements of a program. For example, consider the evaluation of presterilization interviewing that was discussed in the previous chapter (Carey 1976). The policy of the hospital board of trustees was that mandatory interviewing by chaplains or the local clergyman of the patient was required before

any sterilization operation at that hospital. An evaluation of presterilization interviewing was done by randomly assigning couples who applied
for tubal ligations and vasectomies to an interview group and a control
group. Results showed no difference in level of anxiety, guilt feelings,
or marital adjustment between the interviewed group and the control
group. In fact, in some cases hostility was generated in couples who
either had a large number of children or who were near the end of
their child-bearing years and had made a very firm and well thought out
decision not to have any more children. The chaplains themselves felt
that mandatory interviewing in these circumstances was counterproductive. As a result of the evaluation, the hospital policy on mandatory
interviewing was limited to those instances in which the person to be
sterilized was under thirty years of age. This change in policy saved a
good deal of time and money and at the same time preserved the
purpose of the regulation, which was to discourage younger couples
from making a hasty decision in regard to sterilization.

No-difference findings have also been used productively in evaluating
methods of law enforcement and criminal correction. For example, one
feature after another of criminal rehabilitation approaches has been
altered experimentally, and crime and recidivism rates have remained
unchanged. Glass (1976) comments:

> These no-difference findings, the bane of the experimental scientists,
> are grist for the evaluator's mill. If cutting reformatory sentences
> in half does not produce increased recidivism, then shorter sen-
> tences are 100 percent more cost-effective [all other things being
> equal]. . . . Doing as well as in the past but doing it more cheaply
> is a gain in value as surely as is doing better at a great cost (p. 11).

Using no-difference findings in this manner to eliminate costly aspects of a program must be done carefully. It is crucial that the evaluators demonstrate that they used a good research design, had adequate
sampling procedures, and used valid measures of program success.
Obviously, it is possible that no-difference findings can result from a
poor design, from inadequate number in treatment and control groups,
or from inadequate measurement. Nevertheless, with these precautions,
a negative finding can be transformed into a positive impact on the
program.

Finally, even disappointing results can lead to worthwhile changes
and improvement in a program, when evaluation efforts are closely
linked to the decision-making behavior of program planners and administrators. For example, Smith (1975) evaluated the outcome effectiveness of a new clinical care program for seriously disturbed patients from

traditional state hospitals. Outcomes were assessed in terms of social competence and economic cost to the patients and society. The results were very disappointing. Although the increased staff, the increased expenditure, and the community orientation of the new center represented a clear advance in the humanitarian care of the mentally ill, no evidence was found that this new approach substantially altered the social outcome of serious mental disorders or of the disability associated with them. Examination of other outcome studies did not uncover any strong evidence contrary to the negative findings of Smith's investigation. The result of Smith's study was that the center substantially shifted its resources from traditional management techniques (drugs, group psychotherapy) to rehabilitation techniques (teaching useful job skills, skills in daily living, homemaking). Staff were assigned to upgrade community placement facilities and to establish community rehabilitation centers at key locations throughout the region. These new programs were scheduled for another round of evaluation. Unless evaluation had been strongly linked to program planning and administration, as it was at this community mental health center, such shifts in emphasis might well not have taken place.

Even in cases in which results are not negative, experience has proven that a strong link between program evaluators and policy makers is essential if results are to be utilized effectively. This link may take the form of liaison individuals or linking situations that translate the needs of policy makers into evaluation research, and evaluation research into practice. Liaison persons are the bridges that give research results maximum impact for nonresearchers. For example, in the field of agriculture, extension agents act as intermediaries between the agriculture experimental stations and farmers. The agricultural extension agents are one of the earliest examples of liaison persons to translate research results to the ultimate users. In the field of education in public technology, there is also a growing awareness of the need for a liaison role. Public Technology Inc., headquartered in Washington, D.C., and partly funded by the National Science Foundation, transfers research knowledge to such users as urban government, agencies, and organizations who seek to use technology to solve urban problems.

DEALING WITH MIXED RESULTS

The problem of dealing with mixed results, that is, when some findings support a program and others do not, is different from dealing with negative findings, when analysis of the data overwhelmingly indicates that the program or treatment under investigation had no significant effects. When there are mixed results, proponents for a program focus attention on those findings that support the program, and those who would like to see the program terminated focus attention on the negative aspects of the evaluation report. The problem of dealing with mixed results is accentuated when politics are involved, when a large number of jobs hangs in the balance, or when many people are rallied to opposing causes. Four approaches for dealing with mixed results and an evaluation of the appropriateness of each are presented here.

Allow Others to Interpret Mixed Results

First, evaluators can report the findings and leave the interpretation to the readers, that is, policy makers, administrators, or program staff. This can be accomplished by avoiding extended interpretation and discussion of the results in the written report and identifying the difficulties of interpretation only in the oral report, if at all.

This approach may be appropriate in those instances in which an evaluator had an explicit agreement with the sponsors of the research to keep the interpretation of findings to a minimum, and when the role of the evaluator was not to embrace the implementation of the report. However, as we have argued elsewhere, evaluators will ideally have a significant role in program planning. In addition, program personnel correctly expect evaluators to take a position in their analysis and discussion of the mixed results. Evaluators should seldom let the numbers "speak for themselves." Data will be interpreted. If the evaluator does not do the interpreting, others with less objectivity will. The failure of evaluators to take a position and make clear their recommendations suggests either incompetence or a lack of courage.

The Easy Way Out

Evaluators can choose the interpretation they feel is more favorable to the program and emphasize the results in the study that support the favorable interpretation. Where hypotheses in the study were not confirmed or where the effect was weak, evaluators can tone down unfavorable results by: (1) alleging that the outcome measures were unreliable, insensitive, or inappropriate; (2) attributing the lack of statistical significance to the small sample; (3) suggesting that implementation of the program was inadequate due to lack of time, complexity, lack of funds, and so forth; or (4) by putting great weight on measures of consumer satisfaction, which is often surprisingly favorable even when more objective results are marginal.

Choosing the more favorable interpretation may be defended in some instances, for example, when the positive findings concern the more critical issues and there is hope that the program personnel will support a follow-up study to clarify the mixed results if they do not lose confidence in the evaluators. However, to espouse the more favorable position out of fear of being criticized by program sponsors, to avoid hurting feelings, or merely to obtain future evaluation funding is not defensible.

The Adversary Approach

Two other approaches to handling mixed results are more professionally responsible and in the long run more valuable, both to the evaluators and program personnel. The evaluators can use an adversary approach to interpret the results. They can first argue one position and gather all the results in the data that support this interpretation, and then they can take the opposite viewpoint and present the data that support that view. The evaluators can then clearly state which side, if either, they think has the strongest case. If the evaluators cannot decide, they can point this out, along with their suggestions for follow-up research to clarify the ambiguity of the present study.

An alternate form of the adversary style of presentation would be to ask two independent researchers who had not been connected with the report to study the design and the data collected and then write a position paper supporting each side of the issue. These reviews by researchers representing different viewpoints could then be bound with the original report. The evaluators might then choose to evaluate the interpretations of the independent experts and conclude with their own summary and position. The adversary approach has been suggested by some writers (for example, Datta 1976a; Levin et al. 1978); however, this approach is likely to be relatively expensive, making the approach unrealistic for the evaluator working in an institution or government office.

Use the Evaluation to Improve the Program

A fourth approach to dealing with mixed results that seems to be both productive and ethically acceptable is to transform an evaluation originally intended as a summative evaluation into a formative evaluation. For example, suppose that policy makers had commissioned an evaluation to decide whether or not a program should continue to be funded. Evaluators could show how costs might be cut without eliminating the positive results and how the program might be modified to bring about positive results where the impact was minimal. This approach of transforming a summative evaluation into formative evaluation would not be well received by policy makers who were under pressure to make a definitive judgment regarding the viability of a given program. However, if they were not strapped by time or the necessity of cost containment, they might be able to delay a final decision on terminating or extending a program and be willing to entertain suggestions that might change a marginally successful program into a more successful one.

OBSTACLES TO EFFECTIVE UTILIZATION OF FINDINGS

In this section, four of the more common obstacles to the implementation of findings are discussed. Evaluators will not always be in a position to remove these blocks to the effective use of their findings, but at least they can be aware of their existence and try to work around them where possible.

Lack of Respect of Some Evaluators for Their Peers

The first block to effective utilization is the acrimonious battles that occasionally arise in the press between evaluation researchers over the interpretation and application of results to sensitive issues or programs. These battles, which sometimes originate from genuine and honest disagreements between researchers, can be carried to an inappropriate intensity and tend to reduce the credibility of all program evaluators. Public policy makers standing on the sideline tend to be dismayed by the accusations of lack of integrity and competence leveled against researchers by members of their own peer group. As a result, administrators and legislators may question the validity of all evaluation research.

Even when differences of opinion between professionals are expressed with mutual respect, it can result in a loss of confidence among those outside a given profession. For example, when physicians or medical experts give a patient conflicting advice regarding the diagnosis or treatment of a medical problem, the patient begins to wonder whether the doctors really know what they are doing. In reality, some problems are very complicated, and medical science does not have all the answers. One cannot expect all physicians to agree on the answers to certain questions. However, physicians profoundly damage respect toward the medical profession when they express their disagreement with another physician's opinion in such a way as to question the physician's competence or integrity. This can occur when one doctor accuses another as being "too quick to use a scalpel."

In the legal profession, judges do not always interpret or apply the law in the same way. Consider the situation in which a local court convicts a man of being guilty of a certain crime, only to have a higher court reverse the opinion of the lower court. Although one court is usually careful not to impugn the motivation or competence of the other court, nevertheless frequent disagreements among lawyers and courts on a variety of issues and legal decisions tend to create cynicism about the probability of obtaining justice in our present judicial system.

An example of legitimate differences of opinion that have resulted in acrimonious debate between evaluation researchers is the running battle between Pettigrew and Green, on the one hand, and Coleman, on the other, over Coleman's "white flight" thesis and the interpretation of his research on school desegregation in large cities. The highly publicized study, *Equality of Educational Opportunity* (Coleman et al. 1966), popularly called "The Coleman Report," was in essence a favorable evaluation of court-ordered integration and the busing of students to integrate schools. However, some years later Coleman changed his opinion and wrote:

> In school integration, there has been a surprising absence of interest on the part of those formulating and implementing the policy about the overall impact—as opposed to the immediately observable effect—of that policy. The results of these analyses show that the indirect consequences are far from negligible and can sharply reduce or perhaps even in the longer run reverse the intended effect of that policy. . . . The extremely strong reaction of individual whites in moving their children out of a large district engaged in rapid desegregation suggests that in the long run the policies that have been pursued will defeat the purpose of increasing overall contact among races in schools (Coleman, 1976, p. 321).

Pettigrew and Green engaged Coleman in an extended debate over the value of court-ordered school integration. A brief sample of Coleman's remarks about Green and Pettigrew contends that

> . . . on certain questions, there appears to be a kind of conspiracy of silence, and then a rush to the attack when anyone dares to break the silence. I have the impression that if Professors Green and Pettigrew saw the fires in the sky during the riots of 1967, they would have attributed them to an extraordinary display of northern lights. I believe that it does no one any good in the long run for us to blind ourselves to reality, because it is reality, not our fond hopes about it, which measures the effectiveness of government actions (Guttentag, 1977, p. 407).

Pettigrew and Green accused Coleman of incompetence and ignoring methodological problems.

> Unfortunately Coleman does not address an array of problems that have been raised about his research. . . .
> (a) His research on essentially a demographic problem has been conducted in a demographic vacuum. . . .
> (b) His future projections are inflated by unrealistic assumptions. . . .
> (c) An ecological fallacy is involved in his assertions of individual motivation ("white flight") from gross district-wide data (Guttentag, 1977, p. 429).

Need we be surprised if program managers and community representatives hesitate to accept our findings when authorities hold each other in such low repute?

The Weight of Nonempirical Influences

The second obstacle to the effective utilization of findings is the weight of other influences and pressures that compete with the impact of the information in an evaluation report. At times it may seem to evaluators that decision makers are not disposed to give their attention to a report and do not wish to reexamine policy decisions in view of new information received. However, it is possible that decision makers can receive a report with an open mind—even with eagerness—and yet find themselves unable to act because they are constrained by economic realities and political pressures.

Bigelow and Ciarlo (1975) studied the question of what value there was in collecting information and presenting it to human service administrators. Would information improve their decisions? They studied this question in a large community health center which had thirty management and supervisory personnel. They used three different strategies to try to learn how management was using evaluation feedback. First, they conducted interviews with managers using their Information Use and Decision-Making Questionnaire. Second, they interviewed supervisors when a substantial program modification had been made within their jurisdiction. Third, they introduced a body of data bearing on a program management issue during a meeting of supervisors and then tried to trace the effects over a two-week period. They concluded that managers were disposed to use information, that it was perceived and attended to when presented to them, that it affected their intentions to modify programs, and that it resulted in further exploration of a particular management question. The study did not demonstrate that the information resulted in improved performance for the organization. Nevertheless, in the specific instances in which information had, in fact, been introduced, the relative impact of information was appreciable. However, the conclusion that information does have an impact on management had to be qualified by the Heisenberg principle: the very observation of a process alters that process. Changes in management decision making may have resulted in part from participation in the investigation, rather than from the input of the feedback data.

Another instance of how other influences and pressures can have a great influence on decision makers is in the issue of guaranteed income as a form of welfare reform (Haveman and Watts 1976). From the awarding of the original grant for this welfare experiment to submission of the final report in late 1973, a total of six and one-half years elapsed. The four years of the operating phase of the experiment were sandwiched between fourteen months of planning and design and sixteen months of data analyses. The experiment cost about $8 million, about one-third of which went for payments to participating families. In spite of this massive effort, there has been no national movement to modify the present income tax regulation to accommodate a guaranteed income provision. Frankly, no one should have expected a guaranteed income program to develop from the experiment. Public sentiment would have been so overwhelmingly opposed to the idea that legislators would have voted against such a change in the law, even if they were convinced of the merits of the innovation. However, even though public policy has not been changed, the evaluation did alter future debate and discussion of the issue of guaranteed income. Although most economists and politicians would have predicted that even the limited form of guaranteed income used in the study would result in massive malingering and a loss of motivation to work, these theories were not supported. As a result, no longer will the loss-of-work incentives argument occupy the front of the stage in future discussion of the income maintenance policy. Thus, the evaluation did not change income tax law, but it did change the form of the debate.

Preexisting Polarization of Interested Parties

A third block to the effective utilization of findings occurs when opposing factions have been strongly polarized before an evaluation takes place. Recommendations fall on deaf ears when administrators and public representatives have already decided the position they will take, regardless of the results of an evaluation. As a consequence, they miss important nuances in the findings. A clear example of the effect of polarization can be seen in the interpretations of the evaluation research conducted by Zimring (1975) on the impact of the Federal Gun Control Act of 1968. Gun control legislation is a highly emotional issue. It was unlikely from the beginning that any evaluation would materially change the opinions of many of those aligned on both sides of the issue. Zimring comments on this at the beginning of his report:

> The study will be of little use to the most fervent friends and foes of gun control legislation. It provides data they do not need. Each group has already decided that the 1968 Act has failed, and each group uses the Act's presumed failure to confirm views already strongly held. Enthusiasts for strict federal controls see the failure of the law as proof that stricter laws are needed, while opponents see it as evidence that no controls will work. The picture that emerges from available data is more equivocal. There is evidence that the approach adopted by the Act can aid state efforts at strict firearms control, although other resources necessary to achieve this end have never been provided by Congress. There is also reason to believe that the potential impact of the Act is quite limited when measured against the problems it sought to alleviate (p. 133).

Another emotional issue on which some have already decided their position prior to research is the abortion issue. On the one hand, proabortionists place the freedom of the mother above all other values and will not modify this position regardless of the demonstration of harmful effects on society caused by the ready availability of abortion. On the other hand, those who belong to the so-called Right to Life movement place the life of an unborn fetus above all other values and are not about to change this position, even though research shows the harmful effects of back-alley abortions.

The abortion issue is also an example of an issue where the weight of other influences and pressures influence decision makers. It is hard for legislators to objectively weigh the evidence of the studies when they are bombarded by letters and public protests on both sides of the issue. In fact, legislators are doing the correct thing in not allowing themselves to be guided merely by the results of sociological or psychological investigations. Policy makers must be alert to the input from the legal profession, philosophers, and medical experts, as well as input from social science studies.

Costs May Exceed Benefits

A final block to the effective utilization of findings is obvious, but worth singling out because of its importance, namely, the cost of programs. Effective evaluators will not ignore cost-benefit and cost-effectiveness considerations. If the value of a program is measured in terms of its benefits per unit of cost, then it is inadequate for evaluators to pursue evaluation research by measuring either the benefits or the cost alone. Rather, both the benefits and cost must be considered.

Carnoy's (1975) evaluation of the cost effectiveness of educational television (ETV) is an exemplary blend of careful research into both cost and benefits. He concluded that the performance of pupils is not significantly better with ETV as compared to situations in which teachers are retrained to use more effective curricula. At the same time, the cost of ETV schooling is much higher per pupil than classroom teacher schooling, because teacher retraining costs are usually only a small fraction of the cost of operating a traditional school system.

However, ETV does have the advantage of comparatively rapid implementation. Carnoy showed ETV cannot be promoted on the grounds that it produces good outcomes because student achievement in ETV settings, although high, is not consistently better than the achievement levels of students in programs that are less expensive. Policy makers, when faced with careful evaluations such as Carnoy presented, can hardly push hard for ETV, even though it can be demonstrated that it has had beneficial results. This is especially true in periods of tight budgets.

METAEVALUATION

Another way to increase the impact of evaluation is to improve the evaluations themselves. Evaluators will be more likely to see their studies effectively utilized when they demonstrate that their work can stand the test of careful analysis and that they themselves are open to growth through constructive criticism. These goals can be realized in part by the practice of evaluating evaluations, or what has been termed *metaevaluation*.

Various authors have given slightly different meanings to the term *metaevaluation* and have suggested different ways for executing it. For example, Stufflebeam (1978) distinguishes formative metaevaluation from summative metaevaluation. *Formative metaevaluation* is conducted before an evaluation takes place and is intended as a guide to help evaluators effectively carry out their project by improving the evaluation plan. For example, Stufflebeam illustrated an ambitious formative metaevaluation by a National Institute of Education (NIE) project designed to develop a system for NIE's use in evaluating research and development institutions. The NIE project had two teams prepare alternative evaluation plans and then had a third team evaluate the two plans. *Summative metaevaluations* are studies of the merits of a completed evaluation. Both formative and summative metaevaluation assess the extent to which an evaluation is technically adequate, useful in guiding decisions, ethical in dealing with people in organizations, and practical in the use of resources. Stufflebeam suggests thirty-four standards as dependent variables for judging the merit of completed evaluations and presents sixty-eight guidelines as procedural suggestions to help evaluators meet the standards. His work provides a detailed outline for those who wish to conduct a metaevaluation of their own work or someone else's work.

Cook and Gruder (1978) use the term *metaevaluation* in a slightly different sense from Stufflebeam. They use metaevaluation to refer only to the evaluation of empirical evaluations, that is, studies in which data are being, or have been, collected directly from program participants. They exclude from consideration the evaluation of proposed evaluation plans, an activity that Stufflebeam called formative metaevaluation.

Cook and Gruder discuss seven different models of metaevaluation: four that are subsequent to the initial evaluation, and three simultaneous with the initial evaluation. The three simultaneous models (consultant metaevaluation, simultaneous secondary analysis of data, and multiple independent replications) are more complicated and costly and beyond the scope of the present discussion. However, the four models of metaevaluation that can be used subsequent to the primary evaluation are less costly, more practical, and within the consideration of most evaluators. An overview of these four models is presented below.

Model 1

Model 1 is an essay review of an evaluation report. An essay review would include both published reviews and also unpublished documents written by in-house or outside consultants at interim stages before the final report is published.

Published reviews would usually concentrate on technical issues such as sampling, measurement, and data analysis. They are particularly useful if, without questioning the data, they bring fresh interpretation to bear on the study. Pettigrew et al. (1973) did this, in part, when they observed that Armor (1972) judged busing a "failure" because his criterion for success was that integration should reduce racial gaps in achievement. Instead, they demonstrated that the absolute achievement levels of blacks had increased, irrespective of what happened to whites. In this approach, the data and analyses are accepted as valid, and the issue is one of interpreting the findings. Obviously, only major evaluation studies would receive this scrutiny.

Another type of essay review occurs when a prepublication draft is sent to people with technical and substantive skills and to those likely to oppose the major conclusions of a report. People with differing points of view often interpret phrasing differently than the authors of a report intended. Also, they can provide different, valid ways to interpret findings. Their feedback can be used to modify the final report so that discussion of the report is focused on the implications of the results, rather than on secondary or side issues.

Model 2

The second model of metaevaluation is a review of literature about a specific program. For example, there have been multiple evaluations of prison rehabilitation, psychotherapy, and educational programs. Cook and Gruder suggest that the second model of metaevaluation is best used at an early date to identify approaches to program evaluation that are not fruitful. However, the evaluators can also use this model at the conclusion of their own evaluation to demonstrate the extent to which the major conclusions are supported by other similar evaluations and also to indicate the direction that future research should take.

Multiple evaluations permit more valid and credible research conclusions, especially where clear patterns of convergence emerge. However, it is probably more common that inconsistencies will be found among various evaluations. In these instances, no explicit rules exist for combining the results of relevant studies. Light and Smith (1971) have severely criticized the most common method of resolving inconsistencies among different research. They note that most reviewers simply take a vote among the various reports. The "taking a vote" method involves gathering all the studies that have data on a dependent variable and specific independent variable of interest. Three possible outcomes are defined. The relationship between the independent variable and dependent variable is classified as either significantly positive, significantly negative, or neither, that is, as having no significant relationship in either direction. The number of studies that fall into each of these three categories is then simply tallied, and the category with the most votes is declared the winner and is treated as descriptive of that body of research.

Light and Smith propose *cluster sampling* as an alternative approach to the taking-a-vote method. Clusters are not random samples, but natural aggregations within a population. A set of studies investigating a given problem may contain a number of different clusters, not all of which will be present in each study. In the taking-a-vote method, each complete study is the unit of analysis. In cluster sampling, the cluster becomes the unit of analysis. Suppose, for example, that the relationship between nursing turnover and race is investigated and that there are five studies of nursing turnover that include data from thirteen hospitals. These hospitals can be divided into community hospitals, private teaching hospitals, university hospitals, and government hospitals. The clusters in this instance would be the types of hospitals. In the event that all differences among clusters prove to be insignificant, the cluster approach concludes that all data from the studies can be combined into the equivalent of a single large study. This is the assumption with which the other types of metaevaluation often begin. However, if the differences between clusters are significant, then the evaluator can search for an explanation in site differences, unmeasured variables, or population characteristics. Thus, the cluster approach allows for a more careful analysis than simply taking a vote. However, the cluster approach requires access to the original data.

Model 3

The third model of metaevaluation is an empirical reevaluation of a program evaluation and is perhaps the best-known approach to metaevaluation. The third model consists of the reanalysis of another evaluator's data to test published conclusions or to examine new questions. The reanalysis of the Coleman report by Mosteller and Moynihan (1972) and that of the Sesame Street studies by Cook and others (1975) are examples of the third model of metaevaluation. Empirical reevaluation is usually better than an essay review because an empirical metaevaluation includes the reanalysis of raw data. However, there are also some drawbacks. Empirical reevaluation is seldom timely for the needs of decision makers and can be misleading if subsequent analyses are conducted on special samples. Nevertheless, evaluators can often lend a great deal of credibility to their report by making the data available to interested researchers for this type of reanalysis.

Model 4

The fourth model of metaevaluation suggested by Cook and Gruder is an empirical reevaluation of multiple data sets about the same program. This model of metaevaluation has been termed *meta-analysis* by other authors because it consists in the integration of research through statistical analysis of the analyses of several studies. The fourth model is appropriately used in an area that has been heavily researched and where evaluation findings are mixed and controversial. For example, Smith and Glass (1977) conducted a meta-analysis of psychotherapy outcome studies. They coded and statistically integrated the results of nearly four hundred controlled evaluations of psychotherapy. They integrated the magnitude of therapy effects in the various studies by defining the "effect size" as the *mean difference between the treated and control subjects divided by the standard deviation of the control group.* For example, an effect size of +1 indicates that persons at the mean of the control group would be expected to rise to a level equivalent to the eighty-fourth percentile of the control group if they were in the program evaluated. Smith and Glass's findings provide strong evidence of improved adjustment through psychotherapy. On the average, they found that the typical therapy client is better off than 75 percent of untreated individuals. However, they detected only negligible differences in the effects produced by different types of therapy. They concluded that unconditional judgments of the superiority of one or another type of psychotherapy are unjustified. One obvious weakness in this approach is that their sample of nearly four hundred evaluations may not be a representative sample of all the psychotherapy evaluation conducted. It is well-known that evaluations with negative findings have a harder time finding a place in journals than do evaluations with positive findings. It is also possible that psychotherapy provided during evaluations is better than psychotherapy provided routinely when no review or evaluation is being conducted. Therefore, the force of the conclusions might not apply to all psychotherapy.

In summary, metaevaluation will increase the probability of findings being utilized effectively because metaevaluation research is a means of improving the quality of evaluation methodology and indirectly testing whether program evaluation delivers what it promises—namely, the accurate representation of the need for a program, a description of the degree to which a program was actualized, and a documentation of the outcomes and the efficiency of various programs. The benefits that metaevaluation also holds for individual evaluators from the standpoint of improving their skills in methodology and interpretation are obvious. For these reasons, metaevaluation may be a significant factor in increasing the quality of program evaluations and in raising the level of utilization of evaluations in the human services.

STUDY QUESTIONS

1. Discuss some of the negative attitudes that can block the effective utilization of well-conducted evaluation.

2. Should an evaluator argue for the termination of an existing program when the results are predominantly negative? Explain.

Epilogue

This text has sought primarily to provide the groundwork for the development of the technical skills necessary to conduct program evaluations in human service settings. The organization of the book reflects the authors' view of the most useful approach to conducting such research. A brief reexamination of the flow chart in the Preface can give the reader a quick review of the main points of the material covered. The flow chart can also help evaluators explain to staff the services evaluators can provide.

Of perhaps equal importance with technical skills are the evaluator's attitudes and orientation toward the role of program evaluator. There are a number of references throughout this book to these attitudes and to the evaluator's role. It may be of help to draw these themes together in this section.

Humility Won't Hurt. Evaluators work in service settings. These settings are not designed to facilitate the conducting of research. Because of this fact, the evaluator can expect to be seen as filling a marginal role in the service delivery setting. Because the evaluator is always working on someone else's turf, arrogance will effectively block the exercise of even superb technical skills.

Impatience May Lead to Disappointment. Program and facility administrators have many constituencies, all expecting attention. Program evaluation is only one source of information on which decisions and plans are based. Financial concerns, community pressures, political realities, bureaucratic inertia, and so forth, are all powerful influences on program planners and administrators. Evaluators who have patience are less likely to feel ignored and unloved when their recommendations do not receive immediate attention.

Recognize the Importance of the Evaluator's Perspective. Evaluators have some skills that may be lacking in human service settings. Service staffs focus on individuals and often do not picture the overall program. Evaluators have a social orientation that can provide the staff with a new viewpoint. Administrators, on the other hand, do seek an overall perspective. However, administrators have a far better grasp of financial and other tangible matters than of social variables affecting the patient/client/student/trainee population served. Evaluators can provide information to administrators on social variables that are usually unavailable to administrators.

Focus on Practical Questions. People working in human service organizations are seldom concerned about matters solely of theoretical interest. Evaluators can work most effectively when they are oriented toward practical questions about the program being studied. Try not to forget that seeking to initiate and sustain change in people's lives is hard work. Faced with pressing human needs and with criticism from governmental bodies and insurance companies for excessive costs and alleged inefficiencies, agency staff and management desire practical assistance.

Work on Feasible Issues. If an evaluation is not feasible, do not attempt it. Do not waste your time and that of the staff. However, although it may not be feasible to work on a particular issue, it might be feasible to work on a less ambitious question. For example, if outcomes cannot be handled, it may be possible to develop a procedure to monitor the delivery of service.

Avoid Data Addiction. It is tempting to seek to gather a great amount of information about the program or about those served by the program. It might be nice to know everything possible about the program, but there are two compelling reasons to limit the amount of data sought to that which is essential. First, asking for too much information will increase the percentage of potential respondents who will refuse to cooperate and consequently will provide no information. Second, evaluators will often find themselves under too much time pressure to analyze all the data gathered. Thus, the effort of the cooperative respondents will be wasted. If the information is not essential to the evaluation, do not try to gather it.

Evaluators Are Information Channels. There are many things that can get in the way when new information is presented to potential users. Social science jargon and esoteric analyses can reduce the flow of information to those not acquainted with the jargon or schooled in statistics. Readers and listeners will be bored with a presentation that seems planned to display the evaluator's knowledge and technical skills. Save that for meetings of professional societies. To be effective, presentations to staff should be relevant to the program and recommendations should be practicable.

Encourage an Evaluation Orientation. Ideally, evaluation encourages honest relations among staff, clients, administrators, and program sponsors. These groups often act as though all failures could have been avoided. Although all failures cannot be avoided, people can learn from failures. The essence of the concept of the experimenting society is the recognition of the inevitability of failure. Instead of hiding failures or condemning them, help staff and administrators to treat honest attempts as experiments and to learn from failures.

Adopt a Self-evaluation Orientation to Your Own Work. When evaluation results and recommendations seem to be ignored, evaluators will benefit by asking themselves: "Was my presentation clear?" "Did I address the right questions?" "Were my answers right?" At times, the honest answer to these questions will be "No" or "Well, perhaps the evaluation did miss some essential points." Evaluators are like service staff people in some ways; neither can always avoid failures, and both can learn from their errors.

Statistical Appendix:

Worked Examples

of

Statistical Tests

The concepts and statistical tests reviewed and illustrated here are for the purpose of reminding readers of material studied previously. If some of the concepts are new, the reader could profit by referring to a statistics text for a full explanation.

BASIC CONCEPTS

For descriptive purposes, the most basic concepts are the *mean* (X) and the *standard deviation* (s).

For statistical significance tests, the unbiased definitional formula for standard deviation is $\sqrt{\sum_{1}(X_1 - \overline{X})^2/(N-1)}$.

Thus, for the values of 14, 15, 12, 16, and 14 the standard deviation is

$$\sqrt{\frac{(14 - 14.2)^2 + (15 - 14.2)^2 + (12 - 14.2)^2 + (16 - 14.2)^2 + (14 - 14.2)^2}{5 - 1}}$$

which equals 1.48

The *Standard Error of the Mean* ($s_{\bar{x}}$) is an index of how much variation is expected among the means of samples that are repeatedly randomly selected from a population. The formula for $s_{\bar{x}}$ is $s/\sqrt{N}$.

Clearly, the mean is expected to be a more stable figure than the score of a randomly sampled individual. Therefore, it makes sense to see that $s_{\bar{x}}$ is smaller than s. The values given in the paragraph above yield a $s_{\bar{x}}$ of .66. In other words, while raw scores sampled randomly from a particular sample have a standard deviation of 1.48, the means of numerous samples of the same size are expected to have a standard deviation of .66. The formula yields values for $s_{\bar{x}}$ that get smaller as N (the number of scores on which the mean is based) is larger. Once again, this should seem intuitively correct because the mean is more stable when based on a larger sample.

The *standard score transformation* rescales raw scores in a way that is very convenient when the raw scores are normally distributed. To do a standard score transformation, first, each raw score (X_i) is reduced by the mean ($\bar{X}$); second, each difference is divided by the standard deviation (s). This operation is symbolized as $z_i = (X_i - \bar{X})/s$. For the values above, the z of 15 would be $(15 - 14.2)/1.48$, or $+.54$.

The standard scores, z_i's have the same distribution as the X_i's had. The only difference between the original scores and the transformed scores is that the mean and standard deviation of the z scores are 0 and 1, respectively. Some beginning students leave their statistics classes believing that the standard score transformation changes the original distribution into a normal distribution. This is not so! If raw scores are evenly distributed throughout the range of X_i values, transformed scores will be evenly distributed throughout the range of z_i values.

However, if the X_i values are normally distributed, the transformation permits the use of tables for the purposes of calculating the probability of obtaining raw scores between any two specified values of the distribution. For example, if the five scores given above were normally distributed,[1] the probability of obtaining a 15 or more would be .21 because this proportion of a normal distribution of scores lies beyond a z of $+.54$. See a standard normal table to verify these values. This use of z scores and the standard normal table makes it easy to convert normally distributed values into percentiles. If .21 of a distribution lies beyond a given score, then that score defines the seventy-ninth percentile point.

The standard normal table and z scores are useful for more than the calculation of percentiles. The application of the z score transformation to means (in contrast to raw scores) is the first step toward inferential statistics. For example, if the illustrative sample given above

---

[1] For this small a sample, it would be impossible to verify whether a randomly selected sample had a normal distribution.

had included at least thirty scores and had been randomly selected, the table permits the calculation of the probability that the mean is reliably greater than any number smaller than the mean itself. Usually, we want to know if a mean is reliably greater than zero. This statement can be rephrased this way: If we took many random samples, how likely would it be to find a mean that was equal to or less than zero? First, find the z of zero for the above five numbers using the $\bar{X}$ and $s_{\bar{x}}$, $z = (0 - 14.2)/.66 = -21.52$. A z this small or smaller is very unlikely; its probability of occurring is less than .0001. (Again, see a standard normal table to verify this.) Because the probability of finding a mean equal to zero is so small, statisticians will conclude that the true mean is greater than zero.

The line of reasoning just illustrated lies at the heart of all tests of statistical significance. A probability equal to or smaller than .05 is defined as improbable enough to be treated as a statistically significant finding. To summarize, to learn whether a mean is reliably greater than zero, first calculate the standard error of the mean, $s_{\bar{x}}$. Then, calculate what the z score of zero would be using $\bar{X}$ and $s_{\bar{x}}$. Finally, use a table to find what proportion of means from similar samples would equal zero or less. If this proportion is equal to or less than .05, reject the idea (called the "null hypothesis") that the true mean might be no greater than zero. As is reiterated below in reference to other analyses, the statistical test just described does not reveal anything about the reason $\bar{X}$ is greater than zero. The statistical test just says that it is highly probable that $\bar{X}$ is greater than zero.

A HYPOTHETICAL SET OF DATA

Imagine that a program offering training in work skills and emotional support was offered to a group of retarded adults regardless of whether they were currently employed. Suppose that holding a job and increased self-esteem are among the criteria that would indicate the program fulfilled its goals. Assume that both criteria are assessed before and after the program. Job status is fairly objective and easy to measure. Perhaps a self-esteem measure could be constructed from verbal reports of vocational plans and hopes, combined with some nonintrusive observations of how participants conducted themselves during role-played job interviews. Hypothetical data are given in Figure A.1. What analyses of such information can be done? The best way to approach an analysis is by posing and answering questions.

Are more program participants employed after the program than before? Given the above program and available data, this question can

FIGURE A.1: Hypothetical data on a program for retarded adults

Program participants	Job status Before	After	IQ Before	Self-esteem Before	After	Diff.	Regressed change	Units of service
A	E	E	61	24	26	2	− .53	16
B	U	E	72	23	29	6	3.12	18
C	U	E	71	19	26	7	2.73	20
D	U	E	75	18	27	9	4.39	19
E	U	U	63	20	19	− 1	− 4.92	16
F	U	E	65	24	31	7	4.47	20
G	E	U	73	25	22	− 3	− 5.19	15
H	E	E	75	24	25	1	− 1.53	19
I	E	E	74	21	22	1	− 2.58	19
J	U	U	60	14	16	2	− 4.01	14
K	U	E	71	14	26	12	5.99	20
L	U	E	73	21	30	9	5.42	19
M	E	E	64	18	22	4	− .61	19
N	U	U	58	16	15	− 1	− 6.31	13
O	E	E	73	23	26	3	.12	19
P	E	U	56	14	13	− 1	− 7.01	17
Q	E	E	73	23	26	3	.12	19
R	U	E	76	19	29	10	5.73	20
S	U	E	72	17	28	11	6.04	19
T	U	E	68	16	27	11	5.69	18
U	U	U	55	14	15	1	− 5.01	14
V	U	U	52	22	21	− 1	− 4.23	19
W	E	E	68	25	26	1	− 1.19	19
X	E	U	81	23	19	− 4	− 6.88	15
Y	U	E	70	21	27	6	2.42	17
Z	U	E	71	22	29	7	3.77	18

be answered by the *McNemar Test for Significant Changes.* Whenever a criterion is (1) a dichotomous variable and (2) assessed before and after a program, the McNemar test is an appropriate test for statistical significance. Job status is a variable requiring this approach. To conduct the test, it is necessary to classify each participant in one of four categories: (1) maintained employment (N = 7), employed before the program and after the program; (2) showed no improvement (N = 5), unemployed before and after the program; (3) lost employment (N = 3), employed before but unemployed after the program; and (4) improved (N = 11), unemployed before but employed after the program. The important thing to test is whether those who gained employment are more numerous than those who lost employment. Using the McNemar test (see Chapter 5) a χ^2 of 4.57 ($df = 1$, p < .05) was calculated, indicating that more participants were employed after the program than before.[2]

The next question of interest is: *Do the participants have higher self-esteem scores after the program than they did before the program?* An affirmative answer to this question requires that the participants' self-esteem scores should show improvements when scores before the program are compared to those after the program. This comparison requires the *Correlated Groups t-Test.* The amount of improvement for each participant is found by subtracting the pretest from the posttest, as shown in Figure A.1. The crucial question is whether these differences are reliably greater than zero. Some participants lost ground, but most improved. However, is there enough improvement to be sure that the findings are more than just the result of chance variations? To perform a correlated *t*-test simply requires a calculation of $\overline{d}$, the mean improvement, and s_d, the standard deviation of the improvement scores. The *t* is found in this way:

$$t = \overline{d}/(s_d/\sqrt{N}) = 3.92\,(4.66/\sqrt{26}) = 4.30$$

Because the observed *t* has 25 degrees of freedom, the conclusion can be drawn that participants did improve in their observed self-esteem. As in the previous analysis, no conclusion can be made concerning the cause of the improvement.

There are a number of further analyses possible to help understand the data in Figure A.1. *Is amount of exposure to the program associated with employment afterwards?* To answer this requires that the mean number of sessions attended by those employed ($\overline{X}_1 = 18.77$) be compared to the mean of those unemployed ($\overline{X}_2 = 15.38$). The *t* for two separate groups is found as follows:

$$t = (\overline{X}_1 - \overline{X}_2)/\sqrt{\left[\,(s_1^2\left[\,N_1 - 1\,\right] + s_2^2\left[\,N_2 - 1\,\right])/(N_1 + N_2 - 2)\,\right] / \left[\,\tfrac{1}{N_1} + \tfrac{1}{N_2}\,\right]}$$

$$t = (18.78 - 15.38)/\sqrt{\left[\,(1.06^2 \cdot 17 + 1.92^2 \cdot 7)/(18 + 8 - 2)\,\right] / \left[\,\tfrac{1}{18} + \tfrac{1}{8}\,\right]}$$

$$t = 10.94$$

Because the program is offered to help participants to be employed, a one-tailed test is used as before, With $df = 24$, this *t* is statistically significant at the .001 level.

[2] This finding does not tell whether the program was responsible for this improved employment status. Inferences about causality are impossible without a more complicated research design.

One could also ask: *Is exposure to the program associated with improved self-esteem scores?* To answer this question, a correlation could be found between improvement and the number of sessions attended. As explained in the text, the best way to do this is to correlate regressed change scores (rather than raw change scores) with number of sessions attended. Following the methods illustrated in Chapter 7, the residuals of the posttest self-esteem measurement were found by subtracting the predicted posttest value (using the pretest as the predictor) from the actual posttest. These residuals were correlated with number of sessions attended using the following formula:

$$r = \frac{N\Sigma XY - \Sigma X\Sigma Y}{\sqrt{\left[N\Sigma X^2 - (\Sigma X)^2\right]\left[N\Sigma Y^2 - (\Sigma Y)^2\right]}}$$

N is the number of people involved. The number of units of service is X and the regressed change of self-esteem is Y in this example. Substituting into the formula yields the following:

$$r = \frac{(26 \times 163.30) - (461 \times .01)}{\sqrt{\left[(26 \times 8283) - 461^2\right]\left[(26 \times 501.06) - .01^2\right]}}$$

$$= \frac{4241.2}{6079.4}$$

$$= .70$$

This positive correlation supports the hypothesis that participation in the program leads to greater self-esteem, but it is also compatible with a number of other explanations. A review of the threats to internal validity should suggest these to the reader.

A GROUP THAT DID NOT RECEIVE
THE PROGRAM

Up to this point, the example has been analyzed using only one group. Suppose that an additional group of retarded adults, who did not take part in the program, is available. Figure A.2 contains their scores on the variables of interest. Assume that these people were assessed by the same observers as those who assessed the program participants. Further, assume that the information was gathered at the same time as the post-program measures were gathered and that the observers did not know who went through the program and who did not. These data permit the

FIGURE A.2: Scores for retarded adults not in the job skills program

Non-program adults	Job status	IQ	Self-esteem
AA	U	61	16
BB	E	78	19
CC	E	75	22
DD	U	59	17
EE	U	64	18
FF	E	72	21
GG	U	58	22
HH	E	76	23
II	E	78	24
JJ	U	65	22
KK	U	62	19
LL	U	55	15
MM	U	76	18

development of answers to a number of questions that could not be addressed to the data given in Figure A.1.

Is a greater proportion of participants employed after the program than are employed in the second group? To test the data to answer this question requires the use of the *independent proportions test*. This analysis compares the proportion of employed program adults after the program with the proportion of employed nonprogram adults. After the program, over two-thirds of the participants had jobs ($P_1 = .69$), and just over a third ($P_2 = .38$) of the nonprogram adults had jobs. The difference between the proportions employed is divided by the standard error of this difference using the following formula:

$$z = (P_1 - P_2)/\sqrt{PQ/(1/N_1 + 1/N_2)}$$

P is the proportion of people employed if the two groups are combined. *Q* is 1 minus *P*. When the values are substituted into the formula, the following is obtained:

$$z = (.69 - .38)/\sqrt{(.59)(.41)/(1/26 + 1/13)} = 1.86$$

Because the z this large or larger is only likely to occur by chance three out of a hundred times, we may conclude that the program group contains a greater proportion of employed people than the nonprogram group.

At this point, it is not possible to conclude that the program caused the difference found. If the nonprogram group was a randomly selected control group, such a causal conclusion is possibly permitted. If the nonprogram group was merely a group of available retarded adults, this is the nonequivalent comparison-group, quasi-experimental design. If there is reason to believe that the threats to internal validity have been eliminated, then a causal interpretation may be valid.

A second question that can be answered with the inclusion of a second group in the design concerns the self-esteem measure. *Do program participants have higher self-esteem scores than those who do not go through the program?* Because the self-esteem variable is a continuous variable, not dichotomous as the job status variable is, the standard *t*-test can be used to answer this question. The *t*-test formula is made up of the difference of two means divided by the standard error of the difference between two means. The formula for calculating a *t* from data from two groups was given above. Comparing the mean self-esteem scores of the participants with the nonprogram group yields the following value for *t*:

$$(23.92 - 19.69)/\sqrt{[(5.08^{2} \cdot 25 + 2.84^{2} \cdot 12)/(26 + 13 - 2)][1/26 + 1/13]} = 2.25$$

In this equation the program group is group one and the non-program group is group two. The degrees of freedom are $N_1 + N_2 - 2$, or 37. Because the observed *t* is greater than the critical one-tailed *t* at the .025 level, the hypothesis that the participant had higher self-esteem after the program compared to the nonprogram group is supported. Note that the nonprogram group mean self-esteem, 19.69, is nearly equal to the program group pretest mean, 20.0. This near equality increases the evaluator's confidence that the groups are comparable. Furthermore, mean IQ is nearly identical for the two groups. There is one major threat to the internal validity of this hypothetical evaluation. What is it? How can the evaluation be strengthened?

References

ABELSON, P. H. 1977. Commission on federal paperwork. *Science* 197; 1237.

ABT, C. C. 1977. Applying cost/benefit paradigms to social program evaluations. Paper presented at the meeting of the Evaluation Research Society, October, Washington, D.C.

ADAMS, S. 1975. *Evaluative research in corrections.* Law Enforcement Assistance Administration, U.S. Department of Justice.

ADLER, N. E., and STONE, G. C. 1979. Social science perspectives on the health system. In *Health psychology: A handbook,* ed. G. C. Stone, F. Cohen, and N. E. Adler. San Francisco: Jossey-Bass.

ALBRIGHT, E.; BAUM, M. A.; and FORMAN, B. 1973. *Evaluation in criminal justice programs.* Law Enforcement Assistance Administration, U.S. Department of Justice.

ALLPORT, G. W. 1954. *The nature of prejudice.* Reading, Mass.: Addison-Wesley.

ANASTASI, A. 1976. *Psychological testing.* 4th ed. New York: Macmillan.

ANDERSON, J. F., and BERDIE, D. R. 1975. Effects on response rate of formal and informal questionnaire follow-up techniques. *Journal of Applied Psychology* 60; 225–57.

ARMOR, D. J. 1972. The evidence on busing. *The Public Interest* 28; 90–126.

ATTKISSON, C. C., HARGREAVES, W. A., HOROWITZ, M. J., and SORENSEN, J. E. (eds.) 1978. *Evaluation of human service programs.* New York: Academic Press

BALL, R. M. 1978. National health insurance: Comments on selected issues. *Science* 200; 864–73.

BARBOUR, G. P., and WOLFSON, S. M. 1973. Productivity measurement in police crime control. *Public Management* 55; 16, 18, 19.

BERK, R. A. 1977. Discretionary methodology decisions in applied research. *Sociological Methods and Research* 5; 317–34.

BERK, R. A., and ROSSI, P. H. 1976. Doing good or worse: Evaluation research politically re-examined. *Social Problems,* February, pp. 337–49.

BERMAN, J. J. 1978. An experiment in parole supervision. *Evaluation Quarterly* 2; 71–90.

BIGELOW, D. A., and CIARLO, J. A. 1975. The impact of therapeutic effectiveness data on community health center management: The systems evaluation project. *Community Mental Health Journal* 11; 64–73.

BINNER, P. R. 1977. Outcome measures and cost analysis. In *Emerging developments in mental health evaluation,* ed. W. Neigher, R. Hammer, and G. Landsberg. New York: Argold Press.

BLOM, B., and MOORE, M. 1979. Evaluating mental health services through patient care audits. In *Impacts of program evaluation on mental health care,* ed. E. J. Posavac. Boulder, Colo.: Westview Press.

Blue Shield News. 1977. Routine payment to be discontinued for the following procedures. June, p. 3.

BORUCH, R. F. 1975. On common contentions about randomized field experiments. In *Experimental testing of public policy,* ed. R. F. Boruch, and H. W. Riecken. Boulder, Colo.: Westview Press.

BORUCH, R. F., and RINDSKOPF, D. 1977. On randomized experiments, approximations to experiments, and data analysis. In *Evaluation research methods,* ed. L. Rutman. Beverly Hills, Calif.: Sage.

BROWN, F. G. 1976. Principles of educational and psychological testing. New York: Holt, Rinehart and Winston.

BURNS, M. L. 1977. The effects of feedback and commitment to change on the behavior of elementary school principals. *Journal of Applied Behavioral Science* 13; 159–66.

CAIDIN, M. 1960. *Let's go flying!* New York: Dutton.

CAMPBELL, D. T. 1969. Reforms as experiments. *American Psychologist* 24; 409–29.

CAMPBELL, D. T.; BORUCH, R. F.; SCHWARTZ, R. D.; and STEINBERG, J. 1977. Confidentiality-preserving modes of access to files and interfile exchange for useful statistical analysis. *Evaluation Quarterly* 1; 269–300.

CAMPBELL, D. T., and ERLEBACHER, A. 1970. How regression artifacts in quasi-experimental evaluations can mistakenly make compensatory education look harmful. In *Compensatory education: A national debate,* ed. J. Hellmuth, pp. 185–210. Vol. 3 of *Disadvantaged child.* New York: Brunner-Mazel.

CAMPBELL, D. T., and STANLEY, J. C. 1963. *Experimental and quasi-experimental designs for research.* Chicago: Rand-McNally.

CAPORASO, J. A. 1973. Quasi-experimental approaches to social science: Perspectives and problems. In *Quasi-experimental approaches: Testing theory and evaluating policy,* ed. J. A. Caporaso and L. L. Roos. Evanston, Ill.: Northwestern University Press.

CAREY, R. G. 1972. *Hospital chaplains: Who needs them?* St. Louis, Mo.: Catholic Hospital Association.

CAREY, R. G. 1974. Emotional adjustment in terminal patients. *Journal of Counseling Psychology*, 21, 433–39.

CAREY, R. G. 1976. Presterilization interviewing: An evaluation. *Journal of Counseling Psychology* 23; 492–94.

CAREY, R. G. 1979. Evaluation of a primary nursing unit. *American Journal of Nursing*. 79, 1253–1255.

CAREY, R. G. *In press.* Selecting hospital leaders through shared decision making. *Hospital Progress.*

CAREY, R. G., and POSAVAC, E. J. 1977a. *Cancer care center: An evaluation of support to patients and relatives.* Park Ridge, Ill.: Lutheran General Hospital.

CAREY, R. G., and POSAVAC, E. J. 1977b. *Evaluation of the Medical Ecology Program.* Park Ridge, Ill.: Lutheran General Hospital.

CAREY, R. G., and POSAVAC, E. J. 1978. Program evaluation of a physical medicine and rehabilitation unit: A new approach. *Archives of Physical Medicine and Rehabilitation* 59; 330–37.

CAREY, R. G., and POSAVAC, E. J. 1979. Holistic care in a cancer care center. *Nursing Research*, pp. 213–216.

CARNOY, M. 1975. The economic costs and returns to educational television. *Economic Development and Cultural Change* 25; 207–48.

CARTER, D. E., and NEWMAN, F. L. 1976. *A client-oriented system of mental health delivery and program management.* Rockville, Md.: National Institute of Mental Health.

Catholic Hospital Association Study Committee. 1977. *Report of the 1977 CHA Study Committee.* St. Louis, Mo.: Catholic Hospital Association.

CENTRA, J. A. 1977. Plusses and minuses for faculty development. *Change* 9; 47, 48, 64.

CHAPMAN, R. L. 1976. *The design of management information systems for mental health organizations: A primer.* Rockville, Md.: National Institute of Mental Health.

CHAPMAN, L. J., and CHAPMAN, J. P. 1967. Genesis of popular but erroneous psychodiagnostic signs. *Journal of Abnormal Psychology* 72; 193–204.

CHAPMAN, L. J., and CHAPMAN, J. P. 1969. Illusory correlation as an obstacle to the use of valid psychodiagnostic signs. *Journal of Abnormal Psychology* 74; 271–80.

CHELIMSKY, E. 1978. Differing perspectives of evaluation. In *Evaluating federally sponsored programs: New directions for program evaluations*, no. 2, ed. C. C. Rentz and B. R. Rentz. San Francisco: Jossey-Bass.

Chicago Tribune. 1978. Postal Service may dump billion-dollar parcel plan. June 14, Sec. 4, p. 1.

CICARELLI, V. G. 1970. The relevance of the regression artifact problem to the Westinghouse-Ohio University evaluation of Head Start: A reply to Campbell and Erlebacher. In *Compensatory education: A national debate*, ed. J. Hellmuth, pp. 211–16. Vol. 3 of *Disadvantaged child.* New York: Brunner-Mazel.

CICARELLI, V. G.; COOPER, W. H.; and GRANGER, R. L. 1969. *The Impact of Head Start: An evaluation of the effects of Head Start on children's cognitive and affective development.* Westinghouse Learning Corporation, OEO Contract No. B89-4536.

COLEMAN, J. S. 1976. Recent trends in school integration. In *Evaluation studies research annual*, vol. 1, ed. G. V. Glass. Beverly Hills, Calif.: Sage.

COLEMAN, J. S., CAMPBELL, E. Q., HOBSON, C. J., McPARTLAND, J., MOOD, A. M., WEINFELD, F. D., and YORK, R. L. 1966. *Equality of educational opportunity.* Washington, D.C.: Government Printing Office.

Community Mental Health Plan. 1977. Spoon River, Illinois: Spoon River Community
    Mental Health Center.
COOK, T. D., APPLETON, H., CONNOR, R. F., SHAFFER, A., TAMKIN, G., and WEBER, S. J.
    1975. *Sesame Street revisited*. New York: Russell Sage.
COOK, T. D., and CAMPBELL, D. T. 1976. The design and conduct of quasi-experiments
    and true experiments in field settings. In *Handbook of industrial and or-
    ganizational research*, ed. M. D. Dunnette. Chicago: Rand-McNally.
COOK, T. D.; COOK, F. L.; and MARK, M. M. 1977. Randomized and quasi-experimental
    designs in evaluation research: An introduction. In *Evaluation research: A
    basic guide*. ed. L. Rutman. Beverly Hills, Calif.: Sage.
COOK, T. D., and GRUDER, C. L. 1978. Metaevaluation. *Evaluation Quarterly* 2; 5–51.
CRANO, W. D., and BREWER, M. B. 1973. *Principles of research in social psychology*.
    New York: McGraw-Hill.
CRONBACH, L. J. 1975. Beyond the two disciplines of scientific psychology. *American
    Psychologist* 30; 116–27.
CRONBACH, L. J. 1977. Remarks to a new society. *Evaluation Research Society News-
    letter* 1; 1–3.
CULLITON, B. J. 1978. Health care economics: The high cost of getting well. *Science*
    200; 883–85.
DATTA, L. 1976a. Does it work when it has been tried? And half full or half empty?
    Journal of Career Education 2; 38–55.
DATTA, L. 1976b. The impact of the Westinghouse/Ohio evaluation on the de-
    velopment of project Head Start. In *The evaluation of social programs*, ed.
    C. C. Abt. Beverly Hills, Calif., Sage.
DAVID, E. E. 1975. One-armed scientists? *Science* 189; 679.
DAVIS, H. R., and SALASIN, S. E. 1975. The utilization of evaluation. In *Handbook of
    evaluation research*, vol. 2, ed. E. L. Struening and M. Guttentag. Beverly
    Hills, Calif.: Sage.
DAVIS, J. A. 1971. *Elementary survey analysis*. Englewood Cliffs, N.J.: Prentice-Hall.
DAWES, R. M., and CORRIGAN, B. 1974. Linear models in decision making. *Psychological
    Bulletin* 81; 95–106.
DEMONE, H. W. JR., and HARSHBARGER, D. 1973. *The planning and administration of
    human services*. New York: Behavioral Publications.
DENISTON, O. L., and ROSENSTOCK, I. M. 1973. The validity of nonexperimental designs
    for evaluating health services. *Health Services Reports* 88; 153–64.
DICKEN, A. 1978. Why patients should plan their own recovery. *RN* 41; 52–55.
DIXON, M. G. 1977. Medical records guaranteed to ruin any malpractice defense.
    Medical Economics 54; 79–83.
DIXON, R. H., and LASZLO, J. 1974. Utilization of clinical chemistry services by medical
    house staff. *Archives of Internal Medicine* 134; 1064–67.
DRUCKER, P. F. 1954. *The practice of management*. New York: Harper.
EDWARDS, W. 1977. Social utilities. *The Engineering Economist*. (Summer Symposium
    Series) 6; 119–29.
EDWARDS, W.; GUTTENTAG, M.; and SNAPPER, K. 1975. A decision-theoretic approach to
    evaluation research. In *Handbook of evaluation research*, vol. 1, ed. E. L.
    Struening and M. Guttentag. Beverly Hills, Calif.: Sage.
EGDAHL, R. H., and GERTMAN, P. M. 1976. *Quality assurance in health care*. German-
    town, Md.: Aspen Systems.
EGELHOF, J. 1975. Cop layoffs spur slayings. *Chicago Tribune*, July 10, sec. 1, p. 2.
EISENBERG, L. 1977. The social imperatives of medical research. *Science* 198; 1105–10.
ELLSWORTH, R. B. 1975. Consumer feedback in measuring the effectiveness of mental

health programs. In *Handbook of evaluation research,* vol. 2, ed. M. Guttentag and E. L. Struening. Beverly Hills, Calif.: Sage.

ELLSWORTH, R. B. 1979. Evaluating treatment outcomes in mental health services. In *Impacts of program evaluation on mental health care,* ed. E. J. Posavac. Boulder, Colo.: Westview Press.

ENDICOTT, J., and SPITZER, R. L. 1975. Designing mental health studies: The case for experimental designs. *Hospital & Community Psychiatry* 26; 737–39.

ENDICOTT, J.; SPITZER, R. L.; FLEISS, J. L.; and COHEN, J. 1976. The Global Assessment Scale: A procedure for measuring overall severity of psychiatric disturbance. *Archives of General Psychiatry* 33; 766–71.

EVANS, J. W., and SCHILLER, J. 1970. How preoccupation with possible regression artifacts can lead to a faulty strategy for the evaluation of social action programs: A reply to Campbell and Erlebacher. In *Compensatory education: A national debate,* ed. J. Hellmuth, pp. 216–20. Vol. 3 of *Disadvantaged child.* New York: Brunner-Mazel.

FIFER, W. R. 1979. Quality assurance: Debate persists on goals, impact, and methods of evaluating care. *Hospitals,* 53 (April 1): 163–67.

FILSTEAD, W. J., ed. 1970. *Qualitative methodology: Firsthand involvement with the social world.* Chicago: Rand-McNally.

FITZGERALD, J. M. 1973. *Fundamentals of systems analysis.* New York: Wiley.

FLEISS, J. L. 1973. *Statistical methods for rates and proportions.* New York: Wiley.

FOX, B. H. 1976. The psychosocial epidemiology of cancer. In *Cancer: The behavioral dimension,* ed. J. W. Cullen, B. H. Fox, and R. N. Isom. New York: Raven Press.

FOXX, R. M., and AZRIN, N. H. 1973. Dry pants: A rapid method of toilet training children. *Behavior Research and Therapy* 11; 435–42.

FREEMAN, H. E., KLEIN, R. E., KAGAN, J., and YARBOUGH, C. 1977. Relations between nutrition and cognition in rural Guatemala. *The American Journal of Public Health* 67; 233–39.

FREEMAN, R., and HOLLOMAN, J. H. 1975. The declining value of college going. *Change* 7; 24–31, 62.

GARWICK, G. 1973. *Commentaries on Goal Attainment Scaling.* Minneapolis: Program Evaluation Resource Center.

GERSTENFELD, A. 1977. MBO revisited: Focus on health systems. *Health Care Management Review* 4; 51–57.

GILBERT, J. P.; LIGHT, R. J.; and MOSTELLER, F. 1975. Assessing social innovations: An empirical base for policy. In *Evaluation and experiment,* ed. A. R. Lumsdaine and C. A. Bennett. New York: Academic Press.

GLASS, G. V 1976. Introduction. In *Evaluation studies research annual,* vol. 1, ed. G. V Glass, Beverly Hills, Calif.: Sage.

GOSFIELD, A. 1975. *PSRO: The law and the health consumer.* Cambridge, Mass.: Ballinger.

GOTTMAN, J. M., and GLASS, G. V 1978. Analysis of interrupted time-series experiments. In *Single subject research: Strategies for evaluating change,* ed. T. R. Kratochwill. New York: Academic Press.

GRAY, B. H.; COOKE, R. A.; and TANNENBAUM, A. S. 1978. Research involving human subjects. *Science* 201; 1094–1101.

GREELEY, ANDREW. 1972. *American priests: A sociological analysis.* Washington, D.C.: National Conference of Catholic Bishops.

GUTTENTAG, M. 1973. Subjectivity and its uses in evaluation research. *Evaluation* 1 (2); 60–65.

GUTTENTAG, M. 1976. "Future trends in evaluation." Paper presented at the Information and Feedback Conference, November 3–5, Toronto.

GUTTENTAG, M. 1977. Evaluation and society. *Personality and Social Psychology Bulletin* 3; 31–40.

GUTTENTAG, M., and SNAPPER, K. 1974. Plans, evaluations and decisions. *Evaluation,* 1 (1), 58–64, 73, 74.

HAGEDORN, H. J.; BECK, K. J.; NEUBERT, S. F.; and WERLIN, S. H. 1976. *A working manual of simple evaluation techniques for community mental health centers.* Rockville, Md.: U.S. Department of Health, Education, and Welfare.

HANKE, S. H., and WALKER, R. A. 1974. Benefit-cost analysis reconsidered: An evaluation of the Mid-State project. *Water Resources Research* 10; 898–908.

HANSEN, J. B. 1978. The formative-summative dichotomy and the role of description in program evaluation. *Evaluation News,* no. 6 (August); 14–16.

HARGREAVES, W. A.; ATTKISSON, C. C.; and SORENSON, J. E., eds. 1977. *Resource materials for community mental health program evaluation.* Rockville, Md.: U.S. Department of Health, Education, and Welfare.

HARRIS, M. B., and BRUNER, C. G. 1971. A comparison of a self-control and a contract procedure for weight control. *Behavior Research and Therapy* 9; 347–54.

HASTORF, A. H., and CANTRIL, H. 1954. They saw a game. *Journal of Abnormal and Social Psychology* 49; 129–34.

HAVEMAN, R. H., and WATTS, H. W. 1976. Social experimentation as policy research: A review of negative income tax experiments. In *Evaluation studies research annual,* vol. 1, ed. G. V Glass, Beverly Hills, Calif.: Sage.

HAWKINS, J. D.; ROFFMAN, R. A.; and OSBORNE, P. 1978. Decision makers' judgments: The influence of role, evaluative criteria, and information access. *Evaluation Quarterly* 2; 435–54.

HAYS, W. L. 1963. *Statistics for psychologists.* New York: Holt, Rinehart, & Winston.

HELMICK, E.; MILLER, S. I.; NUTTING, P.; SHORR, G.; and BERG, L. 1975. A monitoring and evaluation plan for alcoholism programs. *British Journal of Addiction* 70; 369–73.

HORST, P., et al. 1974. Program management and the federal evaluator. *Public Administration Review* 34; 300–308.

HOUSE, E. R. 1976. Justice in evaluation. In *Evaluation Studies Review Annual,* vol. 1, G. V Glass. Beverly Hills, Calif.: Sage.

HOUSE, E. R.; GLASS, G. V; McLEAN, L. D.; and WALKER, D. F. 1978. No simple answer: Critique of the follow through evaluation. *Harvard Educational Review* 42; 128–60.

Insurance Institute for Highway Safety. 1975. Helmet laws reduce fatalities. *Status Report* 10; 1–3.

ISR Newsletter. 1978. Telephone helps solve survey problems. 6; 3.

JACOBS, C. M.; CHRISTOFFEL, T. H.; and DIXON, N. 1976. *Measuring the quality of patient care.* Cambridge, Mass.: Ballinger.

JACOBS, C. M., and JACOBS, N. D. 1974. *The PEP Primer.* Chicago: Joint Commission on Hospital Accreditation.

JOHNSON, R. A. 1967. *The theory and management of systems.* New York: McGraw-Hill.

KAHNEMAN, D., and TVERSKY, A. 1974. Judgment under uncertainty: Heuristics and biases. *Science* 185: 1124–31.

KANE, R. L., and KANE, R. A. 1978. Care of the aged: Old problems in need of new solutions. *Science* 200; 913–19.

KELLING, G. L.; PATE, T.; DIECKMAN, D.; and BROWN, C. E. 1976. The Kansas City preventive patrol experiment: A summary report. In *Evaluative studies review annual,* vol. 1, ed. G. V Glass. Beverly Hills, Calif.: Sage.

KERSHAW, D. N. 1972. A negative income tax experiment. *Scientific American* 227; 19–25.

KIRESUK, T. J. 1973. Goal attainment scaling at a county mental health service. *Evaluation,* Monograph No. 1, p. 15.

KIRESUK, T. J., and SHERMAN, R. E. 1968. Goal Attainment Scaling: A general method for evaluating comprehensive community mental health programs. *Community Mental Health Journal* 4; 443–53.

KIRK, R. E. 1968. *Experimental design: Procedures for the behavioral sciences.* Belmont, Calif.: Brooks/Cole.

KIVENS, L., and BOLIN, D. C. 1977. Profile of a change(d) agent. *Evaluation* 4; 115–19.

KNAPP, M. 1977. Applying time-series research strategies to program evaluation problems. Paper presented at the meeting of the Evaluation Research Society, October, Washington, D.C.

KREITNER, R. 1977. People are systems, too: Filling the feedback vacuum. *Business Horizons* 20 (November); 54–58.

LANDES, H. R. 1973. Treatment of anxiety in the families of children undergoing tonsillectomy. Doctoral dissertation, Northwestern University. In *Dissertation Abstracts International* 34; 2939B. University Microfilms No. 37–30, 640.

LASKA, E. M., and BANK, R., eds. 1975. *Safeguarding psychiatric privacy: Computer systems and their uses.* New York: Wiley.

LAWLER, E. E., III, and HACKMAN, J. R. 1969. Impact of employee participation in the development of pay incentive plans: A field experiment. *Journal of Applied Psychology* 53; 467–71.

LENIHAN, K. J. 1977. Telephones and raising bail. *Evaluation Quarterly* 1; 569–86.

LEVIN, H. M. 1975. Cost-effectiveness analysis in evaluation research. In *Handbook of evaluation research,* vol. 2, ed. M. Guttentag and E. L. Struening. pp. 89–124. Beverly Hills, Calif.: Sage.

LEVIN, M., BROWN, E., FITZGERALD, C., GOPLERUD, E., GORDON,M. E., JAYNE-LAZARUS, C., ROSENBERG, N., and SLATER, J. 1978. Adapting the jury trial for program evaluation: A report of an experience. *Evaluation and Program Planning* 1; 177–86.

LIGHT, R. J., and SMITH, P. V. 1971. Accumulating evidence: Procedures for resolving contradictions among different research studies. *Harvard Educational Review* 41; 429–71.

LOCKE, E. A. 1968. Toward a theory of task motivations and incentives. *Organizational Behavior and Human Performance* 3; 157–89.

LUBIN, B. 1967. *Manual for the Depression Adjective Check Lists.* San Diego: Educational and Industrial Testing Service.

LUCAS, H. C., JR. 1975. *Why information systems fail.* New York: Columbia University Press.

LUFT, L. L. 1979. The effects of peer review in a community mental health center. In *Impacts of program evaluation on mental health care,* ed. E. J. Posavac. Boulder, Colo.: Westview Press.

LUND, S., and KIRESUK, T. J. 1979. Individualized Goal Attainment as a method of program evaluation in mental health. In *Impacts of program evaluation on mental health care,* ed. E. J. Posavac. Boulder, Colo.: Westview Press.

MAGER, R. F. 1972. *Goal analysis*. Belmont, Calif.: Fearon Publishers.

MARKSON, E. W., and ALLEN, D. F. 1976. *Trends in mental health evaluation*. Lexington, Mass.: Lexington Books.

McCALL, R. B. 1975. *Fundamental statistics for psychology*. 2nd ed. New York: Harcourt Brace Jovanovich.

McCAMY, J., and PRESLEY, J. 1975. *Human life styling: Keeping whole in the 20th century*. New York: Harper and Row.

McCARTHY, M. 1978. Decreasing the incidence of "high bobbins" in a textile spinning department through a group feedback procedure. *Journal of Organizational Behavioral Management* 1; 150–54.

McCONKEY, D. D. 1975. *MBO for nonprofit organizations*. New York: AMACON.

McGREGOR, D. 1960. *The human side of enterprise*. New York: McGraw-Hill.

McKAY, H.; SINISTERNA, L.; McKAY, A.; GOMEZ, H.; and LLOREDA, P. 1978. Improving cognitive ability in chronically deprived children. *Science* 200; 270–78.

McKILLIP, J., and KAMENS, L. 1977. Evaluation of a positive health care program. In *Health Care Research in Illinois*, ed. R. V. Robertson, 2; 352–57.

MEADOWS, D. L., and PERELMAN, L. 1973. Limits to growth. In *The future in the making: Current issues in higher education*, ed. D. W. Vermilye. San Francisco: Jossey-Bass.

MECHANIC, D. 1975. Evaluation in alcohol, drug abuse, and mental health programs: Problems and prospects. In *Program evaluation: Alcohol, drug abuse, and mental health services*, ed. J. Zusman and C. Wurster. Lexington, Mass.: Lexington Books.

Medical World News. May 30, 1977. Hypertension compliance. 18; 20–22; 24–25; 28–29.

MILLER, S. I.; HELMICK, E.; BERG, L.; NUTTING, P.; and SCHORR, G. 1975. An evaluation of alcoholism treatment services for Alaskan natives. *Hospital and Community Psychiatry* 23; 829–31.

MIRVIS, P. H., and BERG, D. N., eds. 1977. *Failure in organizational development and change: Cases and essays for learning*. New York: Wiley-Interscience.

MITLYING, J. 1975/76. Managing the use of staff time: A key to cost control. *Alcohol Health and Research World*, Winter, pp. 7–10.

MORGAN, B. 1968. *An introduction to Bayesian statistical decision processes*. Englewood Cliffs, N.J.: Prentice-Hall.

MORRISSEY, G. L. 1970. *Management by objectives and results*. Reading, Mass.: Addison-Wesley.

MOSTELLER, F., and MOYNIHAN, D. P., eds. 1972. *On equality of educational opportunity*. New York: Vintage.

MUELLER, J. H., SCHUESSLER, K., and COSTNER, H. 1970. *Statistical reasoning in sociology*. Boston: Houghton Mifflin.

National Institute of Mental Health. 1971. *Planning for creative change in mental health services: A distillation of principles on research utilization*. Washington, D.C.: Department of Health, Education, and Welfare. Publication No. (HSM) 73–9148.

National Standards for Community Mental Health Centers. 1977. Rockville, Md.: Department of Health, Education, and Welfare, January.

The nation's toughest drug law: Evaluating the New York experience. 1978. Washington, D.C.: U.S. Department of Justice, Law Enforcement Assistance Administration.

NEWMAN, D. E., and LUFT, L. L. 1974. The peer review process: Education versus control. *American Journal of Psychiatry* 131; 1363–66.

Newsweek. May 9, 1977. Health-cost crisis. 89; 84, 89, 90.

NUNNALLY, J. C. 1975. The study of change in evaluation research: Principles concerning measurement, experimental design, and analysis. In *Handbook of Evaluation, Research,* vol. 1, ed. E. L. Struening and M. Guttentag. Beverly Hills, Calif.: Sage.

PATTON, M. Q. 1978. *Utilization-focused evaluation.* Beverly Hills, Calif.: Sage.

PETTIGREW, T. F., USEEM, E. L., NORMAND, C., and SMITH, M. S. 1973. Busing: A review of the evidence. *The Public Interest* 30; 88–118.

PETTIGREW, T. F., and GREEN, R. L. 1977. The white flight debate. In *Evaluation studies review annual,* vol. 2, ed. M. Guttentag. Beverly Hills, Calif.: Sage.

POPHAM, W. J. 1975. *Educational evaluation.* Englewood Cliffs, N.J.: Prentice-Hall.

POSAVAC, E. J. 1974. *A Study of the coronary classes.* Park Ridge, Ill.: Lutheran General Hospital.

POSAVAC, E. J. 1975. *Survey of past residents in the Clinical Pastoral Education Program.* Park Ridge, Ill.: Lutheran General Hospital.

POSAVAC, E. J. (ed.) 1979. *Impacts of program evaluation in mental health care.* Boulder, Colo.: Westview Press.

POSAVAC, E. J., and CAREY, R. G. 1978. Trading evaluative specificity for statistical power. *Evaluation and the Health Professions* 1; 89–95.

POSAVAC, E. J., and HARTUNG, B. M. 1977. An exploration into the reasons people choose a pastoral counselor instead of another type of psychotherapist. *The Journal of Pastoral Care* 31; 23–31.

RAHE, R. H. 1978. *Life stress and illness.* Presented at the Stress and Behavioral Medicine Symposium, May 20, Chicago, Ill.

RHEINSTEIN, M. 1959. Divorce and the law in Germany: A review. *American Journal of Sociology* 65; 489–98.

RIECKEN, H. W., and BORUCH, R. F., eds. 1974. *Social experimentation: A method for planning and evaluating social intervention.* New York: Academic Press.

ROBERTSON, L. S., KELLEY, A. B., O'NEILL, B., WIXOM, C. W., EISWORTH, R. S., and HADDON, W., JR. 1974. A controlled study of the effect of television messages on safety belt use. *American Journal of Public Health* 64; 1071–80.

ROBINSON, J. P.; ATHANASIOU, R.; and HEAD, K. B. 1969. *Measures of occupational attitudes and occupational characteristics.* Ann Arbor, Mich.: Institute for Social Research.

ROBINSON, J. P.; RUSK, J. G.; and HEAD, K. B. 1968. *Measures of political attitudes.* Ann Arbor, Mich.: Institute for Social Research.

ROBINSON, J. P., and SHAVER, P. R. 1973. *Measures of social psychological attitudes.* Ann Arbor, Mich.: Institute for Social Research.

ROSS, H. L. 1973. Law, science, and accidents: The British Road Safety Act of 1967. *Journal of Legal Studies* 2; 1–78.

ROSS, H. L. 1975. The Scandanavian myth: The effectiveness of drinking-and-driving legislation in Sweden and Norway. *Journal of Legal Studies* 4; 285–310.

ROSSI, P. H. 1972. Testing for success and failure in social action. In *Evaluating social programs: Theory, practice and politics,* ed. P. H. Rossi and W. Williams. New York: Seminar Press.

ROSSI, P. H., and WILLIAMS, W., eds. 1972. *Evaluating social programs.* New York: Seminar Press.

ROTHENBERG, J. 1975. Cost-benefit analysis: A methodological exposition. In *Handbook of evaluation research,* vol. 2, ed. M. Guttentag and E. L. Struening. Beverly Hills, Calif.: Sage.

SALASIN, S. E., and DAVIS, H. R. 1979. Achieving desired policy or practice changes: Findings alone won't do it. In *Impacts of program evaluation on mental health care*, ed. E. J. Posavac. Boulder, Colo.: Westview Press.

SCHNELLE, J. F.; KIRCHNER, R. E., JR.; CASEY, J. E.; USELTON, P. H., JR.; and McNEES, M. P. 1977. Patrol evaluation research: A multiple-baseline analysis of saturation police patrolling during day and night. *Journal of Applied Behavior Analysis* 10; 33–40.

SCHNELLE, J. F.; KIRCHNER, R. E., JR.; MACRAE, J. W.; McNEES, M. P.; ECK, R. H.; SNODGRASS, S.; CASEY, J. D.; and USELTON, P. H., JR. 1978. Police evaluation research: An experimental and cost-benefit analysis of a helicopter patrol in a high crime area. *Journal of Applied Behavior Analysis* 11; 11–21.

SCRIVEN, M. 1967. The methodology of evaluation. In *Perspectives of curriculum evaluation*, ed. R. W. Tyler, R. M. Gagne, and M. Scriven. Chicago: Rand-McNally.

SELIGMAN, C., and DARLEY, J. M. 1977. Feedback as a means of decreasing residential energy consumption. *Journal of Applied Psychology* 62; 363–68.

SELLS, S. B. 1975. Techniques of outcome evaluation in alcohol, drug abuse, and mental health programs. In *Program evaluation: Alcohol, drug abuse, and mental health services*, ed. J. Zusman and C. R. Wurster. Lexington, Mass.: Lexington Books.

SHIPLEY, R. H. 1976. Effects of companion program on college student volunteers and mental patients. *Journal of Consulting and Clinical Psychology* 4; 688–89.

SIEGEL, S. 1956. *Nonparametric methods for the behavioral sciences*. New York: McGraw-Hill.

SINGH, B.; GREER, P. R.; and HAMMOND, R. 1977. An evaluation of the use of the Law in a Free Society materials on "responsibility." *Evaluation Quarterly* 1; 621–28.

SLOAN, S., and SCHRIEBER, D. E. 1971. *Hospital management—An evaluation*. Monograph No. 4. Bureau of Business Research and Service, Graduate School of Business. Madison, Wisc.: The University of Wisconsin Press.

SLOANE, R. B., STAPLES, F. R., CRISTOL, A. H., YORKSTON, N. J., and WHIPPLE, K. 1975. Short-term analytically oriented psychotherapy versus behavior therapy. *American Journal of Psychiatry* 132; 373–77.

SMITH, M. L., GABRIEL, R., SCHOTT, J., and PADIA, W. L. 1976. Evaluation of the effects of Outward Bound. In *Evaluation research studies annual*, vol. 1, ed. G. V Glass. Beverly Hills, Calif.: Sage.

SMITH, M. L., and GLASS, G. V 1977. Meta-analysis of psychotherapy outcome studies. *American Psychologist* 32; 752–60.

SMITH, W. G. 1975. Evaluation of the clinical services of a regional mental health center. *Community Mental Health Journal* 11; 47–57.

SOLOMON, A. 1975. Charges of resigned aide on prisons will be probed. *Madison Capital Times*, September 12.

SPEER, D. C., and TRAPP, J. C. 1976. Evaluation of mental health service effectiveness. *American Journal of Orthopsychiatry* 46; 217–28.

SPEILBERGER, C. D., ed. 1972. *Anxiety: Current trends in theory and research*, vol. 1. New York: Academic Press.

Staff working papers of the Drug Law Evaluation Project. 1978. Washington, D.C.: U.S. Department of Justice, Law Enforcement Assistance Administration.

STOKES, T. F., and FAWCETT, S. B. 1977. Evaluating municipal policy: An analysis of a refuse-packing program. *Journal of Applied Behavioral Analysis* 10; 391–98.

STRAW, M. 1978. Informal presentation delivered at Loyola University, May 22, Chicago, Ill.

STRUPP, H. H., and HANDLEY, S. W. 1977. A tripartite model of mental health and therapeutic outcomes: With special reference to negative effects in psychotherapy. *American Psychologist* 32; 187–96.

STUFFLEBEAM, D. 1978. Meta evaluation: An overview. *Evaluation and the Health Professions* 1; 17–43.

STULL, R. J. 1977. Many concepts mold multiinstitutional systems. *Hospitals* 51; 43–45.

SUCHMAN, E. A. 1967. *Evaluative research.* Englewood Cliffs, N.J.: Prentice-Hall.

SUSSNA, E., and HEINEMANN, H. N. 1972. The education of health manpower in a two-year college: An evaluation model. *Socio-Economic Planning Science* 6; 21–30.

Time. August 4, 1975. More guinea pigs, experiments with LSD. 108; 66.

Time. December 5, 1977. Helping the handicapped. 110; 34.

Time. July 18, 1977. Striking back at super snoops. 110; 16–21.

Time. July 24, 1978. Psst! Wanna good job? 112; 18, 19.

Time. October 9, 1978. "We're taking control." 112; 23–24.

TRIANDIS, H. C. 1978. Basic research in the context of applied research in personality and social psychology. *Personality and Social Psychology Bulletin* 4; 383–87.

TURNER, A. J. 1977. Program goal setting in an evaluation system. Paper presented at the Conference on the Impact of Program Evaluation in Mental Health Care, Loyola University of Chicago, January.

U.S. News & World Report. April 21, 1975. $301 million a day for HEW—and no end in sight. 79: 45–47.

WALDO, G. P., and CHIRICOS, T. G. 1977. Work release and recidivism: An empirical evaluation of a social policy. *Evaluation Quarterly* 1; 87–108.

WARHEIT, G. J.; BELL, R. A.; and SCHWAB, J. J. 1974. *Planning for change: Needs assessment approaches.* Gainesville, Fla.: University of Florida.

WASKOW, I. E., and PERLOFF, M. B., eds. 1975. *Psychotherapy change measures.* Rockville, Md.: National Institute of Mental Health.

WEBB, E. J.; CAMPBELL, D. T.; SCHWARTZ, R. D.; and SECHREST, L. 1966. *Nonobtrusive measures: Nonreactive research in the social sciences.* Chicago: Rand-McNally.

WEISS, C. H. 1972a. *Evaluation research.* Englewood Cliffs, N.J.: Prentice-Hall.

WEISS, C. H. 1972b. Utilization of evaluation: Toward comparative study. In *Evaluating action programs,* ed. C. H. Weiss. Boston: Allyn & Bacon.

WEISS, C. H. 1973. Between the cup and the lip. . . . *Evaluation* 1; 49–55.

WEISS, R. S., and REIN, M. 1970. The evaluation of broad-aim programs: Experimental design, its difficulties, and an alternative. *Administrative Science Quarterly* 15; 97–113.

WERTHEIMER, M. 1978. Psychology and the future. *American Psychologist* 33; 631–47.

WINCH, R. F., and CAMPBELL, D. T. 1969. Proof? No. Evidence? Yes. The significance of tests of significance. *The American Sociologist* 3; 140–53.

YUKL, G. A., and LATHAM, G. P. 1978. Interrelationships among employee participation, individual differences, goal difficulty, goal acceptance, goal instrumentality, and performance. *Personnel Psychology* 31; 305–23.

ZALKIND, D.; ZELON, H.; MOORE, M.; and KALUZNY, A. 1977. A practical reporting and evaluation system for intervention programs: Guiding principles and potential uses. *American Journal of Public Health* 67; 370–73.

ZIGLER, E., and TRICKETT, P. K. 1978. IQ, social competence, and evaluation of early childhood intervention programs. *American Psychologist* 33; 789–98.

ZIMRING, F. E. 1975. Firearms and federal law: The Gun Control Act of 1968. *Journal of Legal Studies* 4; 133–98.

Index

NAME INDEX

343

SUBJECT INDEX